THE QUIET ADVENTURERS IN CANADA

BOOKS BY MARION G. TURK

CRAFTS AROUND THE YEAR
(A booklet for youth leaders, 1960)

THE QUIET ADVENTURERS

(Scottish and Channel Island ancestors,
settlers in Quebec and Ontario, 1971)

THE QUIET ADVENTURERS IN AMERICA

(Channel Islanders in the American Colonies and
in the United States, 1975)

THE STORY OF FISHERS GLEN, ONTARIO, CANADA, 1810-1976
(Booklet, 1976)

THE QUIET ADVENTURERS IN CANADA
(1979)

Reprint......1993

THE QUIET ADVENTURERS IN NORTH AMERICA

(1983)

Reprint 1992

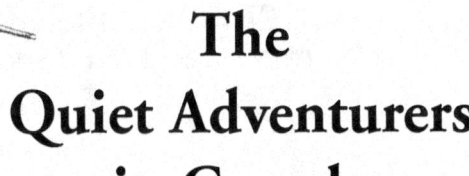

The Quiet Adventurers in Canada

Marion Turk

HERITAGE BOOKS
2019

HERITAGE BOOKS
AN IMPRINT OF HERITAGE BOOKS, INC.

Books, CDs, and more—Worldwide

For our listing of thousands of titles see our website at
www.HeritageBooks.com

Published 2019 by
HERITAGE BOOKS, INC.
Publishing Division
5810 Ruatan Street
Berwyn Heights, Md. 20740

Copyright © 1979, 1993 Marion Turk

Heritage Books by the author:
The Quiet Adventurers in Canada
The Quiet Adventurers in North America (Canada)

All rights reserved. No part of this book may be reproduced or transmitted in any form or by any means, electronic or mechanical, including photocopying, recording or by any information storage and retrieval system without written permission from the author, except for the inclusion of brief quotations in a review.

International Standard Book Number
Paperbound: 978-1-55613-832-4

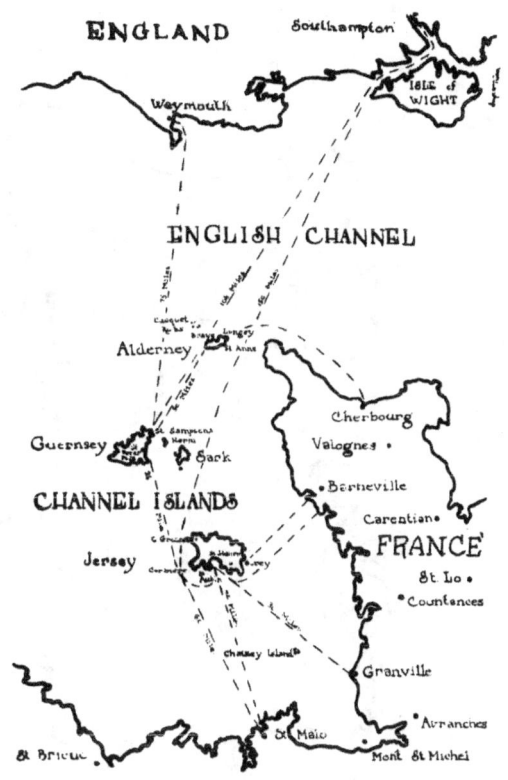

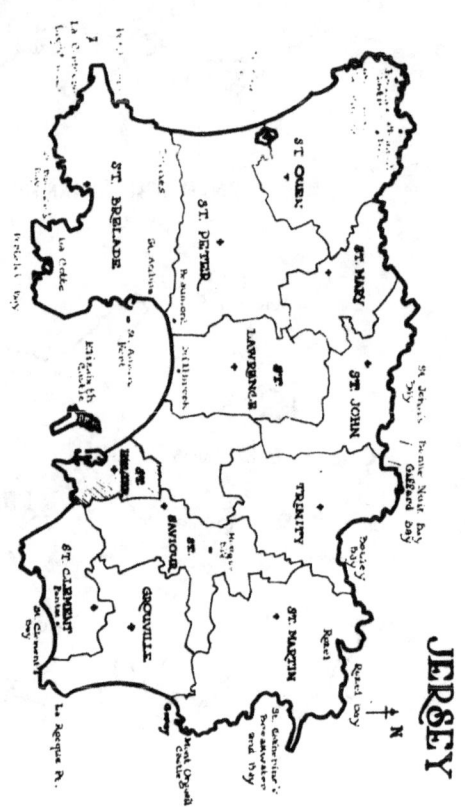

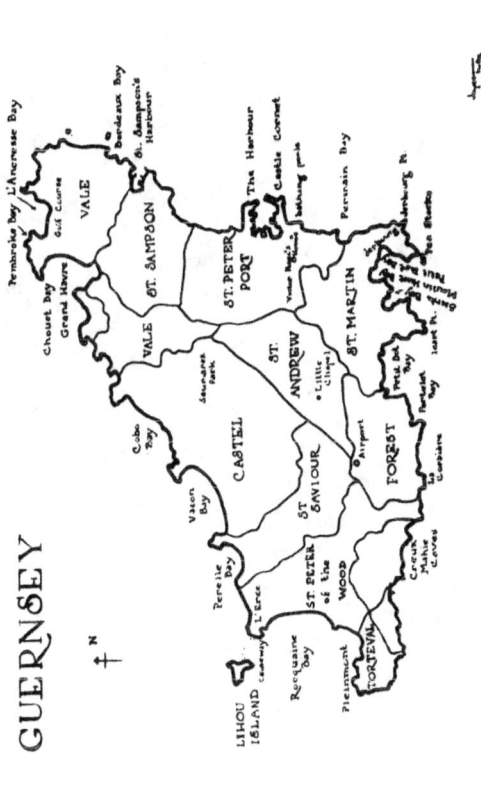

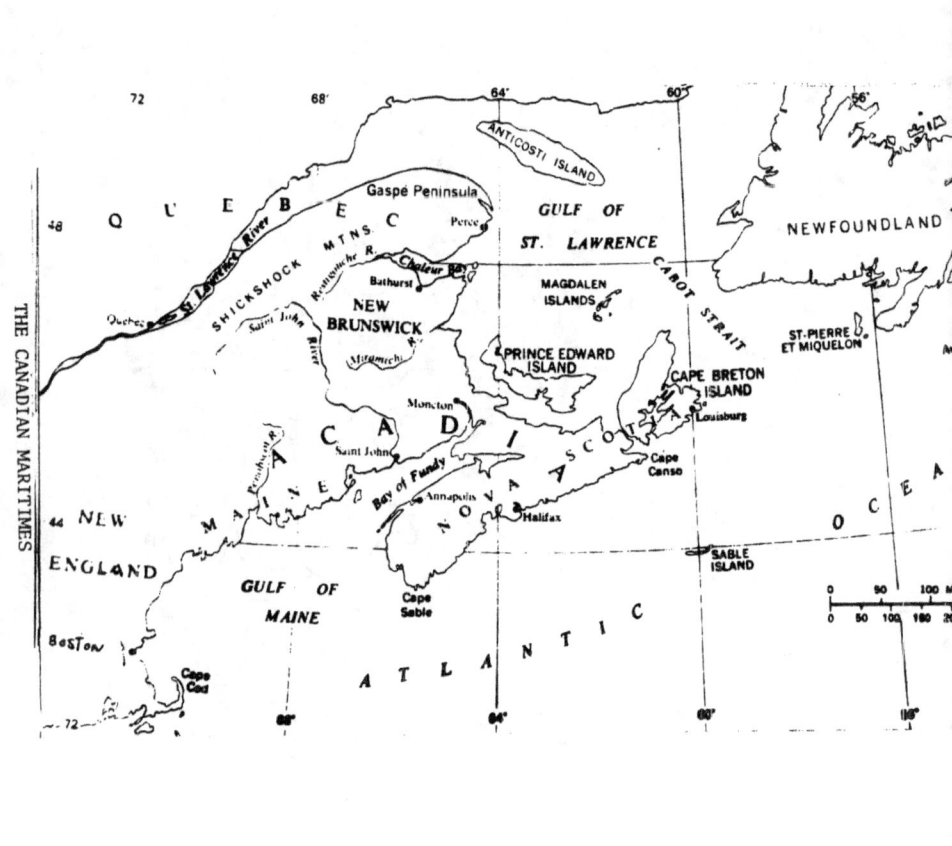

TABLE OF CONTENTS

MAPS: THE CHANNEL ISLANDS
      JERSEY
      GUERNSEY
      THE CANADIAN MARITIMES

ACKNOWLEDGEMENTS

PREFACE
ADDITIONS AND CORRECTIONS
CHAPTER ONE, THE CHANNEL ISLANDERS AT HOME 1
    BIBLIOGRAPHY. 7

CHAPTER TWO, THE CHANNEL ISLANDS AND CANADA. 10
    CHRONOLOGY. 14

CHAPTER THREE, THE ISLANDERS IN CANADA 17
    THE BRIDEAUX INDENTURE. 17
    THE JOURNAL OF CAPTAIN VIBERT 18
    SIR ISAAC BROCK 23
    THE HUDSON'S BAY COMPANY. 26
    NOTABLES. 29
    CHARLES ROBIN 36
    CLERGY. 40

CHAPTER FOUR, NEWFOUNDLAND 47
    CHANNEL ISLAND SETTLEMENTS IN NEWFOUNDLAND. 51
    BIBLIOGRAPHY. 51
    LABRADOR. 53

CHAPTER SIX, NOVA SCOTIA AND CAPE BRETON 57
    CHANNEL ISLAND SURNAMES 61
    BIBLIOGRAPHY. 63

CHAPTER SEVEN, NEW BRUNSWICK 65
    CHANNEL ISLAND SURNAMES 68
    BIBLIOGRAPHY. 68

CHAPTER EIGHT, PRINCE EDWARD ISLAND. 71
    BIBLIOGRAPHY. 75

CHAPTER NINE, QUEBEC 77
    PETITIONERS, 1820 83
    CHANNEL ISLAND SURNAMES 84
    BIBLIOGRAPHY. 86

CHAPTER TEN, ONTARIO 89
    CAPT. POIDEVIN'S JOURNAL. 91
    BIBLIOGRAPHY. 95

TABLE OF CONTENTS, CONTINUED

CHAPTER ELEVEN, THE CANADIAN WEST 96
    CHANNEL ISLAND SURNAMES. 100
    THE BARR COLONY. 101
    BIBLIOGRAPHY 102

CHAPTER TWELVE, BRITISH COLUMBIA. 103
    CHANNEL ISLAND SURNAMES. 111

CHAPTER THIRTEEN, GENEALOGY
    IN SEARCH OF YOUR ANCESTORS. 112
    CANADIAN SOURCES 114
    AMERICAN SOURCES 117
    CHANNEL ISLAND SOURCES . . . .   481F & 118

CHANNEL ISLAND SURNAMES AND FAMILIES IN CANADA. 127

SURNAME INDEX 548

ILLUSTRATIONS

MAPS OF THE CHANNEL ISLANDS, JERSEY, AND GUERNSEY,
   courtesy of Joyce Turk.

MAP OF THE CANADIAN MARITIMES
ST. SAVIOUR CHURCH, JERSEY. 5
GROSNEZ CASTLE RUINS, JERSEY. 5
ST. SAMPSON CHURCH, GUERNSEY. 6
TYPICAL GUERNSEY HOME, LES FORGETTES. 6
The Brig, JAMES 21
THE MEETING OF BROCK AND TECUMSEH 22
THE LETTER, by Edmund Blampied of Jersey. 46
TYPICAL NEWFOUNDLAND SETTLEMENTS. 56
VIEW OF ST. HELIER, JERSEY. 62
PIERCED ROCK AND BONAVENTURE ISLAND, Perce, Quebec. . . . 76
PETIT GASPE, LITTLE GASPE, QUEBEC 88

- Notice -

The original book which was used for this reprint contained some additional handwritten notes which were made by the author. We feel that the contents of this book warrant its reissue despite these blemishes, and hope you will agree and read it with pleasure.

ACKNOWLEDGMENTS

In the preparation of this book a great deal of work was done by persons other than the compiler. Generous donations of information were made by many hundreds of people some of whom went beyond the basic facts of birth, marriage and deaths of their Channel Island families in Canada. I would like to personally thank these charming and generous spirits, but since that is impossible perhaps they will accept here a heartfelt thank you for their great kindnesses to me in aiding the research necessary for this book.

I am greatly obliged to several persons in particular. The speeches and writings of the late Philip Luce of Vancouver, B.C., opened my eyes to the possibility of there being many Channel Islanders in various parts of Canada. This information came to me through Lady McKie of Ottawa, Ontario, for which many thanks! Aldo Brochet, of Perce and Montreal, sent me, literally, thousands of notes on various Gaspe families from his records. A great deal of information in this book was made possible by leads from him and by genealogical research made by him in Quebec. I am greatly indebted to him for the data which would otherwise have been unavailable to me. Max Lucas of Jersey added to and corrected parts of Chapter One for which I am indeed grateful.

The information about many Newfoundland families came to me from Rev. J. W. Hammond of Bell Island, Newfoundland. He copied information about Channel Island families from old records in Newfoundland which I would not have been able to consult.

Another person who was responsible for this book was my dear husband, Edward J. Turk. It would have been impossible for me to finish this volume without his help and constant encouragement.

The following sent material about many families and gave me leads to others. Those who sent information on their own families are identified in the corresponding charts for such families.

The compiler's records will be sent to the Genealogical Society of Ontario and will then be available to all researchers by about 1980. The Society's address is Box 66, Station Q, Toronto, Ontario, M4T 2L7. Arrangements may be made with the Society after that date to examine this Channel Island material some of which is not included in this book. This may be done in person or with the aid of a professional researcher. In the latter case consult the Society's secretary.

BACKHURST, Marie Louise, Grouville, Jersey, for research in Jersey and for the very valuable Jersey name list.
GARRETT, Raymond, Gascons, Quebec, for much information on Ahier and Chedore families.
GOSS, William O., Ipswich, Mass., for information on families in Quebec and N.S.

GRAVEL, Theresa, Montreal, Quebec, for professional research on Quebec families.
JOURNEAU, Nola, St. Eustache, Quebec, for New Brunswick families and friendly encouragement.
KEYHOE, David, Kitchener, Ont., for numerous leads to Channel Islanders in Ontario.
LE FEUVRE, George Francis, of Trenton, Michigan, Texas and Jersey, for the immense number of leads to Channel Island families in his book, JERRI JADIS, in which Gaspe tombstone inscriptions are listed and for encouragement in this endeavor.
LE PAGE, Edward, Grimsby, Ont., for many Le Pages and other Guernsey folk in Canada.
MATHEWS, Dr. Keith, St. John's, Nfld., for early Newfoundland family surnames.
NICOLLE, Leland, Murray River, P.E.I., for families of that Island.
PARKER, Capt. John, of N. Sydney, N.S., for information on Cape Breton Island in his two books about the area.
PATTERSON, Curtis, Harrington Harbor, Duplessis Co., Quebec, who has much unpublished data on Channel Island families in Gaspe.
REMIGGI, Frank, McGill Univ., Montreal, for Gaspe material.
ROBERT, Mrs. Roy, Niagara Falls, N.Y., for much data sent to me on Channel Islanders.
ROBICHAUD, Fr. Donat, of Beresford, N.B., for families of that province in his book.
SEARY, E. R., whose book on Nfld. families has been a fine source of information.
SLOTSVE, Gabrielle Le Rossignol, Estevan, Sask., for much material and loan of books.
STEAD, Mrs. A. C. S., Dorval, Que., for much information on the Carey family.
VIBERT, Mr. & Mrs. Wayne, Burnaby, B.C., for Gaspe families.
WILSON, Sylvia, Medina, Washington, for Gaspe families.

In addition, will the following please accept my warmest thanks for their aid in gathering family records: Eileen Cushing, Lady Richmond of New Zealand, Prof. Stephen White of Moncton, N.B., A. Poidevin, Mrs. A. Balch, Mrs. Philip Piton, Walter Le Courtois, G. Lempriere, Edith Baillie, Gladys S. Lund, Marion Kennedy, Louise Carlson, Dorothy Fairweather, E. J. Le Boutillier, Evelyn Campbell, Arthur Davey, Trudy Mann, Helena Cameron, Richard Gibbons, Richard Spurr, Rev. Gustave Le Gresley, Ivor Le Vesconte, William Swinarton, Florence Ferguson, Alfred Le Mesurier, Dr. Helen Le Vesconte, Ellen Hill, Claudette Maroldo and many, many others.

Finally, my deep appreciation for the manuscript preparation by Sandra Smith-Czinger, of Parma Heights, Ohio, whose generous cooperation and assistance were highly essential to this book.

PREFACE

The magnificent colorful tapestry of Canada's history has been described, explored and expounded by thousands of writers. Nevertheless, while the main picture up to now has been considered almost complete some of the corners, the shadows and fine details need more light to bring out the small truths that lend depth and vitality to the whole.

Among the earliest settlers in the New World were the Channel Islanders, the Quiet Adventurers from the Islands of Jersey, Guernsey, Alderney and Sark. Few Canadian history books mention these seafarers and farmers. They write of the Ukrainians, Germans, Scots, Irish and Welsh, and they write mountains of books on the French settlers. Channel Islanders? A line here, a paragraph there, some books about Gaspe, and that is about all.

Contrary to what most historians appear to think, the Islanders contributed a great deal to Canadian history, and this book will attempt to show the value of their contribution in commerce, in blood lines and in culture.

Island! It's a romantic word with many ideas of adventure, treasure, excitement and far places, but for some an island can be a sort of prison. Some Islanders are content with the quiet of their green fields and pleasant houses and gardens. Others feel chained, bound to the island against their will, yearning for the freedom of the open sea or the green shores of lands on the other side of the world. Political situations, cultural conditions, unfair laws, family quarrels and, very commonly, lack of work were the usual reasons for removal of the Channel Islanders to North America.

In early times Channel Island economy was strictly limited. There were only so many positions to fill, so many fields to farm or pastures to graze. Thus, as families expanded, it was inevitable that the oldest son would inherit most of the property, and that other children in the family would need to pursue their fate elsewhere.

From these Islands in the 18th and 19th centuries poured out a great many young folk for whom no place could be made in the Island economy or by whom the sea's magnetism could not be resisted. These young adventurers removed to many parts of the world, some as indentured servants, others as sailors, clerks and traders. They went to England, France, Spain, Italy, Africa, India, Brazil, Argentina, Honduras, the West Indies, China, Japan, the East Indies, Hawaii, Australia and New Zealand; but most of all they went to Canada.

The first Channel Islanders in Canada were probably those who went to the Grand Banks South of Newfoundland to fish for cod. Through accidents, storms, etc., some of them must have remained over winter at times.

From that period on the Islanders were very active in the Newfoundland, Labrador and other Maritime fisheries. In order to maintain these large and growing businesses it was found necessary to bring Islanders and supplies to hundreds of small ports in Atlantic Canada where men and boys spent the summers fishing and drying fish and who returned, most of them, to the Islands in the cold half of the year. But the fisheries, growing so large and successful, needed settlers to stay the year around to look after the fisheries, the buildings and other property. That was the beginning of the Channel Island settlements in Canada, such as those on Conception Bay in Newfoundland, at Arichat, Cape Breton, Gaspe, Miscou and Shippegan in New Brunswick and countless others.

In these new settlements on the Canadian coast the Islanders fished and farmed just as they had done for centuries in Jersey and Guernsey. Many raised large families and almost to a man left a strong tradition of Jersey and Guernsey origin to their descendants. Some still spoke the Island tongues after three generations in Canada.

The number of descendants of these Channel Island families has, of course, multiplied greatly, and many have prospered. Some of the descendants are becoming interested in their genealogy and family backgrounds, but comparatively few know more than the name of the Island their ancestor left, and fewer still know the story of their ancestors' homeland. Therefore, it seems urgent to record now what can be found of these backgrounds before the information is lost, both in official files and in the memory of the present generations.

If your family line is recorded here I am glad. It was worth the work and the tremendous correspondence involved. If you were queried and declined or neglected to answer I am very sorry that your part of the Island history is omitted here. If I did not reach you with one of the thousands of inquiries I sent out again I am sorry, but due to the physical impossibility of locating all the Channel Island families I did miss out on a goodly number to my vast regret.

Why is this work being done by an American? My ancestors were Canadians: Loyalists, French Canadians, Welsh, Scots and Jerseymen, a fair cross-section of Canadian blood!

ERRORS AND OMISSIONS: Mistakes large and small are inherent in a work of this kind. I apologize to the reader for whatever he finds in this book that is in error. The reasons are manifold: mis-reading of correspondence, difficulties in transcribing old documents, faded ink in old records, confused or incorrect memories of the past, loss of verification such as family Bibles in fires and removals, the constant copying necessary in the production of the book, etc., etc.

Another source of many possible errors in this book is the tendency of the Island families to repeat first names to a surprising degree. Thus there could be in one place at one time 4 or 5 persons with the same full name, a genealogist's nightmare. Clarification in some cases like this was impossible.

Some families remained in one area reproducing in fairly large numbers, and only the work of dedicated correspondents with access to the records of the area and with personal knowledge of the descendants made some of the charts possible.

I hope that the reader will forgive such discrepancies as have occurred. It is most important that the reader take pains to correct his own copy of the book. Also, please notify the members of your family line what and where the error is so that each may correct his own copy of the book. This is a must if future generations are to have a clear and correct version of their family line.

To the French Canadians of Quebec and New Brunswick I give my apologies for two things: the lack of a French version of this book and the omission of accent marks on French words and names. My apologies also to the Channel Islanders for the missing accents.

Queries about this book accompanied by a stamped, self-addressed envelope will be answered by the author-compiler.

Marion G. Turk
5811 Kenneth Avenue
Parma, Ohio U.S.A. 44129

A POEM OF LOVE
by Elsie Rabey Brien, excerpts from.

To the rocky shores of Gaspe Peninsula,
Bleak and dangerous at any time
Came courageous settlers from the Islands
of Jersey and Guernsey, their livelihood to find.

Dauntless in their determination
to harness all problems there,
Caring for one another
Their meager possessions did share.

Pride, dignity and determination
Helped them soon solid homes to build
Friends and families held in together
Until each need was fulfilled.

Being from them closely descended
I write this love poem today.
I still use the crafts they taught me,
Am prouder of memories each day.

XVI ADDITIONS AND CORRECTIONS

Since this book was published in 1979, a rather large amount of data has been sent to the compiler, or has come to her notice in various periodicals, books and letters. Much of this was given to THE CHANNEL ISLANDS COLLECTION. Also the new American and some of the new Canadian data was included in the reprint of THE QUIET ADVENTURERS IN NORTH AMERICA, 1992, by Heritage Books, INC, Bowie, MD.

However, a slightly different situation arose when I considered a reprint of this book. In the 1980s the eagle eye of Aldo Brochet, formerly of the Gaspe area, picked out the numerous typos and other errors made in the Canada book, and also added data which Aldo knew from his Gaspesian connections. He went through the book page by page, and wrote out the changes that were necessary, and sent them to me. This exacting work must have taken a good long time, and I much appreciated it, but did not think that a reprint would be made. Now that this has come about I appreciate even more the hours that Aldo spent. Unfortunately he has moved around, and I have lost track of him. Therefore this acknowledgement will have to do. THANK YOU VERY, VERY MUCH, ALDO BROCHET.

I have gone through the book, adding and changing where possible the errors in the book. In many cases the additions were too voluminous to include, so have notified readers that the data was given to the CHANNEL ISLAND COLLECTION,

In other cases, I have squeezed in directions to consult these added pages. While this detracts from the looks of the book, as a researcher myself, I know how important it is to place related data together where possible.

Also, no source has been given for many of the added items. They were picked out of printed and written material that came to my notice. Not expecting a reprint, I made no note of the source. I am sorry about this.

I would like to draw the attention of Channel Island descendants to some excellent sources of information they may not be aware of.

ADDITIONS AND CORRECTIONS   XVII

Chapter Thirteen, IN SEARCH OF YOUR ANCESTORS, p112 has
some addresses that may now be invalid, since over ten years
have passed. The addresses below are recent. Joining any of
these societies can be extremely rewarding, and their previous
bulletins may possibly hold the answers to some of your genealogical puzzles. In addition, the Societies in the Channel
Islands have organized their Island records in the past few
years, and much improved your chances of locating data on your
Island ancestors. Fall issues of THE GENEALOGICAL HELPER
update each year addresses of hundreds of genealogical and
historical societies.(P.O.Box 368, Logan, UT, 84321)

CHANNEL ISLANDS COLLECTION,
Western Reserve Historical Society Library,
10825 East Blvd., Cleveland, OH, 44106

THE CHANNEL ISLANDS FAMILY HISTORY SOCIETY (CIFHS)
Box 507, St. Helier, Jersey, Channel Islands, UK.

LA SOCIETE GUERNSIAISE,
P.O. Box 314, Candie, St. Peter Port, Guernsey,
Channel Islands, UK

GASPESIENNE CHANNEL ISLANDS SOCIETY,
c/o Dianne Sawyer, P.O. Box 841,
New Richmond, QUE, Canada   GOC 2B0

PEI GENEALOGICAL SOCIETY,
Box 902, 2 Kent St., Charlottetown, PEI, Canada CIA 7M4

NORTH YORK PUBLIC LIBRARY, CANADIANA, 6 TH Floor,
5120 Yonge St., North York, ONT, Canada   M2N 5N9

THE CLEVELAND PUBLIC LIBRARY, MAIN BLDG,
325 Superior Ave.,NE, Cleveland, OH, 44114.
(This library surprisingly has over 50 books listed under
 Channel Islands, Jersey and Guernsey, including old ones)

QUEBEC FAMILY HISTORY SOCIETY, P.O. Box 1026,
Pte. Claire, QUE, Canada   H9L 4H9

GASPE HISTORICAL SOCIETY, Box 680, Gaspe, QUE, has two
 past issues with long and definitive article about the
 Islanders in the Gaspe area. See the 1978 issues, #62 & #63.

ADDITIONS AND CORRECTIONS

FAMILY DATA ABOUT THESE SURNAMES HAS BEEN ADDED TO THE CHANNEL ISLAND COLLECTION THROUGH 1992.

ALLEY, ALLEZ	LE BROCQ	SKINNER
ANEZ, AGNES	LE BRUN	SWARTON
ARMS	LE CORNU	STANNAGE
AUBIN/OBEN	LE CRAW	TORODE
BATES	LE GALLAIS	TOSTEVIN
BIBBER	LE GALLEE	TOUZEL
BIARD	LE GALLIENNE	TUPPER
BILLOT	LE GROW, GROVES	VALPY
BISSON	LE LACHEUR	VAUDIN
BLAMPIED	LE MARQUAND	VIBBER/BIBBER
BRAKE	LE MASURIER, ETC.	WHITELEY
BREHAUT		
BROCHET	LEMPRIERE	
BROWN	LE MUETEL	
BUNTON	LE PAGE	
CHICK	LE VAVASSEUR	
CHURCH	LUCE	
CODY, LE CAUDEY	MACHON	
CONEFROY	MAHY	
CRISTIN	MAJOR	
DE CAMP	MANNING & ROUSSEL	
DE CAEN		
DELAREE	MARRETT	
DOREY	MARTEL	Also included were
DUFFETT	MAUGER	various newspaper
DUMARESQ	MESSERVY	clippings from ass-
FALLE	MOLLET	orted places, Guern-
FERBRACHE	MOULLIN, MILLS	sey Society REVIEWS,
GALLIEN,		CIFHS bulletins, #6,
LE GALLIENNE	NICOLLE	#41, #42, #43, Pic-
GIBAUT	OGIER	tures and other
GODFRAY	PAYN, PAYNE	items about the
GROVES/LA GROW	PINWILL/ PINOIL	Channel Islands.
HAMPTONNE	POINDEXTER	
HAMBLEN	POLLAN, POLEYN	
HAWKINS		
HOTTON		
LA GROW, GROVES	QUEREE RABEY	
LARAWAY	RENOUF	
LARBALESTIER	RICKER	
LANGLOIS	ROBBINS	
LA RUE	ROY	
LAURENS	SARCHET	
LE BOUTILLIER,	SARRE	
BUTLER	SEBIRE	
LE BRETON	SKELTON	

ADDITIONS AND CORRECTIONS XIX
DATA ON THESE CANADIAN FAMILIES IS FOUND IN
"THE QUIET ADVENTURERS IN NORTH AMERICA", 1983.

ALEXANDER	DURELL	LE FEVRE,	PEPIN
AMIRAUX	DUVAL	LE FEVRE	PEZET
ANDERSON	ELSBURY	LE GALLAIS	PITON
ANNET	FALLE	LE GRESLEY	PREVOST
BAILEY	FALLU	LE HUILLIER	PRIAULX
BALLAM	FILLEUL	LE HUQUET	PRICE
BARTRAM	FINDLAY	LE HURAY	QUENAULT
BEASFORD	FRAZER,-SER	LE LACHEUR	QUEREE
BEHAN	FULLER	LE LIEVRE	RAMIER
BELFORD	GALLEY,GALLIE	LE MAISTRE	ROSE
BENEST	GALLICHAN	LE MARQUAND	ROSIER
BERTEAUX	GALUSHA	LE MASURIER	ROUSSEL
BERTRAM	GAUDIN	LE MESSURIER	ROWCLIFFE
BEST	GAVET,GAVEY	LE MESURIER	SANDERS
BIRD	GOSSELIN	LE MOIGNE,	SARCHET
BISHOP	GREFFARD	LE MOINE	SARRE
BISSON	GREY	LEMPRIERE	SAVAGE
BLAMPIED	GRUTE,GRUTT	LE NEVEU	SHORT
BLONDEL	GUIGNION	LENFESTEY	TARDIF
BOURGAIZE	GUNTON	LE PATOUREL	TAYLOR,
BRAY	GUSTIN	LE PELLEY	TAYLER
BREHAUT	GUY	LE SEELEUR	TORODE
BRIARD	HENRY	LE SUEUR	TOSTEVIN
BUESNEL	HERIVEL	LE TOUZEL	TOUET
BULFORD	HOMER	LLOYD	VARDON
BULLEN	HOYLE,HOYLES	LOUGEE	VAUDIN
BUTT	HUNTER	MACHON	VAUTIER
CASSIDY	JANDRON	MAHY	WESTAWAY
CHEVALIER	JEANDRON	MARETT	WHEATON
CLEMENTS	KELLING	MARLEY	WRIGHT
COLLINGS	KEMPSTER	MAY	
COSTER	KIRBY	MCCLOCKLIN	
CURNOW,	LAFFOLEY	MC CULLOUGH	
CURNEW	LAINE	MEAGHER,	
DARBY	LA JEUNESSE	MEGHER	
DE BRODER	LE BAS	MERCER,	
DE CAEN	LE BOUTILLIER	LE MERCIER	
DE GRUCHY	LE BRETON	NAFTEL	
DE LA CROIX/	LE BROCQ	NICHOLSON	
CROSS	LE CAIN,LE QUESNE	NICOLLE	
DE LA MAR	LE CHEMINANT	OXLAND	
DELA PERELLE	LE COCQ	PALLOT	
DE LOUCHE	LE CRONIER	PALMER	
DES LANDES	LE DAIN	PATRIARCHE	
DESPRES	LE DREW	PEDDLE	
DE VOUGES	LEE	PELLEY,	
DU FOUR	LE FAVOR	LE PELLEY	
DUNSTAN	LE FEUVRE	PENNELL	

LATE ADDITIONS

If you are researching your family tree in Jersey, an excellent aid would be the booklet entitled "FAMILY HISTORY IN JERSEY" by Marie-Louise Backhurst, 1991, 56 pages, available from the CHANNEL ISLANDS FAMILY HISTORY SOCIETY, P.O. Box 507, St. Helier, Jersey, CI,GB.

Chapters cover the many sources including census, parish registers, graveyards, Land Registry, Newpapers, Heraldry, etc. The booklet also includes maps and pictures, a glossary and French terms used in Island records, plus useful addresses.

Since this corrected edition was made, more family charts of the Channel Islanders have been received, and some discovered in the files and these will be shortly added to the CHANNEL ISLAND COLLECTION, in Western Reserve Hist.Soc. Library, Cleveland, OHIO. They can then be viewed by interested researchers.

BLAMPIED & LE MASURIER of Trinity Parish, Jersey (H.Palmieri, NY)
BREHAUT of Guernsey (W.Brehaut, Palm Springs, CAL)
DE CARTERET & LE CORNU, LE MASURIER & QUEREE (H. Palmieri,Cohoes,NY)
LE MARQUAND & LE GRESLEY of Jersey (S.Le Marquand, Chatham,NB, Can.)
LE MASURIER of Trinity, Jersey (H. Palmieri, Cohoes, NY)
MACHON of Trinity, Jersey (Palmieri)
MESSERVY of Grouville, Jersey (V. Severeid, Fillmore, CAL)
QUEREE, of St. John and Trinity, Jersey (Palmieri)
PERREE/PERRY & DE GRUCHY of Jersey (Lenore Law, Nepean, ONT, Canada)
ROBERT & GUILBERT of St. Martin and Forest, Guernsey.
                            (Hazel Parkes, London, ONT, Canada)
RENOUF of St. Peter Port, Guernsey (Carl Renouf, St. Samp., Guernsey)
TOSTEVIN of Guernsey (E. Gibbs, Minot, N.Dakota)
VAUTIER of St. Ouen & LE MASURIER Of Trinity, Jersey (H.Palmieri)

An interesting sidelight has appeared in a typescript that contains some excerpts from an article by Claude Laing Fisher. The typescript is named OUR DEAR CHANNEL ISLANDS.

"The Islanders are very loyal to England, and 75% of the males volunteered for active service in the war.(WWI?) Lady Houston of Beaufield, Jersey was a very wealthy widow and in 1926 she gave the British Treasury millions and millions in death duties, purely voluntary, one of the largest windfalls they ever received."

ADDITIONS AND CORRECTIONS   XXI

AMIRAUX, SEE P 59, and OLD CHANNEL ISLANDS SILVER,by R.H. Mayne.
AMIRAUX, Peter, b 1772 J, desc of Hug fam from Saumur,Anjou,France,
    son, 1 of 10 chn, of Pierre A. and Jeanne CANIVET, 2nd wife, of
    St.Sav.J., rem to QUE? d 1856 Kouchibougnac,NB. Mar 1. Magdalen
    PREVOST, QUE city and 2. Patience HAINS, b 1815 Douglas, Keswick Co.
    NB. (Marion Greenwood, Arlington,VA) AMIRAUX also in G.
    A1. Elias, b 1838 NS mar 1860 Patience Shadduck, poss other chn?
        B1. Emma Amiraux, b 1873 Richibucto,NB mar 1911 Horance Greenwood
        and d 1962 Arlington, VA.
ANEZ, AGNES?, George, b1809 J d 1871 Paspebiac, Gaspe,QUE son of
    Francis of J, mar 1836 Pasp. Marie DAY, b Hampshire,Eng. 14 chn.
    (Donald LaLonde, Mt. Iron, MI)   See p. 127.
    A1. Geo. Wm. b 1838 mar Carolyn McCrae, 8 chn
        B1. Mary M., b 1863 mar Don Roth   B2. Lydia mar Richard Tennier
        B3. Francis Ph. b 1873   B4. Christie, mar Geo. Campbell
        B5. Carolyn mar Edmund ALMOND B6. Windham, b 1880   B7. Ellen
        B8. Wm. Geo. mar Jessie Dow.
    A2. Ellen Marie b 1839 mar Jasper C. Kruse, a Dane, 6 chn: John Wm.b
        1866, Geo.F., Alfred, Christian, Edwin, Eliza and Marie Kruse.
    A3. William Geo. b 1841 mar Barbara MOURANT, b 1847, 4 chn
        B1. Alinda, mar.   Underhill.   B3. Emma, mar   Price
        B2. William Philip   B4. Elizabeth mar   Foote
    A4. Marie Louise, b 1843 mar John Hanson
        B1. John Hanson b 1868   B2. Geo. Charles Hanson b 1871
    A5. Lydia b 1845 mar Wm. Thompson. (Donald Lalonde has much more on
        Thompson. Also see ANEZ file in CH.IS. COLLECTION.
    A6. Alinda b 1848, d 1884, mar 1869 Charles Thompson in New Carlisle,
        QUE removed to Bayport, MINN.
    A7. Wm. Alfred b 1850, mar Margaret   ? 7 chn.
        B1. Fred James b 1876   B2. Charles Francis b 1878
        B3. John Henry b 1880   B4. Lottie b 1882, mar   Dodge.
        B5. Mina, b 1884 mar   Anderson B6. Margaret, b 1884 mar
        B7. Mae Claudia b 1892 mar   Conrad.   ____Gagne.
    A8. Francis James b 1852   A9. John b 1854
    A10. Elizabeth Dane b 1855 d 1868
    A11. Charles George b 1858 mar Hannah White, 6 chn: Raymond, Ernest,
        Ira, Allie, Grace Rhines and Eva May.
    A12. Ann, b 1860 mar McGinniss   A14. Amelia Sophia, b 1868
    A13. Henrietta b 1862 mar   Fleming   mar   ____Skill.
ASTEE, Peter, from G to Jenkinstown, PA ca 1834, with Geo.Bates.
AUBIN/OBEN, see Q.A. IN N.Amer., & CHANNEL ISLAND COLLECTION
AUBIN, George was in Philadelphia,PA 1874 (Filby)
AUBIN, Philip of St. Sav. J, mar Eliz. DE STE.CROIX, b ca 1824 J
    and rem to Toronto,ONT 1860s, where part of fam remained. Others to
    BC, Canada. (Linda Bouzane, Gander, Nfld.)
    A1. John   A2. Eliz. Mary b 1852 A3. Ann Webber b 1853 St.Sav.Jersey
    A4. Philippe John Wm., b 1856mar Florence Edith Grant.
    A5. Caroline Julia, b 1858, mar John Scott, Toronto,ONT 1875. Scott
        born 1843? Kent, Eng., son of Wm. and B. Scott.
BAAL, Leslie from J to Peterborough & Guelph, ONT ca 1930s. Two
    sons, both mar, with chn. (Jill Keogh, Trinity, jersey)
BATES, Geo. brought with 6 siblings from G to Phila.PA ca 1817. Chart
    to go in CHANNEL IS. COLL. (H. Evoy, Hudson, OH)

ADDITIONS AND CORRECTIONS

BEAUCHAMP, Jean from J to G age 8, worked later for shipyards in G,
  helped build St. Peter Port Harbor 1885. Mar Jane PHILLIPS COLLINGS,
  Pollet, G.
  A1. Charles Henry, b G mar 15 Oct. 1880 Alice Amy INGROUILLE, rem to
    Milton, then Oakville,ONT ca 1908, 6 sons, 1 dau, 2chn b G.
    (Geo. Beauchamp, Peterborough,ONT)
BIBBER/VIBERT, data in CI COLL FROM Carolyn C. Davis, Oceanside,CAL
BISHOP. This large fam from England to J to New England. See Q.A.
  IN N.AMER. Research on Eng. background by Mr. LeMaitre. and write
  ROOT AND TREE PUBLICATIONS, 18013 Armitage Ct., Homewood,ILL.60430
BREHAUT, See p. 173. Mrs. Effie Ives of Charlottetown,PEI has added
  data on BREHAUT fam:
BREHAUT, Henry mar Marie MAILLARD, St. Peter Port, G. Their son HenryB.
  mar Elizabeth PELHAM of England, 1791-1864. Their son Matthew, 1802-
  1875, was Mrs. Ives' great grandfather. Data below continued fromP173:
  D1. Effie Margaret, mar Stewart G. Ives
    E1. Mary E.L. Ives, b 1946, mar Whitlock
    E2. Lilian M.J. Ives, b 1949 mar White
  D2. Mary Cuyler, b 1921 mar ___ Wilson.
    E1. Barbara Wilson, b 1947 E2. Nora Jean W. b ca 1952
  D3. John William b 1924, 5 chn: Robert, Elizabeth, Mary-Ellen,
    Timothy and James.
BREHAUT data in CI COLL added to by Mrs. H.R. LYle Streight, Ottawa,ONT
BREHAUT REUNION, July 10, 1993, Fantasyland Prov.Park in Gladstone area
  between Murray River and Murray Harbour, in PEI. Write Bill Brehaut,
  1639 Sunflower Ct.No., Palm Springs, CA 92262.
BREHAUT, Charlotte, top of p.174. More data in CI COLL from Ostrander.
  Also note there is some doubt about A1B1 Peter Brehaut, who mar Eliz.
  Ferguson. Poss this is fam of Henry, b 1823 PEI, who mar Maria J.
  MACHON. See orig. records in PEI.
BRIARD, Elias. Good chart of this fam in Q.A. IN N.AMER. from Evelyn
  McClellan and Mrs. A.K. Briard-Smith.
BRIDEAUX, p. 176. A1. Sue Chesley Brideaux mar Charles H. Willett, 8
  sons: Jonathan C. b 1949; James G.; Lorne Edwin, Charles Robert; Her-
  bert Arthur; Victor Alex.; Edwin Allen and Christopher Robin, b 1964.
  (Aldo Brochet)
BRIMAGE, John Le Noury, b 1891 son of Amelia Le Noury, who mar 1st
  Richard Shepard, 2nd Wm. Greening, and 3rd John T. Brimage.
  (Elisabeth Duck, Toronto,ONT)
BUNTON, Margaret, p.270. Gunton is in error. Margaret should have been
  with other BUNTONS on p. 164. (Edwin Lewnard, Mt. Prospect,ILL.
  (See BUNTON data in CH.IS. COLL.
CAREY, top of p. 193:
  C3. Susan Mary Lawrence, b 1940 Winnipeg, mar 1961 Vancouver Paul R.
    Tennant, son of James F.W.T. and Gertrude E. GRAY, b 1938
    Indian Head, SASK.
    D1. Christopher C. Tennant, b 1965 WASH,DC
    D2. Douglas R. Tennant, b 1967 VANC, BC
    D3. Matthew T. Sausmarez Tennant, b 1970
    D4. Jonathan Walton Tennant, b 1971 Penang, Malaysia.
DARBY, fam from England to J to Nova Scotia. See GENEALOGICAL RESEARCH
  IN NOVA SCOTIA, by Terrence Punch, Box 895, Armadale, Halifax, NS.
DAY, James in Gaspe area 1800s, thought to be from CI.
DE BOURSIER, Peter, at Cape Breton 1767, cut wood to be used at Paspe-
  biac, GAspe. Poss from J. (GASPE REVIEW, Apr. 1964)
DE GARIS, research by Russell Sorenson, Glenview, ILL
DE GRUCHY, Eliz. Le B. of J has grdau in CAL.(Gladys Seaman,Ridgecrest,CAL)

ADDITIONS AND CORRECTIONS XXIII

DE LA MARE. Much data in Mormon records, Salt Lake City,UT. Many
from CI, but some from England and France. There is a Hugh Wagner
DE LA MARE pedigree of the English fam. Name in J by 1100s.
DE LA REE/DELAREE, James, b ca 1836 G, to Walters Falls,ONT 1857 from
Meaford,ONT, built 1st blacksmith shop. Mar ca 1858 Susanna, dau
of Henry Smith, she b ca 1842. James became mail carrier then sold
farm implements. He d 22 May 1887, wife in 1939, bur W.Falls, Un.
Ch.Cem. (FAMILIES, of Ontario Gen. Society, Toronto,ONT)
A1. Phoebe Ann, b ca 1861 mar Thomas Barker from brechin, 1877, a
shoemaker, rem to Owen Sound,ONT 1921
A2. Sophia Emily, b ca 1863   A3. Alice mar PERRY
A4. Elizabeth mar Hiram BONNELL   A5. Maud Mary mar Samuel Tucker
A6. Ethel mar Martin Cathrae   A7. Stella   A8. Ernest, setted in West.
DELAREE, John b ca 1845 G, res Walters Falls, mar Ellen English.
A1. Lucy May Proud   A2. John   A3. Walter   A4. Edith Victoria
A5. Grace mar Robert Jerry   E6. Eva d 1944, Anglican.
DE MOUILPIED, Amice, b 29 Nov. 1887 mar Sadie Barbara McClennan,b1891.
Educated J & G, rem to Canada, farmed at Inglis, MAN, 2 sons,2daus.
His bro. Clarence res Roblin, Man. (CIFHS #21)
DESPRES, Helen Esther, dau of Thomas, mar in Alderney? Nicholas BOTT,
rem to Walkerville (Windsor), ONT, d 1884 age 27.
DIELEMENT, see SOC.JERS. BULL. #31, p. 37.
DOREY, several errors in this book re DOREY. Leander Dorey, Hunting-
don Beach, CAL has done much work on this Canadian and American fam.
See also CHAN. IS. COLL.
DRAPER, James Finucane, 1836-1876, b G, res St.Helier J from 1860,
bur St.Sav.Cem. He was an artist and dramatist, had plays performed
in St. Helier. (Soc.Jers. Christmas Card, 1992)
DU FOUR, Hilary, from CI to Chicago,ILL 1800s. Some to Fairoaks,CAL.
DUPUY. One fam said to have come from CI to Canada
DUQUEMIN, a man to US on Titanic, survived, had chn in USA
(Edw. Le Page, Grimsby, ONT)
DUVAL. Much work done on this fam by Aldo Brochet. Some changes made
in this book, pp 234,235. Near top of p.234, Philip, 1771-1839, mar
Marie HUELIN. They had 10 chn. Correct your first edition!
FALLE, see charts in Vol VI, Soc. Jers. Bulletins, and In CH.IS.COLL.
Research also by Virginia Severeid, Fillmore, CAL.
FALLE, Joshua mar Ann Caroline ALEXANDER 1846 J,; he drowned 1853.
Anne mar 2nd Nicolas REMY and d 1865.
FALLE, J.E., son of above, b 1850 J rem to Montreal, QUE by ship ALICE
JANE, mar Jane Louise HOYLES, b 1851 J, dau of John HOYLES and 2nd
wife Marie BERTRAM. 62 plus desc. Both bur Montreal.
A1. Jane Mary Ann Falle, 1871-1946 mar   Knott, no issue and 2nd
Crabtree.
   B1. Berenice Crabtree, b 1911 mar James S. Cameron
      C1. Betty Jane Cameron, b 1938 mar Holly Cameron
         D1. James Eric Cameron, b 1970
      C2. John David Cameron, b 1939
A2. Joshua John Bertram Falle, 1873-1903, drowned, bur Mtl.
A3. William John James Falle, 1874-1939, mar Anne Andrews
   B1. William John b 1906 d 1950 mar Kathleen O'Doherty,bur Mtl.
      C1. Brian Falle, b 1931 mar Therese D'Allaire
      C2. Lorne Falle b 1936 mar Barbara Ferguson, 3 chn:
         D1.Kevin b1961   D2. Cathryn b 1962 D3.Shawn b 1965
      C3. Deane b 1939 mar Nancy Lapierre, res Islington,ONT.
         D1. Linda Lapierre b 1963   D2. Peter b 1966
         D3. Carol-Lyn LaPierre b 1969

ADDITIONS AND CORRECTIONS

   C4. Kerry Falle b 1942, mar Ruth Barnet, res Burlington,
   C5. Carle Falle, b 1945 res Toronto,ONT.   ONT.
  B2. George Falle, b 1909 mar Elise Yvorchuk, 4 chn, res Georgia.
   C1. Gary Falle, b 1939 mar Inga Oldager   USA.
    D1. Gary Richard b 1959 D2. Leah Melinda b 1969
   C2. John Falle b 1942 mar Beverly Anderson
    D1. Jonas Leopold Falle, b 1970
   C3. Barbara Ann Falle b 1945 C4. Cheryl Marie b 1950
  B3. Leonard Falle b 1914 mar Lynne Page, res Beaurepaire,QUE
   C1. Donald b 1952 C2. Robert b 1953 C3. Lesley b 1956
A4. Eleanora Harriet Falle, b 1876 d 1947, mar Edwin S. Crabtree,
 Mt.Royal,QUE.
  B1. . Mona Crabtree b 1909 mar D.S. Abbot, res Beaconsfield.
   C1. . Peter Abbott, b 1933 mar Wade
    D1. Linda Abbot,1960 D2.Peter Abbot 1962
    D3. Kimberly Abbott b 1966
   C2. Edwin Abbott b 1935 mar Ramsay.
    D1. Sarah Jane Abbott, b 1969
   C3. Roger Abbott, b 1942, res Montreal.
  B2. Herbert Crabtree, b 1911, mar Vera Copeman, Westmount,QUE
    D1. Ann K. Crabtree, b 1945 D2. Edwin Crabtree, b 1950
  B3. Marjorie Crabtree, b 1912, mar D. Hooper, res Montreal,QUE
   C1. Jill Hooper, b 1943 mar T.A. Rutherford
   C2. Randall Hooper, b 1946 C3. Virginia Hooper, b 1958
  B4. Eleanor Crabtree, b 1917, mar J. Ross, res Magog, QUE
   C1. Bonnie Ross, b 1942 mar Stephen Wace
    D1. Richard Ross Wace, b 1968 D2.Rebecca Jane Wace,b 1972
   C2. Sally Hope Ross, b 1944, mar Gary Fred.Peterson 1978,
    res Couchenour, ONT
   C3. Michael Ross, b 1948
    D1. Andrew Michael Hope Ross, b 1978
    D2. Martha Jane Hope Ross b 1979
A5. Berenice Caroline Falle, b 1879 d 1880, bur Mtl.
A6. Victoria Alice Falle, b 1881, d 1950, res Montreal,QUE
  B1. Viola Jane Esdon, b 1916   mar Norman Esdon.
  B2. Norman John Esdon, b 1918, d1967, mar Betty Jean VAllance
   Cornwall, ONT.
   C1. Norman S.D. Esdon, b 1944, res Toronto,ONT
   C2. Marjorie Ann Esdon, b 1946, mar Douglas Smith of Pierrefonds,
    D1. Gregory M.A. Smith b 1971,Cornwall,ONT. QUE.
   C3. William Robert Esdon, b 1949
   C4. Roger J. Lindsay Esdon, b 1954
A7. George Hoyles Falle, b 1884 d 1948 mar Janet A. Pettigrew,Toronto.
  B1. George Falle, b 1915, res Toronto
A8. Alexander Stephens Falle, b 1886,, d 1954, mar Owen. QUE.
FAUVEL, Harriet Mary, mar at Perce 1855 Joshua Horatio, son of John
 LE BOUTILLIER and Eliz. ROBIN (Aldo Brochet)
FAUVEL, John?, from CI toPte.St. Peter, Malbay, QUE, 1830s, chn?
A1. Charles, d J A2. Olive d 1833 Perce age 8?
A3. Philip mar Mary BERTRAM?
  B1. Laura
  B2. John, b CI ca 1810, Robin agent at Perce, mar ca 1850 Henri-
   etta Marie, b 1815 St. John J, dau of Jean David LE BOUTHIL
   LEUR and Marie COUTANCHE/COUTANCE?
   C1. George Philip b 1849 Perce, d there 1905, mar Caroline,
    dau of Rev. Lyster.
    D1. John, broker in Montreal 1914

ADDITIONS AND CORRECTIONS XXV

   D2. George Arthur, b 1892 d.y.
   D3. Philip and D4 Henry Wm. both d.y.
  C2. Wm. Le Bouthillier FAUVEL, b 1850 Perce, d 1897 Paspebiac,
   Gaspe, QUE, distinguished Gaspe politician, agent and
   partner in Le Bouth. Bros. fishery. MLA for Bon.Co. Mar
   Emma DU HEAUME of J. Obelisk in New Carlisle,QUE.
  C3. Emily b 1852 Perce C4. Charles David, b 1853.C5. Clara?
FICKET, of New England, research by Joyce Davis, Ellicot City, MD,USA
FILLIATRE, Samuel, son of Francis, from J to Nfld. mar Sarah MESSERVY.
 (A.S. Filliatre, St. Johns, Nfld.)
FILLEUL, SEE Soc. Jers. Bulletin 1976, which takes the family back to
 the Mayor of Rouen, France.
FOZARD, a G family to Canada
GALLEY, LE GALLAIS? from J, ____Mar Florence _____in Salem, MASS
 1635, d Beverly, MASS. (Hazel Hammond, Marcellus, NY)
GALLIENNE, Thomas, p. 248, b 1859 G, mar Mary Ann BOURGAIZE, qv, b
 1860 G, rem to Canada 1910. (Elsie Coniam, Burlington, ONT)
 A1. Alice Mary b 1886 G, mar Albert James MAINDONALD, to ONT 1907.
  B1. Walter, b 1909 mar, a son Frederick b 1941
  B2. Edna May, b 1912 mar   Dauson, d 1937. Son and dau Lillian,
   who was adopted by the Maindonald fam at death of Edna May.
   Lillian mar Gordon Poff.
  B3. Margaret Dorothy, b 1916 mar   Gibbons
   C1.Gary Clark Gibbons, b 1939 C2. Jack Donald Gibbons b 1942
   C3. Jo Anne Gibbons, b 1947 mar Eric Raab
GAVEY, Philip b 1631 J, family charted by author Joseph GAVIT of
 Albany, NY.
GOSSET, mid page 264. (Paul Cleal, Islington,ONT) Add:
 C3. Wm. Duncan Gosset, b 1913 mar Jane Gooch, res Etobicoke,ONT
  D1. James b 1943 mar Agathe Le Bossierre
   E1. Ryan, b 1974 E2. Ursula Janet b 1976
  D2. Selby, mar and div. no issue
  D3. Judith mar Michael Mullen, b 1951 D4. Martha b 1958
GRANDIN, see CI COLL. Amos in Tidioute, PA 1860
GRANDIN, Hannah Jennings mar Wm. BYRD (ca 1610-1672) in Virginia, USA.
 (Dawn Byrd, Sykeston, MO)
GUIGNION, see chart in Q.A. IN N. AMER. and data in CI COLLECTION.
GUIGNION, see p. 269. Nicolas said to have two bros., Elias and Abra-
 ham, poss also a Simon? Fam from G. to Harrington Harbor, QUE.
HARKER, Kesiah, b J ca 1700 mar Barnard Stroud 1722 in Amwell,NJ.Bar-
 nard d Salisbury,PA Kesiah d before 1782.
HARQUAIL/HARQUOIL, ACOW, AOUO, Edouard, a cooper, son of Pierre and of
 Rachel VAUTIER of J, mar 5 Oct. 1792 Angelique Rosalie Robichaud in
 Gaspe area. (ALDO BROCHET)
HELLEUR, William, b ca 1765 poss in CI? rem to near Parrsboro,NS ,
 master shipbuilder. In 1826 to Grand Manan Is.,NB where he with son
 -in-law operated shipyard. D 1828, will prob. 1829 Charlotte Co.,NB.
 Wiliam mar Amy MOSHER/MAUGER?, Anglican. Chn: Elias, Allen, Wm.,
 Charles, Esther b 1803 NS, Phoebe, Lurana, Fanny, Temperance, and
 Mary. (Mrs. Thos. Crawford, Dallas, TX)
HERAULT, prob L'HERAULT to New England 1679 from J.
HOCQUARD, p.277. Two chn named at funeral of their grt.?grandmother,
 Jane SCOTT 1897 at Presb.Ch in Paspebiac,QUE: Rolland and Elizabeth.
 Poss other chn Berta, wife of E.W. Sheppard and Pearly Cuthbert, bp
 1888. Also Charles? Alia? (Aldo Brochet)

ADDITIONS AND CORRECTIONS

HOYLES, William, b 1860s? Devon? England, to J, where he mar Susanne
LE LIEVRE, bp 17 Jan 1768 St. Martin, J, dau of Elie and of Jeanne
NICOLLE. Settled St. Clement J. 3 chn: John below, Marie b 1801,
who mar Pierre LE CORNU of Trinity and Betsy, b 1807.See p.279.
- A1. John, b 1795 J mar 1822 St. Clement J, Anne LE CORNU, dau of Phil.
and of Eliz. HAMON. Anne b 1795. John mar 2nd Marie BERTRAM, & 3rd?
  - B1. Mary Ann Hoyles b 1822 mar Peter Le CORNU, removed to MICH.
    - C1. Anne LeCornu b 1840? d 1898 mar Francois Napoleon Jezequel,
res NYork, Gaspe and Alpena, MICH. (many descendants)
      - D1. Annie Mary Jeqequel d 1893, mar Cevvalen, Louis, Swiss
name=ZWAHLEN.
      - D2. Mary Annie Gezequel, b 1865 bur Alpena,MI mar Claude
DeMarre, b Paris, France.
      - D3. Francois N. Gezequel, b ca 1870, mar ?, a son Francis N.
    - C2. Frank Le Cornu, b 1842?, res Alpena,MI, 8+ chn.
  - B2. Nancy Hoyles, 1824-1898, mar John MACHON, 1824-1901, of Grou.
par. J, son of John and of Sophie AHIER. They rem 1856 from
J to Vittoria,ONT with 3 sons, had 4 chn in Canada.See p.413.
  - B3. John Hoyles, 1825-after 1869
  - B4. Esther Hoyles, 1828-1900, to Port Dover,ONT ca 1865, mar
Thompson, 1 ch d.y.
  - B5. Philip Wm. Hoyles b 1830   A6. Helier, b 1834 by M. BERTRAM.
  - B7. Jane Esther Hoyles 1835-1850 B8. Rachel b 1836
  - B9. Wm. John Hoyles, b 1838 mar at 23 Susan HENRY, res Jersey, a
fisherman, d 1873. (Ancestor of Evelyn Pullin,St.Saviour, J)
    - C1. Wm. John mar Matilda HELLEUR, b 1855. He d 1890s.
      - D1. Emily   D2. Matilda, rem to Canada
      - D3. another dau removed to London, England
      - D4. Wm. John Hoyles mar   fromSt. Lawrence,J.
        - E1.Lily Matilda   E2. Maud Emily
        - E3. Phyllis Elsie
        - E4. George Alfred Helleur Hoyles mar Mabel BUESNEL
4 chn: George, mar M.Le BLANCQ, Cecily M. mar
D.Lovett, & Evelyn M. mar Terrence Pullin
  - B10. Helier John, b 1834, d.y.
  - B11. James Hoyles, b 1845, mar Elvina _____, rem to Chicago,ILL
had Alice Gundlach, Wm.George, Albert, and John b 1872.
  - B12. Eleanor Ann, 1849-1870   B13. and B14. unknown
  - B15. Jane HOYLES, b 1851 J, mar J.E. FALLE, b 1850 J, removed
to Montreal,QUE by ship ALICE JANE, 62 plus desc.
See FALLE family above.

INGOUVILLE. The first winner of the Victoria Cross said to be Capt.
of the Mast, Henry George Ingouville, related to the Philip INGOU-
ville who emigrated to Cape Breton, NS ca 1788. See page 281.
There is a painting in J of the investiture.(R.Gibbons,Scarboro,ONT)

JAMES, Mr.&Mrs. Alfred of Vale, G, res Racine WISC 1800s.

JANVRIN, p. 286. Seventh line from bottom of page is Richard VALPY.
This man was really Richard Francis Valpy DE LISLE, first cousin
to Frederick JANVRIN.

JEAN, pp 287,288. "The males of this fam were typically bp JeanJEAN,
called John John, down to the present day. Luckily for genealo-
gists, some had second names, usually Francis or Wm. John JEAN b
1826 J? His chn are incorrectly listed as chn of John JEAN."
(Aldo Brochet)

ADDITIONS AND CORRECTIONS   XXVII

JOURNEAUX & JOURNEAU. "Francois Journeaux settled at Port Daniel,
    Que in the Gaspe, and mar there, poss 2 or more chn. (P292,293)
    The son John is mentioned in the census of 1871. He mar Sarah
    Travers, bur Shigawake, QUE. William, Cornelius and Herbert would
    be sons of John Cyrus JOURNEAU OF Carlisle, a desc. Re Philippe,
    1778 of Perce, he may be identical with husband of my Moreaux, b
    1704." (Aldo Brochet)
JUNE, poss LE JEUNE?, J fam to Carolina? (Mrs. Wm. Edmund, Broken
    Arrow, OK,USA)
KNIGHT. Near top of p. 296 is Eliz. KNIGHT of Carbonear, Nfld.1755.
    She was Eliz. BUTT, mar 1st Henry KNIGHT. She was dau or grdau of
    Roger BUTT of Carbonear. See Seary's book, FAMILY NAMES OF THE
    ISLAND OF NEWFOUNDLAND.
KRUSE. "Jasper Kruse, b Denmark, bur Paspebiac, QUE, mar in Bona.Co.
    dau of a Jerseyman. See Ray GARRET. Among his chn were 1. Maria,
    who mar Ph. BUTLIN and 2. Alfred C., who mar Philip BUTLIN's Sister
    Rachel Jane, not Eliz. BUTLIN, who d.y. Kruse fam desc. are curr-
    ent in Gaspe Bay area" (Aldo Brochet) See ANEZ addition.
LANGLOIS, mid p.300. Thomas LANGLOIS, who rem from Gaspe to Toronto
    was b G, mar Rachel ROSE, 1810-1892. Add to chn:
    A1. Nicholas mar Jane Emery   A3. James   A4. John
    A2. Rachel mar Jos. LE MESURIER
    A5. Mary Jane, 1851-1930. Mar 1st Roberts and 2. Alex Morrison.
    (Lynn Nye, Corona Del Mar, CAL)
LANGLOIS/ENGLISH, Jane/Jeanne from J, niece of Philip ENGLISH, qv in
    Q.A. IN NORTH AMERICA. She was in Salem,MA 1720, mar John CANN,
    poss DE CAEN? 1731 in Marblehead, MA, later rem to Yarmouth, NS.
    "All the Canns of NS are desc of Jane ENGLISH". (Arthur P. Gottwald
    Alexandria, VA)
LARAWAY/LE RUEZ, research by Carolyn Huyett, Westchester, PA
LE BAS, Charles G., res Cape Cove, Gaspe 1886, was at wedding of
    Drusilla TUZO and Dumaresq VALPY.
LE BOUTILLIER, some from CI to Rhode Island & CT, USA
LE BOUTILLIER, John mar Lydia GAILLARD of Trinity, J, res Trenton,
    ONT, when she d 1882 at 32. (CIFHS)
LE BOUTILLIER, John b 1797 LaChasse, St. John J, see p. 309.
    His son Philip b 1825 Perce mar 2nd and 3rd Susan and Harriet Thorpe,
    daus of Rev. John Thorpe and Harriet ORMANDY.
LE BRETON, p. 315. Near Bottom of page, Philip LE BRETON, b 1827 J,
    d 1897 Perce,QUE, worked for RCC for 50 yrs., mar 3 times, 7 chn.
    Mar 1. Catherine JEAN, who d 1863, dau of John JEAN and Hannah
    Barnes; 2nd, Ellen dau of Mark BUNTON, and 3rd. Mary McNeil, dau of
    Roderick McNeil and Esther GARRET. (Aldo Brochet)
A1. Eliz. Mary b 1860, d 1939 mar F. BOWER
A2. Hannah, 1862-1956, unmar bur Perce
A3. Jane E., 1863-1912, mar Wm. Newberry, res Magpie, QUE
A4. John Philip b 1866, mar?   A5. Philip John, 1869-1915,drowned.
A6. Mary Esther, b 1874   A7. Ellen Jessie, 1878-1939, unmar, burPerce
A8. Catherine, b 1886, wife of A.H. VIBERT
LE BROCQ, Philip of Paspebiac, see near mid p.316, 1885-1975, wife
    Winnifred b 1898 d 1973 Gaspe.
LE CAIN/LE QUESNE, Francis Barkley, p. 318 said to be son of Jean LE
    QUESNE and Eliz. HORMAN, both of J. See LE QUESNE below.

XXVIII   ADDITIONS AND CORRECTIONS

LE COUTEUR, bottom of p.328,then 329. Edward John LE COUTEUR had 1st wife Emma HAMON, 1851-1924.
A1. Delphine Anne b 1912 mar Donald Wright, 4 adopted chn+one.
   B1. Walter Eugene b 1947 mar Mary Stone 3 chn
      C1. Rodney James b 1950 mar Barbara Towne
         D1. Rodney   D2. Veronica
   B2. Daniel Joseph, b 1952 mar Sharon Forbes, 2 son, reside Portage, MICH.
   B3. April Marie, b 1955 mar Randall Lawrentz, a son Jacob res Oregon.
   B4. Edward Joel, b 1965
A2. Edward John, 1913-1930   A3. Charles Philip, b 1915 d.y.
A4. Walter Monroe, b 1917   A5. John Le Grand, b 1920,Toronto.
A6. Wiliam George, b 1921, res ONT, 2 sons, Douglas & Anthony
A7. Robert Arthur, 1923-1967, a son Paul R., and daus Sari and Valerie.
A8. Shirley   A9. Joy   A10. June
LE GARIGNON, Cyril, b 1912 St. Laurens J, to Gaspe 1930 for Wm. Hyman & Sons, there 35 yrs., then with Dept.of Ind.& commerce of QUE. Mar Mae Kennedy, res Gaspe town.(Brochet)
A1. Daniel mar Nicole Mailhot, had 2 daus.
   B1. Sophie b 1975   B2. Marie b 1977
A2. John P., b 1951 Gaspe, a Marist father.
LEGG, see ROUSSEL and p. 338.
LEGG, Thomas mar Louise OZARD in G. (Englert, ONT)
A1. Lily Legg b 1879 G d 1942, mar John Sedgeley ROUSSEL in G. who d 1942 Hamilton, ONT.
   B1. Arthur Willett ROUSSEL b 1905 G, mar 1926 _____Englert?
LE GUEDARD, from CI to Chloridorme, Gaspe area mar Blanche COULOMBE. See p.347.
LE LACHEUR and HAWKINS. See data in CIFHS bulletin #25, article contributed by Sally Lomas of Toronto,ONT. Her data updates and corrects some errors in this book for both LE LACHEUR and HAWKINS families.
LE LACHEUR, p.353, Harriet mar Giles Hawkins
A1. John res PEI   A2. Lost at sea
A3. Charles Augustus Hawkins, res Newport Landing, NS.
LE MARQUAND of Gaspe. See CI COLL., data from sarah Mc Eachern, Loudon, TN and Harry McEachern, Hudson, OH. See also MARQUAND.
LE MARQUAND, John, b J ca 1818. A large corrected chart with added data is on p.361 in THE QUIET ADV. IN NORTH AMERICA.
LE MASURIER, John and Mary Ann res Gaspe area.
LE MASURIER, John Philip mar in J Ann Jane Louisa BUESNEL, sister of Clement and Philip, both of whom rem to Canada, one to BC and the other to Alta. Ann d 3 Mar 1913 Calgary, and John P. returned to J 1914 with their three younger chn.
A1. John Ph., b 1 Feb. 1891 d 1963. To Canada age 18, mar Martha Blake, res Toronto, no issue.

ADDITIONS AND CORRECTIONS   XXIX
LE MASURIER, continued
A2. Elsie b 1894 J mar Alfred Crocker of Devon, rem to Fresno,
   CAL, both deceased, had 6 chn.
A3. Lily, b 1897 J mar Louis Walker 1920, settled Calgary,ALTA
   have 2 mar sons, Cecil and Allen.
LE MASURIER, Philip, see top of p.363, bro of L.Alfred and son
   of Josue Le M. and Mary Jane CLARK of J. Fam rem to England
   1852. Philip was a piano maker ca 1864, mar Sarah ___, b
   1844. Fam res Cannington,ONT 1870. Philip & fam removed to
   St. Vincent, MINN. (Murray Le Masurier, Toronto)
   A1. Ernest b 1866 mar Bertha Grissinger
      B1. Dorothy Mae, b 1898 mar 1.Warren Dayton and 2. W.Howell
      B2. Vera Lanore, b 1899, mar 1. Ralph Gillespie and 2.
         Wayne Thomas.
      B3. Ernest Howard b 1909 mar Virginia May Vanarnum
         C1. Dr.Wesley Ernest   C2. Philip Howard
A2. Philip b 1869
A3. Annie, b 1870 mar Rev. Martin Ray of Canterbury, England.
A4. Alfred mar Margaret Cameron
A5. Florence, mar Kenneth McKenzie, daus Helen and Mildred.
A6. George, mar Ethel ___, son Earl
A7. Arthur, mar Annie Cameron, sons Warren, Philip & Robert
A8. Lucy, mar Wesley Cameron
A9. Charles mar Bertie McKeiver, son Dalton. A10. William.
LE MASURIER, John, b 1826 J, p. 364, res Gaspe, had Emily b
   1858, Anne Mary b 1862, John Thomas b 1864, Susan Jane b
   1869. (Census 1871, Aldo Brochet).
LE MESSURIER, John of G b 1799 mar Eliz.ALLEZ, 3 chn, rem to
   Sauk Prairie,WI then to Wausau, WI 1846, built 4 saw mills.
LE MESSURIER, Melina b 1835 G to US 1842, mar 1st Isaac Coul-
   thurst, 2. Moses Turner, and 3. Solomon TRudeau. 4 chn by
   first husbands. (S. O'Neil, Tualatin, OR)
LE MESURIER, Wm. Fraser, p.365 was son of Charles LeM. of CI.
A1. John, 1884-1941   A2. Mary Anne, 1869-1951.
LE MESURIER, Henry, age 28 of J, son of Francois & Susan
   (Emoss) Le M. was admitted as Henry MEZERAY to Hotel Dieu
   Hospital, QUEBEC City, Dec. 1798.(LOST IN CANADA,#44)
LENFESTEY, P., a merchant on Yonge St.,Toronto,ONT mar June
   Bezeck of Forres, Scotland 22 Sept.1847. (ONTARIO MARRIAGE
   NOTICES, by Wilson)
LENFESTEY, P.380, line 18, add:
   C4. Jessie E. Cooper, b 1894 mar Arthur L. Hodgdon in
      Hoquiam, WA, 2 sons.(A.L. Hodgdon, Sonora, CAL)
      D1. Arthur J. Hodgdon mar Marg. C. Cooney 1948
         E1. Ellen Mary b 1956   E2. Thos. C. b 1958
         E3. Mary C.E. b 1962
      D2. Charles S. Hodgdon mar ?, res Santa Clara area,CAL
         E1. Bruce D.   E2. Eric A.   E3. James A.
LENFESTEY, James, pp 373-375. James was son of Thomas and
   Rachel (nee Lenfestey) of G, b 1786, mar in Perce,QUE 1806
   Susan Dobson, dau of Charles & of Anne Spencer.

ADDITIONS AND CORRECTIONS

LENFESTEY, cont.
  Susan was widow of Elias MAUGER, mother of Ann Mauger, b
  1800. Connections with Dobsons are not too clear.(Brochet)
  A1. James, mar 2nd Amelia LUCAS
    B1. James mar 2nd Catherine MABE
LENFESTEY, see p.378, near top. Chn of Ida May LENFESTEY and
  Edward L. Holden. (Claudette Maroldo, Cherry Hill, NJ)
    D1. Ralph Benj. Holden, b 1907 Eau Claire,WI, a twin, mar
        Ione Clarice Peterson, b 1916, bur Lake View Cem, Eau
        Claire, WISC.
      E1. Helen Mae Holden b 1939, mar John Barstad 1960
        F1. Michael John Barstad, b 1960
        F2. Mark Richard Barstad, b 1962
        F3. Julia Ann Barstad, b 1963
        F4. Brenda Susan Barstad, b 1965
      E2. Richard Peter Holden b 1941, mar Betty Cale, b 1941
        F1. Randy Richard Holden b 1966
    D2. Robert John Holden b 1907, twin, mar 1931 Gladys
        Anderson.
      E1. James E. Holden, b 1934, mar 1955 Nancy Gavry,d1974.
        F1. Steven W.Holden, 1955-1975
        F2. Rochelle A.Holden, b 1957 mar 1974 StevenCraig
          G1. Melissa Beth Craig, b 1976
        F3. Mary Beth b 1960 d.y.
        F4. Anne Marie Holden b 1958 mar Duane Dachel 1975
        F5. James M, b 1962   F7. John Gavre Holden,
        F6. Katherine M. b 1963   b 1967
LENFESTEY, p. 382, top of page.
    F4. Russell Elihu, b 1910 Cape Cove, Gaspe mar Lucinda Anna
        AHIER?, 1909-1977
      G1. Gerald Allan, b 1933   G5. Foster James, b 1944
      G2. Lois Mary b 1935   G6. Carol b 1947
      G3. Winston Wilkie b 1941   G7. Wayne b 1948
      G4. Gordon b 1943   G8. Marylin, b 1953
LENFESTEY, Thomas, b 1809 St.Pierre du Bois, G, mar in NYCity
  Mary Kipp, b 1804, 1 ch. (Wm.R. Lenfestey of Hayward,CAL
  has some data on background family to before the 1600s. See
  chart of his branch in Ch.Is.COLL.)
  A1. Wm.Peter, b 1837 NYCity, d 1920 SanFrancisco,CAL, mar
      Eliz.Gray of Scotland, 1836-1917. 6 chn.
    B1. Wm. Gray, b 1866 NY d CAL 1950, mar Clara M.L.Crosby
        Berkeley,CAL, in 1889, 4 chn
      C1. George Crosby Sr., b 1890 Denmark, d Berkeley,CAL
          3 chn, 3 grchn.
      C2. Marjorie, b 1893 mar Russell B. Adams, 2 chn
      C3. Clara Louisa, b 1900, mar Edward Gallup, 3 chn
      C4. William Robert Sr., b 1903, mar R.B. Kropf, 3 chn
  A2. Helen Marie b 1858 NY d 1941, mar Robert Vail, 3 chn
  A3. Mary Mansell b 1865 d 1924, mar Frank C.Bell
  A4. George b 1869 d 1890 A5. Eliz. d.y.
  A6. Percy Ernest b 1878, mar, no issue.

ADDITIONS AND CORRECTIONS XXXI

LE POIDEVIN, POIDEVIN, James Alex, b J mar Augusta Tope Beatten, rem to Muskoka,ONT 1870, 7 chn: James, Fred.Wm. b1861, John, William, Mary, Minnie and Lena. Fred mar Eliz.Carr, res Gravenhurst,ONT, Canada.
LE QUESNE, Philip Winter and wife Sarah Dearle, bottom of p. 389. H.H. Le Quesne set up a fine chart of his familyLines which unfortunately was not interpreted correctly by M.Turk. If you are of this line, try to locate a copy of the original chart, poss in BC, in North York Library, Toronto,ONT,or at CIFHS, St. Helier, Jersey. Also see CHAN.IS.COLLECTION.
LE SEELEUR. Work done on this fam by Jack Mavins, Anola, MAN., Canada.
LING, Capt. Nicholas, Gov. of G, mar Cecile, dau of Thos. ANDROS & Eliz. DE CARTERET, after 1643. (Wimbush)
LUCAS, Ella mar E.H. Michiel of Paspebiac, Gaspe, QUE.
LUCAS, Philip, Cape Cove, Gaspe was at wedding 1875 of Alice TUZO and Francis GIBAUT of J. (All from Aldo Brochet)
LUCAS, Thomas of Bougerville, QUE mar Rina LE GRESLEY, qv.
LUCE, pp 410,411. This fam incomplete. Philip b J rem to Newport, QUE mar Johanna HELLEYER, HELLIER? HELLEUR?, who d ca 1860. Mar 2nd Anne Ward.
A1. William b 1852 J
A2. Philip Charles b 1864 Newport, mar Georgina MORRISSEY.
    B1. Anne Elizabeth, b 1884 mar John Driscoll
    B2. Philip, with chn as per text.
LUCE, Wm.H. mar Leila _____? Dau mar Eugene BOUILLON
LUCE, Walter George mar Julia, dau of Philip A. MAUGER.
MACHON, See Q.A. IN N. AMERICA, and CI COLL. for more info.
MACHON, p.417, bottom of page. Add to fam of Henry MACHON and Anne LE LACHEUR:
    B6. James, who settled in Phila.PA
    B7. Sarah, who mar 1st ____DAVEY in Pictou, NS
    B8. Margaret, unmar.
MACHON, top of p.420. B1. Esther is given, said to have had 7 chn. B2. Mary, 1841-1927 B3. Emma
MAJOR. See charts in CI COLLECTION, work by Stanley MAJOR, of Toronto,ONT.
MALLET, Ernest, son of A. Mallet of Becquet, Fermain Bay, G, d at San Antonio, TX 1883. (CIFHS bulletin)
MANNAN, John P. from CI, d at 46 in Dighton, MA 1882
MANNING, see chart in CI COLL.
MANNING, James Thomas, b 1784 poss in Kingsbury, Somerset,Eng, mar 24 Dec. 1821 Town Church, G, d 14 Nov. 1836 QUE, Canada, bur bur St.Peters Chapel, occupation butcher. His wife was Mary ROUSSEL, b Mar. 1793, d 1864 Cleveland, OH, bur Monroe Cem. (Susan Cooper, Put-in-Bay,OH, Box 382)
A1. Mary b ca 1823 G, d 1864
A2. Elizabeth, b 23 Aug.1825, G, d 15 July 1876 in Cleveland, bur Monroe Cem. Mar 23 Oct 1856 Alex. Kimberley.

ADDITIONS AND CORRECTIONS

MANNING, CONT.
A3. James Thomas, b 1829, d ca 1859, bur St. Johns,Cleve.
A4. Albert Raleigh Manning, b 1835 England d 1915 Cleve, bur Riverside Cem. Mar 1863 in Cleveland Sarah Harding.
MARQUAND. See CIFHS BULL. #24, refers to a Gen.Chart going back to 1540 about this fam, in Priaulx Library, Guernsey.
MARRET, John, b ca 1766 J d 1843, bur St. Andrews, New Carlisle,QUE. Son Daniel b ca 1802 d 1875, mar 1834 Marcia Assels, dau of James & of Sarah Flowers, had 8 chn, 2 mar Flowers.
See CHAN.IS. COLL. (Bev. Gilchrist, Nanaimo, BC, Canada)
MARTEL, new info. in CHAN. IS. COLL.
MAUGER. "A genealogical line fraught with complexities, poss desc. of Mauger, Archbishop of Rouen, who d 1055, son of Richard II, Duke of Normandy." (Aldo Brochet)
MAUGER, John, p. 427, son of Jacques M., blacksmith, and Marie LE RAY, mar 1828 Malbaie, QUE., Scholastique, dau of Archibald Duncan, called Agapit McNicoll, and of Angelique DALLAIRE. A marriage contract in Greffe office of La Malbaie, Charlevois Co., QUE, not to be confused with Malbay, Gaspe Co. All desc carry name MUNGER. John d Notre Dame de la Terriere in 1861. See E.G. Talbot, GENEALOGIE, CHARLEVOIS_SAGUENAY, 1878, Vol 4,pp 263,265. Roland MAUGER b 1803 had desc. on the Cote Nord, who spell their name MONGER.
MAUGER fams of Bon.Is. called their first sons Philip. Philip Peter, son of Philip mar Ann COUVET, AKA Nancy LE COUVET? or LA COUVEE?
MAUGER, Anne, mother of 11 chn. See TOSTEVIN. Her grandson, Edmund James Flynn was b at Perce 1847, d 1929, elected Deputy for Gaspe 1878-1904. He was a member of many Provincial cabinets, and was Premier of QUE. Given chair of Roman Law at Laval Univ.1874, Judge in Superior Court 1914, no issue.
MAUGER, Richard, p. 429, Ship builder at Hopetown,QUE. No known evidence to connect Richard to others, but may be related to the generations b 1770s.
A1. Charles mar Anna Maria, dauof James Travers and Jane Chatterton.
A2. b 1812 A3. b 1814, mar Molloy. A4. ?
A5. Richard, mar Charlotte dau of Amos Chatterton, U.E.L.. Some desc are called MAJOR.
MESSERVY, data added to CHAN. IS. COLLECTION.
MESSERVY, Sarah Ann mar Samuel FILLIATRE, son of Francis, removed from J to Newfoundland. (A.S. Filliatre, St.Georges, Nfld.)
MOLLET, data added to CHAN. IS. COLLECTION
MOLLET, see p. 436. MOLLET, Jean, bp 1812 Grouville, J, son of Phil. and of Marie D'HORMAN. He d 1896 Salt Spring Is.,BC, mar Marguerite CARTER, b 1807 St. Peter Port, G, d 1889 Albernia, BC, dau of Alex. CARTER and of Marguerite SOHIER, of J. Other chn? More in CI COLL. (Colleen Massabki, Weston, ONT)
A1. Philip C.MOLLET, b 1848 St. Sav. J, d 1940 Arran Twp., Bruce Co., ONT, mar 1878 Ellen Loree, b ca 1860 Bruce Co.
   B1. James Arthur C. Mollet, b 1882 Allenford,ONT, d 1954 Weston, ONT, mar 1929 Naomi R.Graybeal, b 1901 Williamsburg,WVA,d 1962 Weston, ONT.
      C1. Colleen Joyce MOLLET, b 1929 Toronto,ONT mar 1965 Richard Edward Massabki.

ADDITIONS AND CORRECTIONS   XXXIII

NICOLLE, top of p.443. Poss more data available now?
   B1. Ezra b 1862 Georgetown, White Sands, PEI
   B3. Maud, mar Joseph ROBERTS, qv, blacksmith 5+ chn.
NICOLLE, Mary, poss of this fam mar Capt.John McDonald,2 daus?
OLIVER, Thomas, b ca 1806 G, d 7 Feb. 1888 Independence,Iowa.
   (Karen Haas, Maple Lake, MINN)
ORMOND, Lieut.George, Queens Rangers, b 1753 Gramont, FraenchFlanders,
   mar 7 Sept.1783 Elizabeth SMITH, Trinity Ch,NYCity, while on duty
   there. He d 30 June 1802, his widow 1840, bur St.Helier,J.
   (W.O Adams, Vista,CAL)
   A1. Capt. George Richard Smith Ormond, paymaster 86th Regt. of Foot,
      b 1795 Eliz.Castle, J mar Ellen Ruth Howard 1821 at St.Helier,J,
      died 1847 in Guernsey.
   A2. Col. Harry Smith Ormond of New Brunswick, Canada.
PERKINS from CI, researcher Mrs. Stanley Perkins, Vancouver,BC,Canada.
PITMAN, George, b J, age 21 in 1861, res Caraquet, NB.
   (Rev. Le Gresley, Tracadie, NB, census)
PITON/PEYTON, p.474, Victor Emil, b 1901, twin, mar AnnMary Panek.
   D1. Patrick Emil b 1931 Chicago,ILL. (Mary Piton, Bradley,ILL)
   D2. Dorothy Ann, b 1933, mar Clyde R. Sprenger, 1954
      E1. Thos. William b 1955   E2. James S. b 1957
      E3. Patrick R. b 1962 Chicago,ILL.
   D3. Victor Lawrence PEYTON, b 1935 Chicago mar Carol G. Keiper 1959
      E1. Victor T. Peyton, b 1960 E2. Lucille A. Peyton,b 1962
RENOUF. See CH.IS.COLL. Researcher Jack Mavins, Anola, MAN, Canada.
ROBIN, Daniel, b 1801 J, d St. Aug. Duplessis Co, QUE 1876 age 75.
   Mar 1825 Gaspe Jane Cunning, b Haldimand, Gaspe d 1900 Old Fort Bay,
   QUE, dau of James and of Mary L. Kelly. (Curtis Patterson, Coati-
   cook, QUE and Norton, VT, 15907.)
   A1. Henry Robin mar Esther Mary Cunning 1864
   A2. Louise Robin   A3. William Robin
   A4. Josephine Robin mar Francis FEQUET b 1826 J
      B1. Daniel fequet, 1852-1929, mar Emily Baylis Sellinger
      B2. Francis Fequet, 1853-1923
      B3. David George Fequet, 1864-1923, mar Lucy Ann Keats 1898
      B4. John Lewis Fequet, 1864-1948 Old Fort Bay, mar Jane Goddard
      B5. Samuel Butler Fequet, mar 1895 Theresa Annie CHEVALIER
      B6. Henry Fequet, mar Margaret Ellen Robin 1896
      B7. Caroline Fequet, mar Thomas McDonald 1895
      B8. James Fequet, 1865-1942, mar Mary Catherine Leon.
ROMERIL, Matthieu from St.Laurens or St. Peter J to New England before
   1685. Simon was there 1650.
ROUET, Aaron mar Jeanne Sutherland 1812 in J. Their dau Jane, b 1814
   mar Philippe DUVAL of St. Peter J. She d in Grandmere,QUE. Their dau
   dau Esther, b 1815 mar Amice DU VAL, res Jersey. (IDa Duval,Grandmere,
ROUSSEL, see MANNING above.   QUE)
SAVAGE/SAUVAGE data in CI COLL from G.Finch, North York,ONT.
ST.CROIX, William b 1775 J rem to Pte.St.Pierre,QUE where he was bp1803
   (after abjuring?) then mar Marguerite Chicoine, dau of AubinC. and
   Anne DAVID of Pte.St.Pierre. (Remiggi) They mar 30 Oct. 1803 Perce,
   QUE. He d 1815 at Malbaie,QUE.
SCOTT, Francois, b 1854 J d 1921 Gaspe? mar Margaret E.Le GALLAIS,1861-
   1949.
SCOTT, James, 1810-1871, res GAspe. (Aldo Brochet)

ADDITIONS AND CORRECTIONS

SHEPPARD, p. 514. Apparently 3 bros. b Guernsey.
A1. William Grut Sheppard, res QUE city, mar widow BREHAUT
A2. Peter of Quebec city
A3. Martin Sheppard, Sheriff of Bona.Co., 4 chn
    B1. Thomas Grute Sheppard, d unmar   B3. ?   B4. Julia?
    B2. William Mansell Sheppard, Sheriff Bona. Co.,QUE
        C1. Edward Woodburne Sheppard, Sheriff of Bona.Co.,QUE
SMITH, Charles Norton of G mar Jessie Annette COYSH, dau of Frederick, carriage maker and Jessie HILLIER. Mar in Bridport, England, rem to US 1905. (Ruth Smith, Syracuse, NY)
SNOW, many to Nfld. Canada and US. See CHAN.IS.COLL. Much data from James Snow, Brooklyn, NY.
STEELE/STILLE/STEILL, Sire Thomas d Jersey 1542. A son Robert was rector of St. Clement J. This fam res St. Martin J as STILLE. (Soc.Jers.Bull. 1913) Work done on this fam by Mrs. Wm. Strath, Melrose, MASS. A James? Steele mar Mary A. TOURGEE, qv, b 1844, d 1905, dau of Geo. W.T. and Janet McKeleher. See CHAN.IS.COLL.
TAYLOR, Geo.W. of G, to US age 11 with parents from CI 1835. (J.P. Brucken, Brecksville, OH)
TORODE, see p.630 in Q.A. IN N. AMER. Not John but Nicholas had saw mill on Salt Creek,ILL early 1800s. (Ann Fraser?)
Correction re chn:
A1. Nicholas   A2. Peter Richard b 1809
A3. John James b 1810 d 1840 ILL
A4. Charles Wm. b 1812   A5. Daniel H. b 1814
A6. Geo. Fred. b 1818   A7. Philander? b 1824
TOUMINE, THOUMINE, data with Fred Hart, Middlefield, CT.
TUCKER, Murray Stephen, son of Mr. and Mrs. L.G. Tucker, mar Patricia Ann LAMBOTTE of St. Martin G, res Toronto,ONT.
VALPY, Abraham mar Eliz. Fowles 1728 Salem,MASS
VALPY, Abraham mar Lydia Clough 1756 Salem. (1790 Census)
VALPY Richard res Cape Beseau, Yarmouth,NS 1777
    (LOST IN CANADA #39, Poole, pp 14 & 56)
VALPY, work on this fam by Betty McMillan of Wornwall,ONT and mrs. Karen Thompson of Edmonton, ALTA, CANADA.
VAN COURT, see data in Q.A. IN N. AMER. More data with F.V. Fairfield, Pasadena, TX.
VERGE, DU VERGE, VIRGEE, DES VERGES. Name in Grouville J 1716, poss Huguenot? Joseph Verge and Mary Blewett mar in Boston 1755, removed to Liverpool, NS.
WHITELEY, Fred of St. Martin, J had dau b Montreal,QUE 1882
WHITMAN from CI noted in Nova Scotia (Lorway)
WINCY, Dr. George DE JERSEY, p.546, was from St. Peter Jersey.

LE MESURIER, laundry of this name operated in Detroit, MI early 1900s.
    Poss. owned by family from CI, removed first to ONT, then to MICH.

CHAPTER ONE, THE CHANNEL ISLANDERS AT HOME

"The sweet land laughs from sea to sea, filled full of sun."
(E. E. Bicknell, THE CHANNEL ISLANDS)

The Channel Islands lie in the form of a half-circle in the Bay of Mont St. Michel and off the West coast of the Cotentin Peninsula, Normandy. This former duchy was, of course, the motherland of the Islands.

The most northern of the Islands is Alderney which is about 3½ miles long by 1½ miles at its broadest with an area of about 2,000 acres, and some nine miles due West of Cap de le Hague, Normandy. The most exposed of the archipelago, Alderney, which had a population of 1,686 at the 1971 census is about 60 miles South of Weymouth, England, and 24 miles northeast of Guernsey. The latter, the most westerly of the larger Channel Islands, is triangular in shape and approximately 9½ miles by 7 miles in extreme measurements. It has an area of 15,654 English acres (about 24 square miles) and a population at the 1976 census of over 54,000. Apart from Alderney the other main dependencies of the Bailiwick of Guernsey are Sark (7½ miles to the East of the main island), about 3 miles long by 1½ miles at its widest and with an area of over 1,000 acres, about 2 square miles, and a population in 1971 of 590 and Herm (some 3 miles from Guernsey), a mile and a half by half a mile, an area of 320 acres and with a small resident population.

Jersey, the largest and most southern of the main Islands, is some 14 miles from the West coast of Normandy and 30 miles from the northern coast of Brittany. It measures around 10 miles from East to West and nearly 6 from North to South having an area of approximately 28,176 acres or 45 square miles although there are about 62 square miles if all the land to low-water mark is included. Jersey is about 20 miles southeast of Guernsey at the nearest points and some 96 miles South of Weymouth, England. It is divided into 12 parishes, Guernsey having 10 parishes. At the 1976 census Jersey had a population of 74,470 approximately one-half of whom are not of Island descent.

The Channel Islands have been inhabited from pre-historic times and various races have left behind traces of their civilizations, these including many Neolithic megaliths. Gauls preceded Roman and Frankish domination, but the Vikings, progenitors of the Normans, were the greatest of the invaders, and their descendants have influenced the Islands ever since. Many of the older people still speak Norman-French and Channel Islanders of native stock have the same names and characteristics as their Cotentin "cousins". Part of the Duchy of Normandy since about 933, the Islands began their connection with the Crown of England when Duke William II of Normandy assumed the kingship after the Conquest of 1066.

In 1341 King Edward III issued the most important of the charters granted to the Channel Islands. This confirmed the privileges, liberties, immunities and customs granted by his forebears and stated that the Islanders should continue to enjoy them freely without molestation by him, his heirs or officers. This charter has been renewed by successive sovereigns.

As a generality it may be said that the Channel Islands are self-governing although as Charles Cruickshank writes in "The German Occupation of the Channel Islands", acts of the United Kingdom parliament can apply to them but only by express provision.

At various times the French have tried to seize the Islands, the last occasion being in 1781. The Channel Islands were occupied by the Germans from 1940 to 1945, the only part of the British Isles to have fallen to the enemy during the Second World War.

Presiding over both the legislature and judicature of Jersey and Guernsey are Bailiffs, and each island also has a Lieutenant Governor who represents the Sovereign. The legislatures of Jersey, Guernsey and Alderney are known as the States while that of Sark is called the Chief Pleas. A President presides over Alderney affairs and a Seigneur over Sark's. The States of Jersey consist of 12 Senators, 12 Connetables who are elected as head of their parishes, 29 Deputies and the Attorney-General, Solicitor-General and the Dean, the last three having no vote. The Guernsey States of Deliveration are composed of 12 Conseillers, 32 Deputies, 10 Douzaine representatives, 2 representatives of the States of Alderney and Her Majesty's Procureur (Attorney-General) and Comptroller (Solicitor-General). There are 12 members of the States of Alderney, and the Chief Pleas of Sark comprise the Quarantaine, the holders of the original 40 divisions of land and 12 Deputies of the People. Apart from in the courts of first instance Justice is administered by judges known as Jurats, an ancient office, in Jersey, Guernsey and Alderney and by a Senechal in Sark. The ecclesiastical jurisdiction is that of the Bishop of Winchester, England, administered by Deans of Jersey and Guernsey.

Being under the influence of the sea the Islands enjoy a milder climate than either the South of England or northern France and are well suited for agriculture and horticulture. The main exports from Jersey are early potatoes, tomatoes, cut flowers and broccoli while Guernsey's staple industry is the export of glasshouse tomatoes, cut flowers also being exported. Although the Jersey and Guernsey cattle are famous through the world exports of these have declined in recent years. Finance, rich residents and tourism are also very important sources of revenue.

The geological formation of the Channel Islands is to the layman mainly granitic, and the approach to the coasts is rendered difficult by the frequency of outlying rocks and reefs as well as by the great range of the tides, one of the highest in the world, and by strong and diverse currents. The slope of the land is from North to South in Jersey, and the opposite in Guernsey. There are many valleys, and the coastlines are irregular and broken by numerous, mainly sandy bays or coves. Communications by sea and air between the United Kingdom and the Islands, and between the Islands and the Continent, are excellent. (All information above kindly provided by Max G. Lucas, St. Ouen, Jersey.)

North Americans are curious about the people of the Islands. How are Islanders different from those who live on the mainland? Payne's ARMORIAL has put it thusly: "They, (the Islanders) are a capable, knowledgeable and hardworking people with great and proverbial powers of memory, much and genuine hospitality, an innate and Hibernianesque wit with which is curiously blended the phlegm and frugality of the canny Scot ...an incurable mania for petty political intrigue and a native bravery."

In the 1600s the Governor of Cherbourg, France, was deploring the activity of the Islanders as privateers and noted their..."habit of encountering the dangers of the sea renders the natives very brave...excellent marksmen...always in a state of warfare, now against the customs house officers, now against the French commercial marine. A population of this character greatly enhances the natural strength of these Islands." The fact that they were among the very earliest settlers in the New World speaks volumes about their character.

What did the Islanders leave when they signed the indentures and manifests and sailed away from the Islands? They left quiet little towns like St. Peter Port, St. Sampson, St. Helier and St. Aubin or they left ten acre farms or fishing villages like St. Clements in Jersey. Their homes? In Jersey "buildings both in town and country are substantial and strong being all of stone...In the Parish of St. John on a hill called Mont Mado a rich quarry of excellent stone rising in great blocks, cut or shaped, like the Portland stone of England...the Mont Mado stone for corners, doors and windows, the ragstone for filling up the walls...makes a handsome show ...Rich merchants will have theirs faced with Mont Mado or Chausey stone...of a fine grain...a magnificence equal to a capital of a kingdom...Thatching which here is done with long, well-chosen wheat straw...laid on...cut so smooth and even... that the work not only looks good but will resist a storm of wind better than I have observed common tiling to do in England...These Jersey houses with proper care will stand some hundreds of years and would much surpass the slighter buildings of other countries." (Richard Warner) Although written several hundred years ago this is still true, and many Island homes of the 1600s are still in use today.

In Guernsey the homes were built with pink or brownish red stone from Cobo and Albecq, yellowish stone from L'Ancresse Bay, grey, blue and dark stone from other parts of the Island. Caen stone was used for dressing. The standard of workmanship was high. Stucco was also used. Roofs were of slate or red pantiles; galvanized metal was used on later buildings. (C.E. Brett)

What were the occupations on the Islands? They were farmers and fishermen, merchants, clerks, tailors, coopers, boot makers, boat builders, traders, privateersmen, smugglers and Navy men and all the usual occupations of the time were represented there including gold- and silver-smithing and pottery making. On both main Islands the culture was similar although Guernsey's comparative proximity to England made for a certain difference.

At one time in the 1700s the main business of the Islanders was knitting, hence the common term "jersey" for knitted goods. There was a period, too, when many Islanders were involved in some aspect of smuggling. This required casks, barrels and tubs, many of which were made in the Islands. Leather was used in the manufacture of the boots and shoes that were sent in such quantities to the New World. Ship builders, carpenters, sailmakers and smiths all did well in the Islands until the fisheries and boat businesses weakened in the middle 1800s.

Many a fortune was won and lost in the Maritimes by the Island firms. Sometimes the failures were due to the misjudgement of the businessmen in charge or caused by a season of very bad storms. In the times of privateers and pirates vessels might change hands half a dozen times or more in the course of a year or two at sea. No doubt Lloyds of London lost money several times on the ships of the Islands, however, raised to seafaring as the Island men were, there is little doubt that the bold and venturesome captains and the hardy men under them were the main reason for the financial success of many an ocean voyage of Jersey and Guernsey ships.

GROSNEZ CASTLE RUINS, JERSEY ST. SAVIOUR CHURCH, JERSEY

(Courtesy Margaret Turk)

ST. SAMPSON CHURCH, GUERNSEY

(Courtesy GRUT family of Guernsey)

LES FORGETTES, Castel, Guernsey, typical Guernsey house. (Courtesy Mr. Archambault, Racine, Wisc.)

THE CHANNEL ISLANDS, FICTION

BROSTER, D.K., SIR ISEMBRAS AT THE FORK
CLARE, Austin, LITTLE GATE OF TEARS
EDWARDS, W.A., A BLUE STOCKING
FERGUSON, John, DEATH COMES TO PERIGORD
FLETCHER, Inglis, LUSTY WIND FOR THE CAROLINAS
GOUDGE, Elizabeth, GREEN DOLPHIN STREET, and ISLAND MAGIC
HOPPIS, M., THE LOCKET
HUGO, Victor, TOILERS OF THE SEA
KAYE-SMITH, ---, THE GEORGE AND THE CROWN, about Sark Island
MARTIN, ---, CHILDREN OF THE EARTH
MACKENZIE, Compton, FAIRY GOLD
MATURIN, F., PETRONEL OF PARADIS
OXENHAM, John, four romances, including CARETTE OF SARK, and PEARL OF PERL ISLAND
PARKER, Sir Gilbert, A LADDER OF SWORDS, & BATTLE OF THE STRONG
PILGRIM, David, GRAND DESIGN and NO COMMON GLORY
REYNOLDS, Mrs. Baillie, SPELL OF SARNIA
ROBIN, Miss E. Gallienne, several stories
STRETTON, Hesba, DOCTORS DILEMMA
TICKET, Jerrard, ISLAND RESCUE, AN APPOINTMENT WITH VENUS, N.Y. 1952
WALLACE, H., TO PLEASURE MADAME

ARTISTS OF THE CHANNEL ISLANDS

BLAMPIED, Edmund, artist and illustrator of many books including TRAVELS WITH A DONKEY, By R.L. Stevenson; THE BODLEY HEAD LAD, 1931; HAND-PICKED HOWLERS, 1937; BOTTLED TRAVEL AND POLO: THE HOT DOGS: PETER AND WENDY, 1939; THE MONEY MOON, By Jeffrey FARNOL: CHRONICLES OF THE IMP: THE ROAD MENDER, By Michael Fearless; BLACK BEAUTY, By Anna Sewell; THE WAY OF AN EAGLE, By Ethel M. Dell; THE WOULD BE GOODS, By E.E. Nesbit, etc.

LANDER, John Helier, 1868-1944
LE CAPELAIN, Jean, 1812-1848

LE COUTEUR, Sir John, 1885-1925
LE HARDY, Thomas, miniaturist, b. 1771
LE LIEVRE, 1800s

LE MAISTRE, b. 1714

MILLAIS, Sir John E., 1829-1896
MONAMY, Peter, marine painter, 1689-1749
NAFTEL, Paul, 1800s
OULESS, Walter William, 1848-1898

POINDEXTER, Charles Henry, 1828-1905
COURTENAY, Henry, 1802-1890

****

SEE ALSO PAGE 481F, AND OTHER BIBLIOGRAPHY PAGES.

CHAPTER TWO, THE CHANNEL ISLANDS AND CANADA

"To leave your homeland for a better life in a new land doesn't mean that you don't regret the loss of your roots and your history. To want to leave doesn't change the sense of loss, the clinging to all that you once knew." (THE BLOOD RED DREAM, By Michael Collins)

Why did the Islanders leave their homes for North America and other places? The answers to this are many, because the reasons were varied, and differed according to the time, the people and the circumstances of the removal.

Three kinds of emigration were the most common: the men, the boys, and the families. The men were those involved in the fisheries; sailors, fishermen, captains, owners and partners in the fisheries and other businesses of the New World. The boys were lads in their teens, recruited from the quiet little towns and farms, apprenticed or indentured for from 4 to 7 years to a firm or a person in the Maritimes. When their time was up they secured their release and either continued in the fisheries, removed to other work, or sometimes, displeased with the New World, they returned to the Islands, to Great Britain or sailed to New Zealand or Australia.

The families who came over differed in many ways. Some were Huguenots who found the Islands too small for them. Other families were encouraged to come to Canada by sons already settled there in the various ports. Still other families came to recoup fortunes lost in business in the Islands, or to escape petty rivalries. At any rate, listed below are the main causes of Channel Island emigration to Canada.

1. Overcrowding. This has happened and still happens, with lack of lands to till, and other restrictions of the Islands' economy.

2. In the early 1600s, the Govenor of Jersey was Sir Walter Raleigh. He was interested in the development of Newfoundland and Virginia. This focused the Islanders' attention on the possibilities of the New World.

3. In the 1700s there was unrest in Europe. The seas were filled with ships trading and exploring around the world. For this surge of transportation a great many sailors were needed. The Islanders in large numbers joined the British Navy. Some were impressed when caught on ships and in ports out of the Islands, as press gangs were not allowed on the Islands. (Max Lucas)

4. In the late 1600s the Channel Islands began to be crowded with refugee Huguenots from France. This situation continued into the 1700s. Huguenots were being massacred in France after the Revocation of the Edict of Nantes, and the Islands became a much used bridge to safety. Most of the Huguenots

moved to other places, notably America, some taking with them many of the Islanders as friends, spouses and in-laws. While most of the Huguenots were headed for the New England Colonies, Virginia and the Carolinas, a few of them settled in Canada.

5. In the late 1700s oppressive measures were taken by the British Government to stop the enormous smuggling trade that centered in the south of England and the Channel Islands. Those who had profited by this business, even indirectly, were affected by the new laws, and forced to look for other employment. Cask and barrel makers were especially hard hit, as liquor was one of the main smuggled items.

6. By an act of Parliament passed in the 4th year of the reign of George III, it was proposed that vessels sailing from Jersey to Newfoundland and New England should first clear at a British Port. This was considered by the Islanders to be a base infringement of their freedom, unnecessary, and a great injustice. They believed that if carried out, it would hamper the large foreign trade of the Islanders. Several of their vessels were seized for not having carried out the letter of the law. This situation caused the removal of several families, no doubt.

7. In 1816 and 1817 there was a failure of the corn harvest in Europe. This had many repercussions, of course, and could have been for some families the last straw, especially those who had previously considered removal to North America.

8. In the first half of the 19th century, shipping and the North Atlantic fisheries were prospering. They peaked befor 1840, when ships were being built in some numbers in the Channel Islands, and their fisheries were doing a good portion of the North Atlantic business. By 1860, however, steamships had forced the sailing ships out of business in most cases, except for short hauls in the Maritimes. Only a few of the Channel Island firms managed to adapt, such as the Robin firm, which was re-organized several times. In the period from about 1850 to 1880, shipbuilding in the Channel Islands suffered a sharp decline. Many firms being involved in this, metal workers, rope and sailmakers, carpenters, smiths and so on, lost their jobs. Many persons and families then removed to Canada and the United States. Others went farther, to Australia and New Zealand. A banking crisis in 1873 added to the problems.

9. The New World had great opportunities for investment, and many Island families had sizable fortunes. Therefore,

some of the Islanders came to Canada with funds to start
businesses, to buy firms, to go into politics and civic
affairs. A few invested in ship-building and logging firms,
especially in Cape Breton and New Brunswick, where lumber
was readily available, and was low in cost.

Thus it can be readily seen that the reasons for resettlement in Canada depended on varied situations in each family.
Mostly, perhaps, the Islanders saw the opportunity for a fuller and more profitable life, perhaps with temporary hardships.
In the long run, though, a move to Canada promised them a quality of life they may not have been able to achieve in Europe.

Most of us have no idea exactly how our ancestors came to
North America. Via ship, of course, but what kind of vessel?
What year, what season of the year? From what port in Europe?
These details are usually unknown.

The first French and Channel Island ships were very small,
perhaps 30 to 40 feet long. It took a truly courageous sailor
to gamble his life on those huge Atlantic waves in such a vessel. The French ships were fairly high-sided, open decked,
and two or three masted, according to the port they were built
in.

The food was coarse and rough, the shelter minimal. It
boggles the mind, and wrings the heart to think of the many
voyages of Jersey and Guernsey folk that began with high hopes
and ended in the depths of the sea.

On early voyages, ship owners had a practical way to make
the voyage pay both ways. The Islanders left port crowded with
passengers, settlers for the New World, or fishermen, and returned later to Europe with a cargo of fish, oil and rum from
the West Indies.

Later settlers from the Islands went to Liverpool or London,
or other British ports and came to Canada on large steamships.
Small Jersey owned vessels continued to bring Islanders to
Gaspe up to the early years of the 20th century. Some of these
went on to Quebec and Montreal, where those with more distant
goals extended their journeys into the heart of Canada by horse,
railway and by lake vessels. Another route used was by way of
New York City, the Hudson Canal, and then on to Lake Ontario's
northern shore.

From London to Quebec in 1843 the trip took 4 to 6 weeks,
various arrangements being provided by the shipping companies.
First class involved cabins, with bedding and provisions supplied, and cost from 20 to 25 pounds. Intermediate travel,
with sleeping berth and provisions, cost 8 to 10 pounds. Emigrants who took their own provisions were provided with cooking and eating utensils, and could eat at the cost of about 2
or 3 pounds for the entire voyage!

In 1843, if the immigrant had capital, he could stop at the
office of the Crown Land Commissioner, and see what was for

sale. Government agents were stationed at Quebec, Montreal, Bytown (Ottawa), Kingston and Toronto. Quebec to Toronto travel was 590 miles, and was by way of the Rideau Canal, costing under 25 shillings, children under 12 being half-price. From Montreal to Kingston, 258 miles, by canal and river, 10 shillings. Kingston to Toronto was 7 shillings.

"The emigrant before going on board the steamer, should boil as much pork or beef as will serve him for a day or two, which he can do before leaving the ship; in a few minutes he can procure fresh bread; and if he has a large tin tea-pot, with a few tins, he can with ease get hot water in the steamer to make some tea, to refresh the members of his family on the way up."

Also, in 1843, there was estimated to be about 4 million acres of land, surveyed and unsurveyed, considered accessible, and waiting to be granted to settlers in Lower Canada. In Upper Canada, Ontario, 64 million acres were available for grants. The cost of land at this time was about 3 to 12 shillings per acre. A log house cost 20 pounds to build, barns and stables, 35-40 pounds. Workmen cost 2 shillings per day with room and board. There was an annual land tax of a penney an acre in Upper Canada!

There were regulations for the safety of passengers in the small ships of the 1800s. One reads: "No ship carrying passengers from any port or place in the United Kingdom or from the Islands of Guernsey, Jersey, Alderney, Sark or Man, to or for any port or place out of Europe, and not being within the Mediterranean Sea, shall proceed on her voyage with more persons on board than in the proportion of 3 persons to every five tons of the registered burden of such ship, the master and crew being included in such prescribed number, and that no such ship shall, whatever be the tonnage thereof, proceed in her voyage with more passengers on board than in the following proportion to the space occupied by them and appropriated for their use..." The master would be fined for taking more passengers than his ship was allowed. Doubtless this rule was not followed to the letter, as we note in some records of voyages that the ship appears to be heavily overloaded.

Voyages across the ocean lasted a long time. To the east coast of North America averaged about a month, to the West Indies, a little more time, to Central and South America, sometimes as much as three months, according to the currents and winds. To Africa, 12 weeks; to the Falkland Islands, 15 weeks; to Mauritius, 18 weeks; to Western Australia, 20 weeks; to New Zealand, 24 weeks. (This and the other voyage information above comes from A NEW GUIDE FOR EMIGRANTS, by J. Buxton Murray, Glasgow, Scotland, 1843)

The Rev. John Bridger of St. Nicholas Church, Liverpool, England, was the Emigration Chaplain, and encouraged, with the help of a committee of highborn and notable women, the emigration of young women to Canada, protection was given them at all points, "respectible lodgings were promised, jobs, reduced railway fares to get to Liverpool, England, and instructions on what to bring. Recommendations were required from a lady friend, an employer, a doctor and an clergyman."

Some group settlements were successful, some were not. The Barr Colony settlement was not a notable success, but there must have been few settlers who returned to Europe, in spite of the unpromising beginning.

Channel Islanders have acquitted themselves extremely well in Canada, and in the United States. Numbered among their descendants here are a surprising number of professional men, heads of businesses, directors of companies, civil servants, generals, an ambassador or two, a Vice Admiral, authors, mayor, members of parliament, influential persons of every rank, and thousands of "salt of the earth" farmers and fishermen. Count yourself most fortunate if your ancestors came from the Channel Islands to North America!

CHANNEL ISLANDS AND CANADA, CHRONOLOGY

1504 Channel Islanders believed to be on the small Norman sailing vessels that were in the habit of visiting the coast of Newfoundland and adjacent waters from as early as 1504. (ENGLAND IN AMERICA, by Tyler, Vol. 4)

1534 Jacques Cartier of France landed on the Gaspe coase of what is now Quebec. Marguerite Syvret in JERSEY SETTLEMENTS IN GASPE, suggests that among Cartiers' crew were some Channel Islanders. Guillaume de Guernseze represented that Island, and perhaps from Jersey were those named Antoine, Fleury, Olliver, Le Breton and Colas.

1562 Channel Island fishermen noted on the Grand Banks, south of Newfoundland.

1600 Sir Walter Raleigh became Governor of the Channel Islands. He was much interested in Newfoundland and Virginia colonization. No doubt his interest and influence spurred on the Islanders to become more active in the New World.

1608 "Thomas Le Marchant, agent in Spain of James De Beauvoir, . . . later traded on his own account with Newfoundland; for on June 6, 1608, the Royal Court of Guernsey granted him permission to transport out of the Island, as provision for his ship--aux parties de Terre Neuve--ten thousand biscuits; provided that, should during the following summer, the harvest prove poor and the necessity of the island require it, he should supply 80 quarters of wheat, local measure, of good quality, to be sold to the Islanders at the current prive of 12 sous sterling per quarter." (OLD TIME NEWFOUNDLAND, papers of H.W. Le Messurier, edited by C.R. Fay, 1955)

1650 By this time there were a number of ships, manned by

Channel Islanders that sailed between the Channel Islands, Newfoundland and New England. Marblehead, Mass. was their largest settlement in the American Colonies. Many of the Islanders by this time may have settled in small coves around southern and eastern Newfoundland.

1667 This year was formed the Hudson's Bay Company, in London, England. One of the founders and directors was Sir George Carteret of Jersey, "the guiding mind in the beginning of the enterprise." (THE REMARKABLE HISTORY OF THE HUDSON'S BY COMPANY, by George Bryce, London, 1900)

1717 These Channel Islanders, in this year, were involved with the Newfoundland trade and fisheries; Seale, Patriarche, Chevallier, Chastray, Denton, Orengette, Janvrin, Carteret, Dean, Pipon, Lempriere, Auley (or Anley?), Le Bailly, Nicolle, Messervy, Marett, Maugier, Brown, Touzell, Martell, Seward and others." (A.C. Saunders, Co. Jers. Bull)

1750 One hundred and eighty-four persons, Huguenots from Jersey, removed to Halifax, NS.

1769 Philip Messervy, born Jersey mar Suzanne Dennis, and removed to Newfoundland.

1778 Thirteen hundred men in this year left the Channel Islands for the summer to fish on the Grand Banks, and to do other work in the Maritimes.

1788 Philip Ingouville of Jersey settled this year in Cape Breton Island, NS.

1790 William Simon, born in Guernsey, settled before this date near Shipshead, Gaspe, Indian Cove. The land where he lived is now a Park.

1806 A shipload of 73 people from the Island of Guernsey landed at Charlottetown, Prince Edward Island.

1812 Sir Isaac Brock, of Guernsey, the Hero of Upper Canada, died on Queenston Heights, Ontario, near Niagara Falls, after an impressive career in the British Army. He undoubtedly changed the course of history in Canada.

1813 Peter La Serre of Guernsey was a surgeon, and a member of the Council of the District of Assiniboia, in Rupert's Land, Western Canada, where he died soon after at Red River. (THE CANADIAN NORTHWEST, ITS EARLY DEVELOPMENT, by Prof. E.H. Oliver, 1914, Ottawa)

1820 Over 50 Jersey and Guernsey surnames appear on a Petition at Gaspe this year, requesting help from the Government to control American fishing vessels off the Gaspe shore.

1830 Philip Low, a native of Jersey, was the son of an Army officer. He studied law in Toronto, and was called to the bar in 1835, practising in Picton, Ontario.

1845 H.T.D. Le Vesconte, with the Franklin Expedition to Artic Canada, perished near Point Hall, in King William Land.

1854 Sir Gaspard Le Marchant of Guernsey became Lt.-Gov. of Nova Scotia; had been formerly Governor of Newfoundland.

1870 George Machon, resident of Ontario, born in Jersey, served with Col. Wolseley's outfit in Western Canada, passing through the pioneer towns of Fisher's Landing, Brainard, Pembina, Portage La Prairie, and the Battle River District. At about this time there were ten or fifteen other Jerseymen beginning to settle around Winnipeg. Thomas Agnew settled at Ft. Garry in 1876.

1858 David Le Neveu was born in Jersey about 1819. He reached California in a yacht in 1851, in company with some friends and started a business in Marysville, Calif., a Gold Rush town. He later left California and settled in Victoria, BC, organized a grain and feed business. There he also took part in the setting up of Victoria as an incorporated city, whose first election took place in 1862.

The GUERNSEY MILITIA in 1750 includes the following names of members of a troop of horse under Major Peter Carey. (COLLECTIONS FOR THE HISTORY OF HAMPSHIRE, by Richard Warner, an old book possibly printed in the 1700s)

ANDROS, Charles and John
BONAMY, John
BRETON, Nicholas
BROCK, Capt. John
CHIVRET, Hilary, poss SYVRET?
COLLINGS, Edward
DE CARTERET, Charles and Peter
DE GARIS, Nicholas
DE JERSEY, Hilary and Peter
DE PUTRON, Daniel
DOBREE, Isaac, Thomas and John
DOBREE, Peter, son of Nicholas
DU FOUR, Paul
GOODWIN, Samuel
GOSSELIN, John
GUILE, Nicholas
HARRIS, John
KENNET, William
LE COCQ, Peter and Samuel
LE LACHEUR, John
LE MARCHANT, Col. Elisha, William and Thomas
LE MESURIER, John Sr.
LE PAGE, Samuel and Peter
LE RAY, James
MARQUANT, John and Abraham
MAUGER, Nicholas
MELLISH, John
OLLIVIER, Thomas Jr.
PEPPER, Samuel
PRIAULX, Elisha
RETILLEY, Nicholas
RIVOIRE, Simon
ROUGET, Peter
SUTHERN, Henry
TARDIF, Nicholas
TOURGIS, Peter
WOOD, Joseph and John

CHAPTER THREE, THE ISLANDERS IN CANADA

"From Le Vesconte Pt. in the Arctic to Dumaresq River in Australia. . . to Robinstown on Cape Breton, Jerseymen have left their names dotted on all the maps of the world." (G.R. Balleine, Biographical Dictionary)

It seems quite certain that Channel Islanders were in the St. Lawrence Gulf from very early times. Thomas Peddle, of Augusta, Maine, descendant of very early arrivals in Newfoundland from the Channel Islands and Bristol, believes that his ancestors arrived in Cuper's Cove, fished, farmed, made tubs and barrels, and mined coal on a very small scale. The latter trade was thought to have been learned by the Channel Islanders in the mines of Wales. He believes they were only preceded there by the Scandinavians and the Basques. If they did precede Sir John Guy in 1610, as he believes, the Peddles are indeed one of the earliest arrivals in the New World, possibly before the Pilgrims of Massachusetts.

A large proportion of the young men of the Channel Islands went each spring in years past to Newfoundland and other parts of the Maritimes to fish and perform other duties for the Jersey firms. Young lads were signed on with a form called an indenture, an agreement to work for very low wages and their keep, for up to four years, while learning the varied work of the Channel Island firms in North America. These agreements had been in force in the Channel Islands at least as far back as the 1600s. Several are to be found in the papers of the Jerseyman Philippe Langlois, called in Salem, Massachusetts, Philip English. He was born in Trinity, Jersey in 1651.

The use of indentures by Channel Island firms continued until early in the 1900s. One, signed by Wilfred Brideaux, then of Jersey, latterly of Ottawa, Ontario, was signed with the Robin, Jones and Whitman Company, successors to the firm of Charles Robin. Brideaux agreed to serve the company in 1921 for four years, in various places in Atlantic Canada. The language of the indenture is below, slightly condensed:

"This indenture witnesseth that Wilfred Philip Brideaux, age 18, son of Philip Brideaux now residing at Jersey. . . doth bind himself Apprentice, with the consent of his said father. . . unto Robin, Jones and Whitman, Ltd. of Halifax, N.S., Canada, merchants. . . to serve them in Canada from the first day of April next, and during the full term of four years next ensuing. . . during all which time, he the said apprentice his said masters shall and will faithfully serve, their secrets keep, their lawful commands everywhere gladly obey, and diligently and carefully demean and behave himself towards them. He shall not do, or willingly suffer to be done by others, any hurt, prejudice or damage to the goods and merchandises, or other affairs of his said Masters, neither will he waste or lend them unlawfully to others. . . He shall not commit fornication, nor contract matrimony,

within the said term. Without license of his said Masters, he
shall neither buy nor sell. He shall not absent himself by
day or by night from his said Master's service, without their
leave, on pain of making up every day he absented himself, at
the expiration of said term. He shall not haunt ale houses,
taverns, play houses, or any other place of debauchery, but in
all things behave himself during the said term, as a good and
faithful Apprentice ought to do; and the said Masters shall
pay or cause to be paid unto their said Apprentice the sum of
eight pounds for the first year, fourteen pounds for the second year, twenty-two pounds for the third and thirty-six
pounds for the fourth and last year, all in British Sterling
or equivalent in Canadian currency, a portion of which consideration money shall be used to provide sufficient wearing
apparel and necessaries for the use of the said Apprentice
during the said term..." (Wilfred Brideaux, Ottawa, Ont.)

If the lad did not give satisfaction, he was to be returned
to Jersey at his father's expense. A fine of 50 dollars was
to be paid if the lad left the firm before the expiration of
his term. This form of servitude was accepted by thousands
of boys and girls in the Channel Islands, for a chance to
experience the pleasure and problems of the New World. In
1752, an advertisement in a Guernsey newspaper asked for
Guernsey boys and girls willing to go to America.

THE ISLANDERS IN CANADA, JOURNAL OF CAPT. JOHN VIBERT

Jean Vibert, baptized in 1793 in St. Mary, Jersey, removed
to Gaspe with his wife, who is thought to have been Marguerite
Arthur, and his children. One son, John Arthur Vibert, born
1827, was a seaman, and soon progressed to being master of
several vessels. He was employed by the Nicolle Company, by
the Collas Company, and by John Le Boutillier's fishery firm
in Gaspe. His journal shows voyages to nearly all the large
ports on the Atlantic, to the Mediterranean, to Denmark, to
the United States, and to many ports in the West Indies and
South America, in the years from about 1845 on.

His routes led again and again from Newfoundland to Spain
and back to Newfoundland, mostly for the salt necessary to
the cod fisheries, but cargoes also included fish, oil, wine,
molasses, rum, clothing and supplies for the fishermen in
Gaspe, Newfoundland, Nova Scotia, P.E.I. and New Brunswick.

His journal, some thirty pages, is in the Dominion Archives
at Ottawa, Ontario and makes interesting reading. It begins
with the ending of a voyage he had taken, with a landing in
England. By cutter he proceeded to Jersey and looked for a
berth on a ship. He found one on the ELIZA, due to the illness of its mate, and sailed in the early 1840s (?) for Fortune Bay, Jersey Harbor, Newfoundland, one of the Nicolle
establishments. In 20 days they were in port.

From Newfoundland they went to Oporto, unloaded the fish and took in salt, arriving in less than 20 days. After about ten voyages between Cadiz, Spain, Oporto, Portugal, Civita Vecchia and Naples, Italy, and up to Newfoundland, they varied the course to Cape Breton, England, Jersey and Porto Rico. Capt. Vibert finally got to Gaspe, where his family was living, and began to work for the Le Boutillier firm there.

Other ports visited were Rio, Boston, Baltimore, Christiensund (Norway), Havana, Bahia and Malta. One trip to South America and back by way of Chesapeake Bay gave the Captain some anxious moments, but with true Channel Island fortitude and ingenuity he managed to come through safely.

"Next morning we were off Jersey about 10 A.M., took a pilot, and at high water ran in the harbour, discharged the cargo, screwed it in tubs, and sailed for Rio de Janeiro where we arrived after a smart, fine passage. Took in cargo of coffee for Baltimore where we arrived after a smart passage of 38 days, delivered cargo of coffee, and took in cargo of breadstuffs for Trinidad. Four of the crew deserted, having been coaxed or decoyed by the crimps, leaving 3 months' pay behind; so I shipped four more in their place, to whom I had to pay $30 advance before leaving, to the Boarding Master; then made sail and started down Chesapeake Bay. Anchored the first night, the wind being ahead, I noticed that the four men I had shipped were on the watch for a chance to desert the ship, so I kept on deck all night on the watch, and they perceived that. They went below.

The next morning we got under way at daylight to beat down the wind, the wind still blowing up the Bay. At about sunset we anchored in Annapolis Roads, blowing a fresh southerly breeze with squalls of rain at times. I had made up my mind to keep watch myself, being persuaded that the four Baltimore men were still on the watch for a chance to get away from the ship. The weather being warm, I laid down on the skylight, taking a turn on the deck now and then. About 11 P.M. heavy rain squall came on, so I went down the Cabin till it was over, and fell in a doze. When I heard a step on deck, I jumped up in the companion and saw a man near it. I asked him what he wanted...I told him nobody had ordered him to keep watch and to go below, that I was keeping watch...I went off into a doze...I was awakened by the noise of the davit falls lowering the boat which was hoisted on the side...made a start for the companion, which I found closed and fastened from on deck...made a rush for the starboard door; the upper hinge gave way, and the door, so I crawled through and got on deck...I jumped in the boat with the tackle fall on my arm to drive the two men in the boat on board; but, before I could do this, the man at the bow tackle let go by the rim and down went the boat in the water, and then the two who were at the tackle falls, lowering her, both jumped down in the

boat, and there I was with these four rascals alone in the
boat holding her by the stern tackle, and the only one I saw
on deck was my old cook and steward to whom I passed three of
the oars; the fourth was hauled back by the men in the boat
before the cook could get it up.

Two of them came aft and cut the tackle fall over my hands,
and threw me down in the bottom of the boat and the boat was
adrift. When I saw that, I asked them to scull alongside and
put me on board and they could go where they liked with the
boat. "Oh no, Captain, we will put you on shore so that we
will have time to get away from you for if we put you on
board, you would soon have that other boat after us." So I
sat down. . . they tore up one of the bottom boards and tied
a blanket to it for a sail, and steared with the oar, and
this way the boat ran up the Bay at a pretty good rate, blowing a fresh gale. . .

They hauled the boat towards the shore and landed her bow
on the beach. . . put me on the beach clear of the water. . .
shoved off. . . until they disappeared in the darkness of the
night. It was then about 1:30 A.M. . . began tramping along
the beach toward the Annapolis Light which was visible after
tramping for about an hour.

I came to a point and there I discovered that I was surrounded by water and was on an Island without inhabitants.
Then I stood for a few minutes looking toward the Lighthouse,
and the water that separated me from it. . . I noticed a dark
speck on the water. . . could just make out that it was a
boat, and that it was nearing me. . . I jumped into it. . .
a fishing boat which had driven from the opposite shore near
the Lighthouse. . . I found two oars in her, so poled her in
deep water, then began pulling the boat with the two oars
towards the Lighthouse, scrambled up the cliff and knocked. . .
at daylight before sunrise, I was on board (my ship) again and
found the pilot and two mates asleep. They had not stirred a
step to get the other boat out. . . took breakfast, and went
on shore at Annapolis in the Lighthouse boat, and called on
Admiral Porter.

I asked him to assist me to capture my boat back, and he
advised me to wire Baltimore Police to be on the watch for my
boat, giving them a description of her;. . . At 4:00 P.M. I
was in Baltimore and went at once to the Police Station where
they told me that they had received my message. . . Next morning at daylight. . . "Get up, Captain, we have caged the
birds". . . the next morning they were brought by the police
on board in irons. . . I asked them if they were going to do
their duty. . . so pointed out to them what I would do at the
least sign of insubordination, showing them two six chamber
revolvers that I would use without scruple; but on the contrary, if they behaved themselves properly and did their duty

manfully. . . they would be well treated. . ."
The vessel reached Port of Spain, Trinidad, St. Thomas, and then headed for Gaspe, where the four men deserted. The journal is well worth reading in the full.

The brig JAMES, 213 tons, built at Ship Harbour, NS 1826 by Peter John Brouard of Guernsey. F. Polli, artist, Trieste, Italy 1828. (Courtesy of Nova Scotia Museum, Halifax, NS)

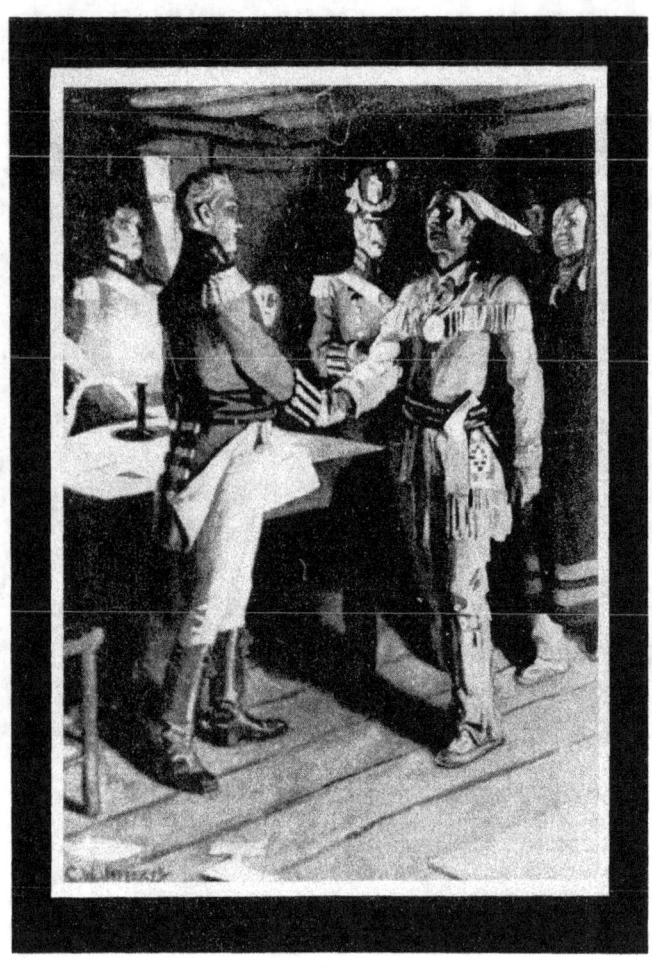

THE MEETING OF BROCK AND TECUMSEH

From a colour drawing by C.W. Jeffreys
(from TECUMSEH, by Ethel Raymond, Toronto, 1915)

General Sir Isaac Brock has been called the Hero of Upper Canada. This great general, born in Guernsey in 1787, also the birth year of Napoleon and Wellington, joined the British Army at the age of 15. The Le Brocq family was long established in Guernsey. (Son of John Brock & Eliz.DeLisle)

"Unlike his predecessor, Sir Francis Gore, Brock was convinced war with the United States was inevitable. There was a hangover of bitterness and rancor from the rebellion of 1776, and there were trade difficulties which the British Government made no serious effort to resolve; England was too busy with Napoleon to concern herself with the affairs of the colony."

"At that period Canada had almost no money with which to meet the expenditures of war. The few fortifications were incapable of resolute siege. The regular troops in Ontario numbered possible 4,000, and these were expected to protect a population of a little over 400,000."

"Somehow, largely through the energy and efficiency of Isaac Brock, these handicaps were overcome. When the American Militia was all set to capture Canada from Detroit, Brock neatly turned the tables by capturing Detroit. For this and his other services he was created a Knight of the Bath, just two months before he fell, mortally wounded on the Niagara frontier..."

"The British House of Commons erected a monument to his memory in St. Paul's Cathedral, and a fine shaft at Queenston Heights was raised in 1824. Sixteen years later this was blown up by the Fenians, but was rebuilt and stands today." (All the above from Philip Luce)

In order to get a fuller picture of the situation it is necessary to go back to August of 1812, when as Governor of Upper Canada, Brock, at the Assembly of Upper Canada, (composed to some extent of American sympathizers) forced through the necessary money bills, and then dismissed the Assembly. Although this appeared to rather high-handed action, the loyal Executive council supported him and he then proclaimed martial law. As General, he assembled troops and supplies which he had brought to Burlington Bay. From the Bay he marched his men across the Niagara Peninsula to the Long Point area, on Lake Erie.

From an historical Atlas of Norfolk County, the following account is taken, being the reminiscences from the life of Col. Titus Williams of Port Rowan, Ontario. Col. Williams was a loyal supporter of Brock, when many of the citizenry appeared to be indifferent whether they preferred to be under the American flag, or to remain British. There were powerful ties between southern Ontario and the United States, ties of kinship and of mercantile interests. Many farmers were highly reluctant to go to war. A few Canadians were working subrosa to deliver the area into American hands. It appears now that the single act of Brock's taking Detroit rerouted the course of Canadian history.

"Colonel Bostwick and Lt. Williams were ordered to return home (from Oxford, Ont) and warn out the Militia, and march them to Dover (Port Dover), where they would be joined by the Regulars. While they were organizing the force, the Regulars and a troop of cavalry (Merritt's) passed them on their way to Dover."

"On the arrival of the Norfolk Militia at that port, they were inspected by General Brock and his two aides-de-camp, after which he delivered a short address, calling on the men to defend their homes and families against the invaders. He stated that he wanted only one hundred men at that time, no married men were to be selected, and only one man from each family. Lt. Williams was requested to select the quota. Among the men who volunteered was a man named Cole, who was blind in his left eye. When objected to, he replied. . . that when taking aim, he would be saved the trouble of shutting his eye, and for that reason could shoot more rapidly than the others! This so pleased General Brock that he allowed him to go. Everything being in readiness, the force embarked in boats for Detroit, but remained at Sandwich two weeks before crossing (the Detroit River)."

"While on parade there one morning the Indians under Tecumseh appeared, and on seeing the Red Coats, gave a yell which made many of the recruits fairly jump. The day after the arrival of the Indians, the force crossed the river, when General Hull surrendered Detroit and the State of Michigan to the General commanding Her Majesty's forces!' (ILLUSTRATED HISTORICAL ATLAS, H.R. Page & Co., Haldimand, Norfolk Counties, Toronto, 1879, reprint by Mark Cumming, Stratford, Ontario)

"Brock had reason to feel elated. Machilimackinac and Fort Dearborn, (Chicago) had fallen to the British, ensuring them all Michigan. The lakes were theirs. Elation, however was shortlived when he (Brock) learned that Governor Gen. Sir George Prevost had arranged an indefinite armistice with the Americans." (Niagara Records, Archives, Ottawa)

This respite, which enabled the Americans to distribute troops and supplies, was nearly a disaster to Brock, with dwindling men and money. After the capture of Detroit, Brock lost no time, but went directly back to the Niagara frontier, where American troops were gathering, and some inroads had been made on Canadian territory.

At three in the morning of Oct. 13, 1813, after writing dispatches till late at night, Brock was awakened by guns. He left Gen. Shaeffe to guard Fort George, and galloped off, resplendant in his gold and scarlet uniform to head his own 49th Regiment at Queenston, Ont. It is said that he stopped for a moment at the home of Sophia Shaw, his fiancee, who was visiting at the Powell home near Queenston. On arrival at the Heights, his men welcomed him, much heartened by his appearance in the face of 4,000 Americans now visible in the early light, embarking in many small boats. They soon stormed ashore.

Brock was shortly felled by an American rifleman, and carried to a nearby farmhouse. . . There he was dressed in a private's uniform to conceal his identity, and the fact that he was mortally wounded.

In spite of their advantage of numbers the Americans were unable to make much headway. They became overwhelmed with confusion in mid-afternoon, when circled and taken in the rear by the forces of Maj. Gen. Shaeffe, which had come to the aid of the Brock forces. The Americans were routed, 958 being taken prisoner, in contrast to the Canadian and British casualties, less than 150.

Soon a temporary truce was called, and General Brock and his aide-de-camp, McDonnell, felled the same day, were buried in the York Bastion at Fort George, where the bodies lay until 1824. They were then transferred to a vault on Queenston Heights, and later to a cemetery on the property of J.M. Bright, the former Alexander Hamilton Mansion. From this cemetery they were finally interred in the present monument in Queenston Heights, a 196 foot stone column topped by the figure of Brock, in 1856.

Although active in the War of 1812 during only its first few months, Sir Isaac Brock set a strong example to the beset territory of Upper Canada. Without his ability and foresight it is quite possible that the border between Canada and the United States might have been somewhat different than it is today.

"In the early 1900s, J.W.L. Forster of Toronto journeyed to Guernsey Island to paint a copy of the portrait of Sir Isaac Brock. The artist was introduced to Brock's nieces and heirs, the Misses Tupper of St. Peter Port. They gave Forster the original chalk drawing, and the only authentic portrait of the general, as well as his uniform, perforated by musket balls, all now in our Public Archives at Ottawa." (Peter Almond, Toronto, Ontario)

There is a great deal of information available in books, manuscripts, etc. on Sir Isaac Brock, including the following short list.

BATTLE OF QUEENSTON HEIGHTS, Leaflet available at the Brock Monument.
GENERAL BROCK, Vol. 9, MAKERS OF CANADA, By Lady Edgar, Toronto, 1906.
TECUMSEH, Vol. 17, CHRONICLES OF CANADA, edited by George Wrong and H.M. Langton, Part V, THE RED MAN IN CANADA, TECUMSEH, by Ethel T. Raymond.
WESTERN ONTARIO AND THE FRONTIER, by Fred Landon, Toronto, Ont., 1941.
LIFE AND TIMES OF MAJOR GENERAL SIR ISAAC BROCK, by D.B. Read, Toronto, 1894.

Carteret, Sir George, was born in Jersey about 1609, one of England's early Empire builders. While he is more frequently written of in connection with the State of Jersey, he was vitally involved in Canada as well, in the organization of the Hudson's Bay Company. He was also treasurer and Navy comptroller under King Charles of England, and had several other irons in the fire, such as flood control in Ireland, mining in Windsor Forest, and dairying settlements on the coast of North Carolina.

Carteret was an able, vigorous and ambitious man, with a thirst for new experiences, if only vicariously. Although it is doubtful that he ever came to North America, except possibly for youthful service in the Newfoundland fleet, he had the vision to see great possibilities for England in the New World.

Foresight, imagination and money are three ingredients necessary for a successful enterprise, in the 1600s as well as today. These three attributes were responsible for the success of many Channel Islanders in Canada. The Hudson's Bay Company today in Canada, is the same company formed in London in 1667, and the original papers of the organization can be seen there. The story of this firm has an intriguing beginning in the very heart of Canada.

The French had been harvesting furs from the eastern half of what was to become Canada for about a hundred years, by then, noting enroute that the more northerly gathered furs were often of somewhat better quality, but they were more than willing to take whatever the Indians brought to them. Young Frenchmen began to take an interest in the sources of these furs, taking up Indian life, as courreurs du bois, woods runners. In large canoes, with the Indians, or alone, they paddled up the streams and lakes of the north, established trading places, bought the furs with trade goods, and brought them back to Montreal. There the furs were taken to the licensees who were allowed to deal in furs. The word licensee is the key to this story.

Exploring and fur gathering seemed to go together, at least they seemed so to Pierre Esprit Radisson and his brother-in-law, Medart Chouart des Groseilliers. These two men were traversing the country west of the Great Lakes to enlarge the area from which furs could be brought to Montreal. They returned triumphantly in 1656 with a tremendous load of furs on 50 canoes. Back they went to the wilderness and began to plot out a plan to get even more of the wonderful furs of the north country, and get them out to the Atlantic without the arduous trip across what is now Northern Quebec and Northern Ontario. Their plan was to use Hudson's Bay. Ships could go directly to a port on the Bay, bringing cheap trade goods, collecting the furs, then go directly to Europe.

In spite of the next great load of good furs brought back by the two, the then governor of New France, Pierre de Voyer, shortsighted and greedy, used their unauthorized departure in 1659 as the excuse for seizing their cargo, and fined them.

Radisson and Groseilliers were furious about this, and attempted through the French government to get redress. This was refused. In Port Royal, Nova Scotia, they secured a New England ship captained by Zachariah Guillaume, Gillam, and persuaded him to take them north past Labrador. At Hudson Strait the captain decided not to risk his ship among the floating icebergs, so turned back, to the disappointment of the adventurers. (Guillaume has been a Channel Island surname, but no verification was found for this Guillaume-Gillam)

The next year, 1664, they were still in New England, no doubt still simmering about their mistreatment in New France, and met up with someone, possibly a Carteret, or another Channel Islander who was interested in their idea.

At this time the Carterets were involved in organizing a settlement in New Jersey, and in order to do this there must have been some agents of the Carterets in New England. (Hundreds of Jersey and Guernsey folk were settled at that time in Massachusetts, Maine and New Hampshire, see QAAM) The Jerseymen in New England were also at this time trying to devise a way to get control of New Amsterdam, New York, from the Dutch.

The two Frenchmen were induced to leave New England and go to London to discuss the project with members of the court. At this time Sir George Carteret of Jersey was the Vice Chamberlain to the King and Treasurer of the Navy. The two men embarked, were captured by a Dutch ship, landed on the coast of Spain, and finally reached England. Through the influence of Carteret they obtained an audience with King Charles in 1666, and he promised them a ship as soon as possible, to proceed with their plan. There was a two year delay, and then an audience was obtained with Prince Rupert, the King's cousin, who was very interested. English Kings in the past were deeply involved in commerce of many kinds, the Duke of York frequently attending directors meetings of various companies, in order to further, of course, the Royal fortunes.

In the stock books that survive of this early Canadian firm, some important stockholders are noted. First on the list is the name of His Royal Highness, the Duke of York. The second stockholder was Prince Rupert, and his stock was paid for in the next two years with the exception of a hundred pounds, which he transferred to Sir George Carteret "who evidently was the guiding mind in the beginning of the enterprise." (THE REMARKABLE HISTORY OF THE HUDSON'S BAY COMPANY, by George Bryce, 1900, and THE ROMANCE OF LABRODOR, by Wilfred Grenfell) Three earls were stockholders. Sir George Carteret had between six and seven hundred pounds worth of stock. Sir John Robinson, Sir Robert Vyner, and Sir Peter Colleton (one of the eight Lords Proprietors of the Carolinas) were some of the other stockholders. Sir Peter made a payment of 96 pounds to the French explorers. Whether this is the sum total they were paid for their ingenious idea is not known.

Two ships were obtained for the first expedition. One, the EAGLET, with Capt. Stannard, proceeded as far as the Hudson Strait, then returned to London, as the captain did not believe the enterprise was a sound one. The other ship was in the command of Zachariah Gillam, Captain several years before of the ship that led the Expedition of 1664. His new ship, THE NONSUCH, ketch, was one of the King's vessels.

"It was in June 1668 that the vessels sailed from Gravesend, on the Thames, and proceeded on their journey. Groseilliers was aboard the NONSUCH, and Radisson was on the EAGLET. The NONSUCH found the Bay, discovered little more than half a century before by Hudson, and explored by Button, Fox and James, the last named less than 40 years before. Captain Gillam is said to have sailed as far north as 75 degrees in Baffin Bay, though this is disputed, and then to have returned into Hudson Bay, where turning southward, he reached the bottom of the Bay on Sept. 29th. Entering a stream, the Nemisco, on the southeast corner of the Bay, a point probably not less than 150 miles from the nearest French possessions in Canada, the party took possession of it, calling it after the name of their distinguished patron, Prince Rupert's River."

Here at their camping place, they met with the natives of the district, probably a branch of the Swampy Crees. With the Indians they held a parley, and came to an agreement by which they were allowed to occupy a certain portion of territory. With busy hands they went to work, built a stone fort, in Lat. 51 degrees, 20 min., Long. 78 degrees W., which, in honour of their gracious sovereign, they called "Charles Fort." (Bryce)

Here the men passed a long cold winter, but in April the weather turned surprisingly good, and they left the bay, sailing south to Boston, from which port they crossed to England and reported to the company on what they had done.

The 400 year history of the Hudson Bay Company, still a big business in western Canada, is well known, fully documented, and written up in countless books. Its amalgam with the Norwesters, its main competition, ensured the continuation of the business. The fur trade, the men who collected the skins, the Indians who did the trapping, the fort built to hold and protect the produce and the men involved in the commerce, the half-breeds who grew up in the trade, all these were very important parts of the growth and settlement of Western Canada. This historical train of action grew from the ideas of two disgruntled explorers, Radisson and Groseillers, and from the farsightedness, imagination and money of Sir George Carteret, a Jerseyman.

ADAM, Graeme Mercer, THE CANADIAN NORTHWEST, Toronto, 1885.
BRYCE, George, THE REMARKABLE HISTORY OF THE HUDSON'S BAY COMPANY, London, 1900.
GRENFELL, Wilfred, ROMANCE OF LABRADOR, and his other books.
KILBOURNE, Wm. Edward, THE WORLD AND ITS PEOPLE, New York and Toronto, 1967.
MCKAY, Douglas, THE HONOURABLE COMPANY.
NUTE, Grace, CAESARS OF THE WILDERNESS, New York, 1943.
WILLSON, Beckles, THE GREAT COMPANY.
WOODCOCK, George, THE HUDSON'S BAY CO., New York.

THE ISLANDERS IN CANADA, NOTABLES

DURELL, Philip, Vice-Admiral in the British Navy.
    Durell was born in 1707 in St. Heliers, Jersey and entered the Navy very young, as was the custom then. He was a midshipman on the frigate SEAHORSE, commanded by his uncle, Capt. Thomas Durell, hero of a famous duel between two ships, the KENT and the Spanish ship, PRINCESA.
    In the middle 1700s, England was in the throes of wresting from France the Canadian Maritimes, now called Atlantic Canada. Louisbourg, the famous fortress of the French on Cape Breton Island, was said to be impregnable. Its great harbour sheltered many privateersmen who preyed on Atlantic shipping. Durell, in command of the ELTHAM, was a part of the first successful attack on Louisbourg. In this connection, see also Nathaniel Messervy.
    Due to political maneuvering, Louisbourg was returned to the French, and was then rebuilt. It later had to be retaken, with great losses. Durell was also on hand for this second reduction of the fortress, along with the New Englander, Messervy.
    Durell's next trial of strength was the taking of Quebec city, and in this campaign, Durell got off to a bad start, allowing a large French convoy to move up the St. Lawrence River three days ahead of his forces.
    Quebec is nearly a thousand miles up the St. Lawrence, whose shoals, reefs, currents and fogs are still snags for the unwary seaman, and pilots are needed. Nevertheless, Durell managed to bring his ships to about 60 miles below Quebec. The outcome of the battle between Wolfe and Montcalm on the Plains of Abraham, of course, made this daring campaign up the river most worthwhile, and on his return to England in 1861, he was appointed Port Admiral of Plymouth. Later he was named Commander-in-chief in the Maritimes, where he died in 1776 and was buried in St. Paul's Church, Halifax, Nova Scotia. He was married three times; to his cousin, Madeleine Sausmarez of Guernsey, ---Skey, and to the widow of Capt. Wittewronge Taylor. His only child, a daughter, mar Rev. Thomas Warwick.

(Balleine, BIOGRAPHICAL DICTIONARY)

DU VAL, Peter John
　　Du Val, of Huguenot stock, was said to have been born in Jersey. He was a captain for the Janvrin company in Jersey, buying salt in Spanish ports, and carrying it to Jersey and other places, where it was much used in the cod fisheries. Du Val received a privateering license against the Republic of Batavia in 1830, which was signed by King George III. He beseiged the Harbour of Bayonne in 1805 and served the British in the War of 1812 by preying on American shipping from a base in Bermuda. Captured by the Yankee privateer ship PAUL JONES in 1812, he was released when the ship was retaken by HMS ORPHEUS in 1813.
　　During the Napoleonic wars, Capt. Du Val commanded a lugger, rigged privateer, the 100 ton VULTURE, with four guns, which plundered the French coast from Normandy to the Bay of Biscay. It is said that the Bayonne merchants, enraged by his continued success against the French, joined together in a project to capture him and his marauders. They fitted out a fine ship, a brig of 180 tons, armed it with sixteen guns, and pursued the VULTURE. Grapeshot from the smaller vessel riddled the French ship on their first encounter, killing and wounding half the crew. The vessel then fled for Bayonne, and Du Val headed thankfully for home.
　　After the war was over, about 1831, Capt. Du Val was granted land on Bonaventure Island off Perce, Gaspe. He died there in 1835, and was buried in the graveyard at Old Christ's Church on Cape Canon. His cutlass, from his privateering days, passed to his descendants. Capt. Du Val married twice, both wives being Spanish. He left five children and many descendants.
　　CENTENNIAL BOOKLET, St. Paul's Church, Perce, Quebec
　　Aldo Brochet, of Perce and Montreal, a descendant.
　　TREASURE TROVE IN GASPE, by Margaret Grant McWhirter,
　　　　New Richmond, Que., 1972.
　　KALEIDOSCOPIC QUEBEC, by Amy Oakley, 1947.
　　MAPLE LEAVES, by James Le Moine, Montreal, 1978.

FALLE, Josue George, 1820-1903
　　Falle was the son of Josue Falle of Hambie, St. Saviours, Jersey, and Ester Bertram. The Falles had been engaged in the Newfoundland Cod Fisheries since the 1700s, and the firm of Richard Falle and Co., Newfoundland ship owners and merchants, was founded at Point George, Little Burin, Nfld., about 1830, by Josue's two uncles, Richard and Elie Falle.
　　In 1838 they took their nephew into the firm, and when both were lost at sea, crossing to Oporto, Spain, Josue remained in charge of the firm. He married Marie E. Godfray, daughter of Jersey Advocate, Francois Godfray. In 1848 he became a

THE ISLANDERS IN CANADA, NOTABLES   31

member for Burin in the Newfoundland Assembly. After he returned to Jersey he entered civic affairs. He left his Pier Road house to the Societe Jersiaise. His son Bertram became Baron Portsea of Portsmouth, England. There were also daughters, Rozel and Lily. (Balleine, G.R., BIOGRAPHICAL DICTIONARY)

FIOTT, Nicholas, 1704-1786
Fiott was the youngest son of Jean Fiott of St. Saviours, Jersey and of Catherine Ahier. He claimed descent from the Fiott d'Arbois family of Burgundy, France. He spent his youth at sea, and in 1740 married Ann Dumaresq, daughter of Edouard Dumaresq and Anne de Carteret, then settled down ashore as a merchant.
In 1743 he was trading with Newfoundland as Fiott and Co. Later, he established a large trading station on Isle Perce Bay, Gaspe. He soon became well-to-do and powerful on his home Island, but a fierce feud developed between him and another Island leader, Philip Lempriere. This became so bitter that at first Fiott, then Lempriere, left the Island. Fiott returned, and later became Seigneur of Meleches in Jersey. He had six children by his first wife. (Balleine, G.R., BIOGRAPHICAL DICTIONARY)

HARDY, Sir Charles
Hardy was a descendant of a long line of Le Hardys in Jersey, many of whom were notables in the British Army, Navy and Government offices. He was Governor of New York in 1756, and that year was in charge of convoying troops intended for the siege of Fort Louisbourg, in Cape Breton. In 1758 he served again in a similar capacity, and joined Boscawen at Louisburg. This action was successful. He later became a Vice-Admiral and a Member of the British Parliament. (Encyclopedia)

HERIOT, Major-General Frederick George. C.B.
Heriot was born in Jersey in 1786. His father was from a French Huguenot family of Nantes, France, and his mother was Irish. At the age of 15, he obtained a commission as ensign in the 49th Reg't., which Brock commanded. In 1802 his regiment was ordered to Canada.
When the War of 1812 broke out, the young officer, now a captain of 26 years, was released from regimental duties to be second in command of a volunteer force of French-speaking irregulars, known as the Canadian Voltigeurs. With these men he fought throughout the war. He was second in command under Col. de Salaberry, holding a joint command with Col. Morrison. He is known to have taken part in the Battle of Crysler's Farm in the War of 1812, for shich he was awarded a gold medal and C.B.

When peace came, he was granted a large tract of land in
the Eastern Townships, and founded there in 1816 the town of
Drummondville, named after his old chief, Gen. Sir Gordon
Drummond. He laid out the city plan himself, and gave the
streets their names.

From 1829 to 1833 Heriot represented Drummondville in the
Legislature Assembly of Lower Canada, and in 1840, he was
appointed Member of the Executive Council. In 1841 he was promoted to Major-General, and died in 1843. He was unmarried.
(G.R. Balleine)

In connection with the above settlement, there is a list
of over 200 names of servicemen who bought or were given land
in Drummondville. Among these surnames of widely varied origins were a few that may have been from the Channel Islands,
such as: ANTOINE, CLERK, CLEMENT, COLLINS, DALLEY, DELANEY,
DU VAL, GODDIN, GREEN, HUDSON, KNIGHT, LANGLOIS, LE FEVRE,
REBY, ROBERTS, ROBINS, SANDERS, SHEPPARD, TURNER, and WAGGONER.
Research on these families might reveal a number of Channel
Island families in Canada that are not covered in this book.

HILLIER, Major George, of the Channel Islands and England.
       Major Hillier, aide-de-camp of Sir Peregrine Maitland,
Lt. Governor of Upper Canada, served there from 1812 to 1828.

LE BOUTILLIER, John, b. 1797 La Chasse, St. John, Jersey, removed to Gaspe in 1812. (See family in last part of book)
       He established his own fishery in 1830, after working for
the Robin firm at Paspebiac and Perce, Gaspe. He bought cod,
"made" fish, and shipped millions of tons to Brazil, the West
Indies, Portugal, Spain and Italy. He represented Gaspe in
the Chamber from 1833 to 1838, and was later named Legislative
Councillor. He died in 1872 leaving many descendants.

LE BRETON, Capt. John, 1780-1848, was born in Jersey.
       As a young man in 1811, he was stationed as Lieutenant in
the Quartermaster General's office at Quebec. "In his office
he seems to have been active and zealous in the performance
of his duties." (Hamnet P. Hill) "On the outbreak of the war
in 1812, between Great Britain and the United States, he was
attached to the Royal Newfoundland Regiment of Fencible Infantry, a regiment which earned an enviable record during the war.
He accompanied the regiment on General Brock's expedition to
Detroit in 1812, and was present at the capture of the city."

In the following spring he took an active part in a battle
with the Americans on the Miami River, being mentioned in
General Proctor's dispatch in these terms: "Lt. Le Breton of
the R.N.F.L. Regiment, Assistant Engineer, by his unwearied
exertions rendered essential service."

"After the disastrous battle at Moraviantown where the British were badly defeated and were obliged to retreat to the

Niagara River, giving up the whole western portion of the Province, Le Breton volunteered and was sent with a flag of truce to General Harrison to arrange for an exchange of prisoners. On his way to Harrison's Headquarters, he was appealed to by numbers of Canadians who had remained on their farms after the British Army had retired, to assist them to join the British Army, which, to quote his report, 'I would have done had it not been for two tribes of hostile savages by whom I was surrounded and who frequently threatened my life, notwithstanding which I would have effected their emancipation as well as several soldiers of the 41st Reg't taken prisoners on the 5th of Oct. 1813, had I been allowed to return by the same route, and which I believe, General Harrison's principal reason for having detained me, and although I regret much having missed the opportunity of bringing these men, yet I am in a great measure compensated by the valuable information I obtained of the situation of the Navy on that lake.'" (OUR FAMILY HISTORY, Vol. 2, H.B. Little, and ROBERT RANDALL AND THE LE BRETON FLATS, by Hamnet P. Hill, Ottaws, Ont., 1919)

Later in the war, Le Breton was badly wounded at Lundy's Lane, near Niagara. Service in the War of 1812 entitled him to a grant of 200 acres near what is now Ottawa. He was unmarried, but the 5 daughters of his sister, Jeanne Le Breton Le Lievre, qv, raised a stone to his memory in Toronto.

LE COUTEUR, John, b St. Aubin, Jersey, 1794, son of Capt. John and of Maria DUMARESQ.

In 1811 he had a lieutenancy in the 104th Foot Regiment, which he joined in New Brunswick. They then saw service in the Niagara district, after a 900 mile march through snow-covered forest. At times, Le Couteur was fighting next to Indian allies, who scalped the slain. In his diary he wrote, "Indians are ticklish friends to deal with. I refused to give a half-drunken Indian a hide he coveted, over and above the meat which had been issued to his tribe. He snatched his tomahawk, and made a motion as if to cut me down. Self-preservation made me place my drawn sword at his throat." He had a distinguised literary and political career later in Jersey, where he died in 1875. (G.R. Balleine, BIO. DICT.)

LE LACHEUR, Rex A. de Putron, musician, vocalist, composer, born 1910 Guernsey, the son of Francis Martin L. and Clarice Marie MARRIETTE.

He is the director and founder of the Rex Le Lacheur singers, a 50 voice mixed choir in Ottaws. He was the composer of at least 120 pieces of music, and wrote songs for John Charles Thomas in 1942, and for Ezio Pinza in 1945. (CAN. WHO'S WHO, XI, also see LE LACHEUR family)

LE MARCHANT, Sir John Gaspard, born 1803 Guernsey, the son of John L. and of Marie Hirzel, was the descendant of an old seafaring family. An ancestor, Thomas Le Marchant, transported out of Guernsey in 1608, a shipload of biscuits, headed for the fisheries in Newfoundland. Sir John became Governor of Newfoundland in 1847-1852. As a young man he had served in Spain and the West Indies, and was Commander-in-Chief in Madras, India, in 1868.

"Le Marchant was an able administrator at a difficult time when the colony was in debt to the tune of $20,000,000, and had but a small population. He encouraged agriculture among the settlers, distributed seeds, fruit trees, potatoes and good bulls, promoted ploughing matches, gave cups and other prizes, and worked hard to establish representative government. However, this did not come about until many years later." (P.M. Luce) Le Marchant also served as Governor of Nova Scotia, 1852-1858, and of Malta. He died in England 1874.

LE MESSURIER, Henry William, born 1848, Newfoundland of an old Channel Island family, son of Henry Corbin L. and Sara Eliza ---.

He was in business, a Customs Officer, editor of the Evening Herald, Imperial Trade Correspondant, J.P., etc. He was also the author of THE EARLY RELATIONS BETWEEN NEWFOUNDLAND AND THE CHANNEL ISLANDS, an article in the American Geographical Society Review of Dec. 1916, Vol. II. Le Messurier died in 1931 in Newfoundland, leaving two sons and two daughters.

LE MESURIER, Henry, was born in Guernsey 1791, the son of Haviland Le Mesurier.

They were Seigneurs of Alderney under Royal Patent. Le Mesurier entered the Army in 1811, went to Spain under the Duke of Wellington, served in Canada in the War of 1812, and resided in Quebec. He married a French-Canadian girl, and had a family of eleven children. (See family in Part Two)

LE PAGE, Bradford William, born in 1876, Rustico, Prince Edward Island, the son of Charles Le Page and Sarah Millicent Woolner.

The Le Pages were descendants of a Guernsey family, in P.E.I. since before 1807. Le Page married Hattie Christie. He was a successful merchant and served as Lt.-Governor of P.E.I. 1939-1945. (Encyclopedia Canadiana) (See Le Page family, Part Two)

LE SUEUR, William Dawson, Civil Servant, Journalist, born 1840 Quebec, died Ottawa 1917, son of Peter Le Sueur and Barbara Dawson.

He was believed to be of a Jersey family. He was the author of COUNT FRONTENAC, in 1906. In 1867 he married Ann Jane

Foster of Montreal. One son, Ernest Arthur, and one daughter were born. Ernest Arthur was a chemical engineer, 1869-1953, educated at M.I.T. He invented the extremely vital process for pulp and paper making, the electrolitic process. In 1893 Ernest married Maud Drummond and they had one daughter. (ENCYCLOPEDIA CANADIANA)

LE VESCONTE, H.T.D., was born in Devon, England, of an old Channel Island family in 1813.
He served in the Navy until the 1840s. In 1845 the British Government sent out an expedition to discover whether there was a passage from the Atlantic to the Pacific, through the northern Canada Islands. This mystery many men had tried to solve, and the truth was not known until the middle 1900s.

For this expedition, two ships were fitted out under the command of Sir John Franklin, who had already led three Arctic enterprises. Le Vesconte was selected as Lieutenant on the EREBUS, commanded by Capt. Fitzjames. The group left the Thames River, England, on the 19th of May in 1845, and on July 4th had reached the Whalefish Islands off the coast of Greenland. On the 28th of July, the Captain of a whaler spoke to them as they were moored to an iceberg in the middle of Baffin Bay. After that, the 129 men were never seen again. A brief report found under a stone cairn chronicled their further desperate adventures. In the summer of 1846 they had tried another channel, but in the summer of 1847 the ice failed to melt. Franklin died, and in April, 1848, it was decided to try to march to the northernmost station of the Hudson's Bay Company, 1200 miles away. Weakened by scurvy they set off.

Le Vesconte reached Point Hall about 150 miles from the ships, where later a skeleton, thought to be his, was found and sent to England. Some relics of this disastrous expedition are in the Societe Jersiaise Museum, and others in the Franklin Expedition Memorial in Greenwich, England. Le Vesconte Point in Baillie Hamilton Land and Point Le Vesconte in King William Land are named for him.

A recent gruesome footnote has been added to this tale. On a fact-finding visit to the grave of Sir John Franklin, specimens were taken from the body. For years there had been a rumour that he had been poisoned, and the laboratory confirmed the truth of this idea. It is thought now that he died of arsenic poisoning, possibly administered to him by the physician of the group, with whom he was at odds.

Over a space of years, more than 40 expeditions were carried out in hopes of finding survivors or records of this trip, one of the most persistent being the researches of Charles Francis Hall, 1821-1871, an American. He found some relics of Frobisher's expeditions, of the ancient dates of 1576, 1577, and 1578. He also found, with the aid of Eskimos, some skeletal remains of the Franklin party.

BIOGRAPHICAL DICTIONARY OF JERSEY, G.R. Balleine, 1945.
HEROES OF BRITAIN IN PEACE AND WAR, by Edwin Hodder,
  London, cr 1900?
CANADIAN ARCHIVES RECORDS
MANY BOOKS ON CANADIAN ARCTIC EXPLORATION

MAUGER, Joshua, 1725-1788, born in Jersey, removed as a young man to Canada.
He was, in 1751, Agent Victualler for the British Navy at Halifax. He was a shipmaster, brewer and distiller, and by 1754 had several shops established at various places in Nova Scotia where he sold goods and spirits to the French and the Indians. He had a rum factory in Halifax, supplying this commodity to the Services. From 1762 to 1768 he returned to England, agent for the Nova Scotia Assembly in London. After making a fortune, he secured a seat in the British Parliament. In 1767 he had a grant on Prince Edward Island also, but appears to have not made use of it. (Nova Scotia Hist. Coll., 1892-1895, Vol. 8, Poole, England Museums Service, Dr. Donald Chard, Dartmouth, NS: NEUTRAL YANKEES OF NOVA SCOTIA, by John Brebner, Toronto, 1969 and other works)

MESSERVY, Col. Nathaniel, born in New Hampshire, the grandson of Clement Messervy, who emigrated from Jersey before 1673 to New England.
He was a prominent shipbuilder at Portsmouth, N.H. In 1745 Nathaniel was Lt. Col. of Colonel Moore's New Hampshire Regiment, (See JEAN family), built up for the reduction of the fortress of Louisbourg, Cape Breton, then held by the French. After this was accomplished, the French again regained it, (See Nova Scotia in Cape Breton section), and a second reduction was necessary, for which Messervy was recalled. While the second reduction was successful, there was a large loss of life, due to small pox, from which both Messervy and his son died.
There are many descendants of this surname in North America, one of whom, a lawyer, spent some time in the Antarctic, and a Glacier was named for him, The Messervy Glacier. (Balleine, Turk, Canadian Archives)

ROBIN, Charles
Below is a condensed and incomplete record of the famous Charles Robin and his Cod fisheries in the Maritimes. A more complete record has been written by Lady Phyllis McKie, of Ottawa, Ontario, called the SEAFLOWER VENTURE. (Also see records at PAC, Ottawa)
Charles Robin was born in Jersey 1745, the youngest son of Philip Robin and Ann D'Auvergne, of St. Aubin parish. The Robins and Pipons had long been connected by marriage and business, and these two families had a firm named Robin, Pipon

and Co., which traded with Newfoundland. In the year that Charles was born, his uncle, a Thomas Robin, had nearly lost his ship, while returning with dried fish, oil and passengers from Newfoundland. (Soc. Jers. Bull, 1928-1931) By the Treaty of Paris in 1765 Canada had passed from French to English hands, and many ambitious firms made plans to enter the cod fishing trade around the Gulf of the St. Lawrence River. "This had largely been in the hands of the merchants of St. Malo, France." (G.R. Balleine)

"When Charles Robin came to Gaspe the fishing was scattered in small establishments and was without organization. Though his purpose was to seek locations for new establishments, the outcome was the development of a concern with interest so wide and influences so commanding as practically to consolidate and control the entire business withoug serious competition for nearly a century." (Clarke)

Robin was well-educated, strongwilled, ambitious, and regrettably, a very real despot. One policy that has probably affected the history of Canada was his ruling that employees may not marry while in his service, or if married, could not bring a wife to Canada. Had the Jersey and Guernsey women come to Gaspe in the same numbers that the men did, Quebec would now be filled with Channel Island descendants, enough to challenge the numbers of the original French of the Province!

Inexperience caused Robin to run into several problems in the first few years. He obtained a permit from the Governor of Quebec to make a treaty with the Indians and to barter some goods for furs. But in May, 1767, his ship, the ENDEAVOR, coming with additional stores, was arrested by the British Government and taken to Halifax. His firm had not taken notice of the New Navigation Act, which required Jersey boats sailing for North America to clear outward from an English port.

Robin claimed in a letter to George Lempriere, in London, that he had first begun operation in the Maritimes when he landed in Arichat, Nova Scotia in 1764, establishing a fishing firm the next year. The Paspebiac location was begun in 1766. A number of other locations were soon added to the Robin chain, as in Perce, Cheticamp, (Cape Breton) Newport, and Caraquet, N.B. A description of Paspebiac nearly a hundred years later shows the strong influence of the Robin firm on the economy of the port.

"Paspebiac, with its roadstead running out to a point in the Bay, is the seaport, the great fishing stand of the Messrs. Robin and the Messrs. Le Boutillier Brothers. The fishing establishment--a crowd of nice white warehouses, with doors pointed red, comprising stores, offices, forges, joiners' shops, dwellings for fishermen, even to a powder magazine-- all stand on a low beach or sand bar, connected with the shore by a ford for horses and a trestlework bridge for foot passengers, which is taken down every fall and restored in the spring at the expense of the Messrs. Robin...Paspebiac is three miles east of New Carlisle...the bar on which the fishing warehouses stand is a triangle formed by sand and other marine detritus. The interior of the triangle is gradually filling up. Here the fishermen dwell in the summer; they remove to their winter quarters on the heights in the rear in December..."

On the green hills in the rear, the great Jersey houses have splendid farms, dwellings, gardens, parks...the winter residences of the managers...are most commodious, most complete...The poor clerks and managers, 'tis true, cannot own wives or families at their residences at Gaspe; the founder of the house ordained it otherwise..." (Le Moine)

The first few years of the Robin establishment were difficult, as the colonists down in Massachusetts were jealous of his trading rights and tried mightily to have him ousted. The Bostonians were still grumbling about him when the Revolutionary War began, and on one occasion in 1778 two American ships looted his port and took his two ships, which were being unloaded. The ships were recaptured by the British Navy, which demanded payment for saving his vessels and a rather unjustified "ransom" was paid. This was a decided set-back, and Robin retired to Jersey for about five years.

While in Jersey, Robin became a Captain in the Southwest Regiment of the Jersey militia, and took part in the Battle of Jersey, 1781. After the battle he was given command of the boat which the States of Jersey bought to watch the French coast, and guard against further surprise attacks.

In 1785 the Robins and Pipons amicably divided their firm. The original part concentrated on the Newfoundland trade, while the Canadian organizations were to be in charge of Charles Robin and Co., upon which change Robin returned to Gaspe. He carried on the business in the ensuing years under French colours at times.

Most of the Robin firm's trade was with the Mediterranean and with South America. Hundreds of Channel Island sailors crewed these ships, as well as men from other nations and places. The best grade of cod went to Spain and Italy, the second grade to Brazil and the third grade to the West Indies. While the ships unloaded at the Italian ports, the Captains would sometimes hire artists to capture the sturdy good looks of their vessels on canvas. These pictures are now highly valued by the descendants of these sailing families.

Robin "introduced the truck system, paying the fishermen for fish caught, half in cash and half in goods from the Company's stores." When the employees rebelled, "and carried their fish to other markets, they are threatened with a summons for debt, and are forced to expiate their bid for freedom by a long penance. The fisherman is always in debt to the proprietors, always at their mercy, liable, whenever his debts reach a point where they cannot be repaid by fishing, to serve without wages on one of the company's ships, and make a voyage to Europe." (Ferland)

Robin settlements were a powerful force in the Maritimes, and a few figures will show the profits involved. In June, 1777, the firm sent home furs worth over one thousand English pounds, ten tons of whale and cod oil, in addition to great quantities of cod fish. In 1786 Robin wrote that he had that year exported 2,200 tons of salt cod, and 1,000 casks of salmon, as just part of his business.

The man, Charles Robin, very similar in character and personality to today's tycoons, realized in 1784 that he was giving too much of his life to the business for what he then considered a small return, but on the whole he must have enjoyed his hard work. He spent much time afloat in small half-decked boats, trading with scattered settlers and Indians, and keeping a close eye on all his affiliated stations. Robin had at one time 800 fishing boats in the Chaleur Bay area alone, and sometimes made 800,000 pounds profit in just one year.

In the autumn of 1802 Robin returned to Jersey "old and fatigued" (letter to his nephew) leaving six commissioners in charge. He settled in St. Aubin, Jersey where he died in June 1824. He left two thousand pounds to build a new wing to the hospital and one thousand pounds to provide a chaplain.

After he left Canada the firm became Robin, Collas and Co., and in 1866 there were still 3500 fishermen working for the company. In 1868 Charles Robin and Philip Gosset of Jersey were partners in the firm. In 1877 the owners of the firm were mentioned as Messrs. Raulin Robin, Philip Gosset, and William Lempriere, all of Jersey. (Le Moine) In 1904, Charles Robin, Collas and Co., transferred their headquarters from Jersey to Halifax, and in 1910 amalgamated with A.G. Jones and Co. of Halifax, and Atlantic Fisheries Co. of Lunenburg to form Robin, Jones and Whitman Co.

Branches of this latter firm are listed as being located in the 1920s at the following places. (This information was printed on the firm's letterhead in 1925, on a recommendation given to Mr. Arthur BAUCHE, qv.)

Head Office, Halifax, N.S. Branches in Quebec: Paspebiac, Bonaventure, Port Daniel East, Gascons, Newport Island, Newport Point, St. Adelaide de Pabos, Grand River, Little River East, Cape Cove, Anse au Beaufils, Perce, Barachois de Malbay, Malbay, Gaspe, Griffin Cove, Fox River, Magpie, Riviere St. Jean, Natashquan.

Branches in New Brunswick: Caraquet and Lameque

Branches in Nova Scotia: Eastern Harbour, Grand Etang, Ingonish, Annapolis, Tiverton, Lunenburg, Petpeswick, Musquodoboit Harbour, and in Jersey.

Subsidiary Companies were: The Lord Bros Co., Portland, Maine and the Bluenose Fish Company, Ltd., West Jeddore, N.S.

BALLEINE, G.R., BIOGRAPHICAL DICTIONARY OF JERSEY, London and New York, 1945.

CLARK, John M, SKETCHES OF GASPE, L'ISLE PERCE , and THE GASPE, New Haven, Conn., 1935.

LE FEUVRE, George F., IMMIGRANTS FROM JERSEY, THE COD AND THE GASPE COAST, Societe Jersiaise Bulletin.

LE MOINE, J.M., CHRONICLES OF THE ST. LAWRENCE, Rouses Pt., N.Y., 1878.

ROMERIL, A.J., FLYING TO THE GASPE COAST, Societe Jersiaise Bulletin, 1963.

SYVRET, Marguerite, JERSEY SETTLERS IN THE GASPE, pamphlet. See also: BIBLIOGRAPHY, QUEBEC.

THE ISLANDERS IN CANADA, CLERGY

Religion has played a large part in the history of the Channel Islands and in Canada. Until the religious unrest of the Middle Ages, the people of the Islands were Roman Catholic. In 1212 Philippe d'Aubigny, the Crusader, was appointed Keeper of Jersey. In 1236 he died in Jerusalem, where his tombstone is still to be seen just outside the entrance to the Church of the Holy Sepulchre.

Changing from Catholic to Protestant was not a matter of days or months, but took many many years, beginning as far back as 1378, the time of the great Schism and the two rival Popes, Urban and Clement. By 1413 the Priories of the Church in Jersey were confiscated by the British Parliament. There was a strong religious feeling in the Islands, shown by the sixty licenses that in 1428 were issued to pilgrims from Jersey who wished to sail to the shrine of St. James of Compostella in Spain.

In 1518 Martin Luther nailed his theses to the church door at Wittenberg, Germany, and gave impetus to the Reformation. By 1528 Protestant martyrs were being burned to death in Normandy, and many French families were fleeing to the Channel Islands, to England, and also to Holland, Germany, Scandinavia and elsewhere. This surge of Huguenots into the Islands often complicated the political, religious and cultural life of the Islanders. Some of the Huguenots settled in Jersey and Guernsey, and other families used the Islands as a bridge to more distant asylums, such as North and South America.

In 1568 all Huguenot ministers were banished from France, and great numbers came to Jersey. French Calvinism was strong in the Islands then, and not until 1620 was the Presbyterian system of church government abolished. In 1637-1639, William Prynne, the Puritan, was imprisoned in Mont Orgueil, Jersey, but was released in 1640.

The regular influx each year of Normans and Bretons to gather the crops was mainly Catholic, and somefamilies remained in the Islands, increasing the number of Roman Catholics there. There were usually a few Jewish families in the Islands also.

While numerous Protestant denominations organized congregations in the Islands during the following centuries, John Wesley stirred the most interest, and many converts were made during and after his visit there in 1787, and in 1790 the first Methodist chapel was opened in Jersey.

Claude Gray of Essex, England, introduced Quakerism to Jersey, which was established there in 1782, followed by adherents to Primitive Methodists, Bible Christians, Baptists, Congregationalists, Roman Catholics and Unitarians.

The rise and fall of these waves of different denominations was not easy to live through, and they were often attended by painful soul-searching, as well as occasional violence. Witch-hunts by over zealous leaders took place here, as they did in Europe and North America. Missionary work stemmed from this strong religious current, and below are listed just a few of those who were called to this courageous work. Also included are a few of the hundreds of priests and ministers in Canada, whose ancestors came from the Channel Islands.

Please note that SPG in the list below refers to the Society for the Propagation of the Gospel, a Missionary Society of Great Britain.

BINET, William, b. 1827 J, d. 1863 London, served in Malbaie, Gaspe 1853, and at Port Neuf 1855, SPG.

BISHOP, A., of Guernsey, missionary in Nfld. 1800s.

BRINE, Robert Frederick, see Brine family in Part Two. There was also a Rev. Richard Brine, and a Rev. Charles Le Vesconte Brine, the latter of Portsmouth, N.H., all believed to be of the same family connection.

BURT, John, not verified as C.I., missionary in Nfld, SPG.

CAREY, Florence Elizabeth, missionary, res Calif.

CARTER, George, and COLLEY, Edward, SPG missionaries, possibly from the C.I.

DE GRUCHY, P., served in Milton, Quebec 1872-1880 for SPG.

DE JERSEY, Methodist Missionary to France, 1822.

DE LA MARE, Rev. Francis, b. 1821 Grouville, J, mar 1. Marguerite GAVEY, qv, of J, and 2. Charlotte DE MOUILPIED of G, 1821-1909. Rev. De La Mare was a minister and missionary in Gaspe, Mauritius Island, and in Natal, South Africa. He died in 1869.

DE MOUILPIED, ---, of the Channel Islands, served in Malbaie, Quebec, 1866-1869, (SPG).

DE PUTRON, John, was named in the first report of the Methodist Missionary Society. He was probably from Guernsey, and conducted the first French Mission, working in Quebec and Ontario. In Canada he served in Quebec City and Ontario.

In Canada he served in Quebec City, Montreal, Kingston, St. Armands, Melbourne, Stanstead, Three Rivers, Shefford, Fort Wellington, and Caldwell Manor, in the early 1800s. A few exerpts from his journal are given here. "Oct. 3, 1820. Established several Sunday schools last May at Quebec and other places, which have been well attended, and I hope very useful to the children. In one of them, the children can repeat large portions of the Scripture. Jan. 1, 1821. Through mercy brought to the beginning of a new year...One of our members in this place announced publicly his intention of gratuitously teaching Canadian children. About 80 immediately came. In a few days they would have exceeded 100. The priest, alarmed, preached against it, and the parents kept their children at home. Jan. 17, 1821. Our new chapel was opened at Montreal; immense congreations attended. The building is very neat, but, as it ought to be, very plain. Jan. 26, 1821. Slept at a distant relation's, who emigrated to this country about 34 years ago. Found them all at a neighbour's wedding. Being pressingly invited, I went, and was soon surrounded. I spoke in plain terms. The young people began to laugh, but soon became serious." (Methodist Missionary records)

DE QUETTEVILLE, Jean, a young French preacher, who brought from France to Guernsey 1700s. He was evidently a persuasive speaker, who brought about the conversion of many in the Islands. He was probably of the same family active in the Newfoundland and Labrador fisheries.

DINGLE, John, Missionary in Newfoundland. Origin unverified. The famous Medical Missionary, Lillian Mary Gradin, of Jersey and China, married in 1812 Edwin J. Dingle. Possibly John was related to this noted cartographer of China.

DOREY, Rt. Reverend George, B.Z., D.D., LL.D., was born in Jersey, 1884, brought out to Canada for the mission field in 1905, to Shellbrook, Sask. He became a circuit preacher, was ordained in 1914, and married Alice Ann Bent, a teacher. In 1929 he was appointed Superintendant of Missions for Southern Sask., and was Assoc. Secretary of the Board of Home Missions of the U.C.C., chosen Moderator in 1954. (The Montrealer, Fed., 1955)

DU VAL, Joshua, SPG missionary in Burgeos, Nfld., 1854, in Channel and La Poele, 1855-1858, unverified.

FALLE, Bessie, of Hespeler, Ont., desc of a Nfld. FALLE family, originating in the Channel Islands. She served in Africa from 1938 to 1971 for the Baptist Mid-Missions.

FILLEUL, Philip James, b. St. Heliers J or Cape Breton, ordained 1843, served the SPG at Lunenberg, N.S., Mahone Bay and Weymouth, N.S.

GAUDIN, Rev. Dr. Samuel, of a J fam, was missionary to the Indians in Northern Canada for more than 40 years, 1800s. (Helen Cameron, White Rock, BC)

GODDEN, John and Thomas, SPG missionaries in Montreal in

the 1850s, and Harbour Grace, Nfld. poss from C.I. fam. Unver.

GODFREY, William Minns, b. St. Clement J 1841, d. 1882. Served SPG as missionary in N.S.

GRUCHY, Florence Evelyn, 40 years a missionary for the United Church of Canada.

HAMMOND, Rev. John, res Bell Island Newfoundland, minister of C.I. descent, researcher.

HILLIER, Daniel, missionary to St. Armands, Que, from C.I.? 1800s?

HOYLES, William, origin unverified, missionary to Ferryland, Nfld. 1843 for SPG.

JEUNE, Francois, resided Les Vaus, St. Aubin J, furnished a shed in his yard for a meeting place for Methodists in Jersey, before they became well-established there. Later he and wife removed to Granda, Windward Isles, as Methodist missionaries to the French-speaking slaves there.

LANGLOIS, Peter , born ca 1794 Guernsey, removed to Canada ca age 33, as a carpenter, fisherman and preacher. His family had been converted by John Wesley. He preached in Gaspe and traveled on horseback throughout the area for a number of years. Previous to his death in 1897 the family removed from Gaspe to Beaverton, Ont. Below is a short exerpt from his interesting memoirs. (Canada Archives) "I arrived in Quebec in 1806 and found that all religious services were performed in the English language, and were held in the following places: The English Church, which had been lately built; the Scotch Church congregation, under the care of the Rev. late Dr. Sparks in a room of the Service barracks; the congregation of the St. Johns Chapel, under the ministry of the Rev. Mr. Dick in the upper part of a house in Hope St. These were the only Protestant congregations which were in existence in that period...As I had then only begun to learn a little English, I could not converse with the few who were members of the society, except a few words and on very few subjects; finding myself in that situation I began in good earnest to apply myself to obtain some knowledge of the English, and though I had no one to instruct me yet in a short while I was enabled to read it so as to derive some benefit from it...In 1815 the first Sunday school was established in the city by a young man named Walker, a pious and active member of the society, and soon after the opening of the chapel in St. Ann St...a good Sunday school was raised and properly organized."

LE FEVRE, C.S., served in Sherbrooke, Quebec, 1820s, SPG.

LE GALLAIS, William Wellman, 1833-1869, was one of 15 children of Richard LE GALLAIS and Susan Nason of Jersey. He removed as a young man to St. John's Nfld., to join his sisters Susan and Mary, who had established a school there. William was ordained an Anglican minister in St. John's, and was sent to Channel, Nfld., with his wife, Fanny Mary Langrish, whose father was at the British Naval Station, St. John's.

Four daughters and a son were born in Channel. In 1869 Rev. Le Gallais was drowned in a storm while on his way to take communion to an ill parishioner. The Royal Canadian Mounted Police of Victoria, B.C., celebrating their 100th Anniversary in 1973, has commemmorated this gallant clergyman with a bronze plaque, mounted in the town of Channel, Newfoundland. (SPG) (E. Le Gallais, Seattle, Wash.; Dict. of Canadian Biography, Vol. 9)

LE JEUNE, William George, ordained 1879, served the SPG in Fort Q'Appele, Western Canada in 1889.

LE SUEUR, Pierre, born Jersey, removed to Newfoundland 1760s as a trader. There, he was converted by Lawrence Coughlan, a missionary. He returned to Jersey in 1775, with an awakened conscience and a message. He became a full time Methodist Missionary, after having served as layman in Harbor Grace, Nfld. A John FENTON, poss a Jersey FAINTON?, was of great help to him, helping to organize a Methodist Society in Jersey in the 1780s, reinforced by the visit of John Wesley himself. According to English Methodist stationing records, Le Sueur was appointed, among other places, to Plymouth Rock (where?), in 1813, and in 1814 to Guernsey, Alderney and Sark, and in 1815-1816 to Jersey. (Shortis-Munn; Arthur M. Butler, Corner Brook, Nfld.; A HISTORY OF WESLEYAN MISSIONS, by Rev. William Moister).

NOEL, John Monk, origin unverified, Methodist Missionary in Nfld. 1864.

SHAW, Rev. James Allen, at Isle Madame in the 1800s. His grandson, a curate at St. Michaels, Toronto, Ontario, was a missionary in Honan, China. This family was descended from the JEANS of Jersey, and were settled in Cape Breton, N.S.

STANNAGE, John, born Jersey, ordained 1834 in Nova Scotia, served St. Margaret's Bay for the SPG, 1834-1857.

TOASE, Rev. W., of Guernsey, did missionary work in France for the Methodist Church, 1818.

TOCQUE, Philip, b J or Nfld., traveler, author and missionary in the 1850s and 1860s. Author of NEWFOUNDLAND AS IT WAS AND IT IS NOW, which gives a fine idea of commerce and culture of the time, not only in Newfoundland but in other parts of the Maritimes. Tocque served the SPG in Hopetown, Gaspe, 1863-1868.

TOURGIS, Philip, of Jersey, was a missionary to France 1882 for the Methodists.

TUPPER. In 1635 Thomas Tupper settled in New England. He came of an English family which had removed to Guernsey in or about 1592. At least one Tupper of those days was an active and successful privateersman. Their parish home in Guernsey was at St. Peters, and many Tuppers are buried there along with the Le Marchants, Le Mesuriers and Careys. In America, Thomas Tupper helped to found the first settlement at Sandwich on Cape Cod. He took over the services when the preacher left, and later, at the advanced age of 90, became a missionary to the local Indians. He died at age 98 in 1676. Some descendants of this family settled in Nova Scotia. (Tupper Family Association)

TUZO, Joseph, said to have come from the Channel Islands in the 1700s as SPG missionaries in the West Indies. Later the family is noted in Gaspe.

WALTERS, John and George Radley, thought to be of Channel Island families, served in Quebec.

WEARY, E., served in S. Riviere du Loup, Gaspe for the SPG, 1889-1892, and had been in Newfoundland in 1882. (SPG records)

OTHER CHANNEL ISLAND MISSIONARIES SERVED ELSEWHERE

BUTT, George, 1842-1844, to New Zealand.
BUTTON, Henry Francis, served 1869, New Zealand.
GRANDIN, Lillian Mary, to China, 1800s, as Medical Missionary.
LEGG, Jacob Philip, to the Cape of Good Hope, d St. Heliers, Jersey.
LE GROS, John S., to Jamaica.
NICHOLLE, Charles H.S., to Whanganue, New Zealand, 1860-1864.
TURPIN, Edmund Adolphus, in Tobago, 1874.
VAUDIN, Adolphe, to Mauritius, 1800s, and many more.

BIBLIOGRAPHY

BALLEINE, G.R., BIOGRAPHICAL DICTIONARY OF JERSEY, 1945.
TUPPER FAMILY ASSOCIATION RECORDS.
FIRST REPORT OF THE METHODIST MISSIONARY SOCIETY.
DIGEST OF S.P.G. RECORDS, by the Society, London, 1893.
MOISTER, Rev. Wm., HISTORY OF WESLEYAN MISSIONS, London, 1871.
SMITH, J.H., NEWFOUNDLAND HOLIDAY.
THOMPSON, Rev. H.P., INTO ALL LANDS, London, 1951.
LANGTRY, THE CHURCH IN EASTERN CANADA AND NEWFOUNDLAND.

THE LETTER, by Edmund Blampied, from MODERN MASTERS
OF ETCHING, London, 1926, by Malcolm Saloman.

CHAPTER FOUR, NEWFOUNDLAND

> "Darest thou now, O Soul,
> Walk out with me toward the
> Unknown region, where neither ground
> Is for the feet, nor any path to follow..."
> (Walt Whitman)

Newfoundland, the Ancient Colony, Great Ireland, that great Island northeast of Canada's mainland, was for several centuries the main source of an important protein food, codfish, needed to supplement the European diet. Fish was then used in large quantities, in part due to the many Catholic fast days. The fisheries, in the hands of the competent and aggressive ship owners of the Channel Islands, were the source of rich income for the businessmen of the Islands.

As early as 1246 it is recorded that ships of Jersey and Guernsey were engaged in the fisheries at Iceland. (Jersey Chronicles in Archives of Jersey) Two hundred more years of experience and improved vessels could have easily seen the Islanders on the Grand Banks.

In the late 1300s and 1400s, vessels of from 20 to 30 tons sailed from Dieppe, St. Malo, France, and from the southern and western ports such as Bristol, in late Spring, and brought back shiploads of codfish from the banks. The Basques believe they were the first to arrive on the Banks. The mixed crews of the French ships undoubtedly included Channel Islanders, known for the centuries-old affinity for the sea and fishing. There was in the 1500s a close association between the French of St. Malo and the Channel Island seamen. The Island ships wintered in the deeper French harbors. From St. Malo in 1534, Jacques Cartier sailed to the coast of Canada. Marguerite Syvret of Jersey, in her booklet, JERSEY SETTLEMENTS IN GASPE, suggests that several of Cartier's crewmen may have come from the Channel Islands. Guillaume de Guerneze was present, and others named Antoine, Fleury, Ollivier, Le Breton and Colas may have been Jerseymen.

Tyler says that "small fishing vessels from Biscay, Brittany and Normandy were in the habit of visiting the coast of Newfoundland and adjacent waters from as early as 1504." The Channel Islands were then called the Norman Isles, and Norman sails are reported by Rut in 1527. "Newfoundland was officially claimed by England in 1583. There were white people unofficially living in Newfoundland before 1583. There were also fishermen from Jersey to fish, and perhaps to stay during the winters before 1583." (Rev. Hammond, Bell Island, Nfld.)

In the old Jersey records it is mentioned that in 1591 John Guillaume was fined by the Royal Court for selling in France the fish which he had brought from Newfoundland. During the 1600s it appears that many of the Islanders were involved in the fisheries, and some, instead of returning home with their catch, went to New England and settled there.

"From the middle of the 17th century down to the close of the colonial period, there was a constant drain of able-bodied fishermen and seamen from Newfoundland to the New England ports. Doubtless, the English shipmasters were parties to the connivances in order to save the cost of their transportation back to England as well as to increase the shares of the voyage for the other members of the crew. The constant harassing of the coastal ports (in Newfoundland) by the French helped to cause the Newfoundland fishermen and planters to cast a longing eye on the colonies on the mainland."

"This continual exodus to New England alarmed the English merchants interested in Newfoundland, and they brought about the passage of an enactment requiring New England shipmasters to be bonded not to carry away from Newfoundland more persons than they had brought in...these different preventive acts did not succeed in halting the traffic, however, as the authorities could not spare the time or the ships to inspect every vessel and many an outgoing vessel when clear of the convoy frigate would return to pick up passengers hidden along unfrequented parts of the coast." (Tait)

In the early 1600s it was forbidden to settle permanently on the Newfoundland shores, in order to maintain the status quo in regard to the fishing industry. There are always those who disregard the law, and fishermen are notably independent thinkers. Many of the seamen and their families must have found handy little hideaway coves by the hundreds along the rocky coasts, where they could grow a few vegetables during the short summer, and fish nearly the year around. So, in spite of the regulations and the cold and foggy winters, these hardy people made Newfoundland their home. Lanctot says that there were at least 400 squatters in and around the Southern coast in 1654, but possibly there were even more than that. By 1660, the ban on settlers was lifted.

In Trinity Bay, Newfoundland, in 1675, the ships of Henry and John Le Cras, and of Nicholas Ballhast, Bailhache of Jersey, were loaded with fish for export to Europe. Thomas Bandinell of Jersey is also mentioned at that time in Harbour Grace, and Abraham Fillett, or Filleul, at Renews.

Carbonear Island, settled by the Channel Islanders, was fortified in the 1600s because of attacks by the French. In 1697 and 1705, 22 plantations went up in flames. The French reported that Carbonear had the best built houses in Newfoundland, and some of its merchants were worth at that time more than a hundred thousand pounds sterling, which is millions of dollars in today's money. (Horwood) Bricks were found in Carbonear with the name of the maker imprinted, firms of the Channel Islands. The stone houses had apparently been built by Islanders who followed their native custom of building with stone.

In 1700 a Guernsey ship stopped in St. John's, Nfld. on its way to Boston. In 1743 Nicholas Fiott of Jersey was trading with both Nfld. and Gaspe. In 1831 there were 17 vessels from Jersey engaged in the fisheries, and by 1732 there were 24. By 1771 there were 45, plus other vessels from Guernsey. In 1778 there were 5678 people in Harbor Grace, a good sized settlement for that day, and no doubt with a large proportion of Channel Island descent. By the 1780s Jersey firms were operating in Battle and Fox Harbors of Labrador. In 1763 a Jersey fishing boat of 560 tons was in Newfoundland ports. By 1765 various Jerseymen and firms were fishing out of La Poile, Fortune Bay, Jersey Bay, Sablon, Placentia and Isle Verte.

From the middle 1700s through the French Revolution was the heyday of the Channel Islands fisheries in Canada. Hundreds of Jersey ships were involved in the business (E.R. Seary) many of the ships being built in the Maritimes for Jersey firms. Ship building also took place on the Channel Islands, in Grouville and St. Aubins Bay, and in Guernsey, too. The West Indies, Rio, Buenos Ayres, Honduras, Spain, Italy, the United States (both Atlantic and Pacific ports), all were known by Channel Island captains. Steam and the emphasis on speed marked the death of the Island fisheries and ship building firms.

It has been estimated that thirty percent of Newfoundlanders are descended from Channel Island families, and many of the old surnames survive to the present time. Moreover, a tradition of Jersey or Guernsey origin persists even now in many of these families.

"I have researched some of the copies of the parish records from Devonshire, England, and have found many names that were Channel Island in origin, not only the surnames, but the Christian names as well. Some of the names went back to the 1600s. Some of the descendants came out here to Newfoundland, became involved in the fishery and stayed." (Rev. Hammond) "Most of the people in St. George's, Newfoundland, were from Jersey." (Francis Marmaud, Bras D'Or, Cape Breton, NS)

Arthur Fuller, researching Fullers in Canada, wrote that "about 1300 men from Jersey and Guernsey went to Newfoundland every year in the fishing industry, many to Placentia." Other historians have noted the similarity of place names and surname in Newfoundland to those of the Channel Islands, including Shortis-Munn, H.W. Le Messurier, and C.R. Fay. "Jersey is divided in 12 parishes...Many of these names are prominent in Newfoundland, especially in the names of bays and inhabited places, such as St. Mary's, St. Lawrence, St. John's, Trinity...Gouffre is a place to be found both in Jersey and Guernsey as Le Gouffre. The harbour now known as Hillier was originally called St. Heliers...The De Quettevilles had an establishment on the south side of Harbor Grace, also known as the "Jersey Room" very early in the 16th century. The house on this property was called Stout House, and was built of freestone quarried at an island in the bay. Only the foundations now remain.

Newfoundland shares with the Channel Islands at least 1000 surnames, some quite close to the original form of the name, others much distorted, such as: Puddister from Poingdestre, Pasher from Perchard, Hookey from Le Huquet, Hawcoe from Hacquoil, Furey from Le Huray, Murrin from Mourant, Cernew from Quenault, Antle from Anquetil, Besant from Bisson, Thomey from Thoume, Bokey from Le Bosquet, and hundreds of others.

"Many locally owned ships had been built in 'British Plantations'...The Jersey firms operating in Newfoundland and North America kept some of their fishermen over winter in the New World to cut trees and build small schooners used on the banks. There was even a (ship) yard discovered in Newfoundland set up by Jerseymen in the 1500s, according to local legend." (Soc. Jers. Bull. 1962)

Thomas Peddle of Augusta, Maine, descendant of C.I. and Bristol families in Newfoundland, writes of early family there. "Cabot knew where he was going because he had Channel Islanders and Bristol mariners aboard as part of his crew...The Jersey people, together with the Bristolmen came over and controlled the inshore fisheries, which produced hard-cured cod put-up on flakes to be hard-dried...William Peddle was in Musketta, Bristol's Hope, in 1510, with some of the Pikes, and other people that were known as Jerseymen. These families naturally inter-married, and I am searching diligently for some of the notes and writings of Nicholas, Nick, Peddle, because he had a direct line from Eli Peddle back to William Peddle...Nicholas was named after one of the families that the Peddles married into. Some of the many names that I recall...are: PIKE, TAYLOR, PENNEY, PIPPY, NICHOLS, WELLS, BUTT, GARLAND, PYNN, NOEL, NOFTLE, SIMMONS, ANDREWS, SHEPPARD, POWELL, HOWEL, HOWELL, TOMS, TILLY, SOPER, TAPP, SQUIRES, DUNCAN." (Ed. note: most of these surnames occurred also in the Channel Islands)

Recently, a number of fine books on the history and origin of Newfoundland settlers has become available. There is still a great deal of research to be done on Channel Island families settled in Newfoundland.

NEWFOUNDLAND, CHANNEL ISLAND SETTLEMENTS   51
Shortis-Munn, C.R. Fay, H.W. Le Messurier, Rev. Hammond, Harold Horwood

ARGENTIA	HARBOUR MAIN
BARACHOIS DE CERF	HARBOUR MILLE
BACCALIEU	HATTENS POINT
BAULINE	HILLIER
BAY L'ARGENT	HUNTS HARBOUR
BAY BULLS	ISLAND COVE
BAY DE VERDE	ISLE AUX MORTES
BAY D'ESPOIR	JERSEY HARBOUR
BAY ROBERTS	JERSEY ISLAND
BELL ISLAND	JERSEYMAN'S BANK
BONA VISTA	JUGLERS COVE
BREAD AND CHEESE COVE	LA POELE
BRIGUS	LITTLE PASSAGE
BROAD COVE	LITTLE ST. LAWRENCE
BUCK COVE	LONG ISLAND
BURGEO	MARQUISE
BURIN	MINT COVE
BURNT HEAD	MOYAMBROSE
CARBONEAR	OLD PERLICAN
CATALINA	PATRICK'S HARBOUR
CHANNEL	PARADISE
COLINET	PETTY HARBOUR
CONCHE	PLACENTIA BAY
CORMORANT	PORT DE GRAVE
CONQUE	AND BAY DE GRAVE
CORBIN ISLAND	PORTUGAL COVE
CRONEY ISLAND	RENCONTRE
COL DE SAC	RICHE'S ISLAND
CUPIDS	SALMON COVE
FORTUNE BAY	ST. AUBIN
FOUNTAIN	ST. CATHERINE'S BAY
GAULTOIS	ST. GEORGE'S BAY
GAUFFRE	ST. HELIER
GREAT JARVIS	ST. SHOTTS
GREAT PLACENTIA BAY	ST. SHORES
GREENSPOND	TRINITY BAY
GUERNSEY	VILLIANEUVE ISLAND
HARBOUR GRACE	WHITE BEAR BAY

NEWFOUNDLAND, BIBLIOGRAPHY

BALLEINE, G.R., BIOGRAPHICAL DICTIONARY OF JERSEY, New York, 1945.
BREBNER, John Bartlet, THE EXPLORERS OF NORTH AMERICA, Cleveland and N.Y., 1964.
BIGGAR, H.C., EARLY TRADING COMPANIES OF NEW FRANCE, 1921.
CARTWRIGHT, John, R.N., EXPLORATIONS IN NEWFOUNDLAND 1768, HIS MAJESTY'S SHIP GUERNSEY.
CARTWRIGHT, George, JOURNAL OF TRANSACTIONS AND EVENTS, 16 years in Labrador.
CELL, Gillian T., ENGLISH ENTERPRISE IN NEWFOUNDLAND, Toronto, 1959.
FAY, C.R., NEWFOUNDLAND AND THE CHANNEL ISLANDS, Cambridge, Eng., 1961.
FAY, C.R., LIFE AND LABOUR IN NEWFOUNDLAND.
GILLEN, Mollie, ST. JOHN'S, NEWFOUNDLAND, article, CHATELAINE, July, 1973.
GRENFELL, Sir Wilfred, many books about Nfld. and Labrador, early 1900s.
HAMMOND, Rev. J.W., researcher, Bell Island, Newfoundland.
HATTON, J. and Rev. M. HARVEY, NEWFOUNDLAND, THE OLDEST BRITISH COLONY,

London.
HORWOOD, Harold, NEWFOUNDLAND, N.Y., 1969.
HOWE, C.D., NEWFOUNDLAND, AN INTRODUCTION TO CANADA'S NEW PROVINCE, Ottawa, 1950.
INNIS, Harold A., THE COD FISHERIES, Toronto, 1954.
LE MESSURIER, H.W., OLD TIME NEWFOUNDLAND, papers, Priaulx Library, Guernsey, 1955.
LE MOINE, J., NEWFOUNDLAND, THE COD FISHERIES AND WHALING, Montreal, 1878.
LOUNSBURY, Ralph, THE BRITISH FISHERIES AT NEWFOUNDLAND, 1634-1763, London, 1969.
LUCE, Philip, of Vancouver, B.C., speeches and writings, some unpublished.
MATHEWS, Keith, St. John's, Newfoundland, ALPHABETICAL LIST OF CHANNEL ISLAND SURNAMES CONNECTED WITH NEWFOUNDLAND, 1660-1840.
MANNION, John, Editor, THE PEOPLING OF NEWFOUNDLAND, Toronto, Ont, 1977.
MOWATT, Farley, THE ROCK WITHIN THE SEA, A SEAL FOR THE KILLING, WAKE OF THE GREAT SEALERS, etc., Boston and Toronto, 1972, 1973.
MUNN, W.A., co-author of JERSEYMEN IN NEWFOUNDLAND, typescript, ca 1915. See Shortis.
PALMER, Rosemary, Researcher, Maritimes Economics. See MANNION'S book.
PEDLEY, Rev. Charles, THE HISTORY OF NEWFOUNDLAND, London, 1863.
ROBERTS, G.G.D., CANADIAN GUIDE BOOK, EASTERN CANADA AND NEWFOUNDLAND, N.Y., 1891.
ROTHNEY, G.O., NEWFOUNDLAND, A HISTORY, Can. Hist. Assn., bklt. #10, Ottawa, 1973.
SAUNDERS, A.C., NEWFOUNDLAND AND THE CHANNEL ISLANDS, Guernsey Soc. Bull., Vol. 12.
SEARY, E.R., FAMILY NAMES OF THE ISLAND OF NEWFOUNDLAND, 1977; PLACES AND NAMES OF THE AVALON PENINSULA, 1971; A NOTE ON JERSEY AND NEWFOUNDLAND, Nfld. Quarterly, St. John's.
SHELTON, A.C., NEWFOUNDLAND, OUR NORTH DOOR NEIGHBOR, N.Y., 1941.
SHORTIS, H.F., with W.A. MUNN, JERSEYMEN IN NEWFOUNDLAND, typescript, ca 1915.
SMALLWOOD, J.R., THE NEW NEWFOUNDLAND.
SMITH, J. Harry, NEWFOUNDLAND HOLIDAY, Toronto, 1952.
STEVENS, Charles, CATALOG OF JERSEY FAMILY SURNAMES, Jersey, Typescript, 1970.
STEWART, Alice R., ATLANTIC PROVINCES OF CANADA, Union Lists of Materials in the Larger Libraries of Maine, Orono, Maine, 1971.
TAIT, R.H., NEWFOUNDLAND, Canada, 1939.
TILBY, H.T., ENGLISH PEOPLE OVERSEAS, Vol. 3, 1916.
TOCQUE, Rev. Philip, NEWFOUNDLAND AS IT WAS THEN, AND AS IT IS NOW, Toronto, 1877.
TUCKER, E.W., FIVE MONTHS IN LABRADOR AND NEWFOUNDLAND, Concord, Mass., 1839.
TYLER, ENGLAND IN AMERICA, Vol. 4.

Two interesting books about the Maritimes:

MY EARTH, MY SEA, by Edmund Gilligan, New York, 1969.

THE BRENDAN VOYAGE, by Tim Severin, New York, 1978.

CHAPTER FIVE, LABRADOR

"In peace they rove along this pleasant shore,
In plenty live, nor do they wish for more."
(Major Cartwright's Journal)

The above quotation does not appear to be written about the same place as Dr. Grenfell writes about! Labrador is not entirely the stony cold desert that some believe it to be. The natives there had adapted to the conditions, but when Europeans tried to conquer the land, not all managed to survive.

Adjacent to Newfoundland, Labrador is the coast of Northern Quebec, and was named after a fifteenth century adventurer from the Azores. It is three times as big as Newfoundland. Some of its fame derives from Dr. Grenfell, who went there on a short survey, and stayed 48 years. The climate is next to Arctic, but the summer is said to be most beautiful. Philip Luce, below, apparently never visited the Labrador.

"Labrador is a grim and forbidding land with a climate that is the very opposite of the long hours of sunshine experienced by the Channel Islands. It is hardly the place to which emigrants could be enticed by a truthful publicity bureau, and yet, toward the end of the eighteenth century there were five settlements in Labrador occupied almost exclusively by men and women from Jersey." (Luce)

These settlements were at Forteau Bay, Blanc Sablon, Isle au Bois, Henley Harbour, and Battle Harbour. They were the northern headquarters of the great Jersey codfish firms of that day, the Quettevilles, the Falla Bros., the Boucher Bros., and Lucas and Robin, plus some other Jersey firms.

Isle au Bois was the largest of these settlements, and it continued in existence long after the others had disappeared. Sir Wilfred Grenfell records in his book, THE ROMANCE OF LABRADOR, that he visited it in 1894 and that the important Jersey fishing rooms and house were then occupied by the leading man of the community, who was merchant, magistrate, and Lloyd's surveyor of the Labrador. Unfortunately, he does not name the man.

Although it was then 125 years since the ancestors of the inhabitants had come from the Channel Islands, their mode of life had undergone little change. They fished for cod, did a little trapping, rarely went out of their district, and they still spoke Jersey French!

Changing conditions eventually forced these transplanted Channel Islanders to seek a livelihood in Newfoundland, Nova Scotia, and Quebec. The settlements have all disappeared, not a house remains, for these were built of wood, and fuel is scarce in Labrador. The town of Brest, once the largest town on the northern part of this continent, close to the Jersey Inlet du Bois, has left not a trace behind. There is a place called Jersey Tickle in Labrador, tickle meaning harbour. (Luce)

In the heyday of the Labrador fisheries women and girls were included in the crews to clean the fish and also the vessels. Some were from Jersey. They received ten pounds for a voyage of 5 months and took care of the heading, gutting, splitting and salting of the fish. (De Boilieu)

From Jersey, the following firms are said to have been active in Labrador in 1806: Robert Berteau, Simon Du Bois, Falle, Durell, De Quetteville. The latter name appeared in several odd forms, such as Kidville!

The Magdalen Islands, in the Gulf of St. Lawrence, belonged to France, but around 1800 a small fishery was established there by John Janvrin of Jersey. He bought a house from Mr. Gridley of Boston, who had been a resident there for many years, since before 1766. Americans were poaching in these waters in the late 1700s, crowding out the British ships.

Other fishery firms in Labrador had posts with wintering employees at Battle Harbour, Fox Harbour, St. Francis and Black Bear Bay. De Quetteville is described as being the most extensive planter on the coast of Labrador. Besides his rooms at Blanc Sablon, he had several other smaller places, and he seems to have been the wholesaler for many other establishments, 'much to his own profit,' (Luce). Le Boutillier also operated in Labrador.

"The summer Labrador settlements are on Islands or outside headlands. In the winter the "Liveyeres," those who stayed year around, moved up the bays and inlets to be nearer wood and game, and the Newfoundlanders returned to their homes. Much of the work was done on shares. Only a small percentage of the liveyeres could read or write. Sometimes visiting clergymen or priests would hold services in as many stations as they could reach in the short summer season. Sometimes the same building would serve in the morning for the Church of England, in the afternoon for Wesleyan, in the evening for the Salvation Army, and pretty much the same congregation attending each." (Grenfell) True ecumenism!

In 1802 there were a thousand vessels on the Labrador. Messrs. Journeaux and George Du Heaume are mentioned as having "rooms" at Chateau Bay in 1840. "By 1850 one quarter of the resident fishermen of Labrador were from Jersey. They had a hard life. Boys from 6 to 10 years were employed in the codfish industry, and Newfoundland dogs were trained to retrieve fish that fell in the water. In the early 1900s there were still a few Jersey descendants on the coast who spoke the Jersey tongue." (Luce)

In 1863 the Labrador salmon trade alone amounted to a million dollars. Also, in that year in Blanc Sablon Harbour were anchored 80 Nova Scotia vessels and ten ships from Jersey.

"One third of the resident inhabitants are English, Irish or Jersey servants left in charge of the property in the

fishing rooms, and who also employ themselves in the spring and fall catching seals in nets...the other two thirds live constantly at Labrador as furriers and seal catchers, on their own account...Half of these people are Jerseymen and Canadians, most of whom have families." (John MacGregor, BRITISH AMERICA)
"After a great deal of disputing and ill-feeling, Labrador, bandied about from pillar to post, was allotted to Newfoundland, much to Quebec's disgust. In 1927, Newfoundland, basing her claims on an early treaty which gave her 'all land drained by the rivers running out the east coast,' was rewarded with no small slice of territory. Hamilton River runs through some four hundred miles, giving a big coastal stretch to Newfoundland, and leaving Quebec with the North Shore of the St. Lawrence and a great inland waste, Canadian Labrador." (Dorothy Hogner, SUMMER ROADS TO GASPE) This land is definitely no longer thought of as a wasteland. Its value is becoming rapidly apparent.

Thousands of men and women over the two centuries from the late 1700s to the late 1900s with Jersey and Guernsey ancestry have been associated with the coast of Labrador, but research from this distance has been most difficult. Perhaps another writer will explore this area of historic interest and write about these hardy Islanders.

LABRADOR, BIBLIOGRAPHY

CARTWRIGHT, George, His Journal, Boston, Estes, 1911.
DE BOILIEU, R., RECOLLECTIONS OF LABRADOR LIFE, 1861.
DUNCAN, Norman, DR. GRENFELL'S PARISH, THE DEEP SEA FISHERMEN, New York, 1905, etc.
GOSLING,W.G., LABRADOR, London, 1910.
GRENFELL, Sir Wilfred, VIKINGS OF TODAY, ROMANCE OF LABRADOR, ADRIFT ON AN ICEPAN, DOWN NORTH ON THE LABRADOR, DOWN TO THE SEA, FORTY YEARS FOR LABRADOR, HARVEST OF THE SEA, LABRADOR DAYS, A LABRADOR DOCTOR, A LABRADOR LOGBOOK, LABRADOR LOOKS AT THE ORIENT, THE COUNTRY AND THE PEOPLE, NORTHERN NEIGHBORS, OFF THE ROCKS, TALES OF THE LABRADOR, etc.
HOGNER, Dorothy Child, SUMMER ROADS TO GASPE, N.Y., 1939.
MAC GREGOR, John, BRITISH AMERICA, Scotland, 1840s.
MERCER, G.A., THE PROVINCE OF NEWFOUNDLAND AND LABRADOR, Ottawa, 1968.
MOWATT, Farley, WAKE OF THE GREAT SEALERS, Boston and Toronto, 1973, and other books.
STEWART, Alice R., ATLANTIC PROVINCES OF CANADA, Union List of materials on, in Maine Libraries, Orono, MA, 1971, booklet.
TUCKER, Ephraim W., FIVE MONTHS IN LABRADOR AND NEWFOUNDLAND, DURING THE SUMMER OF 1838, Concord, Mass., 1839.
VIGNEAU, Elise, HISTORY OF LABRADOR AND THE MAGDALEN ISLANDS.

Typical fishing village of Newfoundland
and
Homestead on Conception Bay
(NEWFOUNDLAND, OUR NORTH DOOR NEIGHBOR, by A. C. Shelton)

CHAPTER SIX, NOVA SCOTIA AND CAPE BRETON 57

"God gives all men all earth to love,
But since man's heart is small,
Ordains for each, one spot shall prove
Beloved over all."
(Will R. Bird)

According to historians of the 1800s, the Channel Islanders were taking an active part in the commerce of Nova Scotia by the middle of the 1700s. This quasi-island is connected to mainland Canada by only a neck of land near Amherst. It is about 500 miles long, and is a rough sausage shape lying tilted to the northeast, just south of the Gulf of the St. Lawrence River. The northern quarter is Cape Breton Island, where Jersey fishing establishments were to be found in the late 1700s, if not before.

Although Bretons, English and Portuguese fishermen frequented Cape Breton Island shores as early as the 1400s, no data found by the compiler mentions Channel Islanders there before the 1700s. Since there were some in Newfoundland and the American colonies in the 1600s, it seems quite likely that Jersey and Guernsey fishermen were there also at that time. R.H. Martin mentions the ruins of Louisbourg, in his HISTORY OF NOVA SCOTIA, "being inhabited by the Acadian-French and frequented principally by Jersey and Guernsey people."

On the south coast of Cape Breton, where European fishermen had come each year for centuries, the French constructed a large fort at Louisbourg, the better to control the fisheries and the settlements. From this fort the French forces set out to harass and capture English and English controlled ships and territory. The New Englanders were indignant, and pressured the British Government to take the Fort. This was done in 1745, but the English traded it back to France in exchange for Madras, India. This single fact was a large contributing cause of the American revolution.

In 1758 the fortress was again taken, at the insistence of the New Englanders. Both captures were credited in part to a descendant of a Channel Island family of New Hampshire, Lieutenant-Colonel Messerve, (see Messervy family), of the New Hampshire Reg't. of the British Army. Messerve was a prominant man, a large landholder, able and innovative, and had been a ship-builder in New Hampshire. The record below is taken from Parkman's A HALF CENTURY CONFLICT.

"The cannon were to be dragged over the marsh to Green Hill, a spur of the line of rough heights that half encircled the town and harbour. Here the first battery was to be planted; and from this point other guns were to be dragged onward to the more advanced stations, a distance in all of more than two miles, thought by the French to be impassable. So, in fact, it seemed for at the first attempt, the wheels of the cannon sank to the hubs in mud and moss, then the carriage, and finally the piece itself slowly disappeared.

Lt.-Col. Messerve, of the New Hampshire regiment, a shipbuilder by trade, presently overcame the difficulty. By his direction, sledges of timber were made, sixteen feet long and five feet wide; a cannon was placed on each of these, and it was then dragged over the marsh by a team of 200 men, harnessed with rope-traces and breast-straps, and wading to the knees. Horses or oxen would have foundered in the mire. The way had often to be changed, as the mossy surface was soon churned into a hopeless slough along the line of march. The work could only be done at night or in thick-fog, the men being completely exposed to the cannon of the town.

Thirteen years after, when General Amherst besieged Louisbourg again, he dragged his cannon to the same hill over the same marsh; but having at his command, instead of 4000 militiamen, 11,000 British regulars, with all appliances and means to boot, he made a road with prodigious labour through the mire, and protected it from the French shot by an epaulement, or lateral earthwork."

The largest number of Jersey and Guernsey settlers here were those in the fishing villages of the coasts, where Jersey firms were established. They brought workers from Jersey and Guernsey, from southern England, and also hired the Acadians.

Annapolis Royal on the west coast, was also a place where a few Channel Islanders settled. Philip Berteaux, a master carpenter, or architect, was in Annapolis Royal before the dispersal of the Acadians. In his will he declared himself a native of St. Heliers, Island of Jersey, the will being dated 1794. Savary says that William, the oldest son of Philip Berteaux, was born about 1745, and died about 1833. "He was therefore about 10 years old when he witnessed the destruction of the French dwellings and barns, which he related to Judge Haliburton." The second son, Thomas Edward, was born about 1770, and descendants still live in Nova Scotia.

During the Huguenot troubles in France, thousands fled from the country, many by way of the Channel Islands. Most of the Huguenots moved on to Great Britain, Scandinavia, North and South America. Joshua Temple de Ste. Croix was from a French Huguenot family. He removed first to New England, and then to Nova Scotia, settling in Bridgetown, Annapolis Co., leaving many descendants.

Le Cains in Nova Scotia and elsewhere are descendants of Francis Barclay Le Quesne, who was born in Jersey, and settled also in Annapolis as Master Artificer or Armourer. He was a noted Mason, belonging to the first lodge in Canada.

Among the Loyalists in Nova Scotia's history are the Balcombs and the Bishops. The Balcombs are said to be descended from Capt. John Balcomb, born about 1697 in Jersey. Descendants of this family removed from New England to Nova Scotia. It is interesting to note that in 1726 in Jersey, Francois

Balcom married Anne Renouf of St. Mary, Jersey, and in 1739 Francois Balcom and Jeanne Hamon were godparents to Elizabeth Ingouville. The Hamon, Hammond, Balcom, Renouf and Ingouville surnames all appeared in Nova Scotia records, and the families were quite likely related to one another in Jersey.

The Le Boutilliers of Nova Scotia came from several different spots in Europe, including probably England and the French-Swiss border province of Mont Beliard. It is believed that other Le Boutilliers of Nova Scotia came directly from the Channel Islands, but coordinating and compiling the Le Boutilliers there was beyond the scope of this book, due to sheer numbers, and the compiler's inability to spend a couple of years in the province.

The Dumaresq descendants in Canada are quite numerous, many descendants of Capt. Philip, born 1695 Jersey. Much work has been done on this family genealogy. The Bishops, another Loyalist family, also originated in Jersey or Guernsey Islands. The first Bishop was apparently kidnapped from the Islands and brought to New London, Conn., and his descendants, or some of them, removed to Nova Scotia. (BISHOP orig. from England)

The Bourinots of Jersey removed to Nova Scotia and produced a number of notable men, M.L.A., Senator, Historians, authors, artists and lawyers. In Uniacke's SKETCHES OF CAPE BRETON, edited by C. Bruce Fergusson of the Nova Scotia Archives, is a description of the Bourinot home in Cape Breton in the last century.

While the Payzant, Paisant family of Nova Scotia was French in origin, Louis, the progenitor, was a Huguenot, and spent 13 years in St. Helier's Jersey, where he and his second wife were married, their seven children being born there. His tragic story is told in THE PAYZANT AND ALLIED JESS AND JUHAN FAMILIES IN NORTH AMERICA.

Cape Breton is divided from Nova Scotia by the Strait of Canso. Arichat at its southern end, plus numerous small settlements, was the home of many families of Jersey folk, associated with shipping and the fisheries. Many old names of Jersey were represented there in the last 1700s and early 1800s, such as Janvrin, Le Vesconte, Jean, Brine, De Gruchy, Belleine, etc.

"Philip Ingouville, a native of Jersey, obtained a grant of 1000 acres of land at Sydney Forks, Cape Breton, eight miles from town...He commenced farming on a large scale...His dairy and farm products found a market not only in Sydney but also in Newfoundland, Halifax and the West Indies. He died in 1818." (Uniacke) Descendants of the Gibbon-Ingouville family are many, in various parts of Canada. The Ingouvilles, according to Soc. Jers. records were closely associated with the silversmiths of Jersey, the Amiraux, Kerby, Aubin and Le Gallais families.

"Arichat was important and prosperous until the late 1800s. Many vessels were registered there and many ships came to refuel and pick up provisions. During the American Civil War, since the British supported the South, Arichat was very busy supplying British ships. When the St. Peter's Canal was built, very few ships came to Arichat, and bad financial times set in. That is when many people went to the U.S. and to other parts of Canada. All my relatives on both sides, except my father and mother, went to the New England states, and I have many relatives there." (Evelyn Campbell, Halifax, N.S.)

"The three Ballam sisters of Jersey, living in Cape Breton, had devoted their entire adult lives to the construction of some magnificent tapestries. Each sister, in turn, had become blind from the exacting needlework required...They covered the walls of the sitting room. In one Biblical scene, the sombre face of Saul seemed to threaten David and the harp. The faces (or so I was told) were worked with German silks and resembled paintings. At home, some time later, we read that 'the representatives of an American collector had paid $50,000 for Tapestries in Cape Breton.' Were they the Ballam tapestries?" (Louise Surgey Brine, typescript, THEY CAME IN SAILING SHIPS)

The author of the above typescript, Mrs. Brine, wrote about several Cape Breton families, including the Brines. William Edward came to Arichat about 1830, but removed to New York, and then to Nova Scotia, where he became Provincial Treasurer. John Jean, descendant of the old Jean family of Jersey, established a firm in Petit de Grat. Six daughters married into the old Jersey families of Brine, De Gruchy, Balleine, Janvrin and Le Vesconte.

Isaac Le Vesconte was born 1822 in St. Aubin, Jersey, and removed to Arichat, where he and his family and partner, a De Carteret, did a large business in shipping. "He shipped dried fish to Brazil in holds that were protected by linings of birch bark. From Brazil the vessels brought cheap wines to England." (Walworth)

SOME CHANNEL ISLAND SURNAMES IN NOVA SCOTIA AND CAPE BRETON

AMEY, AMY	DE GRUCHY	LEGGE	NORMAN
ANLEY	DE LA HAYE	LE GRANDE	NOSEWORTHY
ARTHUR	DE QUETTEVILLE	LE GRESLEY	PAINT
BALCOMB	DE STE. CROIX	LE GRALEY	PEDDLEY, PELLEY
BALL, BAAL	DE VEAU	LE GROS	LE PELLEY
BALLEINE	DE VOUGE	LE JEUNE	PELLIER
BARVIS	DOLBEL	LE LACHEUR	PENNELL, PINEL
BATTYS	DOREY	LE LIEVRE	PERRY
BATISTE	DU HAMEL	LE MAISTRE	PIEROWAY,
BAUCHE	DUMARESQ	LE MARCHANT	PIROUET
BEAUCHAMP	FAY	LE MESURIER	PIPPY
BELL	FILLEUL	LE MOINE	POULAIN, PULLEN
BENNETT, BENEST?	FIOTT	LE MONTAIS	PURCELL
BENOIT	FIXOTT	LE PAGE	RENOUF
BERTEAUX	FRANCIS	LE PATOUREL	RETTIE,
BERTRAND	FULLER	LE QUESNE, LE CAIN	RETTILLIE
BINET	GALLEY	LE ROSSIGNOL,	RICHARD
BISHOP	GALLICHON	NIGHTINGALE	RICHARDSON
BISSETT	GAUVIN	LE RICHE	RIDEOUT
BISSON	GODFREY	LE ROUX	ROBERT, ROBERTS
BLANCPIED,	GOSSE	LE ROY	ROBIN
BLAMPIED	GRANDY, GRANDIN	LE RUE	ROPER
BLANCHARD	GRUCHY, DE GRUCHY	LE SEELLEUR	ROSE
BOSDET	GUSHUE	LE VESCONTE	SALTER
BOURGEOIS	HALLETT	L'HEUREUX	SAMPSON, SAMSON
BOURINOT	HARDY	LONGLEY, LANGLOIS	SAUMAREZ
BOUTILLIER	HAWCO, HACQUOIL	LUCAS	SAVARY, SYVRET
BRAY	HELLIER, HELYER	LUCE	SAVIDENT
BREHAUT	HILL	MAHY	SEALE
BREWER	HILLIER	MALZARD	SERRE
BRINE, BRIEN	HOCQUARD	MANUEL	SHEPPARD,
BRAINE, BRIAND	HUBERT	MARCHAND	SHEPHERD
BROCK	INGOUVILLE	MARSH, LA MARSH	STE. CROIX
BROUARD	JACKSON	MARTEL	STANNAGE
BROWN, LE BRUN	JACQUES	MARTIN	SYLVESTRE
BRUSHETT	JANVRIN	MATTINGLEY	SYVRET
BUFFET	JEAN	MAUGER	TANGY, TANGUAY?
BURT	JOLI, JOLLY	MERCHANT	TILLER, TILLEY
BUTLER, LE	JOURDAIN, JORDON	MERRY	TRAHEY, TRACHY
BOUTILLIER	JOURNEAUX	MESSERVY	TUCKER
CAIN	KEYHOE	MESSURIER	TUPPER
CAREY	LA CROIX	MESURIER	VATCHER, VAUTIER
CAVE	LAFOLLEY	MORRILL	VAUDIN
CLEMENTS	LANGLOIS	MOSER?	WEBBER
CLOUGH	LA VACHE	MOTT, LE MOTTEE?	WHITE, LE BLANC
COISH, COSH	LE BLANC, WHITE	MOUILPIED	WOOTTEN?
CORBET	LE BRUN, BROWN	MULLIN, MOULIN	
COURAGE	LE CAIN, LE QUESNE	MURRAN, MOURANT	
COUTANCHE	LE CLERCQ	NAIDOO	
CROSS, DE CROIX,	LE COCQ	NEVILLE	
de STE. CROIX	LE COUTEUR, CUTOR	NICHOL	
CURNEW, CORNU	LE CRAS	NICOLLE	
CUQUS, CUCU	LE CRAW	NICHOLAS	
DA COSTA	LE DREW	NIGHTINGALE, LE	
DE CARTERET	LEE	ROSSIGNOL	
DE GARRETT	LE FEBVRE	NOBLE	
DE GARIS	LE FRESNE	NOEL	

ST. HELIER'S, JERSEY, early 1900s?

...s town, the capital of Jersey, is the center of government, and the home of the Societée
... and Library, containing records of hundreds of years of Island life and culture. JERSEY
...NS, by Richard Mayne and Joan Stevens, contains many fine pictures of early buildings of
...'s and other parishes of the Island and the people who lived there before 1918.

NOVA SCOTIA AND CAPE BRETON, BIBLIOGRAPHY

ANGIVIN, Joseph, METHODISM IN CAPE BRETON, Sydney Mines, 1912.
ARMSTRONG, G.H., THE ORIGIN AND MEANING OF PLACE NAMES IN CANADA, Toronto, 1930.
ARCHIVES OF NOVA SCOTIA, HALIFAX, N.S., Relevant MSS and books.
BEATON INSTITUTE, Cape Breton, N.S.
BELL, Winthrop P., THE FOREIGN PROSTESTANTS AND THE SETTLEMENT OF NOVA SCOTIA, Toronto, 1961.
BIRD, Will R., THIS IS NOVA SCOTIA, Phila. and Toronto, 1950.
BOURINOT, J.G., a number of excellent books about Canada. See NOTABLES.
BREBNER, John Bartlett, CANADA, Ann Arbor, Mich. and Toronto, 1960; NEW ENGLAND'S OUTPOST, ACADIA BEFORE THE CONQUEST OF CANADA, 1927; THE MINGLING OF CANADIAN AND AMERICAN PEOPLES; THE NEUTRAL YANKEES OF NOVA SCOTIA, etc.
BROWN, Richard, CAPE BRETON, England, 1869.
CALNEK, Wm. A., A HISTORY OF ANNAPOLIS, Toronto, Ont., 1897.
CAMPBELL, G.G., HISTORY OF NOVA SCOTIA, Toronto, 1948.
CHAPIN, Miriam, ATLANTIC CANADA, Toronto, 1956.
CHIASSON, Pere Anselme, CHETICAMP, HISTORIE ET TRADITIONS ACADIENNES, Moncton, N.B., 1962.
CLARK, Andrew Hill, ACADIA, Wisconsin, 1968.
COCHRANE, Rev. Wm., CANADIAN ALBUM OF MEN OF CANADA, Brantford, Ont., 1895, 1925.
COLEMAN, Emma Lewis, NEW ENGLAND CAPTIVES CARRIED TO CANADA, Portland, Maine, 1925.
COLLIER, Sargent F., DOWNEAST, Boston, 1953.
DE BOILIEU, L., RECOLLECTIONS OF LABRADOR LIFE, Toronto, 1861, 1969.
DENNIS, Clara, CAPE BRETON OVER, Toronto.
DOWNEY, Fairfax, LOUISBOURG, KEY TO A CONTINENT. Forts Series of S.H. Holbrook, Englewood Cliffs, N.J., 1965.
EATON, Arthur W.H., HISTORY OF KING'S COUNTY, Belleville, Ont., 1972.
FERGUSSON, F. Bruce, Ed., DIRECTORY OF THE MEMBERS OF THE LEGISLATIVE ASSEMBLY OF NOVA SCOTIA, 1758-1958, Halifax, N.S., 1956; UNIACKES SKETCHES OF CAPE BRETON ISLAND, 1958.
FISHERMAN'S OWN BOOK, Gloucester, Mass., 1882.
FRENCH, Goldwin, PARSONS AND POLITICS, Toronto, 1962.
GILROY, Marion, LOYALISTS AND LAND SETTLEMENT IN NOVA SCOTIA, PANS, No. 4, 1937.
GOSLING, W.G., LABRADOR, London, 1910.
GRANT, Ruth, THE CANADIAN ATLANTIC FISHERY, Toronto, 1934.
HANNAY, James, HISTORY OF ACADIA, Saint John, N.B., 1879.
HARDY, W.G., FROM SEA UNTO SEA, CANADA 1850-1910, Garden City, N.Y., 1959.
INNIS, Harold A., THE COD FISHERIES, Toronto, 1940.
JACKSON, Elva E., CAPE BRETON AND THE JACKSON KITH AND KIN, Windsor, N.S., 1971.
KERR, J. Ernest, IMPRINT OF THE MARITIMES, Boston, 1959.
LE MOINE, J.M., CHRONICLES OF THE ST. LAWRENCE, New York, 1878.
LE VESCONTE AND DE CARTERET BUSINESS PAPERS, Nova Scotia Archives, Halifax, N.S.
LITTLE, Otis, THE STATE OF TRADE IN THE NORTHERN COLONIES, London, 1748.
MACGREGOR, John, BRITISH AMERICA, Edinburgh, 1833, HISTORICAL AND DESCRIPTIVE SKETCHES OF THE MARITIMES, MARITIMES COLONIES OF BRITISH AMERICA, 1828, etc.
MARTIN, R. Montgomery, HISTORY OF NOVA SCOTIA, etc., London, 1837.
MC LENNAN, LOUISBOURG
MC NUTT, Wm. S., ATLANTIC PROVINCES, 1965.

MORSE, Wm. Inglis, GRAVESTONES OF ACADIE, London, 1929.
NOVA SCOTIA HISTORICAL SOC. COLLECTIONS, 1890s, Halifax, N.S.
PLACE NAMES OF NOVA SCOTIA, Public Archives of N.S., 1967.
PICHON, Thos., LETTERS AND MEMOIRS, re Cape Breton and Louisbourg, 1760.
RADDALL, Thomas H., HALIFAX, WARDEN OF THE NORTH.
SAUNDERS, Edward M., HISTORY OF THE BAPTISTS OF THE MARITIMES, Halifax, 1902.
SAVARY, A.W., HISTORY OF THE COUNTY OF ANNAPOLIS, Toronto, 1913, Supplement to the CALNEK book, qv.
STEWART, Alice R., THE ATLANTIC PROVINCES OF CANADA, source list, materials in the larger libraries in Maine, Orono, Maine, 1971
SNIDER, Charles H.J., UNDER THE RED JACK, London, 1928.
SUTTON, Horace, FOOTLOOSE IN CANADA, New York and Toronto, 1950.
TILBY, T.T., ENGLISH PEOPLE OVERSEAS, London, 1916.
TURK, M.G., THE QUIET ADVENTURERS IN AMERICA, Cleveland, Ohio, 1975.
VERNON, C.W., CAPE BRETON, CANADA, Toronto, 1903.
WALWORTH, Arthur, CAPE BRETON, ISLE OF ROMANCE, Toronto, 1948.
WHITE, Stephen, Acadian Genealogies, Centre d'Etudes Acadiennes, U. of Moncton, N.B.
WHITELAW, Wm. M. THE MARITIMES AND CANADA BEFORE CONFEDERATION, Toronto, 1934.
WOOD, Wm., THE GREAT FORTRESS, Toronto, 1915.
TUPPER FAMILY RECORDS, Archives of Nova Scotia, Halifax, N.S.
UNIACKE, see FERGUSSON above.

See GENEALOGICAL RESEARCH IN NOVA SCOTIA by
Terrence Punch, Box 895, Armadale, Halifax, NS, Canada.

CHAPTER SEVEN, NEW BRUNSWICK

"This was the Abenaki land;
Till on a day among the uncounted days,
White in the sunlight,
There came a bark, tiny and frail,
over the sea, threading the island maze,
By ruddy shore and sombre headland veering."
(Henry Milner Rideout)

It was Cartier's frail barque that sailed by Miscou Island in 1534, and he named its Northwest point, Cape of Hope. This was possibly the first notice of what was to be the province of New Brunswick by a European. Micmacs and Abenaquis peopled the deep forests and fished the mighty rivers. In the early years of the 1600s, the French began to settle on a few isolated capes and islands around the coastline. De la Tour appeared in the Bay of Fundy in 1604. Champlain's map of 1632 shows the Island of Miscou and other places on the coast. (Ganong)

The northeastern tip of the province ends in two small islands, Miscou and Shippegan, jutting out into the St. Lawrence Gulf. The charming but luckless Nicholas Denys was living on Miscou in 1645. He was at that time Governor and Proprietor of all the lands from Cape Breton to Gaspe, and in his writings of 1672 tells of his settlement on the south side of the harbour, where he had a habitation and garden. Although the settlement was burned by his enemies in 1647, traces of the place were seen in the early 1900s.

"Probably from 1620 to 1670 Miscou Harbour was an important center of trade and fishery, with a considerable permanent population." (Ganong) While in French hands there were fisheries conducted on the shores, but by the early 1800s they were abandoned. Then, in the 1830s the Jerseymen established a shore fishery on Miscou Point. Peter John Du Val, qv, obtained a grant of the north end of the Island where he established fishery buildings north of the present lighthouse. With him in the business was John Godfrey, another Jerseyman. Du Val was related to the Du Vals of Bonaventure Island, off Perce, Que. Other Jerseymen involved here were John Le Couteur, the Alexandres, Capt. George Syvret, and John Vibert.

"These Jerseymen, of whom there are others at Shippegan, Caraquet, Bathurst and elsewhere, were chiefly Protestants and of a character which has made them an exceedingly valuable element in the New Brunswick population." (Ganong)

About 1817 Capt. George Syvret, a Jerseyman, came from Arichat to Caraquet, N.B. He taught school, was a J.P., and later removed to Miscou, where 'he has left many descendants.'" (Ganong) These many descendants seem to have removed elsewhere. "Samuel Syvret was the builder of the stone church in 1818-1820...The Robins came in 1837...bought land from the Brideaus to establish a fishery." (HISTORY OF CARAQUET, by Ganong) About 1832, the Wm. Fruing Co., competitors of Charles Robin's firm, began a large fishery establishment on the Point, called variously Pt. Alexandre and La Vielle Point. The Alexandre brothers were managers and clerks for the Fruing firm, related to Fruing by marriage. Others who came out in the employ of the Jersey companies were Le Messurier, Luce, John and Thomas Cabot, James Henry, and H. A. Sormany. The latter became a prominent resident and Collector of Customs, of Lameque, and his son, Dr. Sormany, was elected to the local Legislature. (Ganong)

In the early part of this century, Ganong wrote charmingly of the Islands as they were at that time, a rather wild and picturesque corner of the Province, changing slowly but steadily under the force of the ocean currents:

"The Island is slowly sinking beneath the sea, which is eating away the upland, while the beaches are advancing landward over barren and meadow...The Miscou man fishes at the banks for herring and cod, around the shores for lobsters, in the bays for bass, in the brooks for eels, farms a little, shoots ducks and geese and brant in the fall, fishes smelt through the ice in the winter. He thus depends upon the taking of wild game and has much of the joy of the life of the Couriers des Bois, of the uncertainty and charm of the wild life." (Ganong)

A note about the supplies in the Fruing store at Shippegan in 1850 reveals how far-ranging were the Jersey ships. These stores sold stockings from Jersey, butter from Ireland, molasses from Cuba, Naples biscuits, Brazil sugar, Sicilian lemons, American tobacco, and other items from England, Holland, and Germany. The only Canadian items were flour and pork! (Perley)

In the Archives of Canada is a mail route petition of 1834, requesting a mail route between Bathurst and Shippegan, which contains a good many Jersey surnames, but is difficult to decipher. Channel Islanders no doubt gave its name to Sumarez County in New Brunswick.

Continuing and vicious Indian raids into New England from Quebec and New Brunswick resulted in the capture and death of many Channel Islanders settled in the tiny seaports of Maine and New Hampshire. While some of the victims were ransomed, and returned home, others remained in Canada. Some Channel Island families involved were named Durell, Greeley (Le Gresley), Huntoon, Le Montais, Weare, Ricker, and Pendexter. The latter name is a variant of the Poingdestres of Jersey. (See also Puddister of Newfoundland and THE QUIET ADVENTURERS IN AMERICA, by M. Turk)

The Vibert family of Jersey and New Brunswick has flourished and spread to many provinces, and to the States. Some still live in Miscou, though, and Leslie Vibert of Miscou Harbor continues the custom of the family, upholding the old traditions of the Jersey fishermen. He holds the official record for

NEW BRUNSWICK 67

the largest tuna ever caught on sporting tackle. He landed a 1,200 lb. bluefin tuna on Sept. 22, 1976, and this catch was recently recognized as the new world record by the International Game Fish Association. Mr. Vibert was fishing on the boat BABY DOLL, captained by his brother Douglas. The tuna was also the largest game fish of any species caught in the Association's 1976 World fishing competitions. It was caught in Chaleur Bay, New Brunswick, where the world's largest, and the incidence of strikes per boat, per day, is the highest in North America. (See also Capt. Vibert's Journal of the 1800s, and the story of John Vibert's four years as a captive of the Japanese)

Sources of New Brunswick material are plentiful, as this province has a most involved and interesting history.

PUBLIC LIBRARY, Saint John, N.B.
NEW BRUNSWICK HISTORICAL SOCIETY, 120 Union St., Saint John, N.B.
PUBLIC ARCHIVES, Halifax, N.S. (N.B. was once a part of N.S.)
NEW BRUNSWICK MUSEUM, 277 Douglas Ave., Saint John, N.B.
LA SOCIETE HISTORIQUE NICHOLAS DENIS, Bertrand, N.B.
CHALEUR HISTORY MUSEUM, P.O. Box 1717, Dalhousie, N.B.
PUBLIC ARCHIVES OF CANADA, Census records of Gloucester Co., N.B.
MARRIAGE AND PROBATE RECORDS, Prov. Arch. of N.B., Fredericton, N.B.
EARLY MARRIAGE RECORDS OF NEW BRUNSWICK, 1766-1839, by B. Wood-Holt, Saint John, N.B., 1978.

Records compiled by Stephen White, at Moncton Univ., Moncton, NB, Canada
Records compiled by Donat Robichaud, St.Nom de Jesus Parish, CP 90, Beresford, NB, Canada

NEW BRUNSWICK GENEALOGICAL SOCIETY,
P.O. Box 3235, Station B,
Frederickton, NB, Canada   E3A 2W0

The surname list below, like those of the other Provinces, is incomplete. It has been difficult to locate representatives of these families, as considerable movement has taken place in the last fifty years, inland, up to Montreal, and Quebec City, as well as to Ontario and the United States.

AGNES	FALLU	LE MESSURIER
AHIER	FRUING	LE RICHE
ALEXANDRE	GAUDIN, GODIN	LUCE
ANDROS	HACOU, HACQUOIL	MALLETT?
BAUDIN, BEAUDIN	HAMON	MARETT, MARRETTE
BENEST	HEMERY	MAUGER, MAJOR
BISSON	HENRY	PAINT
BRIDEAU?	HILLYARD, HILLIARD	PAINTER
BRIEN	JEAN	RABASSE
CABOT	JANVRIN	ROBBINS
CARON	JOURNEAU	ROBERT
CARR	LA BILLOIS	ROBIN
DE LA GARDE	LA FOLLEY	ROUSSEL?
DE LA PERELLE	LE BOUTILLIER	SAYRE?
DE STE. CROIX	LE BRETON	SIVRET, SYVRET,
DOLBEL	LE COUTRE, LE COUTEUR	SEIVRY
DUMARESQ	LE GALLAIS	SORMANY
DU VAL	LE GRAND	THOMAS
FALLE	LE GRESLEY, GREELEY	VIBERT
FALLA	LE MESURIER	VINCENT

NEW BRUNSWICK BIBLIOGRAPHY

GALLIE, or CALLIE, Michael, NEW BRUNSWICK.
GANONG, Wm. F., HISTORY OF CARAQUET AND POKEMOUCHE, and HISTORY OF MISCOU AND SHIPPEGAN, Saint John, N.B., 1946.
LE MOINE, J., CHRONICLES OF THE ST. LAWRENCE.
MC NUTT, W.S., THE ATLANTIC PROVINCES, Toronto, 1965.
MURCHIE, Guy, SAINT CROIX, THE SENTINEL RIVER, N.Y. City, 1947.
PERLEY, Moses, REPORTS ON THE SEA AND RIVER FISHERIES OF NEW BRUNSWICK, Frederickton, N.B.
ROBICHAUD, Donat, LE GRAND CHIPAGAN, Beresford, N.B., 1977.
SAUNDERS, A.C., CHARLES ROBIN, Gaspe Pioneer.
VROOM, James, GLIMPSES OF THE PAST, Widener Library, N.Y. City, typescript?
WRIGHT, Esther Clark, THE SAINT JOHN RIVER, Toronto, 1949.

John Philip Vibert, born 1898 Miscou, N.B., enlisted in Winnipeg, Man., Sept. 9, 1939, with the Canadian Grenadiers, Company B., H 6355. His report on his four years as a Japanese prisoner is included, in part, below. (Recorded by Nola Journeau, St. Eustache, Quebec)

"We landed in Kowloon before noon and a band greeted us (English and American). Three weeks there, then Japanese came and bombed. We left there, crossed to Hong Kong. Japs started fighting from the mainland over to Hong Kong. Fought for a week. At night the Japs dressed as Chinamen, came across the harbour in sampans. Before we knew they opened fire, then we opened fire on the boats. The Japs were mown down, still advancing until 60,000 Japs landed, cavalry and anti-air craft.

We fought night and day until the Mayor of Hong Kong surrendered, up went the white flag. I was shellshocked, a shrapnel fell on me after I was thrown, and it burned through the flesh. Our officer told us 'every man for himself and God help us all.' Japanese came in and took us prisoners. We thought the Japs never took prisoners, shot them instead.

There were 5 or 6 nurses came with our outfit, also taken prisoner. The Japs cut out their tongues. They put us in big buildings, no beds, then moved 1/2 mile into another building. In the morning they walked us five miles to the harbour, crossed back and marched 3 miles to Kowloon. We were 60 in each hut - floor of cement - no windows, smashed out so boys used brick and red mud to brick up the windows. We only had one blanket and our packs and the clothes on our backs and slept on the floor for 10 months or a year.

...A Canadian officer gave me $10.00 to get 10 chocolate bars,...from the Chinese over the fence. The Japs saw me reaching through the barbed wire fence and a Japanese guard put his gun over my shoulder and shot this Chinese woman who delivered the bars, then he made me lie down on a little table and got the number of my camp and my name, then he slapped me in the face. Then drew off with his fist to hit me in the jaw, but I ducked him. Then he took me by the shoulder and said, 'come with me, I am going to shoot you.' There were three officers coming, American, English, and Canadian, and I sat by the fence. I could hear them talking, they were pleading for me; one officer went in the camp for an interpreter...the guard went on his way and the Canadian came to me and said, 'you're free, go back to your camp.'

...I was so hungry that I often wished I was home in Miscou ...We were fed rice without sugar or salt a teacup full twice a day...Starvation caused malaria which I had three times, also beriberi. Sixty of us in one hut got so sick--they took us out on stretchers to Hong Kong from Kowloon to an English hospital. I was there 8 months. I went blind for 5 months. After regaining my sight another guy and I read the whole of the New Testament. I was 184 pounds when taken prisoner and came out at 80 pounds. When I became well enough I had a dentist remove my gold capped teeth and sold it to a Japanese guard, at midnight, for 1000 yen, then I got the guards to bring cigarettes.

A man from Gaspe, Quebec taught me how to knit, so I knit the Japanese ankle socks and gloves. They went by signs and at midnight they came to buy. I made signs in exchange, such as for salt, eggs, sugar and cigarettes. I got so hungry I didn't care if I got shot or not--I'd roll up some money in anything I could get, and throw it over the barb-wire fence ...the Chinese would roll up bars or anything in a three cornered paper bag, tie it and throw it over to me. I'd get behind the camps so the Japs wouldn't see me then run to camp. I saw then stripping Chinese women and tying them to trees, pouring gas on them, and light cigarettes and burn them all over their bodies, torture them and others. If caught near the fence, they'd unroll a roll of wire 60 feet long, strip the women and girls and roll them over this barbed wire and pick them up all bloody. Then when they were so far they threw gasoline over them and burn them up.

The Japanese asked our Canadian Director how come we were losing so many of our men. The doctor told them we had no medicine and if they got none, all would die. So the Japs got the Red Cross in, and a certain liquid in needle form to administer us guys, 4 needles per day. A boy of 25 years old cried and pleaded with the doctor regarding his feet, the flesh was falling off, two boys like that died from gangrene. Some committed suicide, gave up eating, lost courage.

We got so lousy with bedbugs, we take our iron beds apart and hit them on the cement outdoors and tramp and hammer (the insects)...Some of the prisoners were tied up with barbed wire from one to the other. Any that got too weak they untied them and threw them over the mountain.

When war finished--the guards had left the fence--then we could hear the news on radio, and we sat up all night without sleeping...Next day there was small planes come over, circled around and dripped cigs, bars and food, etc. Each plane loaded with provisions flew very low and waved at us...so glad... ship came to take us to Manilla...To San Francisco...there were all sorts of planes and boats came out to greet us, wharf crowded with people meeting us, with sandwiches and coffee for the prisoners...boat for Victoria, B.C....I caught pneumonia on the way over, 3 died...train to Winnipeg, Man....Home Xmas Eve of 1945. I couldn't work for years afterward...couldn't sleep for nights with pains, nervous, couldn't mix with people, church or crowded places...All the tissues in my fingers, hands, veins and nerves all dried up...feet so tender, can't walk in bare feet."

CHAPTER EIGHT, PRINCE EDWARD ISLAND

> "Can you point me out a corner
> Where his footstep hasn't trod,
> Or a land that has not known him
> For a while,
> Well he can't have heard about it
> Or upon its virgin soil
> At least one man has stood
> From P.E. Isle."
>
> (May Carroll Macmillan)

Low and wooded, Prince Edward Island, formerly called the Isle of St. John, was not much exploited by early settlers. About 34 by 145 miles long, its rich loamy soil, with the gradual clearance of forest from it, has become one huge farm, and the Islanders proudly call it the "Garden of the Gulf." It is known to many of the older generation as the home of "Anne of Green Gables."

Although the fisheries were important there in the earliest years, truck farming quickly became the main source of income. The Acadians came first. In 1714 a hundred families from Placentia, Newfoundland, removed to the Island, probably including some who had come from the Channel Islands. (M.R. Lee, S.E. Placentia, Nfld.) When the British took over from the French in the summer of 1767, the government unwisely handed out in grants and by lottery most of the Island, thus preventing the normal settlement of small landholders. Scots and Americans however soon settled on the unused lands, and late in the 1700s a number of Guernsey families came to the Island. This was a time of troubles for Guernsey, and many left that Island for Gaspe, for Ohio, and for Australia and other places.

The following article printed in the Guernsey Evening Press and Star on Sept. 5, 1972, is included in the form of exerpts, through the kindness of the author, Joan Stockdale and of the publisher.

"When a young Guernsey couple, Robert and Jane Beecher, recently found a place called Guernsey Cove on a holiday in Canada, they were delighted, and wrote to the Evening Press requesting further information.

An article in the Press was immediately followed by a wealth of information about at least one of the families who sailed to a new life in Prince Edward Island in 1806. Mrs. Marie de Garis, of Les Reveaux, St. Peter's, is a descendant of one of the families, the Brehauts. She provides a fascinating story of intrepid Guernsey settlers who chopped down trees in a primeval forest to build their first log-cabin homes...

Henry and Elizabeth Brehaut were the pioneer couple... Henry, described as of medium height, thin, and with quick nervous movements and of a jovial and happy disposition, married Elizabeth Pulham of English parentage in 1791. She was small of stature...very energetic and a good manager...Henry was a Royal Arch Mason...six children born in Guernsey. Then came hard times. The wine industry in Guernsey employed most of the ablebodied men at that time. Wines were brought from France and Spain in large casks, were ripened and later transferred to smaller measures for shipping to ports in the U.K. ...In 1805 trade in spirits and tobacco was placed under restrictions...Henry, with a wife and six children to support, decided to leave the Island. A number of his neighbors and relatives decided to go, also, and they chose Prince Edward Island to be their new home in the New World.

With them went 65 other men, women and children from Guernsey, including Henry's friend, John Le Lacheur and his family, and Elizabeth's sister and her husband, Mr. and Mrs. Daniel Machon. Henry's sister Elizabeth, and her husband, Capt. Fallow (compilers query, Fallu?) went along, and others were the Roberts, Marquands, de Jerseys and Taudvins.

(Upon arrival in P.E.I.) the first on board to greet the Brehaut family was kinsman James Burhoe, a first cousin of Henry's, who told him that the spelling of his name had been corrupted...and he had not troubled to correct it. He had been in Prince Edward Island for about 10 years with his wife and eleven children. His descendants today are still called Burhoe...

Daniel Machon and his family settled on 100 acres on the extreme end of Beach Point, which at one time bore his name. Henry Brehaut took the next 100 acres; the de Jerseys settled on a nearby farm. The Taudvins went across the river and the Le Lacheurs settled at Guernsey Cove. The Roberts went further down the South River, and took up land still owned by their descendants. The Marquands settled on the farm next door to the east...trees were cut down, enormous stumps dug out, the ground levelled...

In winter, the Brehauts and other Guernsey families made barrels, kegs and wooden household utensils and in the spring these were sent by river to Charlottetown, where they found a ready market...

The Brehauts prospered...Aunty Machon kept school...Henry died at 81, his wife...at 96. It was reported in 1906 that their living descendants numbered over 400, some in California...Boston, and Prince Edward Island." (Stockdale)

"Six brothers named Machon were carpenters." (Luce)

"Today there is a huge Guernsey colony there, and place names such as Carey Point, Amherst Cove, Fort Amherst, Crapaud, St. Peter's Harbour, French Village and St. Andrew's. Next year, 1973, a monument is being erected there in memory of the first settlers." (R.W.J. Payne, Guernsey)

"Under the auspices of Lady Fanning, an Englishwoman, who was interested in the development of P.E.I., about 20 Guernsey families emigrated there in the early 1800s. These included Machons, Le Suers, Brehauts, Hamons and one family from Sark named Le Couteur...Most of the sons removed to the States in the early years of this century." (Philip Luce) Lady Fanning owned land around Pisquid, which she sold to the Guernsey folk before they left, saying they were shore farms, which they proved not to be. Complaining, they were given doubled amounts of land, John Le Lacheur then owning 800 acres. Some were still dissatisfied, and sold out, removing to Murray Harbor South. A Mr. John Cambridge had mills and land, and furnished them with food and seed for one year on condition that they would pay him in lumber. He later swapped land with the sons, to their advantage, as the land was more fertile. (PRINCE EDWARD ISLAND MAGAZINE, 1905)

Many Brehaut reunions have taken place in the U.S. The most recent was organized from Shrewsbury, Mass. by Dorothy and Walter Burhoe in 1976. Leonard and Louise Brehaut of Cornwall, P.E.I. are said to have the family Bible.

The Le Page clan is a large one, and it seems few Canadian towns or cities lack members of this surname. Many are descendants of the Le Pages from Guernsey Island. Elisha Le Page, b. 1764 in Guernsey, bought land in PEI in 1807. One of his notable descendants was William Le Page, born 1848 in PEI. He removed to Gloucester, Mass., where he married Ruth Mayo. His inventions were various, but Le Page's glue has a definite place in history. This was, appropriately enough, a by-product of the fisheries at first, and soon became a household word in America. The large and important realty firm of Ontario and elsewhere is also a part of this widespread and flourishing family. (Edw. Le Page, Grimsby, Ont.)

One Guernsey family in PEI, the Le Lacheurs, have hundreds of descendants in North America. One curious note regarding this family is in the female line. Elizabeth Romonof of Guernsey married David Windsor, an Englishman, on the Island of Guernsey. Was she a Romeril, with the name spelled wrongly? Or was she the daughter of a noble Russian family? "Among other children born to them was Elizabeth Windsor, who married John Le Lacheur, sea-faring man, and Commodore of Letter of Marque ships." Evidently a privateer!

In 1806 John Le Lacheur emigrated to PEI together with the other Guernsey families. He and his wife Elizabeth had six children. After arrival in Canada, a pair of twin boys was born, and a daughter, Jane. John, an older son, was a prominent man in Charlottetown, and was elected to the Assembly of the Province 16 times in succession. Some of this family emigrated to Greeley, Iowa, 1850, where John was there elected Iowa State Representative in 1856.

The Pippy family of PEI has had a romantic and adventurous history, with some unresolved questions about their origin. French records show that in the 1600s a Sieur de la Poippe or Poype, was the French Governor of Placentia, Nfld. Apparently the Pippyfamily switched allegiance to the British. It is thought that some of the family lived in Guernsey for a few years.

Channel Island Nicolles have settled in many parts of Canada. One group lived in P.E.I. and has left many descendants. Leland Stanford Nicolle sent the following information on his branch. "John Thomas Nicolle married Elizabeth Clements. Her father William had a general store in Murray Harbor, and also a 100 acre farm. John Thomas had ten children. Louisa never married, lived to 90. William died at 80. Oliver was a blacksmith and foreman in a shop in Boston for some years, then became Fire Chief in Providence. Herbert learned the plaster trade and worked in the U.S. for most of his life... James L...came into possession of a painting of old John Thomas Nicolle on the death of his sister Louisa. I would judge the painting done at age 20, clean shaved, blue eyed, long strait nose. It was painted on the cover of a small ebony case." (L. Nicolle, Murray River, PEI. Much work also done on this family by May Severson, New Brighton, Minn.)

There is information available in the Vital Records on the Robert, Roberts family, but no contributing descendants were located. This is also true of the Taudvin, De Jersey and Le Marquand families. Interested persons with information should see that it goes into the files of the Heritage Foundation, 2 Kent Street, Charlottetown, PEI.

BREHAUT FAMILY

"July 10, 1993 is the date for the Brehaut Reunion. The place is Fantasyland Provincial Park in the Gladstone area between Murray River and Murray Harbour, PEI. If it rains, the following day will be OK...." More information will be found through the PEI Visitors Guide. For more information write Wilfred Brehaut, 1639 Sunflower Ct. No., Palm Springs, CALIF. 92262. Phone 619-327-2179.

ALEXANDRA, THE HISTORY OF, Alex. Women's Institute, P.E.I., 1965.
BREHAUT RECORDS, see mentions of resources in family charts.
CHARLOTTETOWN GUARDIAN, Dec. 10, 1938, BREHAUTS OF GUERNSEY COVE, article.
DE GARIS, Mrs. Marie, of Guernsey, memoirs of Brehaut family.
GRAHAM, Elizabeth of London, Ont., Charts of Le Lacheur and Machon families.
GREENHILL, Basil, and Ann Giffard, WESTCOUNTRYMEN IN PRINCE EDWARD ISLE, Toronto, 1967.
KEEPING, Ewart A., LE LACHEUR CHART.
HARVEY, D.C., editor, JOURNEYS TO THE ISLAND OF ST. JOHN, Toronto, 1955.
LE PAGE, Edward, of Grimsby, Ontario, booklet on various Le Pages, in Guernsey and Canada, and material on the large Le Page family of P.E.I.
LE PAGE, Mrs. G.F., Southbury, Conn. Research on the Le Pages of PEI.
MAC GREGOR, J., MARITIME COLONIES OF GREAT BRITAIN, Ordon, 1828.
MAC QUEEN, Malcolm A., SKYE PIONEERS AND THE ISLAND.
MELLISH, J., HISTORY OF METHODISM IN CHARLOTTETOWN, PEI.
PATERSON, Gilbert, THE STORY OF BRITAIN AND CANADA, Toronto, 1934.
RYERSON, Prof. S., BREHAUT article for Vol. 5, Dictionary of Can. Biog. Univ. of Quebec, at Montreal, ca 1977.
SEVERSON, May, New Brighton, Minn. Research and charts on Nicolle family.
STOCKDALE, Joan, of Guernsey, article in Guernsey Press, as mentioned above, Brehaut family.
WILSON, Mrs. F.G., Fort Stockton, Tex., Le Lacheur charts.

PRINCE EDWARD ISLAND, CHANNEL ISLAND SURNAMES

BISHOP	LE COCQ	PIPPY
BREHAUT	LE COUTEUR	PERREE, PERRY
BURHOE	LE LACHEUR	RICHARDS?
CLEMENTS	LE PAGE	ROBERT, ROBERTS
DAVEY	LE SUEUR	ROBERTSON
DE JERSEY	MACHON	TAUDVIN, TODEVIN,
FALLOW, FALLU?	MARQUAND, MARCHAND	TOSTEVIN
GODFREY	NICOLLE	
HAMON, HAMMOND		
HAWKINS		

THE PIERCED ROCK AND BONAVENTURE ISLAND AT PERCE, GASPE, QUEBEC

(Courtesy Tourist Bureau of Quebec)

CHAPTER NINE, QUEBEC

"But yet, during the days of the Seigneuries, what a luminous procession passed under the shadow of its great Rock, entering by this gate upon their careers of discovery--Marquette and Joliet, La Salle and Perrot, part of a great white galaxy of pioneers on their odysseys to open a vast domain, larger than the Roman Empire." (Montsignat)

These words written to Mme. de Maintenont, point out the early importance of the Gaspe Peninsula in the conquest of North America.

If the reader will look at the map of eastern Canada, Gaspe, the largest promotory in the Gulf will be seen to reach out like a gigantic paw extended to grasp the riches in the waters of the North Atlantic. The position of Gaspe brings it closer to London than New York is, by 600 miles. The distance around the peninsula is about 526 miles, a spectacular drive, with magnificent scenery at every turn of the winding road. The Peninsula is about 170 miles long.

The central portion of the Peninsula, hills, forests, and the Shickshock Mountains, has withstood well the mild pressures of occupation and settlement, and thousands of acres are still as they were before the coming of the Europeans. There are two main reasons for this: first, the mountains lack a good natural pass from North to South; secondly, the fishing and sailing residents of the narrow shelfland on the coasts found travel by boat much more practical than by land. The roadway around the coast was only accomplished in the twentieth century.

The climate is temperate in the summer, but this phrase from MacWhirter speaks volumes: "I have seen the snow so deep in Carlton that we drove over the telegraph wire."

The first Europeans to drop anchor on the coast were probably Basque or French fishermen, who needed repairs to their vessels, wood and fresh water, or room on the beach to dry fish.

Jacques Cartier landed at Gaspe on July 24, 1534. He had sailed from St. Malo, France with probably a few Channel Islanders among his crewmen. Another early explorer in these parts, Verazano, is also said to have had a Norman crew on his voyage in 1524, which may have included Channel Islanders. "For picturesque scenery and quiet beauty Gaspe is unsurpassed by any other locality on the coast." (MacWhirter)

The following years saw the "luminous procession" of great soldiers, priests, courtiers, adventurers, voyageurs, and discoverers past the great Rock of Perce, and up the voluminous waters of the St. Lawrence, the oldest river in the world.

Following Cartier's voyages the French began slowly to settle along the St. Lawrence River, and in the Gulf. French fishermen were known to be on the Gaspe Coast in the 1670s. (Thevet, Tome 48)

It appears that few Channel Islanders were in Quebec before 1700, except for the ones kidnapped by the Indians and brought to the settlements on the St. Lawrence. There they were exchanged for gold promised by the Quebec government for New England settlers. This policy was meant to discourage settlement by the English. This method was also used in Newfoundland, and at least one Channel Islander was captured there by French fishermen and taken to Quebec. (See QAAM by Turk)

In the year 1759 a notable procession of a different kind than that of the explorers took place. General Wolfe and Sir Charles Saunders were in command of a great fleet of 49 ships and 18,000 men. Their first rendezvous was at Louisbourg on Cape Breton Island, and the second at Gaspe Basin. The great flotilla took two days just to weigh anchor in the Basin, and to form the procession on their way to the world-changing battle on the Plains of Abraham, Quebec.

Still another flotilla in Gaspe Bay was gathered there in the summer of 1914, the first contingent of Canadian soldiers headed for Europe, consisting of 32 troop ships, 4 cruisers, and a coast guard ship.

"The Guernsey families which were until ca 1974 at Grande Greve, St. George's Cove, and at Indian Cove, go way back to the 1780s . . . had their own Methodist Chapel, but no records in Gov. Archives." (Aldo Brochet)

Around 1770 Jerseymen began to settle on the Gaspe coast when Janvrin Co. arrived in Grand Greve. At about the same time, the Guernseyman, William Simon settled on Ship Head, the end of the Peninsula. Peter Simon came to Indian Cove about 1817. Also at this time, Charles Robin was enlarging his fishery business and bringing over from Jersey and Guernsey indentured "servants," men and boys who would do the hard work of the fisheries, shoremen to provide food and supplies for the fishing, and to cure the fish. The fisheries also brought young men to do the clerical work of maintaining records of the business. Cartier writes in GASPE DUPUIS, "At this time the Jersiais started to take hold in the Gaspe. The Janvrin, Nicol, Collas, Fruing, Luce, Perchard, Dumaresq, Le Boutillier, de Ste. Croix, Le Quesne, Godfrey, Le Gros and Pinel establishments." (See also Charles Robin's story.)

Paspebiac, whose denizens were once called Paspyjacks, some French, some Channel Islanders, and who were the descendants of blacksmiths, carpenters and fishermen who worked for Charles Robin and other fisheries, was a most important port in the 1700s and the early 1800s. In spite of the Robin ruling, many of these men married French and Indian women. (Le Moine)

Cape Cove was another important port and fishing station with 3 commercial fisheries; De la Perelle, Thomas Savage, and Amice Payne of Jersey. "Pt. St. Peter...its symmetric long rows of boats, anchored at night-fall in a straight line, in view of each fishing-station, all dancing merrily on the crest of the curling billows; its fearless, song-loving, blue smocked Jersey fishermen...Where are the Johnstons, Creightons, Packwoods, Collases, Alexanders of thirty years ago? Gone, one and all...to their long home." (Le Moine)

"Newport is a snug little cove with good anchorage for small vessels. There are two small fishing establishments there, one belonging to Messrs. Charles Robin and Co., and the other to Mr. Philip Hamon of Jersey, who resides here with his family. About two miles beyond are two small patches of rock called the Newport Islands, where Capt. Philip Dean of Jersey once had a fishing stand." (Le Moine)

"Dalhousie...laid out in town lots in 1826...The first settlers were Peter Harquail, (Hacquoil), Dan Roherty, and Alexander Dean." (MacWhirter)

"Cap d'Espoir...west of Cape Cove...Mr. Clement Dumaresq. He lives in a house which is still in perfect repair...there are beautiful old Jersey and Guernsey dishes which are about 200 years old...a large pink lustre jug is intact...old time sampler worked on hand loomed linen by Anne Du Pres, age eleven in the year 1742...old pewter plate still bearing the initials of the owner, from the old Lenfestey house in Guernsey...biography of Philip Dumaresq, written in French and tracing the genealogical descent for many generations." (MacWhirter)

Not all of the Gaspe ships were in transocean service. Some were employed in bringing from the coast to Montreal and Quebec City, cargos of rum, molasses, coffee, sugar, tea, rice, tobacco and wine, in addition to the cod and other fish from the Gulf. In 1832 there were 41 such vessels plying to Quebec City, from Gaspe. This no doubt led to some resettlement from Gaspe to central Quebec.

Two constant changes persisted in Gaspe; a strong increase in the French population and an endless retreat of the Channel Islanders to places farther inland. Many Gaspe families removed to Montreal and Quebec, such as Falle to Montreal, Le Rossignol to Laval, and other families to Levis, etc. These sometimes blended into the French Catholic culture, sometimes maintained their Protestantism. Others went farther, to New England, New York, Ohio, Ontario, Minnesota, Wisconsin and to Western Canada.

Some descendants of the Islanders named Morrissey, Paget, Codey, Hoyles and Le Cornu headed for Alpena and other places in Michigan, but seem to have dispersed from that region fairly soon, as the lumbering industry dwindled.

The Du Vals were a French family settled in Jersey, and were possibly from Rouen, France in the 1500s. Jean Du Val of Jersey married in 1769 Marie Piton, of an old Jersey family also. Du Val is said to have pursued his privateering from a port in Bermuda just before arrival in Gaspe.

Bonaventure Island, like Perce Rock, is an outstanding feature of the Gaspe coast. The Island is only about two and a-half by three quarters of mile across, but was most important in the history of the Coast. It was once the property of Capt. Peter Du Val of Jersey, who in the late 1700s commanded a privateer, lugger-rigged, mounting four guns, with a crew of 27 hands, which was owned by the Janvrin firm of Jersey. The vessel, under 100 tons, was named the VULTURE, and was the terror of the French coast, as it hovered like a bird of prey from St. Malo to the Pyrenees, capturing vessel after vessel.

The city of Bayonne, France, had suffered from these captures, and merchants of that area joined in a venture to produce and arm a vessel that would capture Du Val's ship. This was done, and the brig, about 180 tons, with eighty men, had their chance.

The clever captain of the VULTURE came very close in and pelted the French ship, cutting her rigging, and killing and wounding half the French crew. They in turn, found they were too close to use their guns effectively, and lost the battle. Capt. Du Val must have retired fairly soon after this encounter, and bought Bonaventure Island. Descendants still live in the area, and the local churchyard holds the remains of the doughty captain, who lived to a ripe old age. (Le Moine)

Carrells from the Channel Islands settled in Gaspe, and a picture of the Hon. Frank Carrell, M.L.C., LL.D. is shown in the MacWhirter book. He was Legislative Councillor for the Gulf Division, President of Quebec Telegraph Printing Co., and of Frank Carrell Ltd., a Director of Canada Steamship Lines, Prudential Trust Co., Canada Securities Corp., etc. He was also the author of several travel and Memoir books. (MacWhirter)

The Le Boutilliers had a large fishery establishment on Bonaventure Island, at which 38 boats and about 120 men were employed. This family lived in Jersey since at least the 1500s. John removed to Gaspe at 18 and became an official in the firm. Later, he was owner of his own establishment, with branches along the coast from Gaspe to Ste. Anne des Monts. At these places he bought cod, made fish, shipped to Brazil, the West Indies, Portugal and also to Spain and Italy. He represented Gaspe in the Provincial Chamber from 1833 to 1838, and was later Legislative Councillor. See the Journal of Capt. John Vibert, who was one of his Master seamen.

In 1861, Le Boutillier owned 12 ships and 169 fishing boats, and had 2500 employees. He married Elizabeth Robin, one of the daughters of a Charles Robin family, that removed from Jersey to Switzerland. After Le Boutillier's death, his firm was taken over by the Robin company.

The Maugers of Quebec came from two different places, from the Channel Islands and from Germany. Care must be used in the sorting out of these two large groups. A great deal of genealogical research has been done on these families. Owing to the extremely large numbers of variant spellings, there is as yet no definite work on the subject, although some basic data has been turned up by a Prof. Robert Major.

It seems that Archbishop Rauf Mauger had four children before the year 1100, and lived in Jersey. His children were: Peter, a Guernsey farmer; Michael, the oldest, who was in great favour in English court circles; Etienne, or Steven; and James, who settled in South Wales.

According to D. Munger, there were three branches in Quebec of the Mauger family, of whom the ancestor originated in Jersey; one in Saguenay, one on the Cote Nord, and one in Gaspe. The Maugers of Saguenay are descendants of John, born in Grouville, Jersey in 1797. Most of them use the Munger spelling.

The Quebec North Shore Branch descends from James Mauger, from Jersey, many now calling themselves Monger, although these variations are also known: Mauge, Mauget, Monget, etc. James may have been the brother of John of the Saguenay branch. Other forms of the surname are Malger, de Maugier, Mauge, Mager, Magor, Major, Mougier, Mogier, Munger and Manger.

Channel Islanders settled in Montreal, Quebec, Levis and so on, are difficult to locate, as they have usually melded into the French population with scarcely a hint of their Channel Island origin. Among the English group, a few were found, recruited it is said for the banking business of the large cities. Others in Montreal are descendants of the Gaspe families, removed from the coast in the middle 1800s, when Atlantic shipping suffered a decline on the coast.

There is said to have been a Channel Islands society in Montreal some years back, but the compiler could not find a trace of this group. Also in Quebec Province are the descendants of earlier groups from the Channel Islands, those who came to the small ports of the St. Lawrence River, to make a living in those pursuits that were related to the shipping, fishing and lumbering there. The Price Lumber Company in Lake St. John area was said to be a place where many Channel Islanders settled. It is located approximately 175 miles northwest of Quebec City.

Richard and Philip Mauger settled in Gaspe and retained the original form of their surname. Some descendants of Richard are known.

Owing to the tremendous number of Jersey and Guernsey young men brought to the Gaspe coast to work in the fisheries, a definitive list of their surnames does not seem possible at present. It should be kept in mind that some of the Islanders came to Gaspe, worked a few years, and then returned to the Islands. Others came, and instead of returning to Europe, moved on to the United States, to Australia and to New Zealand.

In other cases, Channel Islanders married in Gaspe, and had only daughters, or had sons who were all lost at sea. Thus the surname has disappeared, although descendants may be quite numerous. In addition, children of Channel Islanders in Gaspe have returned for various reasons to the Islands. In some cases this was owing to their inheritances of Island property or business.

By the early 1800s it was said that four-fifths of the people of Quebec were descendants of the Normans, the Bretons and the (Norman-Breton) fisher-farmer folk of the Channel Islands. Since the French had large families, they soon outnumbered both the British and Channel Island families of the coast.

In 1820 the fishermen of Gaspe signed a Petition to request the Government to take steps against the practices of the American fishermen, who came near the shores to fish, and threw overboard the offal. At least 194 men signed the petition, some unmistakeably French, others believed by the compiler to be from the Channel Islands. These names are listed on the following pages.

Therese Gravel, a Canadian researcher wrote that some Islander names are found in the records of the Congregational French Church at Aux Gres, Trois Rivieres, QUE, from the 1850s: Hammond, Roberts, Tourgis, and Roy, plus Lesbirel and Le Lacheur.

QUEBEC, PETITIONERS, 1820

AHIER, Gideon	HENRY, John
ALEXANDER, Philip	L'ABBE, Jacques and Jean
ALLEYRE, Peter, John and Charles	LAFFOLEY, Philippe
	LE PAGE, Ephraim, and Joseph
BAKER, John Sr. and Jr.	LENFESTEY, James
COUSTANCHE, Philippe	LE SCELLEUR, Philip
CHEVALIER, George	MARCHAND, Nicholas
DE BOIS, Francis	MARETT, Henry
DE CAIN, John	MAUGER, Edward and Richard
DE LA PERRELLE, Elias and George	MCKENZIE, John
	PIQUET, Clement
DESLANDES, Daniel	RENOUF, Philip
DOLBEL, Charles	ROCK, John, Edmunds alias
FRUING, William	ROCK? DE LA ROCQUE?
GALLIE, Jack	SMITH, Francis MOON
GERRARD, John	TAPP, John Sr. and Jr.
GILBERT, John	THELLAND, John and Francois
GOREY, David	TOSVIN, James
HACQUOIL, William	TRACHY, Edward
	TUZO, Joseph

The port of Malbaie supported a rather large number of Channel Island families. Among the members of St. Peters Anglican Church were the following:

BECQUET	HOTTON	LUCAS
CADORET	LE COCQ	SYVRET
ELLIS	LE GRESLEY	TOUZEL
FAUVEL	LE GROS	VARDON
HARQUAIL	LE MARQUAND	VIBERT

These Gaspesians of Channel Island descent served in the Quebec government in the 1800s: Hon. John Le Boutillier, Hon. Frank Carrell, John Gosset, John Le Boutillier, David Le Boutillier, William Le Boutillier Fauvel.

In the counties of Bonaventure and Gaspe, Militia groups were formed in the middle 1800s, and included these Channel Island surnames: Savage, Perree, Le Boutillier, Harbour, Collas, Prevel, Duval, Baker, Couture?, Hamon, Gregoire, Bechervaise, Slous, Smollett, Sheppard, Le Vel, Main, Rosesier, Ste. Croix, Vicq, Le Marquand, Le Mesurier, Hocquard, Gallie, de la Perelle, Le Gallais, Huard, Bean, Flowers, and Renouf.

QUEBEC, CHANNEL ISLAND SURNAMES

Below is a list of Channel Island surnames, of men associated with the old Trading Companies on the Gaspe Coast, and in the Maritimes, mainly the compilation of J.H. Le Breton of Paspebiac, Quebec, with additions by Aldo Brochet of Montreal, Betty Tardif of Gaspe and Lady Phyllis McKie of Ottawa.

AHIER	DE QUETTEVILLE	LA COUR
AGNES	DE STE. CROIX	LAFFOLEY
ALEXANDRE	DESPRES	LANGLOIS
AMY	DE VOUGES	LE BAS
ARNOLD	DOLBEL	LE BELIER
ARTHUR	DU FEU	LE BLANCQ
AUBERT	DU PRE	LE BRETON
AUBIN	DURELL	LE BROCQ
BALLEINE	DUMARESQ	LE BRUN
BANNIER	DU VAL	LE BOUTILLIER
BARRETTE	ELLIS	LE CAUDEY
BAUCHE	ENOUF, ESNOUF	LE CHASSEUR
BAUDAINS	FAUVEL	LE CORNU
BEATON	FLEURY	LE COUTEUR
BECHERVAISE	FIOTT	LE COUVEE
BEQUET, BECQUET	FURZER	LE CRAS
BERTRAM	GALLIE	LE CRAW
BIARD	GALLICHAN	LE DAIN
BICHARD	GAUDIER, GAUTIER	LE FEUVRE
BIGARD	GAVEY	LE FLOCH
BIGEREL	GIBAUT	LE GALLAIS
BINET	GIOTT	LE GARIGNON
BISSON	GIRARD	LE GRAND
BLAMPIED	GODFRAY	LE GRESLEY
BOSSY	GODIN	LE GROS
BOUCHARD	GOSLING	LE MAISTRE
BOUILLON	GRANDIN	LE MARQUANT
BREE	GRUCHY	LE MASURIER
BRIARD	GUERNIER	LE MESURIER
BRIDEAUX	HACQUOIL	LE MOIGNAN
BROCHET	HAMON	LE MONTAIS
BUTLIN	HARRIS	LE MOTTEE
CABOT	HELLEUR	LEMPRIERE
CADORET	HELLYER	LENFESTEY
CAMIOT	HENRY	LE PAGE
CARCAUD	HOCQUARD	LE POIDEVIN
CARRELL	HOCQUOIL	LE QUESNE,
CHURCHWARD	HODGE	LE CAIN
COLLAS	HOLMES	LE RICHE
CORBET	HORMAN	LE ROSSIGNOL
COUTANCHE	HOLT	LE SCELLEUR
DALLAIN	HOTTON	LE SUEUR
DALLAIRE	HUELIN	LE TEMPLIER
DE BOURCIER	HUGHES	LE TOUZEL
DE CAEN	INGROUVILLE	LUCAS
DE CARTERET	JANDRON	LUCE
DE GRUCHY	JARNET	MACHON
DE LA COUR	JEAN	MALLET
DE LA HAYE	JEUNE	MANNING
DE LA MARE	JOUAN	MALZARD
DE LA PERELLE	JOURNEAUX	MARTIN

MARETT	RICHARDS
MAUGER	RIOU
MESSERVY	ROBIN
MILES	ROMERIL
MICHEL	ROPERT
MITCHELMORE	ROUSSY
MORIN	RUCY
MOURANT	ROUTH
MOULIN	SAMSON
NEWBURY	SEALE
NICOLLE	SIOUVILLE
NOEL	SKELTON
OLLIVIER	SNOWMAN
ORANGE	SPRATT
ORVISS	STAINER
PAYN	STENYING
PECHARD	SYVRET
PERREE	TOSTEVIN
PEZET	TOUZEL
PIPON	TRACHY
PINEL	VALPY
POITIER	VARDON
POWELL	VAUTIER
PRIAULX	VIBERT
PRICHARD	VIGOT
RABASSE	VINCENT
REBOURS	WEARY
REMON	WHITE
RENOUF	

Anglican families of Perce, 1862-1962, mostly of Channel Island origin, are listed in a Centennial Booklet, prepared by Floyd Eugene Boys, of Urbana, Illinois, and others:

AGNES	DUVAL	MAUGER
AMY	FERGUSON	MERCIER
ARBOUR	GIBAUT	NEWBURY
AUBERT	GAUDIN	NICOLLE
BENEST	GURNHAM	ORANGE
BIARD	HACQUAIL	PAQUOR
BISSON	HAMON	REMON
BOSSY	JAMES	RENOUF
BOWERS	JEAN	RIVE
BROCHET	KRUSE	ROSS
BROWN	LE BAS	SMITH
BUNTON	LE BOUTILLIER	SMOLLETT
BUTLIN	LE BRETON	SOMERVILLE
CABOT	LE BROCQ	SUMMERHAYS
CANNING	LE BRUN	TARDIF
COLLAS	LE CAPELAIN	THOMPSON
CONWAY	LE COUVIER	THORPE
COWIE	LE DAIN	TUZO
CROWWE	LE FEUVRE	VALPY
DE GRUCHY	LEGGO	VIBERT
DE QUETTEVILLE	LE GRAND	VIEL
DE STE. CROIX	LE GRESLEY	WALTERS
DE VEULLE	LE MARQUAND	WARREN
DOLBEL	LENFESTEY	WESTBROOK
DUMARESQ	LE MOIGNAN	

QUEBEC, BIBLIOGRAPHY

BECHARD, August, LA GASPESIE IN 1888.
BECHERVAISE, John M., J'ASSAYE, Belmont, Victoria, Australie, 1970.
BURT, Alfred Leroy, SHORT HISTORY OF CANADA FOR AMERICANS, Minn., Minn., 1942.
CENTENNIAL BOOKLET, Booklet on members of the Perce Anglican Church, 1965?
CLARK, John M., SKETCHES OF GASPE, L'ILE PERCEE, and THE GASPE, New Haven, Conn., 1935.
DEAN, Sydney and Marguerite Marshall, WE FELL IN LOVE WITH QUEBEC, Phila., 1950.
DAVIES, Blodwen, GASPE, LAND OF HISTORY AND ROMANCE, Toronto, 1949.
DE GASPE, Aubert, LES ANCIENS CANADIENS, LIFE ON A SEIGNEURIE.
DOMINION ARCHIVES, Ottawa, Ontario.
GALLANT, Patrice, REGISTRES DE LA GASPESIE, 1752-1850, Quebec.
HOGNER, Dorothy Child, SUMMER ROADS TO GASPE, N.Y. City, 1939.
JENKINS, Kathleen, MONTREAL, ISLAND CITY OF THE ST. LAWRENCE, Garden City, N.Y., 1966.
LE FEUVRE, George F., IMMIGRANTS FROM JERSEY, THE COD AND THE GASPE COAST, Societe Jersiaise Bulletin, and JERRI JADIS, in the Jersey tongue, Jersey, C.I., 1973.
LENFEST, B.A., GENEALOGY OF THE LENFEST-LENFESTY FAMILY, Brooklyn, N.Y., 1938.
LE MOINE, J.M., CHRONICLES OF THE ST. LAWRENCE, Rouses Pt., N.Y., 1878.
LE MOIGNAN, Michel, GENEALOGIE DES FAMILLES LE MOIGNAN, Gaspe, 1972.
MACKENZIE, John and Marjorie, QUEBEC IN YOUR CAR, N.Y. City, 1952.

QUEBEC, BIBLIOGRAPHY

MAC WHIRTER, Margaret G., TREASURE TROVE IN GASPE, New Richmond, Que., 1919, 1972.
MONTGOMERY, Doris, THE GASPE COAST IN FOCUS, Dutton, N.Y.
MOUNTAIN, George J., VISIT TO THE GASPE COAST, Quebec Archives, reprint, 1943.
OAKLEY, Amy, KALEIDOSCOPIC QUEBEC, N.Y., after 1941.
PETERSON, Roger Tory, A DOZEN BIRDING HOT SPOTS, Edited by George H. Harrison, N.Y., 1976.
QAAM, THE QUIET ADVENTURERS IN AMERICA, by Marion G. Turk
QUEBEC ARCHIVES, Quebec, P.Q.
REVUE D'HISTOIRE DE LA GASPESIE, periodical of the Gaspe Historical Society, Gaspe, Que.
ROMERIL, A.J., PLYING TO THE GASPE COAST, Soc. Jersiaise Bull., 1963.
ROY, C.E., and L. Brault, HISTORICAL GASPE, and GASPE DUPUIS CARTIER, Rev. d' Hist. Bulletin, 1973, and PROFILES LEVISIENS, Levis, Quebec, 1948.
SMITH,---GASPE, THE ROMANTIQUE, Crowell, N.Y.
SUTTON, Horace, FOOTLOOSE IN CANADA, Toronto, 1950.
SYVRET, Marguerite, JERSEY SETTLERS IN THE GASPE, pamphlet, Soc. Jersiaise.
TANGUAY, Cyprian, A TRAVERS LES REGISTRES, Librairie St. Joseph, Montreal, 1886.
THOMAS, C., HISTORY OF THE EASTERN TOWNSHIPS, J. Lovell, Montreal, 1866.
TOME 48, Rapport des Archives Nationales du Quebec, 1970.
TOYE, Wm., THE ST. LAWRENCE, New York, 1959.
TURK, Marion G., THE QUIET ADVENTURERS, Lakewood, Ohio, 1971.
WOODLEY, E.C., OLD QUEBEC TRAILS AND HOMES, Toronto, Ont., 1944.

PETIT GASPE, LITTLE GASPE, QUEBEC
(Courtesy Quebec Tourist Bureau)

e lives of thousands of Channel Islanders centered around the Gaspe Peninsula from the la
gh the early 1900s. They lived along the coast in villages, where, in season, the shores
ed with "flakes," where the cod was dried in the wind and sun. See the Quebec Bibliograp
ames of books about this beautiful coast.

CHAPTER TEN, ONTARIO

> "All that ever I shall desire
> Is in this county, round about me,
> All that ever I shall require
> Is here, and therefore I must be.
> All that ever I shall admire
> Presents itself so splendidly
> That all I ever shall aspire
> I will do here, most happily."
> (Nancy Maki, Berwyn, Ill.)

Although written especially of Norfolk County, Ontario, the verse above could very well speak for residents in most places in the province. Ontario has so much of interest in terms of history, natural beauty, commercial and agricultural assets, that most of the requirements for the good life are indeed there.

In the beginning of Ontario's history the fur trade attracted the French to the northern districts. Explorers and missionaries such as La Roche Daillon, Grenolle, Valle, Champlain, La Salle, Radisson, Joliet, Breboeuf and Thomonet were early visitors. The southern areas were left undisturbed until the latter part of the 1700s, except for the Niagara district. In the late 1700s the United Empire Loyalists crossed the borders in large numbers, and after the War of 1812, many settlers came from eastern Canada and from Great Britain, still more from the United States.

Among the earliest Channel Islanders in Ontario, were Philip and John Low, of Jersey, who were lawyers in Picton, Ontario, in the 1830s. (Firth) A Mr. J.P. De La Haye was teaching in Toronto in 1829. Also, in the 1830s, John Guillet of Jersey settled in Cobourg, Ontario, leaving many descendants. Philip Falle of Jersey was in Oxford Co., before 1850.

Between the 1850s and the 1920s, there was a small but steady stream of Jersey and Guernsey families coming to settle in Ontario. They came to London, Woodstock, St. Thomas, Chatham, Burlington, and Vittoria, Ontario. Many of these families have left descendants, now scattered across the continent.

The surname Gustin is not found in Steven's list of old Jersey surnames, but nevertheless, most Canadian families named Gustin are the descendants of a Jerseyman, who was born in 1647 at L'Etacq, Jersey. His name was then Augustin Jean, and he removed, as did many other Jerseymen, to New England. He served in King Philip's War, and married Elizabeth Browne in Marlboro, Mass. His surname suffered a number of indignities in army records, and ended up as John Gustin, quite different from the original form. Gustins are found in Ontario and several other provinces. (See also QAAM)

The next surge of Channel Islanders to Ontario was in the early years of the twentieth century. Although their numbers have now lessened, each year sees a few more of the Islanders headed for Toronto, Hamilton and other places in Ontario. An estimate of the Islanders and their descendants in Ontario could very well amount to about 20,000 persons.

No doubt many other factors are involved, but two things especially have influenced the Islanders to settle in Ontario. The great Hero of Upper Canada, General Sir Isaac Brock was a Guernseyman, for one. The other might have to do with the good, rather light soil of southern Ontario, which attracted farmers from the Islands who were interested in larger acreages than were available to them in Europe. Glasshouse growing, an important business in southern Ontario, may also have encouraged their removals in the 1900s.

The Gunton family, of Huguenot origin, lived in the town of Matishall, Norfolk, England. In the 1700s, one branch removed to the town of St. Heliers, Jersey. From Jersey in 1858 John Russel Gunton removed to Vittoria, Ontario, where he married and raised a family.

Philip Falle was born in Jersey in 1815, the son of Edward Falle and Rachel de Gruchy, one of nine children. The father died in 1827, and arrangements were made for a job for Philip in Quebec. On the voyage the ship was wrecked near St. John, Nfld. From that place, Philip was finally able to reach Quebec, but found, due to the time lost, the promised position had been filled.

Philip had relatives in Oxford Co., Ontario, and soon engaged in the cutting and clearing of land. He joined the Loyalists in the Rebellion of 1837-1838. Then he removed to Dereham, Ontario, where he bought 100 acres of land, which he cleared and settled on, remaining there for 25 years. In 1866 he retired to Tilsonburg, and bought the local hotel. He served on the school board and the town and county councils. He married Orpha Warden of Trenton, N.Y. (PIONEER CANADIAN FAMILIES, by ?)

John West was born in Cornwall, England in the early 1800s. In old England, a man caught poaching, fishing or hunting without permission of the land owner, was sentenced to death. In the early 1800s it was still considered a serious offense, and John West, caught poaching, decided not to embarrass his father or family, changed his surname to Watts and went to Jersey Island.

Railroads were being built on the Island at this time, and John West Watts became an engineer, and had the honor of driving the Royal Train on the occasion of Queen Victoria's visit in 1840. In Jersey, John, from England, met Mary Ann Dingle, of an old Huguenot family. They were married by the father of Lilly Langtry, Rev. Le Breton and removed to Alderney, where their daughter, Caroline Mary West Watts, was born in 1856. Another girl, Harriet, was born in 1858.

John left the Island for Canada in the 1860s. His wife and daughters soon followed, and the family settled in Coboconk, Ontario, an Indian name meaning "where the gulls nest." John and his wife died when their daughters were under 20. Descendants of this family reside in Chicago, Toronto, and London, Ontario.

John Guillet was born in St. Heliers, Jersey in 1802. His father was Charles Guillet and his mother Marie Thoreau. His grandfather, Pierre Thoreau, was also the ancestor of Henry David Thoreau, American author and naturalist.

When John was a young man he became a clerk for a codfishery firm in Newfoundland, where he sailed each spring from Jersey, and from there shipped cod to the West Indies. In the autumn each year he returned to Jersey. However, he was one of those few Jerseymen who get seasick, and so decided to leave the sea in 1832. He first lived in Quebec, and then removed to Cobourg, Ontario, where he worked first as a Carpenter, both on buildings and on lake ships. He married three times and had fifteen children. George Guillet, the brother of John, also came to Canada, and his widow removed to Akron, Ohio.

"In regard to the Brock family of Guernsey, the Canadian Legislature granted Major-Gen. Brock's four surviving brothers 12,000 acres of land in Upper Canada, Ontario, and in addition were allowed a pension...The four surviving brothers were Daniel Delisle, William, John Savery, and Irving. The four brothers came to Canada in 1817 to see their land. There were 6000 acres in East and West Flamborough at the head of Lake Ontario, 1200 acres in the township of Brock on Lake Simcoe, 3000 acres in Managhan, on Rice Lake, and 800 acres at Murray on Lake Ontario..."

"The brothers sold most of their land, or gave it away to relatives." (Schreiber-Brock-Delisle records, Dominion Archives, Ottawa)

Buffalo Bill, William Cody, was the descendant of a Le Caudey from Jersey and a Le Brocq from Guernsey. His ancestors settled in New England in the 1600s. (Cody Russel, Turk-QAAM) Isaac Cody, Bill's father, was born in Toronto, Ontario, after his family removed to Canada from the United States. They then removed to Cleveland, Ohio, and to Iowa, where Buffalo Bill was born in 1843.

Capt. Edgar F. Poidevin was born in Ontario of a Channel Island family. He lost his mother at age 8, and was raised by relatives on the shores of Lake Ontario. His story about his years on the Great Lakes, contained in a handwritten scrapbook, shows the innate response of Channel Island blood to shipboard life. The following excerpts from the booklet tell a small part of his story.

ONTARIO, FIFTY YEARS ON THE GREAT LAKES

"In 1910 we moved to Toronto from the North...I should have

been born a sea gull, because water seemed to draw me, and had to be part of it...some years later while out on my uncle's fish tug, they had an old blue enamel cup with a length of heavy twine. It was used for many purposes, oil, grease, water pumps, etc. After dipping over the side many times into Lake Ontario, because it was so cold, clear and blue, he would say, 'if you keep that up there won't be any more water left in the lake!'...along with my sister on Sunday we were taken down to the old Western Gap, the new wasn't finished yet. It had two wooden piers with a red lighthouse on the outside Pier. This same light is kept near the Exhibition as a reminder of former days...

In the spring of 1914 I was taken to live with my aunt and uncle, a commercial fisherman at Jordon Harbour...situated on the south shore of Lake Ontario at the mouth of 20 Mile Creek, a natural harbour and refuge for sailing vessels in the early days. A Mr. Oliver was always looking for old Indian relics, many of which are now in the Vineland Museum...One Saturday he passed our house at the harbour to dig in the high bluffs by the bay, so I asked him if it was all right for me to along and help. At the top of Dobsons Hill he started to dig in a sand mound, then knelt down and fingered the sand. I thought it was silly, but finally he came across some burnt wood and a couple of flint arrowheads. He gave me one which I kept for many years. While digging deeper he came across some bones and hair, but when the skull showed up with teeth, it didn't take me long to beat it down the hill and home.

In the late fall, with a gale from the east, just as the ice banks were forming, a small skiff or dory floated against the stone cribs by our wharf, and surely would have smashed up if we hadn't managed to recover it...Notices in the Fishermen's news...I became the proud owner of my very own boat, working whenever I could get away from my regular duties which were enough. I scraped, painted and bothered everyone in order to rig out my ship, even to a pair of oars.

At the harbour, our next door summer neighbor, late spring to early fall, was a Mr. and Mrs. Painter, a high school principal from Hamilton, along with a son Richard, three years older than me, and Grandpa Dick Painter, 96 years old, born 1820. The most outstanding individual, for this was his perfect way of doing everything, a former sailer in the British Navy in his youth.

I bummed a small tarpaulin off the county work gang, and now I was in business...Mr. Painter came to my assistance by marking out in the warehouse the size of sail for my type of boat, also the spar and guy lines, bow sprit. Now sewing in the sidelines around the edges. When I got one side finished, he looked and inspected my work, would take out the jacknife, cut the stitches saying 'Now do it straight, by doing so you could save your life in a storm, if your canvas holds on'...

Everything was perfect...she handled well, and with the help of a false keel could hold very close to the wind...the boat bacame my friend and chum, and would talk to her by the hour...One afternoon late the next summer while tacking across the bay, also running before the wind (I had put some rocks in for ballast, and kept pushing them over to the windward in order to sail close-hauled, with only a couple or three inches of freeboard) A real thrill...we sailed down past our fish wharf, the wind was fresh. I noticed my aunt, waving her white apron...so we put on a few more acts...So tied up and she is yelling and waving her hands and crying, and saying about being drownded!! My uncle...walked to the wood shop... took out the axe, and went to work on my boat, sides and bottom. The end of a wonderful partnership. But years later I got the answer, foolhardiness and ships don't mix."

Capt. Poidevin signed on the lake ships and worked on the Great Lakes and on the St. Lawrence River, and also took a few trips up to Lake Superior. One year he sailed to Newfoundland, "with a full cargo, including 200 drums of gasoline and oil on the top deck. Ran into a gale off Cape Race, lost all the deck load along with a motor truck in just one big sea..."

"...In 1926 we passed the old convict ship SUCCESS, built 1795 on Lake Michigan...In 1927 applied for a transfer to another ship with a pilot house, as I had served on all ships in the past with open bridges...the chief officers were sent to Cleveland, all expenses paid, to Sperry-Rand Tech and Nautical course for the new Gyro patent compasses, operations and maintenance certificate...Chicago and America were dry then, and was approched...to bring in some of that good Canadian whiskey for $125 a case, which was around $45 in Canada. Turned it down, guess I was chicken.

The DELWARNIC had a spare dory on her boat deck...had her rigged out to sail and many hours were spent in her...a small single cylinder Grey gas engine, about 40 rpms. Our engineers installed it in our dory, and that ended the sailing, and we got too lazy to haul the gear...As Depot Harbour was built on an Island of an Indian reserve, and due to a man shortage employment was good. We hired mostly Indians as sailors. They are really good men, so light on their feet. I went many times in the three years I sailed there with other shipmates, to hire help. Always treated with respect...One day while anchored in the Mackinac Strait, noticed two seagulls chasing one another. After a considerable time the older one fell into the water exhausted. Two other gulls set in and began to tear the old one apart. Couldn't believe my eyes, no person I spoke to had seen such action...Received a call from the Coast Guard. A boy was adrift in an open boat...on lookout as we circled around saw a small light. The Indian boy had lit his celluloid comb with a match to attract our attention. This saved his life, as we picked him up and took him to the

Canadian Soo Lock. A 13 year old boy from the Glooscap Reservation. What a frightened kid he was!"

There is a great deal more of interest in this journal. (MS, MY FIFTY YEARS ON THE GREAT LAKES, By Capt. Edgar F. Poidevin, Toronto, Ontario)

As in Gaspe, so many Channel Island surnames are found in Ontario that a full list would number in the many thousands, and they appear in most phone books of the province. The Island of Alderney is represented in Ontario. It seems that before 1900, some of the Alderney families such as Gough, Pezet, Le Messurier and others, settled in Western Ontario. Many of these moved on into Michigan, where some can be found in the Detroit area.

The Guernsey Club of London and St. Thomas, Ontario, had members of the following surnames in 1938: Le Courtois, W. Paul, J. Millard, Le Sauvage, Robilliard, Warren, Le Page, Laraix, Whitchurch, Ruault, Padden, all of whom were officials in the Society. In the same area of Ontario were other Channel Islands surnames, such as Previl, Moon, Mallett, Marchand, Prevost, Noury, Robert, Sylvestre, La Marsh, Le Gros, Lilly, Luce and Batiste.

ONTARIO, BIBLIOGRAPHY 95

CAMPBELL, Marjorie Freeman, NIAGARA, HINGE OF THE GOLDEN ARC, Toronto, 1958.
CHADWICK,---, ONTARION FAMILIES.
COCHRANE, Rev. Wm., CANADIAN ALBUM OF MEN OF CANADA, Brantford, Ont., 1895, Vols. 1-5.
FIRTH, Edith G., THE TOWN OF YORK, 1815-1834, Toronto, 1966.
GUILLET, Edwin C., THE GUILLET-THOREAU GENEALOGY, Toronto, 1960?, PIONEER SETTLEMENTS IN UPPER CANADA, etc.
HARDY, W. G., FROM SEA UNTO SEA, Canada, 1850-1910, Garden City, N.Y., 1959.
HANSEN, M.L., THE MINGLING OF THE CANADIAN AND AMERICAN PEOPLES, New Haven, Conn., 1941.
HERIOT, George, TRAVELS THROUGH THE CANADAS, 1907, and other works, 1800s.
HILL, Hamnett P., ROBERT RANDALL AND THE LE BRETON FLATS, Ottawa, 1919.
LANDON, Fred, WESTERN ONTARIO AND THE FRONTIER, Toronto, 1941.
OWEN, E.A., PIONEER SKETCHES OF THE LONG POINT SETTLEMENT, Toronto, 1898, and reprinted.
PAGE, H.R., HISTORICAL ATLAS OF HALDIMAND AND NORFOLK COUNTIES, Toronto, 1877, reprinted by Mark Cumming, Stratford, Ont., also many other county atlases.
POIDEVIN, Edgar, MS, 50 YEARS ON THE GREAT LAKES.
REAMAN, G. Elmore, THE TRAIL OF THE BLACK WALNUT, Toronto, 1957.
REAMAN, G. Elmore, TRAIL OF THE HUGUENOTS, Toronto, 1963.
REID, Wm. D., editor, THE LOYALISTS IN ONTARIO, Lambertville, N.J., 1973.
ROBERTSON, John Ross, and E.C. Kyte, OLD TORONTO, Toronto, 1954.
SMITH, Wm. H., CANADIAN GAZETTEER, Toronto 1846, and reprint 1970.
STORY, Norah, OXFORD COMPENDIUM TO CANADIAN HISTORY AND LITERATURE, Toronto.
TURK, Marion G., THE QUIET ADVENTURERS, Lakewood, Ohio, 1971.
Periodical: THE ONTARIO REGISTER, Thomas B. Wilson, Madison, N.Y.
DEPARTMENT OF TRADE AND DEVELOPMENT: Govt. of Ontario, Toronto, ONTARIO, THE PLACE AND THE PEOPLE, AND THE POTENTIAL, booklet.
DEPARTMENT OF TOURISM AND INFORMATION: Booklet: HISTORIC ONTARIO

CHAPTER ELEVEN, THE CANADIAN WEST

"In wilderness is the preservation of the world."
(Thoreau)

The enormous Canadian West comprises hundreds of thousands of square miles, even now very thinly populated, except for the cities. The value of this land is incalculable, with its farms, mines, oil and gas fields. Even in the 1600s its value was realized, for the best furs in the New World were collected here and sent to Europe through the attenuated commercial canoe lines, set up by the Scottish and French companies in Montreal.

In the 1700s the British fur trade flourished through the manipulations of the Hudson's Bay Company, with routes by canoe right across the Canadian wilderness, stretching to the Rockies. Farther south the Norwesters pursued their own fur business, with routes from Montreal to Fort William at the head of Lake Superior, and then to the Red River and beyond. The sometimes vicious competition was finally eliminated in 1820 when the two companies merged, and the more northerly route was then most used, as the southern area was becoming depleted, and the northern furs were of a better quality.

The Hudson's Bay Company was then in charge of nearly all movements from Labrador to the Pacific, and settlers were discouraged until about 1850. However, the rivers were full of fish, and elk, bear, deer, beaver and moose were plentiful, as were buffalo and caribou. Game birds were plentiful, and the soil was fertile. The Indian tribes were thinly scattered over the huge domain, and the rich land waited for the eager farmers. (FROM SEA UNTO SEA, Canada 1850-1910, by W.C.Hardy)

The earliest Channel Islander in the compiler's records to show up in the far west was a Le Serre, or Le Sarre, of Guernsey, a surgeon, who appeared in Assiniboia, Rupert's Land, a member of the Council of Miles MacDonell in 1813. He died shortly after this time, and his effects were returned to his executors in Guernsey. (Oliver, Jennings) Another Le Sarre, possibly a brother, was in Ohio in 1806. (QAAM) Le Serre in Assiniboia was called a "superior man in every respect, from Guernsey, related to General Brock...a man of science."

While other Channel Islanders may have been involved in the settlement of the west before the middle 1800s, we know of a few who were drawn there in the boom time of the 1870s and 1880s.

Thomas James Agnew arrived at Ft. Garry, Winnipeg, in 1876. He then borrowed five dollars from the captain of a river boat and started work as French clerk at J.H. Ashdown Hardware. In late April 1879 he and his partner, Arthur Ashdown, son of the company owner, set out for Prince Albert, Sask., with a train of 12 Red River carts drawn by ponies. Each cart carried 1,000 lbs. of merchandise, in this case, hardware. Each man had 4 carts and 4 ponies in his care. Because of an unusually wet spring it took 70 days to travel the 500 miles, as streams became rivers, rivers were wide torrents, and trails were a series of mudholes.

A two foot fall of snow on May 24th stranded the party at Wolverine Creek for several days. At an overnight camp, the Hudson's Bay Company mail packet dogs chewed up the Shaganappi harness of the ponies so the party was stalled until harness could be found and made to replace that ruined by the dogs.

The process of ferrying carts and goods across swollen streams was difficult and dangerous and some stock was lost.

Red River carts were pulled by oxen only when settlers were moving in. For freighting, horses were used. A sturdy type of pony available in the area was most suited to the job of pulling heavy loads in the nail-less squeaking wooden and leather carts. The Ashdown-Agnew party arrived in Prince Albert one evening in late June, 1879. The next day they opened up shop in a small building in the west end of the settlement, which as someone described it--sprawled along the south bank of the river for close to seven miles.

Lots in Prince Albert were river lots, with narrow frontage on the river, and the lots extended back for a mile or two. This had been practical earlier, so that each resident could have access to water. These river lots were one of the points of friction later between the old and new settlers, as roads were needed, and square plots of land were required in the land surveys.

When the telegraph arrived in Prince Albert, the office was midway between the two settlements, so the businessmen moved into what is now downtown Prince Albert. The telegraph line was installed before the 1885 Rebellion, but the line was cut early in the uprising.

Thomas Agnew and his wife and 2 young children were on the homestead on the South Saskatchewan River, just a few miles southeast of Prince Albert when the Rebellion began. "The family,   led by the Northwest Mounted police party under Col. Irvine went into the settlement...as the rebels burned their home."

Later the Agnew family made various trips back to Guernsey to visit, and the descendants have continued this custom, some of the great grandchildren having visited the Island of Guernsey. (Myrtle Lunney, Winnipeg; Man.; Sarah Leppard, Prince Albert, Sask.)

The main part of the settlement of western Canada was compressed, timewise, into about 50 years, from about 1870 to about 1920, mostly Europeans. But surprisingly, in 1911, 120,000 Americans moved north across the border.

Another early settler in the West was George Machon, born in Jersey 1851, raised in Vittoria, Ontario, where his father, John Machon, was a tailor and the town clerk. In the 1870s, George left home, via train to Sarnia, Ontario, via steamer to Thunder Bay, and by horse and foot to the western frontier. His journal reveals some interesting highlights on life in Western Canada at that time, touching the small settlements at Fisher's Landing, Brainard, Pembina, Portage La Prairie and Battle River. He married and settled in Calgary, where he raised a family of six children. His brother Edward also settled in the West. Another brother, John, removed to North Dakota. (See excerpts from diary in QAAM) (Diary in Historical Society files, Calgary, Alta)

Arthur James le Patourel of Guernsey homesteaded at Chinook, Alta., and his brother, J. Lewis came there in 1908.

"When Dad took out his homestead in 1903, there was no province of Alberta, it was the Northwest Territories...The first winter he had no horse and had to walk to Cayley, at that time having a general store, post office and livery barn plus a few houses...There were very few fences and the ranchers cattle roamed at will, often destroying small gardens. The ranchers had come much earlier, and were established, and had no use for the sodbusters, as they were taking up their free pasture. Prairie fires were a great danger and the homesteaders plowed fire guards around their shacks. It was in 1905 that Dad broadcast a gallon of Red Fyfe wheat on his fireguard and it produced well. He knew of no binder in the country so he harvested it all by pulling it up by the roots and beating the heads against his boot. This was done over a blanket and he had two sacks for wheat for the next years seeding.

Hay for the ranchers was a paying crop, and as the wild grass grew tall, it paid well until they could break up more land to grow grain. I have a letter from the Forestry branch in Ottawa, dated April 26, 1905, in acknowledgement of Dad's application for trees for a shelter belt. There were no trees on the prairie, just along the river banks. The government assisted the settlers by sending out, free of charge, trees for shelter belts and wood lots.

A friend of Dad's named Osmond Hocart came out from Guernsey at that time and homesteaded the quarter section next to Dad. He only stayed a few years, and returned to Guernsey. Dad bought his quarter as well as three others adjoining. My oldest brother Jim lived there until he sold in 1967.

Dad helped build the first grain elevator in 1906 in High River, the next town to Cayley. He also worked in the lumber mills in the area of Banff, as did many of the homesteaders, so that they would have money to carry on the next year. Wild game and birds were plentiful then so they never lacked for meat...

Cash was very scarce so neighbors traded labor. In the summer it was difficult to keep meat fresh, except for pork, which they cured and salted. A 'meat ring' was started, each man taking his turn supplying an animal so that each week there was a butchering and the meat distributed among the members. This continued for years until deep freeze lockers became available in the towns and then later the electric power went through the country and the people got their own freezers." (Edith Hunziger, Carlesholm, Alta.)

The Genge brothers and sisters came from Jersey to Western Canada about 1903, associated with a group of other Jersey folk, the De la Hayes and the Le Gallais families.

"The great day when the two girls were to arrive in Moose Jaw came at last, and Charlie and John drove in to meet them. It was in April 1908, and the last of the winter's snow had gone, but unfortunately on this day a delayed blizzard struck the county...nevertheless the party drove out in an open democrat and stopped at my store...We had to fit them out with winter overshoes, woollen mittens and other essentials...they all pitched in with a will and soon had the house looking like a home...they never complained and were invariably cheerful... We headed northwest, much of the way along the route of the old Saskatoon Trail...thousands of square miles of virgin plain, with an isolated homesteader here and there." (D.E. McIntyre)

"We arrived in Moose Jaw, Sask., on March 29, Good Friday morning. It was ten degrees below zero and the sleigh bells were jingling on the streets. From there in a box sleigh, and without old country coats and clothing we drove out to my brother's farm, some 24 miles. We were well wrapped with blankets and rugs and didn't seem to be bothered with the cold. It was the end of a long hard winter and there were several feet of snow for miles around us. I think the last vestige of it remained until May. In our growing up days in Jersey we had only seen snow once or twice and very little at that. I wonder how many war brides and women immigrants have found themselves grappling with the difficulties beset us when we arrived on the prairies." (Mary Genge Ritchie)

THE CANADIAN WEST, CHANNEL ISLAND SURNAMES

Channel Island surnames are very plentiful in the Canadian West; look in any phone book! Most of them are descendants of families who settled there during the 1800s and early 1900s. Some are Channel Island descendants of those who first settled in the Maritimes or in Ontario, and removed westward. This list is far from complete.

AGNEW	LE BRUN	LILLYCROP
ALEXANDRE	LE CAIN	LUCE
ALLEN	LE CLERCQ	MACHON
AMY	LE COCQ	MANSELL
ANLEY	LE DREW	MANUEL
BISSON	LEE	MAINWARING
BRETON	LE FEBVRE	MARKS
COUTANCHE	LE GALLAIS	MARTEL
CURNEW	LE GRAND	MARTIN
DAVIS	LE LACHEUR	MC CLOCKLIN
DE FRAINE?	LE LIEVRE	MERCIER
DE GRUCHY	LE MAISTRE	NICHOLAS
DE JERSEY	LE MARCHAND	NOEL
DE LA HAYE	LE MASURIER	PELLAN
DOREY	LE MESSURIER	RENAUD
EMILY	LE MOIGNAN	RENOUF
FELLE	LE MOINE	RICHARDSON
FALLU	LE MOTTEE	ROBERTS
FLEURY	LEMPRIERE	ROBILLIARD
GAUDIN	LENFESTEY	ROBIN
GENGE	LE PAGE	ROMERIL
HAYNES	LE RICHE	ROUSSEL
HOSKING	LE ROUGETEL	SIMON
LE BEL	LE SAGE	TARDIF
LE BER	LE SUEUR	TAYLER
LE BIHAN	LE VASSEUR	THEOFAIR
LE BLANC	LE VESCONTE	WHEADON
LE BOUTILLIER	LIHOU	

THE CANADIAN WEST, THE BARR COLONY

Settlement in Canada was sometimes accomplished by the formation of groups of people in Europe, as from the Ukraine. This also came about in Great Britain, as for instance, the Barr Colony. Preparations were made in England for the housing and care of these people during their first year in Canada, and to help them establish on grants of land in the West. The carrying out of these plans almost led to a disaster in the heart of Canada, due to less-than-perfect planning and organization. However, this group, through perseverance and hard work, managed to survive the bad beginnings, and added a great variety of good craftsmen and farmers to the Canadian West.

Some Channel Islanders are thought to be included with this group, but identification has been difficult. In 1963 the Lloydminster Times brought out an edition of their newspaper to salute these pioneer families, who began their Canadian lives under such fierce difficulties. The names are listed in that newspaper, and among them are noted quite a few surnames associated with the Channel Islands. While it was impossible for the compiler to locate all these potential C.I. families, an attempt was made to extract from the long list those whose origin might have been the Channel Islands. It is possible that many more could be added, if sources in the Canadian West could have been consulted.

POSSIBLE CHANNEL ISLAND SURNAMES AMONG THE BARR COLONISTS, 1863

ALLEN	DEAN	MILLMAN
ALMOND	DENNIS	MOON
BAKER	DOBREE	NICOLL
BALL	DYER	NORMAN
BARLOW	FRANCIS	OWEN
BECK	GALLON	OZANNE
BELL	GEE	PICKLES
BERRY	GENGE	PIKE
BESSANT, BISSON?	GOSLING	RICHARDSON
BLACKBURN	GRAY	ROBERTS
BODEN, BEAUDIN?	HARDING	ROSE
	HARDY	SALMON
BUTLER	HARDLEY	SALT
COLLINGS	HEADLEY	SHAW
COLLINGWOOD	HILLARY	SMITH
	KELLETT	SYMONS
CASWELL	KING	THOMAS
CLEMENTS	KNIGHT	THORN
ELLIS	LUCAS	WALKER
ENGLISH	MAIN	WHITTLES
DALLAS	MARESH	WOOD
DAVIES	MERCER	WHEELER

BANCROFT, H.H., HISTORY OF THE PACIFIC STATES OF NORTH AMERICA, Vol.27.
BUTLER, Lt. William, THE GREAT LONE LAND.
COOPER, Paul, ISLAND OF THE LOST, 1961
COUES, Elliott, Henry Thompson Journals, 3 vols.
HANSEN, M., and J.B. Brebner, MINGLING OF THE CANADIAN AND AMERICAN PEOPLE.
HEMING, Arthur, THE DRAMA OF THE FORESTS, Toronto, 1936.
HILL, Douglas, THE OPENING OF THE CANADIAN WEST, N.Y. City, 1967.
JENNINGS, John, THE STRANGE BRIGADE, Boston, 1952.
MACHON, George, MS, Journal of trip to Western Canada, 1870s, Historical Soc., Calgary, Alta.
MACINTYRE, D.E., PRAIRIE STOREKEEPER, a booklet, Toronto, 1970.
MC COURT, Edward, SASKATCHEWAN, Toronto, 1968.
MC DOUGALL, ON WESTERN TRAILS IN THE EARLY SEVENTIES.
NUTE, Grace, THE VOYAGEUR.
OLLIVER, Prof. E.H., Ed., THE CANADIAN NORTHWEST, ITS EARLY DEVELOPMENT, Vol. 1, Ottawa, 1914.
OLSON, Sigurd, THE LONELY LAND, New York, 1961.
PATTERSON, R.M., THE BUFFALO HEAD, New York, 1961.
RITCHIE, Mary Genge, PARTNERS IN THE GLORY OF THE GARDEN, booklet.
SHEPHERD, George, WEST OF YESTERDAY, Toronto, 1964.
TANNER, Ogden, Ed., THE CANADIANS, THE OLD WEST, Time-Life Books, Alexandria, Va., 1977.
WOOD, Louis Aubrey, THE RED RIVER COLONY, Vol. 21, THE CHRONICLES OF CANADA, Toronto, 1915.
also, THE LLOYDMINSTER TIMES, July 17, 1963, for information on the Barr Colonists.

CHAPTER TWELVE, BRITISH COLUMBIA

"The most lovely country that
could be imagined." (Vancouver)

This beautiful province has become the home of many thousands of Channel Islanders. Records show that they came here directly from Jersey and Guernsey, but also came from Gaspe, Newfoundland, Ontario, Quebec, Prince Edward Island, the Prairie provinces and from the United States. What drew them? Two things mainly, business opportunities and the fine climate.

A large number of the Islanders settled first in Victoria, then in Vancouver. In both of these cities there was in the early 1940s (and perhaps before) a rather large Channel Islands society, which continued for over 20 years. Active in this group were Philip Winter Luce and his sister, Eva. Mr. Luce was born in Jersey in 1882, and many references in this book came from his speeches and articles, as the gathering of much information on Channel Islanders abroad was his avocation in his later years.

Luce left Jersey for Winnipeg around 1900, and then went to New Westminster, B.C. where he became news editor of the DAILY NEWS. He later left journalism to become advertising manager for W.J. Kerr, one of the leading real estate promoters on the Coast, but returned to the profession some years afterwards to work for both the NEWS-ADVERTISER and the WORLD.

In 1921, Luce became a freelance writer and sold stories, articles and humorous sketches to magazines across the country. When the Channel Islands were occupied by German troops in 1940 he helped organize the Society in B.C., which raised $25,000 to help evacuees from Jersey and Guernsey.

A bachelor, Mr. Luce died at the age of 84, and was survived by two sisters, Eva Luce of Vancouver and Mrs. Frank Renouf of Jersey. Following are quotations from his speeches and writings, about the activities of Channel Islanders in B.C.

"Censorship was strict in Canada when the Germans occupied the Channel Islands in 1940. Very little was known of what happened...Frank Becquet, who had left Jersey during the evacuation, and who had arrived in Vancouver the day before the meeting, July 17th, gave graphic account of the conditions up to June 21st. Extracts from many letters were read, and copies of recent Islands newspapers were passed around.

Realizing that most of the 35,000 evacuees would be in need of help, those present organized themselves into a society which is now one of the largest Channel Islands organizations in the world, and the only active C.I. Society on the American continent. (Compiler's note: This may not be entirely true, as societies were also formed in Montreal and in southern and western Ontario.) It has over 600 members, two thirds of whom live outside Vancouver. A branch in Victoria has about 40 members."

"The membership of the society is made up of approximately 40 percent Jersey folk, 30 percent Guernsey folk, and 30 percent non-natives, chiefly persons who have visited the islands or who have friends or relatives there." (Luce)

The following is from a speech given by F.J. Fleury at one of the meetings of the Society in 1953, which was authored by Philip W. Luce:

"Canada has drawn many Channel Islanders, and British Columbia has had its share. There are now about 300 persons in and around Vancouver who once called Jersey or Guernsey their homeland, and Victoria can boast of perhaps fifty. There are scores or more scattered around the province." (Compiler's note: In B.C. census of 1941, 2,000 Canadians of Channel Island desc.)

"One of the first Channel Islanders to see the coast of B.C. was Capt. James Gaudin, a sea dog, who owned several ships built in Jersey in the 1860s, and who made several voyages to Victoria before deciding to make it his home. He settled there in 1872 and nine years later he arranged for his wife, two daughters and a niece to join him.

The Gaudin family went across the Atlantic in a small sailing vessel, rounded Cape Horn and landed in Victoria six months to the day of leaving Jersey. A stop of a couple of weeks had been made at the Falkland Islands where the party had their first sight of coloured natives in picturesque undress.

Life in a small sailing vessel was bleak and wearisome, and at times dangerous. During the voyage a fire broke out, but this was mastered after most of the clothing and effects had been consumed. Capt. Gaudin continued as shipmaster for some years, and then joined the C.P.R. Coastal service..." (Luce)

James R. Gaudin, of this family, retired in 1952 from a strenuous life in the Far West. He had been Supt. Engr. of the River Div. of the White Pass and Yukon route.

"In July 1897 James Gaudin left Victoria, B.C. on S.S. THISTLE with a crew of men and supplies, machinery and equipment, including a saw mill to build a steamer at Teslin Lake. ...The F.N. York Company...constructed the steamer ANGLIAN, first of the '98 fleet to be built in the North, from native spruce, and started for Dawson, June 20, 1898. (The officers and men were named as McDonald, Gardner, Howatt, Doddridge, Henley, Gaudin). Forty members of the Yukon Field Force were aboard as passengers...Steamer ANGLIAN joined the fleet of the newly organized Canadian Development Co., which was purchased in 1901 by the British Yukon Navigation Co....and operated for several seasons...Mr. Gaudin personally did all the draughting, blue-printing and supervising for the various construction projects of the company, including the Atlin Inn, B.C., the original Whitehorse Inn, which was built by the

White Pass Company, and all other buildings, steamers and barges..." (Whitehorse Star, Whitehorse, Yukon Terr., Oct. 3, 1952)

"Capt. Gaudin's niece, Nancy Renouf, married Henry Anderson, they had one son, who is now editor-in-chief of the Vancouver PROVINCE...Widowed, Mrs. Anderson removed to the Kootenays... lived for a time at Kaslo and Ainsworth, then went to Calgary where she joined the staff of the Western Canada College. In 1915 she married the principal, Dr. A.O. McCrae, and later lived in Vancouver. She died in 1950 at age 88.

Capt. Alphonse D'Allain was for some years accountant in Capt. Gaudin's office. This Jerseyman was in the Victoria 5th Regiment when redoubts were built along the Dallas Road, he was a splendid horseman, but at some time or another every bone in his body was broken. He exercised his horses in Beacon Hill Park.

Very few members of this society know anything about George Fleury, who came to this coast about 1884. He made his home in Comberland, on Vancouver Island, where he married and raised a family. Two of the members are living in Vancouver, the oldest being a Mrs. Thomas.

Four Fleury families came to B.C., three from Jersey, and one from Quebec, the latter possibly from an earlier settler from the Channel Islands.

George Fleury was a versatile man. He learned his trade in Jersey, and worked there as a blacksmith, but this kind of work was lacking in Cumberland. So he blandly took up painting, and made a success of it. He never went back to Jersey, where three brothers remained. Mr. Fleury happened to be in Vancouver on June 13, 1886, when the young town was destroyed by fire...

Walter Fleury came a few years later. He made his home in Vancouver, where he had a furniture repair shop, and a paint shop on Hastings, in the East end. He died more than ten years ago, in his eighties, and his oldest son, now a C.P.R. pensioner, and his widow, are still living. Mr. Fleury attended the first picnic of the Channel Islands Society in 1940 in Stanley Park." (written in the 1950s by Mr. Luce)

"Only two of our active members can boast of having come here before 1900. One of these is Mr. Reginald Hamon, who first sailed up Burrard Inlet in 1896 when he was little more than a boy. He was seventeen, and he was making his first voyage as an apprentice on a sailing ship, the WATERLOO.

Mr. Hamon liked the looks of British Columbia, and he stayed here when the ship sailed away with a cargo of lumber...It is a little difficult for Mr. Hamon to remember all the ways he earned his bread from 1898 to 1900, but his employers were many...He worked ten hours a day six days a week, and his pay was $1.00 a day. A saw mill worker can get ten times that sum now, but there were no unions to help the brawny men of the last century.

For one winter Mr. Hamon made his home in Victoria...driving a baker's wagon,...the pay was $13.00 a month...He went up the Skeena River, and for a time worked from the Hudson's Bay boat CALEDONIA, a stern wheeler that operated on the Northern waters for many years...Sailor, mill hand, teamster, fisherman, jack of all trades, Mr. Hamon can certainly qualify as a real Channel Islands pioneer.

One pioneer who is still active among us is Mrs. J.E. Insley, who has been a resident of these parts since the middle eighties. Her maiden name was Mamie Draper, and she was left an orphan in Jersey at an early age. An aunt adopted her and brought her to the little community on the banks of Burrard's Inlet.

It is on record that the celebrated Lilly Langtry offered to adopt Mamie Draper...but it was felt that she should remain in the family. Her life would certainly have been much more lively if Lilly Langtry had had her wish.

Mr. Charles Pallot and his wife of Pitt Meadows, Mr. Pallot's house was near Trinity Church in Jersey, and Mrs. Pallot came from the same district. Mr. and Mrs. Pallot went in for farming, and made a success of it. One of the sons, Spencer, has made a name for himself as auctioneer, school trustee, real estate agent, and political agent in farm circles...born about 1898 in Maple Ridge...

There are two Channel Islanders who must always be mentioned together for they were inseparable. These were the two brothers Buesnel, John and Walter, who came out from Jersey in the late nineties, and settled in the Kootenays. They both were bachelors, and did their own cooking, washing and housekeeping...On a small farm near Nakusp the Buesnel brothers raised garden stuff and kept a couple of cows, not Jerseys. They sold their garden truck to the little settlements and camps on Upper Arrow Lakes, and it is said that they did very well indeed.

An old trapper and miner by the name of Clement Le Couteur spent his last days in the old men's home in Kamloops. He came from Jersey late in the eighties or nineties, but little is known about him. He died in 1945.

One Jerseyman who came here before Vancouver even had a name was Arthur Le Neveu, who was a young sailor on the sailing ship, CHRISTOBAL. This was in 1882 when the population was only a couple of thousand, and there wasn't much doing. Mr. Le Neveu sailed away with a cargo of lumber after being here a few weeks, and continued life as a sailor for a number of years. Then he came back to B.C. and settled down. He married a girl from Bellingham, who survived him when he died about 1945, after living for many years on Eight Ave., near Granville St. In his little parlour Mr. Le Neveu had a large framed picture of the CHRISTOBAL, and an effort was made to get this for the Museum when he died, but one of his sons had taken it to Toronto.

Although he started life as a sailor, Mr. Le Neveu switched occupations when steel freighters came along, and spent the rest of his life as a carpenter and painter, and he was a remarkably fast worker.

David Le Neveu was born in Jersey about 1819. He reached California by yacht in 1851, in company with some friends, and started a business in Marysville, Calif., a Gold Rush town. Le Neveu left California and came to Victoria, B.C. in 1858, and organized a grain and feed business. There he also took part in the setting up of Victoria as an incorporated city, whose first election took place in 1862. Le Neveu was married in 1867 to a woman from Jersey, who died at the age of 41 in 1880, leaving several children. Le Neveu died in 1885 at the age of 66.

Among the pioneers of B.C. we have the oldest Jerseyman in Canada, who will be 92 next May, and who is still hale and hearty. He is Frederick J. Jeune of Victoria, who has been in business in that city as a sail-maker for 69 years, and who is one of the few men in that trade on the Pacific coast.

Jeune was born in Roseville St., St. Heliers in 1862, and his education was limited....apprenticed to a sail-maker when he was little more than twelve years old...when he first saw Burrard Inlet, in 1881, there were only two lumber mills and forests of pine where Vancouver now stands...On a later voyage, which took six months and ten days, including a hurricane that lasted six weeks, a long delay in the doldrums at the Equator, and three weeks storm bound in the Straits of San Juan de Fuca, the ship caught fire in Victoria Harbour. The vessel was loaded with dynamite and most of the population took to the woods, but the blaze was mastered.

Mr. Jeune decided to stay in B.C. and go into sailmaking... with nine dollars he bought a second hand sailmakers bench... set up in business...did his last bit of sailmaking...(when) over 90 years old...

A brother, W.P. Jeune came out to make sails in a few years, and the firm of Frederick Jeune and Brother was founded...The sealing trade brought much business, and when this was stopped by government treaty, the Klondike gold rush was on. For this business, Mr. Jeune made up 600 tents in one season, innumerable packsacks, tarpaulins, and a large number of collapsable water craft for navigating river rapids...back to sailmaking, but chiefly sails for racing yachts as far south as California, and as far east as the Great Lakes...When the war came... sails were set aside and the firm made life rafts and fender ropes, shipping these east by the carload...a four months visit to Jersey in 1907...many changes. Gone were all the shipyards he remembered, and there wasn't a single sailmaker's loft left in St. Heliers...retired in 1953, age 92.

The oldest member to ever join this society in Canada was Mrs. Thomas Bray. She was 94 when she became a member. She lived in B.C. more than thirty-seven years....Daughter of Judge Aubin of St. Clement's, Jersey...aristocrats...When she was sixteen the girl fell violently in love with the family groom. Her father and mother were scandalized, but could not keep the news from spreading. The girl was shut up in her room, but she managed to evade the family vigilance, and eloped with the groom. She was seventeen at the time and wrote home from England for forgiveness. There was no answer. The girl's name was struck off the family prayer book, and she was left to fend for herself...

A sister-in-law, two nieces, and a nephew of Charles Henry Poingdestre, a celebrated artist of the 1850s, came to Canada in the eighties. The three women came first, one of the girls, Edith, married J.H. Vidal, a son of Senator Vidal, who became News Editor of the BRITISH COLUMBIAN in New Westminster.

Mrs. Vidal was born in 1868, and she celebrated her 87th birthday in White Rock, was 22 in 1888 when she reached New Westminster and she lived there until 1908, when she removed to White Rock, a place which she had first seen in 1903, when it was virtually uninhabited.

Joseph Poingdestre, her younger brother, did not leave Jersey for Canada until 1886...to B.C....He held only one job in New Westminster. He was a bookkeeper for Martin Monk, the fishmonger, and he enjoyed life in his own way...A son of Mrs. Vidal was killed in an air raid over Poland...

There are a number of Channel Islanders who came to B.C. around the turn of the century, but it is not certain whether they were here before 1900. Among these was Walter Vibert, who was a bank manager in Victoria for many years, and who spent his last days at the old Hotel Vancouver. Capt. Le Marquand, too, who had the smelliest job that ever fell to the lot of a Jerseyman, manager of the whaling fleet off Vancouver Island...and three men from New Westminster...Capt. Le Boutillier, who had spend most of his life on the Gaspe coast; Lawford M. Richardson, manager of the local branch of the Royal Bank of Canada, and George Amy, who was clerk at Annandale's grocery store, and who now lives in White Rock." (Luce)

In addition, Mr. Fleury added the names of other Channel Islanders in the area; Capt. George Ferey, survivor of the ISLANDER wreck, Henry Rive, B.C. dairy Supt.; Bob Toneri, Josept Renouf, Joseph Le Sueur, Nicholas Le Couteur, Samuel Le Marquand, Steve Le Marquand.

Others in the same area were John Mollet, who lived in Fulford Harbour, B.C., and came to Albernia in 1900, a pioneer who came to Canada in 1863. Clement Renouf came in the 1800s. Joseph Renouf came in 1889 or a sailing ship. Walter, another brother of the Renoufs came also to British Columbia, and a fourth brother emigrated to Sydney, Australia. John Whittle came later, 1907, and settled in Victoria. (THE COLONIST) Philip Touet settled first in Gaspe 1870, and later came to B.C. His two daughters married two Jeune brothers, of the sail-making firm.

"...my grandfather, Capt. George James Le Marquand...born St. Heliers, Jersey. By his first wife...2 offspring; George Joshua, my father, born St. Heliers 1879, died Victoria, B.C. 1972...second child Lena...Capt. George was lost at sea during a mid-winter storm on the Atlantic. He was coming home to St. John's, Newfoundland, to retire at the age of 48...schooner the DONNA MARIA. My father decided to follow the sea, and at the age of 14 shipped with his father as a cabin boy. He became a Captain at the age of 25. He followed the sea for a number of years, sailing out of St. John's, and New York, U.S.A....graduated to steamers, but not before spending several seasons as Captain of a sealing vessel, taking seals off the Labrador coast. While at the height of his nautical career, he left the sea for a new challenge ashore. His new occupation brought him into the whaling industry."

"A small group of business men organized in St. John's, Nfld., a company of the Newfoundland coast. The station was located at a place called St. Lawrence. My father was the station manager. All this took place in the late 1800s. The company prospered as long as the whales, which were then known as Greenland white whales, lasted. After several years the whales were gone. One of the principals of the company left Newfoundland and went to Victoria, B.C. My father went back to sea."

"He received a call to come to the West Coast of Canada to take over a new whaling station in the Queen Charlotte Islands, off the B.C. coast. The offer was too tempting and my father set out for British Columbia...sent for his family. It was quite a wrench for my mother, who was very well connected in St. John's to pull up her roots and travel over 4000 miles to the rugged Queen Charlotte Islands with her five children, ranging 16 years down to 4 years...When the whaling company opened a new station on the West Coast of the State of Washington in the U.S....was promoted...1916...Gray's Harbor, Wash....promoted to Vice Pres. and Gen. Manager, with headquarters in both Seattle, Wash. and Victoria, B.C....the family moved to Victoria in 1921." (H. Alan Le Marquand, Vancouver, B.C.)

It is very apparent from the above accounts that many in B.C. are descendants of Channel Island families, but memoirs or journals could not be located by this compiler. There is material in the B.C. Archives on some of these families. The Gaudins have a fine booklet, put together by Helena Gaudin Cameron, and a very full chart, the work of W. Allen Briggs of Calgary, Alta. A smaller chart of the B.C. branch of the Le Marquands is also available. Many books about this province

may be found in your local library.
BIBLIOGRAPHY
RYERSON, Stan.BREHAUT, B 1911,THE FOUNDING OF
   CANADA, and UNEQUAL UNION.
HOAGLAND, Edward, NOTES FROM THE CENTURY BEFORE, Toronto, 1969.
PATTERSON, R.M., FINLAY'S RIVER, Toronto, 1968 and TRAIL TO
   THE INTERIOR, N.Y. City, 1966.

SOME CANADIAN AUTHORS AND COMPILERS OF C.I. DESCENT:
ASCAH, Elmer G., Farmington, Ohio, ASCAH GENEALOGY, 1974.
BECHERVAISE, John, b 1910, of Australia, author of more than 18
   books on Antactica, etc., related to the Gaspe Bechervaise
   family.
BRINE, Louise Lowry Surgey, author of THEY CAME IN SAILING
   SHIPS, typescript about C.I. families settled in Cape Breton
   and Nova Scotia.
BROCHET, John Aldo, of Perce and Toronto, author of articles in
   REVUE D'HISTOIRE DE LA GASPESIE, bulletin of the History
   Society of Gaspe.
BOURINOT, Sir John George, 1837-1902, author of many books
   about the Canadian Government, etc.
CAMERON, Helen Gaudin, author of typescript with pictures of
   the Gaudin family of Jersey and Canada. Chart for this re-
   search drawn by V. Allen Briggs of Calgary, Alta.
CARRELL, Frank, business tycoon of Que., author of several
   books, TIPS, CANADIAN WEST AND FARTHER WEST, AROUND THE
   WORLD CRUISE, etc.
DUMARESQ, Emery, of Gaspe. Dumaresq family chart.
GLYN, Elinor, famous actress and novelist of the late 1800s,
   has some Jersey connection, res there for a time in her
   youth. Res Guelph, Ont. Author of HALCYONE and many other
   books.
GUILLET, Edwin C., distinguished historian and author of EARLY
   LIFE IN UPPER CANADA, THE GREAT MIGRATION, etc., and the
   GUILLET-THOREAU GENEALOGY.
HOWARD, Blanche Machon, of Ottawa, and B.C. Author of THE
   MANIPULATOR, current.
HERIOT, Frederick George, 1766-1844, born Jersey, author of
   HISTORY OF CANADA FROM ITS FIRST DISCOVERY, and TRAVELS
   THROUGH THE CANADAS.
KEYHOE, David, of Kitchener, Ont. and of Guernsey, joint author
   with Sybil Leek of STARSPEAK, published New York 1977, and
   author of various educational articles.
KINGSWOOD, Ruby Le Grand, of Toronto, Ont., author of TRUMPETS
   OF DAWN.
LE FEUVRE, George Francis, author of JERRI JADIS, in the Jer-
   siaise tongue.
LE GALLAIS, Maud, author of LURE OF THE LABRADOR, not found.
LE GRESLEY, Gustave, compiler of booklet on LE GRESLEY family.

BRITISH COLUMBIA, CHANNEL ISLAND SURNAMES

Some of the surnames below have only a connection by marriage with Channel Islanders.

AHIER	DEBOICE	LE COUTEUR	QUERTIER
ALEXANDRE	DE BOURCIER	LE FEBVRE	RABEY
AMY	DE CLERCQ	LE GALLAIS	RENOUF
BABBE	DE COU	LE GRAND	RIVE
BAKER	DE COURSEY	LE GRESLEY	ROBILLIARD
BALL	DE FOREST	LE GROS	ROMERIL
BARBIER	DE GRUCHY	LE HURAY	SAVARY, SYVRET
BASHFORD	DE GUERIN	LE JEUNE	SAUVARY
BECQUET	DE HAVILAND	LE LIEVRE	SAVIDENT
BICHARD	DE LA HAYE	LE MARQUAND	SCARISBRICK
BIRD	DE LA MARE	LE MESSURIER	SCOTT
BISSON	DELANCEY	LE MOINE	SELOUS
BLANCPIED	DELANEY	LEMPRIERE	SOLWAY
BLANDY	DE LA RONDE	LE NEVEU	STARCK, STARCH
BLIAULT	DE LA ROCQUE	LENFESTEY	STRATHY
BRAIN	DE LA RUE	LE PAGE	THEOFAIR
BRADFORD	DE LISLE	LE PATOUREL	TONERI
BRAY	DENTITH	LE POIDEVIN	TOSTEVIN
BROWN	DE VEAU	LE QUESNE,	TOUET
BUESNEL	DIVERS	LE CAIN	TOUZEAU
CAIN	DRAPER	LE RICHE	VALLOIS
CAMBREY	DUCHEMIN	LE ROSSIGNOL	VENNEMENT
CANNING	DUKE	(Nightingale)	VIBERT
CANTEL	DUKEMAN	LE ROUX	VINCENT
CAREY	DUTOT	LE SEELEUR	WARREN
CARR	EDMOND	LIHOU	WATERMAN
CARRE	EMILY	LUCE	WELSH
CARRIERE	FAIRWEATHER	MACHON	WHITTLE
CASWELL	FALLE	MAHY	WILLETT
CHICK	FEREY	MAINGUY	YEO
CLEMENTS	FERGUSON	MALTHOUSE	YOUNG
CLERKE	FLEURY	MATTHEWS	
COADE, COADY	FLOOD	MOLLET	
COATES	FROOD	MOSS	
CODY, LE CAUDEY	GAUDIN	MOURANT	
COLCLOUGH	GILLIS	MUGFORD	
COLEBACK	GODFREY	NEEL	
COLEBECK	GODIN	NEWTON	
COLLEDGE	GOLLEDGE	NOURY	
COLLETT	HAMON	OGILVIE	
COLLINGS	HANCOCK	OZANNE	
COURT, A'COURT?	HAYNES	OZARD	
COUTTS	HENDERSON	PAINTER	
COUTANCHE	HULL	PALLOT	
CREASEY	INSLEY	PATRIARCHE	
CROCKER	JAMIESON	PEARSON	
CRONIN	JEUNE	PEDDLE	
CROSS	KIRK	PELLAN	
CROZIER	KITTS	PERREE	
CURRIE	LABEY	PHILLIPS	
CURWOOD	LE BAS	PHIPPS	
DALLAIN	LE BOUTILLIER	PICKLES	
DALY	LE BRUN	POINGDESTRE	
DALTON	LE CLERC	PRENTIS	

CHAPTER THIRTEEN, IN SEARCH OF YOUR ANCESTORS
SEE ALSO "ADDITIONS AND CORRECTIONS"

"Life must be lived forward, but understood backward."
(A WALK THROUGH EUROPE, by John Hillaby, Boston, 1972)

Canadians have recently taken a strong interest in genealogy. Those who have ancestors in the Channel Islands and in North America, and who are beginners in this craft may want to know how to explore their various family lines. For their benefit, some guidelines are included here.

Nearly all experts in this field agree that research on one's family should start with oneself. Therefore, a large notebook and your memory will be the springboard. Write down in a looseleaf book all the things that you do know about your ancestors. Take each parent, grandparent and great grandparent in turn, and record the full names, the years of birth and death, place of marriage and of residence. Examine birth, death and marriage certificates, family Bibles, mortgage and real estate transaction papers, church records, diaries, birthday books, photographs, etc., for vital statistics and background information.

The next step is to tap the memories of all of your relatives, especially the older ones in the family. A family gathering, where much discussion takes place, will reveal a good many things that are vital to your research. Sometimes there is a difference of opinion on dates, places or names. Take down both sets of information, which you can later examine and verify. Do not stop at facts alone, but also include the folklore, tradition, family jokes, ghosts, and stories of past family events. These will be of great interest to coming generations.

Before going any further, locate in your local library, or a bookstore, a good book on genealogical research, to help organize your material, and show you the best methods to obtain more information. Here are three inexpensive and useful booklets to begin with:

1. Send for TRACING YOUR ANCESTORS IN CANADA, from your nearest Canadian Government Book Shop, in Halifax, Montreal, Ottawa, Toronto, Winnipeg, and Vancouver. The cost of this booklet was 25¢ in 1975.

2. Write to the Everton Publishers, P.O. Box 368, Logan, Utah, 84321, for their catalog which describes and pictures various forms of family charts for sale. This firm publishes THE GENEALOGICAL HELPER, a six times yearly bulletin in which, for a fee, you can list the families you are interested in researching. Possibly in this way you can contact relatives who have more information, or who will be able to aid you in your research. There is a small fee for the sampler. A year's subscription will cost at least $20.00, but is well worth it.

3. Send three dollars to the Nova Scotia Museum, 1747 Summer St., Halifax, N.S., B3H 3A6, for a copy of Terrence Punch's article, FIND YOUR FAMILY, Bull. #11 of the Museum's

publications, plus a subscription to the Nova Scotia Genealogical Newsletter. Also see their Bulletin 24 and 25.

City or town records, cemeteries, state and provincial archives, ship lists of passengers, parish and church records, land transfers, probate will records, census records and Dominion Archives, all abound in information that you can use.

Look in telephone books of other cities than your own, often found in libraries, for persons of the surname you are researching. Write to these persons, enclosing a <u>stamped</u>, self-addressed envelope, and ask if anything is known about their ancestors, and what part of the world did they leave to come to Canada, or the United States. Give some details of your own family's origin in an attempt to find common ancestry.

Join your local genealogical society. Take courses in genealogy at local schools and colleges. If you live in a small town, spend a day or two in the nearest large city to explore the information available there. Don't neglect the libraries of colleges and universities.

Investigate the material that the Mormon Church records may hold on your ancestors. It could surprise and please you, as the church has for some years recorded information on hundreds of thousands of families everywhere. This includes the Channel Islands.

Advertise for information on the families you are interested in, perhaps in the Genealogical Helper, or in some of the many other bulletins put out in this field in the United States.

Subscribe to LOST IN CANADA, and include a query about your family puzzles. Join the genealogical societies in the provinces where your ancestors resided. Make use of the query columns in the bulletins. Offer to exchange research in your area for data from other places you are interested in. The more people knowing of your research, the greater possibility of finding more information. Perhaps extensive research has been done on one or more of your family surnames, and this can save a great deal of time and money.

In Channel Island research, the reader should be wary of accepting information as gospel from this or similar books. Certified information must be sought from original sources such as church and state records, census, family Bibles, land agreements, etc. Since it was not possible for this compiler to verify all information in this book, the reader is warned that inclusion of data in this book does not verify the origin of that family or person, or any other family or persons of the same surname.

It is quite possible that a few of the surnames in this book originated in other places than the Channel Islands, such as France and Wales. Inclusion in this book in those cases was accepted for various reasons, such as intermarriage with Channel Island families, long and close association with the

Island families in Canada, or the statement that these persons or families were from the Islands, with no qualifying data to prove it. This was particularly the case with Newfoundland families, where a number are thought to have some early connection with the Islands, but records to prove this are not available.

It is possible that such links to the Islands came through the mother's side of the family, which fact may not be known by the descendant. Also, youths of many different origins were indentured by the Jersey firms, coming from southern England, Scandinavia, Ireland, Brittany, Normandy, Germany, Italy and Spain. Often this came about through the commerce of the Island ships. A lad of 12 or 13 would then take on the language and culture of the firm or group he was with, and would later consider himself a part of the Islanders' culture, although he may not have origins there.

Reasons for inclusion in this book are briefly:

1. The surname has been recorded in the Channel Islands and/or in Canada, in Canadian or American books, and census records, as having originated in the Islands.

2. The family located at a place in Canada where other Channel Islanders are known to have settled, and tradition states they were from the Islands.

3. Some family members married into Channel Island families.

4. The surname is fairly unique to the Islands, and most persons of that surname in the world are said to be from the Islands. Examples would be: Dumaresq, De Jersey, De Guernsey, Vaudin, Torode, Gallichan, Lempriere, Le Mesurier (all forms), De Carteret, De Gruchy, Messervy and Lenfestey, etc.

5. In a number of cases, the surname although British has been known on the Island for a long time, brought about through intermarriage between servicemen stationed on the Islands, and Island women. These marriages have taken place often over the years from very early times.

6. The surname has been included in lists made by Channel Island descendants in Canada, names that were believed to be those of other Channel Island families known to them.

CANADIAN SOURCES OF GENEALOGICAL INFORMATION

ALBERTA GENEALOGICAL SOCIETY, Box 3151 Station A, Edmonton, Alta. T5J 2G7.

BAKER, Eunice Ruiter, SEARCHING FOR YOUR ANCESTORS IN CANADA, Ottawa, 1975, for beginners.

BRITISH COLUMBIA GENEALOGIST, P.O. Box 94371, Richmond, B.C., V6Y 2A8.

BURTON HISTORICAL COLLECTION, Detroit Public Library, 5201 Woodward Ave., Detroit, Mich. 48202 (Houses much information on families of Quebec and Ontario, etc.)

IN SEARCH OF YOUR ANCESTORS   115
  SEE RECENT ISSUES OF"GEN.HELPER" RE:CURR.ADDRESSES.
CANADIAN GAZETTEER, William H. Smith, 1846, reprint.
COWAN, Valierie, 24 Edward Laurie Dr., Halifax, N.S., B3M 2C7,
  DIRECTORY OF CANADIAN RECORDS.
CENTRE CANADIENNE DE GENEALOGIE, C.P. 2234, Quebec, P.Q., Can.
CENTRE DES ETUDES ACADIENNE, Moncton University, Moncton, N.B.
  Attn: Stephen White.
CUMMING ATLAS REPRINTS, Box 23, Stratford, Ont.
GENEALOGICAL COMMITTEE, Subscription, $6.00, Philip Harling,
  3 Scotsburn Ave., Dartmouth, N.S., B2X 1P8, Nova Scotia
  Genealogical Bulletins.
GINGRAS, Raymond, genealogist, 39 St. Cyrille-Quest, Apt. 5,
  Quebec, 6, Quebec, Canada.
  Booklet: HISTOIRE LOCAL ET GENEALOGIE, QELQUE REFERENCES
  ET ADDRESSES, a list of Genealogical Societies, books and
  other resources of French Canada.
GINGRAS, Raymond, MELANGES GENEALOGIQUE, periodical booklets
  with much useful genealogical information on Quebec, etc.
HERALDRY SOCIETY OF CANADA, Norman A. Nunn, 900 Pinecrest Rd.,
  Ottawa, 14, Ontario.
HUGUENOT SOCIETY OF CANADA, Ruth Loft, 136 Tollgate Rd., Apt.
  202, Brantford, Ontario.
INSTITUTE GENEALOGIQUE DROUIN, 4184 Saint Denis, Montreal,Que.
LOST IN CANADA, periodical, excellent, 1020 Central Ave.,
  Sparta, Wisc. 54656. (Much information in back bulletins)
LOVELL, John, ONTARIO, also other provinces. Directories of
  the 1850s and 1860s. Possibly reprints available. See
  also Hunterdon House, 39 Swan St., Lambertville, N.J. 08530.
MAJOR GENEALOGICAL RECORD SOURCE FOR CANADA, by the Geneologi-
  cal Society of the Mormon Church, Salt Lake City. Series B,
  No. 3, 107 South Main St., Salt Lake City, Utah, 84111.
NEWFOUNDLAND HISTORICAL SOCIETY, Room 15, Colonial Bldg., St.
  John's, Newfoundland.
NEWFOUNDLAND ARCHIVES. A soft bound PRELIMINARY INVENTORY,
  compiled by John P. Greene, of historical papers of all
  kinds in the custody of the Archives of Newfoundland and
  Labrador, was printed in 1970, with a promise of further
  records of holdings in the next year or so. These vary
  from sources of one sheet of paper to 72 cartons. This
  sounds most promising for researchers in Newfoundland.
NEWSPAPERS, old issues are excellent sources of information,
  birth and death notices, etc.
ONTARIO GENEALOGICAL SOCIETY, Box 66, Station Q, Toronto,
  Ontario M4T 2L7. Excellent, much information in back bulletins, books for sale, many branches in other Canadian
  cities. See Vol. VII, No. 2, June 1977, and others.
ONTARIO REGISTER, Quarterly, Canadian Genealogy, Defunct, but
  some bulletins available in libraries.
P.E.I. GENEALOGICAL SOCIETY, Donald F. Stewart, 138 Bunbury
  Rd., Charlottetown, P.E.I.(or Box 1000, C'townC1A7M4.)
P.E.I. HERITAGE FOUNDATION, 2 Kent St., Box 992, Charlottetown,

SEE ADDED PAGES, ADDITIONS AND CORRECTIONS.
P.E.I. Some files on Channel Island families in the Island.
QUEBEC, Protestant records. There are unindexed parish registers back to 1820, many of them in the archives of the Anglican Church at Joliette, Que. Some records of the United Church are also at Joliette. Prior to 1925, the United Church records would be listed under Methodist, Presbyterian, or Congregational. In requesting data, the names of the father and mother, the date and year of birth, and the name of the parish are needed. Please write in French. (This information from LOST IN CANADA 1970s!!)
QUEBEC, Presbyterian records, Archives are care of Knox College, 59 St. George St., Toronto, Ontario. M5S 2E6. Please send a donation with your request.
SASKATCHEWAN GENEALOGICAL SOCIETY, P.O. Box 1894 Regina, Sask. S4P 3E1.
SASKATOON GENEALOGICAL SOCIETY, care of Sask. Public Library, Main Branch, Saskatoon, Sask. S7K 0J6.
SOCIETE GENEALOGIQUE DE QUEBEC, C.P. 2234, Quebec, P.Q., Canada.
SOCIETE GENEALOGIQUE DE LA MAURICIE, M. Lucien, 3155 Rue Chambois, Trois Rivieres Ouest, Que.
SOCIETE HISTORIQUE DE LA GASPESIE, Museum and bulletins, C.P. 680, Gaspe Quebec, GOC LRO.
SOCIETE HISTORIQUE NICHOLAS DENYS, Site 19, C.P. 6, Bertrand, N.B. EOB 1J0.
TORONTO, Ontario. Numerous resources here:
Royal Ontario Museum
Registrar General, Bay at Wellesly Sts., Birth, marriage and death certificates
Ministry of Natural Resources, Surveying and Maps for land ownership data
Legislative Library of Ontario, Main Bldg., Parliament Bldgs.
Ontario Archives, 77 Grenville St., Queen's Park, Toronto, M7A 1C7
Metropolitan Toronto Public Library, College and George Sts.
University of Toronto, John P. Robarts Research Library, Harbord and St. George Sts.
Ontario Genealogical Society Library, North York Library, 35 Fairview Mall, Willowdale, a suburb.
City of Toronto Archives, Queen and Bay Sts., New City Hall
Toronto Registry Office, Queen and Bay Sts., New City Hall, North door on Bay
Royal Military Institute, 426 University Ave., Toronto
United Church Archives, Birge Carnegie Library, Victoria Univ., Queens Park Cres. at Charles West, included Methodist and Presb. records prior to 1925 and United Church records since 1925.
Presbyterian Archives, Knox College Archives and Library, 49 George St., Toronto

Anglican Church General Synod., 600 Jarvis St., Toronto, M5C 1L8
Catholic records, Archdiocese of Toronto Chancery Office, 55 Gould St., Toronto, M5B 1G1
Quaker records, Canadian Friends Historical Assn., 60 Lowther Ave., Toronto, M5R 1C7
Mormon, LDS Genealogical Library, 95 Melbert Dr., Etobicoke, a surburb of Toronto
United Empire Loyalists Assoc. of Canada, 23 Prince Arthur Ave., Toronto, M54 LB2
VITAL RECORDS: Located in the Dominion Archives, Ottawa, Ontario. Each province has its own records located in the capitol. Each city and town has its own records. Each county has records at the county seat.

Channel Islanders in Canada organized social groups in various cities such as Vancouver and Victoria, B.C. Also in Toronto, London and Hamilton, Ontario, and a group was mentioned by a correspondent in Montreal. It is possible that records of these groups are still in the hands of older members. During the Second World War, food and clothing was collected by the members and sent to those in Great Britain who were exiled from the Islands due to World War Two.

In regard to early records of Channel Islanders in Newfoundland, Rev. Hammond writes, "Some of the church records here go back before 1750. Most of the Jersey settlers belonged to the Church of England, and are recorded in those older church records."

Regarding the Protestants in the Gaspe Peninsula, Aldo Brochet gives the following information. "The Guernsey families which were until ca 1974 at Grande Greve, Gaspe, St. George's Cove and at Indian Cove go way back to the 1780s. There are many of them, and they had their own Methodist Chapel, but these records don't appear in any government archives, unfortunately. Earliest in Gaspe Co. are for 1825 of the Anglican Church. Methodists were assimilated into the Church of England. In Bonaventure Co. they chose the Church of Scotland, the Presbyterian Kirk."

AMERICAN SOURCES OF GENEALOGICAL INFORMATION

Your best help in this field will be in books especially written about American research. Ask your librarian. Three publishers of genealogical material put out excellent catalogs: (Write for current costs of these)
GENEALOGICAL BOOK COMPANY, 111 Water St., Baltimore, Md. 21202.
GOODSPEED'S BOOK SHOP, 18 Beacon St., Boston, Mass. 02108.
CHARLES E. TUTTLE CO., INC., 28-30 South Main St., Rutland, Vermont 05701.
The Mormon Church Archives in Utah, see your local branch of this church.

Nova Scotia Archives, Halifax, N.S., for Loyalist data.
Canadian Dominion Archives, Ottawa, Ont., for Loyalist and
    other data. SEE "Canadiana",North York Library, N.York,ONT.
Library of Congress, Washington, D.C., Lots of material here.
New England Historical and Genealogical Societies.
Vital Records, in cities, state capitals and county seats.
Booklet, GENEALOGICAL RECORDS IN THE NATIONAL ARCHIVES, General Services Admin., Washington, D.C. 20408, 40¢.

BRITISH SOURCES OF GENEALOGICAL INFORMATION

There are many societies of this kind in England and other parts of Great Britain, and a considerable number of libraries with relevant material. Names and addresses, both of these, and of professional researchers can be located in North American publications and books. Your local library may have copies of bulletins.

THE AUGUSTAN SOCIETY, 1510 Cravens Ave., Torrance, Calif. has genealogical material for the researcher who is working on ancestry in various parts of Europe, Asia, South and Central America. Ask for their International Catalog. This includes special bulletins on Scottish, Irish, English, German and French material available.

Many Channel Island families have Huguenot origins, while others were settled in the Islands before the 1500s. It is sometimes most difficult to distinguish between families of the same surname. Only a great deal of research in depth will provide the answer as to whether or not your family was Huguenot in origin. Kenneth Annett, 1225 Lavigerie, Ste. Foy, Quebec, G1W 3W8, is compiling Huguenot data, and would welcome definite information on your Huguenot family in Canada.

CHANNEL ISLAND SOURCES OF GENEALOGICAL DATA
(Information mostly furnished by Marie Louise Backhurst,
    St.Clement,Jersey. See added pages re: her book.)

There is, potentially, a great deal of information available on Channel Island genealogies. Records back to the 1500s, family histories of dozens of families in manuscript and book form at the Societe Jersiaise Library, in the Priaulx and Guille-Allez libraries of Guernsey, legal papers and wills from the 1700s, all this would seem a rich source and is. The difficulty lies in the lack of someone to research these sources, and to extract information needed. This should be properly done by a trained and meticulous researcher. These are in short supply everywhere.

It is possible that a researcher could apply to the Sociéte Jersiaise and ask for information on an ancestor, giving the full name, the parish, and the years involved. The secretary might write back and say, yes, they have a genealogy on that family in the years back to 1650. This can and has happened. However, for most people, the process is not that simple.

IN SEARCH OF YOUR ANCESTORS

Many families have not been researched, and at first glance there is nothing available about them. Their names and locations are noted in the church and civil records, but no attempt has been made to organize family charts. The family trees that are in print are generally of prominent and/or wealthy families in the Islands. Most of us do not fit into those categories, and are descended from the farmers, fishermen and tradesmen of the Islands.

There is an optimistic side of this however. The Islands are so small that one family could be related to twenty or thirty families of the Island within three or four generations. At least one of these families is quite likely to have genealogical records. With diligent work on church and land records, wills, cemetery stone inscriptions, census and historical records, it is more than likely that at least some information has survived.

One professional researcher is presently working part time on family genealogies in Jersey, and there are two in Guernsey. It is possible that with more demand, perhaps other Islanders will take an interest in this work. The Societe Jersiase does some research on request, usually with volunteer labour, which is not easy to obtain in today's world of working wives and mothers.

The Island societies are at present in the process of organizing their information, which is scattered in a number of locations in the Islands. In a few years, if they are successful, it may be possible to find more easily the requested data.

Join THE CHANNEL ISLANDS FAMILY HISTORY SOCIETY, Box 507, St.Helier, Jersey, CI, UK. Researchers are available for a fee to help you chart your ancestry. Excellent bulletins!

Lawrence R. Burness, in an English Genealogist magazine, gives the following information regarding research in Jersey: No consolidated index books at the Registrars, so search must be made by the staff or by staff of the Societe Jersiaise, who have special access rights.   NOTE! CHARGES HAVE CHANGED
The charge is 5 pounds per hour for research in Jersey.
Certified extracts of any entry can be purchased at 1 pound, short certificates 5p.
Wills are at the probate registry, dating, some of them, from 1660. Hundreds of volumes date from 1775, indexed. Eight volumes of wills date from 1848 to 1964. Since then they are integrated with probate of wills, court house.
Wills of realty are housed in the public registry, open to public inspection, indexed.
Much information is on stones in churchyards and cemeteries. Often the maiden name of the woman is given, which is of considerable help.
IN GUERNSEY:
The Archives are housed at the Greffe, Royal Courthouse, St.

Peter Port, and include, with few exceptions, all births and deaths since 1840, and all marriages, except Church of England, from Jan. 1841 to 1919. Thereafter, C. of E. marriages are included.

IN ALDERNEY:
Some of this Island's records were lost during German occupation. There is a search fee of 50p, and certified copies for 13p. Short birth certificates are 3p each. These costs are remarkably low and may be increased by the time the reader begins his research.

If the reader decides to follow-up on his Channel Island ancestry, it would be well to allow a month or two between the request for information from the sources below, and the expectation of a reply regarding it. The combination of your patience and the generous help of volunteer researchers might result in some interesting and vital information on your forebears in the Channel Islands. Request fee charges for delving into the records.

SOCIÉTÉ JERSIAISE, The Library, The Museum, 9 Pier Rd., Jersey, Channel Islands, Great Britain.
SOCIÉTÉ GUERNSIAISE, P.O. BOX 314, Candie, St.PeterPort, Guernsey, Channel Islands, GB.
GUERNSEY SOCIETY, in England, Mrs. H.B. Roach, 132 Baddow Hall Cresc., Chelmsford, Essex, England CM27BU.
JERSEY SOCIETY IN LONDON, c/o E. Le Maistre, Esq., 8 Hall Close, Farncombe, Godalming, Surrey, England.
CHANNEL ISLAND FAMILY HISTORY SOCIETY, (CIFHS) P.O.Box507, St. Helier, Jersey, GB, has good How-To book by Marie-Louise Backhurst, FAMILY HISTORY IN JERSEY, exellent for researchers.

BIRTH, MARRIAGE AND DEATH RECORDS

Superintendant Registrar, St. Heliers, Jersey, Channel Islands, Great Britain, from 1842.
Superintendant Registrar, St. Peter Port, Guernsey, Channel Islands, Great Britain, from 1840.
The Guernsey records include those of Alderney and Sark, in part, from 1921; marriages from 1912.

CHURCH RECORDS IN JERSEY   CHECK FIRST WITH CIFHS!

At the time of publication, the church records in the Islands are in the possession of the Rector of each church. The correct parish and church must be known in order to locate your records. Application must be made to the Rector, who will appoint an Islander to do the necessary work. Outsiders must not expect to be able to do the research themselves, as is possible elsewhere, as the records are often very old and valuable, and of course, irreplaceable. They must not be jeopardized by careless handling. In some cases, the records are, regrettably, too fragile to handle.

Some church and state records have been filmed, and are available from the Mormon Church Archives in Utah. Research there first might save a great deal of time and money.

There have been churches in the Islands since at least the year 1040. It is believed that there were chapels there by the seventh and eighth centuries. (Raoul Lempriere) Records in most of the parishes date from the 1500s and 1600s, although they are not all complete for all the years since that time.

There are twelve parishes in Jersey, and 12 Anglican parish churches of the same name as the parish. Most parishes have other churches also, some Anglican, Church of England, others are Presbyterian, Catholic, etc. In the Middle Ages the churches of the Islands had other and more ornate names; St. Clement of Pierreville, St. Mary of the Burnt Monastery, St. John in the Oaks, St. Martin of the Bellouse, St. Saviour of the Thorn, St. Andrew of the Sloping Apple Orchard! (Raoul Lempriere, PORTRAIT OF THE CHANNEL ISLANDS) Following is a list of most of the churches of Jersey Island, by parish:

1. St. Helier's Church, baptism records from 1596, burial and marriage records from 1663. In addition: All Saints, St. Andrew, First Tower, St. James, St. Luke, St. Mark, United Reformed Church, Quakers, St. Simon, Reformed Episcopal, St. Columba's, Presbyterian, Baptist, Congregational, Primitive Baptist, and Baptist Belmont Hall. Also, First Church of Christ Scientist, Greater World Christian Spirit Church, Jehovah's Witnesses, and the Swendenborgian Church.

2. Grouville Church, records from 1584, also St. Peter La Rocque, St. Joseph's.

3. St. Saviour Church, records from 1540, also Methodist Churches Eden and Georgetown.

4. St. Clement Church, records from 1623, also Samares Methodist, and St. Nicholas, with records from 1927.

5. St. Peter Church, records from 1626. Also, Mormon, Church of Jesus Christ of the Latter Day Saints. Also, Bethesda and Philadelphie Churches, and St. Matthews.

6. St. Lawrence Church, records from 1654, also St. Matthew with records from 1840; First Tower and Six Roads Methodist Churches, a Congregational Church and Hillbrook Church.

7. St. Mary Church, records from 1647 and 1703, also Bethlehem Church.

8. St. John Church, records from 1594. In addition the United Reformed Church and Sion Methodist.

9. St. Martin Church, records from 1593. Gouray, records from 1834, and St. Martin Methodist.

10. St. Brelade, records from about 1560. In addition churches in St. Aubin, Jersey: St. Matthew Chapel, St. Aubin Methodist, Congregational, Jewish, St. Bernadettes R.C.

11. St. Ouen, records from 1634, St. George's, with records, and also an Evangelical Fellowship Church, St. Ouen

Methodist, and St. Annes.

12. Trinity Church, records from 1612. In addition: St. Matthew, St. George, St. Nicholas, St. Peter, Baptist and Quaker Churches, Ebenezer, Our Lady of the Universe, Sts. John and Anthony. Also St. Thomas, R.C. with records from 1793, St. Mary and St. Peter, with baptisms from 1811.

OTHER CHURCHES IN JERSEY: Grove Place Baptist, records from 1831; Independent Church, on Union St., baptisms 1827 to 1841, records now at Victoria St. Congregational Church.

CHURCH RECORDS IN GUERNSEY, ALDERNEY AND SARK

These records are somewhat incomplete, but some are available from the 1500s in Guernsey. St. Anne of Alderney lacked at times a resident Rector, so has incomplete records, but some date from 1662. Some Sark records exist from 1565. Below are the Guernsey Parish Churches. In addition, there are other Protestant and Catholic Churches on the Island.

1. St. Peter, Cornet St., St. Peter Port, dates at least from 1313. Some records from the 1560s, incomplete.
2. St. Sampson, Grandes Maisons Rd., St. Sampson.
3. Castel, Catel, The Rectory, Castel, Guernsey. This church was named in 1203 OUR LADY OF THE DELIVERANCE OF THE CASTLE (Warner). Records are incomplete, 1674-1714 and 1670 to 1796.
4. St. Saviour Church, dates from 1154. Records from 1582, some missing.
5. St. Peter-in-the-Wood, dates from 1167. Records from 1628.
6. Torteval, originally St. Philip of Torteval, dates from 1130. Records from 1684, some missing others dating from 1660.
7. Forest, originally St. Margaret of the Forest, dates from 1163. Records from 1684, some missing and others from 1700.
8. St. Martin, dates from 1199, records from 1660.
9. St. Andrew, dates from 1284, records from 1573, some missing. Burials from 1728. A census of this parish from 1788 is extant.
10. Vale, L'Abbaye, Vale, Guernsey, records from 1580, some missing.

(Dates of original churches are from COLLECTIONS FOR THE HISTORY OF HAMPSHIRE, a very old book with no date, 6 vols. bound in one, by Richard Warner, Cleveland Main Library.)

In addition to church records, there are in Guernsey similar records to those named in Jersey, relating to property, wills and manorial data, kept at the Greffe, Royal Court House, St. Peter Port, Guernsey. There are also many denominations of Protestant Churches and many Roman Catholic churches. The Societe Guernsiaise bulletins have included some articles about records in the Islands, such as the issues of 1952 and 1953. Cemetery records are also available. A booklet, HOW

TO TRACE YOUR ANCESTORS IN GUERNSEY, by David Le Poidevin, available at bookstores in Guernsey.

OTHER RECORDS OF THE CHANNEL ISLANDS

1. Census records from the 1800s are located in England at the London Record Office.
2. Cemeteries in St. Heliers, Jersey are: Mont a L'Abbe, from 1855; Mont a L'Abbe, (new) from 1880; Green St. Cemetery, from 1881; Surville, from 1850; Almorah, from 1854, with some records missing. Each Jersey parish also has a cemetery.
3. A number of cemeteries in Guernsey.
4. Navy and Army records may be researched in England, by professional researchers. Thousands of Channel Islanders have served in the British forces in the last few centuries.
5. British Civil Service. Many Islanders were in this service also. Possibly information available through the London, England offices.
6. BIOGRAPHICAL DICTIONARY OF JERSEY, by G.R. Balleine, 1945, England and U.S. Many old Jersey families are represented in this fine book.

CAPITALS: All names capitalized have been found at one time or another in the Channel Islands. Possibly others not capitalized have also been found there. Other words and phrases capitalized in this book are names of ships, such as MAYFLOWER, names of books used as references, such as CANADA, by Brebner, names of provinces and states, such as MAN for Manitoba, MASS for Massachusetts, and C.B. or CB for Cape Breton.

CHILDREN: The reader should be aware that lists of children for some families may be incomplete, and the couple may have had other children. This is especially true where the wife or husband was married two or more times. In these cases the children listed may be of only the one marriage. Fairly often it was noted that the first wife died in the Islands, and the husband removed to North America, leaving the children with relatives. The connection broken by time and distance, descendants here are often unaware of their relationship to the Island families.

FAMILY CONNECTIONS: Most families in this book are inevitably related to other Island families. If research on your line is unproductive, there may be more information on collateral lines, or on the maternal side of the family.

FRENCH SURNAMES: A very large number of these names include the articles such as De, De La, Le, La and Du. These articles were often dropped in Canada, or combined with the name, as Du Four to Dufour. Le Poidevin often became Poidevin, De Gruchy became Gruchy, and De la Perelle became Perrelle, etc. Be sure to check for names under all forms.

GASPE: In this book the word refers to the coast of the Gaspe Peninsula from the Bay de Chaleur to about the area of Mont Joli, on the St. Lawrence River. In the early years, most of the Islanders clustered around the end of the promotory from Grand Vallee to New Carlisle, but soon spread out and moved on into other parts of Quebec, and over to New Brunswick. In cases where the town of Gaspe is meant, "Gaspe Town" is used. In the Channel Islands the Gaspe area was referred to as La Cote, and The Coast, and Newfoundland was simply called The Land.

PHONETIC CHANGES TO CHANNEL ISLAND SURNAMES IN NORTH AMERICA: Although these have taken place everywhere in Canada, the most changes, due to special circumstances, took place in the spelling of names in Newfoundland. The Islanders were there very early, when there were few official records made. When names finally were written down, they were often mis-spelled and mis-pronounced in varying degrees. Many of the names were anglicized, often being made to conform with known British surnames; i.e., Ayre instead of Ahier. Poingdestre became Puddester, Bisson became Bessant, and Hookey was easily formed by dropping the article in front of Le Huquet. E.J. Seary's fine book, THE FAMILY NAMES OF THE ISLAND OF NEWFOUNDLAND, touches on some of these C.I. surnames, but there is extensive information awaiting organization and research.

GUIDELINES: In the family charts that follow, numbers and letters have been used. Roman numerals precede the names of brothers and sisters who removed to Canada. Usually the order of their birth is not known, and the numerals are arbitrary. The children of an immigrant to Canada are lettered A, the grandchildren B, and great grandchildren C, and so on. Order of birth in a family is marked by 1, 2, 3, and so on. When birth years are missing, the order is arbitrary, as the actual order is not known at this time, or was not located by the compiler.

Received late: AMERICAN-CANADIAN GENEALOGICAL SOCIETY OF NEW HAMPSHIRE, 587 Rimmon St., Manchester, NH, 03102. Library, photo-copying, researchers available.

IN SEARCH OF YOUR ROOTS: A GUIDE FOR CANADIANS SEEKING THEIR ANCESTORS, by Angus Baxter, Toronto, 1978.

THE CANADIAN GENEALOGICAL HANDBOOK, Wheatfield Press, Box 205, St. James Sta., Winnipeg, Man. $10.00.

1993: Marcel Garnier, P.O. Box 897, Paspebiac, Quebec, GOC 2KO, is available for research on Quebec ancestors.

ABBREVIATIONS USED IN THIS BOOK

- AKA, also known as
- ALD, Alderney Island
- b, born
- bp, baptised
- BC, B.C., British Columbia
- cf, compare with
- ch, chn, child, children
- CB and C.B., Cape Breton
- CI and C.I., Channel Islands
- curr, current
- d, died also dec, deceased
- dau, daughter
- div, divorced
- d.y., died young
- fa, father
- G, Guernsey Island
- Hug, Huguenot
- J, Jersey Island
- J.P., Justice of the Peace
- MAN, Manitoba
- CI COLL, THE CHANNEL IS. COLLECTION, West.Res.Cleveland,O.
- mar, married
- M.L.A., Member of the Legislative Assembly
- M.P., Member of Parliament
- Nfld., Newfoundland
- PAC, Public Archives of Canada
- PANS, Public Archives of Nova Scotia
- par, parish
- poss, possibly
- Prot, Protestant
- QAAM, QUIET ADVENTURERS IN AMERICA, qv, which see (by M. Turk)
- QUE ARCH, Quebec Archives
- R.C., Roman Catholic
- Sask, Saskatchewan
- SPG, Society for the Propagation of the Gospel, of London, England
- Vet, War veteran
- WWI, World War One
- WWII, World War Two
- CIFHS, THE CHANNEL ISLANDS FAMILY HISTORY SOCIETY.

SOURCES, AUTHORS AND RESEARCHERS

ANNETT, Kenneth, St. Foy, Quebec, author ANNETT FAMILY GENEALOGY, and Huguenot research.
ASCAH, Elmer G., author the ASCAH FAMILY GENEALOGY, Burlington, Ont.
BALLEINE, G.R., author of BIOGRAPHICAL DICTIONARY OF JERSEY, N.Y., 1945, and other books.
BOURINOT, Marshall, Arichat, C.B., N.S.
BRIDEAUX, Wilfred, Ottawa, Ont.
BROCHET, Aldo, researcher, Montreal and Perce, Que.
CANADIAN BIOGRAPHICAL DICTIONARY.
CAREY-WIMBUSH, see Channel Islands Bibliography.
Cent. Bklt., see Quebec Bibliography.
COCHRANE, ---MEN OF CANADA, see Ontario Bibliography.
COLEMAN, Emma Lewis, NEW ENGLAND CAPTIVES CARRIED TO CANADA, Portland, ME, 1925.
FAY, C.R., NEWFOUNDLAND AND THE CHANNEL ISLANDS.
FERLAND, Abbe, Canadian writer and researcher.
GALLANT, Patrice, REGISTRES DE LA GASPESIE.
GANONG, see New Brunswick Bibliography.
GARRETT, Raymond, researcher and compiler, Gascons, Que.
GILMORE, Marion, LOYALISTS AND LAND SETTLEMENT IN NOVA SCOTIA.
GLF, George Francis LE FEUVRE, author and compiler, JERRI JADIS, etc.
GINGRAS, Raymond, author and researcher, Quebec, P.Q.
GRAVEL, Theresa, Montreal, Quebec, researcher.
GUILLET, Edwin, author of many books including GUILLET-THOREAU GENEALOGY, Toronto, Ont.
HAMMOND, Rev. John, Bell Island, Nfld., researcher.
LE BRETON, J.H., author of list of Channel Island families in the Maritimes. Res Paspebiac, Que.
LE GRESLEY, Rev. Gustave, Tracadie, NB, author of LE GRESLEY GENEALOGY.
LE MESSURIER, G.W., now dec, of Nfld, writer and researcher.
LE MOINE, J.M., author of CHRONICLES OF THE ST. LAWRENCE, and other books.
LOVELL, J., author of many Canadian Directories of the 1800s.

LUCE, Philip, the late, newspaperman, author and speaker on Channel Island subject. res Vancouver, BC.
MACWHIRTER, Margaret G., see Quebec Bibliography.
MCKIE, Lady Phyllis, Ottawa, Ont., researcher on Gaspe, compiler of booklet on Charles Robin and his Empire.
MATHEWS, Keith, Nfld, researcher, compiler of AN ALPHABETICAL LIST OF CHANNEL ISLAND SURNAMES CONNECTED WITH NEWFOUNDLAND, 1660-1840.
MUNGER, Denys, Quebec, P.Q., researcher, especially of Mauger and Munger families.
OLIVIER, Reginald, YOUR ANCIENT CANADIAN FAMILY TIES, Logan, Utah, 1972.
PARKER, Capt. John, see Nova Scotia Bibliography.
PERLEY, Moses, see New Brunswick Bibliography.
PET 1820. A Petition was signed in Gaspe in 1820, which contained many Channel Island surnames, Dominion Archives.
PUNCH, Terence, researcher, Halifax, Nova Scotia.
REAMAN, G. Elmore, THE TRAIL OF THE HUGUENOTS, Toronto, 1963.
REMIGGI, Frank, Montreal, Que., researcher and compiler, Gaspe surnames and families.
REVUE D'HIST., Bulletin of the Historical Society in Gaspe, C.P. 680, Gaspe, Que.
ROBICHAUD, Fr. Donat, see New Brunswick Bibliography.
SAUNDERS, A.C., JERSEY IN THE 18TH and 19TH CENTURIES, other books and articles in bulletins of the Societe Jersiaise, Jersey, 1900s.
SAVERY, Reginald, Weymouth, N.S., and SEVERY AND SAVARY GENEALOGY, by A.W. Savery.
SEARY, E.R., see Newfoundland Bibliography.
SHORTIS-MUNN, see Newfoundland Bibliography.
SLC, Salt Lake City, records in Mormon Libraries, Salt Lake City, Utah.
STEVENS, Charles, of J, compiler of typescript, CATALOG OF JERSEY FAMILY NAMES, 1970.
SYVRET, Marguerite, author and researcher of Jersey, with articles in Soc. Jers. bulletins, and booklet such as JERSEY SETTLEMENTS IN GASPE, 1963.
TARDIF, Betty, Perce, Gaspe, list of Channel Islanders in the Gaspe area.
TOME 48, 1970 report of the Archives Nationales de Quebec.
TURK, Marion G., books, THE QUIET ADVENTURERS, and THE QUIET ADVENTURERS IN AMERICA. Also, THE QUIET ADVENTURERS IN NORTH AMERICA,1983.
WHITE, Stephen, Moncton, N.B., researcher, Acadian families.
WILSON, Sylvia, Medina, Wash., researcher, Gaspe families.

Compiler's note: If the source you want is not listed above, please consult the other bibliographies in this book.
SEE ALSO PAGES 7 AND 8.

ABBOTT in Nfld. (Seary) Thomas in St. John's 1706. From C.I.? (Rev. Hammond) Cf ABATAFALAIS of J (Stevens)
ACOURT, A'COURT, from C.I. to Ontario, via Lancashire, England?
ACTESON, Philip, 1848-1937, mar Grace LE GALLAIS, 1864-1949. See LE GALLAIS (MacWhirter: GLF)
ADAMS, Zacharie, signed Gaspe Petition 1820 (Dom. Arch.)
ADAMS in Nfld. early (Seary) CF ADAM in J (Stevens)
ADEY in Nfld. Stephen in Bay de Verde 1791 (Seary) Cf ADE in J 1724 (Stevens) ANEZ , SEE ADDITIONS AND CORRECTIONS & CHAN.IS.COLLECTION.
AGNES, C.I. surname assoc. with Robin firm in Paspebiac and with town of New Carlisle, Gaspe (Que. Prov. Arch.)
AGNES, Francis, Frank, from C.I. res Grand Riviere, Gaspe 1921. Later in Paspebiac. (Brideau; GLF; Rev. d'Hist) See ALMOND and BOUILLON. d 1969, bur St. Pauls, Perce.
AGNEW. Three brothers D'Agnelli were with William the Conqueror in 1066. One settled in Galloway, Scotland; one in Lorne Co., Antrim, Ireland, and the third in Hertfordshire, England. The Patrick who founded the Guernsey Agnews was of the Scotch-Irish line. Cousins of this family did a lot of inter-marrying. Thomas Agnew of St. Patrick, Wigtownshire, Scotland, married his cousin, Mary Agnew of Belfast, Ire. They settled there, where Patrick was one of a large family, and was b ca 1720. He was stationed in G in 1740, and remained on the Island. He mar by special license, Mary Gogget, prob Mary GOSSET of G, in St. Michaels Ch, Southampton, England. Their son, Alexander, mar Susan de GARIS of G. Their son, James, mar Mary ARNOLD of G. James' son, Thomas Hillary, mar Mary Elizabeth LE PAGE of G. Of their ten chn, at least 4 rem to Canada. (See Western Canada section, Agnews) Others of this fam rem to Australia, New Zealand and Africa. (Harvey Le Page Agnew, Dorset England; Myrtle Lunney, Winnipeg, Man; Sarah Leppard, Prince Albert, SASK.)
I. Francis Hedley, b G, mar Ada Mary LE CAPELLAIN, qv, his second cousin. Rem from C.I. to Winnipeg and Pr. Albert, Sask by 1882, poss earlier. Francis b 1863.
  A1. Ada Lillian Agnew, b 1893, mar David Earle Steel
    B1. Barbara Helen Steele   B3. Sylvia Mary Steele
    B2. Arthur Reed Steele   B4. David Agnew Steele
  A2. Harold Fletcher, b 1896, d unmar 1940.
  A3. Kathleen Mary Le Messurier, b 1902, mar William Lunney
    B1. Douglas Gordon Lunney, mar ---
      C1. Joanne Susan Lunney   C3. Douglas William Lunney
      C2. Kevin Robert Lunney
  A4. Myrtle Frances Giffard, b 1902, twin of Kathleen, mar Robert E. Lunney
    B1. Belva Jean, mar ---Wilson
      C1. Norma Beth Wilson   C3. Tracey Jane Wilson
      C2. Anne Marie Wilson
    B2. Robert Francis Lunney
      C1. Elizabeth Francis Lunney   C2. Robert Alexander Lunney
IV. Thomas James, b 1855 St. Peter Port, G, d 1942 Medicine Hat, Alta. Left G 1876 for Fort Garry, Winnipeg, Man. Worked in Hardware store, mar 1881 Winnipeg Ida Mary Eliza Hysop, dau of David and Phebe Graham Hysop of Kingston, Ont., later of Killarney, Man. Travelled by buckboard from Portage La Prairie, Man, end of the RR line, to Prince Albert. (See Western Canada section) He was alderman, mayor, Mason, J.P., etc.
  A1. Lily May Agnew, b. 1883, d 1966, mar 1907 Edwin Morley Cawker, who d 1944

B1. Sarah May Cawker, b 1908, mar Victor Alex. Leppard, who d 1957
   C1. Morley Neil Agnew Evans Leppard b 1953
B2. Charles Agnew Cawker, b 1910, mar 1942 Geraldine Mary NORMAN, qv.
   C1. Marilynn Anne Cawker, b 1946, mar 1972 Ross Douglas Erl MacPhee
      D1. Conal Douglas Elliot MacPhee, b 1976
   C2. Gordon Morley Cawker, b 1949, mar 1977 Karen Louise Ranch
   C3. Eileen Mary Michelle Cawker, b 1950, mar 1973 Clark Anderson
      D1. Cameron MacLeod Anderson, b 1975
   C4. John Alexander Cawker, b 1952, mar 1977 Joan Margaret Benson
   C5. Susan Margaret Cawker, b 1956   C6. Noreen Cawker, b 1957
   C7. William Richard Cawker, b 1959
A2. George Patrick Agnew, b 1883, twin of Lily May, d 1944. Mar 1916, Annie MacDonald, who d 1952
  B1. Patrick, b 1917, d.y.
  B2. Thomas Malcolm Alexander, b 1921, mar 1952 Margaret Jane Badham
   C1. Marilyn Anne, b 1953, mar 1973 Harvey Schaefer
      D1. Lance Schafer, b 1974   D2. Bonnie Lee Schaefer, b 1977
   C2. James Malcolm, b 1957
  B3. Katherine Enid, b 1922, mar ca 1951 Ray Johnson, and 2. 1972 Richard L. Buffington
   C1. Dorothy Louise Johnson, b 1955, mar 1973 Reyo Arthur Tywainen
      D1. Daniel Reyo Tywainen, b 1975
A3. Thomas David, b 1884, d 1954, mar Mabel Alberta Kidd, 1907, who d 1952
  B1. Graham Arthur Thomas, b 1908, d 1964. Mar 1945 Jean Newsome, no issue
  B2. Harold Arnold Churchill, b 1910, d 1970, mar 1939 Charlotte Dickson
   C1. Lois, b 1940, mar 1959 Jack Arp
      D1. Valerie Corrine Arp, b 1960   D2. Nancy Arp, b 1971
   C2. David Arnold, b 1941, mar 1973 Lorraine Marie Gareau
      D1. Harold David, b 1976   D2. Joy Melanie, b 1978
   C3. Harvey Harold, b 1943, mar Barbara Gail Zelenski, 1965
      D1. Lisa Dawn, b 1966   D3. Brent Harold, b 1971
      D2. Todd Harvey, b 1966
  B3. Bruce Albert Edward, b 1912, d 1962, mar 1945 Vera----. Widowed, she mar 2. Peche
   C1. Judith, b 1947, mar ca 1967 Carl Ursic
      D1. Cameron Ursic, b 1969   D2. Kara Ursic, b ca 1971
   C2. Mark, b 1948
  B4. Osmir Alan Kitchener, b 1914, mar 1946 Betty Yvonne Pincott
   C1. Marilee Mable, b 1947, mar ---Simms (Alan d Vernon, BC 1978)
      D1. Justin Simms
   C2. Vance Graham, b 1949   C4. Luanne Jean, b 1955
   C3. Gaye Elizabeth, b 1951
A4. Hilary Le Messurier, b 1886, d 1933, mar Winnifred Waddell, d 1956
  B1. Eileen Margaret Le Messurier, b 1912, mar 1936 Liam Patrick Roome. Liam d 1967, Eileen in 1976
   C1. Brien Patrick Agnew Roome, b 1941, mar 1976
   C2. Michael Hilary Roome, b 1946
  B2. Asta Winnifred Agnew, b ca 1917, mar 1940s Frank Fordham
   C1. Basil Fordham, b 1946
A5. Alexander Frederick b 1889, d 1967, mar 1911 Sarah Ellen Doyle
  B1. Phebe May, b 1912, mar early 1940s Joseph Gustave Laurent GOSSELIN, qv.
   C1. Guy Gosselin, b 1945   C3. twin to Lynne, d.y.
   C2. Lynne Gosselin, b 1948

AGNEW

B2. Dorthea Mary, b 1913, mar ca 1940 George PEARCEY Crichton
   C1. Dale Crichton, b 1942, mar ---Shafto, 1970s
      D1. Kiri Shafto, b ca 1974
   C2. Judith Crichton, b 1945, mar John Hay
      D1. Courtney Hay, b 1972   D3. Adam Hay, b 1976
      D2. Joel Hay, b 1974
   C3. Joseph Crichton, b 1946
   C4. Charles Crichton, b 1949
   C5. Frederick Brent Crichton, b 1952
B3. Arthur James Gordon, b 1916, mar 1944 Eleanor O'Brien
   C1. Arel, b 1947, mar   C2. Sharon, b 1949
B4. Frederick Clayton, b 1924, mar Mary Eleanor Craig, 1955
   C1. Brenda Jane, b 1957   C2. Alexander Craig, b 1958
A6. Arnold Le Page, b 1891, mar Sarah Kathleen Dewdney 1916, had 60th wedding anniversary 1976. She d 1977 Victoria, B.C. at age 81.
   B1. Ivan Le Page, b 1918, d.y.
   B2. Mary Kathleen Patricia, b 1920, mar 1940 Harry August Gonneville, who d 1970s. Res Sault Ste. Marie, Ont.
      C1. Sharon Daphne Gonneville, b 1941, mar Randolph Smith 1962
         D1. George Lee Smith, b 1963   D3. Kelly Robert Smith, b 1968
         D2. Randolph Shawn Smith, b 1965
      C2. Maureen Patricia Gonneville, b 1943, mar Edward Jamieson
         D1. Michael Jamieson, b 1964   D3. Aaron Christian Jamieson,
         D2. Sean Jamieson, b 1970   b 1971
      C3. Kathleen Louisa Gonneville, b 1946, mar 1970s Wm. Maguire D1. Shannon
      C4. Patsy Lynn Gonneville, b 1947, mar 1972 Nicholas Chronyz
         D1. Breen Chronyz, b 1973   D2. Trisha Chronyz, b 1976
      C5. Kenneth Arnold Harry Gonneville, b 1949, mar a widow 1976
         D1. Jason, stepson to Kenneth D2. LeeAnn b 1979
      C6. Marion Brenda Gonneville, b 1954
   B3. Thomas Dewdney, b 1924, mar 1947 Christine Hall, who d 1975
      C1. Colleen Daphne, b 1952, mar 1973 Richard Martin Receveur
      C2. Cheryl Anne, b 1955, mar 1974 Scott Bartlett
      C3.   Cathleen Tami Agnew   b 1960
   B4. Arnold Quentin, b 1930, mar 1957 Margaret Lynne England, res Saskatoon, Sask.
      C1. Nicolette Ann, b 1959   C3. Thomas George Arnold, b 1966
      C2. Quentin Douglas, b 1961
   B5. Marion Daphne, b 1937, d 1967, mar 1958 Robert George Burnie, who d 1963. She mar 2. Thor Jacobson 1967. Chn raised by Tom and Holly Agnew
      C1. Patricia Jill Burnie, b 1960, res Prince Albert, Sask.
      C2. Marion Lorraine Burnie, b 1961
      C3. Shari Kathleen Burnie, b 1963
A7. Bertha Ernestine, b 1895, d 1972, mar Harold Stanley Smith 1916, who d 1934. She mar 2. J.J. Murphy 1940, who d 1960s.
   B1. Audrey Elaine Stanley Smith, b 1916, who mar 1. Wm. Joseph McDermott 1935, and 2. in 1956 Jack Owen Smythe, who d 1969. She mar 3. in 1976--Hickey.
      C1. Elaine Noreen Yvonne McDermott, b 1936, mar Donald James Landell 1957
         D1. James Landell, b 1961
      C2. William Stanley McDermott, b 1938, mar ---, a dau
   B2. Yvonne Ida Edna Smith, b 1921, mar 1951 James Patrick Leslie?
      C1. Cameron Patrick Leslie, b 1952, mar 1970s--Leslie Wolfe
         D1. John Leslie, b 1977
      C2. Patricia Arlene Leslie, b 1954

B3. Beryl Noreen Smith, b 1924, mar 1943 Trevor William Pollard
   C1. Cheryl Maureen Pollard, b 1938, mar, divorced, resumed Pollard name
      D1. Brent Pollard
   C2. Garth William Pollard, b 1951
   C3. Gregory Brett Pollard, b 1956
   C4. Grant Trevor Pollard, b 1963
B4. Constance Patricia Hall, b 1934, adopted by Murphys, mar Donald Christopherson
   C1. Glenn Christopherson, b ca 1970
A8. Ida Corrine Edna, b 1897, d 1974, mar 1. 1919, George Francis Whiteman, who d 1928, and 2. in 1939, James Teague Brown, who d 1969. Edna was a nurse trained in Medicine Hat Gen. Hosp.
A9. Terence James, b 1900, mar 1. Bertha McCallum 1929, div. 1942, mar 2. Sheila Margaret Grahame, 3 daus by second wife.
  B1. Josie Coreen, b 1932, mar ca 1961 Robert McDevitt Zoffel, who d 1971
    C1. Robert Zoffel, b 1963   C2. Mark Anton Zoffel, b ca 1965
  B2. Aleda-Mary, b 1934, mar Leigh W. Rabel, 3 daus
    C1. Heather Rabel   C2. Laurel Rabel   C3. Alison Rabel
  B3. Terence Joseph, b 1936, mar ca 1975
  B4. Brenda Margaret, b 1945, mar 1972 Terry Edward Beckstrom
    C1. Matthew Edward Beckstrom, b 1977 C2. David Cameron, b1978
  B5. Sherry Christine, b 1948, mar 1976 Timothy Joseph Lamb
A10. Enid Mabel, b 1903, twin of Hector below, d 1958, mar John Pier Roemer
  B1. John Hector Roemer, b 1924, mar ---
    C1. John Hector Roemer, b 1953   C3. Christopher Allen Roemer,
    C2. James Thomas Roemer, b 1956   b 1966
A11. Hector Lancelot, b 1903, twin of Enid above, mar 1927 Phyllis Lucille Fullerton. Celebrated Golden Wedding Anniversary, 1977. She d 1977.
  B1. Enid Hectorine, b 1927, mar 1. Romeo Masse ca 1947, divorced, mar 2. Fergus Grahame
    C1. Wanda Enid Masse, b 1948, mar 1966 Dale Bigelow, 2 chn
       D1. Teresa Yvette Bigelow, b 1967 D2. another ch
    C2. Linda Rae Masse, b 1951, mar 1968 Graham Lucas
       D1. Bradley Richard Lucas, b 1969 D2. another chn, b 1977
    C3. Ann Margaret Deborah Grahame, b 1964
    C4. Susan Mary Elizabeth Grahame, b 1965
  B2. Margaret Corinne, b 1930, mar 1952 Orest Paul Zuck
    C1. Garry Paul Zuck, b 1952
    C2. Dale Hector Zuck, b 1953, mar ca 1975 Joy Allen
    C3. Bradden Charles Zuck, b 1954
    C4. Lorena Zuck, b 1956
    C5. Sharon Ruth Zuck, b 1959
    C6. Rachelle Zuck, b 1961
    C7. Elizabeth Zuck, b 1964, d.y.
    C8. Tanya Phyllis Zuck, b 1967
  B3. Richard Hilary, b 1932, d 1957. Mar 1953 Shirley Beatrice Ellen White who d 1976
    C1. Elizabeth Mary, b 1954, d 1971
  B4. Donna Phyllis Edna, b 1938, mar 1. 1957 John Charles Klughart, and 2. in 1977, Kenneth Allen
    C1. Michelle Dawn Klughart, b 1961, mar 1975 Lance Krobel
       D1. Michael Lance Krobel, b 1975 D2. Jennifer Lucille Krobel,
       D3. April Krobel, b 1979   b 1977

AGNEW

C2. Richard David Agnew, b 1968
B5. Sandra Lee, b 1944, mar 1963 Walter Joseph McKay, desc of Gentleman Joe McKay, scout-interpreter, N.W.M.P.C3.ShannonLee,1971.
C1. Tammy Lee McKay, b 1963   C2. Walter Joseph McKay, b 1967
V. AGNEW, Walter Giffard, bro of above I, b 1860 St. Peter Port G, d 1897 unmar. Served in Riel Rebellion of 1885, assisted at the settlement, rem to Calif with asthma, returned to G where he d at 37 in 1897.
X. AGNEW, Andrew, b 1865 Hauteville, St. Peter Port, G, rem to Prince Albert, Sask 1882 where he joined the eldest bro in the hardware business. Rem to Saskatoon early 1900s. Mar Laura Pritchard 1896, who d 1932. In 1937 he mar 2. Edith Fish, a widow. D 1956 Victoria BC, ashes scattered over ocean!
A1. Gerald Andrew, d.y.
A2. Willard Victor, b 1897, or 1902, d 1969, mar Marion Beverly Jones in 1930
  B1. Douglas Hilary, b 1944, mar, has son
A3. Gerald William, b 1903, d 1940, mar
A4. Richard John, b 1905, d 1970s, unmar
A5. Christina, b 1909, mar 1933 Ray Hansen, who d 1950. Son Christopher res U.S.
A6. Eleanor Mary Matheson, b 1914, mar 1938 Fred Mills, res South Africa
  B1. Gerald Mills, b 1942   Eleanor d England, 1979.
AHIER, in Nfld, said to be from G (Seary)
AHIER, to Nfld. from C.I., name changed to AYER (Shortis-Munn)
AHIER, Clement, b J in Perce, 1861 (Census) Also, John AHIER.
AHIER, Frederick, b J, mar 1902 St. Philips Ch, Gascons, Que., Susan GAUDIN, qv. (Raymond Garrett, Gascone, Que) Many of this name bur Gascons, Que.
AHIER, Philip, at Grand Greve, Gaspe, 1825 (Brochet)
AHIER, V.W., from J to Victoria BC early 1900s and another to Manitoba
AHIER, Gideon, from J at Bonaventure 1831, prob arrived ca 1800. (Brochet) He was the son of Jean A. and Jeanne ENOUF, ESNOUF, qv, of St. Helier J. Mar 1807 at Carlton, Que 1. Victoire Painchaud, dau of Francois P. and Angelique Drouin. She was the widow of Francois NORMAND. He mar 2. 1815 at Carlton, Rose Bergeron dit L'Amboise, dau of Etienne B. and Claire Courroit. (Gallant, Gravel)
A1. Virginie, b 1808 Carlton, Que.
A2. George Alexis, b 1810
A3. Joseph, b ca 1813, mar 1839 Louise Arsenault, dau of Louis A. and Marie Landry
A4. Marie Anne, twin of Joseph, b ca 1813 Carlton
A5. Guillaume, William, b 1820
A6. Wilhelmine, mar Carlton 1840 Hippolyte Allard, son of August A. and Rose Landry
A7. Rachel, b 1824 mar 1844 Francois Guite, son of Joseph G. and Julie Cyr
A8. Charles Francois, b Carlton 1826
A9. Emilie, b 1827
AHIER, Frederick, b J, age 17 in 1871, employed by Wm. Fruing Co., Caraquet, NB. Prob returned to J. (Census 1871, Robichaud)
AHIER, Thomas, b ca 1846 J, in NB Census 1871, was 24, Mgr. of the Caraquet estab. of Wm. Fruing & Co. Later Mgr. at the main estab. of that firm in NB at Pte. des Alexandres, Shippegan, Island. Anglican, mar in Bathurst, NB 1887 widow Elizabeth McKenzie, dau of John P. Carter, Bathurst. She d ca 1890. Thomas returned to J, d 1909. (Census 1871; D. Robichaud, Beresford, NB)

AHIER, Alfred, b 1857 La Rocque, St. Saviour J, mar Ann Rachel LE ROUGETEL, 1868-1943 to Toronto Ont. ca 1901. Alfred d 1947, at least 11 chn. This fam first rem to New Zealand, then back to J and later to Toronto. (Mrs. D.A. Jaycox, Costa Mesa, Calif.)
A1. Edward, b ca 1888, chn
A2. Charles, b ca 1892
A3. Bertie, b ca 1894
A4. Percy, b 1901
A5. Alfred, b 1907
A6. William, b 1912, no issue
A7. Eileen, b 1899, mar Clifford O'Connell, sea Capt. and interpreter for Cunard Lines, 40 plus desc.

AHIER, Clifford, and others, prob related to above Alfred, rem to Toronto from J, some to Calif.

AHIER, Abraham Philip, b 1890 St. Heliers J, son of Abraham A. and Mary Ann LE COUILLIARD, qv to Canada ca 1912, mar Mabel Alice Taylor, b 1893, dau of James Taylor and Minerva Hunt. Philip, d 1961, WWI vet. (D.A. Ahier, Scarborough, Ont.)
A1. Alan Philip, b 1922 Toronto, mar Doreen Gladys Smith
　B1. Douglas Alan, b 1952 Toronto, mar Donna Agnes Buttle
　　C1. Jeffrey Douglas, b 1977 Toronto
A2. Howard James, b 1925 Toronto, mar Marion Grace Allen
　B1. David James, b 1960
　B2. Gordon Philip, b 1961
　B3. Brian Allen, b 1964

AHIER, James, b J, to Paspebiac, Gaspe, ca 1790, mar Isabella Brotherton, of Loyalist fam from N.Y. state. Settled Gascons, desc there and in Port Daniel, etc. (Gerald Brotherton, Gascons, Gaspe; Raymond Garrett, Gascons, Gaspe)
A1. Martha, b 1803, mar Philippe Chedore, qv, fam of 11 chn. See CHEDORE
A2. Philippe, mar Genevieve Chedore, qv, and 2. in 1840 Rose Duguay, 4 chn, and 3. in 1849 Mary Sullivan, 4 chn (total of 14 chn)
　B1. Mary Jane, b 1828
　B2. Mary, b 1829?
　B3. James, b 1832, mar Ann ALMOND
　　C1. Marguerite, b 1865, d 1867
　　C2. John Alexander, b 1868, d 1895
　　C3. Mary Ann, b 1870, d 1962. Mar Paul Morin
　　　D1. Edmond
　　　D2. Annee
　　　D3. Lily May
　　　D4. Alice
　　　D5. Albertine
　　　D6. Gaven
　　　D7. Lisa
　　　D8. Edna
　　　D9. Omer
　　　D10. Aline
　　C4. James Gaven, b 1872, d 1898
　　C5. Jane Elizabeth, b 1875, mar 1. Dr. Flint, and 2. Alfred Reynolds
　　C6. William Ernest, b 1877, mar Lily STE. CROIX, qv.
　　　D1. Lucinda, b 1910
　　C7. Robert Thomas, b 1879, d 1959, mar Marie Rosalie Chapados, 5 chn
　　　D1. Paul
　　　D2. Ernest
　　　D3. William
　　　D4. Edith
　　　D5. Mrs. Raymond Smith
　　C8. Marguerite Elize, b 1882, d ca 1902
　B4. Philippe, b 1834, mar Elisa ALMOND, 7 chn
　　C1. Edmond, b 1868, d 1895
　　C2. Albert, b 1877, d 1937, mar Annee Chedore, qv, 10 chn
　　　D1. Thelma, b 1907
　　　D2. Aylmer, b 1908-1921
　　　D3. Edwin, b 1910
　　　D4. Hazel, b 1912
　　　D5. Emmely, b 1913
　　　D6. Liliane, b 1917
　　　D7. Harold Maynard, b 1921, d 1925
　　　D8. Harold
　　　D9. Winnie, b 1923
　　　D10. Alice, b 1928

```
        C3. John
        C4. William Alexander d 1896
        C5. Catherine mar 1885 Philip Wm. Chedore, and d 1897, 4 chn
           D1. Mary Jane Chedore, b 1886      D3. Lloyd Chedore, b 1892
           D2. Howard Chedore, b 1889         D4. Julia Chedore, b 1894
        C6. Helene, mar William Hayes, 1883, no issue
        C7. Mary Jane, mar Joseph Morin, 9 chn
           D1. Edmond Morin                   D6. Marie Genevieve Morin
           D2. John Morin                     D7. Elisa Morin
           D3. Philip Joseph Morin            D8. Pearl Morin
           D4. William Morin                  D9. Francis Morin
           D5. Albert Morin
     B5. John Alexander, b 1834, twin         B10. Gregoire, b 1847
     B6. Ann Isabella, b 1836                 B11. William, b 1850, 3rd wife
     B7. Rosalie, b 1841, by second wife      B12. Isabelle
     B8. Joseph, b 1843                       B13. Lise
     B9. Philomene, b 1845                    B14. Catherine, b 1859
  A3. Annabella, mar ---LE GALLAIS, qv.
  A4. Alexandre, mar Suzanne Duguay, 10 chn
     B1. Suzanne, b 1836, mar Louis Gignac, 4 chn, and 2. Richard Molloy
        C1. Marie Genevieve Gignac            C4. Epiphane Gignac
        C2. Hermine Gignac                    C5. Richard Molloy
        C3. Louis Gignac
     B2. Isabelle, b 1838, mar Alexandre Parise, 6 chn
        C1. Louis Parise                      C4. Calixte Parise
        C2. James Parise                      C5. Marie Suzanne Parise
        C3. Timothee Parise                   C6. William Parise
     B3. Genevieve, b 1840, mar Samual HUARD, qv, 7 chn. See HUARD
     B4. Marie, b 1843, mar Louis Fossard, 4 chn
        C1. Saturnin Fossard                  C3. Marie Louise Fossard
        C2. Valentin Fossard                  C4. Georges Fossard
     B5. Alexandre, b 1845, mar Rachel Brotherton, 7 chn
        C1. Elizabeth, mar Michael Lemieux
        C2. Louis, b 1874, d 1926, mar Elizabeth Murray 1907, 7 chn
           D1. Armande, b 1908                D5. Louise, b 1917
           D2. Edgard, b 1909                 D6. Gemma, b 1920
           D3. Alexandre, b 1910              D7. Eugenie, b 1922
           D4. Mercedes, b 1916
        C3. Zenon, b 1877, d 1920
        C4. Suzanna, 1881-1952
        C5. Rachel, Ursulin nun in 1912
        C6. Jacques, 1884-1958, mar Eva Sauvageau in 1914, 8 chn
           D1. Normand, b 1915                D5. Raymond, b 1923
           D2. Rachel, b 1916                 D6. Rene, b 1924
           D3. Fernand, b 1917                D7. Carmen, b 1927
           D4. Gemma, b 1921                  D8. Roland, b 1929
        C7. Normand, Priest at Gascons 1915
     B6. Rosalie, b 1847, mar Paul Chapodos, 6 chn
        C1. Louis Chapados                    C4. Philippe Chapados
        C2. Simon Chapados                    C5. Rosalie Chapados
        C3. Paul Chapados                     C6. Louise Chapados
     B7. James, b 1849, d 1926, mar Julienne Brotherton, 10 chn
        C1. Beatrice, b 1879, d 1958, mar Joseph Hickey, 7 chn
           D1. Stanley, b 1906                D4. Louis Hickey
           D2. Leonard Hickey                 D5. Geraldine Hickey
           D3. Albert Hickey                  D6. Eileen Hickey
        C2. James, b 1880, d 1946, mar Adeline Lemieux, 3 chn
```

D1. Beatrice, b 1915 D3. Julia, b 1918
D2. Yvon, b 1916
C3. Elizabeth, b 1883, d 1965, mar Telesphore Campeau
C4. Rosalie, b 1885, d 1958
C5. Theophile, mar Blanche Rouleau, 1 ch, Rita Rouleau
C6. Regina, b 1890, d 1964, mar Louis Robidoux
C7. Edmond
C8. Yvonne, b 1894, d 1950, mar Romuald Sergerie, 2 chn
   D1. Julienne Sergerie D2. Berthe Sergerie
C9. Clair, mar Eleanore Sergerie, 1 son Robert Sergerie
C10. Romeo, b 1900, d 1953, mar Germaine Savard, 1 ch, Germaine.
B8. Marthe, b 1852, d 1944, mar Louis Brotherton, 3 chn
  C1. Alexandre Brotherton D5. Stella below, b1914 mar BROCHETQV.
  C2. William Brotherton, b 1874, d 1945, mar Angelina Cassivi, 6 chn
    D1. Edmond Brotherton, b 1902 D4. Leo Brotherton, b 1911
    D2. Clarence Brotherton, b 1905 D5. Stella Brotherton, b 1914
    D3. Herbert Brotherton, b 1907 D6. Regina Brotherton, b 1916
  C3. Louis Brotherton, b 1876, d 1942, mar Brigitte Leblanc
    D1. Louis Brotherton, b 1916 D2. Martha Brotherton, b 1921
B9. Philippe, b 1855, d 1932, mar Marie Cyr 1884, 9 chn
  C1. Eugenie, b 1884, mar Adelme Boudreau 1919, 2 chn
    D1. ch, d at birth
    D2. Maurice Boudreau, b 1922, ordained priest 1948
  C2. Jean, b 1886, d 1962, mar Lauria Dugas, 1890-1972, 9 chn
    D1. Gratia, b 1915, mar Rosario Hudon, 1947, 3 chn
      E1. Louise Hudon, b 1950 E3. Ginette Hudon, b 1954
      E2. Helene Hudon, b 1952
    D2. Estelle, b 1916
    D3. Jeanne d'Arc, b 1918, mar Germain Guite, 1944, 5 chn
      E1. Jean Hugues Guite, b 1945 E4. Johanne Guite, b 1952
      E2. Regis Guite, b 1947 E5. Regina Guite, b 1956
      E3. Martine Guite, b 1950 E6. Denis Guite, b 1959
    D4. Germaine, b 1921, d.y.
    D5. Jean Arthur, b 1923, mar Andre?CABOT, qv, 1959, 7 chn
      E1. Richard Cabot, b 1960 E5. Karine Cabot, b 1968
      E2. Danie Cabot, b 1962 E6. Brigitte Cabot, b 1972
      E3. Alain Cabot, b 1964 E7. Sonia Cabot, b 1972, twin
      E4. Eric Cabot, b 1965
    D6. Gerard, b 1925
    D7. Maurice, b 1927
    D8. Marie, b 1928, mar Rene Castets 1964
      E1. Chantal Castets, b 1970
    D9. Simone, b 1930, mar Serge Sasseville 1956, 2 chn
      E1. Lucie Sasseville, b 1957 E2. Marco Sasseville, b 1959
  C3. Arthur, b 1888, d 1952, mar Estelle Savoie, 11 chn, 3 d.y.
    D1. Lionel, b 1916, mar Pearl Hutchinson 1943
    D2. Paul, b 1919, mar Eveline Fournier 1961, 3 chn
      E1. Michele, b 1963 E2. Marc, b 1965 E3. Richard, b 1965
    D3. Gerard, b 1921, d 1977, mar Jacqueline Belliveau 1961
      E1. Carole Anne, b 1961
    D4. Jeannette, b 1922, mar Rodolphe Lavoie, 1943, 5 chn
      E1. Claire Lavoie, b 1944 E4. Louise Lavoie, b 1952
      E2. Paul Lavoie, b 1947 E5. Gilles Lavoie, b 1957
      E3. Marc Lavoie, b 1949
    D5. Gisele, b 1924, mar Roch Bernier 1950, 4 chn
      E1. Pierre Bernier, b 1952 E3. Gilles Bernier, b 1956
      E2. Monique Bernier, b 1954 E4. Lyne Bernier, b 1959

D6. Guy, b 1926, mar Constance TARGETT, 1948, 4 chn
  E1. Lionel, b 1949   E3. Suzanne, b 1953
  E2. Rachel, b 1950   E4. Arthur, b 1964
D7. Pierrette, b 1929, mar Albert Wood 1951, 7 chn
  E1. Michael Wood, b 1952   E5. Christine Wood, b 1958
  E2. Glenn Wood, b 1953   E6. William Wood, b 1960
  E3. Kenneth Wood, b 1954   E7. John Wood, b 1964
  E4. Karla Wood, b 1956
D8. Carmel, b 1931, mar Gerald McNaughton 1958, 6 chn
  E1. Colleen McNaughton, b 1959   E4. Kimberley McNaughton,
  E2. Katherine McNaughton, b 1960   b 1963
  E3. Kenneth McNaughton, b 1963   E5. Gretchen McNaughton, b 1967
                                          E6. Lissa McNaughton, b 1973
C1. Diana, b 1890, mar Edmond ROUSSY, 1913, 10 chn
 D1. Blanche Roussy, b 1914, mar Paul Emile Chapados 1948, 3 chn
  E1. Jean Guy Chapados, b 1949 E3. Giselle Chapados, b 1951,
  E2. Gilles Chapados, b 1951   twin
 D2. Anita Roussy, b 1915, mar Ernest Morin 1945
  E1. Diane Morin, b 1945
 D3. Evangeline Roussy, b 1917, mar Jean Abel Chapados 1943, 9 chn
  E1. Lucien Chapados, b 1944   E6. Jeannine Chapados, b 1957
  E2. Carmen Chapados, b 1945   E7. Jean Chapados, b 1957, twin
  E3. Jeannette Chapados, b 1948 E8. Gerald Chapados, b 1959
  E4. Real Chapados, b 1949   E9. Sylvie Chapados, b 1964
  E5. Evelyn Chapados, b 1951
 D4. Lucien Roussy, b 1919, mar Lauretta Morin, 1949, 4 chn
  E1. Richard Roussy, b 1951   E3. Serge Roussy, b 1956
  E2. Donald Roussy, b 1952   E4. Bruno Roussy, b 1960
 D5. Aline Roussy, b 1921, d 1973, mar Augustin Grenier, 5 chn
  E1. Henri Grenier, b 1954   E4. Adrien Grenier, b 1958
  E2. Therese Grenier, b 1953   E5. Etienne Grenier, b 1965
  E3. Rejean Grenier, b 1955
 D6. Edgar Roussy, b 1923, mar Jeannine HUARD, qv, 1949, 8 chn
  E1. Robert Roussy, b 1950   E5. Solange Roussy, b 1955
  E2. Cecile Roussy, b 1952   E6. Murielle Roussy, b 1956
  E3. Gilles Roussy, b 1953   E7. Julien Roussy, b 1958
  E4. Denis Roussy, b 1954   E8. Remi Roussy, b 1967
 D7. Clarisse Roussy, b 1925, d 1973, mar Edmond Bourque 1958, 3 chn
  E1. Renaud Bourque, b 1959   E3. Gabriel Bourque, b 1964
  E2. Lucie Bourque, b 1962
 D8. Gonzague Roussy, b 1929, mar Rolande HUARD 1954, 10 chn
  E1. Emanuel Roussy, b 1954   E6. Fabien Roussy, b 1963
  E2. Bertrand Roussy, b 1955   E7. Berthe Roussy, b 1964
  E3. Gervais Roussy, b 1957   E8. Mario Roussy, b 1965
  E4. Fernand Roussy, b 1960   E9. Stephane Roussy, b 1968
  E5. Hubert Roussy, b 1961   E10. Marc Andre Roussy, b 1971
 D9. Regina, b 1932
 D10. Rejeanne Roussy, b 1936, d 1937
C5. Simon Ahier, b 1893, d 1957, mar Ida Roussy, 1918, 11 chn
 D1. Leo Ahier, b 1919, mar Louise Morin, 3 chn
  E1. Lyne, b 1961   E3. Johanne, b 1968
  E2. Denise, b 1964
 D2. Adrien, b 1921   D3. Therese, b 1923
 D4. Arthur, b 1926, mar Fernande Morin, 5 chn
  E1. Robert, b 1955   E4. Alain, b 1960
  E2. Bertrand, b 1956   E5. Jocelyn, b 1963
  E3. Nicole, b 1957

D5. Irene, b 1927   D6. Jean Marie, b 1930
　　　D7. Ludger, b 1932, mar Carmen Chapados, 2 chn
　　　　E1. Nathalie, b 1969   E2. Jean Yves, b 1970
　　　D8. Martha, b 1934, mar Wilfrid Marceau, 2 chn
　　　　E1. Andre Marceau, b 1967   E2. Robert Marceau, b 1971
　　　D9. Gervais, b 1937, mar Jeanne Mance Berube, 2 chn
　　　　E1. Rejean, b 1967   E2. Benoit, b 1969
　　　D10. Gilles, b 1938, mar Jeannine Paquin, 1 ch
　　　　E1. Martin, b 1965
　　　D11. Romuald, b 1941
　C6. Marie Anne, b 1894
　C7. Alice, b 1896, mar Bernard Brotherton, 1918, 9 chn
　　　D1. Murray Brotherton, b 1919, mar Gilberte Campeau 1950, 5 chn
　　　　E1. Ginette Brotherton, b 1952   E4. Roger Brotherton, b 1959
　　　　E2. Claudine Brotherton, b 1954 E5. Mariette Brotherton, b 1963
　　　　E3. Michel Brotherton, b 1955
　　　D2. Charles Brotherton, b 1921, mar Eugenie AHIER 1962, 1 ch
　　　　E1. Liette Brotherton, b 1967
　　　D3. Alfred Brotherton, b 1923, mar Blandine Grenier 1949. 7 chn
　　　　E1. Lise Brotherton, b 1950   E5. Louis Brotherton, b 1955
　　　　E2. Jean Marc Brotherton, b 1951 E6. Gilles Brotherton, b 1956
　　　　E3. Bernard Brotherton, b 1953 E7. Marcel Brotherton, b 1958
　　　　E4. Martine Brotherton, b 1952
　　　D4. Georges Brotherton, b 1925, mar Ruth Morin, 1962, 4 chn
　　　　E1. Robert Brotherton, b 1963 E3. Denise Brotherton, b 1965,
　　　　E2. Denis Brotherton, b 1965   twin
　　　　 E4. Paul Brotherton, b 1967
　　　D5. Gerald Brotherton, b 1928   D8. Edwin Brotherton, b 1937
　　　D6. Marie Anne Brotherton, b 1930, D9. Alice Brotherton, b 1940
　　　　d 1974, nun
　　　D7. Geraldine Brotherton, b 1933, nun
　C8. Alma Ahier, b 1899, d 1978, mar Adelard AUDET, 2 chn
　　　D1. Anne Marie Audet, b 1930, mar Joseph C. Bujold 1953, 4 chn
　　　　E1. Christian Bujold   E3. Romain Bujold
　　　　E2. Judith Bujold   E4. Jasmine Bujold
　　　D2. Cecile Audet, b 1937, mar Allan Hogan 1974
　C9. Stella Ahier, b 1904, d.y.
B10. Anne Elizabeth, b 1856, d 1948, mar Alexandre Brotherton, 8 chn
　C1. Alexandre V, b 1879, d 1966, mar Rose St. Pierre, 9 chn
　　　D1. Georges Brotherton   D6. Alberta Brotherton
　　　D2. Ernest Brotherton   D7. Leonard Brotherton
　　　D3. Irene Brotherton   D8. Beatrice Brotherton
　　　D4. Alphena Brotherton   D9. Robert Brotherton
　　　D5. Gerard Brotherton
　C2. Louise Anna Brotherton, b 1881, d.y.
　C3. Louise Anna Brotherton again, b 1882, d 1912
　C4. Elise Brotherton, b 1885, d 1904
　C5. Wilfred Brotherton, b 1887, d 1960, mar Marguerite Rail, 8 chn
　　　D1. Aylmer Brotherton, b 1915 D6. Rose Brotherton, b 1922
　　　D2. James Brotherton, b 1917   D7. Marie Brotherton, b 1923
　　　D3. Marguerite Brotherton, b 1919 D8. Alexandre VI, Brotherton,
　　　D4. Jeannette Brotherton, b 1920   b 1927
　　　D5. Blandine Brotherton, b 1921
　C6. Louis Philippe Neri Brotherton, b 1890, mar Mary Hogan, 9 chn
　　　D1. Inez Brotherton   D4. Phyllis Brotherton
　　　D2. Gertrude Brotherton   D5. Albert Brotherton
　　　D3. Lucy Brotherton   D6. Barbara Brotherton

AHIER 137

  D7. Anne Lavilla Brotherton
  D8. Robert Brotherton
  D9. John Brotherton
 C7. Rachel Brotherton, b 1893, mar John Suchaski
 C8. Alma Brotherton, b 1896, d.y.
A5. Jane, mar William Powers 1830
AHIER, George, b 1832 J, unmar, res 1861 Riviere Madeleine, Que., merchant, res with Francois BRIARD, qv. (Remiggi)
ALBEURY, spelling uncertain, John, origin not ver, in Perce 1863 (Cent. Bklt.) Gaspe and Quebec
ALEXANDRE and LE MARQUAND, fishery firm in Gaspe 1800s. Curr Gaspe Bay, Cross Pt., Que.
ALEXANDRE, fam from J to Pt. St. Peter, Gaspe early 1800s
ALEXANDRE, Amos, Amice?, and wife Felicia M. Trip, d at 55, 1916, bur Sandy Beach, Gaspe
ALEXANDRE, Jacques, b J ca 1801, at Grand Greve, Gaspe 1871, merchant, with wife Eliza age 69, French
 A1. dau Alice R., 20 in 1871, res Malbaie
ALEXANDRE, Francis, d 1913, at 83, bur Sandy Beach, Gaspe, dau Effie Greta, d 1895, at 2.
ALEXANDRE, George, from St. Ouen J. to Montreal, actor
ALEXANDRE, James, from J to Malbaie, before 1836, bro-in-law of Philip PREVEL, qu, of J Poss mar Marie LE MAISTRE?, qv. James b 1801, d 1878
 A1. Louise   A2. Alice, mar Charles LE MARQUAND, qv, 6 chn
ALEXANDRE, Mary Annie Louise, wife of John LE GROS, qv, d 1876 at age 26. Dau Edith Maud d.y. Bur St. Peters, Malbaie, Gaspe (GLF)
ALEXANDRE, Philip, b J to Gaspe before 1820, when he signed the Petition. Mar Jane Elizabeth LE HUQUET, qv, in Gaspe. There was a Philip at Grande Greve, Gaspe 1825, and Philip age 20 b J in Bon. Co. 1871(Census)
ALEXANDER in Nfld., (Seary) Cf ALEXANDRE of C.I. Capt. A. from J in Nfld. (K. Mathews)
ALEXANDRE. There are 87 cards on this surname in the Saint John, NB Hist. Library. Five bros and one or two sisters were said to have come from J to settle in the Gaspe and New Brunswick area, some being employees of the Wm. Fruing & Co. fisheries there. One sister, Jane Elizabeth, mar Wm. Fruing. Poss another sister, Mary. (Robichaud)
ALEXANDRE, George. Mgr. Shippegan Gulley, for Fruing firm between 1842-49. Poss same as Capt. George A.? master of brig MARY ANN, res 26 yrs. in Shippegan, died in Santo Domingo, West Indies of yellow fever 1859. (Robichaud)
ALEXANDRE, Joshua, b ca 1802 J, empl later as mgr for Charles Robin firm at Arichat, C.B. ca 1827 (Robin papers, Paspebiac), then mgr for the Wm. Fruing firm at Pte. des Alexandres, Shippegan, NB. J.P. for Gloucester Co. in Prov. Legis. 1843-1846. Mar Mary Jane LE BROCQ, qv. Joshua d 1859? 60 J men attended his funeral (Robichaud)
A1. Joshua, fish buyer at Grand Anse for Fruing Co. 1849
A2. Mary Ann, mar Nicholas ALLAIN, qv.
A3. Julia, mar John EREAUT, qv.
ALEXANDRE, Francis, b ca 1806 J, ship capt for Robin firm in N.B. Mar Mary Ann ---, b ca 1820. (Estelle de Grace, Athol, Mass.) (Robichaud)
A1. William, b ca 1840, Canada
A2. Francis, b ca 1847, Canada, mar Viatrice, Beatrice, Robichaud
 B1. Francis, Frank, mar Elizabeth MALLETT, qv, rem to Orono, ME?
  C1. Harry?   C2. Helen? mar Peters?
 B2. William, mar Finnish girl from Pokemouche, NB, ---Cullins, rem to Orono, ME
  B3. Vincent, b 1874

B4. James, b 1876
B5. Alice, b 1877?, d unmar Orono, ME
B6. Jane, b 1878, d unmar Orono, ME
B7. George, b 1879, d unmar
B8. Emily, b 1880, mar Denis CLEMENT, qv, of Grand Anse, NB, desc. in Orono, ME
B9. Emma, b 1882
B10. Josephine, adopted by Philippe McNally, mar Louis de Grace, 13 chn
  C1. Estelle, b 1905, mar J. Alfred de Grace, res Athol, Mass.
  C2. Ernestine, b 1907, mar Leon G. Hache, res Shippegan, NB, 3 chn
    D1. Dennis Hache   D2. Bernice Hache   D3. Louis-George Hache
  C3. Oscar, b 1908, mar Helene BRIDEAU, qv, res Shippegan, son Jacques
  C4. Felix, b 1910, mar Pauline Chiasson, res Shippegan, 4 chn
    D1. Jean Camil   D3. Rene
    D2. Clemence   D4. Odette
  C5. Fernande, b 1911, mar Gilas Robichaud, res Marlboro, Mass, 3 chn
    D1. Lucien Robichaud D2. Roger Robichaud D3. Gisele Robichaud
  C6. Irene, b 1913, mar John LUCY, qv, res Shippegan, son Philip
  C7. Lucien, b 1915, d.y.
  C8. Rene, b 1917, d age 29
  C9. Lucienne, b 1919, d.y.
  C10. Yves, b 1921, d.y.
  C11. Jean-Marie, b 1921, twin of Yves, res Shippegan, unmar
  C12. Raymonde, b 1925, mar Charles VASSELIN, res Waltham, Mass.
  C13. Louis-Philippe, b 1927, res Shippegan, unmar
B11. Jeanne, d 1889, age 11
A3. Alice, b ca 1849, Canada
ALEXANDRE, Jane of Sandy Beach mar Geo. G. GALLICHAN, a son of John Abraham, 1840s, Gaspe
ALEXANDRE, John and Frederick, poss bros of George, Joshua and Francis above? to N.B.
ALEXANDRE, Capt. Philip of the brick, PALM, owned by Robin Co.
ALEXANDRE, Jane Elizabeth, mar Wm. FRUING, qv.
A1. Louise Jane FRUING, mar Frederick WARNE, qv.
A2. Amelia Elizabeth Fruing
A3. Jane Fruing
A4. Mary Anne Fruing, mar Philip LE QUESNE, qv.
ALEXANDRE, Mary, sister of Jane one above, mar at Caraquet 1840 John McIntosh
ALEXANDRE, Walter, b 1845 St. Helier J, son of George A., b ca 1810 and Eliza PICOT, qv of St. Peter Port G. Walter was the 7th of 11 chn. He mar Elise Emilie Fredericke de CARTERET 1873, and they emigrated to N.Z. with their chn ca 1890. 6 chn
A1. Walter Henry, b ca 1874
A2. Elise Louise, b 1875
A3. Lucy Agnes, b 1876, to Wailuu, N.Z., some desc
A4. Mabel Mary, b 1880, d.y.
A5. Arthur Herbert, b 1882, rem to Los Angeles, then to Calgary, Alta. where he mar Elizabeth Thomas of Wales. 4 chn
  B1. Walter Daniel, b 1914   B3. Arnold Edward, b 1920
  B2. Rex, b 1918   B4. Arthur H.
A6. Herbert, b 1883, d.y.

COMPILER'S NOTE: Not all ALEXANDERS in the Channel Islands are from ancient families there. "My father's ancestors, the Alexanders who

ALLAIN

came to Jersey Island in the early 1800s, were from Hampstead Heath near London, England, and were expert carvers. I saw some of their carvings in Guernsey in St. Saviour church. My father said his father started in Guernsey making rope, and made enough money to start a farm." (Blanche E. Martin, Sherwood Park, Alberta, Man.)

ALLAIN, see D'ALLAINE also D'ALLAIN curr at Carlisle, Que.
ALLAIN, Nicholas, b J?, mar Mary Ann ALEXANDRE, qv. To Los Angeles from Quebec. Poss son of Joseph John Allain, b 1885, Quebec.
ALLEN in Nfld. (Seary) Cf ALAIN, ALLAIN of J, 1690 (Stevens)
ALLEN, Percy, from Alderney to Moose Jaw, Sask in 1900s, mar Florence JOLLY, qv. He d 1959, 4 sons, 10 granchn. Florence from St. Sampsons, G.
A1. Douglas Allen, Navy, Victoria, BC A3. David, sales in Burnaby, B.C.
A2. Stanley, miller at Moosejaw, Sask A4. Norman
ALLEYRE, Peter and John, from J? signed Gaspe Petition 1820. Cf ALLAIRE of C.I.
ALLEY in Nfld. (Seary) Cf ALLEZ, ALLIX, ALLES in C.I. (Stevens)
ALLEZ, Capt. from G sailed to Nfld., not known to be settler. (K. Mathews) See SEARY
AMOND, ALMOND?, C.I. surnames in Quebec. ALMOND IS PROB.ENGLISH.
An Amy family of Jersey consisting of 8 chn dispersed to other places, London, England; Quebec, and Montevideo, Uruguay. The latter were Henry William, b 1867, who died 1945 in Montevideo, and also, Walter. They both left descendants there. (Ernest Amy, Beauharnois, Quebec)
AMY, Raulin Wm., b 1863 J, son of John and Elizabeth Anthoine Amy. Mar 1888 Matilda Clarke, b 1868 Paspebiac. Matilda d 1912, Quebec and Raulin in 1950, there.
A1. Lillian Elizabeth, b 1889 Grand Bay, Que., mar Ernest H. Woodside 1911, who d 1967 Que. City
   B1. Arnold Raulin Smith Woodside, b 1912 Quebec, killed in action Hong Kong, China, 1941
   B2. Ernest Harold George Woodside, b 1920 Quebec, mar Margery Hesketh 1946
   B3. Marjory Amy Woodside, b 1923 Quebec, mar Wm. Spankre? Kennedy 1954, Que.
A2. Beatrice Jane, b 1890 Grand Bay, Que., mar Ronald Pennington 1924, no issue. She d 1950, he d 1941
A3. Elsie Matilda, b 1891, res Que., mar Albert F. Moore 1914, d 1970 Albert D 1941
   B1. Emma Matilda Moore, b 1915   B5. Thomas Joseph Moore, b 1928
   B2. Albert Raulin Moore, b 1917   B6. Frederick Robert Moore, b
   B3. Edythe Lila Moore, b 1919   1932
   B4. Dorothea Valentine Moore, b 1926, Quebec City
A4. Raulin Anthoine John, b 1893, d in action WWI, 1915
A5. Julia May, b 1895, unmar, d 1964
A6. Mabel Emily, b 1897 Quebec City, mar 1917 Walter A. Kingsland, who d 1942. She d Montreal
   B1. Keith Walter Kingsland, b 1919 B4. Lloyd Francis Kingsland, b
   B2. Helen Dorothy Kingsland, b 1920   1924
   B3. Howard Raulin Kingsland, b 1921 B5. Millicent Amy Kingsland, b
                                                1926
A7. Clara Alice, b 1899, mar Gustavus Seifert 1926, d 1967. He d 1971, Quebec
   B1. Mildred Ruth Seifert, b 1928   B3. Ruth Pricilla Seifert,
   B2. Raulin Edward Seifert, b 1930, res   twin of Raulin, b 1930
       Halifax, NS

A8. John, b 1900, d.y.
A9. Henry Edward, b 1901, mar 1923 Ramah Marshal Ball, Kenogami, Que. He d 1951, She d 1970
  B1. June Marshall, b 1923, Kenogami, Que.
  B2. Joy Harriette, b 1926 St. Joseph de Alma, Que.
  B3. Ida Dawn, b 1928
  B4. Raulin Ball, b 1938, mar Sandra Louise Streeter 1959, res Whitefield, NH
    C1. Raulin William, b 1960, Whitefield, NH
A10. Winter John, b 1903, d 1923
A11. Ernest Payne, b 1905, mar Alice Nadsgood 1936 at Beauharnois, Que.
  B1. Neil Raulin, b 1938, d.y.
  B2. Robert Ernest, b 1939, mar Jessie Katherine Boyd 1962, Cornwall, Ont.
    C1. Robert Keith, b 1954, Montreal
    C2. Victor Graham, b 1964, twin of Robert
    C3. Katherine Joanne, b 1969, Montreal
  B3. Julia Beryl, b 1942   B4. Carol Beatrice, b 1947
A12. Herbert Walter, b 1907, Quebec, mar Genevieve Belleau 1939, no issue
A13. Frederick Keith, b 1912, killed in action, Holland, 1944, WWII

AMY, John, b 1880 J, to Canada, 1901. Mar 1904 Grace Isabel Moorhouse. John was the son of Philip Amy and Anne Jane LESBIREL, qv. (John Amy, Montreal, Que.)
A1. Lily, b 1905
A2. Ethel, b 1907, mar Russell McDowell
  B1. Gordon McDowell, b 1935
  B2. Glen McDowell, b 1936
  B3. Elsie McDowell, b 1941, mar Lionel Fry
    C1. David Fry, b 1963   C3. Jeffrey Fry, b 1967
    C2. Gary Fry, b 1965   C4. Stuart Fry, b 1970
  B4. Grace McDowell, b 1945, mar Spencer Mink
    C1. Timothy Mink, b 1972   C2. Todd Mink, b 1974
  B5. Mary McDowell, b 1946, mar Douglas Warsaba, chn adopted
    C1. Mark Warsaba, b 1971   C2. Paul Warsaba, b 1975
A3. Edward, b 1908, mar Emily Fuller
  B1. Joyce, b 1942, mar Harry Motyka
    C1. Bruce Motyka, b 1966   C3. Stephen Motyka, b 1971
    C2. Gregory Motyka, b 1967
  B2. Gladys, b 1945, mar Claude Lambert
  B3. Douglas, b 1949, mar Gene Seymour
A4. Philip, b 1912, mar Mary Hughes
A5. Ernest, b 1915, mar Olive Bowler
  B1. William, b 1946, mar Charmaine McTeir
    C1. Sherilyn, b 1971   C2. Melissa, b 1974
  B2. Grace, b 1947, mar Charles McNeill
    C1. Randall McNeill, b 1970   C2. Mary McNeill, b 1966, adopted
  B3. June, b 1948, mar Barry Ebata
    C1. Kandace Ebata, b 1972   C2. Karynne Ebata, b 1974
  B4. John, b 1949, mar Glennis Upshaw
  B5. Dorothy, b 1957
A6. Margaret, b 1920, unmar, res Winnipeg, Man.

AMY, Charles, brother of John, above, b 1881 J, mar Estella Leighton, res Grand Rapids, Mich., no issue

AMY, Lydia, b 1889 J, unmar, res New Westminster, BC

AMY, Philip, b 1890 J, brother to above three, mar Daisy Annette REMON, qv.
A1. John C., b 1924, mar Dorothy Eva Schultz

    B1. John Stephen, b 1954   B2. Peter Charles, b 1961
A2. Rozel, b 1925, mar John Evanson, res Penticton, BC
    B1. David Evanson, b 1951   B4. Philip Evanson, b 1961
    B2. Allan Evanson, b ca 1952   B5. Jennifer Evanson, b 1964
    B3. Collin Evanson, b ca 1955
A3. Godfrey Philip, b 1920
A4. Peter Remon, b ca 1922, mar Ruth Tolles, res New Westminster, BC
    B1. Wendy, b 1956   B2. Susan, b ca 1958   B3. Bruce, b 1960
AMY, Several of this surname from J to BC, NS, ONT., NFLD., Gaspe, etc.
AMY, Sylvester Alfred, to Paspebiac early 1800s? Also, Alfred Amy from
    J to Gaspe early 1900s (SYVRET)
AMY, Peter, b J, in Malbaie 1861 with Mary and Elizabeth; both b Lower
    Canada
AMY, some listed in Perce, Gaspe. (Cent. Bklt.) Middle 1800s
AMY, George, from J to White Rock, B.C., 1900s
AMY, Mr. and Mrs. C. from C.I. to New Westminster, BC, 1908?
AMY, Herbert, from J to B.C., 1957
AMY, Edwin C., from J to Winnipeg, Man.
AMY, Mrs. Hilda, nee GOUBERT, from G to Canada, 1900s, cousin of T. DE
    CARTERET, qv of Niagara Falls, Ont.
AMY, in Toronto, 1975
AMEY, J Captain to Nfld. (Mathews)
AMEY, AMY, firm from J estab in Cape Breton, NS 1800s (Mathews) Fam be-
    low may have been connected with some of the Amys mentioned above.
    Philippe of J, mar Elizabeth ANTHOINE, 8 or 9 chn
A1. Philippe, mar Jane LABEY, qv   A7. Julia, b 1832, mar George
A2. Elizabeth, mar John Amy?   Helier LABEY, qv.
A3. Ann, mar Peter LE PELLEY of Sark   A8. William Raulin, or Raulin
A4. John   William
A5. Esther   A9. Henry Helier Anthoine
A6. Jane
ANDERSON in Nfld. (Seary) Cf ANDERSON of C.I. John was a cooper in
    Petty Harb., 1767
ANDRE in Nfld. (Seary) Cf ANDRE, ANDRES, ANDROS in J (Stevens)
ANDRES, later spelled ANDREW from G to the Maritimes Fisheries (K.
    Mathews)
ANDRESS, ANDREWS, Nathan, from C.I. in Salmon Cove, Conc. Bay, Nfld.
    and also William there in 1802, 1804. (Rev. Hammond)
ANDRESS, ANDREWS, Henry, from C.I. in Salmon Cove, Port De Grave, Conce.
    Bay, 1802, 1805, and John in 1763. (Rev. Hammond)
ANDRESS, ANDREWS, George and Richard, from C.I. in Harb. Grace, Conc.
    Bay, Nfld. 1860s
ANDRES, Capt. from G in Nfld. (K. Mathews)
ANDRES, ANDREWS, William in Rock Cove, Conc. Bay, Nfld., 1758
ANDROS, ---Jerseyman in N.B., prob assoc with the fisheries there, 7
    cards in Saint John Museum library.
ANDROS, ANDRES, ANDRE, some in J said to be desc of English fam that
    rem to the Islands and changed surname from ANDREWS to ANDROS
ANEZ, see AGNES, C.I. surname in Gaspe (K.H. Annett)
ANGEL in Nfld. (Seary) Cf L'ANGELE, L'ANGE in J (Stevens)
ANGOT, C.I. surname on the southern coast of Nfld. (G.W. Le Messurier)
    See Seary, also
ANLEY, some in Canada, poss from C.I. where the name is very old
    (Stevens)
ANNETT, Philippe, b G, mar at Perce, Gaspe 1859 Marie Louise, or Eliza,
    Simoneau, dau of Charles S. and Marguerite Methot. See also BOUDREAU,
    BOUDROT, etc. Other Annetts in Gaspe were not from C.I. (M. Fallu,

Quebec)
A1. Rosalie, b 1865 Perce, mar at Carleton, Que. 1889 Abraham BOUDREAU, son of Eric B. and Louise Cyr
  B1. Laurida Boudreau, b 1890 Carleton, mar 1911 Francois Xavier Le Blanc
    C1. Marguerite Le Blanc, b 1914, mar 1942 Arsene FALLU, qv, at Carleton, 7 chn
    C2. Annette Le Blanc, b 1912 Carleton
    C3. Xavier Le Blanc, b 1913
    C4. Rosalie Le Blanc, b 1916
    C5. Napoleon Le Blanc, b 1918
    C6. William Le Blanc, b 1920
    C7. Eliza Le Blanc, b 1921
    C8. Edward Le Blanc, b 1923
    C9. Francoise Le Blanc, b 1926
    C10. Marie Le Blanc, b 1928
    C11. Florian Leblanc, b 1930
    C12. Yvon Leblanc, b 1932
  B2. Helene Boudreau, b 1892
  B3. Eliza Boudreau, b 1894
  B4. Marguerite Boudreau, b 1896
  B5. Esther Boudreau, b 1898
  B6. Melanie Boudreau, b 1900
  B7. Clothilde Boudreau, b 1903
  B8. Hectorine Boudreau, b 1906
  B9. Edgar Boudreau, b 1908

ANQUETIL, Capt. from J in Nfld. early, also agents and ship owners of same surname (K. Mathews, Seary)
ANQUETIL, from J to Chatham, Ont., late 1800s (Luce)
ANTHOINE, Capt. from J, also agent and merchant to Nfld. (K. Mathews, Seary) ANTHOINE, RAchel Hawkes from Mrblhead,MA to Maine.
ANTHOINE,Richard & Sarah, from J to Phila.,PA 1708.
ANTHONY, ANTHOINE?, William, from C.I. in Bay de Grave, Conc. Bay, Nfld. 1788 (Seary) ANTHOINE, from CI to Gaspe, (Syvret)
ANTHONY, Thomas and William in Brigus, Nfld. 1860s (Rev. Hammond)
ANTHONY, J. in Brigus 1775 (Seary) Many in Nfld., some from C.I.
ANTLE, poss variant of ANQUETIL (Seary)
ANTLE, Wm. and widow, Antle in Brigus 1782 (Rev. Hammond) See Seary
APPLEBY, Theresa of J? fam, mar 1898 Charles Nelson PICOT, qv., Gaspe
ARBOUR. This surname poss of Acadian origin, but much intermar with C.I. fams in Gaspe, therefore included.
ARBOUR, Agnes Marguerite LE COUTEUR, b 1846 Bonaventure Island, Gaspe, mar ---ARBOUR
ARBOUR, Agnes, mar Henry, Harry, Clifford VIBERT, qv, who d 1862, age 71, Gaspe. (Cent. Bklt.)
ARCHER, in Nfld. (Seary) Cf ARCHER, and L'ARBALESTIER of J (Stevens)
ARNOLD, from C.I. to Gaspe (J.H. Le Breton list) Cf ARNAULD of J (Stevens)
ARNOLD, Francis of C.I.? and Anne GUILLET, qv., desc said to be in Toronto (Guillet)
ARTHUR, Marguerite, mar ---VIBERT of J 1819, res 1845 Perce, 7 chn, most b J, of whom 4 res in Quebec. See VIBERT
ARTHUR, Charles of Gaspe, from C.I.? mar Selina LE GALLAIS, qv., rem to Duluth, Minn.
ASH, from C.I. to Nfld. (Rev. Hammond, Seary)
ASPELL, ASPLEY, Capt. from J in Nfld. (K. Mathews, Seary)
ASPLET, Aaron, age 25 in 1818, mar, 1 chn, requested a lot at Chebogue on LacBrador, CB (PANS, Robichaud)
ASSEL, see WEARY
AUBAIN, Marguerite, mar Philip MAUGER, qv., of J, in Gaspe 1824 (Gallant) See AUBIN
AUBERT, George? b ca 1805 J, rem to Gaspe. He was poss son of George A. and Marie GALIX?, poss GALLAIS/ or GALLICHAN? He d 1869 Bon. Is. Mar 1829 Mary Ann MORRISSEY, qv. 1812-1846 and 2. Mary Ann LAMB, born PEI?, dau of Patrick Lamb and Sara Jeffroy of PEI (Gallant, Brochet) A George Bon. Is. 1861, age 54 (Brochet)
A1. Angelique, b 1831, mar M. HUARD, qv., of Gascons, Gaspe

AUBERT   143

A2. Ellen-Jane, b 1835.
A3. George, b 1838, d ca 1913, mar Ellen Sadler in England, 1839-1916.
    Worked for Fruing Company (GLF)
    B1. George William, b 1869, d ca 1944, res Bon Island
A4. Susan?, b 1840
A5. Jean Baptiste, b 1843, mar Virginia Paget, d 1885 Bon Is.
A6. Charles George, b 1847, mar Ellen JOURNEAU, qv.
    B1. Hannah, mar ca 1885 Peter BOND of Malbaie, Que.
    B2. Jean   **THIS CHART IS INCORRECT. TRY VITAL RECORDS.**
    B3. Victoria, mar Capt. Basin Boulanger of Perce N.
    B4. Jane, mar James PAGET
    B5. Marie Ann, b 1893, mar Cyril R. Paget, 1873-1921
A7. Pierre-Abel, b 1848, mar 1. 1873 Eliza JOURNEAU, 2 and 3. two Simard
    sisters? and 4. ---Boule. This data not certain.
    B1. Philippe, b 1881, mar Victoria Wall, 9 chn in Montreal and Ont.
        He d Montreal, 1971 (uncertain and unverified)
A8. Sara Ann, b 1850
A9. Margaret
A10. James?, b 1854, d 1933 Perce?, mar 1882 Bridget LE COUTEUR, qv.,
    1869-1939 res Irishtown, Gaspe. Bridget dau of Philip Le C. and
    Jane JOURNEAUX, qv. SEE LE COUTEUR CHART PAGE 327,
    B1. James Jr.
    B2. William, 1897-1967, mar Elgerth Flynn
    B3. Edmond, mar Emma La Flamme
        C1. Agnes, mar Gilbert Simoneau   C3. Ludger, mar Agnes Simoneau
        C2. Erin?, mar Doris Bourget
AUBERT, George, b J, in Perce 1861 with Maria A., b PEI, Suzanne,
    George, Jean Baptiste, Charles G., all b L.C., AUBERT, current Perce,
    Gaspe
AUBERT, Leslie, in Toronto, 1970s
AUBERT, George, b J, in Douglastown, Que., 1861 census
AUBERT, George, B J, d 1904 Riviere Madeleine, Que., age 65, worked for
    Fruing & Co. (GLF)
AUBERT, in Winnipeg, Man.
AUBERT, Michael, b J? at Hopetown, Que. 1825
AUBIN from J in Maritimes Fisheries (K. Mathews)
AUBIN, Francis Alfred, b 1859 J, d 1919, bur Gr. Riv. Gaspe (GLF), mar
    Fanny Florence MALLET, who d 1895, bur Cape Cove Angl. Cem, (Brochet)
AUBIN, Thomas, b 1841 St. Saviour J, d 1869 Montreal, age 28
AUBIN, J.E.A., d WWI, bur Ruville, Normandy, from Canada? (H. Aubin,
    Jersey)
AUBIN, Capt. from J in Nfld (K. Mathews)
AUBIN, John, b J, in Perce 1861, 1871 (census)
AUBIN, Philippe, res Baie Comeau, Que., of J fam?
AUBIN, in Calgary, Quebec, Winnipeg, Man., many from J
AUBIN, Mabel and Belle, from G, cousins of Elizabeth, Laura and Theo-
    dore LE PAGE, qv. See also LE CLERCQ. Rem from G to J, then to Vic-
    toria BC. They were daus of Charles AUBIN, a sea captain. Mabel
    unmar. Belle mar a Rev. Gibson, a widower, and raised his 4 chn.
    Rev. Gibson served in the Queen Charlotte Islands and retired to Vic-
    toria, BC. There may have also been an aunt, Esther Aubin, in BC,
    who mar a Stevens, and had two sons, Richard and Wilfred Stevens.
    Esther's sister was Laura Aubin (Muriel Kidd, Winnipeg, Man.)
AUDOIRE, see LIHOU. From Ald to Owen Sound, Ont.
AUGER, from G? to Ont. AUGRE? Cf Des Augres of C.I.
AULEY, poss ANLEY? of J, involved 1717 with Nfld. Fisheries (C.R. Fay)
AUPIN, from HOPIN, qv, curr at Gr. Riviere, Gaspe. See HOPIN, Samuel.

AUSTIN, from G to St. Thomas, Ont. ca 1900 or before
AVERY, Thomas b ca 1817, said to be the son of a Jerseyman who settled in Nfld., (Compiler's note: poss AVERTY?) Mother of Thomas said to be 103 when she d. Thomas mar Ann Churchill (1815?-1898, a good bonesetter. Thomas d 1899, wife bur Cataline, Nfld. (Pat Hutcheson, Pittsburgh, Pa.) See Seary also
A1. Mary, b 1839 mar Joseph Snelgrove 1863, res Grates Cove
A2. Patience, b 1842, mar James Stringer 1861, res Grates Cove
A3. Simeon, b 1848, d 1932. Taught school at Harbor Grace till ca 1879, rem to St. John's, where he worked for Ayre and Marshall. Manufactured cod liver oil in a plant at Shoe Cove, N.D.B. Methodist lay minister. Later res Bonne Bay and St. John's. Magistrate at Burin, Nfld. Rem to Detroit with son Chesley where he d. Bur Park Lawn, Toronto, Ont. Mar 1. Louisa Ivany, 2. Louisa Trapnell, b 1852, and 3. Sarah Jane Collins of Burin
  B1. Janet, b 1870, d 1953, mar W.J. Hutcheson, rem to Fargo, N.D.
    C1. John A. Hutcheson, b 1905, head of the committee on Ordinance for the National Research and Development Board. Mar Grace Nicholson
      D1. Patricia Hutcheson, b 1932, res Pittsburgh, Pa.
  B2. Minnie, d.y.
  B3. Annie, b 1874, d 1949
  B4. by second wife, Sarah
  B5. Clara
  B6. Thomas
  B7. Bessie
  B8. Edith
  B9. Robert
  B10., 11, 12, other chn
A4. Jonah, b 1854
A5. Lydia, b 1856, mar ---Holmes, res Montreal, d there 1938
A6. William Thomas
A7. Isaac?
A8. Nathan?
AYBORN?. Thomas, b J, in Gaspe 1861 (census)
AYRE, AHIER, C.I. Surname on the S. coast of Nfld. (G.W. Le Messurier, Seary) See AHIER   BAAL, SEE EXTRA PAGES.
BAAL, G.L., from J to Victoria, BC, there in 1940, also res Toronto?
BACHLY, Alfred, from G to St. Thomas, Ont. ca 1904. Related to LE COURTOIS, qv., 2 daus?
BACON, from C.I.? at Barachois, Gaspe, current (Brochet) Cf HAMON of C.I.
BAILEY, BAYLEY, BAYLY, boatkeeper from J in Nfld. (K. Mathews) See also Seary
BAILHACHE, BALLHACHE, BALHASSET, etc., Capt. from J in Nfld. (K. Mathews) See BELHACHE
BAILHACHE, Jos. Guillaume, b 1794 St. Peter J, son of Clement B. and Marie---, farmer res 1861 Mont Louis, Gaspe (Remiggi)
BAILIEU, Judith, from J?, mar Nicholas DE GARIS, a son Nicholas b 1833 Paspebiac, mar Julienne Duguay, res Perce (Brochet)
BAILLIEUL, Capt. from J in Nfld. (K. Mathews)
BAILLIE, see JACKSON and MAJOR
BAINBRIDGE, C. res Victoria, BC member of C.I. Society there, 1940s
BAINBRIGGE, Philip, artist in Ont. before 1830. Origin unknown
BAKER in Gaspe, poss some from C.I., some from Ireland? Related to DE GRUCHY and MAUGER, etc. ONE BAKER/BEAKER FAM. IN GASPE=GERMAN.
BAKER, Capt. John, b 1799 J, d 1884, mar 1880s Domitilda Beliveau, Perce. Poss father and son of same name
BAKER, James, mar Rachel LE MESURIER, a son Edw. James b 1852 Sandy Beach, Gaspe
BAKER, Elisha, res Alderney. Dau Amelia mar Thomas LIHOU, qv., their chn to Canada
BAKER, Hugh, mar Eliz. TRACHY in Gaspe (Brochet)
A1. Aurelia, mar Peter LE MOIGNAN, qv., 1875, Cap D'Espoir, Gaspe

BAKER

(LE MOIGNAN)
A2. Jane, mar 1871 Philip LE MOIGNAN, qv.
A3. Margaret, Maggy, mar Louis Rail 1800s, Cap d'Espoir
A4. Susan, mar Charles Rail of Cap d'Espoir, Gaspe
A5. Mary, mar Joseph ROUSSY, qv. of Grand Riviere, Gaspe
A6. Virginia, mar Victor Bond of Riviere au Renard, Gaspe
A7. Louise mar Narcisse TRACHY, qv. Dau of Hugh Beaker dit Blondin.
BAKER, John, from J? signed Gaspe Petition of 1820
BAKER, Eva, mar 1870 Percy Charles John DE GRUCHY, qv., in Perce, Que.
BAKER, member of Victoria branch of C.I. Society there, 1940s (Luce)
BAKER, Geo from C.I. in Bread and Cheese Cove, Conc. Bay Nfld. 1775
   (Rev, Hammond) Another George in Burin, Nfld. 1860s (Lovell, Seary)
BAKER, Lucy Mary, d 1939, wife of John Abraham LE HUQUET, qv., bur Cap
   OZO, Gaspe (GLF)
BAKER, BEAKER, Christopher, age 30, b Quebec, Prot., Cape Cove, Perce
   1871 (Brochet)
BAKER, Wm. John, of Cape Cove mar Harriet MAUGER 1836, a son John b
   1837, Malbaie
BAKER, Ann, mar Wm. Donohue, a dau Jane Emily b 1846 Gaspe (Brochet)
BALACHE, BALLACHE, BALHAUCHE, BELLEHACHE, Douce, b J, age 65 in 1829.
   Asked for lot in Hawkesbury, CB 1817. Came with husband from J 1788,
   farmed in Gut of Canso. Husband master of vessel on voyage from
   Halifax to Western Islands, bound to Fial, prob lost on return voyage.
   She asked for renewal of husband's lease. Granted (PANS) She also
   asked part of land that John Grant of Ship Harbour owned, as he died
   indebted to her in 1805. (CB Land Papers, PANS). No living children.
BALCOMBE, Capt. John, b ca 1697 J, mar 1. Sarah Jacobs, 1696-1741, dau
   of Joseph and Sarah Lynzey Jacobs 1719. John d 1782 Mansfield, Conn.
   Ten chn by first wife, two by second wife, names uncertain. Prob the
   two Balcoms who appeared in N.S. 1767 to 1770 were desc of this fam.
   In 1726 a Francois Balcam mar Anne RENOUF, qv., of St. Mary, J. In
   1739 Francois and Jeanne HAMON, qv., were godparents to Elizabeth
   INGROUVILLE, qv. (Louise Carlson, Milwaukee, Wisc.; A FIRST BOOK OF
   THE BALCOMB FAMILY, by Frank W. Balcomb, Peabody, Mass., 1942. (Com-
   piler did not see this book)
A1. Sarah, b 1720, mar Nathan SIMONS   A3. John, b 1724
A2. Elizabeth, b 1722, d.y.?   A4. Susannah, b 1726, d.y.
A5. Joseph, b 1728, d Mansfield, Conn., ca 1810, mar Mary King, 10 chn.
   Mary was dau of Samuel and Mary Rose, 1739-1825. Their chn res
   near Otsego Co., N.Y. Poss. another son Horace of Harley, MI?
B1. Azariah, b 1760, mar Deborah Hastings
B2. Elizabeth, b 1762, mar 1784 John MARTIN, son of Elijah
B3. Uriah, b 1764, mar Lucy Webster
B4. Asahel, b 1766, mar Aseneth MARTIN, dau of Robt. and Lydia
B5. Constant, b 1768, mar Anna Crane
B6. Mary, b 1771, mar Elijah MARTIN, Jr.
B7. Sarah, b 1774, d 1864, mar 1800, Ebenezer Gurley
B8. Francis, mar Eunice Lathrop
B9. Daniel
B10. Lucinda, mar Ebenezer Gurley, poss after death of Sarah
A6. Mary, b 1730, mar Joseph Clark   A10. Francis, b 1738
A7. Sarah, b 1732   A11. Samuel, b 1745
A8. Elias, b 1733   A12. Elizabeth, mar 1761,
A9. Susannah, b 1736   Benjamin Jacobs
BALCOM, Henry, mar Elizabeth ---, res Mass. 1668. Two, at least, chn,
Silas and Samuel. It is thought that these brothers came to the head
of the Bay of Fundy in 1755, and may have been among those who

participated in the seizure of Louisbourg, 1768. They settled at Paradise, N.S.
A1. Samuel, b 1745 Conn? (See #11 above?), mar Mary Brigham in Mass and had chn b in N.S.
   B1. Henry, b 1768, d 1850, mar Ann Morse, 1770-1860
      C1. Jonas, b 1797, mar Salome Parker
      C2. Ann, Nancy, b 1799, mar 1. Silas Parker, b 1790, and 2. Joseph Wade
      C3. Elizabeth, b 1803
      C4. Lucy, b 1805, mar Jacob Durland, Jr.
      C5. John, b 1807, mar Margaret Morse, b 1809
      C6. Mercy, b 1809
      C7. James, b 1811
      C8. Lovicy, b 1815
      C9. Mary Ann, b 1818
   B2. Jonas, b 1770, mar Miss McLeay of E. Halifax Co., and had issue. He was the ancestor of Henry Balcom, M.L.A., who mar Mary Quillian. Their son, Capt. Edmund Farrell Balcom, 1833-1898, mar 1862 Catherine O'Leary, 1840?-1897, dau of John O'Leary and his second wife, Ann Lemerill, of Ireland. Bur Anglican Cem. Port Dufferin, Halifax Co., N.S. (Terrence Punch)
   B3. Reuben, b 1772, mar 1796 Phoebe M. McCormich, dau of Ebenezer M. and Margaret HOOPER
      C1. Lydia, b 1797, mar Jacob Durland
      C2. Mary, b 1799, mar Rev. Obed Parker, his second wife, in 1837. He was b 1803
      C3. Samuel, b 1801, mar Lucy Parker
      C4. Ebenezer, b 1803, mar Helen Longley
      C5. Maria, b 1806, d.y.
      C6. Reuben, b 1811, mar Dorcas Emily Longley
      C7. Livicia, b 1814, d unmar
      C8. Eliza, b 1816, mar Obadiah Neily
      C9. William Elder, b 1819, mar in N.B.
   B4. Joseph Brigham, b 1774, mar 1801 Phoebe Tufts
      C1. Silas, b 1802, mar 1. Ann Van Buskirk, and 2. ---Amberman, a widow
      C2. Major, b 1804, mar Mary Roax
      C3. Lavinia, b 1806, mar John Remson
      C4. Aurelia, b 1808, d unmar
      C5. William, b 1810, d unmar
      C6. David Harris, b 1812, mar Mary Willett
      C7. Seraphina Ann, b 1815, mar Paul Amberman
      C8. Phyllis, b 1816, d unmar
      C9. Theresa, b 1819, d unmar
      C10. Leonora, b 1821, mar Jacob Durland, Jr.
      C11. Joseph Allen, b 1823, mar twice
      C12. Samuel Judson, b 1827, mar Elizabeth Banks
      C13. Jonas W.H., b 1829, mar Mary Banks
   B5. Sarah, b 1776, mar George Starratt
   B6. Asa, b 1778, d unmar
   B7. Lucy, b 1780, mar 1803 Abednego Parker, see also Mary, dau of Reuben
   B8. Lydia, b 1780, twin? mar Abijah Parker
   B9. Phoebe, b 1782, mar 1803 John McCormick, 1774-1849
      C1. William, mar Letitia Withers
      C2. Samuel, mar 1850 Elizabeth McDormand
      C3. Maria, mar William Wade
      C4. Lydia, mar Leonard Wade
      C5. Jane, mar John Mills
      C6. Sarah, mar Stephen Troop
      C7. Rachel, mar Joshua Hawkesworth
      C8. George, b 1821, mar Bessie Bent
      C9. John, mar Sarah Calnek

BALCOM   147

  C10. Gilbert, b 1823, mar Martha TUPPER
A2. Silas Balcom, brother of Samuel above, mar Susan ---, chn
  B1. Abel, mar 2. Mary Valentine
  B2. Rachael, mar Benjamin Harris
  B3. John, b 1776, mar 1792 Ellen Gilmore, b 1772, chn
    C1. William, b 1792, d unmar
    C2. James, b 1794, mar 1816 Mary Potter, b 1796
    C3. Mary, b 1796, mar John Potter, b 1792, son of Israel Potter
    C4. Margaret Ann, b 1799, mar Joseph Potter, b 1794, son of I.
        Potter
    C5. Susan, b 1801, mar Ambrose Bent, no issue
    C6. John, mar 1. Catherine Lowe and 2. ---MERRITT
    C7. Eleanor, mar William Lent
    C8. Sarah Ann, mar Jesse WARNE
  B4. Olivia, mar Joseph Potter, b 1773. Also said to have been dau of
      John Balcom!
    C1. Warren, b 1797, mar Martha Lewis of Long Island, N.S.
    C2. Sophia, b 1799, mar Abel Chute
    C3. Eliza, b 1801, mar John Chute, son of Thomas Chute
    C4. Louisa, b 1804, mar 1825 James Purdy
    C5. Joseph Lyman, b 1809, mar Lydia Witt
    C6. William Franklin, b 1809, twin of Joseph, mar 1. Mary Ann Gil-
        liatt, and 2. Mrs. Phoebe Kennedy, nee German
    C7. Mary, b 1811, mar 1. Asahel Howard, and 2. Solomon Bowlby
    C8. Sally, b 1814, mar Israel Gilliatt
    C9. Silas, b 1816, mar Catherine Gilliatt
  B5. Mary, mar John Hardwick   B9. Eunice, d unmar
  B6. Abigail, mar John Carty   B10. Isaac, mar 1808 and had chn
  B7. Lucy, mar ---MERRITT   B11. William, mar 1806 Ruth
  B8. Susan, d unmar   MCKENZIE
  B12. Sarah, mar Abraham Lowe
  B13. Joseph, mar 1808 Sarah Wright and had chn
    C1. Emmeline, b 1809   C5. Joseph
    C2. Wm. Henry, b 1813   C6. Allen, b 1820
    C3. James Stanley, b 1813   C7. Henrietta, b 1822
    C4. John, b 1815
BALCOM, prob of fam above, mar Edward Parker, who d 1876
BALCOM, Sarah, mar 1797 George PICKUP, b 1775, qv., 4 chn, see PICKUP
BALLACHEY, from C.I. to Montreal? Cf BAILHACHE of C.I.
BALLAM, Thomas, age 74 in Arichat 1877. Poss var of BALLEINE? (Robi-
  chaud) "The three Ballam sisters of Jersey, living in Cape Breton,
  had devoted their entire adult lives to the construction of some
  magnificent tapestries...paid $50,000 for tapestries in Cape Breton."
  (See NOVA SCOTIA AND CAPE BRETON, excerpts from Louise Surgey Brine)
BALLAM in Nfld. (Seary)
BALLEINE, BALLAINE, curr at Perce, and Sept-Iles, Canada, old J surname
BALLAINE, John, b 1778 St. Peter J, son of John B. and Marie VALPY dit
  JANVRIN, qv., mar in N.S. Harriet Elizabeth Cutler, Le Couteur?,
  1787-1847, b N.S. (Judy Bingham, Fullerton, Calif.)
A1. Esther Maria, bp 1811 Guysborough, NS, mar 1835 John Joseph Mar-
    shall, 1807-1870, son of Joseph Henry Marshall and Ann RICHARDSON,
    qv. She d 1885, Halifax
  B1. Harriet Ann Marshall, b 1837 Guysborough, mar 1872 Rev. E.H. Ball
  B2. Victoria Marshall, b 1838
  B3. Joseph Ballaine Marshall, b 1839, mar 1865 Susannah Elizabeth
      Oland, dau of John James Oland and Susannah Culverwell. He d 1899
    C1. Esther Oland Marshall, b 1866, d.y.

C2. John Joseph Marshall, b 1867, mar 1897 Marie Cecile Lucy Beaupre. He d 1932
C3. Mary Elizabeth Marshall, b 1868, West River, Pictou, NS, mar 1888 John William Burke Smith. She d 1949
C4. Susannah Carmicle Marshall, b 1870, mar 1898 Francis Walter Rowe Knott. She d 1929
C5. Josephine Ballaine Marshall, b 1871 Truro, NS, mar 1896 John King. She d 1944
C6. Naomi Temple Marshall, b 1872 Truro, NS, mar 1. ---McArthur
C7. Laura Foote Marshall, b 1874, d 1876
C8. Stanley Strongbow Marshall, b 1875, mar Laura Ruttan
C9. Eva Moyle Marshall, b 1877, d 1893
C10. Agnes Zippora Marshall, b 1879, mar Joseph Antoine Aldas Beaupre. She d 1946
C11. Victoria Amanda Marshall, b 1880, mar 1906 James Hugh Heacock, d 1943
C12. Jackson Winterbourne Marshall, b 1882, mar 1. Anna Christine Jonson. He d 1943
C13. Huldah Harriet Marshall, b 1884, mar Edwin HUME, d 1947
C14. Yorke Rowe Marshall, b 1886 Toronto, Ont., mar Margaret Maud King, dau of Francis James K. and Louisa Maud Denny
  D1. Marguerite Elizabeth, b 1907 Calgary, mar 1926 Lloyd Austin Grover
  D2. Florence Pearl Marshall, b 1909 Calgary, mar 1. 1930 John Travat, Weadon, Wheadon?
  D3. Vera Orian Marshall, b 1910, Vera, Sask., mar 1931 Bernard Kissam
  D4. Lyla Evelyn Marshall, b 1912, mar 1936 Hubert Martin Jensen
    E1. Judith Lyla Jensen, b 1940 Hawthorne, Calif. mar Robert Frederick Bingham
      F1. Pauline Ann Bingham, b 1961 Los Angeles, Calif.
      F2. Douglas Marshall Bingham, b 1962
      F3. Stephen Todd Bingham, b 1971 Fullerton, Calif.
      F4. Jonathan David Bingham, b 1973 Orange, Calif.
    E2. Jerry Martin Jensen, b 1944, mar 1968 Melinda M. Zuurbier
  D5. Beatrice May Marshall, b 1914 Vera, Sask., mar 1932 Kenneth William Hackwell of HACQUOIL of C.I.
C15. Charles Evas Marshall, b 1888 Toronto, Ont., d 1916
B4. Mary Elizabeth Marshall, b 1841 Guysborough, NS, mar 1889 David GRUCHY, qv. She d 1904
B5. John George   b 1845
B6. Esther Maria   b 1848, mar 1875 Thomas Henry Blair
B7. James Cutler   b 1849
B8. Francis Le Fevre   b 1852, mar ---McLeod
B9. Stuart Drummond   b 1853, mar Harriet McKeaugh
B10. Stanley Hamilton   b 1855, d 1859
BALLEINE, Edward Frederick, b 1931 St. Peter, J, son of Elias B. and Elsie May LE CORNU, qv. Mar Catherine Beveridge Kirk, rem to London, Ont. 1952, then to Calgary, Alta. 1966 (E.F. Ballaine, Calgary, Alta) (Brochet)
A1. Edward John, b 1971   A2. Alexander Kirk, b 1972
BALLEINE, John James, d 1873 St. Lawrence J, mar ---DE LA PERELLE, qv., 830s sis. of Elias, John & Francois DLP, became partner with John Hardeley in DLP FISHERIES 1860s.
A1. Jennet Susannah, mar Elias COLLAS, of St.Law.Jersey
A2. Adolphus Orange, 1842-1906, Dean of Jersey
A3. John James H., 1843-1929, mar Emily Jane Cass, Gaspe

BALLEINE   149

B1. Maud mar 1900 Charles LE BOUTHILLIER Jr.?
B2. Percy, 1881-1960   B3.Cecil,1890-1969, of Cape Cove? .ce
B4. Leslie Owen, b ?
  C1.John mar 1933 Annabelle, dau of Ph.MAUGER of Gr.
    River, and Rose BEAUDIN.Son.Wm.mar NinonRail.
BALLEINE, George Orange, 1842-1906, in J 1899   2 sons.
BALLEINE, Maude, mar Le Boutillier in Gaspe, 1800s
BALLEINE, Billy, mechanic at Perce, Gaspe, 1976
BALLEINE, D.A., from J fam in Montreal, curr?
BALLEINE, Thomas, b England, Prot. merchant at Petit de Grat, CB 1871
  (Brochet)
BALLEINE, Peter, at St. George's Cove, Gaspe 1831 (Brochet)
BALLAINE, Francois, had a Gaspe land claim in 1819 (Brochet)
BALLEINE, Capt. John Thomas, mar Marie Judith JEAN, qv., 1833 Arichat,
  N.S. She was b 1811, d 1889 (MacDougall)
  A1. Esther   A2. John
BALLEINE, ---father of George Orange BALLEINE, 1842-1906, to Gaspe for
  Robin firm, late 1800s.
BALLEINE, a G firm at Petit de Gras, Cape Breton, was established in the
  middle 1700s by a Balleine. He had 40 shallops fishing in 1761.
  (Lady P. McKie, Toronto, Ont.)
BALLEINE, Doris Mary, b St. Peter J, dau of Elias B. and Marie LE GRAND
  qv., to Canada. Mar 1919 Randolph Remon MICHEL, qv. (E.F. Balleine,
  Calgary, Alta)
BANDINELL, Capt. from G in Nfld. (K. Mathews)
BANDINELL, Thomas. "The same record gives the name of Thomas Bandinell
  of Jersey as one of the principal exporters at Harbour Grace, Nfld."
  (Census of 1675, Nfld.)
BANNIER, John, from J to Gaspe, bro of Winter Bannier of St. Ouen J (GLF)
BANBURY, D.R., of Calgary, said to be from J
BAPTISTE, Daniel, b G, in Perce 1861, (census) See also BATISTE
BARBIER, Walter, newspaperman, from C.I. to Regina, Sask., with the
  Dominion Express ca 1910 (Luce)
BARBINSON, Capt. from G in Nfld. (K. Mathews)
BARETTE, in 1600s in J, curr Gaspe, origin unknown to compiler
BAREFOOT, sometimes a var of BLAMPIED
BARLOW, from G to Gaspe, then to Alpena, Mich. (Alpena Directory, 1905,6)
BARLOW, Ezekiel, poss from G fam was a ship owner in Saint John, NB,
  1800s
BARNES, Hannah and John Jr. at Perce 1824. This surname sometimes from
  LE BAS, qv.
BARNES in Nfld. (Seary) Said to be from C.I. very early as DE BARNEVILLE
BARNES, from C.I. in Trinity Bay, Old Perlican, Nfld. Cf LE BAS?
BARNES, Charles, Giles and Samuel, from C.I.? in Harbour Mille, Nfld.,
  1877 BARON from CI to London, ONT. (DiPiero)
BARRASIN, A., from Ald or G, 1880s to Chatham, Ont., then to Oshawa, Ont.
  Two daus? others to Detroit, Mich? (Helen Dean, Chatham, Ont.)
BARRETT, Douglas, from J to Gaspe late 1800s (GLF) also in Nfld. (Seary)
BARRETT, Sarah, from C.I.? in Bread and Cheese Cove, Conception Bay,
  Nfld. 1755 (Rev. Hammond) and David in 1790 (see Seary)
BARRETT, Abraham, from C.I.? a planter in Bay Roberts, Conc. Bay, Nfld.
  1860s. Others in Otterbury, Jacob and Moses also in 1800s.
BARRETT, from C.I. to Gaspe (J.H. Le Breton, Gaspe)
BARRINGHAM, from J, in Maritimes Fisheries (Mathews)
BARTLETT, Mrs. of St. Aubin J, in 1741 left a fortune to build at St.
  Aubin a poorhouse, which took many years

BARTLETT, Charles, b J?, res Gaspe, 1850-1928, mar Amelia GAVEY, qv.,
   (GLF) (See Seary)
BARTLETT, Thomas, from C.I.?, in Bay de Grave, Conc. Bay, Nfld., 1778
   (Rev. Hammond)
BARTLETT, Frank, from C.I.? in Bay Roberts, Nfld. 1766 (Rev. Hammond)
BARTLETT, John and William, from C.I.?, in Brigus, Conc. Bay, 1780
   (Rev. Hammond)
BARTLETT, Thomas, from C.I., in La Poile, Nfld. 1860s (Rev. Hammond)
BARTLETT, Dorothy Rosina, b G, mar Wm. Cairns, Middleton (where?)
BARTON, Jane, of J, mar 1862 John William MOURANT, qv., rem to Shippe-
   gan, NB 1867. At least 8 chn. See MOURANT (See Seary)
BARTRAM, BERTRUM, Capt. and agent from J in Nfld. (K. Mathews)
   "I do know that there were two families bearing the Bartram family
   name that came from the Island of Jersey. One lived in Grafford,
   Jersey. His coat-of-arms is described as: Azure (blue) an eagle
   displayed, or (gold). The other Bartram lived in Grouville, Jersey.
   His coat-of-arms is described as: Or (gold), an Orle azure (blue).
   The crest is a demi-lion holding between its paws a shield of the
   arms. I have however, no dates as to when these two families lived,
   or if they ever left the Islands." (Michael Bartram, Lethbridge, Alta)
BAS, poss var of LE BAS, qv., Ontario
BASHFORD, 2 fams of this surname belonged to the C.I. Society, BC, 1941
BASSETT, Sgt. William Charles, R.E., of St. Annes, Ald., son of James
   and Margaret Simon Bassett, mar Ella Tinniswood, dau of Arthur T. and
   Harriett Alice AUDOIRE, rem from Ald to Hamilton, Ont. ca 1920 with
   dau E.M. (Ella Doidge, Ancaster, Ont.)
   A1. Ella Margaret Harriett, b 1917 Ald., mar in Canada William Clifford
       Doidge
       B1. William Arthur Doidge, b 1946, mar Jennifer Hazel Wilson
           C1. Julie Christine Doidge, b 1973
       B2. Robert John Doidge, b 1951, mar Maureen ---
           C1. Christin Ella Doidge, b 1972   C2. Katherine Doidge, b 1976
       B3. Bruce Graham, b 1954
   A2. William Jr., d.y., 1916-1917
BATISTE, fam from C.I. in St. Thomas, Ont. related to Robilliards of G,
   Henry, Ernest, Frank   BATES: SEE ADDED PAGES.
BATISTE, Sophie, mar Bill McDonald, res St. Thomas? Ont. (Marlene
   Robilliard, Albion, Mich.)
BATISTE, Jean, John, from G to Elgin Co., Ont. 1880. Fam orig in Lyons,
   France. He mar Rachel MAJOR, MAUGER. Desc in Windsor, Ont. (Walter
   Le Courtois, St. Thomas, Ont., Reaman)
   A1. John, mar Zelphia Ripley, 2 sons, A2. Frank
          Frederick and Earl   A3. Mary, farmed near Toronto, Ont.
BATISTE, John, from G to St. Thomas, Ont., mar Louise LE COURTOIS, see
   LE COURTOIS
BATTEN, Samuel, in Port de Grave, Conc. Bay, Nfld. 1789 (land deeds)
   also in Rock Cove 1768. "The Batten fam came from J and still own
   property in the central part of the Harbor of Port de Grave, Nfld.
   There is a tradition in the family that when their forefathers first
   built their fishing stages there was an encampment of Red Indians
   where their kitchen garden is now. This is one of the most interesting traditions that I know of, as the mention of Red Indians must
   have taken that original settlement back four hundred years or more.
   John Guy arrived at Port de Grave in 1610, before erecting his castle at Cupids. We know from his records that there were no Red Indians in Conception Bay at that time, and he had to go right up to
   the bottom of Trinity Bay before he met them. It shows how long these

Jersey families have been continuous residents in that one spot, and they may well lay claim to the oldest inhabitants of our Island, and the Plymouth Rock aristocracy of the United States are not in it with the Jersey Batten family in Nfld." (Shortis-Munn) The people of this family are said to be blackhaired and with olive complexion. See also Seary on this family.
BATTEN, William, b 1748, d 1824 (Cynthia Batten Stevenson, Mt. Pearl, Nfld.)
A1. John, mar ca 1862, 8 chn: THIS INFO IS UNCERTAIN. Check records. Samuel, Malcolm, Donald, Douglas, Llewellyn, James, Gladys, and Mildred
BATTON, Wm. in Salmon Cove, Nfld. 1798. Samuel in Rock Cove 1789 and 1804.
BAUCHE, Arthur Winter, b 1896 St. Ouens J, son of Arthur Edward B. and Louisa MESSERVY GRUCHY. Left J 1912 to work for Robin, Jones and Whitman in various branches. Rem later to Montreal and Ottawa.
BAUCHE in J 1401, related to LE BROCQ, LE VESCONTE, LE BRUN, LE ROSSIGNOL, BAILHACHE, PROUINGS, SAUVAGE, etc. of J (Chart: Arthur Bauche, Ottawa, Ont.)
BAUCHE, from C.I. in Maritimes Fisheries, 1800s (J.H. Le Breton List)
BAUDAIN, old French for Baldwin. Some in Maritimes fisheries, Cf BEAUDIN
BAUDIN, ---from J to Cap Chat., Gaspe 1861 (census) Gordon bur St. Pauls Perce, Gaspe
BAYFIELD, Capt. from G in Nfld. (K. Mathews)
BEADLE, old C.I. surname, BEDEL? (Stevens) See QAAM, by Turk
BEALE, BALE, BEALES, Capt. from C.I. in Nfld. on ship GUERNSEY (K. Mathews)
BEAMISH, ---, from J. in Maritimes fisheries (K. Mathews) A BEAMISH res Bothwell, Ont. (Rev. Hammond)
BEARD, Innkeeper from J in Nfld. (K. Mathews)
BEAN, John, from J? in Gaspe Militia 1850s (McWhirter)
BEAN, Harriet, wife of Thomas FALLA SAUVARY, qv., to Victoria BC 1920. See LANGLOIS, Lewis
BEASON in Nfld. Prob BISSON of J (Seary)
BEATON, C.I. in Maritimes Fisheries, 1800s (J.H. Le Breton List)
BEAUCAMP, Joseph, son of George B. and Olive Silvray?, mar 1857 Gr. Riviere, Gaspe, Angele Lantin
BEAUCAMP, C.I. surname, south coast of Nfld. (G.W. Le Messurier) See also Seary
BEAUCAMP, Joseph and Charles, b J in Gaspe 1861 (census)
BEAUCAMP, ---, mar Remiggi, thought to have been desc of C.I. fam. Res Quebec. See also LE GRESLEY (Frank Wm. Remiggi, Mtl.) Curr Newport, Gaspe
BEAUCHAMP, to Calgary from C.I. BEAUCHAMP, SEE ADDITIONS & CORRECTIONS
BEAUCHAMP, Fortunate, d 1944 Perce, age 68, wife of Joseph PETITPAS. Name also in Baie Comeau
BEAUCHAMP, Jack, b 1890 St. Peter Port, G, son of J.B. and Mary Richer, RICHARD? Arrived in Canada 1928 . Mar Marguerite Eliza WINTERFLOOD, b St. John G of English fam (Eileen Letson, Toronto, Ont.)
A1. Eileen Mary, b 1926, G, mar George Russell Letson
  B1. Andrea Margaret Letson   B2. Russell John Letson
A2. Audrey Rose, b 1928 Hamilton, Ont., mar George Murray Nelson
  B1. Elizabeth Ann Nelson
BEAUCHEMIN, from C.I.? to Western Canada
BEAUDIN, C.I. surname associated with Robin firm in Paspebiac, Gaspe and with town of New Carlisle, Que. (Que. Prov. Arch.) See also BAUDIN, BODEN, etc.

BEAUMONT from J to London, ONT.
BEAUDIN, Charlotte, b J?, mar Philippe BISSON, qv., res Grande Riviere, Gaspe early 1800s. Also Benoni B. and Elisabth COUL mar Gr. Riv. early 1800s. Their son Francois mar Mary Ann, Nancy, BISSON, qv.
BEAUDIN, many in LE GRAND CHIPAGAN, by Robichaud, res N.B., poss Acadian?
BECHARD, "many Bechards of the Gaspe area said to have been BICHARD, originally from the Channel Islands."
BECHARD, Thomas, of J, rem to Canada, changed surname to wife's name, RICHARD, qv.
BECHERVAISE, current at Gaspe Bay and Carlisle, Que.
BECHERVAISE. A sea-faring and literary fam of J. The two sons of Philippe B. and Marie GASNIER, Philippe and John, were trading in furs in Gaspe and other places in the Maritimes in 1806. John, 1790-1867, was a traveler, trader, author, captain and Master of H.M. Private ship of war, THE LORD WELLINGTON. The father of these two was the author of THIRTYSIX YEARS OF A SEAFARING LIFE, and FAREWELL, published about 150 years ago. Philippe also figures in the book, BEFORE THE MAST, by Henry Baynham.
BECHERVAISE, John, of J, married Charlotte Price, emigrated to Gosport, England, and had 8 chn, three of the sons emigrating to Australia and New Zealand, where a great number of descendants now live. One descendant, John Mayston Berchervaise of Belmont, Victoria, Aust., is an author and explorer, having 18 books in print, in addition to compiling the family tree of the Bechervaises. He is noted for his exploration in, and writings about Tasmania and Antarctica. There is a Bechervaise Plateau in Tasmania and a Mount Bechervaise in Antarctica. The chart below was begun by Douglas Bechervaise, b 1871, and Alice, b 1908. (Tardif list; census; John Bechervaise, Australia; Jessie Coffin, Gaspe)
BECHERVAISE, Philip, b 1787 St. Aubin J, rem to Gaspe 1820, mar Margaret Coffin 1825
A1. Philip, b 1825, mar Eleanor Languedoc, d 1895
  B1. Philip, b 1865, mar Eliza TUZO, qv.
    C1. Drusa, b 1895, mar Jerry Patterson
    C2. Gladys, b 1896, mar Melvin Stewart
    C3. Silas, b 1899, a desc mar Esther Gilliam
    C4. Philip, b 1901, mar Janet Eden
      D1. John Philip, b 1940 D2. Russel, b 1944 D3. Fern, b 1949
    C5. Elias, b 1903, d 1904
    C6. Marjorie, b 1906, mar Lewis Guignon
    C7. Clifton, b 1914, mar Muriet Coffin
      D1. Murray, b 1938   D4. Sandra, b 1945
      D2. Marjorie, b 1942   D5. Keith, b 1948
      D3. Gladys, b 1942, twin
  B2. Edward, b 1868, mar Margaret Patterson
    C1. Godfrey, b 1903 C2. James, b 1905 C3. Albert, b 1908
  B3. Douglas, b 1871, mar Mary Annett
    C1. Melvin, b 1893, mar Jane BECHERVAISE
      D1. Amy, b 1918   D3. Wilson, b 1921
      D2. Ina, b 1919, d 1942   D4. Harold, b 1925, mar Sarah VARDON
                                  E1. Sharon E2. Gail
    C2. Maud, b 1899, mar Hilton Coffin
    C3. Henry, b 1902
    C4. Eva, b 1904, mar Wilfred VIBERT, qv.
    C5. Alice, b 1908, mar Wilbert Eden
    C6. Reginald, b 1910, mar Nellie Coffin
      D1. Joan, b 1937 D2. Shirley, b 1939 D3. Linda, b 1943

C7. Hilda, b 1915, mar Edwin Eden
B4. Angus, b 1874, mar 1. Mora Boyle, 2. Alice Robson, 3. Jane
   Coffin, who d 1967
   C1. Maurice, b 1899
   C2. Pauline, b 1903, mar Gilbert Miller
   C3. Eileen, b 1905, mar Harold Eden
   C4. Leslie, b 1909, mar Etta Coffin
      D1. Ross, b 1936   D2. Lois, b 1938   D3. Elaine, b 1939
   C5. Lulu, b 1912, mar Lewis Patterson
   C6. Mildred, b 1917
   C7. Olga, b 1927, mar Harris Patterson
   C8. Ivy, b 1828, mar Sidney Clark
A2. Benjamin, b 1827, mar Mary Patterson, d 1892
   B1. John, b 1864, mar Annie Wilson, d 1937
      C1. Herbert, b 1893, mar Emily Bevis   C5. Edna, b 1905, mar John
      C2. Helen, b 1894, d 1934   Brown
      C3. Ida, b 1896   C6. Christianna Jean, mar
      C4. Lawrence, b 1903, d 1905   Lloyd Coffin
   B2. Charlotte, b 1862, mar Capt. James Languedoc, d 1921
   B3. Emily, b 1866, d 1910
   B4. Annabella, b 1869, d 1899
   B5. Clarence, b 1873, mar Maud Eden, d 1912
      C1. Dorothy, b 1906, mar Richard McHard
      C2. Lillian, b 1906, twin, mar John TUZO
   B6. Beatrice, b 1875, mar Herbert Coffin
A3. Margaret, b 1829, mar Felix Coffin
A4. Mary, b 1931, mar Frederick DUMARESQ, 6 chn, see DUMARESQ
A5. Ellen Jame, b 1833, mar William Patterson
A6. Jane, b 1835, mar George Coffin, d 1923
A7. Christianna, b 1837, mar John Wilson
A8. John, b 1839, mar Annie Alger, d 1927. Some of this fam rem to
   Oliver, BC and to Calgary, Alta.
   B1. John, d 1920   B4. Helen, b 1884, mar --MacLeod
   B2. Eva, mar ---Cuddy   B5. Jessie, mar George Lundy
   B3. Gertrude, b 1880, mar ---South   C1.Mrs.BJ Williamson,
A9. Sophia, b 1841, mar Benjamin Annett, d 1938   Cornwall, ONT.
A10. Isabella, b 1842   A12. Charlotte, b 1847, d.y.
A11. Emily, b 1845, d.y.   A13. James, b 1848, d 1924
A14. William, b 1851, mar Charlotte Pye, d 1903
   B1. Edith, b 1891, mar Felix Cunning
   B2. Jane, b 1894, mar Melvin BERCHERVAISE, a cousin
   B3. Ada, b 1898, mar Wilson Scott
   B4. Nita, b 1900
   B5. George, b 1902, mar Evelyn Hall, 1937   B6. William, b 1904
BECK. The Beck fam below is probably not of C.I. origin, poss Scottish,
   but they intermarried in some numbers with the C.I. fams, so are here
   included in part.
BECK, Adolphus, In Gaspe mar Esther GAUDIN, b 1866. See GAUDIN
A1. Percy Beck, b 1893, mar Selma Thompson, 2 sons, Gordon and John
A2. Frederick Beck
A3. May Beck, mar 1. Oscar Urquhart? and 2. Nelson Beck?
   B1. Nellie Urquhart, mar Sidney LE GRAND, 2 chn, Winston and Shirley
BECK, associated with Robin firm of Paspebiac and New Carlisle, Que.
   (Que. Prov. Arch., K.A. Annett) Ph.BECK,1885-1975 res.Gaspe.
BECK, Thomas, Prot., mar to Mary O'Hara, late 1700s (Gallant)
A1. Thomas, b 1796 Cap D'Espoir, mar Catherine Biennon, d there 1843,
   poss BRENNAN? 9 chn: Anne, d 1840, Thomas, b 1822, dau, b 1824,

Elisabeth, John David, Edouard, Helen, Suzan, b 1834.
A2. Sarah, b 1797, mar 1813 Charles Bourget A5. Suzanne, mar 1848 Michel
A3. Elizabeth, b 1802, mar Louis Boucher   Louis Bilodeau
A4. Charlotte, b 1800
BECK, Charles, mar 1892 Jane Amelia DUMARESQ, qv., res Gaspe area
   (Emery Dumarewq, Gaspe, Que.)
A1. Janet Esther, b 1893   A4. Roland Philip, b 1899
A2. Charles, b 1895   A5. Alexander Clement, b 1902
A3. Ernest Daniel, b 1897
BECK, Susan Elizabeth of J?, mar T.J. TOUZEL, LE TOUZEL in Barachois,
   Que. 1800s. See TOUZEL
BECK, Mary Laura, 1820-1902, wife of Wm. VIBERT of Gaspe (GLF)
BECK, Mary, mar in J?, George GAUDIN, rem to Canada. See GAUDIN
BECK, Martha Lucy, mar Peter ROBERTS 1831, Murray Harbor, PEI
BECK, Selina Jane, mar John ROBERTS, qv., dau Stella Margaret, b 1882
BECK, Mary, mar John MACHON 1867 Murray Harbor, PEI
BECKETT in Nfld. (Seary) Poss from C.I.
BECKET, BECQUET, John, store mgr., b J, age 70 plus in 1968, res Halid-
   mand, near Gaspe. Two sisters: Evelyn, Mrs. Albert BENEST, qv., and
   Vera BECQUET
BECKET, Capt. from C.I. to Gaspe, 1800s (Syvret)
BECQUET, John C. and Willa Irene of J fam, res Malbaie, Que. 1800s
BECKETT, Hilda, b J, mar Percy WHEADON, qv., to Seattle Wash., early
   1900s
A1. Jack Wheadon, res Kirkland, Wash., Wheadon's Florist shop.
BECQUET, Frank, from J to BC, WWII, BECKETT in Victoria, BC
BEECHAM in Nfld. (Seary) Cf BEAUCHAMP
BEECHER, Mr. and Mrs. Robert, nee Jane MAHY, mar in G 1970, rem to Tor-
   onto. She is dau of Mr. and Mrs. A. Mahy, St. Sampsons, and he is
   son of Mrs. J. Gillman, of St. Peter Port, G. (David Ozanne, Toronto,
   Ont)
BEEHAN, BEHAN in Nfld. (Seary) Cf BIHAN, BEHAN of J, 1593 (Seary)
BEESAW of Nfld., said to have been orig. BISSON of J (Shortis-Munn)
BEGIN in Nfld. (Seary) Cf BEGLIN, BEGHIN of J (Stevens)
BELACHE, BAILHACHE?, Wm., b J in Mont Louis, Gaspe 1861 (census)
BELIVEAU and BECK, J fishery, Cape Cove, Gaspe early 1800s
BELL, "Old G surname of LA CLOCHE often changed to BELL" (Carey-Wimbush)
BELLINJUNE, Capt. from J in Nfld. (K. Mathews)
BELLOT, J surname in Canada?   BELFORD: from CI to Canada.
BENEST, French for Benedict
BENEST, Albert, of J to Gaspe, mar Evelyn BECKET, of J
BENEST, Capt. from J in Nfld. (K. Mathews)
BENEST, fam from J in Gaspe 1861: Michael, Victoire, Paul, Philip,
   Augustine, chn all b Canada.
BENEST, ---, from J to Perce, 1800s (Cent. Bklt.)
BENEST, Philip, Jerseyman whose sister mar Maj. Wm. Shirref, Deputy
   Quartermaster at Boston 1775. Fam rem then to N.B. See letter in
   Dom. Arch. Ottawa, MG 23, B 50.
BENFIELD, ---, mar Maggie LIHOU, b Alderney. Collin and others still
   res there. A son, Hartley, rem to Owen Sound, Ont., then to Hamilton.
   Mar, 2 sons, one named Lee.
BENNETT, John, of BENEST? fam, orig Normandy, rem to J, then to Land's
   End, Cornwall, and to Nfld. Mar Catherine NORMORE, qv., 1822, wit-
   nessed by Mary Squire and Thomas Knight. (See PASQUIRE and CHEVALIER)
   (Rev. Hammond)
A1. Henry, bp 1828, sea captain, settled Cape Breton, N.S.
A2. Edward, bp 1829, d 1890 at 61

BENNETT 155

A3. Oliver, bp 1832, d 1913 age 83, mar Susannah ---
  B1. Oliver   B2. Abraham
A4. Frank
A5. John, bp 1832, d age 89, mar ---
  B1. Reuben   B2. Edward   B3. William
A6. William, b 1845, farmer and surveyor, d 1919 age 74, mar Mary Hiscock, 1852-1907
  B1. Leonard   B7. Lewis
  B2. William   B8. Catherine, b 1883, d 1945,
  B3. John H., b 1879, d 1961 at 82,   mar James Rich Butler
    mar Amice Ann ANDREWS, qv.   B9. Lydia
  B4. Hiram   B10. Elizabeth
  B5. Frank   B11. Mary
  B6. James, d of wounds in France, 1917
A7. Margaret, mar ---Hiscock
BENNETT, John from J, in Bell Island, Nfld., 1820 (Rev. Hammond; Seary)
BENET, poss BENEST?, David, from C.I. in Bread and Cheese Cove, Conc. Bay, Nfld. 1790 (Rev. Hammond)
BENNETT, John, b J, in Perce 1861. John BENNY in Gaspe 1871, from J, 35.
BENNETT, tradesman in Nfld., from J (K. Mathews)
BENOIT, from J to Nfld. (Horwood) Current in Stephensville, Nfld.(Seary)
BENOIT, BENWA, George and Paul, from C.I.? in White Bear Bay, west coast of Nfld. 1860s (Rev. Hammond)
BENOIT, Pascal, owner of the CATHERINE, 20 tons, built at L'Ardoise, C.B. 1864 (Capt. Parker)
BENOIT, BENNOIT, Augustus of Arichat, C.B. had the MARY B of 78 tons built for himself at Port Hawkesbury in 1880. She was lost at the Magdalen Islands in 1894 (Capt. Parker)
BERESFORD, related to Labey fam of London, Ont. (Helen Dean, Chatham, Ont.)
BERNARD in Nfld. (Seary) From C.I.?
BERNARD, Hubert and Isaac, poss from C.I., signed Petition of 1820 at Gaspe
BERNIER, said by Bourgaize to be poss from C.I. at Gaspe
BERRIMAN, Capt. from J in Nfld. (K. Mathews)
BERTEAUX, BERTEAU, from C.I. to St. John's, Nfld. (Shortis-Munn)(Seary)
BERTEAU, F.C., "scion of a worth Jersey family" (Shortis-Munn)
BERTEAU, Robert, of J?, operated Labrador fishery
BERTEAU, le QUESNE and other J fams intermarried extensively in N.S. in 1700s.
BERTEAUX, ---, of Nfld., mar St. John's Nellie V. PIPPY, qv., b 1887
BERTEAUX, Philip, b G, or by another source, St. Helier J, early in 1700s of a Huguenot fam which had fled from France after the Edict of Nantes in 1685. A Master Carpenter in Annapolis, NS, grantee of the Cape Grant. Many desc. in N.A. Mar 1. Mary ---, and 2. Martha? GOULD, qv., d after 1794 date of will. (Calnek)
A1. Philip Edward, son of Philip and Mary BERTEAUX, bp 1770
A2. William, b ca 1745, mar Ann Spurr. At age 10 William witnessed in Annapolis the expulsion of the Acadians, which he related in later life to Judge Haliburton. Ann d 1833 age 81. (Calnek, Savary)
  B1. Charles, b 1773, poss later, mar Mary Robinson
    C1. William, b 1800, mar 1824 Mary Hardwick
      D1. John Henry   D3. Mary Jane
      D2. Emmeline Elizabeth D4. Judson Adoniram, b 1833, d unmar
    C2. Charles, b 1801, mar 1826 Sarah Dunn
      D1. Mary Jane   D3. Sarah Ann
      D2. Charles Wesley   D4. William Henry

```
        D5. Isabel                    D10. Amanda
        D6. Mezelva                   D11. George E.
        D7. Pricilla                  D12. Celia
        D8. Almira                    D13. Sarah, b 1854
        D9. Celenia
     C3. Eliza Ann, b 1803, mar Samuel Wheelock, son of Abel Wheelock.
         Poss incorrect.
     C4. James, b 1804, mar 1829 Parnie Wheelock
        D1. Letitia Salome            D7. Lucinda Jane
        D2. Harriet Ann               D8. James Maynard
        D3. Helen                     D9. Emily Jane
        D4. Parnie                    D10. Leleah
        D5. Samuel                    D11. William Burton
        D6. Ezekiel
     C5. Robert, b 1804, twin, mar 1827 Olivia Wheelock
        D1. Lucinda                   D5. Robert Dickie
        D2. Harvey                    D6. Adoniram
        D3. James Henry               D7. Joseph
        D4. Albert
     C6. Edward, b 1807, mar 1837 Mercy Whitman
        D1. Albert, mar Mary LE CAIN, qv.   D4. Edward
        D2. David                           D5. Laleah
        D3. Maria                           D6. Ada
     C7. John Henry, b 1809, mar Sarah Neily
        D1. Obadiah                   D5. Edwin
        D2. Albert                    D6. Sophia
        D3. Sophronia                 D7. Annie
        D4. Fitch                     D8. Burton
     C8. Mary, b 1812, mar Thomas Baker
     C9. Harriet, mar ---Jones
  B2. Anne?, b 1774, mar Henry Hardwick, d 1848 age 73, unverified
  B3. Philip, b 1780, mar 1808 Catherine Chute, widow of John WEARE, qv.
  B4. Edward, b 1782, d.y.
  B5. Elizabeth, bp 1785, mar William Morehouse
  B6. Edward, bp 1787, mar 1810 Mercy Whitman, dau of Jacob Whitman
     C1. Freeman            C4. Ann Whitman
     C2. Edward James       C5. Louisa, mar Josiah Spurr Potter.
     C3. Benjamin Spinney C6. David, d unmar
  B7. Mary, b 1789, d.y.
  B8. George, bp 1792, mar 1817 Eliza Williams, qv.
     C1. Helen Augusta, mar Alexander Harris,  C7. Henry
           sev sons, incl George B., tycoon    C8. Maria
           of Vancouver, BC (Calnek)           C9. Seraph, b 1835, mar
     C2. Elizabeth                                   George LE CAIN, qv.
     C3. Alfred                                C10. Lucinda
     C4. Sarah Jane                            C11. Caroline
     C5. Charlotte Ann                         C12. George Augustus
     C6. Emily                                 C13. Louisa
  B9. Mary, b 1794 mar William Fairn or Edmund Clark, perhaps both?
  B10. Nancy, Ann, b 1800, mar Henry Hardwick, 1773-1857, she d 1885.
     C1. George, d 1877, his widow at 65 in 1885, 9 chn
A3. poss a son, John
A4. Thomas Edward, by the second wife, mar 1795 Mary Baltzor. Unverified
  B1. Mary, b 1796, mar 1. Thomas Palmer and 2. Samuel Slocomb
  B2. John, b 1797, mar Elizabeth, dau of Peter Baltzor
  B3. Alice, b 1799, mar Thomas Robinson
  B4. Ann Maria, b 1802, mar ---Chipman
```

See Wm. Calnek's book, A HISTORY OF ANNAPOLIS, Toronto, ONT, 1897.

BERTEAUX 157

B5. Philip, b 1804, mar Susan Brown, sister of ---Chipman, 11 chn
B6. Dorothy, b 1806, mar Peter McBride
B7. Elizabeth, b 1808, mar Ezekiel Bent, b 1803, son of Obediah Bent, his second wife
B8. Sarah Ann, b 1812, mar Joseph Dugan
B9. Julia, b 1816, mar William Howell
A5. Margaret   A6. Susan, both d unmar
BERTON, Pierre, Canadian author. Fam name LE BRETON, changed to Breton then to Berton. (Rene Gray, Newmarket, Ont.)
BERTRAM, see also BARTRAM
BERTRAM, Amice John, b 1843, Grouville J, to N.J. 1863, joined Jackson's Forest Rangers, d 1927. Mar Maria Fenton, b 1847 London, d 1928. Mar 1875, Auckland, N.Z.
BERTRAM, listed by Betty Tardif as C.I. in Gaspe, also in J.H. Le Breton List.
BERTRAM, Ernest, b J, manager for Robin firm. From Seymour House, Grouville, J. Mar LENFESTEY from G. (Rev. d'Hist) bur St. Peters, Malbaie (GLF)
BERTRAM, J., fishery firm in Nfld.
BERTRAM, from J in Griffon's cove, Gaspe (Syvret)
BERTRAM, John, of J?, and Eliz. BENNETT, his wife, and son Alex, who was b 1853 Dundas, Ont.
BERTRAND, said to be from C.I. to Canada
BESANT, var of BISSON, qv. John from C.I. said to be in Mint Cove, Conc. Bay, Nfld. 1803 (Rev. Hammond)
BESANT, Patience, mar Benj. LE DREW, Nfld. qv., (Ralph Le Drew, Toronto)
BESSIN, Capt. from J in Nfld. (K. Mathews)
BEST, from England to G to N.Y. city, mar Eliz. Ann RABEY, qv. of Gaspe, 1800s. Susan Eliz. BEST b J mar Pt. St. Peter Gaspe Thomas J. TOUZEL qv.
BEST, George, from C.I.?, in Carbonear, Nfld. 1860s
BEST, merchant and shipowner from J in Nfld. (K. Mathews)
BEVILL, from C.I.?, in St. John's Nfld. 1759 (Rev. Hammond), poss BEAUZEVAL
BEVIS, BEAVIS, Capt. from G, importer in Nfld. (K. Mathews)
BEXFIELD, from C.I.?, res Terrebonne Hts., Que., said to be from C.I.
BIARD, Charles, J fishery at Perce, Gaspe (Oakley, GLF, Dav. Bechard)
BIARD, Charles, 1856-1936, b J, to Gaspe 1885. Mar Mary BUTLIN, qv., ca 1860-1939. Only ch, owner of the DUVAL cutlass, used by Capt. Peter Du Val who commanded the privateer THE VULTURE, which ranged the north Atlantic coase and European waters during the Napoleonic wars. He was killed in an auto accident at age 80. Bur St. Pauls, Perce. NEW CHART FROM: Geo.Thompson, Montreal,QUE in CH.IS.COLL.
BIARD, Jane, b J?, mar Oliver O'Hara at Gaspe early 1800s. Oliver was son of Felix O'Hara, Lord Gaspe, who d 1803. See COLLAS
A1. Mary Ann O'Hara, b 1880, mar Abner Cartwright Huelin BISSON, qv., d 1923 age 43. Bur St. Paul's, Perce. 2 chn
A2. William Charles O'Hara, 1883-1961, mar Nora Ellen Fitzpatrick 1916, (1895-1959) Bur St. Paul's, Perce, 5 chn
  B1. William Percy O'Hara, b 1919 Perce, mar Flora Anderson, 1945, 9 chn, Sheriff of Gaspe Co. 1961
  B2. Abner Raymond O'Hara, b 1925 Perce, mar 1954 Frances Jean Fraser, no issue
  B3. Pearl, b 1917 Perce, mar Thomas Cowie 1939, no issue, res Montreal
  B4. Alma Biard O'Hara, b 1921 Perce, mar George Thompson, res Montreal
  B5. Leonie Biard O'Hara, b 1931 Perce, mar Evans Cowie 1957, res Montreal, 2 chn
    C1. dau, d 1962, bur St. Pauls, Perce

BIARD, see CH.IS.COLL.
A3. Elizabeth, b 1885, mar John BOWER 1909, 4 chn
A4. Ernest, b 1893, mar Muriel BISSON, qv., 1921, 3 chn, 2 in Montreal, one in Cornwall, Ont.
A5. Francis Arthur, b 1895 Perce, mar Agathe LE BOUTILLIER, qv., 1936, no issue
A6. Charles Le Bas, b 1896 Perce, mar Ethel LENFESTY 1934, dau Patsy, res Perce
A7. Elsie, b 1899, mar Thomas BISSON, qv., 1936, 1 ch, res Port Daniel, Que. Mar 2. Lyall Watts, res New Carlisle, Que.
A8. Hilda, b 1901 Perce, mar Edward Acteson 1930, no issue
A9. Herbert, b 1904 Perce, mar Edith Staples 1931, res Lachine, Que., 2 chn
BIARD, Francis, of J fam? Mar Agathe LE BOUTILLIER, qv., b 1866, dau JeanMarieA.Le BOUTILLIER & Georgina Caron.
BICHARD, see also BECHARD and RICHARD. A Capt. from G in Nfld.
BICHARD, John T.G., in Anse aux Sauvages, Gaspe ca 1800. A John at Cape Cove, Perce, 1831 (Brochet)
BICHARD, Mr. and Mrs. John, at Indian Cove, Gaspe. Fisherman ca 1830
BICHARD, Georges, from J, with Robin firm in Gaspe 1768, (John Clarke, THE GASPE)
BICHARD, Thomas, b G, in Cap Rosier 1861 with Ellen, b Gaspe, also Thomas, Mary or Margaret, Jane, Louise, John E., Charles Andre, Mary, all b Gaspe (census)
BICHARD, Ada, dau of Mr. and Mrs. D.H.B. of Les Sauvages, St. Sampson, G, mar A.S. GIBSON, rem to Hamilton, Ont. Three sons: Arthur, Percy and Harold, 1900s.
BICHARD, curr Toronto. F. poss son of James, from G, 1919 to Toronto
BICHARD, James, b 1863 St. Sampson, G, son of Thomas B. and Patty INGROUVILLE, qv., mar Margaret Elizabeth Crothers, b 1874 Plymouth, Eng., in 1894. He d 1933. Fam rem to Parry Sound, Ont., then to Vernon, BC and Queensland, Aust., but returned to Powell River, BC (John Bichard, Powell River, BC; H. Bichard, Victoria, BC) SEE BELOW
BICHARD, John, d Indian Cove, Gaspe 1917. Margaret, Henrietta and John res there 1869. (Brochet)
BICHARD, Eliza and Martha, related by mar to Daniel CORBET of Cap des Rosiers
BICHARD, Ralph John in Indian Cove 1925. Martha B. sold 1904 to Alfred Henry DOLBEL, qv. CHN BELOW BELONG TO JAMES &M.E.BICHARDabove.
A1. Margaret Miriam b 1896, mar George Ewing, a son George res Vancouver
A2. Lillian May, b 1901 Westbourne, England, mar H.N. Davies, dec. Widow res New Westminster, BC
  B1. Frank Davies, killed in an accident
  B2. Robert, res Thetis Island, BC, mar, no issue
A3. John, b 1911 Mackay, Queensland, Aust. Mar Christine Fraser of Powell River, BC
  B1. James John, b 1942, divorced, no issue
  B2. Sandra Louise, b 1949, mar james Karl Williams 1971
    C1. Kara Lynn Williams, b 1974, chn:Steven, Karl, Ryan John
  B3. Vicki Elizabeth, b 1958, mar Cornelius Stroomer 1975 3 daus: Shalane, Kelli,
Above fam related to a HenryRobinson of Oshawa, Ont. and Carrie.
BICHARD, F., Harold B. and Doris B. in B.C. from G fam
BICHARD, James John, from St. Sampson G, ca 1911 to Vict. BC (H.J. Bichard, Vict. BC)
A1. Harold J.   A2. Douce, res Victoria, BC
BICHARD, Louisa Alice, b 1875 St. Sampson G, dau of Jean BICHARD and Betsy MARTEL, qv., mar Thomas John ROBIN, qv., rem to Toronto, Ont. ca 1902, 7 daus

BICHARD, Ivan R., of G Gaspe fam, res Montreal, mar Dorothy May MAUGER,
  qv., b 1921 Bonaventure Is., 2 sons (Brochet)
  A1. Barry, b ca 1953   A2. Wayne, b ca 1956
BICKETT, from C.I. in Trinity Bay, Old Perlican, Nfld., early (Rev.
  Hammond) prob BICQUET, BIQUET, etc. A BIQUET lighthouse in Maritimes.
  See HAMMOND
BIENVENU, Capt. from G in Nfld. (K. Mathews)
BIGARD, C.I. in Maritimes Fisheries 1800s (Le Breton List)
BIGEREL, ditto   BILES data below from
BIGNELL, merchant from J in Nfld. (K. Mathews) Mrs.GF Cassidy,Qual-
BILES, from J to Canada ca 1900, age 18. His bro, George Francis BILES,
  b J, mar --- Seager, rem to Vancouver, BC
BILLARD, Thos. and Wm., from C.I.?, in White Bear Bay, west coast of
  Nfld., 1860s (Rev. Hammond) Cf ROBILLARD, ROBILLIARD (See also Seary)
BILLOT, said to be from C.I. in Maritimes. Surname from dist near
  Lisieux, France
BINET, Richard Edward, 1947-1961, son of Hedley and Ruth LE GRESLEY,
  b J, bur St. Peters, Pasp. (GLF)
BINET, George?, general merchant, 1800s in Arichat, NS (Bourinot)
  thought to be from C.I.
BINET, Martin, in 1790 had crown grants totalling 1200 acres on Isle
  Madame Bay, C.B., and on Southeast end of the Gut of Canso. (Crown
  Grants, Book I, PANS)
BINNET, Edward, (BINET or BENEST, BENNETT?), b J, age 29, mar, 3 chn,
  asked land at Arichat, C.B. N.S. in 1827 (PANS, land papers)
BINET, E.E., owned the DOLPHIN, 103 tons, built 1857 at Janvrin's Har-
  bour, C.B. Sold at Vera Cruz, Mexico in 1863
BINET, William, who had a B.A. degree from Toulouse, b 1827 J, d 1853
  London. He was an S.P.G. missionary in Quebec. At Malbaie 1853, 4,
  and at Port Neuf 1855
BINNEY, Hannah Harriet, of J fam of poss U.E.L. fam b 1798, d 1885.
  Mar Capt. Nicholas Thomas Hill, R.S.C., b Cork Ireland 1792, mar 1817.
  9 chn, including Rev. George Wm. Hill, 1824-1906, d England, and
  Philip CARTERET Hill, 1821-1894, Prime Minister of N.S., 1875-1878,
  d England, no issue (Terence Punch, Halifax, NS)
BIRCH, from J? in Norfolk Co., Ont., 1800s
BIRD, Walter, b G ca 1880, rem to Western Canada, returned to G. A son,
  Donald C.W. Bird in Calgary. Frank BIRD, of G, bro of Walter, res in
  San Pedro, Calif. (C.W. Bird, Calgary, Alta.)
BIRD, Richard, mgr. tourist bureau in Vancouver, from C.I. (Luce)
BISHOP, Capt. and importer from J in Nfld. (K. Mathews)
BISHOP, John, in Rock Cove, Nfld. 1786 (Rev. Hammond)
BISHOP, Joseph, in Buck Cove, Nfld. 1793 (Rev. Hammond)
BISHOP, BISCHOPPE, Eleasar, said to have been kidnapped in J or G in or
  about 1692, poss with 2 other boys, BISSON and SHARPE. The boy or
  boys were brought to New London, Conn. A Richard Dart either took
  his indenture or adopted him, raising him with a dau, Sarah. Sarah,
  1681-1755, and Eleasar married in 1704. His father-in-law died, poss
  at sea, and Bishop inherited. He became very prosperous, had at least
  10 chn, several of whom rem to Nova Scotia in 1700s. (PANS, Mildred
  Jamieson, St. John's N.B.; C. King, Jefferson, Ohio; A. Eaton, HIS-
  TORY OF KING'S COUNTY, N.S., Belleville, 1910, 1972; MS by Boggs and
  Burpee, Acadia Univ., Wolfville, N.S.; Augusta Methune, N.Y., N.Y.;
  Calnek, Savary; BISHOP FAMILIES IN AMERICA, 18013 Armitage, Homewood,
  Ill, periodical.) (BISHOP, AN ENGLISH FAMILY IN JERSEY)
  A1. Timothy, b 1705, d 1720
  A2. Peter, b 1706, d 1722

BISHOP

A3. John, b 1709, d 1785 N.S. Mar 1. 1731 Rebecca Whipple, who d 1751. He mar 2. Mrs. Hannah Allen Comstock, b 1712 dau of Samuel and Lydia Hastings Allen. John rem to Horton, NS with 4 sons ca 1761.
  B1. Col. John Jr., b 1729 or 1731 New London, Conn. d Gaspereau 1815 at 85. He and first cousin George Bishop, had a great amount of land there. He mar 1. 1751 Mary Forsyth Avery, who d 1808 and Ruth Sheffield Harris. 5? chn by Mary, and 4? b Ruth. Ruth d 1827 at 67
    C1. Amelia, b 1754, New London, mar 1772? Charles Dickson, Jr. of Horton, who d 1796 and 2. Joseph McLean. She d 1846
    C2. Hannah, b 1756 New London, mar 1774 Henry, son of Abel and Jean Burbidge
    C3. Charles, b 1758 New London, mar Philander, dau of Ebenezer and Lydia Fish or Fitch
    C4. John, b 1764, Horton, mar prob a dau of Daniel Harris
    C5. etc., other chn
  B2. William, Capt., b 1732, New London, d Horton 1815 at 83, bur Wolfville, NS. Served in American Indian wars, and Amer. Rev. War against the Americans. Mar 1761 Jemima Calkin, res Greenwich
    C1. William, b 1762, mar Hannah Comstock 1788, d 1837
    C2. Samuel, b 1767 Halifax, mar 1798 Anna Jacobs of Halifax, and 2. Bathsheba Fitch
    C3. Rachel, b 1763, mar 1785 Frederick Fitch, of Canaan, N.S.
    C4. Lucy, b 1765,mar1.SamTurner,no issue,2.P.Whittier,4chn.
    C5. Eleanor, b 1770, mar 1797 Rev. Obadiah Newcomb, d 1849
    C6. Joshua, b 1773, mar ---Williamson, d 1848
    C7. Jemima, b 1774, mar 1794 Wm. Best, d 1832 2 chn
    C8. Elisha, b 1777, mar 1816 Eliz. Lovett, d 1864
    C9. Hannah, b 1780, mar Enoch Forsyth, b 1774, see Enoch, grandson of Mary Bishop
    C10. Sarah, b 1782, mar 1. Daniel Chipman, and 2. Deacon Silas Morse of Granville,7 chn by Chipman.
  B3. Peter, Deacon, b 1735 New London, d Horton 1826, res New Minas, bur Wolfville, N.S. Mar 1.---, and 2. Phebe Hamilton
    C1. Simeon B.   C5. Peter, b 1763, mar New London
    C2. Amy   Amy Bowles
    C3. William, b 1780 mar E.Copp   C6. Jonathan, b 1764, mar ---
    C4. GODFREY?   Anderson
    C7. Eliphal, b 1770, mar 1795, John Coldwell
    C8. Phebe, b 1773 mar David Coldwell
    C9. Jeremiah, b 1775, d 1856, mar Keziah Coldwell
    C10. Eleazar, b 1777, d 1865, mar 1803 Hannah Curry
    C11. Esther, b 1779, d 1940, mar at Hopewell NB 1801 John Newcomb
    C12. James, b 1776, d 1856, mar Lydia Martin of Gaspereau 8 chn.
    C13. Harriet, mar James Turner,who d 1863 age 74
  B4. Timothy, b 1740 New London, d Greenwich, Horton, N.S. 1827, mar 1. 1762 Mercy HARDING, dau of Abraham and Mercy VIBBER Harding cf VIBERT, mar 2. Mercy Gore Newcomb of Preston, Conn.
    C1. Abigail, b 1763, mar Ebenezer Fitch of Wilmot
    C2. Silas, b 1764, mar Anna Wells
    C3. Rebecca, b 1766, mar Elijah Calkin,parents from LebanonCt.
    C4. Eunice, b 1768, mar James P. Harris
    C5. Ezra, b 1770, mar Jerusha Newcomb
    C6. Amy, b 1772, mar Oliver De Wolf, son of Jehiel and Phebe
    C7. Timothy, b 1774, mar Eunice Coldwell,2nd Widow West.
    C8. Mercy, b 1776, mar Abraham Seaman, qv.
    C9. Mary, b 1776, twin, mar Newton Wells

BISHOP   161

        C10. Anna, b 1779, mar Samuel Cox
        C11. by second wife, Ebenezer, b 1784, mar Anne Lewis, sev. chn,
             some to U.S. (B5) James Bishop, to US.
        C12. Olive, b 1789, mar George ROY of New Minas, N.S., 5 chn
    A4. Samuel, b 1712, d 1804, mar Elizabeth---, 1711-1756, 7 chn
        B1. Samuel, b 1736   B5. Clement, b 1748
        B2. Elijah, b 1738   B6. Elizabeth, b 1750
        B3. Mary, b 1742, mar Elijah Waterhouse B7. Phebe, b 1752
        B4. David, b 1744
    A5. Clement, b 1714, d 1747, prob at sea. Mar Abigail---. The widow
        mar Samuel CLEMENT of Saybrook, Conn.
    A6. Sarah, b 1718, mar John Shaw, res Niagara Falls, NY, d age 115!
    A7. Mary, b 1720, mar Gilbert Forsythe of Groton, Conn. 1741, rem to
        Horton, NS, one of the orig grantees there.
        B1. Jason Forsythe, mar 1773 Horton, NS, Mary Anderson
            C1. Enoch, b 1774, mar Hannah BISHOP, b 1780, a cousin
            C2. Mary Forsythe, b 1776
            C3. Elijah Forsythe, b 1778
            C4. James Forsythe, b 1781
            C5. Caleb Forsythe, b 1783, mar Charlotte Beckwith
               D1. Mary Eliza Forsythe   D3. Rebecca Julia Forsythe
               D2. Elijah Nelson Forsythe D4. Nancy Matilda Forsythe
            C6. Gilbert Forsythe, b 1786   C8. Rebecca Forsythe, b 1791
            C7. Jason Forsythe, b 1788   C9. John Forsythe, b 1793
        B2. Gilbert Jr., mar 1777 Ruth Kennie, and 2. 1783 Mary Coldwell, 3
            chn by first wife
            C1. James, b 1778   C2. Nancy, b 1779   C3. Ruth, b 1782
        B3. Caleb Forsythe, b 1756, mar 1782 Eunice De Wolf. He d 1816, his
            wife in 1819
            C1. John Forsythe, b 1785   C3. Eunice Forsythe, b 1792
            C2. Elizabeth Forsythe, b 1787 C4. Andrew Forsythe, b 1795
    A8. Nicholas, b 1723, d 1776? Mar 1749 Hannah Douglas, res Montville,
        Conn., where he had a large farm. Second Lieut. at Crown Pt., Capt.
        of the 12th Co., 4th Conn. Rgt. in 1759, d at New London, 1780.
        B1. Sarah, b 1750, mar 1773 Edward Richards (Hannah was dau of
        B2. Ebenezer, b 1751, mar Sally Pierpont, d 1782(Robt&SarahEdge-
        B3. Jonathan, b 1754, mar Anne Allen, d 1840 (comb Douglas)
        B4. Joseph, b 1758, mar Desire Gilbert, d 1834
        B5. Mary, b 1765, mar David Congdon, d 1843
        B6. John, b 1768, mar Mary Kilburn, d 1805
    A9. Eleasar, b 1727, mar 1750 Susannah Whipple, dau of Silas Whipple
        Rgt. Rem to Horton, NS 1760, 10 chn. Another record says 1726-
        1776.
        B1. Susannah, b 1751, mar Confort Davis
        B2. Thomas, b 1752, mar Amy Fargo
        B3. Anne, b 1754, mar Edw. Stebbins
        B4. Simon, b 1757
        B5. Rebecca, b 1759
        B6. Hannah, b 1762, mar Daniel Fargo
        B7. Lydia, b 1764, mar Jonathan Noble
        B8. Eleasar, b 1766
        B9. Mary or Mercy, b 1768, mar Daniel Minor
        B10. George Dolbeare, mar 1770 or 1760. Rem to Horton, NS, with
             uncle, John BISHOP and fam, res Gaspereau. Mar Jane Burbridge,
             relative. Desc now in and around Dorchester, N.B. a book was
             written about this fam ca 1918. Descendants to US.
    A10. Joshua, b 1733, mar Pattie Comstock

BISHOP, Capt. and importer in Nfld. from J (K. Mathews) See also Seary
BISHOP, a John Bishop was in Rock Cove, Nfld. 1786
BISHOP, Joseph, in Buck Cove, Nfld. 1793
BISHOP, from C.I. to Gaspe? unver.
BISSETT, BISSET. Several BISSETTS in Arichat, CB were owners of vessels there. George B. owned the IDA, built in River Bourgeois 1868, by Charles LANGLOIS.
BISSETTE, C.I. surname in Gaspe (K. H. Annett)
BISSON, vars: BEESON, BESOM, BESANT, etc. Current at Carlisle, Shigawake, New Richmond, Que.
BISSON, Philippe, b 1794 J, son of Abraham BISSON and Anne COLLAS of J, d Riviere Magpie, Que., 1883. Mar 1821 Bonaventure Charlotte BEAUDIN, qv., 1807-1855, dau of Jean-Baptiste BEAUDIN and Marie COUTURE, dit Bellerive. (Ronald Methot, Ville St. Laurent, Montreal, Que)
  A1. Philippe, b 1820 Gr. Rivere, Gaspe, mar 1850 Perce, Charlotte---, 1827-1857? Mar 2. Suzanne Duguay who d 1897.
    B1. Marie Odile, b 1851, Gr. Riv., d 1857
    B2. Rachel, b 1853, d 1918, mar 1874 Edouard Joncas, son of Etienne J. and Elizabeth Cyr, b 1847 Perce
      C1. Jerome Joncas   C3. Benoit Joncas
      C2. Joseph Joncas   C4. Zephirin Joncas
    B3. Philippe, b 1855 Gr. Riv., d age 2
    B4. Moise, b 1857 Gr. Riv.
    B5. By second wife Joseph Avile   b 1858 Gr. Riv., mar 1883 Marie MERCIER, dau of Jean Louise M. and Marie HUARD. She d 1916 Riv. St. Jean, Que.
      C1. Philippe
    B6. Jean, b 1860, mar Marie Walsh. He d 1918 Riv. St. Jean, Que.
    B7. Pierre, b 1862 Riv. St. Jean
  A2. Marie Anne, Marie, Nancy, b 1822 Gr. Riv. mar 1838 Francois BEAUDIN, son of Benoni Beaudin and Elisabeth COAL (disp 2/3) Marie d 1852
  A3. Elisabeth, b 1824 Perce, mar 1. 1853 Jean Baptistle Rail, Rehel, his second wife. He d 1869, she mar 2. Filee BEAUDIN? She d 1897
  A4. Jean, b 1825, Perce, d 1826   A5. Jean, b 1827
  A6. Georges Philippe, b 1829 Perce, mar 1850 Charlotte BELLIVEAU, dau of Joseph B. of Cap d'Espoir, Que. and Charlotte PAGE (disp 2/3)
  A7. Jean Elie, b 1831 Perce, d 1893. Mar Euphemie Rail, dau of Antoine Rail and Marie Page, or Pagee, 1831-1896.
    B1. Marie Ann, b 1856 Gr. Riviere, d 1904. Mar 1882 Leandre Methot, son of Dominique M. and Ursule HUARD. He d 1940 Gr. Riviere, Que.
      C1. Marie Euphemie, b 1883 Gr. Riv., d 1884
      C2. Marie Beatrice Victoria, b 1884, d 1885
      C3. Leandre Joseph Leonard, b 1886, d 1888
      C4. Jean Baptiste Elie, b 1888, d 1957 Gr. Riv. Mar there, Marie Eliz. BERTRAND, dau of Philippe B. and Elizabeth BEAUDIN, qv.
      C5. Joseph Adelard, b 1891, d 1892
      C6. Joseph Camille, b 1893, d 1968, mar 1. 1925 Marie Sophie Elisabeth Methot, 1903-1928, dau of Pierre Methot and Agathe Aspireault, mar 2. Georgiana Methot, sister of Marie
        D1. Joseph Leandre Marc, b 1927, d 1928, only ch by first wife
        D2. Marie Georgine Noelline, b 1933 Gr. Riv., mar 1953 Joseph Cyprien Boutin, son of Firmin Boutin and Marie Margaret Cauvier.
        D3. Marie Regina, b 1935, d.y.
        D4. Joseph Gerard Ronald, b 1936, mar 1963 Marie Simone Andree Nicole Brisset des Nos, dau of Andre Brisset and Jeanne Gagne.
          E1. Joseph Ronald Andre, b 1966, N.D. des Agnes, Mtl., Que.

BISSON 163

    E2. Marie Jeanne Nicole Louise Sophie, b 1972 St. Hypolite
- D5. Joseph Leandre Jude, b 1938
- D6. Marie Therese Cecile, b 1940, d.y.
- D7. Joseph Guy, also Jean Guy, b 1941, mar 1969 Ste. Anne de Portneuf, Sagneunay Marie Rose Monette Dube, b 1943, Bic, Que.
- D8. Joseph Eymard Orile b 1942, mar 1969 at Ste. Adelaide de Pabos Marie Jeanne Blais, dau of Pierre Blais and Alberta Leblanc
- D9. Joseph Leo, b 1944
- D10. Anne Marie Cecile, b 1945 Gr. Riv., mar 1965 Joseph Lorenzo Dugauy, son of Edouard D. and Alice Chapados
- D11. Jean Marie, b 1948
- D12. Marie Lise Paulette, b 1950, mar 1972 Joseph Georges Ulric, Michel Gougeon, son of Lucien G. and Gertrude Maloney
- D13. Gilles Methot, b 1951, Gr. Riv.
- C7. Joseph Elie Dominique, b 1896, d 1957 Mont-Laurier, Que.
- B2. Antoine Elie, b 1858 Gr. Riv., d 1918. Mar 1833 Sophie LAMBERT, LAMBRETTE, 1859-1936, dau of Denis L. and Sophie Tremanier.
- B3. Euphemie, b 1860 Gr. Riv., d 1943. Mar 1881 Baptiste Adelard Methot, son of J.B. Methot and Sophie Beliveau, 1857-1891, and 2. Lazare Dube, son of Dorothy Lafontaine, 1901.
- B4. Philippe Albert Edouard, b 1862, d 1903
- B5. Georges, b 1864, d 1942. Mar 1888 Emma Lelievre, dau of Isidore Lelievre and Elisabeth COUTURE, qv., who d 1960, age 93
- B6. Moise, b 1867, d 1962, mar 1896 Marie Philomeme Azilda Joncas, dau of Etienne J. and Elisabeth Cyr. (1872-1945)
- B7. Appoline, b 1870, d 1945. Mar 1896 Constant Joncas, b 1870.
- B8. Jean Baptiste, b 1872, d age 10
- A8. Louis, b 1833
- A9. Marie, b 1835, d 1871, mar Philias BEAUDIN, b 1837, son of Joseph B. and Emerence Blais of Gr. Riv. He d 1908, widower. He mar 2. Marguerite COUTURE, dau of Olivier C. and Veronique Joncas, who d 1908. Two sons, Zepherin and Wilfred.
- A10. William, b 1837, d 1923, mar 1. Marie Rail and 2. Georgina Methot
- B1. Ronald Bisson, b 1936, mar 1963 Montreal, Nicole Brisset
- A11. Genevieve, Jane, b 1839, mar 1858 Philippe Henry LANGLAIS, qv., b 1837. She d 1907. Philippe was the son of Philippe LANGLOIS and Euphemie COUTURE
- A12. Esther, b 1841?, mar 1862 Herman Tetu, 1833-1885. She d 1908.
- A13. Moise, b 1843, d 1908. Mar Celice, Celisse, Lebreux, dau of Alex. L. and Lucie Joncas. She d 1903.
  - B1. Philippe   B2. Jean   B3. Joseph   B4. Arthur
- A14. Charlotte, b 1847, d 1924. Mar Clement Dupuis, son of Clement D. and Esther Duguay. He d 1932.
- A15. Marie Louise?, d 1906 Gr. Riv. Mar 1857 (under name of Elizabeth) Fidele BEAUDIN, son of Benoni Beaudin and Elisabeth Coal. He was b Perce 1806. "It is poss that Marie Louise Bisson was perhaps the ch bp under the name of Louise, 25 Aug., 1833." (Ronald Methot)

BISSON, Daniel, b 1822 St. Brelade J, to Canada 1837 apprentice for Le BOUTILLIER fishery at Paspebiac, Gaspe. Later opened his own business in 1849; farmer, postmaster. D 1881, age 59. Mar Mary Caroline LE GALLAIS, qv., b 1824, dau of Philip LE GALLAIS, who came to Gaspe ca 1780 and Mary Caroline Holmes, of a Swedish fam. She d 1917. (W.S. Bouillon, Montreal, Que.)
- A1. Frank, b ca 1848, rem to South Prairie, Wash., mar ---
  - B1. Newell, res Tacoma, Wash.
  - B2. Dr. Daniel, b ca 1891, res Bremerton, Wash.
- A2. William, rem also to Washington State   A3. Walter, b ca 1865

A4. Daniel, b ca 1852, d 1923. Mar Annie Cuthbert, b 1848, d 1897, bur
   St. Peters, Gaspe. Son? Clarence, d.y.
A5. John Elias. A John was 17 in 1871.
A6. Caroline L., b 1851, d 1941, mar Philip J.L. AHIER, qv., 1849-1952
A7. Mary Elizabeth, b ca 1859, d age 5
A8. Elizabeth Jane, b 1867, mar Eugene Auguste Albert BOUILLON, qv., d
   1942, 7 chn. Bur St. Peter's, Paspebiac, with husband and father
Poss connected with above fam:
BISSON, Walter Giffard, 1864-1950, mar Sarah WHITTON, 1864-1934
A1. unver, James Giffard Bisson, 1896-1961, mar Laura Lalibert
A2. Florence, mar Joseph LE FLOCH, qv.
BISSON, Daniel, 1848-1933, mar Annie Baxter, 1859-1931, bur Port Daniel,
   Gaspe (GLF)
BISSON, John Elias, mar Matilda LE MARQUAND, qv., (GLF)
A1. Adolphus Stanley, 1889-1890
A2. Clarence, 1894-1895
BISSON, Daniel (Cf another Daniel, above) This one at Port Daniel, Que.
   1871, age 48, farmer. Mar Mary Jane ALMOND, b Que. (Census, Brochet)
A1. Daniel, 22 in 1871   A5. William, 14 in 1871
A2. John, 20 in 1871   A6. Thomas, 11 in 1871
A3. James, 18 in 1871   A7. Edward, 8 in 1871
A4. Joseph, 16 in 1871
BISSON, Charles, b J?, 25 in 1871, wife Margaret 26, and son Charles
   Jr., age 2 at Port Daniel, Que. 1871 (Brochet)
BISSON, Abner Cartwright Huelin, b J, to Gaspe 1901 for Robin, Collas
   Co. Mar Mary Ann BIARD, qv., 1911, 2 sons. She d 1923, age 43.
   Bisson built the first hotel in Perce, the PERCE ROCK HOUSE. Widowed,
   he mar 2. Alice Miller, Abner rem to J in 1946, d there 1959, age 72
   (Cent. Bklt., W.C. Bisson, Hull, Que.)
A1. William Charles, b 1912 Perce, educated England, mar in Canada 1953
   Myrtle Davidson of Gatineau, Que.
   B1. Douglas, b 1954   B3. Barbara, b 1961
   B2. Beverly, b 1958   B4. Eleanor, b 1963
A2. Abner Watson, b 1914 Perce, educated England, served in WWII with
   C.A.F. In 1946 mar Montreal Irene Hartery of London, no issue
A3. Robert Chalmers Bisson, son of Abner and Alice, res Jersey
BISSON, Elsie, b J, sister of Abner above, rem to New Carlisle, Que.,
   mar 1. Thomas Bisson, and 2. ---Watt. Res New Carlisle, Que.
A1. Stanley Bisson
BISSON, Ann, b ca 1816 J, mar Francois BEAUDIN, qv., d 1906, N.B.
   (Robichaud)
BISSON, Alfred W., from J to Montreal, commercial traveler, arrived ca
   1901 (Luce)
BISSON, Bessie, 1883-1960, bur Port Daniel, Gaspe
BISSON, Clara May, 1895-1953, bur Gaspe
BISSON, George, d WWI, memorial Port Daniel, Que. (GLF)
BISSON, Henrietta Kate, b J?, mar John Francis LE GRESLEY, 1878-1946,
   bur St. Peters, Paspebiac, Que. (GLF)
BISSON, Herman, 1874-1957, mar Ida Jane YOUNG (GLF)
BISSON, Jeannie C., 1894-1919, res Port Daniel, Que. (GLF)
BISSON, John, 1850-1925, mar Martha AMELIA LUCAS, 1857-1930
A1. Thomas Clair, b 1893, d of war wounds 1923, bur Port Daniel, Que.
BISSON,   Lillian, mar Harold Cleveland LE GRAND, qv., res W.
   Paspebiac, dau of Walter B. of J.
BISSON, Mary Ann, 1877-1960, wife of Edmund YOUNG, 1874-1959, see
   Herman, above
BISSON, Philippe John, b J, in Perce 1861 (census)

BISSON

BISSON, Sydney, 1893-1957, bur Port Daniel, Que.
BISSON, Thomas Byers, 1891-1956, bro of Sydney, above, bur Port Dan. Que.
BISSON, Thomas, 1860-1891, bur Port Daniel, Que.
BISSON, Thomas Clair, d WWI, memorial, Port Daniel, Que.
BISSON, William, 1857-1932, mar Margaret A. Sullivan, 1860-1943, bur Port Daniel, Que.
BISSON, William, 1886-1952, bur Port Daniel, Que. (GLF)
BISSON, Channel Island name on south coast of Nfld. (G.W. Le Messurier) Seary
BISSON, changed in Nfld. to BEESAW (Shortis-Munn)
BISSON, Capt. merchant and boat keeper, from J in Nfld. (K. Mathews)
BISSON, Oswald, from C.I., merchant in Rossland, B.C.
A1. Dr. R.A. Bisson, in Vancouver, BC, 1940 (Chan. Is. Society)
BISSON, Edw. Le Couteur, b 1845 J, mar Sophie GRUCHY, qv., sev chn who d.y. (Dorothy Cushing, Halifax, N.S.)
  A1. Lydia, b J, mar Henry MANNING
    B1. Josephine Lydia Manning, b 1910
  A2. Mary, b J, mar Walter George GREEN
    B1. Gladys Green, b 1893
    B2. Margeretta Green, b 1894
    B3. Dorothy Mary Green, b 1898, mar Reginald V. Cushing, to Canada
      C1. Bruce Cushing, b 1932 Halifax, NS, RCAF pilot, mar Lorraine Champagne, res St. Albert, Alta.
        D1. Carole Daphne Cushing, b 1955 Winnipeg
        D2. Cynthia Denise Cushing, b 1956
        D3. Deborah Louise Cushing, b 1957 Halifax
        D4. Barbara Anne Cushing, b 1959
        D5. David Bruce Cushing, b 1961
    B4. Louise Green, b 1899   B7. Lydia Ruth Green
    B5. Evelyn Lydia Green, b 1901   B8. Phyllis Alma Green, b 1911
    B6. Walter George Green
  A3. Philip, d at sea 1915
BITOT, Adolphus, Doc, b J, to Hamilton Ont. ca 1912, mar ca 1945, no issue
BLACKLER, Mary, b J, related to the MACHONS and/or HOYLES, qv., was in Quebec City ca 1850, later in Vittoria, Norfolk Co., Ont., ca 1880. D Ontario? Unmar?
BLACKLER, in Cap Chat 1861 Census, Quebec
BLACKLER, also noted in B.C. and Nfld. See Seary
BLAKE, Philip, b J, in Gaspe, 1861
BLANCHARD, from J to Nfld. (Horwood) Many in Stephensville, Nfld.
BLAMPIED, also as BLANCPIED, BLANPIED, BLAMPY, WHITEFOOT and BAREFOOT
BLAMPIED, Mr. and Mrs. of Vancouver, BC, from C.I. ca 1910
BLAMPIED, Selma Alexandra, of J, b 1877, mar Francis John HUBERT, qv., rem to Edmonton, Alta. ca 1908, 4 chn

BLAMPIED, Louis Stanley, b 1890 England, raised in J, rem to Canada age 24, res BC, mar ---, 4 chn. Bro and aunt in N. Zealand. A dau b 1920 Ontario. (Margery Kapas, Delta, BC)
BLAMPIED, Jean, b 1720, from St. Peter J, rem to N. Zealand. (John B., Invercargill, N.Z.)
BLAMPIED, from C.I. to Gaspe (Betty Tardif and J.H. Le Breton lists)
BLAMPY, from C.I. to Winnipeg, Man.
BLAMPIED, curr Calgary, Alta
BLANCPIED, C.I. name assoc with Robin firm in Paspebiac, Gaspe and with the town of New Carlisle, Gaspe (Que. Prov. Arch.)
BLANCPIED, Charles, age 21, b J, in Cape Breton 2 yrs. by 1820, mar, 1 ch, had land at Descousse, CB, near Jean JEAN, qv. (PANS, C.B. land papers) See Charles, below
BLANCPIED, P., was part owner of the BARBARA, 108 tons, built in 1857 at Arichat, CB, wrecked at Halifax, 1875
BLANCPIED, Peter, b N.S. of J fam, ca 1839, shipmaster (census)
BLANCPIED, Charles, b 1799 or 1800 J, to Isle Madame, CB, ca 1819, mar, 1 ch. Had land at Descousse, CB, near John JEAN, qv. (PANS, C.B. land papers) Mar Elizabeth LE VESCONTE, qv. Charles was a shoemaker 1828, 1830, and a trader in 1834 (Stephen White, Moncton, N.B.)
A1. Rachel Ann, b 1826, 27, converted to R.C. Ch 1846 at Tignish, PEI, mar there Patrick Power, son of James P. and Mary Lanigan of Indian River, PEI
A2. Caroline Jean, bp 1828 at Arichat, CB, St. John's Angl. Ch
A3. Philip Abraham Joshua, bp 1830 at Arichat
A4. Mary, bp 1832, Arichat
A5. John George, bp 1834, Arichat
BLAMPIED, Charles Jean, of J, res Arichat at the same time as the above Charles. Poss mar 1. Elizabeth JEAN, who d ca 1827, and 2. Charlotte Leblanc, who d 1875, ca age 80, b Arichat, dau of Augustin L. and Anne Bellefontaine (Stephen White, Moncton, N.B.) Charles d 1849.
A1. Charles Jean, b ca 1828, mar 1854 at Arichat Sabine Vigneau, dau of Renaud and Brigitte LANGLOIS. He was a sea capt. in 1866
B1. Marie Elizabeth Athalie, b 1856
B2. Sabine Eugenie, b 1858, d.y., as Eugenie-Henriette?
B3. Charlotte Eugenie, b 1860, d 1934. Mar 1882 at Somerville, Mass., Jean Louis SAMSON, qv., son of Sebastian S. and Rose Hureau of Somerville, formerly of Arichat. Her husband was a plasterer and bricklayer, who d 1929 at Somerville
B4. Louise, b ca 1862, d 1896 Weymouth, Mass., mar Emmeline ---
A2. Henriette, b ca 1803, mar Aime LANGLOIS, son of Jos. L. and Marie Leblanc
A3. Anne Elizabeth, b ca 1831, mar 1857 at Arichat Daniel Forest, son of Hilarion and Adelaide Paon. He was a seaman in 1871
A4. Jean, mar 1861 at Arichat, Louise LANGLOIS, dau of Joseph and Marie
A5. Marguerite Angelique, b 1834 Tracadie, d.y.
A6. Pierre Michel, twin of Marguerite, b 1834, mar 1860 at Arichat, Charlotte NORMAND, qv., dau of Joseph N. and Charlotte Landry. He d 1915 Arichat, a shipmaster in 1871
A7. Charlotte
BLANDY, poss BLANDIN, from C.I. to Ont. and B.C.
BLIAULT, Walter, from C.I. to Peace River Dist., Alberta, and to Vancouver, BC before 1900 (Luce)
BLONDELL, Capt. from G in Nfld.
BLUNDELL in Nfld. (Seary) C.F. BLONDEL of C.I.
BLUNDON, from C.I. in Bay de Verdes, Conc. Bay, Nfld 1860s (Lovell) Poss BLONDEL?

BODEN, fam from ? to Markham Twp., Ont., origin uncertain. Cf BEAUDIN, BAUDIN, etc.
BOGLEJI, from C.I. to Nfld. (Rev. Hammond)
BOALCH and BOARD, from G? to Vancouver, BC
BOGLE, Charles, b Gaspe in 1861 census
BOHEN, from C.I. to Nfld. (Rev. Hammond) BOHAN in Torteval G 1700s, and BOHEN in J
BOHEN, Jonathan from C.I.? was in Harbor Mille, Nfld. 1877. CF BOHON of J, also
BOITEAU, C.I. surname southern coast of Nfld. (G.W. Le Messurier)
BOIT, poss BOITEAU, Richard, from C.I. in Bay Roberts, Nfld. 1790 (Seary) Cf BOY, also in Port de Grave, Nfld. as George BOY 1802. Cf BOY, BOISTE of J (Stevens)
BOKEY, LE BOSQUET, of J?, Philip in Northern Cove, Nfld. 1799
BOLGER, James from C.I. to Nfld. In Harbor Grace, 1860s (Rev. Hammond, Seary) Cf BOLEOR of old J? (Stevens)
BONAMY, from J to Gaspe? "Bon Ami, Cape Point, in Forillon National Park, Gaspe, named for early Guernsey settler." (Clark, HEART OF GASPE, 1913, p 275)
BONAMY, David, son of David Kinsela Bonamy and Eliza Ann, b 1857, Gaspe (Church Reg.)
BONAMY, Capt. from G in Nfld. (K. Mathews)
BONAMY, Helier of G, Cape Gaspe 1777. Also a company. BONAMY AND LE MESURIER, with 58 men
BONAMY, P., in Gaspe (Gravel)
BOND, David, b 1937 St. Martins G, son of Mildred Amelia BOUGOURD, qv., and Harold Wilfred BOND, rem to Canada 1956, mar Ardele--- (David Bond, Willowdale, Ont.)
A1. Brian David, b 1963   A2. James Hedley, b 1965
BONES, Maurice, from C.I. to Great Placentia, Nfld., 1860s. Cf BON or LE BON of J
BONNELL, from C.I. to Nfld. (Shortis-Munn) See also SEARY
BONNER, from C.I.? to Nfld. (Seary) Cf BONHEUR from C.I.?
BONOVIEW? from C.I. in Maritimes fisheries (K. Mathews) Cf LE BONTEVUE in JANVRIN Genealogy
BONOVRIER, Capt. and boat keeper from J in Nfld. (K. Mathews)
BOONE, said by corr to be C.I. surname in Nfld. (Noel) See also Seary
BORDEN in Nfld. (Seary) Cf BOURDON, BORDON of J (Stevens)
BOSDET, J fishery and Hotel operators in Arichat, C.B., N.S. (Bourinot) See Fixott
BOSDET, Peter, from J?, in Richmond Co., N.S. 1861 (census) with son, Peter Cline Bosdet. Conn with BOURINOT family qv.
BOSSY, John, 1840-1920, wife Jane, 1845-1918, bur St. Peters, Pasp., from J? (GLF)
BOSSY, John Philip, 1875-1956, a son? Mar.Mary E.Bunton of
BOSSY, Anne E., 1874-1894   St.Peter, Gaspe.
BOSSY, George W., 1876-1904, and his bro Reginald, who died at 8 mos. All bur Paspebiac, Que.
BOSSY, George, b J, mar Flore Tessier in St. Anne de Beaupre, Que., 1839 or 1899 (Gingras)
BOSSY, from C.I. to Perce (Cent. Bklt., and J.H. Le Breton list)
BOTT, Peter, b ca 1835 J, to Melbourne, Aust., son of Peter BOTT b 1817 and Rachel Mary BENEST, qv., b 1819 Longy, St. Anne, Alderney. Cf BOIT of J. See BOIT, above.
BOTT, John, bro of above, b 1853, to Walkerville, Windsor, Ontario, a maltsman ca 1880 (Fred Bott, Grosse Point, Mich.)
BOTT, Nicholas, another bro, came later, rem to Detroit, Mich., 1898.

Wife, Helena Despres d 1883 Walkerville,ONT.(CIFHS #54)
"Grandfather came to Canada ca 1910, farmed in Michigan before that, went back to Michigan around 1930."
BOTT, current BC, Burlington, Ont.; Edmonton, Alta., Mich. and Salinas, Calif. A Mrs. C.P. Bernacci, of Salinas knows of a book about the Bott fam in England and America.
BOUCANT, Capt. from J in Nfld. (K. Mathews)
BOUCHER, fam from G in St. Thomas Ont. 1800s. See ROBILLIARD fam
BOUCHER Bros. mentioned by Luce as a J fishery firm in Labrador
BOUCHER, merchant from J in Nfld. (K. Mathews)
BOUCHER, also spelled BOUGHE, and BOUCHIE, ship owners in Cape Breton, middle 1800s
BOUDIER, Ann, b St. Helier J, mar Thos. THACKER of Nfld. Also spelled TACKER
BOUDREAU, Charles, b C.I. to B.C., shipyards in Vancouver, BC, WWII
BOUDROT, spelled var ways in Cape Breton, NS early 1800s. Charles BOUDROT owned many ships there middle 1800s (Capt. Parker)
BOUGOURD, Wm. b 1926 G, son of Sidney B., and Lucy M. Bree, rem to Ont., mar June Le FEUVRE, qv., dau of Walter and Sheila Le F. of G 1948, res Aurora, Ontario (Mrs. J. Bougourd, Aurora, Ont.)
A1. David John, b 1949 G, mar Julie Flippin, 1972
    B1. Tara M., b 1974, Newmarket, Ont.
A2. Sheila, b 1954, Canada, mar Harry Turriff 1974
A3. Stephen, b 1962 Canada
BOUGOURD, Valerie, from G to Chatham, Ont. 1900, mar Smith. (E. Robert, Niagara Falls, NY)
BOUGOURD, Mr. and Mrs. John, res Aurora, from G, curr.
BOUGETT, Capt. from G in Nfld. (K. Mathews)
BOUILLON, Eugene Marie, son of Francois Bouillon, b Munneville-sur-Mer, Normandy, 1835, rem 1867 to St. Helier J, mar Marie Euphrosine Le MIERE, b 1848 Cadeville, Normandy. Mar St. Thomas R.C. Ch St. Heliers, J (W. Selwyn Bouillon, Montreal; Walter D. Bouillon, Paspebiac, Que.)
A1. Eugenie Sophie, b 1868 St. Saviour, J
A2. Eugene August Albert, b 1869 St. Saviour, J, rem to Gaspe, mar 1891 Elizabeth Jane BISSON, qv., at St. Peter's Ang. Ch. Paspebiac, Que. 68 yrs. with Robins there
    B1. Harold E., b 1892, d.y.
    B2. Lizzie, Elizabeth Blanche, b 1894, now res Toronto. Mar John R. M. Mackenzie 1922, at St. Peters, Pasp. He d 186, 1973, b Scotland
        C1. Leila Elizabeth, b 1923, mar Forrest Buckingham 1948, 4 chn, res Toronto
            D1. Nancy Lee Buckingham, b 1950 D3. Andrea Lynn Buckingham, b 1959
            D2. John Earl Buckingham, b 1953 D4. Cheryl Gay Buckingham, b 1964
    B3. Albert Howard, b 1895, d 1971. Mar 1924 Helen Mary Hamer, 1902-1971, res Mexico
        C1. Rothwell Howard, b 1927, res Los Angeles, Calif., unmar
        C2. Walter Duncan, b 1931, mar Carol Ann Kyle, b 1935
            D1. Graham Howard, b 1961   D2. Nancy Ann, b 1965
            D2. Heather Gail, b 1963
    B4. Sybil Mary, b 1897, d.y.
    B5. Ernest Linden, b 1899, res Paspebiac, Que., unmar
    B6. Leila Eugenie May, b 1902, d 1932, mar 1927 William H. LUCE, qv., J, who was then working for Robins in Gaspe. No issue. W. Luce res St. Petersburg, Fla.
    B7. Walter Selwyn, b 1904, res Montreal, mar there 1939 Margaret Jean ALMOND, dau of Edmond ALMOND and Caroline AGNES, qv., whose father came from J to Hopetown, Que. late 1800s, mar Marie BUTLIN. See AGNES, BUTLIN

BOUILLON

    C1. Joan Elizabeth, b 1940, mar David Sydney LANGLOIS, Montreal,
        1967. He was of J fam, b 1940 Grand Greve, Gaspe
        D1. David James LANGLOIS, b 1968 D2. Wade Roy Langlois, b 1969
    C2. Carole Diane, b 1943, mar Ronald Dalley, Toronto, 1966, divorced, mar 2. 1970, Richard A. Taylor
    C3. Katharine Margaret B., b 1946, mar 1970 James Peter McIntyre, Montreal
        D1. Ryan Walter McIntyre, b 1973 D2. Peter James McIntyre, b 1975
A3. August Clement, b 1871 St. Saviour, J
A4. Ernest A., b 1873   A5. Blanche, b 1875   (See p.298)
BOURGAIZE, Peter, b ca 1793, G, mar Mary or Margaret COUVET, LE COUVET?
    b G. Fisherman and farmer in Gaspe. This fam incomplete, and partly unverified. (Sylvia Wilson, Medina, Wash.; Census; family Bible)
    Some data may be in error.
A1. Mary, b 1813
A2. Abraham, b 1815 G, mar Mary ---, from Ireland
A3. Peter   mar Mary Court, a Scottish Gaspesienne.
    B1. Elijah, d 1959, mar 1911 ---
    B2. Abraham, b ca 1883 or 1887, poss desc. Stanley and Norman, plus a dau?
    B3. Edmund, d 1917?
    B4. Beatrice, mar Dr. Prescott NOURY, qv., d 1948
    B5. Tilly, Matilda?, d 1928, nurse
    B6. Florence, d 1953, nurse
    B7. Thomas, had 3 sons
A4. John Frederick, b ca 1819 G, d 1899, carpenter, Ship's Head, Gaspe.
    Mar 1843 Elizabeth HAMON, HAMMOND, qv., b Que. She was the widow of LE HUQUET, qv.
    B1. John Nicholas, b 1844, mar Christina MC KENZIE
        C1. Purl, b 1891, mar Minnie ---, res Tacoma, Wash. She was b 1891
            D1. Donald, b 1917   D2. another son
        C2. son
        C3. ---, res Zillah, Wash., 1920s
    B2. Philip Abraham, b 1846, d 1847
    B3. Abraham Peter, b 1848, d 1904, bur Cap aux Os., Gaspe
BOURGAIZE, current Gaspe Bay, Que. and Cap des Rosiers
BOURGAIZE, Enoch Archibald of G fam, res Gaspe, b 1870
BOURGAIZE, John Alexander, b 1872, res Gaspe
BOURGAIZE, ---, mar in Gaspe a Mr. ROBERTS, qv. A son, Joseph ROBERTS mar a cousin of McKenzie GROUCHY, qv.
BOURGAIZE, Peter, b ca 1793 G, mar Mary, b 1813 G
A1. Peter, b 1836 Quebec   A3. Celina, b 1846
A2. Matilda, b 1844   A4. Jane, b 1850

BOURGAIZE, Emily, dau of J. de Garst BOURGAIZE of G, b late 1800s, mar Grauvett, res Toronto, Ont. Had chn. Her bros and sisters:
A2. Basil, res Colorado   A6. Hugh, res New Jersey
A3. George, res Los Angeles, Calif., A7. Wallace, res St. Petersburg,
    d ca 1958   Fla.
A4. John, res Providence, R.I.   A8. Edna, res G
A5. Wilfred, Rev., res Africa   A9. Ida, res St. Peters Port, G
BOURGAIZE, a fam of bros and sisters, prob desc of Peter above, res Gaspe
A1. Peter, b 1836 Quebec   A4. Betsy, b 1845
A2. John, b 1843   A5. Celina, or Selena, b 1846
A3. Matilda, b 1844   A6. June, b 1850

BOURGAIZE, Mary Ann, b G, to Canada 1910, mar Thomas GALLIENNE, qv.
  (Elsie Coniam, Burlington, Ont.)
BOURGEE, Carter, from C.I.? signed the Petetion at Gaspe, 1820
BOURGEOIS, some said to be from G in Canada
BOURGET, Edward, had J fishery in Cape Cove, Gaspe, 1800s. A William res in Grande Riviere, Que.
BOURGET, Olive, mar in Gaspe, Edward LE BOUTILLIER, 1900s
BOURNIEF, ---, from C.I. to B.C., d there 1925
BOURINOT, John, b 1814 Grouville, J, rem to Sydney, NS. Was French-Vice-Consul, MLA, Senator in 1867, etc. Mar Mary Jane Marshall, dau of American Chief Justice Marshall, U.E.L. He d 1884. (A GREAT CANADIAN, article in Dalhousie Revue, Summer 1954, by Madge MacBeth, Can.; Who's Who 1967, John Aylen, Ottaws; Helena Bourinot, Simcoe, Ont.; Nora Bourinot, Ottawa, Ont.; Marshall Bourinot, Arichat, NS; Cochrane; Bruce Fergusson; ATLANTIC ADVOCATE, Aug. 1963)
A1. Sir John George, b 1837 Arichat, CB, clerk assistant in 1879, Clerk of the House of Commons, 1880-1902. Scholar, author, lecturer, Pres of the Royal Soc. of Canada. Mar 1. Delia Hawke, dau of John H. 2. Emily Alden Pillsbury of Belfast, ME, and in 1889 Isabella Cameron, dau of Rev. John Cameron of Toronto.
  B1. a son, d.y.
  B2. Desiree Elise, mar Henry Aylen, 1893, 7 chn
    C1. John Alden Aylen, mar Jean Anderson 1922, lawyer
      D1. John Gordon Aylen, mar Andree Choquette, 3 chn
        E1. John Henry Aylen E2. David Aylen E3. Elsie Aylen
      D2. Pricilla, mar William A. BISHOP, qv., 2 chn
        E1. Diana Bishop   E2. William Bishop, Jr.
    C2. Henry Aldous Aylen, mbr. Superior Court, Ont., res Oakville, Ont.
      D1. Derek Aylen
    C3. Dorthea Elizabeth Aylen
    C4. Lois Aylen
    C5. Gwenneth Marguerite Aylen, mar ---Graham
    C6. Elise Aylen, mar Duncan Campbell Scott, res B.C., 4 chn
    C7. Peter Aylen, mar, Director of United Nations Radio Div., res B.C., 3 daus
  B3. Sydney Philip, b 1891?, by I. Cameron, d 1968. Mar Helena Pepperdene 1914 Toronto, Ont. Res Simcoe, Ont.
    C1. Frances Evelyn, b 1917, mar Virgil Tyrrell, res Fraser, Ont., no issue
    C2. Grace Doreen, b 1919, mar John Schott, res Brantford, Ont. Mar 1. Wesley Weidrick
      D1. Dale Garnet Weidrick, Army Major.
      D2. Patricia Ann, mar ---Clist? 3 sons
      D3. Yvette Helena, mar, 2 daus by 1st husband. Robert and Sally by second husband
    C3. Isabelle Margaret, mar Charles DOREY, qv., res Sarnia, Ont.
      D1. Barbara Lynne Dorey, mar 1. Fern Boyer, 2. Gerald Wilson, res London, Ont.
        E1. Jason John Boger
      D2. John Louis Dorey, mar, res Petrolia, Ont., no issue
      D3. Robin Lee Dorey, mar, res Sarnia, Ont.
      D4. Holley Ellen Dorey, mar Gerry Stover, res London, Ont., 1 dau
  B4. Arthur Stanley, b 1893, d 1969, Vet R.A.F., WWI, lawyer. Mar 1920 Nora, dau of Sir Percy and Lady Sherwood. 2 daus
    C1. Suzette, b 1922, mar Edwin Charles McDonald of Bronxville, NY
      D1. Joan Bourinot McDonald, b 1948? mar Harry Alexander McConnell?
        E1. Alexandra Bourinot McConnell, b 1976

        D2. Heather Elizabeth McDonald, b 1954
    C2. Esme Joan, b 1926, mar R.J.D. Lewis of Pretoria, S. Africa, 2
        daus
        D1. Sarah Ann Lewis, b 1953
        D2. Jacqueline Clair Lewis, b 1956, res outside of Pietermaritz-
            burg, Natal, South Africa
A2. Marshall John, mar 1862 in Arichat, Laura Harrington FIXOTT, qv.,
    dau of Henry F. of Arichat. Marshall was the owner of coal mines,
    Port Morien, C.B. (Stephen White)
    B1. John, b 1863 Arichat, d 1929, Port Hawkesbury, MLA, 1916-1925,
        Collector of Customs, Mayor of Port H. Mar Minnie V. Hunson of
        St. Peters, Cape Breton, who d 1893. John d ca 1929
        C1. John J., res Port Hawkesbury, NS, mar ---
            D1. John C., b ca 1931
    B2. Bertram, b 1864, d 1948, bur Arichat, journalist, Newspaper found-
        er and publisher, RICHMOND CO. RECORD, 1897-1948, mar Carrie Carr
        C1. Marion E., d 1917, age 22 in Bisbee, Ariz., bur Arichat. Mar
            Griffith L. BOSDET, qv., son of Peter Cline Bosdet of W. Arichat
        C2. Earl, mar in Montreal
        C3. Florrie, b 1903, d 1938 bur Arichat, unmar
        C4. Marshall James, b 1904, publ. of Richmond Co. paper, 1948-1970.
            Insurance man, mar 1930 Cape La Ronde, C.B., Ina MAUGER, qv.,
            dau of John M., and Olive Latimer of Cape La Ronde, C.B.
            D1. Muriel, mar Fred McCathy
            D2. Marion, mar ---Dickie, electrician, Port Hawkesbury, C.B.
            D3. Laura, mar ---McCabe
            D4. Lloyd, mar Ruth Nauffts, res Cape La Ronde, C.B.
            D5. Cline
BOURINOT, a Capt. from J in Nfld. (K. Mathews)
BOUTILIER "... there is a Boutilier fortune buried down here in Cape
    Breton. My grandfather had half of the map and the other half was
    never found---ten one-hundred lb. leather bags of gold and sliver...
    in gold bars and candle holders taken from a church where the French
    protestants invaded. Seven priests and one Indian tried to get away
    with it, but were killed except this one Indian boy, who had been kid-
    napped in the first place by the Indians, and wasn't really an Indian.
    He was a Boutilier, he was my grandfather's great uncle, his name was
    Henry." (Henry Boutilier, Glace Bay, N.S.)
BOUTILLIER, from J to Cape Breton Island ca 1800
BOUTILLIER, see also LE BOUTILLIER
BOUTILLIER, Guillaume, son of Jean B. and Marie of G, "France", mar
    1777 at Notre Dame de Quebec to Anglique Guignard, dau of Julien G.
    and Maria Louise MORAND (Olivier)
BOUTILLIER, curr Toronto and Winnipeg, Man.
BOUTILLIER, Florence Catherine, mar Richard Gibbons, VI, qv. See
    INGROUILLE-GIBBONS. She d 1944, Vancouver, BC

Many Boutilliers in Nova Scotia, one said to be from C.I., others from
England via New England. There is a great deal of info. in PANS on the
French Boutilliers who came from Mont Beliard near the French Swiss border. This was a noted Huguenot area but the French Boutilliers in N.S.
were Catholic. The following info. from A. Caroline MacFarlan, Burnaby,
BC and an article in Cape Breton POST, June 19, 1959. "I have a copy
of the original passport issued to my great grandfather in the year 1752.
This man (poss John George Boutillier) his wife and four children, with
the consent of their sovereign (King George II) left Europe in that year,
and as the passport states, they resolved to settle in New England,

under the rule of His Brittanic Majesty,..."Later Calnek states that the family came to Nova Scotia and settled at St. Margaret's Bay. Calnek'sgreat grandfather then came to Cape Breton and settled at old Bridgeport. He had 10 sons and 4 daughters, who married and settled either in N.S. or returned to Britt, Iowa." "One son, Henry, my great grandfather, remained in Cape Breton. I believe most of Henry's family went to Iowa, or Penna. My grandfather Thomas, one of the sons, remained in Sydney, Cape Breton. . . .We always believed that the Boutilliers, Huguenots, either went to Holland or possibly England, the names being quite anglicized. . . .my mother told me that her grandfather Henry lived to be 103 years old. It is quite conceivable that they may have settled in the Channel Islands after fleeing France, and not have been as we supposed, having fled to Holland. D'Auvergnes related. Many in Iowa changed their name to BUTLER. Related to Louis XIV, the Sun King, poss bastard son?"
BOUTON, from J to Cape Breton, NS, also in Nfld. (Seary)
BOWDEN in Nfld. (Seary) Cf BEAUDIN of J (Stevens)
BOYCE in Nfld. (Seary) Cf BOYCE of J (Stevens)
BOWER, from C.I. to Gaspe (Perce Cemetery, Syvret)
BOWER, at Perce, related to Mrs. JEAN of Coin du Banc (GLF)
BOWER, Eliza Jane of Perce, mar William JEAN, qv., res Montreal
BOWER, Cecilia and Lillian, res Montreal, desc of Jerseymen, cousins
  of John BOWER of St. Mathew, J, and of Snowden BOWER of St. Ouen, J
  (GLF)
BOWER, Francis, 1857-1945, bur St. Pauls, Perce, Gaspe, mar Elizabeth
  Mary LE BRETON (Cent. Bklt.)
BOYLE, see BOGLE
BOY, cf BOIS, DU BOIS, George, in Port de Grave, Nfld. 1802, from C.I.?
BRACHE, Miriam, b G, dau of Wm. B., to Canada ca 1924, mar Ernest DENNIS. She d Toronto 1972. He d 1958? (Joan Ingram) See also KEYHO
BRACHE, Zelia, sister of Miriam, b G, mar Wm. de GARIS KEYHO, qv., she
  d Toronto 1971 (David Keyho, Kitchener, Ont.)
BRADFORD, member of C.I. Soc., Victoria, BC 1941
BRADTHRAFT, Bradthaft, Capt. from G in Nfld. (K. Mathews)
BRAIN, BRANE, DE BRANE, BRENNE, BRUNE, BRAME, BRINE, qv., See also Seary
BRAIN, member of Victoria BC Chan. Is. Society, 1940
BRAY, "I do have a Bray family Bible, pictures and the fam tree, but
  it doesn't go back to the Islands. There is just a note that the
  fam came to the USA from the Chan. Islands." (M. Depew, Simcoe, Ont.)
BRAY, Frederick, from J in Burlington, Ont. 1859, farmer and orchardist (Cumming)
BRAY, Thomas, a fishery out of Blanc Sablon 1800s. See Seary
BRAY, gravestone in Annapolis, NS, 1700s
BRAY, Thomas, had land in Cape Breton 1825 (C.B. land papers, PANS)
BRAY, fam from Normandy to Jersey, then to Yorkshire, from where 3 sons
  rem to Canada. This fam connected with DE GRUCHY fam. (Mrs. Ernest
  Bray, Toronto, Ont.)
BRAY, Arthur, mar twice
A1. James, b England, mar, 2 sons, 1 dau in England
A2. Ernest, served WWI or II, d 1968. Mar Marguerite Vivienne DE
  GRUCHY, qv.
  B1. Wm. Ernest, b ca 1914, res Toronto. Veteran
    C1. Robert Wilson, b ca 1950, teacher, mar Kathleen E. Walker
  B2. John, b ca 1928, mar Kathleen M. Harris
    C1. Laura Verna   C2. Sharyn Kathleen, mar Scott Gordon 1972
  B3. Edgar, res Vancouver, BC
BRAY, Harry, official in WW Vet. Soc., Ontario, from C.I.

BRAY   173

BRAY, "His grandfather came from Devon. My grandfather and father came
from Guernsey and Alderney in 1879 and settled in Chatham, Ont."
(LE HURAY, qv.)
BREE, Channel Islanders in the Maritimes Fisheries (J.H. Le Breton List)
BREHAUT, see BURHOE, P.E.I. (Some data in doubt.Check records!)
It is probable that most of the Brehaut descendants in Canada are
from the three or more Brehauts settled in PEI in the late 1700s and
early 1800s. There may be a more complete record with the Brehauts in
Danvers, Mass., or with some families in PEI, but the data below was
all that was available to the compiler at this time. At least three
heads of families were located in PEI. Henry, b 1767 G; James, thought
to have arrived the earliest, and possibly a cousin of Henry; thirdly,
John, b 1757 G. There is a Mary Cornfoot Brehaut History Award given
in PEI, prizes are awarded for the best projects by high school students
on PEI history. (HERITAGE, Arthur Davy, Guernsey Cove, PEI; Susan
Burhoe, Bethesda, Md.; J. Robert Mutch, C'town, PEI; J. Hedley Brehaut,
Danvers, Mass.; Mrs. Cecil Brehaut, Vancouver, BC; Leland Nicolle,
Murray River, PEI; Gary Brehaut, Toronto, Ont.; Joan Stockdale, Guernsey; Mrs. Marie de Garis, Guernsey) SEE LATE ADDITIONS AND CORRECTIONS
BREHAUT, Henry, b 1767 G, son of Henry B. and Elizabeth, nee Brehaut.
  A cooper. Mar 1791 Elizabeth Pulham of England. He had worked at
  his trade in the Islands, in France and in Spain. They sailed with
  a group of about 75 persons, mostly Channel Islanders, from Southhampton, England to PEI in 1806, their vessel being conveyed by a
  man-o-war part way, owing to the war between England and France. He
  is said to have brought 300 guineas as capital to get a start in Canada. See NICOLLE, LE MARCHANT, MACHON, ROBERTS, DE JERSEY, TAUDVIN
  and LE LACHEUR, other members of the same settlement group. Henry d
  1848, his wife in 1864. Said to be of "medium height, thin and with
  quick movements, but of a jovial and happy disposition."
A1. Henry, b 1792 G, mar Frances THORNE, 10 chn, six living in 1906
    B1. Peter, mar Elizabeth Ferguson, of Murray River, PEI(or Henry?
        C1. Roy Clarence, mar, a son, Peter   (b1823, mar MariaMachon)
        C2. Cecil Henry, mar Joan ---, res Vancouver, BC
            D1. Charles Henry, b 1938, mar Jeannie Palycia 1966, res Isling-
                ton, Ont.
                E1. Paul Henry, b 1968   E2. Glen M., b 1970
            D2. William George, mar Janice Mae Nettle 1971, res Powell River,
                BC
        C3. E. Bert
        C4. Leonard, mar Louise ---, res Charlottetown, PEI, a son, Boyd
A2. Daniel, b 1792 G, mar Isabella Bell, 7 chn
A3. Thomas Smith, b 1796 G, rem to Miramichi, PEI, mar Sarah Noble, 8
    chn. Two sons rem to Douglasfield, NB, others to U.S.
A4. Elizabeth, b 1798 G, mar James Laird Noble of Vernon River, PEI, 4
    chn: one dau mar, d.y.; her 4 chn raised by grandmother Brehaut.
A6. James, b 1804 G, mar Elizabeth Bell of Murray Harbour, res Summer-
    side, 9 chn
A5. Matthew, b 1802, d 1875, mar Ann BISHOP, qv, bp 1813. Chn.
    B?. William Bishop, b 1836, mar 1865, Margaret Burke (order of chn
        C1. Burke, d ca 1940, res Toledo, OH and Miami   uncertain)
        C2. Anne, mar --- MacEachern, res Lethbridge, Alta.
        C3. Charlotte, mar --- Snyder, res Nevada   C6. Harry, Henry, res
        C4. Laura, mar --- Spurling, res Burmuda   Toledo, OH
        C5. May, unmar, res Boston and C'town, PEI C7. Frederick, d.y., BC
        C8. William Melville, b 1872, mar
SEE LATE ADDITIONS AND CORRECTIONS PAGES, Also p.418 and 548

A7. Margaret, b PEI, mar Henry Sencabaugh, 7 daus
A8. Joseph, b PEI, mar Susan White of Murray River, PEI, 12 chn, including .Charlotte,below, more in Ch. Island Collection.
   B1. Charlotte, mar ---Murray, res St. Paul, Minn. B2. Bessie
A9. Charlotte, b Murray Harbour PEI, mar James Sensabaugh, 8 chn
BREHAUT, James, said to have met the Henry Brehaut fam when they arrived in PEI, having been there ten years, 11 chn. James and Henry said to be cousins.
BREHAUT, George Hammon, of a PEI fam, mar Margaret McKinnon (Joan Brehaut, Vancouver, BC)
A1. Cora, res Vancouver, BC, McGill degree ca 1910, 86 in 1977
A2. Dr. Lester Brehaut   A3. Ernest   A4. Alder   A5. Hammond
BREHAUT, Judd, res Campbell River, BC, desc of a branch that settled in N. Battleford, son of Judd Warren Brehaut and Betty Rutherford, grandson of Maynard Elijah Brehaut
BREHAUT, Walter George, son of Edwin, b G, rem to BC
A1. Graham W., res Victoria, BC
BREHAUT, Peter, b G, was drown 1817 Quebec. He was merchant there, dealt in gen. goods, but mostly in grain trade. Papers, 1817-1832 in Dominion Archives. (Stanley Brehaut Ryerson, Montreal, Que.) Prob. mar Theresa LE MAITRE 1792? Peter may have been b in G 1764, son of Pierre B. and Marie TOSTEVIN. Widow later mar Wm. GRUT SHEPPARD from G?
A1. Peter Percival, 21 in 1827, left prov. in 1828 and d on a passage of his ship from India to England, 1820
A2. Marie Elizabeth, mar Wm. Crosby Hanson, Capt. in 71st Regt. Que.
A3. Catherine Ester, mar Edmund Wm. Bower Antrobus. A Capt. Brehaut mar E. ANTROBUS ca 1873. He was ADC of the 71st Regt. (MAPLE LEAVES, by J.M. Le Moine, Quebec, 1873)
A4. William Henry, a minor in 1817
BREHAUT, John of Jersey Cove, Gaspe, mar Elizabeth JEUNE, a dau, Mary Ann b 1845, Jersey Cove, Gaspe (Brochet)
BREHAUT, William Freeman, b 1874 PEI, mar 1902 Margaret Jordan, d 1965
A1. Freeman Jordan, b 1918, mar 1946 Ellen May Dulia Dunnington, res Colborne, Ont.
   B1. Gary Jordan William, b 1946, mar 1969 1. Maureen Jane Osborne, and 2. in 1972, Gundula Yolande Ella Wilke, res Toronto, Ont.
   B2. Dale Margaret, b 1948, mar 1975 Orville Broder Morrison, res Toronto
   B3. Virginia May, b 1950, mar 1973 Peter Robert John Raven, res Toronto
   B4. John Philip, b 1951, mar 1975 Susan Ann Hoare, dau Erica Ann, b 1977
   B5. Terry Lee, b 1955, res Colborne, Ont.
   B6. Gloria Sheila, b 1962, res Colborne, Ont.
BREHAUT, John B., rem from G? to Indian Cove, mar Elizabeth SARE, poss SARRE?, a dau, Elizabeth BREHAUT b 1836
BREHAUT, John, b G?, mar Gaspe? Elizabeth LE RHE, qv., a son (Brochet)
BREHAUT, ---, from G? in Cape Gaspe 1819, mar ---LENFESTY. A book publ. 1938 on LENFESTY Family by Charles Bertram LENFEST, U.S.
BREHAUT, P., cooper's apprentice, from G ca 1788, b 1764, son of Pierre B. and Marie ---, to Quebec (Stanley Brehaut Ryerson, Montreal) Also a Brehaut accompanied Gov. Montmagny to Quebec in 1636, commandant at Rois Rivieres, 1638-1640. Brehaut's wharf was near where Montgomery fell in the siege of Quebec, 1775
BREHAUT, Edwin, b G, son, Walter George, b G, rem to Canada (Graham

BRENTON, fam from CI to London, ONT.
(Brehaut, Victoria, BC)
BRETON, see LE BRETON. Also see Seary, re BRETON in Nfld.
BRETON, changed to BERTON, see Seary
BRETT, or BRITT, from G to the Maritimes (K. Mathews, also ship owner in Nfld. See Seary
BREWER, Robert, in Mint Cove, Conc. Bay, Nfld. 1803. This name assoc with some Channel Islanders (QAAM, census, Seary) Cf BRUERY, etc. of J (Stevens)
BRIAND, BRIEN, Capt. from J in Nfld. (K. Mathews)
BRIAND. "The French-speaking Briand group from Edmundston claim that the name was originally BRILLANT, and was found in Bretagne, France in the 13th century. Near about that time France was in the process of becoming a national state under the leadership of Isle de Paris. The Brillant group openly resisted the aspirations of the Paris nobility. They supported a noble from Bretagne, but eventually lost the battle...Their punishment was banishment or flight. Some went to Ireland and others to the Channel Islands. Both groups, however, altered their family name's spelling to BRIAND, though to the French person the pronunciation of that name would have been practically identical to that of Brillant." (Gary Briand, Douglastown, Que.)
BRIARD and BRIAND, sometimes confused in spelling, in 1800s, Canada
BRIARD, M., to Toronto from G
BRIARD, from J to Gaspe, listed by Betty Tardif (Revue d'Hist; Bourgaize, GLF)
BRIARD, Philip Hubert, d 1945 Melbourne, Aust., of C.I. fam, also his bro, Leonard
BRIARD, Alfred E., res West Paspebiac, from J fam (GLF) current Gaspe Bay and Carlisle, Que.   (See Add. & Corr.pages for Briards
BRIARD, Elias J, 1862-1930, res Gaspe (GLF)   below)
BRIARD, Louisa, 1875-1942, wife of Elias Wm. LE GRAND, qv., res West Paspebiac, Gaspe (GLF)
BRIARD, Annie Alma, 1896-1954, wife of Ogilvy McLellan, res W. Pasp. (GLF)
BRIARD, in Gaspe and St. Catherines, Ont.
BRIARD, George, b J, in Gaspe 1861, with Mrs. B., Edward and Anne, both b Canada
BRIARD, agent for Robin firm from J in Perce 1861 (census)
BRIARD, John, b J, in Gaspe 1861 (census)
BRIARD, Stanley J., b J, mar ---LUCE, qv.
BRIARD, Francois, from J?, res Riviere Madeleine, Que., 1861
BRIARD, Capt., master of the CRC, a brigantine of J, from Arichat for Pictou, was driven ashore on the S.E. Point of Pictou Is., 104 tons. This was in the August Gale, 1873 (See Additions & Corrections)
BRIARD, Elias, b 1835 or 1846 J, em to Paspebiac at 13. Ship carpenter for Robins, later res Campbellton. An Elias mar Joanna--- b ca 1851, chn: Elias James, Ann Eliz., Eliza Amelia, Elvina, all under 9 yrs. A1. Walter (More in Q.A.in N.A)   A2. dau, ---, mar John LE GRAND
BRIAND, also spelled BRIARD, petitioner for land in Cape Breton 1815, 1819, Agent for Philip Robin & Co. in Cape Breton (PANS)
BRIDEAUX, Wilfred, ca 1905 St. Mary?, J, son of Philip John B. and Francoise Marie MORVAN, b St. John, J. He was one of 6 chn. To Gaspe, indentured to Robin, Jones and Whitman 1921. See under CHANNEL ISLANDERS IN CANADA, Chapter 3. Mar 1931 Dorothy LE TOUZEL, qv., dau of George Frederick LE T. of Rosebridge and Clarissa Guignion. (Wilfred Brideaux, Ottawa, Ont.)
A1. Wayne, Dr., Ph.D., b 1939 Gaspe, mar Marjorie Bennett, b 1946, res Calgary, Alta.

B1. Philip Lloyd Harold, b 1971   B2. Stuart, b 1973
BRIDEAUX, said by Shortis-Munn to have been from J, settled in Nfld. and changed name to Bridle. See also Seary
BRIDEAUX, Eli Jean, of J, mar Mary Ann PIROUET, qv., 14 chn, several of whom came to North America (Phyllis Brideaux, Sault Ste. Marie, Ont)
  I. Frederick J, b 1874, d 1943   VII. Agnes Jane, b 1882
 II. Florence, b 1876, d.y.   VIII. Eliza Margaret, b 1883, d 1965
III. Winter Philip, b 1877, d 1943
 IV. Annie Mary, b 1879, d 1935   IX. Francis Elias, b 1883, d.y.
  V. John Francis, b 1880, d 1934   X. Marie Rachel, b 1884, d.y.
 VI. Walter Pirouet, b 1881, d 1965,   XI. William Elias, b 1885, d 1921
    in U.S.
XII. Edwin Charles, b 1887 St. Saviours, J, mar Phyllis Marie Chestle in 1926. She was b Portsmouth, England 1905. Edwin came to Canada ca 1910 settled first in Quebec and then in Sault Ste. Marie, Ont. (Phyllis Brideaux, the Soc., Ont.)
  A1. Sue Chestle, b 1928, mar Charles H. Willet (See Additions and
  A2. Charles Edwin, b 1929, mar Elizabeth Draper   Correction
  A3. Richard Arthur, b 1930, mar Sheila Harvey   Pages for more)
  A4. David George, b 1932, mar Joan Coaker
  A5. Colin Robert, b 1933, mar Bernice Lambert
  A6. Philip John, b 1944, mar Marilyn Baker
XIII. Philip Herbert, b 1889, res Jersey
 XIV. Arthur Le Rossignol, b 1892, d 1906
  XV. Francis Elias, b 1883, d.y.
BRIEN, Charles M., b 1868 St. Mary, J, son of Esprit Pierre Marie Brian and Marie Louis LE ROI, both b St. Brieuc, Brittany, France. Charles mar Mary Blanche NIXON, b 1872 Caraquet or Shippegan, NB and d 1922 Gaspe. He d 1933 Kingston, Ont. Worked for Fruing firm at Caraquet, NB then res Miscou, NB, Gaspe and Grand Greve. Traveled much between J, England and Gaspe. Also worked for Des Brisay firm of Petit Rocher, NB. (Kenneth Annett, Ste. Foy, Que.; Donat Robichaud, Beresford, NB; Elsie Brien, Montreal)
A1. Mary Blanche, b 1892, mar Percival Annett, 1913
  B1. Kenneth Hugh Annett, b 1914, mar 1945 Velma Law
    C1. Christopher Annett, b 1946, res Charlottestown, PEI
    C2. Richard Annett, b 1950, mar Carol Mackinnon, res Toronto, Ont.
    C3. Andrew Annett, b 1955
A2. Hugh John, b 1894, d 1914
A3. Charles Archibald, b 1895, d 1917, mar Eva Miller
  B1. Cecil, d 1975, mar Elsie RABEY, qv.
    C1. Wayne, mar res Winnipeg, Alta. C2. Myrna Annett, teacher, Mont.
A4. Jane Gertrude Clara, b 1896, d 1975, mar James Capell, res Kingston, Ont.
  B1. Mary Capell, teacher, mar Anthony Eyton, artist, res London, Ont.
    C1. Jane Eyton, b 1961   C3. Sarah Eyton, b 1964
    C2. Claire Eyton, b 1963
A5. Marguerite, b 1903, d 1960, mar Robert Suddard
  B1. Marguerite Suddard, b 1929   B3. Wesley Suddard, b 1933
  B2. Robert Suddard, b 1931   B4. Vera Suddard, b 1934
A6. Mabel Ethel Helen, b 1905, d 1967, war nurse, WWII, bur with full honors by the Royal Canadian Legion
BRIDLE, of BRIDEAUX of J (Stevens) in Nfld. (Seary)
BRIDLE, George Henry, b 1883 G, one of 3 bros. Wm., rem to Pontypool, Wales ca 1900, had 2 sons, Wm. and Raymond. Thomas res Gosport, England, unmar. A sister, Clara, mar, res Bath, Eng., had chn. George rem to Burlington, Ont. 1903, mar Eleanor Maud SHEPPARD, qv., 8 sons,

BRIDLE 177
  BRIMAGE, SEE ADDITIONS AND CORRECTIONS PAGES.
  4 daus, 2 sons d.y. One son killed in auto accident 1965. (Duncan
  Wm. Bridle, Burlington, Ont.)
  A1. George Wilfred, b 1908   A7. Victor Thomas, b 1921
  A2. Douglas Steven, b 1910   A8. Duncan William, b 1923
  A3. Jennie Isobel, b 1911   A9. Georgina Mae, b 1925
  A4. Gladys Eleanor, b 1912   A10. Bruce Frederick, b 1927
  A5. Garnet, and   A11. Betty Marie, b 1929
      A6. Beryl, d.y.   A12. Donald Harold, b 1931
BRINE, Rev. Robert F., B.A., b St. John's, Nfld., Graduate King's College NS, ordained deacon 1846, priest 1847, by Bishop of NS. Appointed to New Dublin, Arichat, C.B., Cornwallis, and St. George's in Peterborough. (THE CLERICAL GUIDE AND CHURCHMAN'S DIRECTORY, by C.W. F. Bliss, Ottawa, 1877)
BRINE, William Edward, b 1815 St. Aubin, J, son of John B. and Mary Ann BISHOP, qv. Both fams said to have come from Clairmont in Hants, Eng., one or two generations previous to birth of John BRINE. He left J for Arichat in 1830 via brig MARIA, Capt. Breton, for five years, to be a clerk in employ of John JANVRIN, qv., returned to J, then in 1836 took charge of Janvrin estab in Descousse, Cape Breton, rem to New York City. Returned to Halifax where he had a business shipping and selling wood from NS to Boston. He became Prov. Treas. of N.S. and in 1840 mar Mary Tremaine JEAN, qv. of a J fam in Arichat (1820-1888). He d 1903 French Village, Halifax, NS (PANS, Clara Dennis, Louise and Jean Brine Brown, Halifax, NS; L. Surgery, Islington, Ont.; Elizabeth Kirk, Buckingham, Que.; Clara Dennis)
  A1. John Stannage, 1842-1895, see also STANNAGE
  A2. Louise, 1845-1929, mar Rev. Philip Brown, 1835-1892. Desc in Halifax
      B1. Edward Brown   B2. William Esson Brine Brown, d.y.
  A3. Edward Cornwallis, 1849-1930
  A4. William Clement, 1851-1903
  A5. Mary Ann Elizabeth, mar ---Chambers
  A6. Victoria Henrietta, 1858-1934, mar ---Lowrey
  A7. Albert Ambrose
  A8. Charles Le Vesconte Brine, named for an uncle, Isaac LE VESCONTE, qv.
  A9. Sara Jane?, mar in Marblehead, Mass. 1863, John I. Baily
  A10. Rev. Richard, see above, poss only a cousin or other relative
BRINE, Robert Frederick, b 1818, St. John's, Nfld., of J fam?, son of Robert and Elizabeth Brine, ordained 1846 N.S., mar Windsor, NS 1844 Gertrude Rosena Wollenhaupt, 1819-1889, d 1902 PEI (Elizabeth Kirk, Buckingham, Que.) See also Seary
  A1. John Frederick, b Kentville, NS 1845, M.D., Harvard 1868, practiced Canso and Hazel Hill
      B1. Harry T. Brine, telegraphist, Canso, NS
      B2. Maisie, mar Frederick Demont, Canso, NS
      B3. William D., settled Vancouver, BC
          C1. dau   C2. son
  A2. Henry Kenneth, 1848-1909, mar Elizabeth Welling, 1848-1906, merchant, Arichat, NS and Antigonish, NS
      B1. Percival Frederick, emigrated to Boston, Mass. as a young man
          C1. Elizabeth   C2. Robert
      B2. Garnet Reginald, b 1885 Arichat, NS, d Antigonish, NS 1973, mar at Westville, NS 1909, Kathleen MacLeod of Pictou Co., 1882-1969
          C1. Henry Kenneth, b 1910 Inverness, NS, d 1968, mar Arisaeg, NS, Jeannette MacDonald
              D1. Douglas Kenneth, b 1944, mar Linda Fraser 1969
                  E1. John Kenneth, b New Glasgow, NS 1974

D2. Robert Graham, b 1948 Pictou, NS
C2. Alexander Graham, b 1911 Inverness, NS
C3. Elizabeth Welling, b 1913, mar Antigonish 1937, William Burnside Kirk, 1910-1951
  D1. William Brine Kirk, b 1941 Montreal, Que., mar Ottawa, Ont. 1972, Valerie Levecque
    E1. Robert Douglas Kirk, b 1975
C4. Garnet Reid Brine, b 1924 Antingonish, NS, d 1954 Chatham, NB, mar 1947 ---Doris O'Rourke in Joggins, NS
  D1. Kathleen Alsoon Brine, b 1953 Chatham, NB

BRISTOL, Hillyard H., b G, mar 1921 Hamilton Ont. Other relatives of this fam in Norwalk, Ont. or Conn. and in Santa Paula, Calif.

BROCHET, Jacques, James, mariner of Gorey, J, rem to Perce, Gaspe, for Robin firm ca 1829. Poss returned to Gorey. Mar St. Saviour, J, Jeanne, Jane, PHILIPPE. Their son, John James, came to Miscou, NB 1833 on Robin ship DAY. B ca 1803, mar 1843 Henrietta, Harriet, LAWRENCE, qv., 1827-1891. Six Gen. in Bon. Is. He was a merchant, but suffered losses and his property was sold to John HAMON, qv. D 1867 Bon Is., 7 surviving chn. (Aldo Brochet; Rev. d'Hist; Le Moignan, Gallant; Cent. Bklt.; Census) (1993: SOME ERRORS IN THIS CHART!)
A1. Angelique, b 1843, d 1858 Bon. Is., age 15 SEE CH.IS.COLLECTION.
A2. James, b 1845, mar Appoline BERTRAND, qv., worked as fisherman for Le Boutillier Bros and for the FAUVEL firm, qv. Appoline b 1843 Grand Riv., dau of Pierre B. and Therese Bezeau. 7 sons, 1 dau
  B1. James William, b 1870, d 1968. Mar Ellen Jane Morrissey, qv., 1872-1945. He was a story teller and musician, 10 chn
    C1. Appoline, b 1891, d.y.
    C2. Joseph William, b 1895, d.y.
    C3. James Wm., Jr., b 1896, d 1956, no issue
    C4. Angela Bridget, b 1898, res Dunham, Que.
    C5. John Edmund, b 1900, bur Gaspe 1977, no issue
    C6. Joseph Leon, b 1902, res Sudbury, Ont.
    C7. Lydia Jane, b 1904, mar Wm. Beaulieu of Montreal
    C8. Marie Blanche, b 1906, d.y.
    C9. Mary Gertrude, b 1908, d ca 1926 Quebec
    C10. Mary Stella, b 1911, res St. Sylvestre, Que unmar.
  B2. Peter Timothy, b 1872, d 1964, Mont Joli, Que. Lumberman, mar at Bon. Is. 1892 Charlotte Plourde, b 1872 Dalhousie?, NB, d 1897, bur Bon. Is. Dau of Isaac Plourde and Euphrosine GERARD, qv., of Malbay, two chn
    C1. Mary Louisa, b 1896, mar 1929 Patrick Cotton, d 1971 Bridgeville, Gaspe, 5 chn
      D1. Rena, mar Jules DES LANDES, qv., res Acton Vale, Que.
      D2. Arnold Cotton
      D3. Alvin Cotton, mar Gisele Gendreau
      D4. Lenora Cotton, mar Regis Simoneau
      D5. Evelyn Cotton
    C2. Peter Isaac, 1897-1907
  B3. Edward, b 1873, d 1933, Bon. Is., called Edward BROCKETT!, sapper 159th Bttn., WWII, res Ont. 1919-1931, bur Bon. Is.
  B4. Thomas Albert, b 1876, d 1918 of flu at Gr. Riviere, Gaspe. A farmer, mar 1907 Emma Driscoll, b Seal Cove, ca 1876, d 1911 Gr. Riv., dau of E.L. Driscoll and Bridget Delahanty, and 2. in Gr. Riv., Bernadette Belliveau, dau of John, Acadian, and Marie Jeanne FALLU, 4 chn

C1. Ernest Emery, b 1908, d 1933, age 22 Quebec, bur Petit Riv., Gaspe
  C2. James Nelson, b 1914, res St. Eustache, Que., garagist, mar Mary Alice JOURNEAUX, b Bon. Is. 1916, 3 chn
    D1. Lois, mar Raymond Grant, 2 chn, res Mississauga, Ont.
      E1. Lee Grant, b 1967   E2. Tara Grant, b 1969
    D2. John Richard, b 1947, Perce, mar Susanne Pontbriand, res Two Mountains, Que.
      E1. Robert, b 1977
    D3. Linda, or Lynn, b 1952, mar Murray MATSON, res Two Mts., Que.
  C3. Mary Rose Roxa, b 1912 Gr. Riv., Gaspe, mar Montreal 1935 Baptist Church, Marcel Adolphe Brassard, b 1913 Upton, Que., d 1969 Montreal, 6 chn
    D1. Bernice Brassard, b 1936, mar Leonard McNeilly of Montreal, res Zaire, Africa, Salvation Army Missionaries, 3 chn
    D2. Roger R. Brassard, b 1938, mar 1. Louise Auclair, divorced, 4 chn, mar 2. Carmella Trimarchi
      E1. Kathleen Brassard   E3. Elizabeth Brassard
      E2. Jonathan Brassard   E4. Mark Brassard
    D3. David Brassard, b 1942, d 1962, mar Eileen Davison, 2 sons
      E1. Victor David Brassard, b 1960 E2. Carl Wm. Brassard, b 1961
    D4. Claude Brassard, b 1943, mar Nancy Svendsen, 2 daus
    D5. Claudette Brassard, b 1943, mar Arthur Bruce Guthrie, of Scotland
      E1. Paul Guthrie, b Thompson, Man.   E2. Adrienne Guthrie
    D6. Marcel, a fireman, mar Lorraine Auclair of Rosemont, Que., 2 sons
  C4. August, b 1916, d.y., bur Pettie Riviere, Gaspe
B5. Francis de Xavier, b 1878, d 1957 Gaspe, age 79, called Frainque, Frank, bur Perce, no issue
B6. Augustus, b 1880, d 1956 Perce, a fisherman. Mar 1917 Louisa Anna LAURENS, LAWRENCE?, b 1879 Barachois de Malbaie, d Baie des Sables 1960, educator, dau of John LAURENS, qv., and Caroline Maloney, no issue
B7. John Leon, b 1882, d 1951, Gr. Riviere, Gaspe, called Jack, travelling merchant, mar 1905 Kathryne Driscoll, teacher, b 1887 La Breche A Manon, d there 1918, flu. Jack mar 2. Kathryn's sister, Rosalie Victoire Driscoll, 1893-1971, issue by both wives
  C1. Bridget Alma, b 1907, d.y.
  C2. John Arthur, b 1909, Director of Quebec Grocers Assn., Bank President, Knight of Columbus, Chamber of Commerce director, etc., etc. Mar Fox River 1941 Cecile Tremblay, b 1912, dau of Joseph T. and Malvina
    D1. Earl, b 1942
    D2. Carole, mar Demetrios Karathanos of Montreal, a son, John, b 1977
    D3. Andre, B.C.L., mar Francine ---, res Quebec
      E1. Patrick   E2. Vanessa   E3. Justin Andrew
    D4. Claude   D5. Marcel, mar 1974 Diane Cote   D6. Jacques Arthur
  C3. Joseph Walter, b 1911, Gen. Merchant, res Grand Riv., Que., mar at Gascons 1936 Stella Brotherton, teacher, 10 chn, dau of Wm. B. and Angelina Cassivi
    D1. Marquita Anna, b 1937, res Nova Scotia
    D2. Therese Joyce, b 1940, nun, res Barbados
    D3. Peter Winston, res Quebec   D4. Edmund Carl, b 1943, M.D.
    D5. Marie Phyllis, b 1945, RN, mar 1968 George Davis Swan Jr., M.D. of Golita, Calif.

D6. Marion Claire, b 1948, RN, mar Andre Amesse, res Boisbriand, Que, a son, Steven, b 1977
D7. Joseph Leslie, b 1950, teacher   D8. Walter, sports educator
D9. Melvin   D10. Louis Edmond
C4. Percy Edward, b 1913, innkeeper, served R.C.A. Sgt. Royal 22nd Regt., WWII, mar at Wallingford, Eng., 1943 Elizabeth Vita Bates, 5 chn
   D1. Janet, b 1943, England   D4. Anne, b 1950
   D2. Donald, b 1947   D5. Hazel
   D3. Mark, b 1948
C5. Howard James, b 1915, insurance, founder HOWARD BROCHET, INC., res Chandler, Que., mar Mary Sylvia Levesque, b 1922, dau of John L. and Rosanna Wall, at Perce, 8 chn
   D1. Daniel, 1953-1958 D4. Frances, mar Toronto D6. Brian
   D2. John   N.A. Lee of Guyana D7. Caroline
   D3. Theresa   D5. Catherine   D8. James
C6. Stella Louise, b 1917, mar at Pte. Claire, Que. 1943, Joseph Raymond Legault, b 1916, res Pte. Claire, Que.
C7. Louis Ralph, b 1918, mariner, res Bon. Is. and Perce, mar St. Patrick's Montreal, 1946 Edith Anna DU VAL, qv., b 1916, dau of M. Wm. Du Val and Matilda Clara MAUGER, 4 chn
   D1. Lucille Anne, b 1947 Montreal, mar Perce 1969 Gerard Armand Donohue, mechanic, son of John Michael Donohue and Marguerite Gendreau of Perce
   D2. Louis David, b 1948 Bon. Is., biologist, mar New York City 1973 Margaret Louise Loughman Grant, called Madge, b 1942 NYC, dau of Maurice Vivian Grant and Maude Casey, res Guelph, Ont.,   E2. Ariana Maria b 1979 Guelph, ONT.
   E1. Danielle Corinne, b 1976, NYC
   D3. John Ronald, called Aldo, b 1952 Montreal, journalist, res Mtl.
   D4. Constance Ruth, b Perce 1954, amateur astronomer and botanist, mar Perce 1976 Renaud J. Cyr, educator, son of Roderique Cyr and Dorothy Sewell, res Murdochville, Que.
C8. Leon York, b 1920, d.y., bur Petit Riv., Gaspe
C9. Emma Mabel, b 1921, mar 1942 Gr. Riviere Hector NICOLAS, qv., son of Francis X. Nicolas and Helene Duguay, 12 chn
C10. Mildred Beatrice, b 1935, R.N., mar 1952 Maurice Omer Brunet, res Kirkland, Que., 3 daus
   D1. Kathryn Ann, b 1953, mar Pt.   D2. Jennifer, b 1957
      Claire Que., 1978 Peter   D3. Kristine, b 1964
      SMOLEN of Grt. Britain
C11. Normand Gilles, b 1926, town policeman, mar 1958 Delores Boudreau of Mont Joli, res New Richmond, Gaspe, 3 chn
   D1. Diane   D2. Pierre   D3. Denis, b 1971
C12. John Leon, Jr., b 1928, mariner, mar 1955 at Baie Comeau, Patricia Patterson, dau of Henry P. at Wakeham, res Baie-Comeau, 3 daus
   D1. Lynn   D2. Deborah   D3. Susan
C13. Joseph Raymond, b 1930, town policeman, res Schefferville, New Quebec, mar Marie GIRARD, dau of Leon-Druse Girard of Forestville, 3 chn
   D1. Lynda   D2. Richard   D3. Judith
C14. Marie Ada, b 1931, mar 1953 Ralph Keays, son of Joseph K., res Pabos, 3 sons
   D1. Norman Keays   D2. David Keays   D3. Robert Keays
C15. Marie Edith, b 1931, d.y., bur Petite Riviere

BROCHET 181

    C16. Douglas Earl , b 1934, insurance adjuster, mar Gaspe 1966
        Fernandé G. Giffard of Perce
  B8. Mary Alma, b 1884, d 1937 Bon. Is., mar 1907 William Maloney, who
    d 1956, res Barachois, both bur Bon. Is., 7 chn
    C1. Gladys Maloney, mar Rudolphe Flynn, a son
    C2. Richard Gilbert Maloney, d 1942 Sudbury, Ont., no issue
    C3. Sara Agnes Maloney, mar Jeremiah Donohue
    C4. Walter, 1911-1972
    C5. Robert Charles, b 1913, mar Brigit Irene JOURNEAULX, 2 chn
        D1. Anson   D2.Sandra Maloney,   res Verdun, Que.
    C6. Sydney John, b 1923, res Perce Add to this fam:
    C7. James Alfred, d 1939, no issue George Thomas 1853-1891
A4. Mary Rachel, b 1847
A5. Mary Jane, b 1849, mar ---McNulty of Saint John, N.B., son and
    dau, Matilda
A6. John Philip,b 1851 Bon.Is. d there 1924,mar Philamene
A7. Peter Joseph, b 1857, d 1933, no issue   Morrissey,d.y.
A8. Jos.; Alfred, b 1858, d.y.
BROCHET, a fam of Gorey J, at least 6 chn, including Francis, who had
  at least 3 chn
A1. Alfred, rem to Chile, where there are descs A2. Clare
A3. Joseph, b 1906, res Ottawa, Ont., where he was a librarian for
    C.B.C., retired to J. Poss others of this fam in Canada. One
    branch in Vale, G (Brochet)
BROCK, General Sir Isaac, see Chapter NOTABLE CHANNEL ISLANDERS IN
  CANADA
BROCK, Clement Powell, b 1886 St. Peter of the Wood, G, d 1971. He was
  the son of Rev. Henry Walter Brock and Amy Gabrielle Powell, 1857-
  1947, the third of 7 chn. From G to Lacombe, Alberta ca 1905. A son,
  Allan, still farms the place he homesteaded. Clement mar Kathleen
  Maud Ritson, 1887-1972, of Gateshead, England. (T.C. Brock, Sydney,
  B.C.; Dorothy Black, Red Deer, Alta.)
A1. Dorothy Margaret, b 1912, mar 1945 William Black, 1902-1962, res
    Red Deer, Alta.
A2. Thomas Carey, b 1913, mar 1942 Elizabeth Anne Bell, b 1916
    B1. Pamela Ann, b 1948, mar 1973 John Sutherland King, b 1946
    B2. Michael Clement, b 1950, unmar
    B3. Heather Jill, b 1952, mar David Gerhardt, b 1946
A3. Kathleen Marjorie, b 1916, mar William Papineau, res Red Deer, Alta.
    B1. Ruth Marjorie, b 1938, mar Frederick Grant Schneider, res Red Deer
        C1. Bonnie Lauree Schneider, b 1962   C3. Barrie Grant Schneider,
        C2. Barbara Lee Schneider, b 1962, twin   b 1964
A4. Allan Ritson, b 1921, mar 1955 Patricia Gray, res Lacombe, Alta.
    B1. Anita Louise Brock, b 1956   B3. Brenda Joan, b 1959
    B2. Douglas Paul, b 1958   B4. Helen Mary, b 1962
BROCK, Rev. Isaac, b 1828 G, son of either Rev. Wm. or Rev. Thomas
  Brock, rem to Halifax, NS, d 1907. Chn below not verified
A1. Cecil Victor, b 1856, mar M. Jessie Munroe
A2. Arthur Egbert, mar Lizzie Lindsay
A3. Alfred William, b 1859, mar Jessie Burwell
    B1. Ruby, b 1890, mar James Bell   B3. Arthur Stanley, b 1894
    B2. Herbert Alfred, b 1892   B4. Isaac Victor, b 1896, d 1923
A4. Gertrude, b 1860, mar Charles I. Raymond
A5. Kathleen, b 1962   A6. Edith, b 1870, mar Clifford Tufts
BROCK, Catherine Schreiber, b 1835, d 1894. Mar Col. L.W. Lovell, R.E.,
  res Halifax, NS, chn in Eng. (Brock fam chart by Howard G. Schreiber,
  1960, Dominion Archives)

BROCK, George W.J. of the Brock-Saumarez fam of G, mar Mary Emily
   Schreiber, a first cousin b 1827 G? He practised law in Toronto, Ont.
   1848-1851, d England, no issue. See also, Floud, Morrell and DE LISLE
BROCK, Addison Tice, said to be a desc of Sir Isaac Brock's branch of
   the fam. He was the son of Samuel and Almeda Brock. Samuel d Amherst-
   burg, Ont. 1890, born in Canada. Almeda b NY state. Another dau in
   fam b Lindsay, Ont. Almeda d 1908 Medicine Hat, Alta. (Mary Arens,
   St. Louis, Mo.)
   A1. Addison Tice Brock   A4. Annie Elizabeth, mar ---Baker
   A2. Henry Redner   A5. Mary A., mar ---Porter, res Medicine Hat,
   A3. George Wellington   Alta.
BROCK, George, b J, farmer, settled in Carleton Co., Ont. 1872, Glou-
   cester Twp., P.O. Hawthorne (Cumming)
BROCK, John, second cousin to Sir Isaac Brock. Is said to have settled
   in Thamesford, and Ingersoll, Ont. early 1900s (poss related to fam
   above)
   A1. Mary Margaret, mar Thomas Loughheed
      B1. Margaret Jane Loughheed, 1861-1941, mar Edward Browning, 1853-1933
         C1. Edna Browning, b ca 1892, mar Harry Skidmore, res Wallacetown,Ont.
   A2. Samuel
BROUARD, Philip, master and part owner of the brig CAPE BRETON, 114 tons,
   blt at Cheticamp, CB 1812, owned by Robins of J.
BROUARD, Peter, shipbuilder from G blt the GENERAL BROCK, 97 tons, which
   was transferred to J after completion. Blt a number of ships in Ship
   Harbour CB early 1800s: LOUISA, 1833, UNICORN, 1840, etc.
BROUARD, Peter, same as above, or another, built the barque WILLIAM, 288
   tons, the largest to come out of Port Hawkesbury, owned by Thomas
   MULLIN, poss MOULIN? from C.I.? A desc named Arthur J. Langley Sr.
   operated a marine railway most of his life. His mother was a BROUARD
   of Port Hawkesbury, C.B. (Parker)
BROUARD, Thomas, of Grand Greve, Gaspe, mar Sophia Johnston, a son,
   James BROUARD, 1840s. (K.H. Annett, and Ch. Records)
BROWARD, BROUARD, Nicholas N., b 1840 St. Sampson G, son of Nicholas
   Naftel Brouard and Judith ROBERT, mar ---Pearson, who d 1882, leaving
   2 daus. Raised by her sister in N.J., then by Mrs. Daniel LE PATOUREL
   in G. Both returned to N.J. and became nurses (Edith Hunziger, Clares-
   holm, Alta.)
   A1. Edith, b ca 1875, a nurse in the early 1900s but d shortly after
   A2. Bertha Togerson, b 1882 Vineland, N.J., d 1945, mar Arthur James
      LE PATOUREL, qv.
BROWN, Henry Smith, of J, rem to Nfld. Changed surname from Smith to
   BROWN after deserting from HMS RENOWN in Burin, Nfld. Settled Rock
   Harbor 1800s? (Seary)
BROWN, from G to Maritimes fisheries (K. Mathews) John, Bon. Is., 1871
BROWN, from G to Chatham, Ont. Cf also LE BRUN of C.I.
BROWN, BROWNE, boat keeper from G in Nfld. (K. Mathews)
BROWN, Mary Ann Moorish, b 1863 in The House of the Round Chimney, St.
   Sampson, G, mar John ROBERTS, qv., res London, Ont. and Vancouver, BC
BROWN, a Brown fam from the C.I. settled in Falmouth, NS in the late
   1800s (Duncanson)
BRUNET, Capt. from J in Nfld. (K. Mathews)
BRUSHATH, from C.I. to Nfld. (Hug. Soc. letter) Cf also BROCHET, BRU-
   SCHIE, BROUSSEAULT, etc. of C.I. See also Seary
BRUSHETT, James from C.I.? In Burin 1860s (Rev. Hammond)
BRUSHETT. "My father was born in Burin, Nfld. in 1862. He had three
   brothers older than he, which would go back to 1856. I think his fa-
   ther was born there. I understood they came from Bristol, England."

BRUSHETT

Many C.I. had connections with Bristol very early. (Susan B. Brushett, Victoria, BC)
BRUSHETT, d 1891 Collins Cove, Nfld. Mar ---
A1. James Brittle Brushett, b 1856 Nfld., mar 1884 Jemima Brixey Butler, 1862-1940, d Path End, Burin, Nfld.
    B1. Maybill, E.B., 1885-1953, d Lethbridge, Alta.
    C1. James Herbert Inkpen Hollett, mar May Bolger, Chemainus, BC
BRYNE, see BRINE
BUBAR, poss from BUBIER, Hug from C.I. to N.B. (See QAAM)
BUBER, Capt. from G in Nfld. (K. Mathews) (Consider also BUBIER, see QAAM)
BUESNEL, Alfred Stanley, b 1886, J, son of Philip and of Jane MICHEL, qv., rem to Chatham, Ont. 1912, served in Army 1915-1919, rem to Toronto, where there are desc. Related to Buesnels below, and to some in Australia
BUESNEL, R.M., wife of A.S., res Toronto
BUESNEL, John Mitchel, b 1882 St. Heliers J, son of Philip B. and Jane MICHEL, rem to Ont. Mar Annie May LEMPRIERE, qv., b 1886 (Ethel Warwick, Windsor, Ont.)
A1. Vera May, b 1907, d 1948, mar Martin Lizyness (Cf;La Jeunesse)
B1. Dorothy Odette Lizyness, b 1926	B7. Harry Lizyness, b 1938
B2. Donna Lizyness, b 1927, mar Venier	B8. William Lizyness, b 1939
B3. Martin Lizyness, b 1928	B9. Robert Lizyness, b 1942
B4. James Lizyness, b 1930	B10. Janet Lizyness, b 1947, mar Ewaniwick
B5. John Lizyness, b 1932	
B6. Ann Lizyness, b 1935	

A2. John Philip, b 1909, mar Elizabeth Tuck
    B1. Patricia Trudell, b 1939   B2. Karen Weatherhead, b 1943
A3. Ethel Marguerite, b 1911, mar Thomas Warwick
    B1. Norma Crossley, b 1932   B3. Joyce Rundle, b 1942
    B2. Joan Ostren, b 1935, d 1957
A4. Florence Marjorie, b 1912, mar Victor Bowes
    B1. Alan Bowes, b 1937   B2. Carol Bradbury, b 1944
A5. Frederick Martin, b 1925, mar Verna Horton
    B1. Linda McWha, b 1948   B5. Nancy Packham, b 1952
    B2. Barbara McAlpine, b 1950   B6. Carrie Buesnel, b 1964
    B3. Sheila Beintema, b 1951   B7. Freddie Buesnel, b 1968
    B4. Shirley Tope, b 1951, twin
A6. Monica Jean, b 1923   A7. Douglas, b 1927, both d.y.
BUESNEL, Philip and Clement, bros, of J, first cousins of Philip Thomas of Calgary, Alta., rem to Nakusp, BC in 1905. (Helen Dean, Chatham, Ont.)
BUESNEL, Frederick, rem to Chatham, Ont. from J
BUFFET, from C.I.? in Burgeo, Nfld. 1860s, Hug? (Rev. Hammond)
BUFFET, Benj. and George in Channel Nfld., 1860s (Rev. Hammond) See also Seary
BUFFET, James, mar Emma Mary Gwendolyn Ascah, b 1925, Gaspe area (Ascah Gen.)
BULFORD, from C.I. in Ontario, said to be from G
BULGER, cf BOLGER. Origin uncertain to compiler. Cf BOLEOR of J. Occurs in conn. with C.I. fams in NB and Gaspe, as well as Nfld. See Seary
BULLARD, Capt. from J in Nfld. Poss ROBILLIARD, qv. (K. Mathews)
BULLEY in Nfld. (Seary) Cf BULLEN of J (Stevens)
BUNGAY from C.I. to Nfld. (Rev. Hammond) Cf BUNOET of J. See Seary
BUNTON, ---, in Perce before 1829, members of the orig Ch on Cap Canon. One Martha B. d in Perce age 92 in 1942, b ca 1844. Her parents

Large BUNTON chart by Edw.Lewnard,Mt.Prospect,ILL, in CH.IS.COLL.
attended Old Christ Ch.   BUNTON, SEE GUNTON P.270.
BUNTON, Mark, Mbr of the Council of Perce, Gaspe. Origin uncertain
BUNTON, John, people's warden from 1930-1935, bur 1941, b 1859. His
  sister, Maria, said to be b in 1861, d 1924. A Mrs. Fred James of
  Phila., Pa donated the stained glass window in Bunton memory.
BUNTON, Jane, 1838-1907, mar J. F. DU VAL, qv.
BUNTON, Sara, of Gaspe, mar 1. Joseph Cass, and 2. Peter VIBERT, qv.,
  1800s
  A1. Caroline Cass, mar Daniel Mabe, mariner
  A2. Frances Cass, mar Philip VIBERT, qv.
  A3. Joseph Alfred Cass, machinist and artisan, Guelph, Ont.
  A4. Sarah Cass   A5. James Vibert Cass
  A6. Elias Cass, shot while duck hunting, age 16
BUNTON, George, b 1846, d 1946, mar 1. Catherine McTavish, and 2. Mary
  Young, res Perce, bur Anglican Cem., Cape Cove, Gaspe
BURDEN, from C.I. to Carbonear, Nfld., early. Cf BOURDON of J (Stevens)
  (Rev. Hammond)
BURCHART, Capt. from G in Nfld. (K. Mathews)
BURFITT, Joseph, from C.I.? in Nfld. 1860s. Cf BAREFOOT, BLAMPIED,
  MOUILPIED of C.I.
BURGESS, see BOURGEOIS
BURHOE, BREHAUT, John, b G, of fam that left France ca 1572, rem first
  to Gaspe, Quebec, then to Charlottetown, PEI, joined Army. Later
  settled Alexander, PEI. "I saw a brass wine pot that came over with
  the second lot of Brehauts in 1806. Also the Brehaut crest in one of
  the homes, and the cellar of the 1st home built, and site where they
  landed. Also second home built (still standing) of the John Brehaut
  I learned came in 1776. John married Jane Douglas whose father was
  a soldier at Louisbourg. John was her third husband." (Lynne Jenkins,
  Souris, PEI)
BURHOE, BREHAUT, this or another B. fam said to have left France ca 1572
  for G. John, b G, rem ca age 19 in 1776, settled first in Gaspe, then
  rem to Ch'town, PEI. Settled Squaw Bay. (Lynne Jenkins, Souris, PEI)
BURHOE, formerly BREHAUT, John, Jean, b ca 1754, 56 in G, rem to PEI ca
  1786, settled Squaw Bay, now Alexandra, PEI. Had been discahrged
  1784 from Br. Army, and had served in Amer. Revolution. In 1787 mar
  Jane Douglas, who had been widowed twice, Capt. Thomas Mellish and a
  Mr. Gretteau. John joined the Royal N.S. Volunteers Regt. (J. Robert
  Mutch, C'town, PEI) See Mutch's book, MUTCH FAMILY, publ. 1929
  A1. Susannah, b 1789, mar Robert Wood, res Alexandra, PEI. She d 1882
    B1. Jane Wood, b 1819, mar 1840 Robert Peel Jones of Hazelbrook, PEI,
      1818-1897
      C1. Robert Jones, b 1841, d 1926, mar 1873 Elizabeth Mutch, 1846-
        1920
        D1. Belle Jones, 1874-1952, mar Herbert Mason, Bunbury, PEI
          E1. Bertha Mason, b 1896, mar Stanley Matheson, res C'town, PEI
          E2. Alma Mason, b 1898, unmar, res Sea Island, BC
          E3. Mildred Mason, b 1899, unmar
          E4. George Mason, b 1906, mar Minnie MacDonald, C'town, PEI
            F1. Herbert Mason, b 1931, mar Glen Darke
              G1. Allan Mason, b 1952, mar Jean MacDonald
              G2. Sharon Mason, b 1955
          E5. Hazel Mason, b 1910, d 1917
        D2. Lottie Jones, b 1876, d 1953, mar 1900 Ernest Mutch, 1865-
          1945
          E1. Robert Mutch, b 1901, mar 1931 Helen MALLETT, 1907-1972
            F1. Ernest A., b 1932, mar Marion Moore, res Hazelbrook, PEI

                G1. Ernest B. Mutch, b 1955   G4. Kristin Mutch, b 1966
                G2. Lorraine Mutch, b 1956   G5. Tonya J. Mutch, b 1967
                G3. Daniel Mutch, b 1958
             F2. Lloyd Mutch, b 1934, mar Anna Chincilla, res Hamilton,
                 Ont.
                G1. Jonathan R. Mutch, b 1971 G3. Georgina Mutch, b 1975
                G2. Rebecca H. Mutch, b 1974 G4. David L. Mutch, b 1976
             F3. Donald A. Mutch, b 1935, mar Barbara Barton, res Grand
                 Bay, N.B.
                G1. Tiffney Mutch, b 1970   G2. Jason Mutch, b 1972
             F4. George W. Mutch, b 1937, mar Janet Powell, res Kentville,
                 NS
                G1. Robert P. Mutch, b 1962   G4. Janine Mutch, b 1970
                G2. Cheryl Mutch, b 1963   G5. Craig G.A. Mutch, b 1972
                G3. Leanne Mutch, b 1968
             F5. Dorothy E. Mutch, b 1939, mar Albert Stairs, res Kensington, PEI
                G1. Nancy D. Stairs, b 1962   G3. Melanie Staris, b 1967
                G2. Natalie Stairs, b 1964   G4. Michele Stairs, b 1968
          E2. Lois Mutch, b 1904, mar Harry Wood
          E3. Bernice Mutch, b 1909, mar Ernest Smith
       D3. Roberta Jones, b 1877, d 1952, mar John M. Bouyer, res Vancouver, BC
       D4. Hazel Jones, b 1884, d 1959, mar John R. MacGregor, Sea Island, BC
       D5. Amy Jones, b 1888, d 1962, unmar, res Mt. Herbert, PEI
  B2. Charles Wood   B6. Richard Wood
  B3. Henry Wood   B7. Prudence Wood
  B4. Samuel Wood   B8. William Wood
  B5. Joseph Wood   B9. Robert Wood
A2. John, b 1790, mar Sarah Hensley, 9 chn
  B1. John H., school teacher, d ca age 23
  B2. James, mar Mary Wood, 4 chn
     C1. Theophilus   C2. John T.   C3. Abbie   C4. James Ingram
  B3. Thomas, mar Maria Sentner, 5 chn
     C1. Albert C2. Ann C3. Hannah C4. Laverna C5. Maggie
  B4. Sarah, mar James Sentner
  B5. Elizabeth, mar George Sentner
  B6. William, mar Jane Wood, 8 chn
     C1. Albert   C3. Samuel   C5. William   C7. Sarah
     C2. Lucy   C4. Mary   C6. Susan   C8. Martha
  B7. Robert, mar Annie McPherson, 5 chn
     C1. John Thomas   C3. Maxwell   C5. William
     C2. Reuben   C4. Sarah
  B8. Jane, mar Theophilus Wood   B9. Martha, d age 8
A3. Robert, b 1793, mar Nancy Praught, 8 chn
  B1. Susan   B2. Ann   B3. Jane   B4. Mary
  B5. Richard, mar Susannah Wood, 7 chn
     C1. Mary Ann, mar Daniel McClennan
     C2. Theophilus, mar Elizabeth COUSINS
        D1. George   D3. Ethel, mar J. Harold McCabe
        D2. Lottie, mar W. Chester S. D4. Russel, unmar
            McClure   D5. Lena
        D6. Hendley, unmar
     C3. Thomas Knight, mar Elizabeth Ellen Judson, 8 chn
        D1. Lola, mar Mark Enman
        D2. Ella, mar Lee Enman

        D3. Ivan, mar Elva Rafuse, no issue
        D4. Charles, mar Prudence Wood
        D5. Annie, mar Daniel Myers
        D6. Mary, mar James Walker and/or Sterling Walker
        D7. Wallace, mar Islay Jenkins
          E1. Noreen, mar Weldon McCoubrey
          E2. Glendon, mar Anne Tweedy
            F1. Glenda Ann
        D8. Thomas Milton, mar Mildred Olive Tanton, 3 sons
          E2. Darryl Blair Brehaut
      C4. John, mar Margaret Duncan, 4 chn
        D1. Emmeline, mar Emmett Callaghan D3. Richard, killed in WWI
        D2. Shirley, mar Stanley Martin   D4. Sydney, mar Ann Ballingall
      C5. Richard Franklin, mar Jennie Graves, no issue
      C6. William, mar Laura Wood
        D1. Gordon, unmar
        D2. Frank, mar Christina Crossman
          E1. Raymond
          E2. Richard, mar Hazel Porter
            F1. Douglas
        D3. Emma, unmar   D7. Winnie, mar Frank Cass
        D4. Lloyd, mar Lucy MacEachern D8. Merle, unmar
        D5. Chester, mar Marion Beck   D9. Gladys, mar Harold Beck
        D6. Walter, mar Ruby Thorne
      C7. Henry, mar Susan Jardine
        D1. Hilda, mar Harry Dunbrack
        D2. Kelsey, mar Mabel Jenkins
        D3. Elwood, mar Eva Stewart
        D4. Susan, mar Earle Ballem, see BALLAM, BALLEINE
    B6. Margaret   B7. Betty   B8. Robert
  A4. William, b 1795, soldier who left PEI.
  A5. Richard, b 1798, mar Susannah Wood and/or Sarah Young (Sumner Burhoe, Bethesda, MD.)
    B1. John Young Burhoe, mar Thankful Wood, all chn but one to Mass.
      C1. Richard   C7. Eliazbeth
      C2. Theophilus, d age 5   C8. Havelock
      C3. John   C9. Thomas
      C4. William   C10. James
      C5. Mary, mar James Burke C11. George Newton
      C6. Abigail, mar George Joseph Judson C12. George?
  A6. James, b 1802, mar Christie Ross
    B1. dau   B2. dau
BURMAN, Charles Henry, b 1841 J, mar 1868 at Perce, Ellen Lamb, res Malbaie, descendants in Montreal
BURT, John, missionary from C.I.? in Nfld. 1800s, for S.P.G. See also Seary
BURTIN, Charles from C.I. in Harbour Buffett 1860s (Rev. Hammond)
BUSHELL, BUSHALL, merchant from J in Nfld. (K. Mathews)
BUSLEY, 3 sisters from St. Sampson G to Ontario, 1911
BUSLEY, E. May, b St. Sampson G 1890, to Canada, mar W. McIlroy (Mrs. M. Hamilton, Ont.)
BUSLEY, Florence, b 1889 St. Sampson G, to Canada, Pres. Hamilton C.I. Society, mar Fred DAVIS, qv.
BUSLEY, Charles, b 1893, to Ontario, mar, a dau, Grace
BUSLEY, William, b G, to Belfast, Ireland
BUSSEY, John, had land in Rock Cove, Nfld. 1775. Some fams of this and similar surnames are descended from the BYSSE, BUSSY, BUZZELL, BUSSEL,

etc. Fams of J, spelled many different ways. See QAAM (See also Stevens and Seary)
BUSSEY, Joseph in Buck Cove Nfld. 1805, and Thomas in Salmon Cove 1799 (Seary)
BUTLER, agent from G and Liverpool, in Nfld. (Seary) Cf LE BOUTILLIER of J and G (Some translated LE BOUTILLIER to English equivalent in Canada and U.S.)
BUTLER, BOUTILLIER, LE BOUTILLIER, from J in Maritimes fisheries (K. Mathews) See Seary
BUTLIN, Thomas, age 40 in 1871 census, b J, of English fam, farmer and fisherman, d 1902, mar Elizabeth D. SAMSON, qv., age 42 in 1871. Rem to Bon. Is. 1859 or before (Aldo Brochet) 7? chn.
A1. Elizabeth Marie, b 1859 Bon. Is., Gaspe, mar   desc in Gaspe Basin
A2. Mary Elizabeth, b ca 1861, mar Charles BIARD of Perce, see BIARD
A3. George, b ca 1863, mar Elizabeth Saint AMAND
A4. Philip, b ca 1865, mar Maria KRUSE, qv. Desc.in Oswego,NY
A5. Anne, b ca 1868, mar John NOEL, poss desc in J
A6. Jane, b ca 1870 (Some Butlins bur St. Paul Angl. Cem., Perce)

BUTLIN, Maria, b J, mar Frank AGNES of J, teacher at Hopetown, Que. Cf BUTLAND?
BUTT, John, in Northern Cove, Nfld. 1802, said to have been orig BOUTE-VILLON See also Seary
CABLE in Nfld. (Seary) Cf CABELDU of J (Stevens)
CABELDU, Francois, Stonemason, and wife Jeanne GALLIE, mar 1822 St. Heliers J, at least 7 chn: son, d.y., Francois, Jean, Samuel, Philippe, Jeanne, and Francois Joseph. Two of these, at least, came to Canada. (Marion Casselman, Hepworth, Ont.; Frances Edwards, Deep River, Ont.)
II. Jean, b 1826, mar 1852, Jane LE GALLAIS, qv., who d 1889, bur St. Saviours ? J
A1. Jane Emelie, b 1853, mar Eli Cunningham, res Guelph, Ont.
   B1. Maud Cunningham, b Guelph, mar Harry Kitchen
      C1. David Kitchen   C2. Robert Kitchen
   B2. Robert, d.y.?
   B3. Robert Cunningham
   B4. Margaret Cunningham, mar Frank Budd
   B5. Betty Cunningham, mar Louis Morenze
   B6. Alfred Cunningham
   B7. Frank Cunningham, rem to Winnipeg, Man.
   B8. James Cunningham, mar Gladys HAWKINS, rem to Western Canada
   B9. Edward Cunningham, no issue, d Western Canada or U.S.
A2. John Samuel, b 1856 G, d 1926 Guelph, Ont., mar Mary Jane HAWKINS
   B1. dau, d.y.
   B2. Alice Beatrice, b 1883, d 1960, unmar
   B3. Albert Ernest, b 1885, d 1959, mar Lillian Van Orde
      C1. Marion Evelyn, b 1913, mar 1947 James Franklin Casselman, d 1970
         D1. Mary Lillian Casselman, b 1949
         D2. James Franklin Casselman, Jr., b 1952, mar 1976 Corneliske Demmer
         D3. Leah Marion Casselman, b 1954
      C2. son, d.y.
      C3. Frances Jean, b 1924, mar 1947 George Robert Edwards
         D1. George Bruce Edwards, b 1950, mar 1964 Carol Lynn Terris
           E1. James Michael Edwards, b 1976
         D2. Albert David Edwards, b 1953, mar 1976 Lorraine Hickling

D3. Evelyn Jean Edwards, b 1956
B4. Norman John, b 1889, d 1962, mar Marguerite Crowe, res Saint John's, N.B.
  C1. James Norman, killed in action over Africa 1942, RCAF
  C2. Margaret Alice, b 1922, mar Sidney Frost, res Toronto, Ont., 3 chn
  C3. Mary Caroline, b 1926, mar T. McKim, res Halifax, N.S.
B5. Frederick James, b 1893, d 1972, mar Maude KIRBY, and 2. Dorothy Fennell
  C1. Leonard, mar Margaret ---, a son
  C2. Harold, mar Loretta ---, res Guelph, Ont.
  C3. Helen, mar ---Maude, res St. Catherines, Ont.
B6. Clarence Victor, b 1897, WWI vet., d 1920s
B7. Arthur Francis, b 1901, d 1972, unmar
A3. Ann Adelaide, b 1859 G, mar James Cochrane, res Guelph, Ont., no issue
A4. Philip, b 1864, d 1942, res J, mar Alice BLAMPIED, qv., res South Africa
  B1. Alice, mar Arthur RENOUF, qv.
A5. Augustus Francis, b C.I.?, mar Minnie Schier, both d in Canada, 2 daus
  B1. Leonora   B2. Doris
III. Jean, b 1826
IV. Samuel, b 1827, rem to Canada 1850
V. Philippe, b 1831 J, d 1857?
VI. Jeanne, b 1834, mar M.P. DELOUCHE, rem to Canada
VII. Francois Joseph, b 1830
CABELDU, Jean, brother of Francois, above, b ca 1800 St. Heliers? J, mar Jeanne SEBIRE, dau of Pierre SEBIRE and Madeleine de la Fontenelle, a Huguenot. Their chn: John, b 1883, Charles, Frank, Philip (who went to Japan), Frederick and Matilda (who married Philip LE MAISTRE, qv.) were b in J. Frederick mar and had at least 6 chn who res St. Heliers? Philip had at least 5 chn; Arthur, Lettie, Walter, Horace and Evelyn, some of whom settled in Vancouver and Ottawa, Ont.
CABOT, Daniel, b 1837 Greendale, Boulivot, Grouville, J, a shoemaker. Mar Sarah Grace WOOTON, WOTTON, b 1835 Ditshum, near Totness, Devon, Eng., rem to J 1855, mar 1857, 10 chn. She came to Canada with dau Matilda Louise in 1906. Returned to J, but came back to Canada in 1908. Res with dau Mrs. Ridalls, London, Ont., and with Mrs. Baker in Montreal, Que., where she d 1935. Bur Mount Royal Cem., Montreal (Grace Beardsley, Verdun, Que.; Sgt. Jack Cabot, Etobicoke, Ont.)
A1. Daniel John, b 1858 J, mar Louise M. LUET, d in J 1942, a son
  B1. Daniel Alfred Edmont, Kt., b 1888 J, mar Anne LE CORNU BLAMPIED 1949, d J 1974. Titles, M.R.C.V.S. Mbr. and officer of Veterinary Societies, England, Spain, France, U.S.
A2. George James, b 1859, lost at sea on coast of S.A., age 40, unmar
A3. John Daniel, b 1861 J, drown at sea, age 24
A4. Clara Sarah Maria, b 1863 J, rem to St. Thomas, Ont. 1887, mar Charles Thomas Ridalls 1887, d Montreal 1943, bur Mt. Royal Cem.
  B1. William Charles Ridalls, b 1887 St. Thomas, Ont., mar Medira Meecham, 2 chn, divorced, mar 2. Faye ---. D in Ozark area, U.S., 1956
    C1. Harold Ridalls, res Seattle, Wash.   C2. Ruth Ridalls
  B2. Mahala Grace Ridalls, b 1889 St. Thomas, Ont. mar Patrick Desmond 1905, d Toronto 1962, dau, Clara
    C1. Clara Helen Desmond, b 1905 St. Thomas, Ont., mar Edward F. Brown 1930. He d 1954, Clara mar 2. George Wells 1967, who d

1973. She res Cambridge, Ont. No issue
A5. Alice Matilda Cabot, b 1865 J, to St. Thomas Ont. ca 1890, mar Albert J. Beal, d St. Thomas 1930. 4 chn, 2 daus d.y.
  B1. Carle Gordon Beal, b 1901 Brandon, Man., mar Annie Fournie 1925. She d 1927, mar 2. Florence Briggs 1930, who d 1967. He res San Bernardino, Calif., 2 chn
    C1. Joyce Beal, b 1931 Detroit, Mich., mar Bennie Miftaraj 1953, res Ottawa, Ont., 4 chn
      D1. Sandra Miftaraj, b 1954, mar Jeff Warthen 1974, res Detroit, Mich.
      D2. Benji Miftaraj, b 1956, in Can. Navy
      D3. Leon Miftaraj, b 1957, res Ottawa, Ont.
      D4. Andre Miftaraj, b 1958, res Ottawa, Ont.
    C2. Dean Beal, b 1939 Detroit, Mich., mar Janet Witt 1962, res Puerto Rico
      D1. Susan Michele Beal, b 1968
  B2. Albert W. Beal, b 1904 Carlyle, Sask., mar Nellie Brooks, who d, and 2. Gwendolene Goff. He d 1964 Strathroy, Ont., bur Oakland Cem., Glencoe, Ont. No issue
A6. James Wotton, b 1867 J, to St. Thomas, Ont. ca 1892. Mar Mary Smith, d St. Thomas 1943, 4 sons
  B1. Stanley Wotton, b 1898 St. Thomas, mar Nellie Monahan, d 1966, no issue
  B2. William Hamilton, b 1900 St. Thomas, mar Marguerite Dunsheath 1923, res Toronto, 4 chn
    C1. Vera Marie, b 1924 St. Thomas, mar William E. Townsend, Toronto, 1948
      D1. Bradley Wm. Townsend, b 1956, res Toronto
      D2. Lesley Townsend, b 1960
    C2. Jack William, b 1929 St. Thomas, mar Muriel Treble, Toronto 1951
      D1. Richard, b 1952
      D2. Debra Anne, b 1955, mar Kevin W. McCabe, 1975, res Toronto
      D3. Lynn, b 1958
    C3. Ronald James, b 1931 St. Thomas, mar Marilyn Davidson 1957 Missauga, Ont.
      D1. Pamela, b 1960 D2. Jeffery, b 1963 D3. Bruce Alexander, b 1965
    C4. Philip Ray, b 1934, res Toronto, Ont.
  B3. Herbert James, b 1904 St. Thomas, d there 1967
  B4. Lewis Tipton, b 1910 St. Thomas, mar Shirley Skelly 1935. D in auto accident, 1938
    C1. Mary Ellen, b 1937, mar Douglas NORMAN, changed name to Ross 1955, res London, Ont.
      D1. Jeffery Norman, b 1960   D2. Christopher Norman, b 1962
A7. Henry George, b 1869 J, to Canada 1893, d NY City, U.S. 1953, bur Jersey City, N.J.
A8. Matilda Louisa, b 1871 J, rem to Montreal, Que. 1906, mar Frederick George BAKER, qv., 1907, d Montreal, Que. 1952, no issue. Bur Hawthorne Dale Cem., Montreal
A9. William Thomas, b 1872 J, mar Emily CORBIN, ca 1902, d 1936, J
  B1. Dora Patricia, b 1906 J, mar Herbert James SHORT 1929, res St. Heliers, J
    C1. Roy Francis Short, unmar, b J 1936, rem to Rhodesia 1959, died in Salisbury there in car accident, 1966
A10. Grace Eva, b 1874 J, rem to St. Thomas in 1904, then to Carlyle, Sask., 1904, to Montreal 1906, mar William Edward Sullivan, Montreal 1910. D there 1964, bur Memorial Park, Montreal. 4 chn
  B1. Edward John Sullivan, b 1911 Montreal, mar Marguerite Mantha in

North Bay, Ont. 1946, d Montreal 1963, bur Cote des Neiges Cem., Montreal, 2 chn
   C1. Joan Sullivan, b 1947 North Bay, Ont., now res Montreal
   C2. Grant Sullivan, b 1953 Montreal, res there
B2. William Frederick Sullivan, b 1912 Montreal, mar Annie Elizabeth Staines 1937 who d 1969. Wm. now res Hull, Que. 5 chn, 2 sons dy
   C1. John William, b 1939 Montreal, mar Jill Cranston in Kamloops. BC 1964. Res Belleville, Ont., 2 sons
      D1. Steven John Sullivan, b 1971 Belgium
      D2. David Edward Sullivan, b 1974 Belleville, Ont.
   C2. Beverly Ann Sullivan, b 1943 Montreal, mar Ronald Bryan 1963, Ottawa
      D1. Thomas Bryan, b 1963 Moncton, NB
      D2. Janice Bryan, b 1965 Ottawa, Ont.
      D3. Linda Bryan, b 1966 Bermuda
   C3. Daniel Sullivan, b 1966 Montreal, res Hull, Que.
B3. Arthur James Sullivan, b 1914 Montreal, mar Ada Busby 1940, res Pte. Claire, Que., a son
   C1. Barry James Sullivan, b 1947 Montreal
B4. Grace Amelia Sullivan, b 1915 Montreal, mar Cyril Beardsley 1940. Res Crawford Park, Verdun, Que., 2 sons
   C1. Keith, b 1949 Montreal, adopted in 1951, mar Beverly Allen 1973, res Fabreville, Que.
      D1. Christina Beardsley, b 1977
   C2. Glenn Beardsley, b 1952 Montreal, res Crawford Park, Verdun, Que. Mar Dianne King of Williamstown, Ont. 1976

CABOT, current at Malbaie, and Gaspe Bay, Gaspe
CABOT, Philippe, b J, son of Jean C. and Rachel GRUCHY, qv., mar Grande Greve, Gaspe 1821 Mary O'Connors, dau of Pierre C. O'Connors and Angelique Bergeron (Gallant)
A1. Rachel, b 1822 Grande Greve
A2. Felicite, b 1824
CABOT, 17 cards on this fam in Saint John, NB Museum Library
CABOT, Thomas, b ca 1830 St. Helier, J, blacksmith for the Charles Robin firm in Caraquet, NB 1858. In Shippegan, NB 1863, plying his trade with his bro John, b 1828 J, d single 1904. Thomas mar 1866 Annie Sutherland from Pokemouche, NB, no issue, adopted a niece Ellen Morrison. Thomas d 1904 (Donat Robichaud, Beresford, NB)
CABOT, from J to Anticosti Island 1800s (Mrs. Adrien Cabot, Malbaie, Que)
CABOT, Mrs. John, d 1942 in Perce, Gaspe, age 80. Believed to have been members of both Old Christ Ch and the new St. Pauls in Perce. (Cent. Bklt.)
CABOT, John, b 1849 J, d 1913 Perce, mar Rachel LENFESTY, qv.
A1. John, b 1887, mar 1904
A2. Philip Francis, b 1889, mar 1906 (Aldo Brochet)
CABOTS from J in Malbaie, Gaspe (Rev. d'Hist)
CABOT, Arthur George, b St. Helier, J, res Gaspe town, lived to at least 80 years. Mar Empress McCall, b PEI. His parents were from St. Martin, J. His dau mar Lloyd Suddard
CABOT, Thomas, b J, in Gr. Riviere Gaspe 1861 (census)
CABOT, from C.E. to Blanc Sablon, QUE. (Shortis-Munn)
CABOT, a Capt. from J in Nfld. (K. Mathews)
CADEREL, CADORET?, John, b J, age 46 in 1871, at Malbaie
CADORET, Elias and Mary from C.I. to Malbaie, 1800s (J.H. Le Breton List) (GLF)
CADORET, John T., 1848-1923
CADORET, in Lachine, Que.

CAIN in Gaspe, origin unverified. John Joseph or John James, b 1853, the son of Thomas C. Sr. and of Matilda BAKER, qv.
CAEN, see DE CAEN
CAIN, LE CAIN, LE QUESNE .Thos.Cain,Perce, was b Isle of Man,Eng.
CAKE in Nfld. (Seary) Cf CAKETERRE in J (Stevens)
CAMBREY, from G, member of C.I. Soc. in B.C. (Luce)
CAMIOT, John, b ca 1872 J, son of Vincent and Eliza LE BROCQ, of St. Peters and St. Mary, J, rem to Gaspe. Worked for Robin firm in Port Daniel and in Cape Breton, N.S. Mar ---Smith, one dau. Left Robins in 1924, purchased retail bus in N.S. Died early 1940s. (P.C. Camiot, Smooth Rock Falls, Ont.)
CAMIOT, Peter, bro of John above, b St. Mathews, J, to Gaspe ca 1890. Mar ca 1877 ---LEMPRIERE, in Montreal. She later came to Gaspe with his two sons. Another son B Paspebiac, Que. She d 1914. He mar 2. widow with chn. They had 4,5 other chn. He d Montreal 1936 at near 100 years of age
A1. Stanley, b J, d 1925 Gaspe?
A2. George, b J, mar Gaspe to Gertrude Mahan, res L'Anse a Beaufils, no issue
A3. Arthur, b J, d Gaspe? 1927
A4. Cyril, b Gaspe, mar Bernice Rowley, res Murdochville, Que.
B1. Michele   B2. Nancy
CAMIOT, Francis Vincent, bro of above Peter and John, b 1879 J, mar Louisa OUEDART, of St. Mary, J, rem to Gaspe, d 1936, 4 sons, 1 dau
A1. Peter C., b 1911 St. Mary, J, rem to Gaspe and Natashquan on the N shore of the St. Lawrence River, for Robin, Jones and Whitman Co. In 1936 worked for the Hudson's Bay Co., there for 40 years. Mar Helen Landry 1937, she was b 1917
B1. Donald, b 1938, mar Tony Paradis, res Sept Isles, Que., 2 sons
B2. Gerald, b 1941, mar Rosa Reynoso of Chihuahua, Mex., one son
B3. Robert, b 1943, res Willowdale, Ont.
B4. Michael, b 1948, res B.C.
B5. Joan, b 1954, res Toronto
CAMIOT, sister of above 3 bros, b J, mar Francis Therein of St. John, J. 3 sons and 2 daus. A son, Francis, rem to Gaspe, but returned to J ca 1930
CANE in Nfld. (Seary) Cf LE QUESNE of J, pronounced CANE (Stevens)
CANILLE, Capt. from J in Nfld. (K. Mathews) Cf Canaille, Canning
CANTELL, D.B.M., b J?, in Victoria, BC 1940 (Luce)
CARAVAN, Thomas, from C.I.?, res Bay Roberts, Nfld. 1781. Cf CARVANEL, CAUVAIN of J (See Seary)
CARCAUD, Daniel, 29 and Alfred, 40, in Bon. Co. Gaspe 1871, related to SUTTONS and LE BOUTILLIERS of Gaspe (Brochet, B. Tardif, J.H. LeBreton)
CAREEN in Nfld. (Seary) Cf CARREIN of J (Stevens)
CAREY, C.I. family to Nfld. very early (Lady McKie) See Seary
CAREY, Lucius, b 1820 G, d 1884 Ontario, Canada. From G to Goderich, Ont. 1860. Mar Isabel Dobree CAREY, dau of John CAREY and Henrietta TUPPER (Mrs. A.C.S. Stead, Dorval, Que.)
A1. Mary Boleyn, b 1849 G
A2. Henrietta, or Rita Laura, b 1852, d 1927
A3. Robert Dobree, b 1854, d 1878, drowned in boating accident on Lake Huron, Ont.
A4. Oswald Frederick Carey, b 1856, d 1928. Mar 1. 1880 Emily Jane Marlton, who d 1907, and 2. Mary Ann Hamilton, of Goderich, Ont., who d 1933, no issue
B1. Albert Dobree Carey, b 1881, mar 1906 Anna Elinor Downing of Vancouver, BC, res Seattle, Wash.

        C1. Catherine Elinor, b 1907   C4. Emily Jane, b 1913
        C2. George Albert, b 1908   C5. Isabella Louise, b 1919
        C3. William Marlton, b 1911, d 1926 C6. Alice Rosalie, b ca 1921
    B2. Edward Hunsdon, b 1881, twin? mar 1915 Gladys Marie Stafford
        Carey, res Toronto and Montreal
        C1. Elsa Joan, b 1916   C3. Louis Stafford, b 1925
        C2. Rosalie Le Marchant, b 1918
    B3. Rosalie Le Marchant, b 1885, d 1929, mar 1908 Frank Chester
        Neltnor
    B4. Harold de Sausmarez, b 1886, mar Jennie Almira McCullough, real
        estate broker, WWI vet
        C1. Edward Harold, b 1912   C2. Oswald Conrad, b 1928
    B5. Rita Laura, b 1888, mar 1. 1912 Alex Goodwin Nisbet, killed 1917
        Vimy Ridge, WWI, mar 2. John Harry Knight, R.N. Commander
    B6. Robert Dobree, b 1890, mar 1920 Jessie Goldsmith, nee Carter of
        Glasgow. WWI vet, many battles in France
        C1. Robert Oswald John, b 1921
    B7. Conrad George, b 1892, killed in action 1916, WWI. Mar 1915 Ida
        Elizabeth Helen Hambly. Estab a business at Moose Jaw, Sask.
        C1. Conrad Elizabeth, b 1916
    B8. Louis Maitland, b 1893
    B9. Philip Falkland, b 1898, mar 1926 Eileen Victoria Munning. WWI
        vet. In bus with father O.F. Carey & Son, Goderich, Ont.
    B10. Helen, b 1901, mar 1924, Joseph Edward Price.
  A5. Eugene de Beauvoir, b 1858 Cork, Ireland, mar Victoria, BC, Mary
      Eliza Booker, dau of John Lawrence B. and Mary Brown Dawson of
      Scotland, 1871-1945. Eugene d 1950 Winnipeg, Man.
    B1. Isabel Dobree, b 1894
    B2. Florence de Beauvoir, b 1895, mar 1927 Arthur Henry Strafford
        Stead, b 1879 Eccles, England, and d 1963 Montreal
        C1. Arthur Carey Strafford Stead, b 1928 Winnipeg, mar 1960 Mon-
            treal, Margaret Catherine Smith, b 1927 Moncton, NB, dau of
            Bowen Benjamin Smith and Ethel Thomas of Moncton and Saint John,
            N.B.
            D1. Katherine Carey Stead, b 1965 Montreal
            D2. Bowen Arthur Strafford Stead, b 1969 Montreal
        C2. George Eugene Strafford Stead, b 1931 Winnipeg, mar 1957 Mon-
            treal, Amy Jancis Durnford, dau of Elliott Augustus Durnford
            and Amy Maxwell MacKenzie
            D1. Sarah de Beauvoir Stead, b 1958 Montreal
            D2. Jennefer Carey Stead, b 1959 Montreal
            D3. Andrew Durnford Stead, b 1964 Montreal
    B3. Muriel Isabel, b 1896
    B4. Ralph Saumarez, b 1898 Winnipeg, d 1976 Pomona, Calif. Res Van-
        couver, BC, Lt. R.F.C., Cadet and pilot in No. 73 Squadron, law
        and Hudson's Bay Co.
        C1. Carolyn Saumarez, b 1931 Winnipeg, mar John David de Vere Hunt,
            b 1929 son of Wm. Harold Hunt and Pearl ---
            D1. Lauren Elizabeth, b 1951, mar 1975 Barbados, W.I. Warren
                Manning, b Ontario
            D2. William David Carey Hunt, b 1952
            D3. Eric Sausmarez Hunt, b 1954 Winnipeg
            D4. Carolyn Dobree Carey Hunt, b 1964 Winnipeg
        C2. Joselyn Margaret, b 1934, mar 1959 Vancouver, John A. Willis,
            son of Howard W. and Mary, b 1931 Vancouver
            D1. William Willis, b 1961 Vancouver D2. Kathleen Mary Willis
            D3. Christine Joselyn Willis, b 1964 D4. Peter John Willis, b 1966

  C3. Susan Mary Lawrence, b 1940 Winn., mar 1961 Vancouver, BC Paul Richard Tennant. SEE ADDITIONS AND CORRECTIONS PAGES.
  C4. Linda Christine, b 1947 Winnipeg, mar 1. Michael Cleland, and 2. 1975, Vancouver, BC, Peter Stead, b 1930 Leeds, England
 B5. Harold Eric Carey, b 1900, mar 1964 Mary Josephine Merritt Duncan, dau of Maj. Duncan and Jessie McVicar, b 1909 Winn.
  C1. Barbara Joan, b 1943 Winn., mar 1964 Larry Ernst Selk, son of John and Ethel S., b 1942 Estevan, Sask.
   D1. David John Lawrence Selk, b 1966 Estevan, Sask.
   D2. Carey Lynne Selk, b 1975 Winnipeg, Man.
  C2. David Eric, b 1946 Winn., mar 1970 Geraldine Daisy, dau of Gerald and Violet Birch, b 1948 Winn.
   D1. Duncan Gerald Carey, b 1976 Winnipeg
 B6. Godfrey Eugene Carey
 B7. Margaret Elizabeth Dobree Carey, b 1909, res Chicago, Ill.
A6. Lucy Isabel, b 1860, d 1904 unmar
A7. Florence Elizabeth, b 1864, missionary at Long Beach, Calif.
A8. Albert Brock, b 1866, mar 1. Margaret Rodgers, nee Somerville, of Dundas, Ont.
 B1. Richard, b 1907, drown as young man on geological trip, Calif.
CAREY, ship owner in early 1800s, from G in Nfld.
CAREY, Engign Walter of J, 15th Regt., d 1838 at Chambly, Que.
CAREY, William, of Big Bras d'Or, C.B., N.S., 1880s, a ship owner
CAREY, some from Devon, Guernsey and Sussex, settled in Canada (P.W.C. Wake, Brighton, Eng.)
CAREY, Emilie, b J?, mar 1875 Tranquille Duguay, his second wife (Robichaud)
 A1. Dorothy Duguay, b 1876 Shippegan, NB, mar 1901 Domique Gautreau of Tracadie, NB
 A2. Elizabeth, b 1877 Shippegan, mar 1902 Peter Poulin, son of Fidele Poulin and Caroline Robichaud
 A3. Azade, b 1888 Shippegan
CAREY, Marie, of Pokemouche, NB, mar Eugene Duguay, in Shippegan, NB Origin unverified
CARON, from J to Caraquet, N.B. early 1800s (Ganong) DOUBTFUL!
CARON, Georgiana, of Gaspe area, mar Jean Marie LE BOUTILLIER, qv., b Perce 1874, d 1967?
CARR, CARREE?, Jerseyman in N.B. fisheries
CARR, 116 cards and a book in Saint John NB Museum Library
CARRE, from G to Australia, 1800s
CARRELL, from G in Calgary and Ontario
CARRELL, Hug fam from J to Gaspe 1800s (McWhirter)
CARRELL, to Labrador
CARREL, Charles Vincent, d 1939, age 69, bur St. Pauls, Gaspe (GLF and J.H. Le Breton List)
CARRELL, Capt. from J in Nfld. (K. Mathews)
CARREL, John, of J?, mar Malbaie, Judith GIRARD, sons John Jr. and Peter, b 1833 Malbaie (Brochet) Poss dau, Jane, b 1835.
CARRELL fam from J in Canada, Joseph Edward, mar Mary Jane ---
 A1. William John, mar Isabella ---
  B1. William John B2. another son, poss Charles Vincent? see below
CARREL, Josue, of J, mar Sara Elizabeth Baldwin (Frank Remiggi)
 A1. Charles Vincent, b 1887 Clothilde Cote, da of Norbert C. and Genevieve Thibault, res Riv. Renard, Gaspe

CARRIE, Ella, mar John Mignot of Que., origin uncertain. A son, John, mar, res Los Angeles, Calif.

CARRIERE. in Ontario and Western Canada, said to be from G
CARRY, John, poss CAREY? of G, owned two vessels that carried cargo from
   a firm at Bonaventure Island, Gaspe before 1770
CARSWELL, CASSWELL, CASWELL, William, bp 1823 J, res Anse au Griffon,
   Gaspe, mar Mary Ann ---, bp 1827 J. Shoemaker (F. Remiggi) Also res
   Cap des Rosiers, Gaspe
A1. Jane Sophia, b 1849 J   A5. Alice M.M., b 1856 J
A2. Sophia E.V., b 1851 J   A6. Amelia B., b 1858 Canada
A3. Elisabeth, M.A., b 1852 J   A7. Williamina, b 1859
A4. Mary Ann, b 1854 J
CARTER in Nfld. (Seary) Cf CARTER, CARTERET in C.I.
CARTER, Margaret E., b 1834 J, d 1874. Widow of Capt. John VAUTIER,
   qv., Carters from Devon to J. She is bur St. Pauls, Gaspe town (GLF)
CARTER, George, from J or Devon? SPG missionary in Nfld. (SPG records)
CARTERET, DE CARTERET, David from J to Perce 1830s or earlier
A1. Susan, b 1837 Perce, d 1914. Mar Francis LE BRUN, b 1835 J, 10 chn
CARTERET and DE CARTERET, to Nfld. as captains, merchants and ship
   owners from J and G, as early as 1717 or before. (K. Mathews, C.R.
   Faye)
CARTERET, material in Soc. Jers., Jersey. Some detail in North Caro-
   lina Gen. Bull., Fall and Winter 1970, by W.P. Johnson
CASTLE in Nfld. (Seary) Also as CASSEL. Cf CASTELL of J 1668 (Stevens)
CASWELL, from G? to Nfld., or from J (See Seary)
CAVALIA, Augustus, from C.I.? to Burgeo, Nfld. Cf CAVALIER, CARVANELL
   of J (Rev. Hammond)
CAVEY or GAVEY?, Percy, b 1894 St. Heliers, J, rem with fam to Winnipeg
   1909, to Vict., BC 1964
CAWLEY, Harold Ernest, b 1887 J, son of George C., b England, a baker,
   and Julia COWLEY, b England. Mar 1913 Ellen Gertrude JOUAN, qv., rem
   to Regina, Sask. Cawley had worked at Gaspe 9 yrs. as a baker, to
   Canada ca 1903 on FANNIE BRESLER. D 1951, Ellen d, 1960 (Jean Wood,
   Regina, Sask)
A1. Harold, b 1914, mar Lorene---, 2 chn
   B1. Donald, b 1949, mar ---, a son
      C1. Shayne Lindon Cawley, b 1976
   B2. Linda, b 1952, mar W. Potts
A2. Marjorie Ellen, b 1916, mar Ron Ordish, a son
   B1. David Ordish, mar Connie ---, 3 chn
      C1. Tanya Ordish, b 1969   C3. Mathew Ordish, b 1973
      C2. Noni-Leigh Ordish, b 1970
A3. Jean Louise, b 1918, mar J.A. Wood, 4 chn
   B1. John Andrew Wood, b 1973
      C1. Sean Andrew Wood, b 1973   C2. Jason Frederick Wood, b 1976
   B2. Patricia Ann Wood, b 1948, mar Ronald Proctor, 3 daus
      C1. Keri Proctor, b 1970   C3. Jennifer Proctor, b 1976
      C2. Lisa Proctor, b 1973
   B3. Charles Harold Wood, b 1950
   B4. Eric Howard Wood, b 1957
A4. Florence May, b 1920, mar Ross Mitchell, 5 chn
   B1. Douglas Mitchell, b 1943, mar Pat ---
      C1. Trent Mitchell, b 1968   C3. Kim Mitchell, b 1973
      C2. Bradley Mitchell, b 1970
   B2. Shirley Mitchell, b 1945, mar Harvey Peters
      C1. Stewart Peters, b 1973   C2. Paul Peters, b 1975
   B3. Allan Mitchell, b 1947, mar Shirley---
      C1. Rae-Elle Mitchell, b 1968   C3. Tosha Mitchell, b 1970
      C2. Dwayne Mitchell, b 1969   C4. Corey Mitchell, b 1975

B4. Joan, b 1951, mar Duncan Robertson
  C1. Janet Robertson, b 1973
 B5. Donna, b 1952
A5. Arthur, b 1922, mar Helen ---
 B1. Mary Ellen, b 1952, mar Ed Chorney
CERNEW, C.I. surname in Con. Bay, Nfld. (G.W. Le Messurier) Cf CORNU, LE CORNU, QUENAULT of J
CHACHA, Peter, b J, bur at Gaspe, age 46, 1800s
CHALKER, from C.I. to Nfld.? See Seary
CHAMBERLAIN and CHAMBERS, ship capts. in Nfld. (K. Mathews) See Seary
CHAMPION, to Nfld. (Seary) Cf Champion of J
CHANCEY in Nfld. (Seary) Cf CHAUNTZ in J (Stevens)
CHANT, said to be from G to Maritimes fisheries (K. Mathews) See also Seary
CHANT, John in St. John's, Nfld. 1765 (Seary)
CHARDINE, John, from G to Hamilton, Ont. 1927. Mar Helen ---, b England. Sons J.F. and G.H. A grandau, Mrs. B. Paling has two chn, res Scarboro, Ont.
CHARLES in Nfld. (Seary) Cf CHARLES of J (Stevens)
CHASE, from C.I. at Pettye Harbour near St. John's, Nfld. 1860s (Rev. Hammond)
CHASE in St. John, Nfld., ca 1757, said to be of C.I. origin
CHATEL, George Alfred, b 1906 J, to Canada age 6, with parents, George Arthur CHATEL, b France, and mother LOUISE BILLOT, b 1885 J, no issue
CHASTRAY, of J in 1717, involved with Nfld. fisheries (C.R. Fay)
CHEDORE, variants in early documents, Gaspe, were CHADOUR, SHEDOR, CHEDOR, etc., Prot in early records, said to be on the Gaspe coast in 1815. John, "formerly of the Island of Jersey," b ca 1794, d 1864, bur Port Daniel, Gaspe. Burial notice signed by Philip TOCQUE, qv., missionary. One account says fam in Canada 180 years. This fam helped to save 12 persons from shipwreck of the barque COLBOURNE from Hull, England at L'Anse au Gascons 1838. (Raymond Garrett, Gascons, Que.; MacWhirter)
CHEDORE, Philip, b ca 1793 J?, d 1869, mar Martha AHIER, qv., 1803-1882, b Coxtown, Gaspe ca 1803, 11 chn
 A1. Isabella, b 1823, mar Joseph Jones Acteson, b ca 1814 London, England, d 1880, Gascons, mar St. Andrews 1839
  B1. Thomas Penrose Acteson, b 1839
  B2. James Alexander Acteson, b 1842
  B3. Ann Acteson, b 1844
  B4. Joseph Acteson, b 1846
  B5. Philip Acteson, b 1848
  B6. Charles Arthur Acteson, b 1851
  B7. Jane Isabel Acteson, b 1853
  B8. Martha Acteson, b 1855, mar J. A. Chedore
  B9. John Arthur Acteson, b 1857
  B10. William Charles Acteson, b 1860
  B11. Margaret Elizabeth Acteson, b 1863
  B12. Frederick Edward Acteson, b 1867
 A2. John James, b 1825, mar Margaret Ross, dau of Hector Ross and Sarah Huntington of Hopetown, Gaspe 1849
  B1. James Alexander, b 1850, mar Martha Acteson, b 1855
   C1. Arthur, b 1886 in U.S.A.
   C2. Eva Margaret, b 1888 Gascons
   C3. James Earnest, b 1890
   C4. Joseph Henry, b 1892
   C5. Charles Philip, b 1895, d.y.
  B2. Philip, b 1852
  B3. Sarah Ann, b 1854
  B4. Annabella, b 1858
  B5. John Adam, b 1861
  B6. Martha Jane, b 1863
  B7. Barbara, b 1865
  B8. Margaret Amelia, b 1868
  B9. Philip Joseph, b 1871, mar Elizabeth AHIER, dau of Joseph A. 1902
   C1. James Eric, b 1903, d.y.

  B10. Malcolm, mar Flora Jane Chatterton of Hopetown 1877, rem to Alberta
    C1. James Stuart, b 1888   C2. Elvina, b 1891
 A3. Philip, b 1827, mar Sarah Ann Crozier, b 1830 Gascons, dau of Wm. Crozier of Glasgow, Scotland. She d 1896
  B1. James William, b 1853, mar Annabella CHEDORE, dau of John James, 1879
    C1. John James, b 1880   C4. Laura Ida, b 1887
    C2. Margaret Melvina, b 1883 C5. Lynda May, b 1892
    C3. William Ephraim, b 1885   C6. Philip Walter, b 1894
  B2. Alexander Crozier, b 1857, mar Jane Elizabeth Duguay, dau of Daniel and Mary CHEDORE, 1883
    C1. William Alexander, b 1884, d.y. C5. Susan Elizabeth, b 1893
    C2. Sarah Wilhemie   C6. Annie Edith Isabelle, b 1894
    C3. Mary Jane, b 1889   C7. Philip Alfred, b 1896
    C4. Clarence, b 1891   C8. Margaret Ellen, b 1898
  B3. John Thomas, b 1858
  B4. Margaret Isabelle, b 1864
  B5. Philip Robert, b 1867, mar Margaret Sullivan, dau of Daniel Sullivan, 1899
    C1. Annie May, b 1901
  B6. Matilda Ann, b 1869
  B7. George Arthur, b 1872
  B8. Emma Jane, b 1855
 A4. Alexander, b 1830, d 1877 Gascons, mar 1858 Marie Flowers, b 1834 Coxtown, dau of William Flowers and Mary Chatterton. She d 1903, Gascons
  B1. Philip William, b 1859, mar Catherine AHIER, dau of Philip. She d 1897
    C1. Mary Jane, b 1886   C3. Philip Alexander Lloyd, b 1892
    C2. Howard Milton, b 1889   C4. Julia Edna Eliza, b 1894
  B2. Mary Jane, b 1860, d 1884   B5. Susan, b 1869
  B3. Melvina, b 1865   B6. Sarah Elizabeth, b 1871
  B4. Deborah Anna Maria, b 1867   B7. Martha Isabella, b 1862
 A5. Charles, b 1833, mar 1855 Johanne Elizabeth Scott, b 1832 Shigawake, dau of Adam Scott. Charles d 1908 Shigawake, Gaspe
  B1. Charles Adam, b 1856, mar 1879 Christie Malvana McRae, b 1858 Hopetown, dau of Duncan McCrae. Charles d 1908, wife in 1905, Shigawake
    C1. Christina Maria, b 1880   C3. John Arthur, b 1884
    C2. William Vinton, b 1882   C4. Reginald Scott, b 1888
  B2. Martha Isabella, b 1857   B5. Johann Maria, b 1862, d 1933
  B3. Jane Elizabeth, b 1859
  B4. Mary Ann, b 1862, d 1870   B6. Phoebe Margaret, b 1866
 A6. William, b 1835
 A7. Mary, b 1837, mar Daniel Duguay 1860
  B1. Jane Elizabeth, b 1862   B4. Susan Rebecca, b 1878
  B2. Charles Alfred, b 1872   B5. Margaret Eliza, b 1881
  B3. William Alexander, b 1876   B6. Adam
 A8. Jane, b 1840 Gascons, mar 1865 Philip MOURANT, qv., his second wife, 8 chn. See MOURANT
 A9. William Robert, b 1842, mar 1866 Matilda Sullivan, b 1840, d 1894
 A10. Adam, b 1845
 A11. Francis Thomas, b 1847, mar 1869 Susan Allen, b Port Daniel, d 1897 Gascons. She was dau of Samuel William Allen and Nancy Young
  B1. Philip, b 1870 Gascons, mar 1892 Sarah Jane Isabelle Dow, b Port Daniel

CHEDORE

    C1. James Francis, b 1892   C5. Susan Jane, b 1898
    C2. Philip Lyster, b 1893   C6. Thomas Clifton, b 1899
    C3. Susan Isabella Beatrice,   C7. John Frederick Earle, b 1901
        b 1895, d.y.   C8. Annie Laura, b 1903
    C4. Sarah Myrtle, b 1896
  B2. William Edward, b 1871   B4. Martha Clarissa, b 1873
  B3. Jessie Margaret, b 1872   B5. John James, b 1875, d 1896
  B6. Alexander, b 1877, mar Clara Jane Hall 1897, dau of Benj. of
    Port Daniel, she d 1901
    C1. Grace Lillian, b 1898
  B7. Nancy Beatrice, b 1879, d 1883   B9. Charles Arthur, b 1883
  B8. Laura Isabelle, b 1881   B10. Anne Beatrice, b 1886
CHEDORE, Violet, b 1919, d 1976, mar Earl MERCIER of Chandler, poss of
  above fam (Brochet)
CHERRY, Richard Mitchell, Capt. from C.I., to New Brunswick 1800s, mar
  --- (R.M. Cherry, Calgary, Alta.)
A1. Richard Mitchell, mar Jane Rice
  B1. Harry Scott, mar May Ethel Cattle
    C1. Richard Mitchell, res Calgary, Alta.
CHESTER, Mr. and Mrs. David, from G to Pierrefonds, Que., ca 1967
CHEVALIER, Mary, who d 1842, age 78, res Sandy Beach, Gaspe, mar Francois LA FOUR
CHEVALIER, of this period, rem from Gaspe to Labrador
CHEVALIER, CHEVALLIER, Capt. from J in Nfld. (K. Mathews)
CHEVALIER, George, signed the Gaspe Petition in 1820, prob from J
CHICK, from G? to BC
CHINN, from C.I.? to Nfld. (Seary)
CHRISTIAN in Nfld. (Seary) Cf CRISTIN of J 1607 (Stevens)
CHURCHWARD, from C.I. in Maritimes Fisheries (J.H. Le Breton List)
CLANTER, James and Wm. of C.I. fam in Nfld. poss in Cataline, Bonvestia
  Bay, 1860s (Rev. Hammond)
CLARK, Richard, b J, in Gaspe 1871, age 22 (Census)
CLEMENS, CLEMENTS, of J had a fish business in Nfld., trademark being
  G.R.C., and Charles ROBIN, qv., intended to sue them for infringement,
  as C.R.C. was known all over the world. Agents of this firm at several places in South Nfld. CLEMENS Sr. was b J, son Harry, b Nfld.
  Dau, Hope, went to school in N.S., and was a librarian in Ottawa.
CLEMENTS, John, had land at Jugglers Cove, Nfld. 1760, also at Bread and
  Cheese Cove, both in Conc. Bay. Benjamin SQUIRE, qv., bought land
  from John Clements, formerly of Bell Island. Fam at Broad Cove 1806.
  Mar Margaret --- (Hug. Soc., Rev. Hammond, G.W. Le Messurier) Many
  in Nfld. See Seary
A1. Jane Harriet, b 1795   A2. Charlotte, b 1791
A3. William, who mar 1822 Mary Somerton of Portugal Cove, Nfld., res
  Lance Cove and Bell Island
  B1. Elizabeth, b 1827   B2. Ann, b 1830
  B3. William Edward, b 1832, mar Mary Ann Stone of Bryants Cove, Nfld.
    1840-1915
    C1. William, alive at 76, mar Emma Jane Bickford, 1882-1919
    C2. Thomas, mar Mildred Hussey   C5. Emma
    C3. Susie, mar William Hussey   C6. Sarah
    C4. Ann, mar 1898, Albert SQUIRES of Broad Cove, Nfld.
CLEMENT, John, b J, in Gaspe 1871, age 26, cook
CLEMENTS, in N.S., from C.I.?, not verified
CLEMENT, John D. of J fam? husband of Viola Patterson, d 1947 Gaspe
  town, age 39, bur St. Paul's Anglican, Gaspe (GLF)
CLEMENTS, from C.I. to Cornwall, then to Nfld. (Rev. Hammond)

CLEMENTS, H. and J. in PEI 1841 (census) See Nicolle family
CLEMENT, from C.I. to West Coast of Nfld. (Shortis-Munn, K. Mathews) See Seary
CLEMENTS, Capt. John of Marblehead, Mass. 1715-1805, rem to N.S. shortly after the American Revolution. (Robt. J. Frost, Victoria, BC) Poss of C.I. origin
CLEMENT, Catherine, b early 1800s, dau of Thomas C., origin unver., and Elisabeth BAKER, qv., res Malbaie, mar Charles TAPP, qv., 4 chn. See TAPP
CLERKE, CLERK, said to be from C.I. in Canada, orig. LE CLERCQ
CLIFFORD, Capt. and boat keeper from J in Nfld. (K. Mathews) See Seary
CLOADE, COADE, Capt. from G in Nfld. (K. Mathews)
CLOUGH, Thomas, b 1791 G, d Canada. Mar ca 1806 Rachel TUDRAW, TOUSEAU, TOUSSINT?, who was b 1789 G, d Canada. To Quebec during the British early post war immigration of 1815-1820. They had 4 sons and 5 daus, b 1807-1826 (Howard Brown, Ottawa, Ont.)
- A1. Rachel, b 1807 G, d Matilda Twp., Dundas Co., Ont., 1866, mar ca 1830 Andrew Flett, b Orkney Is. 1797, d Haddo, Ont., 1977, bur Iroquois, Ont. She spoke G French. He was a farmer in Haddo from the late 1840s, and a shoemaker at Cornwall, Stormont Co. They had 3 sons and 4 daus b 1831 to 1851
  - B1. Thomas Flett, b 1831, mar after 1871 Marie Glover, 3 sons, 4 daus
  - B2. Marjory, b 1833, d Vancouver, BC 1907, a nurse, unmar
  - B3. Rachel?
  - B4. John, b 1836, d Vancouver 1900, mar twice, 4 sons, 3 daus
  - B5. Margaret, b 1838 Cornwall, d Vancouver 1927, unmar, nurse
  - B6. Mary, b 1841 Cornwall, d 1861, unmar, res Ogdensburg, NY 1961, bur Iroquois
  - B7. Martha, b 1843, mar Samuel Johnson, 2 sons and 2 daus, some in Akron, Ohio
  - B8. Henry, b Matilda Twp., 1851, d Vict., BC 1916, mar, 1 son, 1 dau. Seattle and Victoria
- A2. Mary, b 1809
- A3. Thomas, b 1811
- A4. Elizabeth, b England or G 1814, d Canada. Mar 1837 John Warcup, b 1799 England, res near Montreal 1861, La Prairie. Three sons and 2 daus with them in 1861, b Lower Canada, Ont.
  - B1. Mary L., b 1838, res Goderich, Ont. 1920, unmar
  - B2. Marguerite, b ca 1841, mar late in life, d before 1920
  - B3. Mathew, b ca 1850, d before 1920
  - B4. Arthur, b ca 1853, d before 1920
  - B5. Charles, b ca 1856, d before 1920
- A5. Martha, b 1816, poss as Mary mar ---McNish, res Quebec City 1863, had chn, including 1 dau
- A6. John, b 1819. A.J.A. Cluff in 1904 was a retail merchant at Greenfield, Kenyon Twp., Glengarry Co., Ont.
- A7. William, b 1821, d Victoria, BC 1891, willed his real estate to Henry H.C. Flett, son of his nephew, Henry Flett, 1851-1916
- A8. Henry, b 1824
- A9. Margaret, b 1826 Ontario, living in 1852 Matilda Twp., with the families of Eneas and Nelson TOUSAINT. Mar after 1851, ---McLeod, res Martintown, Glengarry Co., Ont. Mar Cornwall, Ont.

CLOUGH, Jane, b 1791 G, resided with the Cloughs in 1861, unmar, prob sister of Thomas the immigrant. Age 70 in 1861, res near St. Lawrence River with Andrew Flett and Rachel CLOUGH
CLUETT, John, said to be from C.I. in Fortune Bay, Nfld. 1860s, also Samuel, Thomas and William (Rev. Hammond) See also Seary
COADY, See Seary

COBAT, Thomas, b J, blacksmith with Robin firm in Caraquet, NB 1861, age 30 (census)
CODE, CODY, CODEY, COADY, LE CAUDEY. Some confusion on these surnames, especially in Gaspe. "My great-great-grandfather was born a Cody. He left Ireland, changed his name to CODE, and joined the British Army. His son, John William Code, mar a Guernsey girl and settled on the Island after having served in the Army." (Arthur Gadd, Leamington, Ont.)
CODE, Emily, b 1880 Ireland, dau of John William Code, alias CODEY, b 1852 St. Martin's, G, and Emily STAGG, b 1859 G, d Rugby, Eng. 1934. Mar Henry Ernest Gadd, b 1878 Brighton, England, d 1938 Toronto. Gadds rem to Canada 1924
- A1. Henry, Harry, Adames Gadd, b Pt. Royal, Jamaica 1904, d Cobourg, Ont., mar Marjorie, Molly, ---
- A2. Doris Adames Gadd, b 1909, d.y.
- A3. Dorothy Gadd, b 1912 Birchvale, Derby, England, mar 1. Clifford Walker
- A4. John Allan Sydney Gadd, b Birchvale, England 1907, mar Phyllis May Cook
  - B1. Arthur Sydney Gadd, b 1926 Windsor, Ont., mar Gladys Mona Gifford
    - C1. Gail Sharon Gadd, b 1956 Leamington, Ont., mar Dwayne Eldon Mountney, b 1953 Renfrew, Ont.
    - C2. Gordon Neil Gadd, b 1965 Leamington, Ont.
  - B2. Valerie Joan Gadd, b 1931 Toronto, mar Keith Albert McGorlick
    - C1. Keith Allan McGorlick, b 1953 Windsor, Ont., mar Susan ---
      - D1. Heather Elsie McGorlick, b 1975 Trenton, Ont.
    - C2. Deborah Ann McGorlick, b 1956 Windsor, Ont., mar Robert Bondy, b 1954 Windsor, Ont.

CODE, John, bro of Emily CODE above, b 1883 G, d at sea 1905
CODE, William, b 1881 London, Eng. of above fam, d 1958 Toronto, Ont., mar Olive ---
- A1. Alec, killed WWII
- A2. Margaret
- A3. Jean
- A4. William

CODE, Margaret of above fam, b 1895 G, res England, mar Dennis Noon
- A1. Roy Noon, b 1922 Dunchurch, Rugby, England, mar Joan ---
- A2. Leslie Noon, b Dunchurch 1934

CODEY, COADE, a Capt. from G in Nfld. (K. Mathews)
CODNER, GODNER, Henry, in Renews, Nfld. 1676 (Seary) Cf CORDINER, shoemaker of J (Stevens) Also as CORDWAINER
CODY, John, from J?, mar Annie LE MIEUX, res Bonaventure Is. Their son, Francois, mar 1840 Adelaide Simard? (GLF)
CODY, Philippe, b St. Peters, J, 1698, rem to America with wife Martha LE BROCQ, qv. A desc, b Hopkinton, Mass. 1775 rem from Manilus, NY to Newmarket, Ont. ca 1798. Desc in Ontario, and other parts of Canada (Jay Cody, Orillia, Ont.) (See QAAM by Turk)
CODY, CODEY, Peter or Percy?, b 1786, d 1853 Bonaventure Island, mar Mary Horan <u>AN IRISH FAMILY</u>. (Aldo Brochet)
- A1. Catherine, b 1809, mar Daniel Collins (Aldo Brochet)
- A2. Patrick, b 1811, mar 1838 Bon Is. Susanne MORRISSEY, b 1821
  - B1. Mary Margaret, b 1839 Bon Is., d there 1904. Mary John LE COUTEUR, qv.
  - B2. Angelique, b 1841
  - B3. Suzanne, b 1844
  - B4. John, b 1846
  - B5. Patrick, b 1848, mar Anne Hachez
    - C1. Suzanne Codey, b 1882, Grande Riviere, Gaspe

B6. Ellen, mar 1878 Bon. Is. Philip A.DuVAL   chn
A3. James, b 1814 Bon. Is., mar 1844 Mary Mulmichael, b Ireland
　　B1. Adelaide, b 1846   B4. Joanna, b 1853
　　B2. Ellen, b 1847   B5. Mary Ann, b 1856
　　B3. James Xavier, b 1849, d 1924, B6. Catherine, b 1861
　　　　mar Mary Ann Bilodeau   B7. Margault, b 1866
A4. John, b 1816, d 1887, adopted a son, Louis E. Moreau
A5. Edmund, b 1818 Bon. Is.
A6. Margaret, b 1821, mar 1835 William Sheehan, d Grande Riv., Gaspe
A7. Michael, b 1823, d 1840
A8. Ellen, b 1825, d 1915
A9. Lawrence, b 1831, mar Susan JOURNEAU, qv., b 1834. See Le Couteur
　　B1. Laurence, b 1858   B4. Mary, b 1864
　　B2. Susan, b 1860   B5. Ellen, b 1866
　　B3. John, b 1862   B6. Catherine, b 1870
COFFIN, said to be from C.I. in Rencontre Bay, Nfld. 1870 (Rev. Hammond)
　See Seary
COGHLAN, William, b ca 1890 G, mar in Canada Lillian Maud DE BRODER,
　qv. Res Racine and Chicago, Ill., rem to Hialeah, Fla. (Lena Orchard,
　St. Martins, G)
A1. Robert, mar Mary Ellen Kiegan, Irish, 5 chn
　　B1. Mary Ellen   B4. Eileen
　　B2. Robert   B5. Elizabeth Ann
　　B3. Dolores
A2. Dorothy, mar Robert Walsh, who d 1977
　　B1. Kenneth Walsh, mar ---
　　　　C1. Jennifer Walsh
　　　　C2. Colleen Walsh, b ca 1965
A3. Colleen, mar Robert Maxwell, 2 daus
　　B1. Kathleen, mar Robert Rainy
　　　　C1. Robert Rainy   C2. Eric Rainy   C3. Kevin Rainy
　　B2. Patricia, mar, res Illinois
COHU, Suzanne, see Peter ROBIN
COLBECK, members of Vict. C.I. Society 1940
COLBORNE, Capt. and merchant from J and G in Nfld. (K. Mathews)
COLCLOUGH, said to be from C.I. in Canada
COLE, Thomas, a teacher, b G, in Gaspe 1861 (census)
COLINET, from C.I. in Placentia, Nfld. 1877. See also COLLENETTE
COLINETT, COLLINETTE, Capt. from G in Nfld. (K. Mathews)
COLLINGS, said to be from C.I. in Victoria, BC
COLLARD, from C.I., said to be in Ontario
COLLAS, Judith, widow of Abraham LENFESTEY of Grand Greve, Gaspe, sold
　in 1855 lot at Cap des Rosiers to Hilary LENFESTY (Brochet)

COLLAS, James, age 32 in 1871 (census), b J, res Malbaie, Gaspe, had
　fam of 5 in 1831 (Brochet)
COLLAS, Francis, b J, at Gaspe Bay 1871, with wife Jane, age 43, b J
　(Brochet)
COLLAS, James, shipbuilder, with fam of 5 at Pt. St. Peter, Gaspe 1831
　(Brochet)
COLLAS, Francis, b 1829 St. Helier, J, son of Helier C. and Elizabeth
　DE LA PERELLE, qv. Rem as a boy to Gaspe, worked for Robin Collas
　Co., related to the Collas of the firm name. Also taught school.
　Mar 1853, Elizabeth LE HUQUET, qv., 1826?-1915, 3 sons. His brothers
　or nephews?, Elias, John, Helier, and George also thought to have

COLLAS 201

come to Canada. (George Collas, Calgary, Alta.; GLF; Cent. Bklt.;
Census 1861; Le Moine; Brochet, Soc. Jers. Bull. #12; Viola Collas,
Dorvall, Quebec)
- A1. Elias John, b 1858 Gaspe, mar 1887 Agnes PRICE, qv., 1868-1955. He d 1939. 6 sons, 1 dau
  - B1. Elias Abner, b 1890?, mar May or Mary Bebe, of Hug UEL fam, dau of Joshua Bebee, res New Carlisle, Que., 4 chn
    - C1. Percy, mar Geneva ---, son Percy, dau June
    - C2. Fred, unmar
    - C3. Carrie, unmar, res New Carlisle, Que.
    - C4. Ann, mar Lawrence LE GROS, qv., chn
  - B2. John William, b 1893, d 1974, unmar, Vet of WWI (MacWhirter)
  - B3. Amelia May, b 1896, res Montreal, Que.
  - B4. Henry Hubert, b 1896, twin, sailor, d 1923
  - B5. George Reuben, b 1898, res Calgary, Alta.
  - B6. Walter Price, b 1900, mar Jessie Sarah Stanley 1931. She was b 1911, res Pte. aux Trembles
    - C1. Marjorie Ruth, b 1932, mar Lennox Stanley Williams, 1953, b 1926, 3 chn
      - D1. Richard Stanley Williams, b 1954
      - D2. Esther Marjorie Williams, b 1955
      - D3. Allan Warren Williams, b 1957
    - C2. Audrey Marion, b 1934, mar 1958 Henry Adams, b 1933
      - D1. Timothy Charles Adams, b 1964
    - C3. Wesley George Collas, b 1936, mar Soulange Forbin 1956, b 1940, 3 chn
      - D1. Wesley Jr., b 1957
      - D2. Darlene, b 1958
      - D3. Connie, b 1964
    - C4. Robert John Arthur Collas, b 1945, mar Barbara Bartlett 1965
      - D1. Candee Barbara, b 1966
      - D2. Bradley Walter Collas, b 1968
  - B7. Alfred Gordon Collas, b 1901, d unmar 1963
- A2. Francis George Collas, b 1860, drown 1887
- A3. Adolphus, b 1863 J, mar Lucy Nile Handy 1896, 1874-1951, bur Cap aux Os (GLF) He d 1955, bookkeeper at Malbaie 1871, age 25
  - B1. Arthur William, 1897-1944, mar Gertrude Gibbons 1926, res Toronto, Ont.
  - B2. Rufus Lordon, b 1900, mar 1936 Viola May LENFESTY, qv., b 1908, res Dorval, Que.
    - C1. Gloria Ann, b 1937, mar Clifford Hamilton
    - C2. Wanda, b 1947, mar David Craig

COLLAS, Francis of Cap OZO, Gaspe, mar Eliza Jane LE HUQUET of Shiphead, Gaspe, 1853
COLLAS, Harry, from J to Montreal and Vancouver, BC early 1900s

COLLAS, Helier, bro of Elias John above, b 1826 J, may have settled first in Gaspe, then returned to J where he d 1892. Mar Nancy Esther LE GRAND, b 1816, d age 70. Stone in St. Heliers, J
COLLAS, John, b J, d 1904, bur St. Peters, Grand Greve, Gaspe, age 30 (GLF)
COLLAS, John and Elias, prob bros of Francis, above, in Gaspe 1855, and 1867 (Brochet)
COLLAS, James of J, part of reorganized Robin firm, Gaspe 1855, 1861 (census)
COLLAS ---, b J, mar a dau of Felix O'Hara, Seigneur de Pabos.1743- Julia and Louisa were his minor chn in 1819. This fam said to have

rem to N.Y. state ca 1855. Louisa d 1832 Gaspe Basin (Brochet)
COLAS, from J?, one of Cartier's crew, voyage to Canada 1534. (Syvret)
COLLAS, James and Elias met Pierre Fortin at Pt. St. Peter 1858 (Le
    Moine)
COLLAS, Peter, in Nfld. in 1811 (Brochet)
COLLAS, Samuel J., b J, mar ---PERREE, qv., rem to Malbaie 1848, mar
    Charlotte PERREE. He was the agent for Perree Co., which became J.
    and E. Collas Co. (Brochet) He was age 28 at Malbaie, 1871 (census)
    A1. James   A2. Elias
COLLAS, Clarence Hardeley, b ca 1856 J, d St. Mathews J 1881, but
    stone in Malbaie (GLF)
COLLENETTE, found in Catel G 1700s
COLLENETTE, from St. Peter Port, G, to Glencoe and Toronto, Ont. 1914
    "My husband's father came from South Africa in the first world war,
    met and married my mother-in-law in 1916. My husband's father died
    when my husband was a few months old, in London, Eng. He had left a
    family in Port Elizabeth. The wife married again. I married in
    1940...Another person told me his family were from Guernsey, named
    Collenette. He believed they originally came from Brittany to the
    Islands. My husband and I came to Canada in 1957 with our son. A
    Lady who comes from Newfoundland said there is a village of that name
    there." Letter from Cornwall, Ont., with COLLENETTE crest, said to
    be only 50 people in Canada with that surname.
COLLETT, John Isaac from G to Victoria, BC, a sailor, settled in BC
    1800s. B ca 1850, d ca 1920. One dau, Margaret, mar ---ROBILLIARD,
    qv. A sister, Elizabeth, mar J. NOURY. Mother's name thought to be
    RENOUF, qv.
COLLETT, Thomas J, had a store in Bay Bulls, Nfld. 1860s (Lovell)
COLLETT, Richard and Thomas, from C.I. in Harbour Buffett in 1860s
    (Rev. Hammond)
COLLETT. "As a boy I remember my father Edward Collett, who was b in
    Truro, Cornwall in 1865 telling me his great grandparents were garden-
    ers in Guernsey, and that they came to Cornwall for work." (Harry
    Collett, Calgary, Alta.)
COLLIER, COLLYER, Samuel, from C.I. fam? at Hatten's Pt. Nfld., ca 1865
    (Seary, Rev. Hammond)
COLLEY, Edward, from C.I. fam? S.P.G. minister in Nfld. 1800s. See
    also Seary
COLLIN, Caroline, from C.I.? mar 1843 Samuel HOPKIN or HOPIN, qv., of
    G, res Grande Riv., Gaspe, later Qubecois family (AldoBrochet)
COLLINGS, Philip d'Auvergne, from G to Vancouver, BC 1955. Others in
    Nfld. (Seary)
COLLINGS, Francis d'Auvergne from G to Kingston, Ont. 1953, then to
    Wash. D.C., U.S.
COLLINGS, in Western Canada, from G?
COLLINS, Samuel, in Grt. Placentia, Nfld. 1860s, from C.I. fam? (Lovell)
    Also ---COLLINS, from C.I. to Bristol's Hope about 1710, later at
    Spaniard's Bay, Nfld. (Seary)
COLLYER, COLLIER, Charles, from C.I. fam? in Burgeo, Nfld. 1860s (Rev.
    Hammond)
COLOMBE in Nfld. (Seary) Cf COLOMBE of J 1692 (Stevens)
COMBER, C.I. name in Gaspe (K.H. Annett)
CONWAY, from C.I.? to Perce (Cent. Bklt.)
COOMBE, COMBE, COMBES, Capt. and by-boat keeper from J in Nfld. (K.
    Mathews) See Seary
COOMBS, the chn of George Henry Coombs and Rachel Elizabeth CHURCHILL
    of J, several of whom rem to Canada

COOMBS 203

A1. George   A2. James   A3. Amelia   A4. Louise   A5. Florence
A6. Rosana Beatrice, b 1891 J, mar 1913 Allan Lyle LUCE, rem to Canada, 6 chn. See LUCE
COOPER, from J to Douglas town, Gaspe?
COOPER, Mrs. Hazel, arrived in Canada from G in 1953, mother's name being LIHOU, qv., res Scarborough, Ont. (David OZANNE)
COOPER, from C.I. in Carbonear, Nfld. (Rev. Hammond) See also Seary
CORBET, Thomas, b G, in Gaspe 1861 (census) CORBET curr at Paspebiac, Gaspe
CORBET, from C.I. to BC (Bourgaize)
CORBET, Chan. Islanders in the Maritimes fisheries, 1800s (J.H. Le Breton List)
CORBET, Daniel, b G, in Cap Rosier, Gaspe 1861 with Judith ---, Daniel, Henry, Paul and Job (census) Was 72 in 1871 (census) Judith nee LE HARY, or similar surname
CORBETT, James from C.I.?, res Petit Rocher, NB, unver. (Robichaud)
CORBIN, from C.I.? to Nfld. See Seary. See also Clement NOEL
CORBUIS, C.I. firm in Nfld. very early (Lady McKie)
CORCORAN, said to be from C.I. in Nfld. (Rev. Hammond)
COREEN, to Nfld. Said to be from C.I. ca 1750, Cf CAREEN of J (Rev. Hammond)
CORNELL, from C.I.? to Nfld. See Seary
CORNICK, Richard, of Placentia, Nfld. 1794 (Seary) Cf CORNIC of J (Stevens)
CORNISH, Henry, of Fermeuse, Nfld. 1677 (Seary) from southern Eng. or J?
CORNU, from C.I. to Nfld. (Rev. Hammond) Cf LE CORNU of J (Stevens)
COSH in Nfld. (Seary) Cf LE COZ of J (Stevens)
COSH, COISH, to Nfld. Poss from Ald. (Rev. Hammond) Fishermen at Bay de Verdes, Conc. Bay, Nfld. 1860s. John, Joseph, Thomas, Robert and Wm. See also Seary
COSTARD, from C.I. to W. coast of Nfld. (Shortis-Munn) See Seary.
COTTER, Thomas, age 55 in 1877, res Arichat, NS, merchant. Cf LE COU-TEUR? He was mar to Louisa ---, b J ca 1830 (census)
COURAY, from J, in Maritimes fisheries (K. Mathews)
COUDRE, John, b J, in Malbaie 1861 (census) with Hannah, Julia, Eliza, Elvina, Clement, Flora, Amice, all b Canada
COUL. Three COUL bros, nephews of G. PREVEL of C.I., to Gaspe 1840s, then to U.S. (Rev. d'Hist)
COUL, COOK, COAL, Sarah Randall, "On Sat. Dec. 8, 1703, was baptised by me...Marie Therese (Mary) Coal, English, (poss C.I.) girl b at Beverly in New England...1701 of the late Joseph Coal, Eng. Prot. and of Sara Randall, taken at Saco the 21st of Aug. and brought to Canada with her children." This fam was captured by Indians and taken to Canada like so many of the New Englanders at the turn of the century. She was mar in 1718 to Pierre Rougeau, called Berger. The girl's surname is there written as Therese Cool, dau of Joseph Cool and Sere, native of Boston. Her chn were baptized at Boucherville, Que. (Coleman)
COULL, from C.I.? in Gaspe
COULLARD, Pvt. Frank, b J, related to Doris M. Coullard, St. Heliers, J, enlisted 1914, Reinforcements, Princess Pats, Lt. Inf., Ottawa, Ont. (OUR HEROES IN THE GREAT WORLD WAR, by J.H. De Wolfe, Can. 1919)
COUILLARDS, some in Western Canada, from C.I.?
COUILLIARD, Philip, b J, blacksmith, age 28 in 1871 at Perce, Que. (Brochet)
COURAGE, John, from C.I.? in Harbour Grace, Nfld. 1800s (Rev. Hammond)

COURAGE, COURISH?, John and Joseph, from C.I.? in Catalina, Nfld. 1860s
   Cf J surname COURISH. See also Seary
COUTANCHE, Edward, bp 1799 J, res 1861 as carpenter in Anse au Griffon,
   Gaspe, with wife, Nancy, bp 1804 J (Remiggi)
COUTANCHE, Charles, son of Tranquille C. and Mathurine Day of J, mar at
   Carleton, Que. 1844 to Zoe Parent, dau of Francois Parent and Marie
   Veilleux (Gallant)
A1. Rachel, b Carlton 1846   A3. Charles, twin, b Carleton 1849
A2. Francois-Martial, b Carleton 1849
COUTANCHE, COUTANGES, etc., Charles of J?, rem to C.B. mar Euphrosine
   DES ROCHES, qv., dau of Regis DES ROCHES (Stephen White, Moncton, NB)
A1. Philippe, b ca 1822, d 1897, unmar. Res with Charles Forgeron and
   Charlotte Clory, West Arichat, C.B.
A2. Clement, b ca 1829, mar 1855 at Arichat, Angele Quick, dau of Joseph
   Q. and Rosalie GIRROIR, d 1856
A3. Marie-Euphrosine, b ca 1835, mar 1856 at Arichat, Thomas Upton, son
   of John U. and Mary Proctor. He was a laborer in 1871
COUTANCHE, Walter, from J to Manitoba, farmer, came in 1909 (Luce)
COUTANCHE, Philip, signed Gaspe Petition 1820, also in J.H. Le Breton
   List
COUTANCHE, Jane Susan, 1859-1883, res Gaspe (GLF)
COUTANCHE, May, b J?, mar ca 1900 St. John, J, George Joshua LE MAR-
   QUAND, qv., res BC
COUTANCHE, res Thunder Bay, Ont.
COUTANCHE, Edward, b 1799 J, mar Nancy ---, b 1804 J, in Cap Rosier
   1861 (census) Poss related to TOUET fam
COUTANCHE, see DE BOURCIER
                                          COUTURE
COUTURE, on Bonaventure Is., 1831   NOT CH.ISLAND FAMILIES!
COUTURE, of C.I. fam?, Philip, son of Edouard and Nancy Molseur, mar
   1830 Genevieve Flynn, Bon. Is.
COUTURE, Euphrosine, mar 1825 Grande Riviere, Gaspe, Philip LANGLOIS,
   son of Jean-Ely and Marguerite GALLICHAUD, poss GALLICHAN? of J.
   See LANGLOIS
COUTURE, Charles, poss son of above?, wife Marguerite TRACHY, qv., Lou-
   isa, John and Joseph, all b Canada were in Perce 1861 (census), also
   many other COUTURES
COUTURE, some in Cap Chat, Gaspe, 1861 census
COUTURE, Antoine, Edmund, Frederick, James, John and Joseph listed in
   Alpena, Mich. directory 1905,6. Some Gaspe fams are known to have
   rem to Alpena and Mich. in middle and later 1800s
COVIEDUCK, see CABELDU
COWIE, from C.I. to Perce? (Cent. Bklt.)
COWLEY, see CAWLEY (E. Le Boutillier)
COX, LA COX, see LE CAUX, Gaspe fam from J
COVVYDUCK, COBBADUC, etc. "An unusual surname in Nfld. is COVEYDUCK.
   Earlier forms are COBBIDUCK. John, John Jr., Joseph and William
   lived in Salmon Cove, Conc. Bay, in 1870s. (Lovell) Another form was
   COBBADUC, Charles, who lived in Seal's Cove or Indian Pond, Nfld.
   1871...CABELDU has occurred in the Channel Islands, and is listed in
   1972 in Jersey. The name is pronounced by older folk as COVEYDOE."
   (Mary Ann Gallup, Swampscott, Mass.)
COX in Nfld. (Seary) Cf CAUX, DE CAUX, LE COCQ, etc. of J (Stevens)
CRAWFORD in Nfld. (Seary) Cf CRAFFORD of J 1669 (Stevens)
CREASEY, Frank, from G in Victoria, BC 1940 (Luce)
CREIGHTON, fam from J at Pt. St. Peter Gaspe, 1800s (Le Moine)
CRISBY in Nfld. (Seary) Cf CRESPEL of J (Stevens)
CROCKER and CROFT, curr Gaspe and BC, from C.I.?

CRONYN, V.F., from C.I. to BC (Luce)
CRONIN in Victoria, BC, said to be from C.I. (Luce)
CROSS, LE CROIX, DE LA CROIX, from C.I. in Canada
CROSS in Nfld. (Seary) Cf CROIX, CROSS, DE STE. CROIX of C.I. (Stevens)
See Seary
CROSSE, from C.I.?, to Perce, Gaspe (Cent. Bklt.)
CROIX, from J, in Maritimes fisheries (K. Mathews) See DE STE. CROIX
CRUCHET, A.B., from C.I.? to Aurora, Ont. 1800s (Stone)
CUBIT, C.I. surname on S coast of Nfld. (G.W. Le Messurier)
CUQUS (Sic) This surname poss LE CUCU, or similar of G
CUQUS, John, age 29, single, 2 yrs. in Cape Breton 1821, served 6 yrs. in H.M. ships REGULUS and SURVEILLANTE, asked lot in Riviere Habitant, C.B. (PANS)
CURNEW, Jerseymen in Nfld., from LE CORNU, qv., or QUENAULT (Shortis-Munn) See Seary. John from C.I. in Port de Grave, Nfld. 1784. Others in Brigus, etc.
CURRIE, C., member C.I. Soc. 1941 in Victoria, BC (Luce)
CURTIS in Nfld. (Seary) Cf CURTIS of J (Stevens)
CUSTANCE, in Canada, from J? Cf COUTANCHE, COUSTANCHE of J
CUSSION, Gregg, from C.I. to Agincourt, Ont. 1900s
CUTLER, Wm. R., b 1821, mar ---HUBERT, qv., of Arichat, C.B., 4 sons and 1 dau, who mar W.H. PAINT, qv. (Cochrane) Some Cutlers in N.S. are thought to be formerly LE COUTEUR, qv., or desc of ABRAHAM COUTEUR, Hug., res near French Church in Leicester Fields, Eng. (See FOREIGN PROTESTANTS IN THE SETTLEMENT OF CANADA, by Winthrop Bell)
DA COSTA, DE COSTER, ---, "was probably a native of the Channel Islands, and in his early years joined the Board of Artificers (Ordnance or Engineers) and with this corps served in many parts of the world. He was stationed at Annapolis Royal, NS in 1738. While there was a member of the Masonic Lodge formed there in that year by Erasmus James PHILLIPS, qv., son? of Col. Richard Philipps, under a deputation from Henry PRICE of Boston. This was the first lodge on Canadian soil. He had a dau Martha, who lived in Annapolis in 1756, and may also have had at least one son. A Dorothy Jane DE COSTA, b 1797, dau of Mary DE COSTA of Granville was baptized 1798. The baptism was by an S.P.G. Missionary at Granville." "Da Costa was in Boston, Mass. for the preparations for the second reduction of Louisbourg in 1758, and later was in Halifax." (Canadian Masonic Research Assoc. in Halifax, letter to Richard E. Spurr of Arlington, Va 1965) DE CASTRO, Charlotte, mar in N.S. middle 1800s?, Claude Philip LE QUESNE, a son, Colin LE QUESNE (LE QUESNE chart)
DAIN, from C.I. to Ontario? Cf LE DAIN of C.I.
DALEY, DALY in Nfld. (Seary) Cf DALET of J, also D'ALLAIN (Stevens)
DALLAIN, C.I. fishermen in the Maritimes (J.H. Le Breton list)
D'ALLAIN, Adolphus John, Jersey lawyer from J to Montreal ca 1865
DALLAIN, Capt. Alphonse in BC late 1800s from J
DAMPIER in Nfld. (Seary) Cf DAMPIER of J (Stevens)
DANCY in Nfld. (Seary) Cf DANCY of J (Stevens)
DANIEL, merchant from G in Nfld. (K. Mathews) See also Seary
DARBY in Nfld. (Seary) Cf DARBY of J (Stevens) DARBY: SEE EXTRA
D'AUVERGNE, from J to Nfld. (K. Mathews)   PAGES
DAVEY, George William, b 1868 South Petherton, Somerset, England, rem to G ca 1890, where he mar Alice Mary LE PREVOST, 1870-1929, dau of Julia LE PREVOST, qv., 1850-1928. Alice and Julia both b Vale, G. LE PREVOST thought to be Hug fam. Settled Chatham, Ont. ca 1914 (Edw. Davey, Chatham, Ont.; Edwin Hamon, Chatham, Ont.)
Al. Maria, 1892-1973   A?. Also a John DAVEY in this family

A2. George, b 1894 G, rem to Chatham, Ont. mar Maria WRIXTON, b 1891
    G, d Chatham 1973
    B1. Mollie, b 1924, mar Murray French, res Chatham, Ont.
        C1. Brian French, b 1967   C2. David French, b 1971
    B2. Gladys, b 1927, mar Murray ROSE, qv., res Blenheim, Ont.
        C1. Margaret Rose, b 1947, mar ---Brophie, res Lucan, Ont.
            D1. Stephanie Brophie, b 1974
            D2. James Edward Brophie, b 1976
        C2. Diane Rose, b 1949   C3. Janet Rose, b 1951
A3. Nellie, b 1895 G, unmar, res Chatham, Ont.
A4. Eva, b 1897 G, d Chatham 1976, mar Clifford LE BRUN, qv., b 1898 G.
    He d 1966
    B1. Bette Le Brun, mar Hicks, no issue
A5. William, b 1898 G, d Chatham 1963. Mar Marguerite Clark
    B1. Clarke William, b ca 1927, mar Joyce Gordon, res Toronto, Ont.
        C1. Richard, b 1955   C2. Kevin, b 1958   C3. Clarke, b 1962
    B2. Kenneth, b ca 1930, mar Janet Evans, res Toronto
        C1. Christopher, b 1963 C2. Megan, b 1966 C3. Catherine, b 1969
A6. Edward, b 1904 G, mar Gladys LE BRUN, sister of Clifford, above,
    mar 2. Gilberte MAISONEUVE, res Chatham, Ont.
    B1. Donald Elwyn, b 1931 Ottawa, mar Martha Senior, res Cheltenham,
        Glou. England
        C1. Angelina, b 1968 London, England
        C2. Edward Antonio, b 1969, London, England
DAVEY in Nfld. (Seary) From C.I.?
DAVID, Capt. from G in Nfld. (K. Mathews) See also Seary
DAVIS, Fred, b C.I. and wife, Florence---, to Mt. Hamilton, Ont. 1900s
    (Gaudion)
DAVIS, Emma Mary, b 1828 J, nee HOSKING, dau of J blacksmith, mar 1861.
    Widowed young, 8 chn, rem to Edmonton, Alta. 1912 with mar dau Mary
    RODDA, qv. One of Mrs. Davis' brothers went to the Calif. Gold Rush
    in 1849, and d in America. Another bro was a missionary to India.
    (Grace Rodda Beck, Vancouver, BC)
A1. Mary Davis, b ca 1881, mar Richard Elias RODDA, qv., 1903, St.
    Mark's, St. Heliers, J
    B1. Grace Rodda, mar Beck   B3. Florence May, d.y. 1908
    B2. Mary Gladys, d.y. 1904
DAWSON, Roy G., b England, fam rem to G where father was in partner-
    ship with a Mrs. FERBRACHE, in a grocery and general store in St.
    Peter Port. Emigrated to Riverside, Calif. 1958. R. Dawson res St.
    Peter Port and St. Andrews, G, emigrating to Ontario, Canada 1964.
    (R. Dawson, Newcastle, Ont.)
DEAN, Carteret, involved 1717 with Nfld. trade (C.R. Fay) See also
    Seary
DEAN, Capt. Philip from C.I., had a fishery on Newport Islands, Gaspe
    1840s (Le Moine)
D'EANE, Philip, b J, son of Hug fam in Gaspe Basin 1850s, 1860s. (Thos.
    Pye, Brochet)
DEAN, from C.I. in Gaspe and B.C.
DEAN, Andrew, at Bonaventure Is., Que. 1825 (Brochet)
DEAN, John, at Newport 1819
DEARING, see Carole May TRACHY
DE BEAUCAMP, DE BEAUVOIR, DE BLANCHELANDE, G surnames of 1117
DE BOIS, Francis, signed Petition of 1820 in Gaspe. Origin unver.
DE BOURCIER, J, from C.I. to Victoria, BC, there in 1940 (Luce) Poss
    from St. Aubin, J. In 1907, a De B. had a bakery in J. (Soc. J.
    Bull., 1977)

DE BOURCIER

DE BOURSIER, see extra pages.
DE BOURCIER, R.J., b J, son of Francis Philip de B. and Harriet COUTANCHE, qv., of St. Aubin, J, to Boston then to Victoria, BC, descs in BC
DE BOURCHIER, from C.I. in Maritimes fisheries 1800s (J. H. Le Breton list)
DE BRODER, see ROMERIL, and QAAM
DE CANE, DE CAIN, Capt. from J in Nfld. (K. Mathews) See also CANE in Seary, and LE QUESNE
DE CAEN, see LE GRESLEY. Joseph DE CAEN was Charles Robin's firm gardener in Perce, 1800s. Joseph DE CAEN, mar ---ROBIN, dau of Stanislaus ROBIN, all of J stock
DE CAEN, in western Canada and Newport, Gaspe

A Huguenot, Guillaume de Caen, and his nephew, Emery de Caen, ship owners of La Rochelle, Huguenots in Quebec before 1620. (TOME 48, Archives Nationale de Quebec)
DE CAEN, Anna, mar PALMER, qv. a son. She b 1855 Canada?
DE CAEN, Harold Frederick Balleine, b 1887 J?, d 1972, son of George Frederick de Caen 1858-1929, and Dorcas Aimee Stephens, mar Violet Labat (Anderson)
A1. Roland Frederick Balleine, b 1931 Ireland, res Calgary, Alta., mar Alison Errey 1960
B1. Allan Roland Balleine, b 1962 B2. Susan Alexandra Jane, b 1970
A2. Blanche, b 1899, d 1960, mar Gerald Scott, a Col. in Indian Army
B1. Pamela Scott, b 1920, no issue
DE CAEN, George Frederick, poss same as above, left J ca 1880 for England, then Ireland. A son b 1889, served in Br. Army (R.F.B. De Caen, Calgary, Alta., chart)
DE CAIN, John, signed the petition of 1820 in Gaspe. Poss LE QUESNE, or CAIN
DE CARTERET, CARTERET, David from J to Perce 1830s or earlier
A1. Susan, b 1837 Perce, d 1914, mar Francis LE BRUN, b 1835, J, 10 chn. See LE BRUN
DE CARTERET, Thomas, b Vale, G, rem to Niagara Falls, Ont. 1920. His bro John had res there since 1913. Their mother, Mrs. John LE PAGE, qv. joined them after her 92nd birthday. She d there at 95. Cousins to Mrs. Hilda Amy, nee GOUBERT, res Canada. Related also to Mrs. W. George, nee BOUGOURD, of J, res Great Bookham, Surrey, Eng.
DE CARTERET, from C.I. to Perce 1800s (Syvret, J.H. Le Breton list)
DE CARTERET, Yvonne, from J to Portland, Oregon, then to Canada, middle 1900s

DE CARTERET, Joseph, b Sark Island, in Perce 1861 (census)
DE CARTERETS, from C.I. in Trois Rivieres, Que., 1800s? (Wm. Mainguy)
DE CARTERET, David, in Perce, Gaspe, 1845, witnessed a sale of land by John James BROCHET, qv. to John HAMON, qv. of Bon. Is. (Aldo Brochet) Was age 48 in 1871.
DE CARTERET, Peter, b J, age 38 in 1827, mar, 4 chn, had land in Cape Breton, NS (PANS)
DE CARTERET, Peter, with Peter LE VESCONTE, qv. of J, owned several vessels at Arichat, Cape Breton, NS, including the SEAFLOWER, 71 tons, built at Descousses 1835. (Capt. Parker) and the PETER AND JANE, 80 ton brigantine built 1823, transferred to J in 1824, the MARTHA, 28 tons, at River Bourgeois, C.B., the LADY FALKLAND, in 1840, 150 tons or 182 tons, owned by De Carteret and Le Vesconte, transferred to J. Other ships mentioned in Capt. Parker's book, SHIPS AND MEN OF CAPE BRETON

DE CARTERET, Clement, son of John de Carteret and Elizabeth BELIN, mar 1746, rem to Nfld. ca 1776 (Soc. Jers. Bull,. 1897-1901)
DE CARTERET, Peter, b 1786, rem to N.S. where he became a J.P. and Col. in local militia. Mar 1846, he d in Switzerland 1875. He was the son of Jean de Carteret, b 1748 and Rebecca RAULAND, ROWLAND. (Soc. Jers. Bull., 1897-1901)
DE CAUX, DE COX, COX, etc. From Pays du Caux, France. "our ancestors, Huguenots, fled from France at the time of the French Revolution. We know there were ancestors that went to Jersey, and our relatives are in England." (Gregory Lynn DE CAUX)
DE CAUX, William Shakespear, b Norwich, Eng. of J fam in 1860, d 1935. To Canada, res Vict., BC 1909, then to Calgary in 1912. Mar Charlotte GARRETTE
  A1. Harold Walter Cornilius, b 1900 London to Canada 1911, then to Calgary 1912. Mar Rose Matilda Poffenroth
    B1. Edward Harold, b 1934 Calgary, mar Jeneane Young
    B2. Gregory Lynn de Caux, b 1947 Calgary, mar Gail Diane Scott
DE CHESNEY, Eleanor, in G 1359, mar ---WALLIS. Closely associated with early history of C.I., there in 1248. Name noted in Canada
DE COSTER, DA COSTA, qv., to N.S. Gertrude DE COSTER mar in NS 1903 Edward Johnson, res Auburn, Me. (Ryerson Genealogy, by Albert Ryerson, 1916, Chicago) See also Pierre-Jean DOREY of Arichat, C.B.
DEE, Maurice, from C.I.? to Great Placentia Bay, Nfld. ca 1864,5. (Rev. Hammond) Said to be of C.I. orig., poss De Dee of J (Stevens)
DE FEU, John, age 39, b J, blacksmith, at Gaspe Bay 1871. See also DU FEU (Brochet)
DE GARIE, prob DE GARIS, from G? in Richmond Co., NS 1861 (census)
DE GARIS, Peter John, Sr., b G, a carpenter, d Ont. 1956, to Toronto 1907. Built home at 36 Hastings Ave. (C.M. De Garis, Peterboro, Ont.)
  A1. Nellie Green   A4. Peter John, Jr.
  A2. Clara TOSTEVIN, husband from G A5. Bert
  A3. Annie BEAUMONT   A6. Madeline Hornett
DE GALLIE, C.I. surname in Quebec (K.H. Annett)
DE GARIS, ---, wife of ---PRIAULX, to Gaspe early 1800s from G. See MACHON
DE GARIE, curr Gaspe
DES GARRIS, Nicholas, son of Nicholas and Judith BALIN, BALLEINE? of G, mar 1833 Cape Cove, Gaspe to Julienne Duguay (Gallant)
DE GARIS, Job, b G, in Gaspe 1861 (census) with Mary, Lydia, James, Jane and William, all b Gaspe
DE GARIS, John, b G, in Douglastown, Gaspe 1861 (census) with Betsy, b Ireland and Harriette, b Gaspe. A Harriet was born in 1841 in Gaspe (Brochet) Poss Betsy's surname was PRUNTY?
DE GARRETT, fishmerchant, Arichat, also, ship builder, ca 1800, said to be C.I. origin. See also JERRETT (Brouinot, C.B.)
DE GRAVE, Peter, from C.I., Port de Grave, Nfld., Con. Bay, early
DE GRAY in Alderney very early 1226. See GRAY
DE GRUCHY, Charles, b 1845 St. Heliers, J, mar Anna LE BOUTILLIER in J, qv., and d Canada 1910, 4 chn (Kenneth De Gruchy, Gaspe, Que.; GLF)
  A1. Percy Charles John, b 1880 J, d Cape Cove, Gaspe. Mar Eva BAKER, qv., 1879-1946. He d 1953.
    B1. Reginald Percy, b 1905 Gaspe, mar Jean Charlotte LE TOUZEL, qv., no issue
    B2. William Ralph, b 1920, mar Doreen Miller, 2 sons, res Ottawa, Ont.
      C1. John Laird   C2. William Kark
    B3. Doris Joyce, b 1910, d 1975, mar Robert Whitcombe, a son, David, res Batavia, NY.

DE GRUCHY

B4. Charles Kenneth, b 1926, mar Eveline Scott, a son, Richard Charles, Gaspe
A2. Wallace George, d at 3 mos.   A4. Charles James Gerald, b 1913,
A3. another son, res England?   d.y.
DE GRUCHY, listed as J merchant at Woody Point, Bonne Bay, west coast of Nfld. 1800s. (Mannion) William settled at Pouch Cove in early 1800s (Seary) Thomas in St. John's Harbour, 1704. Others named in Seary
DE GRUCHY, RENOUF, CLEMENT ET CIE, of Channel Burgeo, Nfld., 1800s?
DE GRUCHY, ---, grandson of the De Gruchy firm founder, rem to Canada where he d in a railway accident on his own property (Dixon)
DE GRUCHY, Philip, b 1789, Moses b 1791, Abraham, b 1793, and John, b 1795,6. All from St. Saviou, J, rem to Canada.
DE GRUCHY, Jeannette, b 1880 Trinity, J, mar Thomas LE BRUN, rem to Grand Etang, N.S., 4 chn. See LE BRUN
DE GRUCHY, C.I. name assoc with the Robin firm in Paspebiac, and with town of New Carlisle, Que. (Que. Provincial Archives, and J.H. Le Breton list)
DE GRUCHY, John F., from J? to Toronto 1954
DE GRUCHY, Francis P., to Ottawa, 1954, mar ---RENAULT (J. De Gruchy, Don Mills, Ont.)
DE GRUCHY, Philip, b J in Perce 1861 (census)
DE GRUCHY, Charles, b 1853 J, with Robin firm at Cape Cove, Gaspe, d 1908
DE GRUCHY, DE GREECHY, George, b 1700s J, settled N.S. Son, Herbert, had a business in N.S. and PEI. Mar twice: 1. Virginia, a Cree Indian, mother of his sons, and 2. Veronica ---. (R.M. Grinstead, Sarasota, Fla.)
A1. Hubert Albert, mar Malvina Senay, b 1862
B1. Georgiana Mary, mar G.W. Lambert 1919   B3. a son, mar ---Senay
B2. A son, mar ---Senay
DE GRUCHY, to Gaspe (Rev. d'Hist., ARC)
DE GRUCHY, Ellen, at Cape Cove, Perce, Que. 1831
DE GRUCHY, and BOUDREAU, J firm at L'Anse a Beaufils, Gaspe
DE GRUCHY, merchant at Arichat, NS ca 1800 (Bourinot)
DE GRUCHY, Nicolle and Co., J fishery at Little St. Lawrence, Nfld. (Rev. Hammond, Shortis-Munn)
DE GRUCHY, Capt. from J in Nfld. (K. Mathews)
DE GRUCHY, from J late 1700s to Canada, mar Marguerite ---
B1. Philip, d.y.   B4. Dorothy Annie Tighe, b ca 1896
B2. Charles   B5. William Frederick Tighe, b ca 1901
B3. Sara Elsie, b ca 1891
Above are no doubt grandchildren of the first De Gruchy.
DE GRUCHY, ---, b J? ca 1773, mar Ann GALLICHAN, qv., chn b Gaspe area, Data uncertain
A1. Ann   A3. Lillian, mar ?
A2. George or Georgia   A4. Mathew
A5. Mary Ann, b ca 1810, mar Philip LE HUQUET, 7 chn, see LE HUQUET
DE GRUCHY, Jeannette, b 1880 Trinity?,J, mar Thomas LE BRUN, rem to Grand Estang, NS, 4 chn
DE GRUCHY, GRUCHY, David of J, rem to Cape Breton, was merchant, J.P., M.P. and coroner Descousse, C.B., mar Mary Marshall, a JEAN desc, see JEAN
DE GRUCHY, said to be related to the Gibbon-INGOUVILLE fam of Cape Breton
DE GRUCHY, b J, to Perce ca 1885 for Robin, Collas and Co. Was Church Warden at St. Paul's, Perce (Cent. Bklt.)

DE GRUCHY, from J to N.B. (Rev. Le Gresley)
DE GRUCHY, Raoul, or Ray, of Rochester, NY, desc of Canadian DE GRUCHY fam? 1800s
DE HAVILLAND, HAVILAND, etc., old name in G. Some said to have settled on S coast of Nfld. (G.W. Le Messurier)
DE HUME, see DU HEAUME
DE JAUSSERAND, Mr. and Mrs. J., from J to Canada or U.S. in 1920 (Luce)
DE JAUSSERAND, from C.I. to London area 1900s. Ruth DE JAUSSERAND mar Fred Norwood. (Ruth Norwood, London, Ont.)
DE JERSEY, fam from G to Canada. Said to be a book called ANNALS OF GUERNSEY on this fam
DE JERSEY. "In 1327 one of our ancestors, John Rivers, saved King Edward III's life in battle. The king's horse was shot and John Rivers put the King on his own horse and sent him safely away. As a result John Rivers received a coat of arms and an estate in the Island of Jersey, and the name de Jersey." (Harold de Jersey, Winnipeg, Man.)
DE JERSEY, Walter John of G, mar Mary Jane LE MASURIER, and 2. Emily Maud LE BOUTILLIER
A1. Walter Rivers, b 1890, St. Clements J, d 1973, mar Ethel Mary Scott, b ca 1896. Chn by first wife
  B1. Harold R., b ca 1925, Winnipeg B3. Walter, b ca 1923
  B2. John, b ca 1921 B4. Maurice, b ca 1927, res BC
A2. Florence, b 1900, d.y.
A3. Roy, b 1901, living in 1977
  B1. William John, b 1921, mar Gloria James 1943
    C1. Robert Rivers, b 1944
    C2. Joan Elizabeth, b 1948, mar Loren Tyson 1970
      D1. Charles John Tyson, b 1974 D2. Tania Michelle Tyson, b 1976
    C3. Leslie John Stewart, b 1951 C4. Diane Lynn, b 1953
  B2. Walter Scott, b 1923, mar Beryl Janaway 1969
    C1. Doris Irene, b 1970 C2. George Scott Rivers, b 1973
  B3. Harold Rivers, b 1925, mar Margaret Doris Betteridge 1954
    C1. Donald Wayne, b 1956 C2. David James, b 1957
    C4. Maurice Fletcher de Jersey, b 1926, mar Beryl MORRISH, 1951
      D1. Alan John, b 1952, mar Faye Tyler 1973
        E1. Sean Alan, b 1975
      D2. Margaret Anne, b 1953 D5. Yvonne Clair, b 1959
      D3. Silvia Phyllis, b 1955 D6. Joyce Marie, b 1963
      D4. David Maurice, b 1957
A4. Henry de Jersey
DE JERSEY, from C.I. to Cape Breton
DE JERSEY, J.W., prob from G, to Riviere Madeleine, Que., 1858-1928, bur St. Peter's Grand Greve, Gaspe (GLF)
DE JERSEY, some with BREHAUT, qv., to PEI. Settled first next to Wm Sencabaugh at Guernsey Cove, then sold to Thomas and Henry MACHON, qv. Catherine and Thomas were in school in Murray Harbor PEI 1820. Also show in PEI census, 1841
DE JERSEY, Henry, from G in Harbour Grace, Nfld. before 1780 (M.R. Lee, S.E. Placentia, Nfld.)
DE JERSEY, and JERSEY, Capt. from G in Nfld. (K. Mathews) (French Arch.)
DE LA COUR, from C.I. on Bonaventure Is. 1831 (Syvret)
DE LA COUR, in Gaspe (J.H. Le Breton list) John at Bonaventure Is. 1800s (Brochet)
DE LA COUR, C.I. surname on S. coast of Nfld. (G.W. Le Messurier)
DE LA COUR, from C.I. to Harbor Main, Nfld. (Shortis-Munn) COUR, qv., also (Seary)
DE LA CROIX, from C.I.? to Quebec?

DE LA GARDE, Charles D., son of Charles?, and Esther GALLUCHAN, GALLI-
CHAN, of St. Heliers, J, rem to Shippegan, NB early 1800s, mar 1842
Caraquet, Venerande Robichaud. Charles d 1858, and she mar 2. at
Shippegan, William BOUCHER, with whom she had 3 chn; Joseph, Mattie-
Marie and Catherine. Some material below unverified. (J. George de
La Garde, Shippegan, NB; Nola Journeau, St. Eustache, Que.; Aldo
Brochet; Donat Robichaud)

A1. Louise, b 1843, mar 1970 Joseph PAQUET, qv., b 1838 Shippegan, rem
to Mass., d 1912
  B1. Michel Paquet, b 1881 Shippegan, NB
  B2. Venerande, mar William Robichaud, b 1881 Shippegan

A2. Isabella, b 1845 or 1847, mar 1877 James MALLET, b 1847 Shippegan,
NB, d 1929
  B1. James Mallet, d 1908   B3. Marie Mallet
  B2. Joseph Mallet

A3. Venerande, b ca 1849, mar Charles Rochford, res Kingston, Ont., d
1930

A4. Charles, b ca 1852, mar 1. Elmire Rioux, 10 chn, and 2. Louise de
Grace, who d 1974, age 102. 5 chn. Charles d ca age 86.
  B1. Louis Philippe, religious   B3. Marie Louise
  B2. Eugene, diocesan priest   B4. Helene, nun
  B5. Philomene, mar Alphonse G. Robichaud, widower with 3 small chn,
no issue
    C1. Onile, mar Adrienne Mazerolle, res Detroit, Mich.
    C2. Agnes, mar Norman Goodrum (Gooderham?), res Drummondville, Que.
    C3. Marie Alma, mar Pitt MALLET, res Shippegan
  B6. Julienne, d 1919
  B7. Hilaire, b 1882, d 1904, mar 1. Georgiana Brison 1911, dau of
Charles B. and Helene Losier. Helene was his 3rd wife. (Nicho-
las Denys Soc., Caraquet, Vol 1, #5) Hilaire d 1964
  B8. Elmire, by Louise de Grace, unmar, res Moncton, NB
  B9. Alma, mar Raymond BRIDEAU, res NY City
  B10. Joseph
  B11. Imelda, mar Jacques Trottier, res Montreal. Que.
  B12. Venerande, mar Clarence Savoie, res Pointe Verte, NB, b ca 1916,
taught 35 yrs. in Pointe Verte. 8 grandchn
    C1. Reginald Savoie
    C2. Michel Savoie, res Moncton
    C3. Daniel Savoie
    C4. Micheline Savoie, mar Jacques McNeil, res Victoriaville, Que.
    C5. Louisette, mar Vincent Trentadue, res St. Zotique, Que.
  B13. Charles, poss of this fam? b ca 1891 St. Isidore, Shippegan, Que.,
d 1977. Mar Marie Hache? who d at age 90
    C1. Charles Eugene, res Shippegan, NB   C6. Philomene, res Mon-
    C2. Claude, res Tracadie, mar ---Ferguson   treal
    C3. Florina?, res Shippegan   C7. Alfreda, res Ship-
    C4. Stella, mar ---Robichaud, res   pegan, NB
        Inkerman, NB   C8. Rita, res St. Isidore,
    C5. Bertha, res Montreal   NB
    C9. Lea, res St. Isidore, NB
    C10. Irene?, mar Remi JEAN, qv., res Drummondville, Que.
    C11. Ernestine, mar Robert Charpentier, res Drummondville, Que.
    C12. Marie-Ange, mar Piere-Paul ROY, res Drummondville, Que.
    C13. Rose Helene, mar Jack Power, res Bathurst, NB
    C14. Anita, mar ---Hache, res Allardville, NB?
    C15. Jacqueline, mar ---Cote, res Drummondville, Que.

A5. Esther, b ca 1856, mar August Robichaud, b 1849

B1. Venerande, Vinnie, b 1876 Shippegan, NB, mar James De Grace
B2. John, b 1878, mar 1. Marie Hache, no issue, and 2. Odile Boucher
  C1. Linda, mar Leonard LUCE, qv.   C4. August
  C2. Sylvia, mar J. Baldwin   C5. Lea
  C3. Paul, mar Gaston Chiasson   C6. Elda   C7. Estelle
B3. Philippe August, b 1880, d.y.   B5. Germaine, b 1883, d.y.
B4. David Isidore, b 1881   B6. Annee Leonie, b 1884, d 1890
B7. Edmond, b 1886, mar Ida Gallant, res Dalhousie, NB, d 1963
B8. Philippe, b 1888, drown at age 22
B9. Leonie, b 1890, mar Albert Gravet, res Bridgeport, Mass.
B10. Emile, b 1891, mar Josephine Mazerolle, res Bathurst, NB
B11. Augustin, b 1893, d 1964
B12. Edward, b 1897, mar Marguerite Ferguson, res US, d 1974
B13. Charles, b 1899, mar Jeanne St. Charles, res Montreal, d 1960
B14. Anne, b 1901, d 1964
B15. Freda, mar Joseph de Grace, res Bangor, ME
A6. John, b 1855, mar Margaret Cesare PAQUET, 1881, 12 chn
B1. Theodore, b 1881, d 1903, unmar
B2. Charles, b 1883, d 1961, unmar, schoolteacher
B3. Rose Anna, b 1885, mar Arthur Savoy, d 1965 Athol, Mass.
B4. Margaret, b 1887, d 1889   B5. Lucy, b 1889, d 1912, teacher
B6. John, b 1890, d 1957, mar Ida Nelson, 1896-1970, res Dalhousie, NB, 11 chn
B7. Ellen, Helen, b 1892, res Athol, Mass., mar Michel Boccardy, teacher
B8. Joseph Georges, b 1894, unmar, res Shippegan, NB, jurist
B9. Sophie, b 1896, d 1973, mar Evariste de Grace, res Athol, Mass., teacher
B10. Armand, b 1898, d.y.
B11. Lauza, b 1900, teacher, d 1924   B12. Dianna, b 1902, d.y.
DE LA HAYE, of J?, Philip, b Carlisle, Que. ca 1887 (Brochet)
DE LA HAYE, a young man from J to Texford, Sask., poss with Barr Group ca 1903, mentioned in Genge book by LE GALLAIS, qv.
DE LA HAYE, Prof. J.P., at Upper Canada College in 1829. Poss from J?
DE LA HAYE, Jack, b J?, mar ca 1840 Mary QUERREE, qv., rem to Canada. (Mrs. C. Querrie, Toronto, Ont.)
DE LA HAYE, Samuel, b J ca 1885?, to Montreal ca 1900? Lumberman, capitalist! (Mrs. Owen, Peace River, Alta.)
DE LA HAYE, Charles Dickson, to Magpie, Malbaie and Paspebiac 1900s, mar Elsie LE GRESLEY, qv. Charles b 1887 J?, d 1950. Worked for Robin firm, bur St. Peter's, Paspebiac, Gaspe (GLF)
A1. Kingsley   A2. Selwyn
DELAIN and A. MALLOWNEY, said to be J firm at Barachois, Gaspe
DE LA MARE, Chan. Islanders in Maritimes fisheries 1800s? (J.H. Le Breton list)   **DE LA MARE, MUCH DATA IN MORMON RECORDS!**
DE LA MARE, Rev. ---, b 1820 J, to Gaspe. Information incomplete on this fam, but there is more in Salt Lake City, back to 1597 in Guernsey. See QAAM by Turk
A1. Philip Mourant, poss son of above Rev., b 1856 St. Helier, J, to British Columbia, then to Los Angeles, Calif. Mar 1. Louisa Jane Waddington, 1863-1912, and 2. Cora ---
B1. Philip Waddington, b 1889, to B.C.
B2. Winifred Eva, b 1891, Mission City, BC, 2 chn, d 1922
B3. Anita Louise, b 1900 J, to Los Angeles, Calif. with father, mar Adams
DE LA MARE, Rev. Francis, b J, mar 1847 Charlotte ---, in Cap Chat., Gaspe 1861 (census) Some of this fam bur St. Paul's Anglican Ch, Gaspe

DE LA MARE   213

This fam may be related to one above.
A1. Theophilus A2. George Jehosaphat A3. Alma Jane A4. Eva
DE LA MARE, Jean, christened 1766 St. Saviour, G, son of Nicholas D.
  and Jeanne DE GARIS, qv. Jean's fam was living in Gaspe in 1820 (Salt
  Lake City records)
DE LA MARE, James, chr 1766 St. Saviour, G, bro of Jean, above. His
  fam also res in Gaspe 1820
DE LA MARE, Julia Rachel, b 1840 Les Prevosts, St. Saviour, G, rem to
  Canada and mar there, Henry Grimsell. She d 1912 (SLC)
DE LA MARE, James Victor, b 1897 Forest, G, son of James D., rem to
  Hamilton, Ont. 1921, mar ---, returned to G 1943, where he d. Dau,
  Doreen
DE LA MARE, K., b G, father from St. Sampson, and mother from St. Peter
  Port, G, to Scarboro, Ont. 1970 (K.E. De la Mare, Scarborough, Ont.)
DE LA PERELLE, DE LA PARRELLE, etc., Bros. Fishery firm, from J, at
  Cape Cove, Gaspe (J.H. Le Breton list, Rev. D'Hist, Le Moine, Betty
  Tardif list)
DE LA PERELLE, Charles, of J?, signed a petition to the NB Government
  at Bathurst, NB in 1843
DE LA PERELLE, Elias and George, b J, in Perce 1861 (census, Cent.
  Bklt., PET 1820)
DE LA PERELLE, Francois and Edward in Gaspe (Cent. Bklt.)
DE LA PERELLE, Capt. from J in Nfld. (K. Mathews)
DE LA PERELLE BROS. & CO., at Petite Riviere, Gaspe, early 1800s. Bought
  land at Perce, Gaspe from the son of Remi Roussy. Elias and others
  named to Power of Attorney for James Robin, at Gr. Riviere, Gaspe
  (Aldo Brochet)
LE PERELLE, lumber company established at Rimouski, Que. ca 1900
DE LA PERRELLE, John, at Natashquan, Labrador coast of Quebec, in 1873
  (Brochet)   DELAREE OF ONT. SEE ADDITIONS & CORRECTIONS!
DE LA ROCQUE, DES ROCHES, occurs in C.I. Many ROCK surnames in Canada,
  poss some derived from these C.I. surnames
DE LA RONDE in N.A., said to be from ancient fam of J., poss Hug.
DE LA RUE, Capt. from G and J in Nfld. (K. Mathews)
DE LA RUE. One of these fams in G is connected in ancient times to
  the LA RUE, DE LAREAU fam of St. Remi, Dieppe, Rouen, France in the
  1600s (Olivier; Paul Lareau, So. St. Paul, Minn.)
DE LA RUE in Western Canada, origin unverified
DE LA TASTE, John, from J in Harbor Grace, Nfld. before 1780 (French
  Archives, M. R. Lee, S. E. Placentia, Nfld.)
DE LAUNEY, DELAUNEY in Nfld. (Seary) Cf DELAUNEY of J (Stevens)
DE LISLE, Peter, b G, res 3 yrs. in Cape Breton, NS by 1820. Asked
  water lots in Sydney, CB for wharf and stores (Cape Breton land
  papers, PANS)
DE LISLE, Dr. David De Garis, res Assiniboia, Man. 1800s?
DE LISLE, rem from C.I., prob G, to Canada, Japan, Africa, England,
  France, and two to S.A. (Fay, Soc. Jers. Bull., 1977)
DE LISLE, Francis Joseph Peter, from G to Deseronto, Ont. 1886 (F.J.
  De Lisle, Toronto)   SEE DE LISLE FAMILY IN QUIET
DE LISLE, curr Gaspe and BC   ADVENTURERS IN NORTH AMERICA!
DE LISLE, Charles of G to Ont. in middle 1800s, desc in BC
DE LISLE, curr Calgary and Toronto
DE LISLE, Mary Jane, 1814-1873, dau of Frederick DE LISLE, a London
  banker of J fam, and of Elizabeth JANVRIN, qv., mar Thomas Grassie
  of Halifax, NS (Soc. Jers. Bull., 1968)
DE LISLE, data below from chart by Howard G. Schreiber on Brock-De Lisle
  fams

DE LA MARE, SEE EXTRA PAGES.
DE LISLE, Louise, b 1795, d 1875. Dau of John CAREY, qv. of G and Judith MAINGAY, qv. In 1869 she had 150 acres of land in Ontario and deeded these to her niece's three chn: Herbert, Weymouth, and Edith Schreiber, see below. The land had been given to her by Daniel DE LISLE BROCK, bro of Sir Isaac BROCK, qv. of G.
DE LISLE, Harriet, mar 1856 G, d 1861. Mar Weymouth G. Schreiber 1826-1898. She was the dau of Mary CAREY and Capt. Hirzel Frederick De Lisle, both being desc of the fam of Sir Isaac Brock. Res Toronto. Schreiber's first wife was Charlotte Brock MORRELL, qv.
  A1. Edith Harriet Schreiber, b 1857, d 1939. Mar 1880 William Quin, Q. E., res Toronto
    B1. Edith De Lisle Quin, 1882-1959, unmar
  A2. Weymouth De Lisle Schreiber, b 1859, d 1955, mar 1882 Ottilie Graham, res Erindale, Ont.
    B1. Marjorie Schreiber, mar ---BEATTY, res Caledonia?, Ont.
    B2. Marion Schreiber, mar ---Robinson, res Toronto
    B3. Ottilie Schreiber, mar ---Mason, res Toronto, chn, and grandchn
  A3. Herbert Harrie Schreiber, 1861-1940, mar 1. 1882 Beatrice Mary Walker, 2. Olivia Clara Barth, d 1958
    B1. Enid May Schreiber, b 1877, mar Archdeacon Cecil Swanson, res Calgary? 3 mar daus
    B2. Norman De Lisle Schreiber, b 1889, mar Grace Graham, res Burns Lake, BC, son and dau
    B3. Edith Caroline Rose Schreiber, b 1891, mar 1923 a cousin, Cuthbert Charles Schreiber, 1870-1956
      C1. Beatrice Mary Schreiber, b 1924, mar 1947 Commander Neville Geary, res Halifax, NS, 3 chn
      C2. Howard Gibbon Schreiber, b 1925, res Toronto
      C3. Wilfred Weymouth Schreiber, b 1926, mar Audrey Anderson, 7 chn, res Milton, Ont.
      C4. John Harrie Schreiber, b 1929, mar Sally Evans, 3 chn, res Caledonia, Ont.
    B4. Collingwood Schreiber, b 1894, mar Lorna Libby, 3 mar daus in Langley, BC
    B5. Beatrice Mary Schreiber, b 1896, mar Guy Clarkson, res Toronto, 3 chn
    B6. (by Olivia Barth) H. S. Schreiber, mar Ruth Holland
      C1. Mary Ellen Schreiber   C3. Harris, res Pt. Carling, Ont.
      C2. Peter Schreiber
DE LOUCHE, M.P., mar Jeanne CABELDU, qv. of J, 1834, and rem to Canada (Marion Casselman, Hepworth, Ont.)
DE LOUCHE, DE LUCE, in Nfld. 1871 (Seary) Cf DE LOUCHE of J, and LUCE of C.I. (Stevens) DE MOUILPIED TO INGLIS, MAN.CANADA also.
DE MOUILPIED, a parson at Perce, Gaspe in 1861 (census) Rev. Joseph, b G, also Sophia, Emily, Sophie, Francis, Charles, and Walter, b G. Poss S.P.G. Missionary at Malbaie, also. See BAREFOOT and BURFITT
DENNIS in Nfld. (Seary) Cf DENNIS of C.I.
DENNIS, Ernest, from G to Canada, prob Ontario, ca 1924, 1925. Mar Miriam BRACHE, also of G. "My aunt and uncle, Mr. and Mrs. Ernest Dennis, started the Channel Islands relief fund in Ont., and sent clothes to England to the refugees of the Channel Islands there, whose parents were still in Guernsey during the Occupation. A group of devoted ladies collected and repaired and made over clothes. They rented a small room downtown in Toronto. They also raised money to send the parcels overseas." (Keyhoe)
DENNIS, Wm., fisherman at Sandy Pt., Nfld. 1871, from G? (Lovell)
DENTITH, said to be from G in Ontario.

DENTY, in Nfld. (Seary) Cf DENTITH of G
DENTON, Capt. from J in Nfld. (K. Mathews)
DENTON fam, involved with the Nfld. trade in 1717 (C.R. Faye)
DE PRE, see DU PRE and DESPRES
DE PUTRON, John, a missionary of G to French Canada, Methodist, 1818 and later. See NOTABLES
DE PUTRON, Capt. from G in Nfld. (K. Mathews)
DE PUTRON, Nancy of G, mar early 1800s? Capt. Henry KNIGHT of the Brit. Consulate at Boulogne, France. Nancy was b St. Peter Port, G, orphaned early, adopted by Gen. Peter Pickmore Faddy of the Royal Artillery and Knight of St. Ferdinand. Henrietta Ann Knight mar Arthur Handel GEAR. Their son, Henry Handel Gear, b ca 1894 and lived at one time in B.C., N.Y. City, then rem to England. (C.M. Gear, Eastbourne, Sussex, England)
DE QUETTEVILLE, "the most extensive planter on the Labrador coast." (Tocque)
DE QUETTEVILLE, a Capt. from J in Nfld. (K. Mathews)
DE QUETTEVILLE, Jersey fishery in Harbor Grace Nfld. and Blanc Sablon, Lab., early 1800s
DE QUETTEVILLE, "Now on the south side of the Harbor (Harbor Grace?) about 100 yards west of the public wharf the foundation is still pointed out as the STONE HOUSE, which tradition says belonged to the De Quettevilles, another very old Jersey family, that had important fishing establishments in the Straits of Belle Isle." (Shortis-Munn)
DE QUETTEVILLE, agent for Clemens in Nfld. was afraid of ghosts. He slept in a huge wooden box lined with sailcloth, and pulled the lid over him. First he made the cook go all through the agents house and basement with a lantern before he got into the box. Hope, the dau, mar Mr. Robson. Wound up the business in 1951. Clemens Sr. retired to J with dau Hope. (Lady McKie, Ottawa, Ont.)
DE QUETTEVILLE, Clifford Nicolle, 1862-1928, res Gaspe, mar 1890, Julie Vibert Tuzo, qv., 1862-1934, bur St. Pauls, Perce, Gaspe (GLF)
DE QUETTEVILLES in Perce, Gaspe 1800s (Syvret, Bechard, Rev. d'Hist, Cent. Bklt., Tardif, and Le Breton lists)
DE QUETTEVILLE as Codville, in Quebec 1850s. See John Henry LE LACHEUR
DE QUETTEVILLE, Clement, b ca 1885 J, d 1974, rem at age 12 to a farm in Harrow, Ont., later to Grimsby, Ont. Mar Loretta Caroline Hildreth (1892-1962) Both bur Grimsby (Rev. C.W. de Quetteville, Arva, Ont.)
A1. Bernard, or Clarence Osborn, res Cambridge, Ont., mar Helen Jones, b 1914
B1. Allan, mar ---?
C1. Craig Cameron de Q., b 1963   C2. Daryle Alexandra, b 1966
A2. George Alfred, b 1911, mar Jean ---, res Grimsby, Ont.
B1. Gerald, b 1941, mar Edith Turney, b 1940, res Oakville, Ont.
C1. Beverly Jean, b 1962   C2. George William Gerald, b 1964
B2. Rev. Clifford, b 1937, mar Carol Catherine Cook, b 1943, res Arva, Ont.
C1. Michael Todd, b 1967   C2. Mark Thomas, b 1969 C3. Miles
DE QUETTEVILLE, John and William, bros of Clement above, also emigrated. John to Perth in the Ottawa Valley; William rem to Detroit Mich., mar ca 1953, retired to Fla., widow in Tampa, last known.
DE QUETTEVILLE from J to Cape Breton
DE QUETTEVILLE, Jane, b J, ca 1841, mar Emile Marie Joseph Mouchet of West Arichat, C.B. She d 1906 in J, and by her special request, her body was shipped back to W. Arichat, where she was bur with her husband. He was b at Morlaix France 1827, d 1889. A son, Pierre, d

DESPRES, SEE EXTRA PAGES.
1882, age 8. Emile was a school teacher many years at W. Arichat, also had a store and was postmaster. His widow continued as postmistress till ca 1905. (History of W. Arichat, by Sabine Rose LeBlanc)
DE QUETTEVILLE, Elizabeth, b 1794 J?, dau of Francois D.Q, b 1740 St. Martins, J, and Elizabeth SOHIER, qv., b J, mar 1873 Capt. David GAUDIN, qv., rem to Dalhousie, NB and then to Ontario (Helena Cameron, White Rock, BC)
DE ROSIER. Some thought to have come to Canada from C.I. De Rosier in Alpena, Mich. (Mich. 1905 directory) Some Gaspesians known to have settled in Alpena, Mich. DESPRES, SEE ADD. AND CORRECTIONS.
DE RUE, of J, sometimes altered to DREW (QAAM)
DE SAUMAREZ, George, b 1838 J, mar Perce 1882, Susan LENFESTY
DE STE CROIX, Guillaume, b J, mar in Malbaie, Gaspe 1803 Margaret Chicoine (J.H. Le Breton list) William, from J, was said to be son of Moses of J, and brother of Joshua T.
DE STE. CROIX, Ernest, husband of Marie Morin, b St. Helier 1865, d 1947, bur St. Pauls Angl., Gaspe town, Marie b Gaspe? (GLF)
DE STE. CROIX, John, b J, in Gaspe 1861 (census)
DE STE. CROIX, ---, from J, res Sept Isles, Quebec in 1941, ca 76 yrs. old (J.G. de la Garde, Shippegan, NB)
DE STE. CROIX, Dennis, b England of J? fam, rem to Halifax 1954
DE STE. CROIX, Nicholas, from J?, at Shippegan, NB 1800 (Robichaud)
DE STE. CROIX, Charles and James, in Malbaie, Gaspe 1850s, 1871 (Syvret)
DE STE. CROIX, John, 1848-1918, bur St. Andrews United Ch, Port Daniel, Gaspe (GLF)
DE STE. CROIX, Joshua Temple, b 1734 J, of Hug fam. Was in New York City before 1783. Mar 1759, Leah Gallaudet, dau of Dr. G. of New Rochelle, NY. Joshua d 1805 Bridgetown, Annapolis, N.S. He was a Loyalist and Methodist. (Noes; Calnek; Savary; Trudy Mann, Mississauga, Ont.; Syvret; GLF; Morse; Gilroy)
A1. Thomas, b 1760, d 1801
A2. Maryie, Mary, b 1762, mar 1. Caleb Fowler, and 2. Isaac Woodbury. Fowler d 1793.
  B1. Leah Fowler, b 1782, mar Benj. Greene, of Warwick, R.I. fam
    C1. Leah Greene, b 1813, mar 1836, Granville Bevil Reed
      D1. Guilford Shaw Reed, mar Ellen Pauline Berryman of St. John, NB
        E1. Helen Leah Reed, author
  B2. Ann Fowler, b 1784, mar 1805 Seth Chute
  B3. Caleb Fowler, b 1785, rem to N.B., where he may have desc.
  B4. Alexander Fowler, b 1787, mar 1. Ann Sanders, and 2. Ann HICKS. Chn by Hicks
    C1. Priscilla Ann, mar Robert Troop   C3. ?
    C2. Weston Alexander, mar 1861 Mary Ann Hall
  B5. Joshua Temple, b 1780, d 1790
  B6. Gilbert, b 1790, mar Nancy Clarke
    C1. William   C5. Rachel, mar William Gibbon
    C2. Wallace, d unmar   C6. Nancy, mar George E. Chesley
    C3. Gilbert, mar ---
    C4. Eliza Isabella, mar Charles LONGLEY
  B7. Isaac Woodbury, b 1798, d 1863. Mar 1. 1823, Martha Chute, and 2. Elizabeth Brotha, widow of James Orde and of Peter Long
    C1. John Galaudet, b 1825, mar Naomi, dau of John C. Wilson
  B8. Mary, b 1800, mar 1. James DeLancey Harris and 2. William B., son of Rev. Cyrus Perkins. She had 12 chn.
    C1. Elizabeth, mar Charles Goucher
      D1. Mary de Ste. Croix Goucher, b 1878 Annapolis, mar James Avard

DE STE. CROIX 217

    Orde, b 1874 Greywood, N.S.
   E1. Mary de Ste. Croix Orde, b 1903 Annapolis Royal, NS, mar
    Harold Sefton Mann, 1898-1964, b Eng., d Medicine Hat, Alta.
    F1. Avard Sefton Mann F3. Mary Elizabeth Mann
    F2. Lance Edgecombe Mann F4. Fleur Emily Mann
    F5. Edgar Marland Mann, b 1931 Eckville, Alts., mar Gertrude
     Thomason, b 1934 Winnipeg, Man.
     G1. Richard James Mann, b 1959
     G2. Carolyn Joan Mann, b 1962 Winnipeg
     G3. Bruce Douglas Mann, b 1967 Winnipeg
  B9. Elisha, b 1802, mar Nancy C., dau of James Harris
   C1. Rachel Maria, mar Abraham BALCOM, qv.
   C2. Chalmers, mar Sarah Jane Whitman
 A3. Joshua, b 1764, d 1910, unmar
 A4. Peter, b 1766, mar 1795 Euphemia Palmer
  B1. Joshua T., b 1795, d 1914, unmar
  B2. Rachel P., b 1797, d 1799
  B3. Leah Gallaudet, b 1798, mar 1815 or 1820 Thomas Sinclair, Earl
   of Caithness?
  B4. Thomas, b 1801, d 1803
  B5. Peter Louis, b 1803, mar 1828 Philena Hunt, to U.S.?
  B6. Benjamin, b 1805, d 1859, to U.S.?
  B7. Euphemia P., b 1806, d.y.
  B8. Thomas, again, b 1807, d 1810 B9. Euphemia, again, b 1809
  B10. Mary Eliza, b 1811, mar Samuel Goodrich, desc?
 A5. Leah, b 1768, mar 1785, Samuel Willett
  B1. Samuel Willett, b 1787
  B2. Joshua Willett, b 1788, mar 1811, Catherine Durland
   C1. Mary Willett, b 1812, mar ---BALCOM, qv.
   C2. Gilbert Willett, b 1814, d 1817
   C3. Catharine Willett, b 1816, mar Joseph JACQUES, qv.
   C4. Leonora Willett, b 1818, mar ---Ryar
   C5. Matilda Willett, b 1821, d.y.
   C6. Gilbert, again, Willett, b 1822, mar --- in U.S.
   C7. Daniel Willett, b 1824, mar ---Ward
   C8. Famford? Willett, b 1826, mar ---
  B3. Benjamin Willett, b 1789, mar Phebe Woodbury, no issue
  B4. Walter Willett, b 1791, mar Mary Wheelock, dau of Obadiah W.
   C1. Mary Willett, mar John Webster
   C2. Lavinia Willett, mar Archibald Walker, chn
   C3. Rachel Willett, mar Israel Gilliatt
   C4. Selena Willett, mar Samuel PICKUP, qv., 5 chn
   C5. Irene Willett, mar James Palmer C6. Walter Willett, d unmar
  B5. Thomas Willett, b 1793, mar Deborah Wilson, a dau, Ann
  B6. Augustine Willett, b 1795, d unmar
  B7. Lawrence Willett, b 1797, d unmar
  B8. Leah Willett, b 1799, mar John Pittman
  B9. Eliza Willett, b 1801, d unmar
  B10. Caroline Willett, b 1803 B12. Margaret Willett, b 1806
  B11. Temple Willett, b 1806 (Last four chn d unmar)
 A6. Madeleine, b 1770, d 1771 A7. Madeleine, again, b 1772, d 1773
 A8. Benjamin, b 1776, a surgeon, mar Margaret Des Brisay. A dau, Marguerite de Ste. Croix, who mar 1826 John Brechin, was the mother of Frederick de Ste. Croix Brechin, a noted public figure of P.E.I. (Calnek, Savary)
DES GARRIS, DE GARIS?, Nicholas, son of Nicholas D. and Judith Balieu
 of G, mar Cape Cove, Gaspe 1833 Julienne Duguay (Gallant) Poss a son

DIELEMENT, see SOC.JERS.BULLETIN 31, p 37.
Nicholas, b Perce, plus James and Narcisse, b Canada, in Perce 1861 (census)
A1. Julienne, b 1836 Cap d'Espoir
A2. John, b 1839
A3. Jacques, James, b 1842
A4. Marie, b 1844, d.y.
A5. Narcisse, b 1845, in Perce 1861?
A6. Abraham, b 1848
A7. Nicholas, in Perce 1861?
DE SILVER, DE SILVA?, Richard, from J? in Harbour Grace, Nfld. before 1780 (Seary, French Archives; M.R. Lee, Southeast Placentia, Nfld.) Poss Portuguese?
DES LANDES, Jules, mar Rena Cotton, Que. See Peter Timothy BROCHET, qv.
DES LANDES, Daniel, from J?, signed Gaspe Petition 1820
DESPRES, from C.I. to Canada (J.H. Le Breton list) Also noted in Alpena, Mich. ca 1905, poss by way of Gaspe. Christine D. DESPRES mar Elias DUMARESQ 1857, Fox River, Gaspe.
DESTERRE, D'ESTERRE, from France to J ca 1572, from J to Canada ca 1860 and before? Hug (Reaman) Cf DEXTER
DE ST. ESTIENNE of J, sometimes changed to Stephens, Stevens. To Canada?
DE VEULLE, from J to Perce (Cent. Bklt.)
DE VEULLE, F.E., clerk from J in Caraquet 1861, age 17, for Robin firm (Census, Rev. Le Gresley)
DE VEAU, in Cape Breton, some poss ACADIAN. M. Brochet says that many of the De Veau fam in Cape Breton came with the Janvrin ships and the Jersey people, but poss most did not res in Jersey. Peter and Simon De Veau of C.B. built several ships.
DE VIC, Sir Henry, bp 1597 J?, son of John de Vic, King's Procureur, Knight and Baronet, and Elizabeth PAGEOT of G. PAGEOTS settled in England from G, and became very wealthy, changed surname to PAGET. Poss some to Canada. Henry de Vic mar Margaret DE CARTERET, d 1671, bur Westminster Abbey, England.
DEVOE in Nfld. (Seary) Cf above DE VEAU of J and of France
DE VOUGE, from C.I. in Maritimes Fisheries (J.H. Le Breton list) To Cape Breton ca early 1800s (Bourinot)
DE VOUGE, Cecil in Brilliant Cove, Gaspe 1800s, and in Seal Cove, Que.
DE VOUGE in Toronto
DE VOUGE, Peter, b J, in Gaspe 1861 (census) Also Thomas Francis and James, b Canada. Wife was Jane BOULET of Malbay. A dau, Jane, was b 1851 (Brochet)
DEVEREAUX, Jane, b J, in Perce 1861 (census) DEVEREAUX from Gaspe to Alpena, Mich.?
DEWEY in Nfld. (Seary) Cf DEWE of J (Stevens)
DIAMOND in Nfld. (Seary) Cf DIMOND of J (Stevens)
DICK, George, from C.I.? in Fortune Bay, Nfld. 1860s (Rev. Hammond)
DIMOCKE, from C.I.? to Gaspe (Bourgaize)
DINGLE, John, SPG missionary in Nfld. from J? 1800s (SPG)
DINGLE, Richard, from J to Dundas, Ont. 1800s, a son Richard (Russel Dingle, Burlington, Ont.)
DINGLE, Mary Ann, b 1831 St. Peter Port, G, mar John WATTS, qv. She was the dau of Walter D. a stone cutter, and Mary SEARLE. Mary Ann and husband rem to Coboconk, Ont. 1860s. He was a railroad engineer in J (May Stone, Aurora, Ont.) See WATTS
DINNEY in Nfld. (Seary) Cf DENNIS and DESNEY (Silent S) of J (Stevens)
DIOUVILLE, D'IOUVILLE, Francis George John of St. Ouen, J, bur there 1968. Stone in St. Paul's, Perce, Que. (GLF)
DITCHBURN, Herbert, b 1906 G, mar Gertrude RIVE, qv., res Agassiz, BC
A1. Ray, res Wellington, N.Z., 5 chn
A2. Lloyd, res Kamloops, BC, 4 chn

A3. Ann, res Chetwynd, BC, mar R. Parent, 3 chn
DIXON, ---, from J, settled in Harbor Breton, Nfld. ca 1850, rem to Fortune, Nfld. (Seary)
DIXON, see Jane DOREY Latimer
DOBREE, C.I. surname on S. coast of Nfld. (G.W. Le Messurier, K. Mathews)
DOBREE, Dobrey, J fam? Forillon area, Gaspe
DODGE, George, from C.I.?, in Fortune Bay, Nfld. 1777
DOBREE, Isabel, see Lucius CAREY, to Goderich, Ont. 1860 from G (Margaret Carey)
DOLAMOUNT, DOLLIMOUNT, DOLIMOUNT, DIELEMONT, etc., from G to Nfld. 1830 (Seary) (Margaret D. Davis, Port Aux Basques, Nfld.)
DOLBEL, Horatio and Eliza, b J, in Douglastown, Que. 1861 (census), poss returned to J
DOLBEL, Alfred William, b 1844 J, son of William D. and Mary AMY, qv., mar 1871 Fox River, Gaspe, Mary Selina Cote, 1852-1921. He d 1910 Montreal (Ivy Suddard, Dartmouth, NS; Frank Remiggi)
  A1. Alfred Henry, b 1871 England?, mar 1900 Lucy Ada GAVEY, qv., b 1876 Grand Greve, Gaspe. She d 1922. He d 1940 Riviere de la Madeleine, Que.
    B1. Earl Gavey, b 1901 Gr. Greve, mar 1930 Colletta MINCHINTON, qv., b 1904
      C1. Donald Alfred, b 1931 Verdun, Que., mar 1954 Constance Mitchell
        D1. James Early, b 1956 Montreal D2. Randall Donald, b 1962
      C2. Gwendolyn Isabel, b 1933, mar 1953 William Kelly
      C3. Barbara Ann, b 1937, mar 1976 Douglas MacKinnon
    B2. Marjorie Edith, b 1902, mar 1927 Lorne George Patterson, d 1943 Riv. de la Mad.
    B3. Burton Eric, b 1904, mar 1. Cecelia Bowen, who d that year in Montreal. Mar 2. Madeleine Rheaume in 1940.
      C1. Mary Pauline Lorraine, b 1942 Verdun, Que., mar 1962 Jacques Masse
      C2. Mary Linda Ann, b 1945, mar 1964 Thomas Gerry
    B4. Leslie Roy, b 1907, d 1927 Gaspe, or 1929
    B5. Ivy Lucy, b 1909, mar 1931 Charles Kingsley Suddard, b 1907, d 1975
    B6. Alfred William, b 1912, mar 1940 Nancy Drusilla VALPY, qv., b 1919
      C1. Alfred Dumaresq, b 1944, Hamilton, Ont., mar 1967 Elizabeth Ann MacLean
        D1. Alfred Roy, b 1972 Halifax, NS D2. Carol Ann, b 1975
      C2. Stuart William, b 1947 Toronto, mar 1968, Brenda Arlene Lane
        D1. Cari-Ann, b 1968 Hamilton, Ont.
      C3. Drusilla Ann, b 1950 Hamilton, mar 1974 Jorgen Hansen
      C4. Kenneth Valpy, b 1955 Hamilton
      C5. Marjorie Laura, b 1959, Hamilton, Ont.
  A2. William John, b 1874 Griffon Cove, mar 1917 Edith Duchesnay, a son d.y.
  A3. Mabel Selina, b 1977 Griffon Cove, mar 1905 William Baxter Taylor
  A4. Edgar George, b 1879, d 1965 Montreal, Que.
  A5. Maud Alice, b 1882 Fox River, Gaspe, d 1882 Grand Greve, Gaspe
  A6. Eva Maud, b 1885, mar 1921 Arthur RENAULT, qv. D 1941 Montreal
  A7. Amy Alice, b 1894, d 1960 Montreal, Que., mar Alexander Campbell Wood
DOMAILLE, Capt. from G in Nfld. (K. Mathews and C.R. Fay)
DOMINE, from C.I.? to Nfld. (Rev. Hammond) James, Robert and Wm. in Deer Island, Nfld. 1864, 65.

DOREY, SEE EXTRA PAGES,& CHANNEL ISLAND COLLECTION.

DOREY, Rt. Rev. George, D.D., LLD. "Moderator of the United Ch. of Canada. B 1884, brought out to Canada for the mission field in 1905 to Shellbrook Sask. Had at least two bros., of which one, Senator Dorey of J, was presented to Queen Elizabeth in 1957, and the other, Josue, was keeper of a castle on J. Two chn d.y., the girl at 8 and the boy at 21." (Ruth Stewart, Edmonton, Alta.)

DOREY, Hilary, b G, res Lancresse Bay, a stone cutter. Mar Mary Ann MAHY, and in 1900 rem to Hamilton, Ont. with 5 of their 16 chn, some of whom d in G. Chn b Sauvages, St. Sampson, G (Mrs. Arthur Dorey, Stoney Creek, Ont.)
- A1. John, b G, rem to Canada. A son, Jack, had a son David and a dau
- A2. Alice, mar Alfred ROBERTS, res G, 2 daus
- A3. Daniel, mar ? of Alderney, 1 ch, rem to Canada
- A4. Lillian, mar Alfred LE NOURY, qv., rem to Canada, 4 chn
- A5. Alfred, b St. Sampson, G, mar 1. ? Emma OGIER, qv., rem to Canada but returned to G where he d. May have mar 2. Mary LE PREVOST, who d 1972 St. Catherines, Ont.
  - B1. Adele Una, b 1920, mar Harold Eckert, b 1917
    - C1. John Alfred Eckert, b 1944, res St. Catherines, Ont.
    - C2. David Roy Eckert, b 1946, mar Mary Anne Piper, b 1950
    - C3. Una Mary Eckert, b 1950, mar Douglas Byers, b 1948, 1 ch?
    - C4. Bruce Harold Eckert, b 1953
    - C5. Nancy Eileen Eckert, b 1960
  - B2. John Alfred, b 1922, mar Beverly Sandliam, 1961
    - C1. Virginia, b 1965   C2. Steven, b 1968
  - B3. Eileen, b 1926, mar William RODGERS, qv., res St. Catherines, Ont.
    - C1. William Rodgers, b 1955   C2. Joseph Rodgers, b 1957
- A6. Edwin Charles , b 1891 Sauvages, St. Sampson, G, mar 1912 Vale, G Adelaide Alice LE PAGE, qv., to Hamilton ca 1900, res Burlington Ont.
  - B1. dau, d.y. in G   B3. dau, res Hamilton, mar?
  - B2. Edna May, b 1920, mar L. Young B4. dau, res Burlington, Ont., mar?
- A7. Ada, mar Steven MAHY, qv., both dec, 3 daus
- A8. Nicholas, b 1893, mar Margaret PHILLIPS, qv., one dau, dec. He was living in 1977, age 84.
- A9. Elizabeth, mar Charles Bates, no issue
- A10. Arthur Hedley, b ca 1900 G, rem to Canada 1912, mar 1922 Dorothy Sarah Cottrill
  - B1. Stanley Arthur, engineer, mar
    - C1. Richard   C2. Daniel   C3. Nancy
  - B2. Rev. Gordon William, Registrar, Ont. Bible College, Toronto
    - C1. Terry Paul   C2. Linda
  - B3. Merle, mar Harry Sinden, a printer, 3 chn including Susan
- A11. Albert, mar Nellie Riley, no issue, d ca 1970

DOREY, Nicholas, 1844-1910, son of Nicholas D. of G and Rachel LE PAGE, mar Henriette, HAMON, qv., 1849-1918, dau of Charles HAMON and Polly ---, 1811-1882, all in G. 14 chn, several to Canada (Edw. Le Page, Grimsby, Ont.)
- A1. Harriet Mary, b 1868 G, d 1936, res Hamilton, Ont. Mar 1. Nicholas LE NOURY, 1863-1930, and 2. his bro, Thomas Alfred LE NOURY, qv., 3 chn
- A2. Ann Elizabeth, b 1869, mar William DE GARIS, qv.
  - B1. Wilfred   B2. Florence   B3. Nora   B4. Elsie
- A3. John William, b 1870, mar 1. Lillian BISSON, qv. and Alice CORBIN qv.
  - B1. Annie   B2. William   B3. Daisy
- A4. Alice Mary, b 1872, d 1958, mar Eugene LE PAGE, qv.
- A5. Mary Louise, mar Nicholas Alfred TOSTEVIN, qv.
  - B1. Edna   B2. Claudia   B3. Walter   B4. Ronald

A6. Alfred John, b 1877, mar Elizabeth Harriet LE PAGE
  B1. Alfred   B2. Rita
A7. Henry Joseph, b 1879, mar Daisy C. MAHE, qv.
  B1. Edward B2. George B3. Harold B4. Gladys B5. Primula
A8. Joseph Henry, b 1879, mar Louisa BICHARD, no issue
A9. Thomas Henry, b 1882, mar Ada BAILEY, 10 chn
A10. Edwin Wilfred, b 1886, mar Ada PASQUIRE, and 2. Selina DE LA MARE, qv.
  B1. Edwin   B2. Ena, mar ---Young, res Burlington, Ont.
A11. Francis William, b 1889, unmar
A12. Hilda Alice, b 1889, mar Harry OZANNE, qv., and 2. John Frederick QUERIPEL, qv., 2 chn
A13. Walter Eugene, b 1890, unmar
A14. William Cecil, b 1893, mar Elsie BICHARD, qv. Ch, Joan, many desc
DOREY, George, b ca 1810 J, mar Charlotte PETITPAS, who d 1888, prob dau of Louis P. and Charlotte BELLEFONTAINE, bp 1811 Tracadie, N.S. (Stephen White, Moncton, NB)
A1. George William, b 1848, d 1904. Mar 1867 Arichat, Judith Angele Rancon, dau of Charles and Marine Bonin of Descousse, 1844-1942. She d at Janvrin's Harbor, age 109.
  B1. Marie Jeanne, b ca 1868, mar Desire GREY, qv., son of Jean Marie G. and Marcelline Meunier
  B2. Judith or Angelique Anne, b 1870, d 1884, age 13
  B3. Louise Artimise, b 1873
  B4. Pierre Jean, b 1875, d 1974, Janvrin's Island, CB. Mar 1907 at West Arichat, C.B., Marie Bertha de COSTE, qv., dau of Aime DE COSTE and Marine BOUDROT.
A2. Clement Honore Henry, b 1851, mar Adele Landry, dau of Charles and Virginia BOUDROT, 1854-1954?
  B1. Charles George, b ca 1878, mar 1903 W. Arichat, Marie Alma Fougere, dau of Pierre and Catherine Meunier Fougere, b 1882. A mariner in 1907.
  B2. Marie Delvina, b 1883, d 1920. Mar 1911 at W. Arichat, Vincent McNeil, son of Roderick M. and Mary Anne McNamara, b 1887.
  B3. Joseph Alfred, b 1884, mar 1913 at W. Arichat, Virginie BOUDREAU, dau of Alfred B. and Marie Louise SAMSON of Martinique. A fisherman in 1907. She d in Halifax in 1969, age 74.
  B4. Joseph Arthur, b 1886, mar 1924 Lillian GAUDET, dau of Agapit and Marie Boucher of Arichat.
  B5. Marie Jeanne, b 1888, mar 1911 John McIsaac, son of Ronald M. and Mary Gillis of Port Hawkesbury, N.S.
  B6. Marthe, b 1890, mar 1913 at W. Arichat, Daniel McIsaac, son of Allan and Catherine Gillis of Port Hood. Mar 2. at Montreal 1961 Remi R. Terrio
  B7. Clement Henry, b 1893, d.y.
  B8. Joseph Miller, b 1895, mar Marie Marguerite Arsenault
  B9. Dominique Alcide, b 1901, d 1902
A3. Pierre, b 1855, d 1933, mar Marie Emilie Eugenie Morin, dau of Auguste M. and Sophie Chenalle, 1858-1897.
  B1. Joseph Henry, Harry, b ca 1879, mar 1903 W. Arichat, Marie-Catherine McNamara, dau of David M. and Helene Firoir of St. Mary's, 1881-1919. He mar 2. Rose Alfreda Boudreau, dau of Jeffrey and Sara Jeanne Boudreau. Joseph Henry d 1940.
  B2. Colin Jean, b 1880, mar 1. ---, and 2. Florence d'Entremont, dau of Jean D. and Marie ---.
  B3. Joseph Albert Georges, b 1884, W. Arichat or PEI
  B4. Louis Alfred, b 1885

B5. Pierre Alexandre, b 1888, mar 1. 1917 at W. Arichat, Marie Alice
      Forest, dau of Remi and Marie Eugenie Boudrot, 1898-1918, and 2.
      1921 at W. Arichat, Laura May Des Lauriers, dau of Thomas Albert
      D. and Marie Artimise Gorgeron, b 1894.
  B6. Marie Emilie Johanna, b 1890, mar 1917 Joseph Edouard Isaac Fou-
      gere, son of Joseph F. and Anne Drinkwater, b 1895 W. Arichat, CB
  B7. Emile Amable, b 1892, mar 1924 at Descousse, CB
  B8. Walter Augustin, Gus, b 1893, mar Marie Alma Boudreau
 A4. Anne, b 1857 (Some errors below. See DATA IN chan.Is.Coll.)
 DOREY, Jane, dau of George D. and ---LA SALIER, b 1801 J, d 1872. Mar
     Charles Frederick Latimer, b Glasgow, Scotland 1790s who was ship-
     wrecked off Halifax, NS, rem to Isle Madame. They res Arichat, Mass.
     and N.Y. City, where Charles d 1838. Jane taught school in Arichat,
     and d at Cap La Ronde 1872, 9 chn. (LATIMER FAMILY HISTORY, Robert
     Latimer, Tatmagouche, N.S., 1970; Stephen White, Moncton, N.B.)
  A1. Caroline J. Latimer, mar ---Elliott, res Boston
  A2. Charles Latimer, mar Mary MAUGER, qv., and 2. Elizabeth DIXON
    B1. Charles Latimer, a farmer
    B2. Caroline J. Latimer, mar ---Cole, res Boston, Mass.
    B3. Clarissa Latimer, unmar
    B4. George J. Latimer, farmer, mar Sarah Lewis, res Lockside
    B5. William Latimer, farmer, (by second wife), mar Carrie Latimer,
        res Cap La Ronde
    B6. Jack, farmer, mar 1. Libbie Hearn, and 2. ---Kelly, res Rocky Bay
    B7. Saul, farmer, mar ---MacRae, res Barrasois, Richmond Co., N.S.
  A3. George Latimer, mar 1. Jean Shaw, and 2. Elsie Wilson, res Arichat,
      3 chn by each wife
    B1. George P., a mason, mar Eva Fonda, res Somerville, Mass.
      C1. Lloyd C. Latimer, civil engineer, res Somerville, mar ---
      C2. Ruth F. Latimer
      C3. Walter Allen Latimer, b 1896, d 1918, Navy, WWI
    B2. Tillie, Matilda? Latimer, furrier, unmar, res Chicago, Ill.
    B3. Jemima Latimer, dressmaker, unmar, res Boston, Mass.
    B4. Margaret Latimer, mar 1. Wm. Fonda, and 2. B.J. Arnold, res
        Chicago, Ill.
    B5. Jane Latimer, mar ---Tato, res Mass.
    B6. Carrie, Caroline?, Latimer, mar Wm. Latimer, res Cap La Ronde
  A4. Horatio Latimer, merchant, mar ---BARRETT, res Arichat
  A5. Peter Latimer, unmar, res Arichat and U.S.
  A6. Francis Latimer, res Arichat and U.S.
  A7. Elizabeth Latimer, mar ---MacTavish, res N.B. and U.S.
  A8. James Frederick Latimer, mar Jemima Allen Shaw, res Arichat, N.S.
    B1. Charles Frederick Latimer, 1862-1949, contractor, mar Leah Smith
    B2. Rosina, Roxy?, Latimer, 1868-1900, mar Samuel H. Bonner, res
        Galveston, Texas
    B3. James Allen Latimer, 1863-1930, mason, unmar, res Boston
    B4. John Latimer, 1865-1946, contractor, mar Mary, Rosina Robertson,
        res Arichat
    B5. George Albert Latimer, 1871-1946, farmer, mar Mary Doyle, res
        Potty's Lake
    B6. Horatio Edward Latimer, 1867-1875
    B7. Henry Ingles Latimer, 1870-1875
    B8. Martha Ada Latimer, 1873-1926, mar Geo. Crowell, res Gloucester,
        Mass.
    B9. Jamima, 1875-1951, mar 1. ---Meredith, and 2. James Clark, res
        Cape Cod, Mass.
  A9. Clarissa B. Latimer, d.y.

DOREY, Jane, wife of above Charles Frederick Latimer, was one of a Jersey family of four chn, including two doctors and a sea captain named Henry DOREY. They were the chn of George DOREY and ---LA SALIR. Jane's maternal grandmother was a LA BRAVE, of a merchant fam in J. Jane's uncle, named LEEDS was the author of a number of books about insects. He rem to Conn. and became Governor of that state. Jane and her bro Henry rem to Arichat, C.B. (Latimer fam Hist.)

DOREY, (Hug, D'ORE) George, early 1800s, had a son John, a sea captain. John's son, John Thomas, b ca 1860 J, taken to Canada by his father, wintered in the Magdalen Islands. To J in the spring, but rem to Canada, and d in Halifax, NS 1942. He mar 1888, Caroline CROCKER in Toronto. She was b 1862 Nfld., and d 1914 Dartmouth, NS. His sister, Annie, mar Walter CHAMBERS, their dau Muriel res Minehead, Eng. John Thomas res Tuft's Cove, Dartmouth, NS, electrician, 5 chn (Jennifer Sutherland, Brooklyn, NY; Vivian Dorey, Halifax, NS)
- A1. Muriel Annie, b 1889 Toronto, R.N., res NY City, d Halifax 1973, unmar
- A2. Gladys May, b ca 1891 Toronto, d Halifax, 1950s, unmar
- A3. Edwin Walter, b 1893 Halifax, d at Passchendale, Belgium 1917, unmar
- A4. Enid Marguerite, b Halifax 1896, d Arvide, Que. 1948. Mar 1923 Halifax, Walter Clarence Hamilton b 1893 New Carlisle, Que., son of Gavin Hamilton and Edith Borlase, d Cookshire, Que. 1976. Settled Isle Maligne, Que. (Alma), near Lake St. John, 2 chn. Walter mar 2. ---, dau Emily Frances b 1950.
  - B1. Edith Muriel Hamilton, b 1925 Isle Maligne, bp Anglican Ch, Kenogami, Que., mar 1948 John Robert Sutherland, b 1925 near Vegreville, Alta., son of John Walter S. and Margaret Emma, Cora, Moore. Res Toronto, Ont.
    - C1. Jennifer Enid Sutherland, b 1950 Toronto, mar 1973 St. Lambert, Que. Richard James Wight, b 1949 San Diego, Calif., son of Roland Wight and Erma Wildermuth of Paradise, Calif. Res N.Y.
  - B2. Edwin Walter Dorey Hamilton, b 1928 Isle Maligne, mar Marie POULIN 1957, dau of Roland Poulin, res St. Lambert, Que., 4 chn
    - C1. Peter Hamilton, b ca 1958   C3. Steven Walter Hamilton, b ca 1961
    - C2. Anne Marie Hamilton, b 1959 C4. David Roland Hamilton
- A5. Vivien Harriet, b 1897, unmar, res Halifax, NS

DOREY in Nfld. (Seary) Cf DOREY in C.I.

DOREY, Elizabeth, b 1807 J, d Arichat 1870, age 62, widow of Thomas DIXON, qv. Nicholas DIXON, a desc.

DOREY, Jane, b 1801 J?, mar Donald McPherson. See Channel Is. Coll. for much more info. on DOREY FAMILY.

DOREY, Philip, b 1799 J?, d 1863 Arichat. Mar Margaret Leete, b ca 1809.
- A1. Elizabeth, b 1843   A4. Henriette, b 1848
- A2. John James, b 1845, emigrated to Mass. A5. Cyrus
- A3. Andre, b 1848, d.y.

DOREY, Helier, mar Emilie BROCQ, rem to America (Edw. Le Page)

DOREY, Jean, to sea, settled and mar in America (Edw. Le Page)

DOREY, Ann, dau of ?, mar James LE LACHEUR, b 1806, son of emigrant John, qv., and Elizabeth WINDSOR, qv. Rem to PEI. Related to WILLIAMS and ROBBIN fams. (Eliz. Graham, London, Ont.)

DOREY, Adam and Arnold, res Calgary, Alta., from C.I.?

DOUBLET in Canada from J? Cf DOUBLE, DOUBLARD, DOUBLET of J (Stevens)

DOW, Sarah, 1859-1929, of J?, wife of John A. LE GALLAIS, qv., bur Shigawake, Gaspe (GLF)

DOWN, DOWNS, DOWNEY in Nfld. (Seary) Cf DOWNS, DOWNES in J (Stevens) Wm. DOWNE in Bonavista, Nfld. 1681

DOWN, Walter, b 1875 G, rem to Ontario 1921, d 1926. His father came
   from Devon to G. Mar Olive LE PAGE of Vale, G, b 1891, dau of Wm.
   George LE PAGE and Amy FALLA, qv.
   A1. Richard W. Down, b 1915 Vale, G, mar Barbara Morris, b Eng., dau of
       Alfred M. and Harriet LE PAGE, b G (Richard W. Down, Pefferlaw, Ont.)
       B1. Christopher, b 1957   B3. Victoria Mary, b 1961, d car
       B2. Geoffrey, b 1959   accident, 1970
   A2. John William, b 1920 G, res Silver Spring, Md. Mar 1. Thelma Hart,
       and 2. Mabel Nesbitt
       B1. Anne Beverley Down, mar 1. ---, 2 sons, and 2. James Gurba
           C1. Calvin Gurba, b 1962, adopted by Gurba
           C2. Andrew Gurba, b 1964   C3. Joseph Gurba, b 1969
DOWNTON, ---, b G, rem ca 1890 to Hamilton, Ont.
DOWNTON, in Nfld. (Seary) Cf DOWNTON of C.I.
DRAPER, Mamie, b J ca 1870, orphaned early. An aunt adopted her, and
   she was raised at Burrard's Inlet, BC. It is on record that Lilly
   Langtry offered to adopt Mamie. Mar very young to J.E. Insley, a
   former Caribou gold miner, who was quite a bit older than Mamie.
   They had 6 chn, the oldest a boy of 14 in 1907. She ran the Colonial
   Hotel in New Westminster, BC, and was active in the Pioneers Assoc.
   Her name appears on the CADORET fam record of Salt Lake City as Mamie
   Draper MADSEN? (Luce)   DRAPER, SEE EXTRA PAGES.
DREW in Nfld. (Seary) Cf DE RUE in QAAM, LE DREW, DRIEU in J (Stevens)
DREW, DRUE, Thomas, boatkeeper of St. John's Harbor 1682 (Seary) See
   also LE DREW and DE RUE
DROS, LE DROW, LE DROS in Nfld (Seary) Cf LE DROIT of J (Stevens)
DRUGGET, J merchant 1800s at Lark Harbor, Nfld. (Mannion) Poss from
   French DROGUET? (See Seary)
DU BOIS, merchant from J in Nfld.
DU BOIS, Simon, of J?, operated Labrador fishery
DU CHEMIN, Violet, wife of Cecil J. LE POIDEVIN, of Osoyoos, BC, to
   Brockville, Ont. then rem to B.C.
DU CHEMIN, boat keeper from G in Nfld. (K. Mathews) Also a Capt. DU
   CHEMIN (Brochet)
DU CHEMIN, Francois, son of Elie D. and Rachel ROBILLARD of G, mar
   Marie Louise Marcotte in 1793 at Cape Sante, Quebec (Pontbriand)
DU FEU, of J, Ch. Islander in Maritimes Fisheries 1800s (J.H. Le Breton
   list)
DUFFETT, Charles, Henry, James, John from C.I.?, at Bay de Verdes, Conc.
   Bay, Nfld. 1860s (Rev. Hammond, Seary) Poss from Dorset, Eng. if not
   C.I.
DU FOUR, current Gaspe, from C.I.? Also DU FOUR in Baiecomeau, Que.
DU FRESNE, see FRANEY. From C.I. to U.S., poss to Canada
DU HEAUME, George, from J. Had a fishing room at Chateau Bay, Nfld.
   1840 (Tocque)   DU HAMEL from Jersey to BC, Canada.
DU HEAUME, merchant from J in Nfld. (K. Mathews)
DU HEAUME, John, b St. Heliers, J, to Gaspe, then to Corinth, NY. Mar
   there, his wife died. Had a dau, rem to Fox River, Que. Mar 2. Ven-
   etia Ascah, a widow, b 1866, who d 1926 (Doris E. McDougall, Mon-
   treal, Que.)
DUKE in Nfld. (Seary) Cf DUC, LE DUC in J (Stevens)
DUKE in B.C. 1940, desc of OULESS the C.I. painter?
DUKEMAN, poss DUQUEMIN?, of C.I.?, member of C.I. Soc. in Victoria, BC
   1940s (Luce)
DUMARESQ, old and illustrious Channel Island surname. Sev branches
   settled in North America. Descendants widespread, but much more information available with research in Canada and U.S., as well as in

Soc. Jers. files (Margaret Le Breton, Belleville, Ont.; James Dumaresq, Halifax, N.S.; Donat Robichaud, Beresford, N.B.; Rev. Albert Dumaresq, Caraquet, N.B.: Emery Dumaresq, Gaspe, Que; Census, Gaspe, 1861; JERRI JADIS, by Geo. Le Feuvre; BIOGRAPHICAL DICTIONARY OF JERSEY, G.R. Balleine; NEW ENGLAND HIST. AND GEN. BEGISTER, Vol. 17; LE COUTEUR PAPERS, Joan Stevens, Jersey; Nicolas Denys Society, Vol. 1, #5; Soc. Jers. Bull. 11; HISTORY OF HUGUENOT EMIGRANTS TO AMERICA, by C.W. Baird; A SKETCH OF THE FAMILY OF DUMARESQ, by August T. Perkins)

DUMARESQ, Capt. Philip, b 1695 J, son of Elias D. and Frances DE CARTERET, qv., to Boston before 1716, mar Susanne PERRY, qv., as privateer commander took at least 7 ships. D before 1744.
- A1. Edward, mar in Boston, Mass., Mary Boutineau, poss BOUDINOT? BOURINOT? cf
  - B1. Stephen
  - B2. Ann
- A2. Philip, b 1721?
- A3. Elizabeth, b 1730
- A4. Ann, b 1736, mar Nicholas MALLETT of J
- A5. Douce, b 1743, mar George BANDINEL of J. This dau by second wife.
- A6. Susan, mar Mathew SAUMAREZ. They were the parents of Admiral Lord Saumarez of G.
- A7. Philip, b 1737, mar 1763 Rebecca Gardiner, at least 8 chn. Philip, a Loyalist, escaped in 1776 to Halifax, N.S. then was appointed Collector of Customs at B.W.I. where he died. Chn: James of Maine, Capt. Philip, Dr. Francis of Jamaica, Anne, Rebecca, Susannah, Hanna and Abigail.

DUMARESQ, John and Frank in Gaspe 1861. DUMARESQ current at Gaspe Bay, Perce, Fox River

DUMARESQ, Nicholas, b J, mar 1842. With Mrs. D., James and Edward in Cap Chat, Gaspe, 1861 (census) A Nicholas Syvret Dumaresq was mayor of Gaspe, 1863

DUMARESQ, C.I. name on S. coast of Nfld. (G.W. Le Messurier)

DUMARESQ, Capt., merchant and ship owner from J in Nfld. (K. Mathews)

DUMARESQ, from C.I. to Placentia Bay, Nfld. (Shortis-Munn)

DUMARESQ, Daniel and Elizabeth Ann of Les Colombiers, St. Mary, J, had at least 5 sons, Daniel, Clement, George, Frederick and Elias, most of whom rem to Canada in the early 1800s. (GLF; Census; Emery Dumaresq, Gaspe, Que.; Margaret Le Breton, Belleville, Ont.; Claudette Maroldo, Cherry Hill, NJ; Brochet)
- I. Daniel, b 1817 St. Mary, J, mar 1. Mary Ann TOSTEVIN, qv., and 2. Judith LENFESTEY, qv. The latter mar 1860, Cape Cove, Gaspe. Judith, dau of Jacques? L'Enfaite & Susan MAUGER.
  - A1. Daniel, b 1846, mar 1879 Martha LENFESTY, 1847-1920. Daniel d 1909
    - B1. Helene or Ellen, b 1880 Cape Cove
    - B2. Marie Eliza, b 1881
    - B3. Lilian Susan, b 1884
    - B4. Emmeline, b 1886, twin, Cape Cove
    - B5. Daniel George III, b 1888 Cape Cove
  - A2. Susan Rachel, b 1848, d 1886. Mar Alfred LE GRAND, qv. He mar 2. Elizabeth DUMARESQ. See fam under LE GRAND
  - A3. Philip John, b 1861 Perce, mar Maria Charlotte LENFESTEY, first cousin, b 1863, dau of Peter and Margaret Bragg Lenfestey. Philip John by second wife.
  - A4. Edouard de la Perelle, b 1862, d 1863
  - A5. Eliza, mar Alfred William LE GRAND, his second wife, ca 1888, upon death of Susan. See fam under LE GRAND
  - A6. Jane Amelia, mar Charles Alexander BECK, qv., 1892, a farmer
    - B1. Janet Esther Beck, b 1893 Cape Cove
    - B2. Charles Dumaresq Beck, b 1895
    - B3. Ernest Daniel Beck, b 1897

B4. Roland Philip Beck, b 1899 Cape Cove
B5. Alexander Clement Beck, b 1902 Cape Cove
A7. Clement, b 1868, mar Grace Amelia Mahan, 1874-1921, in 1898 Cape Cove. He was a farmer. Both bur St. James Ch, Cape Cove
B1. Claude Elias Dumaresq, b 1899 B2. Daniel Clement Dumaresq, b 1903
A8.?James, mar Hannah JEAN, qv., 1881. She d 1907 Irishtown, Perce.
II. Clement, b 1823 St. Mary, J, bro of Daniel, above, mar Jane LANGLOIS, qv.
III. George, b 1828, bro of above, mar Jane Ellen Coffin, dau of Douglas Coffin, in Gaspe? Poss a son, Daniel, b 1847 J? Merchant in Fox River (Remiggi)
IV. Frederick Marett, b 1829 J, bro of above, d 1902 Gaspe. Mar 1861 Mary Charlotte BECHERVAISE, qv., 1833-1902. Res Gaspe. Charlotte res Fox River.
A1. John Philip, b 1862, d 1948, mar 1892, Julia Maud Boyle, no issue
A2. William George, b 1863, d 1938, mar Sophia Coffin
  B1. Frederick George, b 1904
  B2. Clement John, b 1907, mar Viola Patterson
    C1. Betty C2. S----- C3. Ronald C4. John C5. Barry
  B3. Harold William Arthur, b 1912
A3. Charlotte Sarah, b 1864, d 1955, mar Sydney S. Coffin 1892, a dau, Essie Coffin
A4. Frederick, b 1867, d 1955, mar Carrie Elizabeth Dondiet
  B1. Ross   B2. Rose   B3. Edythe   B4. Francis
A5. Jane Margaret, b 1871, d 1900, mar Andrew Dupre VALPY, qv., two chn, see VALPY
A6. Clement Ross, b 1875, d 1977
DUMARESQ, Elias, b 1832 St. Mary, J, son of David D. and Elizabeth Ann ---, mar 1857 Fox River, Gaspe, Christine Delphine DESPRES, qv., b 1838 Fox River, dau of Jean Baptiste D. and Christine Samuel (Remiggi)
A1. Elisabeth Esther, b 1857, mar Antony NOEL, qv., 1877
A2. Susan Josephine, b 1859, d 1865
A3. Georges Olivier, b 1860, mar Eloise or Louise GIRARD, bp 1867, dau of Charles G.
A4. Charles Elias, b 1862, mar Elvine Element 1886. He d 1926, she d 1896, 6 chn
  B1. Joseph Charles
  B2. Joseph Felix, b 1889, mar 1919 Mary Yvonne Alvina Cloutier, 6 chn
    C1. Mary Delphine, b 1920, mar Romuald CARON 1953, 3 chn
      D1. Joseph Gerard Caron, b 1953 D3. Joseph Daniel Caron, b 1960
      D2. Joseph Denis Caron, b 1955, mar Celine Rancourt 1976, dau
    C2. Philippe Deneri, b 1921, d 1923
    C3. Mary Simonne, b 1923, mar Antoine ROY, qv., 6 chn
      D1. Mary Lise Roy, b 1952, mar Robert Arsenault, 3 chn
        E1. Mary Emmanuelle Arsenault, b 1973
        E2. Mary Stephany Arsenault, b 1975
        E3. Felix Antoine Arsenault, b 1977
      D2. Mary Michelle Roy, b 1953 D3. Joseph Georges Roy, b 1954
      D4. Mary Magdalen Roy, b 1955, mar Rodrigue Paulin 1975
        E1. Mary Chloe Paulin, b 1977
      D5. Mary Martine Roy, b 1960 D6. Mary Charlotte Roy, b 1962
    C4. Mary Anita, b 1926, mar Charles Borromee Verreault, 2 chn
      D1. Mary Claudette Verreault, b 1952
      D2. Mary Denise Verreault, b 1959
    C5. Joseph Emery, b 1928, mar 1976 Monique Roy of Fox River, Gaspe, at St. Mathews R.C. Ch, St. Peters, J.
    C6. Mary Delvina, b 1930, unmar

B3. Mary Alvine, Adelvina, b 1890, d 1894
B4. Joseph Euloge, b 1892, d 1969, Sargeant-Major WWI, D.C.M., unmar
B5. Joseph Eddy, b 1894, d 1963
B6. Joseph Amedee, b 1896, d 1918, WWI, in France
A5. Mary Josephine, b 1866, mar Eugene Francoeur 1884
A6. Susan Euphrasie, b 1868, mar Felix Element 1886
A7. Elias John, b 1870, mar Amerilda Henley, 1890, dau of Pierre Henley and Elisabeth GIRARD
A8. Joseph Philippe, b 1873
A9. Mary Lucy, b 1876, mar 1894 Moise Dufresne
A10. Anne Regina, b 1878, mar 1896 Theotine Theriault
A11. Anny Jane, b 1882, mar Maurice Theriault 1901
DUMARESQ, John and Rachel BANDINELL of J, had at least 7 chn. Philip, of this fam, b 1760, J, rem to Canada. (Desc of Abraham D. and Susan DE CARTERET) Philip was appointed Collector of Customs at Cape Breton before 1800. Mar Jersuah PERRY, qv., of J. Bur St. Paul's Halifax, NS
A1. Perry, b 1789 N.S. Served in War of 1812, captured 3 Amer. ships. Mar 1. Louise Newton?, an American, rem to N.S., then to N.B. where he became Customs Collector at Dalhousie, N.B. Was also J.P. and deputy Treas. at Bathurst ca 1823-1829. Mar 2. Mary Stewart, dau of Charles Stewart of PEI. Active politically. D ca age 50 in Dalhousie, N.B.
B1. John Perry Newton, b ca 1808 N.S., mar 1833 Delphine Arseneau, b 1804, dau of Joseph A. At least 12 chn
C1. Louisa, b ca 1835, telegraphist at Shippegan, N.B., then in Tracadie, N.B. Mar ---Arseneau. No issue. Adopted Louise Anne, her niece, dau of Peter Robichaud and Marie-Therese DUMARESQ, who mar 1897 Augustin Comeau of Petit Rocher, N.B.
C2. Mary Ann, b ca 1837
C3. Sarah, b ca 1839, d unmar at home of John DUMARESQ, St. Isidore, N.B.
C4. Francis, b ca 1841, d 1902, lighthouse keeper at Shippegan, NB. Mar Susanne Leger of Caraquet, N.B.
D1. Marie, b 1867, mar Xavier Robichaud of Pokemouche
D2. Joseph, b 1869, mar Marie Losier, res St. Isidore, N.B.
D3. John, b 1870, mar ---Leger, and 2. Marie Godin
D4. Peter, b 1871, mar 1899 Veronique Albert, d 1957
E1. Bella, b 1900, d 1971, nun
E2. Maria, b 1902, d 1970, mar Theolime Sasier 1943?
E3. Philippe, b 1903, d 1955, mar twice, 1926-1931 and 1935-1955
E4. Albert, b 1905, d 1933, priest
E5. Frank, b 1906, mar Claudia Landry 1935
E6. Emilienne, b 1908, nun in 1926
E7. Diana, b 1909, d 1970, mar 1937 Jim Callaghan
E8. Henriette, b 1911, nun in 1927
E9. Annonciade, b 1913, d 1916
E10. Leo, b 1915, mar Marguerite Brien 1939
E11. Alice, b 1916
E12. Pierre, or Patrice?, b 1918, d.y.
D5. Xavier, b 1873 or 1875, mar 1900 at Lameque, N.B.? Seraphie Paulin
E1. Alphonse   E4. Barceleau
E2. Andre   E5. Francois, father of 8 chn
E3. Alma
D6. Charles, mar ---Rioux, father of 4, d 1902
D7. Philippe, Marist father at Tynshore, Mass.

    D8. Edmond, d unmar   D11. Annee, religious
    D9. Frank of Gatineau, Que.   D12. Louise, religious
    D10. James of New York
  C5. Elisabeth, b ca 1842, mar 1870 Shippegan, N.B. William Robichaud, son of Dosithe R. and Cecile Le Blanc, res Paquetville, N.B.
  C6. Mary, b ca 1843, mar 1870 Peter Robichaud, res St. Isidore, NB
  C7. Philomene, b ca 1847, mar 1874 Shippegan, Charles Robichaud, his first wife
  C8. Joseph, b ca 1849, mar 1875 Pokemouche, N.B. Helene Duke, dau of Samuel Duke and Helen Marooney, rem to Vancouver, BC, 3 daus
  C9. Harriet, or Marie, b Shippegan, a nun, d.y.
  C10. Helene, b ca 1854
  C11. Blanche, b 1856 Shippegan, mar Bobby Bowes of Chatham, N.B. where she d at an advanced age.
  C12. Sophia, b 1860 Shippegan
A2. William Grant, b 181-?, Sydney, N.S., Civil servant, originated paid police force in J.
A3. Charles Wittigan Ferdinand August, b 1806? Sydney, N.S., d 1887, mar Christiana McDonald 1837. 5 sons, 7 daus. (James Dumaresq, Halifax, N.S.)
  B1. John Wittigan, b 1838
  B2. James Charles Philip, b 1840 Sydney, N.S., d 1906. architect. Mar Madeleine McDonald
    C1. Sydney Perry, b 1875 Halifax, N.S., architect, mar Ernestine MacLellan, d 1943
      D1. James Philip Dauvergne, b 1916, architect, Halifax. Mar Leila Suckling
        E1. Sydney Philip, b 1946, architect, Halifax, mar Sandra Schlacter
        E2. Peter   E3. Marc   E4. Daphne
      D2. Jacqueline   D3. Lucille   D4. Antoinette   D5. Dauvergne
    C2. Jean   C3. Anne   C4. Jessie, d 1968   C5. Edna
  B3. William T.C. August
    C1. William, b 1884, d 1967, res Sydney, N.S.
  B4. and B5. Two sons   B6.-B13. Seven daus
A4. Eveline   A7. Harriett
A5. Eliza   A8. Louisa
A6. Suzanne   (All born in Sydney, N.S.)
Other children of John DUMARESQ and Rachel BANDINELL:
II. John, Lt. Col. in Br. Army, mar ---Jones, bro of Philip above, son of John D. and Rachel BANDINELL
A1. Henry, Col. at Waterloo
  B1. Major Henry, Royal Artillery, 1870
  B2. William John, Engineer, worked on the Ottawa Canal, then rem to Australia 1800s, elected to first Parliament there.
  B3. Edward   SARA E. below may belong to fam of
III. Charles, lost at sea   Perry,p.227.(Maroldo + Brochet)
DUMARESQ, Sara Elizabeth, of Dalhousie, NB, mar 1845 at Shoolbred, Gaspe, Mathew Caldwell of New Carlisle, Bona. Co. (Brochet) Poss sister of Daniel, b 1817, J, above?
DUMARESQ, Philip John, b 1860, mar Maria Charlotte LENFESTEY, qv., b 1863 Perce, his first cousin
DU PARC, Capt. from J in Nfld. (K. Mathews)
DUPLAIN, from C.I. to Gaspe (K.H. Annett)
DU PARCQ, Capt. from J in Nfld. (K. Mathews)
DU PONT, Capt. from J in Nfld. (K. Mathews)

DUPRE or DEPRE

DUPUIS IS PROB. QUEBECOIS ORIG.

DUPRE or DEPRE, Capt. from J in Nfld. (K. Mathews)
DU PRE, from C.I., settled in Gaspe (Betty Tardif list)
DU PUIS, from G? to Gaspe, then to Alpena, Mich.?, (Directory, 1905)
DUQUEMIN, ---, b G, uncle of Milicent Roberts Dorey of G, travelled to America on the ill fated TITANIC, was one of the survivors. Has chn in N.A. (Brian Dorey, Guernsey)
DUQUEMIN, Sidney John, b 1901, res Forest Parish, G, son of John D. and Louise ROBILLARD, qv., rem to Canada 1923. Mar Stella May Manley, 1906-1972, no issue. Res Southhampton, Ont. (Sidney Duquemin)
DUQUEMIN, Geo. Henry, b 1906, res G, bro of above, Sidney John. He mar Elise VIDAMOUR, 2 daus, both mar, with 2 chn each.
DUQUEMIN, Marie Louise, sister of above Geo. and Sidney, mar Reg. GENGE, qv., rem to Australia 1926. 3 chn, Reggie, Louise, and John, all mar with chn of their own.
DURAND, see LE MOTTEE. Hug name in G
DURANT in Nfld. (Seary) Cf DURAND in C.I. In J 1668 (Stevens)
DURELL, Bosdet, apprentice to CRC in Paspebiac, d ca 1884 in accident
DURELL, in Maritimes Fisheries (J.H. Le Breton list)
DURELL, Thomas and Philip. Durell Island in the Gut of Canso is called after Thomas.
DURELL, Vice Admiral Philip. See NOTABLES, this book.
DURELL, Philip, from G to New Hampshire, U.S. in 1689. His name then was spelled in an enormous variety of ways: DUDAY, DUBY, DURILL, DUDY, DORRELL, DORRIEL, etc. The fam settled in small coves and was twice victimized by Indian raids. The first time was in 1703, when Mrs. Durrill, her two daus, Susan and Rachel, and two sons, one of them an infant, were captured by Indians. One son drown in the Saco River, the baby son and Mrs. Durrill were allowed to return home. The two daus were carried to Canada and there married Frenchmen. In the second Indian raid in 1726, Mrs. Durrill and Mrs. Baxter, her dau, and Mrs. Baxter's chn were killed. John, a 12 yr old son, was carried to Canada, and later exchanged in about two years. However, he had been "Indianized" to such an extent that he later lived much like the Indians the rest of his life. (DURRELL GENEALOGY, DESCENDANTS OF PHILIP, compiled by Harold Clarke Durrell, Cambridge, Mass. 1918, sent by Mrs. Robert Miles O'Neill, Nebraska)

A1. Joseph, b ca 1685, mar Rebecca Adams
A2. Susan, b ca 1687, taken to Canada by the Indians and married there
A3. Rachel, b ca 1689, taken to Canada by the Indians in 1703, and married there
A4. Benjamin, b ca 1691, taken to Canada 1703, drown in the Saco River
A5. Philip Jr., b ca 1701, mar Keziah Wakefield
A6. Mary, b at Arundel, Me. ca 1703, mar at Wells, Maine 1719, James Wakefield
A7. Sarah, b ca 1705, mar ca 1724 John Baxter. She and her baby son, John, killed by Indians 1726.
A8. Elizabeth, b 1707 Me., mar 1724 John Wakefield
A9. Benjamin, b ca 1711, mar Judith Perkins
A10. Lydia, b ca 1712, mar 1728 Stephen Larribee
A11. John, b 1714, mar Lydia Hutchins Jellison

DUTOT, in Victoria, BC 1940s. Member of C.I. Society (Luce) Poss same fam as D.F. Dutot, cabinet maker, from C.I. to Sask., then to Victoria, BC before 1900
DUTOT, John, son of Daniel Dutot, a Hug refugee from France to J. Daniel's wife, Catherine LE CAUTEUR (COUTEUR?). John was one of 5 chn. Mar Mary Ann NICOLLE, also of Hug parentage. To Quebec in 1862, then to Perth Co. Settled in Tilbury West Twp., Ont., 5 chn (Reaman)

A1. John, a farmer in Tilbury West
A2. Mary Anne, mar Lorne Smith
A3. Elizabeth, b in Canada, mar James Bailey
A4. James, a farmer in Perth Co., mar Mary A. Halliday, 6 chn
DUTOT, C.I. surname on S. coast of Nfld. (C.W. Le Messurier)
DUTOT. "I have no known relations of our name outside the Newfoundland family. My great grandfather, C.J. Dutot died at La Hauteur, Trinity, Jersey." (C.J. Dutot, Montreal) The grandfather settled in Nfld. in the 1800s.
DU VAL, French fam from Rouen? ca 1550. As Hug they dispersed, one branch settling in St. Brelade, J ca 1670. Jean Du Val mar there in 1769 Marie PITON, qv. (Aldo Brochet, Montreal and Perce; Cent. Bklt.; MacWhirter; K.H. Annett of Gaspe) CAUTION! SOME ERRORS BELOW!
A1. Peter, b 1769 St. Brelade, J, d 1851 Bonaventure Island, Perce, Que. He was a capt. for the Messrs. Janvrin Bros. Co. of J for ca 20 yrs. Took part in the wars against the French Empire and the United States. After the war, set up his own fishery, Peter Du Val & Co. in Cape Breton Island and other places in the Maritimes. He took part in the Blockade of Bayonne, France in 1804 for which he received special honors. His wife, Elizabeth HUBERT, d in J, 3 sons. Du Vals said to be a knightly Galician fam.
B1. Peter John, b 1794 St. Brelade, d Bon. Is. 1835. Mar at Santander, Spain 1819, Dona Julia Maria Joquina de Aldana, 1802-1829. Bur St. Brelade, J, 5 chn. Peter John mar 2. 1835 Marguerita de Bartoloma of Spain, who d 4 months later in Canada. She was dau of Dom Pedro de Bartolma Y Pan. Peter John bought the Du Val fisheries from his relatives in 1835 and continued to expand operations in the Maritimes. In 1831, he had a crown grant at Miscou, NB. In addition to being a merchant, mariner, shipowner, he may have been a commissioned officer in the Navy. He is named at various times in Guernsey, Jersey, Spain, Bonaventure Island and Bristol, England. Julia Aldana from Galicia, Spain.
C1. Julia Elizabeth Monica, b 1820 Santander, Spain, d on ship LORD GAMBIA 1833 off Spanish Coast.
C2. Peter Nicholas, b 1821 St. Brelade, J, d Bon. Is. 1889, mar 1842 Cape Cove, Perce, Anne de Mountenay, b 1816 Bon. Is., d there 1894. She was dau of Wm. de Mountenay and Ellen O'Hara. He was beachmaster, bookkeeper, schoolmaster, school commissioner, and J.P. under Queen Victoria. Ann, Nancy, his wife, was an herbalist, medicine woman. At least 8 chn, 1816-1894.
D1. Sophia Louisa, b 1841, d 1926, mar Philippe Abraham MAUGER, qv., of C.I. origin. Res N.Y. City.
D2. Peter John, Pierre-Jean Eusebius, b 1843, d 1929, mar Susan Elizabeth LENFESTEY, qv., dau of Peter L. and Margaret Bragg. Mar 2. Catherine McNeill de Barra, dau of Roderique McNeil de Barra, and Esther   GARRETT, qv., who d 1910. Adopted Leslie Crombie, b 1898, WWI vet.
E1. Mary Anne, b 1870, d 1957, bur Montreal, seamstress
E2. Peter Philip, b 1872 Bon Is., d 1940 Verdun, Que., mar Isabel Tait of Ville St. Laurent, Que., 3 chn
F1. Peter John, 1909-1929 F2. Helen F3. Elizabeth
E3. Julia Margaret, b 1875, d 1951 Van Nuys, Calif. Mar Montreal, Wm. McFetridge, 4 chn
F1. Hector McFetridge
F2. Ailsa McFetridge, mar ---Gibb
F3. Clara McFetridge   F4. Ruth McFetridge, mar ---Watt
E4. Susan Elizabeth, twin of Julia, d 1969, N. Burnaby, BC,

DU VAL 231

    mar 1899 Perce, John LENFESTY, qv., 1875-1939, Montreal,
    2 daus. See LENFESTY
 E5. Arthur Charles, b 1876, d 1955 Pembroke, Ont. Mar at
    Pembroke, Martha de Vine, 2 chn
    F1. Russell   F2. Lillian, mar Alroy Butler, res Toronto
                    G1. Russell Butler or Kingsley?Butler.
 E6. Lillian Elizabeth, b 1879, d 1975 Dorval, Que. bur L'Anse
    du Cap, Gaspe. Mar 1903, Perce, Henry Allen LENFESTY,
    6 chn. See -LENFESTY
 E7. Emily Louisa, b 1881, d Kingston, NY, mar ca 1902 Emory
    Hoyt
    F1. Albert Hoyt   F4. Grace Hoyt
    F2. Harmon Hoyt   F5. Helen Hoyt, res Kings-
    F3. Ambrosia Hoyt, mar V. Chase   ton, NY
 E8. Grace Victoria, b 1884, d.y.
 E9. Harry Archibald William, b 1886, d.y.
 E10. Ernest John, b 1888, d.y.
 E11., 12., 13., all d.y. (A.Brochet says only 10 chn)
D3. Julia Anna Elizabeth, b 1846 Bon. Is., d 1886
D4. Archibald Joseph William, b 1848, d 1923 Brockville, Ont.
    Mar Ottawa 1882, Marcella O'Donoghue.
    E1. Alice Anne Elizabeth, b 1883 Ottawa, d 1959 Ottawa. Mar
        1904 George Claudius Adrian Warren, b 1883, Barachois,
        Gaspe, who d 1953 Ottawa, 6 chn
        F1. Eric, d.y.   F2. Rita, d.y.
        F3. Isabel Marcella Warren, mar 1. Charles Bradwin
        F4. Charles Adrian, mar Joyce Blackwell
        F5. Archibald William, b 1917, d 1970, mar Verna Schwerdfager
        F6. Melville George, mar 2. Claire Perrier
    E2. Rita May, b 1890 Ottawa, d 1973, mar ca 1908 John James LEE,
        1890-1949
        F1. John Lee, 1913-1975, mar Lena ---
        F2. Lois, mar Richard Edward MacDonald, b Scotland 1909
        F3. Eric, mar Frieda Lecuyer
    E3. Mary Ann, d age 28, no issue
D5. Henry Ridley Du Val, b 1850, mar 1. 1879 Flora Jane LE COU-
    TEUR, qv., and 2. her sister, Katherine Hannah LE COUTEUR,
    1849-1895,   and 3. in 1898 Elizabeth Anne de St. Amand,
    dau of Francois and Eliza JOURNEAUX. She was the widow of
    George BUTLIN, qv., of Bon. Is., her father of J fam. 6 chn
    by first wife
    E1. Henry Joseph, Joe, b 1880, d 1899, bur Bon. Is.
    E2. Francis Randolph, b 1881, d 1971 Huntington Park, Calif.,
        boat builder, carver, painter, mar 1. Elsa ---, and 2. Mae
        ---
    E3. Alfred Philip, b 1884, killed Houston, TX ca 1927, mar ?
        F1. Lillian, mar Herschel Stovall in Louisiana F2. John Henry
    E4. Alberta Louisa, b 1887 Bon. Is.
    E5. Lillian Jane, b 1889 Bon. Is., mar 1909 Ottawa, Cyrville,
        James E. Dean, b 1890 Renfrew, Ont., d 1936, Ottawa, engi-
        neer, 4 chn
        F1. Vera Myrtle, 1910-1969, mar Emile Le Roy, dau
            G1. Flora Le Roy, b 1947 Ottawa
        F2. Walter Benedict Dean, b 1912, mar Yvette Oshier, res
            Barrie, Ont. Issue
        F3. Rolland, d 1967, mar Emma Grace O'Neil, d 1977, issue
        F4. Myrtle, mar Peter Zazulak, res Ottawa

                    G1. Gary Zazulak
            E6. Marie Violette, Lucy, b 1890, Bon. Is., d ca 1902 Montreal
        D6. Arthur Philip, b 1853, mar 1878 Ellen Cody, b Bon. Is. dau
            of Patrick Cody and Susannah Morrissey, 3 daus
            E1. Julia Anne Elizabeth, b 1880 Bon. Is., d.y.?
            E2. Sue Ann Louisa, 1879 Bon. Is., mar John Whitaker?, b 1879
                Perce
            E3. a dau, poss an R.C. nun?
        D7. Albert Francis, b 1855 Bon. Is., mar Anna McNeill de Barra,
            1844-1915, mar L'Anse du Cap 1881, he d 1938 Bon. Is.
            E1. John, b 1879? Pabos, d 1969 Perce, farmer, no issue
            E2. Anne Sophia, b 1881, d.y.
            E3. Mountenay William, Will, Capt. Du Val, b 1883 Bon. Is., d
                Mont Joli, Que. 1960. Mariner, naturalist, warden of the
                Bon. Is. bird sanctuary, mar at Perce 1912, Matilda Clara
                MAUGER, qv., 1884-1954, bur Perce (L'ISLE PERCE, J.M. Clark)
                F1. Grace Sophia, b 1912, mar 1941 Montreal, James Robert
                    Carrol, b 1905 Ulster, UK, stationary engineer, 4 chn
                    G1. Robert Wm. du Val Carroll, b 1942, mar 1967 Carol Ann
                        Marcus, res Montreal, with issue
                    G2. Doris Edith, b 1943, mar 1971 Michael Edward Nash, res
                        Rosemere, Que., with issue
                    G3. Howard James
                    G4. Clifford Gerald, b 1947, mar 1976 Jill Cole, res Hia-
                        leah, Florida
                F2. Mildred Lucille, b 1914, d.y., bur Perce
                F3. Edith Anna, b 1916, artisan, mar 1946 Montreal, Louis
                    Ralph BROCHET, qv., b 1918, mariner, 4 chn, see BROCHET
                F4. Howard William, b 1918 Bon. Is., d 1963 Whitby, Ont.
                    electromechanic, artist, archivist, bur Pine Hill Cem.,
                    Toronto, Ont. WWII vet.
                F5. Julia May, b 1920, artisan, mar 1946 Montreal, Clifford
                    George Wilson, b 1924 Montreal, postman at Huntingdon,
                    Que., res Athelstan, Hinchinbrooke Twp., Que., 2 chn
                    G1. Leslie Raymond Wilson, b 1948, mar Beverly Therrien of
                        New Minas, N.S., with issue
                    G2. Catherine Gail Wilson, b 1953, mar 1. Douglas Henry
                        Williams of Dorval, Que., separated
                F6. Elwood Archibald, b 1923, d Agincourt, Scarboro, Ont.
                    1977, engineer, physics, R.C. Army WWII, mar 1950 Doris
                    Everard widow of McCarthney, Albertan pilot killed in
                    action.
                    G1. Richard John, b 1960 Agincourt, Ont.
            E4. Archibald Frederick, b 1884, d.y.
            E5. Julia Ellen Victoria, b 1886, d 1971 Meaford, Grey Co., Ont.
                Mar ca 1916 Montreal, Elwood Dales, 2 chn
                F1. McNeil Dales
                F2. Laura Dales, b 1921, d 1974, mar Rev. John Miller
            E6. Mary Ann, Maria?, b 1888, d 1959 Montreal, mar 1910 Perce,
                Arthur William MAUGER, qv., 1880-1944, 9 sons, 2 daus
        D8. Frederick William, b 1858 Bon. Is., d 1889? Rem to Phila.,
            Pa., no issue
    C3. Charlotte Ramona, b 1823 Santander, Spain, d Portsmouth, Eng.
        ca 1890. Mar ca 1848 St. Brelade, J, Henry John Kelly, pay-
        master in Royal Navy
        D1. Grace Kelly   a mariner.
    C4. Juan Evarist, b 1824 Santander, Spain, drown Bon. Is. ca 1850,

DUVAL   233

C5. Sophie Alexandrine, 1827-1829, St. Brelade, J.
B2. Francis Nicholas, Master Mariner,drowned from
    brig SIREN, 1830,mar Ang.Beaker,res Jersey.
    C1.Hnry   C2. Philip (Beakers=Germany)

B3. Philip J.J.M., b 1806 St. Brelade J, d 1878
    Pasp., QUE. Mar Mar Coxtown,Q.1829 JaneScott,
    dau of James S. & Joanna Brotherstone.9 chn.
    Bur St.Peters, Pasp. Sev.chn mar GALLIEs.
    Jane,1807-1897, from U.E.L. family.
    C1.Jane Eliz., b 1830 Coxtown, Que mar 1851
       Benj. Smith.
    C2.Joanna, b 1832 mar 1852 Richard Smith, Jr.
    C3. Margaret, 1834-1906, mar Francis LE GALLAIS,
        qv, 1834-1883, bur Perce, 9 chn
    C4. Sarah Ann, 1837-1899, mar James P. Gallie,qv
        1834-1906. Sarah twin of Philip.
    C5. Philip, 1837-1918, bur St.James, Hopetown,Q.
        Mar margaret Smith,b Carlisle.Philip a Pvt.
        in local Militia, farmer later with dau Emma
        (W.Scott, Hopetown; Aldo Brochet)
        D1. Phil.Nicolle, 1864 D4. Phoebe Ann,1868
        D2. Jane Eliz. 1864   D5.Margaret J, 1870
        D3.Eliza Jane 1866
        D6. Jane Emma 1874-1967, bur Montreal. Mar
         . Elias Henry MAUGER ,1871-1931,of Montreal
           (3ANGLICAN PAR.BY YEAR OF BIRTH, Notary
           Office at New Carlisle, QUE)
    C6. Celina Eliz, b 1841
    C7. John Francis, Frank, 1844-1925, shoemaker,
        mar Coxtown Jane BUNTON, qv,1838-1907, widow
        of John Henry Newman, no issue
    C8. James, b 1847
    C9. Eliz, b 1851 Cowtown, mar Francis HOCQUARD,
        qv, 9 chn, member of Plymouth BretherenSect.
        D1. Charles HOCQUARD, res Campbellton,NB,
            son in La Chute, QUE.
A2. Jean, b 1769, twin of Peter, mariner, d 1831,
    Lieut.R.N., bur St. Brelade, Jersey.(Brochet)
A3. Nicholas, b 1771, mariner, d after 1819
A4. Francis, b 1773
A5. Marie, b 1775, mar John HUELIN, qv, mariner for
    Chrles Robin firm. Desc. Cape Cove, Gaspe
    B1. John HUELIN jr., merchant
A6. Amice, b 1777, merchant at St.Helier, d?1850 J.

"The Philippic branch of the Du Val family is descended from a Daniel Francois Du Val of St. Peter Parish, Jersey. While an exact connection of this Philippic branch to the Peterian branch is unclear, the similarities are quite evident of consanguinity, occupation, area of migration, and proper names are similar." (Aldo Brochet)

"George Du Val, sailmaker, circumnavigated the globe several times. His dau Mayda and grandsons Arthur and Wilfred Du Val, res at Bathurst, NB. Alfred John, merchant of caraquet, has his family correspondence and ledgers, 1880-1950, preserved at the PANB Bldg., Fredericton, NB. DU VAL-LEIGH line descendants at Montreal, connected to Mignaults. Peter's descendants usually Anglican, and Philip's are Methodist. Du Val-Cormier line is in the Eastern Townships. (Aldo Brochet)

DU VAL, Philip b ca 1771, d1839, of Les marais, St.Peter,J. He mar Marie HUELIN. 10 chn. A family hist.& gen. of this line is being worked on by Fidele Theriault, Caraquet, NB. Desc. in NB, QUE, Iowa, etc. (LE ROSSIGNOL FAMILY, by S.J.Le Ross., Ida Duval, Grandmere, QUE;Brochet; Betty Dolling, Ames, Iowa). This Philip was Capt. of ship ESTHER in 1810. SOME DATA UNCERTAIN OR POSS IN ERROR.
A1. Mary Anne, b 1798
A2. Elizabeth, b 1800, mar Henry MAYNARD?
A3. Anne, b 1802
A4. Jeanne b 1803 mar 1. _____LESUEUR, and 2. Edw. LE BOUTILLIER, desc. in Iowa.
A5. Nicholas, of Portelet, b 1807 J, d 1891, 8 chn. He mar Marguerite LEIGH, who d 1896, dau of Geo. Leigh and _____QUERIPEL, of G.
   B1. Philip Leigh DUVAL, b 1837 St. Brelade, J, d 1916, mar Jane Susan LE BROCQ
      C1. Jane, b 1867 teacher, mar P.LEMASURIER
      C2. Philip b 1869 J, mar Louise FIOTT
         D1. Phyllis, b 1897
   B2. Eliza Leight DuVal, b 1839
   B3. John Leigh DuVal, b 1841 St. Brelade, J, in Militia in Caraquet, NB 1860.Rem to Wisconsin and d by accident there.
   B4. Frederick Leigh, mar _____ASPLET in J
      C1. Anna, b 1869, teacher
A6. Anne (again), b 1810
A7. Philippe, b 1813, mar Jeanne ROUET, res NB?
   B1. John, d ca 1900 Caraquet, NB, a joiner, mar Alice LE COUTEUR, 2 sons
      C1. Alfred John b 1872 d 1951 unmar

```
            C2. Walter, b 1890?
        B2. George, b 1849 St.Peter J, d Bathurst,NB,
            Sailor, mar Veronique PAULIN
            C1. Elias              C3. George
            C2. Mayda, b 1899, mar J.A. PINAULT, who d
                ca 1967
        B3. Philip b 1840 St. peter J, joiner, res NB
            then Grandmere, QUE. Mar Susan Cormier,9 chn?
            He d 1921.
            C1. John b 1869 mar Alice Mary LE DAIN,qv,
                D1. Aylmer, b 1915
            C2. Philip b 1873, mar Anna Harper
                D1. Lydia Anne, b 1901    D3. Albert
                D2. James Philip          D4. Cecile
            C3. George, b 1875 mar Ida ROY, and 2. Clara
                St.Onge.
                D1. Ida, b 1916, The Soo,ONT, res mère Grand Q.
            C4. Emma, b 1876          C5. Jane, b 1880
            C6. Lydia, b 1882
            C7. Alwyn, b 1884, mar Eliz. Forsay
                D1. Lorna, b 1912    D2.Winston, b 1918
            C8. Raymond, b 1886 mar Grace Greene of
                South Bolton, QUE.
    A8. Amice, b 1815, mar Esther ROUET, d Caraquet, NB
        B1. Capt. John, who d at Liverpool, England
    A9. Nancy b 1818        A10. Peter John, b 1821
DU VAL, Philip d 1918 age 80, bur Hopetown,Gaspe.
DU VAL, Capt and ship owner, from J to Nfld.early.
   (K. Matthews, St. Johns, Nfld.)
DU VAL, Joshua, S.P.G. Missionary in Nfld.  At
   Burgeos in 1854.  In Channel & La Poele,1855-8.
DU VAL, Charles, fisherman/SandyPt.Nfld.1871(Lovell)

DYER, appears in cem. in Annapolis, NS 1700s. CF
   DYER in Chan.Islands.
DYER, from Alderney to Chatham, ONT ca 1870-1880.
   (Luce)  One a soldier who mar an Alderney girl.
DYER in Nfld. Philip in St.John's 1705.(Seary)

EBSWORTHY, from G in Nfld. (K. Matthews)
ECOBICHON, Gerald David, b 1950 J, son of Alex.E.
  and Roselle Florence HUELIN, qv, to Toronto 1974.
  Mar Norma Dove NICHOLS, b Eng.  ECOBICHON from
  La Fontaine, Corley Plouec, Cotes du Nord, France.
  (Gerald Ecobichon, Toronto, ONT)
EDMOND, Mrs.,nee LE QUESNE, qv, to Vancouver from
  Jersey, was active in Channel Island Society of
  Vancouver, BC, 1952.(Violet Perkins, Vanc., BC)
```

EDMONDS, EDMUNDS, from G? to Nfld. (Seary) Cf EDMONS of J (Stevens)
EDWARDS to Gaspe from C.I.?
EFFARD, from J?, to Nfld. (Seary) In Perlican 1682. See EFFARD in QAAM, by Turk.
EGRE, William, b J, age 27 in Caraquet, NB 1871 (census) with wife Vitaline, b N.B. He was Presbyterian and a blacksmith.
ELLIS in Maritimes from C.I. (J. H. Le Breton list)
ELLIS, Thomas, b St. Heliers, J, res Gaspe town 1800s
ELLIS, George, b 1809 J, to Canada ca 1845, employed 30 years on the Beauharnois Canal, retired 1875, in Melocheville, Beau. Co., Que. (HIST. ATLAS OF QUEBEC EASTERN TOWNSHIPS, 1881-1972, Ross Cumming, Stratford, Ont.)
ELLIS, Eric John, and Jane Susan, from J? to Malbaie, Gaspe 1800s
ELY, from C.I.? Ann, mar Jean RICHARD. He mar 2. at Perce 1840 Genevieve Desbois. See BEECHARD, BICHARD and RICHARD.
EMERY, Capt. from J in Nfld. (K. Mathews)
EMILY, John A., b Trinity J, rem to Winnipeg, Man. 1889, then to Vancouver, BC 1919. Mar ---?, 2 daus: Mrs. Gwenneth Hodgson, Vancouver, and Mrs. A. Kathleen Cory, Ferndown, Dorset, Eng. 4 grchn, 5 grtgranchn. Had two sisters, Irene and Elsie of J. Mr. Emily d 1972 in Vancouver, in his 90th year.
EMOND, from C.I. to Gaspe
ENEVOLDSEN, from C.I. to Calgary, Alta.
ENGLAND, ENGLISH in Nfld. (Seary) Cf same in J (Stevens)
ENGLISH, from C.I. to Gaspe. Curr at Anse au Griffon, Gaspe. John Jr. mar 1810 Grand Greve, Brigitte, dau of Edouard Sennett and Marie ROBERT. (Brochet)
ENOUE, from C.I. to Gaspe, listed by Betty TARDIF. Prob ESNOUF?
EREAUT, from C.I. to Nfld. (Seary) Cf EREAUT of J (Stevens) (Also noted by K. Mathews)
EREAUT, John of J? mar Julie Alexandre of N.B.
ESCOTT in Nfld. (Seary) Cf ESCOT of J (Stevens)
ESNOUF, from C.I. to Gaspe, a blacksmith. Poss res also at Perce and Malbaie
ESNOUF, Francis, b J, only son of Francis and Mary ESNOUF, d Grande Riviere 1882, Gaspe, age 29 (GLF) A Francis was 18 in 1871 (Census)
ESNOUF-DENIZE, Walter of St. Lawrence, J, mar 1905 Edmonton, Alta., Jane Harriet Hennequin, b 1885 St. Heliers, J. A dau? Jane Harriet bur W. Vancouver in her 99th year. A niece in England and a nephew, Albert Wilkinson, in Vancouver, BC (Eva Luce)
ESNOUF, Charles, b J, in Gaspe 1861 (census) with Jane, a teacher, Jane, Charles, John, Clara, Evangeline, Rachel, b Gaspe
ESNOUF, Martha Pearl, b 1885 J, mar John Philip LE MASURIER, rem to Gaspe, d 1972 (Harold Le Masurier, Forillon, Gaspe, Que.)
ESNOUF, fam in Montreal, one in Quebec City, one in Victoria, one in Vancouver, BC. A cousin of this fam, res Dayton, Ohio, has some gen. data. All from C.I.
ESNOUF, Flight Sgt. L.V., in Claresholm, Alta. in 1951
ESNOUF, Charles, at Cap des Rosiers, Quebec, 1861 (census)
FACEY in Nfld. (Seary) Cf FAESAN of J (Stevens)
FAINTON, surname of J, poss changed to FENTON sometimes in Canada
FAINTON, Capt., master of the BEE, a Robin ship, going between Paspebiac and St. Heliers, J in 1774 (Donat Robichaud)
FAIRSERVICE, Poss BECHERVAISE, BEAUSERVICE, Susie, wife of J.W. Godfray of L'Anse au Griffon, Gaspe, d 1899, age 33. GODFRAY, Mgr. for Robin firm, bur Penouille, Gaspe, St. Mathews Ch (GLF)

FAIRWEATHER, a Mr. and Mrs. from G in Victoria, BC 1940s (Luce)
FALLA, Howard Tardif, b 1928 G, son of Clifford F, and Vera TARDIF, qv.,
   mar Norma Grace PAYNE. To Agincourt, Ont. Vera res N.J. and Mass.
   from ages 6-18, returned to J. See TARDIF. (Howard Falla, Agincourt,
   Ont.)
A1. Steven Howard, b 1955   A3. Kathryn Vera, b 1963
A2. Elaine Norma, b 1956
FALLA, John L., son, also, of Clifford and Vera FALLA, b G, to Ontario
   1970s
FALLA, Bernard, b ca 1900 G, rem to Ontario. Uncle of Howard, above.
   The above FALLa fams related through great grandfather Nicolas FALLA
   and Harriet RENOUF to large FALLA clan of Maine and Mass. (See QAAM)
FALLA, E., b St. Helens, Lancashire, Eng. of G? fam, rem to Canada
   (Mrs. E. Falla, Scarborough, Ont.)
FALLA, Wilson Arthur, b G, left at age 13, served in G Militia, rem to
   Canada 1923. In 1926 mar Doris QUERIPEL, qv., of Bordeaux, Vale, G.
   Res Hamilton, Ont. Related to LE PREVOSTS of St. Peter Port, G.
   (Wilson Falla, Hamilton, Ont.)
FALLA, others in Calgary and Hamilton, Ont., from G
FALLE, in Nfld. A Jersey merchant in Sandy Point, Nfld. 1800s (Mannion, C.R. Fay, Seary)
FALLE, FALLES, Captains and ship owners, from J and G to Nfld. (K.
   Mathews, Robichaud)
FALLE, Richard of Jersey Harbor, Nfld. 1832 (Seary)
FALLE, Josue George, 1820-1903, Jurat in J, son of Josue FALLE of Hambie, St. Saviour, and of Ester, dau of Jurat George BERTRAM. The
   FALLES had been engaged in the Nfld. fisheries from 1795 at least,
   and the firm of Richard Falle & Co., Nfld., ship owners and merchants
   was founded at Point George, Little Burin, Nfld. ca 1830 by Josue's
   two uncles, Richard and Elie Falle. In 1838 they took their nephew
   into the firm, and when both were lost at sea while crossing with cod
   to Oporto, Portugal, he remained in control of the business. In 1848
   he became Member for Burin in the Nfld. House of Assembly.
   Some years later Falle returned to Jersey, leaving two nephews in
   charge of the firm, and married Marie Elizabeth GODFRAY, dau of Advocate Francois GODFRAY, qv. In 1864 he became Deputy of St. Heliers,
   J, and though later a Conservative, he won his seat on a reform program. He was later Constable, encouraged the building of a Museum,
   now the home of the Societe Jersiaise. He left two daus, Rozel and
   Lily, and a son, Bertram Godfray, later created Baron Portsea of
   Portsmouth, England. (G.R. Balleine)
FALLE, Thomas, b 1801 St. Savious, J, cordwainer, mar Susan LE SUEUR,
   b St. John, J. Some members of this fam settled in U.S. and Canada.
   (Betty Wickham, Loveland, Colo.)
A1. Thomas, b 1827 St. Saviour, J, mar Elinor M. LE FEBVRE, qv., b J,
   poss res Lansingburgh, NY, where he d
A2. Susannah, b ca 1830 J, d there 1848, bur St. Saviours
A3. Henriette, Harriet, b 1831 J
A4. Philip, b 1833 J?, d 1862, bur at sea on voyage home from Australia
A5. Marie, Mary Ann, b 1835, mar Philip LE SUEUR, 1828-1866. Mary Ann
   d 1893, Lansingburgh, NY (chn)
A6. Jane, b 1837, rem to Ottawa, Ont., mar ---Fraser
A7. Elias, b 1839 J, mar Mary Ann CHAMPION, qv., of J, d 1904 Troy, NY
   B1. Capt. William Champion   B3. John Edward
   B2. Albert Henry   B4. Eliza May
A8. Rachel, b 1841 J, mar Julius PFAU
   B1. Ida, b Canada   B2. Vida Pfau, b N.Y. state

A9. Ann, b 1843 J, mar John F. PARRETT, 1830-1893. Ann d 1921 Lansingburgh, NY, where grave marker is mistakenly marked BARRETT
FALLE, John, age 32, in 1870, res Troy, NY, mar Frances ---. This FALLE prob related to the other FALLES there.
FALLE, Philip, b 1815 J, one of 9 chn b to Edward FALLE and Rachel DE GRUCHY. Edward d J 1827. Philip rem to Canada age ca 20. Worked in J for brother-in-law, Charles AHIER, qv. Wrecked on ship near St. John's, Nfld., and by the time he reached Quebec, the promised job was gone. Rem to Oxford Co., Ont. where he had connections! Engaged in cutting and clearing of timber lands. Joined the Loyalists in the Rebellion of 1837-8, rem to Dereham, Ont. and bought 100 acres of land which he cleared and settled on for 25 yrs. In 1866, retired to Tilsonburg, Ont. and bought the Hotel there. Served on the school board and on town and county councils. Mar Orpha Warden of Trenton, N.J. (PIONEER CANADIAN FAMILIES)
A1. dau mar William Ferguson of N.S.
FALLE, current at Gaspe and Matapedia, etc.
FALLE, Joshua, b J, rem to Gaspe ca 1840, mar there 1843 ---. In Gaspe 1861 (census) with Elia, Henry, Felice, Edward and Edward, all b Gaspe
FALLE, Joshua Edward, b 1850 J, to Montreal before 1880. Mar Jane Louise HOYLES, qv. FALLE d 1908, bur Montreal, 4 chn See THE QUIET ADVENTURERS for this complete family.
FALLE, Earl W. of Knowlton, Que., d 1971 in his 67th yr., husband of Marjorie Coffin. He was the son of Frederick and Elvena Falle of Gaspe, brother of Clarence of Montreal, Carl of London, Ont.; Charles of Gaspe, Elsie, Anne (Mrs. Louis Le Parneau of Calgary); Alice (Mrs. Archie Le Mesurier of Wallaceburg, Ont.) Pearl (Mrs. W. Le Messurier of Wallaceburg, Ont.) and May (Mrs. Malcolm Hodge of Lennoxville, Que.). Bur Knowlton Cem., Que. (SPEC, Dec. 19, 1977, A. Brochet)
FALLE, Elias Richard, b 1842 Gaspe, son of Joshua Philip FALLE and Margaret Ellen Annett (Brochet)
FALLE, Joshua, age 54 in 1871, ship carpenter, b J, wife, Sophia, 36, b Ireland, mar 1843, with chn Elia, Henry, Felice?, FELIX?, b ca 1851 (census) and two Edwards. (Brochet)
FALLE, Joshua, another record gives the following chn: in 1871, Felix, age 20; Edward, age 17; Alfred, age 8; John, age 7; Henry, age 3; and Margaret, age 10 mos. (Brochet)
FALLE, John, b J, age 31 in 1871, blacksmith, wife Rachel, age 21, at Gaspe Bay with chn; John, age 1 and Alice 2 mos.
FALLE, Thomas, b J, arrived in Shippegan, NB ca 1830, where he became Mgr. for the Godfrey estab. He was prob single in 1848. (Robichaud) Jean VINCENT, qv., built a ship there under his management in 1835. Falle also had a general store in Shippegan and was in civic activities.
FALLE, Thomas, settled in Miscou, NB as Mgr. for Peter John Du Val's fishery. The same Thomas?
FALLE, John William, of St. Georges, Nfld., J fam, rem to Hespeler, Ont., mar Eva Cutler. J.W. b 1865, wife, in 1884
A1. Anne Dorothy, b 1904, unmar
A2. Herbert Chesley, b 1905, mar Sophie Castle, b 1909
A3. Bessie Gladys, b 1908, Baptish missionary from 1938 to 1971
A4. Grace, b 1907, mar William Austin Smith, b 1906, chn
A5. Harold Lester, b 1910, mar Erna Warnholtz, b 1911, chn
A6. Douglas Frank, b 1913, mar Dorothy Kay
A7. Beulah Doris, b 1915, mar John Ody Maron, b 1913, chn
FALLIER, Medart?, b G, in Gaspe Bay South, 1861 (census)
A number of FALLES noted in N.S. and in Western Canada.

FALLOW, FALLON, FOWLOW, etc. in Nfld. (Seary) Cf Luke FALLON in St. John's Nfld. 1850 (Seary) Cf DE FALLONS of J (Stevens)
FALLU, current at Carleton, Nouvelle, Que.
FALLU, Irene Gladys, b J early 1900s? To Canada with mother in 1917. Step-dau of John P. LEMPRIERE, qv. Mar, A. Knowles, res Edmonton, Alta.
FALLU, Monica Maud, sister of Irene, above. Mar, M. Voss. (G. Lempriere and Mrs. Knowles)
FALLU, FALLY, George, b 1809 J, son of Philip F. and Elizabeth LE FEVRE of Notre Dame, St. Mary's, J. Rem to Paspebiac, Gaspe 1826 or before, for Robin firm. Mar 1840, Carlton, Que., Genevieve McIntyre, dau of Jean Baptiste M. and Reine Bergeron of Carlton. Res ca 1843 in Nouvelle, Gaspe, d 1888, 7 chn. (Gaston Fallu, Carlton, Que., Olivier, Brochet) Other chn? Esther, b 1841; Alexander, b 1845; Elias Albert, b 1847.

A1. Philippe, mar Sophie Berthelot
  B1. Eugene   B2. Albert   B3. Marguerite
A2. John, mar Helen Calvert
  B1. James   B2. Peter
A3. James, mar Helene Berthelot
  B1. Flore   B2. Helene   B3. Parmelia
  B4. Marie, b 1870 Nouvelle, Que., mar 1890 Gr. Riv. John Belliveau
A4. Lazare, b 1849 Carlton, mar Tatienne Landry, 1854-1951
  B1. Joseph, b 1883, mar at Nouvelle, Que., Leocadie Leblanc (See Annett)
    C1. Arsene, b 1909, mar Marguerite Leblanc, 7 chn
      D1. Jocelyne, b 1946, mar Pierre Cyr D5. Gaston, b 1953, mar ---
      D2. Denis, b 1947, mar Mary Connors D6. Charles, b 1955, mar
      D3. Roseline, b 1949   Rena Audet
      D4. Jean Marie, b 1950, mar Francoise D7. Guy, b 1958
          MERCIER
    C2. Leandre, b 1910, mar Rose Landry, 6 chn
      D1. Carmelle   D3. Roger   D5. Raymond
      D2. Clement   D4. Rachelle   D6. Francine
    C3. Lea, b 1913, mar Rupert Leblanc, 3 chn
      D1. Esther   D2. Rodrigue   D3. Gerald
    C4. Jeanne, b 1917, mar Antoine Francoeur, 3 chn
      D1. Renald   D2. Louisette   D3. Rejean
    C5. Leopold, b 1919, mar Madeleine Lavoie, 6 chn
      D1. Rejean   D3. Pauline   D5. Rock
      D2. Gilles   D4. Richard   D6. Yvon
    C6. Emerentienne, b 1921, mar Zephirin Parent, son, Marius Parent
    C7. Armand, b 1923, mar Henriette Dufour, 3 chn
      D1. Nicole   D2. Mario   D3. Sylvain
    C8. Rene, b 1926, mar Rita McBrearty, 6 chn
      D1. Alain   D3. Lorraine   D5. Henri
      D2. Gilbert   D4. Micheline   D6. Serge
    C9. Roland, b 1929, mar Janine Dion, 4 chn
      D1. Danielle D2. Gina D3. Luc D4. Nathalie
    C10. Marcel, b 1931, mar Rita Laforet, 4 chn
      D1. Ghislain D2. Cadie D3. Carole D4. Andrew
    C11. Marie Ange, b 1932, mar Bernard PERRIN, 4 chn
      D1. Manon D2. Isabelle D3. Lucie D4. Francis

FALLU, Elie, b ca 1920 Nouvelle, Gaspe, was a Member of the National Assembly of Quebec, for Terrebonne riding, elected 1976. Desc of George FALLU and Mary McIntyre of Nouvelle area. (Brochet) George F. was executor of the estate of Charles LE FEUVRE, dit LE FEUILLATRE of

Nouvelle, Bon. Co., Que. 1849, poss another Jerseyman (Sheppard Notorial Act, Carlisle, Que.)
FALLU, Marie Jeanne, b 1870 Gr. Riv., Gaspe, mar John Beliveau, Acadian, dau of Jacques F. and Helene Berthelot (Brochet)
FARR, Olive, b St. Thomas, Ont. ca 1913, was taken back to G at 3 months. Her father, Arthur Farr, was the son of a sea captain, his mother was Harriet Crabb. Arthur mar ---Paul, from Dorset, Eng. Olive returned to St. Thomas age 6, ca 1918 with her grandmother. Mar 1939 St. Anglican Ch, Frederick Bolter from London, Eng. (Olive Bolter St. John, St. Thomas, Ont.)
A1. Madeline Bolter
A2. Sharon Bolter, mar ---Schuyler, 3 daus
A3. Robert Bolter, mar, a son and a dau
FASHON, FASHION, FACHON, etc., C.I. surname on S. coast of Nfld. Nicholas FOUASCHIN, son of Thomas, Hug?, bought in 1509 the Fief d'Anneville of G, but later rem to England as Fachin or Fashion. Alice, a desc in 1660 mar Charles ANDROS, related to the DE SAUSMAREZ and DE CARTERETS of G and J.
FAUVEL, John, from J?, with Robin firm in Paspebiac, Gaspe and Pt. St. Peter, Quebec, d Paspebiac 1897. SEE EXTRA PAGES.
A1. John
A2. George Philip, b 1849 J?, bur St. Peters, Malbaie, Gaspe 1905 (GLF)
A3. William, fisherman, instructed the Norwegians in drying codfish Gaspe style, was later chief agent for Le Boutillier at Paspebiac, d 1897. Was MP for Bona. Co. 1893. (Rev. d'Hist; Cent. Bklt.)
Wm. b 1850? Bur Newcarlisle, Que.
FAUVEL, Philip Bertram, b J?, d St. Agathe des Monts, Que. 1914, age 19 (GLF)
FAUVEL, George Arthur, d 1893, age 11 mos. (GLF)
FAUVEL, Henry William, d 1896, age 5 weeks, both poss sons of George Philip, bur Malbaie, Que. (GLF)
FAUVEL, Capt. from J to Nfld. (K. Mathews)
FAUVEL, John, b G, with H. Mary Fauvel, E.M. Fauvel in Gaspe 1861 (census) Also with Emily, C.D., Clara, all b Canada.
FAUVRETT, Capt. from J in Nfld. (K. Mathews)
FAWNE, George, son of George Fawne of G, Hampshire, a woolcomber, at age 10 was bound to John BARE (Le BER ?) for 12 yrs. in the Island of Jamaica 1685 (Chirelli)
FEARON, in Canada from C.I.?
FENTON, from C.I. in Canada? Cf FAINTON of J
FEREY, FERRIE, FERRY, from C.I. to Nfld. (Seary) Cf FEREY of J (Stevens)
FEREY, Capt. George, survivor of the ISLANDER wreck in B.C. Poss another George FEREY? in B.C. Cf also FERRY in Victoria and Vancouver, BC (Luce)
FERGUSON, Mrs. Amelia J., from C.I., Director of Music and founder of Nelson, B.C. Boys' Choir (Luce) See also Rex LE LACHEUR
FERGUSON from J in Perce, Que. (Cent. Bklt.)
FEVER, FEUVRE, FEAVER, LE FEUVRE, LE FEBVRE, etc. from C.I. to Nfld. (Seary, Rev. Hammond)
FEWER in Nfld. (Seary) Cf DU FEU, etc. of J (Stevens) or LE FEUVRE
FIANDER in Nfld. (Seary) Poss of C.I. origin?
FICKETT in Nfld. (Seary) Cf FICQUET of J (See QAAM) There was a Thomas FICQUET in St. Clement, J in 1668 (Underhill)
FILLETT, Abram of J, exporter at Renewes, Nfld. (Census of 1675)
FILION from C.I. to Canada? (Max Lucas, Jersey)
FILLEUL, E., in Port de Grave, Conc- Bay, Nfld. 1790 (Rev. Hammond)
Others there as FILLEUL or FILLIER from at least 1760, prob from C.I.
FILLEUL, Eliza, b 1888 J, mar Everard J. LE BOUTILLIER, qv. res

FILLEUL 241
  SEE FILLEUL IN ADDITIONS AND CORRECTIONS PAGES.
Saskatoon, Sask. Sister of Rev. Philip, below.
FILLEUL, Rev. Philip James, b 1817 St. Heliers, J, son of Philip and
  Marie Arrive GUILLAUME, orphaned young, raised by Du Parcqs. Deacon
  1861, priest 1862, (Bishop of Worcester) Curate at Rugby and Lunen-
  burg, N.S. Missionary at Sackville, NS, Rector at St. Peter's, Hali-
  fax 1852-1892., d 1900. Mar 1. Mary Elizabeth Maxwell, and 2. Eliz-
  abeth Scott Bartlett of Round Hill, NS (M.F. Filleul, Weymouth, NS;
  D.F. Filleul, Halifax; Ethel Gilbert, Drexel Hill, Pa.)
  A1. Charles   A2. George   A3., 4., 5., ???
  A6. Gertrude, by second wife, mar Walter McCormick
    B1. Ethel, mar Richard Gilbert, res Drexel Hill, Pa.
      C1. Richard   C2. Patricia   C3. Margaret   C4. Anne
  A7. James
    B1. George   B2. Douglas   B3., 4., 5., daus   MORE FILLEUL
  A8. Henry Philip, mar Mary Jones   DATA IN CHAN.Is.
    B1. Kathleen   B2. Norman   B3. Donald   COLLECTION
    B4. Philip, mar Blanche Gibson
      C1. Blanche, mar Richard Journeay, 2 daus
        D1. Sharon Journeay   D2. Dawn Journeay
      C2. Ethel, mar Stanley Hatt
        D1. Sandra Hatt   D2. Arthur Hatt   D3. William Hatt
      C3. Philip, mar Lilian Allen
        D1. Philip   D2. Lynn
      C4. Kenneth   C5. Margaret
  A9. Richard John, b 1848, d 1951
FILLEUL, Philip Thomas, b 1887 J, d 1965. Mar 1912 Myrtle Myles, set-
  tled ca 1910 Indian Head, Sask, then to Regina Sask till ca 1964, when
  rem to Victoria, BC (H.E. Filleul, Winnipeg, Manitoba)
  A1. Edna, b 1914, mar A.L. Irwin, 4 chn, 9 grchn
    B1. Shirley Irwin, b 1931, mar Hazen Stamford, res Clearbrook, BC
    B2. Darlene, mar Brian Burbridge, 1 ch, res Courtney, BC
    B3. Barrie Irwin, mar, res Victoria, BC, 3 chn
    B4. Sandra Irwin, b 1950, mar John Windish, 2 chn, res Victoria, BC
  A2. Philip Thomas, b 1916, mar Eleanor Baldwin, 2 chn
    B1. Philip Thomas, b 1950, mar, 2 chn, res Victoria, BC   4 CHN
    B2. Joanne, b 1952, mar Joseph Williams, res Nelson, BC   1 CH
  A3. Alfred, b 1920, mar Eunice Fraser, 3 chn, 2 grchn
    B1. Richard, b 1947, mar, 3 chn, res Regina, Sask.
    B2. Randolph, b 1952, res Regina, Sask.   B3. Karen mar David
  A4. Walter, b 1922, mar Eileen Courtney   Parker
    B1. Rhonda, res Regina, Sask.
  A5. Harold, b 1924, mar Alice Huot, 3 chn, res Winnipeg, Manitoba
    B1. Linda, b 1950, mar Stephen Archer, res Regina, Sask.
    B2. Ronald, b 1952   B3. Alan, b 1954
  A6. Edward, b 1926, mar Ruth Kelly, 2 chn
    B1. Deborah, b 1952, res Regina, Sask.
    B2. Sharon, b 1954, mar Richard Hanson, 3 ch, res Mossbank, Sask.
  A7. William, b 1930, unmar
  A8. Yvonne, b 1931, mar Ralph Kleisinger, 5 chn, 3 grchn
    B1. Donald Kleisinger, b 1953, mar, 2 chn
    B2. Denise Kleisinger, b 1954, mar Harold Chupik, 1 ch, res Calgary,
      Alta.
    B3. Angela Kleisinger, mar ---Chupik, bro of above, res Calgary, Alta.
    B4. Martin Kleisinger   B5. Leonard Kleisinger
FILLIATRE, FILLATRE, etc. in Nfld. See QAAM. John JOSSLYN, in his notes
  on early voyages, mentions meeting a ship of a Jerseyman, Abraham
  Phalater, written variously FILIATRE, LE FILLIATRE, LE FILLIASTRE, etc.

FILIATRE, SEE EXTRA PAGES.
This meeting took place off Maine in 1660. Le FILIATRE in St. Lawrence, J 1607, 1669 (Noyes)
FILLIATRE, Francis of Georges Harbor, Nfld. in 1830 (Seary)
FILLATRE, Samuel, mar in Nfld., Sarah Ann MESSERVY, qv., in 1855, dau of John M. of St. George's Bay, Nfld.
FINDLEY, Mrs. N. from G to London, Ont. 1900s (K. de la Mare)
FIOTT. "Capt. John Fiott was lost in 1782. Another John Fiott was in the Navy with Admiral DE CARTERET. Nicholas, a brother, was lost in one of the DE GRUCHY ships...Capt. John Fiott traded to Nfld., on a merchantman belonging to Nicholas Fiott, had a large family. De Gruchy and Fiott had a business at College Hill, Ondon. Nicholas d 1785, a bachelor. De Gruchy bur 1784 in the same vault, St. Stephen's Church, London." (Lady McKie, Ottawa, Ont.) Capt. Nicholas had 9 vessels in the Nfld. trade. (G.R. Balleine)
FIOTT, Bay Chaleur Mystery, a fire ship. "The ship's favorite haunt was Caraquet, Gasport and Sea Gull...In a wooden mansion run by two female descendants...Peter Fiott is now in middle age and is a much respected citizen...gentleman of the old school, born in Jersey. Lived fifty years in Caraquet, manager of Robin, Jones and Whitman, founded by Jerseymen 1766." (Willie Chiasson, Shippegan, NB) Thought to be from a magazine article in June 1951, poss McLean's Magazine.
FIOTT, Peter James of J, d Montreal in the 1860s at 96 yrs. (GLF)
FIOTT, Nicholas, a company from J to Perce, Quebec, under the agency of George LE GEYT, qv., late 1700s.
FIOTT, listed by Betty Tardif and J.H. Le Breton as Jerseymen
FIOTT, from J to Caraquet, N.B., early 1800s (Hist. of Caraquet, Ganong)
FIOTT, John, of London, petitioned for land at Paspebiac, Gaspe in 1787 (Dom. Arch.)
FIOTT, Peter James, b St. Brelade, J, to Canada, son of John Fiott, mar Lillian Blackhall. (Maude Le Selleur, Montreal; James Fiott, Toronto)
A1. James, b 1891, res Toronto 1976, no issue
A2. Sydney, b 1894, res Joliet, Ill., no issue
A3. Maude, b 1893, mar ---LE SEELEUR
   B1. Marjorie Le Seeleur, mar Reginald BLUNDELL, qv.
      C1. Peter Blundell   C2. Rose Blundell
FISHER, C.I. in Gaspe (K.H. Annett)
FISHER, Owen Charles, b C.I., a private enlisted 1915 Universities Co. 4th reinforced draft in Ottawa, Ont. Related to Mrs. Fisher of Clifton, Bristol, England. (OUR HEROES IN THE GREAT WORLD WAR, by J.H. De Wolfe, Canada, 1919)
FISHER in Nfld. (Seary) Cf FISHER of J (Stevens)
I. FIXOTT, Charles, M.D., b ca 1804 J, d 1854 Arichat, C.B., mar Triphosa ---, b ca 1811 England. Charles was the son of Charles F., M.D. and Mary HUBERT, qv., who both d J. (Lois Coates, Sydney River, NS; GLF; Mrs. Walter Grant, Halifax, NS; Stephen White, Moncton, NB)
A1. Laura Harrington, mar 1862 John Marshall BOURINOT, qv., son of the Hon. J. Bourinot, of the Canadian Senate, and Margaret Jane Marshall of Port Morien, C.B., 4 chn, See BOURINOT
A2. Ada, b ca 1836 in N.S., converted to Catholicism, a nun, later a superioress of convent in Montreal
A3. Mary Ann De Carteret, b ca 1836 N.S., d 1907, age 70. Bur St. John's, Arichat, C.B. Mar 1856 Peter BOSDET, qv., b ca 1817 J, merchant at W. Arichat, sold dry goods and groceries, Postmaster, also ran Sea View Hotel. At least 6 chn.
A4. Victoria, b ca 1839 N.S., mar 1874 St. John's, Arichat, John George CLOUGH, qv., b 1838 N.S., merchant at Arichat 1864, 1866, farmer at

FIXOTT

Grandique Ferry, NS 1871, 1890.
- A5. Sophia H.C., b ca 1840 N.S., mar 1876 St. John's, Arichat, Edward Frederick Howell of Carbonear, Nfld., at least one son.
- A6. Triphose, b 1841, d.y.
- A7. Henry James, M.D., b 1843 Arichat, d 1917, bur St. John's, Arichat, mar 1868 Henrietta Maria GRUCHY, dau of David G. and Jane Catherine Robertson JEAN, qv., of Descousse, 1847-1914. Chn below uncertain and unverified, except Harry.
  - B1. ---, mar Brown
  - B2. Sophia, mar Alfred E. BRIARD, qv., d 1934 N.B.
  - B3. Harry, Henry, b ca 1869, mar Marie Annette V. Le Noir, dau of Capt. Daniel H. Le Noir and Sara A. Madden of Arichat, 1876-1969, bur Our Lady of Assumption. Harry was Supt. of the bar mill at Sydney Steel Works.
    - C1. Lois, mar ---Coastes, res Sydney, C.B. 1969
    - C2. Gerald, res Ontario 1969
  - B4. Melville
- A8. Maud E., mar 1886 Arichat, Nicholas WHITE of Charlottetown, PEI. Witnesses: J. George CLOUGH, qv., and Peter BOSDET, qv.
II. FIXOTT, Ann, b ca 1809 J, sister of Charles, above, d 1892 Arichat, age 83. Mar John HUBERT, qv., son of Clement H. John was merchant at Arichat until 1837, when he d. 2 chn, see HUBERT.
III. FIXOTT, Astley Cooper, d.y. in J
IV. FIXOTT, Henry Cline, b ca 1821 J, d 1884 Arichat, M.D., M.R.C.S., London, was Coroner, health officer, J.P. for Richmond Co., unmar. In 1871 his brother Charles' widow and her daus, Ada, Victoria, and Sophia res with him at Arichat. (census)
V. FIXOTT, James, M.D. b ca 1823 J, d 1859 J, physician to the Exeter Disp., Devon, Eng.
VI. FIXOTT, Richard, b ca 1824 J, d 1832 age 7

FIXOTT, Peter, d ca age 96 in Gaspe? Cf Peter FIOTT
FIXOTT, G.L., res Toronto
FLETCHER in Nfld. (Seary) Cf FLETCHER in J (Stevens)
FLEURY, Fred, a carpenter from J to BC 1891 (Luce)
FLEURY, surname in Cartier's crew in 1541, poss from J
FLEURY, listed as Channel Islanders in the Maritimes, by J.H. Le Breton and Syvret
FLEURY, Joseph and Henry, prob from C.I., resided Ottawa, Ont. early 1900s, next door to the BOURINOT fam, qv.
FLEURY, James, res Whitehorse, Yukon
FLEURY, John and D.W., from J? to Manitoba 1800s
FLEURY, ---from J to Cumberland, Vancouver, BC ca 1884, mar. Two chn res Vancouver, one, a Mrs. Thomas
FLEURY, F.J., to BC from J
FLEURY, Francois David, b St. Lawrence?, J, res Mont Louis, Gaspe, farmer, son of Francois F. and Ann DUTOT of J, mar 1879? Anna Marie Isabelle, dau of Dominique I. of Cap Chap and Adeline Dugas (Remiggi)
FLOOD, from C.I. to Nfld. See QAAM and Seary. Cf FLOOD in J (Stevens)
FLOUD, J., from J? to Victoria, BC, there in 1940s (Luce)
FLOUD, Bernard, son of Sir Francis FLOUD, of the Rev. Thomas Brock fam of G. Attended Univ. of Toronto (Brock-DeLisle Chart, by H.G. Schreiber, Ottawa)
FLOWERS, John and Henry, in Gaspe Militia 1850s (MacWhirter) Poss same as Fleury?
FLOWERS, associated with Robin firm in Paspebiac, and New Carlisle, Que. (Que. Prov. Arch. and K.H. Annett)
FOARD, Bert, of J, tobacco merchant, drowned on TITANIC on his way to Canada (F. Le Seeleur, No. Vanc., BC)

FOLEY, see L'AFFOLEY, FOLLEY, FOLLETT, etc. FOLLETT in Nfld. (Seary)
FOLEY in Nfld. (Seary) Cf LAFFOLEY, LA FOLIE of J (Stevens)
FONTAINE in Nfld. (Seary) Cf FONTAIN of J 1668 (Stevens) Thomas in Western Bay, Nfld. 1777
FOOTE, Thomas, fisherman at Sandy Harbor, Nfld. 1871, many in Stephenville, Nfld. Some of this surname said to have come from C.I. (Rev. Hammond, Hug. Soc.)
FORGETT, John, in Bonavista Bay, Nfld. 1860s, poss from C.I. Cf TOURGET, FOURNET of C.I.
FOREMAN, James from C.I. in Nfld. early 1800s (Hammond)
FORSEY, poss FOSSE, in Nfld. (Seary) Cf FOSSE in J (Stevens)
FORSEY, George, from C.I.? at Grand Bank, Nfld. ca 1763. His son, Samuel, at Fortune, Nfld.
FORTIER, C.I. surname in Ont. and New Eng. (Gingras), also Gaspe (K.H. Annett)
FORTIN, Pierre, magistrate, report published 1858 St. Peter Port, Perce, Gaspe, Quebec, origin unknown.
FORTUNE in Nfld. (Seary) Cf FORTUNE in J (Stevens)
FOSSEY in Canada, poss from FOSSE in J?
FOWLOW in Cupids, Nfld. 1799. This surname poss from FOULEAU, or FALLON of C.I./FOZARD, one from G. to Canada.
FOULEAU, John, was in St. John's, Nfld. ca 1754, origin uncer (Seary)
FOURNIER, from C.I.? to Alpena, Mich., via Gaspe?
FRAIZE, FRAISES?, in Nfld. early (Seary) origin uncertain. John, Joseph and Moses at Carbonear 1860s, from C.I. (Rev. Hammond) Cf also FRESNE, DU FRESNE of C.I.
FRANCIS in Nfld. (Seary) Cf FRANCIS of C.I. John in Nfld. 1730 See QAAM
FRANCAIS, LE FRANCAIS, in J 1607 (Stevens) Francis also in G, see QAAM by Turk.
FRANCIS, Elias, at Barachois, Gaspe, from C.I.?
FRANCIS, from G to Gaspe, then to Alpena, Mich.?
FRANCIS, Richard, age 63, b England, at Malbaie 1871
FRECK, FRECKER, from C.I.? to Nfld. (Saunders) L. Frecker was in St. Peter, NB 1851 (Donal Robichaud)
FRECKER, ---, b ca 1868 Brooklyn, dau of George Frecker, b ca 1845 J, and Harriet NORMAN, b G (Robert Scheuermann, Sarnia, Ont.)
FRECKER, John Peter, b G, master mariner, retired to Quebec City. His son of the same name rem to Harbour Breton, Fortune Bay, Nfld., clerk apprentice to Newman & Co., then rem to St. Pierre & Miquelon, to work from the St. Pierre branch of the Boston firm of Atherton, Hughes & Co. He was later a partner in that firm, and owner of the St. Pierre branch. The Frecker business was known as THE AMERICAN HOUSE. Upon his death in 1892, the business was taken over by his son, George Henry Frecker and his son-in-law, George Steer. It remained in the family until 1918, when George Henry died. It was then sold as the eldest son, John Peter, was at that time serving in the French Army in WWI, and the two other boys were still young chn. The fam rem to Halifax, and to Montreal.
In 1934 the second son, George Alain moved to Nfld. to head-up the engineering dept. in the Memorial Univ. He is at present Chancellor of NUN. We have a family of 8, four boys and four girls. All but the youngest boy are married and have families of their own. Grandchildren total 20, scattered throughout Canada, Nfld., Ontario, and Alberta. There are still Freckers in G and many in the churchyard. (Helena M. Frecker, St. John's, Nfld.)
FRENCH, LE FRANCOIS?, William Edward in Bay Roberts, Nfld. 1790 (Seary) Others were in Nfld. earlier.

FREWINS, Channel Islanders to Nfld., early (Lady McKie, Ottawa, Ont.)
  Cf FROUING (Stevens)
FRITOT, see LE QUELENEC
FRIZZELL in Nfld. (Seary) Cf FRIZELL of J (Stevens)
FROOD, Mrs., G., from C.I. in Vancouver, BC, in 1910 (Luce)
FROOME, Nigel, b G, in charge 1970s of Grand Bahama Hotel, Bahama Island (Edw. Le Page, Grimsby, Ont.)
FROUDE, in Nfld., settled early in Trinity Bay, Old Perlican, from C.I. (Rev. Hammond)
FROST, John Dove, b ca 1790 Devonshire, Eng., rem to G where at least 3 of his chn were born, then rem to J, where another son was born. Between 1838 and 1850, his wife Anne died. He and most of his chn and maybe his wife or second wife, rem to Saint John, NB. He d in Westport, NS while visiting or living with his son, William Thomas. Bur Saint John, NB. (May Stevenson, New Brighton, Minn. who has more on this fam)
A1. Henry Dove, b 1823 G, bp 1823 St. Peter Port, res at one time in Gagetown, NB, ca 1849, descendants. Julia A. Frost, his executrix in 1881.
A2. Capt. William Thomas Frost, b 1825 St. Peter Port, G, d 1889 Westport, NS, mar Eunice Evans, dau of Evan Evans, 1823-1916. Capt. Frost brought settlers to PEI, poss from C.I. on his ship, HMS NEW EDINBOROUGH, was a merchant and mariner, and a schoolteacher.
  B1. William Henry Evan Frost, b 1853 Yarmouth, NS, d 1930 Calif. Mar Mary Delilah Stanton.
  B2. Eunice Mary Annie, b 1855 Yarmouth, NS, d 1882, bur Westport, NS, poss unmar
  B3. Emily Laura Julia, b 1859 Gagetown, NB, d 1945 Lakewood, Oh., bur Rocky River, mar 1. Charles Whitfield Denton, and 2. Alvin Codding, farmer of Haydenville, Mass.
  B4. Gohegan Wilmot Henderson, b 1861 Gagetown, NB, d 1903 North Brookfield, Queens Co., NS, mar 1892 Mary Mae Gates, dau Enid and son, Lawrence.
  B5. Richard Albert Edward, b 1864 Westport, NS, d 1878, unmar.
  B6. Annie Edith Victoria, b 1867 Westport, d 1955, mar James William Lock Strickland, Saint John, NB 1891.
A3. Eunice, b 1826 G
A4. Edwin, b ca 1828 or 1838 Jersey, res Saint John, NB, d 1893 Atlantic City, NJ, mar twice, no issue
A5. poss other chn? Anne, Edward, Thomas???
FRUING, William, poss adopted by Charles ROBIN, qv., of Jersey and Gaspe. He signed the Gaspe Petition of 1830. Was b England, but may have had some J connections. To Gaspe with Robin Collas firm 1820, later took over Janvrin Co. in 1852 at Grand Greve. He mar Jane Elizabeth ALEXANDRE of Pt. Alexandre, Miscou, N.B. (Donat Robichaud)
A1. Louisa Jane, mar Frederick WARNE   A3. Jane
A2. Amelia Elizabeth   A4. Mary Ann, mar Philip LE QUESNE
A5. Mary or Margaret, who mar in Caraquet, NB 1840 John McIntosh, local merchant.
FRUING. Cf PROUING of C.I.
FRUING, Philip, poss bro of William?
FRY, Mary Elizabeth, mar ---MAINGUY, qv., in B.C.
FULLER. Origin of these Fullers is not known. John F. and his fam are included because his wife was b in G. The others have some connection or possible connection with the Islands and are therefore included. Much research was done by Arthur Fuller, and by Rev. Kenneth McDonald of Deep River, Conn. on the Fuller line, but only an oral tradition of

origin in J or G was known. However, cf FULLER with common names of
the Islands, FALLE, FALLA, FALLU.
FULLER, Joseph, b 1815 England, rem to J ca 1853. Had 4 daus and son,
Frederick. The girls remained in J, some marrying there, and the son
emigrated to Fullerton, Nebraska where a dau of his eldest son still
lives (1970s) (Arthur Fuller, deceased, resided Los Osos, Calif.)
FULLER, Horace, mar Anne Whelan of Placentia, Nfld. Ten chn b Arichat.
Record below was worked by Arthur Fuller, but some material incomplete and unverified. Horace may have mar 2. in 1810 Margaret Stanley of Catalina, Nfld. Chn below not verified.
  A1. John Edmund, b 1811 Halifax, High Sheriff of Richmond Co. 25 yrs.,
    res Arichat, mar Mary D. Oakley, dau of Thomas and Mary Boyd Oakley
    of Halifax. She d 1878 in Arichat, CB, and may have been b in PEI.
    B1. James, b 1841 Arichat, NS   B4. Mary Ann, b 1851
    B2. Eliza, b 1849   B5. Margaret, b 1854 Arichat
    B4. Louisa, b 1853
  A2. John F., b 1814, d 1886, mar Elizabeth ---, b 1819 G. Chn b Arichat, NS
    B1. Charles, b 1841   B3. Charlotte, b 1853
    B2. Albert G., b 1851, later Sheriff   B4. Eliza E., b 1855
    of Richmond Co.   B5. Catherine, b 1859
  A3. Thomas Horace, b 1817   A4. Mary Ann, b 1818, unmar
  A5. Charles James, b 1822, d 1894, unmar
  A6. Edmund Bennett, b 1823, d 1893, mar ca 1850 Lucy Butler Burnham
  A7. Charlotte, b 1824, d 1894, mar 1848 James McDonnell
  A8. Andrew
  A9. Hyacinth Hudson, b 1828, d 1900
  A10. Martha, mar Sir Richard Hare?
  A11. Eliza Ann, d 1918, unmar   A12. Louisa Ellen, d 1910, unmar
FULLER, Jacob, was in Sackville, NS 1770 (census, PANS)
FULLER, Thomas Brock, Bishop of Niagara. Was the son of Major Fuller,
  Aide de Camp to General BROCK, qv., poss of G fam, like Gen. Brock.
FUREY in Nfld. (Seary) Said to be var of LE HURAY of J. Name in Conc.
  Bay 1750. (G.W. Le Messurier, Lady McKie)
FURNEAUX, John, b J, mar Mary Ann WINTER, qv., of J middle 1800s?
  (Marion W. Stone, Mount Pearl, Nfld.)
  A1. Emily, mar ---Rolls, rem to Calif.
  A2. Richard, mar ---, 3 sons, 2 daus, mar Annie LE SEELEUR, qv., rem to
    North Sydney, NS, where he died
  A3. George, had 3 sons and 2 daus
  A4. Annie, mar Dr. Thomas Malcolm, a Scot, and rem to Denver, Colo.
  A5. Jessie, mar Dr. C.J. Weeks, a Canadian who rem to Boston, d there
  A6. Elizabeth Mary, mar Aaron Stone, had 3 sons and 1 dau, Marion, b
    1901
FURNEAUX, Joseph, from the C.I. in Buck Cove, Conc. Bay, Nfld. 1763.
  Also a John F. to Lamaline, Nfld., mar 1851 (Rev. Hammond, M. Stone)
FURSE, FURZE, ship owner from J in Nfld. (K. Mathews)
FURZER, C. Islander in Maritimes Fisheries (J.H. Le Breton list)
GABOUREL, Capt. from J in Nfld. (K. Mathews)
GABRIEL, Capt. and boatkeeper from J in Nfld. (K. Mathews)
GABRIEL, Thomas in Trinity Harbor, Nfld. 1675 (Seary)
GABRIEL, cf GABOUREL of J in 1528
GAILLE from C.I. in Gaspe (Francis Gibaut list, Rev. d'Hist)
GALE, Annie, b ca 1850 Ald., 3 sisters. One mar a LA VALLEE, qv., and
  had 2 sons, Thomas and Henry LA VALLEE, who lived in London, Eng. then
  rem to Chatham, Ont. Desc in Chatham. Annie mar Thomas PALMER, qv.,
  5 chn. She d in Detroit 1935. (Mildred Chase, Montague, Mass.)

GALE, Thomas, b Que. of G fam?, age 55 in Cape Cove, Gaspe with James, age 37, census 1871

GALE, Rose, mar Peter VIBERT, qv., of the Philippe James VIBERT fam of Gaspe
GALE, Roseanne or Roxanne, said to have mar Philip or Peter VIBERT, see above
GALE, James Francois, bur Cape Cove, Ang. Ch., Gaspe
GALE in Nfld. 1700s, from C.I.? (Seary)
GALE cf LE GALL, LE GALLE of C.I. (Stevens) GALLEY, SEE ADDITIONS
GALLAIS, see LE GALLAIS   AND CORRECTIONS PAGES.
GALLANT in Nfld. (Seary) Cf GALEN of J (Stevens)
GALLIARD, from G, bur at Rosebridge, Gaspe (GLF)
GALLIARD, from C.I. to Gaspe (Bourgaize)
GALLIARD, John, b J, age 40 in 1871, at Gaspe Bay (Brochet, Census) A dau, Eliza, b 1853 was said to be dau of John G. and Euphemia WEST
GALLIARD, John, b G, in Gaspe 1861 (census)
GALLIARD, see GILLIARD of Nfld.
GALLICHAN, current at Sept Isles, and Mutton Bay, Que., also at Gaspe, there in 1781 (Syvret)
GALLICHAN, John, of C.I. fam, res Sandy Beach, Gaspe, mar Mary Janet ---, 1886-1942, bur St. John's Anglican Ch, Sandy Beach, Gaspe (GLF) A1. James Lance, 1917-1938   A2. Mary Ellen, mar Hugh Thompson, d at 33
GALLICHAN, Alice Jane, b ca 1859, d 1941, bur Sandy Beach, Gaspe
GALLICHAN, Mathew William, 1861-1943, bur Sandy Beach, Gaspe
GALLICHAN, Mathew, of Gaspe area, b C.I.?, had son, George, plus Ann, Mary Ann, b ca 1810, Mathew and Amelia (census)
GALLICHAN, Mary Ann of J, mar Philip LE HUQUET, qv., 1836, Gaspe
GALLICHAN, George, b J, in Gaspe 1861, mar Jane ALEXANDRE: Adolphus, John Abraham, all b Gaspe and Alice Jane and James Edward. 1871 census gives George age 47, wife, Jane, 45.
GALLICHAN, Abraham, b J, in Perce, Gaspe 1861 (census), also wife, Elizabeth, b Ireland, plus Elizabeth, Harriet, Emily, Elizabeth, Susannah, Abraham, John, Elias, Edward, Philip and Jane, all b Canada (Census, Aldo Brochet)
GALLICHAN, Francois, b J, in Perce 1861 (census)
GALLICHAN, a young man of this surname whose grandmother was Marguerite DE LA LANDE, visited in Grand Valle, Gaspe, some years ago. (Annette Fournier, Grand Valle, Gaspe)
GALLICHAN, Stephen, from G?, in Yarmouth, NS 1773 (Census, LOST IN CANADA)
GALLICHAN, Capt. from G in Nfld. (K. Mathews)
GALLICHAN, Ann, mar in Quebec? ---DE GRUCHY, qv.
GALLICHAN, GALLUCCI, GALLISON, Daniel, b J, captured by Indians in New England 1706, died later that year in Montreal or Que. (Tanguay, Coleman)
GALLICHAN, Philip, from J, res London, Ont. ca 1874, boarded with a LE SUEUR fam from J. Related to the George LE SEELLEUR fam, qv.
GALLICHAN, Jane, mar Thomas John LE SEELLEUR, b 1852
GALLICHAN, John and Charles, b J, brought by parents to Ontario early 1900s. John, res Weston, Ont.
GALLICHAUD, Francois of J, was mar in L'Islet, Quebec 1839 (Biography and desc in RECUIL DE GENEALOGIE BELLECHASSE-MONTMAGNY, L'ISLET, by Eloi-Gerard Talbot)
GALLIE, John, unver, b 1789, d 1874, mar Ann Maria Scott, 1805-1868, U.E.L. She was dau of James Scott Sr. and Joanna Brotherstone, 7 chn.

(Raymond Garrett, Aldo Brochet)
A1. Joanna, mar Thomas Brock Munro, issue
A2. Margaret, mar Wm. Munro, issue
A3. Mary, b 1819 or 1822, mar 1841 John HOCQUARD, qv., issue, bur St. Peters, Paspebiac
A4. John Francis, mar 1846 Eliz. Whittom, 1825-1908. He was b 1814, d 1889, issue
A5. Jane Elizabeth, b 1822, mar 1855 John LE MASURIER, qv.
A6. Ann Maria   A7. Philip James, mar 1860 Sarah Ann DU VAL, issue
GALLIE, Wm., at Gr. Greve 1806 (Perce Court records)
GALLIE, Susan Isabel, 1872-1894, wife of Adolphus GRANDIN, qv., dau Alice d 1891, age 6 mos. (GLF)
GALLIE in B.C.
GALLIOT in Nfld. (Seary) Cf GALIOT of J (Stevens)
GALLIENNE, Eva LE GALLIENNE, famous actress of Eng., Canada and U.S., descended from "a long line of Guernsey sailors."
GALLIENNE, Rachel, b G, in Perce, Gaspe, 1861. See also LE GALLIENNE
GALLIENNE, Frank, b Torteval?, G, 1848, son of Mathew G. and Marie BREHAUT, to Canada 1861 with father Mathew, mar Bibiane Cummings 1870. Mathew had mar 2? Fanny GODION, GAUDION? 1844 at St. Heliers, J, dau of Nicholas GODION, qv.
GALLIENNE, Frank, b 1873 J? or Canada, mar Elise VIGNEAU, Acadian, writer of the HISTORY OF LABRADOR and the North shore, and Magdalen Islands. "Capt. John Gallienne was the brother of my grandfather Frank. The Capt. died in a wreck in the open sea near New Zealand." (Gerard Gallienne, Sillery, Que.)
GALLIENNE, Clayton, son of Mrs. N.M. Gallienne of G, b in G, recently an instructor in the Grand Bend Yacht Club's Junior Group, sails on Lake Huron. A member of the Canadian Power Squadron. (Ed. Le Page, Grimsby, Ont.)
GALLIENNE, Thomas, b 1859 G, mar Mary Ann BOURGAIZE, qv., b 1860 G, rem to Canada 1910. (Elsie Coniam, Burlington, Ont.)   SEE ALICE'S
A1. Alice Mary, b 1886 G, mar Albert James MAINDONALD, qv.,(chn in
A2. Walter Henry, b 1890, mar Annie Hamilton Dodd, b 1895   added
   B1. Albert Ernest, b 1922   pages)
      C1. William Albert, b 1948   C5. Patricia Ellen, b 1955
      C2. Thomas Paul, b 1949   C6. Laura, b 1958
      C3. Anne Elizabeth, b 1951   C7. Stephen, b 1959
      C4. Catherine, b 1954
   B2. Marjorie, b 1924, mar Peter Reed
      C1. Lynda Marjorie Reed, b 1953   C3. Janice Carol Reed, b 1960
      C2. Donna Mary Reed, b 1957
   B3. Thomas, b 1926, mar, 2 daus:Laurie J. & Jeanne Raye
   B4. Barbara Mary, b 1930, mar Gordon Bennett
      C1. Lori Jayne Bennett, b 1954   C3. Susan Jo Ann Bennett, b 1959
      C2. Jeanne Ray Bennett, b 1958   C4. Terry Richard Bennett, b 1961
A3. Elsie, b 1892 St. Martin, G, mar Alfred Coniam, b 1895
   B1. Albert Robert, b 1933, adopted
      C1. Karen Lynn Coniam, b 1955   C3. Kevin Robert Coniam, b 1958
      C2. Kimberly Hope Coniam, b 1956 C4. Karla Faith Coniam, b 1969
GALLIENNE, fam from J with descendants on the North Shore, Que.
GALLIENNE, Alice Maud, dau of Matt. G. and Fanny GAUDIENNE, mar Patrick Reddy, son of John Reddy, at St. Patricks, Que., P.Q., 1882 (RECUEIL DE GENEALOGIE DE CHARLEVOIX-SAGUENAY, Vol. 1, 1856-1973)
GALLIENNE, Cyra A., b 1925 St. Peter Port, G, son of Cyril A. and Nelly M. LE PREVOST, rem to Canada during 1925-1937. Served WWII, returned to Canada 1950, mar Ivy ---, b 1920.

A1. Susanne, b 1948   A2. Carol, b 1950   A3. Janette, b 1956
GALLON, C.I. name assoc with the Robin firm in Paspebiac and with the town of New Carlisle, Que. (Que. Prov. Archives) Poss Irish name. (Brochet)
GALLON, Elizabeth, 1857-1930, res New Carlisle, Que. Mar Daniel ASSELS, a dau mar John WEARY, qv.
GALLON, appears 1905 in Alpena, Mich., where Gaspesians removed in middle 1800s
GALLON, current at New Carlisle, Que.
GALPIN in Nfld. (Seary) Cf GALOPIN of J (Stevens)
GARDE in Nfld. (Seary) Cf DE LA GARDE of J (Stevens)
GARDEN, GARNIER, GARDNER, Capts from J in Nfld. (K. Mathews)
GARDENER in Nfld. (Seary) Cf GARDNER in J (Stevens)
GARDNER, GARNIER, current in Gaspe
GARIS, Cf DE GARIS, qv. A Capt. GARIS from Alderney was in Nfld. (K. Mathews)
GARNER, Luke, in St. John's, Nfld. 1804 (Seary)
GARNIER, Constant, from C.I. fam?, planter in Sandy Pt., Nfld. 1871 (Lovell, Seary)
GARNIER, Jose, from J, res London, Ont., worked at Cowan's Hardware there, mar, retired in or ca 1935. Dau Mary lived in Detroit, married.
GARRETT, current in Gaspe
GARRETT, Mary Ann, of C.I. fam?, d Little Pabos 1892, mar Philip HUELIN, qv. (Aldo Brochet, Perce, Que.)
GARRETT, from C.I. to Nfld.? (Seary) Cf also JERRETT
GARSIN, to Nfld. (Rev. Hammond) Poss from DE GARIS or GARCELON, Hug fam in J (QAAM)
GASNIER, Thomas, from G to Gaspe. Woodcarver, cabinet maker, inventor of a photo-taking apparatus. Mar Ada HOTTON, qv., a son, F.H.? (Cyril Hotton, Toronto, Ont.)
GAUDIER, poss GAUTIER, qv., listed by Betty Tardif as from C.I. in Que.
GAUDIN. This material taken from an excellent but greatly reduced chart which in a number of places is somewhat hard to interpret. Chart researched by Helena Gaudin Cameron, White Rock, BC, and produced by W. Allen Briggs, of Calgary, Alta. ca 1969. Some data uncertain.
GAUDIN, Capt. David, b late 1700s?, d 1860, mar 1. Elizabeth DE GRUCHY, qv., 1803? and 2. Elizabeth DE QUETTEVILLE, b 1794?, mar 1812. Capt. David rem ca 1830 in his own schooner to Canada with some of his chn. Settled in Port Dalhousie, NB, then in Ontario. 4 chn by first wife.
A1. David, b 1805, supt. of sailors home in Liverpool, England?
A2. George, b 1807, to Australia
A3. Thomas, b 1810, res Manchester, England, sev chn including a dau Christine?
A4. Capt. Philip, b 1808, mar 1. Jane PHILLIPS, dau of Capt. P. and 2. a widow ---Watts. Settled in Rustico, PEI as a young man.
  B1. Elizabeth
  B2. Philip, mar Mary Lowe
    C1. George, d 1916, ship carpenter, PEI, mar Matilda Yonkers, a dau Marion
    C2. Annie, b 1863, mar Jack Elliott
      D1. Bert Elliott, b 1882, mar Henrietta GAUDIN, b 1893
        E1. George Elliott, b 1925, mar Patsy Barnes
          F1. Gerry, b 1950
      D2. Rev. George Elliott, b 1893, mar Pearl Saunders
        E1. Rev. Waldo Elliott, b 1932, mar Mildred GARDNER

                F1. Ron Elliott, b 1958   F3. Timothy Elliott, b 1963
                F2. Jocelyn Elliott, b 1961 F4. Andrew, b 1963, twin
      B3. David   B4. Frederick, mar Emma Smith
      B5. George, ship carpenter, res Georgetown, PEI, town named for him
      B6. Benjamin
      B7. John, mar Jane Pratt
          C1. Alfred   C4. Robert
          C2. Frederick, mar Emma Smith C5. Jane
          C3. Henry, mar Margaret Smith
          C6. William, mar Elmira Smith
              D1. Elizabeth, b 1889, mar Alex McDavid
                  E1. Muriatta McDavid, mar H. Kentnor
                      F1. Pat Kentnor, b 1930   F2. David Kentnor, b 1932
                  E2. William, b 1910, unmar
              D2. Mamie, b 1891, mar George Young, b 1872
                  E1. Weston Young, b 1912, mar Lily Pegg, d 1969
                  E2. Elva Young, b 1915, mar Bert Barnson
                      F1. Brian Barnson, b 1947
              D3. Henrietta, b 1893, mar Bert GAUDIN, grandson of Capt. Philip
              D4. William, b 1895, mar Minnie Coles, b 1893
              D5. Percy, b 1906, mar Mary Belliveau
                  E1. Selina, b 1937, mar Coleman Levin
                      F1. Margaret Levin, b 1964   F3. David Levin, b 1967
                      F2. Sarah Levin, b 1965
      B8. Frank, mar Katherine Dunville
          C1. Henry
              D1. Elmer, res Maple Green, NB
          C2. Jane, mar George Court
              D1. Cyrus Court, mar Melissa Hunter
A6. Elizabeth, b 1815, d Liverpool, England, mar William Thompson
A7. William, b 1816, rem to Canada. Mar 1847 Jane Finnis, 12 chn. Res
    Dalhousie, NB, then Heathcote, Ont. 1873
    B1. Mary, mar Duncan Bole, related to Quinns of the Soo, Ontario?
        C1. Sandy Bole, mar John McPhail, lawyer   C4. Allie, a nurse
        C2. Jeanne, mar W.G. Bowen, res Los Angles C5. Athelyn Austin Bole
        C3. Amy, mar Clarence Adams
    B2. David, mar Mary Foster, no issue
    B3. Elizabeth, b 1852, mar Dick Hewgill
        C1. Norman Hewgill, b 1874, mar Bertha Goodfellow
            D1. Ken Hewgill   D2. Jean Hewgill
        C2. Frederick Hewgill, b 1880, mar Eda Hind
            D1. Stanley Hewgill D2. Frances Hewgill D3. Gordon Hewgill
        C3. Ada Hewgill, b 1884, mar William PERRY, d 1969
            D1. Helen Perry, b 1910, mar Clare Needham
                E1. Karen Needham
                E2. Myra Needham, mar Lorne Leverson
                    F1. Mark Leverson F2. Gregory Leverson F3. Dorothy Leverson
            D2. Doris Perry, b 1914, mar M. Baron Scheurman
                E1. Lynn Schuerman, b 1939, mar Ted Rapley
                    F1. Leanne Rapley   F2. Susanne Rapley
                E2. John Scheurman, b 1943   E3. Perry Scheurman, b 1949
            D3. Wilda Perry, b 1915, mar Gerry Thompson, divorced
                E1. Sharon Thompson, b 1943, mar Ron Nelson
                    F1. Paige Nelson
                E2. Judith Thompson
                E3. Tracey Thompson, b 1948, mar Gordon Switzer
                E4. Tanis Thompson, b 1951, mar Grant Phillips

GAUDIN 251

    D4. Jean Perry, b 1918, mar Joe Bate, res Penticton, BC
        E1. Susan Bate, b 1944   E3. Janice Bate, b 1952
        E2. Sandra Bate, b 1947   E4. Gerald Bate, b 1955
    D5. Lloyd Perry, b 1923, d.y.
  C4. Marion Hewgill, b 1891, mar Jack Hunter
    D1. Bill Hunter, b 1915   D3. Eileen Hunter, b 1924
    D2. Gwen Hunter, b 1923   D4. Beverly Hunter, b 1934
B4. Jane, b 1853, mar Robert McAuslen
  C1. Bertha McAuslen   C2. Jeannie McAuslen, unmar
  C3. Margaret McAuslen, mar Geo. Dinsome, or Dinsmore?
    D1. Grace Dinsom   D2. Robert Dinsom   D3. Ken Dinsom
B5. Agnes GAUDIN, b 1855, mar Tom Hewgill
  C1. Albert Hewgill, b ca 1874, mar Margaret Mitchell
    D1. Harold Hewgill, mar Dora Glen   D6. Florence Hewgill, mar
    D2. Roy Hewgill, mar Dorothy Robinson   Robert Drynes?
    D3. Evelyn Hewgill, mar Lewis Ardiel? D7. Herbert Hewgill, mar
    D4. Robert Hewgill, mar Edna Maxwell   Doris McMurchy
    D5. Opal Hewgill, mar Arle? McNab
  C2. Victor, b 1885, mar Ellen Lougheed
    D1. Elwood Hewgill, mar Cora Rencit?
      E1. Denton Hewgill, mar Marilyn Young E3. Ralph Hewgill
      E2. Vivian Hewgill, mar Antony Kapusta
    D2. Kathleen Hewgill, mar Percy Jarvis, dau, Deborah, d.y.
    D3. Mary Hewgill, mar Wm. Bowens, chn Elwood and Lynn
  C3. Mabel Hewgill, b 1886, mar Wesley Dinsmore
    D1. Elizabeth Dinsmore   D4. May Dinsmore, mar G.
    D2. Stanley Dinsmore, mar Joy Wiley   Cooke
    D3. Harold Dinsmore, mar H. Ramer
  C4. Earl Hewgill, b 1896? mar Mina Short
    D1. Murray Gaudin Hewgill
    D2. Vincent Hewgill, by second wife   D3. Lisa Hewgill
    D4. Frank Hewgill, mar Hilda Bray
      E1. Carolyn Hewgill E2. John Hewgill E3. Gayne Hewgill
    D5. Ruth Hewgill, mar Rev. Babcock
      E1. Raymond Babcock E2. Dean Babcock E3. Ruth Babcock
    D6. Raymond Hewgill, mar K. Glugston
    D7. Grace Hewgill, mar Tom Wilton D8. Alice Hewgill, mar Dr. Hicks
B6. Andrew, b 1855, mar Jane Abercrombie, 1868-1962
  C1. Helena, b 1891, mar Everett Cameron, YMCA Secty., BC
    D1. Gretta Cameron, b 1921, mar T. Wesbrook, Banker, d 1975
      E1. Lee Wesbrook, b 1945, mar E2. David Wesbrook, b 1948
          Susanne B---   E3. Kenneth Wesbrook, b 1951
    D2. Clayton Cameron, b 1923, mar Kay Hughes
      E1. Linda Dale Cameron, b 1949, mar Wm. Chrichton
        F1. Theresa Mary Chrichton, b 1975
      E2. Lorne Cameron, b 1950   E3. Wesley Cameron, b 1954
  C2. Harold Gaudin, b 1893, killed WWI, 1918
  C3. Dr. Frank, b 1902, mar 1. May Zimmerman, 2. Muriel Holt, and
      3. Pierette Lannel, 1918-1967 (order uncertain)
    D1. Gloria Gaudin, b 1941, mar Russell Repp
    D2. Frank Gaudin, b 1943
    D3. Daniel, b 1950, by second wife D7. Joanna Ruth, b 1961,
    D4. Catherine, b 1952   poss by 4th wife?
    D5. Anne, b 1954   D8. Adrian
    D6. Colleen, b 1955   D9. Dean
  C4. Beulah, b 1905, mar Wallace Thorsen
    D1. Keidi, poss Karen Thorsen, b 1946

C5. Dr. Melvin, b 1908, mar 1. Betty Davidson, 4 chn, and by 2. Dorothy Sykes, 2 chn. (Her own chn were Lynn and Barry)
   D1. Pamela, b 1941, mar David Herd
      E1. Kelly Herd, b 1963   E3. Bradford James Herd, b 1967
      E2. Andrew Herd, b 1965
   D2. James, b 1942   D5. Jacqueline, b 1963, by
   D3. Judith, b 1944   second wife
   D4. Jennifer, b 1946   D6. Catherine, b 1965
B7. Janet, b 1858, mar Robert Hall
  C1. Villa, pianist, unmar, d in her twenties
  C2. Marjorie, violinist, mar Harold MARSH
   D1. Stephen Marsh, res Sherman Oaks, Calif.
B8. Rev. William, b 1862, d 1920, mar Margaret GAUDIN, one son a pilot WWII
  C1. Stanley, d 1944, bur Londonderry   C2. Murray
B9. James, b 1864, mar Sophie Shearer, and 2. ---?
  C1. Illa, b 1890, mar G. England
   D1. Marion England, b 1921, mar R.K. Davis
   D2. Dr. Harold England, b 1954, mar Joyce Kwasny
      E1. Connie England, b 1954   E3. Illa England, b 1956
      E2. Myra England, b 1955   E4. Wendy England, b 1960
   D3. Marjory England, b 1930, mar Charles Balding
      E1. Charles Balding, b 1951   E4. Devon Balding, b 1955
      E2. George Balding, b 1952   E5. Judy Balding, b 1956
      E3. Garry Balding, b 1953
  C2. Lavina, b 1891, mar Austen O'Brian
   D1. Austen O'Brien, b 1916
   D2. Helen O'Brien, b 1921, mar Thomas Wherry
      E1. Sandry Wherry, b 1941, mar ---Wallender
  C3. Sophie, b 1894, mar Devereau
   D1. James Devereau, b 1916, mar Irene Ingoldsby, a son, Roy Devereau
   D2. Connie Devereau, b 1929, mar Glen Munro
      E1. Donna Munro, b 1967
   D3. John Devereau, b 1931, mar Nancy Edwards
   D4. Charles Devereau, b 1932, mar Norma Anderson
      E1. Stephen Devereau, b 1958   E3. Deane Devereau, b 1961
      E2. Nelson Devereau, b 1960
  C4. Ashley, b 1896, mar Pearl Stokes
   D1. Dora, mar Geo. Thompson
      E1. Christie Thompson, b 1957 E3. George Thompson, b 1965
      E2. Caroline Thompson, b 1960
  C5. Lorne, b 1900, mar 1. Jean Ennis, and 2. ?, res Vancouver, BC
   D1. Robert, mar Connie Lyle
      E1. Arnold, b 1953   E4. Michelle, b 1963
      E2. Kenneth, b 1956   E5. Patrick, b 1965
      E3. Terrence, b 1957   E6. Lyle?
   D2. Dr. Donald, b 1932, mar Wilma Luome
      E1. Glen, b 1961
   D3. Margaret, b 1933, mar B. Cooke   D4. George, b 1934
B10. Caroline, b 1868, unmar
B11. Amy, b 1869, mar Geo. Kirk
  C1. Ann Kirk, b 1898, mar Sam. Short
   D1. Lois Short, b 1934   D3. Helen Short, b 1943
   D2. Gwen Short, b 1936
B12. Irving, b 1870, mar Elizabeth Porter, founded Beaver Lodge, Alta.
  C1. Darcy, and other desc., res Beaver Lodge, Alta.

GAUDIN 253

A8. Francis, b 1818, mar 1852 Eva Young, b Ireland 1826, sister of Anna Young. See Rev. Dr. Samuel GAUDIN. Res Campbellton, NB, 7 chn, Francis d 1872.
  B1. Mary Ann, b 1855, mar Henry Howe of Yonkers, NY, rem to Restigouche River, Bonaventure Co., Gaspe. A desc in Kimberly, Ont.?
    C1. Percy Howe   C4. Thomas Howe, mar, a son,
    C2. Esther Howe, unmar   Thomas Howe
    C3. Augusta Howe, mar Briggs,   C5. Edith Howe, b 1883
        res U.S.
  B2. Elizabeth or Clara?, b 1856, mar Horace Hurlburt, res Peace River Dist.
    C1. Clifford Hurlburt, b 1880, rem to BC
    C2. May, d.y.   C3. Irvin Hurlburt, mar, a dau Wilma
  B3. Hedley, b 1858, d 1954. Mar 1. Elizabeth Breen 1888?, res Plymouth, NH and 2. the widow of Rev. Wm. GAUDIN, qv., poss more than 6 chn.
    C1. Vera Evangeline, b 1888, mar ---McAuslan, res Clarksburg, Ont., has 2 mar daus, and mar sons
    C2. Leonora Elizabeth, b 1890, res Toronto
    C3. Errol Francis, b 1892, res Portwashington, and Toronto, WWI vet
    C4. John Hedley, b 1894, res Washington
    C5. Valentine Adelaide, b 1896, res Toronto
    C6. Esdale Little, Pat, b 1899, res Fort Lauderdale, Florida
  B4. Minnie, d.y.
  B5. Katherine, b 1859, mar Will. Thurston, Editor of Fleshton, Ont.? She d 1948
    C1. Myrtle, mar ---Shaw?   C2. Arnold, killed WWI
    C2. Florence, mar ---Durant?   C5. Dell, a teacher
    C3. Stanley   C6. Frank, res Fleshton, Ont.?
  B6. Rev. Dr. Samuel, b 1861, d 1948, mar Anna Y. Young, nurse of Campbellton, NB? Samuel was a missionary to Northern Canada 44 years at Cross Lake.
    C1. Irene, b 1896, mar Lawrence Honner?
      D1. Ernest Honner?, b 1922, mar Muriel, sons, Danny and Arnold
    C2. Nelson, b 1907
    C3. Esther, mar I. Ross
      D1. John Ross, b 1935, mar Doris Kail
        E1. Deanne Ross, b 1962   E2. David Ross, b 1965
      D2. Gordon Ross, b 1940, mar Marilyn Newley
        E1. Katherine Ross, b 1961   E2. Gary Ross, b 1966
      D3. Elizabeth Ann Ross, b 1941, mar John Gawryluk
        E1. Ronald Gawryluk, b 1963   E2. Robert Gawryluk, b 1964
  B7. Eva?
  B8. Matilda, Tilly, b 1965, mar James Brown, res Owen Sound and Winnipeg?
    C1. Vera   C2. Zella, mar Shantz, of Peterborough?
    C3. Algretta, b 1895, mar H. Jackson, sons, Herbert and Robert
A9. John
A10. Carolyn, b 1830, mar 1856 Capt. John Armstrong, 8 chn, res Charlottetown, PEI? Many desc to U.S.
  B1. Harry Armstrong
  B2. Robert Armstrong, b 1870, mar Mary Schultz
    C1. Margaret Schultz, b 1877, mar Irving Benson
      D1. Irving Benson
    C2. Lucille Schultz, b 1899
  B3. George Armstrong   B4. Gertrude Armstrong
  B5. Mildred, mar Henry Maynard

C1. Annabelle Maynard, b 1894, mar J. De Winton, b 1893
   D1. Millie Winton, b 1915, mar Maurice Hawkins, res Riverside, Calif.
      E1. Melvin Hawkins, b 1941
   D2. Margret Winton, b 1917, mar Geo. Dressler
      E1. David Dressler, b 1944   E2. George Dressler, b 1945
   D3. Wendal Winton, b 1919, mar Sylvia Bennett, poss 3 chn?
      E1. Dianna Winton, b 1946   E2. Randall? Winton, b 1948
   D4. Warren Winton, b 1922, mar Mary Harris. Data unclear on this fam.
      E1. James Winton?   E2. Thomas Winton
   D5. Lawson Winton, b 1929, mar Jeannette Shadey
      E1. Brian Winton, b 1962   E2. Wendy Winton
   D6. Meriam Winton, b 1931, mar Harold Yoder
      E1. Gregory Yoder, b 1951
C2. Gertrude Maynard, unmar
C3. Allan Maynard, mar Georgia King
   D1. Allan Maynard, mar Gloria Griber
      E1. Catherine Maynard   E2. Janet Maynard
   D2. Henry Maynard, mar Jeannette Kliz
      E1. Henry Maynard   E2. Wade Maynard   E3. Edward Maynard
B6. David
B7. Francois, b 1874, mar Grace Schultz
   C1. Warren, b 1899
   C2. Audrey, b 1902, mar Arthur Anderson   C3. Dorothy, b 1909
      D1. Rodger Keith Anderson, b 1943
B8. Allan, mar Luella Curtis
   C1. Gertrude, b 1888, mar Robert Lewis   C2. Curtis, b 1890
A11. Matilda, b 1838, mar Thomas Hurlburt, 1845-1876, son of Herman H. and Mary Dulmage.
   B1. Minnie Hurlburt, d at age 21
   B2. Carolyn Hurlburt, b 1873, mar ---Hartman
   B3. Frank Hurlburt, b 1876, mar Jenny Walker, 1871-1961. He d 1943. He had the firm of Hurlburt shoes for chn.
      C1. Louise, Anne Louise, b 1908, mar Dr. Ray H. Judge, b 1900
         D1. John, b 1939, mar Mary Jane Price
            E1. Wendy Judge, b 1968
         D2. Ann Louise Judge, b 1942
         D3. Carol Ann Judge, b 1945, nurse
      C2. Gwen Hurlburt, b 1911, mar Charles Corbin, 1902-1967
         D1. Ruth Corbin, b 1934, mar Dr. David Wainwright
            E1. Keith David Wainwright, b 1966
         D2. Mary Louise Corbin, b 1936, mar Paul Wessenger or Messenger
            E1. Christine Marie, b 1965
      C3. Frances, b 1912, mar Roy Burton, b 1915
         D1. Margot Burton, b 1947, gold Medalist, viola
         D2. Gail Burton, b 1950
A12. Amelia, b 1839?, d 1900. She mar 1. ---White? and 2. ---Brown, a jeweler?, res Levis, Quebec
A13. George, b 1842 St. John's?, rem to New Zealand. Mar 1. Clara Vining, dau of James V. and Ella Fitzgerald, 1840-1897, and 2. Anne Brown, a widow with 3 chn. Two sons by first wife and 6 chn by second wife, 12 families in N.Z., some in Oonarama, N.Z.?
   B1. Howard, b 1875, mar Robina Marr, a cousin, 5 chn
   B2. Arthur, b 1877, mar Fanny Cleland, 3 chn
   B3. by second wife, Maude, b 1891, mar R. Vercoe?
   B4. Albert, drowned, twin of Maude?

GAUDIN 255

B5. Ada, b 1893, mar John Cowie, 13 chn
B6. Wilkin, b 1889, mar Ruby Hughes, 5 chn
B7. Sidney, b 1895, mar Gertie Carter, 3 chn
B8. Eric, b 1899, mar Gladys Pledger, no issue
GAUDIN, Gustavus Vincent, b 1880 J, son of Wm. G. and Elise VINCENT, rem to Gaspe ca 1892, d 1964. Mar Mary BAKER, qv., homesteaded in Wildwood, 80 miles west of Edmonton, Alta. (Helena Cameron, White Rock, BC)
  A1. Eva, b 1903, mar John Anderson
    B1. Mary Anderson, b 1924, mar John BEAUCHAMP, qv., res Flin Flon, Man.
      C1. Maurice Beauchamp, b 1946   C4. John Beauchamp, b 1957
      C2. Sharon Beauchamp, b 1951   C5. Robert Beauchamp, b 1963
      C3. Doreen Beauchamp, b 1954
    B2. Vera Anderson, b 1931, mar Don Murchison
      C1. Heather Murchison, b 1949   C3. Clifton Murchison, b 1956
      C2. Carel Murchison, b 1951
    B3. John Anderson, b 1934, mar Thelma G---
      C1. Leslie Anderson, b 1956   C2. Lyle Anderson, b 1960
    B4. David Anderson, b 1934, twin, mar Kitty Cowrie
      C1. Christina Anderson, b 1961   C2. Sharon? Anderson, b 1963
  A2. Vera, b 1904, mar 1. Walter Harold Briggs, and 2. Ernest Pettindale
    B1. Vincent Allen Briggs, b 1930, mar Lois Buchan 1955
      C1. Robert Allen, b 1964   C2. Jason Andrew Allen, b 1966
    B2. Dr. Alice Ethereda Briggs, mar Robert Hodgart?
      C1. Graeme Hodgart, b 1967   C2. Jeffery Hodgart, b 1967, twins
    B3. Janice Elizabeth, mar Parry Routley
      C1. Jason Todd Routley, b 1969
  A3. Mary, b 1905, mar Ernest LE GRAND, 1884-1959, bur St. Peters, Paspebiac, Gaspe (GLF) Three chn, see LE GRAND
I. GAUDIN, George, b 1842 Haut de Rue, St. Martin, J, son of George C. and Esther PAYN, qv., of J. George to Gaspe, mar May BECK, qv., 1839-1898. (Helena Cameron, White Rock, BC)
  A1. Esther, b 1866, mar Adolphus BECK, qv., chn
  A2. Frances, b 1868, mar Eli ROMERIL, qv., no issue? Frances d 1928? bur St. Peter's, Paspebiac, Gaspe (GLF)
  A3. Susan, b 1868, twin, mar Frederick AHIER, qv.
    B1. Charles Ahier, res Gaspe   B3. George Ahier, to Montreal
    B2. Francis Ahier, rem to New Zealand
  A4. Mary Jane, mar George ---?
    B1. Norman   B2. John   B3. Marjorie, 1913-1951
  A5. Charles, 1876-1877
  A6. George Godfrey   A7. Minnie   (Chn A6 and A7, uncertain)
II. GAUDIN, Marie, mar Francois LABEY, qv., in 1867, J. Marie is the sister of George, above. Dau Daisy mar ---LABEY, qv., rem to Canada
III. GAUDIN, Francois, brother
IV. GAUDIN, Elizabeth Jane, sister of I, II, and III, above
GAUDIN, Capt. James, b 1838 J, son of Thomas G. and Jane DE GRUCHY, qv., rem to Victoria, BC in 1860s? Mar Agnes Anderson, dau of James Caufield Anderson, J.P. She d 1929, age 80. He was commander of the LADY LAMPSON ship, d Vict., BC 1913 (Prov. Arch., BC)
  A1. James R., b G?, worked for British Yukon Navigation Co., d 1953, age 76. Worked also on the White Pass Rte., mar Nell Cummins, poss chn.
  A2. Marie, mar Major A.W.R. Wilby
  A3. Beatrice, mar ---Bond, res Vancouver, BC
  A4. Kate, Catherine?
  A5. Mabel, b 1880, mar J.S. Harvey, res Knapp Island, BC

B1. Robert Harvey, b 1900, mar Mary Martindale
  C1. James Harvey, mar Barbara Brown
    D1. Renata   D2. Bettina
  C2. Robert Harvey, mar Mary Ella Cook
    D1. Robert, b 1951   D3. Elizabeth, b 1955
    D2. John, b 1953   D4. Ann, b 1958
A6. Percy   A7. Philip
GAUDIN, Stanley, b 1885 St. Martin, J, to Gaspe 1899, to work for Fruing firm, Mont. Louis, Gaspe (GLF) Mar 1. Laetitia L'Etourneau 1910, who d 1911. Mar 2. Eugenie Dion 1912, 1894-1940. Stanley d at Mont. Louis 1938, 12 chn (Andree Gaudin, Mont. Louis, Gaspe West)
A1. Gabrielle, b 1912, mar Willie Auclair, b 1905, d 1969
A2. Evelyne, b 1914, d 1957, mar Noel Gagne, b 1917
A3. Theodora, b 1916, d 1968, mar Louis Bernier, b 1906
A4. Simone, b 1917, d 1971, mar Georges Element, b 1911, d 1968
A5. Philippe, b 1918, mar Madeleine Deroy, b 1926
A6. Florence, b 1919, mar Jean Baptiste Richard, b 1912
A7. Raymond, b 1921, d 1942
A8. Clement, b 1923, mar Therese Pelchat, b 1926
A9. Lena, b 1925, mar Richard LE PAGE, qv., b 1914
A10. Rodrigue, b 1927, mar Andree PROVOST, b 1927, 5 chn
  B1. Clermont, b 1948, mar Francine B3. Yvon, b 1952
    St. Laurent, 1973   B4. Sylvia, b 1956
  B2. Renaud, b 1951, d 1973   B5. Helene, b 1961
A11. Ghislaine, b 1929, unmar
A12. Reynelde, b 1932, mar Bernardin St. Laurin, b 1929
GAUDIN, Capt. John, b 1847, son of Capt. Elias G., d 1927. He mar Elisa BERTRAM, qv., of Grouville, J. They had sev chn, who came to Canada (GAUDIN chart)
A1. Sylvia, b 1897, mar George Lewis. She d 1959 Montreal
A2. Percival John, d 1947, mar Alice LE GROS, sister of Lucille LE GROS Le Mouton
  B1. Phyllis Gaudin, mar ---Colbourne, res Montreal
    C1. Margaret Alice Colbourne, mar ---Jersey
A3. Wilford Gaudin, d 1960
A4. Reginald Bertram Gaudin, d 1950 Montreal
GAUDIN, May, b J, mar Henry GENGE, qv., rem to Sask., Sask, 1908 (LE GALLAIS book)
GAUDIN, M., res Victoria, BC
GAUDIN, Henry, res Escuminac, Gaspe, Que., 1800s?
GAUDINs to Perce 1800s (Cent. Bklt.)
GAUDIN, M. in West Kildonan, Man.
GAUDIN, Philippa Louise, b 1860 J, mar George Peter DE BRODER of G, qv., 8 chn
GAUDIN, Francois, listed in Gaspe Petition of 1820
GAUDIN, Capt. Philip, ship pilot, son of --- of St. Martins, J, to Gaspe, 12 chn, res Ville d'Anjou, Que.
GAUDION, Marie, from C.I. to Belleville, Ont., recent
GAUDION to Melbourne, Australia
GAUDION, Alice M., b G, to BC 1920 via Montreal, mar Edw. RENOUF, qv.
GAUDION, Wilson Mahy, b 1886 Pleinheaume, Ald., mar Annie Elizabeth Stovin, b Deloraine, Man. 1898 (Mrs. W.M. Gaudion, Trenton, Ont.)
A1. Marie Elizabeth, b 1921, Neptune, Sask., res Belleville, Ont.
A2. Annette Helene, b 1927 Radwille, Sask., res Toronto
A3. Marguerite Lois, b 1929, mar Archie Sillars?, res Willowdale, Ont.
  B1. Belinda Ann Sillars, b 1960   B3. Diane Margaret Sillars
  B2. Deborah Leslie Sillars, b 1962

A4. Frances Beatrice, b 1930 Unity, Sask, mar John Luscombe, res Belleville, Ont.
   B1. John David Luscombe, b 1959   B3. Anne Elizabeth Luscombe, b 1963
   B2. Peter Andrew Luscombe, b 1961 B4. James Robert Luscombe, b 1966
A5. Wilson Horace John G., b 1937 Unity, Sask, mar Susan Jane Niblock, no issue, res St. Clements, Ont.
GAUDION, Ray, wife Olive, emigrated to Canada, 1900s, returned to St. Peter Port, G. (David Keyho, Kitchener, Ont.)
GAUDION, rem from Ald. to Chatham, Ont. ca 1875? (Luce)
GAULTON in Savage Cove, Nfld. early 1800s. Cf GAULTRON of J (Stevens; Seary; Lovell)
GAUTIER, Joseph, signed the Gaspe Petition 1820, sometimes spelled GAUDIER
GAUVAIN, Ann, see DAVEY
GAUVIN, Marie, dau of Charles and Marie Landry G. of Caraquet, NB, mar 1835 Pierre Goulet, 9 chn (See Robichaud) Origin unverified
GAVET, from G to Nfld. (K. Mathews)
GAVEY, Abraham, b G?, mar Esther Rachel LE HUQUET, Gaspe 1867 (Wilson)
GAVEY, Philip, res Fontenelle, Gaspe 1800s
GAVEY, John, b G, also Isabel, in Douglastown, Gaspe 1861 (census) with John, Abraham, Daniel, Caroline, Emilia, Elias, and Joseph, all b Gaspe
GAVEY, George, b G, in Douglastown, Gaspe, 1861 (census)   SEE GAVEY IN ADDED PAGES.
GAVEY, in Gaspe ca 1830 (GLF; Wilson; Bourgaize; Le Breton list)
GAVEY, Daniel, 1844-1926, from J, mar Jemima LE HUQUET, qv., 1852-1918, bur Grande Greve, Gaspe
   A1. Lucy Ada, 1875-1922, b J?, mar Alfred Henry DOLBEL, qv.
GAVEY, Amelia, 1853-1932, bur Gr. Greve, Gaspe, mar Charles P. BARTLETT, 1850-1928 (GLF)
GAVEY, John, b G, d 1869 at age 50, mar Isabella PRICE, who d 1903, age 64, res Gaspe?
GAVEY, Charles Amice, 1855-1946, mar Margaret Jane ---, 1862-1923, bur St. Peters, Paspebiac, Gaspe (GLF) One fam from Paspebiac, rem to Howick, Quebec
   A1. Lorna Margaret, 1895-1918   A2. Charles Robin, b 1896, d.y.
GEAR in Nfld. from C.I. (Rev. Hammond) Also to U.S. (QAAM) Cf also DE GUERRE, GREARE, GEARY, GUEIRR, GUERRE, etc. See DE PUTRON
GEARY in Nfld. (Seary) from C.I.? James, in Carbonear 1785.
GENDRON, John, b J, age 41 in 1871, cooper at Bonaventure Island (Brochet) Cf also JEANDRON
GENGE. A family of six orphaned young people from Jersey to Western Canada, ca the time of the Barr Colony, 1903, 1910. Charles and John came first, Harry in 1908. Charles returned to J to fetch the girls to Sask. They first lived near Tuxford. See PARTNERS IN THE GLORIES OF THE GARDEN, by Mary Ritchie; Elizabeth Le Gallais, Seattle, Wash.)
A1. Anne, b ca 1886, to Canada ca 1910, mar Cecil L'ARBALESTIER, qv., in 1912
   B1. Duncan Philip, 1925-1973, mar Nancy ---, 3 daus
A2. Dorothy, b J, mar Norman LE GALLAIS, celebrated 62nd anniversary 1974, 2 chn
   B1. Elizabeth Le. G.   B2. Norman Hugh, see LE GALLAIS
A3. Harry, b J, mar May GAUDIN, qv., of J, joined his two bros in 1908 in Sask.
   B1. Richard, mar Lucy Barker 1939
      C1. William, b 1943, mar Dorothy ---, dau, Jennifer
      C2. Ann, b 1946, mar John Paton
         D1. Michael Paton   D3. Catherine Paton
         D2. Richard Paton   D4. Kelly, twin of Catherine

    B2. Kenneth, mar Jean ---
        C1. Anthony   C2. Daly, dau
    B3. Marjorie Frances, mar William Forrest, no issue
    B4. Charles, d.y.
A4. John, b J, d WWI
A5. Charles, b J, mar Ethel Hailes
    B1. John Pope, mar Peggy Ross
        C1. Patricia, b ca 1956   C2. Ross, b ca 1960
A6. Mary, b 1884 J, to Halifax 1907 on ship VICTORIAN, mar Jack Ritchie
    B1. Mary, Molly, Asplet, unmar, b ca 1911
GENGE in Nfld. (Seary) Cf GENGE in J
GENGE, curr Toronto and Calgary, Alta.
GENNEAUX, GENOE in Nfld. (Seary) From C.I.? A Hug fam from C.I. to
    U.S. early, same surname in GANO in America. Cf also GERNOUD of J
    (Stevens) Cf GERNEAUX, GANO, GAYNEAU, etc. from France to G, to New
    Rochelle, NY 1661. (QAAM; Howard Le Master, Carlinville, Ill.)
GEOFFREY, LE GEOFFREY, see GODFREY, GODFRAY
GEORGE, from C.I.? said to be in Manitoba and Gaspe
GEORGE, Clement, from C.I.? in Harbor Grace, Nfld. 1860s, also Robert
    GEORGE (Seary, Rev. Hammond)
GEORGLIN, GEORGELIN, GEOGLIN, from J to Moose Jaw, Sask, several bros.
    One was a Vet of Boer War and WWI, prob father of the boys.
GEORGELIN, Cp. Harry, poss son of Mrs. N.E. Georgelin of St. Heliers, J,
    b England. Mbr of Princess Pat's Can. Light Inf. (J.H. De Wolfe,
    OUR HEROES IN THE GREAT WAR, Canada 1919)
GERARD, from C.I. to Western Canada?
GERARD, Nicholas, b G, in Malbaie, Gaspe 1861 (Census) mar Mary LaFlamme,
    1827.
GERARD, Thomas, Mary, Martha, Celina, Isabella, from G? in Gaspe 1861
GERARD, Arthur mar Elsie LE GRESLEY, GASPE.   (Census)
GERARD, Peter, b G, also Ann and Wm. in Gaspe 1861 (Census)
GERARD, others in Gaspe 1800s, see Census
GERARD, to N.B. from C.I., poss a Thomas
GERMAIN, from C.I. to Ontario
GERMAIN, Gilles and wife, Anne LE MOYNE, Hug refugees from Brittany to
    G 1600s, related by marriage to the powerful DE BEAUVOIR and CAREY
    fams in G.
GERRARD, John, signed the Petition of 1820 in Gaspe, and was poss from
    C.I. See also GERRETT, JERRETT
GEZEQUEL, husband of Anne LE CORNU of J, who d 1898 in Alpena, Mich.
    See QUIET ADVENTURERS, and LE CORNU. Napoleon G. of Gaspe was b in
    Paris, France, but this surname was assoc with the Ch. Islands at times.
GIBAUT, Moses, from J, b before 1840, worked for Robin firm in Gaspe
    (Cent. Bklt.)
GIBAUT, Francis, b Gorey, J 1844, cousin of Moses, above, son of Fran-
    cis G. who d 1848 Naples, Italy, and Francoise ASPLET, qv., who d St.
    Brelade, J 1896. Francis rem to Gaspe, mar Alice Louise TUZO, qv.,
    dau of Joseph Eve Tuzo (RD; Syvret; Bechard; GLF; H.H. Gibaut, Que-
    bec; J.H. Le Breton, Gaspe; Betty Tardif)
A1. Alice Frances, b 1879, unmar, bur St. Pauls, Perce, 1967
A2. Francis Moses, b 1881, mar 1915 Lillian JEAN, qv, and d 1973 age
    94. Wrote Memoirs, Rev. d'Hist, 1963.
    B1. Jean, mar R.L. Gourley, 3 sons   B2. Janet   B3. Marie
A3. Edwin James Godfray, b 1883, d.y., killed at Vimy WWI?
A4. Janet Louisa, b 1884, d 1961. Mar Frank E. AGNES, qv, res Paspe-
    biac, Gaspe
    B1. Francis Agnes   B2. John Agnes

GIBAUT   259

A5. Florence May, b 1889, d 1891
A6. Marie Jeanne, b 1888, mar Charles Gyllum Dunn
    B1. Alice Mary Dunn   B3. Timothy Hibbard Dunn
    B2. Helen Margaret Dunn B4. Stewart St. Helier Gyllum Dunn, killed WWI
A7. Major Joseph Tuzo Gibaut, b 1891, mar Edith Bagnall, d 1942, served
    in WWI, WWII, bur St. Pauls, Perce, Gaspe
    B1. Janith   B3. Nanette, b 1932, mar David
    B2. Jo-Anne, b 1929, mar Al. Norris   Casgrain
A8. Victor John, b 1894, d 1896
A10. Harry Helier, b 1898, mar Marjorie Isobel Ross, res Quebec
    B1. John St. Helier   B3. Frederick Philip
    B2. Mary Marjorie   B4. Barbara Anne
GIBAUT, Lewis J, b J, res Cloridorme and St. John, traveled for Wm. Hyman and Son, fishery of Grand Greve, and Gaspe, Que. Retired to J?
GIBAUT, Mrs., b J, ca 1887, res Quebec City
GIBAUT, Addie, of J fam, res Quebec
GIBAUT, Arthur, res Sask, Sask.
GIBSON, Mr. and Mrs. A.S., left G in 1910, having been mar at St. Sampson ca 1906. He was the son of Mr. and Mrs. S. Gibson of the Bridge, St. Sampson. She was Ada BICHARD, qv, dau of Mr. and Mrs. D.H. Bichard of Les Sauvages, St. Sampson, G. Sons Arthur and Percy b G, Harold in Canada. Harold has 12 grandchn and 13 gr grandchn in Canada.
GIFFARD, Philip, from J to Queensland, Aust. 1800s
GIFFARD, Florence Mary, b 1872 J, mar 1. George Francis LE FEUVRE, qv, 6 chn, and 2. Wm. Keys, b England. She d Ottawa, Ont. 1934. Keys died in 1949.(GLF, Trenton, Mich.) See LE FEUVRE for his chn.
A7. Elsie Ann Keys, b 1908 Ottawa, rem to Wyandotte, Mich. 1929, mar John Mercer Trowbridge of Montreal. He d 1964 Montreal. She rem to Ottawa, d there 1970, no issue.
A8. William Henry Keys, b 1910 Ottawa, rem to Wyandotte, Mich. 1929, mar Pearl Matteson, res Detroit, Mich., 6 chn
    B1. James, mar, res Calif.   B5. Elsie, mar Alex Vlad, res Allen Park,
    B2. Frank, U.S. Marine   Mich.
    B3. Edward, res Detroit   B6. Beverley, res Detroit
    B4. June, mar Stanley Bartnicki, res Allen Park, Mich.
GIFFARD, Mr. and Mrs. Henry, from G in 1920 to Canada. Many of this fam in British Army, some in India, a monument in G to this fam. A Dean of G was GIFFARD, 1931-47. Some research done on hist. of this fam (Henry Giffard, Toronto, Ont.)
GIFFARD, JEFFARD, Capt. and boat owner from J and G in Nfld. (Seary, K. Mathews)
GIFFARD from C.I. to Gaspe
GIGUERE, GIGUET in Nfld. (Seary) Cf GIGUET of J (Stevens)
GILBERT, John, signed the Gaspe Petition of 1820, prob from J
GILBERT, F.C., from G to Toronto 1920
GILBERT, GUILBERT from C.I.? to Nfld. (Seary)
GILE, GILES, from C.I. to Nfld. See Seary
GILLAM, GILLIAM in Nfld. (Seary) Cf GUILLAUME of J (Stevens) Charles GUILLAM in Port Aux Basques, Nfld. 1830 (Seary) George at La Poile, Nfld. 1860s (Rev. Hammond)
GILLARD, GILLIARD? in Nfld. (Seary) Cf GALLIARD of J
GILLFILLING, James, in Yarmouth, NS. While the name is Scottish, a GILLFILLAN was b in G and emigrated to Australia.
GILL, GILLES, John, in Channel Nfld. 1860s from C.I.? (Seary, Rev. Hammond)
GILLETT, boat keeper and tradesman from G and J (Seary, K. Mathews)
GILLINGS, GELLONCE, GELLANCE, C.I.? name in Portugal Cove, Nfld. ca

GILLINGS, GELLONCE, GELLANCE
PLEASE NOTE THAT MANY GIRARDS BELOW ARE NOT FROM CHAN.IS.
1800 (Rev. Hammond)
GIOT, C.I.? name in Maritimes Fisheries 1800s (J.H. Le Breton list)
GIRARD, W. and father (poss Guillaume below?) built first chapel in
   Magpie, Cote Nord, Que. ca 1840s (LABRADOR AND ANTICOSTI, by Huard,
   1897; Brochet)
GIRARD, Guillaume, b J ca 1755, d 1845 a Catholic in Malbaie. Mar Mary
   Henly, dau of Jacques Henly and Catherine Chicoine. He was a banker,
   with 17 banks, had 13 chn. (Therese Gravel, Montreal; Reg. by Gallant)
   A1. Jacques, b 1791 Malbaie, mar 1818 Brigitte Maloney, dau of Wm. M.
       and Josette BAKER, qv, dit Blondin
       B1. Marie, b 1819 Barachois, d 1824
       B2. Jacques, James, b 1821 Barachois, mar 1840 Mary TAPP, qv, dau of
           John T. and Angelique Chicoine
           C1. Suzanne, b 1841   C3. Anne, b 1844
           C2. Jean Baptiste, b 1846   C4. William, b 1849 Barachois
       B3. Sophie, b 1823, mar 1845 Charles Rail, son of Sylvestre Rail and
           Julienne Chicoine
       B4. Caroline, b 1825 Barachois   B9. Charles, b 1837
       B5. Patrice, b 1828   B10. William, b 1839
       B6. Frederick, b 1830   B11. William Henry, b 1841
       B7. William John, b 1833   B12. Elisabeth Jane, b 1843
       B8. Brigitte, b 1835
   A2. Pierre, b 1793 Malbaie, poss mar to Sara LUCAS, qv, from J?
       B1. Daniel, b 1828   B6. Pierre, b 1837
       B2. Charlotte, b 1829   B7. Charles, b 1839
       B3. William, b 1832   B8. Guillaume, William, b 1842
       B4. Elisabeth, b 1833   B9. Charlotte, b 1845
       B5. Nicholas, b 1835   B10. Justine Rachel, b 1847
   A3. Nicholas, mar Marie Laflamme, res Barachois?
   A4. Jean, mar 1814 Catherine Maloney, dau of Wiiliam M. and Josette
       BAKER, qv, dit Blondin
       B1. Jean, b 1816 Barachois
       B2. Andres, b 1818, mar 1841 Elisabeth TAPP, dau of John TAPP and
           Angelique Chicoine
           C1. Elisabeth Jane, b 1842 Barachois   C4. Georges, b 1847
           C2. Andrew, b 1843   C5. Emilie, b 1849
           C3. Caroline, b 1845
       B3. Jacques, James, b 1821 Barachois, mar Mary SPRUEN? Malbaie
           C1. George James, b 1846 Malbaie   C3. Caroline, b 1850
           C2. Henry Frederic, b 1848
       B4. Michel, b 1822 Barachois, mar 1844 Mathilde STE. CROIX, b J?, dau
           of Jacques Ste. Croix and Catherine Marthe Element
           C1. James, b 1844   C2. Elisabeth, b 1847   C3. Marie, b 1849
       B5. Guillaume, b 1824 Barachois   B8. Jean Baptiste, b 1832
       B6. Catherine, b 1826   B9. Brigitte, b 1834
       B7. Charles, b 1829   B10. Elisabeth, b 1841
   A5. Judith, b 1797 Malbaie, mar 1. 1815 Matthew Morris, widower of
       Genevieve Hayden? and 2. 1822 in Malbaie, Pierre BRILLANT, son of
       Thomas Brillant and Charlotte Cecile Yvon
   A6. Catherine, b 1799 Malbaie, prob mar William GIRARD, a cousin? He
       d Malbaie 1843, age 48
       B1. Susanne, b 1822 Malbaie, mar 1845 Alexis NOEL, son of Jean N. and
           Euphrosine Bond
       B2. Marie, b 1823 Malbaie, mar 1846 Jacques Bond, son of Pierre Bond
           and Anne Gourdeau (disp 4-4c)
       B3. Justine Rachel, b 1824, mar 1846 John Denis, son of Francois D.
           and Marie Chicoine

GIRARD 261

B4. Sophie, b 1826, mar 1850 Aubain-John TAPP, son of Jean-Baptiste
    Bond   and Marie (disp. 4-4c)
B5. Catherine, b 1827 Malbaie   B8. William, b 1833
B6. Judith Catherine, b 1829   B9. Elisabeth Zoe, b 1835
B7. Henriette, b 1831   B10. Pierre, b 1836
A7. Guillaume, William, b 1802 Malbaie, mar 1822 or 1828 Catherine Morris, dau of Mathew M. and Genevieve Hayden
    B1. Mathias, b 1829 Malbaie   B7. Jeanne, b 1838, twin
    B2. Anne, b 1830   B8. Jacques Edouard, b 1840
    B3. Patrick Charles, b 1837   B9. Edouard, b 1842
    B4. William, b 1834   B10. Caroline, b 1844, d 1847
    B5. Jean Gaspard, b 1836   B11. Alexis, b 1846, d 1847
    B6. Frederic, b 1838   B12. Marguerite Caroline, b 1848
A8. Marguerite, b 1804, Malbaie, mar 1. 1825 Jean Guillat, son of Louis
    G. and Marie Deschamps, mar 2. 1828 Malbaie, Joseph Deraiche son of
    Anastasie Plourde. Marguerite d Malbaie 1843
A9. Patrice, b 1807 Malbaie, d 1827
A10. Charles, b 1809 Malbaie, mar 1831 Genevieve Chicoine, dau of
    Antoine-Michel C. and Henriette Francoise Samuel, Riviere aux Renards. (disp. 3-3c) See Charles, A2., below. Confused.
    B1. Genevieve, b 1832, mar Joseph Synnett 1848
    B2. Elisabeth, b 1834   B6. Caroline, b 1844
    B3. Charles Andrew, b 1836   B7. Guillaume Elzear, b 1847
    B4. Jacques, b 1838   B8. Mathilde, b 1849 Riviere aux Renards
    B5. Primitive, b 1841
A11. Susanne, b 1812 Malbaie, mar 1828 Jean Louis HAMMOND, qv, son of
    J.L.H. and Antoinette Lilois
A12. Marie, b 1814 Malbaie, mar 1834 Antoine Chicoine, bro of Genevieve
    C., above
A13. Mathurin, b 1816, d 1818
GIRARD, Pierre, poss related to above fam
A1. Judith, b 1818 Barachois, mar 1845 Adolphe Derois, son of Jean Marie D. and Madeleine Bernier
A2. Pierre, b 1818 Barachois   A3. Mathieu, b 1820 Barachois
A4. Guillaume, b 1821 Barachois, a dau Marie?, b 1848 Barachois
GIRARD, Philip, b J, at Malbaie 1800s. Also 2 other Philip Girards
    there
GIRARD, Wm. Sidney, mar ---MUNRO, res Malbaie 1800s (GLF)
GIRARD, Bruce, d Malbaie, age 24, 1800s (GLF)
GIRARD, this surname appears ca 1900 in Alpena, Mich. where some Gaspe
    folk removed in the middle 1800s
GIRARD, Jean, John, b J, rem to Malbaie, Gaspe, mar Marie Henley in
    Malbaie (Remiggi) See also p. 260, A6., Catherine, Confused record.
A1. William, b Malbaie, mar Catherine Morris
    B1. Suzanne, bp 1822, mar 1845 ---Noel, qv.
    B2. Marie, bp 1822?, mar 1846 ---Bond, qv.
A2. Charles, bp 1805 Malbaie, fisherman, res Fox River, mar Genevieve
    Coton, bp 1809. See Charles, A10., above. Chn incorrect?
    B1. Marie, bp 1828, d 1918, mar 1848 ---Synot
    B2. Charles, bp 1836, mar 1859 Sedulie Cote, dau of Norbert C. and
        Genevieve Thibault.
        C1. Charles Achille, bp 1859, mar 1881 Celina Blanchet, dau of
            Francois B. and Celina Giasson, Chiasson? of Cap Rosiers
        C2. Andre Francois, b 1861, mar 1882 Dinora Jalbert, dau of Jean
            J. and Elisabeth Caron, qv, of Fox River, Que.
        C3. Marie Zoe, bp 1862, mar 1883 ---Cotton
        C4. Edmond, bp 1864, mar 1885 Nathalie Page, bp 1867, Fox River, dau

of Alexandre Page, and Clarisse ENGLISH, LANGLOIS?
   C5. Marie Selene, bp 1866, mar 1886 ---DESPRES
   C6. Marie Eloise, bp 1867, mar 1886 ---DUMARESQ, qv.
   C7. ---, bp 1869, d.y.? (Chn below poss belong to Charles, A10.,
  B3. Jacques, bp 1838   page 261)
  B4. Primitive, bp 1841, d 1878, mar 1863 ---Bernard
  B5. Caroline, bp 1844, mar 1862 ---Bond, qv.
  B6. Elzear, bp 1847, mar 1873 Mary Cloutier, dau of Theodore C. of
    St. Thomas, Montmagny, Que., and Rose Metivier
  B7. Elisabeth, bp 1848
  B8. Matilde, bp 1849, mar 1890 ---Samuel   B9. Marie Genevieve
 A3. Pierre, bp Malbaie, mar Sarah LUCAS, qv.
  B1. Pierre, mar 1851 Marcelline Duguay of Malbaie, dau of Hubert D.
    and Henriette QUERREE?, qv.
   C1. Hubert, bp 1851   C3. Guillaume
   C2. Francois Xavier, bp 1852   C4. Pierre
  B2. William, bp 1821, mar 1848 Charlotte DAIGLE, bp 1825, dau of
    Charles D. and Victoire LANGLOIS, qv.
   C1. Marie, bp 1849   C5. Jean Baptiste, bp 1859
   C2. William, bp 1852, d 1872   C6. Pierre, bp 1861
   C3. Charles, bp 1855   C7. Georges, bp 1864
   C4. Andre Jacques, bp 1857   C8. Philomene, bp 1866
 A4. Jean, bp Malbaie, mar ---Maloney
 A5. Marie, bp 1813, mar 1834 ---Chicoine and/or Cotton, d 1886
GLYN, James, in Bay Bulls, Nfld. 1653 (Seary) Cf GLYNN of J in 1502
  (Stevens)
GLYN, Elinor, b 1868 England, dau of Elinor Saunders of pioneer English
  and French fam settled in Guelph, Ontario 1830. Elinor's mother,
  second youngest of 8 daus and 1 son, mar Douglas Sutherland, who d 4
  yrs. later leaving her with 2 daus, Lucy and Elinor. The mother re-
  married, to David Kennedy, a Scot, the fam settling for some time in
  J, where Elinor was b in 1864. The two girls spent much time between
  1873 and 1888 in J. They were at one time wrecked on the Casquet
  rocks, being rescued by a Guernsey tug. Elinor mar Clayton Glyn ca
  1892, and had two daus, Margot and Judith. She wrote books, visited
  and lived for a time in U.S., in connection with the films made from
  her books. She traveled extensively, making many friends in high
  society and royalty in Russia, France, Egypt, Hungary, and Spain.
  She was beautiful, talented, a romanticist, and had a compelling personality. She d in 1943, nearly 79 yrs. old, retaining her beauty
  till the last years. She left at least 3 grandsons and a grandaughter.
  (ELINOR GLYN, by Anthony Glyn, her grandson, pseudonym of Sir. G.L.S.
  Dauson, Garden City, N.Y. 1955)
GLYNN, GLEEN. Gleen appears in J records of the PREVOSTS-VAUTIER fam
  tree, Ste. Foy, Que., ca 1700s
GOASDOUE, Ray, of a Brittany fam, to Guernsey. Rem to Canada 1948,
  Pincher Creek, Alta., mar Maxine NEVE
 A1. Dean Kenneth, b ca 1955   A4. Julie Anne, b ca 1967
 A2. Robert Edward, b ca 1962
 A3. Raymond Stanley, b ca 1962, twin of Robert
GODDEN, Albert, b J to Barrie, Ont. 1900, d Canada 1936. Relatives to
  N.Y. City 1907. Mar Sophia ---, who d Canada 1960 (George Godden,
  Hartford, Conn.)
 A1. Albert, b 1896   A4. Reginald, noted pianist
 A2. Trevor?   A5. Grace
 A3. Sydney, b 1899 G, mar ---   A6. Lily
    William Alfred, b 1900 G, d Bronx, N.Y. 1924

. Dorcas Florence, b 1913, mar George Fanning
GODDEN, Geo. Henry, bro of Albert, above, mar Dorcas Caroline THOUMINE, b 1882 G, d Bronx, NY 1948. Son, George, and other chn?
GODDEN, Joseph, in Bonavista, Nfld., 1792 (Seary)
GODDEN, John, S.P.G. minister in Harbour Grace, Nfld. 1873. John and Thomas Godden were missionaries in Montreal 1855-1865 (SPG)
GODFRAY, tombstone in Annapolis, NS 1700s, from C.I.?
GODFRAY, Edwin, b 1894 St. Helier, J, with sister Lillian, bros Charles and Frank. Edwin mar Florence Humberstone. A dau Jean, b 1926, mar ---Duncan. (E.C. Godfray, Toronto, Ont.)
GODFRAY, William, in Petty Harbour, Nfld. 1675 (Seary) from C.I.?
GODFRAY, GODFREY, Jerseymen in N.B. fisheries (J.H. Le Breton list; Saint John Museum)
GODFREY, LE GEOFFREY, fam from G to Ontario 1910
I. Rita, b G before 1890, mar ---Gray and 2. ---Maxwell, res Ont., 4 chn
II. George
III. Lillian, b G before 1890, mar Daniel GRIVEL, 4 chn, res Ontario
IV. Ethel Mae, b 1890 G, mar 1. Arthur Dutch Gray of Portland, ME (Pricilla Leming, Warehouse Pt., Conn.)
A1. Robert Le Baron Gray, b 1921, mar 1942 Florence Vose Rickard, b 1918
B1. Robert Le Baron Gray, Jr., b 1943, mar 1966
B2. Richard Weld Gray, b 1944, mar 1968
B3. Pricilla Elizabeth Gray, b 1948, mar 1971 Paul Lemming
B4. Phyllis Louise Gray, b 1950, mar 1969
B5. Ronald Arthur Gray, b 1951
GODFREY fam from J in Quebec (Brochet)
A1. Philip, a partner 1819 in Peter DU VAL and Co.
A2. John, also a partner, 1830-1860 in Bertram, Godfrey, Grey and Co.
A3. fam from J to Montreal?
GODFREY, Rose, b J, niece of Joshua LE CLERCQ, mar Thomas DE GRUCHY. A dau, Rose GHIGHI, res London, England or Ontario
GODFREY in Nfld. (Seary) Cf GODFREY, GODFRAY of C.I.
GODFREY, Thankful, in Yarmouth, NS 1773 (Census; Lost in Canada) Poss U.E.L.
GODFREY, Wm., S.P.G. Minister in N.S. 1841-1882
GODIN, Stanley, from J to Gaspe ca 1900. See also GAUDIN, GODDEN (J.H. Le Breton list)
GODION, see also GAUDION
GODION, Fanny, mar Mathew GALLIENNE, qv, in 1844 at St. Helier, dau of Nicholas GODION
GOLLEDGE, Mr. and Mrs. Bert. from C.I., prob G, to BC in 1920 (Luce) He was a carpenter
GOLLEDGE, J.B., to BC also from C.I.
GOOBIE to Nfld. (Seary) Cf GOUPY, LE GOUPIL, GUPPY of J 1668 (Stevens)
GOOTE, COOTE, said to be of C.I. origin in Nfld. (Rev. Hammond)
GORDEN, Nicholas, in New Perlican 1708 (Seary) Cf GORDEN of J (Stevens)
GORE, Matthew, at Burgeo, Nfld. 1860s, from C.I.? poss as GORIN? or GOREY?
GOSLING, C.I. in Maritimes Fisheries 1800s (J.H. Le Breton list)
GOSSE, from C.I.? to Nfld. (Seary; Rev. Hammond)
GOSSE, Capt. Thomas of Nfld., bought the JANE in 1856 for about a thousand pounds, and sailed with 45 men in the seal fishery. (Capt. Parker)
GOSSELIN, Gosling in Nfld. (Seary) Cf GOSSELIN of J (Stevens)
GOSSELIN, THE LIFE OF JOSHUA GOSSELIN OF GUERNSEY, by D. McClintock, Guernsey Soc. Bulletin, 1977
GOSSELIN, in Manitoba
GOSSELIN, C.I. surname in Conception Bay, Nfld. (H.W. Le Messurier)

MARIE L.S. MASTERS BELOW WAS MLS LE MAISTRE,OF JERSEY.
GOSSELIN, Capt. from G in Nfld. (K. Mathews)
GOSSET , Richard, b 1822 J, d there 1852. Mar Marie Lucy Smith MASTERS, b 1823 England, d 1904 Canada. He was the founder and editor of the St. Heliers Gazette, a French language newspaper in J. She was the dau of Col. Richards MASTERS, who had served in the garrison of St. John's, Nfld. mid 1800s. After her husband's death she carried on the LA PATRIE, leasing it to a cousin. Widowed, she rem to Toronto, where she operated a dry goods store on Yonge St. for a number of years. (Ruth Garrett, Don Mills, Ont.)(Paul Cleal,IslingtonONT)
- A1. Richard Masters, b 1852 St. Heliers, J, to Canada as a young man, surveyed a RR line through the Eastern Twps., Que., then was a bookkeeper in Toronto. Mar 1878 Sarah Ann Boore, on her 21st birthday, 6 chn
  - B1. Richard Selby, b 1879 Canada, d 1942, mar Janet Wheeler, 3 chn
    - C1. Richard MacKenzie, d 1977, mar Beatrice Bell
      - D1. Patricia Louise, b 1935, mar ---Houghtalin
        - E1. Robin Houghtalin   E2. Richard Houghtalin
    - C2. Mary Alice, b 1910, mar 1. Percival Ross Love, and 2. Kenneth Harrison   WM.DUNCAN BELOW, SEE EXTRA PAGES.
    - C3. William Duncan, b 1913, mar Jane Gooch, res Etobicoke, Ont.
      - D1. James, b 1943, mar Agathe La Bossierre, 2 chn (See addedPP)
        - E1. Ryan, b 1974   E2. Ursula Janet, b 1976
  - B2. Marion Beatrice, b 1880, d 197-. Mar Paul Cleal 1910, living 1977
    - C1. Paul Ethelbert Cleal, Jr., b 1914, WWII Vet, mar Lillian Tetlaw, accountant, Toronto
      - D1. Bruce Paul Cleal, b 1949
      - D2. Mary Ellen Cleal, b 1953, adopted, mar John Ruffolo, of Islington, Ont., 1972. Son, Derek Paul, b 1975.
    - C2. Vivyan Beatrice Cleal, mar Gareth Edgar 1947 Toronto, no issue
  - B3. Ernest Reginald, b 1883, d 1968, mar Greta Lee
    - C1. Lee, mar, res London, Ont.
    - C2. Elizabeth, mar Stewart Laing, b 1912, res Toronto
  - B4. Clara Vivian, b 1885, unmar, Legal Secty, worked till age 89, res Toronto
  - B5. Sarah Lillian, b 1887, res in Toronto 1976. Mar Ernest Edward GARRETT
    - C1. John Douglas Garrett, d.y.
    - C2. Ruth Audrey Garrett, b 1929
  - B6. Ada Masters, b 1890, d 1963, unmar

GOSSET, Capt. Wm., in New Westminster, BC 1860, connected with Gov. James Douglas
GOSSET, boatkeeper from J in Nfld. 1800s? (K. Mathews)
GOSSET, John and Mary Ann, b J, in Cap Rosier, Gaspe 1861 (Census) with Ann Mary, Edward, Jane and Theophile, all b Canada
GOSSET, John, from J to Gaspe. Signed Petition of 1820.
GOSSET, Jean, b J, in Coxtown, Quebec 1871 (Census)
GOSSET, James, age 18, b J, in Bon. Co., Gaspe 1871
GOUBERT, Mrs. Hilda Goubert Amy, from G to Canada 1900s
GOULD, from C.I.? in Nfld. Michael in St. John's, 1682 (Seary)
GOULD, Martha, second wife of Philip BERTEAU, qv, who res Annapolis, NS ca 1745
GOULDRUP, GOLDRUP. Cf GOULDTHRUP, Henry, bp Yorkshire 1731.
GOULDRUP, GOOLDRUP, GOLDRUP, Henry, b J?, served in Br. Army at Plains of Abraham during battle of Quebec, 1759. Mar French Canadian named Jane ---, res near Trois Rivieres. In 1768 had land on P.E.I. near Tryon, and nearly drowned at Crapaud Harbor, near mouth of Tryon River. Jane mar 2. Henry's friend, Capt. William Warren. Henry and

GOULDRUP, GOOLDRUP, GOLDRUP   265

    Jane had 2 chn. (Harold Goldrup, Waterville, ME; Tom Goldrup, Ben
    Lomond, Calif.)
 A1. Charlotte, b 1768, said to be second ch b PEI of English parents.
     Mar John LORD, qv, had large fam.
 A2. John, b 1765 Que., owned first grist mill in Price Co., PEI, gave
     flour to Loyalists to help them through first winter on island.
     Mar 1796 in Prince Co., Mass.-born Judith Partridge. John d Tryon,
     PEI 1843, 6 chn
     B1. Jacob, b 1799 Tryon, PEI, farmer, mar 1. Charlotte DAVIS, and 2.
         Flora McIntyre, 19 chn. Jacob d 1889.
     B2. James Foy, b 1802 Tryon, inherited mill from father and later sold
         it to his cousin, John LORD, Jr. Mar Elizabeth ---, became Bap-
         tist minister, rem to Stoney Creek, NB near Moncton, d 1886, 7 chn.
         Changed spelling to Gooldrup.
     B3. Henry Charles, b 1803 Tryon, PEI, mar 1832 Eunice MacNaught, rem
         to NB, settling at Bathurst, shoemaker and clerk. She d 1875,
         Henry killed in 1876 in duck hunting accident near Bathurst, 6
         chn. Henry changed spelling to Gooldrup.
         C1. Sarah Sibley, b 1838 Tryon, PEI, mar 1873 at Bathurst, NB,
             Thomas Gammon. She was a seamstress. Son, Samuel.
         C2. Ephraim Howard Gooldrup, b 1840 Tryon, poss unmar, rem to
             Marinette, Wisc.
         C3. Elizabeth Ann, b 1842, mar 1868 at Bathurst, NB, William Horni-
             brook, b 1842, NB, carpenter. Rem to Marinette, Wisc., where
             he d 1927. Eliz. d there 1937. 4 chn: Harry, Fred, George
             and Eunice.
         C4. George Edward Gooldrup, b 1844 Tryon, mar at Bathurst, NB 1873
             Nora Hurley, dau of Patric and Julia McCarthy Hurley, b 1852
             Grande Anse, NB. Carpenter and painter. George d 1924, Nora
             1929 at Bathurst.
         C5. ?
         C6. John Milton Gooldrup, b 1847, mar Dora Good, rem to Mass., 6 chn
     B4. Elizabeth Gouldrup, b Tryon, mar James MacNaught, boat builder, rem
         to northern PEI
     B5. Lydia, b Tryon, mar James Hillson, poss rem from PEI
     B6. Charlotte, b Tryon, mar William Wood, res Tryon, 6 chn
GOURBVILLE?, ---, in Malbaie 1825, from C.I.?
GOUSHON, James, from C.I.? at Brigus, Conc. Bay, Nfld. 1785
GOVER, GOUBERT?, GOUVERT?, Capt. Agent and Merchant from G in Nfld.
    (K. Mathews)
GRAHAM in Nfld. (Seary) Cf Graham of C.I., also in Quebec
GRANDIN, Adolphus, b J?, mar Susan Isabel GALLIE, qv. A dau Alice
    Isabel d 1891, age 6 mos. (GLF) GRANDIN, SEE CHAN.IS.COLLECTION!
GRANDIN, C.I. in Maritimes Fisheries (J.H. Le Breton list)
GRANDY, GRANDIN, from C.I. to Nfld. (Hug. Soc.) (Shortis-Munn) See also
    Seary
GRANDY, Capt. from C.I.? in Nfld. (K. Mathews)
GRANT in Nfld. (Seary) Cf GRANT of J (Stevens)
GRANVILLE, from C.I.?, in Harbour Grace, Nfld. 1700s (Seary; Rev. Ham-
    mond)
GRAY, Susan, b G, dau of Francis Martin Gray and Dorothy Mary Townsend,
    rem to Vancouver, BC, mar Marcel Greffard of the French community in
    Sask, 2 chn (Susan Greffard, Vancouver, BC)
GRAY, Nicholas and Thomas of Carbonear, Nfld. 1676, from C.I.? (Seary)
    Cf GRAY in J 1584 (Stevens)
GREALY, GRESLEY, John, in Hibb's Hole, Nfld. 1783, prob from C.I. (Shor-
    tis-Munn)

GREELEY, LE GRIZZLEY, Joseph, from C.I., settled Ladle Cove, Nfld., drowned 1887 (Seary) Cf LE GRESLEY of C.I.
GREEN, Dorothy, b 1898 First Tower, J, dau of Walter George Green and Mary BISSON, qv. Mar Reginald Victor Cushing, rem to Canada. (Dorothy Cushing, Halifax, NS)
  A1. Donald Bruce Cushing, b 1932 Halifax, NS, mar Lorraine Champagne at RCAF Prot. Chapel, Winn., Man. 1955
    B1. Carole Daphne Cushing, b 1955 Winnipeg, Man.
    B2. Cynthia Denise Cushing, b 1956
    B3. Deborah Louise Cushing, b 1957 Halifax
    B4. Barbara Ann, b 1959   B5. David Bruce Cushing, b 1961
GREEN, from C.I.? to Nfld. (Seary) Cf GREEN of C.I.
GREENSLADE in Nfld. (Seary) Cf GREENSLADE of J 1607 (Stevens)
GREGG, John George, son of John Gregg and Rachel PERCHARD of J, mar 1846 Riviere aux Renards, Gaspe, to Sarah BOND, dau of Pierre Bond and Anne Goudreau (Gallant)
GREGORY, John, b J, 1821-1858, bur St. Peters', Paspebiac, Gaspe (GLF)
GREGORY, Nathan, from C.I., in Little Islands, Bonavista Bay, Nfld. 1860s (Rev. Hammond) See Seary. Cf GREGORY in C.I.
GREGORY, Abraham, and Joseph, in Isle aux Mortes, Nfld. 1860s (Rev. Hammond)
GRESHUE, early form of GUSHUE in Nfld. which see
GRESLEY, see LE GRESLEY
GRIMSHAW, in Ontario, said to be from C.I.
GROOM, William of Alderney, mar Evelyn LIHOU, 1800s. A son. The widow to Toronto after WWI, mar 2. William Manger, 7 chn: Harry, Jack, Arthur, Florence, Lillian, Helen and Marie. Some mar, res Toronto.
GROUCHY, DE GROUCHY, DE GRUCHY, in Nfld. (Seary) Cf DE GRUCHY of C.I.
GROUCHY, DE GRUCHY, from C.I. to Pouch Cove, Nfld. (Shortis-Munn; Rev. Hammond; H.W. Le Messurier)
GROUCHY, Marshall, notable in French history, was a Huguenot in G 1815
GRUCHY, David, b 1822 J, rem to Arichat, NS in 1836, mar Jane Catherine Robertson JEAN, qv., 5 chn (Allan G. Gruchy, College Park, Md.)
  A1. John P., b 1849 D'Escousse, CB, rem later to Vancouver, BC. Mar Henrietta Helen Weeks of Sydney, Mines, NS
    B1. Lewis   B2. Frederick
    B3. David, b 1876, Petit de Grat, CB, settled Vancouver, BC, mar Sadie Ann SAMPSON, qv, of Petit de Grat.
      C1. Seymour   C2. John   C3. Robert
      C4. Allan Garfield, b 1906 Vanc., mar Florence K. Schumacher of Batesville, Ind., 1937, rem to College Park, Md.
        D1. Allan Garfield, b 1942
        D2. Katherine Anne
    B4. Roy   B5. Jenny   B6. Mary
  A2. Philip
  A3. Henrietta, mar Dr. H.C. FIXOTT, qv. of Arichat, NS
  A4. Peter, b ca 1839, mar Sophia McClean
    B1. Elizabeth, mar ---FIOTT, rem to U.S.
      C1. Eric FIOTT
    B2. Aubrey, b ca 1868   B3. William, b ca 1869
  A5. David Jr., mar Eva ---
    B1. Irene Mildred, 1890-1968, res with her aunt, Mrs. FIXOTT, mar Geo. Rice of Liverpool, NS
      C1. Howard Rice, res Liverpool
      C2. William Rice, res Saint John, NB
      C3. Helen Rice, mar Edward MacKinnon, res Brooklyn, NY
GRUCHY, Charles, b 1852, St. Saviour?, J, rem to London, mar Mary Ann

GRUCHY
SEE ALSO DE GRUCHY
HICKS. Rem to Asnieres near Paris, France, as Personnel Mgr. for Redfern Clothiers. Ten chn, all b Asnieres, France, 4 boys, 6 girls, all to Canada. (Lydia Gruchy, White Rock, BC)
A1. Charles Herbert, b 1883, unmar, rem to Strasbourg, Sask 1905, killed in WWI, ca 1915
A2. Edith Mary, b 1885, mar John H. Airey, London, d 1961, 4 sons b Acton, England
  B1. John Airey, mar 1965 Hannah, d 1976
  B2. Stanley Airey, mar 1946 Peggy Fenton
    C1. Jennifer Airey, mar Michael Kidd
      D1. Alisdair Kidd   D2. Fiona Jane Kidd
  B3. Raymond Airey, mar Eve ---
  B4. Maurice Airey, mar Margaret ---
    C1. Anthony Airey, mar Susan Wood
A3. Victor Albert, b 1887, mar Maisie Huggard, who d 1973. Rem to Canada 1903. Homesteaded in Strasbourg, Sask. 5 chn.
  B1. Charles, killed WWII, unmar
  B2. Evelyn, mar Albert Keyser
    C1. Charles Keyser, b 1946, mar Barbara Skagen
      D1. Steven Charles Keyser, b 1969
      D2. De Leigh Keyser, b 1973
  B3. Victor S., mar Beryl G. Strickert, 7 daus.
    C1. Becky Ann or Betty Ann, b 1949, mar Arthur G. Schultz
      D1. Michael Arthur Schultz, b 1974
      D2. Tania Faye Schultz, b 1976
    C2. Esther Mary, b 1955   C5. Arlene, b 1960
    C3. Holly Evelyn, mar Terry Birkan C6. Leona May, b 1962
    C4. Diane Lenore, b 1959   C7. Kathleen Faye, b 1967
  B4. Gordon Arthur, mar Deone Geiger. Gordon, minister in the Yukon, 5 chn.
    C1. Valery Jean, b 1960   C4. Lorelei Deone, b 1964
    C2. Verla Christine, b 1961   C5. Linda May, b 1966
    C3. Richard Graham, b 1963
  B5. May, mar William Johnson, 3 sons
    C1. Byron V. Johnson, b 1954, mar Glenda Krupp
    C2. Miles Alfred Johnson, b 1956 C3. Mark Patrick Johnson, b 1959
A4. Arthur Gordon, b 1889, rem to Strasbourg, Sask, 1955, where he homesteaded. D WWI ca 1916.
A5. Stanley, b 1891, to Canada 1903, d in U.S. 1963. Mar May Southward 1919, res California, 2 daus.
  B1. Dorothy, mar Francis W. Hainley, 5 chn
    C1. Francis William Hainley, b 1942, mar Kathleen Crawford
      D1. Erika Hainley, b 1973 D2. Timothy Francis Hainley, b 1975
    C2. Linda Kathryn Hainley, b 1944, mar Patrick Cullen, 2 sons
      D1. Patrick Russel Cullen, b 1966
      D2. Mathew Francis Cullen, b 1967
    C3. Robert Hainley, b 1951, mar Sally Craig
    C4. Mary Hainley, b 1952, mar Christopher Lubner
    C5. Richard Hainley, b 1955
  B2. Grace, mar Bernard Dunbar, d 1962, 2 sons, mar 2. Jack L'Amoreaux
    C1. Dennis Dunbar, b 1942
    C2. Dale Dunbar, b 1946, mar Kathy Lynn Cherry
A6. Cecile Maud, b 1891, twin of Stanley, mar Walker Woodbridge, England, 3 daus
  B1. Winnie, mar Leslie Arnold, 3 sons, mar 2. Eddie Forde
    C1. Rodney Arnold, b 1942, mar Gay ---
    C2. Clive Arnold, b 1943, mar Rosa Prior, 2 sons

         D1. Anthony Arnold, b 1966   D2. Michael Arnold, b 1967
      C3. Malcolm Arnold, b 1947, mar Karen? ---
   B2. Hilda Woodbridge, mar Charles Banks, 5 chn
      C1. Miriam Banks, b 1942
      C2. Michael Banks, b 1944, mar Sandra Cope, 2 sons
         D1. Richard Banks, b 1968   D2. John Simon Banks, b 1971
      C3. Keith Banks, b 1946
      C4. Terrence Banks, b 1950   C5. David Banks, b 1956
   B3. Doreen Woodbridge, mar Herbert James Ford
      C1. Sally Ford, b 1949, mar Richard Walder
         D1. James Walder, b 1974
      C2. Valery Ford, b 1955
A7. Florence Evelyn, b 1893, rem to Canada 1913, missionary of the
   United Church for 40 years, d 1969, unmar.
A8. Lydia Emelie, b 1894, rem to Canada 1913, United Church minister,
   unmar
A9. Hilda May, b 1897, to Canada 1913, mar Ralph Strudwick, 3 chn
   B1. Ruth Mary Strudwick, b 1919, mar William Dunne, res Eng., d 1969
      C1. Michael Dunne, b 1949, mar Veronica Frost, 2 sons
         D1. James Daniel Dunne, b 1974 D2. Joseph Arthur Dunne, b 1976
      C2. Pamela Dunne, b 1952   C3. Gillian Dunne, b 1957
   B2. Philip Strudwick, b 1920, mar Barbara Stevens, 4 chn
      C1. Sharon Strudwick, b 1946, mar Stewart Black
      C2. Linda Strudwick, b 1947
      C3. Larry Strudwick, b 1947, twin
      C4. Eric Strudwick, b 1949, mar Louvain Chalmers
   B3. Sidney Strudwick, mar Dorothy Stevens, 3 chn
      C1. Gary Strudwick, b 1949, mar Althea Snyder
      C2. Jennifer Strudwick, b 1950, mar Gary Gray
      C3. Carol Anne Strudwick, b 1963
A10. Winnifred Elsie, b 1899, to Canada 1913, mar Wilfred T. Sisson
   B1. Enid Sisson, b 1923, mar Arnold Perry, 2 daus
      C1. Christine Perry, b 1951, mar Rick Baker
      C2. Janice Perry, b 1953
GRUCHY, David, b 1822 J, son of Philip G. and Elizabeth ---, was in Ar-
   ichat 1836-1844. A merchant, and in 1860 P.M., Coroner, J.P., Com-
   missioner. Mar Mary Marshall, dau of John J. Marshall, Speaker of
   the House of Assembly. See BALLEINE, John.
GRUCHY, Rev. Edward, Pastor of the First French Methodist Church, Mon-
   treal. B 1850, J, ordained 1876, mar, 3 chn. (Cochran, MEN OF CANADA)
GRUCHY, Henrietta Maria, 1847-1914, dau of David G. and Jane Catherine
   Robertson JEAN of Descousse, C.B., mar Henry James FIXOTT, M.D. See
   FIXOTT, JEAN.
GRUCHY, George, from J to Gaspe later 1800s. Mar, a son Charles, rem
   to Rainy River, Ont. where he was for a time Mayor.
GRUCHY, John, son of Charles, b 1883 J, rem to Canada 1897, mar Jane
   LE GRAND, qv, b 1886 (Mrs. R.G. Gruchy, St. Hyacinthe, Que.)
A1. Reginald George Gruchy, b 1912, mar Adrienne Jodoin, b 1914, no
   issue
GRUCHY, from C.I. in Richmond Co., NS 1861 (Census)
GRUCHY, from C.I., res in Descousse, C.B., NS
GRUCHY, David, Peter and Philip, shipowners in N.S. 1883, THE LENOX,
   THE JUBILEE, etc. The JUBILEE 34 tons, was built 1887 Port Royal, NS
GRUCHY, Peter, b ca 1839, merchant in Petit de Grat 1871, mar Sophia,
   b ca 1845 N.S. (Census 1871)
A1. Aubrey, b ca 1868   A2. William, b ca 1869
GRUCHY, Philip, O.B.E., was part of a delegation in Nfld. in regard to

GRUCHY   SEE   269
        GRUTE FROM CI TO WINDSOR, ONT.   Q.A. IN N.America.
   joining with Canada as a province.
GRUCHY, a Capt. from J in Nfld. (K. Mathews)
GRUCHY, Mathew, poss the son of a Gruchy in Gaspe, was the cousin of
   Mary Ann LE HUQUET, qv. Their mothers were GALLICHAN sisters, and
   Mathew was raised by the LE HUQUETS from the age of 8. Dau, Lillian,
   b 1873, mar ---QUINN, qv.
GRUCHY, Rachel, from J to Gaspe, mar Jean CABOT, 1800s.
GRUCHY, GROUCHY, DE GRUCHY, Channel Islanders in Conception Bay, Nfld.
   and Pouch Cove. (H.W. Le Messurier; Rev. Hammond; Shortis-Munn)
GUEGAN from C.I. in Ontario?
GUEDARD, Jean, from J to Gaspe (Turcotte, Ste. Foy, Que.)
GUERIN, from C.I. to Gaspe? See in Library of Congress, OUR KIN, by
   Wm. C. Guerin
GUERNIER, Channel Islander in Maritimes Fisheries (J. H. Le Breton list)
GUERNSEY. This C.I. surname in U.S. and Canada, poss from early set-
   tler in the American colonies (See QAAM)
GUGE, Ambrose and John, from C.I.?, in Burgeo, Nfld. 1860s (Rev. Hammond)
GUPPY, in Nfld. (Seary) Cf GOUPY, LE GOUPIL of C.I. (Stevens)
GUIGNON, Mary H., b G, in Gaspe or Sydenham 1861 (Census) with Nicholas,
   Elias, Susan, James, Benjamin, Elvina?, and a baby, all b Gaspe.
GUIGNON, Charles Nicholas, b G, in Gaspe Bay 1861 (Census), poss rela-
   ted to TOUZELS, qv.
GUIGNON, Clarissa, b G?, or of above fam, mar in Gaspe, George James
   LE TOUZEL, qv.   (See GUIGNON in added pages)
GUIGNON, Nicholas, from G to Gaspe, there in 1842 (K.H. Annett)
GUIGNON, Hilaria LE MESURIER, 1844-1924, wife of Nicholas, bur Rose-
   bridge, Gaspe (GLF)
GUIGNON, Nicholas, said to have come in 1842 from G (Curtis Patterson,
   Harrington Harbor, Que.)
GUILBERT, GUIBERT, John and Wm. from C.I. in Harbour Grace, Conc. Bay,
   Nfld. 1860s (Rev. Hammond)
GUILBERT, Gilbert, Capt. from G in Nfld. (K. Mathews)
GUILBERT, Marguerite, Margaret, b ca 1823 or ca 1830 G, mar 1853 Martin
   ROBERT, son of Martin ROBERT, to Canada ca 1874, d London, Ont. 1911,
   age 81. She was the dau of Nico. Guibert, Guilbert?, and ---VARIOUF
   of Forest G. See ROBERT for fam.
GUILLAN, Edward and Michael in Channel, Nfld. 1860s, said to be from
   C.I. (Rev. Hammond)
GUILLARD in Nfld. Cf GUILLIARD, GUILLARD, in Stevens. See Seary for
   GILLARD.
GUILLAUME, see GILLAM, etc. Also see GUILLAN in Gaspe (K.H. Annett)
GUILLE, John, from C.I. in Nfld. 1800s (Brochet)
GUILLE, from G in Nfld. (K. Mathews) Guilles were landowners in G since
   1303.
GUILLE, James and Edward, b G, rem to U.S., d at Newark, Ohio 1845 and
   1853, without issue. Henry Stevens-Guille, related to the above, b
   G, son of Hubert GUILLE, Seigneur of St. George, rem to Western Can-
   ada 1928, mar ---, 4 chn, and grchn. (H. Stevens-Guille, Sidney, BC)
GUILLE, Peter, b Sark, C.I., mar Florence LIHOU, qv, rem to Owen Sound,
   Ont., 5 chn, mar and res Ontario (R.R. Lihou, Cornwall, Ont.)
   A1. Peter A2. Frederick A3. Tillie A4. Lillie A5. Evelyn
GUILLET, John, b St. Heliers, J 1802, son of Charles G. and Marie THOREAU.
   His grandfather, Pierre Thoreau, was the ancestor also of Henry David
   THOREAU, the naturalist. In his youth, John became a clerk for a cod-
   fishery in Nfld. He often became seasick, so rem inland, leaving the
   sea in 1832, going first to Quebec, and then to Cobourg, Ont. where
   he at first worked as a carpenter, both on buildings and on ships.

Three wives, 15 chn. Associated with a Mr. Pierce, and later with his father-in-law, John PAYNE. He worked on the steamer, COBOURG, built in 1833. In 1842 he opened a notion ship, soon expanded to crockery and groceries. John mar 1. Hannah PAYNE, b ca 1810, (one ch); 2. Charlotte Payne, b ca 1806, (4 chn); 3. Sarah Catherine Payne, b ca 1828, (10 chn). (See Edwin Guillet's, THE GUILLET-THOREAU GENE-ALOGY, Toronto, 1971)

A1. Mary Ann, 1834-1914, mar Peter Mitchel 1873. One ch, d.y.
A2. Walter John, 1836-1914
A3. Sarah Hannah, 1838-1911   A5. Charlotte, 1844-1874
A4. George, 1840-1926, mar Annie Bickle A6. son, stillborn
A7. Emma, b 1849, mar Jonathan Pettet 1871, 3 chn, 1 stillborn. Descendants.
A8. Albert, 1852-1868
A9. James, 1854-1885, mar Ernestine Bush, descendants
A10. William, 1856-1880
A11. Charles, 1856, twin, d 1902, descendants
A12. Harriet, 1861-1935, mar Lockburn B. Scott, descendants
A13. Edwin, 1863-1936, mar Lula Kemp, descendants (J.E. Guillet, Toronto, Ont.)
A14. Cephas, 1865-1948, mar Alma Clark 1904, descendants
A15. Elise, 1868-1928

GUILLET, George, b early 1800s J, to Canada as a young man and taught school in Baillieboro, near Peterborough, Ont. In early 1860s, was twp. clerk of Cavan, Ont., mar Mary Ann RUSSELL, 5 chn. He d 1865, bur Cobourg, Ont., widow and 3 chn to Akron, Ohio 1866.

GUITON, ---, from J, curate at Anglican Cathedral, Montreal, later a missionary to India, where he died

GUITON, Emily, sister of above, from J to Montreal, author (Rev. d'Hist)
  BUNTON, Margaret, 1856-1918, bur Corner of the Beach, mar George VIBERT, qv, 1842-1916 .Marg.belongs with BUNTON, p.184.

GUNTON, this fam to Norfolk, England, town of Matishall, to J in the 1700s. Some to Ontario. ERNEST, d 1862, son of John and Eliza Gunton, to Ont. B ca 1842 J. John Russel Gunton, his bro, was b ca 1839 and res Vittoria, Ont. Other Guntons to Wisconsin, Montreal and California.

GUNTON, Robert, mar Perry Austin, dau of Maria Ryerse and John Austin (Ryerson Genealogy)

GUSHUE. This fam found in large numbers in Nfld. and elsewhere in Canada. Original surname prob not Gushue, but poss GUIZIOU, GUIZOT, GASHET, GACHET, GASSET, GOAZIOU. A definitive work on this fam said to be begun by sev Americans, but no genealogy found by compiler. Huguenots Henry and David Gachet in Mass. late 1600s. GASSET and GUSHEE said to be American variants. These may be from the same origin as GUSHUE in Nfld. (Hug. info from New Eng. Reg., Vol. 4) Info below not of first generations in Nfld. Prob the first ones came in 1600s or early 1700s. These fams res Port de Grave, Brigus and Cupids, Nfld. (Rv. Arthur Butler, Corner Brook, Nfld.)

I. GOUSHOU, John, b middle 1700s, res Lower Bacon Cove, s of Brigus in 1775
II. GOUSHOU, James, b not later than 1760, prob related to above John, res 1785 Brigus.
A1. John, mar Grace PERCY, qv. Poss some b in Bristol, England
  B1. James, b 1808, mar Charlotte ---. A son James b 1837.
    C1. James, b 1837
  B2. Thomas, b ca 1806 Bristol, England?, d at 54. Mar Amy MUGFORD, b 1809, d 1845

C1. George   C2. Rachel, b 1832, mar 1855 George Morgan
C3. James John, b 1835, mar ---
   D1. Thomas, mar 1889 Mary Elizabeth Whalen
      E1. Mina   E3. Thomas
      E2. Hazel, mar Thomas COKE, COOKE?   E4. Stewart
   D2. John, Jack, mar Mary BISHOP
      E1. Reuben   E2. Gladys
C4. Naomi Susanna, b 1840, mar 1858 Robert Harland Dawe, b 1833
   D1. William Dawe
   D2. John Gushue Dawe, 1863-1939, mar 1. Joanna Atkins, 1872-1902, 2. Mary Ann Wells SEAWARD, who d 1913, 3.? and 4.?
      E1. Emma Dawe, b 1898, mar Robert Henry Butler, b 1898, d 1972
         F1. Rev. Arthur Melvin Butler, b 1920, mar 1944 Margaret Florence Millen
            G1. Michael Donald Butler, b 1945, mar 1966 Arlene Elizabeth Conner
               H1. Gregory Paul Butler, b 1967
            G2. Robert Eric Dawe Butler, b 1948, mar 1968 Christine Birecki
               H1. Holly Lynn Butler, b 1976
            G3. Alison C. Butler, b 1950, mar 1976 Adrian Zagni
         F2. Vida Blanche, b 1922, mar Robert Craig
      E2. Robert William Dawe, mar Jean Simm
      E3. Christopher Dawe, mar Cassie BUSSEY
         F1. Dorothy Dawe   F3. Roy Dawe
         F2. Irvine Dawe   F4. Evelyn Dawe
      E4. William A. Dawe, b 1909, mar Myrtle Hurley, b 1909
         F1. Audrey Dawe, mar Dr. Spurrell
      E5. Jessie R. Dawe, b 1911, mar Rev. A. Spaeder, who d 1975
         F1. Brenda Spaeder
   D3. Elizabeth, mar 1868 Robert GUSHUE
   D4. George Dawe, mar ---HOYLES
      E1. Robert Hartland Dawe, mar Iris Butler
   D5. Bertha Dawe, mar William PERCEY NORMAN, qv, who drowned in the Seal fishery 1914 (Naomi Taylor, Toronto, Ont.)
      E1. Naomi NORMAN, mar Ernest TAYLOR, 1927. He d 1976.
         F1. Vida Pearl Taylor, b 1927, mar Geoffrey Gavin 1961
            G1. Kathryn Rose Gavin   G2. Margaret Ellen Gavin
         F2. Ruby Lillian Taylor, b 1932, mar James BROWN 1956
            G1. David James Brown   G2. Linda May Brown
         F3. Ralph Norman Taylor, b 1938, mar Marian Levy 1970
            G1. Serena Taylor
         F4. Ernest John Taylor, b 1950, mar Olga Furgeson 1975
      E2. John Norman, mar Jean Butler
      E3. Annie Pearl Norman, b 1905
      E4. John Clarence Norman, b 1912, d 1977
   D6. Sarah Dawe, mar John Spooner
      E1. Clarence H. Spooner, mar Mabel Johnston, d 1975
         F1. Joan Spooner, mar Ronald Bark
         F2. Ruth Spooner, mar Warren Scott
   D7. Mary Dawe, mar ---Serrick   D8. Eliza Dawe, mar William Taylor
B3. Ann, b 1810   B7. Mary, b ca 1823
B4. Elizabeth, b 1811   B8. Stephen, bp 1825
B5. Charles, b 1813   B9. Charlotte, bp 1826
B6. John, b 1816
A2. James, mar Ann Spracklin
   B1. Susanna, b 1812

A3. Mary, mar Thomas Spracklin
   B1. James Spracklin, b 1813   B2. Mary Ann Spracklin, b 1814
A4. George, mar Elizabeth ---
   B1. George, bp 1825   B2. Ann, bp 1826
GUSTIN, from J to New England. See QAAM by Turk, some in Canada.
GUY, James and Julio, said to be from C.I. in Carbonear, Nfld. 1860s
   (Rev. Hammond)
GUY. Edward LE GUY AND CO., J firm in Nfld. early 1700s. Cf GUY in G
   and J (Stevens)
HACAULT, Capt. from J in Nfld. (K. Mathews)
HACHE from C.I.? to Canada. Cf BAILHACHE in various forms.
HACKETT, HAGGETT, some in Canada, variants of HAGUAIS and HACQUOIL of
   C.I.
HACKING in Nfld. (Seary) See HACKETT, qbove
HACOU, Pierre, poss HACQUOIL, commis in Pokemouche, NB 1800s (Donat
   Robichaud) Also as ACOU in Gaspe (Brochet)
HACQUOIL, Walter, from J, d Nova Scotia 1971, related to ECOBICHON,
   George, qv. HACQUOIL, MANY IN BATHURST, CAMBELLTON AREA NOW.
HACQUAIL, HACQUOIL, Peter, in Gaspe 1826, also in Dalhousie, NB?
HACQUOIL, fam from St. John, J, the mother named Amelia. The father,
   Capt. H., drowned in storm on voyage between Jersey and Gaspe 1800s.
   Many variants of this name, as HARQUAIL.
HACQUOIL, Jean in Gaspe 1781 (Syvret) A John, age 52, res Gaspe 1871.
   (Census)   HARQUAIL, Edouard, SEE ADDED PAGES.
HACQUOIL, Wm., signed the Gaspe Petition 1820
HACQUOIL, Francis, b ca 1819 J, in Gaspe 1861 (Census) Also listed by
   J.H. Le Breton, Farmer.
HACQUOIL, Philip, b 1813 J, in Perce 1861 (Census; Cent. Bklt.) Poss
   this was the carpenter in Perce who mar Elizabeth LENFESTY, b 1819
   Perce, dau of James L. and Susannah. He d 1871, age 57. His wife
   was then 52, b Que., and Philip Jr. was 15. (Brochet)
HACQUOIL, from C.I. in Nfld., changed surname to HAWCOE (Shortis-Munn)
HACQUOIL in Nfld. (Seary)
HAFEY in Nfld. (Seary) Cf HAFEY of J (Stevens)
HAGGETT, poss HAGUAIS of J? Job and Joseph at Harbour Mille, Nfld.
   1877 (Rev. Hammond)
HAINS, Francois, from J, captured by Indians in Maine and taken to Que.
   See QAAM by Turk (Coleman)
HAINS, HAYNES in Nfld. (Seary) Cf HAINS of J 1607 (Stevens)
HAKE from C.I. to Gaspe
HALENAN, Capt. from J in Nfld. (K. Mathews)
HALLETT in Nfld. (Seary) Cf HALLETT of J
HAMEL, see DU HAMEL
HAMELIN, from C.I. to Canada?
HAMEN in Nfld. (Seary) Cf HAMON in J 1607 (Stevens)
HAMMOND, John Elias, Sr., father of Hammond, below. Was b 1781, and d
   in St. Fabian's Parish, Quebec, bur at Riviere de Loup.
HAMMOND, John Elias, b 1807 J, drowned 1859 at Biquet Lighthouse near
   Bic Island. Mar Elizabeth LANGLOIS, qv of Gaspe, 1834. John's fa-
   ther, also John Elias, was b 1781, d 1850 St. Fabien Par, Que., bur
   at Riv. du Loup, at the side of his grandson, George Douglas Hamon.
   (Wm. Goss, Ipswich, Mass.; Hammond Bible)
A1. John Francis, mar Elizabeth LE LACHEUR, qv, Quebec City 1852?, prob
   dau of John Henry LE LACHEUR, qv, and Elizabeth RIPPEY. John Fran-
   cis prob b 1837 J.
   B1. Elizabeth Rose, mar ---Cook, b 1862 Quebec, PQ, desc.
   B2. Elinor Victoria, b 1865   B3. John Francis, b 1867

HAMMOND 273

A2. Elizabeth Elanore, b 1835 Gaspe, d 1839, christened by Rev. Arnold, godfather. Godmother was LEONORE BENEST, qv, and Louisa LE MESSURIER, qv.
A3. George Douglas, b 1840 at Lighthouse on S.W. pt. of Anticosti Is. Godfather, George SOHIER, qv, and Miss Richards, godmother. He d 1850.
A4. Charles T., b 1847 Isle of Biquet Lighthouse
A5. poss other chn
HAMMOND, John, fam from C.I., res Portugal Cove, Nfld. 1793,4. One son, plus 3 or more daus. (Census; Rev. Hammond, Bell Island, Nfld.)
I. Judith Hammond, mar George Stone 1786, Portugal Cove, Nfld.?
II. Sarah Hammond, mar George Quigley 1797 Protugal Cove?, Nfld.
III. Elizabeth, first dau?, mar John Harvey of Portugal Cove 1782
IV. Mary, mar Charles Brown, Portugal Cove 1783
V. John
A1. Peter, mar Elizabeth SQUIRES, qv, 1801
 B1. John, bp 1802
 B2. Thomas, b between 1803 and 1810, mar Alice Neary
  C1. Stephen, b 1834   C5. William
  C2. Peter   C6. James, b 1844
  C3. Ann   C7. Philip, b 1848
  C4. Mary
 B3. William, b between 1803 and 1810, mar Mary Churchill 1833
  C1. Peter, d 1909, mar Sophia Squires, qv, 1837-1909
   D1-9. William, Eli, Elijah, Andrew, Elizabeth, Martha, Lavina, Jane, Belinda
  C2. John, b 1834, mar Belinda Hanlon, 1839-1888. John d 1924.
   D1. Henry, 1871-1943, mar Sarah Mitchell
   D2. Thomas, 1875-1946, mar Lucy HARDING, 1882-1948
    E1. Henry, b 1900   E5. Victor, b 1912   E9. Thomas
    E2. Wm. John, b 1902   E6. George   E10. Violet
    E3. Walter, b 1905   E7. Clarence   E11. Sadie
    E4. Frederick   E8. Peter
  C3. Thomas, 1835-1919, unmar
  C4. Henry, b 1840, d 1915. Mar Sarah Somerton, 1855-1937
   D1. through D10.: William James, Richard, George, Ambrose, Michael, Peter, Nellie, Ann Heath, Elizabeth, Helen.
HAMMOND, Joseph, b J, in Gaspe Bay 1861 (Census)
HAMMAND, Asa, from C.I.? in Yarmouth, NS 1773 (Lost In Canada)
HAMON, from C.I. to Gaspe, Perce, Paspebiac, Newport, Barachois, etc. (Census; Brochet; etc.)
HAMON, Capt. Daniel, a privateersman in 1799
HAMON, from J to Gaspe (Syvret; Bechard; Wilson; Bourgaize and Le Breton lists)
HAMON, Philip, from J in Paspebiac in 1767, fisherman for Chas. Robin's firm (Revue d'Hist) Philip had grant at Newport, Gaspe 1819.
HAMON, Philip and Eliz. from C.I.? to Newport, Gaspe (Census 1861)
 A Harriet LE FEUVRE was res with them at that time. Chn b Canada (GLF)
A1. Emma
A2. Alice, b J?, mar Stannis Edward HUE, qv from J ca 1880, res New Carlisle Que.
A3. Robert
A4. Lydia, mar John James VIBERT, qv, rem to Montreal A5. Emily
HAMON, Charles, in Gaspe 1861 (Census)
HAMON, Philip Syvret, b 1852 St. Ouen J, d Truro, NS 1927, mar Eva Stow TUZO, qv., 1865-1947, bur St. Paul, Perce. Poss son of Philip S. Hamon of Newport, Gaspe.

(This Francis of Petit Hurel,St.Ouen,Jersey)
HAMON, Francis, b J, son of Francis HAMON and Lydia Ann LE FEUVRE, qv.
Francis Jr. worked for Robin firm, d in N.S. 1918 age 20 (GLF)
HAMON, curr Barachois, Gaspe. Hamon, John E., of Shiphead mar Eliz.
LANGLOIS, a dau, Elizabeth Eleanor, b 1835. (Ch. records)
HAMON, Jean, b Sark, in Perce 1861 (Census)
HAMON, Marie, b J, in Perce 1861 (Census)
HAMON, John, in Malbaie 1831, age 54, with wife Marie, b J, age 33
HAMON, John, b J, age 66, in Bonaventure Island 1871 with wife Jane, b
    J, age 39 (Census)
HAMON, Thomas, the father? of Capt. Jacques Hamon who in 1831 bought cod
    for Fruing Co. He was b 1834 J, son of Thomas. Mar, but wife in J.
    She d and Thomas mar 2. Annie Lawlor, b Cork, Ireland. Ann was a
    telegrapher, well educated. Mar ca 1878 despite her father's strong
    objections. Adopted John Ryan, a relative, when he was about 9 yrs.
    old. Couple retired to North Devon, Frederickton, NB. Thomas d 1921,
    wife in 1930, both bur Sunnybank, Frederickton, NB. No issue.
    (Robichaud)
HAMON, Jean, son of Edward H. and Betsy LE BRETON of J, mar 1827 Angele
    Robichaud, who d 1875. Res N.B. (Robichaud)
HAMON, a fishery firm established at Newport, Gaspe, with his fam ca
    1830 (Wilson)
HAMON, HAMMOND, merchants from C.I. in Nfld. (K. Mathews)
HAMON, Patience, in Canada 1711
HAMON, Reginald, a city worker, in Vancouver before 1900 (Luce)
HAMON, from G to PEI early 1870s?
HAMON, John David, b 1872 St. Heliers, J, mar Emily LE PREVOST, qv, b
    1872 Vale, G. Rem to Canada ca 1902, returned to G with Sidney 1940,
    where John David d ca 1937. Emily and Sidney were evacuated to Eng.
    WWII, and Emily d there ca 1944. (Judy Ogletree, London, Ont.; Ed-
    win Hamon, Chatham, Ont.)
A1. Eva Emily, b 1902, d England
A2. Edwin John, b 1903, to Canada, mar Evelyn F. M. Grimwood
A3. John William, b 1904, to Canada, mar Florence Jones, b 1910. He
    d 1955
    B1. Frances Sue, b 1933, d 1940
    B2. Judith Ann, b 1938, mar John Ogletree, res London, Ont.
        C1. Heather, b 1962   C2. Michael Ogletree, b 1965
A4. Francis, b 1906, d 1920
A5. Arthur, b 1908, d 1918
A6. Sidney, b 1910, res Cambridge, Eng., mar Ruby Forsdyke, 2 chn
HAMPTON in Nfld. (Seary) Cf HAMPTON in J 1668-1749 (Stevens)
HANDY, to Gaspe from C.I.? (Poss--Bourgaize)
HANDY, John, b J, in Gaspe 1861 (Census) With Jane LE MESURIER, John,
    Thomas, and Jane, all b Gaspe
HANDY, HANDEY, Lucy Niles, b 1874, mar Adolphus COLLAS, qv. She d 1955
    Cap aux Os, Gaspe (GLF)
HARCOE, see HAWCOE, HACQUOIL, etc. See ADDITIONS & CORRECTION PP.
HARQUAIL, Peter, from C.I.? at Dalhousie, NB 1826
HARQUAIL, HACQUOIL, HALQUOIL, Peter from J to U.S.?
HARQUAIL, HACQUOIL, Walter J. and Winnifred R. of Malbaie, 1800s? (Cent.
    Bklt.)
HARDY, Admiral, from J, see story of LOUISBOURG
HARDY, Thomas, b J 1787, d 1869 Nouvelle, Quebec (GLF) bur St. Peter's,
    Paspebiac?
HARDY in Nfld. (Seary) Edward in St. John's 1750. Cf HARDY, LE HARDY
    in J (Stevens)

HARDY, LE HARDY 275

HARKER. see ADDITIONS AND CORRECTIONS PAGES.
HARPER, Anthony, in Nfld. (Seary) Cf HARPER in J 1607 (Stevens)
HARRINGTON, Capt. from G in Nfld. (K. Mathews)
HARRIS, from C.I. in Maritimes Fisheries (J. H. Le Breton list)
HARRY, John Edmund from G to Wellington, NZ before WWI, descendants
HARVEY in Nfld. (Seary) Cf HARVEY in J (Stevens) George H. from J at Isle aux Morts. LE ARVIE, Philip, in St. Georges Bay, Nfld. 1819 (Seary)
HASKELL in Nfld. (Seary) Cf HASKELL of C.I. and HACQUOIL of J (Stevens)
HASKETT, from C.I. to Canada?
HATCHER, Annie Nellie, b 1890 St. Peter Port, G, mar in Toronto 1922 Hubert Marshall, b Belfast, Ire., who d 1940. Res Winnipeg, Man. (Pat Carmichael, Winnipeg, Man.)
  A1. Patricia Nina Marshall, b 1923, mar 1946 Wm. George Carmichael
    B1. Richard Wm. Carmichael, b 1953 Winnipeg
    B2. Debra Ann Carmichael, b 1955, mar 1974 David Brent Millar
HAVILAND, HAVILLAND, DE HAVILLAND, etc., most if not all of this surname in N.A. have their origin in a Norman fam that settled very early in Guernsey. In 1497, Thomas De Haviland served at the recovery of Mont Orgueil, Jersey. Of 2 sons, Thomas and James, Thomas d without issue, but James of St. Martins, G, had issue and his descendants rem to England, then in the 1600s to N.A. The Havilands of PEI are from Cirenchester, England, desc of Thomas Heath Haviland, b 1797, who settled there. In 1815 he mar Jane Rebecca Brecken, dau of Ralph Brecken, speaker of the House of Assembly in PEI. His son of the same name, a distinguished public official, was b in Charlottetown, PEI 1822. The Havilands of Norfolk Co., Ont., are an offshoot of the Havilands from G to England in the 1600s, who settled in the American colonies. Some Torreys and Hardings of the American colonies are also descendants of the Havilands on the female side. See HAVILAND GENEALOGY, by Josephine Frost, N.Y., 1914.
HAVILAND, HAVILLAND, DE HAVILAND, etc., surname of C.I. on S coast of Nfld. (G. W. Le Messurier)
HAWCOE, see HACQUOIL. C.I. name in Nfld. Curr in Stephensville, Nfld.
HAWKINS, surname connected to C.I. fams in N.S. and Nfld., etc. Origin unverified .SEE LE LACHEUR & SALLY LOMAS DATA IN CIFHS # 25.
HAWLEY, a G merchant in area of St. Heber, to Bonne Bay, Nfld. 1800s (Mannion)
HAYDEN, Sophia, d 1915 age 79, res Gaspe, origin unverified (GLF)
HAYE in Nfld. (Seary) Cf DE LA HAYE of J (Stevens)
HAYNES, W.J., b 1882 J, son of Sgt. Haynes of St. Brelade, b Northumberland, England, and --- MISSON, of J. W.J. mar Eunice TEOFAIR, dau of George T. and of Amelia HACQUOIL, qv, of St. Johns, J. Her father was drowned between J and Gaspe in the days of sail. To Canada 1894, wife in 1914. Rem 1903 to Lethbridge, Alta., res Vancouver and Edmonton, Alta.
HEAD, either Wm. Joshua Head or his dau left G for Canada in 1905. He was 87 yrs. old in 1977, has grandson Mark Rose in Calif. (G. Soc. Bull., Feb. 1978)
HEANEY in Nfld. (Seary) Cf HENEY of J (Stevens)
HEAUME, sev in Canada, prob from C.I. See also DU HEAUME
HELLEUR, Stanley, b J, mar his cousin Lillian LE RICHE, res Montreal
  A1. Stanley   A2. Irene   A3. Dorothy
HELLEUR, Sidney, b J, rem to Montreal, d 1900s, no issue
HELLEUR, from C.I. in Maritimes Fisheries (J.H. Le Breton list) Some to Cape Breton   HELLEUR, SEE ADDED PAGES.
HELLIER, HELIER, Rachel, b 1831 G, to Cape Breton at 8 yrs. where she

mar George N. LE LACHEUR 1852. They had at least 10 chn. Her father was a ship owner who lost a fortune in ships in the gale of 1873. She d 1890, age 59. One son, George, was b in Cape Breton 1863, d in Danvers, Mass. 1955, age 92. (Goss)
HELLIER, HILLYER, etc., from C.I. to Nfld. (See Seary)
HEMERY, Clement of J, 1811-1877, mar Portia Owen of Cape Bello Island, NB, and visited there 1842. A record of their voyage in 1842 to New York and then to N.B. is contained in a diary, reprinted in the Societe Jersiaise Bull, of some years back. The document belongs to a fam residing in England, a connection of the Hemery fam.
HENDERSON, G.H., from C.I.?, in Victoria, BC 1940 (Luce)
HENRY, an old G surname sometimes changed to HARRIS, qv. (Carey-Wimbush)
HENRY, John, signed the Gaspe Petition 1820, also Amasteur, a son? Origin unverified. A John Henry b G, d 1839 Gaspe.
HENRY, C.I. in Maritimes Fisheries (J.H. Le Breton list; K.H. Annett)
HENRY, James, from J to Shippegan, NB mid 1800s? (Robichaud)
HENRY in Nfld. (Seary) Cf HENRY in J (Stevens) SEE HENRY IN
HENRY, Elizabeth, mar James HERAULT?, Perce, ca 1830 ADDED PAGES
HENRY, James, b ca 1817 J, mar ca 1843 Elizabeth, Betsy, Sara Edwards, Londonian of Welsh ancestry. James was from 1845-1895 master ship builder for Wm. Fruing Co. at Pte. des Alexandre, Shippegan, NB. He d there 1902. In 1843 a Le Mesurier of J was the ship builder there, but died accidentally, leaving a badly needed ship unfinished. Henry finished the ship and replaced Le Mesurier. He finally persuaded his wife to leave J and settle with him in Canada, 1847. After a dreadful passage, she never wanted to go aboard ship again. She was Anglican, tolerant, and had a knowledge of folk medicine. He d 1899, age 82. She d 1902, age 82, bur Prot. Cem., Shippegan. (Donat Robichaud, Beresford, NB)
A1. James, b J, educated London, to Canada, age 21, said to speak 5 languages. Worked for the Mann Co. at Grand Anse, NB, and for Fruing at Caraquet and in Inkerman. In 1892 he bought land from Thomas CABOT. D unmar 1929, age 83.
A2. George, b 1856 Pt. Alex., NB, educated J, farmer, d unmar 1929
A3. Phoebe, b ca 1859, mar Georges GODIN (Cf GAUDIN of C.I.)
A4. Alice, b ca 1862, her fiance drowned, she d unmar
A5. William, b 1865, mar ---Duguay, who d.y., leaving a son John, who d 1932
 B1. John, mar Exilda Guignard of Lamaque, NB. He d Caraquet 1970, leaving fam of Anita, Freddie, Roger, Will, Louis, Odette, Normand and Rheal.
HERAULD, Jean, with Charles ROBIN at Miramichi 1767 (Donat Robichaud)
HERAULT, George, b ca 1861 J, clerk at Petit de Grat, CB 1871 (Census) Cf L'HERAULT of J
HERIOT, Major Gen., Frederick George, C.B., b 1786 J, age 15 obtained commission as Ensign in 49th Reg't. In 1802 his reg't was sent to Canada. See THE ISLANDERS IN CANADA, NOTABLES, page 31.
HENRY, Wm., b ca 1765 CI? res near Parrsboro, NS, mar Amy MOSHER, poss MAUGER?, ship builder, 10 chn. (Mrs.T. Crawford, Dallas, TX) CHN: Elias, Allen, Wm., Charles, Esther, Phoebe, Lurana, Fanny, Temperance and Mary. In 1826 to Grand Manan Is.,NB. He d 1828.

HERITAGE, Douglas Spencer, b J?, ca 1871, mar Mary Eaton, rem from J to Toronto, Ont. ca 1900. A son, Howard Percival Heritage. (T. Heritage, Toronto, Ont.)
HERIVEL, see LE CLERCQ
HERON in Nfld. (Seary) Cf HERON of J (Stevens)
HERPE, Claude and Rita from G to London, Ont. 1900s?
HERRALD, Rebecca, from C.I.? in Harbor Grace, Nfld. 1806. Cf HERAULT in J (Stevens)
HERRO in Nfld. (Seary) Cf HERAULT, HERALD of J
HEULIN, HEULAN, see HUELIN
HEWITSON, James, b ca 1846 J, in Perce 1871 (Census)
HIBBERT in Nfld. (Seary) Cf HUBERT, HEBERT of J (Stevens)
HIBERT, John, signed the Gaspe Petition 1820
HIBBS. This fam in Nfld. (Seary) Some thought to be from C.I. Many intermarried with those from C.I. (Rev. Hammond)
HIBBS, Henry, res Upper Island Cove, Nfld. 1763. In Portugal Cove, his fishing room was taken by Gregory NORMORE, qv, in 1769 (Rev. Hammond)
HIBBS, George, witness at wedding of Peter HAMMOND in 1801
HICKS in Nfld. (Seary) Cf HICKS in J 1668 (Stevens)
HILL in Nfld. (Seary) Cf HILL of C.I.
HILLIER, Maj. George, ADC of Sir Peregrine Maitland, Lt. Gov. of Upper Canada 1812-1828. A township in PEI named for him. He mar the dau of James Givens.
HILLIER, Daniel, a Methodist missionary in 1821 at St. Marmands, Que.
HILLIER, to Nfld. from the C.I. (Hug. Soc.) Curr Stephenville, Nfld.
HILLYARD, Jerseyman to N.B. fisheries
HILLYARD, Lawrence, in Fermeuse, Nfld. 1681, from C.I.? (Seary)
HOBBS, from G to B.C. (E.M. Renouf)
HOCQUARD, also spelled HOCART, HOCQUART
HOCARD, HOCQUARD, Osmond, b G, rem to Western Canada late 1800s, homesteaded next to Arthur LE PATOUREL. Hocart returned to G after a few years, selling to his neighbor.
HOCQUARD, John, b 1815 J?, d 1887, bur St. Peters, Paspebiac. Mar 1841 Mary GALLIE, 1822-1889. A John, age 55 in 1871, b J, res Cox, Que.
HOCQUARD, Francis, b ca 1850 Gaspe, mar Eliza   DU VAL, dau of Philip DU VAL & Marg.Smith. SEE EXTRA PAGES.
HOCQUARD, Berta, 1885-1951, wife of E. Woodburne SHEPHERD, 1885-1943, bur St. Andrews, New Carlisle, Gaspe (GLF)
HOCQUARD, Philip, b 1869 J, wife Annie TENNIER, 1873-1948, bur United Ch., West Paspebiac (GLF)
HOCQUARD, James, b 1871, d 1953, wife Ella ---, b 1888   d 1962
HOCQUARD. Stella, of Cape Cove, Gaspe, mar Ernest Reginald Cass, 1900-
Hocquard, John, b J, d 30 Mar.1887, bur St.Peters, Gaspe. His wife Mary d 13 June 1889.
HOCQUARD, Frank J.1873-1944,wife Aug.BarbaraSmith,1880-1943
HOCQUARD, George M., 1907-1948, husband of Laura MUNRO
HOCQUARD, John and Philip, in the Gaspe Militia 1850s (McWhirter, Rev. d'Hist)
HOCQUARD, C.I. in Gaspe and Maritimes (listed by Betty Tardif and J. H. Le Breton)
HOCQUARD, Mary Jane LE GALLAIS, said to have rem from Gaspe to Alpena, Mich.
HOCQUARD, Francis, had a Crown grant of 214 acres at Arichat, Cape Breton, NS (PANS)

HOCQUARD, Capt. and agent from J in Nfld. (K. Mathews)
HODDINOTT in Nfld. 1827 (Seary) Cf HODINET in J 1340
HODGE, tradesman from J in Nfld. (K. Mathews)
HODGE, C.I. in Maritimes Fisheries (J.H. Le Breton list)
HOLLETT, Philip, from C.I. in Burin, Nfld. 1860s (Rev. Hammond)
  Four Hollet Bros. came from Guernsey Island and settled on the South
  coast of Nfld. in the 1700s. Reuben Hollet was b Nfld. 1854, mar
  1880, Mary Amelia Bonnell?, b 1855 Nfld., d 1931 Halifax. He d 1926
  Halifax.
  A1. James Herbert Inkpen, b 1882 Great Burin, Nfld., mar 1911, Mabel
    Aliez E. BRUSHETT, qv, 1885-1953. They both d in Lethbridge, Alta.
    B1. May Aliez Hollett, b 1912, Fort Pitt, Sask, mar 1942 Thomas
      Patrick BOLGER
HOLLEY, William in Nfld. 1764 (Seary) Cf HOLLY in J (Stevens)
HOLMAN, HOLEMAN, byboat keeper from G in Nfld. (K. Mathews)
HOLMES, C.I. in Maritimes Fisheries (J.H. Le Breton list)
HOLTON, Joseph, b ca 1845 J, in Perce 1871
HOMER, from C.I.? to Nfld. (Seary) Cf HOMMART in J 1668 (Stevens) See
  also QAAM, by Turk
HOOKEY, LEHUQUET, HOCQUET, LE HOUGUEZ? in Nfld. Merchant from J (K.
  Mathews)
HOOPER in Nfld. (Seary) Cf HOOPER from C.I. (Saunders)
HOPIN, HOUPIN, HOPKINS, Aupin, a shoemaker, b G, son of Jean H. and
  Marguerite VIDAMOUR of G, mar 1843 Grande Rivere, Gaspe, Caroline
  COLLINS, b Canada, dau of Jean C. and Marthe Rail (Gallant) Samuel's
  name sometimes spelled HOPKINS. Cf HORPIN in G, old. All chn b
  Canada. This surname now appears as AUPIN in Gaspe. (Brochet)
A1. Jeanne Marguerite, b Gr. Riv. 1844   A5. Mary
A2. Honore Samuel, b 1845   A6. Esther
A3. Caroline, b 1848   A7. Martha
A4. Jean Baptiste, b 1850   A8. Philomena
HOPEN in Nfld. (Seary) Cf HOPIN, HOUPIN of J (Stevens) and HORPIN of
  G, old
HORMAN, C.I. in Maritimes Fisheries (J.H. Le Breton list; Turk)
HORNE, in Canada, some formerly LE CORNU of J
HORRELL in Nfld. (Seary) Philip HORRELL from C.I. in Buck Cove, Nfld.
  1788. Cf LE HUREL of J (Stevens)
HOSKING, Emma, b 1828, St. Heliers, J, mar ---DAVIS, qv, rem to Canada
  1912 with dau, Mary Rodda. Lived to be 102 yrs. old, d Edmonton,
  Alta. 1930
HOSKING, ---, from J to Gold Rush 1849, in California
HOSKING, another bro, missionary to India
HOTTON. Prob all those in Gaspe are desc of a fam or more of this name
  who possibly came from J in the early 1800s. List below is by year
  of birth, where known.
HOTTON, John, b ca 1797 J, farmer, with wife, Marie, b Quebec, at Mal-
  baie early 1800s (Brochet; Census) Poss a son, John, b ca 1826, who
  d 1916, age 90 (GLF)   See GASNIER
HOTTON, Victoria, 1858-1946, of Gaspe
HOTTON, Edward, b ca 1860, res Malbaie, a son, Sydney, d 1921 (GLF)
  Had wife Elizabeth? 1873-1957, nee LAWRENCE, qv.
HOTTON, Edith, 1862-1951, mar Alphonse LE GRESLEY, qv.
HOTTON, William Duncan, 1862-1952, poss mar Maria D., 1872-1940
HOTTON, George Charles, 1866-1944. This may be the one who is bur at
  St. Peters, Malbaie, Gaspe. Mar Annie---, had two sons, one d 1895,
  one d in 1897.
HOTTON, Charles, 1875-1960, mar Mary JOHNSON, 1875-1960, res Malbaie.

Other Hottons listed by GLF in JERRI JADIS, pp. 141-142, relationship not known.
HOUGUEZ. An Alderney fam of this name looked after the beacon lights on Casquet Islands, C.I. ca 1800, man and wife and their 6 chn.
HOUSE, HOWSE in Nfld. (Seary) Cf HOUZE in J, early (Stevens)
HOWARD in Nfld. (Seary) Cf HOWARD of J (Stevens) Edw. in New Perlican, Nfld.
HOWELL, HONEL, HORRELL, from C.I. to Nfld. (Rev. Hammond)
HOWLETT, James, in Nfld. (Seary) Poss from C.I. Cf HOLLETT.
HOYLES, fam in St. Clements, J early 1800s. Sev rem to Canada and U.S. See QUIET ADVENTURERS. Chn of John HOYLES and ANNE LE CORNU of J:
A1. Mary Anne, b 1822 J, mar Peter LE CORNU, rem to Gaspe, then Mich., at least 38 descendants
A2. Nancy, b 1824 J, rem to Ont., wife of John MACHON, qv, 85 desc
A3. John, b 1825, d after 1869
A4. Esther, b 1828, d 1900, rem to Ont. 1865, mar Thompson, 1 ch, d.y.
A5. Philippe Wm., b 1830
A6. Jane Esther Hoyles, dau of second wife, Marie BERTRAM of J, d 1850
A7. Wm. John, b 1838, mar Susan HENRY, res Jersey, dau, Matilda Ellen
A8. Helier John, b 1840, d.y.
A9. Elizabeth, b ca 1841, d 1935, bur Montreal. Mar McWhinney, poss a son, George.
A10. Rachel
A11. James, b 1845?, mar Elvina ---, rem to Chicago, where name is HOILES in census, desc
A12. Eleanor Ann, b 1849 J, d 1870 J
A13. and A14. Unknown
A15. Jane, b 1851, mar J.E. FALLE, qv, b 1850 J. Rem to Montreal, 62 desc plus.
HOYLES, Rev. Wm., in Carbonear, Nfld. 1800s. (TOCQUE, NFLD AS IT WAS)
HOYLES, in Ferryland, Nfld. 1843 (Seary)
HUARD, Mrs. Rose, res Bear Island, Western Canada 1963, has grandchn Nora, Pat, Penny or Kenny, Marilyn Ross, and poss a Gerald and Roy. (Lloydminster Times, Sask.)
HUARD, from C.I. in Gaspe 1781 (Syvret)
HUARD in Gaspe Militia 1850s (McWhirter)
HUARD, Samuel, b J?, mar Genevive AHIER, qv, of Gascons, Gaspe 1800s (Census)
A1. Edmond   A3. Alphonse   A5. Emelie   A7. Marie Martha
A2. Alfred   A4. Samuel   A6. Isabelle
HUBERT, Edward John, b 1856 St. Lawrence, J, son of Edward H. and Carterette Susanne BAUDAINS, qv, mar Susan Newman, rem to Paspebiac, Que. where chn were born. (Wm. David Hubert, Dalhousie, NB)
A1. Harry Jack, b 1884, mar Florine Doberty 1916, d 1948
  B1. Gifford Allison, b 1917, mar Emily Clowater, res Frederickton, NB
    C1. Peter, res Vancouver, BC   C3. Harry, res Frederickton, NB
    C2. Emily, res St. Stephen, NB   C4. Daniel, res Frederickton, NB
  B2. Isobel Alma, b 1919, mar Herbert BISSON, res Port Daniel, Que.
    C1. David Charles BISSON, res Montreal, Que.
    C2. Nancy Bisson, res Frederickton, NB
  B3. Mary Elise, b 1921, mar Frank Caldwell, res Campbellton, NB, no issue
  B4. Harry Edward, b 1923, mar Ruth Hofman, res St. Catherines, Ont.
    C1. Laura, res St. Catherines   C2. Elise
  B5. William David, b 1927, mar Joanne VINCENT, res Charlo, NB
    C1. Wendy, res Charlo, NB
A2. Gifford, unmar, d WWI   A3. Elsie, mar Earl Hill

A4. Mildred, mar Charles KING, res N.Y. state
A5. Lydia, mar Allan Ledingham, res Saint John, NB
HUBERT, Nicholas, was a sponsor at birth of Charles VARDON's son in Gaspe, 1840s
HUBERT, Capt. Clement, b late 1700s, J. During the French Revolution, while still a teenager, he is said to have brought many Frenchmen across the Channel to England, and was offered land in Arichat as a reward. He mar twice, had sev chn. He and his son-in-law, or grandson, Hubert Harrington of Sydney, owned sev ships, the HARRIET, the SEAFLOWER, and poss a hotel, the Caledonia House, and other N.S. enterprises. His first wife may have been a J or G girl. His second wife was said to be a Murchison from Inverness, Scotland, from a family that settled in Grand Riviere, Que.?, and spoke Gaelic. The dau of Hubert and ---Murchison was named Arabella, and fam trad says that she danced with the Prince of Wales when he made his visit to Canada ca 1860. A granddau of Clement was b in 1855. (Mrs. V. McDonald, Medicine Hat, Alta.; Stephen White, Moncton, N.B.) Capt. Clement may have had other chn by first wife.
A1. John, merchant at Arichat in partnership with his father until 1837, when he d, age 26. Mar Ann FIXOTT, qv, b ca 1809 J, d 1892 Arichat, age 83.
  B1. Mary Elizabeth, bp 1833 St. John's, Arichat, d 1921, mar 1852 William Reynolds Cutler, son of Hon. Robert Molleson C. and Sophia Reynolds, b 1822 Guysboro, NS. Seven chn; a dau mar W.H. PAINT, qv, of Hawkesbury, NS (David Hubert, Dalhousie, NB)
  B2. Clement Fixott, bp 1834, d at Halifax 1869, age 35. Grocer at Arichat 1864.
HUBERT, Philippe, worked for Fruings firm at Grande Valley, Gaspe 1800s
HUBERT, Francis John, b 1877 St. Mary, J, then res St. Peter?, J. Rem to Edmonton, Alta. 1908 with wife, Selina Alexandria BLAMPIED, qv, b 1877? He d Nelson, BC 1957. (Geo. Lempriere, Rexdale, Ont.)
A1. Francis John, b 1902, d.y.
A2. Harold Edward, b 1903, d Edmonton, Alta. 1971
A3. Phyllis Maude, b 1908, mar Ebdon, res Chiliwack, BC
A4. Lynden George, b 1910, res Edmonton, Alta.
HUBERT, Eva, sister of Francis John Sr. above, mar John Philip LEMPRIERE, rem to Edmonton, Alta. (Geo. Lempriere, Rexdale, Ont.)
HUBERT, Edouard, b J, in Caraquet, NB 1861 (Census), farmer, age 22, assoc with the ROBIN firm there. (Rev. Le Gresley)
HUBERT, Philippe, worked for Fruing firm at Grand Vallee, Gaspe 1800s
HUDSON, from C.I.? to Adams Cove, Nfl.d (See Seary) Cf HUDSON, HODSON of J (Stevens)
HUE, in Nfld. (Seary) Cf HUE, HUGHES of J (Stevens)
HUE, Stannis Edward, from St. Mary, J to New Carlisle, Que. ca 1880, mar Alice H. HAMON, qv. Hue said to be Hug fam. (Reamon)
HUE, C.I. surname on S. coast of Nfld. (G.W. Le Messurier) See HUE above.
HUE, Edward, b ca 1855 J, in Perce 1871 (Census)
HUELIN, HULAN, HULON, HEWLIN in Nfld. from C.I. (Seary, Shortis-Munn, K. Mathews) John H. was a J merchant in 1800s at Sandy Pt., Nfld. (Mannion)
HUELIN, Isaac and Joseph, on Isle aux Mortes, Nfld. 1860s (Rev. Hammond)
HUELIN, Roselle Florence, see Gerald David ECOBICHON
HUELIN, John, b ca 1800 J, first cousin to Pierre Jean DU VAL, at Bonaventure Island, Perce, Gaspe 1835
HUELIN, John, Capt. in Robin Fleet, seasonally in Nfld. ca 1804-1816, mar Marie DU VAL, b 1775 J. In 1805 master of the TRUE FRIEND.
A1. John, b ca 1800 J, poss 1794-1835, at Bon. Is. 1835 (Brochet, Census)

HUELIN   281

This HUELIN data is incorrect, according to AldoBrochet.
B1. Edward, b 1839, res Paspebiac 1869   For correct info. go
B2. John, master of Bark HOMELY 1849   to original records.
B3. Charles, b 1833, St. Mary's, J, part of crew on HEMATOPE 1851
B4. Clement, b 1839 St. Ouen, J, in Paspebiac 1862
B5. Philip, b 1827? or 1829? J, d 1899 Pabos, bur Cape Cove, Gaspe.
    Mar 1871, Mary Ann GARRETT, b 1829, who d 1893, bur Cape Cove,
    dau of Wm. GARRETT
    C1. Edward Jr., b 1847 St. Peters, J, carpenter
    C2. Francis C., part of the crew of the brig HOMELY 1873
        D1. Livingston, mar Ida LE MARQUAND, qv, sons Sidney?, Bruce
            Brian and William
A2. Francis James, b 1818 J, master of bark NEW BRUNSWICK 1850, HEMA-
    TOPE in 1852, res Perce, Que. Age 60 in 1871.
HUELIN, Thomas, b ca 1811 N.S., fisherman, wife Harriet b ca 1821 N.S.?
    Res 1871 Petit de Grat, C.B. (Census)
A1. Harriet, b ca 1845   A5. Margaret, b ca 1852
A2. Mathilda, b ca 1847   A6. Jeffrey, b ca 1856
A3. Thomas, b ca 1848   A7. Alfred, b ca 1858
A4. Marie, b ca 1849   More children?
HUET, HUOT at Cloridorme, Gaspe, poss from C.I.?
HUELIN in Robichaud book, res N.B.
HULEN, Clem., age 32, b J, in Bon. Co., Gaspe 1871 (Census) Also Char-
    les, age 16
HULL, from J in Victoria, BC
HUNTON, HUNTOON. Ch. Islanders in New England, captured by Indians and
    taken to Canada. See QAAM by Turk.
HURDLE in Nfld. (Seary) Cf HURTAULT of J (Stevens)
HURE, at Gaspe Bay 1871, poss HUREL? (Brochet)
HURDELEY, HURDERY, Capt. from J in Nfld. (K. Mathews)
HURRELL, see HORRELL, cf LE HUREL of J (Stevens)
HUSSEY in Nfld. (Seary) Cf HUSSU of J (Stevens)
HUSTINS in Nfld. (Seary) Cf HASTAIN of J 1607 (Stevens)
HUXTER in St. John's, Nfld. (Seary) Cf HUXTER of J 1800s
HYNES, Henry, fisherman at Sandy Pt., Nfld. 1871 (Seary) Cf HAINES,
    HAYNES of C.I.
INGOUVILLE, Philip d'Auvergne, b 1757 J, son of Philip I. and ? Marie
    LE BOUTILLIER, qv. Mar 1779 Anne MARTIN, qv, of St. Heliers, J, dau
    of Isaac M. Hug? and Anne LE GALLAIS, qv. Philip rem to Sydney Forks,
    NS, in Cape Breton Island, ca 1788 and began to farm on a large scale,
    having over 1000 acres of land and 40 workers. (See Nova Scotia and
    Cape Breton Island) Anne Martin d in 1791, and Philip mar again?, a
    Mrs. Blackburn. Many of the willows in the Bras D'Or area are said to
    be from whips used in making the crates that brought goods from Jer-
    sey to Cape Breton. Philip d 1818, and the farm was subdivided. At
    least 5 chn were bp in St. Heliers, J, but Anne, his dau, was the
    only one to leave descendants in Canada. She mar Richard Collier Ber-
    nard Marshall Des Barres Gibbons in 1805 when he was 26. His father,
    Richard Gibbons, was prob a native of Virginia, as was his mother,
    Susanna Shepherd. The father became Attorney General of N.S., and
    later Chief Justice of C.B. 1784. (Societe Jers. records; Richard
    Gibbons; Scarborough, Ont.; A. Caroline MacFarlan, Burnaby, BC; Jetta
    MacDonald, and Emily MacDonald, Marion Bridge, C.B.: Hortense Steven-
    son, Combermere, Ont.)
A1. Philip, b 1780, in London 1791   A3. William again, b 1784, d 1786
A2. William, b 1783, d 1784   A4. Charles, b 1785, d.y.
A6. Sophia Ingouville, b 1791, Sydney, CB, last ch, d 1808, unmar

A5. Ann, b 1786 J, mar Richard Gibbons
  B1. Portia Gibbons
  B2. Alfred or Ralph?
  B3. Ann Gibbons
  B4. Octavia, or poss 8th ch, Gibbons   B5. Susan Gibbons
  B6. Julian, Amer. Civil War Vet, fought for South, d in New Westminster, B.C.
  B7. Frank, fought in Amer. Civil War, for the North, mar M.E. McDonald
  B8. Richard Napoleon Bonaparte Gibbons, b 1822 Sydney, NS, d there 1881. Was High Sheriff or Richmond Co., mar Mary MARTIN, qv, dau of Nicholas M., Sydney.
    C1. Brigid Ann Cavanaugh Blackador Gibbons, mar F. Rudderham
    C2. Mary Martin Gibbons, unmar
    C3. Catherine Maude, or Winnie Gibbons, unmar
    C4. Richard Bernard Des Barres Gibbons, b 1865 Sydney, C.B., d 1948 Vanc., B.C. Mar Florence Catherine BOUTILLIER 1897 at Sydney. She d 1944 Vancouver, BC, 10 chn
      D1. Mary Florence Gibbons, b 1898, mar John Shore, 2 chn
        E1. Joan Catherine Shore, b 1931
        E2. Ralph John Shore, b 1933, mar Norma Jean Porter, 3 chn
          F1. Kenneth John Shore, b 1961   F3. Andrew Ralph Shore, b
          F2. Brian Robert Shore, b 1962   1972
      D2. Anne Catherine Gibbons, b 1899, mar Patrick Francis O'Flynn, 5 chn
        E1. Patricia Anne O'Flynn, b 1931, mar John Weatherill
          F1. Kenneth Patrick Weatherill, b 1964
        E2. Eileen Frances O'Flynn, b 1932, mar Roland Houde, 6 chn
          F1. Loralee Alexandra Houde, b 1958 F4. James Houde, b 1962
          F2. Shelley Rolande Houde, b 1959   F5. Scott Houde, b 1964
          F3. Yvonne Marie Houde, b 1960   F6. Craig Houde, b 1965
        E3. Kathleen Gertrude O'Flynn, b 1934, mar Arnold George Edgington
          F1. Michael James Edgington, b 1956
          F2. Barbara Anne Edgington, b 1959, mar Richard Ian Jepson
            G. Catherine Denise Jepson, b 1977
          F3. Edward Edgington, b 1960
          F4. Patricia Gail Edginton, b 1962 F6. Karen Marie Edgington,
          F5. Alan George Edgington, b 1964   b 1965
        E4. Marion Shelagh O'Flynn, b 1936, mar Robert Smirl
          F1. Corinda Smirl, b 1965 F2. David Smirl, b 1967
        E5. Maureen Mary O'Flynn, b 1938, mar Wesley John SHARPE
          F1. Francis Patrick Sharpe, b 1956, mar Louise Mallick
            G1. Shane Sharpe, b 1977
          F2. Stephen Sharpe, b 1958 F3. Leonard Sharpe, b 1964
      D3. Helen Gibbons, b 1900, d.y.
      D4. Philip Henry Gibbons, b 1902, mar Mary Gretchen Thorpe
      D5. Agnes Caroline Gibbons, b 1904, mar James Alexander MacFarlan, 2 chn
        E1. Eleanor Caroline MacFarlan, b 1927, mar Wm. James Cadden
          F1. William James Cadden   F2. Lawrence Alexander Cadden
        E2. James David Lyle MacFarlan, b 1936, mar Marilyn Yvonne Johnson
          F1. David Allan Stuart MacFarlan, b 1961
      D6. Delia Maria Gibbons, b 1905, mar John Langley Mosdell, 3 chn
        E1. John Douglas Mosdell, b 1935, mar Orma Ebba Trelvick, and 2. June Miller
          F1. Ronald Kirk Mosdell, b 1956

F2. Kim Lorraine Mosdell, b 1958
   F3. Anna Margery Phyllis Mosdell, b 1970, 2nd wife
  E2. Barbara Lorraine Mosdell, b 1942, mar Norman George Bailey
   F1. Debra Lee Joan Bailey, b 1961   F3. Judith Lynne Bailey,
   F2. Kim Lorraine Bailey, b 1961   b 1967
  E3. Heather Juanita Mosdell, b 1945
 D7. Susanna Young Gibbons, b 1908, mar Norval Stuart Bryson, 3 chn
  E1. Gary Stuart Bryson, 1930-1951
  E2. Helen Diane Bryson, b 1932, mar John Rowan, 3 chn
   F1. Gary Stuart Rowan, b 1955   F3. Susan Anne Rowan, b
   F2. Frederick Mark Rowan, b 1956   1958
  E3. Richard Keith Bryson, b 1934, unmar
 D8. Thomas Samuel Gibbons, b 1910, mar Isobel Thompson, 2 chn
  E1. Richard William Gibbons, b 1951
  E2. Robert Thomas Gibbons, b 1954
 D9. Robert Emmett Gibbons, b 1911 Vancouver, BC, mar Jeanette
   Dorothy Leaman, 2 chn
  E1. Susan Lori Gibbons, b 1948, mar James Lewis, 2 chn
   F1. Daren Lewis, b 1969   F2. Jason Lewis, b 1971
  E2. Karen Gibbons, b 1950, mar Brian Clayton
   F1. Tracy Clayton, b 1971
 D10. Charles Alfred Gibbons, b 1914
C5. Philip Ingouville D'Auvergne Gibbons, b 1869, d 1956, mar 1903
  Henrietta Evalina Huntington
 D1. baby, b 1903, d.y.
 D2. Richard Napoleon Gibbons, b 1904, mar 1952 Doris Evalena
  Beggs, separated
 D3. Henry Hubert Gibbons, b 1905, mar Annie Jane MacKeigan, b 1908
  E1. Albert Henry Philip Gibbons, b 1944, mar
   F1. Caleb John Gibbons, b 1966   F3. Curtis Richard Gibbons,
   F2. Kimberlea Ann Gibbons, b 1967   b 1977
  E2. Philip Henry Gibbons, b 1951, mar Anne Marie Reginatto, b
   1952
   F1. Shalla Lee, b 1977
 D4. Emily Gesner Gibbons, b 1907, mar 1932 Owen William MacDonald,
  1904-1974
  E1. Henrietta Hazel MacDonald, b 1933, mar 1958 Lloyd Roland
   Doncaster, b 1930
   F1. Roland Leslie Doncaster, b 1961   F3. Ellis Cyril Doncas-
   F2. Nadine Emily Doncaster, b 1963   ter, b 1967
  E2. Harvey William MacDonald, b 1934, mar 1967 Gail Synette
   Robison
   F1. Darren Gilbert MacDonald, b 1968   F3. Corine Joy MacDon-
   F2. Lori Wynette MacDonald, b 1969   ald, b 1974
  E3. Owen D'Auvergne MacDonald, b 1936, mar 1958 Marlene Velma
   MacPherson, b 1937
   F1. Debbie Dianne MacDonald, b 1958   F3. Robert Owen Mac-
   F2. Judith Christine MacDonald, b 1960   Donald, b 1965
  E4. Gilbert Gesner MacDonald, b 1941
  E5. Vivian Christine MacDonald, b 1944, mar 1968 John Ronald
   MacKinnon, b 1943
   F1. Vicki Collette MacKinnon, b 1969
   F2. Christa Yvonne MacKinnon, b 1972
  E6. Keith Everett MacDonald, b 1949, mar 1976 Helen Marline
   Lever, b 1953
 D5. Mary Jane, Molly, Martin Gibbons, b 1908, mar 1. 1946 Cyril
  W. Russell, res Sydney, CB, who d 1964. Mar 2. 1973 Hans J.

Doerr, res Dunedin, Fla. No issue.
D6. Portia Ingouville Gibbons, b 1909, mar Donald John MacDonald, b 1911, 6 chn, res Marion Bridge, NS
  E1. Donald Francis MacDonald, b 1931, d.y.
  E2. Stanley Bruce MacDonald, b 1933, mar Meta Witten
  E3. Isobel Frances MacDonald, b 1935, mar Harry Crombie
    F1. Heather Isobel Crombie, b 1965
    F2. Harry Maxwell Crombie, b 1966
  E4. Donald David Lamond MacDonald, b 1936, mar Stella Kiley, b 1935
    F1. David Kiley MacDonald, b 1958
    F2. Victoria MacDonald, b 1963
  E5. Henrietta Marion MacDonald, b 1942, mar John MacKenzie Buchanan, b 1941
    F1. Donald Iain Buchanan, b 1963
    F2. Robert James Buchanan, b 1969
    F3. Henrietta Mira Buchanan, b 1976
  E6. Christene Elizabeth MacDonald, b 1944, mar J. Gordon Lehman
    F1. Steven Troy Lehman, b 1962
    F2. Dale Vincent Lehman, b 1963
    F3. Gillian Christene Lehman, b 1974
  E7. Philip Ingouville MacDonald, b 1946, mar 1967 Betty Ann Watkinson, divorced
D7. Ruth Henrietta Gibbons, b 1911, mar James Vernon Goode, 1906-1971
  E1. Gertrude Lillian Goode, b 1934, mar Harold Fairley Betts, b 1926
    F1. Vernon Graham Betts, b 1953
    F2. Sylvia Ruth Betts, b 1957
    F3. Merrill Harold Betts, b 1960
    F4. Alayne Marie Betts, b 1964
    F5. Lisa Jean Betts, b 1974
  E2. Yvonne Mary Goode, b 1939, mar Walter MacDonald, b 1930
    F1. Miles Richard Walter MacDonald, b 1963
  E3. Alayne Emily Goode, b 1943, mar Fred. MacKee Stassen, b 1941
    F1. Eric MacKee Stassen, b 1969
    F2. Michelle Elizabeth Stassen, b 1973
D8. Gertrude Hortense Gibbons, b 1911, twin of Ruth, mar Thomas Henry Stevenson 1947, res Combermere, Ont.
  E1. Brian Phillip Stevenson, b 1949, mar Nancy Elisabeth Haslam, b 1955
  E2. Ralph Gesner Stevenson, b 1952, mar Cherly Ann Browne, b 1956
    F1. Amanda Melinda Stevenson, b 1974
D9. Caleb Phillip Gibbons, b 1912, d 1956, unmar
D10. Jetta Marion Gibbons, b 1914, mar John MacDonald, b 1920
  E1. John Paul MacDonald, b 1943, mar 1965 Eleanor L. Kendrick, b 1946
    F1. Juanita Louise MacDonald, b 1967
    F2. Kelly Lynn MacDonald, b 1969
    F3. Tonya La Vergne MacDonald, b 1970
  E2. Phyllis Evelyna MacDonald, b 1946, mar 1970 Edward Winsor Kirkpatrick, b 1937
    F1. Lorelei Ann Kirkpatrick, b 1971
    F2. Jennifer Marie Kirkpatrick, b 1974
    F3. Patrick Lee Kirkpatrick, b 1976
  E3. Nelson Caleb MacDonald, b 1949
  E4. Miriam May MacDonald, b 1950
  E5. Kerry Lynn MacDonald, b 1954
  E6. Delia Catherine MacDonald, b 1956
  E7. Bridget Ann MacDonald, b 1966

INGOUVILLE, Elizabeth Anne, b 1848, d 1881, bur St. Peters, Malbaie, Gaspe
INGOUVILLE, Judith, of G, mar Peter VIBERT, qv of J, res Gaspe early 1800s

INGROVILLE 285

INGROVILLE, Henriette, of Vale, G, mar Eugene ROBIN, qv.
INGROUVILLE, Daniel, b 1825 Malbaie, to NS 1800s, and/or res Barachois, Gaspe
  A1. Harry, b ca 1890
    B1. Daniel, res Toronto   B3. Gerard, to Montreal
    B2. Mary, mar ---O'Reilly B4. Connie, res New Jersey, mar A. Drody?
INGROUVILLE, H., mar Catherine Maria Ouillet, Gaspe, a dau, Jane Marie, b 1837
INGROUVILLE, Henry, b J, in Malbaie in 1861 (Census) with Angelique TAPP, qv, b Canada
  A1. Elizabeth Jane A2. Mary or Margaret A3. Danie, b G
  A4. Jane Maria, b 1851 Malbaie
INGROUVILLE, Daniel, of J, in Malbaie, mar Judith ---, who d 1853, age 78
ISABEL, ISABELLE, old J surname in Gaspe
JACK in Nfld. (Seary) cf JACQUES of J (Stevens)
JACKMAN, from C.I. to Canada?
JACQUES from C.I. to Canada (Gingras) At Lark Harbor, Nfld. (Mannion) Also Annapolis, NS and Gaspe (K. H. Annett)
JACKSON, Hughie, lived to a great age at St. Peters, C.V., said to have come out from J on the first voyage with the Marmauds of George's River, C.B. "They sighted Green Island 3 times, and each time the ship was driven back to sea by storms and ice. There was not any food or water left, the rigging and sails were in a sorry state and even their clothes were worn out. After 90 days they got into St. Peter's in an exhausted condition." (Capt. Parker)
JACKSON, John was the first SPG missionary in Nfld., 1703, 1705, poss from J? SEE JAMES DATA IN ADDED PAGES.
JACKSON in Nfld. (Seary) Cf JACKSON of J
JAMES, to Perce from C.I. Poss formerly JACQUES, which is James in French. (Cent. Bklt.) The church in Perce, St. Paul, Anglican, was gifted with a Tiffany window by an American artist named Frederick James. He left it to the church in his will, probated in 1907.
JAMES to Nfld. (Seary) Cf JAMES, JACQUES of J (Stevens) Henry in Harbour Grace 1681.
JAMIESON, G.C., from G to Victoria, BC, member of C.I. Society there
JANDRON, Francis, b J, came from W. Indies with black servant Sowles in 1800s to Perce,Quebec, mar Marie LE MOIGNAN, and they rem to Jersey (Michel LE MOIGNAN GENEALOGY)
JANDRON, Francis Philip MARETT, b 1850 J, to Grande Riviere, Gaspe, at 17, where he mar Marie LE MOIGNAN, sister of June LE MOIGNAN in 1872. The sister rem to Canton, Ohio. Francis Le Moignan res Grande Riviere, worked for Robin 1905. He and his wife returned to J ca 1872, and their 4 chn were born there. He d 1934, age 83; she d 1932, age 82. (Le Moignan; Christian Science records; Gingras)
  A1. Lister, this may have been Francis Lyster Jandron, who was b in J, lived in Canada and Detroit, Mich. He was a Christian Science practitioner and teacher from 1921 to 1964. Poss a son in Boston, F.L.J., Jr.
  A2. Leslie   A3. Mamie
  A4. Hilda, who mar Charles Cash of England. They lived some time in Quebec, and Mrs. Cash lived in J in 1963.
JANDRON, C.I. in Maritimes Fisheries (J.H. Le Breton list)
JANVRIN, this family was represented in the Nfld. trade by 1717 or before, ship owners and business ventures of various kinds. By the late 1700s there were a number of Janvrins involved in all parts of the Maritimes. The following were in the Gaspe area: (Brochet, C.F. Fay,

MANY JANVRIN TO NEW ENGLAND.
K. Mathews, Innis. See "VICTORIAN VOICES" by Joan Stevens.
Mssrs. Janvrin Freres & Cie, 1770-1816
De Lisle, Janvrin and De Lisle, 1800-1820
Francis Janvrin Co., 1816-1851
Francis Janvrin Co., 1837-1851
Frederick Janvrin Co., 1851-1859

SOME JANVRIN DATA BELOW IS IN ERROR.
(Aldo Brochet)
SEE EXTRA PAGES.

In addition, at least five Janvrin men served as managers and proprietors at various establishments in the St. Lawrence Gulf in the 18th and 19th centuries. (A. Brochet) In 1770, one firm of the Janvrin family was at Grand Greve, Gaspe. In 1813, Philip and Francis were active in the firm. Francis petitioned for land at Paspebiac, Que. in 1787. Philip Valpy, dit Janvrin, was involved in the Nfld. trade in 1721, born in Jersey 1677. The Janvrins married into other Channel Island families in Canada, such as Le Boutillier and Jean. (John Le Boutillier of Perce; H. and M. Jean, Arichat)

A Jersey firm of John and Philip Janvrin employed Pierre Du Val, qv, as master of a Privateer, against the Batavia Republic and France, ca 1800, or before.

JANVRIN, Frederick, res Bath Co., Somerset, England, was the desc of a branch of the family settled in southern England and deeply involved with the codfisheries and Canadian shipping. He bought fishing rights from John LE COUTEUR and others at Gaspe Basin, Grand Greve, and Griffon Cove. In 1841 he advertised the businesses for sale. By 1860 the surname had disappeared from shipping lists of Jersey. "Daniel Janvrin was ancestor of a long line of Janvrins whose wealth was derived from shipping in various forms." They were "armateurs" of privateers, merchants in New Brunswick, Nova Scotia and Gaspe, and finally bankers, always with their headquarters in Jersey.

The Societe Jersiaise has the receipt and letter book of Edouard LUCE, who was trading with Newfoundland in the DAUPHIN, shows that in 1743 he had an account with Mrs. Elizabeth ORANGE, widow of Philip JANVRIN of the ESTHER, for oil and quintals of fish. "In the latter part of the eighteenth century the sons of Brelade Janvrin of Le Coin, Jersey, set up as merchants in New Brunswick, Canso, Magdalen Islands and on the Gaspe coast in the fishing industry, but their major activity lay in the arming of privateers during the wars with France and Spain." The diary of Jean Syvret related two voyages which they undertook on corsairs belonging to Janvrin and Co. John Janvrin had a lease of Janvrin's Island, C.B. in 1794. The property and business in Canada gradually went into the hands of Frederick, who advertised for sale the property at Grand Greve, Malbaie, Cap Rosier and Griffon Cove, at Gaspe in 1841. By 1860 the name had disappeared from the shipping lists of Jersey. A stone marked F.J. Janvrin is on his property lot at Gaspe Basin. (Above and other material provided by Jane Neilsen, Danville, Ill, from research done by Marguerite Syvret of Jersey; Societe Jersiaise, St. Heliers, J; Southampton Port books and registers; Balleine's BIOGRAPHICAL DICTIONARY; Joan Stevens, books by; Autobiography of Jean Syvret; CAPE BRETON OVER, by Clara Dennis; Payne's ARMORIAL; Account books of Edouard Luce; and, many Janvrins in England.)

JANVRIN, Philip and John, were established at Grand Greve, Gaspe 1798

JANVRIN, Frederick, is also mentioned in the affairs of a Richard VALPY, poss dit Janvrin? of London, a merchant. He may be bur at Gaspe.

JANVRIN, John, b St. Brelade, J, fishery and shipping at Arichat, mar Harriet JEAN. This firm sent 2 million pounds of codfish to Brazil, etc., in S.A. 1836.

JANVRIN, Philip, owned several ships in Cape Breton, N.S. The GENERAL BROCK, 197 tons, built in C.B. by Peter BOUCHARD, or BURRARD of Ship

JANVRIN 287

Harbour, Port Hawksbury, CB, later transferred to Jersey. BOUCHARD was a noted shipbuilder from G, 1800s.
JANVRIN, Peter, owned in C.B., the BETSY, 84 tons, built 1799, Capt. Abr. LE MAITRE, qv. Taken by the French Navy or a French privateer on a voyage to the West Indies.
JANVRIN, John of Arichat, C.B., owned the brig, BROTHERS, 136 tons, in the 1830s. (Capt. Parker)
JANVRIN, Daniel, barrister, mar 1844 Henrietta JEAN, qv, of Arichat, CB
  A1. Melline? A2. Cecilia A3. Henrietta A4. Percy A5. William
JANVRIN, John, b 1740, had business in Nfld., N.B., Gaspe and Cape Breton, res J
JANVRIN, Francis, Prop. of Francis Janvrin & Co., d J 1837
  A1. Daniel, notary public in St. Heliers, mar Louisa Mary ---
  A2. Harriet, mar John   poss a relative of Philip PERREE, Jr., who d 1848 (LE COUTEUR?)
  A3. Frederick, Prop. of Fred. Janvrin & Co., retired ca 1880, sold to Fruing Co., John Perree and others. Res Bath, England?
JANVRIN, Francis, John and Philip, bought crown lands from Peter Landris LABBE, of C.I.? Lots 23, 33? on N side of Arichat Harbor, 1806, 30 acres.
JANVRIN, in 1791, bought N side of Harbour next to lot 32; 38 acres
JANVRIN, John, W side of Petit de Grat, C.B., 45 acres
JANVRIN, 1788, lots 7-17 E side of Harbour Petit de Grat, 130 acres
JARDIN in Nfld. (Seary) Cf DU JARDIN of J (Stevens)
JARNET, Reginald, son of Charles Jarnet of J, to Sept. Isles, Quebec 1928. (K. de la Haye)
JARVIS, JARVES in Nfld. (Seary) Cf GERVAISE, of C.I. Cf also JARVES of U.S., from C.I., changed name from Gervaise to Jarvis, Jarves.
JEAN, Armand from Normandy to J, 1207. (Louise Surgey, Toronto)
JEAN, John, b late 1700s, St. Ouen, J, rem to Arichat, Cape Breton, NS, and mar 1810, Louisa Moore, dau of an American Colonel, who had come to N.S. with the Cornwallis group. Jean supervised the building of ships for many years in Arichat and "undoubtedly contributed to the gradual rise in class of ships." (Capt. Parker) He supervised the building of the ST. LAWRENCE, 152 tons at Arichat, owner master Hippolye Marmaud. John JEAN and F. LA VACHE, qv, owned the UNION, 34 tons, built 1849 at Arichat. (Allen Gruchy, College Park, MD; Annie Laurie MacDonald, Antigonish, NS; Louise Surgey, Toronto, Ont.; Rev. Kenneth MacDonald, Deep River, Conn.) JEAN, SEE EXTRA PAGES.
  A1. Eliza Louise Cutler JEAN, b 1809? Poss by a first wife?, d 1859, mar 1835 Rev. James Allen Shaw of Scotland, an SPG missionary. Poss birthdate was 1819?
    B1. John Valentine Shaw
      C1. Ethel Shaw, mar William Isaac LE VESCONTE, qv
        D1. Caroline LE VESCONTE, b 1906, mar Fred. MAUGER, qv, rem Cap La Ronde, near Arichat, d 1977
      C2. Eva Shaw, mar Lennon LE VESCONTE, qv
    B2. Eliza Louise, mar George J. Andrew, res Shubenacadie
      C1. George Allen Andrew, b 1883, res Toronto. At one time pastor of Cronym Mem. Ch., London, Ont. Ordained 1907, lived to at least age 91.
  A2. Marie Judith, b 1811, d 1889, mar 1833 Capt. John Thomas BALLEINE, qv
    B1. Esther BALLEINE   B2. John BALLEINE
  A3. Louise Harriet, b 1812, mar 1830 John JANVRIN, and 2. Thomas Cutler, no issue
  A4. George Edward, mar 1838 Mary Lannigan
    B1. George   B2. Tupper, unmar   B3. Thomas Robin   B4. Jane

B5. Catherine
A5. Anne, mar 1838 Henry B. COWLEY, a merchant
  B1. Rose Cowley   B2. Annie Cowley   B3. Clifford Cowley
  B4. Frank Cowley   B5. Cecilia Cowley
A6. Jane Catherine Robertson, b 1818, d 1887, mar 1844 David GRUCHY, qv
  at least 5 chn. See GRUCHY, David.
A7. Henrietta, mar 1844 Daniel JANVRIN, barrister
  B1. Melissa? Janvrin   B2. Cecilia Janvrin   B3. Henrietta Janvrin
  B4. Percy Janvrin   B5. William Janvrin
A8. Mary Tremaine, b 1820, mar 1840 by Rev. Philip FILLEUL, qv, to Wm.
  Edward BRINE, BRYNE, qv. She d 1888, 9 chn. See Wm. BRINE.
A9. Caroline Susan, b 1822, mar 1844 Isaac LE VESCONTE, d 1876
  B1. Caroline Louise LE VESCONTE, mar John L. MacDougall
    C1. Bertram C. LE VESCONTE MacDougall, mar 1917 Helen Jean MACKEN-
        ZIE
      D1. Isaac Lorne MacDougall
A10. John Janvrin, mar 1851 Ann Amelia Lannigan, sister of above Mary
  Lannigan
  B1. John, unmar, d 1930   B2. Margaret, d unmar
  B3. William, mar, had dau Mary, who did not marry
JEAN, John, b ca 1800 J, widower in 1971, carpenter, had chn, res Perce,
  Gaspe. Mar Hannah Barnes, d 1877, age 79. (Brochet, Maroldo)
A1. Sarah, b ca 1846 Quebec 1824
A2. Hannah, b ca 1849   A3. Susan, b ca 1851
JEAN, John Francis, b ca 1826 Jersey mar Margaret or Mary Bragg, who d
  1871 (Brochet, Maroldo)   Possible errors in this chart!
A1. Hannah, b ca 1850 Quebec, mar?   She d ca 1863?
  Perce.   SEE ADDITIONS AND CORRECTIONS PAGES.
A2. William, b ca 1854, mar Eliza Jane BOWERS?, qv, bur St. Lukes, Coin
  du Banc, Gaspe
A3. Ellen, b ca 1857
A4. John, b ca 1860, poss mar Adora TRACHY, qv.
A5. Mary, b ca 1862
A6. Susan, b ca 1865. A Susan bur St. Pauls, Perce.
A7. Francis, b ca 1869. A Francis d 1968, bur Perce.
JEAN, Wm., res Coin du Banc, Gaspe, mar Eliza Jane BOWERS, qv. See
  Wm., above. (GLF)
JEAN, Jean Francois, b J, mar 1845 Julie Belanger   Sainte Foy, Que.
  (Recueil de Genealogy, de Beauce-Dorchester, Frontenac, Vol. II, p.
  27) See also above, John Francis.
JEAN, John Jr., age 45 in 1871, b J, poss same as John Francis JEAN?
JEAN, John Jr., d 1937, age 43 at Perce
JEAN, Frank, d 1975, mar 1933 Ellen Birmingham of Perce. Another Frank
  Jean d 1968, bur St. Pauls, Perce (GLF)
JEAN, Henry, in Alpena, Mich., 1905. Some Gaspesians rem to Mich. 1800s
JEAN, to Nfld. (Seary) Cf JEAN of J (Stevens) Cf also JENNE, JEANNE.
JEAN. "My grandfather had two bros., one named Gustave, the other
  Auguste, who were engaged in the Jersey shipping to Nfld. and who
  settled in Canada ca 1850 or 1860." (Allan Jean, St. Lawrence, Jer-
  sey) This fam from Carteret, France, where John was b 1816.
JEAN, in Miscou, Shippegan, NB 1800s (Ganong)
JEAN, from C.I. or Gaspe to Ontario
JEAN, Lillian M., b 1886 Leoville House, St. Ouen, J, mar 1915 Fran-
  cis Moses GIBAUT, qv, b Gaspe of J fam. See GIBAUT.
JEAN, Francis George, b J, bro of Lillian above, to Gaspe 1910, res
  Grand Riviere.
JEAN, Mr. and Mrs. John of J, settled in the 1800s in Cannes Des Roches,

Gaspe (Bechard)
JEAN, in Gaspe 1777 (Syvret; Rev. d'Hist, etc.)
JEANDRON. See also JANDRON
JEANDRON, John Edward, b 1839 St. John, J, son of John J. and poss ---
CABOT. John d 1924, his wife in 1925, both bur Mt. Pleasant Cem,
Toronto. They res until 1892 in Quebec, then rem to Toronto. His
wife was Anne Hall, b 1838 Ireland. (Florence Waugh, Toronto, Ont.;
Joseph Withrow, Minn., Minn.) J.E. was cousin of Winter LE GRAND.
A1. William John, b 1866, mar Ada Rutledge 1891, d 1930. Res E. Orange,
 N.J.
 B1. Alder, d ca age 20 B2. Aileen B3. Genevieve
A2. Arthur Edward, b 1867, mar Bertha SHARPE 1891, d 1926, res Toronto
 B1. Vere, mar 1. Mary Blackburn, chn, and 2. Mary Keller, no issue
  C1. Lenore   C2. Wesley   C3. Harold
 B2. Zeta, b 1894, mar Lewis Edmonds 1918
  C1. Robert Edmonds C2. Joan Edmonds C3. Paul Edmonds
 B3. Erie, b 1903, mar Ross Smellie 1928
  C1. Gary Smellie, b 1930   C3. Paul Smellie, b 1936
  C2. Jane Smellie, b 1933
A3. Herbert Henderson, b 1869, d 1874
A4. Charles Frederick, b 1871, d 1894
A5. Ida Gertrude, b 1874, mar John Arthur Withrow 1890 Toronto. She d
 1942, John in 1964, bur Mt. Plesant Cem, Toronto.
 B1. Evelyn Gertrude, b 1897, mar Wilfred Forbes Withrow 1924, d 1962,
  Wilfred in 1970
  C1. William John, b 1926, mar June R. Vanoostrom 1948
   D1. John David Withrow, b 1951   D3. Anne Withrow, b 1956
   D2. Stephen Withrow, b 1953
  C2. Terence Withrow, b 1940, d 1941
 B2. Florence Margaret Withrow, b 1904, mar 1928 Freeman D.R. Waugh,
  1904-1975
  C1. Mary Margaret Waugh, b 1930, mar Harold J. Threapleton 1955
   D1. Sarah Threapleton, b 1967
  C2. Nora Elizabeth Waugh, b 1933, mar Arnold R. Brown 1965
   D1. Nancy Ellen Brown, b 1968   D3. Roberta Lynn Brown, b 1973
   D2. Susan Heather Brown, b 1970
JEFFARD, John, of Mathews Cove, Labrador in 1789, and Simon JEFFARD at
 Scilly Cove, Nfld. 1800. Poss same as GIFFARD of J? (Seary)
JEFFERIES in Nfld. (Seary) Cf Jeffries of G
JEFFERY, Jerome, in Gaspe from C.I.
JENKINS, byeboat keeper from G in Nfld. (K. Mathews)
JENNIEX in Nfld. Cf JEAUNAIX, Jean, and Antoine in Gaspe 1820. Signed
 Petition 1820. Also cf JOWINOIX and JEUNAIS of J (Stevens)
JENNINGS, merchant from J in Nfld. (K. Mathews)
JENNINGS in B.C., member of C.I. Society 1940
JERRETT, GARRETT?, C.I. in Carbonear, Nfld. 1700s. (Rev. Hammond)
 Said to be from C.I.
JERRETT, George, a builder in Brigus, Conc. Bay, Nfld. 1860s (Rev. Hammond; Seary) Cf also DE GARRETT, qv.
JERSEY, DE JERSEY, Capt. from G in Nfld. (K. Mathews)   See DE JERSEY
JERSEY in Gaspe, prob DE JERSEY. (Langlois in Toronto)
JEUNAIX, Jean and Anthoine in Gaspe, signed Petition of 1820
JEUNE, Francois, res in Les Vaux, St. Aubin, J, furnished a shed in his
 yard as a Methodist meeting place in 1787, when this sect was getting
 a start in Jersey. He and his wife later became Methodist missionaries to the French speaking slaves of Grenada, Winward Islands. His
 son, Francois, father of Dean Jeune, remained a miller at St. Aubin,

J. He mar Elizabeth LE CAPELAIN, qv, went to Oxford, England and won his DCL in 1834. He went to Canada as Sec. to the Gov. General, Sir John Colburn, then returned to England, and mar Margaret Dyne, only ch of Henry Symons of Axbridge, England. In 1843 he was offered the Bishopric of New Brunswick in Canada. (G. R. Balleine)

JEUNIEX in Nfld. (Seary) Cf JOWINOIX and JEUNAIS of J (Stevens)

JEUNE, see also LE JEUNE

JEUNE, four bros b J, 3 rem to B.C. before 1886. One, William, settled in Boston, Mass. They were the sons of a sea Captain. (Wallace Jeune, Sidney, B.C.) See page 107.

I. Frederick John, b 1862 J, d 1955 BC, mar Emily E. TOUET, qv, 1868-1941
  A1. Frederick P. Jeune, b 1891, d 1960, mar Bernice E. Wood, 1897-1975
    B1. Dr. Ronald F., b 1918, mar Katherine G. Gallaher
      C1. Margot A., b 1947 C2. Frederick A., b 1949 C3. Debora G., b 1954
    B2. Muriel M., b 1920, mar John J. Armstrong, b 1918
      C1. Murray J. Armstrong, b 1948   C3. Jane B. Armstrong, b 1960
      C2. Ross J. Armstrong, b 1958
  A2. Percy W. Jeune, b 1893, d 1975, mar Eva M. McDougal, b 1895
    B1. Kenneth P., b 1922, d 1963, mar Lucy M. Edge, b 1924
      C1. Paul S., b 1950, mar Christina E. Penny, b 1953
    B2. Inez E., b 1920, mar Wm. C. Ord, b 1922
      C1. James G. Ord, b 1947, mar Louise H. Porter, b 1948
        D1. Shawn G. Ord, b 1971   D2. Kelly L. Ord, b 1973
  A3. Herbert H., b 1896, mar Clara H. Gibbens, b 1898
    B1. Vera E., b 1918, mar David B. CROFT, b 1914
      C1. Janis C. Croft, b 1948
    B2. Ila C., b 1920, mar Thomas A. Clegg, b 1921
    B3. Wallace H., b 1925, mar Margaret H. Harrison, b 1927
      C1. Susanne L., b 1950
    B4. Gordon A., b 1931, d 1971, mar Shirley L. Bath, b 1937
      C1. Linda G., b 1955   C3. Daryl G., b 1962
      C2. Dawn P., b 1957   C4. Gary R., b 1966
II. Philip John Jeune, b 1865 J, d 1957, mar Agnes Emily TOUET, qv, 1867-1965
  A1. Lily A., b 1892, mar Harry Clark, who d 1964
    B1. Murial J. Clark, b 1914, mar Ivor D. Hoskin, b 1912
      C1. Ruth C. Hoskin, b 1934, mar Alfred J. Goslin, b 1930
        D1. Sherrie J. Goslin, b 1953, mar Edward Burman
        D2. Linda D. Goslin, b 1953, mar Robert Webster
          E1. Rita Webster, b 1974
        D3. Wayne D. Goslin, b 1957   D5. Nadine H. Goslin, b 1960
        D4. Steven G. Goslin, b 1959   D6. Marilyn P. Goslin, b 1961
      C2. Ethel M. Hoskin, b 1936, mar Jack Morgan
      C3. Harry D. Hoskin, b 1938, mar Shirley A. Reid
        D1. Cheryl A. Hoskin, b 1961
      C4. Eileen L. Hoskin, b 1951
    B2. Edwin H. Clark, b 1920, mar Mabel P. Nottingham, b 1923
      C1. Dorothy P. Clark, b 1946   C2. Donald E. Clark, b 1950
      C3. Lorraine G. Clark, b 1952, mar Lawrence J. Bresson, b 1952
        D1. Jennifer L. Bresson, b 1973
  A2. Arthur P., b 1893, d 1965   A4. Eva M., b 1896, d 1966
  A3. Edith P., b 1894   A5. Laurel E., b 1897, d 1957
  A6. Alma E., b 1902, mar George W. Malcolm, mar 1899, he d 1971
    B1. Dulcie Malcolm, b 1924, mar Angus E. Hamilton, b 1912
      C1. Leslie E. Hamilton, b 1959
    B2. Alma M. Malcolm, b 1925, mar Edgar A. Smith, b 1917

JEUNE

    C1. Edgar M. Smith, b 1950   C3. Roderick A. Smith, b 1958
    C2. Philip G. Smith, b 1951   C4. Douglas P. Smith, b 1960
  B3. Chere L. Malcolm, b 1930
  B3. Julene V. Malcolm, b 1945
III. Hellier Jeune, b J, to B.C., mar Clara Stacey
A1. Walter P., b 1884, mar Jane Harris, b 1884
  B1. Lily E., b 1907, mar Lawrence Mackay, b 1905
    C1. Wallace J. Mackay, b 1931, mar Mildred DAVEY
      D1. Eva L. Mackay
    C2. Eva L. Mackay, b 1937, mar David H. Inglis, b 1934
      D1. Steven H. Inglis, b 1955   D4. Michael D. Inglis, b 1959
      D2. Alan J. Inglis, b 1956   D5. Kim M. Inglis, b 1962
      D3. Ronald T. Inglis, b 1958
  B2. Clare E. Jeune, b 1910, mar William A. McNeill, b 1903 d 1976.
    C1. William R. McNeill, b 1930, mar Myrtel Lainchbury, b 1932
      D1. Glenda McNeill, b 1956   D3. Shawna McNeill, b 1959
      D2. Dianna McNeill, b 1958
    C2. Donald L. McNeill, b 1933, mar Lori Gogo
      D1. Carol McNeill, b 1959   D4. Ronald McNeill, b 1962
      D2. Daniel McNeill, b 1960   D5. Robert McNeill, b 1968
      D3. Suzette McNeill, b 1961
  B3. Martha E., b 1911, mar Norman R. Thompson
    C1. Norman A. Thompson, Jr.
  B4. Mabel E., b 1914, mar Alfred G. Slocomb
    C1. Edith Slocomb, b 1938, mar Leslie L. Grant, b 1936
      D1. Cheryl A. Grant, b 1959   D3. William L. Grant, b 1962
      D2. Robert L. Grant, b 1961
    C2. Linda B. Slocomb, b 1940, mar Robert Clark, b 1929
      D1. Wayne S. Clark, b 1969   D2. Wendy J. Clark, b 1971
    C3. Walter B. Slocomb, b 1943, mar Patricia Brown, b 1943
      D1. Sandra L. Slocomb, b 1966   D2. Richard W. Slocomb, b 1967
A2. Edith, b 1886, mar David H. ENGLAND
  B1. Harold M. England, b 1913, mar Ellis I. Waller, b 1911
    C1. David H. England, b 1941, mar Donna Jensen, b 1940
      D1. Timothy P. England, b 1971 D2. Stephen D. England, b 1973
    C2. Margaret L. England, mar Robert L. Roth, b 1943 D3. Darren,
      D1. Laurene? B. Roth, b 1969   D2. Brent R. Roth, b 1973 1979
    C3. Donald E. England, b 1943 mar Betty Wilson b 1947
      D1. Sherri L. England, b 1968   D2. Julie M. England
    C4. Jeanette A. England, b 1939, mar Kenjiro Yokoyama, b 1939
      D1. Kimeko S. Yokoyama, b 1971   D2. Jenine M. Yokoyama, b 1973
  B2. Evelyn M. England, b 1916, d 1973, mar William Oldnall, b 1907
    C1. Barbara Oldnall, b 1942, mar Desmond Montgomery, b 1939
      D1. Clinton J. Montgomery, b 1962 D3. Michael V. Montgomery, b
      D2. Lance R. Montgomery, b 1965   1966
    C2. Gordon Oldnall, b 1945, mar Victoria E. Sanders, b 1944
      D1. James W. Oldnall, b 1967   D3. John C. Oldnall, b 1973
      D2. Mark H. Oldnall, b 1970
A3. Esther R., b 1887, mar John J. ROBILLIARD, qv, b 1879. Two chn, see ROBILLARD.
A4. Phyllis E., b 1906, mar John W. Yates, b 1896. Phyllis d 1980
  B1. Dr. George R. Yates, b 1927, mar Laura V. Manton, b 1925
    C1. Donald J. Yates, b 1957   C3. Kenneth Yates, b 1960
    C2. Carol Yates, b 1955   C4. Robert G. Yates, b 1961
  B2. Jeune Yates, b 1930, mar Richard J. Bolton, b 1928
    C1. Wyatt M. Bolton, b 1956   C2. Donna L. Bolton, b 1960
JEUNE, William, fourth bro., settled in Boston, Mass.

JEUNE, Edwin, from J to Canada late 1800s, first to Montreal, then to Toronto, Ont. (Mrs. Wm. E. Jeune, Toronto, Ont.)
 A1. Aubrey Edwin, b Montreal, had metal stamping business in Toronto, Jeune Canopy, then as Jeune Metals, 7 chn
  B1. Aubrey Edwin II, mar Alice Maud Macklem-Robert in B.C.
   C1. Robert   C2. Aubrey III
  B2. Arthur Clarence, res Toronto
   C1. Garry   C2. Diane
  B3. Alice Maud Mary, mar ---Stonehouse, no issue
  B4. Herbert Edward, a dau Thelma
  B5. William Edgar, mar ---
   C1. Suzanne Carol   C2. Maryanne Louise
  B6. Arthur
JEUNE, in the Maritimes Fisheries, 1800s (J. H. Le Breton list)
JEZEQUEL, this surname from France to Gaspe. Mrs. Jezequel of Gaspe, 1861 (Census) was b J. See also HOYLES.
JOHNS, Judith?, dau of Francis Johns and Mary Ann Niles, b 1887, the Vale, G, rem to Canada with husband, Alfred LE PAGE early 1900s. See Alfred LE PAGE. (Miriam Russell, Belleville, Ont.)
JOHN in Nfld. (Seary) Cf JEAN of J (Stevens)
JOHNSON, fam from C.I.? at Pt. St. Peter, Gaspe, 1800s (Le Moine)
JOHNSON, fam from C.I. in Malbaie, 1900s (Poss Scottish, See
JOHNSON, Thomas, in Nfld. 1666, from C.I.? (Gaspe Review, 1979
JOHNSON, Mary, mar Charles HOTTON, qv, res Malbaie, Gaspe 1800s
JOHNSTONE, James, from G to Willowdale, Ont. 1900s
JOLI, from J in N.S. ca 1800 (Bourinot) Res Cap La Ronde?
JOLLY, Mr. and Mrs. from St. Sampson, G to Moose Jaw, Sask ca 1919. They brought three daus and a son. Two sons had already settled there. A dau, Florence, mar ALLEN.
JORDAN in Nfld. (Seary) Cf JOURDAN, JORDAN of J (Stevens)
JOUAN, Ellen Gertrude, b 1887 J, mar 1913 Harold Ernest CAWLEY, qv, b J, 5 chn. She was dau of Francis Joseph Touson Laurens J., b Carte de Nord, France, and Louise TURNER, b J. (Jean Wood, Regina, Sask)
JOUAN, Mable Maud, b 1888, sister of Ellen, above. Mar Albert Mathew, b ca 1887 England, rem to Regina, Sask, but returned to J later. 3 chn in J.
 A1. Dorothy Mae Mathew, b 1916 Canada, mar ---RIVE, 3 daus
  B1. Dawn Rive, b 1938 B2. Robin Rive, b 1940 B3. Cleone Rive, b 1945
 A2. Glen Albert Mathew, b 1921, mar, 3 chn. Bricklayer, farmer, Halbrite, Sask.
  B1. Glenn Mathew, b 1945   B3. Mark Mathew, b 1950
  B2. Gaye Mathew, b 1947
JOUAN, from C.I. in Maritimes Fisheries 1800s (J.H. Le Breton list)
JOURNEAU, JOURNEAUX, Francis, b 1810 J, d 1886. Son of James J. Journeaux and Mary HEREAULT, mar Sara MORRISSEY, 1814-1898, dau of John M. and Angelique BAKER, qv. Poss other wife or wives, and other chn. (Brochet; Nola Journeau, St. Eustache, Que.; AUTOUR DE LA FAMILLE JOURNEAUX, Documents Recueilles, L'Islet, Que., 1953 (not seen by compiler); C.E. Roy; Gallant)
 A1. Suzanne, b 1834, mar Lawrence CODY, b 1831 Que. One dau res North Shore
  B1. Laurence Cody, b 1858   B4. May Cody, b 1864
  B2. Susan Cody, b 1860   B5. Ellen Cody, b 1866
  B3. John Cody, b 1862   B6. Catherine Cody, b 1870
 A2. Marie Jeanne, b 1837, mar Philippe LE COUTEUR?, qv

 A3. Francis, mar Mary LE COUTEUR

JOURNEAU, JOURNEAUX

A4. Elisa, Elizabeth, b 1841, mar Francois St. Amant and mar 2.? Peter AUBERT, qv. At least 2 chn, Elizabeth and Francis.
A5. Henriette, b 1844
A6. John James, b 1846. d 1922. mar 1877 Sarah Lamb Morrissey, b 1844 Bon. Is., d 1925. Sarah dau of James Lamb & Ann Brennan. 2 sons
  B1. Francis J, b 1879 Bon.Is. d.y.
  B2. Philip, b 1881 Bon. Is., d 1971, mar Victoria Wall, Irish, b Bon. Is., 1888-1969 POSS.ERRORS IN THIS FAM. CheckRecords
    C1. Theresa, b 1913, mar Wm. BOURGET, b 1907 Newport, Gaspe, rem to Ste. Rose, Que., 7 chn
      D1. Dorinda Bourget, b 1939, mar Dominic Triventi, res Montreal
        E1. Michel Triventi, b 1968   E2. Carmen Triventi, b 1969
      D2. Lorraine Bourget, b 1940, mar Albert Penner, b 1939, res Winnipeg
        E1. Keith Penner, b 1967   E3. Stephen Penner, b 1973
        E2. Sandra Penner, b 1970
      D3. Joyce Bourget, b 1941, mar Eric Gaudet, res Montreal
        E1. Brenda Gaudet, b 1964   E2. Sonia Gaudet, b 1972
      D4. Muriel Bourget, b 1942, res Montreal
      D5. Kenneth Bourget, b 1944, mar Rachel Nash, res Montreal
        E1. Shawn Bourget, b 1970
      D6. Leola Bourget, b 1953, res Montreal
      D7. Marilyn, b 1956, res Montreal
    C2. Irene, b 1914, mar Robert Maloney, b 1915 Bon. Is., res Verdun, Que.
      D1. Anson Maloney, b 1948, mar Wilma Shelley, 3 chn, res Verdun
        E1. Kimberley Maloney, b 1972   E3. Scott Maloney, b 1975
        E2. Lisa Maloney, b 1973
      D2. Sandra Maloney, b 1949, mar Thomas Price, no issue
    C3. Alice, b 1916, mar Nelson BROCHET, qv, b 1914 Bon. Is., res Two Mts., Que. See Brochet, 3 chn.
    C4. Hazel, b 1918, mar Zepherin, Jerry, HAMON, res Two Mts., Que.
      D1. Robert Hamon, b 1940
      D2. Freda Hamon, b 1942, mar ---, res Vancouver, BC, ch b 1976
      D3. Norman Hamon, b 1944   D4. Cleta Hamon, b 1948, mar Brian ---
    C5. George, b 1920, unmar, res Verdun, Que.
    C6. Earl, b 1922, mar Corrinne Pichette, res Niagara Falls, Ont., 5 chn
      D1. Diane D2. Nancy D3. James D4. Sharon D5. Bonnie
    C7. Emily, b 1923, mar Guy McLean, res St. Eustache, Que., 5 chn. She d 1975.
      D1. Linda, mar B. Johnson, res Oshawa, Ont., 2 chn, Tracy and ?
      D2. Allen McLean, mar ---, res St. Eustache, Que.
      D3. Shirley McLean, b 1953, mar Harry Bleeker
      D4. Robert McLean, b 1956   D5. Patty McLean, b 1962
    C8. Ernest, b 1926, mar Nola Myrtle VIBERT, qv, res St. Eustache, Que.
      D1. Gary George JOURNEAU, b 1960, Montreal
    C9. Amanda, b 1928, mar Rex QUINTON, qv, b Nfld., res Toronto, Que.
      D1. Shirley Quinton   D3. Kim Quinton
      D2. Debbie Quinton   D4. Terry Quinton
A7. Angelique, b 1848, mar J.B. Morin Lafrance
A8. James Edward, b 1851 mar Sophronie Vezina, issue?
A9. Mary Ellen, Marie Helene, mar Charles AUBERT, qv.
A10. George Frederick, mar Marie St. Amand
JOURNEAUX, Thomas, b 1816, St. Saviour, J, son of Richard J. and Ester LE BRETON, qv, to L'Islet, Que. Bp there, age 22, in 1838, when he

SEE EXTRA PAGES
mar Monique Gaudreau, who d 1880. He d 1899. (AUTOUR DE LA FAMILLE JOURNEAUX, by Nap. Journeaux, 1953, L'Islet, Que.; Reaman)
A1. Thomas Zepherin, 1841-1916, mar Henriette CARON, 1844-1932
A2. Aurelie, 1842-1925, mar 1868 Ferdinand Gerjeau, 1845-1931
A3. Philippe Zoel, 1844-1894, mar 1. 1877 Vitaline Fortin, 1852-1894, and 2. Georgianna Blanchette
A4. Ignace, 1846-1926, mar 1875 Philomene Guimont, 1854-1930
A5. Hypolyte Milaire, 1847-1918, mar 1874 Hortense Fraser, 1854-1912
A6. Exaree, 1849-1917
A7. Arthemise, 1851-1878   A8. Clarisse Fenoline, 1852?
JOURNEAUX, Philippe, b 1704 J, son of Edward J., b 1678 and Marie de CARTERET, qv, of St. Brelade, J. Rem to Nfld. ca 1732.
JOURNEAUX, Nicholas, b 1742, rem to Gaspe from J, was presumed dead ca 1800. Mar Dina BURT, qv, a dau, Marguerite J. was bp Gaspe 1767, poss d.y.
JOURNEAUX, Philippe, from J, was a signer of the Petition to N. Cox of 1778, against Boston "pirates" at Perce
JOURNEAUX, Philip, b J, mar Betsy Moreaux, rem to Canada (Reamon)
JOURNEAUX, a fishery firm at Chateau Bay, Nfld. 1840
JOURNEAUX, John and Mary, bro and sister from J in Port Daniel West, Gaspe, ca 1800 (C. Journeaux, New Carlisle, Que.)
JOURNEAUX, Claudia Azelia, b J, 1894, dau of Thomas John J. and Esther Azelia HUELIN, mar Alfred John LE RICHE, qv.
JOURNEAUX, Eliza, b 1841, d 1877, mar 1863 Francois de St. Armand, mar 2. 1872, Peter Abel AUBERT. Dau of Francis? See top of page 293.
A1. Eliza Ann, b 1864, who mar 1. George Philip BUTLIN, mar 2. H.R. DU VAL, qv. She d 1921, Ottawa, Ont.
A2. Francis, b 1866, settled Port Daniel, Gaspe.
JOURNEAU, William, 1859-1935, mar Mary Ellen Dea, 1865-1951, bur St. James Ang. Ch, Port Daniel, Que. (GLF)
A1. Olive W., 1855-1901   A2. Stella Sivret?, 1905-1907
JOURNEAU, Cornelius, 1868-1931, mar Annie ---, 1874-1941, bur St. James Angl. Ch, Port Daniel, Gaspe (GLF)
JOURNEAU, Herbert, 1877-1940, mar Amanda Maude, 1876-1955 (GLF)
JOURNEAU, John, memorial at Shigawake, St. Paul's Angl Ch, Gaspe (GLF)
JOURNEAUX, Jane, wife of Eli Scammell, qv. (Florence Ferguson, Strathroy, Ont.)
JOURNEAUX, a Capt. from J in Nfld. early 1800s (K. Mathews)
JOURNEAUX, Philip, b J, cement mill owner, with French Govt. contract. He mar ---, had 2 sons, 2 daus. A son, first name not known, b 1810, mar J, rem to Toronto, Ont. ca 1855, then to Ottawa. Mar Elizabeth MOURANT, qv, dau of Capt. Jacques M. and Jean Maitland, a Scot. (G.F. Peter Journeaux, Willowdale, Ont.)
A1. Sophie, b 1840s J, mar Charles Stanley? of Calif, engineer. She d ca 1878
A2. Philip, b ca 1848 J, rem also to Calif, d there 1940, age 92
A3. Elizabeth, Lizzie, b ca 1858 Toronto , Ont., d Ottawa, 1946, age 87
A4. Henry, b 1862 Ottawa, d Toronto 1924
A5. Frederick Maitland, b 1868 Ottawa, d 1951, age 84. Mar Mary Ellen Dancey, 1867-1951.
  B1. Philip Alexander, b ca 1899 Ottawa, res Kirk's Ferry, Que., mar ---
    C1. George Frederick Peter, b 1934 Ottawa, mar Lorene Brown
      D1. Kari Lorene, b 1967   D2. Kirsten Elaine, b 1969
    C2. Mary Irene, b1935 mar B. Birkabeck Nielsen res Kirk's Ferry, Que.
      D1. Christopher Nielsen, b 1959   D3. Lisa Nielsen, b 1964
      D2. Karen Nielsen, b 1960   D4. Jennifer Nielsen, b 1966

B2. Mary Elizabeth, b 1895, mar Andrew McAnulty, 28 grchn, res Mass.
   Chn: James, Donald, Margaret, Nyal and Frances McAnulty.
B3. Grace, b ca 1904, mar W.L. DE LA RONDE, no issue
B4. F. Stewart, b ca 1900, d 1966, mar Marion McIntyre
   C1. David, res Burlington, Ont.
   C2. Janet   C3. Agnes   C4. Alexander   C5. Sheila
JOWINOIX, JOUINOIX?, a boat keeper from C.I. in Nfld. (K. Mathews)
JOYCE, George Edward, b St. Heliers, J, to Carbonear 1820s (Seary)
KARTELL. Involved in Nfld. trade 1717 (C.R. Fay)
KASTELL, CASTELL?, Capt. from J in Nfld. (K. Mathews) Poss same as KARTELL?
KERAUTRET in Nfld. (Seary) Cf KERAUTRET in J (Stevens)
KERBY, fam in St. Heliers, J 1700s, connected with BALCOM, INGOUVILLE, MAUGER and HAMON families. Poss some of the fam to Canada.
KEYHO, William, from G to Canada 1925, son of Thomas
KEYHO, David W., b 1928 G, mar Heidi Hofer, Swiss, rem to Canada from G, 1959. Mgr. Nissen Trampoline Co., and organizer of Phys. and Health Educ. for Barrie, Ont. Grad 1962 from Univ. of Toronto, later Insp. Ont. Bd. of Education. (Ed. Le Page) A dau, Sally Ann, b 1960 Barrie, Ont. Author, with Sybil Leek, of STARSPEAK. "In the mid 1700s there were two bros. KEOGH, whose Gaelic name means 'horsemen' living in Ireland...They were Protestant in a Catholic Society and were obliged to flee religious persecution in their country. They sailed a boat away from the southern coast of Ireland, intending to sail to Cornwall or Devon, but because of a storm, got driven way beyond their intended landfall and were shipwrecked on the Island of Guernsey. They settled there, changing the spelling of their name to KEYHO, and married local girls. Virtually all of the Channel Island Keyhos are descended from one or the other of these two brothers. I am the 7th generation of Keyhos on Guernsey...our name is pronounced KAY-O." (David Keyho, Kitchener, Ont.) David was raised on G until 1940, rem to England, served in R.A.F., res G 1948-1953, rem to Canada.
KEYHO, Ruby Miriam, b 1918, St. Peter Port, G, dau of Wm. De Garis K., who d 1925, and Zelia BRACHE, d 1969. Ruby mar Elvin Walter Johnson, b 1914 Halls Lake, Ont. Res Minden, Ont.
A1. David William, b 1947, mar Darlene May HAYNES, b 1949
   B1. Kimberley Francine Johnson, b 1972
A2. Ray Ernest, b 1950, mar Candice Ellen Bailey, b 1953
A3. Ralph Walter, b 1958
KEYHO, Joan, sister of Ruby, above, b 1920 St. Peter Port, G, mar Gordon Ingram, res Edmonton, Alta. (Joan Ingram)
A1. Norman Glenn Ingram, b 1959 Edmonton
A2. Bernice Anne Ingram, b 1960 Edmonton
KELLING in Winnipeg, curr, said to be from C.I.
KEMPSTER, Albert Enslin, one of 12 chn, b 1901 St. Clements, J, to New York then Ont. in 1926. Later to Edmonton, Alta. Mar Winnifred Nora BUESNEL, qv, dau of John B. (A.E. Kempster, Edmonton, Alta.)
A1. Kenneth Albert, b 1932, res Edmonton, Alta., mar Jean Robley of Calgary, Alta.
   B1. Lynette, b ca 1957   B3. Susan, b ca 1961
   B2. Wendy, b ca 1959   B4. Carol, b ca 1963
A2. Constance Winnifred, b 1934, mar Donald Colpitts, divorced
   B1. Kathy Colpitts, b ca 1959   B3. Jayne Colpitts, b 1963
   B2. Dean Colpitts, b 1961
A3. Shirley Ann, b 1936, mar John Young, res Penticton, BC
KENNETT, from G to Toronto ca 1920 or 1930

KILNER, in Toronto and other parts of Canada, from C.I.?
KING, variant of LE ROY, old G surname (Carey-Wimbush)
KING in Nfld. (Seary) Cf LE ROY and KING of C.I.
KING, Joseph in Island Cove, Conc. Bay, Nfld. 1793, from C.I.? (Rev. Hammond)
KING, Capt. from J in Nfld. (K. Mathews)
KINSELA, Thomas Nicholas, b G, in Douglastown, Que. 1861 (Census) with Mary or Margaret, Enoch, Harriet, Julia and Caroline, b Gaspe. Poss mar Mary LENFESTY ca 1838 Gaspe Bay (Brochet)
KIRBY, KERBY in Nfld. (Seary) Cf KERBY of J, 1700s
KIRK, M., from G to Victoria, BC before 1940 (Luce)
KNAPP, Capt. from G in Nfld. (K. Mathews) See KNIGHT in added pp.
KNIGHT, from C.I. to Nfld., Elizabeth of Carbonear 1755. See Seary.
KNIGHT in Canada, cf CHEVALIER of J (Stevens) This change took place in New England also.
KNIGHT, Clara, widow of Frank LE NOURY, qv, d 1974, res with niece, Mrs. Hilda Henderson, Burlington, Ont.
KNIGHT, Richard, mar Susanne MAHY, of Hug fam, res St. Peter Port, G. Their younger son, Samuel, with bro-in-law, Richard HOLLAND, emigrated to Queen's Co., NB, petitioned the Lt. Gov. for land grant in 1821, had lived in Sunbury, then Queens, with wife Sophia Holland of UEL fam, mar 1817. Samuel and Sophia had 13 chn. (Arch. Christ Ch, Fredericton, NB; Bertha Wood-Holt, Saint John, NB)
A5. Esther, b 1826, Jemseg, NB, mar there 1844, Charles Henry Wood, son of Moses W. of Eng.
  B1. Stephen Amos Wood, mar Sarah Magowan
    C1. Thomas, d at 22 in 1897
    C2. Ernest Amos, mar Bertha May Graham, Irish
      D1. Bertha Winnifred, mar ---Holt   KRUSE, SEE EXTRA PP.
KRUSE, Alfred C., (Danish fam in J), mar Rachel BUTTON, b J. Their son, b 1901 Campbellton, NB, mar 1928 Gladys LE TOUZEL.
KRUSE, See page 481F, ANEZ-KRUSE MARRIAGE.

KRUSE, Marie, mar Philip BUTLIN, b ca 1865
LABBE, ---, signed Petition in Gaspe 1820, poss LABBE of J (Stevens) Poss also same as LABEY.
LABEY, some in Canada, said to be desc of Pierre L. b 1725, who settled in Canada. Origin uncertain. (Helen Labey Dean, Chatham, Ont.)
LABEY, George Helier, b 1829 J, son of Thomas and Betsy MOURANT, qv, mar Julia AMY, qv in 1859, settled in Belleville, Ont.
A1. George Amy, b 1861 Belleville, mar Addie M. Reed, res Trenton, Ont.
  B1. Gertrude, b 1889, mar B.E. Potts, res Sask, Sask
    C1. Gordon Potts, b 1916, mar Helen Murphy, a dau Sharon Potts
    C2. Dorothy Potts, b 1918, mar Basil Cullen, res Calgary, Alta.
      D1. James Cullen   D2. Judith Cullen, mar ---Sinclair
    C3. John Potts, b 1920, mar Dorothy Bell
      D1. Barry Potts   D2. James Bell Potts
    C4. Audrey Potts, b 1926, mar William Wylie
      D1. Mark Wylie   D3. Pamela Wylie
      D2. Lisa Wylie   D4. Nancy Wylie
  B2. Evelyn M., b 1891, unmar
  B3. Almond Helier, b 1893, mar Beatrice ROBERTS, res U.S., no issue
  B4. Lulu Labey, b 1895, mar John H. Kinney, res Trenton, Ont.
    C1. Douglas Kinney, b 1916, mar Betty Soloman, res Trenton, Ont.
      D1. Ronald Kinney, b 1942, mar Jen. Bonisteel, 2 chn?
      D2. Elwood Kinney, b 1944, mar Lois ---, a dau
    C2. Marjorie Kinney, b 1919, mar Cecil A. Horne, res Dartmouth, N.S.

LABEY

      D1. Margo Lou Horne, b 1942   D4. Ian Douglas Horne, b 1950
      D2. David John Horne, b 1944   D5. Leslie Horne, b 1954
      D3. Stephen Horne, b 1949
   B5. Helen, b 1903, mar Martin Perrin DEAN, rem W. Chatham, Ont.
     C1. Virginia Dean, b 1937, mar Donald D. McGeorge, res Chatham, Ont.
       D1. Heather McGeorge, b 1964   D2. Jean McGeorge, b 1967
     C2. James Dean, b 1942, d of Leukemia, age 25
   B6. Dorothy, b 1909 Toronto, mar Norman Eustace Smith, res Vancouver, BC, separated
     C1. Martha Jane, b 1950, mar Byron? Hill, res Toronto
LABEY, Reginald Mourant, b 1894 J?, rem to Lloydminster, Sask. He was the son of George Thomas L. and Jane Mary MOURANT, qv.
A1. Donald?
A2. Clifford, mar Valerie Johnson, res Mississauga, Ont.
   B1. Clifford James, b 1948   B3. Ronald George, b 1951
   B2. Philip Randolph, b 1949   B4. Murray Reginald, b 1952
A3. Doris, mar Jerry Foster
   B1. Hugh F. Foster   B2. Judith Ann Foster   B3. Jerry Foster
LABEY, Louise, b J, mar D.A. DE BROCQ, LE BROCQ?, rem to Toronto, Ont. early 1900s. Related to George A. Labey, qv. (and below, Violet Robertson, Winterhaven, Fla.)
LABEY, Francis Hocquard, b ca 1875 J, son of Francis Hocquard of J, rem to Paspebiac, Gaspe, then to Stonewall, Man. where he is bur. Mar Adelize LE GALLAIS, qv. (Mrs. Frank Labey, Toronto, Ont.)
A1. Violet, mar Earle Robertson of Winnipeg, no issue, res Fla.
A2. Eileen, b 1907, nurse, unmar, res Fla.
A3. Francis, b 1910, res Toronto, mar Eileen Jones of Wales, England
   B1. Ann Winifred, mar Ken. CLEMENTS, b 1939 England
     C1. Kimberly Clements, b 1962   C2. Lori Clements, b 1964
   B2. Judy, mar Michael Coulter, has adopted son
   B3. Michael David, b 1941, mar Renate Cook, res Lethbridge, Alta.
     C1. David, b 1974   C2. Craig, b 1975
LABEY, banker in Vancouver, BC ca 1940
LABEY, curr Gaspe
LABEE, Jacques, in Gaspe 1820
LABEY, F.P., in Toronto, from C.I.?
LA BARGE, BARGY, sev fams to Canada. One to Ont., poss some to Gaspe. Name in Alpena, Mich. 1905 where some Gaspe people settled in the 1800s.
LA BILLOIS, from C.I. to Gaspe and/or N.B. (John D. Alexander, Campbellton, N.B.)
LA BLANC, from C.I. to Nfld. (Hug. Soc. and G.W. Le Messurier)
LABOU, John Bernard, b 1922 St. Aubin, J, son of John L. and Emma M. Paul of St. Heliers, J, mar Marguerite G. Le Dez, b France. Rem to Ont. (J. Labou, Toronto, Ont.)
A1. John Lewis, b Toronto 1957   A2. Michael Neil, b 1959 Toronto
LA BRUE, Benj. in Cul de Sac, Nfld. 1860s. Said to be of C.I. origin, poss LE BREUILLY, LE BRUN, LE BREU, LA BRIE, LE BREUX, LE BRECQUE? A LA BRU is mentioned as one of the early companies in Canada by H.P. Biggar
LACHEUR, see LE LACHEUR. See also Hammond; Nicolle; and Machon.
LA CLOCHE, old name in J, fisherman in Gaspe early 1800s. This surname often changed in N.A. to BELL
LA COGNES?, fam from C.I. to Ontario. Cf LE COIGNET?
LA COSTA in Nfld. (Seary) Cf DA COSTA
LA COURS, LE COURS, DE LA COUR, DE LA COURT in Nfld. (Seary) Cf same and similar of J. (Rev. Hammond)

LA COUTURE, one of the oldest J surnames, poss in Canada?
LA COUVEE, also LE COUVET, LE COUVEE, etc., in Gaspe. Said to be of C.I. origin. (J.H. Le Breton list) LA COUVEE in B.C.
LA COUVEE, Mary, age 86 in 1861, (Census), widow, nee Appleby. Dau, Anne MAUGER, age 54, was at Bon. Is., Gaspe 1861 (Brochet) Surname curr Gaspe Bay. See P. 169.
LA CROIX, from C.I. to Canada. Name in Alpena, Mich. 1905, where some Gaspe people settled late 1800s.
LA CROIX, LA CROY, boat keeper in Nfld., from C.I. (K. Mathews) Name in BC also.
LA DROS, Mary, in Brigus 1762, said to be C.I. surname (Rev. Hammond) George La Oros there in 1795 and Nicholas in 1788. Others in Cupids, Nfld.
LAFOLLEY, Robert and Edward, twins, to N.B., res Grand Manan Island. (Mrs. Ivan Laffoley and Mrs. Claude Ellis, Gales Ferry, Conn.) There was a ---Lafoley mar in St. Ouen, J 1729, Abraham PITTON, see PITON.
LAFFOLEY, Abbe Louis Nelson, "certainly a desc of Jerseymen, poss son of Nelson L....one of the managers of the Fruing Co. at Mont Louis, Que." (J.H. Le Breton, Gaspe)
LAFFOLEY, Philip T., b J, to Moncton, NB ca 1870
LAFFOLEY, Philip, in Gaspe 1820 (Petition) Mar Mary LE GROS. Philip Jr. mar Perce Oct.1810 Brigit Molloy. Son Philip mar Margaret Shea. (Brochet) Philip Sr. b 1783 G, son of Ph.7 Marie LE GROS L.
LAFFOLEY, Philip, b J, rem to Quebec ca 1812, mar ---De Vere. Hug fam, builders, craftsmen. "Philip came to Canada in a boat he designed and built. Later in Boston he made wood vestibules for the trolley system. Was also a violin maker, made hundreds of them." (Paul Laffoley, Boston, Mass.)

A1. Edmond
A2. Frederick
A3. Percival
A4. Reginald
A5. Alice, mar ---Eichorn?

LAFFOLEY, Charles, b J, son of Charles and of Marguerite DE LA LANDE, to Montreal
  A1. Charles Nelson, b 1874 J, to Mont Louis in Gaspe, age 14. At 28 he mar there, Emma Letourneau, d suddenly in 1912, age 38. (Annette Fournier, Grande Valley, Gaspe, Que.)
    B1. Lilian, b 1906 at Mont Louis, res Cap Chat, unmar
    B2. Louis Nelson, b 1911, priest at Cloridorme
    B3. Annette, b 1909 Mont Louis, mar 1943 Douat Fournier, 4 chn
      C1. Marie Frances, mar Egide Minville, 3 chn; Carmen, Sylvaine, Carleen
      C2. Marie May, mar Lucien Minville, 2 chn, Nelson, Maryline
      C3. Marie Lys, mar Guy Gleeton of Cloridorme, 2 chn, Allen, Guylaine
      C4. Nelson, dentist, mar Colombe Chicoine

A2. Nelson Sydney
A3. Sydney Giffard
A4. Ophilia, mar Henry COOPER
A5. Hilda Marie

LAFFOLEY, Giffard, related to above family, president of the Board of Trade in Montreal, a dau Lois, mar in New York. Giffard b in Jersey.
LAFFOLEY, ---, bro of Philip above, from J, settled Grand Manan Island, desc. Said to have d in Halifax, NS ca 1911 (Paul Laffoley, Boston, Mass.) LAFFOLEY data found in secret drawer in mariner's secretary of George L. "I was married Sept. 24, 1788, my age 24, my wife 28. (Poss Jane ---?, b N.S.)

A1. Saley, Sally?, b May 24, 1790
A2. William, b 1793
A3. Tim, b 1795
A4. Lucy, b 1796
A5. Marier, b 1798
A6. Iney, poss Inez?
A7. Stephen, b 1801
A8. James, b 1804
A9. Benjamin, b 1806
A10. ---tey, b 1808

LAFFOLEY, Robert and Edith, of this fam?, parents of a Mrs. Ellis. Her grandparents were George LAFFOLEY and Mary Elizabeth ---. Robert and Edward, twins of this fam were b 1868. Res Westport, NS? (Mary Ellis, Gales Ferry, Conn.)
LAFFOLEY, George, age 75, mariner, b J, wife Jane, age 76, b N.S., Ch of Eng., res NS 1800s (Lloyd Melanson, Haligax, NS)
LA FLEUR, LA FLURE, in Gaspe and in Alpena, Mich. where Gaspe folk rem late 1800s. LA FLEUR sometimes changed to FLOWERS?
LA FOSSE, C.I. surname on S. coast of Nfld. (G.W. Le Messurier)
LA FOUR, Francois, of J?, mar Mary CHEVALIER, who d 1842, age 78, res Sandy Beach, Gaspe. Unverified
LA FRANCE, George and Prosper in Nfld., said to be of C.I. origin (Rev. Hammond)
LA FRANCE, also appeared on Gaspe Petition 1820 with many C.I. surnames
LAGADU, from J to Cape St. George, Nfld. ca 1900 (Seary, Rev. Hammond)
LA GERCHE, J surname, appeared at St. Peter Pt., Gaspe 1800s. Connected with LE COUTEUR surname of J.
LAINE, C.G., from G to Hamilton, Ont.
LAINEY, LAINEZ, fam from C.I. to Nfld. (K. Mathews, Seary) LAINE, Wm. from G? in Hibb's Hole, Nfld. 1745. A Wm. Laine in Brigus 1768 (Seary) Henry in Hibb's Hole 1759. Cf LAINE, LAISNEY of C.I.
LAKE, Wilfred C., left G to serve with the Royal Field Artillery 1914-1918, later rem to Canada. Visited G at age 82 with dau, Mrs. Winifred Vargo and son, Clifford LAKE. At age 9, Wilfred worked in a quarry in the north of G, was b at L'Islet, G. Mar Mary Frances PHILIPPS of St. Sampsons, G, had 12 chn, five sons and 4 daus, res Canada. The couple celebrated diamond jubilee ca 1975? 40 grchn, 29 grgrchn. (Edw. Le Page, Grimsby, Ont.)
LAKE in Nfld. (Seary) Cf LAKE of C.I.
LAKE, said to be a number of this fam in Ontario, from C.I.
LA MARR, DE LA MARE?, from C.I. to Nfld. (Rev. Hammond) See DE LA MARE
LA MARSH, from C.I. to Ontario and B.C.
LA MASURIER, sometimes noted in Canada. Mistake for LE MASURIER, qv? or another surname?
LAMB, Richard, in Buck Cove, Conc. Bay, Nfld. 1776, said to be of C.I. origin (Rev. Hammond)
LAMBERT, C.I. surname on S. coast of Nfld. (G.W. Le Messurier, Seary)
LAMBERT, Capt., merchant, and boat owner from G to Nfld. (K. Mathews)
LA MONTAGNE, said to be surname of C.I. in Gaspe and elsewhere in Canada
LAMY, L'AMY, several from J to Canada, Quebec and B.C. See AMY
LAMY, Jack, from J to Gaspe early 1900s, returned to J. (J.H. Le Breton; Gerald Le Bas, Toronto)
LANGDON, C.I. in Maritimes Fisheries (J.H. Le Breton list)
LANGIN in Nfld. (Seary) Cf LANGIN of J (Stevens)
LANGLAIS, J.P., b J, rem to Mitchell, Perth Co., Ont. ca 1862. A planing mill operator.
LANGLAIS, Ferris, b J, worked for Robin firm in Caraquet, NB 1861 (Census) age 27. (Rev. Le Gresley)
LANGLAIS, LANGLOIS. "I found mention of this Philippe LANGLOIS, and a note in the registers that they became LANGLAIS. Iwas also told that some LANGLOIS who went to work in USA or English Canada became ENGLISH." (Colette LA CROIX, Ste. Foy, Quebec)
LANGLAIS, poss many desc of Philippe L. son of J. Ely, many fams in Grande Riviere, Que.
LANGLOIS, curr at L'Anse au Griffon, Barachois and Perce, of whom some are French, not from C.I.

LANGLOIS/ENGLISH, Jane mar J.Cann. Many desc.in Nova Scotia(Gottwald)
LANGLOIS, Philippe, b J, son of Jean Ely L. and Marguerite GALLICHAN,
    qv, of J, mar 1825 at Grande Riviere, Gaspe to Euphrosine COUTURE,
    dau of Pierre C. and Marie Leonard.
A1. Philippe, b 1826, Gr. Riviere, d.y.
A2. Marguerite, b 1828, mar 1844 Daniel Blainey, son of John B. and
    Angelique Desnoyers of Riviere de Loup, Gaspe, d Grand Riv. 1850
A3. Marie, b 1829 Gr. Riv., mar there 1848 James Wafer, son of ---Wafer
    and Brigit? LAWRENCE, qv.
A4. Elisabeth, b 1831, d 1836   A7. John, b 1839
A5. Lisette, b 1833   A8. Joseph, b 1841
A6. Philippe Henry, b 1837   A9. Francois, b 1845
LANGLOIS, Peter, of Shiphead, Gaspe, mar Mary BOURGAIZE, a dau Eliza
    b 1843
LANGLOIS, Peter, b 1784 G, d in Quebec City, age 82. (MS Memoirs, re-
    ferring to the RISE AND PROGRESS OF WESLEYAN METHODISM IN QUEBEC FROM
    1800) See NOTABLES, CLERGY, this book. (Dom. Arch.)
LANGLOIS, Margaret?, b G, in Cap Rosier, Gaspe 1861 (census) also Peter,
    Margaret, Elizabeth and John, all b L.C.
LANGLOIS, settled in Port Daniel, Gaspe. One fam to Gaspe 1777 (Syvret)
LANGLOIS, LANGLAIS, poss changed to ENGLISH, J.P., b J, rem to Mitchell,
    Perth Co., Ont. ca 1862, planing mill operator.
LANGLOIS, Louisa, mar John Edward LE HUQUET, qv, in Gaspe, 1860s
LANGLOIS, in Cap Chat, Gaspe, 1861 Census
LANGLOIS, Thomas, rem from Gaspe to Toronto in 1874?, mar Rachel ROSE,
    qv, d 1878. Res Beaverton, Ont. Thomas? b ca 1794 G, to Canada ca
    age 22. Carpenter, fisherman, Preacher. Fam converted by John Wesley
    to Methodism. Locally preached in Gaspe, and travelled on horseback
    through the area for a number of years. (Mrs. G. Langlois, Toronto,
    Ont.) Poss this Thomas with wife Rachel in Gaspe Bay 1871 (Census)
A1. Nicholas   A3. James   A5. Mary Jane,b1851
A2. Rachel   A4. John   See data in added pages.
A6. William, b 1855 Gaspe, mar Jane, Jennie Whitecross Gray
    B1. Mabel, b 1889 Toronto, mar Norman CARTER
    B2. Mary, b 1893, mar Milton Lovering
    B3. Isabella, b 1895, mar Hubert Dundas
    B4. Pearl, b 1898, mar Monte Griffin
    B5. Gordon, b 1900, mar Gladys Booth, 3 chn?
    B6. Evelyn, b 1904, mar Ed. Radke
LANGLOIS, from G to Grand Greve, Gaspe, 1800s
LANGLOIS, prob from J? in Richmond Co., N.S. 1861 (Census)
LANGLOIS, Charles, built the Mary B, 45 ton ship at River Bourgeois,
    NS, later owned in P.E.I. (Capt. Parker)
LANGLOIS, Desire, poss French, owned the LIBERAL, 86 ton ship, 1847, res
    Descousse, N.S.
LANGLOIS, Philippe, b J, a mason, son of Francois and Suzanne ROMERIL,
    qv, to Perce, Gaspe ca 1863. Mar 1869 Genereuse Laflamme, dit Kem-
    neur. She was age 25 in 1861, b Quebec. He was a fisherman and ma-
    son. Poss a widower, as an Edward is listed as b 1863. (Colette
    Lacrois, Sainte-Foy, Que.) (See note on LANGLAIS-LANGLOIS above)
A1. Philippe, b 1870 Perce   A4. William Hypolite, b 1877
A2. Joseph, b 1873 Perce, mar 1899   A5. Francois, b 1879, d.y.
A3. Marie Suzanne, b 1875, d ca 1876   A6. Josephine, b 1880, d.y.
A7. Edouard, b 1863? Fisherman and farmer, poss adopted? Mar 1895
    Marguerite Cronier. He d 1957, age 94.
    B1. Joseph Edouard Donatier, b 1895, d 1900
    B2. Pierre Rodolphe Alexandre, b 1897, mar 1926 Bertha Flynn, d 1976
    B3. Marguerite Marie Anne, b 1898, mar 1928 Robert LAKE, qv.

LANGLOIS   301

  B4. Jean Emilien, b 1901, mar 1937 Annette LAMBERT, d 1974. Barber
      at Grande Riviere 1951.
    C1. Colette, b 1939, mar 1960 Guy Lacroix, Ph.D., Laval Univ.
      D1. Louise Lacroix, b 1962   D2. Dominique Lacroix, b 1967
  B5. Joseph Edmond, b 1905, mar 1950 Lumina Appleby, res Ontario
  B6. Joseph Charles, b 1906, mar 1940 Stella Flynn, not related to
      Bertha Flynn
  B7. Marie Gilberte, b 1909, d 1912
  B8. Marie Berthe Emilie, b 1913, mar 1938 Anthony McKoy
  B9. Joseph Paul Eugene, b 1916, mar 1963 Rita BOURGET, widow of
      ---Sweeney
LANGLOIS, Lewis, b 1884 Pied de Monte, St. Sampson, G, son of James
  Henry L. and Louisa Harriet MAUGER, qv, mar Harriet Olive SAUVARY,
  qv, dau of Thomas Fall S. and Harriet BEAN, rem to Victoria, BC ca
  1906. Wife came in 1910, 6 chn. (Eileen Taylor, Cobble Hill, BC)
  A1. Lewis Thomas, b 1911, mar Marjorie Fletcher
  A2. Leonie Olive, b 1912, mar W. Frank Reeves
    B1. Ronald James Reeves, b 1940
    B2. Janice Marie Reeves, b 1945, mar ---, dau and son
  A3. Eileen Edna, b 1914, mar Geoffrey Taylor
  A4. Marjorie Leah, b 1916
  A5. Henry Hames, James?, b 1917, mar M. Eileen Johnson
    B1. Pamela Eileen, b 1947, mar ---, 2 sons
  A6. Bernice Louise, b 1923
LANGLOIS, Thomas Jr., b G, mar there 1830s, Marguerite FERBRACHE, qv.
  Thomas and his bro Jean owned Upper and Lower Vrangue Mills. Business
  failed after 1850. His widow and dau Julie rem to N.Y. state.
  (Richard Ruggles, Glen Williams, Ont.)
  A1. Marguerite, b 1835 G, res there in 1842, but was in Hamilton, Ont.
      1858. Mar Elias James LE PATOUREL, qv, b 1834 St. Peter Port, G,
      son of Thomas Le P. and Julie LE CHEMINANT, qv.
  A2. Julie Patty, b 1844 Bordage, St. Sampson, G, mar ---Benson, and
      mar 2. ---Cook, a judge in Rochester, N.Y.
  A3. May, mar ---Styles, res Winnipeg, Man.
  A4. Elizabeth (Marie?) who mar Daniel LE MESURIER, qv, res Hamilton, Ont.
  A5. Richard, b 1850
LANGTRY, Lillie Charlotte LE BRETON, The Jersey Lillie, was born in St.
  Saviour Parish 1853. Her beauty, acting and talent for headline
  made her famous in England, Canada and the United States. Her career
  brought her to America many times, and she was a citizen of the U.S.
  for at least five years, residing at times in California. Desc. in
  England and Scotland. (Because I Loved Him, by Noel Gerson; and
  other books)
LANNON, John, in Great Placentia Bay, Nfld. 1860s, said to be of C.I.
  Poss LANYON, of LANNOY of J (Rev. Hammond)
LA PERELLE, forestry lumber firm, established at Rimouski, Que. ca
  1900, thought to be owned by the C.I. family DE LA PERELLE, qv.(Aldo
  Brochet) Elie, age 60 in Bon. Co. 1871.
LA PIERRE, from C.I. to Gaspe (K.H. Annett) <u>LARAWAY,SEE LE RUEZ</u>
LARAIX, Mrs. D., a Guernsey Club member in London, Ont. early 1900s
LARBALESTIER, Cecil, b ca 1890 J, rem to Western Canada. Mar Ann GENGE,
  qv. Later res B.C.
  A1. Duncan Philip, b 1925, d 1973. Mar Nancy ---, 3 daus. He was an
      engineer.
L'ARBALESTIER, b J, rem 1955 to Vancouver, BC, married, 4 chn.
L'ARBALESTIER, Dorothy Rebecca, sister of Bernard, b 1903 St. Heliers,
  J, dau of Walter L. and Rebecca LE CRAS, who was one of the 6 chn of

Francis BISSON LE CRAS. To Canada, mar --- Shield, res Kingston, Ont.
(D. Shield, Kingston, Ont.)
LARRAWAY, LARROWAY, appears in Ont. 1783 to 1823 in THE LOYALISTS IN
ONTARIO, by Wm. D. Reid, Lambertville, N.J., 1973) These are poss
desc of Philip LE RUEZ, b 1757 J, who became LARAWAY in Poultney,
Vermont late 1700s. A Lydia LARROWAY mar John Keller of Fredericksburg, Ont. LARAWAY, RESEARCH BY C. HUYETT, WESTCHESTER, PA.
LORWAY, poss variant of above corrupted surname?
LA RUE, Capt. and boat owner from J in Nfld. (K. Mathews) Cf DELARUE
LA SERRE, LA SERRA, LE SERRE, LE SARRE, ---, Hug surname in J. A surgeon of this surname of G, was a member of the council of the Dist.
of Assinboia, in Rupert's Land, northwestern Canada in 1813. "A
superior man in every respect, from Guernsey, related to Gen. Brock."
"A man of science." He d shortly after this in 1813 at Red River.
Effects sent home to his executors. (THE CANADIAN NORTHWEST, ITS EARLY
DEVELOPMENT, Vol. 1, edited by Prof. E.H. Oliver, Univ. of Sask.,
Ottawa, 1914; THE STRANGE BRIGADE, by John Jennings, Boston and Toronto, 1952)
LE SUEUR, Daniel, from J?, was in Bon. Is., Gaspe 1824 (Brochet)
LATIMER, see Jane DOREY
LAUGA, a Capt. from J in Nfld. (K. Mathews) This surname also seen as
LAUGEE and LOUGEE, LAUGIER, etc. See QAAM. LOUGEE in J 1692.
LAURENCE, Wm. from C.I.? to Port de Grave, Nfld. 1676 (See Seary)
LAURENS, LAWRENCE in Nfld. (Seary) cf LAURENS of J (Stevens)
LAURENS, from C.I.? in Gaspe (Brochet)
LAURENS, John, of J?, at Bon. Is., Gaspe 1825, 1831 (Brochet) In Census, John was age 26 in 1871, with wife Caroline Maloney, age 37 and
4 chn in Malbaie, Gaspe. SEE BOTTOM OF PAGE.
LA VACHE, Alex. owned the ELIZABETH, 66 tons, at Arichat, middle 1800s.
This surname could be French, but also occured in J early.
L'AVENTURE, William, b J, foreman at Gr. Riviere 1871
LA VALLEE, from C.I.?, curr Gaspe. See also LE VALLEY
LA VALLEE, ---, b ca 1851 Alderney, mar ---GALE, rem to London then
Chatham, Ont., desc Thomas and Henry res Chatham
LA VALLEY, Susanna, wife of Jeremiah Sabin. Their dau, Diedamia Sabin
mar 1785 Nathan SAVARY, qv, in Digby, NS. Susanna was a desc of the
Hug fam of Levalley or Lavallee, which came to Marble head, Mass.
from France or from the Channel Islands. Evidentally, a Levalley was
a U.E.L. and rem to Nova Scotia, as did Nathan SAVARY. (New England
Register ca 1924)
LA VALLEE, from C.I.? to Nfld. ca 1800? (Seary)
LA VIELLE, Pierre, a butcher, res Toronto then Florida 1950s, thought
to be from G.
LAW. A man of this surname and his wife named ---Waterman came from G
to Ontario, 1800s? (Gladys Smith, Ingersoll, Ont.)
A1. Gladys, mar ---Smith, res Ingersoll, Ont.
A2. ---, mar LE POIDEVIN, rem to Western Canada
LAWRENCE, LAURENS?, several in Gaspe intermarried with the Channel Island families in Gaspe and thought to be mostly from J.
LAWRENCE, John, or LAURENS, John, mar Elizabeth Maloney, b Perce 1803,
dau of Wm. M. and Johanna BEAKER, BAKER? (one Irish,wife German)
A1. Jane, b Bon. Is. 1822, mar there 1840 Alexandre CAMPION, b France
A2. Peter, b 1823, d 1825   A3. Elizabeth, b 1825
A4. Harriet, b 1827, mar J.J.Brochet. MANY DESC. OF THIS FAM.
A5. Julie b 1830 Bon.Is.   A6. Katherine, b 1831 IN MALBAY. QUE.
A7. Margaret, 1833-1836   A9. Philip, b 1841, d.y.

A8. John b 1867 mar cousin Caroline Maloney. 6 chn.
A10. Patrick, b 1842 Bon.Is.
A11. Adelaide, b 1844 cousin Michael Maloney
LAWRENCE, Elizabeth, wife of Edw. HOTTON, qv, 1873-1957, at Malbaie,
   Gaspe
LAWRENCE, Louisa Anna, 1877-1960, mar 1917 August BROCHET, qv. She was
   desc of John and Caroline L.
LAWRENCE, Agnes, 1883-1918, wife of Philip LE GALLAIS, qv. Bur St.
   Andrews United, Port Daniel, Gaspe (GLF) Agnes poss Scottish, not
   from C.I. (Brochet)
LAWRENCE, John, estab in Bonaventure Island 1803
LAWRENCE, Arthur, 1874-1952, b J? or Gaspe, mar Susan LE GRAND, qv,
   bur St. Andrews United, Port Daniel, Gaspe (GLF) Arthur poss Scot-
   tish, not from C.I. (Brochet)
LAWRENCE, T., at Barachois, Gaspe 1800s
LAWRENCE, Thomas, in La Poile, Nfld. 1860s From C.I.? (Rev. Hammond)
LAWRENCE, Francis, bro of John above, mar Catherine Maloney
A1. Maria, b 1819 Bon. Is., mar ca 1840 Abraham GALLICHAN, Jr., qv.
A2. Caroline, b 1822 Bon.Is., d 1823?
LAWTON, Sydney Corsellis, b J, and his brother Richard John, b in Eng.,
   are mentioned in OUR HEROES IN THE GREAT WORLD WAR, by J.H. De Wolfe,
   Canada 1919, as enlisting from Ottawa, Ont. in Dec. 1914. They were
   related to Isabella Lawton, res Hastings, Eng.
LEADBEATER, Gertrude, b G, mar ---TOWER in Canada 1912. (Edw. Le Page,
   Grimsby, Ont.)
LEALE, a Miss ---, from G, mar Rev. Cecil Swanson, Christ Ch Cathedral,
   Vancouver, BC. Year not known.
LEAMY in Nfld. (Seary) Cf LEMME of J (Stevens)
LEAMON, LEAMAN, prob from LE MOINE in Nfld. Said to be of C.I. origin
   (Rev. Hammond) Poss also LEMAN of J. (Stevens) See Seary
LEAR in Nfld. (Seary) Cf LERE, LERRIER of J (Stevens; Shortis-Munn)
LEARNING in Nfld. (Seary) said to be from G, at Cartright, Labrador
   before 1852. Cf LAURNEYS of J (Stevens)
LE BAIRE, LE BER?, Capt. from G in Nfld. (K. Mathews)
LE BAILLY, involved in 1717 in Nfld. trade from J (C.R. Fay)
LE BARGE, LE BARGY, Albert, b G, mar there Maria PRIEST, half sister
   of Edith RIPLEY, qv, COURTOIS, qv. First to St. Thomas, rem to
   Flint, 3 girls, and a boy. (Rita Roberts, Pontiac, Mich.) See also
   LA BARGY
LE BAS, see also BARNES
LE BAS, Capt. William, and his wife Elvina Sophia LE QUESNE, res J.
   He was a sea capt. and vessel owner. Three of their sons, of 7 chn,
   rem to N.A. Wm. to Gaspe ca 1900; Roland, who changed his name to
   Barnes; Spencer, also Barnes, Margaret who res J, and 3 other bro-
   thers who were in Canada, but returned to J. (Mabel Le Bas, Toronto,
   Ont; Marion Hawkes, N. Vanc., BC)
I. William C., b 1886 St. Helier, J, to Canada 1900 to work for Robin
   Collas Co. until 1943, when he was killed in an accident. Mar 1892
   Mabel Gertrude Glover.
A1. Margaret Gertrude, mar John Howe
B1. Mark Le Bas Howe, b 1955, res London, Ont.
II. Roland, changed name to Barnes, res Seattle, Wash. Mar Marion ---,
   no issue and 2. Ruth ---.
III. Spencer, changed name to Barnes, res Vancouver, b 1898 St. Helier,
   J, rem to Gaspe age 14, d 1971. Served with Black Watch Highland-
   ers during WWI, age 16. Rem to U.S., mar 1. Eileen Ella Nesbitt
   who d 1975, age 80. Divorced. Mar 2. 1925, a widow in Vancouver,

BC with 4 chn.
A1. Marion Louella Barnes, b 1927 Vanc., mar Clifford Wm. Hawkes
   B1. Michael William Hawkes, b 1951 Vancouver, BC
   B2. Mark Spencer Hawkes, b 1957
A2. Roland Frank Barnes, Col. and Assistant Judge Advocate for the Can.
   Forces in Ottawa, Ont. Mar 1954 Dorothy Dugdale
   B1. Alan George Barnes, b 1956 Edmonton, Alta.
   B2. Barbara Eileen Barnes, b 1958 Germany
   B3. Linda Joy Barnes, b 1959 Germany
   B4. David Barnes, b 1962 Ottawa
IV. Margaret Le Bas, res J, mar, 2 sons, Donald and George
V, VI, VII, brothers, to Canada, but returned to J
LE BAS, involved in the Maritimes Fisheries, from J (J.H. Le Breton list)
LE BAS, see added data in Additions and Corrections pages.
VALPY and LE BAS, fishery firm in Gaspe, 1800s (Brochet)
LE BAS, from J, settled Perce (Cent. Bklt.)
LE BAS, Capt. from J and/or G in Nfld., early 1800s (K. Mathews)
LE BASS, two sisters, Ann and Elizabeth, b St. Heliers ca 1820, daus
   of Francis LE BAS and Mary DURELL, were wives of Peter ROMERIL, qv,
   and rem to Utah, middle 1800s. (See QAAM)
LE BASTARD, from C.I., in New Westminster, B.C.
LE BASTARD, from C.I., in New Brunswick (Robichard) Origin not verified.
LE BEL, from C.I.? occurs in New Carlisle, and Bonaventure, Gaspe and
   in Toronto and Vancouver, B.C. Origin unverified.
LE BELIER, C. Islanders in Maritimes Fisheries (J.H. Le Breton list)
   Also as LE BELLIER?
LE BELLIER, Percy Albert, b 1893, St. Peter, J, son of John Albert Le
   B. and Mary Ann GIBEAU of J, to Canada 1908, res Newport, Gaspe. Mar
   1920 Yvonne Dupuis, b Gr. Riv., Gaspe 1900. She d 1976. (Mrs. C.
   Filion, Montreal, Que.)
A1. Lloyd John, b 1920 Newport, mar 1943 Therese Legruiec of Cap
   d'Espoir
   B1. Vyola, b 1945 Chandler, Gaspe, mar Jean Paul MAINVILLE
      C1. Nolleen, b 1966
   B2. Lloyd, b 1946, mar Rena Leblanc 1966, son Lloyd b 1976
   B3. Mona, b 1950, mar Renald Lemieux, Cap Chat, a dau
   B4. Diana, b 1954
A2. Doris, b 1922, mar 1948 at Chandler, Que., Alphonse Ouellette of
   Cacouna, Que., res Chandler
   B1. Charlotte Ouellette, b 1953   B3. Claudine Ouellette, b 1957
   B2. Suzanne Ouellette, b 1954   B4. Jacques Ouellette, b 1961
A3. Percy Romeo, b 1923, mar 1949 Chandler, Que., Edith Mahler, b
   Germany
   B1. Manfred, b 1950, mar Melba Fahye 1973 B2. Peter
A4. Reginald, b 1925, d 1966
A5. Doreen, mar Charles-Auguste Filion of Limoilou, Que. 1950. A dau,
   Audrey, b 1955, Three Rivers, Que.
A6. Nolleen, b 1932 Chandler, Que., d 1974
LE BER, William, b ca 1824 Ald?, mar Maria OLIVER, qv. William was a
   cattleman, taking stock to a French port for sale. Said to be Hug.
   fam. To Ont. ca 1877. (Maurice Le Ber, Sharon, Ont.; Rosaline Aus-
   tin, West Hill, Ont.; Irene Grey, Newmarket, Ont.; Luella Grey,
   Toronto, Ont.)
A1. Mary, b 1850 Ald., mar ---QUESNEL, remained in C.I. At least 1 son.
   B1. Nicholas William, b 1872 St. Annes, Ald., rem to Toronto, Ont. in
      1884, age 12, prob lived with grandparents LE BER, above. Worked
      for John Inglis & Son Co. Mar ---? A dau Marion mar William

LE BER

Imrie. Poss another dau Margaret, or ch of Marion Imrie, res Toronto.
A2. Harriet, b 1852 Ald., d 1892 Ontario
A3. Susan Oliver, b 1855, d.y. in Ald.
A4. William John, b 1857 Ald., mar Elizabeth Stone
  B1. William, mar Elizabeth?, Lizzie, Roach
    C1. Isobel, b 1903, mar Walter Annandale, 3 chn?
  B2. Henry, Harry, b 1874, mar Frances Fallows, poss FALLU? qv.
    C1. William John Henry, b 1908, mar Rosaline Austin, res West Hill, Ont.
      D1. William John Thornton, b 1927, mar Jane Sword, res St. Catherines, Ont.
        E1. Mary Suzanne, b 1952   E3. Elizabeth Jane, d.y.
        E2. James Alan, b 1958
      D2. Robert Austin, b 1933, mar Eleanor Rooney?, res Ottawa, Ont.
        E1. Richard, b 1958 E2. David, b 1964 E3. Catherine, b 1968
      D3. Barbara Gail, b 1935, mar Victor HIBBS, qv, res West Hill, Ont.
        E1. Andrea Gail Hibbs, b 1962 E2. Carolyn Anne Hibbs, b 1964
    C2. Audrey?
  B3. Charles
    C1. Charles, b 1912
      D1. Brian, b 1940s   D2. Eric   D3. Charles
    C2. Dorothy, mar Johnson
  B4. George, b 1875, d 1912 B5. Pearl B6. Oliver, b 1880
A5. Nicholas Thomas, b 1862, mar Margaret Williamson
  B1. Harriet Beatrice, d.y.
  B2. Margaret Louise, b 1890, mar 1918 Robert Leslie Wright, b 1884, res Bobcaygeon, Ont.
    C1. Margaret Louise Wright, b 1925, mar Lloyd Bruce Ingram, b 1927
      D1. Stephen Lloyd Ingram, b 1953 D2. David Bruce Ingram, b 1956
    C2. Roberta Wright, b 1920s, mar William Robertson Kennedy, in 1957
      D1. Leslie Garfield Kennedy, b 1959
      D2. Laura Marie Kennedy, b 1961
      D3. William Nicholas Kennedy, b 1962
  B3. Stanley Nicholas, b 1896, mar Hazel Josephine Ada Broad. He d 1946, she d ca 1976 in Edmonton, Alta.
    C1. Dr. Stanley Marshall, b 1921, mar several times, no issue, res Houston, Texas
    C2. Maurice Nicholas, b 1923, mar Barbara Wilson, res Sharon, Ont.
      D1. Michael Norman, b 1951   B4. Kelly Maurice, b 1958
      D2. Timothy Mark, b 1953   B5. Allison, b 1961
      D3. Stanley Nicholas, b 1956 B6. Nicole, b 1965
    C3. Katherine Mary, b 1925, mar Ernest Frieson
      D1. Joanne Elizabeth Frieson
      D2. Mona Elizabeth, Betty, Frieson, b 1929, mar Kenneth Cartwright, res Vancouver, BC, no issue
A6. Susan Anne, b 1866, mar Joseph Gray, b 1864, d 1943. Susan d 1897, res Toronto.
  B1. Luella Mary Marie Gray, b 1892, d 1976 Toronto, Ont.
  B2. Norman Joseph Oliver Gray, b 1895, d 1955, mar Luella Augusta May Pletzer, b 1895, res Toronto
    C1. Norman Howard Gray, b 1921, mar Irene Evelyn Martin, b 1919, res Newmarket, Ont.
      D1. Douglas Howard Grey, b 1956
    C2. Gladys Luella, b 1928, mar Walter Barlow Whitelaw, b 1924, res Weston, Ont.
      D1. Wendy Ann, b 1949, mar Brian Denton Riddell, b 1945
        E1. Sarah Jane Riddell, b 1973

         E2. Michael Denton Riddell, b 1974
      D2. Susan Rose Whitelaw, b 1959 D3. Walter Barlow Whitelaw, b 1961
   B3. Harold George, b 1897, d.y.
 A7. Ann Maria, b 1872, d 1949, mar William Alfred Caldwell, 1869-1961
   B1. Lorne Andrew Caldwell, b 1905, mar Christina McLachlan, res Cornwall, Ont.
      C1. Cairine Elizabeth Caldwell, b 1938, mar John Glenn Scott, res Islington, Ont.
      C2. John Ross Caldwell, b 1941, mar Barbara Jane Park, res Markham, Ont.
         D1. Scott Andrew Caldwell, b 1966 D2. John Douglas Caldwell, b 1968
   B2. Ethel Olive, b 1909, d.y.
LE BEUF, LE BUFF, LA BUFFE, etc. Capt. from J in Nfld. (K. Mathews) See also LE BOEUF.
LE BLANC, to Nfld. from C.I.? (Seary) Cf LE BLANC of C.I. (Saunders)
LE BLANC, C.I. in Maritimes Fisheries (J.H. le Breton list)
LE BLANC, or LA BLON, ship owner from J in Nfld. (K. Mathews) Cf also LA BLONDE
LE BLANC, Capt. Allen, a ship captain from J in Gaspe 1900s (Capt. Poidevin, Toronto)
LE BLANC, many in Cape Breton, mostly from France. See CAPE BRETON SHIPS AND MEN, by Capt. John P. Parker.
LE BLOND, or LE BLANC, ship owner from J in Nfld. (K. Mathews)
LE BOEUF, Th., was in Gaspe 1820 and signed the Petition
LE BOEUF, fam from Bordeaux, France, to Brittany, then to C.I. ca 1520, and to Virginia, U.S., and to Gaspe as UEL's? ca 1800. (W. Willett, New Richmond, Gaspe)
LE BORGNE, from C.I. to Gaspe (Dom. Arch. and K.H. Annett list)
LE BOSIGNET, merchant from J in Nfld. (K. Mathews)
LE BOSQUET, Capt. from G in Nfld. (K. Mathews) This fam somehow assoc with VIBERT fam.
LE BOURVEAU, from France ca 1685 to C.I., to England, to America (Homer Le Bourveau, Calgary, Alta.)
LE BOURGNON, LE BOURNON?, ---, age 22, blacksmith for Robin firm in Caraquet 1861 (Census) (Rev. Le Gresley) See data in added pp.
LE BOUTILLIER. See THE INTERNATIONAL BUTLER FAMILY, by --- Des Brisay. Not available to compiler. See also LE BOUTILLIER FAMILY CHART by Gertrude Le B., Gaspe, Que., enlarged by Mabel Dunn Le Boutillier, Gaspe; Gordon and June Pimm, Coral Gables, Fla.; and others in Jersey and England. Gen. research on this fam also done by Barry Le Boutillier of Beckenham, Kent, England.
LE BOUTILLIER, found everywhere. While the origin of some in N.S. is definitely from France, others are from the Channel Islands. No definitive study recently as far as this compiler knows, but would be in great demand, as this is a most interesting and prominent family in many places.
LE BOUTILLIER, Charles, b 1888 Meadow Bank, St. Lawrence, J, mar Florence Murley RENOUF, rem to Montreal 1913 (Ivy O'Reilly, S. Portland, ME)
   A1. Florence V.I., b 1909 St. Aubin, J, mar 1931 John V. O'Reilly, 3 chn. To Canada 1920, rem to N.J. 1924, then to Maine 1928.
      B1. Charles W. O'Reilly, b 1932, mar Norma McGlinn
         C1. Michael O'Reilly, b ca 1955   C4. John O'Reilly, b ca 1959
         C2. Colleen O'Reilly, b ca 1956   C5. Erin O'Reilly, b ca 1961
         C3. Patricia O'Reilly, b ca 1957, res Va. Beach, Va.
      B2. Patricia A., b 1936, mar Marvin A. Clifford, res Topsham, ME
         C1. Scott A. Clifford, b ca 1959 C2. Sheryl Clifford, b ca 1963

C3. Laurie Clifford, b ca 1965
B3. John R. O'Reilly, b 1950, divorced, dau Stephanie, b 1972
LE BOUTILLIER, Everard, Sr., served with Brit. forces in WWI and WWII, in Jersey, India, Mesopotamia, Persia, Alexandria and France, then was in the Regina Rifle Reg't, and Legion of Frontiersmen. He was b 1890 St. Aubin, J, son of Everard John of St. Heliers and Mary Jane BATES. Res St. Brelade, St. Heliers, rem to Regina, Sask. 1929. Mar Eliza M. FILLEUL. He d 1938 Regina. (John Le Boutillier, Sask, Sask.)
A1. Everard John, b 1916 St. Heliers, J, to Canada 1929, mar 1943 in England, Kathleen Livingston, b 1917 Mid. Eng. Vet WWII.
B1. John Everard, b 1945, mar Margaret A. Mitchell, res Turna Valley, Alta.
C1. Curtis Mitchell, b 1971   C3. Trevor Peter, b 1976
C2. David Everard John, b 1973
B2. Elizabeth Carol, b 1949 Regina, res Calgary. Mar R. Kelsey, divorced 1974.
C1. Jostin R. Kelsey, b 1968   C2. Leith Adele Kelsey, b 1971
A2. Rozelle Beatrice, b 1922 St. Heliers, J, mar 1949 Thurston Talbot, res Melfort, Sask.
B1. Thurston Graham Talbot, b 1951
LE BOUTILLIER, Walter Alfred, b 1924 St. Helier, J, son of Francis James Le B. and Gladys Maud BAKER? A cousin of Everard, above. Mar Lilian May VIBERT, qv, b ca 1925. Rem to Canada 1952, res Sask, Sask. (Lilian Le B., Sask, Sask.)
A1. Anne Lilian, b 1947 J, mar 1970 Sask., William Hoffman, res Regina, Sask.
B1. Jonathan William Hoffman, b 1973 Winnipeg, Man.
B2. Joanne Sara Hoffman, b 1974 Regina, Sask.
A2. Jane S., b 1949 J, mar 1972 Lloyd Kenneth Moker, res Prince Albert, Sask.
A3. David Walter, b 1960 Sask, Sask.
LE BOUTILLIER, Capt. Oliver Colin, b 1900 in Canada of J fam. Pilot in WWI, who witnessed the shooting down of the "Red Baron," now res Las Vegas, Nevada, U.S. His father d in East Orange, N.J. 1933.
LE BOUTILLIER, Philip, mar in Perce 1866, Harriet Ormandy. He d 1914, age 88. Poss mar also sister of Harriet, Susan Maria. (Brochet)
LE BOUTILLIER, many of this surname came to Gaspe area, some spelled variously BOUTILLIER, LE BOUTHILLIER, BUTLER, BUTTLER, LE BOITILLIER, etc. (Syvret, Arch., Mountain, Bechard, Cent. Bklt., Brochet) The following were noted in Gaspe records, but may have been part of other families established there, and charted below.
LE BOUTILLIER, John, appointed to the vacant estate of the deceased Theophilus Fox, of Perce. Fox signed the 1820 Gaspe Petition. (Dom. Arch.)
LE BOUTILLIER, David, res Paspebiac, and bought lot No. 1, of Bonaventure Island, site of Peter Du Val and Co. fishery operation, from John GODFRAY, merchant in J.
LE BOUTILLIER, David, Amy and Mary Anne, together with John MOURANT, General Merchants, by their agent Abraham LE BRUN, bought lot No. 13, Bon. Is. from the heirs of the deceased John Everest, Evariste, DU VAL, qv. Indenture dated 1852. David was M.P. for Bon. Co. 1851-1854.
LE BOUTILLIER, Laura, had dealings in property in Bon. Is. 1870s re: David Le B.
LE BOUTILLIER. One business was sold to another company, 1800s, owned by the same or another family, LE BOUTILLIER, LTD. Philip GOSSET, qv, and Clement NICOLE, qv, of J were connected with this Liquidation at Bon. Is. 1888, also Joshua ALEXANDER, qv, John Wright, and William

LE BOUTILLIER, SEE ADDED PAGES.
LE BOUTILLIER FAUVEL, qv. (Brochet)
LE BOUTILLIER, Philip, mayor of Perce 1800s (Cent. Bklt.)
LE BOUTILLIER, from C.I. to Newport, Gaspe
LE BOUTILLIER, Charles, b 1841 Gaspe, in Perce 1861, d 1909 Montreal (Syvret)
LE BOUTILLIER, from C.I. to Miscou Island, NB, to Isle au Bois, Labrador, straits of Belle Isle
LE BOUTILLIER, Capt. from J in Nfld. (K. Mathews)
LE BOUTILLIER, Herbert John, b ca 1890 St. Mary, J, son of John and of Clara Jane Wilbecque L. He d 1972 at age 87, Cheticamp, C.B. To Canada for Robin, Collas and Co. 1905, rem to Cheticamp 1910, employed by Robin, Jones and Whitman. Was later a grocer there. Mar Ruby May LE BRUN, 8 grchn, 4 grgrchn. (MAIL STAR, Halifax, NS; Lloyd Melanson, Halifax, NS)
A1. Herbert, res Cheticamp   A3. Gertrude, mar ---Mabey, res Halifax
A2. Clifford, res London, Ont.
LE BOUTILLIER, Lillian and Gertrude, sisters of above Herbert John, remained in J
LE BOUTILLIER, Philip Henry, b ca 1865 J, rem to England, mar, poss returned to J. At least 4 sons and a dau (Jack Boutillier, Vict., BC)
I. Philip Henry, b Liverpool, Eng., rem to Gaspe then to Minneapolis, Minn. where he d.
A1. Edward, d age 12 in Minneapolis, Minn.
A2. Thomas Henry, b 1891 at Paspebiac, Que., mar Hyla Stanforth, res Minn.
  B1. Philip George, b 1920, mar Irene Staiton, Stanton?, res Stillwater, Minn.
    C1. Marc, b 1947
  B2. Joan, b 1922, mar Merril Fox, res Wash., D.C.
  B3. Gordon, b 1927, mar Patricia Leeper, res Rock Rapids, Iowa
    C1. Linda, b 1952   C3. Steven, b 1955
    C2. Cynthia, b 1954   C4. Paul, b 1957
  B4. Jean, b 1931, mar Kenneth Anderson, res Minn.
  B5. John E., b 1931 Montreal, mar Barbara Anderson
    C1. Kent, b 1956   C4. Jeffrey, b 1962
    C2. Scott, b 1958   C5. Renee, b 1963
    C3. Lynn, b 1959
A3. Gertrude, b 1892, mar William F. Ewe, res Minn.
II. Thomas Cecil, bro of Philip Henry above, b ca 1874 Liverpool. Eng., raised in J, rem to St. Malo, France. Sailed ca 1890 from St. Malo to Gaspe, age 16, employed by Le Boutillier Bros of Halifax, N.S. Mar Eva Jane LE GALLAIS, qv, dau of Edmund Le G. and Martha MILLER. Rem to Quebec City, then to Montreal.
A1. William, b 1904 Quebec, mar Nell Stewart 1931 of PEI. He d ca 1972. Nellie res Ottawa, Ont., no issue. Wm. was a Jap. prisoner in Hong Kong for 3 years. See New Brunswick section re John Vibert, prisoner of the Japanese.
A2. John E., b 1906 Montreal, mar Jean Ballantyne of Montreal 1941. He was a WWII Vet. Res Victoria, BC. 6 chn.
  B1. Gary, b 1942, mar 1. ---, and 2. Roni Richter, in 1972
    C1. Richard, b 1965   C3. Curtis, b 1976, by 2nd wife
    C2. Cynthia, b 1964
  B2. Bobby Jean, b 1943, mar Colin Tennyson
    C1. Troy Tennyson, b 1963   C2. Lisa Tennyson, b 1966
  B3. Willa Gay, b 1944, mar Thomas Leason
    C1. Paul Leason, b 1972
  B4. Ian, b 1953, mar MichellePare, son, Jess

LE BOUTILLIER   309

   B5. Glen, b 1956   B6. Anthony, b 1968
III. Ernest Le B., brother of above two, b St. Malo, France, d Minn.,
     Minn., mar Lillian ---. Widow res New Brighton, Minn.
IV. Madeline, d in Paris, France
V. Frank, brother of above four. D in France WWII. His son res La
   Rochelle, France, 1968
LE BOUTILLIER, John, b 1797 La Chasse, St. John, J, to Gaspe in 1812.
He was the son of Jean-David Le B. and Marie BAUDAINS, first wife.
In 1830, John estab his own company at Gaspe, which extended along
the coast to St. Anne des Monts, where he bought cod, made fish, and
shipped to Brazil, the West Indies, Protugal, Spain and Italy. (See
Capt. Vibert Journal) He represented Gaspe in the Chamber from 1833-
1838, 1844-1847, 1854-1867. Named Legislative Councillor 1867 and d
in 1872. The Hon. John was Protestant, mar Elizabeth Robin, of a J
fam in Switzerland, dau of Philip Robin of Berne? and of Martha
ARBOUR, qv of Gaspe. Several Le B. boats sailed between Jersey and
Gaspe. Later, his son Charles and dau Eliza, wife of Antoine Pain-
chaud, took over the business in Gaspe and L'Anse au Griffon. Pain-
chaud constructed the home in Guernsey Harbour, Gaspe, where Miss
Gertrude Le B. lived recently. (Gordon and June Pimm, Coral Gables,
Fla.; Aldo Brochet, Perce, Gaspe; Mabel Dunn Le B.; Rev. d'Hist,
Winter 1972 article;Dictionaryof Can. Biog.)
A1. Philip, b 1825 Perce, mar 1. Victoria Sutton of J. After the birth
    of her two sons, she rem to J with her chn, fell ill and d there
    1861. The two sons lived there for several years with their grand-
    mother Sutton, then returned to Gaspe. Philip mar 2. Susan Thorpe
    of Oxford, England, and 3. Harriet Thorpe, sister of Susan. 7 chn,
    2, 1, and 4, resp. See also p.307, re Thorpe.
  B1. John, b ca 1855 Perce, rem to U.S. later d age ca 40, unmar, in J?
  B2. Charles Sutton, b 1857, res France, where he lived with his aunt,
      Mme. de Gaudement. Educated in France, rem to Gaspe, mar Zoe
      Belleau of Quebec City.
    C1. Gertrude Mary, b 1883, res Gaspe
    C2. Zadie, Zoe Mary, b 1885, mar Robert Pimm, res Cornwall, Ont.
        Desc Gordon Pimm of Fla.
    C3. Marion, b 1887, mar Moise Brassard, dentist at Gaspe, who d 1958
    C4. Herbert Sutton, b 1888, d 1964, mar Helen Neif, 3 chn
      D1. Kathleen, b 1927, mar Dr. J. McCarthy 1953
      D2. Lois Mary Helen, b 1930 Gaspe, mar Francis Tuffy Ireland 1963
      D3. Charles Sutton David, mar Betty Mullin 1958, res Montreal,
          succeeded his father in their company
        E1. Michael, b 1959   E3. Charles Sutton, b 1965
        E2. Steven   E4. Louise Suzanne, b 1968
    C5. Stella Mary, b 1890, d 1970, mar Joseph Grogan who d 1969
    C6. Leo Belleau, b 1889, d 1917 France
    C7. Lauretta Alma, b 1896, d 1966, mar Thomas Whalen, b Boiestown,
        NB
    C8. Horace, b 1899, d 1906
  B3. John, d.y.
  B4. Susan Victoria, b 1865, by Suzan Thorpe, mar Alphonse CARON, qv.
      Susan d 1936 Cape Cove, Gaspe. Sev. chn including Sister Stella
      Caron of the Quebec Ursulines, 3 other nuns and 3 pastors.
  B5. Philip, 1866-1940, customs collector at Perce, son of Harriet
      Thorpe
  B6. Ethel, b 1876, d.y.
  B7. Mary, 1877-1965, mar Joseph Wm. Pidgeon of Perce, 8 chn
    C1. M. Terence Pidgeon, lawyer at Gaspe C2. Gregory, of Perce

  C3. John C5. Kathleen C7. Veronica
  C4. Marion C6. Lauretta C8. Joseph, d at Hong Kong during WWII
 B8. Susan H., b 1868, mar Dr. Simon Grenier, rem from Perce. She d
  1951
  C1. Regis Grenier, pastor St. Jules, Chandler, Que.
  C2. Emilien, doctor at Sherbrooke and Gaspe
  C3. Harriet C4. Marguerite, res Montmagny, Que. C5. others?, d.y.
 B9. Harriet, 1880-1939
A2. Horace, 1828-1925, better known as Horatio. Ship captain, and
 director of the company affairs at Ste. Anne-des-Monts and at Mont
 Louis. Mar Harriet FAUVEL, qv, of J, no issue. D at Dalhousie,
 NB, bur Gaspe. His wife returned to J and d there 1915.
A3. Charles, b 1841 Gaspe, d 1909 Montreal. Res Quebec City, returning
 to Gaspe each spring. He mar Helene Tetu of Trois-Pistoles 1871,
 6 chn.
 B1. Helene, 1872-1912, singer, mar Arthur Lavoie, MD, res Sillery, Que.
  C1. Eva Lavoie, Sister of Jesus Mary of Sillery, b 1902
  C2. Germaine Lavoie C3. Arthur, priest in James Bay since 1933
  C4. Marcelle C6. Paul Andre C8. Marcel, d at age 16
  C5. Rene C7. Helene, d at age 32 C9. Jules, d at age 2
 B2. Eva Marie Louise, b 1874, d 1965, mar Jean-OMER MARCHAND, architect, d 1936
  C1. Raymonde, mar Richard Pane, d Montreal
   D1. Marie-Claire Pane, mar Peter Holland, res Toronto
 B3. Alice, b 1877, d 1954, mar Oliver Asselin, editor of Le DEVOIR
  of Montreal (1874-1937), 4 chn
  C1. Claude Asselin, d.y. C2. Jean Asselin, engineer
  C3. Paul Asselin, journalist
  C4. Peter Asselin, Consul in New Orleans from 1962-1972, now Ambassador in Cameroun, Africa
 B4. Jean Charles Joseph, b 1879, d Contrecoeur 1910, belonged to
  65th Regt.
 B5. Marie Therese Hermine, b 1885, drowned 1892 in Gaspe
 B6. Elizabeth, b 1881, d 1970. Mar Jules Boisvert 1917, b in Bordeaux, France, 1867, d 1955.
A4. John William, b Perce, res Gaspe 1873. A John at Cap Rosiers 1871
 (Brochet)
A5. Georges, b 1829 or 1830 Gaspe, d 1879. Mar Josephine Tremblay 1858,
 (1834-1893). Georges was customs collector at Perce, and Josephine
 was the dau of the first registrar of the County of Gaspe, 10 chn.
 B1. Jean Georges, b 1859, mar Marie-Renee Lemieux, of Que. 1888, 9 chn
  C1. Corrine, b Ile de la Madeleine, d Manchester, NY 1946
  C2. Marie Jeanne, mar Alva Fournier, d 1969
  C3. Marmel, mar Philippe Cote, d 1965
  C4. Leonce, d 1904 C5. Charles Edward, d in Calif.
  C6. Hermine, sister of St. Luke, a missionary in the Indies,
   motherhouse in NY
  C7. Arthur, d 1925
  C8. Jean Pierre, mar Yvette Salvas, d 1960 C9. Eugenie, d.y. 1913
 B2. Marie Josephine Elizabeth, b 1861 Perce, mar Narcisse Emile Roy,
  doctor of Gaspe. A son d.y. She mar 2. Notary Alphonse Dumais
  of Karmouaska, who d in 1914. She d in New York 1941, no issue.
 B3. Marie Bertha Eugenie, b 1862, Sister in Sillery. She d in New
  York 1913.
 B4. Edouard Augustin, surveyor, b 1864, res Rimouski. Mar 1. Alice
  Letourneau, who d in 1902 leaving 5 chn. Mar 2. Ursule St.
  Laurent, a son Jean-Marie. Mar 3. Blanche Bouillon, and 4. Adelia

Rious in Trois-Pistoles, where she lived recently. Edouard Augustin d 1942.
  C1. Marie Alice Eugenie, b 1890
  C2. Charles Edouard, b 1892 Matane, Que., d 1943 Conn. Mar Doria Charron 1917, (1893-1939), rem to Mass.
    D1. Irene, mar Alphonse Lapierre 1942 Mass.
    D2. Edward, b 1919 Conn., mar Anna Beatrice Clark 1948
      E1. Cynthia Carol, b 1950, mar 1965 Gary Wayne Giles, Oklahoma
      E2. Elaine Kay, b 1953 Indianapolis, Ind.
    D3. Lilian, b 1921   D4. Doria, b 1921, d 1937
    D5. Gloria, b 1922, mar 1942 R. Loren Vilnent Bandagriggt
    D6. Marie Blanche Catherine, b 1924, mar 1945 Leon Francis Livernois
  C3. Mimie Clara Leontine Elise
  C4. Joseph Alphonse Henri, b 1895, d 1937 at Matane, Que. Mar 1925 Jeanne Rioux, b 1904 Ste. Felicite, Que.
    D1. Jean Yves, b 1928 Matane, mar 1957 Clemence Philibert, b 1927
      E1. Line, b 1958   E2. Pierre, b 1963
    D2. Joseph Ernest Daniel, b 1930 Ste. Felicite, mar 1958 Matane, Marielle Gagne, b 1938 Ste. Luce, Que.
      E1. Andre, b 1958   E3. Paul, b 1963
      E2. Claude, b 1960   E4. Danielle, b 1965
  C5. Joseph Antoine, b 1898, d.y.
  C6. Jean Marie, mar Gertrude ---, res Hull, Que. 1970
B5. Marie Elizabeth Agathe, b 1866, d 1893 in U.S. unmar.

      (B11. Alex, below, belongs after MaryM.I., top of
B11. Alexandre, b 1879, d 1956 N.Y., mar Lydia Flynn   (page 312)
B6. Charles Albert Narcisse, b 1867, d 1880 Perce
B7. Marie Napoleon Michel, b 1869, d 1882 Perce
B8. Marie Georgianna, b 1872, mar August Roy, jeweler, d 1967. She d 1960, 4 chn.
  C1. Charles August Roy, b 1903, missing in Madagascar
  C2. Marguerite Roy, b 1905, res Montmagny, Quebec
  C3. and 4. two infants, d.y.; one named Eugenie
B9. Charles Borromee, b 1874, d 1917 N.Y. City, mar Mary Mulcahey, who d 1896 Conn.
  C1. Eugenie, mar Eugene Meyer, res N.Y. City in 1972
B10. Jean Alphonse, b 1876 Perce, d 1959 Perce, mar Georgiana CARON, qv, 1906, (1878-1967)
  C1. Marie Agathe Georgiana, b 1906, mar Francis A. BIARD, son of Wm.C.Biard &NoraEllen Fitzpatrick. No issue.
    D1. Jean Guy Bond, b 1943, mar Janine LANGLOIS, 1970, CHN OF
      E1. Anne Evelyn Bond, b 1972 Rimouski. Edw.BOND,1910-1964
    D2. Paul, b 1949   D3. Marc Bond, b 1954   D4. Gilles Bond, b 1956
  C2. Jean Charles Horace, b 1908, d.y.
  C3. Joseph Edward Cyrille, b 1910, d 1964. Mar 1939 Oliva BOURGET, b 1915
  C4. Alma Marie Evelyn, b 191-, d 1969
  C5. Alphonse Narcisse, b 1913, mar Mary Mabel Dunn 1942, b 1912
    D1. John Arthur, b 1944
    D2. Joseph Herbert Alphonse, b 1947 Lamaque NB, mar Ginette Mattheau 1970 at Sherbrooke, Que.
      E1. Patrick Herbert, b 1973
    D3. Mary Margaret Susan, b 1948 Lamaque, NB, mar Christian Lucien Esculier 1971 Paris, France, b 1946

D4. Mary Mabel Irene, b Palos, 1952
A6. Marie Elizabeth, b Perce, mar Antoine Painchaud, Surveyor
A7. Edward, b 1838, d 1873, Perce, a lawyer
LE BOUTILLIER, David, b 1812 St. John, J, half-brother to above John, b 1797, son of Jean David and second wife, Marie COUTANCHE. Rem to Paspebiac with Robin, helped set up the Le Boutillier firm at Paspebiac, bought lot No. 1, Bon. Island, site of Peter Du Val fishery, from John Godfrey. He was MP for Bon. Co. 1851-1854.
LE BOUTILLIER, Stanley, to B.C.
LE BOUTILLIER, Anna, mar Charles DE GRUCHY, qv, rem to Cape Cove, Gaspe, 4 chn
LE BOUTILLIER, a captain, from J to Gaspe then to New Westminster, BC (Luce)
LE BOUTILLIER, Philip, b Gaspe, there in Perce 1861 with Victoria, b J and Charles and John, b Canada (Census)
LE BOUTILLIER, Edward, mar Jeanne, dau of Philip DU VAL and ---HUELIN, emigrated to Caraquet, N.B. (Brochet) 1800s. Desc. in Iowa.
LE BOYER, Ernest, b 1892 J, son of Pierre Paul and of Anne Marie LE TIRANT, b Brittany, rem to Ontario. Pierre Paul was b ca 1867 Normandy, France. Ernest d 1964 at 72. He mar Elizabeth, or Lizzie, GAUTRON, GAULTRON, b 1885 St. Laurence, J, who was 91 in 1976. (Rozelle Collins, Sarnia, Ontario)
A1. Rozelle Agnes, b 1920 Hamilton, Ont., mar Charles Bignie Collins, b 1910 Ont., d 1969
  B1. Rozelle Charlene Collins, b 1944 Oshawa, Ont., mar Stephen John Vokes, b 1945
    C1. Stephen John Vokes, b 1968   C2. Charles Collins Vokes, b 1972
  B2. Cecille Anne Collins, b 1945 Oshawa, mar Yvon Joseph Beauregard
  B3. Pamela Michelle Collins, b 1951 Sarnia, Ontario
  B4. Frieda Edith Collins, b 1960
  B5. Elizabeth Casell Collins, b 1962
A2. Cecille Ernestine, b 1923, mar Earl Skinner, res Hamilton, Ont.
  B1. Beverly Skinner, b ca 1956 Hamilton
  B2. Roderick Skinner, b 1960 London, England
LE BOYER, Henry, bro of Ernest above, b 1891 St. Ouen, J, rem to Canada ca 1913, then returned to J in 1932. Mar in J before 1912 a widow with 3 chn surnamed RENOUF, qv. (Agnes Noel Renouf) Res Hamilton, Ont.
LE BOW, LE BEAU?, Capt. from G in Nfld. (K. Mathews)
LE BRASSEUR, C.I. surname assoc with Robin firm at Paspebiac, Que., and with town of New Carlisle, Que. (Que. Prov. Archives; K.H. Annett)
LE BRASSEUR, James, in Port Daniel 1884, witness at wedding of his cousin's son. His cousin was Sarah Douglas PREVOST, qv. The son was Samuel PREVOST, who mar on that day, Jane Day, or Dea.
LE BRETON, old surname of J since at least 1236. (Societe Jersiaise, Vol. XXXI) In 1309 a Le Breton owned the famous Mont St. Michel. Many of this surname removed from J to North America.
LE BRETON, Capt. John, b 1780 J, joined the British Army, poss while he was in Nfld. He was stationed in 1811 at Quebec and attached during the War of 1812 to the Royal Nfld. Reg't of Fencible Infantry. Accompanied the Regiment on General Brock's expedition to Detroit and was present at the capture of the city. Took park in a battle with the Americans on the Miami River, Ohio. Wounded at Lundy's Lane, Ont. 1814, rem to England. Returned to Canada as Capt. and obtained a grant of land in 1819 of 200 acres at Brittania, near Ottawa, where he lived in 1827. Some talk of illegal land purchase (see ROBERT RANDALL AND THE LE BRETON FLATS, by Hamnet P. Hill, Ottawa, 1919). Fine war record, unmar. He d 1848 Toronto, age 69, headstone being

LE BRETON   313

erected in his memory by 5 nieces, daus of his sister. See below.
(OUR FAMILY, by Harold Butler Little, Vol. 2; Henry Ross, Toronto,
Ont.; E.C. Little, Fonthill, Ont.; Dorothy Fairweather, Albany, N.Y.
and Lakefield, Ont.) The entertainer, Rich Little, is a member of
this family.
LE BRETON, Jeanne, b 177-, sister of John above, mar 1798 in St. John's,
Nfld., Francois Tito Le Lievre, thought to have been born in France.
However, Le Lievres res in the same parish as LE BRETONS in J at that
time, and were established in J from the 1300s to the 1750s, at least.
Jeanne and Francois settled in Perth, Ont. At least 7 chn. She d
1841, he 1830 in Pt. Claire, Que.(K.LeLievre, NSW, Australia)
A1. Julius Skerrett? LE LIEVRE, d 1828
A2. Henry F. Le Lievre, b ca 1800?, d Austr. 1882
A3. Sophe Charlotte Le Lievre, b 1804 Nfld.
A4. Emily Le Lievre, mar Dr. Henry MOUNT, chn
  B1. Emily, b 1847, d Toronto? Poss mar Pfluger?
A5. Louise Hermine Le Lievre, b 1808, D Austr. 1889.
A6. Jeanne Le Lievre, b 1811 Quebec, d 1888 Toronto, mar Henry Eccles

A7. Marie Elizabeth Ursule Le Lievre, b 1812 Montreal, mar 1845 William
Chisholm Ross, b 1805 Tain, Scotland, d 1856. She was his second
wife. Order of chn uncertain. At least 8 chn.
  B1. John Le Breton Ross, b 1836, d 1880, mar Maria Louisa Peniston,
  b 1837 Bermuda, d 1910 Ottawa, 5 chn
    C1. Henry Le Breton Ross, b 1863, d 1954, mar Mary Lois Murford?,
    1864-1939
      D1. Fenwick Le Breton Ross, b 1890, d 1970, mar Alice Sara Mac-
      Quarrie, who d 1942
        E1. Margaret Lois Ross, b 1920, mar Erling Knudsen?
          F1. Merite? Lois Knudsen, b 1960
      D2. Gordon Le Breton Ross, b 1896, d 1972
    C2. Clara Le Breton Ross, b 1865, d 1869
    C3. John Walter Le Breton Ross, b 1866 Ottawa, d 1946, mar 1898
    Mary Ethel Mattice, b 1867 Cornwall, d 1942 Ottawa, Ont., 4 chn
      D1. Dorothy Elizabeth Ross, b 1903 Morrisburg, Ont., mar 1925
      Sault Ste. Marie, Ont., Edgar Daryl Fairweather, 5 chn
        E1. Ross Hunter Fairweather, b 1926, mar Frances Eileen Titus
        1953
          F1. Ross Le Breton Fairweather, b 1955
          F2. Mark David Fairweather, b 1958
          F3. James Fairweather, b 1958
        E2. Barbara Jean Fairweather, b 1927, mar 1955 Herbert Hutton
        Insley
          F1. Barbara Marie Insley, b 1959
          F2. David Insley, b 1961   F4. Marcia Louise Insley,
          F3. Peter Insley, b 1964   b 1965
        E3. Donald Harry Bryant Fairweather, b 1929, mar Joan Elizabeth
        McMillan, or McMullen, divorced
          F1. Wendy Elizabeth Fairweather, b 1960
          F2. Laura Fairweather, b 1961
        E4. Mary Daphne Fairweather, b 1930, mar Frederick Charles
        Case 1963
        E5. Dorothy Sandra Fairweather, b 1939, mar Kenneth Ian McKenzie
        1965
          F1. Elizabeth McKenzie, b 1967   F2. Rebecca McKenzie, b 1974
      D2. John Arthur Ross, b 1906, mar 1930 Mary Alice Beckwith, b
      Halifax, NS, 3 chn

E1. John Beckwith Ross, b 1931, mar Ann Tracy
   F1. Wendy Ann Ross, b 1956   F2. Tracy Le Breton Ross, b 1958
E2. Barbara Ann Ross, b 1933, mar James Ronald McMurrich
   F1. Judith Beckwith McMurrich, b 1954
   F2. Susan Davis McMurrich, b 1960
   F3. Barbara McMurrich, b 1961
E3. Judith Le Breton Ross, b 1937, mar Robert Wm. Korthals
   F1. Lisa Korthals, b 1968
   F2. Christopher Ross Korthals, b 1971
   F3. James Korthals, b 1973
D3. Arthur Le Breton Ross, b 1910 Sault Ste. Marie, d 1876 Toronto, mar Anne Boggs 1935, or poss Anne Lawrence?
  E1. William Arthur Ross, b 1941
D4. Henry Urquhart Ross, b 1912, mar 1940 Jennie Mildred Caughill, b 1914 Little Current, Ont.
  E1. Henry Ian Le Breton Ross, b 1946 Victoria, BC, mar 1969 Kathryn Pottle, b Nfld.
    F1. Kathryn Elaine Ross   F2. Craig Ian Le Breton Ross, b 1973
  E2. Kenneth Allan Le Breton Ross, b 1947 Toronto, mar Judy Mountjoy
    F1. Jeffrey Daniel Mountjoy Ross, b 1976
C4. William Le Breton Ross, b 1868, d 1964. Mar Caroline Stewart Lampman, 1868-1962, 6 chn
  D1. John Roderick Ross, b 1893, mar Elsie Marion Hooker, b 1893, 3 chn
  D2. Phyllis Isabelle Ross, b 1894, d 1970
  D3. Elsie Stewart Ross, b 1896, mar Arthur Larmour, 2 chn
    E1. Robert Warren Larmour, b 1933, res Victoria, BC
    E2. Michael Larmour, b 1937
  D4. William Ernest Ross, b 1900, d 1965, mar Julie Moore? 3 chn
    E1. Timothy Arrowsmith Ross, b 1936   E3. Mark Ross
    E2. Matthew McMillan Ross
  D5. Hilda Catherine Lillith Ross, b 1902
  D6. Richard Henry Charles Le Breton Ross, b 1907, mar Elizabeth Maud Huld?, 4 chn
    E1. Carol Ann Ross   E3. Roderick Andrew Ross
    E2. Patricia Evelyn Ross, b 1942   E4. Lynn, twin of Roderick?
C5. Mabel Gertrude Ross, b 1870, d 1947 Ottawa, Ont., mar William Caruthers Little, 1860-1935
  D1. Edward C. Little, b 1893, mar 1920 Anna Mary Johnston, b 1891
    E1. Edward C. Little, b 1924, mar Frances Ann Clarkie?, b 1929
      F1. Edward C. Little, b 1955   F3. John Butler Little,
      F2. Margaret Rosalie Little, b 1956   b 1960
    E2. Barbara Mary Frances Little, b 1926, mar Vernon St. Clair Simpson, b 1923
      F1. Rosemary Elizabeth Simpson, b 1951, teacher, mar David Shea 1977
      F2. Janet Margaret Simpson, b 1953, mar James Roy Finlay, b 1950
      F3. Katherine Joyce Simpson, b 1955
      F4. William James Frederick Simpson, b 1958
    E3. Robert Harward Little, b 1928, mar Zoe Audrey Birch, b 1928
      F1. James Johnston Little, b 1954   F3. Robert Bennett Little,
      F2. John Simpson Little, b 1958   b 1964
  D2. Harold Butler Little, b 1894, mar 1927 Eileen Picard, who d 197-
    E1. John Caruthers Little, mar Doris Lorraine McMahon, b 1936

LE BRETON 315

```
            F1. Brian Caruthers Little, b 1968
            F2. Roger Craig Little, b 1959
      D3. Gurney Palling Little, b 1896, mar 1927 Alice ---, res Ottawa
         E1. Mary E. Little, mar Donald Baxter, res Ottawa
            F1. Doborah Baxter, b 1958
            F2. Ross Lawrence Baxter, b 1961
      D4. Ethel Gertrude Little, b 1897, d 1961, unmar
      D5. Lawrence Peniston Little, b 1899, d 1959, mar 1934 Elizabeth
          Maud Wilson, b 1903
         E1. Frederick William Little, b 1935, res Ottawa
         E2. Richard Caruthers Little, b 1938, res California, a dau.
             (Rich Little, entertainer)
         E3. Christopher William Little, b 1948, res Scarborough, Ont.
            F1. Judith      F2. Jeanne       F3. Joyce
(The other chn of A7. Marie Eliz. Ursule Le Lievre, b 1812, Montreal
and Wm. Ross)
   B2. Frances Ross      B5. William Ross      B8. Louise Ross
   B3. Emily Ross        B6. Elspeth Ross
   B4. Catherine Ross    B7. Mary Jane Ross
```

LE BRETON, Thomas Charles, b 1887 J, son of John Le B. and Marie PEPIN, qv. His first wife, A. DU FEU, d.y. He mar 2. Margaret May Caldwell, U.E.L. desc 1890-1938, and 3. Jennie VALPY, qv, res Belleville, Ont. (Dorothy Sheehan, Ste. Foy, Que.; John H. Le Breton, Paspebiac, Que.)

```
A1. John Hugh, b 1914, mar Eva L. LE RICHE, qv, b 1907, res Paspebiac?,
    Que.
   B1. Doreen E., b 1942, mar John Haydon
      C1. Bruce Haydon, b 1964         C3. Elizabeth Haydon, b 1972
      C2. Geoffrey Haydon, b 1965
A2. Dorothy M., b 1915, mar John F. Sheehan
   B1. Michael Sheehan, b 1940, mar 1967 ---
      C1. Martin Sheehan, b 1968       C3. Cynthia Sheehan, b 1975
      C2. Philip Sheehan, b 1970
   B2. Brian Sheehan, b 1942
   B3. Veronica Sheehan, b 1945, mar Joseph Crozier 1974
      C1. Richard Crozier, b 1975
   B4. Humphrey Sheehan, b 1952        B5. Kevin Sheehan, b 1954
A3. Helen M., b 1918, mar Maurice Fiset, res Casgrain, Que.
A4. Ruth, b ca 1920 Paspebiac, Que., d.y.
A5. Harold A., b 1923, mar Mary Jess, res Toronto
```

LE BRETON, M. Jeremie, of St. Isidore, Que? (Robichaud) Origin unver.

LE BRETON, Julian, b ca 1787, res in Shippegan, NB 1861 (Census)

LE BRETON, res J, rem to Wales 1913, a son b Swansea Wales 1928, rem to Canada 1957 (Vit. Le Breton, Vict., BC)

LE BRETON, John, of London, in 1766, petitioned the Privy Council in London, together with Joshua MAUGER, qv, and Gregory OLIVER?, about trade in St. Pierre, Magdalen Islands. LE BRETON was in business with Charles Robin in trading to Gaspe 1786. (H. Townley Douglas, Ottawa, Ont.) See ADDITIONS AND CORRECTIONS PAGES.

LE BRETON, Philip, from J to Perce, for Robin, Collas and Co. A sister, Miss A. Le B., d in 1946, age 84, b 1862. A son of Philip, also Philip, served overseas in WWII SEE EXTRA PAGES

LE BRETON, Jane E., widow of Wm. Newberry, 1863-1912, b Perce, d at Magpie, Gaspe, bur St. Pauls, Perce. Husband b England 1856, d 1889. (GLF)

LE BRETON, Hannah, aunt of Jane above, b J?, res Perce, Que., middle 1800s (Margaret Valpy Le Breton, Belleville, Ont.)

LE BRETON, Philip, b Canada, and Catherine, b J, also Elizabeth, b Canada, in Perce 1861 (Census) See Philip, above.
LE BRETON, Elizabeth Mary, 1860-1939, wife of Francis BOWER, qv, 1857-1945, bur St. Pauls, Perce, Gaspe (GLF)
LE BRETON, Thomas C., branch mgr. of Robin firm, retired. A son, John H. LE BRETON worked for Robin firm, res Paspebiac, Gaspe (GLF)
LE BRETON, Thomas and John, curr Paspebiac, Gaspe
LE BRETON, with Cartier's crew in 1534
LE BRETON, Rev. Corbet, the father of Lilly Langtry, qv. He married many couples who emigrated to Canada, according to data received from many sources.
LE BRETON and LE FEUVRE, partners in a smithy in Perce, late 1800s (GLF)
LE BRETON, Capt. of the 60th Rifles of Canada, mar a Miss George, ca 1873 (MAPLE LEAVES, by J. LeMoine)
LE BRETON, Charlotte, origin unver. Poss b C.I. She mar 1789 Caraquet, NB (rehab. of the marriage) Prosper Losier. He was the son of Augustin ROY, so called Losier and Desjardins, and of Marie Angelique Lizot, dau of Francois Rene LE BRETON and of Marie-Therese Boissel (Jean-Guy Poitras, Edmundston, N.B.)
LE BRETON, Abraham and Sara, were in Tracadie, Caraquet, N.B. middle 1800s. Abraham mar ca 1858 Genevieve ROUSSEL and died shortly after. (D. Robichaud)
LE BRETON, Sara, res Tracadie, mar Eugene Comeau
A1. Jean Batiste Comeau, mar Celina BULGER, qv. (Robichaud)
LE BRETON, Marguerite, mar Rene Duguay. Origin not verified.
A1. Francois Duguay, mar 1761 Madeleine Chapados, who d 1814, ten chn. Origin not ver. on sev other LE BRETONS noted in Robichaud's book.
LE BRETON, Capt. from J and/or G in Nfld. early (K. Mathews)
LE BREUX, from C.I. to Gaspe (Bourgaize) Cf also LE BRU, LE BREUILLY
LE BROCQ, LE BROCH, BROCK, etc. C.I. surname assoc with Robin firm in Paspebiac, Gaspe and with town of New Carlisle, Que. (Que. Arch.)
LE BROCK, C.I. in Maritimes Fisheries (J.H. Le Breton list)
LE BROCQ, Philip, in Paspebiac, Gaspe   SEE ADDED PAGES
LE BROCH, Capt., mentioned by Syvret
LE BROCK, Albert, b J, to Gaspe and to Saguenay, Que., in partnership with George LE FEUVRE of J, early 1900s
LE BROCK, Philip, of St. Ouen, J, whose dau mar John LE BOUTILLIER of Grand Greve, Gaspe (GLF)
LE BORCQ, Mrs. James, b J?, nee LE GRESLEY, res Gaspe (GLF)
LE BROCQ, George, and wife Elisa Marie LE HUQUET, b 1844?, mar 1867, no issue   (Sylvia Wilson, Medina, Wash.)
LE BROCQ, Capt. from J in Nfld. (K. Mathews)
LE BROCK, LE BROCQ?, son of John and Heloise LE MONTAIS of J, mar Rosalie Beauchamps 1899, Notre Dame, Que.
LE BROCQ, John, at Perce 1825
LE BROCQ, LE BROCK, from C.I. to Ontario
LE BROCQ, LE BROCK, from G to Cape Breton early 1800s? Unverified
LE BROCQ, Mary Jane, b J, wife of Joshua ALEXANDER, qv, chn
LE BROCK, James of Gaspe, mar ---LE GRESLEY, sister of Frank LE G. of New Carlisle, Quebec, 1900s
LE BROSSAULT, C.I. name assoc with Robin firm at Paspebiac and with town of New Carlisle, Que. (Que. Prov. Arch. and K.H. Annett) See also BRUSHATH, BRUSHETT.
LE BRUN, Jean, b ca 1819 J, mar Antoinette, b ca 1821 Que., res Port Daniel, Gaspe. With Philippe, age 20, mar; Flora, age 18, mar; and Pierre, 5 months. (Census)
A1. Jean, b ca 1845 A2. Antoinette, b ca 1850 A3. Elizabeth, b ca 1853

LE BRUN 317

A4. Edouard, b ca 1855   A6. Rachel, b ca 1859   A8. Alfred, b ca 1865
A5. Pierre, b ca 1856   A7. Louise, b ca 1861   A9. Philippe
LE BRUN, William, age 60, b J, carpenter, in Maria, Bon. Co., Gaspe 1871 with Phoebe, age 60, b Que., also William, age 19 and Betsey, age 13
LE BRUN, Thomas John, b 1888 G?, son of Lewis Orange LE B. and Theresa Buckley?, rem to Canada 1904-5. Res Milton, Ont., mar Winifred Bolander, Toronto. An adopted son, Gordon Ray. (Gordon Le Brun, Toronto, Ont.)
LE BRUN, from C.I. to Port Daniel and/or New Richmond, Gaspe (J.H. Le Breton, Gaspe)
LE BRUN, John, from G to PEI 1890s
LE BRUN, Abraham?, a J fishery, to Perce, Gaspe through 1871 (Cent. Bklt.; Syvret, Bechard)
LE BRUN, Dora, mar John P. LE MOIGNAN, qv in 1912, to Vict., BC, then to J, Mont Mathew, St. Ouens, J
LE BRUN, J., to Cape Breton Island, ca 1800 (Bourinot, C.B.)
LE BRUN, Francis, b 1825 J, mar Susan DE CARTERET, qv, bur St. Pauls, Perce. Poss from J ca 1850, 10 chn. (Census 1861; Cent. Bklt.; Brochet)
A1. Edith May, 1858-1935, mar James Thomas TUZO, qv.
A2. Ada Mary, b 1862, d 1866
A3. Lydia, mar 1883 Simon Grenier, M.D. She soon d and he mar 2. Susan LE BOUTILLIER, 1888, a son
   B1. Regis Grenier, R.C. priest, b Perce ca 1893
A4. Douglas De Carteret, b 1866, d 1913, bur Kenora, Ont.
A5. Adela Maud, b 1868, d.y.   A6. Albert Francis, b 1872
A7. Elsie Elizabeth, b 1874
LE BRUN, Charles, of St. Peter, J, related to Benj. TRACHY, qv, res Perce 1800s (Gallant)
LE BRUN, a Capt. from J and/or G in Nfld. (K. Mathews)
LE BRUN, Abraham, b J, in Perce 1861 (Census)
LE BRUN, John, vicar of St. Annes, Ald., b 1887, d 1945. Mar Henrietta Proctor McCormick, at least 7 chn (Anne Le Brun, Vancouver, BC)
I. Henry, in Navy, d England 1974   II. John Leslie, d 1972 Ald.
III. Mark, res Bromley, Kent, England
IV through VII, 4 daus, res Alderney, 3 rem to England (Mrs. Cairns-Forsythe, Ald.)
VIII. Ernest Winter Vernon, b 1889 Ald., to Montreal 1910 then to Vancouver, BC, mar 1905 Anne Lydia Horwood
A1. John Desmond, res Chateauguay, Que., mar Doreen Jenkins
   B1. David John, b 1957   B3. Douglas Edward, b 1961
   B2. Donald Robert, b 1959   B4. Sarah Luane, b 1967
LE BRUN, Clifford, b 1898 G, d Chatham, Ont. 1966, mar Eva DAVEY, qv, b 1897 G, d 1976
A1. Bette, b 193-, mar Fred. Hicks, no issue, res Chatham, Ont.
LE BRUN, Gladys, sister of Clifford, above, b 1905 G, mar Edward DAVEY, qv, d 1933 Ottawa, Ont. Son Donald Elwyn res Eng. (Ed. Davey, Ont.)
LE BRUN, George, son of John L. and Jane DUMARESQ, res Malbaie 1850s (Brochet)
LE BRUN, Thomas, b 1869 Beaulieu, J, son of John LE BRUN. From J to Gaspe, age 14, worked for Robin, Collas and Co. Mar Jeannette DE GRUCHY, b 1880, in 1900, from Benelais, Trinity, J. Res Grand Etang, NS, 4 chn, 2 d.y. (Gerald Le Brun, Bedford, NS)
A1. Charles Thomas, retired judge, Bridgetown, NS
A2. Gerald Jersey Le Brun, res Bedford, NS. Mar Barbara Longmire, b 1913, Bridgetown, NS

B1. Gerald Paul, M.D., F.R.C.S., (C), b 1941, res Halifax, NS, mar
   Janet McEvoy, b 1942
   C1. Danielle Suzanne, b 1970   C2. Stefan Paul, b 1973
B2. Suzanne Marie, b 1945, mar John Malcolm MacKeigan, MD, F.R.C.S.
   (C), res Grand Rapids, Mich.
   C1. Sara Elizabeth MacKeigan, b 1971 C2. Daniel MacKeigan, b 1972
   C3. Jeffrey Paul MacKeigan, b 1972, twin
LE BRUN, George, b J?, res Cheticamp, Inverness Co., NS (Gerald Le
   Brun, Bedford, NS)
A1. Stanley, d ca 1918, unmar   A2. Phyllis, res Cheticamp
A3. Ruby, mar Herbert LE BOUTILLIER, qv, res Cheticamp, C.B., N.S.
LE BRUN, William, b J, son of Philippe and Suzanne of J, mar Cascape-
   dia 1833 Phebe Cormier, dau of Aime and Brigitte Leblanc (Gallant)
LE BRUN. Some persons of this surname in Scotland 1296, later changed
   name to BROUN. Still later one branch changed surname to Moor and
   Muir. (Hist. of Brantford, Ont.) Cf LE BROUNE of J. (Stevens)
LE CAIN, LE QUESNE, Francis Barkley, is thought to have been born in J
   of the Le Quesne fam there, and appeared in Annapolis Royal, N.S. ca
   1738 or before. He was an armourer for the Board of Ordnance stationed there. He mar 1745 Alicia Maria Hyde, dau of Thomas Hyde, who
   was a Master in the Ordnance Dept. She d 1858, and Francis mar 2.
   Elizabeth Foster, dau of Benjamin F. and Sarah Woodward. Much inter-
   esting material held by descendants. (Calnek; Savary; Wayne W. Walker,
   Ottawa, Ont.; H.H. Le Quesne, Vancouver, B.C.: Richard Spurr, Alex-
   andria, VA; G. Kenneth Robb, Hampton, N.B.; Mrs. Fred Schneider,
   Fresno, Calif.; HISTORY OF NOVA SCOTIA, by Barnes)
A1. John, b 1746, mar Sarah Providence. He was accidentally shot,
   leaving a small family, not traced, but poss these were his chn
   B1. Letitia Maria, bp 1786   B3. Alice, bp 1794
   B2. Mary, bp 1788   B4. Susan, bp 1794
A2. Alicia Maria, b 1748, mar John Ritchie, M.P. Grandparents of a
   Chief Justice of Canada, and several other notables. More data in
   N.S. records.
A3. Elizabeth, b 1750, mar Thomas Harris ca 1775, oldest son of Thomas
   or John Harris. More data in N.S. archives.
   B1. Capt. John, b ca 1775, mar 1799 Mary Shaw
      C1. Thomas Harris, res Eastport, N.S.   CAUTION!
      C2. Henry Harris, d at sea, unmar   SEVERAL ERRORS IN
      C3. Nelson Harris, d at sea, unmar   THIS CHART!
      C4. Charles B. Harris, d in Ontario
      C5. John McNamara Harris, mar Diadema McDormand
      C6. Moses Harris, mar 1. Rachel Rice, and 2. Sophia Rice
      C7. Isaiah Harris, d unmar
      C8. Mary Harris, mar George Ryerson. More info in N.S. on Ryersons
      C9. Susan, d unmar
   B2. Capt. Thomas Harris, b 1777, d unmar, abroad
A4. Annie, b 1752, mar John Skelton, rem to mainland Canada
A5. Mary, b 1754, mar Abraham, son of Michael Spurr and Jane Shippe.
   B1. Mary Spurr, b Annapolis Royal, N.S., mar 1791 George Davis
   B2. Michael Spurr, b 1775, mar 1798 Elizabeth Roach, d 1804
   B3. Elizabeth Spurr, mar 1791 Christopher P. Harris, d 1864
   B4. Jane Spurr, mar 1799 Benjamin Potter
      C1. Thomas Potter, b 1800, mar 1823 Sarah Ann Smith, dau of Jeremiah
         S., Jr. Thomas d 1881, bur Smith's Cove, N.S. Sarah Ann d 1885.
         D1. Henrietta Jane Potter, b before 1827
         D2. Charles Thomas Potter, b 1826, mar Susan Ann Chute, 1836-
            1909. He d 1895

        D3. Eliza Abigail Potter, mar Benjamin Potter Sulis
        D4. Oratia Adelia Potter, d 1853, age 23
        D5. Sarah Ann Potter, mar James R. Bryant, she d 1866, age 34
        D6. Amelia Emma Potter, mar 1870 Jonas Wellington Rice
        D7. Cynthia Potter, mar 1868 James R. Bryant, his second wife,
            see Sarah Ann, above
        D8. Jeremiah Smith Potter, b 1844, mar 1870 Margaret Bryant
        D9. Louisa Maria, b 1847, d 1948, age 100 plus. Mar 1870, Deacon
            Jonas W. Rice. See Amelia Emma, above. No issue.
    C2. John Lawrence Potter, b 1802, mar 1840 Caroline Hunt, dau of
        Elijah Hunt. John d 1867, age 65. She d Boston, Mass., 10 chn.
    C3. William Franklin Potter, b 1804, mar 1827 Abigail O. Simpson,
        dau of Capt. S. Four chn, no data on other three.
        D1. William Edwin Augustus Potter, b 1840, mar 1870 at Digby, NS,
            Hattie Camp Chute, age 16, dau of Joseph and Maria Chute
    C4. Henry Potter, b 1806, mar Margaret Rice, dau of Silas R., 5 chn
    C5. Mary Eliza Potter, b 1809, d 1848. Mar Caleb Sulis 1829, his
        first of three wives. Caleb d 1899, bur Smith's Cove, N.S.
        D1. Benjamin Potter Sulis, b 1830, mar Eliza Abigail Potter,
            cousin
        D2. Cynthia Sulis, b 1831   D3. Henry Harris Sulis, b 1833
        D4. Eliza Deborah Sulis, b 1835, d 1848, age 13
        D5. John Lawrence Sulis, b 1838, d 1933, mar Diadamy Rice, 1837-
            1921
        D6. James Albert Sulis, b 1839
        D7. Amanda J. Sulis, b 1841, mar George Welch
        D8. Mary Emily Sulis, b 1843, mar 1873 James Emry Turnball
        D9. Annetta Sulis, b 1845, d 1847
    C6. Cynthia A. Potter, b 1811, mar William Jones, Jr., d 1843
    C7. Jane C. Potter, b 1813, mar 1833 John Ditmars, son of Jeremiah
        Ditmars, 3 chn
    C8. Emmeline Potter, b 1816, mar George Samuel Sulis, b 1819, in
        Smith's Cove, N.S., son of Daniel Sulis, Jr. She d 1859, age
        44. He mar 2. Minerva Sypher.
        D1. Laura Sulis, b 1846, d 1847 D2. Mary Emma Sulis, b 1848, d.y.
        D3. Robert Sears Sulis, b 1850, mar 1873 Laliah Sulis
        D4. Arthur E. Sulis, b 1853, mar Iona? Sulis
        D5. Laura Emma Sulis, b ca 1856, mar 1874 Charles E. Bent
        D6. by second wife, Allice, b 1862 D7. Avery Sulis, b ca 1865
        D8. Bessie Jane Salisbury, b 1874, d 1960
    C9. James M. Potter, b 1818, mar ca 1842 Elizabeth J. Shay, rem to
        Fonthill, then to St. Catherines, Ont., and to Calif., 6 or
        7 chn
    C10. Edward W. Potter, b 1820, mar Eliza Abigail Sulis
  B5. Thomas Spurr B6. Anne Spurr, mar Henry Hennigar, d 1871
  B7. Abigail Spurr, b 1785, mar Thatcher Sears, d 1870
  B8. Rev. Gilbert Spurr, b 1787, d 1870, mar Esther Chute, 6 daus
  B9. Diademia Spurr, mar 1808 Elijah Hunt
    C1. Rev. Abraham Spurr Hunt
  B10. Maria Spurr, mar Samuel McColly, res Ontario
  B11. Alicia Spurr, mar John Sulis
  B12. Abraham Spurr, bp 1796, mar 1820 Ann Harris, dau of Capt. John
       H. of Digby, NS
A6. Thomas, b 1756, mar Martha Wilkie
  B1. David, mar 1868 Ann Le Cain Dickson, also called DIXON
    C1. Thomas Henry, b 1809, living in 1831, d unmar
    C2. Mary Jane, b 1811, mar Silas Hancock

C3. Frederick, b 1813, d 1888, mar Mary, dau of Peter Le Cain, qv.
　　D1. William?, b ca 1832, d 1888?
　　D2. Robert Dixon, master mariner of Annapolis, mar there 1874, at
　　　　age 25, Amelia Hope Baker, age 23, dau of Henry and Eliza Lake
C4. Margaret Eliza, b 1816, d unmar
C5. Walter William Wilkie, b 1818, mar --- Ross in Batavia, in N.Y.?
B2. Frederick, mar 1. Ann Davies and 2. an American, rem to U.S.
　　C1. Charlotte, b 1816　　C2. Ann Martha, b 1819　Poss other chn
B3. Walter, poss bp 1793, mar Frances Thomas, res St. John, Nfld., d
　　there
B4. Francis, unmar　　　　　　　　B5. Maria Lavinia, bp 1796
A7. Francis, first ch by second wife, b 1762, mar Margaret McNeish
　　Ritchie, who d 1843
　B1. Charles, b 1785, mar 1820 Maria Eliza Mence
　　　C1. Margaret, b 1826, mar Robert James Spurr, b 1824
　　　C2. Barclay Farquarson, b 1829
　B2. Elizabeth, b 1786, mar David Fleet, 2 sons, 2 daus
　B3. Andrew Ritchie, b 1788, d unmar
　B4. James, b 1790, mar 1817 Frances Ryerson, dau of Francis R.
　　　C1. Anna Maria, b 1818, mar Avard Gates
　　　C2. Margaret Eliza, b 1821, mar John L. Rice
　　　C3. James Francis, b 1823, mar 1850 Sarah Morse, dau of James, res
　　　　　Annapolis
　　　　　D1. Oscar R., b 1853　　　　D4. Andrew, bp 1859
　　　　　D2. Ella Maria, b 1855　　　D5. George, bp 1861
　　　　　D3. James, bp 1859　　　　　D6. Frances, b 1862
　　　C4. Sarah Ann, b 1825, mar Isaiah Potter, b 1814
　　　C5. John M., b 1827, mar Adelaide Durkee, d Yarmouth, N.S., res
　　　　　Hillsburgh and Bear River, N.S., 7 chn
　　　　　D1. Charles Edward, bp 1858　　D5. Anne Blanche, bp 1862
　　　　　D2. Frances, bp 1858　　　　　　D6. John Turnbull, bp 1862
　　　　　D3. Alva, bp 1858　　　　　　　D7. Franklin Clements, bp 1867
　　　　　D4. Edgar Athelstane, bp 1859
　　　C6. George, b 1829, mar Agnes Hoyt, dau of James Fred. Hoyt, farmer
　　　　　in Annapolis area
　　　　　D1. Mary Hoyt, b 1864, mar William Horsefall at age 22
　　　　　D2. Millidge De Lancey Hoyt, b 1865
　　　　　D3. James Alfred Hoyt, b 1867
　　　C7. Amasa, b 1831, d unmar　　　　C8. Thomas, b 1833, d unmar
　　　C9. Mary, mar Albert BERTEAUX, qv, son of Edward B.
　B5. Margaret McNeish, b 1791, mar Joseph Wells
　B6. John, b 1794, mar 1828 Maria Eliza Stewart, Stuart. He d 1869
　　　C1. Elizabeth Georgina, b 1832, d 1848
　　　C2. Maria Louisa, b 1835, mar Elisha L. Bancroft, b 1831, son of
　　　　　Wm. B.
　　　C3. George Augustus, b 1839, mar Saraphina BERTEAUX, qv, dau of
　　　　　George B.
　　　　　D1. George Augustus, b 1862, mar 1893 Annapolis, NS, Blanche Ame-
　　　　　　　lia BERTEAUX, qv, dau of Albert and Mary Elizabeth B.
　　　　　D2. John, b 1865, mar 1891 at Le Quille, Addie Hardwick, age 17,
　　　　　　　dau of William and Margaret Hardwick
　　　　　D3. Louisa Victoria, b 1867　　D4. Bessie Marie, b 1871
　　　C4. Georgina Mence, b 1849, mar William M. Bailey
　B7. Nicholas, b 1796, mar 1840 Margaret Lucretia Williams
　　　C1. Francis, b 1840, d 1856?
　　　C2. William, b 1844, mar Zeruiah Williams
　　　　　D1. Ralph, at 25 mar Ida Mabel Spurr, 28, dau of Alfred and Ellen

C3. Andrew, b 1845, mar Emma Sanders
  D1. Minnie, mar at age 21 in 1891 at Roselle, James Primrose
  C4. Margaret McNeish, b 1847, mar William Hardwick
B8. Alicia Maria, b 1797, d unmar 1815   B9. Benjamin, b 1800, d 1801
A8. Benjamin, b 1764, mar Mary Winchester, no issue
A9. Nicholas, b 1765, a merchant in Halifax, mar Catherine Jost and poss mar 2. Elizabeth Beale?
  B1. Francis Barclay, mar Margaret Bond, no issue
  B2. John William, d unmar   B3. Arthur Walter Wilkie, d unmar
  B4. George Frederick Augustus, mar Susan B. Oxner, res Halifax and Berwick, 10 chn
    C1. Catherine Elizabeth, mar Felix King of H.M. dockyard, Halifax, 2 daus; one mar Rev. Arthur W. Cook of Kingston, Ont.
    C2. Eliza, mar Rev. John STANNAGE, qv.
    C3. Ann, mar James Cameron   C4. Alicia Maria, d.y.
    C5. Sophia Edwina, mar Joshua Kaulbach, merchant at Lunenburg
    C6. Susan Parker, mar Edward Pierson Archbold, son of Capt. P. Archbold, Royal Meath Reg't. Susan was the tenth ch.
      D1. Edward Thorn Ambrose Archbold
      D2. Rev. Francis H.W. Archbold, Hon Curate of St. Paul's, Halifax, NS
  B5. Benjamin, b 1792
A10. William, b 1767, mar Sarah Henshaw. Res Annapolis, d 1830. 3 sons, 4 daus.
  B1. Peter, mar 1824 Sarah Tomlinson. Blacksmith in Annapolis.
    C1. Mary, mar Frederick LE CAIN. A son Wm. res Vermont, U.S.
    C2. Elizabeth, mar James Edward CORBETT 1847
    C3. Eliza, mar James Wright
    C4. Margaret Almira, bp 1834, mar Andrew Hogan
    C5. Sarah, mar Duncan Miller
    C6. Susan Jane, bp 1836, mar George Stailing, d Digby, N.S.
  B2. Thomas, b ca 1805, mar Sarah and/or Elizabeth Orde. Res Guinea, near Clements, NS, farmer. Order of chn uncertain, record unclear.
    C1. William, b 1831, mar Margaret Sweeny of Yarmouth, NS in 1853. Mariner in 1877. Poss mar 2. in 1886 Jeanette Hudson, Clementsport, NS, and 3. Sarah Williams in 1889.
      D1. Thomas, b 1854,5
      D2. John, b 1857, mariner, mar 1881 Louisa BERRY, dau of James and Rebecca B.
      D3. Edward, b 1859,60   D6. William, b 1864.5
      D4. Mary E., b 1861,2   D7. Charles, b 1868,9
      D5. Amelia, b 1864,5
    C2. Thomas, b ca 1839, bp 1843, mar Minetta RHODDA. Cf RODDA
      D1. Charles, b 1864,5
    C3. John, b ca 1839, bp 1843, mar Rebecca Hannan, Hain? 1869, dau of Daniel Hain? In 1871 he was a master mariner and res with him were Frances, 23; Armanda, 21; Phebe, 4; and Armanda, age 1.
    C4. James, bp 1848-50, mar 1872 Samantha BERRY, dau of Jesse Berry
      D1. Jessie, at 18 mar in 1892, Ansley Fraser, 21, son of Wallace and Mary Ann Fraser
    C5. Frank, Francis Nicolas   C6. Colin, mar Rachel MERRITT
    C7. Elizabeth, mar 1. 1843 Joseph Jestings of Annapolis, mar 2. Thomas F. BERRY, and 3. Nathaniel Mott. Cf MOTTEE of C.I.
    C8. Mary Hester, bp 1843, fourth dau, mar Edward C. BERRY
    C9. Ann or Susan, mar 1847 John Purdy in Clements, NS. A Susan bp 1843. A Susan Le Cain, widow of a Philips, age 30, res in Bear River, dau of Thomas and Elizabeth LE CAIN, mar 1873 in Bear

River John Isles, age 42, seaman, b Halifax, son of William Isles and Susan I.
    C10. Martha, bp 1843, mar William Milner, son of Thomas M.
    C11. Sarah, mar --- Long   C12. Dau, mar Joseph Rawding
    C13. Another Thomas?, mar Elizabeth ---, res Clements, N.S.
        D1. Pheobe, b 1854   D2. Francis Nicolas
        D3. James Bernard, b ca 1850, mar Samantha BERRY, age 20 in 1872. She was dau of Jesse and Charlotte BERRY.
        D4. Samuel Caldwell, b ca 1850, mar 1873 Letitia MERRITT, age 16, dau of George and Emmeline MERRITT, Baptish
  B3. William, mar 1824 Ellen Ritchie, dau of Robert R., a shoemaker in Annapolis, NS
    C1. John, d unmar before 1827   C4. Davis, bp 1837, d unmar
    C2. David Alexander, d unmar, bp 1846 C5. Malvina
    C3. Sarah, d unmar   C6. Charlotte, d unmar bp 1837
    C7. Frances, Fanny, bp 1846, mar Israel Young, son of Robert Young
    C8. Harriet, bp 1846, mar Daniel Dukeshire
    C9. Mary Eliza Ritchie?, bp 1851. The last two chn uncertain.
    C10. George Washington Ritchie?, bp 1851
  B4. Elizabeth Mary, mar 1831 Alexander Easson Ritchie, bp 1799, son of Robert Ritchie. He d 1834. She mar 2. Thomas Roach Spurr
    C1. William A. Ritchie, b 1831, mar 1857 Fannie Foster
    C2. John Moore Campbell Ritchie, b 1832, mar Joanna Daly
        D1. Mary   D2. Bessie
    C3. Anna Ritchie   C4. George Ritchie C5. poss other chn by Spurr
  B5. Mary Ann, mar 1831 William R. Webb, son of Robert W.
    C1. William Le Cain Webb, c 1832 C3. Sarah Ann Webb, b 1834
    C2. Robert Webb, b 1833   C4. John Webb, b 1835
LE CAIN, John, and wife, Harriet, and/or 2. Margaret? in N.S. Placement uncertain.
A1. Arthur, bp 1871, age 6   A2. Richard, bp 1871, age 5
LE CAPPELAIN, also LE CAPELAIN and LE CAPELLAIN, etc. Cf CAPLAN often found in the Maritimes.
LE CAPELLAIN, George, b 1850 St. Peter, J, son of Samuel Le C., d 1935 North Bay, Ont. Mar 1880 Susan WHITE, qv, b 1864 Alice Twp., Ont., d 1946 Toronto (Richard Le Capellain, Bloomfield, NJ; M. Vandray, Montreal, Que.)
A1. George William, b 1882, d 1883 Papineau, Ont.
A2. Mary Ann, b 1884, d 1924 Eau Claire, Ont. Mar Francis Joseph Moore, b Shawville, Que., who d 1926 Eau Claire, Ont. Mar 1913.
  B1. a son, b 1914, d.y.
  B2. Marjorie Isabel Moore, b 1915, mar Clarence W. Allison, res Toronto
  B3. Mary Agnes Moore, b 1916, Eau Claire, Ont.
  B4. Florence Moore, b 1918
  B5. Frances Susan Moore, b 1920, mar Andrew John Scott
  B6. Margaret Lillian Moore, b 1922, mar William Haddon Schaefer, res Toronto
  B7. dau, b 1924, d.y.
A3. Jane Rebecca, b 1886, d 1966 North Bay, Ont. Mar Richard Fleming, 1888-1920.
  B1. James Bertram Fleming, b 1914, d 1916
  B2. Thelma Muriel Fleming, b 1915, Kirkland Lake, Ont., mar Allan Bud James
  B3. George Richard Fleming, b 1918, North Bay, Ont., mar Edna Alice Diggles
A4. Susan Jessie, b 1888, d.y.

A5. Samuel Jacob, b 1889, d 1962 North Bay, Ont., mar Edith Gertrude Saunders, b 1887 London, England, res North Bay, Ont.
- B1. Gertrude Florence, b 1918, mar Harold Alcorn
- B2. Constance Victoria, b 1920, mar Lou Batchelor, res North Bay
- B3. Haroldine Rebecca, b 1921, mar William KNIGHT, res Scarborough, Ont.
- B4. John Milton, b 1924, mar Alice Ferris
- B5. Albert Howard, b 1926, mar Rhoda Vaught, res Capreol, Ont.
- B6. Richard Samuel, b 1929 North Bay, mar Jean Quinn, res Bloomfield, NJ
- B7. Dorothy Edith, b 1931, mar William Snoddow, res Whitby, Ont.

A6. Agnes Georgina, b 1891, d 1972 Ottawa, mar John Martin Shoup, 1893-1968
- B1. John Murray Shoup, b 1917 Coniston, Ont., mar Mary Marjorie Williams, res Dusbury, Ont.
- B2. George Gordon Shoup, b 1920 Sudbury, Ont., mar Lois Elizabeth Pratt, res Ottawa, Ont.
- B3. Robert Manley Shoup, b 1921 Little Current, Ont., d 1935
- B4. Mary Elizabeth Myra Agnes Shoup, b 1931 Chapleau, Ont., mar Donald Kenneth McNab Brownlee

A7. Bertha Julia, b 1893 Papineau, Ont., mar Harold G. Deutsch, no issue

A8. Albert James Eska, b 1895, d 1962 North Bay, Ont., mar Betsy Victoria MacBeth, b 1902 Widdifield Twp., Ont., res North Bay, Ont.
- B1. George Duncan, b 1927, mar Christina Hastings, res Sudbury, Ont.
- B2. Alton MacBeth, b 1929, mar Marie Simm, res North Bay, Ont.
- B3. Beth, Florence, b 1932, mar Ellard Mousseau, res North Bay, Ont.

A9. Ida Susan, b 1897, mar 1923 Little Current, Ont., William F. BROWN, b 1896 Hanover, Ont. Res St. Petersburg, Fla.
- B1. Doris Julia Brown, b 1924 Detroit, Mich., mar James William Holmes, res St. Petersburg, Fla.
- B2. Betty Brown, b 1926 Detroit, mar Arvin Doyle Riddle, res Fla.
- B3. Shirley Brown, b 1929 Detroit, mar Merlin Early Whitley, res Fla.

A10. Julia Regina, b 1898, d 1923

A11. Georgina Victoria, b 1900 Papineau, Ont., mar Clifford Shaw, b 1897, Detroit, Mich., res Englehart, Ont.
- B1. Kathleen Joyce Shaw, b 1930 Allen Park, Mich., mar Richard Fick
- B2. Susan June Shaw, b 1931 Detroit

A12. Marjorie Ellen, b 1901 Papineau, Ont., mar 1922 Carl Henry Vandray, b 1894 Pembroke, Ont., d 1962 Beloiel, Que.
- B1. Carl Wallace Vandray, b 1923, North Bay, Ont., mar Anita Louise Corinne, res Montreal, Cartierville, Que.
- B2. Dorothy May Vandray, b 1927 Waltham, Que.
- B3. June Arlene Vandray, b 1936 Pembroke, Ont., mar Carl Joseph Ashton, res Ottawa

A13. Eva Florence, b 1907 Mattawa, Ont., mar 1928 Niagara Falls, Ont., Franklyn John Crawford, 1905-1964, res Toronto
- B1. Patrick Franklin Crawford, b 1929 Toronto, mar Jean Whalen and 2. Eunice Eileen SHEPHERD, res Toronto
- B2. James Ferguson Crawford, b 1930 Toronto, mar Helena Sulatycka, res Toronto
- B3. Robert Allan Crawford, b 1932, res Toronto

A14. George William, b 1903, d 1904

A15. Eva Florence, b 1905, d.y.

LE CAPPELAIN, Herbert Dupre, also a desc of Samuel Le C. of J, as above, and his bro John, came to Canada from J in 1871. Herbert mar Clarisse Fletcher of Montreal. John rem to Winnipeg. Herbert lost 3 boys in the plague in Montreal, and rem west, said to have descendants there.

LE CAPPELAIN, John, also a son of a Samuel Le C. in J, was a noted J artist who d age 36. His father, Samuel, d 1850 age 62. (M. Vandray, Montreal, Que.) Album in Soc. Jers., Jersey.
LE CAPPELAIN, see also AGNEW fam
LE CAPPELAIN, Ada Mary, b ca 1850s G, mar her second cousin, Francis Hedley AGNEW, qv, and rem to Winnipeg and Fort Albert, Sask. Ada's aunt or gr aunt, Mary AGNEW, sister of James AGNEW, mar John LE CAPPELAIN of J, and rem to Costa Rica.
LE CAPPELAIN, from J to Perce 1800s (Cent. Bklt.)
LE CAPPELAIN, in N. White Rock, BC, curr
LE CASSE or LA CASSE?, from C.I. to Gaspe (Annett)
LE CAUDEY, Sylvestre, from J to Bonaventure Is., Gaspe 1800s (Syvret)
LE CAUDEY, see CODY LE CAUDEY DATA INCORRECT. (Aldo Brochet)
LE CAUDEY and CODY, Ellen, mar Arthur Philip DU VAL, b 1853, See DU VAL. This CODY-LE CAUDEY fam was from J and was R.C.
LE CAUX, John, from J to Gaspe 1768, drowned at Caraquet, NB 1773. Cf LA COX, and Cox of the Maritimes.
LE CAUX, John, at Isle Madame, CB 1768-1769
LE CERF, surname of J. Cf BARACHOIS DE CERF, where Jerseymen settled in Nfld.
LE CHASSEUR, Channel Islanders in the Maritimes Fisheries (J. H. Le Breton list)
LE CHASSEUR, from C.I. to Gaspe (Ascah)
LE CHEMINANT, G., from St. Peter Port, G to Glencoe, Ont. then to Toronto ca 1914. Wives surnames TRACY? and COLLENETTE?
LE CHEMINANT, Norman, from C.I. to Whitehorse, Yukon 1900s?
LE CLAIR, poss LE CLERCQ?, from C.I. to Nfld. (Rev. Hammond)
LE CLAIR, several in Ontario, source unknown
LE CLERC, D.A., from G to Victoria, BC before 1940
LE CLERC, curr Gaspe
LE CLERC, E., in Dufferin, Ont.
LE CLERCQ, from J to Vancouver, BC (Andrea Le Clercq, Walnut Creek, CA)
LE CLERCQ, Joshua Frederic, b J, son of Alfred Le. C. and Margaret HERIVEL, qv, who res St. Clement, J. Joshua's bro Alfred lost at sea, and a sister mar a LE BRUN, qv. Joshua mar 1889 J or G, Elizabeth Rachel LE PAGE, poss at St. Heliers, J. He traveled a great deal, trying to conquer his asthsma. A lay preacher, bilingual, preached in both French and English. The fam has letters from all over the world in the 1800s. Finally settled in Victoria, BC
  A1. Laura Agnes, b 1890, court reporter and private secretary to Attorney General, d 1955 Victoria, BC, mar Rev. Ebert Charles Curry of Somerset, England
    B1. Muriel Gene Curry, mar James Robert Kidd, agrologist
      C1. Patricia Gene Kidd, b 1963 C2. David James Ebert Kidd, b 1962
    B2. Lawrence Edward Curry, res Calgary, Alta., mar Sylvia ---
      C1. Leanne Nadine Curry, b 1956, mar 1975 Garry Ralph Jones
      C2. Janine Denise Curry, b 1958 C3. Vanda Lynn Curry, b 1962
    B3. Eberta Gertrude Curry, mar Imre Dobi, Hungarian Orchardist, res Okanagan Valley, Naramata, BC
      C1. Attila Dobi C2. Arpad Dobi C3. Maria Dobi C4. Scaba Dobi
  A2. Donald Alfred, b 1892, mar Victoria, BC 1946 Eleanor or Elizabeth McCormack, d 1969
    B1. Donald Allan, b 1947, res Brandon, Man.
  A3. Evelyn Beatrice, Nina, b 1893, mar Thomas Arthur Brown of Durham, England, res Chilliwack, BC
    B1. Maurice Donald Brown, b 1922, mar 1. Kathleen Ruth East, b 1948, and 2. Saralie Routledge in 1971

C1. David Allen Brown, b 1951, d 1974
C2. Eric Douglas Brown, b 1954   C4. Timothy Sandor Brown, b 1958
C3. Gordon Donald Brown, b 1955 C5. Casey Thomas Brown, b 1962
B2. Andrea Audrie Erica, b 1927, mar 1950 George Leo Burke, b Ireland, who d 1966. He had two chn by a previous marriage. Andrea attended Diablo Valley College, Walnut Creek, Calif.
B3. Gordon Keith, b 1936, d 1952, shot by person unknown
A4. Percy, d.y.   A5. Cecily, d.y.
LE COCQ, Philip, b J, d in Africa ca 1893. He had mar Rachel RENOUF, qv of G, 5 chn. (Le Moignan; Marie Le Cocq, Dalhousie, NB)
I. Philip Renouf, mar, no issue
II. Walter Renouf, mar St. Heliers, J, 1931 Ellen FAUVEL LE SUEUR, b 1885, a son, Philip
III. Alfred Renouf, b 1876 Trinity, J, to Belle Anse, Gaspe ca 1889, then to Cap d'Espoir. Mar 1. Amelia LE COCQ, dau of John Le C. and Alice LE MOTTEE, qv. She d.y. and Alfred mar 2. Ida Ethel LE GRESLEY, b 1892 Malbaie. He d at age 80.
A1. Alfred Renouf, b 1930, mar Marie Francoise Vermette of Campbellton, N.B.
B1. Rachel Blanche, b 1955, mar Cornelius Machulson of Holland, res Antigonish, N.S.
B2. Deane Ida, b 1956, mar Denzil HARQUAIL, qv, res Bathurst, NB
C1. Deny HARQUAIL, b 1974
B3. Stephen Daniel, b 1957 Saint John, N.B.
B4. Brian Alfred, b 1958   B6. Donna Gail, b 1964
B5. John Timothy, b 1962, d.y.   B7. Marie Sharon, b 1966
B8. Vance Francis, b 1969
IV. Eva, d.y.   V. Rachel, d.y.
LE COCQ, William Lucas, b 1877 Raleigh Twp., Kent Co., near Fletcher, Ont. and Chatham, Ont. Son of Lucas LE COCQ of J? Wm d 1936 Windsor, Ont., bur Valetta, Ohio, Stewart Cem. Mar Christina LE COCQ, b 1888 Raleigh Twp., res Fletcher, Ont., then in 1919, Windsor, Ont. (John A. Lecocq, Burlington, Ont.)
A1. John, b 1913 Raleigh Twp., mar Lorraine Goulet 1943, b 1915 Belle River, Ont.
B1. Linda Lee, b 1944, mar Barry Headon
C1. Brian Headon, b 1975
A2. Dorothy, b 1915, d 1975 Windsor, Ont. Mar Howard Burdette 1937 Windsor, and 2. Louis Lajoie in 1945.
B1. Roxene Burdette, b 1938, mar Keith Mifflin 1957, res Port Alma, Ont.
B2. Robert Lajoie, b 1946, res Toronto, Ont.
A3. Garnet, b 1916, mar 1945 Mildred ---, res Windsor, Ont., then Hawkesbury, Ont., near Ottawa
B1. Bonnie, b 1946, res Windsor
B2. Michelle, b 1948, res Thompson, Man., mar ---
A4. Margaret, b 1921 Windsor, d 1970, mar William Reid
B1. William Reid Jr., b 1948   B3. Daniel Reid, b 1955
B2. Michael Reid, b 1950
LE COCQ, William, b J, rem to Paspebiac, Gaspe in 1880s, mar --- (Lady McKie, Ottawa)
A1. Thelma, author, mar Winston McQuillan, res Toronto, Ont.
B1. Janet, mar, res Ottawa
LE COCQ, Clifford John, b J, bro of William above, mar Gertrude Mary Vickery (Mrs. C. Le Cocq, Toronto, Ont.)
A1. Thomas, d.y.
A2. Clifford P., b Lachine, Que., at death of mother, father and son

returned to J. Clifford mar Alice Amelia Keates, b Plymouth, Eng.
Settled England. Dau, Patricia Ann.
LE COCQ, Morris, son of George Le C. of Malbaie, Gaspe, b Trinity, J,
mar Alice LE MOTTEE, qv of St. Mathew, J. He was mgr at one time of
Royal Hotel, Gaspe (GLF)
LE COCQ, John, and Alice, from J on DAWN, to St. Peters, Gaspe, 1901
LE COCQ, John Frederick, beachmaster for Robin firm, b St. Martin, J,
to Malbaie, Gaspe (Syvret)
LE COCQ, cooper in PEI, 1841 census
LE COCQ, Alfred Renouf, 1876-1961, bur Cape Cove Angl. Cem. (Brochet)
LE COCQ, ---, second cousin to George Cousens OZARD, qv, from J to
Ontario, to Gordon Head, BC (E.G. Ozard, Vict., BC)
  A1. Lillian, a school teacher, mar Ray Hollins, Vanc., BC. 3 chn including Barbara and Ardell Hollins.
LE COCQ, Lucas, from C.I. to near Chatham, Ont. ca 1860 or 1870 (John
Le Cocq, Burlington, Ont.)
  A1. William Lucas, a son b 1877
LE CONTE, from C.I. to Canada? Surname in Ald. 1309
LE CORE, LE CORRE, from C.I. to the Maritimes? (Francis Marmaud, Cape
Breton, N.S.)
LE CORNU, Elizabeth, mar Thomas PITON 1782. See PITON, she was 2nd wife
LE CORNU, see THE QUIET ADVENTURERS, and THE QUIET ADVENTURERS IN
AMERICA, by Turk
LE CORNU, see Edward BALLEINE, Ontario
LE CORNU, John, at Bonaventure Island 1850s and in Maritimes Fisheries
(Le Breton list)
LE CORNU, Peter, b J, settled Bonaventure Island for a few years ca 1840.
Mar Mary Ann HOYLES, qv (Brochet)
LE CORNU, Philip Elias and Edward, were on the brig PATRUUS, the Robin
ship, sailing from J to Gaspe 1844, 1845. (Brochet)
LE CORNU, Peter of J, to Gaspe, then to Alpena, Mich. where he is bur.
Two chn (Turk)
  A1. Ann, b ca 1840?, d 1898, mar Francois Napoleon Gezequel, b Paris, France. Res New York, Gaspe and Alpena
    B1. Ann Mary Gezequel, mar Christ, Louis, Cevvallen, Zwahlen, of Switzerland. Desc
    B2. Mary Annie, b 1865, bur Alpena, Mich., mar --- De Marre, res Michigan. Desc
    B3. Francois, Frank, Napoleon Gezequel, mar, a son, Francis, b ca 1890, desc in Michigan
  A2. Frank, b 1842, desc poss in Michigan
LE COURTOIS, Francis, b ca 1854 G, mar Eliza PAUL, qv, rem to St.
Thomas ca 1890, bringing Ada and Charles Henry. (Mrs. W.H. Le Courtois, Brentwood Bay, BC)
  A1. Ada, b before 1890, mar Frank BERRY
    B1. Francis Berry B2. Lila Berry B3. Mabel Berry B4. Malo Berry
  A2. Charles Henry, b 1884 G, mar Edith Adelia Ripley, 1886-1945. Charles d 1949.
    B1. William Henry, b 1908, mar 1. Edna Smith, and 2. Barbara Rhodes, b 1922, no issue by second wife.
      C1. Marilyn Dorene, b 1931, mar D. Fred Cohoon, b 1931, mar 1952
        D1. Stephen Cohoon, b 1955   D3. Kelley Jo Cohoon, b 1961
        D2. Scott Cohoon, b 1957
    B2. Walter Charles, b 1911, mar 1935 Mabel Hawley, b 1912
      C1. Gary Francis, b 1938, mar 1959 Ann Morse
        D1. William Alan, b 1961   D2. Joan Marie, b 1965
      C2. Alan William, b 1941, mar Donna Mae Rodgers

LE COURTOIS 327

       D1. Anne Marie, b 1968   D2. William Alan, b 1970
     C3. Jeanne Elaine, b 1943, mar 1969 John Hobbs, divorced 1975, no
        issue
  B3. Gordon Francis, b 1914, mar 1. Muriel Thomas, dec, and 2. Gertrude Williamson, no issue
     C1. Joanne, b 1946, mar Paul Dunn
        D1. Shawn Dunn, b 1966   D3. Jody Dunn, b 1969
        D2. Peter Dunn, b 1967   D4. Carrie Dunn, b 1971
     C2. Mary Jane, b 1948, mar Gary Castellan, divorced
        D1. Jennifer Castellan, b 1968
  B4. Arthur Joseph, b 1916, mar 1937 Gwendolyn Smith, b 1916
     C1. Marie Joanne, b 1939, mar Kenneth Turnbull, b 1938
        D1. Kevin Turnbull, b 1965   D3. Scott Turnbull, b 1971
        D2. Darryl Turnbull, b 1967
     C2. Carol Ann, b 1943, mar 1962 George Chilton, b 1940
        D1. Michael Chilton, b 1963 D2. Connie Lyn Chilton, b 1968
LE COURTOIS, Henry Philip, b 1865 G, bro of Francis, above, d 1939.
Mar in St. Stephens, G, Emma PAULE, qv, rem to St. Thomas, Ont. ca
1890 (Walter Le Courtois, and Alice Stone, St. Thomas, Ont.)
A1. Edith Ann, b ca 1892, d 1968, mar Leroy WALKER, res Sparta, Ont.
A2. Henry Travers, b 1894, d 1934 or 1964, mar Florence Rayner
A3. Walter Charles, b 1896 St. Thomas, Ont., mar Catherine Kay, b 1898
    London, England
  B1. Dorothy Jean, b 1919, mar John Herbert Taylor, b 1918 Montreal,
     Que.
     C1. Karen Jean Taylor, b 1949, mar --- Cresswell
  B2. Kenneth Walter, b 1921, mar Marjory Phyllis Rose, b 1921
     C1. Susan Lynne, b 1954
A4. Emma Louise, b 1898, mar 1. Harry Menzies and 2. Ernest Rouse of
    Pontiac
A5. Alice Mary, b 1900, mar Alfred Stone, res St. Thomas, Ont.
A6. John Frederick, b 1902, d 1960, mar Audrey Skellding
LE COURTOIS, Louise, sister of Henry and Francis, to Ont., mar John
    BATISTE, qv
LE COUTEUR, Philip, son of Edward Le C. and Nancy MOLSEUR or MOISEUR,
    b 1805 J, d 1892 Bonaventure Is., Gaspe. Mar Hannah Jane Flynn, b
    1816, dau of John Flynn and Katherine Henley or Hendy, 9 chn.
    (Gallant, Brochet)
A1. Philip, b 1831 Bon. Is., d there 1863. Mar Jane JOURNEAU, qv,
    1837-1913.
  B1. Bridget, Minnie, b 1864 Bon. Is., d 1939 Perce, or 1882 Bon. Is.
    Mar James AUBERT, qv, 1854-1933, at least 3 sons
  B2. Philip, b 1874, d 1950 Perce
  B3. Jane, b 1869, d 1945 Perce. Mar 1907 Perce, Joseph PROULX Sr.,
    b 1873
  B4. Lydia Jane, b 1870, d 1948 Perce. Mar 1901 at Perce, John
(B1.? Alice,b1863 d Saskatoon 1944)   La Flamme.
     C1. Winnifred La Flamme, mar ---Cain   C3. Emma mar Edmond
     C2. Bridget Laflamme mar CliftonFlynn   AUBERT.

  B5. Edmond LE COUTEUR, b 1872 d 1900s Bon.Is.
  B6. George LE COUTEUR b 1877, d 1900 Perce. Mar 1894 Ellen Cahill
    D1. Walter, b ca 1897, mar 1926 Mont., Laura Normandeau
    D2. John Clarence, b ca 1898 Perce, mar 2. Montreal, Marianne
        Normandeau of Perce
    D3. Edith, b ca 1900 Perce, d Montreal 1976. Mar 1. Alfred O'
        Leary of Perce and 2. Arthur Donohue of Perce. Bur Perce.

        E1. Brian O'Leary, res Kingston, Ont.
A2. Eliza Jane, b 1833, d 1850   A3. Edward, b 1835 Bon. Is.
A4. John, b 1837 Bon. Is., d there 1900. Mar Mary or Margaret CODEY,
        qv, 1839-1909.
    B1. Alice, b 1863 Bon. Is., mar Louis E. Moreau, who d Bon. Is. 1922,
        9 chn
    B2. John Philip, b 1864   B4. Edward James, b 1870 Bon Is, d there 1885
    B3. Ann, b 1867 or Maria B5. Ellen Flora, b 1872 Bon Is. Mar ---Jessup
    B6. James Adolphus, b 1874   ?Son George Jessup? Que.city.
A5. George, b 1839, d ca 1900 Que., mar Catherine Farman, fam in Montreal
    B1. William Rowland, b 1872 Bon. Is., a soldier
A6. Mary Ann, or Anne, b 1841, d 1930 Cape Cove, Gaspe. Mar Francois
    JOURNEAU, qv, who d Bon. Is. 1871. She mar 2. James Wall 1877, and
    3. in 1895, Edward BECK, qv.
A7. Elizabeth Jane or Genevieve Elizabeth, b 1843, d 1850
A8. Agnes Margaret, b 1846 Bon. Is., mar ---ARBOUR, qv.
    B1. Alfred Arbour?, b ca 1870?
A9. Catherine Hannah, or Anne Catherine, b 1849 Bon. Is., d ca 1920.
    Mar Henry Ridley DU VAL, qv, 1893, his second wife.
A10. Flora Jane, b 1853 Bon. Is., d 1891, mar 1879 Bon. Is., Henry
    Ridley DU VAL, qv, who mar 3. Elizabeth Anne de Saint Amand.
LE COUTEUR, Henry and John, from J, were in Bon. Is. in 1831, poss bros
    of Philip. Also a John res in Miscou, NB ca 1830. With 6 in the fam.
    (Ganong)
LE COUTEUR, Harold Adrian, b J, d 1908 Gaspe at age 27, bur St. Pauls,
    Gaspe
LE COUTEUR, John Arthur, from J, res Fox River, Gaspe, a cod merchant.
    His dau, Florence, d ca 1871
LE COUTEUR, Sir John, heir to Francis JANVRIN, qv. in Canada. See
    Notables chapter.
LE COUTEUR, Susanne, b J?, mar Francois PERCHARD, qv, by Bishop Mount-
    ain ca 1852 Quebec?
LE COUTEUR, Philip, b J, Jeanne b Perce, in Perce 1861 (Census) with
    Philippe, Jean, George, Marie Ann, Agnes, Anna Flora, all b Bon. Is.
    Same as Philip's fam above?
LE COUTEUR, Maria Anne, mar Peter Chiasson at Shippegan, NB before 1878.
    (Robichaud)
LE COUTRE, a resident of Pt. Miscou at Grand Plaines 1850 (Journal
    Assembly 1850, N.B.)
LE COUTEUR, LE COUTRE, Capt. from J in Nfld. (K. Mathews)
LE COUTEUR, COTTER, in Cape Breton, N.S. census 1871. Thomas at that
    time a merchant in Arichat, and wife Louise, b ca 1820 J.
LE COUTEUR, from Sark to PEI 1870s (Luce)
LE COUTEUR, Nicholas, from J to B.C. (Luce) Also a Clement Le Couteur
    to B.C.
LE COUTEUR, to N.S. Mrs. Ross Taylor, N.E. Margaree, NS, a desc as
    well as Clifford Le C. of Sidney, NS, Laura Cutler, Hilda Robertson,
    Mrs. J.C. Their father was Dauvergne Cutler. (Lady McKie, Ottawa)
LE COUTEUR, from J to Ontario
LE COUTEUR, Ruby, dau of Francis Le C., wine merchant in St. Helier, J,
    and Alice LE GROS. 4 chn: Gertrude, Ruby, Dorothy and Frank. Ger-
    trude's son, Peter, res U.K. Dorothy unmar. Frank's 2 daus res U.K.
    He mar May Campbell, a famous preacher. Ruby mar Louis NEEL of J,
    rem to Ontario. A son, Dr. Boyd Louis Neel, res Toronto.
LE COUTEUR, Edward John, b J, mar 1. ---, and 2. Florence May Monument
    1924. She d 1968, he d 1970. (June Keasey, London, Ont.)
    A1. Shirley Winnifred May, b 1925 (See LATE ADDITIONS AND CORRECTIONS)

LE COUTEUR

Note that LE COUTEURS OF Miscou had desc. in New Hampshire
- A2. Joy Irene Ethel, b 1926 Pelee Island
- A3. Joan Amelia June Phoebe, b 1929 Pelee Island, Ont., mar 1. Robert Charles Egelton, divorced, mar 2. Frank Denis Keasey, 1970
  - B1. Pamela Lynne Egelton, b 1949
  - B2. Charles Robert Egelton, b 1951
  - B3. Wendy Winnifred Egelton, b 1954, all res Windsor, Ont.
  - B4. Joy Charmaine Egelton, b 1956
  - B5. Debra Anne Egelton, b 1958

LE COUVET, Mary, b J, in Perce 1861 (Census) Also spelled LE COUVIER (Cent. Bklt.) and LA COUVEE See also pp 169,298,427.

LE COUVET, C.I. in Maritimes Fisheries (J.H. Le Breton list)

LE CRAS, LE CRAW, fam of J. Frank rem to Australia

LE CRAS, LE CRAW, Henry, b 1841 J, bro of Frank, above, poss sons of Francis BISSON LE CRAS of J who d 1928, age 83. Poss also from fam of Les Platons, Trinity, J. Henry rem to Laxton Twp., Norland, Ont. ca 1865, boot and shoe maker, farmer. Mary Mary Alice Campbell, 1853-1942, youngest dau of George and Catherine Campbell, from Island of Islay, Scotland who came in 1840s to Argyle, Ont. (F. Vernon Le Craw, and others in family, Norland, Ont.)
- A1. Edwin Francis, b 1875, d 1943, merchant and postmaster in Norland. Capt. 109th Regt. WWI. Mar Mary Littlejohn of Edinburgh, Scotland, 1898-1975 in Canada.
  - B1. Lachlan Augustus, b 1920, d.y.
  - B2. Francis Vernon, b 1921, R.C. Artillery, WWII, merchant, clerk-treasurer 1969 of Norland. Mar 1953 Eleanor Currie, b 1935
    - C1. Edwin Vernon, b 1957
    - C2. Heather Mary, b 1960
    - C3. John Lachland, b 1962
- A2. Frederick Campbell, b 1877, d 1965. Farmer, mar Olive Paulson of Head Lake, Ont. who later rem to Calif.
  - B1. Verna Marie, mar Gerald Robertson, b ca 1940
    - C1. Gerald Robertson
    - C2. Rick Robertson
- A3. Perle, b 1882, mar cousin, Harry LE CRAW, b 1843 St. Heliers, d 1941. No issue
- A4. James Alexander, b 1883, d 1962, merchant and cattleman, res Norland, Ont., mar Edith Louise Adair, 1887-1963
  - B1. Jean, b 1914, d 1959, mar Keith Henderson of Toronto
    - C1. Beverly Henderson, mar, res England
  - B2. Lorne Hughes, b 1921, d 1970, R.A.F. WWII. Merchant in Norland, mar 1944 Enid Walker, b 1923 Carlisle, Eng. Widow res Norland.
    - C1. Gary Stuart, b 1945, teacher, mar Carolyn Wilson, b 1946 of Hudson, Que., res there.
      - D1. Darren J., b 1974
      - D2. Brent R., b 1976
    - C2. Robert A., b 1951, Civil Engineer, res Toronto
    - C3. James A., b 1953
- A5. Dossie, b 1886, d 1968, teacher, unmar, d in Norland
- A6. Aldwin Bruce, b 1893, d 1966, hunter, trapper, guide, trucker, mar Estella, Ethel Hunter, 1897-1973, res Norland, Ont.
  - B1. Ausburn, b 1917, d 1976, mar Olive Baker of Rosedale?
    - C1. Anthony, res Toronto, mar Margaret ---, issue
  - B2. Gladys Mary, b 1923, mar William Pollard of Gooderham, Ont., b 1912, res Norland. Real estate agent.
    - C1. William Pollard Jr., b 1947, unmar
    - C2. John Pollard, b 1948, unmar
    - C3. Ricardo Pollard, b 1952, unmar
  - B3. Gordon Aldwin, b 1932, res Lindsay, Ont., baker. Mar 1957 Ann Povey, b 1937, of Coboconk, Ont.
    - C1. Lynn Heather, b 1959
    - C2. Bruce Emerson, b 1961
  - B4. Colin Campbell, b 1924, trapper, guide, marina operator, Vet of WWII, RCAF. Mar Shirley Perryman of Fenelon Falls, Ont., res

Norland
  C1. Brenda Alldean, b 1952, mar Bernard Greer, of Miners Bay, Ont.,
      res Norland
    D1. Toni Greer, b 1973
  C2. Debra Darlene, b 1954, mar Peter Magee, b 1946, of Dongola, Ont.
    D1. Robin Lynn Magee, b 1972   D2. Peter Daniel Magee, b 1974
  C3. Brian Campbell, b 1955, mar Ruth Ferguson?, b 1955
LE CRAS, LE CRAW, to Bon. Is., Perce, Quebec 1831
LE CRAS, from C.I. to N.S. (Lorway)
LE CRAW, from C.I. to Maritimes Fisheries, also noted in Nfld.
LE CRAS, "In the census of 1675 of Newfoundland, I find that several vessels were loaded between Trinity and Bonaventure by prominent Jersey firms of Henry LE CRAS, John LE CRAS and Nicholas BALLHAST" (BAILHACHE), "who exported their fish"..."This old record mentions these firms particularly as Jerseymen, and proves that it was the Jersey people who carried on the principal business in that locality over two hundred and fifty years ago." (Shortis-Munn)
LE CRAS, Henry, from J? or from Nfld., joint owner with John Lorway of British built brigantine MATILDA in 1864, Cape Breton. Lorway bought out LE CRAS in 1865. (Capt. Parker)
L'ECRIVAIN, poss as SCRIVEN? to Canada from C.I. (Stevens)
LECRONIER, LE CRONIER, in Canada. Cf LE CRONIER of J (Stevens)
LE CRONIER, Capt. from J in Nfld. (K. Mathews)
LE CROS, poss LE CRAS?, LE CROIX, LA CROIX?, Capt. from J in Nfld. (K. Mathews)
LE DAIN, Thomas, age 36 in 1871, b J, blacksmith at Perce, with Jane, bur St. Pauls, Perce (GLF)
LE DAIN, Capt. from C.I. in Gaspe 1800s (Syvret; J.H. Le Breton list; Cent. Bklt.)
LE DAIN, Edmund John, b 1862 St. Heliers, J, son of Capt. John Le D. and Annie ---, indentured for five yrs. to CRC in Gaspe beginning in 1876. Worked in Douglastown, Sandy Beach, Perce and Gaspe. Mar Jane Elizabeth Clark from 6 miles up the York River, bur Anglican Cem., Wakeham, Que. (P.J. Le Dain, Sidney, BC)
A1. Annie Florea, b 1889
A2. Percy John, b 1892, mar 1823 Eileen Clare O'Brien, no issue
LE DREW and LE DROW. "Talking with a cousin who lives in the city I told her about you and she told me that there were DROWS in a part of Brigus, but there was no relationship with the LE DREWS. In the old cemetery at Cupids which dates back to about 1846 the name LEDREW is spelt as one word." (Rev. Ralph Le Drew, Toronto, Ont.)
LE DREW, Tobias, son of Benjamin and Patience BESANT (BISSON), qv, mar Emma Marie Ellsworth. Fam in Cupids 1846. (Rev. Ralph Le Drew, Toronto, Ont.)
A1. Frank, d ca 1956
A2. Ralph G., b 1912 Cupids, Nfld., rem to Halifax, Montreal, Sask. and Toronto. Mar Alice M. Smith from Random Isl., Trinity Bay, Nfld. She was b 1915.
  B1. Ellsworth Frank, to Boulder, Colo., Ph.D. 1947, mar 1972
  B2. Stephen Ralph, b 1950, in law school, Toronto, mar 1976
LE DREW, to Nfld. (Hug. Soc. letter; E.R. Seary, etc.) Cf LE DRIEU, LE DREW of J. (Stevens)
LE DREW, to Gaspe
LE DREW, in Conception Bay very early, Nfld. (G.H. Le Messurier; Shortis-Munn) Curr Bell Island.
LE DREW, James Samuel, b Nfld. late 1800s. He had 3 bros and 2 sisters: Thomas, John, Isaac, Laura and Agnes, all b Nfld. (Ernest Le Drew of

this fam, b Nfld. 1904)
LE DROW, said to be of C.I. origin in Nfld. Prob from LE DROIT of J (Seary)
LE DROW, Edward, ship carpenter, Brigus, Conc. Bay, Nfld. 1860s (Rev. Hammond)
LE DROW, John, ship owner, Brigus, Nfld. 1860s (Rev. Hammond)
LE DROW, Thomas and Tobias, planters in Brigus, Nfld. 1860s (Rev. Hammond)
LE DROW, many in Cupids, Nfld. 1762, 1780, etc.: Samuel, May, George and Nicholas
LE DUC, from G to Toronto, 1900s?
LEE, from C.I.? to Nfld. See Seary. A Lee said to be from C.I. settled in Petty Harbour, Nfld. 1780. (Rev. Hammond)
LEE, Richard, b J, retired to U.K. from Canada
LEE, John, bro to Richard, b ca 1825 J, mar, said to have drowned in Toronto Harbour as a young man. (Olive Lee, Donsview, Ont.; Wm. Lee, Brampton, Ont.; D. Dewar, London, Ont.)
A1. Dolphus T. Lee, b J, brought to Canada as a boy
  B1. Eileen M. Lee, res Toronto, Ont.
  B2. Phyllis Lee, mar ---Baldwin, res Chatham Head, N.B.
A2. John Philip Lee, b 1856 J, d 1902 Toronto, mar Harriet Jane MACHON, qv, 12 chn, Mar.3Feb.1877 in Toronto by Rev. Lovell.
  B1. Edwin John Lee, b 1876, d 1879, bur Toronto
  B2. Percival John Lee, b 1880, d 1961, mar ---Storey, bur Ottawa, Ont. 48 years in YMCA work in Toronto, Ottawa and in Detroit, Mich.
    C1. Dorothy Ethel Lee, b 1905, mar ---Dewar, res London, Ont., retired principal
  B3. Lillian Lee, b 1881, d 1908, bur Toronto
  B4. Amy Lee, b 1882, res Toronto, Ont.
  B5. Elsie Lee, b 1884, d.y.
  B6. Harry Lee, b 1886, d 1967, mar ---McMahon, bur Toronto, Contractor at Port Credit, Ont.
    C1. Frances Harriet Lee, b 1911, mar ---KNIGHT, pharmacist, res Barrie, Ont.
      D1. Dora May Knight, b 1933, mar ---Harris
        E1. Debra May Harris, b 1956   E2. Jennifer Harris, b 1961
      D2. Charles Victor Philip Knight, b 1942
    C2. Thomas Norman Lee, b 1913, mar ---Tout, res Erindale, Ont.
      D1. Kathy Frances Lee, b 1965
    C3. John Philip Lee, b 1916, mar ---, res Beaconsfield, Que.
      D1. Carol Ann Lee, b 1948   D2. Gail Lee, b 1951
    C4. Lewis Lee, b 1923, d 1960, postal service, Oakville, Ont.
    C5. Gordon Stuart Lee, b 1923, twin, mar ---Lightfoot, res Port Credit, Ont.
      D1. Lydia Lee, b 1951   D3. Robert Lee, b 1956
      D2. Douglas Lee, b 1954
  B7. Arthur Lee, b 1887, d 1957, bur Pomona, Calif, mar ---Dyce
    C1. Arthur E. Lee, b 1911, d 1970 San Clemente, Calif, mar 1. ---Weinmann and 2. ---Dauks
      D1. Doris Jean Lee, b 1941, mar ---West, res Burbank, Calif
      D2. Larry Dean Lee, b 1943, mar ---Glawenwhite, res Visalia, Calif
        E1. Bryan Lee, b 1964   E2. Dean Arthur Lee, b 1966
    C2. Helen Amy Lee, b 1916, d 1964, mar ---McWherter, bur Pomona, Calif
    C3. A. Howard Lee, b 1916, twin, mar ---Patterson, res Visalia, Calif, Dry Cleaning service
      D1. Robert A. Lee, b 1939, mar ---Harmon, res Visalia, Calif

            E1. Kari Lee, b 1960   E3. Robert Lee, b 1964
            E2. Shari Lee, b 1962
         D2. Charles H. Lee, b 1939, twin of Robert, mar ---Dewlaney
         D3. James Marvin Lee, b 1945, d 1961, bur Pomona, Calif
    B8. Lewis Lee, b 1889, d 1908
    B9. Edgar Lee, b 1891, mar ---Chisholm, res Toronto, Ont.
    B10. Albert Lee, b 1894, d 1940, mar ---Weatherell
       C1. Albert J. Lee, b 1927, d 1962, mar ---Perrin. Widow mar ---
          Hay, res Weston, Ont.
          D1. Linda Lee, b 1952   D3. Carolyn Lee, b 1959
          D2. Barbara Lee, b 1953
       C2. William H. Lee, b 1929, mar ---Luyben, in sales, res Toronto,
          Ont.
          D1. Sharon D. Lee, b 1960   D3. Robert W. Lee, b 1963
          D2. Glenn D. Lee, b 1961
    B11. John Lee, b 1895, d 1922, mar ---Feast, res Toronto, Ont.
    B12. Walter Lee, b 1898, d 1899
LE FEBVRE, Charles, bp 1810 Jersey, rem to Cap Rosier, d 1898. Mar
    Elizabeth JACQUES, qv, pb 1831, d 1874. Charles mar 2. Marie Riffou,
    bp 1828, d 1907, dau of John R. and Elizabeth Whalen, of Cap Rosier.
    (Remiggi)
LE FEBVRE and LE FEUVRE of C.I. to Nfld. See FEAVER, FEVER (Seary)
LE FEBVRE, Ernest, from C.I. to Langley, BC
LE FEBVRE, to Ft. Garry, Man.?
LE FEUVRE, C.I. surname on S. Coast of Nfld. (G.W. Le Messurier; Rev.
    Hammond; Hug. Soc., and K. Mathews)
LE FEUVRE, from C.I. to Gaspe early 1900s. (G. Le Bas, Toronto, Ont.;
    J.H. Le Breton list)
LE FEUVRE, Capt. and agent from J in Nfld., also from G. (K. Mathews)
LE FEUVRE, b J, in Malbaie, Gaspe 1861 (Census), also in Perce (Cent.
    Bklt.)
LE FEUVRE, Harriet, b J, in Newport Gaspe 1861 (Census) apparently res
    with Philip HAMON fam
LE FEUVRE, Charles, b J, in Cap Rosier, Gaspe 1861, also Betsy (Census)
I. LE FEUVRE, Frederick Charles, b G, mar Elsie Parnal, b 1896, rem to
    Canada. Confectioner in Toronto, Ont. (Fred. George Le F., Toronto,
    Ont.)
   A1. Frederick George, b 1922, mar Audrey Rosina Leaman
      B1. Frederick George, b 1950, unmar
      B2. Joan Lois, b 1953, mar Carman Thompson, res Willowdale, Ont.
         C1. Jared Thompson, b 1974   C2. Sean Thompson, b 1976
   A2. Dr. Albert Richard, b 1927, mar Audrey June Hillis, b 1925, res
       Burlington, Ont.
      B1. Bruce Douglas, b 1955   B3. Gary David, b 1965
      B2. Donald Gordon, b 1952
II. Richard, bro of Frederick, above, b G, res Toronto, no issue
III. Clifford, b G, brother also
   A1. Kenneth, res Oakville, Ont.   A2. Shirley
IV. Clemence, b late 1800s, mar ---Giles
   A1. Robert, res French River area
      B1. Robert Giles, Jr., mar, chn
LE FEUVRE, George Francis, b 1869 J, mar Florence Mary GIFFARD, qv, 1887.
    Blacksmith in J until 1901, when he and wife and sons, Sydney and John
    rem to Paspebiac, Que., via brigantine DAWN. Soon rem to Perce, Gaspe
    then to Ottawa, Ont. 1907. Accidentally killed North Bay, near Sud-
    bury, Ont. 1907. Widow mar 2. William Henry Keys, b England. See
    GIFFARD, Florence. (G.F. Le Feuvre, Trenton, Mich.; S.G. Le Feuvre,

Ottawa, Ont.)
A1. George Francis, b 1891 J, remained in J with grandparents, served in WWI. Mar Marguerite Forgeard of France in 1916, who d 1919. Author, see Acknowledgements.
  B1. Reine, b 1917 France, mar William Voigt, res San Antonio, Tex., mar Wm. Voigt.
    C1. Glenn Voigt, b 1944 Detroit, Mich., mar Carla Clemens
      D1. Trenton G. Voigt, b 1953
    C2. Carol Voigt, b 1948 San Antonio, Med. Research Tech., res Lubbock, Tex.
A2. Sydney George, b 1892 J, to Paspebiac, and Ottawa, Ont. Mar May Isabelle North, b 1893 Canada, 5 chn
  B1. Grace Isabelle, b 1914, mar Arthur Relf, Ottawa, Ont., no issue
  B2. Sydney George, Jr., b 1915, mar Margaret Eileen Wilson in 1940, WWII Vet. Dept. of Ext. Affairs.
    C1. Margaret Joan, b 1943 Ottawa, mar Dr. Bruce Wallace Wilton
      D1. Catherine Joan Wilton, b 1964 D3. Stephen John Wilton, b 1969
      D2. Michael Bruce Wilton, b 1965 D4. David William Wilton, b 1971
    C2. John Sidney, b 1946, mar Susan Gail Barlowe of Chatham, Ont., res Brampton, Ont.
      D1. Andrew John Frederick, b 1969 D2. Heather Michelle, b 1972
    C3. Geoffrey, b 1951, mar ---
  B3. Frank Henry, b 1916 J, mar Shirley Grace Campbell, b 1920 Canada. He is WWII Vet, in Internal Rev. Dept.
    C1. Richard Wayne, b 1942 Ottawa, mar Marilyn Ruth McLeod, res Waterloo, Ont.
      D1. Catherine, b 1968   D3. Erica Paulette, b 1976
      D2. Kenneth James, b 1971
  B4. Henry Flood, b 1919 Ottawa, d 1945. Mar Florence Agnes Tildesley, 2 chn, adopted by her second husband, William West, who d 1974.
    C1. William Henry Hamilton (Le Feuvre) West, mar ---, res Coquitlam, BC
      D1. Mark West   D2. Jennifer West
    C2. Patricia Grace West, mar Nigel Trevor Ackerman, res Vanc., BC
      D1. Benjamin Ackerman   D2. Roberta Ackerman
  B5. Joan Hope, b 1927 Ottawa, mar Edward Harvey Wright, 3 chn, res Kirkland, Que.
    C1. Cynthia Holley Wright, b 1954, mar Kenneth Peters, a ch? Res Amherstburg, Ont.
    C2. Elizabeth Ann Wright, b 1958
    C3. Robert Edward Harvey Wright, b 1960
A3. Frank, b 1895 J, raised there, served in France and Belgium WWII. Retired 1962. Mar 1928 Gertrude Mary STOODLEY, b 1895 J. Res Trenton, Mich.
  B1. Frank George Stoodley, res Wyandotte, Mich.
A4. John Giffard, b 1899 J, to Canada 1901, served in WWI, res Detroit, Mich. Mar Dorothy Flynn of Wyandotte, Mich. John d 1973 Fla. No issue. She d 1967.
A5. Percy Charles, b 1902 Perce, Que., to Ottawa, and Detroit, mar Bertha Michniak, b N.S. Res Utica, Mich.
  B1. Nancy Ann Caroline, b 1930 Detroit, Mich., mar John Edward Forester, b 1927 Bowling Green, Ohio
  B2. Ruth Yvonne, b 1933 Detroit, mar 1955 Linwood F. Strauss, b 1934 Detroit, res Sterling Hts., Mich.
  B3. Florence Ione, b 1938 Detroit, mar Dr. Sheldon Martin Epstein 1959, res Indianapolis, Ind.
  B4. George Allen, b 1946 Detroit, mar 1966 Colleen Belanger, res

Rocher, Mich.
A6. Emily Georgina, b 1906 Ottawa, mar Lewis A. Burke 1925, who d 1954
   B1. Arnold Frank Burke, b 1926, mar Winnifred Draper 1948, who d 1975 Ottawa
      C1. Debra Burke, b 1949, mar Robert Richer, 1970, res Ottawa
         D1. Chantal Richer, b 1971   D2. Lisa Richer, b 1972
      C2. Kevin Burke, b 1954   C3. Laurie Burke, b 1957
   B2. Elsie Gifford Burke, b 1928, mar Maurice Jean-Louise 1946, res Scarborough, Ont.
      C1. Cheryl Janice Jean-Louis , b 1947, mar Gary Beamish, 1972
      C2. Pierre, Peter, Jean-Louis , b 1949, mar Hillary Reid 1974, res Aylmer, Que.
         D1. Devin Victor Jean-Louis , b 1975
      C3. Rodrigue, Roddy, Jean-Louis , b 1950, mar Joan Baldwin, 1969
         D1. Timothy Travis Jean-Louis , b 1970
LE FEVRE, C.S., SPG missionary, was stationed in Sherbrooke, Que. 1821
LE FEVRE, John and Jane, b J, were in Gaspe 1861 (Census)
LE FEVRE, Philip Alexander, b J, with Esther LE FEVRE, in Gaspe 1861 (Census)
LE FEVRE, from J to Cape Breton
LE FEVRE, from J to B.C. (Luce)
LE FEVRE, Henry John, b 1852, St. Peter?, J, settled Lakefield, Ont. 1870. Mar Agnes Strickland Tully ca 1872. Both d Lakefield ca 1909. Henry poss son of George William LE FEUVRE and Jeanne LE BROCQ? Data below incomplete and some uncertain. (Phyllis Evans Atwood, Toronto, Ont.; Mrs. H. Raymond Pocock, Jersey; Gladys Atwood, Toronto, Ont.)
   A1. Alfred George Tully, b 1874, mar Gwyneth Tate, dau of Wallis Tate?, rem to Chili, S.A. for 30 yrs., then returned to Lakefield, Ont.
      B1. William, b ca 1913, mar Elizabeth ---
      B2. Elizabeth, Peggy, b 1907, mar Roy Pocock, res J
         C1. Anne Pocock, mar, 3 chn, all res England
         C2. Jennifer Pocock, mar ---   C3. Mark Pocock
   A2. Daisy Clemence Lucy Belfield, b 1878, d 1967. Mar 1898 George Evans Atwood, 1869-1954, bur Toronto, Ont.
      B1. Henry Le Fevre Atwood, b 1899, d 1965. Mar Jean Gladys McCorkingdale, res Toronto
      B2. Phyllis Clemence Evans Atwood, b 1901, unmar
      B3. Betty Le Brocq Atwood, b 1910, unmar
      B4. Hugh Kivas Atwood, b 1915, mar Constance Knox 1942, res Williams Lake, BC
         C1. Harry Knox Atwood, b 1943, d.y.
         C2. Hugh Knox Atwood, b 1947, mar Diana Hunt, 1973
         C3. Michael Le Fevre Atwood, b 1949
   A3. Helen Mary Strickland, b 1876?, d 1945. Mar Thomas William Berchall Marling 1911, no issue
   A4. Emily Louise Beresford Le Fevre, b ca 1880, mar William Robert Grieve 1908
      B1. Norman Le Fevre Grieve, b 1909, mar ---
         C1. John Grieve   C2. Dophne Grieve
      B2. Verite Grieve, b 1911, mar Glendon Jackson
         C1. Gillian Jackson   C2. Ann Jackson
      B3. Daphne Grieve, mar Harry Byatt
         C1. Susan Byatt   C2. Sarah Byatt   C3. Monica Byatt
LE FEVRE, Francois or Francis of J, mar the dau of Col. Moore. See BRINE. After the wedding the vessel they sailed on was boarded by a French privateer, England being at war with France, early 1800s. Le Fevre was carried to France, imprisoned there for 5 months. The bride

LE FEVRE   335

died at sea. Le Fevre retired to Arichat, NS and d there. (Arichat WARDEN)
LE FEVER, LE FEVRE, or LE FEUVRE, Jean, d Paspebiac, Gaspe early 1800s. Bro Charles returned to J, bro Francois d abroad.
LE FILLIATRE, Samuel, fisherman off Sandy Pt., Nfld. 1871 (Lovell)
LE FILLIATRE, LE FILIASTRE, PHALATER, Abraham, a Jerseyman, met in Maine 1660s by John JOSSLYN, noted in his TWO VOYAGES TO NEW ENGLAND. LE FILIATRE in St. Lawrence J 1607, 1668. FILLASTRE curr J. (Noyes; QAAM)
LE FLOCH, Joseph, b 1890 Brittany, France, his fam rem to J in 1880. Indentured to Robin firm for five years, sailing in brigantine FANNY BROSLAUER from J in 1907. Mar 1919 Florence BISSON, qv, of Paspebiac, Gaspe. Retired from Robin firm 1964 after 57 yrs service. Manager at Natisquam and Paspebiac. Res Chomeday, Laval, Que. (J. Le Floch, Chomeday, Laval, Que.) Fam said to be from Pomerche-LeVicomte, Brittany.
A1. Gerald J, b 1920, RCAF WWII, res Rimouski, Que., mar Rebecca Bowman 1944, 3 chn. Mar 2. Mary Scott, a son, Wayne.
   B1. June, mar ---Da Encarnacas, res Sydney, Aust. (Spec., Gaspe newsp. 12/22/77)
   B2. Allan   B3. Heather   B4. Wayne, by second wife
A2. Roy W.F., b 1921, mar Lillian Stack 1949, 3 chn. She was killed in car accident 1957, mar 2. Anna Connors 1959, 3 chn. Roy, Vet WWII, res New Castle, NB.
   B1-3. names not known by compiler   B5. Tamara
   B4. Harold   B6. Elizabeth
A3. Eileen J., b 1923, mar Gerald Cote 1946, 3 chn
   B1. Rene Cote   B2. Marc Cote   B3. Paul Cote
A4. George H., b 1925, mar Clara Scott 1952, 2 chn. Vet paratroopers WWII
   B1. Judy   B2. Deborah
A5. Leila M., b 1926, mar Scott Duncan 1953, mgr. wholesale groceries, Robin, Jones and Whitman, Gaspe?
LE FRESNE, C.I. name on the S. coast of Nfld. (G.W. Le Messurier)
LE GALLAIS, Philip, b 1818 St. John, J, son of Judge Le G., mar Mary Caroline Holmes of Danish ancestry. Philip d 1897 age 89. (Reta Le Gallais Gallup, Campbellton, NB; Violet L. Robertson, Fal.; Francis Arthur, Duluth, Minn; Mrs. Walter Currie, St. Catherines, Ont.)
A1. Mary Jane, mar ---HOCQUARD, res Boyne City, Mich.
A2. Margaret Elizabeth, mar Francis Scott, res and bur Paspebiac
A3. Emma, unmar, bur Paspebiac
A4. Adelize, mar Francis LABEY of C.I., rem to Paspebiac, then to Stonewall, Man. where they are bur. See fam under LABEY.
A5. Selina, mar Charles ARTHUR of Duluth, Minn.
A6. Herbert, mar Alma Draper of Sutton Jct., Eastern Townships, where they res
A7. Walter, unmar, res Winnipeg, Man., where he d
A8. Francis, b 1832, mar Margaret DUVAL, 1834-1966, d 1883, bur St. Peters, Paspebiac, Gaspe, res Coxtown 1871
   B1. Francis, b 1870, d 1938, mar Jessie Miller of Port Daniel, Gaspe, 1873-1954
      C1. Reta   C3. Francis   C5. Bertram, had a son, Boyd
      C2. Howard, desc   C4. Eva
LE GALLAIS, Edmund, b 1838 J?, mar 1. Mary Ann Munro of Paspebiac 1864 who d 1874, 5 chn and 2. Martha Miller, 1847-1936, 5 chn. (Freda Le Gallais, Whitby, Ont.; GLF)
A1. William, 1866-1890, bur St. Peters, Paspebiac, Gaspe
A2. Mary Ann

A3. Edmund. An Edmund W. 1858-1939, mar Ann Mary LE MASURIER, qv, 1863-1942, bur St. Peters, Paspebiac. (GLF)
  B1. Emily Grace, 1890-1938   B2. Alice Edna, 1893-1945
A4. Drucilla
A5. Frederick, poss the Rev. Frederick G., 1871-1926, bur St. Peters, Paspebiac (GLF)
A6. Eva, poss Eva Jane, res Gaspe, mar Thomas C. LE BOUTILLIER, qv, 2 sons
A7. James
A8. Evelyn Miller, b 1882, d 1939, mar Edith Travers, 1883-1967, mar Shigawake, Gaspe by Rev. Ernest ROY. Bur St. Andrews, New Carlisle, Gaspe. (GLF)
  B1. William Evelyn, b 1909 Paspebiac, Que., mar Freda French, b 1918, dau of Charles D. French and Mehitabel Bowen, Eastern Townships, Que.
    C1. Randall William, b 1940, mar Janet Hazelton
      D1. Michael Jason, b 1968   D2. Kimberly Anne, b 1970
    C2. Bryan Travers, b 1945, mar Joan Webb
      D1. David James, b 1971   D2. Jennifer, b 1973
    C3. Wendy Marian, b 1947, mar Richard Roney, Rochester, N.Y.
      D1. Jeffrey Patrick Roney, b 1975
A9. Jessie May, b ca 1886, d.y., bur St. Peters, Paspebiac (GLF)
A10. Percy, poss Percy Clement, b 1888, d 1916, bur New Carlisle, Gaspe (GLF)
LE GALLAIS, Mary Caroline, b 1824 J?, sister of Philip, below?, mar Daniel BISSON, Gaspe
LE GALLAIS, Edward, 1830-1904, mar Margaret SMITH, 1829-1919, bur Port Daniel, Gaspe (GLF)
LE GALLAIS, Philip, 1827-1889, mar Rebecca SMITH, 1834-1874. These three poss brothers and sister. Poss Edmund also belongs to this fam, along with a Jane and Francis.
LE GALLAIS, Charles and Isabella, res Gaspe
A1. Harold G., d 1918, age 23, from WWI, bur New Carlisle, Gaspe (GLF)
A2. Stanley, d from wounds in WWI, bur Paspebiac
A3. Leslie P., b 1892, d.y., bur Paspebiac (GLF)
LE GALLAIS, Jane, 1844-1876, mar Hugh Miller (GLF)
LE GALLAIS, C.I. name assoc with the Robin firm Paspebiac, Gaspe and New Carlisle, Que. (Prov. Archives)
LE GALLAIS, Edwin, war victim, bur St. Pauls Anglican, Shigawake, Gaspe (GLF)
LE GALLAIS, 1929, 1934, bur Port Daniel, Gaspe (GLF)
LE GALLAIS, Jennie Ida, 1893-1954, mar James W. MacKenzie, bur Shigawake, Gaspe (GLF)
LE GALLAIS, E.A., from C.I. fam, res Campbellton, NB
LE GALLAIS, Norman, b J, rem to Sask late 1800s. Mar Dorothy GENGE, qv. See also (his uncle) Wellman William LE GALLAIS. (Eliz. Le Gallais, Seattle, Wash.)
A1. Elizabeth Dorothy, b ca 1913, mar John Denis Walsh
  B1. Robin John Walsh, d.y.
A2. Norman Hugh, b 1920, mar Margaret Elford
  B1. Judith, b 1955   B3. Peter, b ca 1958
  B2. Christopher, b 1955   B4. David, b ca 1960
LE GALLAIS, Geoffrey, bro of Norman, farmed in Sask, then in BC
LE GALLAIS, Eva Jane, b J?, mar ---LE BOUTILLIER, b Liverpool ca 1874. Raised in J, res St. Malo, France. Le B. sailed ca 1890 to Gaspe when ca age 16.
LE GALLAIS, Wellman William, b 1833 St. Heliers, J, son of Richard Le G.

and Susan Nason. To Nfld. as a young man to join his sisters Susan and Mary, who had a school there. (15 chn in this fam) Mar there, Fanny Mary LANGRISH, 5 chn b Channel, Nfld. Le Gallais was an Anglican minister and drowned in 1869 on a visit to a parishioner. Plaque installed by RCMP to commemorate this man's life. (E. Le Gallais, Seattle, Wash.; Dict. of Can. Biog. IX)
A1. Isabell A2. Maud A3. Esther A4. Susan A5. John
LE GALLAIS, from J to Ontario
LE GALLAIS, Jane, b ca 1826 J, mar Jean CABELDU, qv, rem to Guelph, Ont. 2 chn
LE GALLEZ, from G to Hamilton 1900s
LE GALLEZ, Thomas, b J, in Perce, Gaspe 1861 (Census)
LE GALLIENNE, old G surname, some from G in N.A. See QAAM. See also GALLIENNE.
LE GALLEE, from C.I. To Assiniboia, Man.
LE GALLIS, ---, b Nfld. of J fam, mar Sir Edward Morris, a son educated there (Shortis-Munn)
LE GALLOIS, from C.I. to Gaspe (K.H. Annett)
LE GARIGNON, Cyril, b J, to Gaspe 1930 for Wm. Hyman and Sons Company, worked there 35 years, then with Dept. of Industry and Commerce of Que. Mar Mae Kennedy, res Fox River. SEE ADDED PAGES!
A1. ---, mar Nichole Mailhot, had dau A2. John P., a Marist father
LE GASSE, C.I. surname assoc with Robin firm at Paspebiac and with town of New Carlisle, Que. (Prov. Arch.; Annett)
LE GELLUS, Capt. from J in Nfld. (K. Mathews)
LE GEOFFREY, Ethel Mae, b 1890 G, to Ont. 1910, later to Portland, ME. Mar 1. ---Gray and 2. ---Maxwell. Name modified to GODFREY. See GODFREY, GODFRAY.
LE GEYT, LE JEATT, LE GAYT, etc. Merchant from J in Nfld. (K. Mathews)
LE GEYT, two genealogies listed in Library of Congress, U.S.
LE GEYT, Capt. Edward of the brig MOLLY, acting for John LE GEYT of J, merchants, fished on coast of Labrador at a place called Red Bay in 1783, a cod salmon and seal fishery. (Papers of H.W. Le Messurier)
LEGGETT, americanized form of LE GEYT
LE GEYT, Daniel, involved with the fisheries at Bon. Is., Gaspe middle 1800s
LE GEYT, Daniel Edward, b 1868 J, son of Daniel Mathew L. and Victoria DU HEAUME, mar Eliza Aris 1900, b 1873 Cork, Ireland, d 1951. 8 chn including a set of triplets. (Jers. Soc. Bull., 1904; John A. Le Geyt, Esquimalt, BC)
A1. Barbara Nancy, 1900-1977, no issue
A2. Ashley Hubert, 1902-1948, no issue
A3. Edward Gerard, b 1904, mar 1947 Susanne Philipps Strickland, b 1901, no issue
A4. George Janvrin, b 1907, d 1954, no issue
A5. John Aris, b 1912, mar 1940 Elizabeth Marion Rothera, b 1914, 5 chn
  B1. John, b 1941
  B2. Christopher, b 1943, mar 1967 Judy McNab
    C1. David, b 1972   C2. Peter, b 1975
  B3. Ashley Peter, b 1945, mar 1969 Marjorie Ann MacCallum
    C1. Christopher Ladd, b 1974   C2. Michael Joseph, b 1975
  B4. Michael Robert, b 1948   B5. Philip Francis, b 1955
A6. Mary Victoria, b 1914, no issue   A7. Anthony James, b 1914, no
A8. Philip, b 1914, d.y.   issue
LE GEYT, Charles Mathew, b 1863 St. Heliers, J, son of Philip John Le G. and Mary Ann Susan LE GALLICHAN, qv, rem to Calgary, Alta. Mar Mary Sarah PARKER, b 1871 St. Heliers, J. This fam not verified.

(Jean Le Geyt, Calgary, Alta.)
A1. Charles Philip, b 1893 St. Heliers, J, mar Emily Snow DURMAN, b 1887 St. Saviours, Guernsey
  B1. Reginald Charles, b 1913, mar Dorothy Buckhart, b 1916 Calgary, Alta.
    C1. Julia Margaret, b 1937, mar Earl Clifford Logan
      D1. Debra Lee Logan, b 1957, mar David John Eide
      D2. Lori Joy Logan, b 1958   D4. Bonnie Gail Logan, b 1965
      D3. Sherry Lynne Logan, b 1962 D5. Dean Early Robt. Logan, b 1968
    C2. Barbara Joan, b 1940, mar Donald Thomas Copeland, b 1941, res Edmonton, Alta.
      D1. Bradley Kevin Copeland, b 1961
      D2. Scott Thomas Copeland, b 1962
    C3. Eleanor Joyce, b 1942, mar Angus Campbell Chalmers, b 1940
      D1. John Paton Chalmers, b 1964 D2. Brenda Lee Chalmers, b 1966
    C4. Ross Reginald, b 1957
  B2. Philip James, b 1916, mar Margaret Jean Bailey, b 1921 Calgary
    C1. James Allan, b 1946, mar Janet Ruth Anderson, res Sexsmith. Alta.
      D1. Katharine Jean, b 1972   D2. Jason Philip, b 1974
    C2. Linda Margaret, b 1948, res Calgary
  B3. Thomas Albert, b 1920, mar Agnes Maley Dunnett, b 1915, no issue
  B4. Charles Haig, b 1927, mar Iva Elizabeth Pigden
    C1. Gregory Scott, b 1963   C2. Graham Charles, b 1965
  B5. Edward Albert, b 1930, mar Lorraine Haroldine Digney, b 1933
    C1. Leslie Lourine, b 1958   C3. Melanie Jean, b 1962
    C2. Shelley Snow, b 1960   C4. Nicole Lorraine, b 1964
LE GEYT, George, agent of Nicholas FIOTT Co. at Gaspe late 1700s (Luce)
LE GEYT, Daniel of J, a fishery at Bon. Is., Gaspe 1800s
LE GEYT, res Manotick, Ont.
LE GEYT, Jack, b J, rem to Ontario, then to B.C. Mar, two sons in Ontario, one in Alta, two in B.C. Divorced
LE GEYT, Sophie MILLMAN, qv, from C.I. to Red Deer, Alta.
LEGGETT, LE GEYT, to Canada and to Calif. Clement at Rexdale, Ont.
(Soc. Jers.)   <u>LEGGO BELOW PROB.FROM CORNWALL</u>!
LEGGETT, curr Gaspe, origin unverified.
LEGG, Sophie, b G, rem to Alberta ca 1900
LEGGE, Isaac, from C.I. in Cataline, Nfld. 1860s (Rev. Hammond)
LEGGO, Jennifred, b 1899 Gaspe, mar Henry Theodore SNOWMAN, 3 chn
LEGGO, Mansell, from G? early 1920s, settled first in Gaspe, then in Perce. Employed by Robin, Jones and Whitman. Mar Lena BOWER, qv, no issue.(Cent. Bklt.) A.LEGGO MAR LAURALeGRESLEY,GASPE.
LE GRAISEY, prob LE GRESLEY, Philip, mar Mary PICCOT, PICTO?, qv, of Portugal Cove, Nfld. 1774. Res Pouch Cove near St. John's, Nfld. (Rev. Hammond)
LE GRALEY, from C.I. to NS ca 1800. To Cap La Ronde?
LE GRAND, C.I. surname in S. coast Nfld. (G.W. Le Messurier)
LE GRAND, from C.I. to St. George's Bay, Nfld. (Shortis-Munn)
LE GRAND, Capt. from J in Nfld. (K. Mathews)
LE GRAND, Alfred William, b 1845 St. Brelade, J. Mar 1. Susan Rachel DUMARESQ, 1848-1886, and 2. Elizabeth M. DUMARESQ, 1864-1952, both of G. (Ida Brunet, Port Daniel, Quebec; Aldo Brochet, Perce, Que.) 15 chn, 7 by first wife.
A1. Alfred Dumaresq, b 1873 Cape Cove, Gaspe, mar Maida Susan Kerr, 1868-1953. He d 1942. Two chn: Julia Alberta, 1905-1923, and Ernest Roy, b 1916, d.y.
  B1. Ida May, b 1897, mar Dr. Omer Brunet, b Clarence Creek, Ont.
    C1. Mariette Fernande Therese BRUNET,b 1922, mar James Edward

Flynn of Perce, res Verona, N.J. 2 sons
   D1. Kevin James Flynn, b 1957   D2. Edward Wayne Flynn, b 1960
C2. Beryl June Lorraine, b 1923, mar Elbert John Wormington of Prescott, Ont., res Picton, Ont.
   D1. Susan Gail Wormington, b 1952   D3. Judith Lorraine Wormington,
   D2. Nancy June Wormington, b 1954   b 1956
   D4. Robert John Wormington, b 1958
C3. Corinne Iris Elaine, b 1925, d.y.
C4. Marie Elise Ida Brunet, b 1926, mar Arthur William Housemant of Central Butte, Sask, res Livittown, Pa. No issue.
C5. Emeric Omer Brunet, b 1928, mar Georgette Ouellet 1956, res Port Daniel, Que., 4 chn
   D1. Barbara Brunet, b 1964   D3. Shirley Brunet, b 1967
   D2. Susanne Brunet, b 1965   D4. Martin Brunet, b 1969
C6. Daphne Laura Natalie Brunet, b 1930, mar 1952 Richard Sabourin, Montreal, Que., 4 chn
   D1. Andrew Richard Sabourin, b 1953   D3. Robert Peter Sabourin,
   D2. Ronald Michael Sabourin, b 1955   b 1957
   D4. Roger Norman Sabourin, b ca 1959?
C7. Miriam Nadine Roberta Brunet, b 1932, unmar
C8. Margaret Ardath Doreen Brunet, b 1934, mar 1956 Russel Wallace Wilson III of Lachine, Que., no issue
C9. Darcy Osborne Yves Brunet, b 1935, mar Marthe Perron of St. Quentin, NB 1960
C10. Marilyn Janet Andrea Brunet, b 1937, mar 1954 Kenneth Anthony Shea of Montreal and Lake Connelly, Que., 1954. 5 chn
   D1. Steven William Shea, b 1955   D4. Thomas Joseph Shea, b 1964
   D2. Sandra Lynn Shea, b 1957   D5. Kathryn Marilyn Shea, b 1966
   D3. Natalie Anne Shea, b 1959
B2. Susan Esther, b 1899, mar Walter Wieland, chemist
   C1. Carrol Lola Wieland, b 1925   C3. Kathleen Elizabeth Wieland,
   C2. William Walter Wieland, b 1930   b 1936
B3. Herbert Lauder, b 1901, mar Empress Glover, no issue
B4. Laura Alice, b 1903, mar John Alfred AUBIN, qv.
   C1. Maida Diane Aubin, b ca 1925 C2. John Godfrey Aubin, b 1927
B5. Julia Alberta, b 1905, d 1922
B6. Lewis Dumaresq, b 1907, mar Edna Gammon
   C1. Janice, b 1938
B7. Marion Stella, b 1909, mar Ernest BOWER, chemist. See BOWER
   C1. David Ernest Bower, b 1935   C2. Mark Bower, b ca 1936
B8. Ethel Mildred, b 1912, teacher, unmar
A2. William George, b 1875, d ca age 5
A3. Susan Amelia, 1877-1935, mar Arthur LAWRENCE, qv, 1874-1952, bur St. Andrews United Ch, Port Daniel, Gaspe (GLF)
A4. George Ernest, b 1879, d 1884
A5. Esther Mary, 1881-1937, bur Cape Cove, Gaspe
A6. Ernest, 1884-1959, mar Mary GAUDIN, qv, chn. Bur St. Peters, Paspebiac, Gaspe
  B1. Marjory, b 1927, res Gaspe, mar David Doherty 1946
    C1. Marjorie Ann Doherty, b 1947, mar Ralph GALLON, qv, 1966
      D1. Marlene Gallon, b 1967
    C2. Sharon Doherty, b 1948   C5. Will Doherty, b 1957
    C3. Mona Doherty, b 1951   C6. Susan Doherty, b 1959
    C4. Steven Doherty, b 1955   C7. Karon Doherty, b 1963
    C8. Maureen Doherty, b 1964
  B2. Arthur Ernest, b 1929 Toronto, mar Margaret Johnson 1954
    C1. Robert Arthur, b 1959   C2. James Allen, b 1963

B3. George Stanley, b 1938 Gaspe, mar Evelyn Thompson 1958
   C1. Glenn, b 1962   C2. Gregory, b 1963
A7. Jane, b 1886
A8. Charles Daniel, 1889-1914, first ch by second wife
A9. Francis James, b 1889, mar Widow Eulalie Cote, widow of Charles V.
   CARRELL, qv., d 1952
A10. John Albert, unmar, bur Cape Cove, Gaspe 1892
A11. Arthur Philip, b 1894, lost in WWI
A12. Sydney Clement, b 1895, d Paspebiac
A13. Edwin Victor, b 1897, res Wilcox, Sask.
A14. Eva Louise, mar Arthur OLLIVIER, qv, res Paspebiac, no issue
A15. Walter Edward, mar twice. Res New Carlisle, Que., has 2 sons,
   one by each wife.
   B1. Winston   B2. John
LE GRAND, in Gaspe from C.I. (Rev. d'Hist; Que. Arch.; Cent. Bklt.;
   Census; GLF; Brochet)
LE GRAND, Elias William of J fam in W. Paspebiac, Gaspe 1900, mar Louise BRIARD, qv. Had 22 chn, of whom 14 lived. (GLF; Ida Brunet, Port Daniel, Que.)
LE GRAND, Sydney, b mid 1800s St. Brelade J, half bro of Alfred Wm., above. Had son, Winston and dau, Shirley?
LE GRAND, Harold Cleveland, 1886-1935, mar Lillian BISSON, qv, bur United Ch, W. Paspebiac, Gaspe (GLF)Son of John&Elvina below.
LE GRAND, George E., b J, d 1884, res Cape Cove, Gaspe (Census, 1861)
LE GRAND, Louis, res Port Daniel, Gaspe (GLF)
LE GRAND, John Philip, b J?, d 1911 age 64, mar Sara Jane LE BRUN.
   d 1886, age 57 (GLF)
LE GRAND, John LE COUTEUR, son of John LE GRAND and Elvina BRIARD, d age 8 mos., 1897, bur Zion Ch, Carlisle, Que. (GLF)
LE GRAND, Jules Pierre Aimable, b 1874, son of Julius and Rosalie LE GRAND of Cobo, Guernsey. Rem to Pine Grove, Ont. 1913, a harness maker and shop owner. Rem to Woodbridge, then Weston, Ont. Jules d 1957, age 83. Mar Ella Louise TORODE, qv, b 1873 G, d 1950, age 77. (Doreen Kilpatrick, Vancouver, BC)
A1. Leila Ella, b 1898 G, mar Daniel John MUGFORD 1919 Vancouver, BC
   B1. Phyllis Joyce Mugford, b 1920, mar Norman J. Goode, Vancouver
      C1. Barbara Louise Goode, b 1954   C2. Murray John Goode, b 1956
   B2. Doreen Leila Mugford, b 1925, mar Alexander Graham Kilpatrick
      C1. Diane Lee Kilpatrick, b 1947
      C2. Maureen Joan Kilpatrick, b 1948, mar Lorne James of Vict., BC
         D1. Mia James, b 1968   D2. Ericka James, b 1971
      C3. Rosalyn Joy Kilpatrick, b 1950 C5. Alexander Bruce Kilpatrick,
      C4. Susan Ellen Kilpatrick, b 1952   b 1957
A2. Reginald George, b 1899   A3. Alfred Edmund, b 1900
A4. Mabel Louise, b 1901, mar ---Hand
   B1. John Hand, res Ontario   B2. Joan Hand, res Ontario
A5. George Alfred, b 1902   dau Julie Duke in ONT.
LE GRAND, Winter John, b 1852 St. Heliers or St. John, J, son of Amice
LE GRAND, d 1922, bur Mt. Pleasant, Toronto, Ont. Mar Charlotte Hiram SHARPE, b 1856 Quebec City, bur Toronto. This fam related to JEANDRON, qv. (Ruby Kingswood, Toronto, Ont.)
A1. Walter Sydney, b 1879 Quebec City, mar Carolyn COWLEY, d 1947 Vancouver, BC
   B1. Walter, b 1900? B2. Florence May, b 1902 B3. Frederick, b 1904
A2. Edna Idonea, b 1881 Quebec City, unmar, d 1961, bur Mt. Pleasant, Toronto
A3. Violette Isabel, b 1883 Quebec, mar Frederick Charles Bell 1907,

res Hamburg, NY
B1. Evelyn Sylvia Bell, b 1907   B4. LLoyd George Bell, b 1914
B2. Constance Isabel Bell, b 1909   B5. Julian Le Grand Bell, b 1916
B3. Edward Charles Bell, b 1912
A4. Alberta Florence, b 1886 Toronto, mar 1910 Murray Hartwell, d 1965, bur Mt. Pleasant, Toronto
  B1. John Murray Hartwell, b 1915
A5. Pearl Veron, b 1888 Toronto, mar 1912 Richard Clarence Hornibrook, d 1968, bur Mt. Pleasant, Toronto
  B1. Ruby Veron Hornibrook, b 1913   B3. Richard Alexander Horni-
  B2. Marjorie Claire Hornibrook, b 1915   brook, b 1926
A6. Ruby Irene, b 1888 Toronto, mar Arthur Clarence Kingswood 1914, res Toronto. She is author of TRUMPETS OF DAWN, 1972, etc. See Authors.
LE GRAND, from J, to B.C., John W., New Westminster, BC
LE GRAND, Philip, b J, in Caraquet, NB 1861 (Census) a joiner, age 23
LE GRAND, John, desc of above?, mar ---BRIARD, qv, dau of Elias BRIARD. She d 1927, Campbellton, NB
LE GRAND, from J to Cape Breton, NS
LE GRAND, from J? to St. Boniface, Man.
LE GRAND, C.I. surname on S. coast of Nfld. (G.W. Le Messurier; Shortis-Munn)
LE GRANDAIS, J merchants said to have been located at Sandy Point, W. coast of Nfld., 1800s (Mannion) Prob LE GRANDAIS, Jos (Lovell)
LE GRESLEY, Philip, claimed land at Petit Riv., Gaspe 1819
LE GRESLEY. "Sir Roger de Toeny, living in 1000, came from France with William the Conqueror. His son William took the name de Gresley from CASTEL GRESLEY. Man of the Norman nobles of that time took the name of their estate, and dropped their family names...One Lord Le Gresley, Baron, Knight of the Bath under Edward II, living about 1285. There is no doubt that they came from England to Jersey...Sir Robert Gresley of Drakelowe is 24th in direct descent from Robert de Gresley, grandson of Nigel, who was a kinsman of the Conqueror. Nigel's son William built and lived at Castel Gresley in Derbyshire. After three centuries the family moved to Drakelow in the same estate, which has been their seat since the time of the Conqueror." (Sophia R. Le Gresley, via C.E.B. Le Gresley, Toronto, Ont.)
LE GRESLEY, Philip Perree, b 1841AugresFarm, Trinity, J, son of Philip and Anne PERREE
A1. Philip Frederick, b 1867 Trinity, J, rem to Paspebiac, Que. 1889, mar 1901 Mabel Amelia Balfour of Acton Vale, Que. Worked first with the LE BOUTILLIER BROS., Paspebiac, Gaspe, rem ca 1921 to Newcastle, Ont. to farm.
  B1. Reginald Balfour, b 1902, mar Helen Jane Farmcomb, 1899-1975
    C1. Alfred Philip Farncomb, b 1926, mar 1956 Nancy Wonnacott of Oshawa, Ont. He is a science teacher. 4 daus.
      D1. Patricia, b 1957, also Sarah, Joanne and Cathy
    C2. Charles Ernest Balfour, b 1929, mar Hildegarde Mathilde Emma Vierkoetter, physician, b 1926 Germany. He is a science teacher.
      D1. Susan Marcia Louise, b 1955 D3. David Malcolm Balfour, b 1959
      D2. Karen Laurel Joy, b 1957   D4. Michael Stuart Karl, b 1960
A2. Jack, John?, emigrated to Nfld., mar a widow, has chn
A3. Alice, mar ---LE BOUTILLIER, rem to Canada, res Haliburton, Ont.
  B1. Gerald Le Boutillier   B2. Roy Le Boutillier
A4. Laura, mar ---MANNING, qv, poss in J. A son Bert MANNING res Paspebiac
A5. Louisa, mar ---RENOUF?, 2 sons and 2 daus, rem to Australia
A6. dau, rem to England, had dau Ada, mar LESBIREL.A7.son,d.y.

LE GRESLEY. "The first LE GRESLEY to have settled in Newport, Gaspe was Philippe, who came from J and settled on the coast ca 1850s. He mar a Cyr from the coast and rem to Newport Centre...sent for his two unmar sisters, names unknown, one of whom also mar a Cyr, the brother of Philippe Le Gresley's wife." (Frank Remiggi, McGill Univ.)
LE GRESLEY, curr at Pabos, Newport and Paspebiac, Gaspe
LE GRESLEY, John Francis, 1880-1918, mar Henrietta Kate BISSON, qv, 1876-1946, bur St. Peter's, Paspebiac, Gaspe. Worked for C.R.C. at Cape Cove, Gaspe
A1. Florence M., b 1903, res Penouil
A2. Marjorie Eleanor, b 1905, mar John Hilton MUNRO, bur St. Peters, Paspebiac
A3. John Arthur, b 1907
A4. Percival F., b 1908
A5. Ralph Montgomery, b 1911
A6. Leonard Gordon, b 1912
A7. Hedley Ernest, b 1913
A8. Kenneth Bertram, b 1919
A9. Kathleen Vivian, b 1917
LE GRESLEY, Philip, b ca 1817 J, mar Marie---, age 53 in 1871, b Que., res Malbaie, Gaspe. (Brochet)
A1. Maria A., b ca 1843
A2. John, b ca 1845
A3. Philip, b ca 1846
A4. Judith
LE GRESLEY, Philip, b ca 1828 J, mar Anne---, age 49 in 1871, Swedish, res Malbaie, Gaspe
LE GRESLEY, John Jr., b J, mariner and merchant at Petit Rivere 1819, mar Mary Boyle, res Malbaie, Gaspe
LE GRESLEY, Henry, minor son of Capt. John, d 1863 Perce, Gaspe, connected with Perree family? (Brochet)
LE GRESLEY, Edith Emily, widow of John James LE GROS, qv, 1871-1945, res Gaspe (GLF)
LE GRESLEY, Elsie, mar Charles Dickson DE LA HAYE, res Malbaie and Paspebiac 1900s, 2 sons, Kingsley and Selwyn, qv.
LE GRESLEY, Isabella Victoria, 1859-1927, res Gaspe (GLF)
LE GRESLEY, Ida Ethel, b 1892 Malbaie of J fam, mar Alfred RENOUF LE COCQ, qv.
LE GRESLEY, Charles, b J, 1860-1921, bur St. Peters, Paspebiac, Gaspe (GLF)
LE GRESLEY, Eli, in Gaspe 1820, where he signed the Petition
LE GRESLEY, Francis Steven, b 1849, d 1940 Gaspe
LE GRESLEY, Frank, of St. Ouen, J, served in WWI, sheriff at New Carlisle and County Judge. Mar Queenie Cook. His sister was Mrs. James LE BROCK. (GLF)
LE GRESLEY, George, b Gaspe, in Malbaie 1861 (Census)
LE GRESLEY, Harold, b Gaspe, son of Capt. Black Jack LE G., once a mgr for the Robin firm at Malbaie, later civil servant (GLF)
LE GRESLEY, Henry, 1840-1863, son of Capt. John Le G. of J, bur St. Paul's, Perce, Gaspe (GLF; Cent. Bklt.; Census 1861)
LE GRESLEY, John, b J, in Malbaie 1861, with Mary, Mary Ann, John, Philip, Judith, Francis, James, Edward, Elizabeth and Eliza, all b Que. (Census 1861)
LE GRESLEY, Philip, b J, and Anne, b Gaspe in Malbaie 1861 (Census)
LE GRESLEY, LE GRAISY, in Nfld. from C.I.
LE GRESLEY, LE GRISLEY, Philip, mar Mary PICCOT, PICOT? of J, res Pouch Creek, Nfld. 1774
LE GRESLEY, LE GREELEY, Capt. from J and G in Nfld. (K. Mathews, Shortis-Munn)
LE GRESLEY, Francois, b 1805 St. Ouen, J, son of Josue Le G. and Elizabeth DE CAEN, qv, rem to Canada ca 1820. Mar Marguerite Landry, dau of Simon Landry and Marguerite Hache, 1827 Caraquet, NB. One of his

LE GRESLEY

brothers settled in New Carlisle, Que., worked for Robin firm. Francois disinherited by his father when he converted to Catholicism. An official in local affairs, Grande Anse, NB. Will dated 1878. At least 11 chn. (Rev. G. Le Gresley, Tracadie, NB, family Gen.)
- A1. Jean, b 1830, mar 1856 at Caraquet 1. Rachell Theriault, and 2. Justine Leger. Jean d 1908 at 78 yrs., Grande Anse, NB
  - B1. Edouard, b 1856 Grande Anse, unmar, cook, merchant marine, d St. Leolin 1928
  - B2. Marguerite, Maggie, d 1914. Adopted by Jean, mar 1905 Antoine LE GRESLEY, qv.
- A2. Josue, b 1834, mar Judith Theriault, 1839-1926, sister of Marcel Theriault. Josue d 1892 Caraquet.
  - B1. Frederic, 1866-1953 Grande Anse, NB, mar 1900 Marie Albert (1871-1942)
    - C1. Leo, adopted, d 1902
    - C2. Georges, b 1903, unmar
    - C3. Louis, b 1905, unmar
    - C4. Elizabeth, b 1907, mar 1934 Fred Larocque
    - C5. Marie Anne, b 1910, mar 1947 Emile Chiasson
    - C6. Cecile, b 1912, mar 1942 Emile Landry
  - B2. Simon, b 1870, mar Emilie Cormier Godin, widow, b 1873. Simon d 1938 at St. Paul, NB
    - C1. Marie Anne, b 1899, mar 1920 Anthony? Downing
    - C2. Alma, b 1900, d 1928, mar 1919 Fred Larocque
    - C3. Leon, b 1905, unmar
    - C4. Amedee, b 1908, mar 1936 Alice LE GRESLEY
    - C5. Aldea, b 1913, d 1916
  - B3. Frederic, b 1877, d 1936, unmar
  - B4. Helene, b 1878, d 1951, mar 1901 Manuel Landry
    - C1. Ida Landry, mar Alphonse Blanchard
    - C2. Arthur Landry, mar Laura Cormier
    - C3. Florence Landry, mar Arthur Landry
    - C4. Yvonne Landry, mar Leo Chiasson
    - C5. Bertha Landry, mar Wilfred Landry
    - C6. Malvina Landry, mar Edward Dugas
    - C7. Honore Landry, unmar
    - C8. Bibianne Landry, mar Alfred Degrace
    - C9. Leonie Landry
  - B5. Madeleine, b 1881, unmar, d 1958
  - B6. Antoine, b 1883, mar 1905 Marguerite LE GRESLEY, 6 chn, and 2. 1916 Sara Duke, 8 chn. He d 1968.
  - B7. Joseph, unmar, res Lowell, Mass., U.S.
  - B8. Elie, unmar, rem age 17 to England, d Bristol 1949
  - B9. Pierre, mar, res Thurso, Ont., 6 chn
- A3. Charles, b 1839, mar Delphine Pitre, living in 1887. Charles d Grande Anse 1903
  - B1. Francois, b 1862, mar Maggie Bertin, no issue, d 1930. Adopted Albina 1891 who d at 3 mos. and Leo, b 1901, d 1903.
  - B2. Luce, dit Lucie, mar 1. Eugene Doucet and 2. in 1908 Sylvain CLEMENT who d 1918, and 3. Patrick Landry in 1920.
  - B3. Edouard, b 1873, mar Marie Anne Legace, 1882-1940, Edouard d 1947 at Neguac, NB, 14 chn
  - B4. Marie, b 1877, d 1895, unmar
  - B5. Michel, b 1882, mar Lumina ---, d ca 1950, res Maine, US, 4 chn
  - B6. Maggie, unmar, res with cousin, Edouard at St. Leolin, who also raised Lauza LE GRESLEY
  - B7. Francois, mar Fidele ROY, res Bathurst. A dau, Minnie Roy, mar at Lavigne, Que.
- A4. Rachel, b 1841, mar widower Pierre Blanchard, 1883-1943. Rachel d 1924.

B1. Honore Blanchard   B5. Marie Blanchard
  B2. Joseph Blanchard   B6. Pierre Blanchard
  B3. Romain Blanchard   B7. Edouard Blanchard
  B4. Monique Blanchard   B8. Racquel Blanchard
A5. Monique, b 1845, mar 1906 widower Pierre Hache, no issue, 1842-1928.
  Monique d 1920. Pierre's first wife had been Marguerite JEAN, qv.
A6. Philippe, b 1849, mar ca 1873 Marie Dumas, 1855-1913. Philippe d
  1924, Grand Anse, NB
  B1. Francois, Francis, b 1875, mar 1908 Anna Theriault, dau of Severin
    T.   Francis d 1944, 4 chn.
    C1. Francoise, d.y.   C3. Edouard, mar Marcelle Allard
    C2. Anita, mar Maurice Gagne C4. Louis Phillipe, mar Marcelle Proulx
  B2. Gertrude, b 1877, religious, Notre Dame
  B3. Elie, b 1878, mar 1907 Christine Theriault, b 1883. He d 1967,
    11 chn
  B4. Alphonse, b 1880, mar 1907 Phoebe Theriault, he d 1919, 7 chn
  B5. Elizabeth, b 1882, mar 1917 Antoine Theriault, 1876-1949, 5 chn
  B6. Lucie, b 1883, unmar, d 1914
  B7. Lea, b 1885, religious
  B8. Helene, b 1886, d 1914, unmar. Frederickton, NB
  B9. Gustave, b 1887, unmar, res Bathurst 1914
  B10. Joseph, b 1889, Eudist pastor, director Juvenat, Bathurst, and
    Montreal
  B11. Philomene, b 1891, mar 1911 Pierre Rioux, 16 chn
  B12. Josue, b 1892, unmar, merchant
  B13. Azade Omer, b 1894, d 1895
  B14. Omer, b 1896, Eudist preacher, priest at Bathurst West 20 yrs.
    D 1963, Quebec.
A7. Marie Salome, mar Bastien Theriault, res St. Paul, NB
  B1. Philippe Theriault
  B2. Jean Louis Theriault of Robertville, NB?
    C1. Lionel Theriault   B4. Marguerite Theriault, mar
  B3. Bastien Theriault, d at 15 yrs.   Jerome H. Doucet
A8. Anastasie, mar Pierre Theriault, res Anse Bleue, NB
  B1. Rachel Theriault   B3. Elizabeth Theriault
  B2. William Theriault   B4. Joseph Theriault
  B5. RoseAnna Theriault
  B6. Felicite Theriault, mar Moise Porier, of St. Leolin, NB
A9. Elizabeth, prob d.y.
A10. Marguerite, ill in 1879, unmar A11. Elie, d 1859
LE GROS, John James, b ca 1866 Malbaie, Gaspe, son of John LE GROS, b
  ca 1840 J, and Mary Anne, b ca 1849 J. John J. d 1923. Mar Edith
  Emily LE GRESLEY, qv, b 1871 Pt. St. Peter, res Malbaie, Que. (Doris
  E. Ward, St. Thomas, Ont.; Sydney Le Gros, Ottawa, Ont.; GLF)
  A1. John Arthur, b 1897, mar Muriel LE HUQUET, qv, res Pt. St. Peter,
    Que.
    B1. Joyce Lillian, b 1934, mar ---Huddleson, res Montreal?
      C1. Catherine Anne Huddleson
  A2. Gladys Muriel, b 1904, mar James Ralph COOPER, res Port Stanley,
    Ont., no issue
  A3. Doris Emily, b 1906, mar Rev. Edward Cecil Ward, res Port Stanley,
    Ont.
    B1. Rev. David Edward Ward, b 1936, mar Janet Elizabeth Thom
      C1. James Thomas Ward
    B2. Rev. Robert Grant Ward, b 1938, mar Donna Lee Reed
      C1. Crista Mary Ward   C3. Teen Lee Ward
      C2. Anita Ruth Ward   C4. Stephen Paul Ward

LE GROS

    C5. Robert Edward Craig Ward
  B3. Edith Joy Ward, mar Stephen Voeth
    C1. Teresa Lynne Voeth
  B4. Peter John Ward, mar Margery Anne Smith
    C1. Jonathan Bruce Ward   C2. Rosalie Anne Ward
  B5. Mary Elizabeth Ward
A4. Sydney, b 1907, mar Margaret Ellen Bathurst, res Ottawa, Ont.
  B1. Veronica Evelyn, b 1937, mar Robert Kendall
  B2. Jane Margaret, b 1939, mar Robert Richard O'Reilly
    C1. Andrew Robert O'Reilly, b 1974 C2. Janet Evelyn O'Reilly, b 1976
  B3. Rev. John L., b 1943, unmar
  B4. Peter Ross, b 1946, mar Heather Kerr
A5. Winnifred, b 1910, unmar, res Pt. St. Peter, Que.
A6. Harold, b 1912, d age 9 accident, bur St. Peters, Malbaie, Gaspe
  (GLF)
LE GROS, John Philip, age 25 in 1871, b J, merchant in Bon. Co. 1871
  with sister? Sarah, age 20. (Census)
LE GROS, Arthur Gordon, b 1898 St. Martin, J, d 1978 Montreal, bur St.
  Peter Cem, Paspebiac, Gaspe, retail merchant, historian, mar Jessie
  Isabel Mahan, b 1904 Cape Cove, Gaspe, 3 chn
A1. Lawrence, mgr. Robin Jones and Whitman, Gaspe. Mar Ann COLLAS.
A2. Peter, res Paspebiac   A3. Enid, well known potter of Gaspe
LE GROS, Gervaise, owned the SWALLOW, built in Cheticamp, CB 1851
LE GROS, Gervaise, of reorganized Robin firm in Gaspe 1855 (Rev. d'Hist)
LE GROS, Helen M., dau of Peter and Eliza LE GROS, 1877-1888, bur St.
  Paul's, Gaspe (GLF)
LE GROS, Hilda Celina, nee LE FEUVRE, dau of Peter LE FEUVRE of Villa
  La Bas, St. Ouen, J, d a widow in Gaspe 1967, age 85 (GLF)
LE GROS, John, b J?, mar Mary Annie Louisa ALEXANDRE, of Malbaie, Gaspe
A1. Edith Maud, b 1874, d.y. (GLF)
LE GROS, Leslie, b ca 1905 Barachois, d there 1964 (ARC; Wilson; GLF)
LE GROS, Thomas ALEXANDRE, 1871-1952, bur St. Peters, Malbaie
LE GROS, John, James and R.G., from J, rem to Blenheim, Ont.
LE GROS, Rex, b Barachois, Gaspe, of J parents, rem to Leamington, Ont.,
  bro of Leslie LE GROS of Barachois, above
LE GROS, Thomas, a merchant from J to Saskatoon, Sask. His dau a
  school teacher (Luce)
LE GROS, George H., b St. Heliers, J, in BC 1906. D 1963, plumbing
  contractor in N. Vanc.
LE GROS, Thomas in Bauline, Nfld. 1800 (Rev. Hammond)
LE GROS, James in La Poile, Nfld. 1860s (Rev. Hammond)
LE GROS, LE GROW, in Conception Bay and Burin, Nfld. early (K. Mathews;
  Seary)
LE GROS, Susanna, mar a Nicholas LE PELLEY, qv, in Nfld. early 1700s,
  both from C.I. She was the dau of Judge John LE GROS (Gallup)
LE GROW, Thomas, b J?, mar Charlotte---
A1. Henry Thomas, d 1900, bur St. Peters, Malbaie, Que.
A2. Frederick, b 1908, d 1929
LE GROW, Peter of J, a trader, sold his business at Eskimo Pt., Que.
  LE BOUTILLIER bought him out at St. Peters, Que. Mrs. LE GROS,
  LE GROW, res Gaspe
LE GROW, Nathaniel, mar Mary PIPPY, b 1838, her first husband. She mar
  2. Solomon or Joseph Butt, Pouch Cove, Nfld.
LE GROW, Levi, mar Elizabeth Jane PIPPY, qv, b 1876, d 1922
LE GROW, Peter, mar Maude Gertrude PIPPY, b 1881, d 1970. She was b
  GreenHarbour, Nfld.
LE GROW, James Gideon of Nfld., mar Selina Gertrude LE GROW. One of

these two was the ch of Mathew LE GROW. (Spurgeon Le Grow, Cobourg, Ont.)
LE GROW, Newman, mar Eliza LE GROW of Nfld.
A1. Wesley LE GROW, Scarboro, Ont.
LE GROS, LE GROW, fisherman in Broad Cove, Bay de Verde, Nfld. ca 1870. (Lovell) Many marriages between the LE GROW and SQUIRES families. Some of each fam rem to Boston and the North Shore, Mass. Said to have once had the title to Bell Island, Nfld.
LE GROW, in Nfld. middle 1800s: Broad Cove, Bay de Verde; Adam, Benjamin, two John's, Josiah, Mathew, Moses, Nathaniel, Nicholas, two Peter's, Philip, Samuel, Simon, Solomon, two Thomases', and William
LE GROW, Joseph, a planter, res East Cul de Sac, S. Coast, between Burgeo and La Poile, ca 1870
LE GROW, Henry, fisherman, res Madox Cove, south of St. John's, ca 1870
LE GROW, Peter, res Broad Cove 1836
LE GROW, John, res 1776 in Broad Cove. Had 5 chn, including John and Thomas.
LE GROW, Thomas, son of John, received land from his father in 1779. (Vol. 13, Folio 39, Broadcove, Nfld.)
LE GROWS, in Conception Bay and Burin, Nfld. very early (K. Mathews)
LE GROW, ---, mar Dorothy, who lived to be 90. He was Pres. of the Nfld. Assoc of Toronto in 1934.
A1. William, mar Louisa THISTLE, qv (William Le Grow, Toronto, Ont.)
  B1. Edward Lewis, mar Lilian Beatrice KING, dau of John and Emily KING, qv., b Nfld. He d 1970.
    C1. William, res Toronto, Ont.
LE GROW, William, desc of early LE GROS-LE GROW fam, prob in Broad Cove, Bay de Verde, Nfld. Mar Dorothy Butt, at least 5 chn. (Susan Squires, Newburyport, Mass.)
A1. Samuel, mar 1869 Mary Ann KING
  B1. Jessie, b 1871, mar Silas THISTLE, qv.
    C1. Samuel Thistle
      D1. Robert Thistle   D2. Carol Thistle
    C2. Cary Thistle
    C3. Jack Thistle
      D1. Ella Thistle   D2. Jack Thistle
  B2. Bertha, b 1872, mar 1900 William Squires, b 1874
    C1. Allan, b 1905, mar Marion Parker, dau Virginia
    C2. James, b 1912, mar Sadie LE GROW, daus Dorothy Ann, Mary Lou
    C3. William Squires, b 1916, res Boston, Mass., mar Dorothy Gertrude Pulaski, Polweski, b 1923
      D1. Susan Squires, b 1946, mar William Marion Bates, Jr., b 1951, no issue
      D2. William Squires, b 1948, mar Etsuko Kagihari 1972
        E1. Polly Anna Reiko Squires E2. Edmond Squires, b 1977
      D3. Rosemary Squires, b 1951 D4. Kathy Squires, b 1958
  B3. James, b 1874   B4. Moses, b 1877, unmar
  B5. Dorothy Jane, b 1880, mar Allen LE GROW
    C1. Bessie, mar George KING, no issue   C2. Stella, unmar
    C3. Herbert, mar Dorothy Whitehead
      D1. Donald   D2. Ruth
  B6. William, b 1883
    C1. Arthur   C2. Harold   C3. Dorothy   C4. Winnie
  B7. Hannah, b 1885, mar ---Janes?
    C1. May Janes?, mar ---Taylor   C2. Jack
  B8. Maria?
A2. James, b 1843. A James LE GROW res La Poile, Nfld. 1860s (Census)

A3. William, b 1846. A Wm. LE GROW res in Bay de Verde, Nfld. ca 1870
A4. Sarah Jane, b 1848   A5. Hannah, b 1852
LE GROW, Thomas, desc of John LE GROW, like John above, res Broad Cove, Nfld. (Spurgeon Le Grow, Cobourg, Ont.) Mar Julia KING.
  A1. Simon, mar ---, had Allan, Walter, Miriam, Beatrice and Newman
  A2. Mathew, mar Selina Gertrude LE GROW, not related, b Bauline, St. John's East, ca 1880, Nfld.
    B1. Gideon, d 1966, mar Gertrude LE GROW, not related
      C1. Matthew Hudson, b 1910, mar Maude Green 1944
      C2. Spurgeon, b 1913, mar Arline Dorothy Pearson 1943
      C3. Miriam Jane, b 1920, mar Roy Moores 1939
    B2. Elsie Ann   B3. Chesley
  A3. Samuel, mar ---, had chn; John, Nicholas, Eleazer and Miriam
  A4. John, mar ---, had chn; George, Sophie and Katie
  A5. Sarah, mar ---, had chn; Bertha, Hettie, Thomas and Sandy
  A6. Betsy, mar ---, had chn; Willis, Thomas, Tobias and Michael
LE GUEDARD, John, b 1891 St. Mary, J, son of John Le G., rem to Canada at 16 in 1907, d age 58. Mar Blanche COULOMBE of Gaspe, living at age 80. (Francois Turcotte, Ste. Foy, Quebec)
  A1. Roland, b 1920, mar Rose Aimee Cote, res Ancienne Lorette, Que.
    B1. Clermont, b 1946 B3. Murielle, b 1950 B5. Denis, b 1955
    B2. Blanche, b 1950   B4. Lynda, b 1953   B6. Carole, b 1956
  A2. Francois, b 1921, mar F.L.G. Turcotte, res Ste. Foy, Que.
  A3. Julien, b 1924, mar Gaetane Chicoine, res Cloridorme, Que.
    B1. Gaetan, b 1947   B5. Gerald, b 1952, a son
    B2. Claude, b 1948, mar, a dau Josee   Israel
    B3. Rejean, b 1950, mar, a dau Nathalie B6. Leger, b 1954
    B4. Rejeane, b 1951   B7. Alain, b 1958
  A4. Clement, b 1925, mar Antoinette Froment, res Repentigny Co. Assomption, Que.
    B1. Sylvie, b 1958   B3. Lucie, b 1963   B5. Guy, b 1969
    B2. Helene, b 1960   B4. Jean, b 1965
  A5. Florian, b 1928, mar Jeanne Ouellet, res Murdochville, Que.
LE GUILCHER, Louis, from J to Baie Comeau?
LE GUYADER, C.I. in Canada?
LE GUY, Edward, from J in early Harbour Grace, Nfld. (French Archives)
LE HARDI, HARDY, Thomasine of J, mar there Daniel LE MESURIER, res Riviere au Renard, Que. early 1800s. LE MESURIER mar 2. Symphorose BOND 1844, Riv. aux Renards, Que. (Gallant)
LE HERISSIER, Royston G., b 1943 St. Heliers, J, son of Clarence and Luce Le H., rem to Toronto, Ont. 1974. A Percy Le H. res Trinity, J 1932. (Mrs. Le Herissier, Cambridge, Ont.)
LE HERON, from J to NB (Rev. Le Gresley)
LE HOUILLIER, at Gr. Greve, 1798, origin unknown
LE HUQUET. Several persons of this surname rem to Gaspe from the Channel Islands in the late 1700s and early 1800s. Others came later. The immigrants listed first below may have been siblings or cousins, but please note that some are said to have come from Jersey and some from Guernsey. (Census; GLF; Sylvia Wilson, Medina, Wash.; L.L. Le Huquet, Calgary, Alta.) Some data below is unverified and some have not been fully identified in records.
  I. John, b ca 1786 J, res 1861? Gaspe Bay North, unmar, d 1876? (Census)
  II. Abraham, b ca 1787, in Gaspe Bay 1861 (Census)
  III. Marie, b ca 1790 J, unmar, res 1861 Gaspe Bay North, d 1876?
  IV. John, b ca 1796 J, in Gaspe Bay 1871 (Brochet)
  V. Abraham, b ca 1797 G, res 1861 Gaspe Bay North, mar Judith LE PELLEY, qv, 1829

VI. Francis, b ca 1803 J, rem to Grand Greve, Gaspe, mar Elizabeth Susan HAMMOND, HAMON, qv.
VII. Abraham, b ca 1804 G, unmar, d 1877 (Census)
VIII. Philip, b ca 1808 J, mar 1836 Mary Ann GALLICHAN, qv, rem to Gaspe (Sylvia Wilson)
IX. John, b early 1800s St. Helier, J, mar Marie C. LE MESURIER of G

LE HUQUET, Abraham, b 1832 Gaspe?, son of Abraham L. and Judith LE PELLEY. Mar Mary LE LACHEUR, qv. He d 1908, she d 1914, at least 9 chn.
A1. Jemima Jane, b 1869, mar John Arthur Ascah, 1871-1953. She d 1918, bur Gr. Greve, Gaspe
   B1. John Watson Garland Ascah, b 1900, mar 1926 Leila May Willett, d 1948. He mar 2. Constance Gwendolyn Thompson, nee Bagnold.
      C1. Evelyn Mary Ascah, b 1927, mar 1. Walter COOPER, who d 1965 and 2. Joseph De Laurentis 1967
      C2. Bernice Willett Ascah, b 1929, mar Clyde NICHOLS, res Detroit, Mich.
      C3. Lewis Watson Ascah, b 1931, mar Judith Dymtryshak
         D1. Heather Ascah, b 1963   D3. Lewis Scott Ascah, b 1971
         D2. Kelly Ascah, b 1965
   B2. Evelyn Kathleen Ascah, b 1902, d 1936, mar 1926 Robert Ernest Horner
   B3. Eileen Campbell Ascah, b 1904, mar Arthur Lockwood
   B4. Audrey Violet Ascah, b 1906, d 1954, mar Alex Wadleigh
A2. Samuel Benjamin, b 1868?, mar Agnes Palfrey 1910, 1876-1923. He d ca 1936 (GLF)
   B1. Margaret, b 1911, mar Lloyd Annett, res Gaspe, Que.
      C1. Elaine Margaret Annett, b 1942, mar Roy ALMOND
         D1. Christopher Almond, b 1967   D3. Dean Almond, b 1970
         D2. Michael Almond, b 1969
      C2. Colin Watson Annett, b 1948, mar Leonie Jalbert
         D1. Tashia Annett, b 1977
   B2. Mildred, b 1916, mar Henderson Stanley, res Fontenelle, Gaspe
A3. John Abraham, b 1871 Gaspe, mar Lucy Mary BAKER, qv. He d 1941, bur Cap aux Os, Gaspe (GLF)
   B1. Lillian, b 1902, unmar, res Montreal
   B2. Muriel, b 1903, mar John LE GROS, qv, res Montreal
      C1. Joyce Lillian LE GROS, b 1934
   B3. Adeline, mar George COLLAS, qv, res Calgary, Alta.
A4. Walter May, b 1873, d 1876
A5. Nelson William, b 1875, d 1905, unmar
A6. William Henry, b 1878, d 1883
A7. Elizabeth, b 1880, mar Lawrence RICHARDSON, qv, 6 chn
   B1. John Richardson   B4. Benjamin Richardson
   B2. Donald Richardson   B5. Audrey Richardson
   B3. Reginald Richardson   B6. Rita Richardson
A8. Emmeline, b 1882, mar Herbert Harison
   B1. Gordon Harrison, b 1899, d 1959
A9. Alpheus, b 1885, d 1967, mar Belle Annett, no issue
A10. Charles Gordon Neil, b 1889, d 1959, mar Muriel Eden
   B1. Thelma, mar ---Ivers   B2. Blair   B3. Watson

LE HUQUET, Francis, b ca 1803 J, rem to Grand Greve, Gaspe, mar Elizabeth Susan HAMMOND, HAMON?, b 1810, widow of ---, widowed again, she mar John BOURGAIZE, qv in 1843. This fam or part of it, rem to Iowa. See BOURGAIZE.
A1. Elizabeth, b 1828, mar Francis COLLAS, qv, who d 1955, age 89. At least 3 sons.

B1. Elias Collas   B2. Francis Collas   B3. Adolphus Collas
A2. Mary Ann, bp 1830, d 1845
A3. William John, bp 1833, mar 1856 his first cousin, May Ann LE HUQUET, dau of Philip Le H. and Mary Ann ---. He d 1909 and she d 1908. Celebrated 50th wedding anniv. in Chariton, Iowa 1905.
  B1. Francis Philip, b 1857, mar 1884 Margaret B. Huyck, d 1893
    C1. William Eugene, 1885-1967, res Iowa. Started the first weekly newspaper in Bellevue, Wash. 1918. Mar Lillian M. CLEMENTS, b 1891 Jordan, NY, who d 1949.
      D1. Sylvia E., b 1912, mar 1936 Donald A. Wilson, res Medina, Wash.
        E1. Albert Wilson
      D2. Gloria M., b 1913, mar Charles Anderson, and 2. Robert Vosika, res Portland, Ore.
      D3. Cherie E., b 1914, mar E.D. Dodson, a son and two daus. Mar 2. Andrew Doyle, res Colton, Calif.
        E1. Donna Diane Dodson, b 1947, mar ---Anessi
        E2. Harold Emil Dodson, b 1948
        E3. Colleen Rochelle Dodson, b 1952
      D4. Wynn E., b 1914, twin of Cherie, res Portland, Ore. Mar Eloise Dreyer
        E1. Wendie A., b 1952   E3. Wynne S., b 1960
        E2. Lori M., b 1953   E4. Brian W., b 1963
      D5. Robert E., b 1915, mar Leah Lord, res Asotin, Wash.
        E1. Robert Jr., b 1943, mar Linda ---
          F1. Britta   F2. Spencer Todd
        E2. Ted W., b 1945, mar Dana Marie ---
          F1. Theodore Brian, b 1969 F2. Danielle Marie, b 1971
        E3. Karen Dorene, b 1947, mar Robert Michael Stephens, b 1942
          F1. Robert Michael Stephens F2. Andrew Anthony Stephens
        E4. Bruce Dee, b 1948, mar Connie ---
          F1. Bradley Dee   F2. Katrina Dion
      D6. Pricilla M., b 1916, mar Robert Burdett, and 2. C.P. Decker, res Bathell, Wash., a son and a dau
      D7. Roger B., b 1918, d 1949, mar Georgia Satterlee, dec.
        E1. Nancy
        E2. Alan D., both adopted by Georgia's sister and brother-in-law named Sprut?
      D8. Ruby M., b 1919, mar James S. Erven, res Kirkland, Wash., no issue
      D9. Janice J., b 1921, mar H. La Ville, res San Diego, Calif. Mar 2. Richard Palmer. One dau by each husband.
    C2. Burton V., b 1888, d 1970s, res Syracuse, NY, no issue
  B2. Edward Peter, b 1859, mar 1881 Celestia Sheffer, d 1893
    C1. Earl James, res Fort Worth, Tex, a son, Clifford Francis, mar Bertha Sheiman
    C2. Iva, mar Frank Stock   C3. Leola, unmar
  B3. Ophelia Alice, b 1861, mar 1882 John G. Smith in Iowa
  B4. Kesia Ida, b 1863, d 1879 B6. Abner Isaac, b 1869, mar Minnie ---
  B5. John William, b 1867   B7. Eunice, b 1871, d.y.
  B8. Philip George, b 1873, d 1899
  B9. George Abraham, b 1878, d unmar Denver, Colo.
  B10. Anna Elizabeth, b 1880, mar in Colo, Carl Kendall, d 1843, Denver, Colo.
A4. Amelia Matilda, b 1835 Indian Cove, Gaspe
A5. Francis Peter, d 1864   A6. Philip
LE HUQUET, Philip, b ca 1808 J, mar 1836 Mary Ann GALLICHAN, b ca 1810.

Res Cap Rosier, Gaspe 1861.
A1. Mary Ann, b 1837, mar 1856 William John LE HUQUET, d 1908, 11 chn
A2. Philip Abraham, b 1839, mar Mary Ann Parsons
A3. John Edward, b 1841, mar 1861 Louise LANGLOIS, qv, mar 2. Mary Ann ---, 1868, res Idaho ca 1900.
  B1. Edward, b 1871
  B2. Josephine, b 1875, mar ---Morton, res Sequim, Wash.
    C1. Alvin Morton
  B3. Frank, b 1878
  B4. Gertrude, b 1881, unmar, Univ. of Wash., Admin. Supt., Idaho
  B5. Pearl, b 1884, mar C.P. Stackhouse, res Pierre, S.D., no issue
  B6. Carrie, b 1888, no issue   B7. Jack, d.y.
A4. Jane Elizabeth, b 1843?, mar 1868 Philip ALEXANDER, qv, who d 1929
  B1. Edna Alexander
  B2. Ernest Alexander, mar ---McColloch and d 1927
    C1. Margaret Alexander, mar 1932, Thomas D. Campbell
      D1. Margaret Ann Campbell, b 1934
  B3. Eunice, mar Thomas Breeze, 3 sons
    C1. Ernest Breeze   C2. Kenneth Breeze   C3. George Breeze
A5. Elisa, Eliza, Maria, b 1845, mar 1867 George LE BROCQ, qv, no issue
A6. Esther Rachel, b 1847, mar 1867 Abraham GAVEY, qv, no issue
A7. Jemima Rachel, b 1852, mar 1873 Daniel GAVEY, qv, 1844-1926. She d 1918, 6 chn?
A8. Francis William, b 1854, mar 1875 Margaret Jane PRICE. Res Grand Greve, Gaspe
A9. Blanche, mar Stanley HOTTON of J. Two sons? Cecil and Brian?
LE HUQUET, John Francis, b 1850 Indian Cove, Gaspe, son of John F. Le H. of St. Heliers, J, and Marie C. LE MESURIER, qv, b G, rem to Gaspe. Mar Sarah Jane PRICE, qv, b 1853 Gaspe, rem with 8 chn to Toronto, d there 1926. Widow d 1929.
A1. John William, b 1873 Gaspe, mar 1900 Mary C. Harrison, b Parry Sound, Ont. 1872. Res Victoria, BC where he d 1937, the widow in 1969.
  B1. John L., b 1901 Toronto, mar 1925 Joyce Wormold, b 1904, Liverpool, England. Res Victoria, BC.
    C1. Dr. John R., b 1927 Victoria, BC, mar 1952 Mary F. Bowkett, M.S.W., b Trail, BC 1927
      D1. Dr. John B., b 1953 Vancouver, BC
      D2. Cynthia J., b 1955 Victoria, mar 1977 Thomas M. Wells, b Sheldon, Iowa
    C2. Jacqueline A., b 1929 Victoria, mar Robert F. Sails, b 1914 Winnipeg, Man. Res Victoria, BC.
      D1. Jennifer Susan Sails, b 1954 Vancouver, BC
A2. Alma G., b 1875 Gaspe, d 1897 Toronto, Ont.
A3. Albert Wilfred, b 1878 Sandy Beach, Gaspe, d 1928. Mar Mae Estelle Tuck 1909, b 1885. Res Sunnydale, Ont. Res Toronto, Vancouver and Calgary.
  B1. Meredith Ivan, b 1910 Toronto, mar 1937 Frances L. Crawford, b 1915, Vancouver, BC, res Calgary, Alta.
    C1. Thomas Albert, b 1938 Vancouver, BC, mar 1964 Kathleen Mae Heppner, b 1938 BC
      D1. Cheryl Diane, b 1965 Vancouver, mar De Grant Allen?
A4. Nicholas R., b 1880 Gaspe, d 1963 Toronto, mar Edna E. Wills 1923, no issue
A5. Mary J., b 1882 Gaspe, d 1936 Toronto. Mar Wm. R. Plummer 1921, no issue
A6. Ada B., b 1885 Gaspe, d 1970 Toronto, mar J. Norman Campbell 1907

LE HUQUET 351

B1. Norman Campbell, b Toronto, res Vermont, US
   C1. Judith Campbell, b Toronto
A7. Emma G., b 1887 Gaspe, res Mississauga, Ont. Mar Eric G. Wells 1914, no issue
A8. Eleanor M., b 1893 Gaspe, d 1969 Toronto, mar Albert E. McCartney 1922, d 1975
A9. poss other chn such as Reginald, Blanche and/or Nellie?
LE HUQUET, Elizabeth, b ca 1845, schoolmistress in Bon. Is. 1871 (Brochet)
LE HUQUET, Edward, b G, to Gaspe, b ca 1806, widower
LE HUQUET, Thomas, bro of John and of Capt. Philip of Les Champs, St. Brelade, J, b 1820. Son, John Jr., b 1844, grson John III, b 1874. to San Francisco.
LE HUQUET, name changed to HOOKEY in Nfld. (Shortis-Munn)
LE HURAY, Theodore Victor, d age 75 in 1972, b Torteval, G, son of Wm. Le MESSURIER LE HURAY and Kathleen FOWLER. Rem to BC with bro William to Farm near Kamloops, BC. Both served in Can. army in France, WWI. (K. A. Le Huray, Vict., BC)
LE HURAY, John Nicholas George, and son from G and Alderney in 1879 to Chatham, Ont. (Mrs. Reginald Bray of Hatley, Que. She was Olive Le H, b ca 1891)
LE HURAY, Henry, b G, in Sydenham, Que. 1861 (Census)
LE HURAY, L. from St. Peter Port, G to North Vancouver, BC 1900s?
LE HURAY, Robert Spencer, b 1915, mar Norma Berwick, res Dartmouth, NS
LE HURAY, Stephen Bartlett, b 1918, mar Mona Dunn, res Middletown, N.Y. Above two are brothers.
LEIGH, said to be J surname in Canada (Saunders)
LEIGH, John, SPG missionary in Nfld. (1817-1818) (SPG records)
LE JERSEY, from C.I. to Maritimes (J.H. Le Breton list) Poss DE JERSEY?
LE JEUNE, William George, from J?, ordained 1879, was in Fort Q'Appelle 1889 for SPG
LE JEUNE, from C.I. to Ontario?
LE JEUNE, to Gaspe?
LE JEUNE, to B.C. See also JEUNE
LE JEUNE, from J to Nfld. (Horwood)
LE JEUNE, Marie Henriette, poss from C.I., widow, res Northeast Margaree, NS, mar Lemuel Briand DE JONG, DE YOUNG? 1786. She mar as Marie Henriette YOUNG, qv, 1793, James Ross, 2 chn bp 1799. At this time the Channel Islanders were becoming very involved in this part of N.S. Poss C.I. or from France. (MacDougall's History of Inverness, N.S. from Elva E. Jackson, N. Sydney, NS)
LE LACHEUR. !ERRORS BELOW! SEE NEW DATA BY SALLY LOMAS IN CIFHS BULL.#25. Jean, John, b 1768 G, was the son of Elize and of Martha LE VALET. He d age 98 (92?) Rem from G to Murray Harbor, PEI. Jean and Elize said to have been smugglers on G. Jean traded in 1805 2 homes in St. Peter Port for 570 acres of farmland in Kings Co., PEI. Jean mar Elizabeth Windsor, 1773-1849, dau of David Windsor and Elizabeth RENOUF qv. Jean said to be captain and privateersman at times. They had at least 9 chn; 5 sons and 4 daus. Chn not in order of birth. (Eliz. Graham, London, Ont.; Doris Le Lacheur, Burlington, Ont.; Edith Le Lacheur, Guelph, Ont.; Mrs. F.B. Wilson, Fort Stockton, Tex; Rev. Dan Le La Cheur, Des Moines, Iowa; Mardell Le La Cheur, Des Moines, Iowa; Jean Ward, Granville Perry, NS; P.E.I. MAGAZINE, 1905)
A1. John Windsor, b 1793 G, d age 86. Mar Sarah Sencebaugh, rem to Iowa 1851, wife d age 62. John served in Iowa State Legislature, bur Oakland Cem, Delaware Co., Iowa
   B1. William, b 1821

B2. Elizabeth, mar L.J. Penny, res Greeley, Iowa, and 2. ---. Harris d age 84
B3. Windsor, b 1828   B4. Mary Ann, b 1830, mar James Martin
B5. Margaret, b 1833
B6. Elisha, b 1839, mar Mary Jane Bliss, who d 1910 age 63. Rem to Mullen, Nebr, where he d in a prairie fire, 1894.
  C1. Phoebe Elizabeth, mar Clarence, Kit, Gay
  C2. Frank Windsor Le La Cheur, b 1873, d 1955, mar Ella Wickham, 1875-1975
    D1. Alta, b 1896, d 1977, mar Clarence Pecht
    D2. Clarence, b 1898, mar Catherine Harding, b 1902. Cowboy, preacher.
      E1. Evelyn Claire, b 1923, mar Ray Van Antwerp, b 1925
      E2. Mildred Carol, b 1927, mar Monroe Arne, b 1927
        F1. Steven James Arne, b 1952, mar Debra Johnston, b 1951
          G1. Jolene Renae Arne, b 1974 G2. Ryan Douglas Arne, b 1976
        F2. David Monroe Arne, b 1954   F4. Blair Verdon Arne, b
        F3. Judith Melanie Arne, b 1956   1962
      E3. Norman Orvel, b 1929, mar Norma Jean Johnson, b 1930
        F1. Daniel Norman, b 1954, mar Brenda Laughlin
        F2. Scott Allan, b 1954, not a twin
        F3. Monte Joel, b 1956   F4. Ruth Ann, b 1958
      E4. Viola Catherine, b 1931, mar Gerald W. Wood, b 1929
        F1. Carol Lynn Wood, b 1953, mar David H. Hozen, b 1954
        F2. Anita Kay Wood, b 1954, mar David Schreder, b 1952
          G1. Joel David Schreder, b 1976
        F3. Gerald Daniel Wood, b 1959
        F4. Shirley Mardell Wood, b 1958
        F5. Donald Wallace Wood, b 1956, mar Kimberly Jo ---, b 1958
          G1. Candice Mae Wood, b 1977
        F6. Julie Ann Wood, b 1962
      E5. Daniel, b 1933, mar C. Mardell Varney, b 1934, minister, res Des Moines, Iowa
        F1. Danell Sue, b 1955   F3. Mark, b 1963
        F2. Lynne Marcene, b 1957, mar Jonathan L. Smith, b 1956
    D3. Violet, b 1900, res Vancouver, BC
    D4. Elva, b 1903, mar Russell Phipps, b 1897, res Mullen, Nebr
    D5. Frank Orvel, b 1906, mar Ivoretta Wood, b 1906
    D6. Mary Ella, b 1907, d 1938, mar Charles Anderson, b 1907
    D7. Hazel Olive, b 1909, mar Clarence Anderson, b 1912
  C3. John Ross   C4. William Horton
B7. John Horton, b 1842, drowned in Mississippi River during Civil War
B8. James Richards, b 1844, d 1926, mar Fanny E. Woodward
  C1. James Asa, b 1867, d 1951, mar Rose Holroyd, 1872-1950
    D1. Esther, b 1894, d 1973, mar Harry J. Drennttel
      E1. Lorraine Drennttel, mar Curtis WALTERS
        F1. Ronald C. Walters   F4. William H. Walters
        F2. John H. Walters   F5. Ann M. Walters
        F3. Marilyn J. Walters
      E3. John Drennttel, mar Shirley ---
        F1. William Drennttel   F2. Bradley Drennttel
    D2. Fred, Frederick or Alfred, b 1897, mar Ada ---
      E1. Harold J., b 1922   E2. Darlene, b 1924?
      E3. Leo R., b 1924, mar Lela Willis, res Great Falls, Mont.
        F1. Carolyn, b 1953   F3. Merna, b 1957
        F2. Lucy, b 1955   F4. Nancy, b 1959

LE LACHEUR 353

   F5. Eric, b 1961   F6. Fred, b 1964
  E4. Vivian, b 1926, mar Waldo Cranston
   F1. James A. Cranston, b 1950 F2. Sandra Cranston, b 1952
  E5. Edith, b 1928, mar John B. Jones, 8 chn
   F1. Steven Jones, b 1951 F5. Thomas Jones, b 1960
   F2. Dan Jones, b 1952   F6. Joanne Jones, b 1960, twins
   F3. Catherine Jones, b 1955 F7. Christine Jones, b 1965
   F4. Barbara Jones, b 1957 F8. Gregory Jones, b 1971
  E6. John W., b 1931
 D3. John, b 1898, mar Ruth Winfield, d 1927
  E1. Rosemary
 D4. Helen, b 1901, mar Edward Edson
 D5. Edith, b 1903, mar Frank B. Wilson
  E1. Frank B. Wilson, Jr., mar Edna Faye Southern
   F1. Rhonda, b 1954 F2. Gregory, b 1955 F3. Helen, b 1958
 D6. Mary, b 1905, mar Vernon R. Guthrie, d 1967
 C2. Raymond C3. Stella C4. Elsie C5. Charles C6. Mildred
A2. Jane, mar Thomas ROBIN, qv. A son John res Castlerock, Wash.,
 Mayor. See Robin
A3. Harriet, b 1798, d 1883, mar Giles Hawkins, 1799-1875, res Guernsey
 Cove?, PEI. A son, John. SEE EXTRA PAGES.
A4. Elisha, emigrated to Australia, mar Englishwoman, no issue.
A5. David, rem to Nova Scotia, mar ---Simpson, blacksmith, a son, May-
 nard, res Amherst, NS.
A6. Elizabeth, mar Henry MACHON, qv, several chn? or mar Ben Sencabaugh
A7. Bartholomew, b 1802, d 1877, mar Margaret Jennings or M. Hawkins?
 Order and number of chn uncertain. See John, b 1829 at end of Le
 Lacheurs. Poss son of Bart?
 B1. Rev. David Windsor, ordained Halifax, NS, bur Africa, after work-
  ing in Tibet and China. Supt. International Missionary Alliance.
 B2. Matilda, mar John Cowan, a dau Jemima who mar ---Johnston?
 B3. James, b 1839, d 1920, mar Sophia MACHON, qv, 1843-1925
  C1. Fred W., mar Emily Murley C3. Lillian, mar Will Hugh
  C2. Cyrus, mar Lizzie Hooper C4. Rose, mar George MacDuff
 B4. Bartholomew, b 1843, d 1932, mar Mary Herring?, 1846-1910, res PEI
  C1. James, b 1881, d 1947, mar Cecilia Maria MACHON, qv, 1883-1932
   D1. Bessie, Elizabeth, mar Wallace PERRY, a son, Carmen Machon
    Perry
   D2. Machon, unmar, res Edmonton, Alta.
   D3. Lois, mar Percy Bell, no issue
   D4. Aubrey Foch, mar Doris Peardon, res Burlington, Ont.
    E1. Faye, b 1953 E2. Brent E3. Brian, b 1973?
   D5. Genevieve, mar Blaine Atwell, res Nova Scotia, 7 chn
   D6. James Daniel, b 1928, mar Victoria Ann Downs of Eng., res
    Burlington, Ont.
    E1. Leslie Ann, b 1955 E2. Jo Ann Gail, b 1957
   D7. Florence, d 1961
  C2. Frank, rem to U.S.   C3. Lewis, rem to U.S.
  C4. Angus, mar ---Ferguson, res U.S. C5. Nettie
 B5. Giles, rem to N.S., then to U.S., 2 sons, Frederick and Arthur
 B6. Margaret, b 1847, d 1908, mar William MACHON, qv, 1834-1933
 B7. Elizabeth, mar James Bell
  C1. Jane Bell, mar W. BECK
A8. Charles, b 1806, drowned in Chaleur Bay, N.B.
A9. James, b 1806, twin, d 1868, mar Anne DOREY, qv, 1816-1857, of Cape
 Breton, N.S. Bur Murray Harbor, PEI, 3 sons, poss other chn. A
 Blacksmith

B1. Charles, b 1841, d 1902, mar 1. Charlotte Jane Sencabaugh, 1837-1877, and 2. Maria McLeod, 1849-1893, and 3. Mrs. ---Maclure, no issue
  C1. Embert, mar June Beaton, res U.S.
    D1. Embert, mar Gertrude Westwood, res Washington
    D2. Lewis, res U.S.   D3. Gladys   D4. Jessie
  C2. Maria, 1865-1953, mar Wm. Keeping, 1853-1938, 7 chn
    D1. Kimball Fletcher Keeping, b 1886, killed WWI, 1917, no issue
    D2. Olive Charlotte, b 1888, d 1976, no issue
    D3. Benjamin Charles, b 1891, d 1951, mar 1920 Doris Stickings
      E1. Kimball Keeping, b 1921   E3. Olive Keeping, b 1925
      E2. Dorothy Keeping, b 1923
    D4. Minter Frederick, b 1893, mar 1928 Margaret McWilliams
      E1. Frederick, b 1929   E2. Marion, b 1931   E3. Donald, b 1933
    D5. Ewart Allan, b 1896, mar 1919 Florence Jorden
      E1. Beatrice Olive Keeping, b 1920, mar 1950 Gus Arsenalt
        F1. Linda Florence Arsenalt, b 1954
        F2. Theodore Calais Arsenalt, b 1955
      E2. Eileen Marguerite Keeping, b 1921, mar 1950 Lloyd Nicholson
        F1. Ian Lloyd Nicholson, b 1951   F3. Eileen Inman Nicholson,
        F2. Fraser Lea Nicholson, b 1953   b 1959
      E3. Vivian Dolores Keeping, b 1923, mar 1949 Lorne Parker
        F1. Carl Lorne Parker, b 1951
        F2. June Louise Parker, b 1952, mar 1970 Ray Szezech
          G1. Erica Laine Szezech, b 1972
          G2. Ross Edward Szezech, b 1975
        F3. Glen Allen Parker, b 1952, twin
        F4. Kenneth Donald Parker, b 1953, mar 1972
          G1. Michael Kenneth Parker, b 1973
        F5. Joan Dolores Parker, b 1954
        F6. Roy Alfred Parker, b 1956
      E4. Bess Keeping, b 1925, mar 1958 Norman Birt
        F1. Alan Ewart Birt, b 1959
        F2. Angus Norman Birt, b 1962   F3. Florence May Birt, b 1963
        F4. Carolyn Olive Birt, b 1963, twin
      E5. Ruth Alberta Keeping, b 1927, d 1967, mar 1948 Keith Carmichael
        F1. Jennifer Marlene Carmichael, b 1950
        F2. Beverly Joanne Carmichael, b 1953
        F3. Dennis Keith Carmichael, b 1957
        F4. Lynn Anne Carmichael, b 1962
      E6. Inez Keeping, b 1928, mar 1954 Douglas Slaughter
        F1. Susan Elaine Slaughter, b 1955   F6. David Slaughter,
        F2. Ellen Larraine Salughter, b 1956   b 1965
        F3. Peter Slaughter, b 1957   F7. Mark Slaughter,
        F4. John Paul Slaughter, b 1958   b 1971
        F5. Gordon Slaughter, b 1963
      E7. William Ewart Keeping, b 1934
    D6. Florence Mary Keeping, b 1898, d 1938, mar 1920 Francis Drake
      E1. Evelyn Adelaide Drake, b 1921   E3. Perle Wm. Drake, b 1925
      E2. Lorne Minter Drake, b 1923   E4. Donald Drake, b 1927
    D7. Bessie Le Lacheur Keeping, b 1900, d 1925, no issue
  C3. Margaret, b 1869, d 1916, mar Elisha BECK, qv.
    D1. Chester Beck   D2. Lillian Beck   D3. Grace Beck
  C4. Frederick, b 1875, mar Margaret MACHON, b 1910, res Guernsey Cove, PEI
    D1. Ruth, mar Ray Brooks, no issue

LE LACHEUR 355

D2. Chester, b 1904, mar Margaret MACHON, b 1910, res Guernsey Cove, PEI
  E1. Keith, mar Lorraine Buote, res Charlottetown, PEI
    F1. Stephen, b 1955   F2. Holly, b 1965
  E2. Elizabeth, b 1932, mar Kenneth Graham, b 1924
    F1. Kathryn Graham, b 1960   F2. Mathew Graham, b 1973
  E3. Ralph, b 1935, mar Ethel Jenkins
    F1. Ann, b 1957   F3. Douglas, b 1960
    F2. Charles, b 1959   F4. Margaret, b 1965
  E4. Edythe, mar Kenneth MacLeod
    F1. Alan MacLeod   F3. Jean MacLeod   F5. Robert MacLeod
    F2. David MacLeod   F4. John MacLeod
D3. Cecil, b 1910, mar Catherine Macpherson, b 1914
  E1. Jean Elizabeth, b 1941, mar Russell Ward
    F1. Marianne Ward, b 1965   F3. Bruce Ward, b 1968
    F2. James Ward, b 1967   F4. Joy Ward, b 1971
  E2. Ruth Christine, b 1944, mar Donal Croswell
    F1. Jeffrey Croswell   F3. Heidi Croswell
    F2. Peter Croswell
  E3. Mary Katherine, b 1945, mar Standord Peardon
    F1. David Peardon   F2. Cathy Peardon
D4. Kimball, b 1919, mar Florence Gosbee
  E1. Thane, b 1947, mar Elizabeth Carter
    F1. Clare C.
  E2. Donna, b 1951, mar James Butter
    F1. Josie Butter   F2. Gineen Butter
  E3. Scott, b 1956
C5. by second wife, Bessie, b 1878, d 1947, mar Lorin BREHAUT, qv.
C6. Percy, b 1880, d 1934, mar Minnie Bell, 1881-1933, res Guernsey Cove
  D1. Seton, mar M. Jackson, res Mass. Chn, Sharon and Seton.
  D2. Grace, mar E. McKinnon
    E1. Barbara Anne McKinnon, mar J. MacPherson
      F1. Sandra Lynn   F2. Scott MacPherson
  D3. Helen, mar Roy NICOLLE, qv.
    E1. Margaret, mar W. Chapell
    E2. Minnie, mar E. Carver, chn Donna and Scott
    E3. Kay, mar H. Glover?   E4. Kenneth
  D4. Mildred, mar H. Harvie
  D5. Roma, a dau, Thelma, mar Ken. Daly, a son, Ken
C7. Charlotte Jane, mar Rev. T. Hodgson
  D1. Margaret, mar A. Robinson, chn Frederick and Mary
C8. Ella, mar James Boone
C9. Garnet, mar Margaret Murray, res Sackville, NB
  D1. Robert, res Penna, mar Elizabeth---, a son, Bruce
  D2. Arthur, res Sackville, NB, mar Dorothy McLaren
    E1. Nancy   E2. David   E3. Kathy
  D3. John, res Ottawa, Ont., mar Margaret Mueller
C10. Silas, mar Mildred Latimer, res Western Canada, poss mar 2. Louise?---
  D1. James, mar Shirley Easterbrook
    E1. Richard E2. Ken E3. Ted E4. Candy
C11. Herman, res Western Canada, mar ---?
B2. James, b 1851, d 1874 of T.B.
B3. John, mar 1. ---, and 2. ---Macaulay
  C1. Emerson, mar ---McIntosh
    D1. Kenneth, mar Eve Wilson, chn James and Wendy

D2. Margaret, mar D. ---, chn Dina and Heather
D3. Mary, mar V. Drake, chn Margaret, Barbara and James
C2. Lorne   C3. Sadie, mar Ronald Slocum?, res New England?
C4. Roland, res Murray Harb., PEI, a son, Clayton C5. Windsor
A10. Anne, mar Henry MACHON, qv, res Guernsey Cove, PEI. Sons Charles and Daniel, and several daus, among them a Mrs. Wm. Howe and a Mrs. Clements of Murray Harbor South.
LE LACHEUR. This group must belong to the above family, but exact connection not known, and combined info does not match. (Jean Kennedy, Saint John, N.B.)   Three brothers: SEE PAGE 358
A1. John, b 1829, d 1913. Mar Margaret ---, 1840-1923.
  B1. John Jr., b 1871, d 1939, mar Anna Mowatt, of Irish fam (1874-1956). Although badly injured in WWI, and lamed, John led active, full and rich life.
  B2. Marion   B3. Margaret
A2. Giles, b 1837, d 1928, age 91. Mar Mary Cooper, 1844-1882.
A3. David, first Methodist minister in Advocate Harb., Cumberland Co., NS on the Bay of Fundy, a circuit preacher. On March 29, 1868, bp 9 adults. David b PEI?
LE LACHEUR, John Henry, b 1798 Sir William Place, G, mar 1823 Margaret Codville. Poss LE QUETTEVILLE?, 1800-1826, at St. Andrews, Quebec City. Witnesses were Esther LE VALLEE and John CODVILLE, poss DE QUETTEVILLE. He mar 2. 1833, Elizabeth Rippey, half sister to Margaret, his first wife, 1810-1849. (Wm. O. Goss, Ipswich, Mass.)
A1. and 2. Margaret and Elizabeth, both d.y.
A3. Rachel, b 1826, by 1st wife, mar Robert Rickaby, Inverness, Que. 1842 at Wesleyan Methodist Ch, Quebec City. Robert,   farmer and J.P. Inverness, Que., read law with Sir Wilfred Laurier, P.Min. of Canada. The Rickabys thought to be Hugs from France to G to Ireland, to Canada early 1800s from Wicklow?, Ireland.
  B1. Hamilton Rickaby, 1844-1878
  B2. John Henry Rickaby, 1846-1920, mar Alice Caroline Stone
  B3. Jeremiah Rickaby, 1848-1911, mar Nellie McCutcheon
  B4. Alice Maria Rickaby, 1850-1920, mar Andrew Patterson
  B5. Margaret Ann Rickaby, 1852-1921, mar 1. Cyrus L. Angier and 2. Beauchesne
  B6. Leah Jemima Rickaby, b 1854, mar John Smith
  B7. William Robert Rickaby, b 1856, d 1917
  B8. Theophilus Rickaby, b 1858, mar Ida M. BARRETT
  B9. Benjamin Rickaby, 1860-1871
  B10. Rachel Warren Carleton Rickaby, 1862-1934, mar Loring Chandler Baldwin
  B11. Albert Edmund Rickaby, 1864-1922, mar Sarah Jane Parker
A4. John, b 1835, mar Jane Graham
A5. James, b 1836, d 1837
A6. William Charles, b 1838
A7. Elizabeth, b 1839, mar John Francis HAMMOND, qv.
A8. James Henry, b 1842   A9. Mary, bp 1846, d 1926, mar ---SEARLE, qv.
A Mary LE LACHEUR, mar 1870 Helier LESBIREL, qv, b J, son of Jean Daniel LESBIREL of Trinity, J, and of Nancy GALLICHAN, GALLICHON, of St. Saviours, J at The Congregational Ch, Eglise Evangelique Francaise, Pte. Aux Trembles, Que.
LE LACHEUR, Pierre, cooper and shoe maker, res in Que. City 1821-1830s
LE LACHEUR, Capt. William, in Quebec 1786   (C.R. Fay)
LE LACHEUR, Pierre, b 1807 G, d 1889 Arichat?, son of Peter LE L. of G and Miss LA RUE of Quebec City. Mar poss 2. Christina McKinnon?
A1. Pierre, b 1826, d 1906, mar Rachel J. HELIER, qv, 1852

LE LACHEUR 357

B1. Peter Matthew Joseph, b 1852, d 1935
B2. George N., b 1854, d 1855   B3. Matthew M.L.J., b 1856, d 1935
B4. Rachel Jane, b 1858, d 1922, mar ---Hurst
B5. Judith Louise, b 1860, d 1947, age 83, Boston Mass. Mar John NICOLLE, qv, son of J. Nicolle and Jane ---. He was b Cape Breton 1857.
B6. Ellen Elizabeth, b 1863, d 1895
B7. Henry William, b 1865, d 1955, mar Mary ---, who d 1954
B8. John James, b 1867, d 1951 B9. Josephine Annie, b 1870, d 1895
B10. George Nicolas, b 1883, d 1955 Danvers, Mass. Mar 1. Mary Margaret ---, and 2. Sarah Joudrie?
A2. James?, owner of the ANNABELLA, 69 tons, built at Grand Ruisseau, C.B., middle 1800s. (Capt. Parker) Poss this was the James b ca 1837, a Scottish wife Mary, b 1836. (Chn below from Arichat Census 1871)
B1. Mary Jane, b ca 1858   B3. James   B5. Peter G., b ca 1867
B2. Laughlin   B4. Carolina M.
A3. William?, b ca 1844, N.S., seaman, wife Elizabeth b ca 1845?
B1. Flora Jane, b ca 1863   B3. Anne E., b ca 1869
B2. Judith E., b ca 1865
A4. Collin?, became Collector of Customs, Arichat and general merchant, b ca 1862? (from Prof. Stephen White, Moncton, NB)
A5. Maria S., age 13 in 1871 (Census)
An Ester Nicole, age 6, was living with the above family in 1871.
LE LACHEUR, H., owned the KATIE, 11 tons, built in French Cove, CB. (Capt. Parker)
LE LACHEUR, James and Peter, from G or from the above family, were in Richmond Co., N.S. middle 1800s. (1861 Census)
LE LACHEURS to Cape La Ronde, NS early 1800s
LE LACHEUR, Rex A. DE PUTRON, qv, musician, baritone, b 1910 G, son of Francis Martin L. and Clarice Marie MARRIETTE, qv. Mar Marjorie Lucile Penman of Fla. in 1933, a dau, Rive Reine. Director and founder of the Rex LE LACHEUR SINGERS, in 1956; a 50 voice mixed choir in Ottawa. Composer of at least 120 pieces. Wrote songs for John Charles Thomas in 1942 and for Ezio Pinza in 1945. A sister, Ruth Le L., res B.C. (Can. Who's Who, XI)
LE LACHEUR, Francis, present at a RABEY-MACHON wedding, Roseville, Gaspe 1869
LE LACHEUR, John, d 1867 Gaspe, age 71, poss of Sir Wm. Place, G?
LE LACHEURS in Gaspe, Census 1861
LE LACHEUR, John, b G in Malbaie, Gaspe 1861 with Hannah Sara, Mary Jane, both born Canada, and Mary Jane VARDON, qv. (Census 1861)
LE LACHEUR, Peter, b G, in Gaspe Bay 1861 with Mary Ann, Eliza, b Canada, and John, Peter, Enoch and Abraham, all b G
LE LACHEUR, Henry?, b G, in Gaspe 1861 with John and William, b Canada
LE LACHEUR, Francis and Thomas, b Canada, res Douglastown, Que. 1861 (Census)
LE LACHEUR, Robert J., 1871-1921 (GLF)
LE LACHEUR, Mary S., b 1877, d 1950, wife of Wm. LE TOUZEL, qv, and daus Ruth and Elise, all bur United Ch Cem, Rosebridge, Gaspe (GLF)
LE LACHEUR, Martha Lydia, 1853-1928, bur United Ch, Rosebridge, Gaspe, with William David, 1884-1894, and Hubert D., 1889-1959 (GLF)
LE LACHEUR. Three Captain Le Lacheurs are noted in C.R. Fay's THE CHANNEL ISLANDS AND NEWFOUNDLAND. One was Capt. William, in Quebec in 1786. Another was connected with SEWARD AND PIPON, shipbuilders from Jersey in Southampton, England. The third, another Capt. William of Guernsey, d 1863, age 60. He had sailed to Valparaiso, Costa Rica,

South America, etc. in the coffee trade. SEE PAGE 356
LE LACHEUR, John Jr., b G, son of John, rem to Saint John, NB, mar 1894
Anna Evesia Mowatt, 1874-195-. (Joan Kennedy, Saint John, NB; Edith
Le Lacheur, Guelph, Ont.)
  A1. John Louis Mowatt, b 1895, d 1967, mar 1. Grace COOPER who d 1925,
    2 daus. Mar 2. Margaret Louise Evans, 1898-1963, res Wolfville, NB.
  B1. Louis Maurice, b 1927, mar Edith Florence Simmons, res Guelph, Ont.
    C1. Margaret Louise, b 1948, mar Michael Garfield Floto, b 1949
      D1. Richard Michael Floto, b 1967
      D2. Brian Garfield Floto, b 1973
    C2. Judith Ann, b 1950, mar Gary Alan Campbell, b 1950
      D1. John Chadwick Campbell, b 1972
      D2. Margaret Jane Campbell, b 1976
    C3. John Maurice, b 1956   C4. Thomas Gordon, b 1961
LE LIEVRE, see TITO, in record of LE BRETON fam, Nfld. and Ontario
LE LIEVRE, curr at Grand Riviere, Quebec, poss French
LE LIEVRE, John, signed Petition at Gaspe 1820
LE LIEVRE, Charles, age 26, b J, farmer in Perce 1871, also Edw., age
50, b J
LE LIEVRE, John, 1837-1910, b J, and Mary Ann PAYN, buried Baptist Cemetery, Vittoria, Ontario, Norfolk Co., desc
LE LIEVRE, in Toronto, origin not ver.
LE LIEVRE in Nfld. (Seary) Cf Le Lievre of C.I.
LE LIEVRE, Pt. Clarence Dalton, b C.I. Related to Thos. Francis Le
Lievre, St. Heliers, J. Enlisted 1915 in Univ. Co., 3rd Reinforcement Draft, Can. Army, Ottawa, Ont. (OUR HEROES IN THE GREAT WORLD
WAR, by J.H. De Wolfe, Canada 1919)
LE MEE, LEMEE, in Nfld. from C.I.? Cf LEMME, in J (Stevens)
LE MAISTRE, Francis, Lt. Governor of Gaspe, b J, a Colonel under General
Carleton, who was Gov. of Que. 1786-1796. LE MAISTRE had been secretary and aide de camp to the celebrated Gen. Halimand. Prob named Lt.
Gov. in 1785. A letter is known addressed by him to the inhabitants
of Gaspe, requiring them to treat the Indians fairly and honestly and
show them a good example. Le Maistre mar a Catholic named Stuart in
Quebec. He was probably from St. Ouen, J, and was bur Paspebiac,
Gaspe. (Les Lieutenant--GOUVERNEURS DE GASPE, Recherches Hist., Vol.
V, 1899; and MERCURY, Quebec City, 1805)
LE MAISTRE, M. and Isabelle of J, mar two LE ROSSIGNOLS. See fam of
Pierre Nicholas.
LE MAISTRE, Philip Thomas, b 1845 St. Heliers, J, a sea captain, later
captained boats on the St. Lawrence River between Quebec City and
Pictou, NS. In 1900 wnet down with his boat on a bad storm on the
St. Lawrence, mar Matilda CABELDU, qv, desc. (Mrs. F. Wm. Long,
Niagara Falls, Ont., Canada)
LE MAISTRE, William, b J, d 1826 age 77, bur St. Peters in Paspebiac,
bro of Francis above? Poss worked for Robin firm. (GLF)
LE MAISTRE, Charles Philip, Jr., 1923-1962. His father b J in 1895, d
1962. Charles is bur St. James Angl. Ch, Port Daniel, Gaspe, and
his father bur West Paspebiac United Ch Cem, worked for Robin firm.
A widow and 2 daus res New Carlisle, Que. One dau, Lydia, res St.
Martin, J.
LE MAISTRE, Philip, b J, in Gaspe 1861 (Census)
LE MAISTRE, Charles, b J, in Perce 1861 (Census)
LE MAISTRE, in Maritimes Fisheries (J.H. Le Breton list)
LE MAISTRE, Wm., signed the Gaspe Petition 1820. Jean signed also.
LE MAISTRE, J. Le B., of reorganized Robin firm in 1855
LE MAISTRE, in Bonaventure Island 1831 (Syvret)

LE MAISTRE 359

LE MAISTRE, Marie, was in Cap des Rosier 1800s
LE MAISTRE, Edward Joshua, b St. Ouen, J, blacksmith, at 13 to Malbaie for Robin firm, early 1900s.(GLF) Later res Almonte, Ont, with 6 chn.
LE MAISTRE, from J to Canada 1870, a son Frederick John, res Ridley Park, Penna.
LE MAISTRE, Harold of J, his grandfather to Australia 1870s
LE MAISTRE, Jane, wife of Capt. Amice LE MOIGNAN, who was master of several Robin ships sailing to the Mediterranean in the 1840s. (Le Moignan)
LE MAITRE, Zepherin?, from J? to NB (Gordon Le Maitre, Campbellton, NB)
LE MAITRE, Capt. Abraham, master of the BETSEY, 84 tons, built 1799 in C.B., owned by Peter JANVRIN, qv, and taken by the French on a voyage to the West Indies.
LE MAITRE, LE MAISTRE, LE MASTRE, etc., Capt., agents, and merchants from J in Nfld. (K. Mathews)
LE MAITRE, Jules, from J to Gaspe ca 1900 or before
LE MAITRE, from J to BC?
LE MAISTRE Francis, 2nd Lt. in Gaspe and Supt. at Labrador Fisheries, 1794-1821, succeeded by Alexander Forbes. (Rev. d'Hist)
LE MAITRE, Bellenoy, Therese, widow of Peter BREHAUT, qv, of Quebec City, mar Wm. GRUT SHEPPARD, poss also of G. See BREHAUT, Peter.
LE MAITRE, Maive?, b C.I.?, mar Kester in Canada
LE MAITRE, from C.I. to Chatham, Ont.
LE MAITRE, in western Canada, poss from C.I.
LE MARCHAND, Nicholas from C.I.?, in Gaspe 1820, signed Petition
LE MARCHAND, see MARCHAND of Cape Breton, N.S. Sometimes changed to Merchant in N.A.
LE MARCHANT, Gaspard. In 1854 Great Britain, needing more servicemen, enacted a law to permit foreign enlistment and sent recruiters to the United States. There was a depression at that time, and many applied. Joseph Howe of Canada, told to check into the possibilities, unwisely jumped the gun. Instructions had been given to him by Sir Gaspard Le Marchant of a C.I. fam, then Lt. Gov. of N.S. Recruiting pamphlets were circulated. Since this was all illegal, indictments were prepared and his agents arrested. The British consul in Cincinnati thought a thousand men could be raised on the western frontier. He commissioned a Hungarian nobleman to command a regiment of 600 Kentucky riflemen. Few recruits got as far as Halifax, NS, and those who did were persuaded to take other work.
The venture had a comic opera aspect, and Howe's actions, his fierce and ill-considered drive for American recruits lasted only a few months, and was then dropped. Howe was subsequently defeated in Nova Scotia elections in 1855 by Dr. Tupper. (FROM SEA UNTO SEA, Canada 1850-1910, by W.G. Hardy, Garden City, NY, 1959)
LE MARCHANT, Gaspard, was Gov. of Nfld. from 1847-1852, was also Gov. of N.S. and Gov. of Malta. He d 1874 in London, England.
LE MARCHANT, Capt., agent, and merchants from J and G in Nfld. (K. Mathews)
LE MARQUAND, John, b J, age 53 in 1871, res Bon. Co., Gaspe. (Census) Wife, Mary, age 43, was Catholic.
LE MARQUAND, Charles, b 1849 J, to Canada age 13, worked for James ALEXANDER and Co., whose firm was begun in 1847, Gaspe. Charles mar Alice ALEXANDRE and d at 58, 1907, 6 chn. (Cecil Le Marquand, Malbaie, Que.) MORE ON THIS FAM. IN CI COLL, FROM MC EACHERN.& FROM
A1. Edith, mar Philip PAYNE, qv, 4 chn   Sydney LE MARQUAND, of
   B1. Lillian Payne   Chatham, NB, Canada.
   B2. Gladys Payne   B3. Stuart Payne
                                          B4. Reginald Payne

LE MARQUAND, SEE EXTRA PAGES & CHAN.IS. COLLECTION.
A2. Herbert, Herbert Charles?, 1879-1925, bur Malbaie, mar twice, no
   issue
A3. James, 1880-1929, mar Effie Caldwell, 1881-1974, in 1905, 4 chn.
   James drowned?
  B1. Cecil, b 1906, mar ---Douglas 1946, dau, Wendy, b 1949
  B2. Sydney, b 1908, mar twice, no issue
  B3. Irene, b 1910, mar ---, 3 chn; Faye, Fern and Ernest.
  B4. Melbourne, b 1920, mar a Scot, 3 chn. He won the Military Medal
   in Holland 1944, WWII. 3 chn; Elaine, Derrick and Glenda.
A4. Maude, mar Paul Morin, qv, no issue
A5. Ida, mar Livingston HUELIN, qv, 1 son
  B1. Sydney Huelin. Sons, Brian and William.
A6. May, unmar, d 1963
LE MARQUAND, Francis, b J, in Gaspe 1861 with Mary Catherine, Francis
   Elias, and Mary Ann, all b J. (Census)
LE MARQUAND, Charles P. of St. Peter, J, 1882-1926, bur St. Peter's
   Paspebiac, Gaspe died Sept Iles, QUE.
LE MARQUAND, Pierre, Sr. and Jr. with a family of 10 in Bonaventure
   Island 1831 (Syvret; Cent. Bklt.)
LE MARQUAND, Capt. Pierre, b J, d 1901 Eskimo Pt., now Havre St. Pierre
   on the north shore of the St. Lawrence, age 83 at death. (Que. Arch.)
LE MARQUAND, firm of Alexandre and Le Marquand in Gaspe 1800s. (Rev.
   d'Hist)
LE MARQUAND, Mary Ann, of St. Ouen, J, wife of Thomas LE PAGE, qv. Bur
   Malbaie, 1800s.
LE MARQUAND, from J to Toronto in 1904
LE MARQUAND, Nicholas, age 64, b G, farmer in Gaspe Bay 1871
   Three sons of James LE MARQUAND of St. Peter's Jersey, came to N.A.:
Ernest Philip, Elias John, and Judge Samuel James, who made his fortune
in New York with the Pullman Co. (GLF)
I. Elias John, b 1855 J, d 1931 Newport, Gaspe, mar ---
  A1. Edgar, mar ---
    B1. Edgar Gerald, d.y.   B2. Lorne Nelson, d.y.
  A2. Elias Perceval, d 1888, age 5   A4. Hazel, b 1902, d.y.
  A3. Lewis Elias, b 1899, d.y.   A5. Adolphus Stanley, b 1889, d.y.
  A6. Clarence, b 1894, d.y.
  A7. Irene, b 1900, d 1953, mar Reginald TUZO, qv, bur Perce, Gaspe
  A8. Ida?, mar Charles MARETT, qv, unverified
    B1. Maud Marett, mar Harold LE GRESLEY, qv.
II. Samuel James
III. Ernest Philip, b 1862, d 1925, bur Newport, Gaspe
  A1. Ernest John, b 1892, d 1925, mar Margaret Myrtle MacPherson, 1895-
   1935, bur Port Daniel, Gaspe
  A2. Gordon, mar Mary Huntington, d 1964   A3. Jeffrey, 1906-1943
  A4. Victor Samuel, d 1897, at 10 mos.
  A5. Corrinne, d.y., bur Newport, Gaspe
LE MARQUAND, James, res Malbaie, Quebec   IN Q.A. IN NORTH AMERICA
LE MARQUAND, SEE BIG CORRECTED CHART   IN John was b J ca 1818, rem
to Nfld. then Cape Breton, and settled in New Carlisle, Que. before
1846. He mar Marie E. Castillon. At least 11 chn. (Mary Sullens
McEwan, Salt Lake City, Utah) (This fam uses MARQUAND)
  A1. John, b ca 1846 New Carlisle, Que.   A3. Mary Jane, b ca 1850
  A2. Frank, b ca 1849   A4. Philip, b ca 1853
  A5. Marie, b ca 1855, mar Stanley McCoubrey, son of Richard McCoubrey.
   Rem to Cloquet, Minn., had 6 chn. Later rem to Spokane, Wash.,
   where they are buried.
    B1. Ethel McCoubrey   B2. Alice Ann McCoubrey, d.y., 1888

LE MARQUAND 361
LE MARQUAND data in CI COLL. from Sydney LeM.,Chatham,NB.
  B3. Edward McCoubrey   B4. Bertha McCoubrey, mar?
  A7. Peter, b ca 1859 New Carlisle, Que.
  A8. Edward, b ca 1862, rem to Mason Co. Mich. where he mar Mary B.
      Keson 1890. Poss other chn. Edw. d Scottville, Mich. 1944
    B1. Caroline, b 1891, Lundington, Mich.   B4. Raymond, b 1903
    B2. Ruth E., b 1897, Amber, Mich.   B5. Kenneth, b 1905, un-
    B3. Gertrude, b 1900, Amber, Mich.   certain
LE MARQUANDS from C.I. to Prince Edward Is. with the BREHAUT fam 1806
LE MARQUAND, John, of J, manager ca 1891 of Wm. Fruing Co., Goulet de
  Shippegan, N.B. (Robichaud, has picture)
LE MARQUAND, from J to St. John's, Nfld. (Shortis-Munn)
LE MARQUAND, George Joshua, b 1870, St. Heliers, J, rem to Nfld. See
  George James LE MARQUAND.
LE MARQUAND, William George, b 1908 J, son of ---Le M. and Marie RICH-
  ARD, latter born France. Wm. and bro George rem to Gaspe then to
  Western Canada in 1920s. Homesteaded in Thorhild, Alta. and in 1949
  to Peace River country for 16 yrs. William was carpenter in Sexsmith,
  Alta. 11 yrs. See Chap. Western Canada. Sisters in J, Mrs. Lily
  GAUTRON, and Mrs. Lucille JEAN of Trinity, and bro Edwin LE MARQUAND
  of St. Lawrence, J. William "farmed with the moon,...tries to get in
  tune with the natural rhythms of the earth and to live in harmony
  with it, instead of fighting it...the big farms are ruining everything. Too much bush is taken off, causing drought conditions...the
  thing I regret now is that people don't leave room for a fence. We
  used to leave 8 feet and the road allowance was another 8 feet. Eventually we will have created another drafty desert, and there will be
  famines...It won't be because the earth cannot produce the desired
  crops, (because we) don't treat it right....Bill contends that a one
  acre farm garden allowed people to feel that their life comes from
  the soil, not the department store...Bill keeps an inner peace that
  radiates outward. Perhaps it's called perspective. He would call it
  faith." (Clipping from Western Canada newspaper, name unknown)
LE MARQUAND, Capt. George James, in the Nfld. trade, settled there.
  Mar 1. Mary Ann COUTANCHE, qv, a son and dau, and mar 2. ---, 2 sons.
  Capt. G.L. was lost in a storm at age 48, schooner DONNA MARIA.
  George Joshua sailed at age 14 with his father, as cabin boy, became
  a captain at age 25, sailing out of St. John's, Nfld. and New York.
  See his story in Chapter on B.C. (H.A. Le Marquand, White Rock, B.C.)
  A1. George Joshua, b 1870 St. Heliers, J, mar 1. Sarah MILLEY, poss
      MILLAIS?, and 2. Christina MOON, qv. Chn by first wife.
    B1. James Maxwell ACOURT, b 1897 Nfld., rem to Vancouver Island, BC.
        Mar 1. Gertrude Beaty, 2 chn, mar 2. Edna Kilvington.
      C1. Edna, b 1937, mar Vernon Ganz, res Parksville, BC
        D1. Gary Ganz, b 1961   D2. Cynthia Ganz, b 1964
      C2. Beverly Joan, b 1942, mar James Sherry, res Fremont, Calif.
        D1. William Sherry, b 1971
      C3. James Sidney, b 1952, mar Joan Pearl HILLIAR, qv, no issue, res
          Sidney, BC
    B2. Olive, b 1897, mar Ivan Shearer, res Port Angeles, Wash.
      C1. Dwayne Shearer, adopted
    B3. George R., d 1964, mar Blen Alsbert, res Santa Cruz, Calif.
      C1. Victor, adopted
    B4. Hubert John Millais, changed from Hubert Keslake Millais, b 1906,
        d 1967. Mar 1. Vera Voise and 2. Margaret Betty Inglis. Data
        below uncertain.
      C1. George, b 1930, Vancouver, BC
      C2. David Bennet, b 1932, res Winnipeg, Man.

        C3. Ruby, married, 5 chn
        C4. Elizabeth, b 1937, mar Douglas Gilbert
    B5. Harry Alan, b 1907, mar Mary Wilson, res Vancouver, BC
        C1. John Alana, mar Elaine --- C2. David George, mar Leslie Porter
LE MARREC, Peter, b 1902 J, son of Emile Le M. from Brittany and Jeanne
    MARGUER, related to ROMERIL fam? Peter was an engineer, and rem to
    Vancouver, BC 1924. He mar 1932 Jessie Pinkerton of Scotland. Re-
    turned to J for recuperation, but came to Canada again in 1954, re-
    settled in Vancouver. Hug fam. (P. Le Marrec, Vancouver, BC)
    A1. Jeanne, b 1934, mar Edw. Villette, res Surrey, BC
        B1. Gary Villette, b 1959?   B2. Michael Villette, b 1960
    A2. Pauline, b 1939, mar John PARSONS, res Kelowna, BC
        B1. Kathy Parson, b 1959   B3. Judy Parsons, b 1960?
        B2. Susanne Parsons, b 1960   B4. John Parsons, b 1963?
    A3. Jacqueline, b 1944 J, mar Gerry Kingsley, Burnaby, BC
        B1. Robert Kingsley, b 1967   B3. Brian Kingsley, b 1971
        B2. Lynda Kingsley, b 1969
LE MARSH, from C.I. to Canada?
LE MARSH, E., owned the ACTIVE, 40 tons, built in 1847 at Arichat, CB
    with partner, W. Boudrot
LE MASURIER, and other spellings. Some material in Guildhall, London;
    Priaulx Library, G. LE MASURIER, LE MESURIER, SEE EXTRA PAGES.
LE MASURIER. (Compiler's note: Aug. Le Messurier, R.E. of the Indian
    Army, by 1922, had gathered and printed a history of both private and
    public records on these numerous families of the Channel Islands, Le
    Masurier, Le Mesurier, Le Messurier, particularly of Guernsey fam-
    ilies, which included the explanation for the variations in spelling)
I. LE MASURIER, L. Alfred, b 1853 Clapham, Eng., son of Joshua Le. M.,
    and Mary Jane Clark. This fam had rem to England 1851. Alfred rem
    1870 to Cannington, Ont. with his bro Philip, and Philip's family
    noted below. Alfred mar 1871, Henrietta Elizabeth Burgis, dau of
    Cornelius Burgis and Louise Grove of Cannington, Ont. Alfred was
    a successful cabinet maker there, and retired to Toronto 1909,
    where he d in 1932. 8 chn. (Murray Le Masurier, Toronto, Ont.)
    A1. Florence Ada, b 1872, mar 1897 Richard G. Smith, of Unionville, Ont.
    A2. Alfred Henry, b 1874, mar 1. ---Ford, and 2. Bertha L. Gibson. D
        1951 Toronto, no issue.
    A3. Marion Edith, b 1875, mar 1898 John G. Robinson
        B1. Harold Robinson B2. Frederick Robinson B3. Elroy Robinson
    A4. Clarence Theodore, b 1879, mar Myrtle McNabow, res Duluth, Minn.
        No issue.
    A5. Henry Sinclair, b 1882, mar 1906 Eva M. Stoner of U.E.L. fam, b
        1888 in Toronto. Had carpenter business with bro Alfred in Toronto.
        D Langstaff, Ont., 2 sons.
        B1. Harry Edward, O.B.E., b 1907 Toronto, mar Hilda L. Braid. Lt.
            Col. 15th Gen. Hosp. Admin. of Sunnybrook Military Hosp. 1946-
            1952.
            C1. Harry S.   C2. Peter J.
        B2. Alfred Henry, b 1915 Toronto, mar 1938 Eleanor Wilson Groves, b
            1916. He was founder of Langstaff Card Co., Reeve of Markham,
            various civil service offices, Toronto and Ont. govt. Res Kettle-
            by, Ont. Executive Director, Ont. Housing Authority.
            C1. Murray Alfred, res Toronto, Ont.
    A6. Ethel May, b 1886, mar Thomas BLACKBURN, res Thornhill, Ont.
        B1. Earl Blackburn B2. Wesley Blackburn B3. Ross Blackburn
    A7. Ernest Edward, b 1888, mar 1. Edith Crosier, and 2. Katherine Baker.
        Restaurant owner. Res Fenelon Falls, Ont.

LE MASURIER 363

    B1. John Montgomery, b 1914, d 1939
    B2. Kenneth, b 1941, mar 1965 Carol Fuller, res Fenelon Falls, Ont.
       C1. Craig, adopted   C2. Sherry
A8. Greta, b 1892, d 1906
II. LE MASURIER, Philip, b 1845 J, bro of Alfred, above. Philip
    was a piano manufacturer ca 1864, mar Sarah ---, b 1844. Rem to
    Cannington, Ont. 1870. See LATE ADDITIONS AND CORRECTIONS pages.
A1. Ernest, b 1865   A2. Philip, Jr., b 1868   A3. Annie, b 1869
LE MASURIER, William John, b 1878 England, raised in J, rem to Canada
    early 1900s. Mar 1910, Harriet Rhoda WATTS, qv, of West Bromwick,
    Stafford, Eng. (Peter R. Le Masurier, Toronto, Ont.; Doris Hooper,
    Brussels, Ont.)
A1. Doris, b 1912, mar Francis Egbert Hooper, res Downsview, Ont.
    B1. Helen Ann Hooper, b 1938, mar Leslie de Finta
       C1. Alexander de Finta, b 1963   C3. Rebecca de Finta, b 1969
       C2. Michael de Finta, b 1966
    B2. James S.M. Hooper, b 1941, mar Carolynne ---
       C1. Stuart Ian James Hooper, b 1966   C3. Scott Eric Adam Hooper,
       C2. Craig Andrew Thomas Hooper, b 1970   b 1974
    B3. Muriel Eileen Hooper, b 1944, mar Malcolm Stead
       C1. Gregory Malcolm Stead, b 1962
    B4. Valerie Hooper, b 1949, mar ---Chalmers
    B5. John Francis William Hooper, b 1955
A2. William, b 1915, mar Edna Lindsay, res Toronto, 2 chn
A3. Clifford Joseph, b 1916, mar Dorothy Phyllis Freeborn, b 1918
    B1. Paul, b 1940, res Montreal
    B2. Peter Robert, b 1944, mar Diane Heather McDonald, b 1947, res
        Toronto
       C1. Andre Justin, b 1973   C2. Lise Nicole, b 1976
LE MASURIER, John Joshua, mar Harriet OAKES, both of J, and two of
    their chn rem to Canada. Chn: Albert, Lilian, John Philip, Bertram,
    Percy and Clive. John Philip settled in Gaspe, Clive somewhere in
    Canada. (Harold Le Masurier, Forillon, Gaspe; Keith Le Masurier,
    Hannon, Ont.)
I. Albert
II. Lilian, res Greystones, St. Ouen, J
III. John Philip, b 1883 J, to Nfld. in sailing ships, then to Gaspe,
     where he worked for the Fruing firm at Grand Greve until 1917, and
     was appointed a fishery officer, later chief tech. Mar Pearl
     ESNOUF, qv, bur St. Peters, Little Gaspe, Que. 1967.
A1. Roy Philip, b 1911 Grand Greve, Gaspe, res Espanola, Ont.
A2. Harold Bertram, b 1913, mar Hazel Olive ROBERTS, qv, b 1911 Gaspe
    B1. Audrey Pearl, b 1936, mar Roy Miller of Farewell Cove, Gaspe
       C1. George Roy Miller, b 1960   C2. Donna Marie Miller, b 1963
    B2. Keith Harold, b 1938, mar Leona ---, res Hannon, Ont.
    B3. Mansel Gregor, b 1940
    B4. Linden Philip, b 1942, mar Otilia Boulay of Gaspe
       C1. Linda, b 1961   C2. Thomas Le B., b 1963
    B5. Judith Hazel, b 1945, mar Warren Patterson, res Wakeham, Gaspe
       C1. Michael Warren Patterson, b 1966
       C2. Fay Judith Patterson, b 1971
    B6. Wendoline Caroline, b 1951, mar Remi Boulay, res Forillon, Gaspe
       C1. Raymond Harold Boulay, b 1970   C2. Nancy Caroline Boulay, b 1974
    B7. Spencer Norman, b 1953, of J
A3. Herbert Eric, b 1927, res Grande Greve, Gaspe
IV. Bertram C., unmar, res J, b 1885
V. Percy, res Vincheles, St. Ouen, J   VI. Clive, to U.S.?

LE MASURIER, Harriet, mar Henry Ramsden in Gaspe, a son, Samuel Adolphus George, b 1841
LE MASURIER, Charles and Peter in Gaspe 1838, signed a petition
LE MASURIER, Thomas, b Gaspe or G, mar Elizabeth LENFESTY, qv
    Poss error here. See below Thomas and Elizabeth LE MESSURIER.
  A1. John, bp 1828, witnesses, J. Le Mess. and Mary.
  A2. Caroline, bp 1839 at Indian Cove, Gaspe
  A3. Abraham, bp 1841 Grand Greve, Gaspe
LE MASURIER, Alfred, 1874-1956, b J?, mar Mary E., 1880-1957, Gaspe (GLF) Bur St. Mathews, Penouille, Gaspe.
LE MASURIER, Ann Mary, 1863-1942, wife of Edmund W. LE GALLAIS, qv, Gaspe (GLF)
LE MASURIER, Jane, 1903-1920, bur Paspebiac, Gaspe (GLF)
LE MASURIER, John, b 1826 J, d 1901, mar Jane E. GALLIE, qv, bur St. Peters, Paspebiac, Gaspe (GLF) SEE EXTRA PAGES.
LE MASURIER, John T., 1894-1908, bur Paspebiac, Gaspe (GLF)
LE MASURIER, John E., 1906-1925, bur Paspebiac, Gaspe (GLF)
LE MASURIER, John, b J, in Malbaie 1861 (Census), with Betsy, Martha, John, Robert, Hannah, Charles and Margaret, all b Canada
LE MASURIER, Mary L., b 1909, d.y., bur Paspebiac (GLF)
LE MASURIER, Peter, b Gaspe, in Douglastown, Que. 1861.(Census) Also John and Thomas, b Gaspe, and Rachel, b G
LE MASURIER, Rachel, b G, in Gaspe 1861 with George, b Gaspe
LE MAY, ship owner from J in Nfld. (K. Mathews) Cf also LEMEE, LEMME of J (Stevens)
LE MERCIER, Hug surname. Some settled in C.I. then rem to New England. Some also settled in N.S. See Mercier.
LE MESSURIER, see note before LE MASURIER
LE MESSURIER, Thomas, from C.I.?, prob G, res Hamilton, Ont. Mar Phoebe Livinia BAKER. This fam poss first in Gaspe area. Rem 1900 to B.C., res Vancouver. Joined Irish Fusiliers in WWI. Artist, cartoonist, res Toronto, then Montreal, and in New York for a few years. Mar 1928 in Montreal, Elizabeth Olive Dawes, dau of Norman Dawes and Olive Grace Claggett. Musician and amateur actor. Died young at age 38 in 1932. Bur Mt. Royal Cem. (K.H. Annett, Gaspe, Quebec)
LE MESSURIER, John, age 45, b J, was in Bon. Co., Gaspe 1871 with Jane, age 42, b Que., Emily age 13, Ann Mary age 9, John Thomas age 7, and Susan Jane age 2. (Census)
LE MESSURIER, Thomas, b G, mar Elizabeth LENFESTY, rem to Gaspe (Esther Le Messurier, Honeoye, New York) Error? See Thomas and Eliz., above.
  A1. Thomas, b 1836, d 1923, mar Charity Gunby 1963
    B1. William John, b 1867, d 1942, mar Margaret Campbell 1894, who d 1934
      C1. Clyde, b 1895, mar Esther Bentley 1921, res Honeoye, N.S.
        D1. Robert, b 1924, mar Esther Hollon 1946
          E1. Suzanne, b 1947, mar David Lippert
            F1. Keith Lippert, b 1969
          E2. Barbara, b 1948, mar Thomas Walker 1973, a ch b 1975
          E3. Matthew, b 1953?
        D2. Bruce, b 1926, mar Jean Klein 1949
          E1. Carol, b 1952, mar Robert Marryman   E3. Sandra
          E2. Nancy   E4. Scott, b 1956
LE MESSURIER, Lilly of Toronto, rem to San Francisco, Calif.
LE MESSURIER, a G fam settled at St. John's, Nfld. ca 1800
LE MESSURIER, Peter and Co., had a whale fishery at Hermitage Bay, Nfld. 1797 (H.S. Le Messurier)
LE MESSURIER, Maria, to Gaspe 1869

LE MESSURIER, Ada, in Gaspe 1878
LE MESSURIER, Jean and Mary, were sponsors at the birth of John LE
     MASURIER in George's Cove, Gaspe 1828
LE MESSURIER, Henry William, b 1848 J, son of Henry Corbin Le M. and
     Sara Eliza---. Was elected to the Nfld. House of Assembly for Burin
     dist. 1885. He was J.P., Minister of Customs, etc. Mar 1872, Eliz-
     abeth Arnott of Oban, Scotland, died 1931, bur St. John's, Nfld., 2
     sons, 2 daus. (C.R. Fay, papers of H.W. Le Messurier)
LE MESSURIER, Peter, merchant in St. John's, Nfld. in 1815
LE MESSURIER, Nicholas, in Nfld. 1811 (Brochet)
LE MESSURIER, Nicholas, of C.I., settled in Cape Breton, NS. Owned a
     ship, the brig BROTHERS, 136 tons, built at Arichat or Port Hawkes-
     bury, sold on completion to John JANVRIN, qv, or Arichat. In 1832 it
     was bound for New York with 130 cauldrons aboard. In 1833 the brig
     was sold to Jersey traders. (Capt. Parker)
LE MESSURIER, from C.I. to B.C.
LE MESURIER, see note before LE MASURIER, regarding sources of data for
     this and other similar surnames.
LE MESURIER, Henry, b 1791 G, son of Haviland Le M. (Had bros, at least
     Paul and Haviland) Henry entered the Army in 1811, and lost his right
     arm at the Battle of Salamanca 1812. He was sent to Canada and took
     part in the War of 1812. Mar Julie, dau of Pierre Guillaume Guerout
     and J---, in 1815 at St. Denis, Que. by special permission. He was
     Lt. Col. of the Militia, magistrate of Dist. of Quebec, deputy master-
     paymaster of the Trinity House, and merchant at Quebec. Between 1818
     and 1823 res Quebec, agent for export of squared timbers. His firm,
     LE MESURIER, TILSTONE & CO., later, Le Mesurier, Routh and Co., had
     4 ships built Quebec, 1825-1847. A Quebec Committee of Trade member,
     also of several insurance, navigation and mining companies, a director
     of Grand Trunk Railway in 1852. He welcomed the Prince of Wales on
     his visit in 1860. D in Quebec, age 69, I 61. His wife d Quebec
     1869, bur Anglican Cathedral of Quebec. One dau mar Col. Clifford,
     Royal Artillery. (Dict. of Can. Biog., Vol. IX; Memoires de la
     Societe Gen. Can. Francaise, Vol. VIII, MAPLE LEAVES, article by
     J. M. Le Moine 1873; Therese Gravel, Montreal, Que.)
A1. Julie, b 1816 St. Denis, Que., bp Anglican Ch of Sorel, Que.
A2. William Henry, b 1819, merchant in Quebec. Mar 1843 at Quebec
     Metro. Ch, Mary Frances Stewart, who d 1902. He was bur at age
     52, 1871.
   B1. Henry Stewart, b Quebec 1844
   B2. William Guerout, b 1846, mar Maud Stewart, dau of Sir Andrew
        Stewart, or Stuart, Judge and Charlotte Elmire Aubert de Gaspe.
        He d 1909 at 63.
      C1. Charles Stuart, mar at St. Andrew's Presbyterian Ch at West-
           mount, Que. 1919 to Beatrice Mary Ross, dau of James Ross and
           Beatrice Graham
         D1. Marguerite   D3. James
         D2. Andrew   D4. Mary
   B3. Arthur Graves, b 1848 Que., d 1852
   B4. James Morrin, b 1851
   B5. Joseph Dobree, b 1851 Que.   B6. John Clifford, b 1852, d 1853
   B7. George Geddes, b 1856 Que., living in 1909. Res Toronto, Ont.,
        mar Wilhelmina Elizabeth Todd 1885, connected with the LE MAITRE
        and GRASETT fams. (Chadwick, ONTARIAN FAMILIES)
A3. Haviland, b 1820, St. Denis, Que., d 1832
A4. James, b 1826, Que.
A5. Harriet Amelia, b 1826, twin of James

A6. Edward, b 1828 Quebec, mar there St. Matthew's Chapel 1872, Jane Rogers. She d 1888, age 50. He was bur Que. 1896. Had firm with bro Henry at Sillery Cove, Que.
   B1. Maud Mary Constance, b 1875 Que., mar in Angl Ch, Quebec, Charles Stanley Smith 1898. 4 sons, 1 killed in WWI. Mrs. Smith d at Montreal.
A7. Frederick, b 1829   A8. Anne Ruth, b 1831 Quebec
A9. Amelia Jane, b 1832 Que., mar there Anglican Cathedral in 1857 Robert Herbert Smith, merchant of Que. where he d in 1895. She was bur 1917, 12 chn. Poss mar 2? Carrington?
   B1. Robert Harcourt Smith, b 1858 Quebec   B7. Charles Carrington, b 1867
   B2. Edith Elizabeth Smith, b 1862 Quebec
   B3. David, b 1863   B8. Edmund, b 1869
   B4. Amelia Blanche, b 1863   B9. George Carrington, b 1870
   B5. Amelia Blanche again, b 1864, bur 1927 Quebec
                                      B10. Edmond Harcourt, b 1874
   B6. Herbert Carrington, b 1866   B11. Arthur Carrington, b 1875
   B12. Arthur again, b 1876, d 1952 at 77
A10. Haviland, b 1835 Quebec, bur 1836
A11. Louisa Elizabeth, b 1846 Quebec, mar 1862 William Henry CARTER, who d 1918 Quebec. She was bur 1929, 9 chn.
   B1. Ethel Maud Carter, b 1869, bur 1898
   B2. Lilian Mary Carter, b 1870   B5. Basil Brooke Carter, b 1874
   B3. Arthur Butler Carter, b 1872   B6. Bowan Buthie Carter, b 1876
   B4. George Herbert Carter, b 1873   B7. Agnes Mabel Carter, b 1876, d.y.
   B8. William Carter, b 1877 Quebec, mar Muriel Olive Duffus, he d 1954
      C1. William Owen Le Mesurier Carter
      C2. Kenneth Le Mesurier Carter, mar Rebecca Marshall Murdoch
         D1. Paulding Carter
   B9. May Florence, bur Quebec, 1923
A12. Thomas Augustus, b 1837, mar Lucy Evelyn Darling
   B1. Maud, b 1868 Quebec
LE MESURIER, in Gaspe East when Bishop Charles Inglis visited there in 1789. "There are several bros of this name, natives of Guernsey, who deal in this business. They generally catch from 10,000 to 12,000 quintals of fish every year, and sometimes bring over 100 fishermen from Guernsey for the season." (Bishop Inglis diary; Yvonne Le Mesurier, Barachois, Que.)
LE MESURIER, John, b ca 1830 G, mar Elizabeth GIRARD, qv. At least 7 chn.
A1. Zerobabel, b 1860 Gaspe, mar Margaret Rehel
   B1. Randolph, b 1888, mar Yvonne ROUSSEL, res Barachois, Que.
      C1. Earl, b 1930, mar Mariette Picard, res Hearst, Ont.
         D1. Paul, b 1967   D2. Linda, b 1969
      C2. Carl, b 1931, unmar, dec
      C3. Mary, b 1932, mar Ernest Henley, res Barachois, Que.
         D1. Maureen Henley, b 1952   B4. Heather Henley, b 1957
         D2. Brian Henley, b 1953   B5. James Henley, b 1959
         D3. Colleen Henley, b 1955   B6. Iola Henley, b 1962
      C4. Ralph, b 1937, dec
      C5. Kevin, b 1938, mar Verna Walsh, b 1940 Douglastown, Que.
         D1. Anthony Gavin, b 1962   D2. Joseph Lorne, b 1963
      C6. Alma, b 1939, mar Bona Donahue, res Perce, Que.
         D1. Lynn Donahue, b 1961   D2. Lisa Donahue, b 1965
      C7. Stella, b 1942, mar Carl ROUSSEL, res Barachois, Que.
         D1. Karen Roussel, b 1968
      C8. Rosalee, b 1943, mar Marcel Proulx, res Perce, Que.

           D1. Nathalie Proulx, b 1967   D2. Linda Proulx, b 1968
        C9. Anora, b 1946, mar David Gorman, res Cape Cove, Que.
           D1. Mathieu Gorman, b 1968   D2. Dean Gorman, b 1970
        C10. Valerie, b 1950, mar Eugene Rooney, res Douglastown, Que.
           D1. Amanda Rooney, b 1977
     B2. Lorne, b 1889, mar Exhilda Savard, no issue, res Tupper Lake
     B3. Charles Philip, b 1891, mar Mary Fayie
        C1. Opal, b 1929, mar Ernie Glass, res Manitoba
        C2. Clifford, b 1926, mar Corinne Johnson, res Campbellton, NB
        C3. Lorne, b 1935, mar Shirley Fayie, res Longuil, Que.
     B4. Lilly Ann, b 1893, mar 1912 Herbert Dart, res Toronto, 12 chn, 39 grchn
        C1. Joseph, b 1915, mar 1939 Ella Cowling, 8 chn, 13 grchn, res Scarboro, Ont.
        C2. Hannah, b 1917, mar 1953 Edward Fleming, res Scarboro, Ont.
        C3. Margaret, b 1919, mar 1942 Fred Cowling, 4 chn, 2 grchn, res Scarboro
        C4. Walter, b 1921, mar 1949 Isobel ---, 4 chn, 6 grchn, res Scarboro
        C5. Delia, b 1923, mar 1946 Jack Wright, 5 chn, 3 grchn, res Scarb.
        C6. Douglas, b 1925, mar 1952 Shirley Prentice, Scarb., 5 chn.
        C7. Edward, b 1927, mar 1949 Irene Keats, res Newfoundland, 3 chn
        C8. Lillian, b 1929, mar 1949 Frank O'Hara, res Detroit, Mich, 2 chn
        C9. Earl, b 1931, mar 1953 Anetia Cicerella, res Scarboro, Ont., 1 ch
        C10. Lorne, b 1921 or 1931?, mar 1953 Barbara Albright, res Toronto, 6 chn
        C11. Lorraine, b 1932, unmar
        C12. May, b 1937, mar 1964 Albert Dornbourgh, res Scarboro, Ont., 1 ch
  A2. Philip, unmar

A3. John (A John, son of John, mar Eliz. VIBERT, qv.)
A4. Martha, mar Wm. Bouchey, res Barachois, Que.
A5. Maria, mar Octave Henley, res Barachois, Que.
A6. Nancy, mar Arthur King, res Toronto, Ont.
A7. Hannah, mar Thomas VIBERT, qv, res Perce, Que.
LE MESURIER, Elsie Joyce, b ?, mar in Gaspe?, Hubert Leigh Ascha, 1884-1963. (Ascah Family Genealogy)
A1. Willa Joyce Ascah, b 1931, mar Dennis Cluley
A2. Allan Henry Ascah, b 1932, mar Sheila Mullin
   B1. Stacey Ascah, b 1963   B2. Kimberley Joy Ascah, b 1966
A3. James Watson Ascah, b 1934, mar Ruby Miller
   B1. Peter Gordon Ascah, b 1962   B2. Geoffrey Leigh Ascah, b 1966
A4. Paul Hubert Ascah, b 1937, mar May Mullin
   B1. Wayne Ascah, b 1963   B2. Wendy Susan Ascha, b 1965
LE MESURIER, Edith Fairbairn, b 1899, mar 1926 Robert James Ascah, d 1972
A1. Royce Kingsford Ascah, b 1928, mar 1952 Helen Elizabeth Gabriel
   B1. Robert Brookes Ascah, b 1953   B4. Margaret Ann Gabriel Ascah,
   B2. Elizabeth Hope Ascah, b 1955   b 1963
   B3. Jeffrey Karl Ascah, b 1959   B5. Catherine May Ascah, b 1969
A2. Elizabeth Veronica Ascah, b 1929, mar Barry Jones
LE MESURIER, John, from G to Gaspe (Peter Le Mesurier, Scarboro, Ont.)
A1. John, mar Elizabeth or Eliza VIBERT, qv.
   B1. Archibald, mar Annie Brown of Gaspe

C1. Sydney Peter, mar Ruby Elaine HOTTON, bur Barachois West, Gaspe, fam rem to Toronto
   D1. Julia, mar Lorenzo Chicoine of Gaspe, 7 chn, res Toronto
   D2. Harold, mar Sybil Chicoine, 1 ch, res Toronto
   D3. Helena, mar Don McMillan of Montreal, 3 chn
   D4. Guy, mar Bessie Boucher of Gaspe, res Scarborough, Ont.
   D5. Dolly, mar Osborne Mitchell, res Barachois West, Gaspe, 2 chn?
   D6. Peter Alvin, mar Shirley Irene Gill, res Scarboro, Ont.
     E1. Ruby Elaine, mar Brian Bond of Gaspe, res Scarboro
     E2. Lorrie Anne   E3. Peter Shane
   D7. Howard, mar Lynn Mander, divorced, 3 chn, res Scarboro, Ont.
   D8. Henry, mar Leona Prentis, 2 chn
C2. Francis, mar Belle Cartier of Douglastown, Que. Some desc in Penetanguishine, Ont. All mar but Alvin.
   D1. Lloyd   D5. Mary   D9. Lindsey
   D2. Mabel   D6. Ross   D10. Margaret
   D3. Leona   D7. Edwin
   D4. Winston   D8. Alvin, unmar
C3. Dolly, mar Reuben Hotton of Barachois, Que.
   D1. Lorne Hotton   D2. Beulah Hotton
B2. John, unmar

LE MESURIER, Daniel, (also as MELLON DIT LE MESURIER), b St. Heliers, J, in Fox River, Gaspe before 1849, mar 1. Thomasine LE HARDY, b St. Heliers, J, and 2. Symphorose Bond of Malbaie, dau of Jean Bond and Sophie Larue, qv. Daniel res Douglastown also. (Remiggi)
A1. Mary Elvina, b 1839, bp 1845, by first wife
A2. Marie Philomene, bp 1845   A3. Georges Seraphin, bp 1847
A4. Sophie Judith, bp 1848
LE MESURIER, Abraham, also William?, tinsmith, res with SIMON fam, poss from G, 1800s
LE MESURIER, May, b J, mar John Francis LE HUQUET, bp 1855 Indian Cove, Gaspe
A1. John Francis LE HUQUET, d Toronto, Ont., at least 6 chn, see LE HUQUET
LE MESURIER, Philip, b ca 1825 C.I.?, mar Jane PYKE, whose father had been lost at sea 1831 Gaspe (Ascah Genealogy)
LE MESURIER, Pierre, b J?, mar at Cap Rosiers, Gaspe, Rachel GARE (Remiggi)
A1. Anne, bp 1822, mar 1845, ---MALOUIN
LE MESURIER, John and James, were sponsors of a John LE HUQUET, Indian Cove, Gaspe mid 1800s
LE MESURIER, Thomas and Nicholas, were signatories of the petition to retain Rev. E. Cusack at Gaspe 1838. A Thomas is said to have mar an Elizabeth LENFESTEY, b 1819 Perce.
LE MESURIER, Susanna, mar Joseph JEAN, or Joseph JEAN LE HUQUET, in Indian Cove, Gaspe 1853. Minister: F.S. DE LA MARE, qv, and present were John FALLE, qv, and Wm. Hyman.
LE MESURIER, John, mar Eliza GIRARD, a dau, Hannah Eliza, b 1846, Gaspe, poss Malbaie
LE MESURIER, Margaret, mar John Fry at Indian Cove, Gaspe, a dau, Margaret, b 1831
LE MESURIER, Charles, b J, served under Nelson for 9 years in the Navy, and was present when Nelson fell at Trafalgar. Charles arrived in Quebec in 1821, and mar soon Mary Thompson, an Irish woman. (K.H. Annett, Gaspe, Que. and An. Bio. Dict. 1881)
A1. John, b 1826 Gaspe, was a sailor, and wrecked twice around the

Gaspe and St. Lawrence shores. Rem to Quebec city, and worked in a bank until he was able to buy the business. He was elected to city council 1859 and in 1867 was Mayor of Quebec. He mar Mary Sylvain and d at age 55. Five chn. MORE DATA IN CI COLL.
LE MESURIER, Nicholas, b G, age 35 in 1830, single, asked land of the government at Ship Harbour, Cape Breton. (PANS)
LE MESURIER, ---, in Miscou and Shippegan 1840s, d accidentally in 1843
LE MESURIER, Capt. and agent from the C.I. in Nfld. ca 1800 (K. Mathews)
LE MESURIER, George, in Nfld. 1871 (Lovell)
LE MESURIER, George, in Twillingate, Nfld. before 1871 (Seary)
LE MESURIER, Pierre, noted in Gaspe?
LE MESURIER, Alfred and Henry of Barachois, Que., curr. Some of this fam from Alderney to Gaspe. (GLF)
LE MESURIER, Mary, of Gaspe, mar 1. John LE HUQUET, qv, and 2. John Domelle?
LE MESURIER, C.I. name assoc with the Robin firm in Paspebiac, Gaspe, and with the town of New Carlisle, Que. (Que. Arch.)
LE MESURIER, John, in the Gaspe Militia 1850s (MacWhirter)
LE MESURIER, Jack, from J to Gaspe ca 1900 or before
LE MESURIER, ---, mar Col. Clifford of the Royal Artillery, stationed at that time in Canada, ca 1873, or before. (La Moine, MAPLE LEAVES, Que., 1873)
LE MESURIER, Daniel, b G?, mar Elizabeth Maria LANGLOIS, qv, dau of Thomas L. and Marguerite FERBRACHE. Res Hamilton, Ont.
LE MESURIER, bros and sisters, from C.I. family:
I. LE MESURIER, Peveril Charles Kincaid, b 1912 India , son of Charles Andrew LE M and Clarice Evelyn Bridgnell of England and India. Mar Helen Eddie of Windsor, Ont.
A1. Carolyn Anne, b 1948 Toronto, mar 1974 Calgary, Alta.
A2. Cleveland Peveril, b 1954 Markham, Ont., mar 1976 Calgary, Alta.
II. LE MESURIER, Joyce Ethel, b 1915 India, mar 1945 Francis Kuit Randles of Sydney, Australia
A1. Frances Evelyn, b 1949 NSW Aust., mar Anthony Vickers, res Syndey, Aust.
A2. Elizabeth Joyce, b 1951 Aust., mar Rodney ---, res London, Eng.
III. LE MESURIER, Denise Margaret, b 1918 India, mar 1940 Twonbey Morris, b England, res Notts, England
A1. James Edward Morris, b 1945   A2. Jonathan Charles Morris, b 1948
IV. LE MESURIER, Cleve Arthur, b 1919 Eng., mar in Australia 1951, Alice Doreen Moore of Sydney, b 1928, rem to Canada 1957
A1. Andrew Arthur, b 1952 Geelong, Aust.
A2. Simon Christopher, b 1952, twin, res Calgary, Alta.
A3. Jacqueline, b 1956, Perth, Aust., res Weston, Ont.
A4. Kim, b 1957, Peterborough, Ont., res Toronto, Ont.
LE MOAL, from G to Western Canada, poss Winnepeg, MAN?
LE MOIGNAN, Pierre, b 1816 St. John, J, bp Angl Ch there, son of Amice Le M. and Marie LE ROSSIGNOL. To Canada ca age 14 to work for Robin firm. Carpenter, ship bldr. Converted to R.C. and mar at Grande Riviere 1837 Salome Dupuis, dau of Germain D. and Louise Bloid. Peter was Mayor of Gr. Riv. in 1866. He d 1907, age 90, and Salome in 1908. (A fine genealogy of this fam both in Canada and Jersey, by the Rev. J. Michel LE MOIGNAN, of Gaspe, Quebec, 1972, gives a great deal more information on this family.)
A1. Louise, b 1838 Gr. Riv., mar Napoleon Bernard 1860
B1. Edward Napoleon, b 1861, at Maria, Gaspe, d 1871
A2. Philippe, b 1840, mar Jane BAKER, dau of Hugh B. and Elizabeth TRACHY, qv, at Cap d'Espoir 1871. Ten chn.

    B1. Edward Amice, b 1871
    B2. Philippe, b 1873
    B3. Malvina, b 1875
    B4. Pierre Louise, b 1877
    B5. Jean Abraham, b 1879,
        d 1901
    B6. Joseph B., b 1881, mar Clara Gasseault
    B7. Marie Louise, b 1883, worked in Quebec, Montreal
    B8. Jean Vincent, b 1886, mar Bridget Sullivan
    B9. Jean Francois, b 1888, mar Ellen Sullivan
    B10. Salome, b 1891, mar 1. Francis Shannon. See bottom of page.
A3. Jean Baptiste, b 1841, Grand Pabos, mar Elizabeth NICHOLAS, dau of Charles
    B1. Charles   B4. Joseph   B7. Marie Anne
    B2. Baptiste   B5. Peter   B8. Adelaide
    B3. Octavie   B6. Marie Louise   B9. Salome
A4. Olive, b 1843, mar 1. James Morris 1863 and 2. John Johnson. 11 chn by No. 2, in Maine.
    B1. Peter James Morris, rem to Canton, NY, mar Emilia Plants in 1889, 3 daus
A5. Esther, b 1846, mar Moise Gauthier, 1871, res Grand Riv., 7 chn
    B1. Aurelie   B3. Laura   B5. Edmont   B7. Leda
    B2. Hermine   B4. Georges   B6. Adolphe
A6. Sylvain, b 1847, d 1875
A7. Marie, b 1848 Gr. Riv. Mar Francis Philip Maret JANDRON, qv, and returned to J where she d 1932, age 82. Jandron d 1934, age 83.
A8. Jeanne, Jane, b 1851, d 1941. Mar 1877 at Gr. Riviere, Narcisse Lapierre, rem to Canton, NY with chn, celebrated 70th wedding anniversary!
    B1. Eva   B3. Harry   B5. Mabel   B7. Frank
    B2. Marie   B4. George   B6. Louise   B8. Violet
A9. Peter, b 1853, farmer and sailor. Mar Aurelie BAKER, dau of Hugh B. and Elizabeth TRACHY, qv at Cap d'Espoir 1875. Peter d 1942 at Gr. Riv. His wife d 1902, 7 chn.
    B1. Joseph   B3. Joseph, again   B5. Narcisse
    B2. Louise   B4. Arthur   B6. Marie
A10. Salome, b 1856, d 1863
A11. Francois, b 1858, d at age 16
A12. Amice Joseph Antoine, b 1861, mar Rose Peloquin, and rem to Duluth, Minn. 4 chn, including a son Arthur, grandchildren also.
LE MOIGNAN, Amice, Capt., b 1831, mar Jane LE MAISTRE, sailed for Robin firm to Medit.
LE MOIGNAN, John Philip, b 1884 G, mar Dora LE BRUN, of St. Ouen, J, rem to Victoria, BC, 1912, d 1963. He was the son of John Le M. and Louisa Jane FEREY, mar 1881. (Rev. Le Moignan)
LE MOIGNAN, Charles, master mariner, b 1814 St. John, J, son of Amice Le M. and Suzanne LE MAISTRE, mar Anne HOCQUARD. They d in St. Mary, J 1879. He prob worked for the Robin firm in Gaspe between the years 1834 and 1853. (Rev. Le Moignan)
A1. Philip, b 1943, carpenter, d unmar 1932
A2. Charles Jr., b 1846, d 1963
A3. Caroline Jane, b 1848, mar William John Germain of Grouville, J 1879
A4. Anne, b 1849, mar George PICOT of Trinity, J 1869, d 1920
A5. Jane Denize?, b 1853, mar Richard Gould Gallaway
LE MOIGNAN, Canon Alfred Stanley, b 1894 St. Mary, J, to Gaspe 1910 to work for Robin firm, also worked in Labrador. D 1953 in New Carlisle, Que. where he was rector of St. Andrews Anglican. (Le Moignan)
LE MOIGNAN, Salome, poss dau of Jean Baptiste?, b 1891, d 1968, mar 1. Frank Shannon, and 2. Louis Zenon LE LIEVRE, widower of Lisa Ann

LE MOIGNAN

LE MORVAN, SAID TO BE FROM CI TO MANITOBA, CANADA.
Driscoll, Petit Riv., Gaspe (Brochet)
LE MOIGNE, also as LE MOINE, curr Gaspe
LE MOINE, a Channel Island fam settled at Channel Nfld. (Shortis-Munn)
LE MOINE, on S. coast of Nfld. (G.W. Le Messurier). John in Lower Burgeo 1842. (Seary)
LE MOINE, sometimes changed to MONK
LE MONNIER, from C.I. to Canada?
LE MONTAIS, John, b J of fishery firm at Pt. St. Peter, Que., ca 1800. (Innis; J.H. Le Breton list)
LE MONTAIS, see also QAAM
LE MONTAIS, Philip, owned the SWALLOW, 62 tons, built at Cheticamp, CB 1888, later transferred to J in 1910. (Capt. Parker)
LE MOTTEE, Herbert Durand, b J?, Col. in the Med. Serv. India, mar Clara DE LISLE, qv, b St. Peter Port, G, 3 chn (Catherine Salter, Vict., BC)
- A1. Caroline, b 1891 India?, mar Evan Maberly Byrde, b Celon 1878
  - B1. Ella Mary Bryde, b Ceylon 1914, mar Robert Spiers
    - C1. Elspeth Speers, b 1947 Kenya
    - C2. Jean Speers, b 1949 Kenya
  - B2. Charles Maberly De Lisle Byrde, b Ceylon 1915
    - C1. Evan Byrde, b 1946 Paris, France   C3. Pauline Byrde, b 1951
    - C2. Maurice Byrde, b 1947 Paris, d 1957   Paris
  - B3. Major Henry Evan Byrde, b 1917 Ceylon, d 1957, mar Sheila Christie
    - C1. Penelope Byrde, b 1948 Wales
    - C2. Prudence Byrde, b 1951 Wales
  - B4. Catherine Galira? Byrde, b 1918 Ceylon, mar 1943 England, Wm. John SALTER, b 1910 Toronto, d 1972. Res Westmount, Que., Ottawa 1950, Aylmer, Que., then to BC 1974.
    - C1. Carolynne Salter, b 1944 London, Eng.
    - C2. Melodie Ann Salter, b 1948 Montreal
    - C3. William Peter George Salter, b 1950 Ottawa
    - C4. Gillian Clare Salter, b 1956 Ottawa
    - C5. Rosemary Kim Salter, b 1956 Ottawa
  - B5. Michael Herbert Durand Byrde, b 1926 Guernsey, mar Ann ---
    - C1. Lisa Byrde, b 1952, adopted   C2. Vanessa Byrde, b 1954
- A2. Olive LE MOTTEE, b 1893 India?, mar Lancelot FEARON
  - B1. Hope Fearon, b 1927 Oxford, Eng.
- A3. Herbert, b ca 1895 India?, d.y.

LE MOTTEE, from C.I. to Ontario, Western Canada and B.C.
LE MOTTEE, in Annapolis Royal, NS. Cf MOTT who was MLA in NS 1800s.
LE MOTTEE, from C.I. to Gaspe   (J.H. Le Breton list)
LE MOTTEE, James from J?, to Gaspe, mar Emelie POINGDESTRE. He was b ca 1844. (M.W. Le Mottee, Willowdale, Ont.)
- A1. Adolphus, b J?
- A2. Alice Emelie, b 1875 St. Mary, J, mar J.F. LE COCQ, qv, d 1950, bur Malbaie, Gaspe (GLF)
  - B1. Amelia, b ca 1895, mar Alfred LE COCQ, a cousin, d age 24 (GLF)
  - B2. Morris John, b 1903, d 1961
- A3. Laura LE MOTTEE, b ca 1884 J, mar George Irwin, d 1911 age 27, bur St. Peters, Malbaie

LE MOUSTRE, Thomas, age 23, b J, in Bon. 1871
LEMPRIERE, information in Soc. Jers. Bulls. 1915-1918. Library of Congress has LEMPRIERE GENEALOGY, #10368.
LEMPRIERE, W.C., b J, mar Agnes LE NEVEU, qv. At least 5 chn, one at least to Canada. This was prob. Walter Charles.
- I. William ?   II. Marjorie
- III. Guy, mar in J, a son in Ireland, a dau in Scotland.

    IV. Beatrice   V. Victor Frederick, who d 1950
    A1. John, b 1931, res Vancouver, BC, mar Jean Stewart
       B1. Julie, b 1956   B3. Shirley Jayne, b 1961
       B2. Christine Ann, b 1959   B4. David, b 1963
    A2. Brian Michael, b 1932, mar Shirley Cherie Curward?, res Seattle,
        Wash.
       B1. Evelyn Diane, b 1958   B2. Michael Edward, b 1960
LEMPRIERE, John Philip, b ca 1888 St. Mary, J, son of George L., mar
    Eva HUBERT. She rem to Canada 1917, while J.P. in Edmonton 1914
    served in WWI, returned to Canada 1919. Shoemaker, retired 1951, d
    1954. Eva d 1964, almost 84 yrs., bur Edmonton, Alta. (G. Lempriere,
    Rexdale, Ont.)
    A1. Jack, b 1908 J, res Calgary, Alta., mar Nellie ---, no issue
    A2. Bernard, b ca 1911 J, res Edmonton, Alta., mar Joyce Carpenter 1934,
        divorced, 2 chn. Joyce remar ---Metcalfe, chn adopted named Met-
        calfe. Bernard mar 2. Betty, no issue, res Edmonton, Alta.
       B1. Dale, b ca 1935   B2. Cara Lee, b ca 1937
    A3. George Hubert, b 1920 Edmonton, mar Rosemary Dionne, air traffic
        controller, served with R.C.A.F.
       B1. Patricia Anne, b 1945, mar Robert Robichaud
          C1. Michelle Patricia Robichaud, b 1972
          C2. Danielle Catherine Robichaud, b 1974
       B2. Brian Philip, b 1947, mar Christine Swanek
          C1. Stephanie, b 1972   C2. ---, b 1976
       B3. Catherine Mary, b 1949, res Rexdale, Ont.
    Note: Two stepdaughters of this fam also came to Canada and settled
           in Calif.
    A4. Irene Gladys FALLU, mar ---Knowles
    A5. Monica Maude FALLU, mar ---Voss
LEMPRIERE, Capt. from J to Nfld. (K. Mathews)
LEMPRIERE, in the Nfld. trade by 1717 (C.R. Fay)
LEMPRIERE, Charles Philip, b 1807 J, son of Philip L. and Marie ESNOUF,
    qv, rem to Canada
LEMPRIERE, Abraham George, b 1836 J, son of above Charles Philip, and of
    Rachel Ann GAUDIN, qv. Unmar. (Raoul Lempriere, Jersey)
LEMPRIERE, Dr. W.W., res Australia, current
LEMPRIERE, ---, mar Peter CAMIOT, qv, of Paspebiac. She d 1914.
LEMPRIERE, Annie May, b 1886 J, mar John M. BUESNEL, qv, rem to Ontario.
    7 chn.
LEMPRIERE, to Australia, Daniel Matthew, b ca 1830, John Daniel and
    Charles William
LE NEVEU, Godfrey, b ca 1855 J, son of Rev. Thomas L. (1882-1902), of
    St. Martin, J, and wife Anne Godfrey of Le Hocq House, who d 1862.
    At least 7 chn. Godfrey rem to Vancouver, BC 1886. (Harold Le Neveu,
    W. Vancouver, BC: Guy Lempriere, Jersey)
    I. Henry Godfrey, mar, Rector of Tavistock, Eng., 1915, one dau
    II. Herbert Godfrey, res J, unmar   III. Hannah, d.y.
    IV. Arthur Godfrey, b J, to Canada 1886, d 1946, 3 sons
    A1. Allan
       B1. Arthur, res Ottawa, Ont., one son, two daus
       B2. Ronald, res Toronto, one son, one dau
    A2. Donald   A3. Harold, res W. Vancouver, BC, a son, Gordon
    V. Agnes, mar J. LEMPRIERE, qv, 5 chn   VI. Lucy   VII. Lilly
LE NEVEU, Thomas, related to Rev. Thomas, above, rem to Victoria, BC
    1850, mar ?, dau mar ---Dumbleton in BC. A son d in Duncan, BC.
LE NEVEU, David, b J, mar 1867 Victoria, BC an Englishwoman, who d 1880.

He had arr in Calif in a yacht 1851, rem to BC 1858, had a large business there and sev chn. (THE COLONIST, Jan. 9, 1955; Philip Luce, Vancouver, BC)

LE NEVEU, to Gaspe, Toronto and to Manitoba

LENFESTEY, LENFESTY, LENFEST, L'ENFETE, L'AFETE, etc. This fam in Canada consists of the desc of several persons, families and groups of this surname, coming from Guernsey Island. The following are known to be emigrants from the Island to Canada and the U.S. There were perhaps several others also, this being a very vigorous line. Information below on the first family is based on a chart by Edmund Lenfestey of G, with additional data from the Census of 1861, Gaspe, and the records of J.L. Jenkins, New Westmister Bay, BC. (Other data from Aldo Brochet; Claudette Maroldo, Cherry Hill, NJ: Cent. Bklt.; Frances Parry, Port Alberni, BC: Chadwick's ONTARIAN FAMILIES; Pat Vibert, Burnaby, BC: Lenfestey Genealogies, Library of Congress; GLF; Gaspe Petition; LENFESTEY GENEALOGY, by Fred. Priaulx and Bertram Augustus Lenfestey, based on C.I. records) SEE ADDED PAGES.

LENFESTEY, James, b 1745 G, Le Pomare Branch, son of Pierre L., b 1694 and Elizabeth ROBILLIARD, qv. He mar Judith PAINT, qv. James was the first cousin of Pierre L. who emigrated to Maine, US. See QAAM. James and Judith had at least 3 sons: Jean, James and Nicholas, and poss some daus.
I. Jean, b 1777, mar Elizabeth PAINT, of Torteval, G
  A1. Jean, b 1807, to USA or Canada
    B1. John, his son or grandson?, b 1868 Que., rem to Mt. Clemens, Mich.
      C1. James, to US, had son, Frederick J. C2. Frederick, to US
      C3. John, to US
        D1. Gladys, mar J. Lathmer
        E1. John K. Lathmer, curr Prof., Columbia Univ., N.Y.

LENFESTEY, James, b 1786 G, d 1865 Perce, Gaspe, bur St. Paul's Ang. Ch., Perce. Mar Susanne MAUGER Dobson, a widow, b 1784 Perce, d 1876. See MAUGER fam. James may be a part of above Jean LENFESTEY family.
  A1. James, b 1807, d 1862, mar Elizabeth Ferguson, b 1817 Perce, Gaspe
    B1. James, b 1835 Perce, mar 1860 Sara Cass, 1835-1878, and 2. ---
      LUCAS. (No issue with second wife.)
      C1. Eliza, Elizabeth?, b 1860 Perce, mar James TOSTEVIN, Jr., 1861-1926. She d 1951, both bur St. James Angl. Ch. 9 chn, see TOSTEVIN.
      C2. Laura, mar Robert C. LORD of Montreal
        D1. Arthur James Lord, 1889-1890   D4. Reginald Lord
        D2. Mabel Lord   D5. Emily Lord
        D3. Percy Lord   D6. Eva Lord
      C3. Harold   C4. Frederick
      C5. Robert James, b 1868 Cape Cove, mar Emma Mahan 1897, 1870-195-. He d 1930, bur St. James, Cape Cove, Gaspe.
        D1. Edith May, b 1899 Cape Cove   D3. Allan Ernest, b 1904, bur
        D2. Sarah Hilda, b 1902   1933 St. James, Cape Cove
      C6. Elias Daniel, b 1872, mar 1. Emily Mahan, 1876-1909, dau of James M. of Perce. He mar 2. Ida Ethel LE GRESLEY ca 1912.
        D1. Sarah Isabelle, b 1914 Cape Cove
        D2. Ethel, b 1915, mar Sydney Lorne Cass, son of Minnie Alicia Lenfestey and Elias Cass
        D3. Cora Emily, b 1917
        D4. Francis James, b 1919 Cape Cove, killed WWII 1944
    B2. Susanne, b 1836 Perce
    B3. Judea, b 1838, mar James Cass 1860. (b 1831 Perce)
      C1. James Elihu Cass, b 1861 Perce

B4. Thomas, b 1840 Perce, mar Elizabeth Rebecca Cass, 1839-1913. He was a farmer, d 1916, bur St. James Ang. Ch, Cape Cove.
  C1. Euphemia, b 1868, unmar
  C2. Minnie Alicia, b 1871 Perce, mar Elias Cass
    D1. Ernest Reginald Cass, b 1900   D2. Lewis Philip Cass, b 1903
    D3. Sydney Lorene Cass, b 1907, Cape Cove, mar Ethel Lenfestey, 2nd cousin, d 1973, bur St. James, Cape Cove, Gaspe
  C3. James Elihu, b 1875 Cape Cove
  C4. Henry Allen, b 1878, mar Lilian Eliza Du Val in 1903, 2nd cousin, 1879-1975, dau of Susan E.L. and Peter John DU VAL. Henry d 1955.
    D1. Muriel Blanche, b 1906 D4. Russell Elihu, b 1910, res Gascons
    D2. Charles Ford, b 1907   D5. Phyllis Rena, b 1917 Cape Cove
    D3. Viola May, b 1908   D6. Gerald Gordon, mar, chn.
B5. Mary, b 1843, mar Arthur Cass, a planter
  C1. Claudius Merrin Cass, b 1875 C3. John Elihu Cass, b 1880
  C2. Edward Joseph Cass, b 1878   C4. Philip Cass, b 1882
B6. John A., b 1845 Perce, mar Elizabeth BAKER 1878
  C1. John James, b 1878 Cape Cove
B7. Martha, b 1847 Perce, mar Daniel DUMARESQ, 1st cousin, a merchant, son of Daniel D.   5 chn, see DUMARESQ.
B8. Liza, Eliza Ann, b 1850 Perce, mar Edward Mabe of Corner of the Beach 1880, a farmer
B9. Andrew, b 1851 Perce   B10. Peter, b 1852 Perce, d 1857
B11. Philip, b 1856 Perce, res Minn.
B12. Adelaide L., b 1862 Perce, d unmar
A2. Rachel, b 1810 Perce
A3. Abraham, b 1812 Perce, d 1893 Red Head, near Perce. Mar Mary Bragg, b 1810 Devon, England, d 1888 L'Anse au Beaufils, bur St. Paul's Ch, Perce, Gaspe.
  B1. Abraham, b 1838 Perce, mar Mary Ann McDonald, 1849-1922. He d 1915, bur St. Paul's.
    C1. Emily, b 1874, mar ---Bunton, d 1933
    C2. Wm. Donald Barnabas, b 1876 Perce, mar Margaret Fanny Barners 1906, 5 chn. Joined the Gold Rust of 1898, traveled up the famed Chilkootin Pass, and knew some of the celebrities of the time such as Diamond Lil. Donald d 1953, Margaret in 1972.
      D1. Ida Margaret, b 1908 Vancouver, mar Stanley Everett Weismiller, 1893-1956, in 1926
        E1. Kenneth Stanley Weismiller, b 1928 Vancouver, mar Sue De Long, 1952
          F1. Suzanne Winnifred Weismiller, b 1952 Victoria, BC, mar Robert Meyers, 1977
          F2. William Stanley Weismiller, b 1956 Victoria
          F3. Paul Ronald Weismiller, b 1959 Victoria
          F4. Miriam Ida Weismiller, b 1961 Victoria
        E2. Grant Emerson Weismiller, b 1930, New Westminster, BC, mar Shirley Cammiade 1953, divorced, mar Wilhelmena Vander-byle 1957
          F1. Stanley Emerson Weismiller, b 1958 Victoria
          F2. Carol Anne Weismiller, b 1959
          F3. Norman David Weismiller, b 1960
          F4. Glen Allen Weismiller, b 1962
          F5. Michael Martin Weismiller, b 1964
        E3. Doreen Margaret Weismiller, b 1931 New Westminster, BC, mar Carlton Luther Whitaker, Vict., BC 1958
          F1. Robert David Whitaker, b 1960 Chicago, Ill.

F2. Raymond Luther Whitaker, b 1962 Morocco
F3. Mark Leine Whitaker, b 1964 Morocco
F4. Brent Whitaker, b 1966 Victoria, BC
E4. William John Weismiller, b 1934, d 1938 Duncan, BC
E5. Douglas Norman Weismiller, b 1937 Duncan, BC, mar 1. Johanna McNair 1955 in Victoria, BC, divorced, mar 2. Joyce Holland
F1. Marie Ann Weismiller, b 1958 Victoria, BC
F2. Douglas John Weismiller, b 1960 Victoria, BC
E6. David Roy Weismiller, b 1943, mar Sharon Williams 1965, Vancouver, BC
F1. Sylvia Janine Weismiller, b 1966 Vancouver, BC
D2. Donald William Lenfesty, b 1909, mar Leona Hatch, d 1976
E1. Shirley
D3. George Bertram, b 1910, mar Viola Ardath Anderson 1937, d 1947
D4. Frances Mabel Kathleen, b 1913, mar Harry Melvin, Robert, Parry 1940
E1. Marilyn Joanne Parry, b 1942 N. Vancouver, BC
E2. Dianne Carol Parry, b 1943, mar 1964 Michael Gerald Bullock
F1. Tara Michele Bullock, b 1969
F2. Todd Michael Bullock, b 1971
E3. George Henry Parry, b 1947
D5. Roy Edwin, b 1918, mar Patricia Shirley, divorced
C3. Mary Ida, b 1884 Perce, mar Charles William Ferguson 1874. He d 1951, she d 1964, bur Perce.
B2. James, b 1840 Perce, d 1919 L'Anse au Beaufils, mar Charlotte Dobson, 1837-1913. He was a farmer, bur St. James, Cape Cove.
C1. John, b 1875, mar Elizabeth Susan DU VAL of Bonaventure Is., 1898. A farmer.
D1. Doris Grace, b 1901 D2. ---, mar Wm. Divens, res Montreal
C2. Susan Mary, b 1876 Perce, d 1877
B3. Elizabeth Mary, b 1842 Perce, d 1867
B4. John Peter, b 1844 Perce, Gaspe, mar Emily Erickson 1882, changed name to Linfesty, res Highland, Calif, in charge of 40 acres of orange groves for L.C. White. He d 1928, she 1858-1913, bur San Bernardino, Claif.
C1. William Linfesty, b 1882 Calif
C2. John Howard Linfesty, b 1884, d 1928, bur San Bernardino, Calif
C3. Charles Linfesty, b 1887, mar 1. Laura ---, 3 chn, div and rem to Wash. ca 1925. Mar 2. Florence ---. Laura d 1965, bur San Bernardino, Calif
D1. Eric Linfesty, b 1911, architect in Ariz. or N.M.
D2. Lorraine Linfesty, b 1913, mar Les. Salm, fire chief at Lake Arrowhead, Calif
D3. Marguerite Linfesty, b 1915   D4. dau by second wife
C4. Fred Linfesty, b 1888, mar Maude ---, d 1966, bur San Bern., Calif
C5. Harry Linfesty, b 1890, mar Emma ---, who d 1961. He was cremated, ashes to sea, 1973?
D1. Loretta, nurse in northern Calif
D2. Harry Linfesty, Jr.   3. ch, d 1922, bur San Bernardino
C6. Lyman Linfesty, b 1895, mar Zona, both d 1942
C7. Milton Linfesty
C8. Martha, Mattie Linfesty, b 1892, mar Bob Bromilow, both d 1960s
D1. Barbara Bromilow, res Arizona, 5 chn
C9. Milton, b 1897
C10. Ralph Linfesty, b after 1900, mar 2. Janie---, 1905-1974, bur

San Bernardino
- D1. Ralph Linfesty Jr., mar Barbara ---div, mar 2. Linda ---
  - E1. John, d 1975
  - E2. dau, b ca 1959   E3. dau, b ca 1961
  - E4. Ralph Linfesty III, res San Bernardino, Calif, has a son
- B4. John Peter, b 1844 Perce
- B5. William, b 1847 Perce, a farmer, mar Margaret McDonald, d 1901 L'Anse au Beaufils
  - C1. William Allen, b 1880 Red Head
  - C2. John Cameron, b 1881, mar Annie Marie Ferguson, who d 1935, in 1904 Perce. He d 1945 Vancouver, BC
    - D1. Ida Lillian, b 1905 Perce   D2. Winnifred, b 1906
    - D3. Violet Helen, b 1907, mar ---Stewart
    - D4. Allan Reginald, b 1910 L'Anse au Beaufils, Gaspe, mar Marian ---
    - D5. Cameron Joseph, b 1911
    - D6. John Cameron, b 1912, mar Ethel Nancy Barnes, d 1955 Vancouver, BC. She was b 1913 Todber, Dorset, Eng., dau of Alfred B. and Annie Violet Goodwin.
      - E1. Charles Cameron, b 1941 Vancouver, mar Marjorie Ruth Harvey, 1963. She was b 1941.
        - F1. Jason Cameron, b 1964 Vancouver, BC
        - F2. Kurt Darnell, b 1966
        - F3. Evan Morgan, b 1969 Bella Bella, BC
        - F4. Omar Hunter, b 1969 Bella Bella, BC
        - F5. Azure Lota Nanci, b 1972 Korea, adopted?
    - D7. Charles   D9. Grant, res Calendar, Ont.
    - D8. Harold   D10. Gordon, mar Edna ---?
  - C3. Mary Ellen, b 1883 Perce, mar 1903 Thomas Hugh Mahan, 1871-1950. Mary Ellen d same day, 1950.
    - D1. Wilbur Ernest Mahan, b 1904
    - D2. Bertha Lenfesty Mahan, b 1907 L'Anse au Beaufils
    - D3. Mary Margaret Mahan, b 1912
    - D4. James Ralph Mahan, b 1914, killed WWII, 1944
  - C4. James Abraham, b 1885 Red Head, Perce
  - C5. Frederic, b 1887, mar 2nd cousin, Sarah Eliza TOSTEVIN, dau of Eliz. Lenfestey and James TOSTEVIN, 1917, Cape Cove
  - C6. Ernest McDonald, b 1890 Red Head, Perce
  - C7. Grant, b 1892 Perce
- B6. Ann, b 1849 Perce
- B7. Mary Susan, b 1852 Perce, mar John McDonald of Port Daniel, Bona. Co., Que. 1876
- A4. Charles, b 1814 Perce, mar ca 1841 Susan ---, b 1817 Perce. He d Perce 1881, fisherman and farmer.
  - B1. James Philip, b 1842 Perce, mar Annie Ferguson of Cape Cove 1880. Rem 1882-3 to Eau Claire, Wisc., rem 1899 to Hoquiam, Wash.
    - C1. Wilfred Edmund, b 1881 Irishtown, Perce, d Eau Claire, Wisc. as child
    - C2. Charles Thomas, b 1884 Eau Claire, d.y.
    - C3. Susan A., b 1886 Eau Claire   C4. Myrtle, b 1889 Eau Claire
    - C5. Irving James, b 1893, d 1897, bur Eau Claire, with the other chn
    - C6. another ch, d.y.
  - B2. Thomas, b 1844 Perce   B3. Elizabeth, b 1847
  - B4. Susan, b 1849 Perce, mar George Summerhayes of Irishtown, Perce, a widower in 188s
    - C1. Susan Diana Summerhayes, b 1883

B5. Abraham, b 1851 Perce, d 1899 Eau Claire, Wisc., unmar
B6. William, b 1853 Perce
B7. Judith, b 1856 Perce, mar Mark Moir of Red Head 1881, b 1854, son of Robert and Margaret Moir of Scotland, and Perce
 C1. William Alexander Moir, b 1882 Red Head
 C2. Susan Ethel Moir, b 1883
A5. Thomas, b 1817 Perce, d 1896 Whitehead, Perce, mar ca 1845 Ann ---, b 1821 Perce
 B1. Thomas, b 1846 Perce, d 1875 Red Head
 B2. Martha, b 1848 Perce, d 1896, unmar
 B3. Philip, b 1850, mar Marthe TOSTEVIN, qv, 1863-1920, in 1886, dau of John T. and Eliza Collin of Cape Cove. He d 1928, bur St. Paul's
  C1. Susan, b 1886, d 1890 Red Head, Perce
  C2. Eliza Jane, b 1888
  C3. Jania, bur St. Paul's, Perce, with parents
 B4. Mary Jane, b 1853 Perce, d 1875
 B5. Alfido, b 1857 Perce. (An Alfred L. of Whitehead mar Rachel TOSTEVIN, 1898)
 B6. Elias, b 1860 Perce, d 1895, fell off a cliff at Perce
A6. Elizabeth, b 1819 Perce, d 1907 Cape Cove, bur St. Paul's Angl., Perce. Mar Philip Hacquoil, carpenter, b 1813 J, d 1871 Perce. SEE HARQUOIL.
A7. Peter, b 1821 Perce, d there 1877, mar 1844 Margaret Bragg, b 1825 England, d 1888 Eau Claire, Wisc., dau of Wm. and Eliz. Bragg.
 B1. Susan Elizabeth, b 1845 Perce, mar Peter John Eusebius DU VAL, 1843-1929, of Bonaventure Island in 1869, son of Pierre Nicolas and Anne. Peter John mar 2. in spring of 1903, Catherine McNeil, 1842-1914?, dau of Roderick McNeil. See DU VAL and Henry Allen LENFESTEY.
 B2. Emily Jane, b 1848 Perce, mar John Scott 1880 Perce
 B3. Peter James, b 1850 Perce, mar Mary Jane Slaughter, 1860-1952, 1878 in Eau Claire, Wisconsin, dau of Stokely and Henrietta Beckwith Slaughter. To Wisc. 1870, d 1931 Eau Claire.
  C1. Elizabeth Mary, b 1878, mar John Mooney in Eau Claire, bp R.C., St. Patrick's
   D1. Lavern Thomas Mooney, res St. Paul's, Minn., mar twice
    E1. Thomas, has two sons, Michael and Thomas Mooney
   D2. Mary Mooney, dau from second mar, mar --- Loftgren
  C2. George J., b 1880 Eau Claire, mar Mary Whitman, b Germany, d 1942
   D1. Peter Joseph, b 1901, d 1933, unmar
   D2. Margaret, b 1902 Superior, Wisc., mar Clarence Shurr, no issue
   D3. Evelyn Mary, b 1908 Superior, mar 1. John S. Lewis 1927, and 2. Iler Jensen in 1950. No issue by second mar. He d 1972 Wisc.
    E1. John R. Lewis, b 1927, d 1948, auto accident
    E2. Robert E. Lewis, mar Jean Sheridan
     F1. Cathy Lewis, mar Robert Sollom, 2 sons, Hugh and Clare
     F2. John Lewis, mar Nancy Saunders, 3 sons, John, Robert, and William Lewis
     F3. Martin Lewis   F5. Patricia Lewis
     F4. Mary Jo Lewis, mar John Keikken   F6. Laurie Lewis
   D4. Lavern G. Lenfestey, mar, no issue, res Milwaukee, Wisc.
  C3. Minnie, Amelia, Jane, b 1881 Eau Claire, mar Charles Botsford, RR conductor, res Long Beach, Calif
   D1. Mildred Ruth Botsford, b 1902 Altoona, Wisc, mar --- Smith

D2. Phyllis Jean Botsford, b 1906   D5. George Botsford
D3. Geraldine Lucille Botsford, b 1910
D4. Charles Jones Botsford, b 1913 Altoona, Wisc.
C4. Ida May Lenfestey, b 1883, Eau Claire, mar Edward L. Holden, 1880-1950, son of John P. Holden, worked in paper mill. She d 1933. See LATE ADDITIONS AND CORRECTIONS pages.
  D1. Ralph Benjamin Holden, b 1907, mar Ione C. ---, d 1969 of Leukemia
  D2. Robert John Holden, b 1907, twin
C5. Ethel Victoria, b 1885, mar Hans Erickson, d 1976
  D1. Harold Emanuel Erickson, b 1908 Eau Claire, mar Mildred Kosmo, b 1908 in 1938. He d 1960
    E1. Stephen Harold Erickson, b 1946, mar Linda Nelson in Ogema, Wisc.
      F1. Stephanie Erickson, b 1971   F2. Mathew Erickson, b 1974
  D2. Paul Francis Erickson, b 1912, mar Thelma Christeson, b 1914, in 1939
    E1. David Erickson, b 1941, mar Janice Robinson 1961
      F1. Brenda Joy Erickson, b 1962
      F2. Kim Marie Erickson, b 1966
    E2. Donald E. Erickson, b 1941, twin, mar Susan O'Donahue 1974
      F1. Brian Douglas Erickson, b 1975
    E3. Diane Marie Erickson, mar Daniel Campbell, b 1948
      F1. Sandra Jean Campbell, b 1971
      F2. Cynthia Lynn Campbell, b 1973
  D3. Marian Vivian Erickson, b 1921, mar Eugene Merritt Morse, b 1918 in 1941
    E1. Eugene Pierre Morse, b 1946, mar Julie Thur 1974
      F1. Heidi Jeanne Morse, b 1975
    E2. Marilynn Kay Morse, b 1949 Eau Claire, Wisc.
C6. Irvine, b 1888, d.y.
C7. Benjamin Clark, b 1889 Eau Claire, mar 1909 Emily Mable Block, 1891-1957. He d 1960 Superior, Wisc.
  D1. Frederic Jerome, b 1910 Eau Claire, mar Mary Jane Arceneau 1939
    E1. Marie, b 1946 Superior, Wisc., res Oklahoma City, Okla.
  D2. Ramona Lucille, b 1911 Superior, mar 1. Clifford Christianson, divorced, mar 2. Lawrence Thomas Duret, b 1901. Mar 1939 Duluth, Minn.
    E1. Ramona Marie Christianson, b 1931 Superior, mar Blair Cadotte, divorced 1964, d 1969 Texas
      F1. Myrna Marie Cadotte, b 1950 Superior, Wisc., mar in Texas, d 1969 of diabetes
      F2. Stephen Blair Cadotte, b 1959 Superior
      F3. Paul Cadotte, b 1964 Superior
    E2. Jeanne Anne Duret, b 1939 Superior, mar John Glenn Jensen 1962, res West Carrollton, Ohio
      F1. Robert Thomas Jensen, b 1963 Kettering, Ohio
      F2. David John Jensen, b 1965 Kettering, Ohio
      F3. Michael Edward Jensen, b 1970
      F4. Valerie Ann Jensen, b 1974
    E3. Mary Catherine Duret, b 1943 Superior, Wisc.
    E4. Claudette Lucille Duret, b 1947 Superior, Wisc., mar Anthony Edward Maroldo, Jr., St. Anthony Cath. Ch, Superior, Wisc. 1969
      F1. Michelle Catherine Maroldo, b 1970 Camden, N.J.
      F2. Mark Anthony Maroldo, b 1972 Camden, N.J.

F3. Todd Lawrence Maroldo, b 1975 Camden, NJ
E5. Thomas Lawrence Duret, b 1948, d 1960 in car accident
E6. Joan Lee Duret, b 1954 Superior, Wisc.
D3. Clyde Lyman, b 1915 Superior, Wisc., mar Olive Sorenson
E1. Sandee, b 1939, mar Morris Carlson, St. Albans Episc. Ch, Superior
F1. Nickolas Carlson   F3. Jennifer Carlson, adopted
F2. Christopher Carlson
E2. Paul, b 1941, mar 1. Patricia Arness, divorced, 2 chn, and mar 2. Mary Smith in 1977 St. Paul, Minn.
F1. Camille   F2. Jennifer
E3. Jill, b 1943 Superior, mar Larry Stone 1961
F1. Cole Stone   F3. Craig Stone
F2. Cindy Stone   F4. Chad Stone
D4. William Benjamin, b 1918, killed by a train 1920
C8. Charles Louis, b 1891 Eau Claire, Wisc., mar Jennie Kristina Beata Johnson, 1899-1964, dau of Cornelius and Christina Lien Johnson of Norway. Mar 1915 Duluth, Minn., RR man, both bur Montecito, San Bernardino, Calif. He d there in 1967.

This fam complete, but omitted by request. 6 sons, 2 daus, mostly res in California.

C9. Mary Margaret, b 1893, Eau Claire, mar 1. Reuben Arthur Mooney, b 1893, son of James and Lydia Mill Mooney in 1915. He was killed by a train, she mar 2. Clifford McMahan, a farmer, b 1895.
D1. John Howard Mooney, b 1917 Ashland, Wisc.
D2. Clifford Jones McMahan, b 1919 Clear Creek, Wisc.
D3. Marjorie Jeane McMahan, b 1921, mar Frank Matz
D4. Dorothea Lucille McMahan, b 1922
D5. Bernice Irene McMahan, b 1924 Clear Creek, Wisc.
D6. Betty McMahan
C10. William John, b 1895, mar 1. Emilienne Moreau, div 1923, mar 2. Lydia Lissack 1925 in Eau Claire, Wisc., no issue, d 1976
C11. Edward Ralph, b 1898, mar Gertrude Marie Braun, b 1902 in 1923
D1. Edward Arthur, Bud, b 1923 Eau Claire, mar Arlene Marie Gort, b 1926 in 1945
E1. Larry Edward, b 1946, mar Lucy Anne Hunt, b 1948 in 1967
F1. Devin Edward, b 1968 Eau Claire
F2. Tammy Anne Lenfesty, b 1970
E2. Suzanne Marie, b 1947, mar Gordon Lavern Gullikson, b 1942 in 1967
F1. Timothy Gordon Gullikson, b 1970
F2. Mikel Edward Gullikson, b 1972
E3. Mary Jo, b 1954 Eau Claire
C12. Esther Henrietta, b 1901, mar Joseph Lahner, d 1975
D1. Mary Ann Lahner, mar Pat Shiels
E1. James Shiels, b 1941, mar Elizabeth Lambert
E2. Paul Shiels, b 1942   E3. Richard Shiels, b 1943
E4. Patricia Shiels, b 1946, mar Floyd Carr
E5. Kathleen Shiels, b 1948, mar Gary Larson
E6. Mark Shiels, b 1951   E7. Mary Shiels, b 1962
C13. Earl Thomas, b 1902, mar Alice Nora Johnson, div., mar 2. Ruth Mabel Bethanke
D1. Thomas Vernon, b 1917 Eau Claire
E1. Thomas Vernon, Jr., b 1945
F1. Thomas Vernon Lenfesty III, b 1975

  E2. Kenneth Allen, b 1948
   F1. Kenneth Allen Lenfesty, Jr., b 1968
  E3. Frank Earl, b 1950
   F1. Frank Earl Jr., b 1969 F2. Abraham Xavier, b 1975
  D2. Donald Norman, b 1924, d 1925 D4. John Norman, b 1928, d 1970
  D3. Mary Jane Isabelle, b 1925 D5. Gary James, b 1942 Eau Claire
 C14. Mildred Ruth, b 1906, d.y.
 B4. George Francis, b 1853 Perce, mar Lydia Cass 1880 Cape Cove
  C1. Emma Helen, b 1881 Eau Claire, Wisc.
 B5. Charles Moses, b 1858 Perce, mar Hannah Tilly 1885
  C1. Adelaide, b 1886 Eau Claire C2. John Albert, b 1889
  C3. Charles Lester, b 1891 Hoquiam, Wash., mar Ann Burrows in 1917
 B6. Eliza Harriet, b 1862 Perce, mar 1884 James G. Cooper, b 1862, son
  of Joseph Cooper and Sarah McFarland, to U.S. 1880
  C1. Lillian M. Cooper, b 1887 Eau Claire, Wisc.
  C2. Charles A. Cooper, b 1890 C6. another ch d.y.
  C3. James G. Cooper, b 1892 C5. Percy J. Cooper, b 1896
  C4. Hessie E. Cooper, b 1894, MORE DATA IN ADDED PAGES.
 B7. Maria Charlotte, b 1863 Perce, mar Philip John DUMARESQ, qv., b
  1860, 1st cousin
 B8. Frederick Thomas, b 1866 Perce, d 1915 Hoquiam, Wash., unmar,
  cigarette merchant, to U.S. 1880
 B9. Mary Ann, b 1868 Perce, unmar, d 1952 Hoquiam, Wash.
 B10. Julia Victoria, b 1871, mar ca 1888 James Tilly, who d ca 1892.
  Mar 2. 1892, William Clarence Pettit, b 1859 Missouri, son of
  Jonathan P. and Mahala Coolman of Missouri.
  C1. Adda Tilly, b 1889 Hoquiam, took name Pettit
  C2. Albert Tilly, b 1891, doctor in San Francisco
  C3. Minnie Pettit, b 1892, dau of first husband
  C4. Clarence Pettit, b 1893 Hoquiam, res San Pedro, Calif
  C5. George Pettit, b after 1900
A8. Mary, b 1823 Perce
A9. Martha, b 1825 Perce, mar Philip James VIBERT, qv, b J 1825. See
 VIBERT fam.
A10. Judith, b 1828 Perce, mar Daniel DUMARESQ, b J 1817. See DUMARESQ.
 B1. Philip J. Dumaresq, b 1860 Perce
III. Nicolas, b 1798 G, d 1878. Mar Marthe BLONDEL, qv, res St. Saviour,
 G. At least 6 chn. This chart unverified.
A1. Nicolas, d 1925 England
A2. James, mar Anna S. Thompson of Tampa, Fla.
 B1. George S., mar Lena ---
  C1. Elizabeth, b ca 1876, res Tampa, Fla. 1960s
A3. Jean, b G, rem to USA, res Detroit, Mich. ca 1874
 B1. William Nicholas, res 1927 Victoria, BC
  C1. John, Jack, res Brentwood Bay, BC
 B2. Barbara, b 1875, mar David Jenkins, res 1927 BC
  C1. John L. Jenkins, b 1904 Victoria, BC, mar Ethel Hassard, b 1906
   Enderby, BC
   D1. David John Jenkins, b 1938 Nelson, BC, mar Marlene Deitrick,
    2 sons
    E1. Reid Jenkins, b 1970 E2. Blake Jenkins, b 1973
  C2. Roy W. Jenkins, b 1906 Dawson, Yukon Terr., mar Rosabelle Lock-
   hart
   D1. dau?   D2. son, res Nanaimo, BC
A4. Louise, d.y.   A5. Pierre, d.y.
A6. Marthe, mar Nicholas DE LA MARE, qv, of St. Saviours, G
 B1. Nicholas DE LA MARE

LENFESTEY 381

C1. Nora DE LA MARE, mar Edmund DE LA RUE, res G?
  D1. Leonard DE LA RUE, has chn, res G?
  D2. John DE LA RUE, has chn, res G?
A related branch of this fam; Nicolas LENFESTEY, b 1808, mar Martha GALLIENNE, has desc in Calif and Wisc. Other distantly related fams settled in the early 1800s in Guernsey Co., Ohio, also related BLONDEL families. (QAAM; LENFEST and LENFESTEY GENEALOGIES, in Library of Congress, Nos. 10370 to 76; Petition of 1820; Cent. Bklt.; GLF; Syvret)
LENFESTEY, Hilary, b G, d 1903 age 94, bur Grand Greve, Gaspe. Wife, Judith, b G, d 1936. Another Judith Lenfestey was living in 1861, d 1886 (Census). 2 sons, Abraham and John. (GLF)
LENFESTEY, Charles and Lydia, b Gaspe, in 1861 census
LENFESTEY, Peter, d 1928, age 87, bur Grand Greve, Gaspe (GLF)
LENFESTEY, Syria C., d 1923, age 75, sister of Peter, above (GLF)
LENFESTEY, Elias Daniel, mar Emily Mahan, 1876-1909, bur Cape Cove, Gaspe (GLF) Poss mar later? Ida Ethel LE GRESLEY?, qv, 1873-1919, bur Cape Cove, Gaspe. (GLF)
LENFESTEY, Adelaide, b 1865 St. Paul, Minn, mar George Albert Keefer, and of the same fam, John mar Annie Cook. This fam res Ont. or Que.
LENFESTEY, Henry, b G, in Gaspe 1861 (Census)
LENFESTEY, Thomas, James and Abraham, had land grants in Perce, Gaspe 1856-1885
LENFESTEY, Dr. James Percy, b 1873 Strathroy, Ont., rem to Mich. 1891. A desc, James L., is said to be the 13th James L. in the fam line, res De Pere, Wisc. Res Penetanguishene, ONT, CANADA.
"Peter Lenfestey, 1821-1877, had 2 bros come down the St. Lawrence River from the Gaspe to the U.S., one founding a flour mill in the Chicago area." (Claudette Maroldo, Cherry Hill, N.J.)
LENFESTEY, curr Gascons, Que. and other parts of the Maritimes
LENFESTY, Frederick, mar Sara Eliza TOSTEVIN, qv, b 1891, d 1972. Frederick d at Perce, Gaspe, age 83.
LENFESTY, Mary Ellen, 1884-1950, mar Hugh Mahan, 1871-1950
LENFESTEY, Sarah Jane, mar 1897 John Henry BAKER, of Cape Cove. (C. Maroldo, Cherry Hill, N.J.)
A1. Winston James Baker, b 1900 Cape Cove   A3. Mildred Lenfestey Baker,
A2. John Henry Baker, b 1902   b 1905
LENFESTEY, Rachel, mar John CABOT, carpenter and mariner of Red Head, 1849-1913, mar 1886 Perce. 2 sons, see CABOT.
LENFESTEY, Elizabeth Mary, mar George LUCAS of Cape Cove 1903. 2 chn, see LUCAS.
LENFESTEY, Susan, mar 1906 Robert William Mahan, Perce, Gaspe
A1. Walter Raymond Mahan, b 1907 Red Head
A2. Annie Laura Mahan, b 1910 L'Anse au Beaufils
LENFESTEY, Henry and Herbert, both mentioned as witnesses in early 1900 records. (Claudette Maroldo, Cherry Hill, N.J.)
LENFESTEY, John, 1875-1939, poss b Gaspe, res Montreal, mar Susan Elizabeth DU VAL, qv, 1899. 2 daus. Uncertain which branch of the L. fam this belongs with.
    F1. Edna May, b 1900 Perce, mar William O. Divens 1928, res Montreal
    F2. Doris Grace, b 1901, d 1903
LENFESTEY, Henry Allen, res Perce? Mar 1903, there, Lillian Elizabeth DU VAL, qv, b 1879, d 1975 L'Anse du Cap, Gaspe, 6 chn
    F1. Murial Blanche Lenfesty, b 1906, mar 1. Francis GUIGNON
    F2. Charles Ford, b 1907
    F3. Viola May, b 1908, mar 1936, Rufus Lorden COLLAS, qv.

F4. Russell Elihu, b 1910, mar Lucy AHIER of L'Anse aux Gascons See LATE ADDITIONS AND CORRECTIONS pages.
F5. Phyllis Rena, b 1919, mar George Robinson
F6. Gerald Gordon, b 1921, res Nitro, Quebec

LENFESTEY, Capt. John, of "The lugger INTREPID, of Guernsey. Here we have the craft beloved of French and English smugglers, and extolled by Cooper in WING AND WING. The rig was ever rare on this side of the Atlantic. How an English lugger came to seek letters of Marque in Halifax is not known to the writer, but on Oct. 10, 1813, Capt. John Lenfestey, a British subject and native of Guernsey, obtained from the Nova Scotia Court of Vice Admiralty, a commission for the lugger, INTREPID, which he commanded and which was owned by Peter Le Lacheur of Guernsey, merchant."
"The INTREPID was of 67 tons and had 6 six-pounders, and a dozen muskets and cutlasses. A Channel Island lugger, possibly, which had crossed the Atlantic in search of prizes, and registered in Halifax so as to qualify for the captures made in America. The INTREPID had a large supply of shot, 1,000 rounds, and but sixteen hands. No prizes were reported at Halifax." (UNDER THE RED JACK, by C.H.J. Snider, London, England, 1928)

LE NOURY, James and Betsy (poss nee ROBILLIARD?), res near Sparta, Ont. Fam rem to BC, poss dropped LE of name. (Marlene Robilliard, Albion, Mich.)
A1. Thomas, killed in hunting accident   A3. William   A5. Amy, b 1878
A2. Walter   A4. Edward
A6. a dau of Edward's, also raised by James and Betsy

LE NOURY, family below from G to Ontario. (Edw. LE PAGE, Grimsby, Ont.)
A1. LE NOURY, Edwin, b 1889 G, son of Harriet Mary DOREY and Nicholas LE NOURY. Edwin d 1972 Hamilton, Ont. Mar Jessie Wilson, b 1888, d 1969 Hamilton.
A2. Frank, b 1892 G, d 1963 Hamilton, Ont., mar 1. Ada TOSTEVIN, b 1891, d Ont., mar 2. Clara KNIGHT, b 1891, d 1964 Hamilton, Ont.
   B1. Joyce, b 1912, res B.C., mar Carl Parsons, b 1913
      C1. William Parsons, b 1935, res BC, mar Loraine Gillies, b BC
         D1. Patricia Lynn Parsons, b 1958
         D2. Elizabeth Ann Parsons, b 1960
A3. Hilda, b 1897 G, d 1962 Burlington, Ont., mar Wilfred PRIEST, b 1894, who d 1960
   B1. Doris May Priest, b 1914, res Milton, Ont., mar Harry OGIER, b 1910 Ont. See Ogier for chn.
   B2. Lloyd Priest, b 1915, res Burlington, mar Marian LAWRENCE, b 1919
      C1. Lauraine Priest, b 1941, res Brantford, Ont. Mar Wayne Laux, b 1936
         D1. Catherine Louise Laux, b 1975 Brantford, Ont.
      C2. Linda Priest, b 1949, mar David Jacklyn, b 1947
      C3. Louise C. Priest, b 1957
   B3. Harriet Barbara Priest, b 1918, Burlington, Ont., mar Herbert Wignall, b 1918
      C1. Robert John Wignall, b 1942, mar Ann Elizabeth Willis
         D1. Bonnie Elizabeth Wignall, b 1969
         D2. Geoffrey Robert Wignall, b 1971
      C2. Joyce Sheila Wignall, b 1944
      C3. Susan Lynn Wignall, b 1949, mar Robert A. Anderson
   B4. Amanda Rhoda Priest, b 1921, d.y.

LE NOURY, Nicholas, 1863-1930, mar Harriet Mary DOREY in G. The widow mar 2. his bro, Thomas Alfred LE NOURY, to Hamilton, Ont.

LE NOURY, Frederick, b ca 1910 G, rem to Canada 1936. Mar Ada LE PREVOST

qv. Two sons and a dau, all mar, res Ontario? (Edw. Le Page, Grimsby, Ont.) One son, Harold Frederick, d 1944 on Halifax bomber misson.
LEONARD, in Nfld. (Seary) Cf LEONARD in J (Stevens)
LE PAGE. Many of this surname came to Canada from the Island of Guernsey, where the HOUSE OF THE ROUND CHIMNEY, built in the year 1111, is said to be still inhabited there by descendants. See JOHN HEMSTREET, by Winnifred M. Rosewarne, Ottawa, 1962, for fuller and more accurate information on the P.E.I. family. (This book not found by compiler)
LE PAGE, Elisha, b 1764 G, mar Margaret ---. They came to PEI sometime in the early 1800s. Their son, Elisha, b 1787 in G, also settled in PEI. The older Elisha and an Andrew Le Page, poss a relative, both bought land in PEI in 1807. The senior Elisha d in 1813, and his wife, b 1735, d in PEI, age 99, 1834. They are bur in St. Pauls, Charlottetown. Many of this fam were merchants and ship builders.
A1. Elisha, b 1787 G, mar Margaret Du Frecy, settled in PEI. He d 1813. Chn?
    B1. Margaret   B2. Elisha   B3. Alfred
A2. John Nicholas, b 1792, d 1824, bur Elms St. Cem, C'town, PEI
A3. Margaret, b 1793, d 1848, mar Richard Rollings, 1775-1852, bur So. Rustico Cem, PEI. She was mar in England, and brought her brother Elisha Christopher with them when they came to Canada in 1816. He was then 8 yrs. old. The information about the two Elishas in this family is confusing. Perhaps the first Elisha was born of another wife; or, Elisha Christopher may have been the son of her brother, Elisha, b 1787?, or Margaret's own child.
    B1. Elizabeth Rollings, mar George MacNeill, 10 chn. Poss also mar 2. Artemus McNeill?
    B2. Mary Margaret Rollings, mar George Woolner
        C1. Emily Woolner, mar Murray Robertson
        C2. Rachel Woolner   C3. Lavinia Woolner, mar ---MacLeod
        C4. Richard Woolner, at least 4 chn
            D1. Mildred, mar Lionel Robinson
            D2. Irene, mar ---Hickox
            D3. Carl Richard Woolner, mar Florence Laird
            D4. Dora Woolner, mar Clive MacNeill
    B3. Richard Rollings, drowned 1858
    B4. John Rollings, b 1825, mar Mary Margaret Harker, d 1905
        C1. George Rollings, mar Jane Smith
        C2. Artemus Rollings, b 1852, d 1935, mar Eliza Parkman, had at least 3 sons, Elmer, Willis and Edward
        C3. Jeanette Rollings, mar 1. ---Anderson, and poss ---Ward, chn John and Garfield Anderson
        C4. Elisha Rollings, mar Jennie ---
        C5. Rilla Rollings   C6. Josey Rollings
        C7. Margaret E. Rollings, mar Wm. COURT. A son, Beecher Court, res No. Rustico, PEI, 6 chn
        C8. Aquilla John Rollings, b 1868, d 1935. Mar Mary Houston, 1871-1942. Poss also mar 2. Pearle Robinson. A son, Fulton, mar Marjorie Johnstone, and 5? other chn.
A4. Octavius, b 1808, d 1878   TAKE CARE! ERRORS IN CHART HERE!
A5. Elisha Columbus, or poss Elisha Christopher?, b 1808, d 1885, mar Maria Blatch, 1807-1885
    B1. Louisa   B2. Elizabeth   B3. Eliza
    B4. Emma, mar --- Buntain
        C1. Robert Buntain
        C2. Lettie Buntain, mar ---MacLellan, res Calgary, a dau
        C3. Walter Buntain, mar Margaret Clark, res New Glasgow, a son Roland

C4.   CAUTION! POSS.ERRORS IN CHART BELOW.
C5. Marie Buntain, mar Dickieson, res New Glasgow
C6. Gordon Buntain, mar ---Victorson, res Calgary, Alta.
C7. Granville Buntain, mar Laura Bernard, res New Glasgow, 2 chn
   D1. Granville   D2. Ruth
B5. Christopher, b 1845, d 1928, mar Sarah Millicent Woolner
   C1. Oliver Cromwell, 1874-1928, mar Amelia Bell MacMillan, 1875-
       1954, 3 chn, Emma, Edna, Jane
   C2. William Bradford, Lt. Gov. of PEI, 1876-1958, mar Harriett
       Edna Christie, 1875-1961, 7 chn including Reuel and Hilda
   C3. Clara Woolner, 1878-1948, mar ---Dupee
   C4. Elisha Chester, 1879-1948, mar Bessie MacKenzie, 1884-1960
   C5. Emma May, b 1888, d.y.
   C6. James L., b 1892, mar Lucy MacKenzie
   C7. Garfield, 1881-1962, mar Martha Bulman, 1883-1937, mar 2.?
       Mary Bernard, chn: Helen, Frederick, Elwell, Weston
A6. Alfred, b 1810, d 1883, mar Emma Spratt, 1814-1890. Dates on first
    two chn uncertain.
   B1. Ellie, 1836-1900, mar Dawson. Chn: Fred, Beatrice, and Erna, d.y.
       Will Dawson, (mar Inez Mitchell), Glendon, Ernest, and Laurie.
   B2. Louisa, 1836-1859
   B3. Frederick, 1838-1910, mar Elizabeth Passmore, 1841-1907
      C1. Annie Louise, 1867-1933, mar Charles Black, bur Bedeque, PEI
      C2. Bessie Emma, 1869, d.y.
      C3. Arthur Frederick, 1870-1954, mar Agnes Caw Smith, 1877-1970,
          bur Edmonton, Alta. Chn: George, Arthur, Betty, Alex, Keith.
      C4. Fannie Laura, 1872-1953, bur Burnaby, BC
      C5. Frank C., 1873-1898
      C6. Aubrey Johnson, b 1875, d 1942, mar Florence Maude Armstrong,
          1880-1944, bur Medicine Hat, Alta. Chn: Muriel, Cecil, Helen,
          Gerald, Raymond.
      C7. Mary Passmore, 1878-1928, bur Winnipeg, Man.
      C8. Elsie Elizabeth, b 1880, mar Gladstone MacDonald, res Calif?
      C9. Ella Georgina, 1882-1953, bur Burnaby, BC
      C10. Abbie Ellen, 1884-1950
   B4. Lemuel, 1840-1914, mar Mary Snelgrove, 1842-1906, bur Vict., BC
      C1. Connie, 1868-1937, mar ---MacNamara, bur Winnipeg, Man. Chn:
          Edna, Douglas, and Allen.
      C2. Ethel Lucretia, 1869-1956, mar Herbert Wheeler, res Victoria,
          BC. Chn: Mary and Herbert.
      C3. William Morley, mar Jessie Broatch, dau, Ethel Irene, mar ---
          Irish, 5 chn, res Glendale, Calif
      C4. James Harold, 1885-1944, mar Nellie Rushworth, res Victoria,
          BC. Chn: David, Doris, Morley and Marilyn.
      C5. Mary, d ca 1938, bur Victoria, BC
   B5. William Nelson, b 1849 PEI, d 1919 Vancouver, BC, mar 1875, Ruth
       Abbey Mayo, 1854-1923, bur Vancouver, BC
      C1. Nelson Spratt, 1876-1950, mar Ellen Mabel Le Page, 1876-1940
          and 2? Elizabeth Florence Russell. Chn: Theodore, Marion,
          Alfred.
      C2. William Havelock, 1877, d.y.   C4. Wilbur E., b 1879, d.y.
      C3. Ernest B., 1878, d.y.   C5. Ethel May, b 1881
      C6. Alfred Wolseley, 1883-1956, mar Madge Blackman, b 1904. Alfred
          was boat builder in Vancouver, BC.
   B6. Rev. Alfred E., 1842-1916, mar Helen Taylor, res Woodstock, NB
      C1. Alfred, b 1870, mar ---, chn: Ellen, Catherine, Lillian, Ruth,
          res U.S.

LE PAGE

C2. Emma Jane, b 1872, d.y.
C3. Hattie Louise, 1874-1909, mar Rev. G.C. Pringle, 1865-1952, chn: Helen, Mary, Dorothy, Hattie, Rev. Gordon
C4. Ellen Mabel, 1876-1940, mar Nelson Spratt, see above, 1876-1950, chn: Theo., Marion, Alfred
C5. John Taylor, 1878-1965, mar Minnie Ethel Burtt, who d 1959, res Woodstock, NB. Two daus, Inez in Vancouver, and Minnie in Winnipeg, Man.
C6. Eva Ernestine, 1881-1887
C7. Martin Lemont, 1883-1884   C8. Charles Spratt, b 1887
B7. Henry T., 1854-1943, mar Margaret A. Moore, 1866-1939, mar in Hamilton, Ont. Bur Toronto, Ont.
  C1. Albert Edward, 1887-1968, mar 1. Louisa Arnott, 1887-1936, and 2. Florence Johnston, b 1892
  C2. Bessie Louise, 1888-1956, mar Norman COLLETT, 1887-1946, a son, Charles, desc in Ontario
  C3. Herbert Moore, 1891-1898
  C4. Dorothy Margaret, 1892-1922, mar Douglas Chrighton, 1891-1954, a dau, Margaret, mar ---Campbell
  C5. Harry Eylesworth, 1894-1922, mar Marjorie Bickel, b 1897, 7 chn: George, Donald, Elizabeth, Mary, Peter, Larry, David
  C6. Lillian Irene, b 1896, mar 1. Cecil Brydon Wood, 1892 and 2. Walter Twigg, 1889-1927, chn Margaret and Charles
  C7. Anna Emma, b 1900, d.y.
  C8. George Morley, b 1902, mar Evelyn Carter, b 1902, 5 chn: Margaret, Joan, Thomas, Patricia, Lynda, some res Ontario
B8. Emma Lucretia, 1844-1934, mar John D'Orsey, 1835-1884, chn: Alfred, Frederick, Hensley, John Ezra James, 1880-1946 (mar Olive Shaw, 1904-1958, bur Toronto, Ont.). Sons of John?, Seldon Edward, John Alfred, Lawrence, also Olive.
B9. Elizabeth T., 1845-1922, mar C.M. Atwood
B10. Julia J., 1852-1921
A7. Napoleon?, poss a brother of the A chn in above fam
LE PAGE, Andrew, not known if he was related to the LE PAGES, above, but he bought land in PEI 1807, the same year as Elisha Sr. bought land there. He was b 1785 in G and d PEI 1849. Mar Elizabeth Mellish, 1776-1863. Andrew was a Squaw Bay farmer.
A1. Jane, b 1809
A2. Thomas, b 1810, mar Jane---
  B1. John, b 1844   B4. Charlotte, b 1850
  B2. Elizabeth Jane, b 1846 B5. Samuel, b 1855
  B3. Andrew Thomas, b 1850
A3. John, b 1812, d 1886, mar Alice LE PAGE, 1823-1851, and 2. Charlotte MacNeill, 1825-1889
  B1. Chester Woolner, 1853-1921 B4. Sarah Elizabeth, 1863-1888
  B2. Jane Murray, 1868-1892   B5. George Campbell, 1865-1882
  B3. Thomas Alex., 1857-1889   B6. Malcolm William
LE PAGE, John, of PEI, called THE ISLAND MINSTREL, wrote two books of poetry, 1860-1863. He was a school master in what is now Prince of Wales College. It is not known if he was related to Elisha and Alfred LE PAGE, but he was b 1812, d 1886. His wife, Charlotte McNeill, 1825-1889, bur in PEI.
LE PAGE, John Nicholson, 1792-1824, is bur next to Elisha LE PAGE, 1764-1813. Origin unknown. Many other Le Pages are bur in Elm St. Cem, C'Town, PEI and also in Sherwood Cem and Peoples Cem there.
LE PAGE, Elisha. The ILLUSTRATED HISTORICAL ATLAS OF PEI, published in 1880, has a picture of the home of Elisha LE PAGE.

(Contributors to the above information, according to the manuscript copy the compiler saw, were primarily Edward Le Page, Grimsby, Ont.; Mrs. G.F. Le Page, formerly of Southbury, Conn.; and numerours Le Page descendants in PEI, US, surnamed Wonnacott, Rollings, Le Page, MacDonald, Irish, Graham, Maynard, MacCormac, Fidler, Robinson, and Mrs. Lillian Twigg, Toronto, Ont.)

LE PAGE, in Nfld. (Seary) prob from G?

LE PAGE, Elizabeth, b J, age 52 in Malbaie 1871 with son, Thomas, age 30. (Census)

LE PAGE, Joseph and Ephraim, from G to Gaspe early 1800s, signed 1820 Petition

LE PAGE, Thomas, from C.I., mar Mary Ann LE MARQUAND, qv, b St. Ouen, J, bur Malbaie, Gaspe 1800s

LE PAGE, Samuel, in Perce, Gaspe 1863 (Cent. Bklt.)

LE PAGE, Thomas, of Belle Anse, Gaspe, mar Betsy MISSIN, MISSON?, a son, John Philip

LE PAGE, Olive, b G, dau of William George Le P., b 1858, and Amy FALLA, qv, b 1860, mar Walter DOWN, had 2 sons. See DOWN.

LE PAGE, David, b 1930s, son of George LE PAGE and Amy TOURTEL, b G, to Canada, mar, with chn

LE PAGE, Betty, sister of David, to Canada (Edw. Le Page, Grimsby, Ont.)

LE PAGE, Henry, from G to S. America, married, d 1944

LE PAGE, Edward, from G to Scotland, then to Vancouver, BC, 1879-1963, unmar, retired to G in 1960, in Canada 18 yrs.

LE PAGE, Julia, mar ---LE PREVOST, to Canada ca 1920 with dau, Emily
LE PREVOST, who mar John David HAMON, qv.

LE PAGE, Adelaide Alice, mar Edwin C. DOREY, qv.

LE PAGE, Alfred, b 1881 L'Islet, G, son of Alfred John Le P. and Mary Louisa BISSON, qv, mar Anna JOHNS, b 1887, The Vale, G, dau of Mary Ann NILES and Francis JOHNS, qv.

A1. Miriam A., b 1914 Toronto, mar Gordon Russell, res Belleville, Ont. (Miriam Russell, Belleville, Ont.)
   B1. Kenneth John Russell, b 1946
A2. Ruth Mary, b 1918 Toronto, mar Roland Miller
   B1. Mark Miller, b 1951
A3. George, b 1926 Toronto, mar Noreen Foster, res Agincourt, Ont. Adopted chn:
   B1. Robbie, b 1960   B2. Carol, b 1962   B3. Laurie, b 1964
A4. Alfred G., b 1916 Toronto, d 1970, mar Vera Smith
   B1. Philip, b 1948   B2. James, b 1952
A5. Edna Niles, b 1919 Vale, G, d 1925

LE PAGE, Theodore, and wife, Elizabeth Boyer AUBIN, of Bosq Lane, St. Peter Port, rem to Victoria, BC (Mrs. Floyd Snodgrass, Stamford, Conn)
A1. Theodore   A2. Elizabeth Rachel, orphaned at 5 yrs.
A3. Laura Ester, b 1867, d 1958, mar J. Llewellyn Leigh
   B1. Victor Llewellyn Leigh, b 1895, d 1969
   B2. Edna Mabel Leigh, b 1897, d 1967
   B3. Byron Theodore Leigh, b 1900, d 1973
   B4. Laura Llewella Leigh, b 1905 Victoria, BC, mar Floyd Snodgrass, b 1904
      C1. Michael Dale Snodgrass

LE PAGE, Eugene, b 1874 G, mar Alice Mary DOREY, qv, 1872-1958. Eugene d 1923. He was the son of Abraham BLONDEL LE PAGE, 1830-1885, and Nancy LE PELLEY, 1843-1932. Rem to Toronto via Halifax, NS 1916. (Edw. Le Page, Grimsby, Ont.)

A1. Eugene, b 1896 G, unmar, Vet WWI, res Hamilton, Ont.
A2. Alfred, b 1898 G, mar 1. Lila Felker, b 1904, divorced. Mar 2.

Eileen? Smith, b 1916. 4 chn.
B1. Jean, b 1925, d 1970, mar Wallace ROBIN, qv, b 1914
B2. Raymond Alfred, b 1928, mar Joyce C. Weil, b 1932, res Portland, Ore.
   C1. Joseph Perry, b 1954   C3. Joann Joy, b 1960
   C2. Peggy Jean, b 1955   C4. David Ray, b 1966
B3. Eugene Alfred, b 1945, mar Nancy Jacqueline Horrill, b 1946
   C1. Karen Elizabeth, b 1969
B4. Margaret Ann, b 1951, mar Douglas Gordon Roy LAWRENCE, b 1951?
A3. Edward, b 1900, mar Gladys Margaret Kinnear, b 1901, d 1968
B1. Marie Victoria, b 1926, d 1974, mar Carl Mathal Gerdes, 1926-1969. Gerdes mar 2. Dorothy Hansen, a son, Dennis, b 1945.
LE PAGE, Edmond Joseph, son of Thomas BLONDEL LE PAGE, b 1816 G, mar Betsy Louise MARQUIS, qv. Some chn settled in Canada.
LE PAGE, William, son of William LE PAGE and Clara Rachel FERBRACHE of Catel, Borne Fosse, Gorban, G. William was b 1884, mar 1. Elise RENOUF, qv. Ronald J. OZARD was the nephew of Wm. LE PAGE and came to Canada about the time Mr. Le Page died, ca 1958. (Hazel Parkes, London, Ont.)
LE PAGE, Mrs. John, from G to Niagara Falls, Ont. in 1960, age 90, where she d in 1963. She was the mother of John and Thomas DE CARTERET, qv.
LE PAGE, ---, rem from G in 1906 to Halifax, NS, then to Grimsby, Ont.
LE PAGE, Capt. from G to Nfld. 1800s (K. Mathews)
LE PATOUREL, from G to B.C.
LE PATOUREL, James MESSURIER, and wife, Elizabeth GARGET, from G to Wallaceburg, Ont. 1900s. (J.E. Le Patourel, Wallaceburg, Ont.)
A1. Herbert James, mar Gertrude Kathleen Horn
LE PATOUREL, Elias James, b 1834 St. Peter Port, G, son of Thomas Le P. and Julie LE CHEMINANT, qv, mar Marguerite LANGLOIS, dau of Thomas L. and Marguerite FERBRACHE, res Hamilton, Ont. (Richard Ruggle, Glen Williams, Ont.)
LE PATOUREL, J. Lewis, b G, homesteaded at Chinook, Alta. 1908, d Cayley, Alta. 1920. (Edith Hunzinger, Claresholm, Alta.)
LE PATOUREL, Arthur James, b 1881 St. Peter Port, G, d 1962 Cayley, Alta., bro of J. Lewis, above, son of Jean James Le P. and Julie LAINE. Mar Bertha Togerson BROWARD, poss same as BROUARD?, dau of Nicholas NAFTEL BROWARD, and Judith ROBERT, qv. Bertha d at birth of second dau. Chn raised first in N.H. by an aunt, then returned to G, in care of Mrs. Daniel LE P., a relative. The two girls returned to N.J. and both became graduate nurses.
A1. John James, b 1914, mar Edith Stephenson?, 1963, Nanton, Alta.
A2. Edith Mary, b 1915, mar Wilfred HALLETT 1937, divorced 1955, mar 2. Herbert Hunzinger
   B1. Harry Douglas Hallett, b 1940 B2. Richard Arthur Hallett, b 1941
A3. Daniel Frederic, b 1916, mar Gwen Hallett 1941 High River, Alta.
   B1. Gerald, mar Millie ---, 1971, a dau, Nancy
   B2. Patricia, mar Barry Findlay 1967, 2 sons and a dau
A4. Robert Louis, b 1918, mar Marion Nussey 1972, no issue, res near Longview, Alta.
LE PELLEY, PELLEY, from C.I. to Hants Harbor, Trinity Bay, Nfld.
LE PELLEY, Capt. John, in Nfld. early 1800s for Carteret-Priaulx Co. (Brochet; K. Mathews; C.R. Fay)
LE PELLEY, to Gaspe ca 1830 (Wilson)
LE PELLEY, Alfred, son of Steven L. and Mary Ann ROBERT, qv, b 1883 G, d Vancouver, BC. A sister, Mabel, res Castel, G.
LE PELLEY, from G to Pefferlaw, Ont.

LE POIDEVIN, SEE EXTRA PAGES.
LE PELLEY, Judith, b G?, mar 1829 Abraham LE HUQUET, qv. (Wilson)
LE PELLEY, R., his grandfather and father came from G and settled in Toronto
LE PELLEY, Guernsey, noted Christian Science Monitor cartoonist, was the son of Franklin LE PELLEY, who d 1944 Toronto, Ont.
LE PENNEC, Toussaint, from J to Gaspe ca 1900 or before
LE PETIT, in Alderney 1309, desc in Canada?
LE POIDEVIN, Wm. Sir., b ca 1801 G, res Bon. Co., Gaspe 1871, with Mary, age 54, Catholic, Jane age 25, Ellen age 20, Melvina age 15, and Charles Alfred age 1. (Census)
LE POIDEVIN, Alfred John, b 1881 G, d 1968. Son of Alfred John Le P. of Les Rouvets, G, (4th son and 8th ch). Mar Rachel LE POIDEVIN, no relative, b 1882 G, d 1958. Fam from St. Sampson, G, to Stanstead, Que. then to St. Catherines, Ont. Ten chn, all b G but Donald Franklin, the last. (Alfred Le Poidevin, St. Catherines, Ont.; Miriam Osborne, Stanstead, Que.)
  A1. Miriam, b 1905 G, mar Alfred Edward Osborne
    B1. Donald Sefton Osborne, b 1942, mar Dyanne Linda McComb 1970, res Quebec
      C1. Terri Ann Osborne, b 1972   C2. Jodi Dyanne Osborne, b 1975
    B2. Mary Rachel, b 1946, mar James Ralph Cooke, 1967, res Quebec
      C1. Amy Marie Cooke, b 1968   C2. Christopher James Cooke, b 1973
  A2. Reginald, b 1906 G, unmar
  A3. Osmond Thomas, b 1906 G, unmar   A4. Annette, b 1909 G, unmar
  A5. Helene, b 1910 G, mar Finley K. McLeod
    B1. Alfred Allan McLeod, mar ---
      C1. Sandra McLeod, b 1965   C2. Nancy McLeod, b 1968
  A6. Harold, b 1911 G, mar Jean McKean
    B1. Nancy Carol, b 1949   B2. Ronald, b 1955, adopted
  A7. Hilda Maude, b 1913, unmar
  A8. Alfred, b 1914 G, mar Beatrice G. BARLOW, no issue
  A9. Irene, b 1920 G, mar Roland Drew
    B1. David Richard Drew, b 1947, mar Lynn Margaret Belknap
      C1. Bonnie Lynn Drew, b 1970   C2. Stacy Dawn Drew, b 1972
  A10. Donald Franklin, b 1922 Canada, mar Patricia Sangster
    B1. Steven Andrew, b 1851, mar Nicole Charpentier
    B2. Karen Elizabeth, b 1953, mar Roderick James BISHOP
    B3. Gary Michael, b 1957
LE POIDEVIN, Emilie Patty, G, dau of Nicholas Le P. and Sophie LE MAITRE, mar Samuel John MILLMAN, qv.
LE POIDEVIN, Jack, from G to Red Deer, Alta. ca 1900, bro of Emilie
LE POIDEVIN, from G to Mass., then to Queen Charlotte Island, BC
LE POIDEVIN, from G to Gaspe
LE POIDEVIN, ---, from G to Arvida, Quebec, 12 chn, mostly b G
LE POIDEVIN, from G to London, Ont. ca 1900 (Savary)
LE POIDEVIN, Henry, b G, rem to Limehouse, Ont. 1865, desc in Ontario
LE POIDEVIN, Frank, b G, to Victoria, BC 1906, d 1970 (B.C. Archives)
LE POIDEVIN, Thomas Henry and wife, from G to Toronto. A son, Ernest, a Poiatrist, res Toronto, was b 1914
LE POIDEVIN, Cecil, from G at age 17 in 1929 to Canada, returned to G for 5 yrs. ca 1933, mar Violet DUCHEMIN, dau of Helier D. of La Ruette, Castel, G. Mr. C. Le P. crossed Canada by motorcycle from BC to Montreal in 1929, worked on farms. After marriage, farmed 50 acres in Brockville, Ont. In 1945, rem to Oscoyos, BC. (Ed. Le Page)
LE POIDEVIN, ---, mar G. Law, rem to Western Canada (Gladys Smith, Ingersol, Ont.)
LE POIDEVIN, from G to Ontario, Capt. Edward J, with a bro and sister.

LE POIDEVIN

See FIFTY YEARS ON THE GREAT LAKES, Ontario Chapter.
SEE POIDEVIN IN EXTRA PAGES

LE POIDEVIN, William Sr., age 70, b G, in Bonaventure, Gaspe 1871 (Census)
LE PREVOST, Ada, b G, mar Fred. LE NOURY, qv, rem to Canada ca 1936. 2 sons, 1 dau. (Edw. Le Page, Grimsby, Ont.)
LE PREVOST, Mary, b G, mar John DOREY, qv, who d St. Catherines, Ont. 1959. Mary d there, age 75. See DOREY. Had sisters, Mrs. Thomas DOMAILLE of G, Mrs. Linda REAGAN of G; bros, Edwin Le P. of G, and John Le P. of New Zealand.
LE PREVOST, William, b Vale, G, mar Julia LE PAGE, rem to Canada (Edwin Hamon, Chatham, Ont.; Judy Ogletree, London, Ont.)
A1. Julia, d 1928, mar Jack LE QUELENEC, qv, 4 chn. See LE QUELENEC.
A2. Alice, b 1870, d 1929, mar George DAVEY of G, rem to Chatham, Ont. 1914, 6 chn. See DAVEY, George.
A3. Emily, b 1871, d 1943, mar John David HAMON, qv, to Canada 1919, to Chatham, Ont. 1920, 6 chn. See HAMON, J.D.
A4. Adelaide LE PREVOST, mar Jack Jones, 2 chn
B1. Jack Jones   B2. Florence Jones
LE PREVOST, a British Captain, James PREVOST was in Esquimault Harbour, BC in 1872
LE QUELENEC, Mrs., nee FRITOT from G to Rexdale and/or Beaton, Ont.
LE QUELENEC, Jack, b G, mar Julia LE PREVOST, qv, b G, rem to Canada, settled in Ontario. (Edwin Hamon, Chatham, Ont.)
A1. Annie   A2. Frederick   A3. Nellie   A4. Jack
LE QUESNE, see also LE CAIN, from C.I. to Canada
LE QUESNE, Walter P., b J, to Gaspe, bur Riv. aux Renards, a cousin of John BAUDAIN and of Lydia LE MAISTRE of J
LE QUESNE, Rupert, to Gaspe from C.I. (J.H. Le Breton list; GLF)
LE QUESNE, Albert, to Victoria, BC, there in 1940
LE QUESNE, C.I. name on S. coast of Nfld. (G.W. Le Messurier)
LE QUESNE, Capt. from J in Nfld. (K. Mathews)
LE QUESNE. "My husband was Ernest Frederick, who d 1957. As far as I know the family came to Moncton, NB about 1900. They lived in the Maritimes for several years, then rem to Alberta, for a short time, then back to Nova Scotia, I think. My husband joined the R.C.R.'s and served with them in France. In 1920 the family rem to the Okanagan Valley remaining there for 4 years before coming to Victoria, BC." (Mrs. E.F. Le Quesne, Victoria, BC) Ernest F. was the son of Frank Herbert Le Q, b J, one of four chn. (Herbert Frank, Blanche Mary and Mary Ellen) Mar Catherine ---, a son, C. Herbert Le Q. res Wilts, England) POSSIBLE ERRORS HERE. SEE EXTRA PAGES.
LE QUESNE, John, a merchant from G in Quebec City 1765
LE QUESNE, Philip Winter and wife Sara Dearle, rem to Eastwood, NSW, Aust. before 1888. He was b 1838 J, both bur Aust. Their desc in England, Aust., South Africa and Canada. (Le Quesne Chart, by H.H. Le Q., Vanc., BC: Ont. Gen. Soc., Toronto, Ont.) Children of the family b J. Leonard Winter, Gertrude Mary, Philip Herbert, George, Robert, Jesse Laura.
I. LE QUESNE, Eric George, son of Philip Winter Le Q. and Sarah Dearle, b 1909 NSW, Aust., mar May Marshall, desc in Aust.
II. LE QUESNE, Harold Harvey, b 1911 Lindfield, NSW, Aust., mar 1938 Katherine McLellan Black, a Scot, at Notre Dame de Grace, Montreal, Que.
A1. Virginia Catherine, b 1942 Halifax, NS, mar Vancouver 1965 Alex. David Bell, b N.S.
B1. Derek Alex. Ball, b 1968 Peterborough, Ont.
B2. Heather Lynn Bell, b 1972

RE: LE QUESNE, SEE EXTRA PAGES.
   B3. Scott Jeffrey Bell, b 1976 Pt. Claire, Que.
 A2. Philip James, b 1945 Halifax, NS, mar Sandra Gail Clark 1970, Vanc.,
   BC
   B1. Scott Wynter, b 1976 Vancouver, BC
 III. Alan Wynter, b 1912 Chatswood, NSW, Aust., mar Jean Davidson 1939
  A1. Janine Davidson, b 1940 Burwood, NSW, Aust.
  A2. June Wynter, b 1943 NSW Aust., mar Robert James Bell, Islington,
   Ont. 1939
LE QUESNE, Philip Winter, son of Leonard Winter Le Q. of St. Saviour, J,
 who d 1938 NSW, Aust., mar Sarah McLennan 1933
 A1. Pamela Heather, b 1934 NSW, Aust., mar Arthur Allen 1955
   B1. Tracey Evol Allen, b 1961 Vancouver, BC   B3. Allison Heather Allen,
   B2. Deneen Meridith Allen, b 1964 Vanc., BC   b 1965 Vanc., BC
LE QUESNE, ---, dau of Edward G., and --- Le Montais of St. Ouens, J.
 Rem to Winnipeg, Man., mar John Edmond, banker.
LE QUIN, C.I. surname associated with Robin Co. at Paspebiac, Gaspe and
 with town of New Carlisle, Que. (Prov. Arch.)
LE RAY, in Torteval, G 1700s, poss to Canada as ROY and/or KING
LE RENDU, Anne Elizabeth, b 1942 St. Saviour, J, to Cambridge, Ont.,
 mar ---Finlayson, Cambridge, Ont. (Le Herissier, Toronto)
I. LE REVEREND, Alfred William, from G to Canada 1920s, mar Dora ---.
  (Peter Le Reverend, Niagara Falls, Ont.) At least 2 bros and a
  sister, noted below.
 A1. Alfred Jr., spent his 16th birthday in German Prisoner of War camp,
   escaped, served in Armed Canadian forces until retirement 1973. Now
   in RCMP, BC, mar Isabel, 4 daus.
   B1. Patty   B2. Fern   B3. Cathy   B4. Margaret
 A2. Peter, a signpainter, mar Shirley ---
   B1. Diana   B2. Elizabeth   B3. David
 A3. Robert, a computer programmer, mar Susan, res Ajax, Ont.
II. William, trainer of race horses, at one time trainer of the Bally-
  mena stables of the Governor-General of Ontario, Ray Lawson. A
  dau, Pat.
III. Harold, had a son, Bruce
IV. Louisa, mar Bert Weeks, b G, rem to Orangeville, Ont. Bakery
  operator, no issue.
LE RHE, C.I. name assoc with Robin firm at Paspebiac, Gaspe, and with
 town of New Carlisle, Quebec. (Prov. Arch.)
LE RHE, James and Hugh, in Seal Cove, Douglas, Que., 1825
LE RHE, also LA RHE, Elizabeth, mar John BREHAUT, qv. A son, John
 Frank Brehaut, b Gr. Greve, Gaspe 1832.
LE RICHE, ---, of St. Lawrence, J, rem ca 1892 to St. Clement, J. At
 least 6 chn, some of whom came to Canada. (George E. Le Riche, Man-
 otick, Ont.) Some data below is uncertain.
I. George, b J, rem to Hamilton, Ont., a partner in a chemical business.
 Mar Louise Blackhall, res Gaspe and Ont.? 3 sons, 1 dau.
II. Philip, farmer in J, mar, 2 sons, both farmers
III. Peter, b J, at least 6 chn
 A1. David, a farmer in J, rem to Montreal 1904, mar Elizabeth CARTERET
  HELLEUR of J. David d 1918, age 55.
   B1. Edwin, b 1884, rem 1902 to Montreal, later to Fort Saskatchewan,
    Alta. D ca 1955.
     C1. Milton, res Edmonton, Alta. Mar Violet ---, a dau, Camille,
      mar Martin Woolf
   B2. George, b 1886, rem to Montreal 1899, worked there for dry goods
    firm, retired 1955. Mar 1910, Ada Carden ROWE, who d 1948, no
    issue. Mar 1950 Ella Le Riche, res with dau in Manotick, Ont.

Ella was his brother's widow, no issue.
B3. Philip, b 1888 J, rem to Montreal 1902, d 1949, mar Ella Wood
  C1. Arthur, b 1917, mar Jean Armerod
    D1. Arthur Frederick, Fred, b 1949, mar Betty Fay Brooks, res West Hill, Ont.
      E1 Vincent, has son b ca 1970
    D2. Janice, b 1950, mar John Magill. Her twin sister Judith d.y.
      E1. Colleen Magill, b 1973   E2. Tara Magill, b 1974
    D3. Melanie, b 1960
  C2. Phyllis, b 1918, res Kitchener, Ont., mar Edward Saunders
    D1. David Saunders, b 1947   D3. Rick Saunders, b 1954
    D2. Ward Saunders, b 1949   D4. Nancy Saunders, b 1959
  C3. Eleanor, b 1927, mar Donald Coombs, 4 daus, res Manotick, Ont.
    D1. Andrea Coombs, b 1954   D3. Julia Coombs, b 1958
    D2. Pamela Coombs, b 1956   D4. Stacia Coombs, b 1961
B4. Walter, b 1890, d 1962. Rem to Montreal 1904, worked for Brewery there, mar Marjorie BAKER, a dau, Joan, mar --- Groves, fam res W. Palm Beach, Fla.
B5. Lilian, b 1894, to Montreal, 1904, mar Stanley HELLEUR, qv, a cousin, has 3 chn
  C1. Stanley Helleur, b 1918, mar Beth Cavanaugh
  C2. Irene, mar Bertram Smith
    D1. Ian Smith   D2. Lynne Smith
  C3. Dorothy, unmar
B6. Stanley, b 1898, d 1974, rem to Quebec, in insurance field, mar Bertha Hoult.
  C1. Roberta, res Vancouver, BC, mar William Gilmore
    D1. David Gilmore   D2. Lesley Gilmore
  C2. Jeanne, res Beaconsfield, Que., mar John Osler, 4 chn
    D1. Robin Osler   D3. John Osler
    D2. Marilyn Osler   D4. Andrew Osler
A2. George, b J, rem to New Brunswick, store mgr in Lameque, NB
  B1. George, mar?, res near Chicago, ILL?   B2. Stanley, rem to U.S.
  B3. Verne, res St. Lambert, Que., mar May ---
    C1. Gordon, res St. Lambert
  B4. Dalton, d.y.   B5. Eva   B6. Ada   B7. Ethel
A3. John   A5. Anna, remained in J
A4. Frank, unmar   A6. Ada, rem to Hamilton, Ont.
IV. a sister nad V. a sister, remained in J and mar farmers
VI. a sister, married in J, a tradesman
LE RICHE, Alfred John, b 1867 St. Heliers, J, son of Jean Edouard Le R. and of Anne Rachel AHIER, qv. Rem to Winnipeg, Man. 1912. Mar Claudia Azelia JOURNEAUX, qv, of J, b 1894, dau of Thomas John J. and of Esther Azelia HEULIN, qv. (Grace BAETZ, London, Ont.)
A1. Gerald, b 1899 St. Heliers, rem to Toronto. In 1921, ill with TB, rem to Denver, Colo. and d there.
A2. Snowden Ahier, b 1903 J, mar 1940 Elizabeth Alice Gilson, dau of Robert C. Gilson and Elizabeth Hurst. Res Langstaff, Ont. 18 yrs., rem to London, Ont. He was a salesman, and she was a teacher.
  B1. Grace Elizabeth, b 1944 Toronto, mar Charles David Baetz, res London, Ont.
    C1. Michelle Huelin Baetz, b 1968 London, Ont.
  B2. Judith Lynn, b 1946 Toronto, mar ---, res Idon?, Ont.
    C1. Carrie Elizabeth, b 1973   C2. Tracy Lynne, b 1973, twin
A3. Mavis Claudia, b 1912 St. Heliers, J, has worked 30 plus yrs. for the Pentecostal Assemblies of Canada, res Toronto, Ont., unmar.
A4. other sisters?

LE RICHE, James, of C.I., was on Isle au Mortes, Nfld. 1860s (Rev. Hammond)
LE RICHE, C.I. name on S. coast of Nfld. (G.W. Le Messurier)
LE RICHE, Capt. and agent from J in Nfld. (K. Mathews)
LE RICHE, John?, in Port de Grave, Nfld. 1778 (Seary) prob from J
LE RICHE, George, mgr of Fruing Co. at Lameque, NB, lived with his sister-in-law, Maude LE SEELLEUR, qv, a dau of Mrs. A.T. ALEXANDER, who res in Montreal, a desc of the Doran family. (Donat Robichaud)
LE RICHE, a fam from J to Cardiff, Wales 1800s. The father of Arthur James was a shipper-owner, or a trader, running between J and Gaspe. Arthur James, b Newport, Monmouth, was chief officer of TWYFFORD, or similar name of vessel, salvaging in the Gaspe area 1855, 1856. (Frank Le Riche, Burnaby, BC)
LE RICHE, harbour master at Gaspe, 1955, 1956, b J
LE RICHE, curr Ont.
LE ROSSIGNOL, many variants: RACIGNAL, RACINAL, RUSENALL, NIGHTINGALE, etc.
LE ROSSIGNOL, in J since 1608 or before, poss Hug. Re Lake Rossignol, in NS, the following narrative of Capt. Wm. Owen, by Victor Palsits, N.Y. 1942, "Pierre Fritot, known as Rossignol, was an involuntary participant in the building of the settlement, having been captured by De Monts ca 1604 at Port Rossignol." The surname Fritot has also appeared in J.
LE ROSSIGNOL, Edouard, 1763-1820, and wife, Esther ---, had a son, Edouard. Edward mar Elizabeth ESNOUF, qv, a cousin. Their seven chn are listed below, several having settled in Canada. (James Le Rossignol, Calgary, Alta.; Gabrielle Slotsve, Estevan, Sask.; MS-1932, Inst. of Amer. Gen. for Mrs. Horace Baker; Violet L. Matte, Kelowna, BC; S.J. LE ROSSIGNOL, family Genealogy; Roger and Mavis Gray, Indian Head, Sask.)
Chn of Edouard and Elizabeth ESNOUF LE ROSSIGNOL of J: Edouard, b 1817, Elizabeth, John, Nicholas, Peter, Esther and Mary.
I. Edouard, Edward, b 1817 J, mar ---
A1. Edward Nicholas, b 1845 St. Mary, J, mar Elizabeth COLLAS, qv.
A2. Louisa, b J, mar Alfred DE CAEN, qv.
A3. Mary, b J, mar Philip LE MARQUAND, qv, d 1916
A4. Elizabeth, mar T. Charlton   A7. Peter, res Mt. Tolmie, BC
A5. Ann   A8. Philip John, 1855-1867
A6. John, d at sea   A9. Francis
                                        B1. Edward, res NB
                                        C1. William, res NS
II. Elizabeth, b 1819, mar John ESNOUF, qv. a son, John, res St. Mary's, J
III. John, b 1820 J, rem to Canada. Mar a widow with 5 chn, Mrs. Sara GIRARD, qv. John designed and built St. Martins Ch. at St. Brigette de Laval, Que.
A1. John, b ca 1845?, mar Georgianna Thibault, or Thibeau, 9 chn
   B1. Georgianna, b 1875 Laval, Que., mar 1894 Charles Clavet, 1871-1951. She d 1956, 9 chn.
      C1. Paul Clavet, 1894-1975, mar 1914 Corine HAMEL, 1892-1951
      C2. Omer Clavet, 1897-1972, mar 1920 Regina Hibert, 1895-1947, and mar 2. Stella Harrisson Godbout, 1917-1966
      C3. Alexandre Clavet, b Laval, d 1963, mar 1924 Eleanore Hibert, b 1899, Laval
      C4. Amedee Clavet, b 1901 Sillery, Que., d 1967, mar 1923 Berthe Simoneau, b 1901, Laval
      C5. Aline Clavet, b 1903 Les Saules, Ancienne Lorette, Que.

C6. Blandine Clavet, b 1905, mar 1930 Emile Fortier, b 1903
C7. Rene Clavet, b 1911, mar 1939 Patricia Beaumont, b 1915, Ste. Catherine, who d 1966. Mar 2. Therese Boisvert, b 1931.
C8. Rosaire Clavet, b 1913, mar 1940, Yvette Touchette, b 1918
C9. Bella Clavet, b 1915, mar 1941 Jean Paul Menard, 1917-1970, Courville, Que., res Beauport, Que.
B2. Alfred, b 1876 Laval, Que., mar Albertine Perrier 1906 Port Arthur, Ont. He d 1948, wife in 1960.
  C1. Ida, b 1907, mar Armand Carriere, and 2. Bernard Gardner 1974, res Kelowna, BC
    D1. Germaine Carriere, b 1929, mar Patrick Gleason
      E1. Marie Gleason   E2. Timothy Gleason
    D2. Lorraine Carriere, b 1931, mar Stewart Thomas, 6 chn
      E1. James Thomas   E4. Anne Marie Thomas
      E2. David Thomas   E5. Daniel Thomas
      E3. John Thomas   E6. Lee Anne Thomas
    D3. Evelyn Carriere, b 1935, mar Richard O'Rourke, 5 chn
      E1. Jerry O'Rourke   E4. Daniel O'Rourke
      E2. Lynn O'Rourke   E5. Michelle O'Rourke
      E3. Jackeline O'Rourke
  C2. Georgina, b 1909, mar Harry Peel
    D1. Charlotte Peel, mar Ronald WALKER
  C3. Armand, b 1911, mar Ruby Proctor 1933
    D1. Muriel, mar W. Faloona
      E1. Thomas Faloona E2. Danniel Faloona E3. Debbie Faloona
    D2. Joyce, mar R. Savoie
      E1. Raymond Savoie E2. Denise Savoie E3. Christine Savoie
    D3. Glen, mar Clara Lambert 1963
      E1. Brian   E2. Wendy   E3. Donna   E4. Curtis
    D4. Norman, unmar
    D5. Doreen, mar Paul Fisher
      E1. Sherri Lynn Fisher
  C4. Bertha, b 1914, mar Arthur Black
    D1. Maureen Black   D2. James Black
B3. Sarah, b 1977 Laval, mar 1901 Joseph Isaie Thomassin, 1879-1945. She d 1941.
  C1. Leopold Thomassin, 1903-1974, mar 1926 Rosy St. Laurent, b 1902 Val Briand
  C2. Dora Thomassin, b 1904, mar 1931 Roasire Perron, 1877-1957
  C3. Aline Thomassin, 1906-1954, mar 1932 Gerard St. Laurent, b 1906
  C4. Laureat Thomassin, 1907-1973, mar 1937 Dolores Perron, b 1913
  C5. Julienne Thomassin, b 1910, d 1928
  C6. Irene Thomassin, 1912-1955, mar 1931 Charles Eugene Paradis, 1905-1976
B4. Pierre Joseph, b 1882, blacksmith, carpenter, mar Marie Desanges Gervais, b 1899 Casimir, Que. Rem to Indian Head, Sask 1898, age 16.
  C1. Alexander Joseph, b 1911 Bienfoit, Sask, mar Bridgette Ann McKelvey 1935. She was b Carrickbeg, Ire., 1914.
    D1. Allan, b 1938 Marwayne, Alta.   D4. Semone, b 1945
    D2. Marion, b 1940   D5. Joanne, b 1948
    D3. Lorraine, b 1941 Vermilion, Alta.
    D6. James Patrick, b 1950 Vermilion, Alta., mar Dolly Elizabeth Avramenko, b 1954 Drumheller, Alta.
      E1. Alain James, b 1974 Calgary, Alta. E2. Kelsi Dawn, b 1976
    D7. Bernadette, b 1955
  C2. Gabrielle Blanche, b 1916, mar Louis Slotsve 1946, res Estevan,

Sask
- D1. Gayle Marie Slotsve, b 1947, mar Mervin Philip Goens, res Pasedena, Calif.
- D2. Patricia Lou Slotsve, b 1950, mar Ronald Morley 1977
- D3. Joslyn Semone Slotsve, b 1951, mar William Cofre 1977
- D4. Eric Pierre Slotsve, b 1957

C3. Yvonne, b 1917, dec. Mar Lt. Albert Charette.
- D1. Gerald Charette
- D2. Priscilla Charette

C4. Lorraine Mary, b 1919, mar Anton Leo Bonokoski 1941, 3 adopted chn
- D1. Richard Francis Bonokoski, b 1952
- D2. Marian Laura Bonokoski, b 1954
- D3. Hilary Anthony Bonokoski, b 1955

C5. Henry, b 1920, mar Anita PITON, qv, 1947
- D1. Joan, b 1956, adopted

C6. Semone Mary Jean, b 1925, mar 1. Edward J. Schwegman 1946, and 2. in 1969, Clayton Thom
- D1. Louise Marie Schwegman, b 1947, mar Robert Olmsted 1966
- D2. Elaine Semone Schwegman, b 1949, mar Kevin Bieth 1973
- D3. Mark Edward Schwegman, b 1950, mar Candie La Vallee in 1968
- D4. Larry Agustin Schwegman, b 1952, mar Gerry Routante, b 1952
  - E1. Melissa Marie Schwegman, b Metairie, La.
- D5. Susan Elizabeth Schwegman, b 1954, unmar
- D6. Randal Peter Schwegman, b 1957, mar Charlene McCleary, 1977

B5. Jacques, b 1884 Laval, d 1971, mar 1911 Clara Giroux, 1891-1958, 4 chn
- C1. Rolland, 1915-1974, mar 1937 Albertine Giroux, b 1918
- C2. Georgette, b 1923 St. Therese Lisieux, d.y.
- C3. Jacqueline, b 1924, d.y.
- C4. Rose, b 1926, mar 1945 Roger Thomassin, b 1924 Laval, Que.

B6. Edouard, b 1886 Laval, d 1954, mar 1908 Virginie Thomassin, 1886-1949
- C1. Edouard, b 1909, d 1970, mar 1938 Marie Jeanne Vallee, b 1915
- C2. Lorenzo, b 1911, mar 1943 Georgette Thomassin, b 1918 Laval, Que.
- C3. Georges, b 1913, mar 1955 Leonelle L'HEREAULT, 1912-1974
- C4. Jean Baptiste, b 1915, d 1919
- C5. Paul, b 1918, mar 1956 Laura Verret, b 1932
- C6. Wilfred, b 1920, d.y.
- C7. Madeleine, b 1921, mar 1942 Joseph Arthur Thomassin, b 1913 Laval
- C8. Laureanne, b 1923, d 1970, mar 1947 Jean Baptiste Thomassin, b 1921
- C9. Wilfred, again, b 1925 Laval, mar 1954 Berthe Alice Verret, b 1934

B7. John, said to have d in Tacoma, Wash. ca 1975, no issue

B8. Francois, Francis, b 1888 Laval, d 1968. Mar 1910, Philomene Thibeault, b 1891, 5 chn
- C1. Jules, b 1912, mar 1938 Anna Marie Bedard, b 1912
- C2. Juliette, b 1913, mar 1948 Adolphe GUILLET, qv, b 1913
- C3. Raymond, b 1914, d 1918
- C4. Cecile, b 1916, mar 1940 Robert H. Graham, b 1916
- C5. Helene, b 1921

B9. Leda LE ROSSIGNOL, B 1891 Laval,QUE mar Eli Matte, rew KelownaBC.
- C1. Wilfred Louis Matte, b 1910, mar Juliette Beatrice Douville of Ponteix,SASK, dau of emery Douville, mar Ft.William,Thunder Bay,ONT, res Ottawa,ONT.
  - D1. Richard Wilfred Matte, b 1945, unmar
  - D2. Terrence Emery Matte, b 1949 unmar

LE ROSSIGNOL 395

    C2. Laureanne Matte, b 1912, mar Bernard Viens, res Ft. MacLeod,
        D1. Colette Genevieve Viens, b 1938 mar Harvey Dersch ALTA.
            E1. Connie Dersch, b 1954 mar Denis Nathe
                F1. Amber Nicole Nathe, b 1974
                F2. Dennis Bradley Nathe b 1978
            E2. Linda Dersch, b 1956 mar Darwayne Claypool
            E3. Sharon Dersch, b 1958   E4. Colleen Dersch, b 1962
            E5. Jody Dersch b 1969
        D2. Laureen Bernadette Viens, b 1941 mar Lionel Simpson, res
            Calgary, ALTA.
            E1. Katherine Simpson, b 1963   E3. Nadine Simpson, b 1966
            E2. Stuart Simpson, b 1964   E4. Gregg Simpson b 1971
        D3. Paul Montgomery Viens, b 1942,mar Elizabeth Hogsteen, res
            Fort MacLeod
        D4. Paulette Violet Viens, b 1942, twin, mar Richard Webb, res
            Three Hills, ALTA.
            E1. Byron Webb b 1966   E3. Charlotte Webb, b 1969
            E2. Carmen Webb, b 1967
        D5. John Bernard Viens, b 1943, mar Donnalea Hayes
            E1. Colin Viens, b 1943,   E2. Jeffrey Viens, b 1974
        D6. Gisele Laureanne Viens, b 1948, mar Wayne Gregory, res
            Lethbridge, ALTA.
        D7. Denise Florence Viens, b 1952, mar Alan LE BRUN, Calgary,
            E1. Damon LE BRUN, b 1975, Calgary.   ALTA.
    C3. Violet Lillian Matte, b 1925, unmar res Kelowna, BC.
A2. Elizabeth, b 1833 J?, mar Joseph Gray, res Indian Head, Sask., 3
    daus, 1 adopted son. (Gabrielle Slotsve, Estevan, Sask.; Roger
    and Mavis Gray, Indian Head, Sask.)
    B1. Agnes Mary Gray, b 1880, mar 1. Theophilus SHARP, 4 chn, and 2.
        Wm. Price, 1 ch
        C1. Hazel Sharp   C2. Tilly May Sharp, d.y.   C3. Joseph Sharp, dec.
        C4. Ethel Sharp, mar Arthur Benton
            D1. Shirley Benton, mar --- Bolton, 3 chn
        C5. Robert Price, mar Margaret Waddell
            D1. Elsie Price, mar ---
                E1. Ronald   E2. dau
            D2. Margaret Price, mar ---
                E1. James
    B2. Bertha Isabella Gray, b 1882, mar Wm. Prior
        C1. Victor Prior, d.y.
        C2. Ernest Prior, b 1900, mar Muriel Bray
            D1. Lois Prior, b 1944, mar James Weisbrodt
                E1. Paul Weisbrodt, b 1965   E2. Todd Weisbrodt, b 1970
            D2. Russell Prior, b 1947, mar Shirley Stehr
                E1. Tany Marie Prior, b 1969 E3. Tyler Prior, b 1973
                E2. Tera Leigh Prior, b 1971
            D3. Cathy Prior, b 1955
        C3. Stanley Prior, b 1902, mar Myrtle Brewitt
            D1. Dora Prior, b 1933, mar Fred. Nichols 1928
                E1. Leslie Nichols, b 1954, mar Gwen Burwell, b 1954
                    F1. Sherilyn Nichols, b 1977
                E2. Ken Nichols, b 1956
            D2. Frances Prior, b 1935, mar Bert Dodman
                E1. Debbie Dodman, b 1955   E3. Mark Dodman, b 1956
                E2. Penny Dodman, b 1956   E4. Judy Dodman, b 1958
            D3. Lawrence Prior, b 1937, mar Joan Kelly

          E1. Deanna Lynn Prior, b 1961   E3. Terry Jason Prior, b 1973
          E2. Kelly Edward Prior, b 1963
      D4. Christine Prior, b 1941, mar Guy Blair, divorced
          E1. Mitchel Blair, b 1967
      D5. Elaine Prior, b 1947, mar Gordon Wells
          E1. Michelle Wells, b 1968
    C4. Stephen Prior, b 1904, mar May McGregor
        D1. Georgina Prior D2. Dale Prior D3. Leslie Prior, mar Joan ---
    C5. Elizabeth Prior, b 1906, mar Cecil Jeffers
        D1. Joyce Jeffers, mar Kenneth Ellery, divorced
            E1. Brian Ellery   E2. James, dec.
        D2. Unis, Eunice? Jeffers, mar --- Anderson
            E1. Andrea Anderson   E2. Arlene Anderson
    C6. Carl Prior, b 1908, mar 1936 Constance Brewitt
        D1. Robert Prior, b 1937, mar Shirley Hind
        D2. Joan Prior, b 1944, mar Jerry Mitchell
            E1. Len, Leonard?, Mitchell, b 1962 E2. Robert Mitchell, b 1965
    C7. Alice Prior, b 1910, mar Carmen Thackery
        D1. Joy Thackery, mar Roy Cameron
            E1. Robert Cameron   E2. dau
    C8. Melvin Prior, b 1915, mar Ruth McClenehan
        D1. Ronald Prior, b 1942, mar Pat Kirkpatrick
            E1. Christopher Prior, b 1970 E2. Thomas Prior, b 1972
    C9. Winston Prior, b 1915, twin, mar Eileen ---
        E1. Gary Prior   E2. Daniel Prior
  B3. Catherine Gray, mar William Sharp
    C1. Gray Sharp, mar Gertrude ---, a son, William?
    C2. Beatrice, mar Austin Alexander
        D1. Linda Alexander   D2. a son?
  B4. Theresa Gertrude Gray, b 1887, mar 1909 Arthur E. Prior, who d
      1972
    C1. Tilly, Matilda? Prior, b 1910, mar John Booth
    C2. Dorothy Prior, b 1914, mar George Kurtz
        D1. Dennis Kurtz, b 1946, adopted
        D2. Sharon Kurtz, b 1944, adopted, mar Ted Murray
            E1. James Murray   E2. Lori Murray   E3. Amber Murray
    C3. Arthur Prior, b 1916, mar Jean McIntosh
        D1. Ross Prior, b 1952, mar Debra ---
            E1. Graham Prior, b 1970, adopted
    C4. Catherine Prior, b 1922, mar Harold Freeman
        D1. Linda Freeman, mar Garnet Schultz
            E1. Rodney Schultz
        D2. Gayle Freeman, mar Bruce Welsh
            E1. Michelle Welsh
        D3. Garth Freeman
  B5. Wallace Gray, d.y.
  B6. Mabel Louise Gray, mar Gilbert Prior
    C1. Joseph Prior, mar Beth Allen
        D1. Josephine Prior, mar Ken Mader
            E1. Bradley Mader   E2. Lyle Mader   E3. ?
        D2. Eleanor Prior, mar Gordon Graham
            E1. Sherri Graham   E2. Timothy Graham
        D3. Kenneth, mar, 2 chn
    C2. Garfield Prior, killed in R.A.F., WWII
    C3. Gilbert Le Rossignol Prior, mar Elsie Twells
        D1. Melanie Prior, mar Gerry Beattie

                    E1. Jean Beattie   E2. Tracy Beattie   E3. Kelly Beattie
                D2. Alice Prior, mar --- Cox
                    E1 Douglas Cox   E2. Susan Cox   E3. James Cox, adopted
                D3. Laura Prior, mar Ronald Thompson
                D4. Doris Prior, mar --- Bishop?
            C4. Ralph Prior, mar Kay ---
                D1. Merle Prior   D2. Keith Prior   D3. Dean Prior
        B7. James Gray, d.y.
        B8. Thomas Gray, 1883-1964, adopted, son of Thomas Malcolm and
            Catherine Craig, (both of Scotland)
            C1. Elizabeth, b 1914, mar Walton Tennant
                D1. Paul Tennant, mar Susan CAREY
                    E1. Douglas Tennant   E3. Christopher Tennant
                    E2. Matthew Tennant   E4. son
                D2. Barbara, adopted, mar James Mahon, divorced, mar 2. Chet
                    Simpson
                D3. Bruce, adopted, mar ---, a son
                D4. Susan Tennant, b 1954
            C2. Isabel Gray, b 1916, mar Ivor Korvin
                D1. Ross Korvin, mar Helen ---
                    E1. Barry Korvin   E2. Kim Korvin   E3. Rhonda Korvin, adopted
                D2. Roberta Korvin, mar Donald Shinski
                    E. Scott Shinski   E2. J. Shinski, a son
            C3. Ruth Gray, b 1918, mar Harry Bateman
                D1. Leah Ann Bateman, mar William Woodard, divorced
                    E1. Kent Woodard   E2. Penny Woodard
            C4. Roger Gray, b 1921, mar Mavis Guest
                D1. Douglas Gray, b 1948, d 1973
                D2. Margaret Gray, b 1951, mar Leslie Anderson
                D3. Janet Gray, b 1955
                D4. Richard Gray, b 1957, mar Sydna Joan Stilborn
                    E1. Kara Michelle Gray, b 1977
            C5. David Gray, b 1924, mar Hazel Gilbert
                D1. Thomas Gray, mar Jackie ---   D4. Ian Gray
                D2. Stephen Gray   D5. Caroline Gray
                D3. Michael Gray
    IV. Nicholas, b 1822, poss the winter man at Perce for Charles Robin,
        middle 1800s?
    V. Peter, b 1826, St. Mary, J, rem to Ottawa, Ont., mar Mary Gillespie,
        and rem to Lincoln, Nebr. Desc in Nebr. and Colo. She mar 2. Rev.
        Henderson
        A1. Peter, Analyst, experimental farm, Ottawa, Ont.
        A2. James Edward, b 1866, mar 1898 Jessie Katherine Ross, 2 chn. He
            was the author of several books in various fields, Dean at Univ. of
            Nebr., lecturer, economist, etc.
            B1. Edward Ross, b 1902 Lincoln, Nebr.   B2. Helen Marian Henderson?
        A3. Dr. Walter J., of Rifle, Colo, mar Laura Mabery, b 1870
            B1. Mary Alice, b ca 1900   B2. Annie Elizabeth, b ca 1903
        A4. Annie Elizabeth   A5. Mary, mar A.O. Dawson, 5 chn
    VI. Esther, b 1830
    VII. Mary, b 1833, mar Philip TOUET, res Mt. Tolmie, Vict., BC, 4 chn.
        See TOUET.
LE ROSSIGNOL, Pierre Nicholas, b 1810 J, d 1885. Son of Pierre Le R.
    and Esther Jeanne LE REGLE of J. Mar Nancy Hardeley, who d 1905, age
    95. (Le Rossignol Chart) Poss connected with Peter Le R. of Levis,

Que., below.
A1. Pierre Philip, b 1845, d 1916 St. Ouen, J. Mar M. LE MAISTRE, qv.
  B1. Peter, b 1877, rem to Montreal, mar Jeanne Gaspard
    C1. Isabelle   C3. Marguerite
    C2. Edgar, res Montreal, Que.   C4. Roger, b 1914
  B2. Philip, b 1880, mar F. HUBERT, qv, res J
    C1. Nancy Hardeley, b 1914 St. Ouen, J
A2. Frederick John, b 1845, res St. Ouen, J, mar Isabelle M. LE MAISTRE
A3. John, b J, rem to Lawrence, Mass. where he d 1873
A4. Inkerman?
A5. Louisa, b J, mar John ALEXANDRE, qv, of J
  B1. Louisa ALEXANDRE
A6. Mary Ann, b J, mar John LE MOTTEE
  B1. Mary Ann LE MOTTEE, mar Francis LE FEUVRE, qv, of St. Ouen, J
LE ROSSIGNOL, Peter, b J, Protestant, and English speaking proprietor of a fabric store in Levis, Que. He had a partner named Davidson. Peter d 1874, his widow mar 2. --- HENDERSON? Left MEMOIRS? (Profile Levisiens, by Pierre Georges Roy, Levis, 1948) Desc in U.S.
LE ROSSIGNOL, Peter, of crew on ship HEMATOPE 1846 and 1873
LE ROSSIGNOL, Gilbert was on the 1871 Census in Pabos, Gaspe, mar to Felicite, age 40
LE ROSSIGNOL, John, b 1845 St. Peter, J, a blacksmith, to Paspebiac, Que. 1865
LE ROSSIGNOL, Edward, on the crew of the Robin ship REAPER in 1873
LE ROSSIGNOL, John, a whaler from J at Gaspe Basin 1807
LE ROSSIGNOL, John, b J, res 1815 Isle Madame, Cape Breton, asked for 500 acres on Lac Brador, CB. He was Janvrin agent, had 2 chn on the 1811 census.
LE ROSSIGNOL, John, b ca 1847 J, was in Petit de Grat, CB 187I (Census)
LE ROSSIGNOL, John, b ca 1841 J, carpenter at Petit de Grat, 187I (Census)
LE ROSSIGNOL, C.I. surname on the S. coast of Nfld. (G.W. Le Messurier)
LE ROSSIGNOL, LE ROSIGNOL, NIGHTINGALE, several captains, merchants and boatkeepers in Nfld. 1800s and before (K. Mathews)
LE ROSSIGNOL. The widespread GUSTIN, qv, fam of N.A. is descended from this family, as the first GUSTIN was Augustin JEAN, whose mother was a LE ROSSIGNOL. (QAAM)
LE ROSSIGNOL, Edward, to BC, park caretaker 1907, from J. Other Le Rossignols also in BC
LE ROCHE, LE ROCKE, LE ROCK, LERROCK, LE ROCQUE, in various forms many places in the maritimes. LE ROCK, LE ROCQUE, old J surname (Stevens)
LE ROCQUE, LE ROCKE, Isaac, Henry, and two Michaels were in Shippegan, NB 1861 (Census)
LE ROUGETEL, Ann Rachel, b J, 1868-1943, rem to Toronto ca 1901. Mar Alfred AHIER, qv, 7 chn. (Mrs. D.A. Jaycox, Costa Mesa, Calif.)
LE ROUSSET, from C.I. to Gaspe? Wm. of Grand Greve, had son, John, b 1843
LE ROUX, from C.I. to Nfld? Charles in Lower Burgeo 1861
LE ROUX, from C.I. to Gaspe, to Alpena, Mich?
LE ROUX, Edward and Peter, fishermen at Sandy Pt. Nfld. 1871 (Lovell)
LE ROUX, Thomas, fishery firm out of Blanc Sablon 1800s, and at Forteau Bay
LE ROUX, curr Stephenville, Nfld. (G.W. Le Messurier) (Tocque)
LE ROUX, Capt. from J in Nfld. (K. Mathews; Seary)
LE ROUX, from J?, in Richmond Co., NS 1861 (Census)
LE ROUX, Mark, b ca 1930 J, rem to London, Eng., then to Canada in 1963, settled Charlottetown, PEI. Mar Petra ---, specialized in conducting. Has organized 4 choirs in PEI with outstanding results,

LE ROUX 399

taking 110 chn from 7 to 14 yrs. old on tours all over Canada, to Bermuda and to the U.S. He is the son of Mr. V. Le Roux, dec and of Mrs. H. LE ROUX, who res St. Helier, J.
LE ROUX, George, b Cote Du Lac, near Three Rivers, Que., son of Xenon LE ROUX, b there 1870. Fam rem to Bay City, Mich. area 1879, origin unknown. (Mrs. Lambert Le Roux, Caquitlam, BC)
LE ROY, old G surname often changed to KING (Carey-Wimbush)
LE ROY, from C.I. to Nfld. LE ROY, SHIPMASTERS OF GUERNSEY.
LERRIER, J surname (Saunders) said to be modified to LEAR in Nfd. (Shortis-Munn)
LE RUE. in Nfld. (Seary) Said to be from C.I.
LE RUEZ, John, with fam of 6 at Bon. Is., Gaspe 1831. See LARROWAY.
LE RUEZ, curr Ontario, from C.I. & LARAWAY
LE RUCY? Poss LE ROUSSET or LE RUEZ?, Judith, mar ca 1830 Abraham LE HUQUET, qv, of St. George's Cove, Gaspe (Brochet)
LE SARRE, LE SERRE, LA SERRA, Peter. This man from G was a surgeon, member of the Council of Assiniboia, in western Canada, Rupert's Land, in 1813. See THE CANADIAN WEST. He came to Canada via the ship, PRINCE OF WALES, to Fort Churchill, and his party walked the 200 miles to York Factory in the winter. Only half of the group survived. See SARRe in QAAM, and SARE.
LE SAUTEUR, Harriet Eleanore, mar Charles Ernest PALLOT, qv, 4 chn, rem to BC. Curr Halifax.
LE SAUVAGE, Clifford from G, settled in London, Ont. Desc known of, but not located.
LE SAUVAGE, in Torteval, G, 1700s
LE SAUVAGE, Eva Jane Elizabeth, b J, mar Philip George LE GRESLEY, settled in Newmarket, Ont. 1913. 7 chn, 4 b Jersey.
LE SAUVAGE, Hilda, sister of Eva Jane, a dau, Marjorie Hilda Toop, res Grouville, J
LE SAUVAGE, Marjorie, b J, a dau, Myrtle BLONDEL, res St. Clements, J
LE SAUVAGE, Edith, mar ---. Dau, Mrs. E. THOREAU, res St. Peters, J.
LE SAUVAGE, L., from G to Toronto (Mrs. A. Symes, Toronto, Ont.)
LE SAVAGE, Elizabeth, b G, in Cap Chat 1861 (Census). See also SAVAGE.
LE SEBIRE, also as SEBIRE and SEBIREL, etc. See SEBIRE.
LESBIREL, J.W., from G to London, Ont. 1929 (Parents and grandparents b Liverpool, Eng.)
LESBIREL, LESBOREL, C.I. name on S. coast of Nfld. (G.W. Le Messurier)
LESBRIL, Peter, b J, in Gaspe Bay 1861 (Census)
LESBIREL, from C.I. to West Coast of Nfld. 1800s? (Shortis-Munn)
LESBIREL, Helier, clerk, b J, son of Jean David L. of Trinity, J, and of Nancy GALLICHON of St. Saviour, J, mar 1870 in Pte. Aux Trembles, Que., Mary LE LACHEUR, dau of John Henry LE LACHEUR, qv, and of Elisabeth Rippey, b Ireland. Witness, Eliz. HAMMOND, sister of the bride. See LE LACHEUR, GALICHAN, HAMMOND. (Gravel)
LESBIREL, Anne Jane, of J, mother of John Charles, Lydia and Philip AMY, all of whom came to Canada early 1900s. (J.C. Amy, Montreal, and Margaret Amy, Winnipeg, Man. She was dau of Clement LESBIREL and Nancy BLAMPIED, qv.)
LE SCELLEUR, Roger, at L'Anse au Griffon, Gaspe 1800s (J. H. Le Breton list)
LE SCELLEUR, Philip and James, signed Petition 1820, Gaspe
LE SCELLEUR, Charles, from J to Gaspe ca 1900 or before, mar J 1876, Sophie Lendreau. A son, Charles, see page 400.
LE SCELLEUR, C.I. name on S. coast of Nfld. (G.W. Le Messurier; Seary)
LE SCELLEUR, C.I. surname associated with Robins in Paspebiac and with town of New Carlisle, Gaspe (Prov. Arch.)

LE SEELEUR RESEARCHER: JACK MAVINS, ANOLA, MAN. CANADA.
LE SCELLEUR, LE SELLEUR, from J to Nfld. via Quebec? (Seary)
LE SCELLEUR, current, Riv. aux Renards, Gaspe
LE SCELLEUR, Charles, b St. Heliers, J, son of Charles Le S. and Sophie LENDREAU. res Grande Vallee, Gaspe 1876, where he mar Josephine CARON, dau of Jean-Batiste Caron and Marcelline Fournier
LE SEELLEUR, Thomas Edmund, with wife Florence Maude ---, from J to Winnipeg, Man. 1914. Wife's surname poss FOARD, qv. (F. Le Seelleur, No. Vancouver, BC)
  A1. Edmund Thomas, mar Evelyn Matilda ---?
LE SEELLEUR, Louis Alfred, b 1928 J, from there in 1950 to Toronto, mar, 3 sons, res London, Ont.
LE SEELLEUR, ---, mar Maude FIOTT, dau of Peter James FIOTT and Lillian Florence Blackhall, b Canada, of Scots ancestry. Res Montreal. See FIOTT. Also see George LE RICHE, who mar Louise Blackhall.
LE SEELLEUR, Thomas John, b 1852, res London, Ont?
LE SEELEUR, George, b J, ship captain, made sev voyages to Montreal. Mar Jenny NOEL, qv, of St. Martin, J. He was the son of Thomas Le S. and Susanne ---. She d 1881, he in 1889, J. Sev of their chn to Canada. (G.C. Le Seelleur, Winnipeg, Man.; Nicol Le Seelleur, Ottawa, Ont.) Susanne above may have been Susanne CABOT
  A1. George, b 1845 St. Clement, J, mar Susan CABOT, qv, 1861-1918, 5 chn
    B1. Clarence, 1885-1963, to Robins at Gaspe ca 1900, rem to Brantford, Ont. and to Winnipeg, Man. Mar Mabel Sanford of NS, b 1891.
      C1. Edna Lois, b 1915, mar Donald W. Davidson 1914-1976
        D1. Bruce Davidson, b 1944
        D2. Patricia Davidson, b 1943, mar Ed Kemens, 2 chn
          E1. Debra Kemens   D2. Dale Kemens
      C2. Gordon Cabot, b 1922, mar 2. Joyce MOON, qv, b 1924. Gordon, a civil servant.
        D1. Gordon Robert, teacher, b 1941, by first wife
        D2. Lorie Marie, 1953-1965
        D3. Geraldine Florence, b 1949, mar Ralph Riter, b 1947
    B2. Helena, 1888-1959, unmar   B4. Margaret, 1891-1944
    B3. Maude, 1889-1971   B5. Eva, 1893-1944
  A2. Thomas John, 1852-1929, mar 1. Jane GALLICHAN, qv, d ca 1877, and 2. Isabella NICOL, 1868-1962, dau of James Y. NICOL, qv. Mar 1898. T.J. in London, Ont. 1874. Worked for Grand Trunk RR, cabinet maker, ship carpenter.
    B1. Thomas Nicol, b 1904, mar Anne Brown, b 1906, Irish. Thomas worked for Ont. Board of Education, Dominion Bur. of Stat., and was on Unesco Mission twice to No. Africa. Retired 1969.
      C1. Thomas John, b 1943, design engineer, mar Anne Simpson, b 1947, res St. Lambert, Que.
      C2. Lynda Ann, b 1945, mar Thos. G. Ellacott
        D1. Curtis Ellacott, b 1966   D2. Patrick Ellacott, b 1967
  A3. Jane, 1857-1910. After father's death in 1889, res in J, to Canada ca 1900, res London, and Brantford, Ont., then taught French in private school, Buffalo, NY, bur London, Ont.
LE SEELLEUR, LE SEELER, etc., John, who was 85 ca 1966, wrote on the subject of Cloridorme, Gaspe (Rev. D'Hist, Vol. 3, No. 1)
LE SEELLEUR, Charles Wilfred, 1924-1960, bur St. Peters, Paspebiac, Gaspe (GLF)
LE SELLEUR, LE SCELEUR, John, worked for the Fruing Co. at Cloridorme, Que.
LE SCELLEUR, Capt., master of the SWIFT, a barque of J, from Blanc Sablon for the Magdalen Is., was driven ashore at the entrance of Amherst Harbour, and sold at Auction Sept. 1873, after the famous Gale of 73,

154 tons, built 1826.
LE SEELLEUR, Edward, b J?, res St. James, Winnipeg, Man. 1930s
LE SHANE, from J to Nfld. Cf LE CHESNE, or LE CHANU? (Stevens) 1700s
LESLIE and LE VESCONTE, J fishery in C.B. or Nfld.
LE SUCCEUR, Capt. from J in Nfld. (K. Mathews) Poss LE SCELLEUR?
LE SUER, LE SUEUR?, Joseph J., from J to Victoria, BC before 1940 (Luce)
LE SUEUR, from C.I. to PEI 1870 (Luce)
LE SUEUR, Peter, from J to Nfld. and back to J, became a Methodist missionary to the French. See chapter on Clergy, and Missionaries. Peter had Nfld. fishery ca 1770. (Le Messurier)
LE SUEUR, from C.I. to Ont.
LE SUEUR, Capt., ship owner and merchant from J in Nfld. (K. Mathews)
LE SUEUR, in Maritimes Fisheries (J.H. Le Breton list)
LE SUEUR, William Dawson, civil servant, journalist, b 1840 Quebec, d Ottawa 1917, son of Peter LE SUEUR and Barbara Dawson. Author of COUNT FRONTENAC 1906. In 1867, mar Anna Jane Foster of Montreal. One son, Ernest Arthur, and a dau. Ernest was a chemical engineer, 1869-1953, educated MIT. Invented electrolitic process for pulp and paper industry. In 1893 he mar Maud Drummond, a dau. (Ency. Can.)
LE SUEURS, from J, had a business in London, Ont. late 1800s
LETACNOUX, from J? to Nfld. (Seary)
LE TALIVERE, Geo., from C.I.?, signed Gaspe Petition 1820
LE TEMPLIER, from J to NB (Rev. Le Gresley)
LE TEMPLIER, in Maritimes Fisheries (J.H. Le Breton list)
LE TEXIER, from J?, to Vancouver, BC
LE TISSIER, Walter, from G?, a dau in Winona, Ont., to Hamilton from G. Desc in Fruitland, Ont. (Edw. Le Page)
LE TISSIER, Hilda Alice of Le Houmet, Catel, G, rem with husband, John Wm. Peter ROBIN, qv, and sons to Ontario 1912
LE TIEC, from J to Nfld. (Seary)
LE TOURNEAU, of Gaspe, from C.I.? Sarah, of St. Paul River was b 1829.
LE TOUZEL, see also TOUZEL
LE TOUZEL. Several of this surname from G and from J to Gaspe. Curr in Carlisle and Sept. Isles, Quebec. (GLF; Mrs. Florence Le Touzel, Rosebridge, Que.; Wilfred Brideaux, Ottawa, Ont.) Little verification of fams and dates below.
LE TOUZEL, Adolphus, mar Mary Jane RABEY of G, res Gaspe, there in 1860
A1. William, mar Mary LE LACHEUR, qv.
  B1. Earl   B4. Denton, mar Anne FOURNIER, 2 chn, res Montreal
  B2. Dawson   B5. Herbert, b 1898
  B3. Hartley   B6. Marjorie, unmar, res Montreal
A2. ---, bro of Wm., mar Effie WEST, b 1889, d 1952
A3. Henry, mar Maggie Suddard, res Gaspe?
A4. Malcolm, mar Charlotte Suddard. A dau mar Reg. P. DE GRUCHY, qv.
  B1. Jean   B2. Gladys   B3. Maude   B4. Mable
  B5. Ella   B6. Ruby   B7. Maynard
A5. Amy, mar?   A6. Letitia, mar?

LE TOUZEL, George Frederick of C.I. fam in Gaspe, mar Charlotte RABEY, qv, nee ROSE, qv. Data uncertain on this fam (GLF; Mrs. F. Le Touzel, Rosebridge, Que.; Wilfred Brideaux, Ottawa; Brochet)
A1. Mildred   A2. Otis, unmar, res Rosebridge, Gaspe
A3. Francis, mar --- BRETON? A son, Wayne, mar, has 1 ch
A4. George James, mar Clarissa GUIGNION, sev chn
  B1. Louis?, mar Beatrice GALLIARD, 2 chn including dau, Anita
Mildred, Francis, Otis and Wayne may be chn of G &Clarissa.

B1. Patricia, mar Geral Skene, res St. Lambert, Que.
   C1. Lana Skene   C2. Geoffrey Skene   C3. Rodrick Skene
LE TOUZEL, James, b J, res Barbadoes and Goderich, Ont., 2 daus, 1 son
LE TOUZEL, George, b J, mar 1.?, and 2. Maria RABEY, qv.
LE TOUZEL, Henry, b ca 1818 J, to Gaspe Basin (Brochet)
LE TOUZEL, ---, mar Florence RABEY, b 1878, d 1957. She mar 2. Coxon, res Rochester, NY
A1. Herbert D. LE TOUZEL, b 1898, d 1959, mar?
  B1. Dolores B., b 1924, mar --- HARDING
    C1. Christine Arlene Harding, b 1950, mar Mesiti
      D1. Rocco Mesiti, b 1968   D3. Michael Mesiti, b 1970
      D2. Stephanie Mesiti, b 1969
    C2. Barbara Ann Harding, b 1952 C4. Betty Delores Harding, b 1955
    C3. Edward Wm. Harding, b 1954
  B2. Harold Austin, b 1900, mar?
    C1. Betty Le Touzel, b 1941
  B3. Roland Maynard, b 1902, d 1968
  B4. Evelyn Ireine, b 1903, d 1967, mar --- McCarthy
  B5. Kingsley Rabey, b 1905, mar ?, res Rochester, NY
    C1. Kingsley A. LE T., b 1942, mar ---
      D1. Timothy Alan, b 1965   D2. Kristin Mary, b 1967
    C2. Katherine Florence, b 1945, mar --- Albert
LE TOUZEL, Edward C., 1878-1954, son of Charles LE TOUZEL, to Gaspe before 1860s, and son of Martha RABEY, qv. Mar Sarah ROSE, qv.
A1. Ralph, mar Ann HALE, no issue
A2. Dorothy, mar Raymond LE MESURIER, no issue, res Windsor, Ont.
A3. Howard, mar Florence WILLIAMS, res Rosebridge, Que.

LE TOUZEL, Leyland, 1842-1955, Gaspe (GLF)
LE TOUZEL, Blanche, sister of George, unmar, 1877-1936 (GLF)
LE TOUZEL, Douglas, 1896-1953 (GLF)
LE TOUZEL, Walter, bro of George, mar Mary Jane Clark, 1866-1952, bur Rosebridge, Gaspe (GLF)
LE VAILLANT, Henry A., b J, to Canada 1921, homesteaded at Porcupine Plain, Sask. in 1928. Rem to Toronto 1942, a roofer. Retired 1965, rem to BC 1970. Mar in Toronto, Evelyn Stevenson, no issue. Bro and other relatives in J. (H.A. Vaillant, BC)
LE VAILLANT, from J to Nfld., Fred, who d 1942 at Port Aux Basques, Nfld. (Seary)
LE VAIN, Marguerite, wife of John LE SUEUR, qv
LE VAIN, John, see Jean PALLOT
LE VAINE, from C.I. to BC?
LE VALLEY, LA VALLEY, in Nfld. Cf LE VALLEE, LA VALLEE in J (Stevens)
LE VALLEY, some from C.I. to Marblehead, Mass. and desc to Canada as U.E.L.'s
LE VAVASSEUR DIT DURELL, from J to Canada as DURELL? See NICOLE
LE VASSEUR, curr, sev placed in Canada, poss from J, origin unknown
LE VATT, Capt. from C.I. in Nfld. (K. Mathews)
LE VATTE, included by Lorway in his list of C.I. in N.S.
LE VAVASSEUR, Capt. from C.I. to Nfld. Cf VAVASOUR in Canada (Rev. Hammond)
LE VEILLEZ, curr Gaspe. Cf LE VEILLEZ of J (Stevens)
LE VER, LEVER, Charles, of Marsoui , Que., in 1876, where he mar Marcelline Henley, bp 1854, dau of Patrice Henley, and Basilice Lafontaine. Charles, the son of Desire Lever, of St. Peter, J, and Malanie Lemoir. (Remiggi)
LE VESCONTE, Peter and Isaac, b J. They were very active in boat

LE VESCONTE 403

building and shipping at Descousse, West Arichat, Riviere Bourgeois,
Lennox Passage, Poulamont, Little River, and other towns in Cape
Breton, NS, in the early 1800s.

LE VESCONTE, Peter, b ca 1788 St. Aubin?, J, mar Jane MALZARD, qv, and
rem to Cape Breton, NS, where his firm, DE CARTERET AND LE VESCONTE,
was involved in numerous enterprises. (Letters in NS Arch., 1830-
1860, Caroline MacDougall, Halifax, NS; Peter Le Vesconte, Dartmouth,
NS: Soc. Jers. Bull, 1974 and 1932; Wm. Le Vesconte, E. Hampton, NY:
Lester Le Vesconte, Elmhurst, ILL; Ivor Le Vesconte, Lanigan, Sask;
Balleine's Bio. Dict.; Census 1871)

A1. Jane, mar Peter DE CARTERET, res Cape Breton. De Carteret had been there since ca 1809.
  B1. Peter DE CARTERET, mar a Miss CAVE, 2 chn, Elizabeth and Harold

A2. Elizabeth, known as Livy, mar in Switzerland to a Mr. Roger. The ROBIN family also had connections in Switzerland.

A3. Isaac, b 1822 St. Aubin, J, d Arichat, NS 1879, mar 1843 Caroline Susan JEAN, qv, b 1822, dau of Louisa Moore and John JEAN, qv. Isaac was a sailor, merchant, Spanish consular agent at Arichat, legislator and financial secretary. Elected to House of Commons, Ottawa, 1869 and 1872. Went to England 1864 as a representative of the NS government.
  B1. James Isaac, 1844, d.y.   B5. Isaac, b 1852, d 1877, post
  B2. Peter John, 1846, drowned   office clerk
  B3. William Henry, b 1848, d.y. B6. Jane Malzard, 1854-1898
  B4. John, b 1849, shipmaster
  B7. Caroline Alberta Louise, b 1858, d 1935. Mar John L. MacDougall, barrister of Inverness Co., NS
    C1. Claire   C3. Kenneth Joseph, d.y.
    C2. Lachlan Gordon, b 1885, d 1949, unmar
    C4. Bertram Camillus, b 1892-1967, mar Helen Jean MacKenzie, res Strathlorne, NS
      D1. Caroline Cameron MacKenzie, b 1918
      D2. John Lachlan, b 1920, mar Sarah McFarlane, 2 adopted chn
      D3. Isaac Lorne, b 1922, mar Kathleen MacPherson, 5 chn, res Halifax
      D4. Alice Claire, b 1923, d.y.
      D5. Beatrice Claire, b 1925, mar Charles MacLean, no issue
      D6. Bertram Gerald, b 1927, mar Harriet MacLeod, Assessor, NS, 3 daus
      D7. Kenneth George, or George Kenneth, b 1929, mar Catherine Rebecca Finn, 2 daus, 3 sons
    C5. John Cameron, b 1894, d 1969, unmar
    C6. Isaac Duncan, b 1896, d 1969, mar Winnifred MacDonald of Port Hood, NS. Isaac was a Member of the House of Parliament, Ottawa, representing Inverness Co.
      D1. Kelvin Joseph, b 1930, lawyer, Montreal, mar Frances Dohm of U.S., 2 sons, a dau
      D2. Angela, mar Louis Forsa of El Cerita, Calif., dau, Angela Sharon
    C7. Caroline Jane, d.y.
  B8. Florence, Gertrude, b 1865   B9. Florence Eliz., b 1859, d.y.
  B10. Clarissa Harriet, b 1860, d 1926, res Boston, Mass., no issue
  B11. Louis St. Germain, b 1867, d 1934

A4. William, b 1831 St. Heliers, J, mar Caroline Horton Cutler, qv, of Guysborough, NS. This Cutler said to be originally LE COUTEUR of J.
  B1. Frances Jane, b 1856, d 1923   B2. Letitia, b 1858, d 1866
  B3. William Isaac, mar Ethel Shaw

          C1. Caroline Margaret, mar Frederick MAUGER, qv.
             D1. Eva Mauger, mar Douglas Landry
             D2. George Mauger, mar Ann SAMSON, qv, chn
                E1. Olla Mauger   E2. Kimberly Mauger
          C2. Peter, mar Christine Dunphy
             D1. Laleagh, mar Yvon TANGUAY
          C3. John Cutler, mar Ada Mable MAUGER
             D1. John William, mar Jesslyn MacLeod
             D2. Kenneth Howard, mar Marilyn DOWNING
                E1. Dawn   b 1961   D3. Robin, b 1971
                E2. Daphney, b 1969
             D3. Roy?
          C4. Eva Leila, mar Clive Clare
             D1. David Kerry Clare, mar Catherine Nichols
                E1. Patrick Clare   E2. Brian Clare
          C5. Charles Malzard, mar Lucille Osborne, a son, Robert
       B4. Peter, b 1861, unmar
       B5. Lennox, b 1864, d 1933, mar Eva Shaw, sister of Ethel Shaw, above.
          Res C.B.
          C1. Clement, b 1904, d 1973, rem to Long Island, no issue
          C2. William, b 1906, mar Helen LE BRUN, of Arichat, NS, rem to Long
             Island, no issue
       B6. Alice May, b 1867, mar Henry Moreau McCallum 1896
          C1. Moreau McCallum, b 1897, d.y.
          C2. Caroline Marie, b 1899, d.y.
          C3. Kenneth Malzard McCallum, b 1907, d 1977, mar Eva ---, no issue
LE VESCONTE, Daniel, bp 1828 J, son of Daniel LE VESCONTE, b 1792, and
   of Elizabeth Esther NICOLLE. Owner of the TOWER SHIP YARDS, in J,
   which closed down in 1867. Mar 1863 Alice DESLANDES, qv, dau of Sir
   George DESLANDES, also called DELON? His wife had 3 daus by a pre-
   vious marriage, poss Hilda Huges Abel, Lily Maud Rogers, and Gladys
   Mary Cahil. (Ivor Daniel Le Vesconte, Lanigan, Sask)
A1. Louisa Deslandes, b 1865 J, mar Stanley BROCK
A2. Jessica Nicolle, b 1866 J, mar G. Leary
A3. Alice Esperanza, b 1868, Bristol, England
A4. Romulus Horatio, b 1871, Bristol, d 1948, manager Trafalgar Iron &
   Coal Co., Cardiff, Wales. Mar Janet Ann WILLIAMS, b 1874, d age 98.
   B1. Arthur, b 1893 Caerleon, Eng., mar, no issue
   B2. Ernest, b 1894 Cardiff, Wales, to Canada ca 1910? Served in WWI
      and WWII. Mar Olive Hallam, b 1901, 5 chn, res Calgary, Alta.
      (Some data on chn uncertain)
      C1. Jeannet, b 1924, mar Ross Stanfield, who d 1966, res Calgary
         D1. Ralph Stanfield   D2. Diane Stanfield
      C2. Noreen, b 1927 Calgary, mar John Kayter D1. Fay Kayter mar Rich-
         ard Berglof D2. Donna Kayter D3. Barbara Kayter D4. Kathy Kayter
      C3. Ruth, b 1929, mar John Henderson, res Calgary, Alta.
         D1. Stewart Henderson D2. Debbi Henderson D3. Susan Henderson
      C4. Dorothy, b 1934, mar Gerald Kernaghan, and 2. Buck Kim, res
         Calgary
         D1. Loren Kernaghan D2. Karen Kernaghan D3. Larry Kernaghan
      C5. Kathleen, b 1936, mar Jack Schafer, res Victoria, BC
         D1. Donald Schafer   D2. Leona Schafer
   B3. Ivor, b 1899, d 1934
      C1. Ivor John Raymond, b 1928   D2. Mollie, b 1931
   B4. Harry, b 1902 Wales, mar Lily Simpson Laing
      C1. James Henry, b 1934 Calgary, Alta., mar Sharon Thompson 1956
         D1. David D2. James D3. Judy D4. Debbi D5. Sharon

```
       C2. Gerald Arthur, b 1935, d.y.
       C3. Kenneth, b 1937 Calgary, mar Evelyn Price 1956, res Edmonton,
           Alta.
           D1. Kenneth      D2. Gerald      D3. Ronald
       C4. Brian, b Calgary, mar Susan Ireland
           D1. Philip       D2. Stephen, res Edmonton
       C5. Ian, b Calgary, mar Beverly Coderre, res Calgary
           D1. Ian                          D2. Daniel
   B5. Albert, b 1905, d 1976, mar Gladys Jones
       C1. William, b 1930, mar --- Jones
           D1. Albert Lewis, b 1965   D2. David, b 1968   D3. ---, b 1970
       C2. Albert Neville, mar Paula Holmes
           D1. Stephen                      D2. Michella
   B6. William, b 1907 Newport Wales, mar ---
       C1. Colin     C2. Diane     C3. Paul, b 1953
   B7. Daniel, b 1910, d 1955, Vet WWII, res Calgary. Mar Iris Nellie
       Adrienne Tucker, 1908-1976, b Kent, England
       C1. Yvonne, b 1931 Calgary, mar Walter Bilozir, and 2. Kenneth Ark-
           ley
           D1. Randal Stephen Bilozer, b 1954   D3. Kenneth Arkley, b 1967
           D2. David Bilozer, b 1956 Calgary           Calgary
       C2. Ivor Daniel, b 1934 Calgary, Navy, retired. Mar 1954 Norma
           Gwendolyn Cooke of Innisfail, Alta.
           D1. Clair Estelle, b 1955 Calgary, mar Murray D. Gibney, res
               Lanigan, Sask.
           D2. Daniel Bradley, b 1956
           D3. Lois Adriann, b 1958, Innisfail, Alta., res Fort McMurray, Alta.
           D4. Alan Ivor, b 1960 Victoria, BC, res Lanigan, Sask.
       C3. David, b 1936, mar 1965 Marion Webb
           D1. Sandra Webb, b 1965          D2. Leslie Webb, b 1967
       C4. Michael, b 1939, res Lanigan, Sask. Mar Patricia Dennis 1962
           D1. Philip Richard, b 1964       D2. Michele Lynn, b 1967
   B8. Alice Hetty, b 1913, Cardiff, Wales, mar Ernest Dauger?, no issue
   B9. Percy, d.y.
   B10. Herbert, b 1915 Cardiff, mar Margaret Mary Catto, to Canada ca
        1953
        C1. Caroline, b 1947, mar David Ens  C4. Ann, b 1958
        C2. Rosalyn, b 1950, England         C5. Elizabeth, b 1963
        C3. Paul, b 1955, Calgary
   B11. Janet Ann, b 1918 Cardiff, mar Leslie Sims
        C1. Philip Leslie Sims, b 1946, mar Wendy ---
            D1. David Sims                   D2. Joanne Sims
A5. Percival Alexander, b 1874, d 1953 Calgary, to Canada 1890, a but-
    cher, res Alberta and Kamloops, BC. Mar Kitty Damon, a dau, Alice
    Giesler, res Kamloops.
A6. Linda LE FEUVRE, b 1875 Bristol, England
A7. Gerda Victoria, b 1878 Bristol, mar G. DAVIS
LE VESCONTE, Capt., owned land at Port de Grave, Nfld. 1784, see PICCOTT
LE VESCONTE, John, in Harbour Grace, Nfld. 1700s and also other LE VES-
   CONTES (K. Mathews)
LE VESCONTE, fam from Grouville Parish, J, to Minnesota 1872
LE VESCONTE, Philip, b ca 1760 J, res at Descousse, C.B., NS 1818. At
   that time, mar and had 2 chn in J, but expected them the coming year.
   He asked for lots at False Bay, west of River Bourgeois on the N side
   of Lennox Passage, CB. (PANS, C.B. land papers)  Poss desc of Philip
   are C. John, John W., Kenneth H., Roy G., and P. LE VESCONTE, current-
   ly res Cape Breton, NS, or poss desc of Peter, and his sons Isaac and
```

Peter?

LE VESCONTE, Capt., agent, merchant, ship owner, from J in Nfld. (K. Mathews) A John, was in Harbor Grace, Nfld. 1700s.

LE VESCONTE. "Philip Le Vesconte was born in Jersey 1740, and his eldest son was born and baptized in Grouville, Jersey in 1778. Between 1778 and 1781, Philip left Jersey and settled in Devonshire where his other children (4 sons and 2 daus) were born. Three of his sons, including Henry (my great grandfather) served in the Royal Navy, as well as Philip, who continued to serve until 1794.

The son of Philip, Capt. Henry Le Vesconte, served at Copenhagen and Trafalgar. He married, and his seven children were all born in Devonshire. His eldest son, Henry Thomas Dundas Le Vesconte, born in 1815, was serving in the Navy when his family came to Canada, ca 1832. He saw service in the China war, and was present at the ceding of Hong Kong. On his return to England, he joined the Sir John Franklin Expedition to the Arctic, and was lost with the Expedition. His name appears with the Officers of the H.M.S. EREBUS. His handwritten diary which he kept during the China War came to my father, and three or four years ago we deposited it with the Royal Maritime Museum in Greenwich. Thus, my father's generation were the first of the Le Vescontes (of this family) born in Canada." (Helen Le Vesconte, Toronto, Ont.) (See also, HEROES OF BRITAIN IN PEACE AND WAR, by Edward Hodder, 1900?)

LE VESCONTE, Philip, 1740-1807 of J, mar Rose Maxwell, b Ireland, but a Scot. Eight chn of whom one rem to Canada, Capt. Henry, b 1782 Devon, who mar Sara Wills. He served under Nelson at the battles of Trafalgar and Copenhagen. Around 1832 he and a number of retired Navy officers settled on Crown grants of land in Seymour Tshp., Ont. He d 1850. 7 chn.

A1. Rose Henrietta, b 1809, mar Rev. Macauley of Picton, Ont. On her death, he mar 2. Charlotte Sarah, Rose's sister, b 1815.

A2. Henry Thomas Dundas, b 1813, d 1848. See above account of family in quote from Helen Primrose Le Vesconte.

A3. Charlotte Sarah, b 1815, d 1884, mar Rev. C. McCauley, res Picton, Ont.

A4. Dr. Philip John, b 1816, d 1894. Mar Amelia Whalen, res King's Cove, Nfld. late 1800s
  B1. Rose
  B2. Julia, b 1831, mar Patrick Murphy
  B3. Dr. Charles
  B4. Henrietta, mar P. Ryan
  B5. Sarah
  B6. Philip
  B7. Henry

A5. Charles George, b 1818, d 1867 Belleville, Ont. Served with the First Belleville 49th Regt. during the rebellion, later commanded his regiment.

A6. James Maxwell, b 1821, d 1888, mar 1852 Margaret Cleugh, 1832-1901, 8 chn. James d Campbellford, Ont.
  B1. Sarah, b 1855, d 1946, mar 1874 Edmund Buller, rem to San Jose, Calif. and later to Vancouver, BC.
    C1. Francis Buller
    C2. Dr. Frederick James Buller, mar Sarah Howard
      D1. Arthur Howard Buller   D3. Margaret Buller, mar Stephen
      D2. Frederick Buller   Randall?
    C3. Eva Buller, mar Stanley Barwick
      D1. Evelyn Barwick, mar James Wright
        E1. Carolyn Wright
    C4. Lillian Buller, mar --- Rhodes, a dau
    C5. Marion Buller, mar James Wright, no issue

LE VESCONTE 407

B2. Margaret, b 1855, d 1918
B3. Charles James, b 1856, d 1875, unmar
B4. Adelaide Mary Elizabeth, b 1859, d 1927, unmar
B5. Robert Cleugh, b 1861, d 1945, mar Margaret Helen Ross, 1863-1960
   C1. Dr. Helen Primrose Le Vesconte   C2. Lilian Le Vesconte
B6. Henry, b 1864, d 1872
B7. Philip Maxwell, b 1868, d 1948, unmar
B8. Henrietta Maria, b 1873, d 1953, res Vancouver, BC
A7. Anna Maria, b 1826, d 1907, mar Thomas Wills, 1834-1861, of Aust. Explorers family
  B1. Henry, mar ---, a son, Philip   B3. Dr. Alfred Wills
  B2. Frank Wills, 2 sons, Thomas and George B4. Anna Wills
LE VESCONTE. The chn of Michel Le Vesconte and Marguerite Lael, LISLE?, res Les Buis, St. Mary, J in 1708, then rem to St. Brelade, J, Devon and Canada. Some reference to Capt. Jean Le Vesconte, Capt. Raulin Le Vesconte and Capt. Michel Le Vesconte in Soc. Jers. Bull. 1932.
LEWIS, LOUIS, in Nfld. (Seary) See LOUIS
L'HERAULT, see HERAULT
LIEVRE, see LE LIEVRE
LIHOU, Peter, b 1823 St. Martin, G, son of Thomas L. and M--- MOLLET, mar 1848 Susan PRIAULX, qv, dau of Jean P. and Catherine RABEY, qv, b 1830. At least 6 chn in Canada. (R.R. Lihou, Cornwall, Ont.; Ruth Blight, Oshawa, Ont.)
I. Harriet Kate Susan, b 1849
II. Rachel Mary, b 1851, mar Thomas Henry ROBILLIARD, qv.
A1. Thomas Philip Robilliard, b 1872
III. Peter Thomas, b 1853
IV. Maria Elizabeth, b 1855, mar Philip Daughlrey 1872
A1. Bertha Maria Daughlrey, b 1872, d.y.
V. Thomas Martin, b 1858, mar Amelia BAKER, qv, dau of Elisha B. of Ald. in 1882. At least 15 chn, b Ald.
A1. Thomas Elisha, drowned on H.M.S. GOOD HOPE 1914
A2. Harry   A3. Jack
A4. Alfred George, b 1893, d 1965. To NY with J and G cattle, then to Chesley, Ont. to AUDOIRE, qv, farm, relative by marriage. Rem to Owen Sound, Ont., mar Laura Blanche Osborne, nee Bullock 1916, 7 chn.
  B1. Alfred George, b 1917 Owen Sound, mar Thelma Cowie of Midland, Ont. 1941, 3 daus
    C1. Brenda, b 1945, mar Arthur Cruickshank 1965, 3 sons
      D1. Keith Cruickshank, b 1966   D3. Kevin Cruickshank, b 1972
      D2. Kent Cruickshank, b 1968
    C2. Barbara, b 1948, mar 1970 John Bye, 2 daus
      D1. Melissa Bye, b 1975   D2. Amy Bye, b 1977
    C3. Beverley, b 1956
  B2. Marguerite Laura, b 1921 Owen Sound, mar Cecil Vanslyke 1939, and 2. John James Hopkins, 2 sons
    C1. Robert Alfred Vanslyke, b 1941, mar Judith Helson 1964
      D1. Bernadine Annette Vanslyke, b 1969
      D2. Paul Allan Vanslyke, b 1972
    C2. Richard Cecil Vanslyke, b 1946, mar Victoria Whiteside 1970
  B3. Beatrice Ellen, b 1923, mar 1. MacKenzie BISHOP, qv, and 2. Melvin Cummings
    C1. Marilyn Elizabeth Bishop, b 1938, mar David Quinlan 1958, foster parents of 4 chn, nieces and nephews of D. Quinlan
    C2. Patricia Ellen Bishop, b 1940, mar Wayne Fox 1960, 4 daus
      D1. Joanne Fox, b 1961   D2. Julie Fox, b 1962

            D3. Jennifer Fox, b 1963   D4. Jasmine Fox, b 1965
    B4. Reginald Roy, b 1925, mar Dorothy Elizabeth Owen 1945
        C1. Terry Bruno, b 1948, mar Valerie Margo Jeaurond 1971
            D1. Todd Mathew, b 1974   D2. Tyler Sean, b 1977
        C2. Shirley Anne, b 1950, mar Richard Harper 1972
            D1. Stacey Lynn Harper, b 1974
        C3. Sheila Susan, b 1952, mar Paul Hercules Payette 1977
        C4. Penny Elizabeth, b 1953, mar George Bernard Lafave 1976
    B5. Lloyd George, b 1930, mar Una Slingerland 1953, 3 chn
        C1. Lloyd Arthur, b 1955, unmar   C3. Christine Anne, b 1964
        C2. Gregory Thomas, b 1962
    B6. Laura Matilda, b 1932, mar William Childs 1950, 5 chn
        C1. Carey Childs, b 1952   C4. Kelly Ruth Childs, b 1961
        C2. Montgomery William Childs, b 1957 C5. Kim Ruth Childs, b 1961,
        C3. Mitchell Donaldson Childs, b 1958   twin of Kelly
    B7. Ruth Gladys, b 1933, mar Donald Blight 1956, 2 chn
        C1. Jody Elizabeth Blight, b 1962
        C2. Theodore Donald Blight, b 1966
A5. Morris, res Alderney   A6. Charles, res Alderney, mar Maggie ---
A7. Edward, to Canada late 20's, returned to G, mar, no issue
A8. Alexander, to Canada after WWI, mar Myrtel Hooey, Owen Sound, Ont.,
    9 chn (Lorraine Parry, Agincourt, ONT)
    B1. Thomas, mar, res Ont.   B3. Bert, mar, res Ont.
    B2. Wally, mar, res Ont.   B4. Kenneth, mar, res Toronto?
    B5. Audrey, mar Alexander Miller, res Angus, Scotland, 2 chn
        C1. Sandra Miller   C2. Pamela Miller
    B6. Dorothy, mar Charles RICHARDSON, res Markham, Ont.
A9. Lillie, mar Ernest PHILLIPS. Widowed, mar 2. --- MAHY, widowed
    again, rem to Owen Sound, Ont., then to C.I. with her mother,
    Edward L., and Audrey, her niece, mid 1930s.
    B1. Ernest PHILLIPS, to Canada after WWI, joined R.C.M.P. Mar, res
        Toronto
A10. Pauly?, mar PARMEITIER? A dau mar Stanley KEMISH, res Ald.
A11. Maggie, Margaret?, mar --- BENFIELD
    B1. Colin Benfield, res Ald.
    B2. Hartley Benfield, to Owen Sound, Ont., late 1920s, mar, res
        Hamilton, Ont., 2 chn
A12. Florence, mar Peter GUILLE, qv, of Sark, C.I. to Owen Sound, Ont.,
    5 chn
    B1. Peter Guille   B3. Tillie Guille   B5. Evelyn Guille
    B2. Frederick Guille   B4. Lillie Guille
A13. Susan, mar Charles AUDOIRE, qv, 4 chn, res Guernsey
    B1. Billy, William, AUDOIRE, unmar
    B2. Lawrence Audoire, mar Pansy ---, res Ald.
    B3. Linda Audoire, mar Patrick Murphy, res G, 2 sons
        C1. Martin Murphy, unmar   C2. Michael Murphy, mar Maureen ---
                            D1. Lorraine Murphy
A14. Evelyn, rem to Toronto, Ont., mar William GROOM in Ald., a son.
    Widowed, rem to Toronto after WWI, mar 2. William Manger, 7 chn.
    Res Toronto area.
    B1. Harry Groom   B3. Arthur Manger   B5. Lillian Manger   B7. Marie
    B2. Jack Manger   B4. Florence Manger B6. Helen Manger   Manger
A15. Edythe, rem to Owen Sound, Ont., mar William Charlton, 8 chn
    B1. Grace Charleton   B5. Marguerite Charleton
    B2. Joy Charleton   B6. Marie Charleton
    B3. Dorothy Charleton   B7. James Charleton
    B4. William Charleton   B8. Victoria Charleton

LIHOU   409

LONEY FAM. FROM CI TO ONTARIO, CANADA.
LIHOU, Edgar, from G to Hamilton, Ont. 1917 with wife, a LE COCQ from
   Alderney. A barber for 67 yrs., till he d at 93 in Ont. A sister d
   1972, another res Detroit, Mich. A bro also was a barber in Hamilton.
   Al. Aline, mar C-- Smith. Clifford Smith was the VP of the G Society
   in Hamilton. Desc in Ontario.
LIHOU, Thomas, b G, in Gaspe 1861 (Census)
LIHOU, in Langley, BC. A Mr. and Mrs. L from G in Vanc. early 1900s.
LILLY, from C.I. to Gaspe?
LILLY, from G to Chatham, Ont?
LILLY, Wm., in Bay Roberts 1785, from C.I.?
LILLY, a William also in Bay Roberts in 1766 and 1805 (Census) See
   SEARY.
LILLYCROP, in Canada, origin unknown   (H.P.RENOUF, see p.484)
LINDSAY, Ethel Scott, 1881-1956, wife of man from C.I. in Gaspe (GLF)
LITTLE, Pvt. Albert Murray, b J, related to Mrs. L. Little of St. Hel-
   iers, J, in Princess Pat's Lt. Infantry, from Ottawa 1919. (OUR
   HEROES IN THE GREAT WORLD WAR, by J.H. De Wolfe, Canada, 1919)
LOCKE, John, b ca 1843 J, rem to Shippegan, NB as a clerk, there in
   1861 (Census) See also Robichaud, LE GRAN CHIPAGAN.
LONG, J surname (Saunders) LONEY, to ONT from CI
LANGLEY, LONGLEY, gravestone in Annapolis, NS 1700s. Poss LANGLOIS
   from C.I.?
"LORD, Hiram, fanatic, appeared at Grande-Greve, Gaspe at the head of a
   good number of fanatics like himself, nearly all from Jersey..."
   (Rev. d'Hist, Vol. 7, No. 1, 1969, p. 23; Raymond Gingras, and K.H.
   Annett list)
LORD, from C.I. to Canada.1821, Report of Dr.AntonVon Iffland.
LORWAY, LARAWAY, LE ROY, LE RUEZ. There is a curious resemblance in
   sound in these various surnames. LORWAY is the name of a big shipping
   firm in Nova Scotia, which was owned by a man who was connected with
   the various firms of Cape Breton, and the shipping there. LE RUEZ,
   Philip, was born in J 1757, his father being a soldier with Lafayette.
   The surname shortly became LARAWAY, LARROWAY, and possibly those in
   Ontario were U.E.L.'s of this line. (QAAM) LE ROY's of J are known
   to have settled in U.S. also. (See Capt. Parker re LORWAY)
LARAWAY, Maria, bp 1767 at Schoharie, NY, mar Richard Stanley of Pratts-
   ville, dau of Peter LARROWA, bp 1734, son of Peter LAROWA, bp 1704
   at Kingston, MD., son of Jonas LORWA, b 1674 at St. Joseph, near Que.
   bp Catholic under the name of Leonard LE ROY 1764 at Que. As Jonas
   LE ROY, he was mar at Kingston NY Dutch Ch 1703, Marie Uzille of
   Poughkeepsie, a Huguenot, and died in Scoharie ca 1750, a deacon of
   the Dutch Church there.
Only two records of LE RUEZ were found by compiler, but the family was
   a sea-faring one in Jersey, and it is possible that others of this
   surname have descendants in Canada, poss those in Hamilton, Ont.
LOUIS, Philip, from J to Ower Island Cove, Nfld. ca 1785 (Seary)
LOUVEL, Benjamin, from J? to Grand Bank, Nfld. 1817. Cf LOUVELL, LOVELL,
   in J. (Stevens)   LOUGEE, SEE CHAN. IS. COLLECTION.
LOVERIDGE, in Nfld. (Seary) From C.I.?
LOW, Edward S., in Nanticoke, Ont., b J, a farmer, settled there 1854.
   (See Page's HISTORICAL ATLAS)
LOW, Philip, b J, son of an Army officer, studies law in the offices of
   H.J. Boulton and Marshall Spring Bidwell, Toronto, Ont. Called to
   the Bar in 1835, practised in Picton for many years. Another Low,
   John, was called to the Bar in 1827. (TOWN OF YORK, by Edith Firth,
   Toronto, Ont.)
LOWE, Lt. Joseph, was in the British Navy 1815-1925. One of his sons,

LUCAS, SEE EXTRA PAGES
John Goldie LOWE was b J 1862?
LOWE, in Nfld. (Seary), poss from J? Also LOW.
LOWTHER, Capt. from G in Nfld. (K. Mathews)
LUARD, Capt. from G in Nfld. (K. Mathews)
LUCAN, in Nfld. (Swary) Cf LUCAS of J? (Stevens)
LUCAS, to Nfld. from C.I.? Peter was in St. John's Harb. 1682 (Seary)
LUCAS, Samuel from J?, at Pt. St. Peter, Quebec 1825 (Brochet)
LUCAS, John, was part owner of the AMELIA, 61 tons, built in 1860 at Grand Ruisseau, Cape Breton, NS. (Parker)
LUCAS, George, of Cape Cove, Gaspe, mar Dec. 1903, Elizabeth Mary LENFESTEY (Brochet)
   A1. Susan Charlotte Lucas, b 1905   A2. James Howard Lucas, b 1906
LUCAS, in Gaspe, poss Irish, but much intermarriage with Malbaie Channel Islanders. (Brochet)
LUCAS, in Nfld. (Seary) From C.I. (Rev. Hammond)
LUCAS, a J fishery in Labrador
LUCAS, Mary, wife of William Hunt, d 1863, age 55, bur Malbaie, Gaspe (GLF)
LUCAS, Eliza Sophia, wife of Obadiah Lot VARDON, qv, b 1876, bur Malbaie, Gaspe (GLF)
LUCAS, Martha Amelia, 1857-1930, mar John BISSON, qv. A son, Thomas Clair, d of war wounds in 1923, bur Port Daniel, Gaspe. (GLF)
LUCAS, Agnes, widow of George HOTTON, qv, d 1924, age 75, bur St. Peters, Malbaie
LUCAS, Elizabeth, 1847-1909, wife of Alexander Duncan, 1837-1893, bur St. Peters, Malbaie
LUCAS, Ansel Irwin, 1914-1950, husband of Ethel Sweetman (GLF)
LUCAS, Hilton E., son of Walter Lucas, d 1932, age 12, bur Malbaie (GLF)
LUCAS, Howard Duncan, 1882-1918, bur Malbaie (GLF)
LUCAS, a large fam in Malbaie 1861 (Census) all b Canada, from C.I. family (J.H. Le Breton)
LUCAS, from C.I. to B.C.   LUCE, SEE ADDED PAGES.
LUCE, Francis, b 1859 J, son of Jean LUCE, shipright and Ann CORBEL, mar Jane Elizabeth BISSON, qv, b 1859 St. Andrew, J. Both d 1935 St. Catherines, Ont. Francis was a ship captain assoc with Fruing Co., Gaspe. (Cyril Luce, and Robert Aiken, St. Catherines, Ont.; Clifford Luce, Cambridge, Ont.)
   A1. Alfred, b 1885, mar Alice Parsons, res St. Catherines, Ont.
      B1. Oswald Alfred, b 1919, res Thorold, Ont., mar Eleanor Berge, who d 1973. Mar 2. Ida Brocolo, res Thorold, Ont.
         C1. Carl Alfred, b 1947, mar Darlene Hatt
            D1. Heather Ann, b 1973
      B2. Dorothy Maude, b 1915
   A2. Clarice or Clarissa, b 1887, mar Stanley J. BRIARD in J
      B1. Alfred
         C1. Kerry, Capt. in Can Armed Forces
   A3. Allan Lyle, b 1892, d 1971. Mar Rosana Beatrice COOMBS, qv, of J, b 1891
      B1. Alma Rose, b 1914, mar 1941 Frank J. Brown, 1909-1969, res St. Catherines
         C1. Janet Yvonne Brown, b 1943, mar Anthony Wolanski, b 1939 Poland
            D1. Dana Marie Wolanski, b 1970
            D2. David Anthony Wolanski, b 1972
         C2. Alan Arthur Brown, b 1942, mar Vickie Smye, b 1950
            D1. David Allan Brown, b 1971   D2. Erin Rachel Brown, b 1975

LUCE 411

B2. Yvonne, b 1918?, mar 1944 William Heard Hull, b 1920, res Oshawa, Ont.
    C1. Brian William Hull, b 1950, res St. Catherines, Ont.
    C2. Martha Yvonne Hull, b 1953, mar Randy Scott
B3. Phyllis Louise, b 1920, mar 1942 Robert V. Aiken, b 1919, res St. Catherines
    C1. Jane Louise Aiken, b 1947, mar Michael Robert Wilson, b 1946
        D1. Rachel Alexandra Wilson, b 1977
    C2. Marianne Lisbeth Aiken, b 1943, mar Alexander Reid Hart, b 1947 Scotland
        D1. Reid Christopher Hart, b 1976
    C3. Robert Judson Aiken, b 1952, res St. Catherines, Ont.
B4. Allan Maurice, b 1922, mar 1948 Shirley Smith, b 1923, res Ottawa, Ont.
    C1. Mary Elaine, b 1950, mar Donald Heaton, res St. Catherines, Ont.
        D1. Jennifer Heaton, b 1974   D2. Mark Heaton, b 1976
    C2. David Maurice, b 1952, mar Marilyn McManus, res Ottawa, Ont.
    C3. James Gregory, b 1955, res London, Ont.
    C4. Kathryn, b 1961, res Ottawa, Ont.
A4. Cyril, b 1896, mar Margaret MacLachlan, res Niagara Falls, Ont.
    B1. John Francis, b 1930, res Montreal, mar Betty Thomson
        C1. Moira Jane Luce, b 1964   C2. Carol Ann Luce, b 1968
    B2. Barbara Gene Luce, b 1934, mar Gordon Mumford, res Kenya, S. Africa, in Post Office Communications
        C1. David Mumford, b 1963   C2. Gregory Mumford, b 1965
A5. Clifford, b 1904, mar Margaret Selby, res St. Catherines, Ont.
    B1. Cyril George, b 1919, res St. Catherines, Int., mar 1947, Helen Carvana
        C1. Wendy, b 1953, mar Edward Meyer 1973
            D1. Jeffrey Edward, b 1977
    B2. Shirley Eileen, b 1923, mar 1943 James Campbell Joynt, who d 1966
        C1. James Gray Joynt, b 1945, mar Susan Crapper, res Port Credit, Ont.
            D1. Jason Campbell Joynt, b 1975
        C2. Margaret Susan Joynt, b 1949, mar Ronald Kerr, 1972, res London, Ont.
            D1. James Campbell Kerr, b 1975
        C3. Leslie Ann, b 1953, res Port Credit, Ont.
    B3. Clifford Lyle, b 1927 St. Catherines, Ont., mar Hazel Ruth McNab, b Orillia, Ont., res Cambridge, Ont.
        C1. Kenneth Lyle Luce, b 1952, Galt, Ont.
        C2. Clifford Michael, b 1954
        C3. Catherine Ruth, b 1958   C4. Donald Stephen, b 1961

LUCE, John, b ca 1816 J, a fisherman and seaman at Petit de Grat, C.B., (Census, 1871)
A1. John, b ca 1848 A2. Sarah A., b ca 1851 A3. Margaret, b ca 1843

LUCE, Mary, b ca 1844, in Arichat in 1871

LUCE, Inez? E.S., age 14, b J, with Daniel BISSON fam, Bon. Co. 1871 (Census)

LUCE, Philippe, from J, with Robin firm in Gaspe 1800s (Carmel Luce, Grand Pabos, Gaspe)
A1. Isaac Luce   A2. Raoul Luce   A3. Carmel Luce

LUCE, Moses, b ca 1802 J, mar Sabine Fougere, dau of Joseph Hilarion F. and Adelaide Forest, 1842, Arichat, NS. (S. White, Moncton, NB)
A1. Philomene, b 1845, mar 1871 Arichat, Thomas Rancon, son of Charles R. and Marine Bonin, res Lowe Descouse, CB 1871
A2. Daniel, b 1847, mar 1872 Arichat, Marie Anne Boudrot, dau of Aime B.

and Brigitte Martel
A3. Marine, b 1850 Arichat, d 1860
A4. Desire, b 1856, d 1938, unmar, a shoemaker
A5. Isaiah, b ca 1859, or 1857?
LUCE, curr Pabos and Newport, Gaspe
LUCE, John M., b J, to Grand Greve 1861, d 1884, age 39? Travelled for Fruing firm, mar sister of William Hyman. His widow and son, Philip, rem to J and res in La Grand Maison, near Sion in St. John parish. P.M. Luce, the son, returned to Gaspe for the Fruing estab at Grand Greve, Cap des Rosiers and Cloridorme. He later retired to England in 1956, and d at Worthing, England, 1967, age 91.
LUCE, Philip Mauger, son of John Luce, manager for the Robin firm, later settled at Riviere aux Renards, Gaspe. Prob same as above.
LUCE, Philip, b St. Lawrence, J, 1878, wrote for the Jersey papers in his teens, and left in the early 1900s for Winnipeg, where he worked for the French weekly newspaper there, L'ECHO DE MANITOBA. Later rem to BC and sent for his sister, Eva, who kept house for him in Vancouver. They became much involved in the Channel Islands Society there in the 1940s. Luce worked for several papers, then freelanced. He d at the age of 84 in 1962. He was the author of an article in the 1940s, JERSEY AS A HOME FOR THE LEAGUE OF NATIONS, an admirable idea that did not succeed!
LUCE, Philippe, age 46, b J, Catholic, in Hamilton, Bon. Co. 1871, with Anne, age 27, Philip, age 6, Alice, age 5, Elie Jean, age 3, Francois, age 2, Homar, age 5 mos., and with William, a fisherman, age 17 (Census)
LUCE, a Captain from J in Nfld. (K. Mathews)
LUCE, fisheries in NB and Gaspe (Robichaud; J.H. Le Breton list)
LUCE, Philip, came with the Robin firm ca early 1800s to Gaspe from J (Carmel Luce, Chandler, Quebec)
LUCE, Benjamin, president of the Thunder Bay River Boom Co., a logging business in Alpena, Michigan 1868. Many Gaspesians rem to Alpena district in Mich. about this time.
LUCE, Mrs. and Mrs. J. de G., in Alberta, 1904, them rem to BC
LUCE, re PM Luce in Gaspe. "Our first stay at the Caribou Inn was soon after its opening, ca 1932. Philip Luce, who is an inimitable raconteur, his wife, no less so, held us spell-bound with tales of his ancestor from the Isle of Jersey, a privateer, who became a captain in the navy after the Napoleonic wars. His grandfather, who established the codfish business in Riviere aux Renards; his father who d young after marrying a girl from Quebec; himself, born at Grand Greve, an isolated cove on the Bay of Gaspe, educated in England, later meeting aboard ship a Shropshire lass bound for New Zealand, whose proposed visit was forgone in order to accept another proposal. From shipwrecks and other disasters they lost cargoes of cod worth thousands of dollars. It was then, to retrieve their fortunes that the teahouse, at first a hobby of our hostess, became the Caribou Inn. In those days flakes along the beach front were covered with drying cod to be shipped wholesale to Italy." (Amy Oakley) The Ethiopian War brought disaster to Fox River, as Mussolini would not permit dealings with the British. The Luce coat of arms shows an anchor and 3 pike. "The sister of the Duke of Normandie married a soldier named Luce, who added his wife's name, becoming MAUGER-LUCE, to distinguish him from other Luces." (Oakley)
LUCE, Capt. Edward, was sailing a Jersey "snow," the DOLPHIN, from St. Peter's, Nfld. to Poole, England, when he was taken by a Spanish privateer, 1740s. (Soc. Jers. Bull., 1928-1931)
LUCE, Wm. H., res Paspebiac, then Outremont, Que. in the 1930s (Soc. Jers

LUCE, William, b J, mar 1. Leila BOUILLON, qv, mar 2. ---
LUCE, John, was involved in Crown Grant of land to the Channel Islander John BALLEINE, in Arichat, CB, NS, late 1700s (PANS)
LUCE, John, agent for John Robin in Arichat, Conway Harbour, NS late 1700s (PANS)
LUDD, Capt., from J in Nfld. (K. Mathews)
LUDLOW in Nfld. (Seary) Cf LUDLOW of J (Stevens)
LYS, J name (Saunders) Cf LILLY
LUSH; LUCE, in Nfld. from C.I.? (Seary) LUSH poss LYS? Cf also LOUGEE, of J. See QAAM.
MACE, said to be from G, curr Montreal, Que.
MACE, a Mace's Bay in southern NB. 8 cards in Saint John NB Museum Library.
MACHON, Philip, b 1826 J, d 1895 Gaspe, mar Elizabeth PRIAULX, qv. A carpenter, bur Rosebridge, Gaspe, Que. Philip the son of John MACHON and Sophie AHIER of J. See also THE QUIET ADVENTURERS, by Turk. Bro John listed below.
A1. Elizabeth Sophia, b 1848, d 1935, bur Rosebridge, Gaspe. Mar Nicholas Mauger RABEY, qv. in 1869, at least 8 chn.
A2. Harriet Jane, b 1856, d 1932, bur Toronto, Ont. Mar John Philip LEE of J fam, 12 chn. See J.P. Lee for chn.
A3. Laura Ellen, b 1857, d 1936, bur Rosebridge, Gaspe. Mar William RABEY, 11 chn. See Wm. RABEY.
A4. Peter John, b 1859, d.y.
A5. James Henry, b 1862, d 1895, bur Rosebridge, Gaspe. Mar Jane Patterson, 1858-1905 who is bur Toronto.
  B1. Jessie, b 1887, d 1956, mar --- Cassie
    C1. Jean Cassie, b 1918, d 1939 Cobalt, Ont.
  B2. Ellis Roy, b 1889, d 1939, bur Toronto, mar Gertrude Thompson
    C1. Irma, b 1913, mar --- Milton, RR machinist, res Aurora, Ont.
      D1. Gary Milton, b 1951
    C2. Aileen Machon, b 1916, mar Dalton Saunders, res Richmond Hill, Ont.
      D1. Roy Dalton Saunders, b 1939, mar Ruby Buelow, res Calgary, Alta.
        E1. Philip Saunders, b 1974
      D2. Robert Allen Saunders, b 1945, mar Diane Himburg, res Elmira, Ont.
        E1. Michelle Yvonne Saunders, b ca 1972
        E2. Sandra Lee Saunders, b ca 1976
      D3. Lynne Darleen Saunders, b 1955, mar Paul McMurchy, res West Hill, Ont.
        E1. Sarah Lynne MacMurchy, b 1978
    C3. Elva Machon, b 1918, res Richmond Hill, Ont.
  B3. Hilda Florence, b 1890, d 1923 B4. Myrtle Caroline, b 1895, d 1965
  B5. Henry Allen, b 1893, d 1895, bur Rosebridge, Gaspe
A6. Maud Mary, b 1864, d 1939, bur J. Mar James MAILLARD of J.
  B1. Sydney J. Maillard, b 1884, d 1957, mar Laura Jane RICHARD in J.
    C1. Joyce Laura Maillard, b 1916, mar John LE MARQUAND, Advocate, Senator, J
      D1. Shirley Joyce LE MARQUAND, b 1941, mar Brian DOWNS, res J
        E1. Victoria J. Downs, b 1969
      D2. Graeme J. LE MARQUAND, b 1944, mar Sheila Jackson-Clarke res J
      D3. Joan M. LE MARQUAND, b 1949, mar Alex. James WHITTON, res J
        E1. Shona L. Whitton, b 1969
      D4. Marian LE MARQUAND, b 1954
  B2. Ada Maud Maillard, b 1887, d 1930, mar John Elias QUEREE, res J

            C1. Douglas J. Queree, b 1923, mar Olive COLLINGLY, res J
        B3. Hedley William Maillard, b 1890, res J, mar Florence PINEL LE
            BRUN, d 1967, auctioneer
            C1. Hedley J. Maillard, b 1913, mar Marjorie Beryl DE GRUCHY, res J
                D1. Beryl Marjorie Maillard, b 1936
                D2. Dulcie Marguerite Maillard, b 1940, mar Brian Francis DE
                    GRUCHY, res J
                    E1. Andrea De Gruchy, 1962-1965   E3. Ian De Gruchy, b 1968
                    E2. Kevin De Gruchy, b 1966
            C2. Delphine Florence Maillard, b 1916, mar Thomas John CABOT. res J
    A7. Elfeda Thulia Machon, b 1866 Gaspe, rem to J as a young woman to
        take care of an aunt. At age 22 she mar George Hamptonne LE GRES-
        LEY of St. Saviour parish, son of John LE GRESLEY. Philip LE BRUN
        and Harriet LE SUEUR were witnesses, no data.
MACHON, John, b 1824 J, son of John MACHON, 1801-1863 and Sophie AHIER,
    1797-1883, of J. John was the older bro of Philip John, above. He
    rem to Vittoria, Ont. 1854, with his three sons, and wife, Nancy
    HOYLES, qv. John was town clerk and tailor and 5 more chn were b in
    Vittoria. Nancy was b 1824, St. Clement, J.
    A1. John, b 1847 J, d 1913, bur Calgary, Alta., accountant, res Langton,
        ND, unmar
    A2. Edward, b 1949 J, d 1914. Bur Sprague, Man., mar --- Crockett, se-
        parated.
        B1. Garnet Wolseley, b 1890   B2. May Machon   B3. Pearl Machon
    A3. George M., b 1851 J, d 1909, bur Calgary, mar Charlotte McFarland,
        who d 1889, 2 sons. Mar 2. Sara Jane McLeod, 4 chn. George was an
        adventurer, fisherman, harness maker, and fire fighter.
        B1. Ernest, b 1884, d 191t WWI, bur Paschendale, France. Mar ---
            Davidson, separated.
        B2. Everade, b 1886, d 1948, bur Calgary, Alta., a WWI veteran. Mar
            Margaret McEachern. He was a stockkeeper.
            C1. Gordon, b 1912, d 1962, mar Lillian Swiffen, bur Calgary
                D1. Robert Bruce, b 1948
        B3. John Lawrence, b 1892, d 1961, merchant. Mar Olive McIntosh, bur
            Calgary
            C1. Jeanette, b 1930, mar Gerald Wright, accountant, res Canoga
                Park, Calif.
                D1. Douglas Wright, b 1951   D3. Jacki Lynn Wright, b 1955
                D2. Brent Wright, b 1952   D4. Paul Wright, b 1956
            C2. George A., b 1933, res Calgary
            C3. John Edward, b 1940, mar ---
                D1. John Robert, b 1964   D2. James Edward, b 1965
        B4. George Edward, b 1895, d 1965, mar Florence Lambey
            C1. Kenneth Edward, b 1933, mar Olga Nettie Solojuk
                D1. Carolyn Gaye, b 1964   D3. Douglas Gordon, b 1970
                D2. Patricia Lynne, b 1968
            C2. Arnold Alexander, b 1937, d 1973
        B5. Douglas Machon, b 1896, d 1957, oilman, mar Alice Heald
            C1. Alice Blanche, b 1923, mar Bruce Howard, M.P., res Ottawa, and
                Penticton, BC
                D1. Allison Howard, b 1949   D3. Leslie Howard, a dau, b
                D2. Stephen Howard, b 1951   1953
            C2. Douglas Roy, b 1927, mar Muriel Coultry, a stockbroker, res
                Calgary, Alta.
                D1. Wayne, b 1951   D4. Brian, b 1955
                D2. Dale, b 1953   D5. Deanna, b 1965
                D3. Deborah, b 1954

C3. Maxine Marie, b 1929, mar William Edmonson, draftsman, res Calgary
    D1. Barry Edmonson, b 1952   D2. David Edmonson, b 1954
C4. Shirley May, b 1932, mar Robert Hawkins, accountant, res Calgary, who d 1975
    D1. Patsy Hawkins, b 1951, mar John Wisener
    D2. Robert Daniel Hawkins, b 1953   D4. Edward Hawkins, b 1963
    D3. Carolyn Hawkins, b 1960   D5. Marie Susanne Hawkins, b 1969
B6. Sarah Blanche, b 1902, retired teacher, Calgary, Alta.
A4. Annie, b 1856, Vittoria, Ont., d 1900, bur Pt. Dover, Ont. Mar Wm. Laing, b Scotland, 1855-1928
  B1. Roy Laing, b 1880, d 1924, mar, res Cleveland, Ohio
    C1. Ruby Ellen Laing, b 1912, d 1962, mar McDonald, res Calif.
      D1. J. Ronald McDonald, b 1945, marine D2. Bonnie McDonald, b 1951
    C2. Byron Roy Laing, b 1914, d 1960, mar Frances Harvey, res Parma, Ohio
      D1. Kathleen Laing, b 1943, mar P. Conn, res Brunswick, Ohio
        E1. Timothy Conn, b 1964   E2. William Byron Conn, b 1965
      D2. Terry Ellen Laing, b 1946
  B2. Pearl Erie Laing, b 1882, d 1961, mar C.C. Varey, res Port Dover, Ont.
    C1. Brian Mills Varey, b 1912, mar Almeda Rosalie McGill Dugit, res Port Dover, Ont.
      D1. Robert Brian Varey, b 1945, mar --- Henning
    C2. Ellinor Ann Varey, b 1914, mar David, (Ben), Gilbertson, town clerk, res Simcoe, Ont.
      D1. David Terrence Gilbertson, b 1942, insurance. Mar Johanna Cornelia Sloot.
        E1. Trent David Gilbertson, b 1963   E3. Laura Johanna Gilbertson, b 1976
        E2. David Dominic Gilbertson, b 1975
      D2. Martha Jane Gilbertson, b 1946, teacher. Mar Morley Scott Mossing, b 1945
        E1. Susan Brie Mossing, b 1976
  B3. Ruby Edna Laing, b 1885, d 1911
  B4. Alberta Annie Laing, b 1888, d 1968, mar Carl Ryerse, divorced
    C1. Victor Carl Ryerse, b 1916, mar Whitnum, res Port Dover, Ont.
      D1. Peter Scott Ryerse, b 1944   D3. Cynthia Lou Ryerse, b 1952
      D2. Vicki Leith Ryerse, b 1947
    C2. Harry Vernon Ryerse, b 1917, mar --- Siscoe, res Port Dover Ont.
      D1. Jan Stephen Ryerse, b 1945, mar --- Cameron
        E1. Tashya Lyn Ryerse, b 1969
      D2. Michael James Ryerse, b 1948
      D3. Barbara Jane Ryerse, b 1950, mar Brian W. Uloth, of Peterborough, Ont.
    C3. William Ryerse, b 1926, res Simcoe, Ont., unmar
  B5. John, Jack, Laing, b 1899, mar Agnes Smith, res Port Dover, Ont.
    C1. John Laing, b 1931, mar --- Abbott, res Simcoe, Ont.
      D1. Mary Anne Laing, b 1956 D2. Joseph William Laing, b 1959
  B6. William Douglas Laing, b 1900, d 1918, unmar, bur BC, raised by Durkee family
A5. Georgina, b 1860, d 1901, mar Donald Fisher, 1849-1927, res Vittoria, Ont.
  B1. Vivian Ethel Fisher, b 1886, d 1930, bur Vittoria, unmar
  B2. Estella Grace Fisher, 1888-1937, mar Russell David Break, res Detroit, Mich., bur Vittoria, Ont.
    C1. Evelyn Victoria Break, b 1911, mar Edwin Sales, divorced, res Detroit, Mich.

MORE DATA ON PEI MACHONS IN Q.A. IN NORTH AMERICA
   C2. Vera Donalda Break, b 1913, d.y.
   C3. Marion Georgina Break, b 1914 Detroit, mar Edward Turk, res
      Parma, Ohio
      D1. Laraine Diana Turk, b 1950, res Colton, CAL.
      D2. Steven Darrell Turk, b 1951, res Sewickley, PA, US
  B3. Christina Lea Fisher, b 1890, d 1970, bur Vittoria, Ont., unmar
A6. Sophia, b 1862, d.y., bur Fisher's Glen
A7. Albert, b 1865, d 1922, mar Mary Elizabeth Rombough, no issue, bur
   Toronto
A8. Susan Machon, b 1867, d 1926, mar Daniel McKnight, widower with
   two sons, Alonzo and William. Bur Simcoe, Ont.
  B1. Bertha McKnight, b 1900, schoolteacher, res Simcoe, Ont.
MACHON. A rather large family of this surname, poss including 5 or 6
brothers, from Guernsey in 1806, to PEI, in a shipload of 73 men, women and chn, being convoyed over part way by a man-o-war, owing to
the war between France and England at that time. Daniel, wife and
chn settled on 100 acres at end of Machon's Point. Brought at least
four chn with them, and others were b in PEI. (See PEI chapter)
(Herbert Machon, Bristol, NH: Leland Nicolle, Murray Harb, PEI: Roberts fam typescript, Heritage Foundation, PEI; Doris Le Lacheur, Burlington, Ont.; Elizabeth Graham, London, Ont.)
MACHON, Daniel, b ca 1767 G, d 1828 PEI. Mar Frances Pullem, Pullen,
Poulain?, Pulham in G? She was the sister of Mrs. BREHAUT, qv.
Some data below is uncertain.
A1. Daniel, b ca 1800 G, mar Elizabeth TAUDVIN (Cf TOSTEVIN). She was
   b 1804, d 1883. He d 1876 PEI.
  B1. Henry, b 1826
  B2. Elizabeth, b 1827, mar Alex. Van Iderstine, res Gladstone, PEI
    C1. William, mar Sarah MacLennan   C3. Bessie
    C2. Peter, mar Lavenia Beare and Christine MARTIN
  B3. Mary Ann, mar Henry Sencabaugh. She was b 1829 PEI, res Guern-
     sey Cove. See Calnek and Savary for more on Sencabaugh fam.
    C1. Mark Sencabaugh, mar Nancy Horton, res M.H. PEI
    C2. Silas Sencabaugh, mar Eleza Beck , res Cape Bear, PEI
    C3. Solomon Sencabaugh, mar Lilliam Watson, res Prov., RI, US
    C4. Maria Sencabaugh, mar Sam. MacLeod, res Machon PT, PEI
    C5. Matilda Sencabaugh, mar John Horton, res Murray Riv.,PEI
    C6. Frances Sencabaugh, mar Hugh JACKSON , res Cape Bear, PEI
    C7. Adelaide Sencabaugh, mar August Fletcher, res N.S.
    C8. Olivia Sencabaugh, mar John E. Winslow, res G.Cove, PEI
  B4. Daniel, b 1833, mar Barbara Sencabaugh. Chn Alex. and Harriet
  B5. John Thomas, b 1837 PEI, mar Mary Ann Darby BECK, qv, b 1847 PEI.
    He d 1927 Providence, R.I. Mary Ann d 1916.
    C1. Francis, d.y.
    C2. Charles Vere, b 1870 PEI, mar Euphemia MacKay, res Prov., R.I.
       She d 1913 Saskatoon, Sask. He was a contractor in Prov.,
       where he d 1956.
      D1. Archibald T., b 1894 Prov., mar Gertrude Smith
        E1. Charles V., mar, 4 chn   E3. Archie, no issue
        E2. Elizabeth, mar, 1 ch
      D2. John T., b 1897, mar Ethel Ayer, d Kingston, RI 1975
        E1. John T.   E2. Norman A.
      D3. Charles Vere, b 1898, d Prov. 1972. Mar Lillian Hunter.
        E1. Euphemia, Effie, res Attilboro, Mass.
      D4. Norman H., b 1900, mar Elsie Knowles, res Bristol, NH
        E1. Norman H. Jr., mar Edna ---
          F1. Norman   F2. David   F3. Glen

MACHON   417

        E2. Lolita, mar 1952 Robert W.P. Williams, res Bristol, NH
          F1. Robert P. Williams Jr. b 1955   F3. Bruce Williams, b 1961
          F2. Steven Williams, b 1958
      D5. Euphemia, Effie, b 1902 Prov., RI, mar Nelson Hoxsie, res
        Bristol, NH
        E1. Russell Hoxsie, b 1928, mar Mary Ann ---, 5 chn, res Martha's Vinyard
          F1. Deborah Hoxsie   F4. Russell Jr. Hoxsie
          F2. Steven Hoxsie   F5. Christopher Hoxsie
          F3. Pamela Hoxsie
        E2. Donald Hoxsie, mar Silvia Carlson, res Buffalo, NY
          F1. Erice Hoxsie   F2. Susan Hoxsie   F3. ?
        E3. Joan Hoxsie, mar William BELL
          F1. Wm. Jr. Bell   F3. Donald Bell   F5. Cynthia Bell
          F2. David Bell   F4. Douglas Bell
      D6. Herbert W., b 1911 Victoria, BC, mar Dorothy Howard, res
        Bristol, NH
        E1. Stephen H., b 1943 Bangor, ME, mar Cely, res Philippines
          F1. Virginia, b 1973   F2. William Charles, b 1977
        E2. Janet D., b Hartford, Conn, mar 1. Lisle Gilbert and 2.
          Richard Foster, res Waitsfield, Vt.
          F1. Lisle Gilbert, b 1969
        E3. Emily M., b 1957 Hartford, Conn, res Bristol, NH
      D7. Ruth, b 1913, d.y.
    C3. William, d.y.
    C4. Maude Mary, b 1875 Providence, RI, d 1960, unmar
    C5. Herbert J., mar Margaret Murphy
      D1. Herbert J. Jr., b 1917 Prov. RI, res Barrington, RI
    C6. Asa, d.y.
    C7. Stella, b 1878 Prov., RI, d there 1957, mar William BERRY
      D1. Hope Berry, b 1917, mar Raymond Stockley, res Bristol, NH
        E1. Raymond Jr., b 1940   E3. Jane Stockley, mar ---
        E2. Nancy Stockley, b 1943   dau, Kristen
    C8. Lillian, d 1974, Prov., unmar
  B6. William, mar Emily Campbell, res Providence, RI
    C1. Ethel, mar Frank Marr   C3. Bertha   C5. Sydney
    C2. Ernest   C4. Cecil   C6. Percy
  B7. Sophie, b ca 1843 PEI, d 1925, res Murray Harbor, PEI, mar James
    LE LACHEUR
    C1. Frederick Le Lacheur, mar Emily Murley
    C2. Cyrus Le Lacheur, mar Lizzie Hooper, res Prov., RI
    C3. Lillian Le Lacheur, mar Will Hugh   C4. Rose, mar George MacDuff
  B8. Mary Jane, mar --- Boyce, b 1835 PEI
  B9. and B10. ??, Charlotte and Abraham?   Rachel?
A2. Henry, b G, mar Anne LE LACHEUR. In 1841 there were 8 in the house,
  including servants, 6 under age 16, 3 boys and 3 girls. Sons, Charles and Daniel, and several daus including a Mrs. Wm. Howe and a
  Mrs. Clements.   (PEI MAGAZINE, 1905)   SEE ADDED PAGES
  B1. Charles, mar Elizabeth MacIntosh, and 2. --- Tweedy
    C1. Henry Alex., b 1863 PEI, mar? C4. Penzie, mar Hampden Hawkins
    C2. Charles Herbert, b 1872 PEI   C5. Cedric, d.y.
    C3. Benjamin?   C6. Drosilla, d.y.
  B2. Elizabeth, b 1831 PEI, mar William Clements
    C1. Albert Clements, mar Jane MacLeod, res Murray Harbor, PEI
    C2. Cecelia Clements, mar I.J. Kier, res USA
    C3. Charlotte Clements, mar --- MacMillan
  B3. Frances, b 1836 PEI, mar George Harris

SEE B6, B7, and B8 OF THIS FAM. IN EXTRA PAGES.
  C1. Perley Harris, mar Barbara MacLeod
  C2. Harry Harris   C3. Nettie Harris, mar --- Lemon
  C4. Lizzie or Elizabeth?
 B4. Marie, mar William Howe, res Guernsey Cove, PEI
  C1. Milton Howe, mar Ethel BREHAUT, qv.
  C2. Blanche Howe, mar Fred LE LACHEUR, res Guernsey Cove
  C3. ---, d.y.
  C4. Myrtle Howe, mar Carl Spaulding, res Beverly Hills, Calif.
  C5. Ella Howe, mar Charles Wadey, res Vancouver, BC
  C6. Hattie Howe, mar William Brodie, res Los Angeles, Calif.
 B5. Daniel, b 1834 PEI, mar Isabel MacLeod, res Guernsey Cove
  C1. Reuben, b 1870, mar Belle Hyde
  C2. Cecelia, b 1853, d 1932, mar James LE LACHEUR, qv.
  C3. Daniel Walter, b 1871 PEI, mar Jane Harris Dan.d 1936 bur
   D1. Daniel Walter, mar ---?, res Maine Glastonbury,CT.
    E1. Karen, res Agoura, Calif., worked in TV
    E2. Marc, mar Christina Frick, res Los Angeles, Calif.
  C4. Fred Seymour, b 1874 PEI, mar ?, res Hartford, Conn.
  C5. Gower? Eng. in LosAng,CAL   C6. Minnie, b 1878 PEI, mar ?
A3. William, b G, mar Caroline or Charlotte Reid. Wm. a sailmaker,
  res Lot 64 in 1841, White Sands, PEI. 8 chn
 B1. William, b 1839 PEI, d 1933 PEI, mar Margaret LE LACHEUR, qv,
   1847-1908
  C1. Gertrude, b 1873 PEI, mar John Herring, res Murray Harbor, PEI
   D1. Stanley Herring, d 1976   D3. Margaret Herring, d age 7
   D2. Harold Herring, d 1934
  C2. Lebert, b 1877 PEI, d there 1942, mar Elsie PENNY, res White
   Sands
   D1. Freeman, mar Alleyne ROWLAND, res Park Ridge, Ill.
    E1. Robert   E2. Gary   E3. Barbara
   D2. Robert, mar Christine Blue, res Montague, PEI, a son, Ray
   D3. Margaret, b 1910, mar Chester LE LACHEUR, 4 chn. See LE
    LACHEUR.
  C3. Penelope, b 1870, mar Freeman Reynolds, res Murray Harbor, PEI
 B2. Maria Jane, b 1831 PEI, mar Henry BREHAUT, qv, res Guernsey Cove,
  PEI
  C1. Charlotte Brehaut, mar Andrew Miller, res Murray Harbor
  C2. Frances, mar John Hill   C5. Bessie Brehaut, mar James Reid,
  C3. Priscilla, unmar   res Prov., RI
  C4. Peter Brehaut, mar Elizabeth Ferguson C6. ---, d.y.
 B3. Elizabeth, mar Daniel BREHAUT, res White Sands
  C1. Albert Brehaut, mar ?, res B.C.
  C2. Lucy Brehaut, mar Ambrose Gordon, res Prov., RI
  C3. Maria, unmar, res Prov., RI
 B4. Charlotte, b 1833, mar Charles Brehaut, res Murray Harbor, no
   issue
 B5. Kathrine, mar George White, res White Sands, PEI
  C1. Fred White, mar Ida BREHAUT, res White Sands (more data)
  C2. Harriet White, mar Charles Brookes, res White Sands
  C3. Mathilda White, mar Herman Wright, res N.S.
 B6. Margaret, b 1837 PEI, unmar.
 B7. Daniel Benjamin, b 1846 PEI   B8. Peter James, b 1849 PEI
A4. Elizabeth, d 1838 PEI, mar John NICOLLE, qv, res Gladstone, PEI.
  Some data uncertain. See John NICOLLE.
 B1. John Nicolle, mar Elizabeth Clements B4. Margaret, mar Thomas
 B2. William, mar Arnett   HENRY
 B3. Isabel, mar Neil Penny

MACHON

MORE DATA ON PEI MACHONS IN Q.A. IN NORTH AMERICA

    B5. Mary Ann, mar Charles Cupps   B6. ?, mar --- Clark
A5. Thomas, b 1807 PEI, d 1894 PEI, mar Rachael TAUDVIN, cf TOSTEVIN, qv
    B1. Mary, unmar   11 chn.
    B2. Margaret, b 1833 PEI, mar John ROBERTS, qv.
        C1. Mark Roberts, unmar
        C2. Alice Roberts, mar John MACKENZIE, res Cape Bear
        C3. Anne Roberts, mar John Penny
        C4. Jane Roberts, mar Joseph Sutcliffe
    B3. John, b 1834, mar Elizabeth Roberts and 2. Mary Moore
        C1. Sarah, mar William Glover
        C2. Thomas, mar Mary MacLeod, 3 chn; Grace, Mildred and Olive, res Prov., RI
        C3. Joseph, b 1865, d 1966, mar Mary Sooner, and 2. Emily Craven
        C4. Daniel, mar Janet Marshall, res Prov., RI
        C5. Mathilda, mar William Byrne, res N.S.
        C6. Peter J., b 1876, d 1968, res Prov., RI. Mar Sarah Glover, sons, John and Leon   (more data from John HB Machon,
        C7. Mary Ellen, mar Albert Stuttard, res Prov., RI Warwick,RI)
        C8. Rebecca, mar Thomas Booth
        C9. Lauretta, mar David Brooks, res Murray Harbor, PEI. A son, John Brooks, another named Ray?
    B4. Daniel, b 1837 PEI, mar Anne ROBERTS, qv, no issue, res C'town, PEI and Michigan (Bay City?) Adopted 2 chn.
    B5. Henry, mar Margaret MacDonald, res Machon Pt., PEI
        C1. Horatio, mar Edith Penny
            D1. John, mar Frances MacKay
        C2. Alfred, mar Nellie ---, res Winnipeg, Man.
    B6. Thomas, b 1839, mar?
    B7. William, b 1841, mar Susan Sensabaugh, res Providence, RI
        C1. Elizabeth, mar George Jenks, res Prov.
        C2. Sarah, mar Ban? MacLeod and 2. Arthur Fielder, res Prov., RI
        C3. Bertha, mar Byron Reid, res Mich.
        C4. Maria, mar Thomas Jenks   C6. William, mar Ann Browning
        C5. Albert, mar ?   C7. Clarence, mar Abbey, res Prov.
    B8. Samuel, mar Emily Davey
        C1. Lydia, mar Leroy Morrel, res Prov.
        C2. Jane, mar Robert MacDuff, res Prov.
        C3. Rosa May, mar Neil Crawford, res Woods Is.
        C4. Hubert, mar Lena MacKay, res Woods Is.
    B9. Anne, mar 1. James DAVEY and 2. John Hingley, res Murray Harbor
        C1. John, mar Christine MacDonald, res Murray River
        C2. Thomas Davey or Hingley, mar Elizabeth Richards, res Guernsey Cove, PEI
        C3. Maria, mar Wallace Singleton, res Belle River
A6. Nancy Ann, b 1810 PEI, mar Matthias Hawkins, res Murray River, PEI
    B1. William Hawkins, mar Sarah MacLeod (Matthias 1804-1864)
        C1. David Hawkins, mar Annie MacLeod   C3. Albert, mar ?
        C2. Louise Hawkins, mar Gavin MacLeod
    B2. Elizabeth, unmar   B3. Charlotte, unmar
    B4. Maria, mar Thomas ROBERTS, qv, res Boston, Mass.
    B5. Priscilla, mar Henry Beare. Poss more chn than 5?
        C1. Lavenia Beare, mar Peter Van Iderstine, res Gladstone
        C2. Cyrus Beare, mar Olive Nickolson, res Boston, Mass.
        C3. Sydney Beare, mar Della Jordon, res Gladstone
        C4. Annie Beare, mar Ezra HENRY, qv, res Boston, Mass.
        C5. Ralph Beare, mar Cassie Hume. Poss other chn.
A7. John, b 1816 PEI, mar Mary Buchanan, res Machon Pt. (mar 1838)

B1. Esther, mar Joseph Thompson, b 1839 PEI, res Milltown. 7 chn.
  C1. Annie Thompson, mar Will Reynolds, res Murray Harbor
  C2. Mary, b 1841, d 1927, unmar
  C3. Emma Thompson, b 1855, d 1905, unmar
  C4. John Thompson, mar Frances Brooks, a son, Ira, who mar Lucille ---, res Boothbay, Maine
MACHON, David, b J, in Malbaie 1861 (Census) with Jane, Jane, Elizabeth, and John, Thomas and Francis, all b Canada
MACKENZIE, James W., of J?, mar Jennie Ida LE GALLAIS, 1893-1954, bur Shigwake, Gaspe (GLF and Gingras)
MACKENZIE, John, mar Blanche BOUILLON of Gaspe, res Toronto
MACINTOSH, Mrs., was a member of the Channel Island Society 1941, in BC
MAGER, a form of MAUGER, noted on Bon. Island 1831 (Syvret)
MAHY, Edmund Thomas, b 1892 Cap du Roi, Vale, G, son of Thomas Henry M. and Louisa Elizabeth LE TISSIER, qv. Mar Elsie Emmeline RUGG in 1921. To Hamilton, Ont. 1913, served in WWI until 1917, retired with total war disability. Elsie came to Canada in 1919. (Phyllis Mahy, Willowdale, Ont.)
  A1. Claude Edmund, b 1922 Toronto, mar Phyllis Winnifred Edmonson 1951, res Toronto
    B1. Kenneth Edmund, b 1953   B3. Linda Karen, b 1960
    B2. Douglas John, b 1955   B4. Christopher Bruce, b 1962
MAHY, Hilda, sister of Edmund, above, b G, mar --- Reid, Madeira Park, BC, 7 chn
  A1. James Reid, Garden Bay, BC
  A2. Marion, mar Bileick, res Madeira Park, BC
MAHY, M., b G, in Vancouver, BC 1970
MAHY, Peter, from G to Vancouver, BC. Fam came in 1906.
MAHY, Valerie, b Catel, G, res Vale, G, mar --- MORRELL, res Guelph, Ont.
MAHY, "My father-in-law and his wife (Ernest John MAHY, b 1870 G, and wife Marie Louise MARQUIS, b 1871, mar 1892) brought his herd of registered Guernsey cattle from the Island all the way to Oregon City, Ore. without first visiting this country, in 1923. My wife and I accompanied them and worked for them for many years. Because of the hoof and mouth disease in England, the cattle had to be shipped directly to the London docks by a special small steamer, hoisted onto the deck of the SS PRESIDENT VAN BUREN without touching land, then across the Atlantic to Hoboken, N.J. where the animals were lowered into a barge and towed up to the Hudson River to the quarantine dock. Then hauled in a special rail car to the quarantine station in Athenia, N.J., where I took care of them. As soon as the animals were given a clean bill of health, they were shipped in an 80 foot Amer. Express car direct to Clackamas, Ore., via passenger train, then trucked to the farm Mr. Mahy had already picked out. (Lloyd Wheadon, San Luis Obispo, Calif.)
MAHY, Janet, from G, 1970, to Toronto, from St. Sampson, G, mar BEECHER
MAHY, John, b G, to Hamilton 1912
MAHY, Nicholas, master and part owner of the brig, JAMES, built in 1826 in Cape Breton by Peter BROUARD, qv. There is a picture by F. Lollie of Trieste, Italy, date 1828, of this ship. (Capt. Parker)
MAHY, Capt. from G in Nfld. (K. Mathews)
MAHY, fam from G to Vancouver, BC, ca 1906 via Salvation Army ship, KENSINGTON, 5 sons
MAIN, John, from C.I.?, in Gaspe Militia 1850s (MacWhirter)
MAINDONALD, Albert James, b 1885 G, mar Alice Mary GALLIENNE, qv, b 1886, Toronto, Ont., on honeymoon 1907. (Elsie Coniam, Burlington, Ont.)

A1. Walter, b 1909, mar ---
   B1. Frederick, b 1941
A2. Edna May, b 1912, mar Robert Dauson
   B1. a son   B2. a dau, Lillian, adopted by the grandparents
A3. Margaret Dorothy, b 1916, mar Clark Gibbons
   B1. Gary Clark Gibbons, b 1939   B3. Jo Anne Gibbons, b 1947,
   B2. Jack Donald Gibbons, b 1942   mar Eric Raab
A4. Lillian Mary, b 1930, the adopted ch, mar --- Poff

MAINGUY, MAINGY, MAINGI, etc. Many variants of this surname.
MAINGUY, Daniel Wishart, b 1842 England, raised in G, one of the 13 chn of James MAINGUY and Charlotte Beckwith. He d at age 64 in Cowichan, BC 1906. From G to the Valley in 1863, then farmed at Chemainus. Sailed from Gravesend in the STRATHALLEN 1863, bound for Victoria, BC. The Cariboo Gold Rush was on. D.M. took land at the mouth of and along Chemainus River on Vancouver Is., some 50 miles north of Victoria. The first year he started building a home, living alone for 20 years, and then for the next ten years with his wife and family. "He described himself as a farmer, but never really worked at it. From time to time he took up various jobs, overseeing road work gangs, building the CPR Railway east of Vancouver, and was Constable at Chemainus for some years. But mostly I think he liked visiting people or having them visit him. He was 42 when he married. He died from a shooting accident when he was alone in 1906, but was able to get home, about a mile, before he died." (E.R. Mainguy, Qualicu, Beach, BC) He married Elizabeth Fry. (Can. Who's Who, 1958) (Mainguy documents at Ottawa)
MAINGUY, of the above family, Ferdinand stayed in G, as did James and Wm. Henry. George S. was in India with the Hyderabad contingent, 1875. Others are known of in Holland, Ceylon, South Africa, Brazil, New Zealand, etc., mostly desc of Capt. Nicholas Maingy, b 1747 G, and Peter Maingy, b 1743 G, brothers.
A1. Harold Wishart, b 1884, d 1964, no issue. Res Williams Lake, BC.
A2. Richard Cecil, b 1886, d 1946. Mar Aileen ANKETELL-JONES 1913. Began surveying at age 15 at Cowichan Lake and Nitinat in 1902. Served in WWI, wounded at Paschendale, 1917.
   B1. Richard Patrick, b 1916, d RCAF during WWII. Mar Jeanne Holmes 1939.
      C1. Paul Wayne, b 1940, mar Ellen Koen
         D1. Steven Richard Patrick, b 1962 D3. Daniel Scott, b 1965
         D2. Mark Tyler, b 1964
      C2. James Wishart, b 1919, mar Lorna Castley 1942
         D1. Alison Aileen, b 1945, mar Thomas Francis MACE, qv, 1969
            E1. Emily Margaret Mace, b 1975
         D2. Diana Margaret, b 1950, mar John David McMahan 1974
A3. Barbara Edith Mary Charlotte, b 1887, d 1946. Mar Francis Barber-Starkey 1911.
   B1. Daphne Aimee Barber-Starkey, b 1912, mar Arthur M. Field
      C1. David Field, b 1941, mar Elizabeth Annabelle Allen, 1966
         D1. Rhonda Field, b 1968
      C2. Barbara Field, b 1946, mar John M. Creighton 1972
         D1. Tyler Stanley Lowe, b 1976
   B2. Mary, Molly, Bannon, b 1914
   B3. Joseph William Mainguy Barber-Starkey, b 1918, mar Felicity Aldersey 1947
      C1. Michael Francis Barber-Starkey, b 1951, mar Sherry Frenette 1973
      C2. Andrew Paul Barber-Starkey, b 1952
      C3. Rosemary Elizabeth Barber-Starkey, b 1954

        C4. Susan Polin Barber-Starkey, b 1960, adopted
    A4. Roy Beckwith, b 1890, d 1891
    A5. Edmond Rollo, b 1901, mar Maraquita Frances Cynthia NICHOL 1927.
        (Admiral E.R. Mainguy, O.B.E., C.D., R.C.N., retired)
        B1. Daniel Nicholas, b 1930, mar Susan Wainwright, Commodore D.N.M.
            C1. Sarah, b 1956   C2. Barbara, b 1958   C3. Peter Nicholas
        B2. Christopher David, b 1932, mar Geraldine Burns
            C1. Edmond James, b 1966
        B3. Quita Elizabeth, b 1942, mar Robert A. Longmore
            C1. Darrell Bruce Longmore, b 1966
            C2. Tamara Elizabeth Stinson Longmore, b 1968
MAINGUY, William Anstruther, b 1807 G, son of Peter Nicholas MAINGAY and Euphemia, b Scotland. This fam retained MAINGY spelling, but the son, William, reverted to MAINGUY, the original Breton spelling. William A. mar Helen McLeod, 1813-1892, settled first in NSW, Australia, where his oldest dau was born, then rem to Ont. 1831. Bur 1886 Beechwood Cem, Ottawa, Ont. (Can. Who's Who, 1958; William F. Mainguy, Ottawa, Ont.)
    A1. Euphemia Mary, 1830-1895, mar Charles Pope, 1834-1869
        B1. Helen Pope, 1880-1895, mar E.Y. Steele
            C1. Clarence Steele   C2. Eric Steele
        B2. Charles Pope, 1858-1934
            C1. Cecil Pope, b 1913
            C2. Charles Anstruther Pope, b 1915, mar Ruth McKenzie, b 1918
                D1. Charles A. Pope, b 1946
        B3. Norman Alexander Pope, 1862-1887
    A2. Martha LE FEVRE, 1832-1916
    A3. Isabella Georgina
    A4. William McLeod, 1843-1904, mar Laura Neville, 1844-1938, and 2. in 1913, Jessie May Spaulding, 1882-1976. William a Civil Engineer.
        B1. William Anstruther, b 1874, d 1889
        B2. Philip Neville, b 1881, d 1958, mar 1904 Phyllis Checkley, 1882-1911, res Minneapolis, Cincinnati, Montreal, Windsor, Ont.
            C1. William Francis, b 1905, mar 1929 Dorothy E. Neeve. He was VP and Dir. of many Power firms.
                D1. Wm. Neville Kilbourn, b 1933, mar 1958 Sylvia Arlene Johnson, b 1934
                    E1. Peter William, b 1961   E3. David Gregory, b 1975
                    E2. Robert Thomas, b 1965
                D2. Joan Patricia Anne, b 1939, mar Hendrik Westra
                    E1. Frederick William H. Westra
            C2. Donald Neville, b 1911
        B3. Philip Spalding
        B4. Robert Edgeworth, b 1919, d 1966, mar Caroline E. MacKenzie, b 1922
            C1. Philip Neville Ross, 1945-1974
            C2. George Robert Kirby, b 1947, mar 1968 Kathryn Small
                D1. Christian, b 1969   D2. Jeffrey Campbell, b 1974
    A5. Helenus Gilbert
    A6. Lefevre Anstruther, mar A.M. Layton
        B1. Guy Wilson   B3. David Anstruther   B5. Nora, mar Morton
        B2. Roy Lefevre   B4. John Gregory   BRAY, qv.
    A7. Philip, mar Rose Layton
        B1. Clifford   B4. Herbert Anstruther, res Ottawa
        B2. Frederick   B5. Helen McLeod, twin of Herbert
        B3. Gertrude
MAINGUY, bur Richmond, BC, poss from England or C.I.

MAINGUY   423
            MAJOR, SEE CHARTS IN CI COLL.
MAINGUY, Harold W., 1884-1964 and Kezia, 1895-1950. Origin unknown,
   bur BC.
MAINWARING, found in early records of C.I., some in Canada, Gaspe, and
   Nfld. Origin unknown. See Seary.
MAINVILLE, Edgar, from C.I.? Some rem to Alpena, Mich., 1800s
MAJOR, Rachel, of G?, wife of Jean BATISTE, from G to Elgin, Ont. 1880
MAJOR, C.I. name associated with Robin Co. at Paspebiac and with town
   of New Carlisle, Que. (Prov. Arch.) Majors bur Hopetown, and Shig-
   awake, Gaspe. (GLF)
MAJOR, Elizabeth, 1874-1908, bur Gaspe? (GLF)
MAJOR, Gladys, 1921-1922, bur Gaspe
MAJOR, Charles P., 1888-1962, mar Mary E. Ross, b 1893 (GLF)
MAJOR, sometimes variant of MAUGER. Shipowner from J and G in Nfld.
   (Seary; K. Mathews)
MALLARD, in Nfld. Cf MAILLARD of J. In Placentia 1820. (Seary)
MAJER, MAUGER?, David, b J, age 40 in 1861, farmer at Inkerman, NB, mar
   Elizabeth ---, b NB, age 34. With James, age 14, William, age 12,
   David, age 10, Jane, age 8, Anne, age 5, and Joseph, age one and a
   half years. (Gloucester Co., BROCHET)
MALLETT, Clement, manager of Philip NICOLLE fishery at Jersey Harbor,
   Fortune Bay, Nfld. in 1740
MALLET, Fanny Lawrence, wife of Francis Alfred AUBIN, b 1862 J, d Grand
   Riviere, Gaspe 1893. Also in J.H. Le Breton list, of Channel Island-
   ers in the Maritimes. ERNEST, SON OF A.Mallet of Becquet,Fer-
MALLETTES, from Gaspe to Alpena, Mich. 1800s?   (_main Bay, G, d at
MALLETT, D.G., from C.I. to Chatham, Ont.? (San Antonio TX 1883.
MALLETS of the Shippegan, NB area, intermarried with Jersey and French
   families. Origin not known to compiler. MALLET, James, b 1849, mar
   in Shippegan 1877, Isabella DE LA GARDE, qv.
MALLET, Heloise, mar 1883 Isidore MERCIER of Newport, Que. (Robichaud)
MALTBY, MALTHOUSE, and MALTWOOD, all noted in C.I.; have occurred in
   Gaspe and BC, origin unverified
MALYARD, MALGARD, Capt. from J in Nfld. (K. Mathews) Cf MALZARD, below.
MALZARD, Francis Langlais, b 1854 St. Aubin, J, d Arichat, NS 1901. Mar
   Anne Marie LE NOIR, dau of Elizabeth and Charles Lenoir. (Elsie
   McTague, Oromocto, NB)
   A1. Leila Elizabeth, mar Frederick V. Kelly, 4 chn
      B1. Francis B2. William B3. Charles, twin of Wm. B4. Leila
   A2. Charles Stanley, mar Elmira Sylvania Wilson 1916
      B1. Lelia Elsie, b 1917, mar Major Maurice Alfred McTague, of the
         Can. Black Watch
         C1. Anne Marie McTague, b 1958
      B2. Jean Emily, b 1919, mar William James Wright, b 1913
         C1. William James, b 1953   C2. Barbara Jean James, b 1954
      B3. Helen Frances, b 1921, mar George Arthur Cox 1948
         C1. Susan Jane Cox, b 1949, mar Kenneth Daley 1970
            D1. Andrew Liam Daley, b 1977
         C2. Patricia Diane Cox, b 1951, mar Brian Kane 1973
         C3. Jeane Elizabeth Cox, b 1961
   A3. Alva Vladimir, unmar
MALZARD, Channel Islanders in Maritimes Fisheries (J.H. Le Breton list)
MALZARD, from C.I.?, in N.S.   MANNING, SEE CI COLLECTION.
MANNING, in Nfld. (Seary) Cf MANNING of C.I.
MANNING, one in Paspebiac, said to have mar Laura LE GRESLEY, with a
   son, Herbert   MANNAN, FROM CI TO DIGHTON, MASS 1800s?
MANSEL, said to be from C.I. in Gaspe. Name also in various parts of
   Canada, from C.I.?

MANSHELL, poss MANSELL, Capt. from G in Nfld. (K. Mathews)
MANUEL, Benjamin in Channel Nfld. 1860s (Rev. Hammond, Seary)   Cf MANUEL, MENUEL of J
MARCHE, LA MARCHE, in Nfld. (Seary) Cf LA MARCHE in J (Stevens) Also LA MARSH
MARCHAND, D., owned the BARRACHOIS, a ship of 21 tons built in 1840 at Poulamon, CB. Origin unverified. Cf MARCHAND of C.I.
MARCHAND, Nicholas, from C.I.?, signed the Gaspe Petition in 1820. Cf LE MARCHAND, LE MARCHANT of C.I.
MARCHAND in eastern Ontario, from C.I.?
MARDELEY, Capt. from J in Nfld. (K. Mathews)
MARETT, C.I. in Maritimes, curr Gaspe (J.H. Le Breton list)
MARETT, MARETH, Capt. John R. of the ship UNION, from J to Gaspe in the 1800s (Syvret)   MARRET, SEE EXTRA PAGES.
MARETT, Charles, of J, mar Ida LE MARQUAND, dau of Elias John LE MARQUAND, qv. She was the sister of Maud LE MARQUAND, qv, who mar Harold LE GRESLEY, res Gaspe. (GLF)
MARETT, involved in 1717 with the Nfld. trade (C.R. Fay)
MARETTS from J or from Gaspe, rem to Dover, N. Hampshire, U.S.
MARETT, Elias, was in Channel Nfld. in the 1860s (Rev. Hammond)
MARETT, James LEMPRIERE, of St. Aubin, J, died in Que. 1830, age 56
MARIE, Mary, b J?, mar in Gaspe area,   John BROWN in 1851
MARIE, P.C., raised Bellozanne Valley, St. Helier, J, rem to Toronto
MARIE, Percy Cecil, b 1920 St. Peter Port, G, son of Percy Marie and Beatrice Sarah ---. The father was French and the mother was a Poindestre of J. Percy mar Patricia Doreen, b 1929 England, rem to Toronto, Ont. (P.C. Marie, Rexdale, Ont.)
A1. Peter Paul, b 1950 London, Eng.   A3. Raymond Charles, b 1957 Toronto
A2. Philip Stephen, b 1952 Toronto
MARION, Thomas Henry, son of Wm. Ch. M., was b 1846 Malbay, Gaspe. Origin unverified.
MARQUAND, see LE MARQUAND
MARRIOTTE, Capt. from J in Nfld. (K. Mathews)
MARKS in Nfld. (Seary) Cf MARKS in J (Stevens)
MARKS, John, from C.I., with fam of 6 in Little Shippegan, NB 1860s, origin unverified
MARKS, Michael Joseph, b Tunbridge Wells, Eng., mar in J to Ellen CORBIN, qv. Rem to Montreal. (Dorothy Hampshire, Pt. Claire, Que.)
A1. John Edward, b China Quarries, St. Lawrence, J, 1889, rem to Que. 1909, mar Jane Cotnam, 1888-1950.
B1. Dorothy Ellen Patricia Marks, b 1920, mar Leslie Elton Hampshire, 1912-1972
C1. Robert Elton Hampshire, BSC, DDS, b 1942 Montreal, mar Lucia Federico, b 1946 St. Valentine, Pescare, Italy
D1. Jonathan Matthew Hampshire, b 1975 Montreal
C2. Sandra Patricia, b 1944 Montreal, mar Gordon Charles Alexander Bryan, b 1944 Ayre, Scotland
D1. Andrea Patricia Bryan, b 1969 Montreal
D2. Judith Elizabeth Bryan, b 1972
B2. Lillian Elizabeth, b 1923 Montreal, mar James Stephen Jamieson, 1917-1962, res Campbellton, NB
C1. Marcia Joan Jamieson, b 1945, mar Thomas Wesley Dixon
D1. Christina Marie Dixon, b 1965 Montreal
D2. James Wesley Dixon, b 1970
C2. James Stephen Jamieson, b 1947
C3. David Edward Jamieson, b 1948
C4. Kathrine Gail Jamieson, b 1951 Campbellton, NB mar Gerard Bureau

        D1. Lee Ann Bureau, b 1972 Montreal
    C5. Wayne Gregory Jamieson, b 1950 Campbellton, mar Marie Rita Danielle Leblanc, b 1952 Laverne, Que.
        D1. Mitchel, b 1972 Montreal
    C6. Timothy William Jamieson, b 1952
    C7. John Brian Jamieson, b 1955
    C8. Deborah Lee Jamieson, b 1956   C9. Alan Bruce Jamieson, b 1958
  B3. Doris Gwendolyn Jane, b 1928 Montreal, mar Reginald George Wiltshire, b 1924
    C1. Douglas Ronald Wiltshire, b 1950 Montreal
    C2. Mark Brian Wiltshire, b 1952, mar Vivian Buker, b 1953 England
        D1. Susanne Wiltshire
    C3. Thomas Gary Wiltshire, b 1957
    C4. Geoffrey Allan Wiltshire, b 1963
MARKS, Christopher, in 1788 had lot 81 or 61 in Arichat, CB, origin unknown. Shoemaker there in 1811, no chn listed.
MARMAUD, MARMO. The father of Hipolyte, (Hipwell), and Francois, Francis Marmo res in Bordeaux, France. The two sons rem to C.I. to establish a fishery and/or ship building firm ca 1800? Thought to have mar two Island girls and rem to Arichat, CB, Francis in his ship PAULETTE MARMAUD and bro in ship named H.H. Their intent was to get a load of fish to take back to J, but it was late in the season when they arrived, so sailed up to Caribou Cove and anchored there for the winter. The two ship crews made a large log cabin and spent the winter, returning to J in the spring. In July they were back in Arichat, and worked at fishing, ship building and also had 3 or 4 stores in and around Cape Breton. Brought back to CB from C.I. two extra captains to take the ships back to J. They are said to have built at least 9 vessels in addition to the first two, a couple being the brigantine LEADER, and the ST. LAWRENCE. Their descendants also built ships, such as the GOOD HOPE in the 1850s. The wife of Francis d ca 1833 in J. The two sons of Francis, Francis and James, built ships for J owners. They rem to Lynn, Mass. where Francis retired when he was very old. Hipwell retired to J. (Francis Marmaud, Bras D'Or, Cape Breton, NS)
MARQUAND, see also LE MARQUAND
MARQUAND, Fanny, Elizabeth and Susannah, daus of a G fam, rem to PEI 1806 with the ship load of other G fams
MARQUAND, Mrs. Charles of England, res Charlottetown, PEI in 1848. There were six in the house, including servants, 4 men between the ages of 16 and 45, and one woman between 45 and 60.
MARQUAND, Henry, Census of 1841, Murray Harbor, PEI, a farmer. 14 in house, including servants; 3 girls under age 16, two women between 16 and 45, 8 men between 16 and 46, and one man between age 45 and 60.
MARQUAND, Nicholas, b G, mar, 1840, in Gaspe Bay 1861 (Census)
MARQUIS in Nfld. (Seary) Cf MARQUIS of C.I.
MARQUIS, curr Gaspe, from C.I.? Also in Western Canada, origin not ver.
MARRETT, also MARET, Ann, see PERREE
MARRETT, in Gaspe (K.H. Annett)   <u>SEE EXTRA PAGES</u>.
MARRETT, Elias, in Channel, Nfld. 1860s (Rev. Hammond) From C.I.?
MARRETT, fisheries in N.B. Origin unverified.
MARRETT, MARETT, James Lempriere, of St. Aubin, J, d in Quebec City 1830
MARRIE in Nfld. Cf MARIE of J (Stevens)
MARRIETTE, John, b St. Sampson, G, to Vancouver, BC ca 1908, mar Ada Harriette MAHY, qv. (W. J. Marriette, Powell River, BC)
    A1. John Sidney, b 1907 G, mar   A2. Edward Henry, b 1911 Vanc., BC

MAUGER, SEE EXTRA PAGES.
A3. Wilfred James, b 1913 Vancouver, BC   A4. dau?
MARRIETTE, John H, or H., b late 1800s, St. Sampson, G, rem to Canada
   1908, mar 1920 Janetta May DIXON, b 1901 Canada. He was son of James
   Joseph Mariette and Mary Ann ROUSSEL, qv. (John Marriette, Dundas Ont)
   A1. James Henry, b 1921 Ontario, mar Doreen Kent
      B1. Daryl, b 1946, mar, a dau, Allison
      B2. Wayne, b 1948, two sons
   A2. Glenn Richard, b 1924, mar Elizabeth Doherty
      B1. Deloris, b 1948, mar --- Ziegler, a son and dau
      B2. John, b 1949   B3. Robert, b 1953
   A3. Gordon Dixon, b 1924, twin, mar Georgina Wyatt, no issue
   A4. Marjorie Irene, b 1932, mar --- Kolenski
      B1. Catherine Kolenski, b 1957   B3. Gail Kolenski, b 1964
      B2. Kenneth Kolenski, b 1959
MARSH, in Nfld. (Seary) Cf MARSH of C.I.
MARSHALL, in Nfld. (Seary) Cf Nicholas Marshall of J 1670
MARTEL. Many French and a few Channel Island Martels in Canada, Gaspe,
   Ontario and the West   MARTEL: SEE CHANNEL ISLAND COLLECTION.
MARTELL, Capt. from J in Nfld.
MARTEL, many in Cape Breton, associated with the Channel Islanders, poss
   some intermarriage
MARTIN, Henry, b J, in Douglastown, Gaspe 1861 (Census, J.H. Le Breton
   list)
MARTIN, Anne, dau of Isaac MARTIN of J and Anne LE GALLAIS, mar Philip
   INGOUVILLE, qv, settled Cape Breton. Her mother, widowed, mar Wm.
   THACKER, TACKER of J.
MARTIN. "They are a well known Jersey family. The name was originally
   St. Martin, an historic old family of the Channel Islands. This fam-
   ily has dropped the saintly characteristic since settling at Harbor
   Grace!" (Shortis-Munn)
MARTINEAU, from C.I. at Harbor Grace, shortened to MARTIN (Seary)
MARTRET, from C.I. to Nfld.? Cf MARTRET in J (Stevens)
MASON, J. Amice, signed the Gaspe Petition of 1820. Origin unverified.
MASTEL, Capt. from G in Nfld. (K. Mathews)
MASTERS in Nfld. (Seary) Cf LE MAITRE, LE MAISTRE of C.I.
MATHEWS in Nfld. (Seary) Cf MATHEWS, MATTHEWS of C.I.
MATTHEWS, Emily, from Old Street, Jersey to BC, mar --- Pickles. Sold
   seed of the famous 10 foot high cabbages of J in the 1900s.
MATHEW, Albert, b J, rem to Regina, Sask. Mar Mable Maud JOUAN, qv.
   To Canada 1913, farmer, bricklayer. Farmed Halbrite, McLean area,
   Sask. (Jean Wood, Regina, Sask)
A1. Frieda, d 1917
A2. Dorothy, rem to J 1935, mar there ---
   B1. Dawn, b 1938   B2. Robin, b 1940   B3. Cleone, b 1945
A3. Glenn, rem to J 1935, builder
   B1. Glenn, b 1945   B2. Gaye, b 1947   B3. Mark, b 1950
MATTINGLY, James, in Yarmouth, NS 1773, poss from J? (Census) This sur-
   name appears in sev places in N.A. Surname in J through 1600s and
   1700s. Sometimes shortened to TINGLEY.
MAUGER, MOGIER, MANGER, MUNGER, DE MAUGIER, etc. of J, involved in 1717
   with the Newfoundland trade. (S.R. Fay, Seary)
MAUGER. M. Denys Munger, of Quebec City, has researched the Channel
   Island families named MAUGER, etc. that settled in Quebec province
   in the 1700s and 1800s. Their names were changed in various parts of
   Quebec, according to the sound, and to the ear of the census taker,
   but thousands of Canadians named MAUGER, MAUGET, MONGET, MAUGE, MUN-
   GER, MAJOR, etc. are all descendants of several families of Maugers

MAUGER   427
        SEE MAJOR FAM. IN EXTRA PAGES   ALSO SEE MAUGER.
   originating in the Islands of Jersey and Guernsey. At times, it is
   not certain which of the Islands was the birth place of the first
   immigrant to Quebec, because of the loose use of the term, Jerseyman,
   which encompassed at times, and in certain areas, both Jersey and
   Guernsey folk settled in the Maritimes.
        Three of the Jersey Island Maugers removed to Canada, and settled
   in Quebec:
I. John, b 1797 Grouville, J, removed to the "Kingdom" of the Saguenay,
   Que. He married 1823 at Malbaie, Gaspe, and raised 7 chn at Ste.
   Agnes. About 1841, he was firmly established in Saguenay, and had
   many descendants. Take care to distinguish these Jersey folk from a
   German MAUGER family, also settled in Quebec. (Prof. Robert Major,
   Malibu, Calif; Raymond Gingras, Quebec City; Denys Munger, Quebec
   City; Aldo Brochet, Perce, Gaspe, Que; Ruth Mauger, Toronto, Ont.;
   LE MUNGERS DE SAGUENAY, in LE PROGRES DU SAGUENAY, Mar 17, 1971;
   HISTOIRE MILLENAIRE DES FAMILLES MUNGER, Cahier C., Mar 1972, Societe
   de Genealogie de Quebec; Gallant; Therese Gravel, Montreal, Quebec)
II. MAUGER, Rolande, a descendant of James M. of J, poss settled for a
   short time at Petite Peche, about 30 miles to the west of Blanc
   Sablon, later established at Whales' Head, Quebec, where there are
   still descendants. He may have been a brother of John, above.
        The third brother, James, had many changes made to his surname;
   MAUGER, MAUGE, MAUGET, MONGET, and now, usually written MONGER.
MAUGER, two settled on the Gaspe coast and were possibly related,
   Philip Abraham and Richard. Philip mar 1824 at Pt. St. Peter, Que.,
   Marguerite BOND, dau of Aubain Bond and Elisabeth O'Conners. Those
   below marked I through V are believed to be of the same family. (Bro-
   chet) P.P., below, son of John M. and Jane BUTLIN of J? (Brochet)
I. Peter Philip, b 1802 J, d 1866, known also as Philip Peter, and
   Philippe Pierre, mar Nancy and Mary Ann or Marie Anne LA COUVET, qv,
   b J, res Chien Blanc and Bonaventure Island, Gaspe. She d 1865,
   dau of Mary Applebay, 1784-1861.
 A1. Philip Abraham, b 1847 Bon. Island, d there 1904. Mar 1867 Sophie
     Louise DU VAL, qv, res NY City and Bon. Island, 12 chn, all b Bon.
     Is., Anglican Ch members. Sophie b 1841 d 1926.
   B1. Peter Philip, b 1867, mar Rachel DEAN of NY, res Chicago, Ill,
       desc.
   B2. Mary Ann, b 1869, d 1941 Montreal, bur Perce, Que.
   B3. Amelia Charlotte, b 1871, mar James DEAN, bro of Rachel, above,
       res NY City, d and bur there 1937, 5 chn
      C1. James Dean Jr., d age 20   C4. Ethel Dean, twin of Jessica,
      C2. Ernest Dean   mar NY, --- Conklin
      C3. Jessica Dean, mar --- Kakuk   C5. Walter Dean
   B4. Sophia Alice, b 1872, mar T. Ro gers, NY City, d U.S. early
       1900s, bur Perce. He was a minister, of the famed Rogers Silver
       Mfg. Co.
   B5. James Archibald John, called Jim, b 1875, res Fernie and Vanc.,
       BC, mar Mabel PHILIPS, b Gaspe?
   B6. John Henry, b 1875, d.y., bur Perce
   B7. Herbert Edward Thomas, b 1877, res Kenora, Ont., desc in Thunder
       Bay, Ont., died Lake of the WOODS, Ont., mar Mabel Thompson of
       Baie de Chaleur, Que., 4 chn
      C1. Albert   C2. William   C3. Clarence   C4. Evelyn, mar Beaudry of
                                                             the Soo
   B8. Arthur William, b 1880, d 1944 Bon. Is., mar at Perce 1910, Mary
       Ann Marie DUVAL, qv, 1888-1959, dau of Albert Francis Du Val and
       Anna McNeil de Barra, 11 chn

C1. Philip Abraham, b 1911 Bon. Is., fisherman and boat builder, served WWII, mar in Montreal 1942, Isabel Caines, b ca 1914 Port aux Basques, Nfld., res Perce, 3 chn Philip d 1979.
  D1. Philip Arthur, b ca 1944, mar Jocelyne Berthelot of Petite Riv., Gaspe
    E1. Marc Eric, b 1969   E2. Isabel, b 1976
  D2. Gary, b ca 1946, mar Margaret Ann Sweetman of Port Daniel, dau of L. Sweetman and Eva LAWRENCE, 3 chn
  D3. Barbara, b 1953, mar Daryll McNeil, b Cape Breton
    E1. Miranda McNeil, b ca 1975 Cambridge, Ont.
C2. Arthur Irving, b 1912 Bon. Is., d 1972 .   Ont., boat builder and carpenter, Vet WWII, mar 1954 Leonie Nowland?, b PEI, 5 chn Art.d 1972 Cambridge,ONT
  D1. Linda, b 1955, mar Roy Chicoine, res.Scarboro,ONT.
  D2. Brenda, mar   Boyle
  D3. Velma   D4. Glenda   D5. James, b 1964
C3. William Walter, b 1914 Bon. Is., mar Maude Foote, b Nfld. res Toronto, twin sons. Uses MAJOR, 3 sons,Dalton,Davy,Peter
C4. Herbert James, b 1915 Bon. Is., mar at MTL,QUE.. Gladys Butler, b Nfld., res Cambridge, Ont., issue: Allan & Wayne MAJOR.
C5. Henry Percival, b 1917 Bon. Is., res Gaspe d 1978
C6. John Timothy, b 1918 Bon. Is., bricklayer, res Montreal, mar there 1950, Lorna Brown, b 1927 Montreal, no issue
C7. Dorothy, b 1921 Bon. Is., mar Montreal 1950, Ivan R. BICHARD, qv, stationary engineer of a Gaspe fam from G, res Montreal, 2 sons
  D1. Barry Bichard, b ca 1953, Montreal, chemist
  D2. Wayne Bichard, b c a 1956
C8. Lloyd Jasper, b 1924, d 1950 Verdun, Que., bur Perce, no issue
C9. Gordon Lancelot Aldana, b 1926, Bon. Is., res Gaspe
C10. Arthur Frederick William, b 1929, drowned at Bon. Is., bur Perce 1941
C11. Mildred Grace, b ca 1930 Bon. Is., mar Galt, Ont., 1955, Hewlett LANGLOIS, qv, b Grande Greve, Gaspe of G fam, res Cambridge, Ont., issue
B9. Julia Ann Edith, b 1881, mar 1916 Walter George LUCE, qv, 1877-1974, res Bridgeport, Conn. She d in fire 1922, U.S. He was from St. Aubin, Jersey.
  C1. Alice Edith LUCE b1917,NY. C2. Elsie Louise LUCE b 1919,mar
B10. Raymond Duval, b 1883, res Vancouver, BC (EricLundgren ofL.A.
B11. Matilda Clara, b 1884, mar 1912 Perce, William Mountenay DU VAL, qv, res Bon. Is., 6 chn. She d Montreal, Que. 1954.
B12. Frederick Percival Wallace, b 1886, d Montreal 1944
A2. John Timothy, b 1848, mar Emily Goodenuff, returned to G, 2 chn
  B1. Herbert Edward   B2. Gertrude Emily ? or
A3. Mary Anne Jane, b 1850, d 1965   Emily Jane?
II. MAUGER, Philip, b 1799?, d 1835, mar 1824 Marguerite Bond of Chien Blanc
A1. Susanna M., b 1824, d 1874 Perce,
                          SEE EXTRA PAGES.
III. MAUGER, Jean, John, settled Chien Blanc, Gaspe, then Bon. Is. in 1831
IV. Edward,b1819 res Bon. Is. 1837
V. Ann, mar 1. Jacques TOSTEVIN, qv, and 2. Daniel O'Sullivan, and 3. in 1841, Michel Bilodeau. Several TOSTEVINS at Gaspe, qv. Jacques, James, signed the Petition at Gaspe 1820. (Gallant) 11 chn.
A1. Elizabeth TOSTEVIN, b 1825, d 1902. Mar 1847 Edw. Jos. Flynn d 1882

MAUGER 429
      Richard MAUGER also called R. MAJOR, b J 1771.
  B1. Judge Flynn
MAUGER, Richard, b J, mar 1. Polly FLOWERS, and 2. ca 1810 at Paspebiac,
  Angelique Loiselle, b 1796, 13 chn. Angelique was the dau of Robert
  L. and Anne Elizabeth ROUSSY, b ca 1796. Richard d Pabos 1860, age
  95. Relationship to other MAUGERS uncertain.
  A1. Charles, b 1811 Paspebiac, mar 1833, Anne Travers, dau of James T.
     and Genevieve Chatterton(called Jan?)
  A2. Angelique, b 1812
  A3. Elizabeth, b 1814, mar 1834 Michel Molloy, son of Hugh MALLOY and
     Catherine Devlin
  A4. Susanne, mar 1830 in Paspebiac, Isaac ROUSSY, qv, son of Pierre R.
     and Genevieve Parise. (Disp 2/2) She d 1885.
     B1. Robert Roussy, b 1834
  A5. Richard, mar Paspebiac, Gaspe 1842, Charlotte Chatterton, dau of
     Amis Chatterton and Nancy Huntington Some MAJOR descendants.
     B1. Anne M., b 1843 Paspebiac, mar B3. Amedee Elie, b 1845
     B2. Richard, b 1844   Poss. also chn: Florence, Sophie,
  A6. Jean, b 1817   William and Marguerite?
  A7. Angelique again, b 1819
  A8. Jane, mar 1844, Charles Bourget, son of Charles B. and Sara BECK, qv
  A9. Marguerite, b 1829 Paspebiac
  A10. Robert, b 1833 Paspebiac, mar Sarah McGinnis?, age 37 in 1871,
      English, RC. Merchant in L'Anse aux Basques, Gaspe. (Census)
     B1. John George, b ca 1860   B2. Robert Richard, b ca 1862
     B3. Peter, b ca 1863, mar Mary Brotherton, dau of Wm. B. and Mary
        Flynn
        C1. Bernadette, b 1884 Grand Riviere
     B4. Charles Robert, b 1866 Pabos, Gaspe
     B5. Anna, b 1868   B6. Simon, b ca 1871
  A11. Guillaume Honore, b 1837, d.y.   A12. Florence, b 1839
MAUGER, Mary Jane, b 1845 Gaspe, proxy sponsors for baptism for Thomas
  LE GROS and Mary ESNOUF were James   and Judith LENFESTEY
MAUGER, John, b 1801 J, son of Jacques M. and Marie LARAY, poss LE RAY,
  LE ROY?, mar 1828 Malbaie, Que., Scholastique McNicholl, dau of Arch-
  ibald M. and Angelique Dollaire. Cf DALLAIRE.
MAUGER, Richard, d 1860 Grande Riviere, Gaspe, mar to Judith Aspirot
MAUGER, Philip, son of Philip and Mary, mar 1899, Rose Selina Beaudin,
  qv. He d 1941. (Brochet)
  A1. Annabelle, b 1907, mar 1933, John BALLEINE, qv.
MAUGER, Adolphus, mar Rosanne Gagnon
  A1. Alfreda, b 1931, mar 1960 Wm. Legace
  A2. Jane, b 1939, mar 1960, Claude GIRARD, qv.
  A3. John Francis Robert, b 1942, mar 1970, Lorraine BEAUCHAMP, qv
MAUGER, Philip, son of Zepheryn M. and Berthe Irene COLLIN, mar 1960,
  Celina Wall, at Grande Riviere, Gaspe
MAUGER, Sophia, 1875-1925, bur St. Pauls, Perce, Gaspe (Cent. Bklt.)
  Poss this was Sophia who mar Wm. Rodgers of NY City. (GLF)
  A1. John Henry Rodgers
MAUGER, Arthur W., 1880-1944, res Bonaventure Island, mar Mary Ann
  Maria DU VAL, 1889-1959.
  A1. Arthur F., 1929-1941, bur St. Pauls, Perce, Gaspe (GLF)
MAUGER, ---, from St. Mathews, J?, mar --- Landry, res Grande Riviere,
  Gaspe (GLF)
MAUGER, Henry, husband of Emma DU VAL, d 1931, age 60, bur Hopetown,
  Gaspe (GLF)
MAUGER, many desc at New Carlisle, St. Peter Point, Malbaie, Anse aux
Basques, Chien Blanc, Bonaventure Island, Cape Cove, Petite Riviere

and Pabos, of Gaspe
MAUGER, from Channel Islands in Nfld. early, there in 1773 (Seary)
MAUGER, John, James, and Philip from J to Arichat, Cape Breton, NS
   (Ruth Mauger, Toronto)
MAUGER, in Cape La Ronde, NS, 1800s (Bourinot)
MAUGER, John and Philip, in La Poile, Nfld. 1860s (Rev. Hammond)
MAUGER, MAJOR, agents from J and G in Nfld. (K. Mathews)
MAUGER, in the New Brunswick Fisheries, MAUGERVILLE,NB?
MAUGER, MAJER, David, b J ca 1821, res Inkerman, NB 1861
MAUGER, John, of J fam, d approx 1921 in Cap La Ronde, CB, NS, mar Olla
   Latimer, who d 1962, 7 chn   (Ruth Mauger, Toronto, Ont.)
A1. Warren   A2. Frederick. Poss. desc. of Joshua Mauger?
A3. Lloyd Mauger, b 1919 Cape La Ronde, CB, mar Jeannette RUSSELL, dau
   of Laurie RUSSELL and Vivian Latimer, who d 1918. The father d
   1940s. Lloyd and Jeannette were related through their grandparents.
   B1. Kevin, b ca 1944, mar Helen Clark, res Ontario
      C1. Steven   C2. Linda   C3. Ryan
   B2. Frank, b ca 1945, mar Sarah Johnson, res Nova Scotia
      C1. Paul   C2. Christopher
   B3. Roger, b ca 1949, mar Virginia Hickey, no issue, res Ontario
   B4. Ralph, b ca 1950, mar Catherine Hickey, res N.S., a son, Callum
   B5. Barbara, b ca 1947, mar Stanley Hynes, res Nfld.
      C1. Ian Hynes   C2. Jason Hynes
   B6. Ruth, b ca 1955, unmar, res Ontario
   B7. Anna, b ca 1957, unmar, res Ontario
   B8. Vivian, b ca 1958, res Manitoba
A4. John   A5. Ada   A6. Bertha   A7. Ina
II. George, res NS, made spinning wheels, shipped them to the States
   and England
III. James, a carpenter in NS   IV. Howard, res NS   V. Jane, res NS
MAUGER, Joshua, "One of the most influential Nova Scotia merchants in
   the first few decades after Halifax was established." See Channel
   Island Notables in Canada.
MAUGER, Edward, was a prisoner of the Algerian Corsairs, in the reign
   of Wm. III. Ransomed by his sister, he named his home in Guernsey,
   LA BARBERIE, for the Barbary Coast.
MAUGER, these of J and G are said to be desc of MAUGER, uncle of Wm.
   the Conqueror, Archbishop of Rouen, banished to Guernsey 1055. Mau-
   gers have been landowners in G since 1303 or before. (Carey-Wimbush)
MAXWELL, Mrs. Ethel M., b G 1890 to U.S., her sisters to Canada. (P.
   Leming, Warehouse Pt. Conn.)
MAY, Alderney surname
MAY, in Nfld. (Seary) Cf LE MEE of J (Stevens) and MAY of Alderney.
MAYBEE, MABILLE, said to be from France to Nfld., to G to N.A. Cf
   MABILLE in J (Stevens) Cf also MABE of Corner of the Beach, Gaspe,
   much intermarried with C.I. fams.
MAYNE, MAINE, from J? to Nfld. (Seary) Cf MAYNE, MAINE in St. John's
   1680.
MAYO, in Nfld. (Seary) Cf MAHAUT, MAYO of J (Stevens)
MC CLOCKLIN, Thomas, b J, to Ontario 1854, farmer and Mason in Usborne,
   Twp., near Farquahar, Huron Co., Ont. (Cumming, C.R. McClocklin,
   Calgary, Alta.) Mar Helen Smith. 3 or 4 chn at time of arrival in
   Canada.
A1. David, b J?, worked on Grand Truck RR, carpenter, res Rockwell,
   Guelph, Usborne and Durham, Ont. Had niece, Mrs. Caldwell, d 1913.
   (Methodist)   A dau Louisa.
A2. Thomas, b J?, mar Ellen or Helen Morrison, poss in Hamilton, Ont.

MC CLOCKLIN

Mason, farmer.
- B1. Elspeth, b 1860, unmar, d 1920s
- B2. William, b 1862, mar ---
    - C1. Thomas Roy, b 1897, mar Edith Henshaw
        - D1. Thomas, b 1920, mar Edith Lillian Cook, res Calgary?
            - E1. Douglas Roy, b 1946, Calgary, mar Karen Grant
                - F1. Laurie Lynn, b 1976
            - E2. Donald Thomas, b 1950, mar Patricia Anne Schell
            - E3. Leslie Edith, b 1952, mar Michael Steven Bristowe
            - E4. James Arthur, b 1956
        - D2. Douglas, b 1929, mar Doreen McGuire, res Calgary, Alta.
            - E1. Cheryl Doreen, b 1951, mar Gregory Wolcott
            - E2. Douglas Laurie, b 1953   E3. Wendy Jane, Janie, b 1955
    - C2. Christine, b ca 1899, mar Alex Ledgerwood
        - D1. Donald Ledgerwood
        - D2. Dorothy Ledgerwood, mar Douglas Pountney
    - C3. John, b ca 1902, mar Jean Acton
        - D1. Orville, mar ---
            - E1. Brenda   E2. Diane   E3. Barbara
- B3. David, b 1863, d.y.
- B4. Ella, b 1865, mar William Cook
    - C1. dau, mar Frederick Hall
- B5. Charles, b 1868, d 1946, mar Alice May Dykeman, b 1879. Charles in real estate, a merchant in Moose Jaw, Regina, Sask.
    - C1. Nita, mar Herbert Crosbie
        - D1. Dorothy Patricia Crosbie, mar Gordon Thompson, engineer
            - E1. Joanne Thompson   E2. John Thompson, lawyer
        - D2. Eric Desmond, mar Lynne Walker
            - E1. Michael   E2. Carolyn   E3. James Eric
    - C2. Charles Randolph, b 1906, lawyer, Calgary, Vet WWII, officer RCN
- B6. David Thomas, b 1872, a son and dau
- B7. Frederick, b 1875
    - C1. Homer, mar Emma ---   C2. Goldie, nickname?, wife named Myrtle
- B8. Thomas, b 1877, res Saskatoon, real estate promoter
    - C1. Clifford, mar Violet
        - D1. Thomas   D2. Marcia, b 1938, mar --- Goodwin, 2 daus
    - C2. Osborne, officer RC Navy, mar Helen Peterson
        - D1. Peter, b 1940, mar Lorraine Florence Mill, b 1943
            - E1. Brent Reynolds, b 1963   E3. Wendy Joan, b 1969
            - E2. Margo Lynn, b 1966
        - D2. Margo Joan, b 1944, mar Ian Rayburn, 3 chn
    - C3. Everett   C4. Eva
- B9. Albert, sons, Ross and Arthur
- A3. a son, name unknown, rem to St. Paul or Minneapolis, Minn., a mason
- A4. dau, name unknown, poss the mother of the Mrs. Caldwell mentioned in A1. David, above. Possibly a Randolph, Nella and Charles McClocklin also belong in this fam.

MC KAIN, MC KANE, from G to Australia. This surname also found in Canada, poss also from Castel, G.
MC KENZIE, C.I. surname associated with Robin firm in Paspebiac and with town of New Carlisle, Que. (Prov. Arch. of Que.)
MC KENZIE, old J surname, poss some of them to Canada
MC KINNELL, member of C.I. Society in Victoria, BC 1941
MENCHINTON, in Nfld. (Seary) Cf MINCHINTON of J (Stevens)
MERCER, Benjamin, b 1813 G?, mar Sarah Trenchard, b 1818 Devon. Benj. said to have come from G, settled in Devon, and then rem to Nfld. Orig surname thought to be MESSERVIE. (Phyllis Mercer, St. John's

MORE MESSERVY DATA ADDED TO CI COLL. 1992, 1993
Nfld.)
A1. Isaac Mercer, b 1844 of Bay Roberts, Nfld. Mar Alice Maude TAYLOR,
b 1875 Nfld. He was the second son in his fam.
 B2. Roy Mercer, b 1902 Bay Roberts, mar Phyllis Clayton COUSENS, b
 1908 St. John's
  C1. John Clayton Mercer, b 1937, d.y.
  C2. James Clayton, b 1939, mar Lillian F. JACKMAN
   D1. David Clayton, b 1964   D2. Ann Jillian, b 1966
  C3. David William, b 1940, mar Stella Regina Martin
   D1. Susan Regina, b 1966   D3. Donald Christopher, b 1970
   D2. Stephen Geoffrey, b 1967   D4. Andrew Paul, b 1974
  C4. Lois Manston, b 1945, mar Robert Bannatyne of Paisley, Scotland
   D1. Leslie Bannatyne, b 1968   D2. Ian Bannatyne, b 1971
 B1. Chesley Mercer, b 1900, mar Annie Millicent Lodge, b 1898
  C1. Elizabeth June, b 1930
  C2. Allison Mary, b 1935, mar Harold Jameson Todhunter, Jr., b 1933
   D1. Stuart Jameson Todhunter, b 1960
   D2. David William Todhunter, b 1962
   D3. Andrew Mercer Todhunter, b 1965
   D4. Sarah Elizabeth Todhunter, b 1970
MERCHANT, to Nfld. (Seary) Cf MARQUAND, MARQUANT of C.I. (Stevens) and
 MARCHAND of G
MERCIER, from C.I.? to Gaspe, then to Alpena, Mich? Cf LE MERCIER of J.
MERCIER, Philip, 1859-1938, of C.I.?, mar Eliza Jane TOSTEVIN, qv, 1870-
 1947, bur Cape Cove, Gaspe (Brochet)
MERCIER, several mar into Cape Cove TOSTEVIN and LENFESTY fams, Gaspe
MERCIER, Simon, mar Rebecca Mahon, in Gaspe area 1840s?, a son, Joseph
MERCIER, Earl, of Chandler, Que., mar Violet CHEDORE, qv, b 1916, d
 1976, bur Angl. Cem, Cape Cove, Gaspe (Brochet)
MERCIER, MERCER, METSERVY, MESSER, all said to be variants of MESSERVY,
 from J and G in Nfld. (Canadian Directory; C.R. Fay; Dr. Mannion;
 Rev. Hammond; Shortis-Munn; K. Mathews; Biographical Dict. of J, by
 G.R. Balleine; Chesley Mercer, Lafayette, Calif; E.R. Seary)
Charles in Bay Roberts and Port de Grave, Nfld. 1770, 1775, 1790, 1797,
 1804, and 1871.
Daniel in Nfld. Fisheries 1717, and 1720-1775
Edward and George in Bay Roberts 1790   John in Bay Roberts 1795
James in Port de Grave 1781   Jonathan in Bay Roberts 1765
 Others in Nfld. in the 1800s were Alexander, Benjamin, Philip, Robert,
Samuel, Thomas, and William.
MERRY, from J to Cape Breton, NS ca 1800 (Bourinot)
MESSERVY, Daniel, b St. Helier, J, involved in the Nfld. fisheries, but
 resided in J, where he mar Jeanne VALPY DIT JANVRIN, of St. Brelade,
 J, and d 1775. 5 chn, b early 1700s? (BALLEINE, Bio. Dict.)
I. Daniel, Seigneur of St. Ouen, J
II. Francois, in the British Navy
III. Philippe, officer in the 18th foot Reg't.
IV. Jeanne   V. Elizabeth
MESSERVY, Capt. in Harbor Grace 1760, from J? (Seary; K. Mathews; Shor-
 tis-Munn)
MESSERVY, from C.I. to Gaspe (Betty Tardif list and J.H. Le Breton list)
MESSERVY, Philip, b St. Saviour, J, mar 1769, Suzanne DENNIS, dau of
 John D., rem to St. George's Bay, Nfld. on the CORSAIR. Some of this
 fam settled at Sandy Pt., Nfld. 9 chn, including second ch, John.
 (Lady Jessie Richmond, Whangarei, New Zealand; MESSERVY GENEALOGY, by
 Jurat Messervy, ca 1900; Grace Marr, Waterloo, Ont.; Messervy booklet
 or book, by John A. Messervy of C'town, PEI; HAZARD FAMILY OF RHODE

ISLAND, 1634-1894, copy owned by Pat Hazard of Burlington, Ont; Beth Oldring, Edmonton, Alta.)
A1. John, b 1826
A2. William Henry, mar Jane PENNEL, PINEL?, qv.   A3. Abraham, b 1833
A4. Sarah, b 1833, twin, mar 1855, Samuel FILLATRE, qv.
A5. Charles Robert, b 1834, mar Jane Marie PARSONS
A6. Marcella Mary, b 1835 Nfld., d 1911 Auckland, N.Z. Mar 1860, Capt. Alexander Campbell, b 1833, res Pinette Farm, PEI, d Auckland, N.Z. 1916.
  B1. Annie Wilson Campbell, b PEI, rem to Edmonton, Alta., mar Thomas Walter Haszard, son of George H. and of Margaret Owen. She d 1953.
    C1. Allan Campbell Haszard, d 1941, mar Lena Mabel Davidson of Orangeville, Ont., who d 1955
      D1. Allan Davidson Haszard, mar Mabel Elizabeth Jacobs, b 1910
        E1. Julia Lee Haszard, mar 1968, Acheson Lucey, res Vancouver
        E2. Margaret Laele Haszard, mar 1966, R.S. Parrott
          F1. Laele Parrott, b 1972   F2. Tanie Lea Parrott, b 1976
      D2. Margaret Anne Haszard, mar Robert Carson Hodsmyth, res Calgary, no issue
    C2. Jean Douglas Haszard, b 1885, d 1915, mar William Charles Lawson of C'town, PEI, who d 1965
      D1. Dorothy, b 1906, mar James Albert Farquharson of Capreol, Ont., b 1905
        E1. Allan Farquharson, b 1931, mar Shirley Rose Wilson of Ont., b 1934
          F1. James William Farquharson   F3. Wendy Ann Farquharson, b 1960
          F2. David James Farquharson, b 1958
      D2. Mildred, b 1908, mar 1. Edward Kondey, and 2. John J. Beasley, and 3. in 1949, William Gorski, res Boston, Mass.
        E1. William Kondey, b 1934, res near Boston
        E2. Robert Lawson Kondey, b 1935, res Bahamas
      D3. Jessie Norah, b 1909, mar Reginald E. Kemp, b 1908, d 1975, res PEI
        E1. Harold Kemp, b 1937, mar 1969 Sheila Sangster, b 1950. Harold a pilot and schoolteacher.
        E2. Katherine Kemp, b 1945, adopted, mar 1967, Roderick Mackinnon, b 1943
      D4. William, b 1913, mar Jean MILLMAN of PEI, b 1918
        E1. Lorna Ann Kemp, mar R. Michael La Fortune, res Brighton, Ont.
          F1. Gordon M. La Fortune, b 1957   F3. Shari Anne La Fortune, b 1962
          F2. Lori Lynn La Fortune, b 1959
    C3. Arthur Alexander Haszard, b 1886 PEI, d 1967, mar Teresa Kurz, b Austria, both d 1959, Long Beach, Calif.
      D1. Jessie Craig Haszard, 1912-1972
      D2. Hazel Delores Haszard, b 1914, mar Verginus Dermont Gale
        E1. David Wayne Gale, adopted
      D3. Arthur Alexander Haszard, b 1920, mar 1942 Ernestine Woods, res near Wash. D.C. Space Flight Eng., Goddard Space Center.
        E1. Arthur Alexander Haszard, b 1943, mar 1967 Elaine VINCENT
          F1. Arthur Alexander Haszard, b 1968
          F2. Rebecca Dawn Haszard, b 1973 Seattle, Wash.
        E2. John Roy Haszard, b 1946 Seattle, Wash.
        E3. Timothy Roy Haszard, b 1949, mar Sharon Lynn Elkins at Bowie, Md.
          F1. Shannon Marie Haszard, b 1974   F3. Carmen Christina Haszard, twin, b 1976
          F2. Megan Diane Haszard, b 1976
        E4. Allan Eugene Haszard, b 1953

D4. Allan Campbell Haszard, b 1917 Merchantville, NJ, res Long Beach, Calif.
C4. Marcella Marguerite Haszard, b 1889, d 1963, mar Daniel Davis Harris, who d 1963
D1. Ada Elizabeth, Beth, Harris, b 1909, mar 1. Ernest V. Dyer, who d 1944, 2 chn. Mar 2. Harold Oldring, b 1904, d 1968, no issue. Children renamed Oldring
E1. Anne Marguerite Oldring, mar 1. Robert Allen Phillips, killed in air crash Montreal, 1963, and 2. in 1968, Hans H. Kurz
F1. James Allan (Phillips) Kurz, b 1957
F2. Judith Phillips Kurz, b 1962
E2. Walter Haszard Oldring, mar 1968 Charlene Gilbert of Edmonton, Alta., dau of Charles G. and Evelyn F. GREGG
F1. Richard Charles Oldring, b 1970
F2. Greg Harris Oldring, b 1972
D2. Williston Douglas Harris, mar Doreen Rogers, no issue
D3. Walter Davis Harris, d unmar 1944
D4. Helen Marguerite Harris, mar Edward Donnelly Hill, 5 chn
E1. Carolyn Evelyn Hill, b 1941, mar Merrill Archibald Hamilton
F1. Tara Dawn Hamilton, b 1963
F2. Darby Cole Hamilton, b 1971
E2. Barbara Joan Hill, mar 1. Raymond Jewel, no issue, and 2. Gordon C. Card
F1. Gordon Bruce Card, b 1968   F2. Shandy Marie Card, b 1973
E3. Rosemary Lea Hill, b 1948, mar William Bruce Kyle
F1. Amber Lea Kyle, b 1965
E4. Patricia Louise Hill, b 1951, mar Peter Barry Ness, 2 chn
F1. Patrick Shane Ness, b 1969   F2. Joel Scott Ness, b 1971
E5. Katherine Anne Hill, b 1952, a son, Jake, b 1973
D5. Pauline Harris, mar Dean Godfrey Johnson, res Clearbrook, BC
E1. Vance Neil Johnson, b 1950
E2. Corinne Anne Johnson, b 1953, mar 1973, Richard Henry Pearson
F1. Filisa Dawn Pearson, b 1976
E3. Garth Daniel Johnson, b 1961
E4. Glen Lee Darryl, twin of Garth, b 1961
C5. Williston Haszard, b ca 1897, mar 1967 Edythe G. Bird, res Edmonton, Alta. He d 1970.
C6. Jessie Craig Haszard, b 1895, d 1964, mar Arthur Maurice Smith of Alberta, no issue
C7. Walter McNair Haszard, b 1899, mar Charlotte Kurtz. He d 1949.
D1. Arthur Craig Haszard, b 1937, unmar
B2. Jessie Campbell, b 1868 Auckland, NZ, d 1951, mar Joseph James Craig, 1860-1916, of Oamua, Epsom, Auckland, NZ. Chn b there.
C1. Hilda Craig, 1889-1894
C2. Hazel Marcella Craig, b 1890, d 1974, mar 1912 Alexander Kinder, F.R.C.S.
C3. Constance Jessica, b 1892, d 1976, mar 1919 Wendell Alfred Langevin Phillips
C4. James Campbell Craig, b 1892, d 1976, mar Bessie K. Sweet Munro-Wilson
C5. Alexander Campbell Craig, b 1895, d 1919. Lt. in Royal Flying Corps
C6. Jessie Messervy Craig, b 1899, mar Vice Admiral Sir Maxwell Richmond, K.B.E., C.B., R.N., retired
C7. Marjorie, b 1904, mar Stewart Parnell McGuigan

C8. Selwyn Campbell Craig, b 1902, d 1924, mar Vera Jones, d in U.S.
   C9. Joan Messervy Craig, b 1910, mar Walter Francis Smith, and 2.
       John Allen WEBBER, qv.
  B3. Marcella Campbell, mar Ernest Laurie of Maxwellton, Mt. Eden,
      Auckland, NZ
  B4. Sarah Ann Campbell, b 1903 Auckland, d there 1953. Mar 1. Arthur
      Henry Brabant, son of Judge Brabant of the Native Land Court, and
      2. Buxton Arthur Laurie, no issue by second mar.
 A7. Mary Jane Messervy, mar Edward LE ROUX, qv
 A8. Benjamin Thomas Messervy, b 1837, d 1873, mar 1861, Martha Julia
     Maratt Bagg, dau of John Bagg, rem to PEI
  B1. John Albert, b 1861, mar 1888 Carrie Augusta Wade, dau of Robert
      W. and --- Coles ROBERT. Rem from J to Nfld., then to PEI.
   C1. Harold, b 1889, mar May Nicholson, no issue, d ca 1969
   C2. Adelaide Gertrude, d.y.   C4. Carrie Augusta, d.y.
   C3. Robert, d 1947, Rhodes scholar, mar Phyllis, dau of Sir Henry
       Drayton, no issue
   C5. Grace, b 1896, mar Bruce Robert Marr, who d 1973, res Waterloo,
       Ont.
    D1. Ian Messervy Marr, mar ---, 2 adopted chn, Patty and Robert
    D2. Sheila Wade Marr, mar C.R. Baleman, res Kitchener, Ont.
     E1. David Baleman   E2. Robert Baleman E3. June, twin of Robt.
   C6. Ethel, d 1937, mar Cecil Lomb, a son, John Alexander Lomb, d.y.
  B2. Benjamin Franklin Wade, b 1864
  B3. Isobel, b 1867, mar 1889, Daniel Gordon of Charlottetown, PEI
   C1. William Gordon, unmar
   C2. John Gordon, mar Myrtle MacKendrick, 3 chn
    D1. Joan Virginia Gordon, b 1922, mar Thomas Love, no issue
    D2. John Gordon, mar Carol Teed, no issue
    D3. Sylvia Janet McKendrick Gordon, b 1935, mar Wayne Muirhead
     E1. Kendrick Wayne Muirhead, b 1959
     E2. Glendon John Muirhead, b 1965
   C3. Adele Gordon, res 1970 Selena, Ala., mar 1924, Dr. William F.
       Harper, who d 1954, age 27
   C4. Edna Gordon, unmar, res Charlottetown, PEI   d 1944
   C5. Robert Gordon, mar Dorothy ---, res Chicago, Ill√, 2 sons; one
       res Quebec, P.Q.
   C6. Dorothy Gordon, mar --- Goldie, a son, Gordon, res Quebec
MICHAEL, Francis, b J, age 34 in 1871, wife Mary Ann, age 33, chn,
  Francis John, age 14, Elias James, Mary Ann, Elizabeth, Susan Amelia,
  Rachel Ann and James Philip, 6 mos., res Bon. Co.Coxtown. (Census)
MICHEL, from C.I. to Gaspe (Betty Tardiff list) Poss related to REN-
  AULTS of B.C.
MICHEL, MICHAEL, in Nfld. (Seary) From C.I.?
MICHEL, John, at Hermitage, Nfld. 1710 (Seary)
MICHEL, Randolf, b J, to Montreal 1919, mar Doris Mary BALLEINE, qv.
 A1. Brian Michel, b 1919, res Montreal
  B1. Danica Michel, b 1964
 A2. Beryl, mar Lyall Lang, res Courtney, BC
  B1. Kenneth Lang, b 1944   B3. Karen Lang, b 1952, mar ---
  B2. Keith Lang, b 1947   Brennand?
MICHEL, Alfred, 1878-1956, mar Elizabeth B. TAYLOR, bur United Ch, W.
  Paspebiac, Gaspe (GLF) Edwin H.MICHEL,b1920 mar Ella LUCAS.
MICHEL, Ernest and Hedley of St. Peter, J, worked for Robins in Paspe-
  biac (J.H. Le Breton list) Hedley b 1893 d 1986,mar Florence
MIDDLETON, in Nfld. and Gaspe, poss from C.I. See Seary.
MILES, in Gaspe from C.I. (J.H. Le Breton list)

MIGNOT, Peter, b J, poss a missionary to Brantford, Ont., returned to C.I. Related to the Ontario LE BER fam, qv
MILES, in Nfld. (Seary) Cf MILES of J (Stevens)
MILLER, Martha, 1847-1936, from J?, mar Edmund LE GALLAIS. A dau, Jessie May, d 1886, bur St. Peters, Paspebiac. (GLF)
MILLER, Hugh, husband of Jane LE GALLAIS, qv, mid 1800s (GLF), bur Paspebiac
MILLER, Jessie, 1873-1964, of Port Daniel, Que., mar Francis LE GALLAIS, 5 chn
MILLER, in Nfld. Cf MILLER of J (Stevens)
MILLEY, in Nfld. Cf MILLAIS of J (Stevens) Also spelled Millay, Melay, in Nfld.
MILLMAN, Samuel John, b ca 1870 G, son of Martha and Samuel M. of Eng., mar Emilie Pattie LE POIDEVIN, qv, rem to Canada 1906. Settled Red Deer, Alta., 24 grandchildren. Jack LE POIDEVIN, bro of Emilie, had settled there previously. This fam to Canada under the auspices of the Salvation Army, which chartered a ship, the KENSINGTON. Most of the settlers went to Toronto, and to Vancouver, BC. (Edgar Millman, Calgary, Alta.)
II. Millie, sister of Samuel John, b ca 1890, of Brooklyn, L'Islet and Le Houmet, G, mar in Canada 1915, --- Herron, had two sons, and 3 grandchildren, res Red Deer, Alta.
III. Elsie, a sister also, b G, rem to Canada 1906, descendants.
IV. Winnifred, b G, rem to Canada
V. Edgar, b 1900 G, res Canada? or G, 9 chn; Florence, Pearl, Ruth, Lois, Margaret, Earl, Ronald, Carl, and Kenneth, twin of Carl.
VI. Sophie, another sister of Samuel, mar --- LEGG, rem to Red Deer, Alta.
MILLS, from C.I. to Gaspe (K.H. Annett)
MINCHINTON, fam at George's Cove, Gaspe 1800s (Brochet) Laura May, 1880-1967, mar --- BOURGAIZE
MINCHINTON, Coletta M., b 1904, mar 1930, EarlGavey DOLBEL, Gaspe
MINSHINTON, at Cooper's Head, Nfld. 1801, from J?
MISCHAUD, MICHAUD, in Nfld. (Seary) Cf MICHAUD of J (Stevens)
MISSIN, MISSON, David from J?, mar Jane Element at Belle Anse, Gaspe. He was b 1804, d 1879. She was b 1828, d 1908. (Le Moignan; GLF)
MISSON, Calvin, res Belle Anse and Barachois, Gaspe
MISSON, Betsy, mar Thomas LE PAGE of Belle Anse, Gaspe, a son, John Philip, in the 1840s.
MITCHELL, C.I. surname associated with Robin firm at Paspebiac, Gaspe and with town of New Carlisle, Que. (Que. Prov. Arch. and K.H. Annett)
MITCHELMORE, from C.I. to Maritimes Fisheries (J.H. Le Breton list)
MOFFET, several mar into Le Lacheur fam in Que. Original surname MAUFETTE, from France? MOLLET: SEE PAGE 401F
MOLLETT, John Carter, b J ca 1849, to Canada 1863, to Alberni, BC then in 1900 to Saltspring Island, BC. Mar ---, a dau, Mrs. J.H. Lee, two sons, P.C. Mollet and A.J. Mollet, who res in Fulford, BC. (B.C. Archives) John also had a dau. MOLLET, SEE CHAN.IS. COLLECTION.
MOLLET, Esme Patricia, b 1918 St. Saviour, J, mar John Philip RENOUF qv
MOLLET, to Toronto from C.I.
MOLLETT, Philip, b J, to Ontario, bro of John Carter Mollett of B.C. Related to AMY fam, qv. (Helen Dean)
MONAMY, Thomas, in Perce 1863 (Cent. Bklt.)
MONAMY and AHIER, owners in Gaspe area of 133 ton brig, St. E----, 1800s
MONAMY, George, b J, rem to Fox River, Que., mar Anne CABOUR, who d 1868 in J (Remiggi)
A1. Jean, bp 1854, res Fox River, Gaspe

MONET, Philip, b J, in Caraquet, NB 1861, a plasterer, age 30, also a cook? (Census; Rev. Le Gresley)
MONGER, John, b 1801 J, son of Jacques MAUGER, qv, blacksmith and of Marie LA RAY. He abjured protestantism and was bp at Malbaie, Gaspe 1828. He mar there Scholastique McNicoll, dau of Archibald and of Angelique DALLAIRE, qv. D at Notre Dame de La Terriere 1861. His desc carry the name of MONGER. (Olivier) SEE MAUGER.&XTRA PP.
MONNIER, MONIER, from C.I. in St. John's, Nfld. 1759 (Rev. Hammond; Seary) Cf LE MONNIER of J (Stevens)
MONSTER, in Nfld. (Seary) Cf DE MONSTRE of J (Stevens) See also LE MOUSTRE
MONTAYE, Philip Joseph, prob LE MONTAIS, b St. Ouen, J, was taken captive by the French at Port de Grave, Nfld. 1705, and taken to Montreal where he was baptised and lived with a M. Jacques Tetard. He was the son of Philippe Montaye and of Jeanne TOURGIS. (A TRAVERS LES REGISTRES, Cyprian Tanguay)
MOODY, in Nfld. (Seary) This is said to be a form of LE MOTTEE of J at times. John Moody at St. John's Nfld. 1753. See also QAAM.
MOON, from C.I. to Canada?
MOORS, James, from G, mar at Ragged Harbor, Nfld. 1818 (Seary) An Isaac was at Twillingate, Nfld. 1808.
MORANT, see MOURANT
MORCOMBE, G.W., from G to Ontario
MOREL, Jean, from J?, merchant at Louisbourg, C.B., dealt with Peter Faneuil, Hug, merchant at Boston 1740s. (Navy records)
MOREL, see MORRELL. Thomas was a clerk at Shippegan, NB ca 1835. Another in Forillon ca 1850.
MORICE, MORISSEY, in Nfld. (Seary) Cf MORICE MORISSE of J (Stevens)
MORIN, C.I. surname associated with Robin Co. at Paspebiac and with New Carlisle, Que. (Que. Prov. Arch.; J.H. Le Breton list; K.H. Annett list)
MORIN, Daniel, b 1939, poss of C.I. fam, Gaspe
MORIN, Paul, mar Maud LE MARQUAND, qv, ca 1900, no issue, res Gaspe
MORIS, John, fisherman in Sandy Pt., Nfld. 1871. Hubert MORIS b J, age 17 in 1861 in Caraquet, NB. (Census)
MORRELL, Charlotte Mount Brock, b 1834, d 1922, dau of Mary Mount BROCK, of Brock-Saumarez fam of G, and Rev. P. MORRELL. She mar in England 1875, Weymouth George Schreiber, his second wife, rem to Canada, became a well-known artist, chapter-member and founding member of Royal Canadian Academy. MORRELL, MOREL in C.I.
MORRELL, MOREL, in Nfld. (Seary) Cf MOREL of J 1668 (Stevens)
MORRISSEY, in Nfld. Some from Ireland, but also in J 1576.
MORRILL, from C.I.?, in Richmond Co., NS 1861 (Census)
MORRISSON, William, b J, in Malbaie 1861 (Census) with Susan, Elizabeth, William, Mary, Henry and Drusilla?, Thomas and Elias, all b Quebec.
MORRISAY, William, from J?, a landowner on Bon. Is. surrounded by Channel Islanders in 1845 MORRISSEY, SEE EXTRA PAGES.
MORRISSEY, 1812-1846, mar 1829, George AUBERT, dau of John MORRISSEY and Angy BEAKER de Blondin
MORRISSEY, Ellen Jane, b 1870, mar James Wm. BROCHET, Perce?
MORRISSEY, Susanne, b 1821, mar 1838 Patrick Cody, b 1811, res Perce?
MORRISSEY, fam from Southern Ireland, settled Southampton, Eng., early 1800s, rem to J. One branch apparently to Gaspe. (Doris Morrissey, St. Helier, J)
MORRISSEY, Edward Graeme, b 1937 J, mar Christine ROSS 1959, rem to Mc Gill Univ., Montreal, then to Goose Bay Labrador, and recently in Willowdale, Ont.

A1. Edward Ross   A2. Timothy John
MOSER, MOSHER, in Nfld. (Seary) poss from C.I.? Moser also to Ohio.
   (QAAM)
MOSER, Michael, of G?, in NS, owned the MARGARET, 40 tons, 1819, Ari-
   chat, NS (Parker)
MOSER's River, port in N.S. Moser is also German.
MOSES, J surname, to Canada? As MOSES and MOYSE to Nfld.? (Seary)
MOSS, from C.I. to Gaspe? and/or to Vict., B.C.?
MOTT, in Nfld. (Seary) Cf LE MOTTEE (Stevens) MOTTY, Nicholas in 1824.
MOTT, M.L.A. in N.S., poss LE MOTTEE?, of Annapolis Royal, early N.S.
MOUILPIED, see DE MOUILPIED
MOUILPIED, from C.I. to Gaspe
MOULAND, in Nfld. (Seary) Cf MOULIN of C.I.
MOULIN, to Gaspe from C.I. (J.H. Le Breton list)
MOURANT, Joseph, age 34 in 1871 (Census) res Gaspe, with John, age 29,
   both b J, in same house with Dumaresq Valpy 22, George Bosdet, 20,
   Philip Le Gresley, age 30, Edward Hue, age 16, and Joseph Holton,
   age 26, all b J. (Census)
MOURANT, Philip, b 1796 J, d 1878, Gascons, Que. Mar 1. 1841, Barbara
   McRae, b Hopetown, Que., d 1854, 4 chn. Mar 2. Jane CHEDORE, qv, 4
   chn. Philip was a shoemaker.
A1. Peter Philip, b 1844, d 1876. Mar Ann Acteson, b 1844 Gascons, dau
   of Joseph A.
   B1. Philip Joseph, b 1867   B4. Beatrice Maude Arthur, b 1878,
   B2. Barbara Isabella, b 1869   d 1879
   B3. Jane Elizabeth, b 1871, d.y.   B5. Charles Robert, b 1872, d.y.
A2. Charles Robin, b 1850, d 1858   A6. John Christopher, b 1868
A3. John Christopher, b 1852   A7. Mary Cahterine, b 1871
A4. William Duncan, b 1854, d.y.   A8. Ann Eliza, b 1872
A5. by second wife, Jane, William Charles, b 1866
MOURANT, John William, b 1844 Havre des Pas, St. Helier, J, son of
   John M. and Marie Esther ---. Blacksmith, to Canada for the Alexan-
   der firm, then Fruings in N.B. Worked in Shippegan, N.B., then re-
   turned to St. Helier and mar 1869, Jane Isabella BATTAM?, BALLAM?, qv.
   She was the dau of John BARTON and Eliz. Rachel LE MONTAIS. Rem to
   Caraquet, had 10 chn. (Adrienne Gionet, Caraquet, N.B.)
A1. John Andre, b 1874, mar ---, d 1948
   B1. William, unmar   B2. Rebecca
A2. Philippe Thomas, b 1876, d 1969, age 93, mar ---
   B1. James, b 1900, mar Jeanne CORMIER, 2 daus
   B2. Xavier, b 1902, mar Lucienne Cormier, a son
   B3. Adelard, b 1904, mar Liza Hache, 2 daus
   B4. Adeodat, b 1906, unmar
   B5. Wenceslas, b 1911, mar Yvonne Albert, 5 chn
   B6. Cajetan, b 1913, mar Josephine Legere, 2 chn
   B7. Emile, b 1915, mar Hedwidge Lanteigne, 7 chn
   B8. Julien, b 1916, mar Jeanne Robichaud, 7 chn
   B9. Carmleia, b 1918, mar Simon Legere, no issue
   B10. Jean, b 1920, mar Melina Boucher, 14 chn
   B11. a baby, d.y.   B12. Adrienne, b 1937, mar Livain Gionet, no issue
A3. Jacques Georges, b 1977, drowned at Bangor, ME, age 21, unmar
A4. Eliza Jane, b 1878, mar Yvano Beaulieu, 3 chn, all with desc.
   B1. Joseph Beaulieu   B2. Jeanne Beaulieu   B3. Leon Beaulieu
A5. Charles William, b 1882, d age 19, unmar
A6. Marie Louisa, b 1884, mar Honorius Le Guerrier, d 1967, age 73, 6
   chn
   B1. Honorius, mar chn   B2. Claude, mar, chn

```
    B3. Gerard, mar, chn   B4. Cecile, mar, chn   B5. Claire, unmar
A7. Francis Alfred, b 1885, mar, 5 chn, with desc.  Francis d 1917, RR
    accident in Shippegan, N.B., age 32.
    B1. Jeanne, d 1968     B3. Alexandrine        B5. Germaine
    B2. Estelle            B4. Bertha
A8. Pierre, b 1886, mar ---, d 1957, 9 chn
    B1. Charles, mar, chn              B6. Henry, mar, chn
    B2. Audard, d 1972, mar, chn       B7. Armand, mar, chn
    B3. Imelda, d 1973, mar, chn       B8. Yvonne again, mar, chn
    B4. Valmond, d 1935, no issue      B9. Cecile, d 1961, no issue
    B5. Yvonne, no issue
A9. Joseph, b 1889, mar, 10 chn, res Montreal, most are mar and have chn
    B1. Lucien, d.y.                   B5. Martin
    B2. Lucienne                       B6. Roland
    B3. Lucien again                   B7. Gisele
    B4. Edith                          B8. other chn, d.y.
A10. ch, b dead
```

MOURANT, Capt. from J in Nfld. (K. Mathews)
MOURANT, a J fam in Nfld. which changed name to MURREN, MURREY (Shortis-Munn)
MOURANT, A.E., from C.I. to Victoria, BC, there in 1940
MOYSE, see Moses, above
MUGFORD, in Nfld. from 1725 on. John and Wm. at Port de Grave. This fam also connected with C.I. in Mass. See LE GRAND.
MULLAN, MOULIN, John, from G, age 20 in 1818, in Cape Breton (Census)
MULLET, in Nfld. (Seary) Cf MOLLETT of J (Stevens)
MULLEY, in Nfld. (Seary) Cf MOULEY, DE MOULEY of J (Stevens)
MUNGER, a form of MAUGER in the Maritimes. See MAUGER and MONGER
MUNRO, Mary Ann, 1841-1874, of C.I. fam?, mar Edmund LE GALLAIS. A son, Albert, d.y. 1874, bur St. Peters, Paspebiac. (GLF) Also MUNRO, Laura, mar George M. HOCQUARD, qv, res Paspebiac.
MUNRO, John Hilton, 1897-1959, husband of Marjory E. LE GRESLEY, qv, bur Paspebiac (GLF)
MURCELL, in Nfld. (Seary) Cf MORSEL of J (Stevens) Cf also MUNSELL of C.I.
MURREN, MURRIN, Wm., in Bay Roberts, Conc. Bay, Nfld. 1804. Daniel in St. John's 1796. Some MURRAY in Nfld. All three names thought to be originally MOURANT. (Rev. Hammond; G.W. Le Messurier, Shortis-Munn)
NAFTEL, ---, of La Vrangue, G, with wife Caroline COLLINGS, 1775-1851, and sons, Abraham, 1814-1898, and John, b 1816, to Gaspe.
NAFTEL, NOFTAL, from C.I. to Nfld. (Rev. Hammond)
NASTEL, poss NAFTEL?, Capt. from G in Nfld. (K. Mathews)
NAIDOO, from C.I. to Ontario?
NEEL, Dr. Boyd Louis, musician, conductor of orchestra founded 1933, known all over the world, and has made sev hundred records. He was b London, Eng., 1905, son of Louis Anthony NEEL and Ruby LE COUTEUR. (Can. Who's Who, Vol. XI) He has much information of the Neels of J. See also QAAM for other Neels.
NETTOT, Jos., signed the Petition at Gaspe 1820, origin uncertain
NEVEU, see LE NEVEU
NEVELL, NEVILL, NEWELL, in Nfld. (Seary) Cf NEVILLE of C.I. John Neville in Greenspond, Bon. Bay 1860s from C.I. (Rev. Hammond) NEVELL in J 1607 (Stevens)
NEWTON, J, member of Ch. Is. Soc. in BC 1941
NICHOL, NICHOLLE, Ch. Is. surname in Carbonear, Conc. Bay, Nfld. very early. (Rev. Hammond; Seary) A NICHOLL from J at Grand Bank early 1800s. George from C.B. came to Deer Lake, Nfld. ca 1870. See SEARY.

Also see NICOLL, NICOLLE, etc.
NICHOL, ---, from J to Cape La Ronde, N.S. ca 1800
NICHOL, in Gaspe, from C.I.?
NICHOLAS, Gravestone in Annapolis, N.S. 1700s, from C.I.? This surname in G, 1117, and in Ald., 1309.
NICHOLL, in Carbonear, Nfld. (G.W. le Messurier)
NICHOLLE, fam in Nfld., desc in Nfld. and U.S. (Edw. B. Thornhill, St. John's Nfld.) Edward Aaron b 1830 Grand Bank, Burin Pen., Nfld. Fam from Jersey, 4 sons.
A1. Philip
  B1. Edward, killed WWI, unmar
  B2. George, d in Calgary, Alta., unmar
  B3. John, d in Grand Bank, Nfld., mar
A2. Joshua, d 1929, unmar
A3. Edward, b 1857, d 1919, mar Elizabeth Maria PARDY, qv, of Jersey Harbor, Nfld.
  B1. Dinah, b 1887, d 1968, mar Isaac THORNHILL, qv, 1920
    C1. June Thornhill, b 1921, mar Harvey CHAFE, no issue
    C2. Edward, b 1923, mar Carmel Ryan, 2 chn
      D1. Heather Gail Thornhill, b 1964
      D2. Pamela Ann Thornhill, b 1966
    C3. May Thornhill, mar Charles Young
      D1. Cathy Diane Young, b 1961
    C4. Irene, b 1932, unmar
  B2. Irene Bell, b 1896, d 1974, unmar
A4. Betty, mar ---, no issue, d in Grand Bank
NICHOLL, John Sr., b ca 1772, res Crocker's Cove, near Carbonear. John mar 1797, Mrs. Mary Kennedy, b ca 1776, d 1853. This J fam settled in Nfld. prob in 1700s, or poss in late 1600s. (Earl W. Kennedy, Orange City, Iowa)
A1. Edward, of Crocker's Cove, mar 1823, Prudence DEAN, qv.
  B1. Richard, 1823-1872, mar Elizabeth ---
  B2. Ann Maria, b ca 1828   B6. Joseph Sampson, qv, b 1840
  B3. John, b ca 1830   B7. Mary Jane, b 1840, twin of Joseph
  B4. Nicholas Kennedy, b ca 1831 B8. Albert Moses, b 1844
  B5. Edward, 1836-1881   B9. Joshua Mark, b 1847
A2. John Jr., b ca 1800, d 1872, mar 1825 Harbour Grace, Diana Wagg. Active in Labrador fishery, res Carbonear. Mar 2. Mrs. Noseworthy.
  B1. Amelia, b ca 1827, mar --- Kendall
    C1. - C5. sons, 3 of whom d.y.
    C6. Ann Kendall, mar William Stubbs, 3 sons
    C7. Belle Kendall, mar George Lietjen, 2 sons, 2 daus
  B2. Mary Jane, 1833-1913, mar 1857 George Richard DAVIS, qv. Res Carbonear, rem 1865 to Bay of Islands, W. coast of Nfld., 9 chn.
    C1. Edward Pakenham Davis, 1858-1923, mar, chn
    C2. John Nicholl Davis, 1859-1934?, mar twice, one dau survived
    C3. Susannah King Davis, 1861-1951, mar twice, many chn
    C4. Jane Davis, 1863-1937?, mar, one dau
    C5. Mary Davis, 1864-1950?, mar, adopted chn
    C6. Isabel Davis, 1866-1880?, unmar
    C7. George Apsey Davis, 1869-1943, mar, 2 sons, 3 daus
    C8. Florence Pamela Davis, 1872-1969, mar Horace Kennedy, 1878-1948, Halifax, NS in 1897. Rem to Los Angeles, Calif 1924.
      D1. Edith Mary Kennedy, 1898-1943, mar George Roy Inglis, 1899-, no issue
      D2. Earl Carleton Kennedy, b 1901, mar Eleanor Harris GREGG, qv, 1931 Santa Ana, Calif
        E1. Earl William Kennedy, b 1932, Los Angeles, mar 1960,

             Cornelia Breugem, b 1937 Rotterdam, Netherlands, 2 sons
         F1. James Carleton Kennedy, b 1963 Orange City, Iowa
         F2. David Harris Kennedy, b 1966 Orange City, Iowa
      D3. Ralph Davis Kennedy, 1905-1975, mar Blanche Marie Metz, no
          issue
      D4. Clyde Johnstone Kennedy, 1907-1962, mar Dorothy Goodner, 3
          daus
         E1. Mary Carolyn Kennedy, b 1939, mar Carl Thomas McIntire, 2
             chn
         E2. Kathleen Davis Kennedy, b 1950, mar Jacob Ellens
         E3. Janice Lynne Kennedy, b 1953, unmar
   C9. James Faulkner Davis, b 1873, d 1937, mar, had adopted son,
       res Toronto
B3. Louisa Sophia, 1836-1920, mar 1863, Edmund Eli PELLEY, qv, chn
   C1. Dianna PELLEY   C3. Martha PELLEY
   C2. Sarah PELLEY   C4. Mary PELLEY
   B4. Moses Clark, b 1838   B5. John Nicholl, b 1842
B6. James Faulkner, 1843-1971, lost at sea?, prob unmar
B7. Anna Dow, 1847-1917, mar Richard Weir, d 1911, age 64, chn
   C1. Ida Maud Weir, b 1869, mar Charles F. Smith, d 1927, a son
   C2. Edith May Weir, b 1871, mar James Henry Shurman, no issue
A3. Maria? Kemp, mar 1826 Harbour Grace, Nfld., Edward TAYLOR, qv.
A4. Nicholas Kennedy, b ca 1810, d 1887?, postmaster of Carbonear. Mar
    1. Susannah ---, 1813-1838, and 2. Tryphena ---, 1810?-1875, chn
   B1. Naomi Ann, b 1833   B5. Tryphena, 1843-1904, postmaster of
   B2. Sarah Maria, 1835-1840   Carbonear, d in P.O. fire, unmar
   B3. Jane Shepherd, 1837-1840   B6. George Apsey, 1845-1915
   B4. John Elson, 1841-1861
A5. Mary Ann, b ca 1811, d 1899, mar 1833, George Apsey, 1797?-1869, chn
A6. Esther?, mar 1834 William BUTT
A7. Catherine?, mar 1846, Mark TAYLOR
NICHOLS, George Aaron, b N.S., farmer, of J fam?, rem with wife and 2
   sons from N.S. ca 1870 to N.shore of Deer Lake, Nfld. with other fams,
   FISHER, BAGGS, FARNELLS. George was a farmer; his sons, hunters,
   fishermen and farmers. This fam may be related to previous NICHOLLE
   fam, Edward Aaron. George Sr. "no ordinary man, a born pioneer, tall,
   lithe, alert, with long black beard and mustache, and an eye denoting
   unlimited pluck and energy..." (Chris Dennis, Hampden, White Bay,
   Nfld.) George d ca 1910. (Thomas Peddle, Augusta, Maine)
A1. John   A2. Fred
A3. George A. Jr., b 1864 N.S., mar Catherine Maria PEDDLE, qv, of
    Bristol Hope, in 1875. Res Deer Lake, 17 chn. He was a sportsman,
    hunting and fishing guide, "knowledgeable about the forests, rivers
    and animals of the west coast. Much of this knowledge came from a
    friend of theirs, Mattie Mitchell, a full blood Micmac Indian."
NICOLAS, see also NICHOLAS
NICOLE, J., in PEI 1841 census
NICOLE, Clement, b J, bur Harbour Grace, 1778 (Earl   Kennedy, Orange
    City, Iowa) He was a Methodist.
NICOLE, Percy, d 1894 Perce, Quebec
NICOLL, James, b St. Peter Port, G 1798, rem to N.S., d 1877 Gabarus.
    He was a British soldier with the Royal Vet. Batt., stationed in CB
    early in the 1800s. Mar a Sydney girl, Lucy Morley, 1794-1875. (A.
    D. MacDonald, Sydney, NS; Stella Brown, Halifax, NS)
 A1. Ann, b 1827, d 1906, mar Abraham HARDY, son of Charles HARDY, of
     Greenwich, Eng.
    B1. Samuel? Hardy, res Gabarus, NS B2. Charles Hardy, res ditto

NICOLLE, SEE CHANNEL ISLAND COLLECTION.
- B3. James Hardy, b 1850, d 1906
- B4. Elizabeth Hardy, b 1852, mar Jos. BROWN, dau, Stella, mar Michael BROWN
- B5. Leah M. Hardy, b 1855, mar James W. Grant, from Ohio, rem to N.N.B.
- B6. Alex Hardy, b 1856, d 1937, mar Margaret Bagnell, 1843-1938
  - C1. Annie E. Hardy, b 1882, d 1972, mar Charles Lyman Smart
  - C2. Leah F. Hardy, b 1889, mar Dr. D. MacDonald, 1886-1965
    - D1. Alexander D. MacDonald, b 1922, mar Minnie A. O'Hara, b 1930
      - E1. Daniel S. MacDonald, b 1949, mar Heather E. Mann, b 1954
      - E2. Donna L. MacDonald, b 1955, mar Barry E. Grossett, b 1953
        - F1. Denis Michelle Grossett, b 1975
        - F2. Tanya Christina Grossett, b 1976
      - E3. Eldon C. MacDonald, b 1957   E5. Noel D. MacDonald, b 1960
      - E4. Karen A. MacDonald, b 1959
    - D2. Christina M.R. MacDonald, b 1927, mar John U. MacIntyre, 1923-1975

NICOLL, NICHOLL, b ca 1772, d 1848, res Carbonear, Nfld. A son, John NICHOLL, b 1800?, d 1872, res Carbonear, poss also sons Nicholas and Edward. Nicholas was said to have inherited property in J in the 1800s. (Earl Wm. Kennedy, Orange City, Iowa)

NICOLL, ---, mar in White Sands, PEI, a sister of Daniel MACHON, and later mar --- Sullivan

NICOLL, Rev. ---, from G to Lennoxville, Que.

NICOLL, John, b 1789, bp by Rev. T. Desbrisay, St. Paul's Ang. Ch, C'town, PEI, son of Alexander NICOLL (May Severson)

NICOLLE, from C.I. to Manitoba?

NICOLLE, ---, of J, involved 1717 with the Nfld. trafe (C.R. Fay)

NICOLLE, Philip, a fishery at Jersey Harb., Fortune Bay, 1740, Clement MALLETT, mgr., also at St. Mary's Harb., Bargea Island and Poele. The then bailiff of J was a partner in this firm. (Balleine Bio. Dict.)

NICOLLE, from C.I. to Perce, Gaspe (Rev. d'Hist; Syvret)

NICOLLE, Clement, worked for Robin firm 1772 Paspebiac (Rev. d'Hist; Syvret)

NICOLLE, ---, from C.I., 1886-1894, bur St. Paul, Perce, Gaspe, also Frederick and Rachel (GLF)

NICOLLE, from C.I., fisherman, res Bay of Quinte, Ont.

NICOLLE, Sophie Arthur, wife of John Arthur LE COUTEUR, merchant in Gaspe, he d 1871, age 39 at Fox River, Que. Their minor dau was Florence LE COUTEUR. (Brochet)

NICOLLE, Alfred Aubin, b J, son of Jean Philippe N. and Jane LEVASSEUR, res L'Anse Griffon, Gaspe 1885, mar Emma Boulay.

NICOLLE, John Thomas, b ca 1795 G, farmer, sailmaker, rem to Guernsey Cove, PEI 1806, d 1856 at White Sands, PEI, bur Murray Harbour Cem. Mar 1. Elizabeth MACHON, qv, 1807-1838, and 2. Margaret Irving, b ca 1803, who d 1885, age 82, bur Murray Harb., PEI. 8 chn, 6 by E. Machon. "John Thomas had several brothers and brothers-in-law in PEI... It is said that one of his younger bros mar an ALEXANDRE and had 14 chn. They were located in Truro, NS. Some of the others rem to U.S. ...The Sullivan homestead was deeded to John Thomas after Widow Sullivan died, called Aunt Mame." (Leland Stanford Nicolle, Murray River, PEI; May Severson, New Brighton, Minn; Carol Warnsdorfer, Pt. Pleasant, N. Jersey) Some NICOLLES of G or J on GAUDIN chart. Some uncertain data on this family. See MACHON fam for record of John NICOLLE of Gladstone, PEI and Elizabeth MACHON, b 1838, and 5? chn.
- A1. Margaret, b 1822 Kings Co., PEI, mar Thomas HENRY, qv, sailmaker, farmer. Sold farm in M.H., rem to Georgetown, farmed there and

NICOLLE

operated a sail loft. SEE EXTRA PAGES.
- B1. Ezra   B2. Nettie, mar John Millford of England, 2 daus
- B3. Maud, mar Joseph ROBERTS, qv, blacksmith. At least 5 chn.
- A2. Mary Ann, b 1824, d.y.? or mar Charles Cupps?
- A3. John, b 1826, d.y.   A4. Frances, b 1828, d.y.
- A5. John Thomas, b 1833, d 1914 White Sands, PEI. Mar Elizabeth Horton CLEMENTS, qv, 1837-1925. She was dau of William CLEMENTS, qv and Mary Ann Sencabaugh.
  - B1. Mary Ann, Mae, mar 1. Capt. John R. Bailey and 2. John Van Iderstine, res Kings Co., PEI. 5 chn by Bailey.
    - C1. Hattie Bailey, mar Dr. Coffin, 2 sons   C2. Minnie Bailey
    - C3. Lois Bailey, mar a detective, res U.S.
    - C4. a son, d.y.   C5. Nina Bailey, mar, rem to B.C.
    - C6. Alexander Van Iderstine of this fam, Mary Ann's stepson.
  - B2. Jane, mar Alexander D. MacDonald, 1862-1942, bur Murray Harb. She d in middle age, when he mar 2. Ade E. Penny, 1879-1948.
    - C1. Loren MacDonald, drowned young   C3. John Milton MacDonald, b
    - C2. Clifford MacDonald, rem from PEI   1889, d 1973, unmar
    - C4. Percy L. MacDonald, b 1897, d 1969, unmar
    - C5. Merland MacDonald, by second wife, unmar
  - B3. Louise Margaret, b 1862 PEI, d 1955 Guernsey Cove, PEI, unmar
  - B4. William John, b 1864 PEI, d 1942 White Sands, a farmer. Mar 1. Elizabeth Jane Bull, 1869-1899, dau of David Bull and Eliz. White, mar 2. Margaret Jane Phillips, dau of John P. and Annie Ferguson. She d 1927.
    - C1. Florence Edith, b 1892, d 1964 Melrose, Mass., mar Elmon Bradford Grover, 1889-1928, WWI Vet, 2 chn
    - C2. Ella May, b 1893, rem to Medford, Mass., Ohio and Minn. d1971. New Brighton, Minn. Mar James Arnold Denton, b 1885 N.S., d 1971 Minn., 1 ch.
    - C3. Ethel Elizabeth, b 1895 PEI, mar William Spencer Sharam, farmer, 5 chn, d 1979.
    - C4. Jeremiah, Jerry, b 1897, fisherman, d 1973 Beach Pt., PEI, mar Ethel MacNeill, 1903-1966. He was a WWI Vet, 2 chn
    - C5. William Earl, b 1899, d 1900, bur Murray Harbor, PEI
    - C6. William Earl again, b 1901, d 1969, farmer, mar Lucille May White, 3 chn. He was first ch by second wife.
    - C7. Lulu Sarah, d.y.   C8. Irene Chapman, b 1906, unmar, d 1925
    - C9. Laura Cecilia, mar Samuel J. BECK, qv, farmer, no issue
    - C10. Roy, b 1910, d.y.   Samuel b 1898 d 1978.
    - C11. Roy again, b 1913, farmer, carpenter, Little River, PEI, mar Helen Margaret LE LACHEUR, qv, 4 chn
    - C12. Arnold D., b 1915, farmer, Murray River, PEI, WWII Vet, mar Mina MacFarlane, 3 chn
    - C13. Violet Annie, d.y.
  - B5. Oliver Cromwell, b 1867 Kings Co., PEI, d 1949 Boston, Mass., blacksmith and city fireman, Medford, Mass. Mar Dora Augusta Joudrey of NS, 1874-1955.
    - C1. Albert Earl, b 1899, d 1962, mar Louise ---, 2 chn, mar 2. Doris ---, no issue
    - C2. Elsie Laura, b 1900, mar 1. Warren Raymond French, 2 chn, and mar 2. John Stanley of Cambridge, Mass., d 1973, no issue
    - C3. Elva Louise, b 1904 Mass., mar Malcolm Gilson, res Lexington, Mass., 3 chn
    - C4. Arnold Oliver, b 1906, mar Thelma Wheeler, 1 ch, res Medford, Mass.

SEE NICOLLE IN EXTRA PAGES.
- C5. Gladys Dora, b 1914, mar Michael Di Pesa?, res Revere, Mass., d 1971, 1 ch
- B6. Herbert Howard, b 1871 PEI, d 1952 Providence, R.I., bur Highland Cem, Warwick, RI. Mar Margaret M. Campbell of Bonshaw, PEI. He was a plasterer.
  - C1. Eathon John, b PEI?, jeweler in R.I., mar Muriel --- of PEI, 1 ch
  - C2. Ivan Melbourne, b ca 1909, d 1957 R.I., mar Lillian Hames, 1908-1967, 3 chn
  - C3. Glenn Herbert, b Providence?, mar 1. Virginia Miller, 1 ch, and mar 2. no issue
  - C4. Etta J., unmar   C5. Kathryn, b R.I.?, dec
  - C6. Marion J., b R.I., mar Axel Carlson, painter, no issue
  - C7. Elizabeth C., b Prov., R.I., unmar
- B7. Laura Cecilia, b 1874, d 1896, mar Capt. Reuben W. PENNY, who remar after her death.
  - C1. Alonzo, b 189-, served in WWI, d shortly after in his 20s
  - C2. son, d.y.
- B8. Albert and B9. Alberta, twins, d.y.
- B10. Lucious James, b 1877, d 1961, age 84 in Maryland, where he lived with his dau. He was a blacksmith in Melrose, Mass., mar Eliz. J. (Ida) Philpot of Melrose, who d 1947.
  - C1. Lester J., d 1972 Melrose, WWII Vet, unmar
  - C2. Audrey, mar J. Paul Bateman, who d 1962. Adopted dau. This fam had a small wood case with picture of John Thomas NICOLLE II, ca age 20, painted on it. He was cleanshaved with a long straight nose and blue eyes.

A 6. William Pullem, b 1835, rem to U.S. ca 1871, date and place of death unknown. Mar Janet Eliza, Jane, Arnett, b 1837, dau of Thomas Arnett, 1792-1871. She was b Kings Co., PEI, d age 33, bur Crapaud Cem, PEI.
- B1. William Henry, b ca 1857 PEI, d ca 1950, age 95 plus in Providence, R.I. Mar 1. in his teens, ---, N.B. girl, who d leaving 6? small chn, who then res with their grandparents. They grew up and mar. Wm. Henry, rem after his wife's death to U.S. and mar 2. Anna Rossiter. Chn 1, 2, 3, a son Henry, who rem to Natick, Mass. and 2 daus.
  - C4. Howard, b Providence, R.I., by second wife
  - C5. William   C6. Chester
  - C7. James Wallace, mar Elsie ---, b 1902, a son
  - C8. Harold, b Prov., RI   C9. Agnes   C10. Violet
- B2. John Thomas, b 1859 PEI, d 1939, a lobster canner, bur Murray Harb. Cem, mar at age 18. Inez Kennedy, and 2. Catherine, Katie A. MacKay, 1870-1933.
  - C1. Inez, mar --- PHILLIPS. Raised by grandparents who rem to Sydney, NS
  - C2. Mame, b 1890, by second wife, 2 sons and a dau mar Ezra BECK.
  - C3. Lulu, b 1893, d 1976, mar 1. Joseph Livingstone, d 1919, a son. Mar 2. Bert Lumsden, WWI Vet, who d in Trenton, N.S.
  - C4. Margaret, b 1895, mar George COOPER, CNP empl., a son and dau
  - C5. Harry Gladstone, b 1897, mar Ann DAVEY, 1 dau. He d 1978
  - C6. Beatrice, b 1899, d 1974, mar George MacKenzie, 4 boys, 2 girls
  - C7. Edna, or Eda L., b 1903, d 1916
  - C8. Charlotte, mar ?, res Montague, PEI, mar, 2 sons
- B3. Emma Jane, mar James SHAW, qv
  - C1. James Shaw, b before 1885, rem to U.S.
  - C2. Arnett Shaw, b ca 1886, d 1976, farmer, res C'town, PEI

NICOLLE 445

   C3. Edward Shaw, d 1975, res C'town, PEI
   C4. Hooper Shaw, wheat farmer, Canadian West
   C5. Pansy, rem to U.S.
   C6. Janet, Jennie, Shaw, d 1976, mar Jack MacLure, Vet WWI, a son and dau
   C7. Nellie Shaw, d 1976, res St. John's
 B4. Hammond Johnston, b 1868 Kings Co., PEI, d 1958 Montague, bur Murray Harb. Fisherman and farmer of White Sands, PEI, mar Mary Ann MacLeod of High Banks, 1872-1954.
   C1. Leland Sanford, b1892, farmer, res Murray River, PEI, mar Pearl Evelyn McKinnon, b 1903, 12 chn
      D1. James Arthur, b 1922, d 1936
      D2. Evelyn Mae, mar Emmerson K. Johnstone, a son and 2 daus
      D3. Audrey Irene, mar Howard Rafuse, WWII Vet, retired
      D4. Norma Eileen, mar Allan Pryne, Fleet Air Arm
      D5. Judson Bennet, mar Mary Butler, 2 sons, 4 daus
      D6. Lois Isabelle, mar Lewis Jenkins, 2 sons
      D7. Joann, mar Lloyd Higgins, no issue
      D8. Hammond L., mar Eva Bearse, 2 daus and 1 son
      D9. Mary Ann, twin of Hammond, mar Thomas Fraser Jr., 2 sons
      D10. William Blain, mar Suzanne Reid, 3 daus
      D11. Darlene Lee, mar Waldo Lowe, 3 daus and a son
   C2. Clarence Oliver, b 1895, mar Ella Bearse, 4 sons, 1 dau
   C3. James William, b 1896, d 1910
   C4. Arnett Lowell, b 1899, mar Sara Isabelle Steward, b 1911 White Sands, PEI, dau of Alex. Stewart and Caroline J. MacLean, res Newton Ctre., Mass.
      D1. Carol, b 1937 Brooklyn, NY, mar Frank Warnsdorfer
      D2. Janet, b 1941 Jackson Hts., NY, mar Joseph FUREY
      D3. Betty, b 1947 C'town, PEI, mar Donald Harris
   C5. Audrey Alexandra, b 1902, school teacher, d 1923
   C6. Emma Isabelle, mar Ray Steward, 3 sons, and 1 dau
   C7. Hammond Floyd, b 1911, mar Kaye Stewart, no surviving chn
 B5. Oliver, rem to U.S., mar, 1 dau
 B6. James   B7. Gertrude   B8. William
A7. Elizabeth, b ca 1838, mar Neil PENNY, dau, Mary Eliza PENNY. Eliz. mar 2. James Clark. MORE IN CI COLL.
A8. James Henry, b 1842, d 1927, mar Mary Harris, 1845-1930, no surv. chn
A9. John Hill, foster son, an orphan, b 1846
NICOLLE fam from St. Heliers, J, chn of Philippe Clement N. and Marie Louise Kercheval, of Louisburg, Queens Rd., St. Heliers, rem to Canada. (Ph. Nicolle, Vancouver, BC; Rosina Eger, Fife Lake, Sask.)
I. NICOLLE, Harvey
II., III., IV. 3 sisters, including Irene, who mar --- LE GROS qv, res J
V. NICOLLE, Clement Dring Kercheval, b J, homesteaded south of Alexander, Man. Mar Florence Eva Aconby Husband 1915, fam in BC and West. Canada.
 A1. Philippe Clement, b 1917, mar Helen Katie Wood 1944, Vet of WWII, RCAF.
   B1. Shelley Devon, b 1946 Vanc., mar Arnold Walker, res Winnipeg, Man.
   B2. Kerry Kendall, b 1948, mar John Cranstone, res Calgary, Alta.
   B3. Dr. Lindsay Ellen, b 1949, unmar
   B4. Gayden Sidney, b 1953, mar James PAYNE 1977, res Calgary, Alta.
 A2. Irene, b 1918, mar Frank Sinden, res Vict., BC
   B1. Marilin Irene Sinden, b 1942, mar Richard A. WAGONER
      C1. Bonita Lynn Wagoner, b 1960 C2. Kelly Deanne Wagoner, b 1963

B2. Rosalie Carol Sinden, b 1944, unmar
B3. Leroy Gordon Sinden, b 1948, mar Jean Meier
   C1. Brett Allen Sinden, b 1967   C2. Shaun Michael Sinden, b 1970
B4. Kenneth Owen Sinden, b 1952, mar Marjorie Orson
   C1. Charlene Dawn Sinden, b 1971   C2. Darren Evan Sinden, b 1974
A3. Rosina Mae, b 1919, mar John Richard Eger, res Fife Lake, Sask., 9 chn, 11 grchn
   B1. Allan Richard Eger, b 1938, mar Lorraine Mertle Booth, res Winn., Man., no issue
   B2. Grace Florence Eger, b 1940, mar Rodney Petford, res McLean, Sask, 5 chn
      C1. Lyle George Petford, b 1958   C4. Bradley Robert Petford, b 1963
      C2. Darwyn Rodney Petford, b 1961 C5. Rhonda Mae Petford, b 1973
      C3. Kevin Petford, b 1962
   B3. Larry Robert Eger, b 1942, mar Shirley Sorsdahl, res Radville, Sask.
      C1. Geoffrey Walter Eger, b 1967
   B4. George Brian Eger, b 1946, mar Jeanette MORCOM, res Regina, Sask., 2 chn
      C1. Terry Lance Eger, b 1970   C2. Leila Maureen Eger, b 1972
   B5. Fern Mae Eger, b 1947, mar Brian McMillan, res Prince George, BC, and Swift Current, Sask., 2 chn
      C1. Tracie Dawn McMillan, b 1973   C2. Grant Brian McMillan, b 1975
   B6. Dean Harvey Eger, b 1949, mar Pat Hand, res Irma, Sask., 2 chn
      C1. Tammy Patricia Eger, b 1973   C2. Karen Elizabeth Eger, b 1976
   B7. Lynn Russell Eger, b 1952, mar Denise Therrien, res Regina, Sask., no issue
   B8. Brent John Eger, b 1960   B9. Dawn Rosina Eger, b 1968
A4. Wilson Raymond, b 1922, mar Hazel Hall
   B1. Raymond George, b 1947, mar and div., res Vanc., BC
   B2. Katherine Laura, b 1949, mar Dennis RICHARDSON, no issue
   B3. Douglas Clement, b 1952
   B4. Victor Wayne, b 1955   B5. Carol Florence, b 1967
A5. Edith Agnes, b 1925, mar Ralph Eugene Starks, res Prince Albert, Sask.
   B1. Ralph Eugene Starks, b 1952   B3. Susan Celia Starks, b 1957
   B2. Stephanie Ann Starks, b 1954
A6. Harvey Donald, b 1927, mar Patricia Gilmore, res Delisle, Sask.
   B1. Russel, adopted, son of wife's first mar
   B2. Heather Marie, b 1962   B4. Cameron Alexander, b 1965
   B3. Trudy Rosina, b 1963   B5. April Alma, b 1967
NICOLLE, Charles, b J, in Douglas town, Gaspe 1861 (Census)
NICOLLE, Ester J., 6 yrs. old in 1871, was living with the Peter LE LACHEUR fam in Arichat, CB, NS. (Census)
NICOLLE, from J to Ottawa, Ont.
I. NICOLLE, Albert Winter, son of Charles N. and Mary LE GRESLEY, qv, one of 8 chn, b 1862 J. An accountant with a J company, to Nfld. very young. Mar Jessie Meagher, 1866-1945 in Nfld. 1887. Rem to Mulgrave, NS 1924, had a grocery store until his death in 1949, 5 chn. (Mildred Huntington, Sydney, NS)
A1. Herbert Winson, b 1888   A2. Clement Charles, b 1890
A3. May Louise, b 1893, res Mulgrave, NS, mar 1. John Frederick Barrie 1920, a son. Mar 2. Murdock MacLeod 1926, 3 daus.
   B1. Albert Winter Barrie, b 1921, d 1976, mar Amelia MORRISON 1949, dau, Jean Elizabeth, b 1962
   B2. Mildred Christina MacLeod, b 1927, mar 1945, Hector Huntington, res Sydney, NS, no issue.

B3. Alice Louise MacLeod, b 1932, mar 1961 Donald Curry, res Mulgrave,
      NS, 2 chn
      C1. Glenn Curry, b 1962   C2. Pamela Curry, b 1973
  B4. Jessie Marina MacLeod, b 1935, mar 1963, Cullen MacLeod, res Port
      Hawkesbury, NS, 3 chn
      C1. Ian MacLeod, b 1964   C3. Sheena MacLeod, b 1970
      C2. Elaine MacLeod, b 1966
II.   Walter A., bro of Albert, above, to Nfld., then Halifax, and finally
      settled in Mulgrave, NS
III. Louise, remained in J, mar --- JANVRIN. Poss desc, Warwick Nicolle
      Dupre.
NICOLLE family. "There were three Nicolle bros, and their brothers-
      in-law, Machon and Sullivan. John Thomas Nicolle, George Washington
      Nicolle, his bro who later went to Scotland, and John Henry Nicolle,
      another bro who also mar a Machon girl and went to Truro, NS. It was
      John Thomas' sister who mar Sullivan. Sullivan was drowned around
      Prim Pt., while taking a load of sails to C'town. A Roberts, learn-
      ing the trade, died with him. According to Leah, the name was origin-
      ally Siliphant and changed to Sullivan---The Nicoles were red-bearded
      and red-haired and very fair complexioned. Were very easily sunburned.
      The red veins in their faces were seen through the skin. James Ni-
      colle and wife were the best looking couple for miles around. He had
      a red curly beard. Beards were the fashion in my boyhood days."
      (Leland Nicolle, Murray Harb., PEI)
NICOLLE, Capt., agent, merchant and ship owner from J in Nfld. (K.
      Mathews)
NICOLLE, at Jersey Harbour, Nfld. (C.R. Fay)
NICOLLE, John, from C.I.?, in Richmond Co., NS 1861 (Census)
NICOLLE, John, in Valois, Que., from C.I.?
NICOLLE, in Maritimes and Gaspe (Betty Tardif)
NICOLLE, John, b Cape Breton 1857, son of John N. and Jane ---, mar
      Judith or Julia LE LACHEUR, qv
NICOLLS, Jasper Hume, b 1818 G, son of Gen. Gustavus NICOLLS and Heriot
      Frances Thomson. He d Lennoxville, Que. 1877. Spent youth in N.S.
      where his father was an engineer. Educated at Oxford, and in 1845
      became first principal of Bishop's College in Lennoxville, related to
      Bishop Mountain. Mar his first cousin, Harriet Mary Mountain and had
      2 sons and one dau.
NICOLS, Edward, book keeper in Carbonear, 1860s (Rev. Hammond)
NICOLS, George, in Carbonear, Nfld. with George A. (Rev. Hammond)
NICOLS, John and Charles in Harbour Grace, Nfld. 1860s (Census)
NIGHTINGALE, in Nfld. (Seary) Cf LE ROSSIGNOL of J (Stevens)
NIGHTINGALE, in Canda, some said to be formerly of C.I.
NILES, see Hacker and Alfred Le Page
NOBLE, in Nfld. Cf LE NOBLE of J (Stevens) See Seary
NOEL, from C.I. to Carbonear, Harbour Grace, Brigus, Port de Grave,
      etc. in Nfld., there in late 1700s. (The following were copied from
      old registers, etc. by Rev. Hammond, Bell Island, Nfld.)
NOEL, Clement in Carbonear 1785; Clement and Richard in Carbonear 1860s;
      J. at Burnt Head 1790; John Monk, Missionary in Nfld. 1864 (SPG);
      Clement and Frederick in Harbor Grace 1860s; John in Brigus, 1786;
      Isaac in Brigus 1790; John in Brigus 1785; Philip in Port de Grave
      1786.
NOEL, Asenath, b Nfld., rem to Lisbon Falls, Maine, mar John Moores,
      some desc. (John K. Butts, Augusta, Maine)
NOEL, Clement from J to S. side of Houhan? Cove, Nfld. Nathaniel and
      Thos. Noel, (St. John's Nfld.), CORBINS in this fam, from C.I. to

Poole, England, then to Nfld.
A1. John Frederick   A3. Ambrose   A5. Mary Ann, and other chn
A2. Martin   A4. Elias
A6. Nathaniel, mar Susannah Catherine Thompson, dau of James King Thompson
  B1. Isabelle Noel, mar James PIKE, son of Charlotte Pike
  B2. Clement, lost at sea   B3. Stuart, mar Elizabeth JEUNE?, qv
  B4. James Archibald, b 1860, d 1917, mar Sarah CORBIN, qv.
     C1. Thomas Corbin, b 1890, mar Flora May WINSOR. He d 1968.
        D1. Nathaniel Stewart, b 1920   D4. Alexandre Clement
        D2. John Winsor   D5. Mabel Louise
        D3. Thomas Corbin   D6. June Pauline
     C2. Nathaniel Stewart, mar Elsie Hyde
     C3. Lillian, mar Henry Stead
     C4. Susannah?, mar William Monroe   C5. Mabel, mar William Crone
NOEL, Dr. Anthony, res in Arichat, NS, from C.I.?, mar ---
NOEL, from C.I. in Cap Chat., Gaspe 1861 (Census)
NOEL, John, mar Anne BUTLIN, qv, res Perce, Gaspe
NOEL, from C.I. to Ontario?
NOEL. "The Noels and other descendants of Jersey family are still living in this vicinity...(South side of Harbour Grace) (Shortis-Munn). Noels, Le Huquets, and Le Scelleurs were close neighbors and friends in St. Martins, J, 1800s.
NOEL, David Philip, b 1892 St. Martin, J, son of Capt. David Philip N. and Jane Eliza BUESNEL, b 1866, mar 1890 St. Saviours, J. Capt. Noel, with 6? of his sons was lost on his ship in the Mediterranean during the first WW. David Philip, the younger, with his twin, Renouf Noel, rem to Winnipeg, 1911. Worked in flour-milling, then grain growing, and were sales managers in Milling Co., etc. Worked until age 75. David was Pres. of Winnipeg Philosophical Soc. Mar Edith Auth, b Sweden, no issue.
NOEL, Renouf, b 1892 J, twin of David, above, rem to Winnipeg, served in both Wars, res Montreal, bur Pte. Clair, Que. Renouf and David had at least two sisters, Dora and Lillian Becquet and a bro, Edmund, of J. Dora and Edmund d of T.B. (Edith Noel, Winnipeg, Man.)
NOEL, James and Paul, signed in 1834, the Petition for mail route requested by New Brunswickers, to run between Bathurst and Shippegan. (Archives) These Noels were prob from J.
NOFTAL, FOFTALL, etc., in Nfld. (Seary) Cf NAFTEL of C.I. Peter was in Broad Cove, Nfld. 1783 (Seary) See Naftel. Gilbert was in St. John's, Nfld. See Seary for more.
NORMAN, Clifford, from C.I. to Edmonton, Alta. 1926, harvester, farmer. Worked in 1927 at Whiskey Gap, Alta. for a 14 team outfit, 4 horses hauling water and 4 horses to haul coal from Woodford for the steamer. One of the fields covered 1260 acres. See ALEXANDER. (Blanche Martin, Alberta)
NORMAN, Clifford Alexander, b 1901 St. Peter of the Wood, G, son of Francis John N. and Mary Ann ALEXANDER, qv. Mar Blanche Eleanore PLEVEN, qv, b 1902 St. Clements, J, dau of Maturin Francis P. and Melanie Rosealie GROSVALET.
A1. Blanche Elaine, b 1925 St. Clements, J, mar Wilfred James MARTIN 1948, res Sherwood Park, Alta., 6 chn
  B1. Rozanne Blanche Martin, b 1949 Edmonton, Alta., mar Victor Unguran 1969, res Alta.
     C1. Melanie Rose Blanche Unguran, b 1972
  B2. Elaine Jeanette Martin, b 1950 Spirit River, Alta., mar 1973, Roger M. Brassard, res Calgary, Alta.

C1. Kevin Leroy Brassard, b 1974
C2. Michelle Bambi Brassard, b 1975
B3. Wayne Wilfred Martin, b 1952, res Edmonton, Alta.
B4. Marilyn Louise Martin, b 1953 Edmonton, mar James Douglas Kaulbach 1971, res Sherwood Park, Alta.
C1. Kimberly Louise Kaulbach, b 1971   C3. Jennifer Ann Kaulbach,
C2. Douglas James Kaulbach, b 1974   b 1977
B5. Lucille Melanie Martin, b 1957 Edmonton, mar Alvin A. Brudnicki
C1. Tennille Lee Brudnicki, b 1977
B6. James David Martin, b 1963 Edmonton
A2. Roselle Ena, b 1927 Edmonton, mar Harold James Davison, 1952, res Fourth Creek, Alta.
B1. Sandra Roselle Davison, b 1956 Ponoka, Alta., mar David James Lindsay 1975, res Wembley, Alta.
B2. Clifford James Davison, b 1957, res Grande Prairie, Alta.
A3. Sylvia Florence, b 1928 Edmonton, mar John Alexander Klienschroth, 1950
B1. John Melvin Klienschroth, b 1952 Edmonton
B2. Barbara Jean Klienschroth, b 1953
B3. Donna Lynn Klienschroth, b 1955
B4. Lennard George Klienschroth, b 1956, mar Janet Irene Lewis 1975, res Morin, Alta.
B5. Arlene Sylvia Klienschroth, b 1960
B6. Brian James Klienschroth, b 1963, res Edmonton
A4. Norman Clifford Pleven, b 1929 Edmonton, mar Joan Elizabeth Thackray 1954, res Sherwood Park, Alta.
B1. Janice Isabel, b 1956, mar Dennis Paul Newman, res Sherwood Park
B2. Karen Elaine, b 1958
B3. Douglas Clifford, b 1960   B4. Susan Eliz., b 1970
A5. Maxwell Francis, Mac, b 1931, mar --- Klienschroth, res Calgary, Alta.
B1. Faye Denise, b 1956
C1. Shannon Gail, b 1975, Calgary
B2. Dean Maxwell, b 1958, Edmonton   B3. Marie Ann, b 1963 Calgary
A6. Katherine Iris, b 1935 Edmonton, mar Carl Horton, 1960, who d 1968
B1. Carlene Blanche Horton, b Salmon Arm, BC 1961, res Edmonton, Alta.
A7. Alexander Frank, Sandy, b 1937, mar Joan Ingram 1960, res Sherwood Park
B1. May Beth Marie, b 1961, Drayton Valley, Alta.
B2. Sheryl Joan, b 1963   B3. Patricia Alexander, b 1965
A8. Jeannette Avis, b 1943, Edmonton, mar Michael Cholowsky 1963, res Edmonton
B1. Christine Catherine Cholowsky, b 1965   B3. Michael Andres Cholow-
B2. Amy Jeannette Cholowsky, b 1967   sky, b 1970
A9. Walter John, b 1945, mar 1973, Geraldine Fay, res Calgary
B1. Kara Lee, b 1975 Calgary   B2. Ryan Trevor, b 1977
NORMAN, C.I. name in Con. Bay, Nfld. early (Rev. Hammond; G.W. Le Messurier; Seary) David in Bay Roberts, 1802; James and Wm. in Brigus, 1774; Grace in Brigus, 1786; Christopher, a watchmaker, in Brigus, 1860s; James, A Capt. and planter in Brigus, 1860s; Lorenzo in Brigus, also Nathan, a planter at that time. John in Port de Grave, 1783. Ernest in Thornhill, Ont., desc from fam in Bay Roberts. "The Normans of Brigus who were pioneers in our seal fishery, and took a prominent and worthy part in building up our Labrador industry were from Jersey. It is said that when they settled at the Battery head in Brigus, it was because of its great resemblance to their old home in the Channel Islands." (Shortis-Munn typescript) Cf Le Normands in

St. Peter Port, G, 1750.
NORMAND, NORMAN, Joseph, b ca 1790 or 1782 in J, poss conn with the
   NORMANS from J in Nfld. settled in Arichat, CB, mar Charlotte Landry,
   dau of Jean Baptiste L. and Ann Pitre. He d 1872 at Arichat, age 90?
   He called himself Scottish, but the census of 1871 says that Marie
   and Sabine, his daus, were Jersey French! Joseph's son, Georges, and
   dau, Charlotte, are simply called French in the census. (Stephen
   White, Moncton, NB)
A1. Charlotte, b ca 1834, mar 1860 at Arichat, Pierre Michel BLANCPIED,
   qv, son of Charles J. and Charlotte LE BLANC., qv. Her husband
   was a shipmaster, 1871.
A2. Georges, b ca 1833, mar 1861 in Arichat, Sabine Leblanc, dau of
   Polycarpe and Archange Theriault. He was a seaman. Mar 2. 1866,
   Emilie MARCHAND, dau of Pierre.
   B1. Marie Elizabeth, b ca 1862, d 1878   B2. Delvinia, b ca 1863
A3. Marie, mar 1866 at Arichat, Angus McDonald, son of Austin and Anne
   McDonald of Little Arichat, a farmer. She was b ca 1838.
A4. Sabine, b ca 1840?, mar 1875 at Arichat, Edouard MARCHAND, son of
   Pierre and Charlotte Fougere. Edward, or Pierre, had mar previous-
   ly, Adele Theriault, dau of Pierre-Paul Theriault and Sara Paon
   1867 at Arichat.
NORMAN, Wm. Percey, b ca 1890?, mar Bertha Dawe. He was drowned in the
   seal fishery 1914. Had 3 chn, res Nfld. Bertha Dawe was the dau of
   --- Dawe and Naomi GUSHUE, qv, her mother a Mugford desc. See GUSHUE
   chart.
NORMAN, LE NORMAND. The Le Normands were in St. Peter Port, G in 1750,
   related to the MARQUANDS, ROBIN, LE WEG, WAGNER, WAGGENER, GRUTE, and
   LGALLIENNE families.
NORMORE, Gregory, from C.I.?, had right to a fishing room in Portugal
   Cove, Nfld. 1769, formerly owned by Thomas Hibbs, who had died. Mon-
   ument at Portugal Cove: "In memory of Gregory Normore of Great Belle
   Isle, who died the 14th of July, 1785, age 66 yrs." He mar Catherine
   White, LE BLANC?, dau of an English planter living at Harbor Grace.
   See also PIPPY. (Rev. J. Hammond, Bell Island, Nfld.; Seary)
A1. Ann, mar John ROBERTS, ROBERT 1780
A2. Mary, mar Joseph PIPPY, qv, 1783
A3. Robert, b 1764, d 1831. Mar Mary Kent of Great Belle Isle 1880
A4. Henry, b 1772, d 1860, mar Margaret Ryan
   B1. Elizabeth, b 1800
   B2. Catherine, mar John BENNETT, qv, 1822
   B3. Solomon, b 1803, mar Joanna SEARLE, qv, who d 1899 at 96, a son,
      Robert, b 1832
   B4. John, b 1804   B6. Ann Frances, b 1813   B8. Frances, b
   B5. Thomas, b 1810, d 1888   B7. Jane, b 1815   1820
A5. Gregory, referred to in some Ch records as Penegaive?, mar 1.
   Frances ---, and 2. Mary ---, ca 1812
   B1. Agnes, b 1798   B3. Gregory, b 1802   B5. Alice, b 1815
   B2. Robert, b 1801   B4. Richard, b 1813
NORMORE, some recent desc of this fam bur St. Boniface Ang. Cem, ---,
   Nfld. are Henry, d age 81 in 1926; John, d 1907 age 55; Thomas, d
   1888 age 78; Thomas J., d 1913 age 94; James, d 1916 age 81; Thomas,
   d 1919 age 79; and Frank, grandson of Henry, b 1859, d 1952.
NORSWORTHY, NOSEWORTHY, of Nfld., much intermarriage between this fam
   and other C.I. fams of Nfld.
NOURY, Mrs. J. Elizabeth, from G to Victoria, BC late 1800s. Nee
   ROBILLIARD. (Collett, BC)
NOURY, Amy, from G in 1910, mar Jack SAVIDENT, qv, res Victoria, BC,

no issue. See also LE NOURY.
NOYON, some to Canada from C.I.
OAKES, Harriet, b J, mother of John Philip LE MASURIER, qv.
ODLUM, Capt. Abraham, b Tullamore, Ire., 1785, met Elizabeth Lovat-Fraser at a military ball. She was the dau of the Lord Lovat-Fraser and b Scotland 1797. They eloped to marry because of religious differences, he being C. of E., and she, Catholic. Capt. Odlum fought in the Napoleonic War at Waterloo. He may have been stationed in G, as several chn were b there over a six year period before coming to Canada. He was granted land in Toronto, Gore Co., and Albion. Eliza, Elizabeth, d in Tullamore, Ont. 1836, and Capt. Odlum d there in 1838. (Trudy Mann, Mississauga, Ont.)
- A1. Charlotte Francis, b 1819 G, d 1902 Orangeville, Ont. Mar Nichols BERRY, qv, b 1812 Ire., d 1882 Orangeville. Inn Keeper and farmer.
  - B1. Eliza Ann, b 1836 Tullamore, d 1924 Toronto, unmar
  - B2. James Berry, b 1838, d 1924, unmar
  - B3. John, b 1842, d 1843
  - B4. Joseph, b 1843, d 1929, mar --- Walker, a dau, Jennie, also mar a Walker, no issue
  - B5. Charlotte, b 1847, d 1902 Tullamore. Mar Richard Thompson, 1851-1902. He was a councillor, farmer, and Reeve.
    - C1. Annie, b 1878, d.y.   C2. Isaac Bertram, no issue
    - C3. Charlotte Lillian Thompson, unmar
    - C4. Richard Alwin Thompson, mar ---. Chn: Jane, Edward, Ruth, Charlotte, Richard, and Neal, all res U.S.
    - C5. Ivan James, b 1887 Tullamore, Ont., d 1968 Winnipeg, Man. Mar Elsie Batty, b 1897 Harney, Man., d Winnipeg 1975.
      - D1. Joan Eloise, b Winn., mar Ronald Collins, a son, Stephen
      - D2. Richard David, mar Isla Putnam, Chn: Debra, Gail, David, Craig, and Bruce.
      - D3. Gertrude Lillian, mar E. Marland Mann. Chn: Richard, Carolyn, and Bruce.
- A2. Edward Daniel Henry Odlum, b 1820 G, mar Sarah Thompson, Tullamore, Ont., 1844. He d 1886 Brampson, Ont. She d 1909 MacVille, Ont.
  - B1. Eliza Jane, b 1846, mar Robert Kerr. She d 1908, he 1912 in Brampton, Ont.
    - C1. John, b 1849, d 1854
  - B2. Leonard, b 1854, mar Elizabeth Coulter, who d 1942. He d 1930.
    - C1. Robert, b 1887, d.y.
    - C2. Edward, mar Jessie Steels
      - D1. Elyn Leonard, b 1902, d 1903
      - D2. Sarah Ethel, b 1905 Ont., mar Earl Small, Bolton, Ont.
    - C3. Isaac Thompson, b 1856, mar Liza Margaret PIERCEY, d 1896, no issue
  - B3. Edward James, b 1860, mar Liza Lougheed
    - C1. Sadie, d.y.   C2. Norman, d.y.
    - C3. Milford, mar Viny Bellas, a dau, Betty, res Brampton, Ont.

ODOIRE, Harriet Alice, b 1875 Alderney?, d 1911. Mar Arthur Inniswood, b 1863, Norwich, Eng., d 1897, Alderney.
- A1. Reginald Inniswood, b 1895, d 1917
- A2. Ella Inniswood, b 1896, d 1958, mar Wm. James Bassett, rem to Ont.
  - B1. Ella Margaret Harriett Bassett, b 1917, mar 1. Wm. C. Doidge, res Ancaster, Ont.
  - B2. William James Bassett, b 1916, d 1917

ODONOGHUE, listed as Jersey merchant, St. Heber to Halfway Point, Nfld. 1800s. (Mannion)
OFFRAY, in Nfld. (Seary) Cf D'AUFRESNE of J (Stevens)

OGIER, Harry, b 1910 G?, mar Doris May PRIEST, qv 1914, res Milton,
  Ont. See LE NOURY and PRIEST. (Edw. Le Page) OGIERS also to Ohio.
  See QAAM. OGIERS ALSO SETTLED IN ROBLIN, MAN., CANADA.
A1. Floyd, b 1934, res Burlington, Ont.
A2. Raymond, b 1937, res Milton, Ont., mar Geraldine Lundy, b 1936
  B1. Steven, b 1959   B2. Greg, b 1962   B3. Wayne, b 1963
A3. Michele, b 1955, res Burlington, Ont.
OGILVIE, M.L., res Vict., BC 1941, where he was a member of the Channel
  Islands Society
OLESEN, Mrs. Carl, res Vancouver, BC, there by 1920?, poss from G
OLIVER, OLIVIER, to Gaspe from C.I. (Rev. d'Hist)
OLIVIER, Herbert J., in Griffon Cove, Gaspe 1926. Name also assoc with
  Robin firm in Paspebiac and with town of New Carlisle, Que.(Que. Arch.)
OLLIVIER, Arthur, b St. Brelade, J, mgr of Robin Co., Barachois and/or
  Paspebiac, Gaspe. Mar --- LE GRAND, early 1900s? (GLF)
OLIVER, OLIVIER, ship owner from G in Nfld., Bay Bulls in 1681 (Seary;
  K. Mathews)
OLIVER, Maria, b ca 1820 Ald.?, mar Wm. LE BER, qv, rem to Ontario
ORANGE, Daniel, age 27, b J, had 6 chn, was merchant at Caraquet, NB
  1861 (Census) D 1877?, bur St. Paul's Ang. Cem, Perce. (Oakley)
  Poss d age 43. (Syvret; Oakley)
ORANGE, Clarence, from Hug fam of France that rem to J in 1574. To
  Gaspe 1913.
ORANGE, Bud, said to be from C.I. in Yellowknife, NWT. Others in
  Western Canada? ORMOND, SEE ADDITIONS AND CORRECTIONS PAGES.
ORGAN, in Nfld. (Seary) Cf ORGAN of J (Stevens)
ORVIS, fishing firm from C.I. in Gaspe. (J.H. Le Breton list) ORVIS in
  Peterborough, Ont.
ORVIS, Harold GOSSETT, 1855-1951, bro of an ORVIS, merchant in St.
  Heliers, J. Was also a Robin mgr. (GLF) Mar Josephine MacCartney,
  1877-1951, bur Gaspe. (GLF)
OSBOURNE, in Nfld. Cf same in J 1749 (Stevens)
OSMOND, in Nfld. (Seary) Cf same in J (Stevens) Job in Fortune Bay
  1860s. (Rev. Hammond) This name also appears as OSMENT and OSMAND of J
OTIS, in Nfld. (Seary; Rev. Hammond) Said to be of C.I. origin
O'TOOLE, Mollie and Terry, in London, Ont., from G, this century
OUGIER, or LOUGIER, or LOUGEE?, Capt. from G in Nfld. (K. Mathews)
OUVEN, or DUVEN?, said to be of C.I. origin in Nfld. (Rev. Hammond)
  Poss same as OWEN, OUEN or OVRAY of J?
OUEDART, Louisa, b St. Mary, J, mar Francis CAMIOT, qv, rem to Gaspe,
  chn
OZANNE, Peter Gavet, b 1885 St. Peter Port, G, son of Henry O. and
  Louisa GAVET, rem to Sask, ca 1905, then to BC 1933, d 1962. (Marie
  Chase, Surrey, BC) OZANNE in Torteval, G, 1700s.
A1. Marie, b 1915, mar Richard Chase
  B1. Arlene Chase, b 1944, mar Thomas Darby
    C1. Gordon Darby, b 1964   C3. Linda Darby, b 1969
    C2. Teresa Darby, b 1967
A2. Gertrude, b 1917
A3. Emily, b 1924, mar Frank Farley
  B1. Janice Farley, b 1947, mar David Bartels
    C1. Ann Marie Bartels, b 1967   C2. Dirk Bartels, b 1969
  B2. Donald Farley, b 1951
A4. Roy, b 1926, mar Eva ---
  B1. Paul, b 1955   B3. Mark, b 1958
  B2. Dean, b 1956
A5. Kenneth, b 1931, mar Elizabeth ---

OZANNE 453

B1. Ronald, b 1953 B2. Michel, b 1955 B3. Jay, b 1958
OZANNE, Mary, mar Peter LE LACHEUR, Shiphead, Gaspe, a son, Peter Helier, b 1842 (Brochet)
OZANNE, fisheries in NB? OZANNE, see DOREY
OZANNE, David, from St. Peter du Bois, G, to Canada in 1970. His mother, a LE POIDEVIN, of Vale, G.
OZANNE, Charles, b G, and Margaret, b Gaspe, in Gaspe 1861 (Census)
OZANNE, listed as Barr Colonist, to Western Canada. Family noted as being farmers in 1963 Lloydminster newspaper.
OZARD, Louise mar Thomas LEGG. SEE EXTRA PAGES.
I. OZARD, William Henry, b 1875 G, son of Wm. Nicholas O. and Elizabeth J. SIMON, qv, mar Rhoda Rose Emma WALKER, 1879-1964. Poss mar in Ald. Related to HOUGEZ fam of G.
  A1. William Charles, b 1905 Winnipeg, Man., mar Evely Royal Georgina Bonavia ca 1934, and 2. in 1963, Kathleen Anne Kerr, widow with 2 daus. (E.G. Ozard, Vict., BC)
    B1. William Wakefield, b 1938, Depty. Min. Dept. of Tourism, N.S.
    B2. Martin Joseph, b 1936, d.y.
    B3. Stepahnie Wakefield, b 1941, mar, a dau, Rachel Rebecca, b 1971
  A2. John Harold, b 1920, mar 1940, Thelma Elizabeth Rolfe, b 1919, res Vict., BC
    B1. John Clifford, b 1944, mar 1967, Judith Annette SIMON, qv
      C1. Tracy Marie, b 1969   C2. Shannon Elizabeth, b 1972
    B2. Jerome Rolfe, b 1946, mar 1968, Susan Emily Albion, b 1950
      C1. Dean Jerome, b 1968   C3. Holly Elizabeth, b 1973
      C2. Janetta Sue, b 1970
    B3. Joel Barry, b 1947, mar 1970, Cheryl Leslie Barnes, b 1948
      C1. Justin Joel, b 1973   C2. Bradley Jonathan, b 1975
    B4. Julie Elizabeth, b 1959
II. Marguerite Jane, b 1876 G, sister of Wm. Henry, above, d ca 1950, Vict., BC, school principal
III. Walter John, b 1870, unmar
IV. Henry MacDonald, b 1882, unmar. Carpenter, patternamker.
V. George Cousens, b 1888 G, mar Hazel Petherick, who d ca 1922. Customs officer.
  A1. Elmore G., b 1914, mar 1. Marjorie Margison, who d 1969, auto accident. Mar 2. Arlene Marie, b Alberta. E.G. served with Navy WWII.
    B1. Ardath Hazel, b 1943, mar --- MacLaren, a son, Michael, a dau, Laura
  A2. William Harvey, b 1916, mar Sheila ---, who d 1969. He served in WWII. Mar 2. Kay ---
    B1. Maureen, b 1940, res Vancouver
OZARD, William, from J to London, Ont. 1800s?
OZARD, Pierre, b 1873 C.I.?, d 1943, settled Windsor, Ont. Mar Rosanna LEVASSEUR, 1880-1923. (Norma Ozard, Toronto)
  A1. Alfred, b Canada, mar Blanche Meunier, 3 chn
    B1. Ronald, b 1937   B3. Maryanne, b 1940
    B2. Roy, b 1939, mar Norma ---
OZARD, Ronald, b G, mar Adele LE PAGE?, qv. To London, Ont. ca 1958 with 3 sons. He was the son of --- Ozard and --- Le Page. Mrs. Ozard was the sister of Wm. LE PAGE who came to Canada ca 1912 with wife, Elise RENOUF, qv. (R. Ozard, London, Ont.)
OZONG, poss OZANNE?, John, a fisherman in Sandy Pt., Nfld. 1871. (Lovell; Seary) Cf OZANNE of G.
PACKWOOD, early settlers from Ireland at Pt. St. Peter, Gaspe, but some desc are also of J origin. This fam intermarried with such fams as VIBERT. (GLF)

PACQUET, Francois, of C.I.?, signed Gaspe Petition 1820
PADDE, a member of the Guernsey Club in St. Thomas, Ont. 1938
PAGET, see DE VIC

PAGE, in Nfld. (Seary) Cf LE PAGE of G
PAGE, Thomas, b J, and Elizabeth, also b J, in Malbaie, Gaspe 1861 (Census, with Mary or Margaret and James, b Canada) Poss another Thomas PAGE also at the same time.
PAGE, E.L., from G to London, Ont. 1900s
PAIN, poss PAYN or PAYNE, Jean, age 47, b J, joiner, with John, his son, age 18, b J, a joiner, were in Salmon Beach, NB 1878 (Census)
PAINE, Jersey merchant listed in Nfld. 1800s at Cowhead (Mannion)
PAINT, Alan, b G, rem from there in 1938 and went to Brisbane, Aust. Mar Aust. girl. Has mar son, and 22 yr old dau, Jane. Mr. Paint was b at St. Saviours, G. (Ed. Le Page, Grimsby, Ont.)
PAINT, Henry Nicholas, from G, had a crown grant near Arichat, NS late 1700s (PANS)
PAINT, Nicholas, b G, age 26 in 1816, res Arichat, asked for 2 town lots in Hawkesbury, CB, where he intended to become a merchant. Granted. He also, on behalf of the firm of THOUME, MOULLIN AND CO. of G, asked land in Hawkesbury, 1817. (PANS) He later became M.P. for Cape Breton, and promoted a town named Guernsey at Point Tupper. The streets were Guernsey names such as Saumarez, Tupper, Guille, Dobree, Le Marchant, Mander and Paint. Paint had at least 2 chn by 1817. (Guernsey Society, Summer, 1975 Bull.) In 1832, the brig, LORD SAUMAREZ (154 tons), was built for him by G. Billows. He d about this time, and the vessel was registered in the name of his widow. He also had the Unity built, 131 tons in 1823, for a Jersey trading company. The PAINT fam had a general store, fishing and trading vessels, fish and cooperage plants, shipyard and ship chandlery. (Capt. Parker) Another ship was named ANNIE E. PAINT, 82 tons, and was built in 1887 at Port Hawkesbury, CB for Peter PAINT, poss a son. In 1831, the REWANO, 121 tons, was launched by Thomas Embre at Port Hawkesbury for Nich. PAINT Jr. Nicholas mar Mary LE MESSURIER, qv, and resided for some time in Buenos Ayres, S.A. He rem to Cape Breton 1816. He also, at one time, represented JANVRIN & CO.
  A1. Henry Nicholas, b 1830 Bellevue, Strait of Canso, d 1921. Lt.-Col. in militia, and conn with marine railways for repairing ships at the Canso Strait and N. Sydney. Mar 1856 at Halifax, Christina St. Clair, dau of Donald McVean of Oban, and Islay, Scotland. Two daus and a son. Both daus mar, res England. He mar 2. 1892?, Ella Marie Cowdrey of N.Y.
    B1. ---, by first marriage, mar Sir Charles Mander or MAUNDER, of Wolverhampton, England
    B2. ---, by second mar, mar Bowman Rafuse of Bridgewater, N.S.
    B3. Mander, res Annapolis area
PAINT, W.H., res Hawkesbury, N.S., mar --- HUBERT, qv. W.H. and Fred. were bros
PAINT, Frederick L.M., Mayor of Port Hawkesbury, N.S., merchant, b 1853, son of Peter Paint, who d 1883. He mar 1894, Eleanor Skimmings of Halifax, NS (Cochrane)
PAINTER, Harry Emanuel, b 1891 St. Luke, J, son of Adolphus P. and Marie Louise ---, mar 1914, Lilian Maud THOMAS, of St. Helier, J. Res N.B. (Lillian Painter, McAdam, NB)
  A1. Evelyn Maud, b 1914, mar Everett Dixon Taylor
    B1. Darlene Lorraine Taylor, b 1942 B2. Corrine Louise Taylor, b 1950

PAINTER   455

A2. William Henry Victor, b 1916, mar Rita Mary McDade
    B1. Carol Ann, b 1948   B4. Gregory James, b 1952
    B2. Joseph William, b 1950   B5. Christopher John, b 1959
    B3. Theresa Mary, b 1954
A3. Charles Ronald, b 1918, mar Mary Elizabeth Robinson
    B1. Janet Elizabeth, b 1948   B3. Joyce Eileen, b 1951
    B2. Ronald James, b 1950   B4. James, b 1953
A4. Dorothy May, b 1920, mar Robert Newton RICHARDSON, qv
    B1. Robert Harry Richardson, b 1947 B4. Neil Thomas Richardson, b
    B2. Lorne James Richardson, b 1952   1959
    B3. Mary Elise Richardson, b 1954 B5. Karen Lynn Richardson, b 1961
PAINTER, Richard, b 1820 G, served in Brit. Navy, mar --- (Edgar Poide-
    vin, Toronto, Ont.)
    A1. ---?, mar, a high school principal, res Hamilton, Ont.
        B1. Richard, b ca 1899?
PAISNEL, from J to Ontario? This is one of the oldest J surnames (Soc.
    Jers.)
PALET, from J to Ontario
PALFREY, Agnes Ann, 1876-1923, b J?, bur Cap aux OS, wife of Samuel
    Benj. LE HUQUET, 1869-1933 (GLF)
PALFREY, from J? to Nfld. (Seary)
PALLAH, in Nfld. (Seary) Cf PALLOT of J (Stevens)
PALLOT, A.W., from J to B.C., mar --- RICHARDSON, related to GIBEAUT of
    J, a dau, Margaret
PALLOT, Charles Ernest, b 1871 Trinity, J, worked for LE GALLAIS & SON,
    auctioneers, St. Heliers, J. Mar Harriet Eleanor LE SAUTEUR, 1896,
    dau of Philippe Le S., 1876-1948. Rem to Canada 1904. Harriet ran
    a drygoods store in St. Heliers, followed her husbant to Vancouver
    in 1907, carrying a tiny pistol to protect her from the wild Indians!
    Ernest a carpenter at Fort Langley, then a farmer. Rem to Pitt Mea-
    dows, BC, where they managed Pitt Polder, later bought a large farm
    named Sunnybrook, establ. a prize-winning herd of pure-bred J cattle.
    Ran a dairy business selling in Burnaby and Vanc. until 1935. Ernest
    remar after wife's death, as a widower again, rem to Haney, BC, where
    he d 1960. (Billie Jo Imlach, Denman Is., BC: Rebecca Pallot, Paquet-
    ville, NB)
    A1. Charles Spencer, b 1897 J, mar 1928, Juliet MORRIS, b 1904, 6 chn.
        Auctioneer, res Haney, BC, then the west coast of Vanc. Island.
        He d 1970. Juliet res Tofino, BC.
        B1. Billie Jo, b 1929, mar 1949, Desmond McLoughlin, 1919-1964, and
            2. in 1968, Robert Imlach, b 1926
            C1. Lois McLoughlin, b 1951   C3. Grant McLoughlin, b 1957
            C2. Bruce McLoughlin, b 1953
        B2. David, b 1930, mar 1957, Mary Radcliff, b 1935, 5 chn
            C1. Paul, b 1958   C3. Denise, b 1961   C5. John, b 1965
            C2. Linda, b 1960   C4. Wendy, b 1964
        B3. Jacquelyn, b 1932, mar 1953 Walter Hansen, b 1929
            C1. Stanley Hansen, b 1954   C3. Phyllis Hansen, b 1958
            C2. Lorraine Hansen, b 1955   C4. Ole Hansen, b 1963
        B4. Dorothy, b 1936, mar 1956, Kenneth Gibson, b 1935, res.Tofino,BC
            C1. Bradley Gibson, b 1957   C3. Roger Spencer T. Gibson,
            C2. Rodney Wayne Gibson, b 1959, d.y.   b 1963, d 1972
        B5. Kathleen, b 1939, mar 1959, Frederick Ladoucer, b 1934
            C1. Bernice Ladoucer, b 1960   C2. Dwayne Ladoucer, b 1962
        B6. Ernest, b 1944, mar 1968, Linda Vader
    A2. Philip, b 1909 Canada, mar 1939, Isobel Lovely, res Vancouver, BC
        B1. Gary, mar Marilyn, 2 chn, Carolyn and Michelle

B2. Sharon, mar Lawrence Winship, 2 chn, Jeff Winship and Lorne Winship
  A3. John, b 1911, mar Annie Hazelwood
   B1. Lillian, b 1942, mar 1961, Jack MacDonald, b 1937, 2 sons
   B2. John Laurie, b 1947, mar 1969, Karen Shaw, b 1950, 2 daus
  A4. Rhoda, b 1912, d 1973, mar 1932, Frank Cobbaert, div, and mar 2. Reuben Metzger 1950, who d 1970s
   B1. Broe Cobbaert, b ca 1933, mar Jacqueline, 2 chn, Amber and Robert Cobbaert
   B2. Allison Cobbaert, b ca 1936, mar Valerie Gomm, 2 daus
   B3. Nelda Cobbaert, mar Nick Kulhawy, 4 chn
PALLOT, some from Trinity, J and some from St. Martin, J to Canada.
 C. Pallot from J to Fraser Valley Dist., BC. (Luce)
PALLOT, Mr. and Mrs. A.J., from St. Martins, J, a druggist, to BC 1911 (Luce)
PALLOT, Mr. and Mrs. Jack, from J to Hamilton 1900s. She was a Miss NOEL, qv. A son, Owen, settled in Anaheim, Calif. (Rozelle Collins, Sarnia, Ont.)
PALLOT, John Charles, b 1859 J, to Canada ca 1876, son of Charles P. and Anne GAUDIN, qv. Settled N.B. (Rebecca Pallot, Paquetville, NB: Lucie Cormier, Notre Dame des Erables, NB)
A1. William   A2. Florence
A3. John Charles, b 1859 J, mar Marguerite Marie BRIDEAU at Inkerman, NB 1887
  B1. Charles Georges, b 1888, d 1945, mar 1917, Ida Ross, b 1894
   C1. Marie Sophie Leona, b 1918, mar 1938 Frederic Pinet
   C2. Jean Charles, b 1919, mar 1945, Marie Reine Pinet
   C3. Guillaume, Willie, b 1921, mar 1946, Noella Pinet
   C4. Amanda, b 1923, mar 1939, Antoine Legere
   C5. Alphonse, b 1925, mar 1951, Valeda Pinet
   C6. Albert, b 1927, mar 1951, Therese Paulin
   C7. Arthur, b 1927, twin, mar 1955, Alfreda Gagnon
   C8. Aurelie?, b 1929, mar 1951, Simonne Theriault, b 1931
   C9. Georges, b 1921, mar 1953, Rebecca Theriault, 9 chn
    D1. ---, b 1954, mar Donald Cormier, 1970
     E1. Bobby Cormier, b 1971   E2. Anne Cormier, b 1974
    D2. Lucie, b 1955, mar Donat Cormier, 1974, dau, Nadie
    D3. Daniel, b 1956   D6. Donald, b 1962, d.y.
    D4. Raoul, b 1960   D7. Carole, b 1963
    D5. Linda, b 1961, d.y.   D8. Rejean Joel, b 1965
                                  D9. Yves, b 1967
   C10. Lea Paul, b 1933
  B2. Philomene Alma, b 1889
  B3. Marie Marguerite Edwige, Dora, b 1892, d 1932, mar 1922, William Lavigne
  B4. Marie Florence, b 1894, mar 1914, Albert Lavigne
  B5. Marie Elisabeth Alice, b 1896
  B6. James Joseph Francis, b 1900, d.y.   B8. Amanda, b 1904, mar 1924,
  B7. Marie Anne Regina, b 1901   Gilbert Christy
PALMER, Thomas, b ca 1850 Ald., mar ca 1870, Anne GALE, qv. Rem to J then to Alton, Ont. in 1872, res Toronto, Chatham and Detroit, Mich., where Thomas d 1884. Anne d 1935, Detroit. (Mildred Chase, Montague, Mass.)
A1. William, b 1872 J   A4. Anne
A2. Louise   A5. son, d.y.
A3. Ethel, b Toronto, mar ---, a dau, Mildred, mar Charles Chase
PALMER, Charles, son of T.N.?Palmer and Anna De Caen. Charles to

Canada. Anna was b ca 1855 J. (R.F.B. de Caen, Calgary, Alta.)
PALMER, in Nfld. (Seary) Cf PALMER of C.I. (Stevens) James P. was in Harbor Grace 1677.
PAQUET, also PACQUET, in Gaspe and in J, 1749. Francois signed the Gaspe Petition in 1820. Origin unverified.
PAQUOR, occurs in Perce, origin unverified. (Cent. Bklt.)
PARDY, said to be of C.I. origin in Nfld. (Seary; Rev. Hammond) See also NICHOLLE in Nfld.
PARODY, Joseph, in Burin, Nfld. 1860. Cf PAROUTY of J (Stevens)
PARES, Capt. from J in Nfld. (K. Mathews) PARRIS, PARIS?, in J 1300s
PARKER, in Nfld. (Seary) Cf PARKER, PASQUIER, DU PARC of J
PARRELL, PARELL, in Nfld. (Seary) Cf DE LA PERELLE of J
PARROT, in Bonavista, Nfld. 1792 from C.I.? Cf PAROUTY, and PARROT of J
PARRY, in Nfld. (Cf LE PARY in J, and other forms, PARRY, PERRY, PERREE, etc.)
PARSONS, listed as J merchant at Sandy Point 1800s, W. coast of Nfld. (Mannion) John and John H. Parsons in Sandy Pt., Nfld. 1871. (Can. Directory; Lovell; Seary)
PASCAL, Capt. from G in Nfld. (K. Mathews)
PASHA, PASHER, forms of PERCHARD in Nfld. esp Conc. Bay. (Seary; Shortis-Munn; G.W. Le Messurier) In Carbonear 1820.
PASQUIRE, Cf SQUARE and SQUIRE of Nfld. Poss from J. See also E.W. DOREY, for Ada Pasquire.
PATEY, in Nfld. (Seary) Cf PASTEY, PATIER of J (Stevens) Interior s is silent.
PATRIARCHE, Capt., agent, merchant, and ship owner from J in Nfld. (K. Mathews)
PATRIARCHE, from C.I. to Western Canada
PATRIARCHE, Wm. and Co. of J, 1770, Maritimes Fisheries, data in J with Soc. Jers.
PATTEN, Mr. and Mrs., with Sidney, age 9, to Burlington, Ont. ca 1911. Sidney mar, a dau, Gloria, and a granddau.
PAUL, C.I. fam to Gaspe from Ch. Is.
PAUL, Eliza, b G, mar Francis LE COURTOIS, qv, from G
PAUL, Emma, mar Henry Philip LE COURTOIS, Western Ontario, late 1800s?
PAUL, W., of C.I. fam, res St. Thomas, Ont. 1928, was V.P. of G club there. Many Pauls in St. Thomas.
PAUL, Charles Wm., b C.I., d ca 1972 (Richard Paul, St. Thomas, Ont.)
A1. Wilfred, b 1914 St. Thomas, d ca 1973, mar Margaret ---
A2. Alice, mar --- Ward, res St. Thomas
A3. Richard, res St. Thomas, Ont.
PAUL, in Nfld. (Seary) Cf PAUL of J and G
PAWLEY, in Nfld. (Seary) Cf PAVEILLEY of J (Stevens)
PAYN, a whole colony at Cow Head, also Burin and Harbor Grace, Nfld. (Shortis-Munn)
PAYN. "My husband's people originated from the Channel Islands. His grandfather, James Payn, a Victorian novelist and at one time Editor of the Illustrated London News, lived in England and had a large family. Possibly his father William? emigrated from the Channel Islands." (Molly D. Payn, Annapolis Royal, N.S.)
PAYN, Mary Ann, wife of John LE LIEVRE, qv, of Vittoria, Ont., Canada
PAYN, Jersey fishery in Nfld. South Coast (G.W. Le Messurier)
PAYNE, in Perce 1861 (Census and Syvret, also Betty Tardif)
PAYNE, Amice, b J, age 49 in 1861 (Census) Was in Cape Cove Gaspe, and in Perce 1861 (Le Moine)
PAYNE, Ernest A , civil servant of J fam in Nfld. (Shortis-Munn)
PAYNE, W.B., of J, to Burin, Nfld. 1866 (Seary)

PAYNE, PAINE, PINE, PYNE, Capt., tradesman, agent, merchant from J in Nfld. (K. Mathews)
PAYNE, Philip, in Gaspe late 1800s. Mar Edith LE MARQUAND, qv, b ca 1880.
  A1. Lillian   A2. Gladys   A3. Stuart   A4. Reginald
PAYNTER, in Nfld. (Seary) Cf PAYNE and LE PEINTEUR of J (Stevens)
PAYZANT, PAISANT, Louis, a Huguenot, was a silk merchant in Caen, France, who rem to J, poss after his first wife died. His dau, Susanne, b ca 1724, was taken to Jersey ca 1738. A son, Philip, was sent to an uncle James in England. A third child, Anne, was christened 1737. Louis settled in St. Helier, where he and his second wife, Anne NOGET? were mar. They remained in J for 13 years and seven chn were born there. Louis was a prosperous merchant and ship owner, and decided to rem to N.S. He had 3 ships, sold two, and came to N.S. on the third, where he set up a trading post on Covey's Is. in Mahone Bay. Captured by Indians and massacred before the eyes of his fam. Mother and chn were taken on a canoe trip to Quebec, but separated before they arrived there. General Montcalm intervened and the chn were re united with the mother. The war over, she and the chn returned to Hants Bay, where Marie received a large grant of land. For more info see THE PAYZANT AND ALLIED JESS AND JUHAN FAMILIES IN NORTH AMERICA, by Marion M. Payzant, Wollaston, Mass., 1970. (Lewis Paisley Jr., Oak Ridge, Tenn; Joan Payzant, Dartmouth, NS)
PEACH, PECHE, of the Maritimes and of New England said to be C.I. origin (La PERCHE? Stevens)
PEARCE, PEARSE, PIERCE, PIERCEY, etc., tradesmen from J and G in Nfld. (K. Mathews)
PEARCE, PIERCE, in Nfld. (Seary) Cf PIERCE, PIERCEY of C.I. (Stevens)
PEARL, in Nfld. (Seary) Cf DE LA PERELLE of C.I.
PEARSON, a member of the C.I. Society in Victoria, BC 1941
PEARSON, in Ont. from C.I.?
PEATTY, in Nfld. (Seary) Cf PETIT, LE PETIT of C.I. (Stevens)
PECHARD, poss PERCHARD? of C.I. in Maritimes Fisheries (J.H. Le Breton list)
PEDDLE, PEDELL, PEDDELL, BEADLE, BIDDLE, etc. Also PETEL of J 1668? "Mariners and Marines, English and French Huguenots, in South Somerset, England and Jersey. Exploiters of the Cabot Charter in Labrador and Nfld. 1510. Wm. Peddel was a Governor-General. Some settled in N.J. and Pa. Some who went to Barbadoes later rem to U.S. A cooperage in Penna, late 1600s. Some in Trinity Bay, Nfld. 1529." Capt. Nicholas Peddle also told us of traditions from his forefathers about the Jersey houses in that old settlement with red brick tiles for the roofs, in Bristol's Hope. (Thomas Peddle, Augusta, Maine)
PEDDLE, William, son of Eli Peddle, direct descendant of Wm. Peddle, Old Bill Peddle, fishing governor or admiral, approx. 1510, of Mosquito or Musketta, Nfld. Among first settlers of Carbonear Island, Conception Bay, Nfld.   SEE BUTT, p.187
  A1. James?
    B1. Nicholas, b 1830s, Bard of Musketta   B2. William
    B3. Thomas, mar Markarla? Wells, 12 chn
      C1. Alethia, mar John A. BUTT
        D1. Stephen Butt, mar, res Mt. Pearl, St. John's, Nfld.
        D2. Jerry Butt, mar Marion ---, res Jeffersonville, Vermont
        D3. Florence Butt, mar Llewellyn Hefford, New Harbor, Trinity Bay, 3 chn
        D4. Jean Butt, mar Raymond PENNEY, res Norris Pt., Bonne Bay. Wilson from New Perlican, Nfld.

E1. Jean Peddle, b 1943, mar Walter Mitchell, res Cornerbrook, Nfld.
   F1. Colleen Mitchell, b 1963   F3. Darlene Mitchell, b 1974
   F2. Tony Mitchell, b 1966
E2. Daphne Peddle, b 1951, mar Anthony Spurrell 1975, res Cornerbrook
C2. Henry, mar Elizabeth Ralph
   D1. Alice, mar Fred Cumby, res Whitbourne, Nfld., 6 or 7 chn
   D2. Henry Jr., res Canada
   D3. George Eleazer, res Walcott, Iowa, mar Bessie ---, of Harbour Grace, a dau
   D4. Julia, mar Joseph Pynn
      F1. Margaret Pynn, mar Frank Leonard, res Bell Island, 7? chn
      F2., 3., 4., etc.
   D5. Thomas, b 1907 Chelsea, Mass., Organizer, President and owner of several N.E. businesses, mar Dorothy Milson, 3 chn, and 2. Maxine M. Denno
      E1 Charles, Vet. Marine Corps, Physicist, scientist, res Phoenix, Ariz.
      E2. Marthalie A. Furber, Boston Univ.
      E3. Duncan Peddle, Vet. U.S. Marine Corps, West Gardiner, Maine
      E4. Douglas W. Peddle, U.S. Marine Corps
      E5. Shelton T. Peddle, student
   D6. James, mar 1. Anne Noseworthy, and 2. Mary Jane Smith Goss, 17 chn, res Bell Island, Nfld.
      E1. Donald Peddle, mar, res Bell Island, 4 chn
      E2. Frederick Peddle, mar ---, 2 children, res Sussex, N.B., at Parlee Brook
   D7. Bridget Young, res Toronto, Ont., 6 chn
      E1. Andrew   E2. Donald
C3. Lucy, mar Bert Sheppard, bro to Alice M. Sheppard Peddle, b Harb. Grace
   D1. Thomas, officer in Dupont de Nemours, res Ohio?
   D2. Charles, in U.S. Post Office
   D3. Roy, a broker   D4. Walter, an artist
C4. Katie, Catherine Marie, mar George Nichols, Jr. of Deer Lake, Nfld., 17 chn. See NICHOLS, George Aaron.
C5. Elwood, mar Tresia Higgins of Harb. Grace, Nfld., 11 chn including George, Beatrice, H. Earl, James, Frank, Ruth Mahala, Roy, and Vera
C6. Duncan, no issue, had adopted chn
C7. Mary Ann, mar Charles NOEL, qv, carpenter and bldr. of Fresh Water, Carbonear, Nfld., no issue
C8. John, mar ---, died in the Mines
C9. Lavinia, mar Edward Butt of Fresh Water, Carbonear, carpenter
   D1. Claude   D2. Joseph
   D3. Pearl, mar 1. --- Cook, 2 sons, and 2. John Young, res Everett, Mass.
   D4. Leslie   D5. Frank   D6. Edgar   D7. Thomas, all b Chelsea, Mass
C10. Wilson, mar Beatrice French, of Bristol Hope, no issue
C11. Julia, mar John TAYLOR of Bristol Hope, sev chn, b Chelsea and Revere, Mass.
C12. Beatrice, mar Rev. Richard Babcock, of Bay Roberts, Nfld. Both d there, 2 chn. Babcocks were leaders of the Pentecostal denomination movement in U.S.

PEDDLE, Elijah, of Nfld., mar Mary Brazil, six chn: John James, Joshua, Francis, Mary and Susan, early 1800s? See Elijah, below, poss same.

(Grace Peddle, Corner Brook, Nfld.)
PEDDLE, Elijah, thought to be brother of James or William of previous PEDDLE fam. (Thomas Peddle, Augusta, Maine; Grace Peddle, Corner Brook, Nfld.)
A1. Joshua, b Tilton, Spaniards Bay, Nfld., 1865, d 1917 Shelburne, mar Susannah Byrne, English, b 1864, d 1938, age 74
  B1. John
  B2. Edward William, mar Martha Hannon, 10 chn
    C1. Joan, b 1940   C6. Thomas, b 1951
    C2. James, b 1941   C7. Leo, b 1953
    C3. Elizabeth, b 1943   C8. Robert, b 1956
    C4. Katherine, b 1944   C9. Mary, b 1959
    C5. William, b 1948   C10. Carla, b 1962
  B3. James, d.y.   B4. Lawrence
  B5. Mary, b 1887, mar Charles Perry, no issue
  B6. James E., b 1896, mar Grace McCarthy, dau of Wm. M. and Julia. Grace b 1897, res Corner Brook, Nfld. James a locomotive engineer, retired in 1959.
    C1. Edward William, b 1917, mar Martha. He was CNR engineer, 10 plus chn, res Corner Brook.
    C2. Andrew Joseph, b 1919, mar Olive Hilliard, 2 chn, WWII Vet, res Corner Brook
      D1. Terrence, b 1951   D2. Bonita, b 1955
    C3. Joshua Kevin, b 1922, farmer, unmar
    C4. James Clarence, b 1924, unmar, RR engineer, res Corner Brook
    C5. Mary, b 1926, stillborn
    C6. Ambrose Hubert, b 1928, mar, Eliz. Legge, former Mbr. Parl., res St. John's Nfld., a son, David Ambrose, b 1950
    C7. Leslie Aloysius, b 1930, mar Loraine Doucette, res Corner Brook, 7 chn
      D1. Susan Ramona, b 1961   D5. Jan Benedict, b 1970
      D2. Cynthia Maria, b 1962   D6. Desmond Walter, b 1972
      D3. Ann Bonita, b 1964   D7. Francis James, b 1974
      D4. Roland Jude, b 1965
    C8. Bernardine Felicitas, b 1933, mar Patrick Cavanagh, div., 3 chn
      D1. Yvonne, b 1953   D3. James Cavanagh, b 1961
      D2. Patrick Cavanagh, b 1956
    C9. Gerard Roland, b 1938, mar Madolyn Jones, Corner Brook, 2 chn
      D1. David, b 1965   D2. Joanne, b 1971
    C10. Sylvia Ann, b 1941, mar Eric PENNELL, 8 chn, see PENNELL
  B7. Joshua L., b 1900, mar Mame Buckle, 6 chn: Teresa, Rita, James, Laura, Joseph and Mary.
  B8. Susannah, b 1903, mar Francis FOLEY, 9 chn: Thomas, Madonna, Joshua, Mary, Kevin, Patricia, Edward, Elica and Francis FOLEY.
  B9. Frances, b 1909, mar Michael CAREY, 11 chn: James, Rosalie, Joshua, Mary, Jack, Michael, Wilfred, Charles, Anne, Gerald, and Donald CAREY.
A2. James   A3. John   A4. Frances
PELLAN, from C.I. to Victoria, BC and to Western Canada
PELLEY, see Louisa NICHOLL
PELLEY, or LE PELLEY, Philip, from C.I., had fishery in Hant's Harbor, Trinity Bay, Harbor Grace, Carbonear early 1800s or earlier. (Rev. Hammond; Seary)
PELLIER, Daniel, age 32, b J, asked land at Descousse, CB, NS, 1820 (PANS)
PENNELL, Thomas and two bros, "came to America from the Isle of Jersey...about the year 1740." Hug fam, settled Maine, some rem to

Kingston, Ont. (Turk)
PENNELL, Mathew, b J, rem to Marblehead, Mass. where he mar 1743, Agnes Trefry. From either Cornwall or C.I. (QAAM) This surname prob PINEL in C.I. (Libby Logan, Denison, Texas)
A1. Mathew, bp 1744, d.y.?
A2. Thomas, bp 1746, d 1827 Lunenburg, NS. Mar prob 1770, Lunenburg, Abigail Crosby, who d ca 1813. (More data available from source)
  B1. Abigail, b 1771, mar --- Finner
  B2. Lucy Catherine, b 1774, mar John Eisenhaur, d 1864
  B3. Elizabeth, b 1777, mar 1800, Jacob Beohner
  B4. Matthew, b 1780, d 1818?
  B5. Thomas, b 1783 Lunenburg, mar 1806, Sarah Rockland, d 1870
  B6. Capt. John, b 1786 Lunenburg, mar 1810, Francesca Elizabeth Rudolph, d 1819 St. Lucia, West Indies
  B7. Mary, b 1789, mar 1807, Calvin Wheelock
  B8. Sarah, b 1794, mar 1817, Joseph Felt
A3. Matthew, bp 1748, d 1816?, mar perhaps 1772, Jane Brooks
  B1. Jane, b 1773   B3. Agnes, b 1777   B5. Henry, b 1782
  B2. Matthew, b 1775 B4. Charlotte, b 1780 B6. Elizabeth, b 1785
A4. Eliza or Elizabeth Hagar, bp 1750 Marblehead, Mass., mar 1769, prob in Lunenburg, Cornwallis Moreau
A5. John, bp 1753, Marblehead   A6. Anise, bp 1758, Marblehead
A7. Rebecca, bp 1763 Ch of Eng., Lunenburg, NS, poss mar John HOMER of Barrington, N.S., poss also mar ca 1781, Samuel Hopkins of Barrington, who d 1840, age 83. Her tombstone reads, Rebecca Hopkins, d 1838, age 77. A son, Elisha, plus other desc.
PENNELL, Thomas and bro Clement, sons of Philippe PINEL and Anne LE MONTAIS, of J, rem to Gloucester, Mass. in the late 1600s. Desc of this fam are said to have settled in Kingston, Ont. See also PENNELL fam, above.
PENNELL, Eric, desc of C.I.? fam in Nfld., mar Sylvia PEDDLE, qv, res Nfld.
A1. Joseph Eric, b 1961   A5. Wm. Eric, b 1966
A2. Michael Eric, b 1962   A6. Grace Erica, b 1969
A3. Daniel Eric, b 1964   A7. Stanley Eric, b 1971
A4. Robert Eric, b 1965   A8. Gordon Eric, b 1975
PENNEY, PENNY, PINNEY, ship owner from G to Nfld. (Seary; Mathews) Poss from PENNEC or LE PENN of C.I. Wm. PENNY, b 1745, cooper in Mosquito, Nfld. (T. Peddle, Augusta, ME)
PENNY, PINNEY, Oliver, from C.I.?, in Carbonear, Nfld. 1700s (Seary) See LE LACHEUR
PENT, see PAINT
PEPIN, Francis, of Gorey, J, in 1850 settled in Gillingham, Kent, Eng. A number of his bros and sisters also left J at this time or later, going to various places. Helier PEPIN son of Francis, came to Ont. 1912. Fam in Vancouver, BC. PEPIN in Mich., Windsor, Ont. and Ottawa, origin unver. Florence PEPIN, b ca 1818 Canada, to U.S. (V. de Marce, Arlington, VA)
PEPPER, in Nfld. (Seary) Cf PEPPERELL of J (Stevens)
PEPPIN, Peppy, Charles, fam from France to C.I., rem to Harbor Grace, Nfld. ca 1750, Hug. (Reaman) See PIPPY.
PERCEY, John, from C.I.?, in Bread and Cheese Cove, Conc. Bay, Nfld. 1763. (Rev. Hammond)
PERCEY, Wm., in Brigus 1770, and Stephen, in 1797. Cf PIERCE, PIERCEY of J (Stevens)
PERCY, Edward, in Brigus, Nfld. 1769. See also Seary. Origin unver.
PERCHARD, Francois, fam from France to St. Heliers, J to Canada in

1852. Mar Susan LE COUTEUR, qv, mar by Bishop Mountain, desc in
Whitby, Norwood and Hastings, Ont. (Reaman)
PERCHARD, Capt. R., of Hug fam, was harbor master in Montreal, early
1900s?
PERCHARD, John, in Bay Roberts, Nfld. 1794. (Rev. Hammond) "The best
waterside property there (Bay Roberts) owned by C.A. and A. Dawe can
show its title deeds back to the Perchard family, well known Jersey
people. " (Shortis-Munn)
PERCHARD, in some cases changed to PASHER in Nfld. (Shortis-Munn; Seary)
PERCHARD, James, b J, mar 1852, Mrs. P., b Gaspe. In Gaspe Bay South
1861 (Census) with James Jr., b J, Henry and Etienne, b G.
PERCHARD, James, b J, rem to Gaspe, mar Jane CHEVALIER, qv, a son, Edward Chevalier, b 1840s? (Church records)
PERELL, PEREL, forms in Canada of C.I. surname DE LA PERELLE, qv
PERCHARD, Nicolas, son of Ph. of Midvale Rd.,J, d 1881 at
Santa Clara, CAL.
PERKINS, Stanley, M.D., b St. Heliers, J, 1921, served in RAF 8 yrs.,
to Canada 1947. Mar Violet M. McConaghy (Victoria, BC), who was b
Chinwangtao, North China. (Violet Perkins, Vancouver, BC)
A1. Melanie Anne, b Victoria, BC, 1955, civil engineer, Vancouver, BC
A2. Stephanie Elizabeth, twin of Melanie, civil engineer, Vanc., BC
PERREE, PERRY, John, b ca 1834 J, res Ste. Anne, Que., son of Jean
PERREE of St. Mary, J, and of Anne MARETT, mar ca 1845 Sara Lepage,
bp ca 1827, d 1882, 14 chn (Remiggi)
A1. Sara, bp 1846, mar 1872, --- Gauthier, and d 1890
A2. Caroline Aimee, bp 1848, mar 1865, Antoine Pelletier, and d 1879.
Antoine mar 2. her sister, Emma Perree.
A3. Jean Jacques Arthur, bp 1850   A4. Marie Louise, bp 1851
A5. Gustave Adolphe Gabriel, bp 1853, mar 1874, Marie Delia Pelletier,
bp 1857, dau of Magloire P. of Ste. Anne, Que., and Catherine Labrie
A6. Pierre Alfred, bp 1855
A7. Joseph Adolphe, bp 1857, mar 1881, Marie Louise D. Lepage of Rimouski, dau of Honoras L. and Julienne Odruit. Res St. Anne des Monts.
A8. Marie Emma Adeline, bp 1858, mar 1880, Antoine Pelletier, his second
wife. See Caroline, above.
A9. Francois Ernest, bp 1859   A12. Charles Francois Auguste, bp
A10. Marie Anne Angelique, bp 1861,   1866
mar 1882, --- Gagnon   A13. M. Eugenie Elianne, bp 1867,
A11. Stanislas Georges, bp 1865   d 1880
PERRY, MORE IN CI COLL.   A14. M. Alice Amanda, bp 1869
PERREE, PERRY, John, b J, mariner and partner in various Gaspe ports
ca 1800. Mar in J. Partner in Peter Du Val and Co., and founded
with John Perry Jr. John PERREE and Son, a fishery at Malbaie, Gaspe,
had 4 sons. John Sr. bought the Janvrin fishery room at Malbaie in
1851 from John LE COUTEUR LA GERCHE of J. (Remiggi) Some data uncertain.
A1. Edward, b J, mar Jane LE BROCK, qv.
  B1. John, b 1830 _ca 1779-1874_   B2. Edward, b 1833 Perce
A2. Philip, b J, mar Elisabeth BOND, qv, res Cap des Rosiers d 1874,
  B1. Elisabeth, b 1814, mar 1832, Daniel ROBERT, qv   age 95.
  B2. Philippe, b 1816, mar Charlotte Packwood, qv, and 2. in 1855,
    Marie DUMAS
    C1. Marie Melinda, bp 1846, mar 1871, --- Fergusson
    C2. Appolline, bp 1848, mar 1868, --- Chouinard
    C3. Georges, b 1845, mar 1878, Celina Boulet, bp 1861, dau of Paul
      B. and Marie Marin? Res Cap des Rosiers. Both d 1893.
    C4. Joseph, bp 1849, mar 1874, Susanne Fortier, of Cap Rosiers,

PERRÉE, PERRY 463

  dau of Aubain F. and Marguerite STE. CROIX
 C5. John, bp 1852, mar 1883, Jane Whalen, dau of James W. and Julie
  BOND, qv
 C6. Edouard, bp 1855, mar 1879, Malvina English, of Anse Griffon,
  dau of Martin English and Henriette Whalen
 C7. Narcisse, b 1851
B3. Jane, Genevieve, b 1819, unmar
 C1. Mary, b 1853
B4. Marie, b 1821
B5. John, b 1824, mar Sophie Smith, bp 1829 Canada, d1894 at 70.
 C1. John, b 1848, mar 1871, Sara Poitras, dau of Michel P. of Mont
  Louis. A son Nazaire, and grson Hector,& sonMichael.
 C2. Philip, bp 1853   C3. Elisabeth, bp 1855
B6. Sophie   B7. Henriette, b 1829
PERRY, Francis, connected with above fam?, b J, in Gaspe
PERRY, John, connected with above fam?, d 1845 Malbaie, Gaspe, leaving
 4 daus in J
A1. Rachel, b J, mar Thomas LUCE, qv A3. Anne, b J, mar Philip LE
A2. Henriette, b J, unmar in 1851   GRESLEY, qv
A4. Charlotte, b J, mar Edward LE GRESLEY, qv
A5. ---, another dau, mar Samuel J. COLLAS, agent of John PERREE AND
 SONS. (Perce documents of 1851; Brochet; poss more data with
 Packwood fam)
PERRÉE, Edward and Mary Ann, b Gaspe, there in 1861 (Census) Packwood
 fam, Gaspe, may have more info.
PERRÉE, from St. Ouen and St. Saviour, J to Canda (S.R. Le Gresley)
PERRY, in Fogo, Nfld. late 1700s (Seary) From C.I. (Rev. Hammond)
PERRY, current Gaspe, New Richmond and Cap des Rosiers, Que.
PERRY, Jersuah, b J, wife of Philip DUMARESQ, qv, res Halifax and Sydney, NS, early 1800s, 8 chn, see DUMARESQ
PERRY, James, age 32 in 1871, res Arichat, a seaman
PERRY, Edmund, from J?, to Toronto, Ont.
PERREY, Moses and John, from C.I.? in Yarmouth, NS 1773
PERRÉE, George Joseph, b 1869 J, rem to Edmonton, Alta. 1908, wife and
 2 sons and dau came in 1909. Two sons drowned in boating accident.
 A mar sister or dau res in Vancouver, BC, widow.
A1. George Henry P., b 1892 A3. George Herbert, b 1898, res Victoria
A2. a son   A4. dau
PERRÉE, William, b 1870s, bro of above, George Joseph, from J to Edmonton, 1908. (G.H. Perree, Victoria, BC)
PERRETT, in Nfld. (Seary) Cf PERROT of J (Stevens)
PERREWAY, formerly PIROUET, qv, of France and C.I.
PERRIER, in Nfld. (Seary) Simon and Dominick in Sandy Pt., Nfld. 1871
 (Lovell). Cf POIRIER and PERRIER of J (Stevens)
PERRIN, Gladys, b ca 1897 Vale, G, mar Chicago widower, Frederick John
 DE BRODER, qv, 6 chn, res Denver, Colo. See DE BRODER. She was the
 dau of David S. Perrin and Harriet Ann BRICE.
PERRIN, from Vale, G to Western Canada
PERRY, Joseph and Noah in Cataline, Bonavista Bay, Nfld. 1860s, from
 C.I.?
PERRY, Thomas in PEI, 1841 census, from J?
PERRY, Daniel in Nfld. early 1800s, from C.I.? (Brochet)
PERRY, in Gaspe, poss desc of PERRÉE, qv
PESET, from Ald. to Ontario. See PEZET
PETEL, PESTEL, in J 1600s, 1700s, poss original surname of PEDDLE in
 Nfld. (s is silent) See PEDDLE
PETHIC, D.W. from C.I. to Victoria, BC

PETITE, LE PETIT?, PETITPAS?, Jeremiah and Wm. in Moyambrose, Nfld.
  1870s (Rev. Hammond)   Cf LE PETIT of J (Stevens)
PETITPAS, in Nfld. (Seary) Cf same in J (Stevens)
PETTEN, PATTEN, William, son of Wm. and Christianna, b 1812, St. John's,
  Nfld. (J. Bowes, Brockton, Mass.)
PETTES, Ed, in Hibbs Hole, Conc. Bay, Nfld. 1781 and 1800 (Rev. Hammond)
  said to be of C.I. origin
PETTIS, William, in Bucks Cove, Conc. Bay 1793 and 1797, said to be of
  C.I. origin (Rev. Hammond)
PETTON, PETTEN, PETON, poss PITON?, Wm. in Bay Roberts, Conc. Bay,
  Nfld. 1765, said to be of C.I. origin (Rev. Hammond)
PEYTON, see PITON
PHILLIPS, merchants from J and G in Nfld. (K. Mathews and Seary)
PHILLIPS, Ernest, son of E.P. and Lillie LIHOU, qv, to Canada 1900s
PHILLIPS, Mary Frances, of St. Sampson, G, mar Wilfred C. LAKE, left G
  for Canada, 12 chn (Edw. Le Page, Grimsby, Ont.)
PHIPPERD, Richard, (prob VIBERT?), in Great Placentia, Nfld. 1860s
  (Rev. Hammond)   Said to be of C.I. origin
PHIPPS, E.H. from Alderney, member of the C.I. Society in Vict., BC 1941
PICCO, Abraham, prob b J, res Portugal Cove, Nfld. 1755, where his son,
  Elias, was b (Seary; Rev. Hammond; K. Mathews; Census)
  A1. Elias, b 1755, owned, with William and Elias PICCOTT of J, in 1784,
    a piece of property at Bearn Head near Port de Grave. Elias pur-
    chased from Capt. Le Vesconte in J, a piece of land, also at Port
    de Grave. There is a small pond there that is known as Picco's
    Pond. Elias res Port. Cove, mar Elizabeth Bradbury 1783. He d
    1818, age 63, gravestone in Piccott Cem, Port. Cove. Census of
    1793 shows 8 in fam.
    B1. Abraham, b 1780s, at least 4 in fam, 1793
    B2. John, b 1783   B3. Thomas, b 1788
  A2. William
  A3. John, mar Mary, a son Abraham, b 1803. See other Johns, below.
  A4. Abraham
  A5. Mary, mar Philip LE GRAISY, prob LE GRESLEY, of Pouch Cove 1774
PICCOTT, John, mar Susan, a dau, Elizabeth, b 1811, and Rebecca, b 1814,
  Nfld.
PICCOTT, John, mar Rebecca Earle, Eade?, 1809, sons Nathan, b 1813, and
  George, b 1819, Nfld.
PICCOTT, James, 1797-1883, wife, Ann Neary, 1801-1883, recorded in
  Portugal Cove, Nfld.
PICCOTT, James, and Jane Allen, mar 1790 Nfld.
PICCOTT, Roger, mar Jane SQUIRES 1801, Nfld.
  A1. James, b 1802   A2. William, b 1814   A3. Tryphene, bp 1831
PICCOTT, Mary, of Portugal Cove, mar George Stone of Bell Island 1772
PICKETT, in Nfld. (Seary) Either same as PICCOTT or PICQUET of J?
  (Stevens)
PICKUP. Was this name in N.S. orig PICOT, from J of Nfld.? "Samuel
  PICKUP served in the 38th Reg't, from which he retired in 1783 and
  threw in his lot with the Loyalists. At the time of his arrival
  here, he had been married eight years and had four chn." (Calnek)
  Res Annapolis, N.S. 1792, prob d in Clements, where his son, George,
  married and settled. Farmers, merchants, shippers and ship builders.
  Samuel the Loyalist, mar 1774, Mary BROWN and had chn.
  A1. George, b 1775, mar 1797, Sarah BALCOM, qv
    B1. Susan, b 1798, d 1833, mar ---   B3. Elizabeth, b 1803, mar Wm.
    B2. Mary, b 1800, mar James RANDALL   Jones
    B4. George, d unmar

PICKUP

A2. William, b 1777, mar 1803, Sarah Timberlake
A3. Margaret, b 1780, mar --- Morgan
A4. Samuel, b 1783, mar 1810, Jane Delap, 5 chn
   B1. Sarah Ann, b 1811, mar John Roop, Jr.
   B2. William D., b 1813, d unmar in Eng.
   B3. James, b 1815, d unmar abroad   B4. George, b 1817, d unmar
   B5. Samuel, b 1818, mar 1. Rachel Ray, LE RAY? and 2. Celina Willett
A5. James, b 1780, d unmar   A6. Jane, mar John Roop, Sr.
PICOT, Charles of J, mar at Perce, Gaspe, 1809, Louise McGinnis, dau of Ignace M. and Louise ARBOUR, qv. (Gallant)
PICOT, John, b 1865 J, d 1882, bur St. Andrews, New Carlisle, Gaspe (GLF) Poss. son of John of St.Sav.Jersey.
PICOT, John, b 1849 Trinity, J, son of Charles P. and Susan Anne MARETT, qv, rem to Caraquet, NB, mar 1871, Adeline Mailloux, 1853-1913 (J.E. Picot, Bathurst, NB)
A1. Marie Adeline, b 1872 Caraquet, mar Baird Burgess 1891, bur Chatham, NB 1893
A2. John Philippe, b 1874, mar Elizabeth Theriault 1911, d 1946 Niagara Falls, Ont.
A3. Charles Nelson, b 1877 Caraquet, mar 1898, Theresa APPLEBY, qv, d 1960 W. Bathurst, NB
   B1. Joheph John, b 1899 W. Bath., mar 1. 1926, Winnifred Payne, and 2. Gladys Hennesy. D 1969, bur New Glasgow, NS.
   B2. Charles Alexander, b 1901, mar 1924, Agatha De Grace, d 1974 Stoneham, Mass., U.S.
   B3. Mary Alma, b 1903, mar 1935, Telesphore Tremblay
   B4. Joseph Ernest, b 1906, mar 1933, Marie Blanche Lebel, b 1906 St. Syprien, Que.
      C1. Patricia Therese, b 1931, Edmundston, NB, mar 1951, Wm. James Gillis, res Westmoreland, NB. 7 chn: Diane Joan, (mar Eric Prosser), Donald William Gillis, Daniel James, Mary Kathleen, Patricia Elizabeth, Michael Charles and Joseph Peter.
      C2. Jules Jean Charles, b 1932, mar 1956, Carol Creaghan, res Frederickton, NB
         D1. Nicole, b 1960   D2. Andre, b 1962
      C3. Marie Jeannine, b 1933, Bathurst, NB, mar 1957, William Cochrane, res Calgary
         D1. Louise Cochrane, b 1958   D3. Claire Cochrane, b 1961
         D2. David Cochrane, b 1959
      C4. Marie Claudette, b 1936 Bathurst, mar 1963, Basil Lang, res Edmonton, Alta.
         D1. Timothy Lang, b 1964   D3. Robert Lang, b 1970
         D2. David Lang, b 1967
   B5. Joseph Philip, b 1908, mar 1935, Blanche ROUSSEL
   B6. Mary Beatrice, b 1911, mar 1. 1936, Ulric Hachey, and 2. 1967, Licourt Boudreau
   B7. Mary Stella, b 1913, mar 1941, Arthur Doucet
   B8. Joseph Adolphus, b 1915, mar 1937, Mercedes Landry
   B9. Theresa Bernadette, b 1917, d 1918
   B10. Joseph Alexander, b 1918, d 1919
A4. Joseph Alfred, b 1879, d.y.
A5. Joseph Alfred again, b 1882, W. Bathurst, mar 1900, Sarah Doucet, d 1946
A6. Susan Ann, b 1887, mar Richard Landry, d 1955 Niagara Falls, Ont.
A7. Marie Josephine, b 1889, mar Theophilus Hachey, d 1962
A8. Marie Beatrice, b 1892, Bersinis, Que., mar 1. Adolphus Landry, and 2. Marjorique Theriault, d 1971?, Niagara Falls, Ont.

A9. Anna Isabella, b 1897, W. Bathurst, NB, mar 1914, Edmond Landry, d 1918 Montreal
PIDDLE, Wm., in Green Head, Nfld. 1803. See PEDDLE, poss PETEL of J.
PIDDLE, Francis, in Bread and Cheese Cove, Nfld. 1775. See PEDDLE.
PIDGEON, in Nfld. (Seary) Cf PIGEON of C.I.
PIEROWAY, Philip in Nfld. at Sandy Pt. 1871. Cf PIROUET of J.
PIERPOINT, in Nfld. early (Seary) Cf PIERPOINT of J (Stevens)
PIERSON, Edna Hazel, mar Louis LE GRAND, bur St. James Anglican, Port Daniel, Gaspe (GLF)
PIKE, from C.I. in Carbonear, Nfld. "The name of the school mistress, who should be remembered in our histories, was Mrs. Catherine PIKE... 'Jersey Kitty.' She was one of those martial dames, who inspired the spirit of war and adventure amongst her young pupils. Here are some of her sayings still repeated today. 'Ye sprang from a race of heroes, be slaves to nobody!' She was married into the well-known Pike fam of that town and it was likely to her own crowd she told, 'Ye are Pikes by name and Pikes by nature.' The old lady would get warmed-up and stamp her feet like a war-horse anxious for the charge, as she told her young heroes how their forefathers fought at the Crusades...How they carried all before them at Cressey and Agincourt. Richard Strongbow was one of her favourites that she liked to tell about, and she always ended up with 'the blood of these heroes flows in your veins.' She lived to the ...age of 97 and left many descendants, one of which was Claudius Watts. Another was Capt. Frank Taylor of sealing renown, and if you wish to know more about her, ask the genial Capt. Jimmy Pike, now living in Carbonear." Capt. Pike is no doubt long deceased. (Shortis-Munn)
PIKE, Henry, bur Channel, Nfld. 1853 (NEWFOUNDLAND HOLIDAY, by Smith)
PIKE, ---, several in Trinity, Old Perlican and Carbonear very early (Rev. Hammond) See also Seary.
PINABEL, Amice, b St. Peters, J, d Pabos, age 50, in 1856 (Brochet)
PINEL, PENNEL, Jane, mar Wm. Henry MESSERVY, of St. George's Bay, Nfld.
PINEL, Arthur, b J?, raised Gravenhurst, Ont., mar. A son, Wm. Gordon, b 1897? and 6 other sons and 2 daus. (Mary Pinel, Toronto, Ont.)
PINEL, later PICKNELL, Thomas, b J, rem to Gaspe. He was said to be the son of Thomas PINEL and Sara BOOLARD of England or J. He mar in Perce 1826, Catherine Enright, dau of Patrick Enright and Mary Barth of Ireland. They had been mar 2 yrs. previously in the Prot. faith. Thomas d at Douglastown, Que. (Gallant)

A1. Maria, b 1824 Perce
A2. Mathilde, b 1826 Perce
A3. Thomas, b 1828
A4. Annabella, b 1831, mar F. Couture
A5. Richard, b 1834
A6. Anatasie, b 1836 Perce
A7. Sara, b 1839
A8. James, b 1841
A9. John Thomas, b 1844
A10. Agnes, b 1847 Perce

PINEL, Philippe, second son of Eli P. and Marguerite LE QUESNE of J, (see Thomas above), mar Modeste PAQUET, from G?, in Anse du Cap, Gaspe, and 2. in 1826, Louise Chouinard in Gaspe, (Gallant), dau of Pierre Chouinard and Louise Dunn. 2 chn by first wife.
A1. Jean, b 1819 Anse du Cap, bp 1821, d 1839 Anse du Cap (Gravel)
A2. Marguerite, b 1818, mar 1832, Charles Dugas, son of Tranquille Dugas and Theotiste Gautier
A3. by second mar, Philippe, b 1827 Anse du Cap
A4. Daniel, b 1829, poss mar Martha Duguay, and was the merchant at Pabos?
A5. Charles, b 1832
A6. Thomas, b 1838
PINEL, PENNELL, J merchant listed at Sandy Point, W. coast of Nfld. 1800s (Mannion)

PINEL, Daniel, merchant at Pabos, 1800s. (GLF) Mar 1852, Martha Duguay?
PINEL, C.I. name on S. coast of Nfld. (G.W. Le Messurier)
PINEL, Capt. from J in Nfld. (K. Mathews)
PINEL, William Gordon, b ca 1897 Toronto, of J? fam, brought up in Gravenhurst, Ont., seven bros and 2 sisters. Two brothers mar, one with a dau, res Vancouver, BC. Involved in gold mining near Kirkland, Ont. (Mary A. Pinel, Toronto, Ont.)
PINK, in Nf.d (Seary) Cf PINGLAUX of J (Stevens)
PINOS, Capt. from J in Nfld. (K. Mathews)
PINSENT, PINSON, in Nfld. (Seary) Poss PINCHARD of J, or PYNCHON, Hug. Wm. Pinsent in Port de Grave, Nfld. 1787, also in Brigus. Samuel mar Mary Glavine, a son Tobias, mar Mary Ann BLUNDON, a son b St. John's, Nfld. (S.E. Pinsent, St. John's, Nfld.)
PIPON, Philippe Gossett, b 1824 J, a general in 1842, entered the Royal Artillery. His battery went to Canada, where he mar 1849, Sophia, dau of John Ashworth, Dept. Assistant Commissary General of Quebec. He served in Cylon and was awarded the Fenian medal for his part in the suppression of that raid in 1866. His two sons settled and mar in Canada. (Balleine Bio. Dict., and P.R. Pipon. Toronto, Ont.)
A1. Capt. John Hodges, of the Royal Engineers, drowned in the Restigouche River, NB, saving the life of a young boy. Mar E. Louisa Rutherford.
   B1. Edward Philip, b 1891, widower, no issue
   B2. John Rutherford, b 1893, d 1919, unmar
   B3. Margaret Phyllis, b 1899, d 1975, unmar
A2. Charles Ashworth, mar 1892, Maude Rutherford, sister of Louisa, above. He d 1906 on a trip from Toronto to Jersey.
   B1. Philip Rutherford, b 1894, unmar B3. Margaret Rozel, b 1902,
   B2. Charles Arthur, b 1899, unmar unmar
PIPON, PIPPON, John, bp 1829 J, son of Jean P. and Jeanne SLOUS, in Anse au Griffon 1853, mar 1853, Justine Synnett, bp 1835, dau of Edouard Synnett of Anse Griffon, and Francois Francoeur. Two sisters of this fam mar two brothers. (Remiggi)
A1. ch, b 1853, d.y.   A2. Elisabeth, bp 1854, mar 1872, --- Chouinard
A3. Jean, bp 1856, mar 1882, Adele LABBE, LABEY, dau of Joseph Labbe of Anse Griffon and Felicite Synnett
A4. Philippe, bp 1858, mar 1888, Anasthasie Jalbert, dau of Victor J. and Marcelline Lemieux
A5. Josephine, bp 1860, mar 1897, --- Goulet
A6. Pauline, bp 1862, d 1919, mar 1881, --- Chouinard, brother of Elisabeth's husband
A7. Esther, bp 1864, d 1866
A8. Esther, bp 1866, d 1889, mar 1886, --- Godreau
A9. ch, b 1868, d.y. A10. Alfred, b 1868, d 1918, mar --- JALBERT
PIPON, Thomas, Jr., merchant, carpenter from J in Gaspe 1787, petitioned for land at Paspebiac. (Can. Arch.)
PIPON, agent from J in Nfld. early BK. Mathews)
PIPON, from J to Cape Breton
PIPON, involved 1717 with Nfld. trade from J (C.R. Fay)
PIPON, ---, mar in Canada, --- Braithwaite. (Joan Stevens, Jersey)
A1. dau, mar ---
A2. Douglas Braithwaite, res Montreal, desc Montreal and Ontario
PIPPY, PIPPIN?, POYPE, POIPPE, etc. Cf Samuel Peppys, the English diarist, whose name is also thought to have a Channel Island origin, and preceding that, French. The PIPPY fam of Canada is thought to be derived from a --- Pippy, Poippe, etc., a French Naval officer, believed to be from a family settled for a while in the Channel

Islands, probably Guernsey. "In 1670 Sieur de la Poippe or Poype was the Governor of Placentia. King Lewis (sic) gave him 10,000 livres to repair the forts (1670-1685). In 1674 Poippe petitioned the King for a ship with food which did not come. Ships from New England came to Newfoundland and started a trade there. In 1675 the Basque began to use Placentia." On old Land Grant records, Geo. Pippy had land in Harbor Grace, Nfld. 1790. (M.R. Lee, Southeast Placentia; June Middleton, Lasalle, Que.; Elizabeth Pippy, Mt. Herbert, PEI; Paul Easterbrook, Fresno, Calif; Georgie Day, Lake Annis, NS)

Although French, it is possible that the Naval Officer married a Channel Islander, and his sons may have done this also. The connection with Channel Islands was further reinforced by the marriage of Joseph H. Pippy and Mary NORMORE, qv, in 1783. There were at least 5 sons in this family: William, Joseph H., George, Charles and Peter.

A1. William, b between 1750 and 1760, returned to England, poss settled in Liverpool
A2. Joseph H., b 1754, d 1827. Rem from Harbor Grace, Nfld. and St. John's, to Charlottetown, PEI, with wife, Mary NORMORE, qv, (1760-1839). He was a property owner and shipwright. His will left everything to his wife and after her death to son Joseph, and dau Catherine, with a fishing room in Blackhead, Nfld. left to son Gregory. No mention of Mary or John.
  B1. Gregory, b 1784, d 1863, mar Mary Hillman 1813, 1798-1882. Shipbuilder, farmer in Mt. Herbert, PEI, still in family hands this century. Ten chn:
    C1. Edward, b 1814, mar Matilda Lowry 1840, rem to USA. Shipwright, 1 dau.
    C2. William, b 1816, d 1893. Mar Flora Hillman 1856, who d 1888. Farmer. Ch records show Wm. b or poss bp 1823, not 1816. 4 chn:
      D1. Mary Alice, Polly, b 1858, mar William MacGregor, Cross Roads, PEI
        E1. Susan MacGregor, b 1892, d 1968
        E2. Percy MacGregor, b 1897, res Glasgow, Scotland, d 1960
      D2. William, b 1859, d 1944, mar Mary Praught?, who d 1924. Res on orig fam farm, Mt. Herbert, PEI. 6 chn:
        E1. Minnie, b 1892, d 1973, unmar
        E2. Roy, b 1893, unmar, res Mt. Herbert, farmer
        E3. John, b 1898, d 1969, mar Irene or Rena Coffin, 5 chn
          F1. Phyllis, b 1938, mar Fred McQuillan, res Ont.
            G1. Theresa, b 1949   G4. Matthew   G6. Kim
            G2. Michael   G5. Martin   G7. Kelley, b 1961
            G3. Mark
          F2. Harold, b 1929, mar Faye Johncox 1967, res Ont., son John
          F3. George, b 1932, mar 1. Barbara Cormier, res Moncton, NB, div., mar 2. Elizabeth Matheson, res Milton, PEI, then Mt. Herbert
            G1. George Arthur, by first wife   G3. Patricia, b 1962
            G2. Kathryn, b 1961   G4. Linda, b 1964
          F4. Denise, d.y.   F5. John, b 1938, unmar, res Mt. Herbert
      D3. George, b 1861, d 1941, mar Amelia Carver Morris, 1866-1937, farmer
        E1. Sylvan Chester, b 1891, d 1959, mar Doris Mutch of Keppoch 1925, res Southport. Farmer, ran sawmill, fox ranch, etc. 4 chn.
          F1. Pearl Maud, b 1926, unmar, res Halifax
          F2. Sylvia Ruth, b 1929, mar George McDonald 1947, 3 chn
            G1. George, b 1951   G2. Kathleen, b 1956

```
            G3. Marjorie McDonald, b 1958
        F3. Margaret Adele, b 1931, mar Ira Craswell, S. Rustico, PEI
            G1. Clifford Craswell, b 1952    G4. Alan Craswell, b 1957
            G2. Gary Craswell, b 1955        G5. Bonnie Craswell, b 1961
            G3. Alan Craswell, b 1957        G6. Dean Craswell, b 1966
        F4. Lena June, b 1934, mar Robert Middleton, Sligo, Ireland,
            1958, res Lasalle, P.Q.
    E2. Lena May, b 1893, mar Aubrey Oxner, Mahone Bay, NS, res Mt.
        Herbert
    E3. Pearl, b 1895, d 1918, mar Cecil Stewart, Cross Roads, PEI
    E4. Percy Wilbur, b 1897, d 1962, mar Myrtle Farquharson, Mt.
        Herbert, 1931, carpenter and farmer, 2 chn.
        F1. George Ernest, b 1934, mar Hazel Myers, Hazelbrook, 1953
            G1. Dale, b 1954    G3. Lorna      G5. Tracy, b 1966
            G2. Gale, b 1954, twin    G4. Kimberly
        F2. Ruby Murtle, b 1942, mar Loran Peters, Digby, NS 1968,
            res Mass.
            G1. Gardiner Peters, b 1969 G2. David Peters, b 1973
    E5. Willard Lawson, b 1900, d 1973, mar 1. Mary Adams, who d
        1933 and 2. Flora May MacPherson, 1935, Bellevue, PEI, 7 chn
        F1. dau, b 1933, d.y.
        F2. Helena Ruth, b 1937, mar Rev. F. MacKinnon, C.B., N.S.,
            res London, Ont., 2 chn by second wife
            G1. Brian MacKinnon      G2. Melody MacKinnon, b 1962
        F3. Willard Aubrey, b 1938, unmar, res Mt. Herbert, PEI
        F4. Kathryn Florence, b 1940, mar Wendell Jeffrey, Alberton,
            PEI, res Ont., 3 chn
            G1. Deborah Jeffrey, b 1960  G3. Kimberly Jeffery, b 1966
            G2. Kevin J.
        F5. Bruce MacPherson, b 1944, mar Carol Herman, Pownal, PEI
            1966, res Mt. Albion, PEI, 4 chn
            G1. Darlene, b 1960         G3. Denise
            G2. Diane                   G4. Doreen, b 1976
        F6. Norman Wayne, b 1945, mar Donna Jenkins 1965
            G1. Robert Wayne, b 1966    G2. Norma, b 1970
        F7. Nancy Elizabeth, b 1951, mar Chris. Jenkins, Mt. Albion,
            bro of Donna, above, 1967, res Hazelbrook, PEI
            G1. William Jenkins, b 1967 G2. Michelle Jenkins, b 1969
    D4. Charles H., b 1863, d 1940, mar 1. Mary Carver, 1868-1912,
        mar 2. Abigail E. McWilliams Atherton. No issue, res Lynn,
        Mass. A stepson, Ray Atherton.
C3. Eliza Jane, b 1816, mar Alex Stewart, 1848
C4. Henry Joseph, b 1819, no trace, may have d.y.
C5. Mary, b 1821, d 1894, mar William MacKenzie 1847
C6. John James, b 1826, d 1859, mar Sarah Moody 1947. Printer and
    publisher in Ch'town, PEI of the ADVERTISER from 1843 to 1854,
    which he inherited from his father-in-law, for whom he had
    worked as a printer. Charter member, Sons of Temperance. Rem
    to Mass, where he d. Fam rem to N.Y., 4 chn.
    D1. Mary Catherine, b 1848, mar Prof. Serena Shine of Savannah,
        Ga. 1886 in NY, no trace
    D2. John James Jr., b 1849, his wife or mother visited PEI 1890s
    D3. Eleanor Sarah, b 1851, went to France and Germany for educa-
        tion, visited PEI 1890s
    D4. Sarah Templeton, b 1854, d 1899 N.Y. Visited PEI 1890s.
C7. Clementine, b 1828, mar Duncan MacGregor 1864
C8. Elsie, b 1832, d 1905, mar Daniel Kennedy 1853
```

  C9. Emily, mar Alexander MacGregor 1854
  C10. Caroline, b 1839, d 1917, mar David MacLeod?
 B2. Mary, b 1788, d 1850, mar Samuel Street, blacksmith 1817, chn
 B3. John, sea capt., ship builder, mar 3 times. Rem from C'town, PEI to San Francisco, Calif after third mar. Mar 1. 1822, Louisa Augusta Nelson, 1801-1824. A son of this mar was prob John Samuel Nelson, poss raised by his aunt, Mary Street, and listed later among her chn, drowned. Might be the John who mar Matilda Haskins or Hawkins in 1861. John, the father, mar 2. Eleanor Edwards, 1825, who d 1831. Poss 3 chn including Richard Edward and Caroline, both of whom d.y. Maybe a Ben or Harry who survived and was raised by his uncle, Gregory Pippy. John mar 3. in 1831, Elizabeth Yeo Watts, widow from Cornwall, Eng. At least 10 chn.
  C1. John Samuel Nelson, b 1824, by first wife
  C2. Richard Edward, d.y., by second wife C3. Caroline, d.y.
  C4. Harry, or Ben, by second wife. A Harry Pippy d 1890, Calif. See above data.
  C5. Robert Normore, b 1832, d 1913 San Fran. by third wife
  C6. Benjamin Yeo, b 1834, d 1900, N.Y.
  C7. Edward Walter, b 1836, d 1923 Yountville, Calif.
  C8. George, b 1838, d 1855 London, Eng. PEI newspaper notice.
  C9. Wm. Frederick, b 1841
  C10. Louisa Elizabeth Eleanor, b 1845, d.y.
 B4. Joseph, b 1798, d 1872. Mar Eunice Gardiner 1843, 1810-1864? Shipwright, poss built ship FANNY, which sailed from C'town, PEI around Cape Horn to Calif in the 1849 Goldrush. 3 chn.
  C1. Joseph Thomas, b 1835, d 1882, prob unmar, no will
  C2. George Henry, b 1835?, d.y.
  C3. Charlotte Eliza, b 1845, mar Charles Hughes 1867
 B5. Catherine Normore, b 1802, d 1891, mar Henry Stamper, no issue but raised her husband's 2 nieces. Henry d 1859, age 70. She had the fam Bible with ancestors and places or origin, which has since disappeared.
A3. George, b 1757, rem to Harbour Grace, Nfld. Had land grant there in 1790. A desc is Baxter Pippy of Sydney, N.S.
 B1. George, b 1782, mar Mary ---
  C1. George, b 1807, mar Amelia ---
   D1. Thomas, mar Jane ---
    E1. Frank, rem to Yarmouth, N.S.
    E2. Annie, mar Herbert Froude?, an adopted son
    E3.,4, 5, three sons
   D2. Bessie? (1829-1903)
   D3. George Augustus, 1832-1899, mar 1857 Mary A. MERCHANT, qv.
    E1. William Merchant, b 1859, mar --- Rolitez? at Lima, Peru, S.A. 1883, a son, no trace.
    E2. Anna Bella, b 1861, mar Clarence Leighton Miller 1891 at Truro, NS
    E3. Frank, b 1863, d 1967
    E4. George Baxter, b 1865, d 1941. Mar Eva Treen 1894 at Malagash, NS. She d 1934.
     F1. Mary Greta, b 1895, d 1963
     F2. George Treen, b 1896, mar Irene McKenzie MacLeod, who d 1963
      G1. Isobel Eva, b 1938
    E5. Elizabeth Anne, b 1867, d 1872
    E6. Fannie Parsons, b 1874, adopted, mar Frederick A. Casson

PIPPY 471

   1893, Truro.
A4. Charles, b 1765, d 1849, settled Broadcove, Nfld. (Paul Easterbrook, Fresno, Calif)
 B1. George, b 1795, d 1880, mar Dinah THISTLE, qv, 1822. She d 1873. They res Baddeck, NS.
  C1. Mary Evans, b 1825, d.y.
  C2. Joseph, b 1826, d 1870?, drowned
   D1. Maggie, b 1849, res St. John's, Nfld.
   D2. William George, b 1850, res St. John's, mar Jessie Louise Lindsay, 5 chn
    E1. Roy, b 1884
    E2. William, b 1886, res St. John's E3. Pearl Ebsary?, b 1888?
    E4. Rita, or Areta, b 1890, mar St. John's, Wallace R. Coobie
    E5. Chesley A., b 1894, d 1971, mar St. John's, Edna M. Hill 1920
     F1. Chesley A., b 1932, mar Sharon Palmer, a son, Douglas J.
  C3. Henry, b 1828, d 1870?, drowned
  C4. Adelaide Condon, b 1833, rem to Liverpool, NS
  C5. Mary Jane Boyd, b 1835, d 1867, res Broadcove, Nfld.
  C6. Louisa, b 1837, d Baddeck, N.S.
  C7. Charles Henry, b 1846, mar Mary MacDonald of C.B.
   D1. Mamie, b 1882, d 1953
   D2. George Henry, b 1884, d 1952, res Sydney, N.S.
   D3. John, b 1891, d 1954   D4. Albert, b 1899, d 1965
   D6. Adelaide Power, b 1900, d 1960, Sydney, N.S.
 B2. Jane
 B3. Joseph, b 1800, mar Julie ---, res Broadcove, Nfld.
  C1. George, b 1834, res Springhill, Nfld. 1885
   D1. William Joseph, b 1860
    E1. William, b 1907, res Halifax
    E2. Doris Bennett, b 1915, res Calif.
   D2. Charles, b 1865, res Springhill, Nfld., a son, George, d 1962
   D3. Frederick? or Alfred, b 1875
   D4. Maria House, b 1858, res Springhill, Nfld.
  C2. Maria, b 1836 C3. Dorcas, b 1839 C4. Julia, b 1839?
  C5. Joseph, b 1846, owned Bell Island, was in partnership with a company named Sherran and Pippy
   D1. Wilfred, b 1880, res St. John's D2. Olive, b 1885, an M.D.?
   D3. Vater? Walter?, b 1890, res St. John's, Officer WWI, Nfld. div
 B4. William, b 1811, d 1899, rem to Pouch Cove, Nfld. 1850, mar Elizabeth Butt, b 1815, 10 chn
  C1. James?
  C2. William Thomas, b 1836, d between 1914 and 1926, res Pouch Cove 1850
   D1. Dorcas, b 1858, d 1950 at Yarmouth, N.S.
   D2. Joseph, b 1860, d 1950 Glace Bay, C.B.
   D3. William T., b 1879, res St. John's
   D4. Reuben, b 1881, res St. John's
   D5. Maud Strom, b 1883, d 1900 Halifax, NS
   D6. Charles, b 1886, res St. John's
  C3. Polly, Mary, b 1838, d before 1926. Mar 1. Nathaniel LE GROW, qv, and 2. Soloman or Joseph Butt
  C4. Sarah Jane Delaney, b 1840, d before 1926
  C5. Charles, b 1843, d 1923. Mar 1870, Jessie A. Williams of Pouch Cove, Nfld. She d 1937, 10 chn.
   D1. Lucy Marion, b 1871, mar 1899, Clement Hudson Easterbrook
    E1. Paul, Fresno, Calif.   E2. Charles

D2. Harry or Henry William, b 1874, d 1964, res Pouch Cove, Nfld. and Vancouver, BC
D3. William, b 1876, d 1952, Methodist minister in Helena, Mont. Mar 1913, Sarah ---, 3 chn.
D4. Nathaniel, b 1879, mar 1908   D5. Maud Julia, b 1881, d 1885
D6. Charles, b 1883, d 1884
D7. Elizabeth May or Mary, b 1885, mar 1916, Earl McKnight, res Santa Cruz, Calif.
   E1. Charles   E2. Marian Harlow   E3. William
D8. Jessie Mildred House, b 1888, mar 1925, res St. John's, Nfld.
D9. Frederick, b 1890, d 1970, mar 1917, Ida Everson, who d 1971, San Jose, Calif.
D10. Herbert Harold, b 1893, d 1917
C6. Nathaniel
C7. Reuben, b 1846, d 1936, mar Miriam Baggs or Briggs, res Moncton? 1904, 7 chn
   D1. George Edwin, b 1878, res St. John's, Nfld. and Glace Bay, CB. Mar Elizabeth BISHOP 1901, 6 chn.
      E1. Marguerite Annette, b 1902, res Glace Bay, CB
      E2. Reta Oliva, b 1904, mar Daniel MacKeigan, res Glace Bay
      E3. Laura Evelyn ROBERTS, b 1905, d 1941
      E4. Miriam Francis MacKenzie, b 1908, mar Charles MacKenzie
      E5. Georgie Marie Day, b 1913, res Yarmouth, NS, mar Donald Day, teacher
      E6. Harold Edwin, b 1918, res Burlington, Ont., teacher, Harley or Harlan?
   D2. Arthur Bertram, b 1884, d 1904
   D3. William John Raymond, b 1887, druggist in Moncton
      E1. Barbara May, b 1920
   D4. Charles, b 1889, d.y.
   D5. Frederick Theodore Dunn, b 1896, Hant's Harbor, Nfld., res Moncton. Mar Viola Purdy of Saint John, b 1926, 3 chn.
      E1. Norma F., b 1927 E2. Joan Marie, b 1939 E3. Ralph T., b 1942
   D6. Maude Gertrude, b 1881, Green's Harbour, Nfld., d 1976, mar Peter LE GROW
   D7. Winnifred, b 1890, d 1946
C8. Levi John, b 1848, d 1928, rem to Toronto 1887. Mar Jessie Moulton, 10 chn.
   D1. William   D2. Charles, d.y.
   D3. Mary Amelice, b 1964, mar Thomas Fraser
   D4. Ada Bertha, b 1874, d 1950 or 1966, res Pouch Cove, Nfld. Mar Peter Mitchell.
      E1 Harold Mitchell, res Toronto   E2. Thelma Mitchell, res Tor.
   D5. Elizabeth Jane, b 1876, d 1922, mar Levi LE GROW, qv.
   D6. Samuel George, b 1877, d ca 1957, res Pouch Cove, mar Lillian Avery, 3 sons
   D7. Walter Harris, b 1880, d 1968, res Pouch Cove and Toronto. Mar Susan Jones, a dau, Audrey Travis.
   D8. Minniver, b 1882, d 1960
   D9. Harry, poss Henry Thomas, b 1884 or 1890?, d 1969 Toronto, mar Ellen Quigley
   D10. Archibald Reuben, b 1891, d 1968. Optometrist, Winnipeg, Man. Mar Nina Macklem.
      E1. Murray G., United Ch. Chaplain, C.A.F., Ottawa, Ont.
      E2. Norma Moore, res Los Alamitos, Calif.
      E3. Bruce, mar Alma Wallberg, Winnipeg, 1968
      E4. dau, res Vancouver, BC

C9. Maria Easterbrook, b 1851, d 1928. Mar John Bowden Easterbrook
      1876. Many descendants in this fam.
   C10. Amelia Butt, b 1853, d 1912, known as Minnie. Mar Tom Hudson,
      lighthouse keeper at Cape St. Francis.
 B5. Sarah, b 1815, res Broadcove, Nfld.
 A5. Peter, b 1768, res Blackhead, Nfld., mar Dorothy ---? Desc, a son,
    John, b 1822. Rem to Australia or N.Z. Peter also had 6 daus.
PIQUET, Clement, of J?, signed the Gaspe Petition 1820
PIROUET, PERRIWAY, PERROWAY, PIEROWAY, PARAWAY, etc. Said to be from
   Birou?, France, Hug, to J, then to N.A. A Philip rem to Boston ca
   1707, mar Johanna MARINER, or LE MARINEL (QAAM) and they or their
   descendants rem to Liverpool, NS. James, Abraham and John b early
   1700s in Boston. Pirouet, Philip, was a Jersey Diarist. (Soc. Jers.
   Bull. 1977)
PIROUET, see BRIDEAUX   PITMAN, SEE EXTRA PAGES
PITON, Jean and Rachel LAFFOLEY, mar 1798 J, had at least 6 chn: Lucy
   or Lucq, unclear, b 1802; Philippe, b 1804; Francois, b 1807; Abra-
   ham, b 1809; see below; Rachel, b 1812; and Nicholas, b 1816, to
   Gaspe, then to Levis? Some material below is unverified.
 I. PITON, Jacques Philippe, b 1820, and several bros: Jean, Philippe,
    Nicholas, all mariners. "They sailed to all parts of the world,
    Montevideo, Leghorn, Australia, London, but chiefly Gaspe." "Accord-
    ing to the log books she has, the cargoes on these voyages were cow-
    hides, tallow, salt, and ...salted cod. One ship was the brig MARIA.
    Joshua PITON was commander of a ship named DE JERSEY, and John com-
    manded also a ship named JANVRIN in the year 1839. She has several
    framed pictures of these vessels. The name of PITON dates back to
    1625 in Jersey." (Mary Piton, Columbus, Ohio)
II. PITON, Nicholas, d at St. Davis of Levis in 1890. "He frequented
    the Anglican Ch there of Holy Trinity, Wolfe St., and was the only
    man in the village to wear his hair down to his shoulders. He was
    from Jersey and it was thought that might have been the custom in
    the Island. M. Piton, desc of Nicholas, lived in Levis in 1850,
    and worked for the Canadian National Railway. He was, for a long
    time, in charge of painting the Bridge at Quebec." (PROFILES
    LEVISIENS, 1949, by Pierre-Georges Roy) Nicholas was b 1816 J, son
    of Jean PITON and Rachel LAFFOLEY, of St. Brelade, J. He first
    went to Gaspe, and later res Levis, Que. Mar Elizabeth Arless, b
    1853? Yorkshire, Eng. The fam had a quarry, from which block was
    taken for part of the Canadian Parliament Bldgs.
 A1. Martin, see above, poss the M. Piton in Profiles Levisiens
 A2. Nicholas, mar, res Texas?
 A3. William John, mar, bur Magnolia Cem., Charleston, S.C. Had step-
    son in Norwood, Mass.
 A4. Guy, b Quebec, bur Toronto? Poss desc in Ottawa?
 A5. Francis Frederick, d Toronto 1902 and bur there
    B1. William Henry
    B2. Letitia, mar Albert Vierin, a chef, res Toronto
    B3. Frederick Francis   B4. Reginald Guy
    B5. Vera Isabel, mar Clarence Hall
 A6. James, b 1852, bur Eng. ca 1927. Mar 1. Dunn? and 2. ---, b Eng.,
    a son d.y.
 A7. Septimus Arless, d Levis, Que. 1910. Champion of Canada at snow
    shoeing. Bur Mt. Hermon Cem, Quebec City. Mar --- Robinson.
    B1. Edwin Septimus, unmar, d 1972, director CNR, res Levis, Que.
    B2. Una Helena, mar Joseph Bouchard, no issue, d 1975, bur Mt.
       Hermond, Que.

B3. Viola, unmar, d 1971 B4. Gladys, mar ---Weller, no issue d ca 1969
B5. Harold Henry, mar, served WWI, res Whawnigan Lake, BC. A son, Harold.
   C1. Harold, b ca 1910, a son and 2 daus
      D1. Richard, Bud, mar, has 4 chn
      D2. and 3. twins, Sherry and Shelly.
B6. Hinda Frances, mar Frank McDeen, a dau Margaret said to res NY city
A8. Elizabeth Frances, Lillie, unmar, d 1929, bur Mt. Hermon, a music teacher
A9. Ernest Henry Newrick, b 1865, d 1923, civil engineer, and Provincial land surveyor. Mar 1903, Ethel Jane Craig of Stoneham, Que., 7 chn. Bur Quebec City.
   B1. Lillie Elizabeth, b 1904, res Buffalo, NY and Vancouver, BC
   B2. Mildred, b 1906, d.y.
   B3. William Ernest, b 1909, unmar, res Stoneham, Que.
   B4. Violet Grace, b 1910, mar Leslie H. Lambley, res Vanc., no issue
   B5. Ethel Stella May, b 1913, mar Wm. Coutts, res Vanc., a dau, Randy Mae, mar Craig Robinson, a dau, Jennifer Robinson
   B6. Walter James, b 1915 Stoneham, Que., mar Alice Nadeau, 6 chn
      C1. Judith, mar Fred Crowley, 2 chn, res Ottawa
      C2. James, mar Nicole Nadeau C3. Nancy, mar Yvon Lavoie, res Quebec
      C4. Esther, unmar C5. Cynthia, mar J. PROULX C6. Jean, b 1958
   B7. Muriel Helena, b 1918, mar M. Konar, and mar 2. Walter Isinger of Vancouver
      C1. Tanya Helene, mar Andre Regan, 3 chn: Moya, Erick, and Noni
A10. Priscilla Helena, b 1866, d 1949, mar Germain Simeon Marceau, a widower with 3 girls and two boys. Two chn d.y., bur St. Valier Cem, Quebec City.
   B1. Paul, a doctor, sev chn   B4. Angeline, mar Dr. Trudel,
   B2. Joseph, unmar, res Montreal   Regina, Sask, 3 sons
   B3. Marguerite, nun in Montreal   B5. Anna, unmar, d 1972

PITON, PEYTON, Philippe, b 1772 J, son of Abr. and Susanne LE PORCQ. SEE EXTRA PAGES for Victor Emil's family. Fam being researched now. Philip PEYTON, age 32, single, res Beaumont, Que., mar Marie Henriette Filion of St. Pietre, St. Paul's Bay, dau of Zacharie Filion, blacksmith, age 19, July 1808, Cathedral of Holy Trinity, Que. (Mary Piton, Columbus, OH: Violet Lambly, Vanc., BC)
A1. Marie Sophie, b 1811 Que.   A2. Marie Henriette, who d 1912
A3. Philippe, b 1813 Baie St. Paul, Que., d 1962 St. Roch, Que. Mar 1836, Flore Allard, and 2. in 1848, Luce Casgrain-Gagnon, b 1824, Canada. Philippe res Quebec City, then rem to Brooklyn, NY. Grocer and merchant-furrier.
   B1. Marie Emma Sarah, b 1849 Que., d Chicago, Ill. 1897, mar George Simard
   B2. Edmond Noe, b 1850, d 1851 St. Roch B3. Marie Lucy, 1851-1853
   B4. Honorene, b 1853, d 1920s, mar Joseph Kalotte, res Wisconsin
   B5. Jean-Philippe, b 1856, d between 1860 and 1870
   B6. Joseph George, b 1856, twin, d.y.
   B7. Harriet, b 1858 Brooklyn, NY B8. Abraham, b 1859, Brooklyn, d.y.
   B9. George, b 1860, Brooklyn, d 1918 Chicago, Ill., mar Sophie Baliff
   B10. Emile George, b 1862 Brooklyn, d 1952 Chicago, Ill. Mar Margaret Dempsey, b Ireland 1868, d Chicago 1958.
      C1. George Joseph, b 1901 Chicago, mar Catherine Burns
      C2. Victor Emil, b 1901, a twin, mar Ann Mary Panek **MORE IN**
         D1. Patrick   D2. Dorothy   D3. Victor L.   **EXTRA PAGES**.

        C3. Peter Phillip, b 1903 Chicago, mar Mary D. Brady, a dau Margaret, b 1946
        C4. Theodore Michael, b 1904, d 1960
        C5. Marie Lucille, b 1906 Chicago
A4. Francois, b 1815 Quebec   A8. Etienne, b 1821, d.y.
A5. Marie Florence PITHON, b 1816   A9. Caroline, b 1822, d 1824
A6. Jean Hercule, b 1818, d.y.   A10. Marie, b 1825
A7. Jean Taouse, b 1819   A11. Marie Elionore, b 1828, d.y.
PITON, Abraham, age 42, b J, mar 1841, Eliza Anne Hayden, b Quebec, age 49, were in Malbaie 1871 (Census)
PITON, Albina, Mrs. John, was in Gaspe area 1927 with John Jr., Mildred, Frank and Edward (Brochet)
PITON, Mrs. Edmond, res Montreal. Her husband from Gaspe and Jersey.
PITON, sev at Campbellton, NB
PITON, a Capt. from J and/or G was listed by K. Mathews in early Nfld. records
PITON, William, b J, in Malbaie 1861 with Eliza, John, Alfred Philip, George, Selena, Samuel, Joshua, and Rachel L., all b Lower Canada (Census)
PITON, some settled at Lauzon, Que.
PITON, Alan, res Forillon, Gaspe early 1900s?
PLEVEN, Blanche, b J, mar Clifford NORMAN, qv. Her grandfather came to J from PLELON, France some generations back. Current. (Blanche Martin, Sherwood Park, Alta.) Some PLEVENS in BC.
PLOWMAN, some from C.I. to Nfld. (Shortis-Munn) Unverified. (Seary)
POIDEVIN, James Alexander, b J, ca 1830?, mar Augusta Tope Beatten, rem to Muskoka, Ont. ca 1870 with 7 chn. This name shortened from LE POIDEVIN, qv. (Catherine Poidevin, Winnepeg, MAN)
A1. Frederick William, b 1861 J, mar 1881 Elizabeth Carr, res Gravenhurst, Ont., to Winn., Manitoba early 1900s. (Desc: Edith
    B1. May, b 1882, d 1911   B3. Lyda,1890. (MCLeod,Ft Worth,TX)
    B2. Frederick Burlington, b 1885, d 1966, mar Asenath HILLIS 1906, 4 chn. She d 1916. He mar 2. Catherine Whibley. 1919.
        C1. Lloyd, b 1907   C5. Josephine, b 1920, by second
        C2. Millicent, b 1909   wife
        C3. Hilton, b 1912   C6. Clifford, b 1927
        C4. Elizabeth, b 1916   C7. Earl, b 1928
A2. James   A4. William   A6. Lena
A3. John   A5. Mary   A7. Minnie
POIDEVIN, James Elias, b near St. Helier, J 1853, mar Lena Tailley?, son of Elias P., rem to Collingwood, Ont. late 1800s. James was the grandson of Jacob Poidevin. (Capt. Edgar F. Poidevin, Toronto)
A1. Henry, b 1883
A2. Edith, b 1885, a nursing supt., mar McLeod?, Fort Worth Army Hospital, 40 years of service
A3. Jacob, 1887   A4. Elizabeth, b 1895, mar --- MASSON?
A5. Edgar Fulton, b 1902, mar Estelle Maud NICHOLS, b 1906 (See FIFTY YEARS ON THE GREAT LAKES).
    B1. Marion, b 1926, mar Desmond Thomas Quinn, res Fort McMurray, Alta., works in the Athabasca Oil Sands Recovery fields
        C1. Michael Quinn, b 1950   C4. Cathy Quinn, b 1960
        C2. Desmond Quinn, Jr., b 1952 C5. Thomas Quinn, b 1967
        C3. Robert Quinn, b 1954
    B2. Audrey, b 1929, mar John Flint, res Toronto, Ont., engineer
        C1. John Flint, Jr., b 1953   C2. Debra Flint, b 1958
"I did hear my grandad talk of playing in the brickyard where it was warm when they lit the fires, and about playing on the commons below

Fort Elizabeth castle, also about a great uncle who lost a leg in the Crimean war. I regret the loss of our family Bible." Capt. Poidevin has heard that one of his family came with the British forces of Halifax, N.S. in 1790. His grandfather, Elias P. came from J to Canada in 1853 and was master in 1873 of the brig MINERVA that ran ashore and sank in the Gulf near St. Paul's Island, all crew saved. This information in Canadian Coastal Manual of 1900.
POINDEXTER, Emilie, b J, mar James LE MOTTEE qv. Bur St. Peters, Malbaie, Gaspe. She d 1916, age 72.
POINDEXTER, John, of J, a merchant or carpenter, petitioned for land at at Paspebiac, Gaspe 1787
POINDEXTER, Mr. and Mrs., from J to New Westminster, BC (Luce) with his sisters, late 1800s. This fam related to the VIDALs, qv.
POINDEXTER, POINGDESTRE, in J, Capt. from J in Nfld. (K. Mathews)
POINGDESTRE, Bertha Rachel, mar Peter John RENAULT. She was b 1887 J, to Canada 1914, d 1957 Montreal?
POIRIER, Mayas, signed Gaspe Petition of 1820 in Gaspe, from J?
POIRIER, in Nfld. (Seary) Cf POIRIER of J (Stevens)
POITIER?, C.I. in Maritimes Fisheries (J.H. Le Breton list)
POLLARD, Capt. from G in Nfld. (Stevens, K. Mathews)
POLLIS, in Nfld. Cf DE POILLEY of J (Stevens)
POLLETT, poss PAULET?, C.I. surname in N.S. (Lorway, Sydney, N.S.) Cf PAULET in Stevens.
POLLOCK, current Gaspe, from C.I.?
PONCARD, Boat keeper from C.I.?, in Nfld. (K. Mathews)
POND, in Nfld. (Seary) from C.I.?, Cf DU PONT in J
PONTSORM, Agnes, from C.I. to Chatham
POPE, Richard, in Bread and Cheese Cove, Nfld. 1775, from J? Cf PAPE of J (Stevens) Said to be of C.I. origin (Rev. Hammond)
PORTER, PORTIER, Richard, in Hibbs Hole, Nfld. 1774 and William in 1777. Said to be of C.I. origin (Rev. Hammond) Mary P. in Cupids 1783, James and Thos. in Hants Harbor, Nfld.
POTTER, in Nfld., said to be of C.I. origin (Seary) Cf PORTIER of J (Stevens)
POTVIN, see POIDEVIN and LE POIDEVIN
POULE, in Nfld. (Seary) Poss as PAULET, or POULIN of C.I.?
POULIN, in Nfld. (Seary) Cf POULAIN, etc. of J (Stevens)
POULAIN, Pierre, was a J servant 13 yrs. old in 1871, with the James HENRY fam at that time, in Gaspe
POULSON, Capt. from G in Nfld. (K. Mathews)
POWELL, Charles, b J?, d 1952, age 85, husband of Marie Boutin, bur Cape Cove, Gaspe, has nephew Philip, and 6 chn, who mar French Canadians. He res Grand Riviere, Gaspe. (GLF; J.H. Le Breton list)
POWELL, from J to Newmarket, Ont. early 1900s. A dau, Hilda, in Uxbridge, Ont.
POWELL, in Nfld. (Seary) thought to be from J
POWLEY, poss PAULET of J? in Nfld. (Seary)
POYNES, Capt. from J in Nfld. (K. Mathews)
POYNTER, in Nfld. (Seary) Cf PYNTRER, PEINTEUR of J (Stevens)
PRATT, in Gaspe and Nfld. poss from J? (Stevens)
PREAUTY?, PRUNTY?, Elizabeth P., mar John DE GARIS, Grand Greve, Gaspe 1832 (Brochet)
PREAUTY, Wm., in Bay de Grave, Nfld. 1788 (Rev. Hammond) Thought to be from C.I.
PREDHAM, PRIDHAM, in Nfld. Thought to be PREUDHOMME, LE PRUDOMME of J.
PRESHYON, in Nfld. Cf PERICHON, PERROCHON of J (Stevens) also mentioned by Saunders of Soc. Jers. Bulletins.

PRESS, in Nfld. Cf DES PRES of J (Stevens)
PRENTIS, Dorothy, of C.I., in Victoria, BC 1940
PREVIL, PREVILLE, Albert, from G to St. Thomas, Ont. with LE COURTOIS fam, qv, as a teenager ca 1890. Mar, 4 sons and a dau. Youngest son Earl, a farmer near Belmont, Ont. Dau mar --- Stafford, res London, Ont.
PREVEL, Georges, b St.Helier 1823, poss son of Ph.& Anne Le.M.? son of Jacques and Suzanne LE MAISTRE of J, mar in Grande Greve, Gaspe 1844 to Emilie Cassivi. No chn listed (Gravel; Gallant; Census) 3 nephews, named COUL, to Gaspe, then to U.S. (Rev. D'Hist)
PREVEL, also in Malbaie, Gaspe
PREVEL, Philip, father of George? to Canada 1836 from C.I.
PREVOST, Lt. de J., from G?, of the 4th Can. Reg't, mar a Miss DOW in Que. 1873. (MAPLE LEAVES, by J.M. Le Moine, Que.)
PREVOST, George, b J, widower of Modeste Anglehart, mar 1831 in Anglican Ch, New Carlisle, Que., Sarah Douglass. He was a ship carpenter, she res Paspebiac, Bon. Co. At least one ch, Samuel. (Jeanne Prevost, Ste. Foy, Que.) Geo.b St. Ouen, J, Val de la Mare.
  A1. Samuel, res Paspebiac, mar Jane Day, or Dea, in Port Daniel, Que. 1884. Witnesses were 2 cousins of Sarah, David Dea and James LE BRASSEUR, qv. Jane was the dau of James Dea and Lea Duguay.
    B1. Jack, res Pitt Meadows, BC
    B2. James, a farmer, res Port Daniel, Que., mar 1909 in St. Godefroi Cath. Ch, New Carlisle, Que., Julia VAUTIER, qv.
      C1. Omer, b 1910 Port Daniel, mar 1940, Jeanne Ouellet
        D1. Edward James, b Baie Comeau, Que. 1941, mar Anna-Marie Murphy of Kingston, Ont. 1964. Res Mt. Royal, Montreal.
          E1. Mark, b 1965   E3. Eric, b 1969
        D2. Louise, b 1967   E4. Lucq, b 1971
      C2. Viola, mar Berbard Dansereau of Outremont, Que., no issue
      C3. Estelle, mar Hans Lenger of Amsterdam, Holland, no issue
      C4. Elger, mar Lucie Cyr from Maria, Bona. Co., Que., res Baie Comeau, later Ville Lasalle, Montreal
        D1. Violet   D3. James   D5. Elizabeth
        D2. Marie-Julia   D4. Paul   D6. Charlotte Ann, res England
      C5. Reginald, mar Elsie Thompson of Scotland, res Ste. Foy, Que.
        D1. Sandra   D2. Linda   D3. Gregory
      C6. Raymond, mar an English girl, had sev chn, res Port Daniel, Que.
PREVOST, Sir George, 1767-1816, Governor and Commander in Chief of the Canadas in 1811. Origin unverified. (See Edith Firth, THE TOWN OF YORK) Mar Catherine Phipps, 3 chn.
PREVOST, from J to Gaspe, to Alpena, Mich.?
PRIAULX, PROULX, Orig form DE PREAUX? A Seigneur of that surname was at Hastings with the Conqueror. Wm. de Preaux, was with Richard the Lion-Hearted, went to the Crusades and saved the King's life. In 1200, King John nominated Pierre de Preaux, Seigneur of Jersey, Guernsey and Alderney, plus other lands in England and Normandy. He married Marie de Vernon, of the ruling family of the Isle of Wight. Pierre died ca 1210 and his bro Guillaume inherited. These brothers were remotely connected to King John and to the Plantagenets. Thomas PRIAULX sold the Fief Le Comte of Guernsey to Eleazer LE MARCHANT in 1722. Many of this surname lived in Forest, Guernsey 1700s.
PRIAULX, John, age 61, b G, in Gaspe Bay 1871, mar Eleanor LE LACHEUR, Methodist, b G, age 45 in 1861. Dau, Caroline, b 1841, and dau, Eleanor, b 1853 Gaspe. (Brochet; Census)
PRIAULX, Agent, merchant, ship owner and boat keeper from J or G in Nfld. (K. Mathews)

PRIAULX, Eleanor, Methodist, 45, in Gaspe Bay 1861.
PRIAULX, Elizabeth, in Gaspe 1864, from G, mar Philip John MACHON, qv
PRIAULX. "My great grandfather left Guernsey in the mid 1800s and settled in Gaspe. My grandfather, a printer, was William Arthur P. He migrated to Rochester, and Buffalo, then to Pasedena, Calif, and finally to Oregon. My father, Arthur William, who mar DE GARIS?, was a newspaper publisher in Oregon until the 1940s, and then became a public relations consultant. We had cousins in Calif, name of Percival P. until their deaths recently, (1965). I have one cousin, son of my late uncle Edward, living some place in Oregon."
PRIAULX, Adolphus, b 1858 St. Peterport, G, a tailor, d 1936 Toronto. Mar Sarah Bondy, b England. To Canada ca 1878 poss first to Gaspe. (H.A. Priaulx, Toronto, Ont.)
- A1. Harold Arthur, b 1893 Toronto, d 1958, mar Ruth Harriet Mathews, b 1899, res Toronto
  - B1. Harold Arthur, b 1916 Toronto, mar Kathleen Florence Brown, b 1922 London, England
    - C1. Michael Charles P., b 1945 England, mar Sheila Fallon
      - D1. Gregory Harold, b 1971   D2. Tammy Ann, b 1974
    - C2. Helen Joyce, b 1948 Toronto, mar Joseph Howell, no issue
    - C3. Paul Arthur, b 1951 Toronto, mar Lorraine Maich
      - D1. Nicole Renee, b 1973   D2. Shawn William, b 1974
  - B2. Charles Stanley, b 1917 Toronto, mar Eileen Warner, London, Eng. Dau, Margaret, b 1954
  - B3. Helen Ruth, b 1918, mar Robert Morrison. Chn: Robert, June and Helen Morrison.
  - B4. Norman Howard, b 1921, res Detroit, Mich., mar Peggy ---. Chn: Peggy Ann and Jack.
- A2. Ethel, mar --- Carlile, poss older than Harold Arthur, 3 chn
- A3. Bertha, mar --- Wardell, 3 chn
- A4. Norman MacDonal, b 1898 Toronto, d 1974, mar Margaret Dumbleton, no issue
- A5. Harry, mar Vera ---, 13 chn

PRICE, some in Gaspe, not C.I., prob from Britain or U.E.L., 1760s (Brochet)
PRICE, Isabella, from J?, wife of John GAVEY, qv.
PRICE, Hug, to J, one associated with Charles Robin in the Maritimes
PRICE, Edward, b G, in Gaspe at Cap Rosier 1861 (Census) with Marguerite, b Ireland, Edward, Elizabeth, James, Christie, Thomas, Rosanne, b Gaspe, Nicholas, b G, Jane and George, b Gaspe.
PRICE, John, b G, in Gaspe with Martha, John, Marguerite, William, Martha, Georgina and Charlotte, b Gaspe, 1861.
PRICE, Susan, of Gaspe, mar John Francis LE HUQUET, b 1850, see LE HUQUET.
PRICE, Margaret Jane, mar 1875, Francis Wm. LE HUQUET, qv.
PRICE, Frederick, b G, in Gaspe at Douglastown? 1861 (Census) with Kitty, b Scotland, Robert, George, Frederick, Edward, Flora, Peter, Margaret?, and Daniel, b Gaspe.
PRICE Bros., a forestry company established at Rimouski, Que., poss connected with the Price fam of C.I., poss also in New Brunswick
PRICE, from C.I. to Gaspe, to Alpena, Mich.? (Directory, 1905)
PRICE, in Nfld. (Seary) From C.I.
PRIDDLE, in Nfld., orig. PRIDEAUX from C.I. or from Wales (Rev. Hammond)
PRIDEAUX. "The most commanding view of Bay Roberts, Nfld. is Prideaux Hill, where the telegraph station is now built...we have undoubted traditions that this locality was called after a Jerseyman." (Shortis-Munn; Seary) Cf also PRINCE from PROUINGS of J.
PRIEST, Wilfred, b 1894 G, d 1960, res Burlington, Ont. Mar Hilda

LE NOURY, qv. (Edward Le Page, Grimsby, Ont.)
A1. Doris May, b 1914, mar Harry OGIER, qv, 3 chn
A2. Lloyd, b 1915, mar Marian LAWRENCE, b 1909
  B1. Lauraine, b 1941, mar Wayne LAUX, b 1936
    C1. Katherine Louise Laux, b 1975 Brantford, Ont.
  B2. Linda, b 1949, mar David Jacklyn, b 1947   B3. Louise C., b 1957
A3. Harriet Barbara, b 1918, mar Herbert Wignall
  B1. Robert John Wignall, b 1942, mar Ann Elizabeth Willis, b 1942
    C1. Bonnie Elizabeth Wignall, b 1969 C2. Geoffrey R. Wignall, b 1971
  B2. Joyce Shelia Wignall, b 1944
  B3. Susan Lynne Wignall, b 1949, mar Robert Alex. Anderson
A4. Amanda Rhoda, b 1921, d.y.
PRIEST, Maria, b G, mar Alfred LE BARGY, res Canada? Related to LE COURTOIS fam.
PRINCE, George, b Vale, G, mar Philippa Georgina DE BRODER, rem to Edmonton, to Vancouver, then to Racine, Wisc. His brother Jack also rem to England.
A1. Phyllis Maud, b 1909, mar Clarence Knudsen, the widow res Madison, Wisc. A dau d.y.
A2. Nellie Gaudin, b 1916, a widow, mar Arnold Kelm, res Racine. Son is mar, 3 chn.
PRINCE, from C.I. to Alpena, Mich., via Gaspe? (Directory, 1905)
PRITCHARD, from C.I. to Gaspe, listed by Betty Tardif
PRITCHETT, John in Greenspond, Bon. Bay, Nfld. 1860s (Rev. Hammond) Said to be from C.I.
PROPERT, in Nfld. Said to be from C.I. Cf PROPERT of J (Stevens)
PROWINGS, PROUINGS, Capt. from J in Nfld. (K. Mathews) This name also assoc with Robin firm.
PUDDESTER, PUDDISTER, variants of POINGDESTRE, (right fist, old French) of Western Bay, Nfld. 1770. From Jersey, C.I. early, to Nfld. (Hon. Harold G. Puddester, St. John's, Nfld.; Census; Mannion; Seary; G.W. Le Messurier)
PUDDESTER, or PODDISTER, George, planter of Broad Cove, Bay de Verde, 1816
PUDDESTER, John, planter of Northern Bay, 1818
PUDDESTER, Stephen, Blackhead, Bay de Verde, 1827
PUDDESTER, George, Harbour Grace, 1834
PUDDESTER, Thomas, St. John's, 1843
PUDISTA, Thomas, Kings Cove, 1871 (Lovell)
PUDISTER, George, Bay Bulls, 1871 (Lovell)
PUDDESTER, John, res Northern Bay early 1800s. His brother said to have rem to Bay Bulls. John mar Anne Whelan, sev chn:
A1. Mark, b 1855, poss the youngest, mar Sarah Sellers 1880
  B1. John Charles, b 1881, mar 1902, Mary Elizabeth Moores of Northern Bay, b 1880, 9 chn, fam res St. John's, Nfld.
    C1. Clayton Wright Wallace, b 1904, mar Susanna Pelley, he d 1949, 2 sons
    C2. Harold George, b 1905, mar Gwenyth Pratt, 1 son
    C3. Robert Percival, b 1907, mar Ann White, 1 son, 1 dau, res Moncton, N.B.
    C4. Stephanna Adelaide St. Clair, b 1909, mar Herbert Coombs, a son
    C5. Marjorie Jean, b 1911, d 1946, unmar
    C6. Arthur Clyde, b 1912, mar Gladys Lush. He d 1973, 2 sons, Corner Brook, Nfld.
    C7. Marion Beatrice, b 1915, mar Cyril Press, 1 son, 2 daus
    C8. Enid Clarice, b 1918, mar Lloyd Rose. Lloyd d 1946, a son, res Williamsport, Pa.

C9. Vivian Mary, b 1920, mar Joseph Josephson, 2 sons
B2. Ann   B3. Chesley   B4. Cecil, b ca 1896
PULLEN, in Nfld. (Seary) Cf POULAIN of C.I., also as PULEN, PULEYN, etc. (Stevens)
PULSFORD, Alfred Wm., b ca 1870 G, a helmsman, then shipmaster, working on ships from and to Sweden, France, the U.K. and Baltic. In 1912, rem to Hamilton, Ont. 8 chn, 2 res G. B St. Peter Port, to sea at age 11 on his father's cutter. "I must have been 18 or 19 at the time, and the 500 ton brig FAITH was plowing through a raging blizzard about 3 miles south of Sark..." Mr. Pulsford was helmsman. "Suddenly, the brig shuddered as she struck a notorious submerged rock known to mariners as BLANCHARD. There was a tearing of timbers and the FAITH began to founder bow first. The crew of seven had barely rowed clear in the ship's boats when the brig disappeared. Then it was discovered that the jollyboat, one of the two craft used to escape, was leaking. Mr. Pulsford tore the cravat from around his neck and plugged a hole with it. Then they began to bail...Just when it seemed that both boat and seamen would be lost, a French steam vessel appeared. We bailed like fury to keep afloat until the Frenchmen could rescue us." (R.L. Pulsford, Hamilton, Ont.)
PURCELL, at Portugal Cove, Nfld. 1793, said to be of C.I. origin (Rev. Hammond)
PYNN, Capt. from J in Nfld. (K. Mathews)
QUEENTON, at Griffon Cove, Gaspe, said to poss be QUINTON of J, qv
QUENAULT, from J to Nfld., early, changed name to CURNEW? (Shortis-Munn) See also Seary.
QUENALT, Henry, who was 22 in 1871, a J servant to James HENRY, qv, NB
QUERIPEL, Doris, of Bordeaux, Vale, G, mar 1926, Wilson Arthur FALLA qv
QUERIPEL, Daniel, b G, in Gaspe 1854, 1861 (Census) with Maria, Rachel, and John, b Gaspe
QUERIPEL, John Frederick, see Hilda Alice DOREY (Curtis Patterson, Harrington Harb., Que.)
QUERRIE, QUARRE?,Geo. b 1810-1871, mar Mary Laurens, b 1811-1872? of Hug fam of J, ca 1845, rem to Victoria Square, near Markham, Ont. with at least 2 chn. (Charles Querrie, Toronto, Ont)
A1. Mary, b ca 1840 J, mar Jack DE LA HAYE, had chn in Ontario
A2. George Joseph, b 1844 J, mar in Canada, Margaret Jane Cook, b 1854 of Scot-Eng. fam
    B1. Charles, b 1887, mar Edna Bell   B2. Hattie Marion, d 1959
A3. Philip, b Markham Twp., mar Jane ---?
    B1. Charles Laurens, b Vict. Square, Ont., famous Lacrosse player, Capt. Tecumseh Ont. team, involved in Hockey and the theatre, mar ---, who d 1956, no issue.
    B2. Harry, killed WWI. Grdau? Viva Waite
A4. Jack, mar, with chn   A5. Charles, d age 18
A6. Ann, school teacher, unmar, d 1936
QUERRY fam of Riviere Caplan, Que., origin unverified
QUERTIER, Dr. and Mrs. of G, were in Vict., BC 1940
QUERTIER, Alfred Hilary, b 1840 G, son of Hilary Q. of Pedvines Farm in G. To NZ 1860, ship KINNAIRD. Fourth ch, Hilary, rem to Canada, an inventor, returned to NZ 1932. (Doris Adams, Gore, N.Z.)
QUESNEL, Nicholas William, b 1872 St. Annes, Ald., son of Mary LE BER, qv, and --- QUESNEL. Rem to Toronto 1884, res there with LE BER fam. Worked for John Inglis and Son Co. Mar ---, a dau Marion mar --- Imrie. Poss other chn. (Margaret Imrie, Toronto, Ont.)
QUINN, see GALLICHAN, Gaspe
QUINN, in Nfld. (Seary) Cf QUINN of C.I.
QUINTON, 50 cards on this fam at St. John, NB Museum. Cf also QUEENTON.

QUINTON, Rex, b Nfld., mar Amanda JOURNEAU, qv, b 1928, 4 chn. See JOURNEAUX.
QUINTON, fisheries in N.B. (Seary) Poss J firm
QUINTON, in Nfld., at Redcliffe Island before 1806 (Seary) Cf QUENTIN, etc. of J (Stevens) RABASSE, fromGranville, France 1780.
RABASSE, REBASS, etc., C.I. surname in Maritimes Fisheries (J.H. Le Breton list) See REBASS, John, res Bathurst, NB.
RABBITS, in Nfld. (Seary) Cf RABASSE of J (Stevens)
RABEY, see first book of this series, THE QUIET ADVENTURERS, by Marion Turk   RABEY, SEE AMENDED CHART FOLLOWING THIS PAGE!
RABEY, David, b 1809 G, was in Gaspe Bay 1861, or poss his son? David mar 1835, Charlotte ROSE, qv. List of chn uncertain and incomplete?
A1. Marie Charlotte, b 1836, mar --- SIMON?
A2. Sophia, b 1839, mar Frank LE LACHEUR   A3. Susan, b 1840
A4. Mary Jane, b 1843, mar Adolphus LE TOUZEL and 2. Thomas LE LACHEUR
A5. David JANVRIN, b 1845, mar 1. --- MAUGER, and 2. Lucy Patterson
  B1. Stillman Patterson, b 1888, mar --- Hodgins
    C1. Frederick, b 1910, mar --- Miller, and 2. --- Hatfield, res Cornwall, Ont.
      D1. Roderick
    C2. Olive, b 1911, mar --- Coffin and 2. R. RABEY, res Fontenelle, Gaspe
      D1. Beatrice Coffin, b 1944, mar --- Jeanotte, res Gaspe
        E1. Wayne Jeanotte, b 1962   E2. Claude Jeanotte, b 1965
      D2. Thelma Coffin, b 1945, mar --- Bernie, res Forillon, Gaspe
        E1. Mark Bernie   E2. Mona Bernie   E3. Monica Bernie
      D3. Earl, mar --- Coffin, 3 chn: Linda, Stella, Darlene
  B2. John, mar Beatrice May Rabey, see Q.A., p. 30
  B3. Alice, mar --- Doggett, a dau mar --- Spinney, res Hunt's Pt., Queen's, N.S.
A6. Nicholas Mauger, b ca 1850?, mar Elizabeth MACHON. See Q.A. by Turk.
A7. Patty   A8. Thomas
A9. Maria, mar Simon LE TOUZEL, and 2. George LE TOUZEL
A10. William Anthony, mar Laura MACHON. See Q.A. by Turk.
RABEY, Mr. and Mrs. P.G., were in Victoria, BC from G (Vict. DAILY COLONIST, 1972)
RABEY, Marion, b Gaspe, in Gaspe Bay 1860 (Census)
RABEY, Nicholas, age 23 in 1871, b G (Census), mar Eliza GUIGNON, Gaspe Bay
RABIN, Capt. from G in Nfld. (K. Mathews) Poss same as ROBIN?, qv
RADFORD, from C.I. to Ont. and W. Canada
RAMIER, RAMIE, John, age 48, from J?, of C.I. fam, carpenter at Pt. Daniel, Que. 1871 (Census)
RANDALL, RANDELL, in Nfld. (Seary) Cf RANDELL of G
RATTIE, RATTUE, RATTEW, RETTIE, in Canada from C.I.? Cf REITILLEY, etc. of C.I. See QAAM by Turk.
RAULT, from G to St. Thomas, Ont. ca 1900
RAWLINS, Capt. from G in Nfld. (K. Mathews)
RAYMOND, in Nfld. (Seary) Cf REMON of J (Stevens)
READ, in Nfld. (Seary) Cf READ of J, 1749 (Stevens)
REBASS, John, res Bathurst, NB, mar --- Hotton of Barachois, Gaspe. A son, Jack, mar Sheila MARKS of Miscou, NB, res Bathurst, 2 chn. (Geo. De la Garde, Shippegan, NB)
REBIC, in Nfld. (Seary) Cf REBOURG of J (Stevens)
REBOURS, from C.I. in Maritimes Fisheries (J.H. Le Breton list) Cf REBOURG of J (Stevens)
RECCORD, RECORD, in Nfld. (Seary) Cf RICORDEAU of J (Stevens)

RABEY, David, Sr., b ca 1809 G mar Charlotte ROSE, 10? chn. Earlydata poss not verified. Later data from many descendants. See also p. 481.
A1. Marie Charlotte, b 1836 mar   SIMON.
A2. Susan, mar CharlesSimpson
A3. Mary Jane, mar Adolph LE TOUZEL & Thomas LE LACHEUR
A4. David Janvrin Rabey b 1845 mar 1.   MAUGER, and 2. Lucy Patterson.
   B1. Stillman Patterson Rabey b 1888 mar Stella Hodgins
      C1. Frederick R. b 1910 mar Ida Miller, and 2. Georgette Hatfield
         D1. Roderick Rabey, resCornwall,ONT.
      C2. Olive Pearl Rabey, b 1911, mar Kenneth R. Coffin and 2nd Russell C. Rabey, res Fontenelle,QUE
         D1. Beatrice Coffin, b 1944 mar Leo Jeannotte, GAspe,QUE
            E1. Wayne Jeannotte, b 1962 E2. Claude, b 1965
         D2. Thelma Coffin, b 1945, mar Velmont Bernie
            E1. Mark Bernie E2. Mona Bernie E3. Monica Bernie
         D3. Earl Rabey, mar Daisy Coffin
            E1. Linda Rabey E2. Stella Rabey E3. Darlene Rabey
   B2. John Rabey mar Beatrice May Rabey, qv.B8.
   B3. Alice Rabey mar Alex Doggett
      C1. _____Doggett, mar Louis Spinney, Hunts Pt.,QueenCo.,NS.
A5 Nicholas Mauger Rabey mar Elizabeth Sophia MACHON,1848-1935, dau of Philip J. MACHON of Gaspe & Eliz.PRIAULX, qv.
   B1.Beatrice,d.y.   B2. Selena/Lena, mar Alf. Tilly, no issue
   B3. Letitia, b 1875 mar C. Gooderham, farmer (Charles)
      C1. Charles Gordon Gooderham, b 1896, mar Janet Shirra
      C2. George, b 1899 d 1900
      C3. Clarence Gooderham, b 1901 mar Mary Burfield
         D1. Ross   D2. Edith   D3. Gordon
      C4. Letitia Mabel, b 1903 mar Walter Thornton
         D1. Betty, adopted, res Cooksville,ONT, mar   Smith.
      C5. Eva Gooderham, b 1905 mar Charles West   has Barbara, Ralph,Gary.
         D1. Charlene June West b 1930 mar Peter Saxton
            E1. Katerina Saxton b 1956
            E2. Paul, b 1958   E3. Robin Ann b 1962
         D2. Charles James West, mar Wilma Callen
            E1. Charles Adam West, b 1963 E2. Ellen Jane (adopted) West, b 1966.
      C6. William John Gooderham, b 1907, mar Alice Helm
         D1. Anthony Gooderham, mar, at least 4 chn
         D2. Paul Gooderham, mar, at least 6 chn
      C7. Dorothy, b 1909, and others, d.y.
   B4. Chloris Rabey, b 1876, mar Albert Gooderham, shipper
      C1. Lena Gooderham, b 1902, mar Albert Jones,Weston,ONT.
         D1. Marion Lena Jones, b 1924
      C2. Frank Gooderham, b 1904 mar Emma Webb, res Toronto,ONT
      C3. Herbert Gooderham, b 1906 mar Charlotte Cowper, res Toronto
      C4. Thomas Gooderham, b 1907, mar Isabell Smith
   B5. Ethel Rabey mar Edward Watkins, res Downsview, ONT
      C1. Ella Watkins, mar Nelson Stalford, a son and dau.
   B6. Florence Rabey, 1878-1957, mar Henry LE TOUZEL and 2nd. Coxon, res Rochester, NY. Chn by 1st mar.
      C1. Herbert LE TOUZEL, 1898-1959, mar ?
         D1. Dolores B. Le Touzel, b 1924 mar   Harding
            E1. Christine A. Harding, b 1950 mar   Mesiti
              3 chn: Rocco, Stephanie and Michael

　　　　　　　　E2. Barbara Ann Harding, b 1952　E4. Betty Delores
　　　　　　　　E3. Edward Wm.Harding, b 1954　　 Harding,b1955
　　　C2. Harold Austin Le Touzel b 1900
　　　　　D1. Betty Le Touzel b 1941
　　　C3. Roland Maynard Le Touzel, 1902-1968
　　　C4. Evelyn Ireine Le Touzel, 1903-1967, mar　　McCarthy
　　　C5. Kingsley R.Le Touzel, b 1905, mar　　　　res Rochester.
　　　　　D1. Kingsley A. Le　Touzel b 1942 mar ?
　　　　　　　E1.Timothy Allen, b 1965　E2.Kristin M. b 1967
　　　　　D2. Kathrine Florence Le Touzel b 1945 mar　　　Albert.
　B7. Clarence Rabey, 1885-1965, mar Minnie ? Olsen and Hilda Simpson.
　　　C1. Evelyn Eliz. Rabey, b 1910 mar Herbert Rex Coffin.
　　　　　D1. Walter Raymond Coffin, b 1930 mar Kathleen Coffin.
　　　　　　　E1. Debra Coffin, b 1955　E2. Gary, b 1956
　　　　　　　E3. Beverly b 1960　　　　E4. Donna b 1964
　　　　　D2. Elizabeth M. Coffin, b 1932 mar Stanford J. Stanley.
　　　　　　　E1. Terence Stanley b 1956　E2. Michael b 1961　QUE.
　　　　　　　E3. Jane L. b 1965　　　E4. Curtis b 1967
　　　　　D3. Marjorie Rhoda Coffin b 1934 mar Paul Foley, 7 chn
　　　　　　　E1. Barbara　E2. Mary Ellen　E 3. Pauline E4.Joseph
　　　　　　　E5. Elizabeth　 E6. John Foley　E7. Evelyn Foley
　　　　　D4. Vernon Coffin, b 1936 mar Joan LA COUVEE, res Murdochville, QUE
　　　　　　　E1. Heather Coffin　E2. Dale Coffin b 1959
　　　　　　　E3. Morgan Coffin b 1965　E4. Tracy Ann Coffin b 1967
　　　　　D5. Nona L. Coffin, b 1937 mar Wm. Burness,res CaledonE.ONT
　　　　　　　E1. Ronald Burness b 1961　E3. Linda Burness,b 1968
　　　　　　　E2. Sheila Burness b 1964
　　　　　D6. Murray H. Coffin, b 1939 mar Cora Clark
　　　　　　　E1. Monica Coffin b 1960　E2. Valery Coffin b 1966
　　　　　D7. Evelene Coffin, b 1941 mar Edw.J. Harvey, res Ottawa.
　　　　　　　E1. Edward J.Harvey Jr.b 1962
　　　　　　　E2. Kathryn M. Harvey b 1964
　　　C2. Letitia Jane Rabey, b 1911 mar Alfred Hunt, res Calgary,ALTA
　　　　　D1. Alfreda Jane Hunt, b 1939, mar 1.　　Haight, 2. Stan.
　　　　　　　Black, res　　　　Water Valley,ALTA
　　　　　　　E1. Cathy Mae Haight, b 1959　E2. Janet Lee Black,1968
　　　　　　　E3. Karen Joyce Black b 1970
　　　　　D2. Alan StevenHunt, b 1947
　　　C3. Nona Rabey, b 1913 Fontenelle,QUE
　　　C4. Ina R. Rabey, b 1914, d 1952, mar Ludger Blanchette
　　　　　D1. Harold Blanchette, b 1935 mar Angele Pelletier
　　　　　　　E1. Caroline Blanchette, b 1961 Laval, QUE
　　　　　D2. Albert Blanchette, b 1937, res Montreal
　　　　　D3. Louise Blanchette, b 1941 mar　　　Tremblay
　　　　　　　E1. Dominique Tremblay, b 1967
　　　　　D4. Angeline Blanchette, b 1945, mar Richard Robinson
　　　　　　　E1. Stevens Robinson, b 1967　Gros Morne, QUE.
　　　C5. Sydney Clarence Rabey, b 1916 mar Gladys Miller,resPeninsula.
　　　　　D1. Nora Ellen Rabey, b 1949 mar Vincent LaVail,Fontenelle.
　　　　　　　E1. Mona　.　　　, b 1970
　　　C6. Maynard Henry Rabey, b 1917 mar Pamela Shepherd,Pierrefonds.
　　　　　D1. Brent Rabey, b 1942
　　　　　D2. Grant Rabey, b 1945 mar Jane Patricia Wheeler
　　　C7. Willis Charles Rabey, b 1919, mar Sadie LANGLOIS,Brampton,ONT
　　　　　D1. Dennis Rabey b 1940　D2. Ross Rabey 1941-1962

```
            D3. Verna Rabey, b 1944 mar Wayne GAVEY, resFlorillon,QUE
                E1. Bradley Gavey b 1968
        C8. Kingsley Olson Rabey, b 1921 mar Annie McAfee,res Ottawa,QUE
            D1. Donna Rabey b 1948 mar Brian Cunningham
            D2. Deborah Rabey b 1949 mar James Farrell, res Ottawa.
        C9. Gerald Edgar Rabey, b 1922 mar Luella Davis, res CalgaryALTA
            D1. Lenwood G. Rabey b 1947 mar Patricia Kelly
            D2. Betty Lou Rabey, b 1949 mar         Shaw
                E1. Darren John Shaw, b 1968
    B8. Beatrice May Rabey, 1887-1958, mar John RABEY, bur Rosebridge,
        Gaspe, QUE.
        C1. John?   C2. Nona Rabey, b 1908, d.y.
        C3. Lena Rabey (Selena?), b 1910 d 1937, mar Alphus Hargrove
            D1. Eva Grace Hargrove, b 1932 mar Edward Brock
                E1. Violet Elaine Brock b 1942
                E2. Shirley Ann Brock b 1953  E3. Arnold L.Brock, 1956
            D2. Ruby Mae Hargrove b 1933 mar Hugh McGown
                E1. Hugh McGown b 1951  E2. Richard L.McGown, b 1952
                E3. Wendy Louise McGown, b 1954  E4. Patricia A.b 1956
        C4. Etta May Rabey, b 1913, mar Victor Marskell, res Islington,
            D1. Kenneth Marskell, b 1942 mar Sharon Thomas        ONT.
            D2. John Marskell, b 1947  D3. David Marskell, b 1955
        C5. DAvid G. Rabey, b 1915 mar Evelyn Mullin, resFarewellCove,
            He d 1989 Simcoe,ONT had 12 grandchn.                  QUE.
            D1. Eric Rabey b 1938 mar Betty Reader
            D2. Barbara Ann Rabey, b 1942 mar Arnold Jacques, and 2nd
                Lloyd Inwood of Nixon,ONT.
                E1. Melvin Jacques,1963  E2. Lana Jacques, b 1971
            D3. Hugh Rabey, b 1948 mar Lila West of Simcoe,ONT.
            D4. Wanda Rabey b 1949 mar Mervin Jacques, of Fontenelle,QUE
                E1. Connie Lee Jacques,1967  E2. Patsy Luella, b 1968
            D5. Janet Rabey b 1953 mar Jean-Guy Dion
            D6. Dwight Rabey, b 1955 mar Vera Ann      , res Delhi,ONT
        C6. Eileen Pearl Rabey, b 1918 mar Percy Coffin, resBronxvilleNY.
        C7. Lila Kate Rabey, b 1920 mar 1. Geo. Patterson,2. James
            Patterson.  Issue by 1st husband
            D1. Albert Patterson, b 1939 mar Elaine BECHERVAISE.
                E1. Stacy Shawn Patterson b 1969
            D2. Bruce Patterson, d.y.  D3. Kenneth Patterson, d.y.
            D4. Edith May Patterson, b 1947 mar Roy TURRIFF
                E1. Darlene May Turriff, b 1967
            D5. Beatrice Patterson, b 1948, mar Alfred Thompson, resMtl.
            D6. Ruth Olive Patterson, b 1957
        C8. Major C.Rabey, b 1922 mar Jean Lewis &      Patton,McKellar,
            D1. Kenneth Rabey b 1947 mar Dinah Fortier            ONT.
                E1. Michael James Rabey b 1971
        C9. Edward C. Rabey, b 1923, d.y.
        C10. Lloyd A. Rabey b 1930 mar Ethel Pratt
            D1. Eileen Pearl b 1953    D5. Lewis b 1956
            D2. Stephen Daryl b 1954   D6. Keith      D7. Kirk
            D3. Sandra Ann,b 1954,Twin D4. Linda b 1955
A6. Thomas Rabey ?
A7. William Arthur Rabey, b 1857, d 1911, 11 chn. Mar Laura MACHON,dau
    of Philip J.Machon and Elizabeth PRIAULX, qv.
    B1. William David, 1878-1881
    B2. Elsie Jane, 1880-1906, mar Daniel Rabey, a son Ralph d.y.
    B3. Arthur Wilbert Rabey b 1883 mar Alice Ann COMBER, 1883-1970 ,
        d Laval, QUE. 6 chn.
```

```
        C1. Mabel,b 1911, mar Fred Linnington, no issue
        C2. Ida, b 1914 mar Ralph Pink, 2. Guy ROSE, resMontreal
            D1.Richard,b1943, a son D2.Brian,b1948, 2 daus
        C3. Ellen Rabey,b 1918, mar Geo.Mitchell,sonsJames & David.
        C4. William Rabey b 1919 mar Rachel Gravel, res Montreal
            D1. William b 1948, has 2 daus.
            D2. Robert, b 1950, has dau, and a son who mar NoraRamsay
        C5. Ernest, b 1921, has son Douglas b 1956
        C6. Gordon Rabey b 1927 mar Barbara Liddell, 4 chn:
            D1. Catherine b 1957    D2. Richard b 1959
            D3. Lynn b 1963         D4. Robert b 1969
    B4. Thomas M. Rabey b 1885 mar Muriel Sarah McAfee
        C1. John William Rabey b 1911, dau Linda b 1952
        C2. Tessie Rabey b 1913, unmar, res Toronto, ONT
        C3. Cecil D. Rabey b 1915 res Rosebridge,QUE
        C4. Russell C. Rabey, b 1919 mar Olive Rabey Coffin,
        C5. Greta R. Rabey, b 1922, mar Harold Jewell, res Toronto,ONT
            D1. Douglas Jewell, b 1950
            D2. Beverly Jewell, b 1954    D3. James Jewell, b 1955
        C6. Annie Verna Rabey, b 1925, mar Chas. Burnie, resVirginia,ONT
            D1. Wayne Burnie, b 1956  D2. Judy Burnie b 1957
            D3. Brenda Burnie, b 1958 D4. Donna Burnie b 1965
        C7. Edison K. Rabey, b 1927, engraver
        C8. Marvin W. Rabey, b 1932, of Toronto,ONT
    B5. Percival Rabey, b 1887, d 1940, marCarrieSimpson, res Montreal.
        C1. Austin Rabey, b 1910
        C2. Elsie M. Rabey b 1912 mar Chas. Brien
            D1. Wayne Brien, b 1940 marSheila Wilkes
                E1. Maureen E. Brien, b 1966
                E2. Richard C. Brien b 1969  E3. Robert M. Brien b 1971
            D2. Myrna B. Brien, b 1944
        C3. Graeme G. Rabey, b 1915 d.y.
        C4. Lorne R. Rabey, b 1917 marNicole Bissette
            D1. Marilyn Rabey b 1966
        C5. Ola B. Rabey, b 1919 mar    Guy ROSE
            D1. Marilyn I. Rose b 1938 mar Roland Parris
                E1. Mark R. Parris, b 1958
                E2. Paul Parris b 1961  E3. Amanda Parris, b 1962
            D2. Gordon P. Rose, 1943-1960
            D3. Brenda Rose, b 1950 marFrank Kapasi
        C6. Chester W. Rabey b 1920 marEvelyn Coffin
            D1. Stephen C. Rabey b 1951    D4. Neil G. Rabey b 1960
            D2. Daniel P. Rabey b 1952     D5. Ruth K. Rabey b 1963
            D3. Keith A. Rabey b 1957
        C7. Merle R. Rabey, b 1922 mar Sydney Miller
            D1. Sydney A.Miller b 1949   D2. Anthony R. Miller b 1952
            D3. Harvey A. Miller, b 1955
            D4. Audrey Rabey, mar George Pullen, 3 sons
                Michael, John and Bruce Pullen
        C8. Ruth D. Rabey b 1927, d.y.
        C9. Leona L. Rabey, b 1929 mar Blair Bartlett.
            D1. Barbara Bartlett, b 1953  D2. Beverly, b 1953,twinD.Y.
        C10. June E. Rabey b 1931 mar GabrielMaioni
            D1. Terence Maioni, b 1949
        C11. Elmer W. Rabey, b 1932 mar Faye Burnett
            D1. Lorraine A. Rabey, b 1967
        C12. Murray G. Rabey b 1936, mar Lise _____?.
            D1. Joyce Rabey, b 1958
```

- B6. William Hampton Rabey, b 1889 d 1917 Vimy Ridge, France.
- B7. Elflida Julia Rabey, 1891-1949
- B8. Reginald James Rabey, 1893-1956, mar Jenny Guignion
  - C1. Marguerite Rabey, 1918-1949
  - C2. Reginald B. Rabey, 1919-1967 mar Muriel G. Forsyth
    - D1. Andrew Gary Rabey b 1947 mar   Day, res Calgary,AL.
    - D2. Reginald Donald Rabey b 1952
  - C3. Patricia Rabey, b 1925 mar Allen Goodman, St.Hilaire, QUE
    - D1. Derek R.Goodman,1958 D2. DAvid A.Goodman, b 1960
  - C4. Wendel James Rabey b 1927 mar Mary Eliz. Smyth
    - D1. Brian Rabey b 1956   D2. Diane Rabey b 1958
    - D3. Lynn Rabey b 1960
- B9. Gordon Peter Rabey, b 1896 mar Lily Guignion, Fontenelle,QUE
  - C1. Ralston Rabey, b 1922 mar Stephanie Cheop, b Manitoba.
    - D1. Wayne Rabey, b 1953
  - C2. Yorston Rabey, b 1926 mar Lucia Hadlock, Brossard, QUE.
    - D1. Donna Rabey, b 1958   D2. Graham Rabey b 1963
  - C3. Lesley Rabey, 1931-1948
  - C4. Vesta Rabey, b 1933 mar Gerald Smith, res Murdochville,QUE.
    - D1. Loren Smith, b 1959   D2. Linda Smith b 1963
- B10. Albert Garfield Rabey, b 1899 mar Edna Guignion, Gaspe,QUE.
  - C1. Ruby Rabey, b 1932 mar Elmer Mullin
    - D1. Brenda S. Mullin, b 1951 D2. Judy A.Mullin b 1953
    - D3. Jean Eliz. Mullin b 1953, twin
    - D4. Donald R.G. Mullin, b 1957
- B11. Donald Russell Rabey, b 1902, mar Edith Smith, res Hopetown,QUE
- A8. Martha Rabey, mar Charles LE TOUZEL and John LE LACHEUR
- A9. Sophia Rabey mar Frank LE CHOUR, prob. also LE LACHEUR
- A10. Maria Rabey, mar Simon and George LE TOUZEL, George's 2nd wife.

RECENT BOOKS ABOUT THE CHANNEL ISLANDS,
            (Courtesy of Harlene Palmieri, Cohoes, NY)

AHIER, Philip, JERSEY SEA STORIES, La Haule, Jersey, 1984
ANQUETIL, Audrey F., WARTIME MEMORIES, Landscape View, Les Augerez, St. Peter, Jersey
BACKHURST, Marie-Louise, FAMILY HISTORY IN JERSEY, 1991, available through CIFHS. See pages 120 and 124. (An excellent HOW-TO book)
BALLEINE, G.R., THE BAILIWICK OF JERSEY, revised by Joan Stevens 1970
            ALL FOR THE KING, Life Story of Sir Geo.CARTERET, 1976
            La Societe Jersiaise
BOIS, Elizabeth, H.M. DE STE. CROIX, Alan YOUNG, JERSEY THROUGH THE LENS AGAIN, 1989, La Societe Jersiaise.
BURGESS, Wilfred DeL., VICTORIAN VERSES AND RANDOM RHYMES, 286 Highland Drive, Jamestown, RI, USA 02835.
EDWARDS, GErald, EBENEZER LE PAGE, 1981, enjoyable fiction about a Guernseyman.
HILLSDON, Sonia, JERSEY WITCHES, GHOSTS AND TRADITIONS, 1987.
JOHNSTON, David E., THE CHANNEL ISLANDS, AR ARCHAEOLOGICAL GUIDE,1981
JEAN, John, JERSEY SAILING SHIPS, 1982, Phillimore, Sussex, GB.
            STORIES OF JERSEY'S SHIPS, 1987, La Haule, Jersey.
LAKE, Chris, THESE HAUNTED ISLANDS, Witchcraft in the Channel Islands, 1986, Redberry Press, St. John, Jersey.
LE MOIGNAN, Luke, GLIMPSES OF JERSEY'S PAST, 1990, La Haule, Jersey
LEMPRIERE, Raoul, JERSEY IN OLD PHOTOGRAPHS, A SECOND SELECTION, 1989.
            THE CHANNEL ISLANDS, 1990.
LE SCELLEUR, Kevin, CHANNEL ISLANDS RAILWAY STEAMERS, 1985, GB.
LLOYD, Beth, EXPLORE JERSEY, ITS COAST, COUNTRYSIDE AND HERITAGE. 1989.
MARETT, Robert, THE MARETTS OF LA HAULE, JERSEY, 1982, La Haule, Jersey.
PAGET-TOMLINSON, Kit, RAMBLING AROUND JERSEY, 1991.
PHILLIPS, Mary, TRACKS AND TALES, 21 Coastal Walks, BBC radio, jersey.
PLATT, Veronica, Colin & Anthony, IN A JERSEY GARDEN, 1990, La Haule,J.
ROBINSON, G.V.S., GUERNSEY, ISLANDS SERIES, 1977, Vancouver and Utah.
RYBOT, N.V.L., THE ISLET OF ST. HELIER & ELIZABETH CASTLE, 1986 (1934) La Societe Jersiaise.
SAXTON, Judith, THIS ROYAL BREED, 1991, Godd fiction about orchid growing and WWII in Jersey. NY,NY,USA.
STEVENS, Joan, VICTORIA VOICES, 1969, La Societe Jersiaise.
STEVENS, Charles, Jean Arthur and Joan Stevens, JERSEY PLACE NAMES, Vol.I, 1985, La Societe Jersiaise, Jersey.
STEVENS, Charles and Collette, JERSEY PLACE NAMES, Vol. II, 1985.
STEVENS, Joan, OLD JERSEY HOUSES AND THOSE WHO LIVED IN THEM, 1980, Vol.I, 1550-1700, Vol.2, 1700 on, La Societe Jersiaise.
THOMAS, Roy, LEST WE FORGET, Escapes from Jersey during WWII, 1992, La Haule, Jersey.
VIBERT, Ralph, MEMOIRS OF A JERSEYMAN, 1991, La Haule, Jersey
WALMESLEY, Gerard, A PEDESTRIAN TOUR THROUGH THE ISLANDS OF GUERNSEY AND JERSEY, 1992, Phillimore, Sussex, GB.
WILSON, Francis R., THE INFLUENCE OF THE CARTERET FAMILY IN THE ENGLISH CHANNEL ISLANDS, 1955, Thesis for M.A. at Occidental College Los Angeles, CAL.,USA.
Many other books about the Islands are available through bookstores in Jersey and Guernsey, through the Channel Islands Family History Society, and through the Societe Jersiaise, and Guernsey Society.
See pages 112 - 124.

REDMOND, in Canada from C.I.?, REDMAN, Capt. from J in Nfld.(K. Mathews)
REGULAR, in Nfld. (Seary) Cf REGLE, LE REGLE of J (Stevens)
REMON, James M., 1824-1904, from C.I., bur St. Pauls, Perce (GLF; Betty Tardif list)
REMON, James and Thomas C., J merchants at Pabos, Gaspe (GLF) A James Remon mar Alice Jane ANTHOINE, a dau, Daisy Annette, b 1890, mar Philip AMY, res Canada 1907, desc, see AMY.
REMON, Thomas, b J, age 42, merchant at Pabos 1871 (Census; Brochet)
REMON, Capt. and ship owner and merchant from J in Nfld. (K. Mathews)
REMON, Joseph M. and Thomas, b J, in Perce, Gaspe 1861 (Census)
REMPHREY, William, from Sark? in Saskatoon, Sask., 1900s (E. Le Boutillier)
REMO, RENO, Peter, in Little Le Poile, Nfld. 1860. Cf REMON of J or RENAUD, qv (Stevens)
RENAUD, from C.I. to Gaspe (K.H. Annett)
RENAULT, Mr. and Mrs. in B.C. from C.I.
RENAULT, Henry, Jack and Arthur, from late 1800s in some of the last sailing vessels settled in Canada. Related to MICHEL, qv. (Mrs. L. Renault, Montreal)
RENAULT, Peter John, b 1890 St. Helier, J, son of Peter Alexander R. and Mary Francoise Derrien, rem from J to Plymouth, Eng., then to Canada. Mar Bertha Rachel POINGDESTRE, dau of Mathew P. and of Annie Bertha BISSON, qv, 1887-1957. (H.J. Renault, North Bay, Ont.; Janet Renault, Hamilton, Ont.; Barbara Dixon, Burlington, Ont.; Eileen Crawford, Montreal, Que.)
A1. Annie Bertha, b 1911 J, mar 1937 Montreal, Henry G. Armstrong, b 1911, no issue
A2. Eileen Elsie, b 1913 Plymouth, Eng., mar 1937 Montreal, James S. Crawford, b 1908 Scotland, d 1973, res Montreal
  B1. Marilyn Gayle Crawford, b 1945, mar Owen Patrick Adams
    C1. Andrew Gordon Adams, b 1968 Montreal
A3. Harold John, b 1914 Canada, mar 1938 Toronto, Margaret Eleanor Bullett, b 1915, res North Bay, Ont.
  B1. Winona Eleanor, b 1939, mar Wm. Ashley Schorse, res North Bay, Ont.
    C1. Peter William Schorse, b 1961 C2. Timothy George Schorse b 1965
  B2. Douglas John, b 1941, mar Susan Wood, b 1944, 3 chn, res Barrie, Ont.
    C1. Paula, b 1969 C2. Jacqueline, b 1970 C3. Angela, b 1974
A4. Lillian Maud, b 1916, unmar, res St. Hubert, Que.
A5. Douglas Francis, d.y.
A6. Phyllis Joyce, b 1920, mar Clarence Brennen of Montreal, res Bramalea, Ont.
  B1. Neill Brennen   B3. Garry Brennen
  B2. Maureen Brennen   B4. Sharon Brennen
A7. Rev. Leslie Reginald, b 1922, mar in Montreal, Jenny Kerr, 3 chn, res Hamilton, Ont.
  B1. Wendy Janet, b 1956 Montreal   B3. Daniel Paul, b 1968,
  B2. Stephen Bruce, b 1968 Sarnia, Ont.   Brockville, Ont.
A8. Marguerite Gladys, b 1923, mar in Montreal, Ronald Webb, 4 chn, res Kitchener, Ont.
  B1. Carolyn Webb, b 1945, mar David Laskey, res San Diego, Calif
    C1. Lillian Marguerite Laskey, b 1974
  B2. Beverley Webb, b 1947, mar Wayne Williams
    C1. Richard Charles Zelenski, b 1971
  B3. Heather Webb, b 1951, res Montreal B4. Deborah Webb, b 1955
A9. Barbara Winnifred, b 1927, mar Montreal, Robert Dixon, 2 chn, res Burlington, Ont.

RENAULT 483
RENHUFF/RENOUF?, Nicolas, Quaker from G early 1800s,toPHILLY
  B1. Wayne Robert Dixon, b 1950, mar Lillian Grant, b 1952
    C1. Carrie Anne Michelle Dixon, b 1973
    C2. Richard Grant Dixon, b 1975
  B2. Lynn Barbara Dixon, b 1952, mar Wayne Douglas Vervoorn, b 1945
    C1. Clayton Wayne Vervoorn, b 1974 C2. Tara Lynn Vervoorn, b 1977
RENAULT, Wm., age 14, in Cose, Bon. Co., Gaspe 1871, apprentice blacksmith with SIMMONS, qv
RENOUF, George P. "I hired with Robin, Collas and Co. in 1896 as a carpenter at 1 pound per month for 18 months. We sailed from Jersey in April, 1896 about 12 young chaps, some as clerks, some farmers, and some carpenters. We went on board the brigatine ROBIN, Capt. LE RUEZ, and it took us 47 days from Jersey to Paspebiac. We had better sleeping quarters than Mr. Romeril, as we had bunks in the fo'c'sle but the food was the same hard tack, with a few weevils in some of the monster biscuits and fat pork, some rough weather and fog but all healthy when we landed. I weighed codfish at Little River West that summer and was sent to Perce as carpenter in the winter. In the fall of 1897 I went home on the FANNY BRESLAUER, Capt. LE DAIN. We had a very rough trip, lost two masts the first night out from Paspebiac and had to throw two-thirds of the cargo overboard, tubs of dry codfish, then man the pumps in two hour shifts night and day to keep her afloat; no gasoline pumps in those days. We arrived home on Christmas Eve. In the spring of 1898 I hired again for another 18 months at 1 pound, 15 shillings per month; left Jersey on the ROBIN, Capt. BECQUET, in April and made a quick trip, 35 days. In the fall of 1899 instead of going home, I saved enough out of my wages to buy a ticket to Winnipeg, where I arrived with two dollars, got a job on a railroad bridge gang, worked in the bush that winter, came to work on the Canadian Northern RR in the spring of 1900, got a homestead, 160 acres in Swan River Valley in the fall, and have lived here ever since, except for a few trips to Jersey." (Jersey Society in London Bulletin, January, 1953)
RENOUF. "My mother's father was Capt. LE SEELLEUR and my father's father, was Capt. RENOUF, both sailing ship captains." (Frank G. Renouf, St. Boniface, Man.)
RENOUF, from J to Cape Breton
RENOUF, Ernest John, b St. Sampson?, G, mar Helene ROBIN, rem to Hamilton, Ont. ca 1920, 8 chn b G. (Kathleen Souder, Whitesville, NY)
  A1. Adele, b G, remained there
  A2. Kathleen, b 1906, mar Ralph Souder, b 1906, who d 1975. She res Whitesville, NY.
    B1. Jean Souder, b 1929, mar Stanley Paluszak
    B2. Roya Souder, b 1930
    B3. Nannette Souder, b 1932, mar Wm. McNeill
    B4. Darcy Souder, b 1936   B5. Gerald Souder, b 1937
    B6. Joel Souder, b 1937, twin
    B7. Penny Anne Souder, b 1941, mar Edw. Dyttmer
    B8. Judith Kay Souder, b 1943, mar J. Rautenstrauch
RENOUF, Nancy, to B.C., mar Henry Anderson, late 1800s
RENOUF, Philip, son of Philip R. and Agnes NOEL, b St. Helier. This fam related to PALLOT fam, a cousin being Owen PALLOT, res Calif.
RENOUF, Agnes Maude, b 1903, St. Helier, J, mar in Hamilton, Ont., Alfred G. Adams, b 1902 (Alfred Adams, Hamilton, Ont.) Sister of Philip, above.
  A1. Marie Eva Agnes Adams, b 1922, mar --- Hutchinson, a pilot, and 2. Norman Adams, bricklayer
  A2. Arnold Renouf Adams, b 1925, mar Jane McPetrie, b 1926, 4 chn

    B1. Janet Gail Green, b 1946, 2 daus
    B2. Thomas Wayne Adams, b 1949, mar Sandra ---, b 1950
    B3. Gordon Adams, b 1952   B4. Scott Adams, b 1961
  A3. Alfred Philip Adams, b 1927, mar Lillian Varley, b 1929
    B1. Bonnie Victoria Gravelle, b 1948, 3 chn
    B2. Robert Craig Adams, b 1951, mar Sharon ---
RENOUF, Dr. Charles, of Nfld., mar Anne ---. "My great grandfather was a corsair doing business between St. Malo and the Channel Islands."
  A1. Charles H., mar Maude ---
    B1. a son, res Berwick-on-Tweed, N.S.
RENOUF, Thomas, in St. John's, Nfld. 1778 (Seary) Prob from J (G.W. Le Messurier)
RENOUF, H.P., d 1959 Perce, wife d 1958 Perce. He was agent for Robin, Jones & Whitman. Hug. SEE HERBERT PHILIP BOTTOM OF PAGE.
RENOUF, in Nfld., Capt., agent, and merchant from J (K. Mathews) Current Stephenville, Nfld.
RENOUF, from C.I., res at Grande Riviere, Gaspe (GLF) Francis Jean R. at Gr. Riv.
RENOUF, Sara, 1830-1910, wife of John A. Dobson?, 1827-1911, bur St. Andrews, New Carlisle, Que. (GLF)
RENOUF, Charles, in Gaspe Militia 1850s
RENOUF, Philippe, signed the Gaspe Petition of 1820
RENOUF, 2 fams from G to Victoria, BC ca 1910
RENOUF, Edward M., b G, mar Alice M. GAUDION, qv, rem to Montreal 1920 then to Sydney and Victoria, BC
RENOUF, Thomas, from G, a bro of above, to Revelstoke 1907, returned to G 1937
RENOUF, Ralph, b 1886 St. Helier, J, d St. Sav., J 1954. Had rem to NY City 1912. Mar Florence Eugenie LUCE, b St. Helier 1888, d there 1937. This couple retired to J in 1931 (related to Helen Juby, qv) (J.P. Renouf, Don Mills, Ont.)
  A1. John Philip, b NY City 1917, mar Esme Patricia MOLLET, qv.
    B1. Andrew John, b 1948 England   B4. Anne Romaine, b 1955 Tor.
    B2. Simon Mollet, b 1950 Berkshire, Eng. B5. Patrick Joseph, b 1963,
    B3. Catherine Mary, b 1953 Toronto   Toronto
  A2., 3, and 4. half bros Ralph, Michael, and half sister Mary, all b England
RENOUF, in Quebec, see pp. 17-22, BULLETIN DES RECHERCHES HISTORIQUES, 1939
RENOUF, John Sr. and Jr. and Philip, traders and fishermen, Sandy Pt. Nfld. 1870s (Lovell)
RENOUF, George of J, to Canada 1897, M.L.A. for Minitonas, Man.
RENOUF, Philip, of J, rem to Hamilton, Ont., related to LE BOYER fam. A son, Victor.
RENOUF, Clement E., b J, to Vancouver, BC after 1880, in business, RENOUF AND NICHOLLS. Alderman in Victoria, customs officer in Vancouver and Yukon, retired, d 1924 Oakland, Calif. A sister mar A.O. McCrae of Vancouver, BC
RENOUF, Joseph, b ca 1865 St. Helier, J, to Victoria, BC. Retail grocer at 1501 Douglas St., later on Gladstone Ave. Went into the customs service, mar ---, a son Clifford and two daus, Mrs. B. Lindsey and Mrs. Earl W. Farr, both of Seattle, Wash. D 1926 Victoria, age 61, bur Ross Bay Cem. (Luce)
RENOUF, Walter, b J, bro of Joseph, rem to Victoria, BC 1800s. Another bro, Frank, rem to Sydney, Aust. Three sisters remained in J.
RENOUF, Herbert Philip, b J, to Perce as apprentice for Robin firm mar Ethel Scott Lindsay,   , bur St. Pauls, Perce, d 1959 Paspebiac.

RENOUF, Mary, b Canada and Hugh, b J, in Gaspe 1861 (Census)
RENOUF, Peter, Pierre, b J, son of Pierre and of Anne LE BRUN, mar 1775 J, was apprenticed to someone in N.S. late 1700s (Jersey Society records) A Peter, b J, in 1820 had been 20 yrs. in Cape Breton, the last two at Mabou, where he asked for land, granted. (PANS) He was a trader, and by 1811 had 8 chn in Arichat.
RENOUF, Nelson, b 1906, son of Philip James R. and Alice Mary LE COULLIARD of Trinity, J, mar Lucille R. Lapointe, a son Richard, b 1945, mar Shirley Dross, rem to Ontario?
RETTIE, RETILLEY, etc. RETTIE, Samuel, 1818-1883, b Pictou, NS, son of John R. and Christine GALLIE, qv. Samuel was M.L.A. of NS. RETILLEY, to Ohio early 1800s from G. (Fergusson's MLA DIRECTORY)
REVANS, Capt. from J in Nfld. (K. Mathews)
REVENU, Capt. from J in Nfld. (K. Mathews)
REYNARD, REGNARD, ship owner from J in Nfld. (K. Mathews)
REYNOLDS, in Nfld. (Seary) Cf RENAULT, RENAUD of C.I. also (Stevens)
RHODDA, Minetta, wife of Thomas LE CAIN in LE CAIN GEN. Cf RODDA
RICH, William and Nicholas in PEI, 1841 Census, from C.I.?
RICH, in Nfld. (Seary) Cf LE RICHE of J (Stevens) Arthur in Salmon Cove 1805 (E.R. Seary)
RICHARD, Thomas, b G, rem to Anse au Griffon, Gaspe, mar Marguerite RICHARD, who d before 1848. Thomas was son of Thomas BICHARD of G and Marguerite. Note change of surname by Thomas Jr. from BICHARD to RICHARD. (Frank Remiggi)
A1. Thomas, bp 1804, b 1796, mar Cap des Rosiers, Gaspe, Helene Henley, bp 1828, res Mont Louis. She was dau of Patrick H. and Mary Anne ARBOUR of Cap Rosier.
   B1. Thomas, b 1843, mar 1873, Georgianna Letourneau, dau of Jerome L. and Louise Pelletier
   B2. Marie Jane, bp 1845, mar 1869, --- Daraiche
   B3. Heloise, bp 1847
   B4. Jean Chrysostome, bp 1850   B5. Charles, bp 1852
   B6. Andre, bp 1855, mar 1873 Magdaleine Daraiche, bp 1852 Riv. Madeleine, dau of Jos. D. and Euphrosine BOND
   B7. Marie Anne, bp 1858, mar 1873, --- Laflamme
RICHARD, RICHARDS, from C.I. to Gaspe and the Maritimes (J.H. Le Breton list)
RICHARD, RICHARDS, John and Isaac, in Port de Grave, Nfld. 1782, from C.I.? Cf RICHARD, RICARD of J (Stevens) RICHARDS, Abraham in Rock Cove 1775 (Seary)
RICHARDSON, Jos. and Thomas in Brigus 1803 (Seary) Cf RICHARDSON of J (Stevens)
RICHARDSON, Abraham of J, refused to obey council orders, and in 1738 rem to Kingston, Jamaica (Soc. Jers. Bull., 1897-1901)
RICHARDSONS, in Alpena, Mich., poss from Gaspe late 1800s

RICHARDSON, tradesman from G in Nfld. (K. Mathews)
RICHARDSON, Lawford M., b J, Bank Mgr in Vancouver or Vict., BC 1900s
RICHARDSON, John, b G, in Gaspe 1861 (Census) with Charlotte, b Canada
RICHARDSON, Marcelline of J fam, second wife of Edmond Duguay, b ca 1860, res N.B. (Robichaud)
RICHARDSON, Joseph and Thomas in Brigus 1803 (Seary)
RICKABY fam, said by Mrs. Eliz. Rose Hammond Cook to have gone from France to Guernsey, then to N.A. Huguenots. Thought to have fled from France 1500s, also rem to Ireland. (Wm. O. Goss, Wenham, Mass.)
RICKER, Noah, son of George R. of J, captured by Indians in N.H.,

taken to Canada, where is said to have become a Catholic priest. (New England Register, Wentworth, Bell, Coleman, Noyes, Turk, etc.)
RICO, C.I. surname connected with Robin firm in Paspebiac and with town of New Carlisle, Que. (Que. Prov. Arch.) Poss another form of RICOU? of C.I.
RIDEOUT, RIDOUET, John, in Bonavestia Bay, Nfld. 1860s, said to be of C.I. origin (Rev. Hammond)
RIEVE, from J to Cape Breton, poss same as RIVE, qv.
RIOU, Channel Islanders in Maritimes Fisheries (J.H. Le Breton list)
RIPLEY, Edith Amelia, b G?, mar Charles Henry LE COURTOIS, qv.
RITHET, C.I. in B.C.?
RIVE. Those below may all have been related, and may have come from St. Brelade, J. There are said to have been three RIVE bros in J in the late 1800s, b St. Helier. Desc scattered to Ontario, BC, NB, and New Zealand.
RIVE, Philip?, to N.Z. A desc rem to Calgary, Alta. but also had lived in Salisbury, Rhodesia. Another desc, Thomas Rive, Prof of Music, res Wellington, N.Z.
RIVE, ---, of J, mar Margaret THOREAU, qv, rem to New York. Desc, Leonard Kleinfield, in Forest Hills, NY.
RIVE, Peter, of J, said to have settled in Gaspe, there in 1861 (Census; Cent. Bklt.) Another settled in Caraquet, NB. A Harry, res Moncton and Caraquet. Josephine and Albert res Caraquet. A James R. was witness to the mar of Wm. and Mary Ann BEATTY in 1810, N.B. (Hist. of Caraquet, by Ganong)
I. Elias, son of Elias?, b 1871 St. Helier, J, rem to Guelph, Ont. ca 1896. Mar Edith LE FEUVRE, qv, in St. Heliers. He d Canada 1954. To Vancouver 1909. (Dorothy Rive, Chilliwack, BC)
  A1. Alfred, b 1897, d Ottawa 1970, High Commissioner to N.Z. and Ambassador to Ireland. Mar Harriet Hopkinson of Manchester, Mass. Harriett res Ottawa.
    B1. Harriet, res Seattle, 3 chn B3. Edith Jane
    B2. Elias B4. John
  A2. Charles, b 1899, d 1975 N. Vancouver, BC, mar Kathleen Elliott, widow
    B1. Elliott, b 1929 Vancouver, mar with 5 chn
    B2. Douglas Edwin, mar, res Winnipeg, Man., 2 chn
  A4. Edwin, d.y.
  A5. Gertrude, b 1906, mar Herbert DITCHBURN, qv, b 1906 G, res Agassiz, BC
    B1. Ray Ditchburn, res Wellington, N.Z., 5 chn
    B2. Lloyd Ditchburn, res Kamloops, BC, 4 chn
    B3. Ann Ditchburn, mar R. Parent, res Chetwynd, BC, 3 chn
II. Edward, b J, rem to Toronto, Ont., bro of Elias above, poss desc in Brantford?
III. Henry, b ca 1878, res Victoria, BC, mar Edith Henry.
IV. Louise, b 1878, twin?, d 1966, unmar
V. Mary, d ca 1904 in Guelph, Ont.
ROBBINS, Nicholas, a shoemaker in G early 1600s, emigrated to Cambridge, Mass in 1634, then rem to Duxbury, Mass 1638. Mar Ann ---. Later, his desc were UEL's and emigrated to Yarborough, N.S. 1760s. A son, John, mar Jehosabeth Jourdaine. (Blanche Dickover, Tenmile, Oregon; see Turk, QAAM) More re this large fam from Mrs. W. Nagle, Yarmouth, N.S. and Mrs. John Wade, Llano, Texas.)
ROBBINS, ROBINS, RABIN, merchants from G in Nfld. (K. Mathews)
ROBBINS, Fisheries in N.B.
ROBERGE, George, from C.I. to Canada, 1900s (Le Huray, Middleton, NY)

ROBERT, from C.I. to Nfld. (Seary) "Bay Roberts was originally Bay de Roberts, the Roberts being a Jersey family." (H.W. Le Messurier)
ROBERT, Martin, b ca 1832 St. Martin, G, son of Martin and Rachel R., mar 1853, Marguerite GUILBERT, qv, b ca 1830 or 1823, dau of Nico. GUIBERT or GUILBERT, and --- VARIOUF of Forest, G. Marguerite came to Canada 1874, a year after her husband. He was a gardner, d 1904, age 72. She d 1911, age 81, 9 chn. (Hazel Parkes, London, Ont.) Part of fam uses ROBERTS.
A1. Martin, b 1854 G, d 1925, mar Susan Lagden, b England, 1856-1937
  B1. Charles, b 1886 London, Ont., d 1918 Vancouver, BC, mar Ruby Gray
    C1. Vivian Irene Bessie, b 1911 Vancouver, BC, d 1963. Mar Leslie Revel, 2 adopted sons, Keith and George Revel.
    C2. Charles Martin, b 1914 Vanc., res Brampton, Ont. 1976, mar Helen McClure
      D1. William Gordon, b 1949 Brampton, mar Karen Bridgen
    C3. William Lorne Robertson Roberts, b 1916 Vanc., mar Ethel Porter
      D1. Betty, b 1940, teacher, traveler
      D2. William Martin, b 1949 Vancouver
        E1. Cari-Anne, b 1969   E2. Cindy, b 1972
  B2. Isabella, b 1888, mar 1912, Chester Smith, d 1970, 3 chn
    C1. Gladys Jean Smith, b 1914, mar 1937, Albert Hilary Bartley 5 chn
      D1. Richard Paul Bartley, b 1940, mar 1960, Dorothy Jean Cartright, 5 chn
        E1. Michele Colette Bartley, b 1960
        E2. Steven Paul Bartley, b 1964
        E3. Linda Ruth Bartley, b 1966   E5. Richard Kevin Bartley,
        E4. Angela Coleen Bartley, b 1968   b 1971
      D2. Marian Yvonne Bartley, b 1943, mar 1969, Gary MacKinnon
        E1. Meleta Michele MacKinnon, b 1971
      D3. Patricia Anne Bartley, b 1947, mar 1963, Blaine Jefferson
        E1. Kevin Max Jefferson, b 1965 E3. Lianna Jefferson, b 1971
        E2. Keith Jefferson, b 1969   E4. Trevor Jefferson, b 1973
      D4. Arnold Carl Bartley, b 1947, mar Janice Thompson, 1970
        E1. Andrea Louise Bartley, b 1971 E2. Sandra Bartley, b 1975
      D5. Frances Ruth Bartley, b 1948, mar 1968, John Sorensen
        E1. Christine Frances Sorensen, b 1968
        E2. Dena Louise Sorensen, b 1974
    C2. Vaughn Robert Smith, b 1915 Toronto, mar 1940, Helen Seipp
      D1. Paul Ross Smith, mar
    C3. Kenneth Frank Smith, b 1918, mar 1939 London, Ont., Mildred Glaholm, 5 chn
      D1. Stephen Wayne Smith, b 1944 London, mar 1969, Marion Joyce Potter, 3 chn
        E1. Samuel Joseph Chester Smith, b 1970 London, Ont.
        E2. Matthew Stephen William Smith, b 1975
        E3. Shelley Anne Smith, b 1977?
      D2. Judith Anne Smith, b 1946, mar 1973, Ross Douglas Hofstetter
        E1. Todd Smith Hofstetter, b 1968 London, Ont.
        E2. Alison Faye Hofstetter, b 1974
        E3. Nathan Philip Hofstetter, b 1976
      D3. Barbara Jean Smith, adopted, b 1949 Nfld., mar 1973, Paul McCaffrey, 2 chn
        E1. Jacob McCaffrey, b 1973 E2. Tina J. McCaffrey, b 1976
      D4. Ross Muttart Smith, adopted, b 1951
      D5. William Joseph Smith, b 1954, London, Ont.
  B3. Bessie, b 1890, d 1974, mar Charles Barker
    C1. Betty Barker, b 1924, mar 1942, Charles Siegrist, res Colpoy

Bay, near Wiarton, Ont.
  D1. Eric Siegrist, b 1944
  D2. Joel Siegrist, b 1949, mar 1973, Cheryl Hibbert
    E1. Shawn Elizabeth Siegrist, b 1974
    E2. Kathleen Joan Siegrist, b 1976
B4. Martin, b 1891, d 1911 hunting accident, age 22
B5. Eunice, b 1893 London, d 1929 Toronto, mar Henry William Plumridge
  C1. Ruth Isabelle Plumridge, b 1919 Toronto, d 1976 Sudbury, Ont., mar 1946, George Andrew Martin
    D1. Sandra Ann Martin, b 1950, mar 1970 Sudbury, Ont., Thomas Trainer
      E1. Sean Trainer, b 1972
    D2. Susan Martim, b 1955, mar 1975 Oakville, Ont., Michael Dorion
      E1. Monica Ruth Dorion, b 1976
  C2. Grace Ethel Plumridge, b 1921, Toronto, mar 1947 London, Orval Hilliard Ternan
    D1. William Leslie Ternan, b 1951 Galt, Ont., mar 1974, Kitchener, Margaret Ann Bursey
      E1. Laura Grace Ternan, b 1977
    D2. Muriel Dianne Ternan, b 1954 Galt, Ont.
  C3. Helen Irene Plumridge, b 1922 Toronto, mar 1950, Vanc., BC, James Albert Stewart
    D1. Robert James Stewart, b 1953 Vancouver, BC
    D2. Margaret Helen Stewart, b 1957 Redwood City, Calif.
B6. Frank, b 1896, d 1898
B7. Gladys, b 1898, mar Charles Petrie 1918, res Grafton, Mass.
  C1. Donald Charles Petrie, b 1920, mar June Martha Moffitt, b 1922
    D1. Brooke Susan Petrie, b 1949, mar John David Sullivan, b 1948
      E1. Shane Patrick Sullivan, b 1973
    D2. Christopher Scott Petrie, b 1953, mar Jane Brennon, b 1954
      E1. Jason Scott Petrie, b 1972
      E2. Essek Brennon Petrie, b 1975
    D3. Laurel Linna Petrie, b 1956
  C2. Robert William Petrie, b 1924, mar Mary Joyce Vickers, b 1924
    D1. Joy Elizabeth Petrie, b 1951, mar David Blanchet 1975
      E1. Elizabeth Joy Blanchet, b 1977
    D2. David Christopher Petrie, b 1953, mar Audrey Lee Seravo, 1977
    D3. James Green Petrie, b 1957   D4. Rebecca Anne Petrie, b 1964
  C3. Edgar Harold Petrie, b 1927, mar 1951, 1. Nancy Gordon, b 1929, and div 1973. Mar 2. Barbara ---, 1974.
    D1. Caroline Elizabeth Petrie, b 1953, mar Kevin Smith 1974
      E1. Brian Michael Smith, b 1975
    D2. Martha Susan, b 1953, twin, mar Gene Tyre
    D3. Leslie Gail Petrie, b 1956, mar ---, two daus
    D4. Charles David Petrie, b 1957, mar Nancy ---
    D5. Lois Anne Petrie, b 1959, mar, a dau D6. Janet Lynn, b 1961
A2. Thomas H.L., b 1855 La Fosse, St. Martin, G, mar Eliza BROWN 1975, Kingston, Ont., res London, Ont., 12 chn
  B1. Nellie Roberts, b 1877, mar Harry Dyson, b 1877
    C1. Marguerite Dyson, b 1900, mar 1924, Harry Stabler, res London, Ont.
      D1. Donald Garthwaite Stabler, b 1925, res Barrie, Ont., mar Floris Shenck, 2 daus
        E1. Cheryl Anne Stabler, b 1952, mar Bob Flook
        E2. Pamela Marie Stabler, mar Richard Buchanan
    C2. Verna Dyson, b 1903, mar Donald Soper, a dau
      D1. Donna Soper, mar Gene Pineo, 2 sons, Steven and Larry Pineo

C3. Henry Dyson, b 1905, mar Marguerite CORDERY of St. Thomas, Ont., res London, Ont.
   D1. Virginia Dyson, b 1930, mar James Dale, res Belmont, Ont.
      E1. Marilyn Dale, mar John Willsey, res Belmont, Ont.
         F1. Alison Willsey, b 1976   F2. April Lynn Willsey, b 1977
      E2. Jeffrey Dale   E3. Vicky Dale   E4. Scott Dale, b 1963
   D2. Karen Dyson, b 1940, mar and div. --- Evans, a son, John Evans
C4. Charles Dyson, b 1906, mar Dorothy Robinson, res St. Thomas Ont.
   D1. Barbara Dyson, b 1936, mar Ed. Hearn, res Exeter, Ont.
   D2. Heather Dyson, b 1944, mar Fred. Sweeney, res London, Ont.
      E1. Jeff Sweeney, b 1967   E2. Erin Sweeney, b 1974
B2. Ernest, b 188-, mar 1. Martha ---, and 2. Mary Malloy
   C1. Louis, optometrist, res Detroit, Mich.
   C2. George, wanderer, saxophonist, res Detroit
B3. Winnifred, d.y. of T.B.
B4. Pansy, b 1900, d 1945 Windsor, Ont. Mar George Kirk, d early leaving a large fam. George d Wallaceburg, Ont.
   C1. George William Kirk, b London, Ont., mar Leona RICHARDSON
      D1. Gary Kirk, b 1940, mar Georgina Anderson 1968
         E1. Gary Kirk, b 1969   E2. Michael Kirk, twin to Gary
      D2. Vonnie Ann, b 1948, mar Arthur Ramsay 1973
      D3. Richard Ross Kirk, b 1952, mar Gayle Martin 1974
   C2. Woodrow W. Kirk, b 1918 London, Ont., mar 1941 Lincoln Park, Mich., Jean Meggison
      D1. Randolph Michael Kirk, mar Jean Klitte 1970
      D2. Raymond Ward, unmar
      D3. Mary Jeanette, mar James Bargert, a son Scott, b 1969?
      D4. Robert Douglas Kirk, mar Eva Matigian, a son, Jason Douglas, b 1970s
      D5. Susan Rae Kirk, mar Wayne Ambrose
   C3. Virginia, mar twice, mar 3. Ron McRaild
   C4. Herbert Kirk, mar Jean ---, 4 chn
   C5. Robert Kirk, mar June ---, 6 chn
      D1. Jimmy Kirk, mar, 1 ch   D3. Nancy Kirk   D5. Mack Kirk
      D2. Patsy Kirk   D4. Bobby Kirk   D6. ?
   C6. Myrtle Kirk, mar Walter Ivey, 2 chn
      D1. David Ivey   D2. Rusty Ivey
   C7. Margaret Kirk, twin of Myrtle, mar Fred. Seed, 2 chn
      D1. Jeannie Seed, mar, 2 chn   D2. Jane Seed, mar, 1 ch
   C8. Dennis Kirk, mar, St. Thomas, Ont., Caroline ---, 2 chn
      D1. Denise Kirk, b 1968   D2. Benjamin Kirk, b 1970
   C9. Edward Kirk, b 1939, mar Patricia ---, 4 chn
   C10. Ida Kirk, mar, 2 chn
   C11. Sandra Lee Kirk, b 1943, mar, 2 chn, plus twins
B5. Chesley, a wanderer, residence unknown
B6. Thomas, mar twice, no issue known, res Buffalo, N.Y.
B7. Alfred, Frederick or Fred, res Montreal, mar twice, a son and dau
B8. Edward Martin, b 1890, d 1920, mar Mary Katherine Gatecliff
   C1. Evelyn, b 1912, mar 1. Ruben Smith, and 2. James ROBERTS
      D1. Donald Smith   D2. Sherry Roberts
   C2. Edward Martin, b 1920, mar Mildred Edith Kilpatrick
      D1. Edward Martin, mar Judy Mitchell, res Bright's Grove, Ont.
         E1. Mary Kate, b 1964   E2. Heather Shannon, b 1970
      D2. Lorne Milton, mar Leslie Speight, Kenora, Ont., res Thessalone, Ont.
   C3. Marjorie, mar Albert Waterman, a son, Kenneth Waterman
   C4. Frances Rita, mar 1. Alfred Waterman, and 2. Ed. Green

      D1. Robert Waterman
         E1. Ann Marie Waterman   E3. William Waterman
         E2. Barbara Jean Waterman
  B9. Harry, rem to New Orleans, U.S.
  B10. Myrtle May, b 1891, mar Thomas William Pepler
      C1. Winnifred, b 1912, d.y.
      C2. Thomas Albert Pepler, b 1914, d 1977, mar Alma Barns
         D1. Thomas Harvey Pepler, mar Betty June Scott, 2 sons
            E1. Thomas Scott Pepler   E2. Steven Michael Pepler
         D2. Margaret Joan Pepler, mar David Jackson
            E1. David Jackson, Jr.   E2. Tracy Alma Jackson, b 1977
      C3. Robert Douglas Pepler, mar 1. Irene Ellis, div., and 2. Marjorie MacDonald who had 3 chn. Robert and Irene had 2 chn; Robert Douglas and James.
      C4. Donald James Pepler, mar Kathleen Tupholme, a dau
         D1. Kathleen Iris Pepler, mar 1. Stephen McLeod, and 2. Wm. Landry
            E1. Stephen McLeod, d.y. in accident E2. Deborah McLeod
      C5. Shirley Gretta Pepler, mar Allen Lynn Redhead
         D1. William Allen Redhead, mar Rosemary McAuley
            E1. Carry Lynn Redhead   E2. Renee Marie Redhead
         D2. Glen Paul Redhead
      C6. Elda Marguerite Pepler, mar John Stewart Wright, no issue
  B11. Margaret, mar Kenneth Penoyer, Grand Rapids, Mich.
      C1. Kenneth Penoyer, res Wyoming, Mich., mar Olga Hugen of Seattle
         D1. Kent Penoyer D2. Kimberley Penoyer D3. Karen Penoyer
A3. Albert Edward, b 1856 St. Martin, G, mar Mary Emilie CAVANAGH, 1867-1926. Albert was a baker in London, Ont. 1912.
  B1. Minnie Emilie, b 1885, d 1965, mar Thomas Edward White, 1883-1948, 3 chn
      C1. Vera Dorothy White, b 1906, mar Arthur Saull, res Ferndale, Mich
         D1. Thomas Arthur Saull, b 1936, mar 1963, Barbara Nicoll, res Denver, Colo., 2 chn
            E1. David Arthur Saull, b 1965 E2. Michael James Saull, b 1965
         D2. Sharon Ruth Saull, b 1940, mar 1964, Thomas Dale Sawyers, res Royal Oak, Mich.
            E1. Ross Sawyers, b 1967   E2. Paul Sawyers, b 1969
      C2. Albert Edward White, b 1908, mar Willa Lackie in Brantford, Ont. Res Santa Barbara, Calif, 2 chn
         D1. Willa Ann White, Binnie, b 1942, mar 1964, Jerome David Kennedy, res Plainsville, NJ
            E1. Cathleen Kennedy, b 1971 E2. Jerome David Kennedy, b 1975
         D2. Christine Ruth White, b 1948, mar 1971, Dennis John Amicis, res Santa Barbara, Calif
      C3. Ruth Irene White, b 1929, unmar, res Brantford, Ont.
  B2. Alice Maud, b 1887, d 1903 in factory accident
  B3. Coryell Albert Edward, b 1896, d 1969, mar 1921, Vera Annie Saich, b 1898, res London, Ont., 4 chn
      C1. Hazel Constance Roberts, b 1922, mar Harold Ewart Parkes, b 1925, Windsor, Ont., res London, Ont.
         D1. Dian Lynn Parkes, b 1950 London, mar 1969, Robert Edward Miller, b 1947 Dashwood, Ont., res Port Elgin, Ont.
            E1. Joel Ryan Miller, b 1975 Arnprior, Ont.
         D2. Barbara Dale Parkes, b 1953 London, Ont., mar 1975, Michael Alex. J. Frankovitch, res St. Catherines, Ont.
         D3. Jill Ann Parkes, b 1956 Montreal, Que., mar 1976, Stephen Alex. McDonald, res London
         D4. Bryan Robert Parkes, b 1969 Montreal

C2. Kenneth Donald, b 1926, d 1975, mar Margery Clare Bartlett
      D1. Sandra Margery Roberts, b 1946 London, mar 1964, Robert Ronald Campbell, Ph.D, res Guelph, Ont.
         E1. Rhonda Elizabeth Campbell, b 1965
      D2. Darlene Clare, b 1956, res London, Ont.
   C3. Jack Coryell, b 1932, mar Doreen BENNETT, res Oakville, Ont.
      D1. John Cameron, b 1956   D2. Judith Gail, b 1959
   C4. Marilyn Ann, b 1936, mar Gerald Robson Ferrington, res Winnipeg, Man.
      D1. David Richard Ferrington, b 1962
      D2. John Ross Farrington, b 1968
  B4. Evedna Lucy, b 1900, d 1967, mar Charles Gilmore
   C1. Ronald Gilmore
   C2. Camilla Gilmore, mar Rev. Laursen, res Michigan
  B5. Irene, b 1905, d 1972, res St. Claire Shores, Mich., mar James Franklin TURPIN, 2 chn
   C1. Coryell Franklin Turpin, b 1927 Detroit, mar 1958, Roberta Swanders, res Grosse Pt., Mich.
      D1. Kevin Richard Turpin, b 1954, adopted, son of Roberta's first husband, mar Judith Gallagher 1976, res Des Plaines, Ill.
      D2. Terri Lynne Turpin, b 1959 D3. Scott Coryell Turpin, b 1966
   C2. James Colin Turpin, b 1934, mar 1956, Lorraine Dutka, res Croswell, Mich., 3 chn
      D1. Deborah Ann Turpin, b 1957
      D2. James Wm. Turpin, b 1965   D3. Dawn Marie Turpin, b 1966
A4. John, b 1857 La Fosse, St. Martins, G, d 1935 Vancouver, BC, mar London, 1880, Mary Ann Moorish BROWN, b G, qv
  B1. Walter William, b 1884 London, res BC, then Calif where he d 1971. Mar 1. Winnifred Petrie, and 2. Eunice Wetmore in 1918.
   C1. Russel W., res Phoenix, Ariz. Wife had 3 chn from prev. mar.
      D1. Patricia, mar Frank Gallo, res Los Angeles, 2 chn
   C2. Donald F., res Placentia, Calif, no issue. Wife has 2 daus from prev. mar.
   C3. Patricia W. Roberts, b 1912, mar 1934, Robert Adair, Vanc., BC
      D1. Phyllis Mary Adair, mar 1957, James Killeen
         E1. Michael Killeen   E2. Bruce Killeen
      D2. Susan Margaret Adair, mar 1961, Klaus Ostrinski
         E1. Juergen Ostrinski   E3. Sarah Ostrinski
         E2. Troy Ostrinski   E4. Tyler Ostrinski
   C4. Doris Edna, mar --- NICOL, res Vancouver, 2 adopted chn
   C5. Walter W., son of second wife, Eunice Wetmore, mar ---, 2 chn. Wife had 3 chn from previous mar.
      D1. Walter, b ca 1955   D2. Pamela, b ca 1957
   C6. Keith W., res San Carlos, Calif., no issue. Wife has 3 chn from prev. mar.
  B2. Elzina Gilbert, b 1887, mar Walter Harry Parlett 1922, res New Westminster, BC, no issue
  B3. Ervin John, b 1890 London, Ont., mar Florence ROBERTS, res Vancouver, BC. Electrocuted on utility pole as a young man, 1918, 2 chn.
   C1. Stanley Milton, res San Diego, Calif, mar Jenny Law
   C2. Merle Edna, mar Edward Steppler, res Coquitlam, BC
  B4. Edna Edith, b 1893 London, d 1917 Vancouver, BC
  B5. Marjorie Mary, b 1900 London, Ont., mar Norman Wigglesworth, res San Diego, Calif, d 1949 Los Angeles.
A5. Henry Alfred, Harry, b 1858 La Fosse, St. Martins, G, mar Jennie Fennell, d London, Ont.

B1. John Edward, b 1883, d 1971 London, 4 chn
   C1. Jack E., res St. Thomas, Ont.   C3. Janet
   C2. Iona, mar --- Loveday, res Winnipeg, Man.   C4. Norman
B2. Maybelle
A6. Frederick W., b 1859, d.y.
A7. Frederick Nicholas, b 1861 La Fosse, St. Martins, G, mar Lizzie Maidens, sev chn, only 1 lived
   B1. Minnie, mar Wallace Child
      C1. Wallace Child, mar Mabel North, res Port Huron, Mich.
         D1. James Wallace Child, b 1937, mar Janet Southall, res St. Clair, Mich.
            E1. Deborah Lynn Child, b 1961   E3. Robert Child, b 1965
            E2. Diane Child, b 1963
         D2. Robert Marie Child, b 1939, mar Hubert Blom, res Royal Oak, Mich.
            E1. Craig Daniel Blom, b 1958   E2. Julia Louise Blom, b 1960
A8. Ellen Mary, b Calais, St. Martin, G, 1863, mar James Meecham, d London, Ont., 4 chn
   B1. Elzina Meecham, mar 1. --- Gilpin and 2. --- Dempsey
   B2. Louise Meecham, mar Edward John Westley Griffith
   B3. Warren Meecham, res Vancouver, BC, mar
   B4. Percy Meecham, mar Gladys Osborn, res London, Ont., a son, Spencer
A9. George Wm., b Calais, St. Martin, G 1865, mar 1. Jane Lagden, who d in childbirth. Mar 2. Alice or Sarah?
   B1. Roy, son of Jane
ROBERTS, John of Portugal Cove, mar Ann NORMORE, qv, 1780. In the 1793 census, John was mar, with 2 girls, 4 boys and 4 servants. (Rev. Hammond, Bell Island; Hug. Soc. of Canada)
A1. Catherine, bp 1790   A2. Sarah, bp 1801
ROBERTS, John, Isaac, Thomas, Dinah, in Brigus 1771, chn of --- Roberts
ROBERTS, James and Thomas, in Brigus, Conc. Bay, Nfld. 1745
ROBERTS, Wm., in Brigus, 1801. Ann in Brigus 1772.
ROBERTS, Edward, a planter, also John, Nora and Thomas, in Brigus 1860s
ROBERTS, a J fam in Bay Roberts, Nfld., early (G.W. Le Messurier)
ROBERTS, manufacturer, from J in Nfld. 1800s (K. Mathews)
ROBERTS, poss from C.I., were in Richmond Co., NS 1861 (Census)
ROBERTS, were said to have a fishery in NB 1800s. Peter Robert signed the mail route petition in 1834 to request service between Bathurst and Shippegan, NB
ROBERT, in Gaspe Bay 1871
ROBERT, Martha, b G, in Gaspe 1861 (Census)
ROBERT, Jane and Maria, b G, in Gaspe 1861, also John, Phoebe, James, b Gaspe, and Julia, b G
ROBERT, Philip Francis, Philip, William, Mary and Elizabeth Jane, all b Gaspe 1800s
ROBERT, some still in Little Gaspe, Belle Anse, Paspebiac, etc. Quebec
ROBERTS, Joseph of PEI, a blacksmith, mar Maud Henry, qv, b ca 1850, of Georgetown, PEI.Maud was dau of Marg.Nicolle &Thos.Henry.
A1. Oscar   A2. Otto   A3. Maxwell
A4. Maude, mar Rev. Murdoch of Murray River, PEI   A5. Hazel
ROBERT and ROBERTS, C.I. fams to Gaspe Bay and North Shore, Que. (Brochet)
ROBERTS, Nicholas William George, b G, mar Maria Emilia ROBERTS of Alderney, res Trois Rivieres, Que.
A1. Adelaide Agnes Roberts, b 1855, aux Gres Dist. of Trois Rivieres, Que.   or Aux Grux?
ROBERTS, many in PEI of this name. Some to Murray Harbour early 1800s.

ROBERTS

Roberts,Hilary, Hilary Jr. and Susannah are known to have emigrated from G to PEI in or before 1820. Another said to have been there since 1806. (HERITAGE FOUNDATION Bull.)
ROBERTS, William, mar Elizabeth MCKENZIE, qv, lot 54, Murray Harb., PEI 1827
ROBERTS, Thomas, mar Elizabeth BAKER, in Murray Harb., PEI 1830
ROBERTS, Peter, mar Mary Lucy BECK, in Murray Harb., PEI 1831
ROBERTS, John, and Caroline WHITE, res Murry Harb., poss he mar 2. Hannah McLeod
A1. Fanny, bp 1853   A5. Uriah, bp 1861
A2. Hannah Elizabeth, b 1857   A6. John Wesley, bp 1863
A3. Elias James, bp 1859   A7. Anna Eliz., bp 1866
A4. Emily, bp 1859
ROBERTS, Elias and wife, Ann MacMillan, res Rustico, PEI, French or French speaking, poss from C.I. Two sons, Hector, bp 1856 and Edward Irving, bp 1858.
ROBERTS, Daniel Jackson, bp 1838, son of Thomas R. and Jane ---, Murray Harbour, PEI, First Methodist Ch and Trinity Ch.
A1. Margaret Jane, bp 1856, dau of D.J. and Fredy Rankin, St. Dunstans Basilica
A2. Georgina Maria B., dau of D.J. and Catherine Marie Louisa, Ch'town, PEI, St. Pauls
A3. Margaret Anna Edith, bp 1860   A5. Catherine H.F., bp 1862
A4. Frances Elizabeth, bp 1861   A6. Ernest, bp 1864
ROBERTS, H. and J., in PEI 1841 (Census) Also Thomas.
ROBERTS, Capt. John of N.S., was a privateer, early 1800s. (CHJ Snider, UNDER THE RED JACK)
ROBERTSON, from C.I.? to Ch'town, PEI 1808 (Leeson, Francis, English genealogist)
ROBERTSON, Mary, wife of Thomas J. LE TOUZEL, 1865-1937, Malbaie, Gaspe
ROBERTSON, John, Scottish, mar --- BOWER of old J fam in Gaspe, res Barachois
ROBICHAUD. This was an Acadian French fam. Jean-Baptiste was b in Truro?, NS, rem in the expulsion to PEI, then to Brittany, where he mar Felicity Sire, Cyr, 1773. He later was brought back to Canada by the Robin firm to Paspebiac, then to Shippegan, NB. (Rev. Donat Robichaud, see also his book, LE GRAN CHIPAGAN)
ROBILLIARD, Arthur, of C.I. fam, b ca 1820 Montreal, d in Poughkeepsie, NY, mar Susan Weaver. Unverified. (Mrs. Hoey, Encino, Calif.)
ROBILLIARD, John, Jack, to Alert Bay, Victoria, BC, with mother and brother 1880s, from C.I. (Alan Robilliard, Victoria, BC)
ROBILLIARD, to Victoria, BC via Port Arthur in the late 1800s
ROBILLIARD, ---, mar a Mr. COLLETT, qv, rem to BC
ROBILLIARD, from C.I. to Gaspe
ROBILLIARD, John Isaac, a sailor, from G ca 1850 to BC, a dau in BC
ROBILLIARD, from G? to London, Ont., ca 1900 (Savary)
ROBILLIARD, Thomas, b Ald., to BC from C.I. ca 1916, age 30, res New Westminster, BC 1973
ROBILLIARD, Joseph and Rose, to Canda, poss father of Arthur, above
ROBILLIARD, A., has a jewelry store in Christ Church, N.Z., (GLF) Ancestors from C.I.
ROBILLIARD, from C.I. to Western Canada
ROBILLIARD, Daniel Hocart (cf HOCQUARD), b 1850 G, a sailor on London to Aust. route. Son of Isaac R. and Margaret RENOUF, qv. Isaac from Ville es Pies, Vale, G, mar Henriette Louise MARTIN, 7 chn, and 2. Rachel David, b 1864 Eng., with a dau, Bertha. This fam related to COLLETT, RENOUF, LE NOURY and BATISTE fams of Ont. (Marlene Robilliard,

Albion, Mich.)
- A1. Henriette Maria, b 1874 G, mar Harold BOUCHER, 3 chn
  - B1. Myra Boucher, mar Bernard BUTTON, a dau, Jane
  - B2. Helen Boucher, mar --- COLE, 4 chn
    - C1. Thelma Cole   C2. Doris Cole   C3. Donald Cole   C4. Arnold Cole
  - B3. William Boucher, mar 1. Dorothy Parker, and 2. ?
    - C1. Janis Boucher   C2. Robert Boucher
- A2. Elisabeth Marguerite, b 1875 G, mar Kenneth Lawrence Allen, b 1870-1948
  - B1. Leroy, d.y.
  - B2. Harry Lawrence, mar Sadie Susan ---, 5 chn
    - C1. Bernice Margret Allen, b 1914   C4. Jean Mildred Allen, b 1921
    - C2. Harry Leroy Allen, b 1916   C5. Kenneth John Allen
    - C3. George William Allen, b 1919
  - B3. Gordon Allen   B4. Russel Allen   B5. Alice Allen, mar Holness
- A3. Thomas William, b 1876
- A4. Amy Louise, b 1878 G, d 1965, mar 1900, Harry Buckman Tummon, 1874-1933
  - B1. Olivia Lillian Tummon, b 1901, res St. Thomas, mar 1922, Gordon Wm. Gaughell, b 1900
    - C1. William Harry, b 1923, mar Bertha Craig, 2 chn
      - D1. Timothy Caughell, b 1952
      - D2. Jill Ann Caughell, b 1954, mar James Burton Crosby 1978
    - C2. Eileen Louise, b 1928, mar 1. 1948, Allan Raymond Wicks, 1924-1957, and 2. Albert Mycroft in 1959
      - D1. Brian Raymond Wicks Mycroft, adopted by Mycroft
      - D2. Robert Evan Wicks Mycroft, adopted
      - D3. Jay Richard Mycroft, b 1962 D4. Colleen Louise Mycroft, b 1966
    - C3. Shirley Grace Caughell, b 1931, mar 1950, John Richard Park, 4 chn
      - D1. Denise Muriel Park, b 1951 D3. Arlene Louise Park, b 1953
      - D2. Gordon James Park, b 1952 D4. John Richard Park, b 1958
    - C4. John Gordon Caughell, b 1943
  - B2. Harry John William Tummon, b 1903, d 1939, unmar
- A5. Alice Maude, b 1880 Cardronet, G, mar Bert Bedell, 3 chn, Samuel, or Pete?, Harold and Edith, res first in B.C.?
- A6. Daniel Isaac, b 1880 St. Thomas, Ont., d 1941, mar Ada Lily Watkinson, b 1881, 4 chn
  - B1. Ernest John, b 1907, mar Mary (Millie) ROSE, b 1912, 2 chn
    - C1. Janet Marylin, b 1940, mar Williams
    - C2. Daniel Robert, b 1942, mar Joanne Kathleen Brown, b 1946, 3 chn
      - D1. Donna Kathleen, b 1965   D3. Brad Alan, b 1971
      - D2. Laura Jean, b 1968
  - B2. James Arthur Russell, mar Myrtle May, b 1918, no issue
  - B3. Lillian Evely, b 1915, mar Roy Edward Lankin, a son
    - C1. James Arthur Lankin, b 1942, mar Beverly Mote
  - B4. Gertrude May, b 1919, mar Wm. George Marshall, b 1921, dau
    - C1. Karen Ann, b 1947, mar James Allan Gilchrist, b 1947
      - D1. Todd Allan Gilchrist, b 1968   D3. Derek James Gilchrist,
      - D2. Farrah Alissa Gilchrist, b 1975   b 1976
- A7. John William, b 1882, d 1956, mar 1911, Caroline Jane Studwick, 1888-1978, 2 chn
  - B1. Nora Florence, b 1912, mar 1942, John Ernest Green, b 1915, no issue
  - B2. Robert, mar Evelyn ---, 2 daus, 2 sons
- A8. Bertha, b 1864, dau of second wife, <u>not ch</u> of Robilliard, mar John Connell, 2 chn

    B1. Etoile Connell, no issue
    B2. Vern Connell, mar 1. ---, 3 chn, and 2. ---, 2 chn
      C4. Elaine Connell, b 1940, mar Lorne Douglas McCaig, b 1938, 3 chn
        D1. Stephen Douglas McCaig, b 1961   D3. Dale Wm. McCaig, b 1966
        D2. Charlene Laverne McCaig, b 1964
      C5. Pat Connell, sons
A9. by second wife, Pearl Victoria, b 1893, mar 1927, John Percival Asher, b 1891, 4 chn
    B1. John Winslow Asher, b 1929, mar Grace ---, sons
    B2. Donald James Asher, b 1931, mar Kristine Elsie Madsen, no issue
    B3. Jean Elenora Asher, b 1933, mar Edwin Montgomery, 2 chn
    B4. Dorothy Mae Asher, b 1937, mar Glenn Rigg, chn
A10. Walter, d.y.
A11. George Frederick, b 1895, mar Elva Davis, 4 chn
    B1. Pauline, b 1916, mar Hugh Waud, 2 or more sons
    B2. Thelma, mar Alex McGinnis, 6 chn
      C1. Timothy McGinnis   C3. Robert McGinnis   C5. Gary McGinnis
      C2. Donald McGinnis   C4. Sylvia McGinnis   C6. ?
    B3. Clifford George, mar Evelyn ---, 2 daus
    B4. Donald, mar Amy ---
A12. Myrtle, mar 1. Wm. Morrison, of St. Thomas, a son, and 2. Herman Greenman
    B1. William Morrison, mar Dora ---, res Detroit, d 1970s
      C1. David Lee Morrison, b 1939 C2. Carol Ann Morrison, b 1944
    B2. Theodore Greenman, res Albion, Mich., mar 1. Naomi ---, and 2. Dorothy ---
      C1. Charlotte Marie Greenman, b 1940
      C2. Nancy Carol Greenman, b 1942
A13. Edith Ellen, b 1899, mar Edward Joseph Irwin, and d 1953, 2 sons
    B1. Edward Joseph Irwin, b 1930, d 1962, unmar
    B2. Patricia Irwin, b 1935, mar Dennis ---, no issue
A14. Arthur, d.y.
A15. Charles Delbert, b 1902, d 1972, mar Dora Bowlby of St. Thomas, 2 chn
    B1. Vern, b 1929   B2. Robert
A16. Ralph Eric, a.k.a. Ralph Harry, b 1907, St. Thomas, mar 1925, Jennie Alice Burkwalt, b 1904
    B1. Richard Lee, b 1927 Albion, Mich., mar 1956, Marlene Joyce Holmes, b 1937
      C1. Teresa Leigh, b 1960 Albion, Mich.
      C2. John Richard, b 1962 Albion
    B2. Wayne Ralph, b 1929, d 1950, unmar
ROBIN, Thomas John, b 1874 Banques, St. Sampson, G, son of William R. and Marguerite Nancy LITTLE. Rem to Toronto, Ont. ca 1898, but returned several times to G. Mar Louise Alice BICHARD, dau of Jean and of Betsy MARTEL, qv. She d 1960. (Wm. R. Swinarton, Scarboro, Ont.)
A1. Ida Matilda, b 1897, d 1975. Mar Joseph Vincent Bero.
    B1. Audrey Isobel Bero, b 1919, mar Joseph Frederick McCabe
      C1. Joseph Robert McCabe, b 1939
      C2. Mary Ellen McCabe, b 1942, mar Christo Steve
      C3. Margaret Louise McCabe, b 1943, mar Thomas Artandi
        D1. Richard John Artandi, b 1967
        D2. Jacqueline Patricia Artandi, b 1973
    B2. Alan George Bero, b 1926, mar Fern Adelaide Hunt, 1927-1977
      C1. Margaret Eileen Bero, b 1947, mar Arvo Merela
        D1. Michele Ann Merela, b 1971

D2. Sean Arvo Alex. Merela, b 1973 D3. Robert Alan Merela, b 1976
  C2. Alan Charles Bero, b 1948, mar Elizabeth Farr
   D1. Jason Scott Bero, b 1973
  C3. Deborah Ann Bero, b 1952, mar Dennis Philip Lacroix 1978
  C4. Lynda Lee Bero, b 1954, mar John Grant
   D1. John Michael Grant, b 1972
  C5. Joan Bero, b 1956, mar Sheldon Francis
  C6. Nancy Patricia Bero, b 1958, mar Wayne Arsenault
   D1. Bobbijean Arsenault, b 1977   D2. ?, b 1978
  C7. Stephen Douglas Bero, b 1962   C8. Tracy Lynn Bero, b 1964
 B3. Robert Alexander Bero, b 1930, mar Georgina Elkington
  C1. Joseph Frederick Bero, b 1963
 B4. Joan Theresa Bero, b 1931, mar James Joseph McKenna
  C1. James Joseph McKenna, b 1951
  C2. Karen Ann McKenna, b 1954, mar Michael Orren Day, b 1953
   D1. Lisa Mary Day, b 1975   D2. Michelle Nicole Day, b 1977
 B5. John Vincent Bero, b 1933
A2. Louise Elizabeth, b 1898 G, d 1938, mar Herbert Barker
 B1. Lois Madeline Barker, b 1920, mar Charles Henry Rae
  C1. Carol Ann Rae, mar Robert Timlock
   D1. Lois Ann Timlock   D2. Alan Robert Timlock
  C2. Charles Leonard Rae
 B2. Allen Herbert Barker, b 1922, mar Marjory McGrath
  C1. Ann Louise Barker   C3. Brian Barker
  C2. Paul Parker   C4. Susan, twin to Brian
 B3. Norma Louise Barker, b 1925, mar Jack Ray King
  C1. Graham Paul King   C3. Catherine Elizabeth King
  C2. Phillip Scott King
 B4. Shirley Elizabeth Barker, b 1928, mar Joseph T. Flint
  C1. Edgar Joseph Flint   C2. Louise Elizabeth Flint
 B5. Dorothy Ann Barker, b 1931, mar Richard James Copley
  C1. Judith Ann Louise Copley, mar Benjamin Carlyong, dau, Robin
      Louise
  C2. Richard Scott Copley   C3. Michael Drew Copley
 B6. Bruce Thomas Barker, b 1933, mar Barbara BROWN
  C1. Robert Barker   C3. Cheryl Barker
  C2. Darlene Barker   C4. Kenneth Barker, adopted
 B7. Mary Catherine Barker, b 1936, mar Robert Ernest Waddingham
  C1. Sherrilyn Waddingham   C2. Brent Waddingham
A3. Winnifred Mary, b 1900 G, mar 1. John Joseph Sullivan, b 1897, and
    2. Arthur West
 B1. William Alan Robin, b 1918, unmar
 B2. Helen Winnifred Sullivan, b 1920, mar Sidney Keith Ormerod, b 1917
  C1. David Keith Ormerod, b 1942
  C2. Carol Jean Ormerod, b 1947, mar John Parnell
 B3. Marjorie Gertrude Sullivan, b 1921, mar Cecil F. Fitzgerald,
     1910-1974
  C1. John Frederick Fitzgerald, b 1943, mar 1. Mary Lou Sullivan,
      b 1945, d 1974 and 2. Janie Gill, b 1946. Chn by first wife.
   D1. John Fitzgerald, b 1967   D2. Kenneth Fitzgerald, b 1970
  C2. Sandra Lee Fitzgerald, b 1946, mar Christopher Thomas Preston,
      b 1945 Dagenham, England
  C3. Michael Richard Fitzgerald, b 1947, mar Donna Tracy, b 1949
   D1. Jennifer Fitzgerald, b 1970 D2. Jeffrey Fitzgerald, b 1975
 B4. Bernice Frances Sullivan, b 1924, mar Norman John Feeney, 1921-
     1973
  C1. Patricia Ann Feeney, b 1943, mar Frank Ernest Babcock

                D1. Theresa Lee Babcock, b 1959   D3. Shirley Ann Babcock, b
                D2. Patricia Ann Babcock, b 1961   1963
            B5. Gerald John Sullivan, b 1925, mar Beatrice Theresa Beaune, b 1926
                C1. Gerald Stephen Sullivan, b 1945, mar Victoria Bernard, b 1950
                    D1. Steven Douglas Sullivan, b 1972
                    D2. Tracy Lynn Sullivan, b 1969
                C2. Douglas Ronald Sullivan, b 1946, mar Marie Morgan, b 1939
                    D1. Teresa Marie Sullivan, b 1974
                C3. Catherine Jean Sullivan, b 1950, mar Gerald Caissie, b 1949
                    D1. Laura Caissie, b 1968   D2. Edward Levi Caissie, b 1970
                C4. Richard Dale Sullivan, b 1951, mar Wendy Passfield, b 1952
                    D1. Kari Ann Sullivan, b 1970 D2. Sean Michael Sullivan, b 1974
                C5. James Michael Sullivan, b 1953, mar Shirley Stephens, b 1955
                    D1. Richard James Sullivan, b 1972
                    D2. Lisa Marie Sullivan, b 1974
                C6. Victor John Sullivan, b 1954, mar Sandra Channon, b 1955
                C7. Brad Lee Sullivan, b 1958   C8. Barry Robert Sullivan, b 1960
            B6. Florence Marion Sullivan, b 1927, mar Germain Rodolphe Hogue
                C1. Sharon Katherine Hogue, b 1947, mar John Hunt
                    D1. Kelly Anne Hunt, b 1971   D3. John James Hunt, b 1973
                    D2. Colleen Patricia Hunt, b 1972 D4. Jason Robert Hunt, b 1975
                C2. Diane Marie Hogue, b 1949, mar John Lovell
                C3. Germaine Rodolphe Hogue, b 1953   C6. Cheryl Anne Hogue, b 1963
                C4. Leo Christopher Hogue, b 1954 d.y.   C7. Donna Elaine Hogue, b
                C5. Lynn Theresa Hogue, b 1959   1964
            B7. Robert James Sullivan, b 1928, mar Lillian Gertrude Carswell, b
                1928
                C1. Debra Joyce Sullivan, b 1956 C3. Pamela Jane Sullivan, b 1961
                C2. Sharon Lee Sullivan, b 1959 C4. Diane Lynn Sullivan, b 1962
    A4. Violet Gertrude, b 1901 Camp du Roi, Vale, G, mar William Joseph
        Shanahan, 1895-1950
        B1. Joan Marie Shanahan, b 1933, mar David Franklin Richards, and 2.
            J.A. Moni
            C1. William David Richards, b 1956   C3. Michelle Frances Moni, b
            C2. Robin Durelle Richards, b 1957   1960
        B2. Durelle Margaret Shanahan, b 1938, mar Frederick Holland
            C1. Joann Durelle Holland, b 1965
            C2. James Frederick Holland, b 1968
    A5. Eva Margaret Robin, b 1906 Toronto, mar 1932, William Allen Swinarton, b 1905, d 1971
        B1. William Robin Swinarton, b 1934, mar Anne Elizabeth Baker, b 1936
            C1. Carole Anne Swinarton, b 1956
            C2. Katherine Lynn Swinarton, b 1958, d.y.
            C3. Kelly Lynn Swinarton, b 1961 C4. Laurie Robin Swinarton, b 1965
        B2. Carole Doreen Swinarton, b 1936, d 1937
        B3. John Joseph Swinarton, b 1938, mar Victoria Dora Katcher, b 1935
        B4. Harold Lloyd Swinarton, b 1939, mar Patricia Isabella Milligan,
            b 1950
    A6. Ethel May, d.y.
    A7. Dorothy Muriel Robin, b 1914 Toronto, mar 1. Wm. Clifford Mitchell
        and 2. Reg. Hutchinson
        B1. Barbara Louise Mitchell, b 1936, mar James Harrison
            C1. John Wm. Harrison, b 1959   C2. David James Harrison, b 1969
        B2. Robert Thomas Mitchell, b 1938, mar Sandra Friend, and 2. ---?
            C1. Scott Mitchell, b 1960   C2. Blair Mitchell, b 1964
            C3. Brent Thomas Mitchell, b 1974
        B3. Linda Marie Mitchell, b 1945, mar Colin Tucker

    C1. Andrea Leigh Tucker, b 1975
ROBIN, Ezekiel, b 1835 G, son of Pierre R. and Susanne COHU, res Grand
   Clos, Castel, G. Master mariner, age 20 to sea, settled London, Eng.
   1859, mar Clementina Anne Bourne. (Some data unclear, poss in error)
   (Ivy Erwin, Pensacola, Fla.)
A1. Peter Francis, mar 1887, Sarah-Sylvia Gibson, b 1868, Irish, family
   had rem to Australia 1881 then to U.S. He d Mobile, Ala. 1929, 3
   chn
   B1. Victor Francis   B3. Harold Ernest, twin of Elsie,
   B2. Elsie Sylvia   d.y.
   B1. Alfred Edwin, b 1889 Brisbane, Aust, d 1950, Prince Rupert, BC.
      Mar Clara Nelson in 1916 at McBride, BC, who d 1968.
      C1. Ernest Clarence, res Ft. St. James, BC
      C2. Margaret Sylvia, mar Dennis Charles Smith, res New Westminster,
         BC, mar Orrice ---
      C3. Clara Linnea, mar Chris MANSELL, res Edmonton, Alta.
      C4. Edwin Peter Robin, M.D., mar Rose ---, res Surrey, BC
      C5. Anna Marie, res New Westminster, BC, unmar
   B2. Robin Peter, b 1903, Alford, Essex, Eng., mar Mobile, Ala. 1930,
      res Port Arthur, Texas
      C1. Robyna Carleen, mar James W. Prescott, res Garfield Groves, Tex.
      C2. Harral Timbes Robin, unmar, res Muncie, Ind.
   B3. Ivy Gibson, b 1908 Manson, Man., mar Mobile, Ala. 1928, Winfred
      Alexander Erwin, b 1906
      C1. Robin Winfred Erwin, b 1929, mar Budenia Jacobs, 4 chn
         D1. Robin Winfred Erwin Jr., mar Juanita Haight 1974
         D2. Dian Erwin, mar Richard Campbell, 1972
         D3. Phyllis Jean Erwin   D4. David James Erwin
      C2. Dorothy Joan Erwin, b 1931, mar 1956, Lawrence E. McGlone, res
         Chula Vista, Calif.
         D1. Karen McGlone D2. Cynthia McGlone D3. Mark McGlone
      C3. Marian Virginia Erwin, b 1935, res Stony Brook, NY
      C4. Patricia Helen Erwin, mar 1959, Lester W. Wolf, res Gulf
         Breeze, Fla.
         D1. Jeffrey Wolf   D2. Jenifer Wolf
A2. Victor Francis   A3. Elsie Sylvia   A4. Harold Ernest, twin, d.y.
ROBIN, ROBINS. Fam below has tradition of French name, DE ROBON, ROBON.
   ROBIN and ROBINS used by the fam in PEI and U.S.
This family apparently came to PEI either at the same time as the other
Guernsey folk in 1806, or possibly earlier. Since three families ap-
pear in Methodist church records in Murray Harbor, and since they
intermarried with the other Guernsey folk there, it seems quite like-
ly that they were also from Guernsey. Some used the name ROBINS.
ROBIN, John, b C.I.?, mar Susannah ---. At least 3 chn.
A1. John James, b 1825 Murray Harb., Methodist, mar Elizabeth Hawkins
   LE LACHEUR 1852
A2. Elizabeth, b 1828   A3. William Nicholas, b 1832
ROBIN, Thomas Robin, mother's name not given in Bedeque Un. Ch records
   in PEI.Mar Jane LE LACHEUR 1836
A1. Thomas, bp 1845   A4. Isabella, b 1845
A2. Mary, bp 1845   A5. Elizabeth, bp 1845
A3. Martha, bp 1847   A6. William, bp 1853
ROBIN, John, Elizabeth and Mary listed on Wesleyan Meth. Soc. records,
   Murray Harbor, 1822
ROBIN, Thomas, b 1804, mar Jane LE LACHEUR 1836 (Laura Barnhart, St.
   Charles, Mich.)
A1. John, b 1837, d 1923 Castle Rock, Washington, age 86. He mar 1.

ROBIN 499

A2. Daniel b 1838   A3. Windsor b 1840.
Martha Ellen Stock 1865, who was b Ill. 1847, brought to Wash. 1853.
He mar 2. Margaret M. LE LACHEUR, brought from PEI 1907.
B1. Frederick Ulysses, b 1866, res Portland, Oregon
B2. Mary Eliza, b 1869, mar --- Thayer
B3. Thomas Winsor, "Win," b 1869, res Castle Rock
B4. John Charles, or Charles, b 1874, res Bellingham, Wash.
B5. George Ernest, or Ernest, b 1877, res Castle Rock, Wash., mar Clara Leffler 1894
  C1. Joseph Roy Robin, b 1895, res St. Charles, Mich. where he mar Florence Boist 1917. He was a dairy farmer and she taught school. He d 1964.
    D1. Laura Eleanor, b 1918, a principal, author of historical subjects, mar Wm. E. Barnhard, res Bradenton, Fla. and Mich., a dau
      E1. Susan Marie, b 1956
    D2. Kenneth Roy, b 1920, res Port Huron, mar Dorothy O'Connor 1940
      E1. Sandra Robins Naascho, b 1942   E3. Sally Robins Fiche, b
      E2. Sharon Robins Kraft, b 1946   1947
    D3. Arlene, b 1926, mar Edward Charles Carden, res Ann Arbor, Mich.
      E1. Catherine Carden, b 1955   E3. David Carden, b 1958
      E2. Robert Roy Carden, b 1957 E4. Daniel Carden, b 1958, twin
ROBIN, Eugene, b 1892 St. Sampson, G, Rue Colin, rem to Grimsby, Ont.
Mar Henrietta INGROUVILLE of Vale, G, in St. Martins, 1911. (Gladys Alexander, Ithaca, NY)
A1. Wilson, b 1911 G, res Kings Ferry, NY, mar Florence Briggs 1937
  B1. Donald, b 1942, mar Lucille Quick, 3 chn
  B2. Janet, b 1945, mar Jeffrey Crandall
A2. Gladys, b 1914, mar Ralph W. Alexander 1937, res Ithaca, NY
  B1. Ralph W. Alexander, b 1941, mar Janet Bradley, 2 chn
    C1. Ralph William Alexander III, b 1968
    C2. Margaret Alexander, b 1970
  B2. Robin Judith, b 1943, mar Lindsay Goodloe
  B3. Anne Louise Alexander, b 1944, mar Peter Koehler, 2 chn
    C1. Michael Friedrich Thomas Koehler, b 1970
    C2. Richard Paul Martin Koehler, b 1973
  B4. Nancy Jean Alexander, b 1947, unmar
  B5. David Wilson Alexander, b 1957
A3. Beulah Harriet, b 1915 Winona, res Rochester, NY. Mar John Janowisc 1939
  B1. Judith Janowisc, b 1943, mar William Keys, 2 chn
    C1. Barbara Jean Keys, b 1964   C2. Kathleen Marie Keys, b 1966
  B2. John Janowisc, b 1945, mar Patricia Autovina, 2 chn
    C1. Jennifer Susan Janowisc, b 1971
    C2. Jeanne Catherine Janowisc, b 1974
  B3. Barbara Janowisc, b 1946, mar Thomas Erdle, 2 chn
    C1. Timothy James Erdle, b 1972 C2. Cynthia Ann Erdle, b 1973
ROBIN, Mary Ann Eugena, b 1882 Houge du Valle, G, dau of John William R. and Mary Ann TOSTEVIN, qv, d 1968 Ontario. Mar Alfred Ernest ROUSSEL, qv, 13 chn. She mar 2. Wm. Booker, who d 1953. (J.A. Robin, Stoney Creek, Ont.) Below are her bros and sisters.
II. Amy Mary, dec
III. John William Peter, b Le Sauvage, St. Sampson, G, to Canada 1911, mar Hilda Alice LE TISSIER, qv, of Le Houmet, Catel, to Canada 1912 with 3 sons:
A1. John Arthur, b 1907, mar Jean McConnell, b 1906
  B1. Sheila Margaret, b 1941
A2. Cyril George, b 1908, mar Evelyn Schurcotte

B1. Carol Ann, b 1935, mar Bruce Dingle
      C1. Cameron Dingle, b 1961   C3. Robin Dingle, b 1954
      C2. Allan Dingle, b 1962   C4. Shelly Dingle, b 1967
   B2. Hilda Evelyn, b 1940, mar P. Bidwell
      C1. Martin Bidwell, b 1955   C3. Timothy Bidwell, b 1971
      C2. Diana Bidwell, b 1967
  A3. Harold Douglas, b 1912, d 1937, unmar
  A4. Stanley William, b 1919, mar Thelma May Ball, b 1924 Brantford,
      Ont., res Linden, Ont.
   B1. Sandra Gail, b 1952 Hamilton, Ont.
   B2. Carrick Stanley, b 1945, res Glace Bay, NS
   B3. Derrick George, b 1956 Hamilton, Ont.
   B4. Candace Helen, b 1957, res Brantford, Ont.
  IV. Walter   VI. Samuel, rem to Boston, Mass. area   VIII. Daisy
  V. Elsie May   VII. Lisette   IX. Frank, and or Frank Albert, to U.S.
ROBIN, Raulin, in Perce, Gaspe 1863 (Cent. Bklt.)
ROBIN, Charles Maingay, in Paspebiac 1800s (Syvret)
ROBIN, Charles, b G, mar 1840 at Perce Monique Boulet, a son, Charles, and dau, Genevieve, b 1840s (Rev. d'Hist)
ROBIN, Helene, b G, mar Ernest John RENOUF, rem to Hamilton, Ont. See RENOUF.
ROBIN, Eva Margaret, b G, dau of Thomas John R. and Louisa Alice BICHARD, qv, mar in Canada. Thomas John rem to Canada ca 1901, and mar 2.? Eva Margaret ROBIN, b G, several daus, some b G, some in Canada. (Wm. Robin Swinarton, Scarboro, Ont.)
ROBIN, Arthur Vavassor, 1858-1859, bur St. Peters, Paspebiac (GLF)
ROBIN, Lewis, 1865-1957, bur Sandy Beach, St. John Anglican church.
ROBIN, Evangeline, 1871-1963, bur St. John's? (GLF)
ROBIN, Jacques, or James, brother of John, bp 1774, rem to Canada but returned to J
ROBIN, Charles. See page 36. Others of this same family involved in various ways with Canada were the following: "Claim of Charles Robin, Philip Robin, Philip Robin, the younger, John Robin, James Robin, Elizabeth Robin, widow of John Robin, Thomas Pipon, Francis Janvrin and John Poingdestre, merchants, trading under the firm and style of Charles Robin & Co., for lands at Paspebiac, Hopetown, etc. Claim taken before Gaspe Land Commissioner at New Carlisle, Dist. of Gaspe on 19 August 1819, and considered by Commissioners in Quebec on 20 December 1821." (81838-18148, Dominion Archives)
ROBIN, James, Philip, and John, dated Quebec, 1828, Petition: "legal representatives of the late Charles Robin, in his life time formerly of Paspebiac, and at the time of his decease resident in the Island of Jersey...Presented themselves as the just and lawful owners and proprietors of the Seigniory of Grande River on the Bay of Chaleur," petition has letters patent for the seigniory attached. (81787-1791, Dominion Archives)
ROBINSON. "In 1769 Elie Robinson, ROBISSON, of G, mar Mathe BIARD." Apparently, Robisson became at times Robinson in G.
ROBINSON, Patric H., b G, rem to Fullerton, Ont. Internationally known breeder of Guernsey cattle. Showed first Guernseys at the Allentown Fair 61 years ago. Raised on G, PRINCESS, a cow whose equal has never been found, and whose daus have been prize winners throughout the world. Brought his cows to Phila. in 1884, showed them in many fairs, including the famous C.N.E., the 'Ex.' Took a consignment of his famous Guernsey cattle to Japan, as well as to many other countries in Europe and Asia." (H.A. Giffard, Toronto, Ont.)

ROCK, John, signed the Petition in Gaspe 1820. Another John Rock appeared in Nova Scotia. Some Rocks in Canada might be descendants of Channel Island families named DE LA ROCQUE, LAROKE, and ROCK. John Gruch ROCK appeared in Marblehead, Mass. 1774, at the time many Channel Islanders were coming to N. America. Edmond, alias Rock, also appeared in J 1607.
ROCHE, in Nfld. (Seary) Cf ROCHES, etc. of J (Stevens)
ROCHE, Barbara, of the Channel Island Society, in Vancouver 1952. (Lady McKie)
RODDA, Richard Elias, b 1872 St. Helier, J, a Salvation Army Officer in J and Edmonton, Alta. Rem to Edmonton in 1911, mar Emma Mary DAVIS, qv. Came with her mother, Mrs. Emma Davis in 1912. "...nearly went aground in Nfld., 6 weeks aboard ship, then by train to Edmonton." Mrs. Davis lived to age of 102. (Grace Rodda Beck, Edmonton, Alta.)
A1. Grace M., b 1886, mar Beck, a dau res Edmonton, Alta.
A2. Mary Gladys, d 1904   A3. Florency May, d 1908
RODDA, Bertram, a cousin, res Oakland, Calif.
RODGERS, now ROGERS, from C.I. in Carbonear very early from G? Cf RODGERS of G (Rev. Hammond)
RODGERS, in Trinity Bay, Old Perlican, Nfld., from C.I.?
ROSSIER, John, from J 1862, farmer, Conc. 1, Lot 7, W. Nissouri, London, Ont. (Norfolk Atlas, reprint by Cumming) See also ROSSIER, p. 502.
ROLAND, in Nfld. (Seary) Cf ROLLAND of J (Stevens)
ROLLAND, Peter, from G to Toronto 1900s. (Eliz. Robert, Niagara Falls, NY)
ROLLAND, some to W. Canada from C.I.
ROMAINE, in Nfld. (Seary) Cf ROMAINE of J (Stevens)
ROMERIL, see Soc. Jers. Bull. of 1929, related to PINEL fams?
ROMERIL, Edwin, b 1911 Four Cabot, St. Andrews, G, mar St. James, G, 1931, Linda DE BRODER, qv
A1. Allan Brian, b 1932, mar 1960, Jeannine Darlyne Hahn
   B1. Margaret Claire, b 1961 Pomeroy, Wash.
   B2. Barbara Linda, b 1962 Pomeroy, Wash.
A2. Philip Robert Francis, b 1936 St. Peter Port, G, mar Jackie Skull, Racine, Wisc. 1958
   B1. Catherine Jane, b 1959   B4. Paul Christopher, b 1963 Eng.
   B2. Mark Philip, b 1960   B5. Jennifer Bell, b 1965 England
   B3. Bruce Allan, b 1961
ROMERIL, Elias, age 28, b J, agent at Grand Riviere, Gaspe 1871/1861?
ROMERIL, Elias, age 38, b J, agent at Perce 1871. (ROMERIL also listed by Betty Tardiff and by J.H. Le Breton)(One Eli b J 1868 d at
ROMERIL, A.J., alderman in Prince Albert, Sask., 1900s   Paspebiac)
ROMERIL, C.I. name associated with Robin firm in Paspebiac, and with town of New Carlisle, Que. (Que. Prov. Arch.)
ROMERIL, Alfred, b St. Peter, J 1881, to Gaspe 1895, d Vancouver, 3 sons and a dau
ROMERILS, res Lethbridge, Alta, from J
ROMERIL, George, b J, 1842-1896, bur St. Peters, Paspebiac, Gaspe (GLF)
ROMERIL, Albert J., b J, to Long Island, NY ca 1908, mar, 3 sons, 8 grandchildren, bro of Alfred of Vancouver
ROMERIL, Edward Philip, b J middle 1800s, son of Capt. Edward, b 1829, who died on a voyage to the South China Sea. His widow remar, and had another son. Edward Philip rem from J to Perce ca 1882, and had a fishery there. (Alan Romeril, Toronto, Ont.)
A1. Gordon William, b 1891 Westmount, Que., d 1952. Mar Mary Minerva Waterton, b 1896 Balaclava, Ont.
   B1. Alan Gordon, b 1934, unmar

ROMERIL, Mathieu & Simon, TO NEW ENGLAND 1600s.
A2. Alexander Edward, b 1893 Quebec, mar ?. and 2. Margaret MACKENZIE
  B1. Beryl Arlene, mar --- CORBET, res Australia
  B2. Derek Alexander, by second wife
ROMERIL, John Philip, b 1853 St. Helier, J, rem to Liverpool, Eng. late 1880s. Mar 2. Eliza Donaghy of Donegal, Ire. 1892. (Rev. John Philip Romeril, Sudbury, Ont.)
A1. Philip, b 1896
  B1. Rev. John Philip, b 1931 Scunthorpe, Eng., to Canada 1950, Sudbury, Ont. 1972
    C1. David James, mar Jeanette ---, res Lynn Lake, Man., 3 chn: Paul, Noel and Jonathan
    C2. Mary Isabel, res Salmon Arm, B.C.
RONDEL, from C.I. to Canada and to N.A. (GLF) One in Tauranga, Bay of Plenty, N.Z.
ROPER, in Nfld. (Seary) Cf ROPERT of J (Stevens)
ROPERT, Frank, from J to Gaspe (GLF) 1900s. (J.H. Le Breton list) At one time, Francis James Alexandre R., b St. Peter, J, bur Sandy Beach, Gaspe, was Postmaster at Gaspe. Mar Nita Muriel Williamson. He d 1958.
ROSE, John, from G, was at Grand Greve, Gaspe 1825, mar 1832, Charlotte Simpson. Chn b Gaspe. Charlotte, widow?, mar again? A son, Joshua MAJOR, MAUGER?, b 1832.
ROSE, Charlotte, mar 1. --- RABEY, and 2. G.F. LE TOUZEL, qv. Uncer.
ROSE, Charlotte, mar 1835, David RABEY, Sr.
ROSE, chn of John and Charlotte? Rachel, Jane, William and Sarah, all b Gaspe, in Gaspe Bay 1861 (Census)
ROSE, Sarah, mar Edward C. LE TOUZEL, qv.
ROSE, John, present at a wedding in Roseville, Gaspe 1869 (QAAM, Turk)
ROSE, Harriet, mar Nicolas GUIGNION, Sr., qv
ROSE, John, mar Mary MAUGER, MOSHIER, chn:
A1. Peter, b 1830   A3. George, again, b 1835
A2. George, d 1831   A4. Elias, b 1834
ROSE, Rachel, b 1810 J, mar 1829, Thomas LANGLOIS, qv, b 1794 G. She d 1892, a son, John LANGLOIS. (Mrs. G. Langlois, Toronto, Ont.)
ROSE, Murray, husband of Gladys DAVEY, qv.
ROSE, in England and J. Thomas ROSE, 1801-1880, owned Cowley Hall in Middlesex, Eng. and property in St. Brelade, St. Helier, and St. Saviour, J. Mar Sarah Eves, 1811-1894. Cf EVE, of TUZO fam. QV.
ROSE, Jeremiah, in Fortune Bay, Nfld. 1860s (Rev. Hammond)
ROSE, George, in Jersey Harbor, Nfld. 1877, and James in Burgeo 1860s
ROSE, James Sr., b G, in Gaspe Bay N. and Sydenham, 1861 (Census) with Mary ROSE, b G, Nicholas b G, Hannah, b England, and Nicholas, Hannah, Henry and Emilie. (Census)
ROSE, Helier and Rachel, b G, in Gaspe Bay 1861 with Emily and Elias, b Gaspe (Census)
ROSE, from C.I. to Ont.?
ROSIERS, Wm., in Gaspe Militia 1850s. Cf ROSSIER
ROSS, Christine of J?, mar 1859?, in J, Edward Graeme MORRISSEY, qv
ROSS, in Perce 1800s (Cent. Bklt.) One Ann Ross mar a MERCER.
ROSIER, ROSIERRE, ROISSIER, etc. Huguenots in the C.I. and Eng. 1600s
ROSSIER, ROSIER, John, of Hastings Co., Ont., translated name to Rosebush, rem to Central Michigan and changed name again to BUSH. (Marion Van Dingstee, Duarte, Calif.) "ROSIER, ROSIERE, of the Hug. Soc. of London, Deacons from 1658 to 1691, Reg. of the Church of the Walloons and Isle of Jersey, Guernsey and Sark, established at Southampton Abraham Rosier 1581, aliens in London." (Van Dingstee)
ROSSIGNOL, from J to Cape Breton. See also LE ROSSIGNOL
ROSSIGNOL, John, b J, age 30 in 1871, res Petit de Grat (Census) N.S.

ROUET 503

ROUET, SEE ADDITIONS AND CORRECTIONS PAGES.
ROUET, Jane, b 1814 J, mar P. DU VAL, d Quebec. See p. 549.
ROUGET, a pilot from St. Sampsons, G. Caroline, mother of James, of St. Sampsons, G, mar Thomas BICHARD, res Victoria, BC, 1940. (Luce)
ROUNDS, ROUND, ROUNDIE, ROUNDY, LA RONDE. "Forefathers of the ROUNDY family in America came from Ardennes, France to the Island of Guernsey...to Colonial America in the middle 1600s." (A.C.M. Palmer, Sturgis, Sask.)
ROUNDS, James, b R.I. ca 1760, mar Weltha Fletcher, rem to Burford, Ont., poss desc of Philip ROUNDY of Salem, Mass., 1628-1640, who mar Ann Bush
ROUSSEL, Mary Ann, of J, see John MARIETTE
ROUSSEL, Stephen, Etienne Ferdinand, b 1832 G, mar Mary Ann SEDGELEY, b 1836 G, dau of Wm. S. and Judy MAHY, qv. Several chn to Canada (Lillian Roussel, Stoney Creek, Ont.; Ida Woods, from Stoney Creek; John Roussel, Burlington, Ont.)
I. Mary Ann, b 1860 G, d G II. Stephen James, b 1862 G, d G
III. Thomas James, b 1864 G, rem to Canada 1907, where he d
IV. Amelia, b 1866 G, d G
V. Eliza, b ca 1870 G, mar John SEBIRE, qv, rem to Ontario, 7 chn. See SEBIRE
VI. John Sedgeley, b 1872, mar Lily LEGG, b 1879 G, d 1942, ONT.
A1. John Thomas Roussel, b 1895, mar ---   SEE EXTRA PAGES
B1. Aline, b 1920 B2. John William, b 1927
A2. Arthur Willett, b 1905, mar ---
B1. Audrey Lillian, b 1928 B2. Beverley Joan, b 1934
A3. William George, b 1909, mar ---
B1. Diane, b 1936 B3. Brian, b 1944 B5. Stephen, b 1951
B2. Roy, b 1940 B4. David, b 1948 B6. Richard, b 1953
VII. William Henry, b 1875 G, d G
VIII. Alfred Ernest, b 1881 St. Johns, G, mar Mary Ann Eugena ROBIN, qv, 1882-1968, b Houge Du Valle, G, 12 chn. Alfred E. d 1930. (John Roussel, Burlington, Ont.; Eleanor Roussel, Hamilton, Ont.; Mrs. A. Roussel, Dundas, Ont.)
A1. Mary Elsie, b 1905
A2. John William Henry, b 1906, mar Blendina Eliz. McFayden 1935, 2 chn
B1. Elizabeth Doreen, b 1938, mar Harold Barnett Jervis 1964, 2 chn
C1. Linda Rose Jervis, b 1966 C2. James William Jervis, b 1969
B2. Alfred Walter, b 1941, mar 1965, Diane Lynn Weaymouth, 2 chn, res Stoney Creek
C1. Kathryn Ann, b 1968 C2. Jason Bradley, b 1969
A3. Ernest Alfred Sedgley, b 1908, res Hamilton, Ont., mar Edna Kirkham
B1. Anita Anne, b 1939, mar 1960, Robert H. Love, res Calgary, Alta.
C1. Rose Anne Love, b 1962 C2. Ruth Anne Love, b 1966
B2. Frederick Ernest, b 1943, mar Eleanor Phyllis York 1964, res Hamilton, Ont.
C1. Phyllis May, b 1965 C2. Jacqueline Christine, b 1967
B3. Edna Lynne, b 1948, mar 1968, Winston Williams, res Ancaster, Ont.
A4. Albert Edward, b 1909, mar Ivay Baker, res Dundas, Ont.
B1. Rose Marie, b 1935, mar 1955, Charles Thompson, b 1927
C1. Charles Douglas Thompson, b 1957, mar 1977, Debra Lynch, Belleville, Ont.
C2. Eric Scott Thompson, b 1959
C3. Heather Thompson, b 1961 C4. Bruce Edward Thompson, b 1963
B2. Ivay May, b 1936, mar James Missen, 1959, res Ancaster, Ont.
C1. Donna Carol Missen, b 1964 Hamilton, Ont.
C2. Nancy Ellen Missen, b 1968
B3. Elsie Jean, b 1939, mar 1962 Dundas, Ont., Norman Chambers, b 1928

        C1. Rosemary Hope Chambers, b 1963 Hamilton
        C2. Susan Valerie Chambers, b 1965 Hamilton
     B4. Patricia Joyce, b 1945, mar Douglas Wilson, b 1928 Port Dover,
        Ont.
        C1. Daniel Gordon Wilson, b 1973
A4. Lisette Eugenia, b 1911, d 1913   A6. Eva May, b 1913 Ont., d 1914
A7. Amelia Bertha, b 1915, mar Sidney G. Chasty, b England
   B1. Alfred George Chasty, b 1938
      C1. Devin George Chasty, b 1963   C2. Darrin Pearce Chasty, b 1966
A8. Frank, b 1916, d 1917
A9. Lillian Daisy, b 1918, mar 1. Verner Le Claire Arnold, b 1915 and
    2. Elmer Ray Dunham, 1945
   B1. William Alfred Le Claire Arnold, b 1936, mar Vivian Barbara Ann
       Jefferies 1957
      C1. Daniel William Le Claire Arnold, b 1958
      C2. Barbara Ellen Lee Arnold, b 1959, mar Richard Ver Heul 1977,
          res Lynden, Ont.
      C3. Jefferie Ray Arnold, b 1961
      C4. James Todd Arnold, b 1964   C5. John Walter Arnold, b 1965
   B2. Marjorie Elsie Arnold, b 1937, mar William Edward Jefferies 1955,
       res Waterford, Ont.
      C1. Edward William Jeffries, b 1956
      C2. Teresa Marjorie Jefferies, b 1957, mar Ronald Howard Thorne
          1975
         D1. Tracy Lea Ann Thorne, b 1973   D2. Howard Jason Thorne, b 1975
      C3. Beth Ann Jefferies, b 1959, mar William Bakker 1976
         D1. William Richard Bakker, b 1977
      C4. Harvey Coleson Ray Jefferies, b 1963
   B3. Frederick Lloyd Arnold, b 1939, mar Sandra MALLETT 1963, res Mea-
       ford, Ont.
      C1. Colleen Lynn, b 1963   C2. Robert Land Arnold, b 1965
   B4. Ada Eugenia Arnold, b 1941, mar 1959, Eugene Neil Lambert, res
       Hamilton, Ont.
      C1. Michelle Lillian Lambert, b 1959
      C2. Sheila Elsie Lambert, b 1961 C3. Shari Lynn Lambert, b 1962
   B5. Patricia Marie Dunham, b 1946, mar John David Dockree 1964, and
       2. John M. Birdsell, res Lynden, Ont.
      C1. Penny Marie Dockree, b 1965   C3. Dustin Robert Lawrence
      C2. Clinton David Ray Dockree, b 1966   Dockree, b 1969
   B6. Lawrence Ray Dunham, b 1951, mar Donna Marie Hill, 1972, res
       Lynden, Ont.
      C1. Deanna Marie Dunham, b 1975 C2. Steven Dunham, b 1977
   B7. Robert Guy Dunham, b 1955, mar Linda May Frankum 1976, res Dun-
       das, Ont.
      C1. Robert Michael Dunham, b 1976
A10. dau, b 1918, stillborn   A11. Gertrude, b 1921, d.y.
A12. Walter Frank, b 1922, mar Margaret Higginson, res Waterdown, Ont.
A13. Charles Lewis, b 1924
ROUSSEL, from J to N.B. (Rev. Le Gresley) Some in NB may be French,
not C.I. See LE GRAN CHIPAGAN, by Donat Robichaud.
ROWE, in Nfld. (Seary) Cf ROWE of C.I.
ROWE, ROW, boat keeper from J in Nfld. (K. Mathews)
ROWE, George, in Fortune Bay, Nfld. 1860s, also fam in Carbonear, Nfld.
ROWE, Eva Mary, b 1882 G, dau of Charles LE BOUTILLIER ROWE, b 1856 J,
   res G, and Ellen THOMAS of G, mar Alfred Edward Salway, b Eng., rem
   to Cardston, Alta. ca 1918. (MALLET GEN., INSTITUTE OF AMER. GEN.)

A1. Alfred Edward Charles Salway, b 1901 England
A2. Eva Ellen May Salway, b 1903 J, mar Robert H. Tagg
   B1. Velma Rose Tagg, b 1924 Cardston, Alta.   B2. Dale Salway Tagg
   B3. Melvin Tall Tagg   B4. Barbara Fay Tagg
A3. John BARLOW Salway, b 1905 England, mar Martha Magdelina Helm
   B1. Milicent Alfreda Salway, b Calgary, Alta.
   B2. Alfred BARLOW Helm Salway
A4. Millicent Ada Salway, b 1907 Wales, d 1918
A5. Harold Alfred Salway, b 1912 England, mar Eunice Sherwood
A6. Hope Rita Mary Salway, b 1916 England, mar Lloyd John Purnell
   B1. Robert Holman Salway Purnell, b 1937 Calgary, Alta.
A7. Holman Rowe Salway, b 1921 Cardston, Atla.
A8. Rowe Salway, b 1922   A9. Morton Salway, b 1925
ROWLAND, Capt. from G in Nfld. (K. Mathews)
ROWSELL, cf ROUSSEL of J (Stevens)   ROY, SEE CH.IS. COLL.
ROY, Francis Philippe, b J, mar Esther TOURGIS, qv, res Pointe aux
Trembles, near Montreal
A1. George Peter Roy, b 1855 bp by Rev. J.E. Tanner, Congreg. Ch.
   (Theresa Gravel, Mont.)
RUALT, RAULT, ---, from G, with G club, St. Thomas, Ont. 1938, mar
Clementine BACHLEY, qv.
A1. a son, mar Dorothy Connoy?
   B1. Jack Rualt, res St. Thomas, Ont.
RUDD, from G to Ontario (Soc. Jers.)
RUGG, Elsie Emmeline, b 1887 Mont Morin, St. Sampson, G, or Devon, dau
of Frederic RUGG of G, 1864-1931, and Emmeline Ada SMITH, b 1866 Les
Canichers, St. Peter Port, G, d G. Elsie mar Edmund Thomas MAHY, qv,
and d Willowdale, Ont. 1975. (Phyllis Mahy, Willowdale, Ont.)
RUMSEY, from C.I. to Bay de Verde, Nfld. (Shortis-Munn)
RUSHTON, from C.I.?, in Winnipeg
RUSSEL, Edward, in Bay Roberts 1798, from C.I.? Cf ROUSSEL (Stevens)
SACKETT, Michael, b G, son of Dulcie KEYHOE, qv, and Leslie Sackett, to
Canada ca 1975
SACREY, C.I. name south coast of Nfld. (G.W. Le Messurier; Seary) Cf
SACRE of J. Two bros said to be from J to Harbour Grace and Twilin-
gate, Nfld. 1800s (Seary)
SAINT, in Nfld. (Seary) Cf SAINT of J (Stevens)
ST. CLAIR, in Nfld. (Seary) Cf DE STE. CLAIR of J (Stevens)
SAINTE CROIX, DE STE. CROIX, many at Murdochville, Que. and Cap de
Rosiers, unver. Rose St.CROIX mar 1863 Gaspe CharlesH.BOND.
ST. CROIX, and SAINT CROIX, DE STE. CROIX, CROSS, etc., early settlers
in Malbaie, Que. from J (Father Ste. Croix; GLF) Also at Annapolis,
NS, current Stephenville, Nfld.
ST. CROISE, ST. CROIX, from C.I. to Nfld. (G.W. Le Messurier, Hug.
Soc., Seary)
STE. CROIX, listed as J merchant, area of St. Heber to Bonne Bay, Nfld.
1800s (Mannion)   ST.CROIX-SEE EXTRA PAGES
ST. CROIX, Christopher, in Great Placentia, Nfld. 1860s (Shortis-Munn)
also in St. Mary's Bay. Also ST. CROIX, boat keeper from C.I. in
Nfld. (K. Mathews)
STE. CROIX, and CROSS in Perce, Gaspe from C.I. (Cent. Bklt.)
ST. CROIX, Thomas, postmaster, Fox River, Gaspe, prob from J (GLF)
STE. CROIX, ST. CROIX, Grace Lillie, 1881-1917, wife of Ernest AHIER,
qv (GLF)
ST. CROIX, John D., b J, rem to Fox River, Gaspe, a merchant, unmar
ST. CROIX, Guillaume, b 17 , J, rem to Pt. St. Pierre, Que., where he
was bp 1803, and then mar Marguerite Chicoine, dau of Aubin C. and

GUILLAUME STE.CROIX, SEE EXTRA PAGES.
Anne David, of Pt. St. Pierre (Remiggi)
- A1. Jacques, b 1802 Malbaie, mar there 1826, Catherine Marthe CLEMENT, dau of Thomas C. and Elizabeth BAKER, qv, mar 2. Malbaie 1836, Marthe McCoy, dau of Richard M. and Ellen Redfoot?
- A2. Aubin, b 1804, d 1888, mar Genevieve O'Connors, bp 1809, who d 1888, and was bur Cap Rosiers, Gaspe. She was the dau of Pierre C. and Angelique Bergeron.
  - B1. Michel, b 1829, mar 1849 Sophie LaFlamme, dau of Etienne L. and Marie COULOMBE
    - C1. Michel, bp 1851, d 1870   C2. Malvina, b 1853, mar --- Cavanagh
    - C3. Etienne, bp 1855, mar 1976, Matilde Giasson, dau of Magloire G. and Elizabeth Packwood, and 2. Marguerite Fournier, and 3. Emma Bond, dau of Isaac B.
    - C4. Joseph Stanislas, b 1857, mar 1880, Victoire Fortin, dau of David Fortin and Rosalie Jacques
    - C5. Salomee, b 1859, mar 1879, --- Cavanaugh
    - C6. Ferdinand Desire, b 1861   C7. Magloire, b 1863, d.y.
    - C8. Marie Anne, b 1865, mar 1889, --- Packwood
    - C9. Zoe, b 1866, d 1894, mar 1884, Cavanagh
  - B2. Aubin, b 1830, mar 1858, Elmire Bond, dau of John Bond and Marie Rinfret-Malouin
    - C1. Marie, b 1859   C5. Genevieve, b 1867
    - C2. Florestine, b 1860   C6. Frederic, b 1869
    - C3. Jean Aubin, b 1864   C7. Elmire, mar 1887, --- Dufresne
    - C4. Susanne, b 1866
  - B3. Marie, b 1830, mar 1851, --- Coulombe, d 1896
  - B4. Elisabeth, b 1832
  - B5. Marguerite, b 1835, mar 1856, --- Fortier, d 1911
  - B6. Henriette, b 1837, d.y.   B7. Emilie, b 1838, d.y.
  - B8. Nicholas, b 1840, d.y.
  - B9. Marceline, b 1841, mar 1857, --- Rifou, d 1874
  - B10. Marcel, b 1843   B11. Esther, b 1844, d 1859
  - B12. Joseph, b 1846, mar 1871, Euphemie Morin, dau of Mellon Morin and Marie Michaud
  - B13. Susanne, b 1848, mar 1868, --- Samuel
  - B14. Angelique, b 1851, mar 1869, --- Coton
  - B15. Jeanne, b 1855, mar 1878, --- BRIARD
- A3. Marie, mar Malbaie 1825, Jacques Dumas, son of Jean Baptiste D. and Marie BOND, qv. Disp, 3-3c
- A4. Susanne, b 1807
  - B1. Marguerite, dau of Suzanne, mar Malbaie 1846, Jean B. Carbonneau, son of J.B. and Louise
- A5. Elisabeth, b 1815, mar 1831, Louis Brient, son of Thomas B. and Cecile Yvon
- A6. Guillaume, b 1816
- A7. John, mar Douglastown, Que. 1833, Anne McGrath, dau of John M. and Helene Hayden

ST. GEORGE, SAINT GEORGE, in Nfld. (Seary) Cf ST. GEORGE of J (Stevens)
ST. JOHN, in Nfld. (Seary) Cf ST. JOHN in J (Stevens)
SALLE, in Nfld. Poss SALLENEUVE? of J, there in 1749, said to be connected with J fisheries in Nfld.
SALMON, ---, in Norfolk Co., Ont., middle 1800s, said to be mar to a Mr. Southern
SALMON, Clement, b J, res Isle de la Madeleine, Gaspe 1861 (Census) with wife Luce Chiapon, b Isle de la Madeleine, with ch Luce, Eugene, Chloraine? and Marie. Poss. that CHIAPON was CHIASSON?
SALMON, Pierre, in St. Peter du Bois, G 1614

SALT and SALTER, in Nfld. (Seary) Cf same in J (Stevens) Also cf
LA SALIER, DOREY fam.
SALTER, ---, mar John Albert FALLE, qv, from C.I. ca 1860, res Belleville, Ont.
SALTER, Daniel, b J, also Jane, b J, in Gaspe 1861 (Census) with Francis, b Gaspe
SALTER, Rachel, b J, husband Wm. b Grt. Britain, with William Philip and Rachel, all b G, in Cap Rosier 1861 (Census)
SALTER, Joseph and sons, ship builders from Moncton, NB to Cape Breton early 1800s (Capt. Parker)
A1. Joseph Jr., mar dau of John Nesbitt
A2. Vibert, a desc named Roy Salter is current
SALTER, William, bp J, farmer and fisherman, poss b Isle of Wight? (Remiggi) Mar Rachel ---, bp J, 1818, res Anse au Griffon, Gaspe.
A1. William F., b 1846 J   A4. Harriet L., b 1851 J
A2. Philip, b 1848 J   A5. Jane, b 1854 J
A3. Rachel A., b 1850 J   A6. Francis P., b 1859 Canada
SALVIDOR or SAVIDENT, John, had grant of land 1819 at Gaspe Basin. Origin unver.
SAMPSON, SAMSON, in Nfld. (Seary) Cf same in C.I.
SAMSON, Wm. in Greenspond, Nfld. 1860s (Rev. Hammond and Cannon Smith) from C.I.?
SAMSON, some located in C.B. Island early 1800s (Holland's Description of Cape Breton Island) Origin unver.
SAMSON, Anne, see George MAUGER in LE VESCONTE fam
SAMSON, Elizabeth, b J, d Bon. Is. 1912, wife of Thomas G. BUTLIN, qv.
SANQUA, see ST. CROIX
SANS SANS, Louis, b J, of French origin, fisherman, mar Deborah English, res Port Daniel, Gaspe 1871 with two chn, Maryann and Sarah (Census)
SARCHET, Algie Marquand, b 1883 U.S., of C.I. fam in Ohio, Guernsey Co., d 1952. Rem 1912 to Sask, then in 1941 to BC, mar Magdalena Maldaner, 9 chn. He was the desc of Thomas S. and Catherine Marquand, who rem from G in 1806 and settled in Ohio. Hundreds of desc in Ohio. Sarchets all over U.S., many in Canada. (Sarchet Genealogy, Fred. Sarchet, Detroit; Mrs. E. Mae Wildy, Delta, BC: QAAM, by Turk; Kenneth Sarchet, Indian Harbor Beach, Fla.)
A1. Addy Mark   A4. Victor Bert   A7. Lenora
A2. Bud Elden   A5. Magdalene   A8. June Violet
A3. Gary Lyle   A6. Anne   A9. Edith Mae
SARCHET, John, who d in G 1861, was the second of four Sarchet bros who came to Guernsey Co., Ohio 1806. A John res in London, Ont. a few yrs. ago. Others claim fam rem to Philadelphia. Chn: John, Joseph, Moses, Albin, Harriet, Helen, Marie, Sophia, Eliza and Ann. (Sarchet Genealogy)
SARGENT, in Nfld. (Seary) Cf SERGENT of J (Stevens)
SARK, in Canada. Poss very old DE SERQ, SARK of C.I.
SARRE, in G from 1100s, some in Torteval Par.
SARRE, Wilfred Herbert, b G, son of Hilary Martin S. and Rachel DE CARTERET, one of six chn, res Kitchener? 1932. Came on the ASCANIA, settled first in Prince Rupert, B.C., returned to Montreal. (Grace Schmearer, Kitchener, Ont.) (Arrived in Canada 1808)
A1. George De Carteret, b 1916, mar 1. Florence Irene Knell, 4 chn, and 2. Alice Simpson, one son. He d 1968, res Kitchener, Ont.
   B1. Beverly Jane, mar Richard Gilbert Freed, 2 chn, res Kitchener
      C1. Elizabeth Jane Freed, b Winterhaven, Fla.
      C2. Richard de Carteret Freed, res Alsomonte Springs, Fla.

       B2. Barbara Joan, mar Gary Reuben Falhaber, 3 chn, res Kitchener
          C1. Sheila Joan Felhaber   C3. Shelly Ann F lhaber
          C2. Randall Reuben Falhaber
       B3. George de Carteret Knell, mar Patricia Ann Grace, 2 sons, res
          Kitchener
          C1. Bradley Patrick   C2. Christopher de Carteret
       B4. Florence Irene, mar Kim Bryant, no issue
       B5. Wilfred Herbert, mar Marion de Weerd, 2 chn
          C1. Scott de Carteret   C2. Steven de Carteret
    A2. Wilfred Robert, b 1918, mar Olga Louise Olsen, 2 daus. Wilfred in
       C.A.F. WWII. Res Galt, Ont.
       B1. Susan Elizabeth, mar Richard Demarse, 2 chn
          C1. Richard Robert Edward Demarse, b London, Ont.
          C2. Tammy Chantise Demarse
       B2. Karen Olga Sarre, mar David Dietrich, 3 chn
          C1. Jason Edward Dietrich   C3. Amanda Marie Dietrich
          C2. Nathan David Dietrich
    A3. Grace Rachelle, b 1922, mar F. Kendall Schmearer, 2 chn
       B1. Elizabeth Mae Schmearer, mar David James Maxwell, a son, Christopher Michael
       B2. Kendall Andrew Schmearer, unmar
    A4. Elizabeth Ethel, b 1925, mar Robert Bruce MacLeod, 3 chn, she d 1966
       B1. Edna Frances MacLeod, b Peace River, Alta., mar Bruce Hill, 2 chn
          C1. Jeffrey Hill, b Brantford, Ont.   C2. Craig Hill
       B2. Jane Elizabeth MacLeod, unmar   B3. Roderick A. MacLeod, unmar
    A5. Annette, b 1930, bur Mt. Royal Cem, Montreal, Quebec
SARRE, Adolph, from C.I. to Hamilton, Ont. Second cousin to Wilfred
    above.   Arrived 1908?
SARRE, from G to Canada (Tanna Savident, Muriel Walsh, Victoria, BC;
    James Savident, San Mateo, Calif.)

SARRE, SARE, SAYRE, said to be forms of SARRE in Canada. Poss from
    SAIRE, east of Cherbourg, France
SARTIN, in Nfld., said to be of C.I. origin. (Rev. Hammond)
SAUMAREZ, fisheries of Channel Islanders in Maritimes, N.B. and N.S.
    (Soc. Jers. Bull. 1951)
SAUMAREZ, Durell, 1776-1799, served with the 8th Kings Reg't as ensign,
    Lt. from 1780, Capt. from 1790. Regiment posted at Niagara Falls,
    Ont., left Canada 1785. 80 pages in Canadian Archives.
SAUMAREZ, some work on the English form of this name done by William
    Saltmarsh of Clearwater, Minn. Sir Lionel Saltmarsh knighted in 1067.
    Some SALTMARSH now in N.A., may have been SAUMAREZ of C.I.
SAUVAGE, Thomas, b J, in Fox River 1831, mar Helene Henley (Remiggi)
    Some Prot., some R.C.
    A1. Henriette, b 1832, mar 1849 --- Dunn
    A2. Thomas, b 1834, mar 1854, Victoire Ouellet, bp 1834, dau of Andrew
       Ouellet and Victoire ENGLISH or LANGLOIS. Res Fox River, Gaspe.
       B1. Marie Victoire, bp 1855, mar 1874, --- Daraiche
       B2. Natalie, bp 1857, mar 1878, --- Francoeur
       B3. Thomas, bp 1858, mar 1833, Obeline Dufresne, of Fox River, dau of
          Michel D. and Obeline Cotton
       B4. Guillaume, William, bp 1860, mar 1886, Aurelie Cotton, dau of
          Pierre Cotton and Victoire Lemieux
       B5. Andre Guilbert, bp 1862, mar 1883, Marcelline Fortier, dau of
          Aubin F. and Marguerite STE. CROIX, qv. Poss known as Albert,
          not Andre Guilbert.
       B6. Jean, bp 1865   B7. Jacques, bp 1867

SAUVAGE

SEE SAUVAGE DATA IN CHANNEL ISLAND COLLECTION.
B8. Charles, bp 1868, d 1886
B9. Helene Rebecca, bp 1870, mar --- Daraiche
A3. Helene, bp 1937, d 1861, mar 1856, --- Synett
A4. John, b 1839, mar 1854
SAUVAGE, Ch. Is. fam in London, Ont. 1938, belonged to G club. Poss Thomas? Surname G 1117.
SAUVARIN, from G in Victoria, BC 1941, C.I. Society
SAUVARY, Samuel in Vale, G 1615. Cf also SAVARY, SYVRET
SAUVARY, Thomas J., from G to Victoria, BC 1906, unmar
SAUVARY, Thomas Falla, b 1858 G, mar Harriet BEAN, b 1860, rem to Victoria, BC 1920
  A1. Harriet Olive, b 1885 G, mar Lewis LANGLOIS, qv, 6 chn (Mrs. G.A. Taylor, Cobble Hill, BC)
  A2. Thomas John SAUVARY, b ca 1887 G
  A3. Leah OZANNE, b 1892 G, to Victoria 1912, mar Edwin ROWBOTHAM
    B1. Edwin Thomas, b 1915   B3. Frances May, b 1927
    B2. Olive Marie, b 1919
SAUVARY, James George, b 1893 G, son of James Henry S. of St. Peter Port, and Ellen BROWN, b 1859, rem to Toronto, Ont. in 1906, mar Gertrude Grace Malins, b 1895 Ireland (Hazel Scrutton, Scarboro, Ont.)
  A1. Grace Ellen, b 1925, mar Lloyd George Harry Young, b 1920, a son, Brian Thomas, b 1946
  A2. Hazel Gertrude, b 1927, mar Richard Henry Scrutton, b 1920
    B1. Susan Hazel, b 1949, mar Robyn Benton Marshall, b 1944
      C1. Adam Benton Marshall, b 1974
SAVAGE, Jean, of C.I.?, from St.Mary,Jersey?,, mar Elizabeth DE GRUCHY   SEE SAVAGE DATA IN CHAN.IS. COLLECTION.
  A1. Thomas, b 1808 J, mar Julie COLLIN dit La Liberte of Perce. Thomas was MLA of Quebec, merchant, miller, partner with John J. LE GROS of Malbay in Fishery. Thomas d ca 1890s. (Brochet)
    Mar 2. Agnes McSweeney?
  A2. Charles, mar Margaret Fermet, poss Fennet?
    B1. Anne Jane, b 1845 Perce
    B2. Charles Jr., mar 1863, Elizabeth Mahan, a son, Philip John, b 1866
    B3. Thomas Narcisse, mar Mary Ann Caulfield, a dau, Winnifred, b 1889
SAVAGE, Philip, age 55, b J, master mariner at Cape Cove, Gaspe 1871 (Census)
SAVAGE, Charles, son of John, b 1799 J, d 1869, bur Cape Cove Anglican Cem. Gaspe
SAVAGE, Philip, of Gaspe, mar Anna Eliza NICOLL, a dau, Anna Eliza, b 1864 (Brochet)
SAVAGE, Thomas, from J, shipowner and fishery at Cape Cove, Gaspe 1800s (Le Moine) and Fishery at Grand River, Gaspe 1880s. A Thomas S. b J, age 62 in 1871, at Cape Cove
SAVAGE, Capt. Francis Philip, b J, 1841-1893, bur Cape Cove, Gaspe(GLF)
SAVAGE, Sophia, wife of Charles S., b 1843 St. Mathew, J, d 1962, bur Cape Cove
SAVAGE, Charles, son of John, b J, 1799-1869, bur Gaspe
  A1. Charles N., 1823-1915, mar Elizabeth Mahan, prob Irish, 1831-1917
SAVAGE, Philip J., 1866-1935, mar Edith Beck, 1869-1942, bur Cape Cove, Gaspe (GLF)
SAVAGE, LE SAVAGE, Elizabeth, b G, in Cap Chat, Gaspe 1861 (Census)
SAVAGE, Francis Sr., b J, age 50, in Perce 1861 (Census) with Charles, b Canada and Sophie, b J
SAVAGE, Charles, b J, wife, Marguerite Fennet?, b Canada, with Marguerite, Elizabeth and Mary, b Canada, all in Perce 1861 (Census)
SAVARY, Judge W., helped to raise St. Luke's Church at Annapolis, NS

1815. He was poss a desc of the Thomas who was in the Plymouth colony in 1634. A desc, Nathan, rem to N.S. after the Rev. War. "At Digby, NS he mar 1785 as his second wife, Diadamia Sabin, dau of Jeremiah S. and Susanna LE VALLEY, a desc through her mother of the Hug fam of Le Valle, or Le Vallee, which came to Marblehead, Mass. from France or from the Channel Islands." (New England Register, ca 1926) Nathan d 1826, father of 17 chn, 5 by first wife Elizabeth Nye, and 12 by Diadamia Sabin. Second ch and oldest son Sabine Savary, b 1788, d 1878, mar 1821, Olive Marshall, b at Yarmouth, NS, dau of Samuel and Olive Haskell Marshall. Olive's father Will Haskett, Jr., came with his father, Wm. Sr. from Beverly, Mass ca 1767. See also QAAM, by Turk.

SAVIDENT, James S., of Marette, St. Saviour, J, 1856-1886, mar Lucie LE MAITRE, 1855-1945, of Vale, G?, to Canada ca 1912, settled Victoria, BC (Tanna Savident, Powell River, B.C.)
A1. James E., b 1880 G, mar Eliza Jane TOSTEVIN, 1882-1956
  B1. James E., b 1900 Vale, G, d 1976, mar Winnifred Louise Craven, 1902-1975
    C1. Winnifred, b 1924, mar --- Morgan, res San Mateo, Calif.
    C2. Verna, b 1930, mar --- Bomont, res Redwood City, Calif.
    C3. James H., b 1933, mar ---, res Campbell. Calif.
  B2. Ernest Peter, b 1901 Vale, G, to Vict., BC, mar Elizabeth Stewart 1925, 2 chn, and 2. Tanna W. Hooft, 1947, 2 chn, res Powell River, BC
    C1. Gordon, b 1926, mar Eileen Lewis 1946 Nanaimo, BC
      D1. Kenneth, b 1948, mar, a dau
      D2. Guelda, mar ---, res Nanaimo, BC
    C2. Jean, mar Leslie McKenzie 1950, separated 1973, 5 chn, res Powell River, BC
    C3. Marguerite Kathleen, by second wife, b 1949, mar Davis Brooks, 1975
      D1. Nicole, b 1969   D2. Michael Davis Brooks, b 1976
    C4. Loren, b 1953, mar Darlene Cosgrove 1972
      D1. Karen Janice, b 1973   D2. Paul James, b 1976
  B3. Arthur J., b 1902 Vale, G, d 1965, rem to Calif. 1923,4, d 1960 Victoria, BC
A2. Jack, b 1882 Mielles, Vale, G, mar Amy NOURY, qv, res Vict., BC, no issue
A3. William, b 1883 G, d 1955, res Vancouver, BC, unmar
A4. Ernest, b 1884 G, d 1940, unmar, res Powell River 1930, bur Vanc.
SAVIDENT, Calvin, res Gaspe
SAVIDENT, John, from G, in Gaspe 1880 (Curtis Patterson, Harrington Harbor, Que.)
SAWYER, see SOHIER. SAWYER also found in C.I.
SAYRE, John, S.P.G. minister in N.B. 1800s, poss from C.I. SAYRE from G to Ohio.
SCAMMEL and JOURNEAUX
SCAMMEL, Eli, b 1817 Wiltshire, Eng., son of Thomas S. and Hannah LUSH, LUCE?, mar 1. Mary Ann PIKE, who d ca 1860, 8 chn; 3 d.y. Eli rem to J ca 1839, all chn b St. Helier, J. Mar 2. 1863, Jane JOURNEAUX, qv, b 1829 St. Helier, J, dau of Charles J and Anne RENOUF, qv. Fam rem to Brantford, Ont. 1871. At least one of first wife returned to J. (Florence Ferguson, Strathroy, Ont.; Jane Bixby, Columbus, Ohio)
A1. Jane, b 1864, mar George Johnston, d 1950 Galt, Ont., no issue
A2. Lydia, b 1865, d 1923, unmar, res Brantford, Ont.
A3. Charles, b 1866, mar Lillian Eliza Sommerville 1890 and d 1944 Brantford, Ont.

B1. Lillian Hope Scammel, b 1897 Brantford, mar 1920 Archibald Shuert? She d 1927.
  C1. Ruth Shuert, b 1921, mar David Cleaves C2. Trevor Shuert, b 1923
B2. Florence Jean Scammel, b 1899 Brantford, mar Frank Riley, who d 1977
  C1. Florence Jean Riley, b 1925, mar James Patton Ferguson
    D1. Wm. Riley Ferguson, b 1958, res Strathroy, Ont.
    D2. James Douglas Ferguson, b 1960, d.y.
    D3. David Somerville Ferguson, b 1962
    D4. Robert Scott Ferguson, b 1964
  C2. Helen Marguerite Riley, b 1932 Goderich, Ont., mar David Howard Jaccki, res St. Catherines, Ont.
    D1. Frank Howard Jaccki, b 1963 D2. David Keith Jaccki, b 1968
B3. Ethel Marie Scammel, b 1900 Brantford, Ont., mar David Rutherford
  C1. Mary Jean Rutherford, b 1926 Brantford, mar Kenneth Heyden 1950
    D1. Jayne Heyden, b 1950, mar David Lane
      E1. Scott Lane, b 1971   E2. Jennifer Lane, b 1974
    D2. Lynn Heyden, b 1950, mar Richard Lewis 1977
    D3. Craig Heyden, b 1964   Katherine Hilda
  C2. Eric David Rutherford, b 1929 Brantford, mar RICHARDSON 1953
    D1. Lorie Ann Rutherford, b 1957
    D2. Janice Rutherford, b 1959 D3. Tod Stephen Rutherford, b 1963
B4. Marjorie Ruth Scammel, b 1900, twin, mar Nelson Campbell, d 1968
  C1. Joyce Marie Campbell, b 1930 Brantford, mar Ronald M. Brown 1957
  C2. Ross Nelson Campbell, b 1931 Brantford, mar Marian Ruth McClellan 1957
    D1. Jeffrey Campbell, b 1959   D3. Stephen Campbell, b 1964
    D2. David Campbell, b 1960
  C3. Marjorie Rosalyn Campbell, b 1933 Brantford, mar Heinz-Gugern Peper 1956
    D1. Erhardt William Peper, b 1961 Kitchener, Ont.
    D2. Marjorie Ann Elizabeth Peper, b 1963
A4. Martha, b 1868, mar Denoice Hadcock, d 1962 Detroit, Mich., no issue
A5. Emelie Scammel, b 1870, mar 1893, George Dixon, d 1953 Detroit, Mich.
  B1. Clarence Scammel Dixon, b 1896, d 1897
  B2. Edith Madeline Dixon, b 1898 Detroit, mar Frank Keller, res New Orleans, La. Div.
    C1. Kathryn Jane Keller, stillborn 1919
    C2. Thomas Dixon Keller, b 1922, mar, with chn
  B3. George Dixon, b 1906, d ca 1973 Fla. Mar Jane Oostema 1936, res Birmingham, Mich.
    C1. David George Dixon, b 1938   C3. Peter Fuller Dixon, b 1945
    C2. John Roelof Dixon, b 1940   C4. Vivien Jane Dixon, b 1947
  B4. Jane Elizabeth Dixon, b 1915, mar 1941, Albert Tilton Bixby, son of Geo. and Carrie Bixby, b 1909 Indianapolis, Inc.
    C1. James Albert Bixby, b 1943 Detroit, Mich., mar 1966, Linda Lou Eagle, dau of John Eagle and Deloris Cannon, b 1947, res Westerville, Ohio
      D1. William Edward Bixby, b 1968 Columbus, OH
      D2. Jill Anne Bixby, b 1972
    C2. Linda Jane Bixby, b 1945, res Columbus, OH
SCARISBRICK, Mrs., member of C.I. Soc. in Vancouver, BC 1945
SCHREIBER. Not a C.I. name so far as the compiler knows, but the Schreiber fam intermar several times with old G families, and may have been resident in the Islands for some time. Schreiber, Weymouth George, b England, mar 1. Harriet De Lisle, desc of Daniel Delisle. She was related through her mother to the fam of Sir Isaac Brock.

This Schreiber family has many connections in Ontario and other provinces. Chart in Ottawa Archives. SCOTT: SEE EXTRA PAGES
SCOTT, member of C.I. Society in B.C. 1940s
SCOTT, ship owner and shop keeper from J and G in Nfld. (K. Mathews)
SCOTT, Elizabeth, 1811-1857, wife of Elias DE LA PERELLE, qv, bur St. Peters, Paspebiac, Gaspe (GLF)
SEALE, to Gaspe 1800s. (Rev. d'Hist; Betty Tardif's list; J.H. Le Breton list)
SEALE, John A., 1874-1921, mar Annie C., 1878-1963, bur St. Peters, Paspebiac, Gaspe. Prob from C.I. (GLF)
SEALE, of J, in 1717 was involved with the Nfld. trade and fisheries (C.R. Fay)
SEALE, in Nfld. (Seary) Cf SEALE of J (Stevens)
SEARLE, in Nfld. (Seary) Cf SEARLE of J (Stevens)
SEAWARD, SEWARD, Exporter and merchant from J in Nfld. (K. Mathews) Involved in Nfld. trade and fisheries in 1717 (C.R. Fay)
SEBIRE, John Alfred, b G, mar there, Eliza ROUSSEL, qv, b 1870, rem to Canada, 7 chn (Ida Woods, Stoney Creek, Ont.) Cf SEBIREL and LESBIREL.
A1. John Nelson, b G, d.y., mar in G, Ellen DE CARTERET, qv.
  B1. John Alfred, res Vale, G, d Canada
A2. Eliza Amelia, b 1893 G, d 1969 Canada. Mar Harold Sykes
  B1. Marion Sykes, mar Hugh Towner, Canada, res Calif.
    C1. Fred. Sykes, res Ottawa, Ont.
    C2. Donna Sykes, res Calif., mar, 2 sons
    C3. Alan Skyes   C4. Caroline Sykes, res Calif.
  B2. Eileen Sykes, b 1916, mar Duncan Macmillan
    C1. Wm. George Macmillan, b 1936, mar Elsie Walleghan
      D1. William Jesse Macmillan, b 1959
      D2. Catharine Evelyn Macmillan, b 1959, d 1972
      D3. Kim Irene Macmillan, b 1955
      D4. Elaine Mae Eileen Macmillan, b 1961
    C2. Elaine Susanne Macmillan, b 1947, res Hamilton, Ont.
    C3. Vernon Leslie Macmillan, b 1943, mar Marie Bulleyment
      D1. Theresa Marie Macmillan, b 1961
      D2. Catherine Louise Macmillan, b 1962
      D3. Faith Eileen Macmillan, b 1964
  B3. Harold Sykes, b 1918, res Stoney Creek, Ont., mar Ida Fern Merritt
    C1. Stephanie Lynn Sykes, b 1948, res London, Ont.
  B4. Vernon Douglas Sykes, b 1924, mar Norah Kemp, res Dundas, Ont., no issue
  B5. Stanley Earl Sykes, b 1930, mar Shirley Joyce Wilson, Burlington, Ont.
    C1. Ross Harry Skyes, b 1956   C2. Neil Stanley Sykes, b 1959
A3. Lena Sebire, b G, d.y.
A4. John William, b G, mar Mattie Elliott
  B1. Rachel Sebire, b 1925 Hamilton, d 1966
A5. Reginald, b 1899 G, d 1967, mar Jean Anderson in Hamilton, Ont.
  B1. Robert Sebire, b 1926 Hamilton, mar Jacquelin Norton, res Cedarburg, Wisc.
    C1. Sandra Jean, b 1954, res Mich.   C3. Gail Ann, b 1961
    C2. Robert John, b 1958
A6. Edgar Alfred Sebire, b 1905 G, d 1936 Canada, mar Aileen Smith
  B1. Donald Charles, b 1929, mar Jean Corbeit?, res Oakville, Ont.
    C1. Dawn Elizabeth, b 1956   C3. Deborah Jean, b 1959
    C2. Kimberley Louise, b 1957   C4. Jason Robert Charles, b 1973
  B2. Beverly Joan, b 1931, mar James Lennard Myall, res Hamilton, Ont.
    C1. Michael James Myall, b 1956

A7. Ida Maud, b 1909 Canada, mar Norman Woods 1934
  B1. Lennard Alan Woods, b 1936, mar Marjorie Saunders, 3 chn
    C1. Thomas James Woods, b 1959   C3. Brian Edward Woods, b 1966
    C2. Brenda Lynne Woods, b 1961
  B2. Ralph Herbert Woods, b 1937, mar Patricia Beamer
    C1. Cynthia Jo-Anne Woods, b 1957   C3. James Albert Woods, b 1961
    C2. Ronald Ralph Woods, b 1959

SEDGELEY, SEDGLEY, see BROUARD, MAHY, ROUSSEL

SEIVRY, variant in N.B. of desc of Capt. George Syvret of Jersey, who settled in Miscou, N.B. (Ganong, Wm. Francis, THE HISTORY OF MISCOU AND SHIPPEGAN)

SELOUS, Harold, first Mayor of Nelson, B.C. "English soldier Philip Slow, in 1650, mar a Jersey girl and settled in the Island. The family name became later jersified into Selous, and from them descended Selous the Painter and Selous the Mighty Hunter." From BAILIWICK OF JERSEY, by G.R. Balleine. Book written on hunting, etc. by SELOUS.

SELOUS, John, b J, in Gaspe Bay 1861

SENNOTT, SYNNOTT, in Gaspe and Nfld. John and Michael SENNOTT in Placentia Bay, Nfld. 1860s. Said to be of C.I. ancestry. (Rev. Hammond)

SERELLE, poss PERELLE?, agent and boat keeper from J in Nfld. (K. Mathews)

SERGEANT, SARGENT, boat keeper from G in Nfld. (K. Mathews)

SERRE, from G to Gaspe to Alpena, Mich?

SEVRET, George, from C.I., res Pt. Miscou, NB 1850, fam of 6 (Census) Cf SYVRET

SEWARD, SEAWARD, exporter and merchant from J in Nfld. (K. Mathews, C.R. Fay)

SHANNEY, Capt. Earl of Gaspe, recent, said to be of C.I. Origin. Poss CHENEY, CHESNEY, etc., of J (Capt. Poidevin)

SHAW, William, b J, in Cap Rosier, Caspe 1861 (Census) with Henrietta, b G, Adeline, John, Jane, Abraham, Mary Ann, all b Gaspe (Ernest Shaw, Gaspe Harb., Que.)
  A1. Adeline   A2. John   A3. Jane
  A4. Abraham, mar Susanne BAILEY of Cap Rosier. He is said to have had other chn, who remained in J. Order of chn below is not certain. An Abram Shaw left J in 1861, settled Cap Rosier, mar Victoria Smith, b Fox River.
    B1. Arthur, b ca 1893   B2. Archie, b ca 1897
    B3. Thomas, b 1898, mar ---?
      C1. Reglis?   C3. Edwin   C5. Harold?
      C2. Guilbert   C4. Cecil   C6. Norman
      C7. Ernest, b 1949, mar Pierette Element
        D1. Daniel, b c 1969   D3. Devin, b 1973
        D2. Sylvia, b 1972   D4. Jino, b 1975
      C8. Abraham C12. Mabel C16. Joyce   C20. Pearl
      C9. Andrew   C13. Georgiane C17. Angeline
      C10. Gary   C14. Gertrude C18. Geraldine
      C11. Charles C15. Louise   C19. Eveline
  A5. Guy, b ca 1907   A8. William A11. Louise
  A6. Edward, b ca 1909 A9. Eveline A12. Mary
  A7. Elfonce, b 1913   A10. Susan   A13. Ethel

SHAW, James, Thomas and William, planters and fishermen in Sandy Pt., Nfld. 1871 (Lovell) Said to be C.I. desc.

SHEPHERD, E. Woodburne, 1885-1943, of C.I.?, mar Berta HOCQUARD, qv, E.W. bur St. Andrews, New Carlisle, Gaspe

SHEPHERD, SHEPPARD, SHIPPARD, SHEPPERD, etc., tradesman from G in Nfld. (K. Mathews)

SHEPPARD, SEE EXTRA PAGES.
SHEPPARD, Martin, b J, to Quebec 1818, where he had two bros. Became sheriff of Gaspe 1825-1884. (Rev. d'Histoire) Sept. 1975
SHEPPARD, John, in Mint Cove, Nfld. 1783. Also in Cupids, in 1802 (Rev. Hammond)
SHEPPARD, H. in Mint Cove 1797 and in Brigus 1787. The chn of Frank were in Mint Cove, Conc. Bay, Nfld. 1783.
SHEPPARD, in Paspebiac, Gaspe and in New Carlisle, Que. (Que. Prov. Arch.)
SHEPPARD, M., age 69, b G, with Jane, age 60, b Quebec, were at Coxtown 1871. See Martin below.
A1. William, age 32   A2. Ann, age 31   A3. Julia, age 29 (Brochet)
SHEPPARD, William GRUT, 1838-1925, prob b G, mar the widow of Peter BREHAUT, qv, of Quebec, Therese Lemaitre Bellenoy? in 1818. 4 step-chn? Issue not known. (32 pages of agreement under Brehaut papers, Archives, Ottawa). William G. was poss the son of Martin below.
SHEPPARD, Martin, b 1800 G, d Carlisle, Que. 1884. Sheriff and Notary public, 59 yrs. Mar Jane Adams, 1811-1896. (Census; Maroldo)
A1. Thomas Grut, b 1837, d 1860
A2. William M., b 1838, mar Jane Blaylock, 1847-1886, bur St. Andrews, Carlisle, Que.
A3. Anne, b ca 1840   A4. Julia, b ca 1842
SHIELDS, Mrs. Dorothy, of London, Ont., related through sister to Carters of J
SHOESMITH, J surname (Saunders) Some to Canada?
SIEVRY, see also SEVRET, SYVRET, SAVERY, SEVERY, SIVERT, SIVRAIS, etc.
SIEVRY, SYVRET, Capt. George, from J to Miscou Island, NB 1830s. George d in NB ca 1846, a "tidewaiter." Was witness to an indenture in Saumarez, Northumberland Co., NB 1827. (N.B. Archives) (See also A GENEALOGICAL AND BIOGRAPHICAL RECORD OF THE SAVERY AND SEVERY FAMILIES, by Judge Savary of Annapolis Royal, NS and Lydia Savary of E. Wareham, Mass., Boston, 1893)
SIGNAC, Capt. merchant, boat keeper from J in Nfld. (K. Mathews)
SIMMONDS, SYMONDS, SIMONS, byboat keeper from J in Nfld. (K. Mathews)
SIMMONDS, Gerturde, from G, settled in Toronto, or poss her parents
SIMMONS, James, b J, age 31 in 1871, farmer in Cose, Bon. Co., Gaspe, with a houseful of young blacksmith apprentices, named STRONG, HULEN, LE BOUTILLIER, BROWN, LE MOUSTRE, and RENAULT, age 14 to 20. (Census; Maroldo)
SIMON, in Nfld. (Seary) Cf SIMON of J (Stevens)
SIMON, Mary, wife of John Richard GAUDION. They settled Detroit then Rochester, NY. (See QAAM, by Turk)
SIMON, Austin, from G to Ont., dau mar T.C. Morrison, res Toronto
SIMON, wife of Wm. Nicholas OZARD, qv
SIMON, William, said to be first fisherman from G to settle near Shiphead, Gaspe. Was in Indian Cove 1790 or before. This land is now Forillon Park. (Innis)
SIMON, Peter, settled in Indian Cove Gaspe 1817, and his bro in 1815 (Irwin Simon, Fontenelle, Gaspe)
SIMON, Nicholas and Rachel, b G, in Gaspe Bay 1860 (Census) with Emile, b Gaspe
SIMON, William, a teacher, b G, also Peter, John and Margaret, b G, and Marguerite, Hellier, William, and William, all b Canada (Census 1871)
SIMON, Mary M., 1843-1895, wife of John Simon, her sister Amelia, 1844-1917
SIMON, Watson Fairfield, 1902-1960. This fam bur at Rosebridge, United Ch Cem., Gaspe
SIMON, Nicholas A., 1874-1947   ONE SIMON TO BC CANADA 1800s.

SIMON, Priscilla, 1870-1934. Also Priscilla, wife of Elias P. GAVEY, bur St. George's Cove 1925, age 84. (Brochet)
SIMPSON, Charles Jr., of C.I.?, present at a wedding in Roseville, Gaspe 1869. Origin unver.
SIMPSON, tradesman from G in Nfld. (K. Mathews)
SINNOT, in Nfld. (Seary) Cf SINATT of J (Stevens) Cf SENNOTT and SYNETT
SIOUVILLE, Channel Islanders in Maritimes Fisheries (J.H. Le Breton list)
SIVRAIS, SYVRET, Joseph, age 26, b Que., in Newport, Gaspe 1871 (Census)
SIVRET, SYVRET, Capt., ship owner and merchant, from J in Nfld. (K. Mathews)
SIVRET, James, George Sr. and George Jr., signed a mail route petition in Shippegan, NB 1834
SIVRET, George, age 35, b J, since 12 yrs. old res in Arichat, NS, 1817, 3 chn with him. Asked for lot in Arichat Harb. This may be the one that later appeared in N.B.? (PANS)
SIVRET, Pierre, son of George S. and Appoline Chiasson, res Miscou, NB, mar 1857, Ursule Chiasson (Robichaud)
SIVRET, Honore, res Miscou, son of Gedeon S. and Marie Forbes, mar 1901, Henriette Chiasson, b 1874 Shippegan, NB (Robichaud, p. 320)
SKELTON, Channel Islander in Maritimes Fisheries (J.H. Le Breton list)
SKETTON, poss SKELTON?, Philippe, steward, son of Philip and of Ann ANUF (ESNOUF) of J, mar Charlotte JEWELL at St. Patrick, Que. 1883
SLEMAN, SLEEMAN, Capt. from J in Nfld. (K. Mathews)
SLOUS, John, b J, age 34, Methodist, merchant in Gaspe Bay 1871 (Brochet)
SLOUS, SELOUS, SLOW, see also SELOUS
SLOUS, Major, Gaspe Militia, 1860s from J
SLOUS, Brigadier W.J., res Victoria, BC, had 2 bros. Father from England, who d when son was 14 yrs. Not ver.
SLY, Capt. from G in Nfld. (K. Mathews)
SMITH, this name found in J and G. Prob many more in Canada from C.I.
SMITH, Margaret, b 1829, d 1919, mar Edward LE GALLAIS, bur St. Andrews Angl. Cem, Port Daniel, Gaspe (GLF)
SMITH, Rebecca, poss sister of above, b 1834, d 1874, bur St. Peters, Paspebiac. Mar Philip LE GALLAIS (GLF)
SMITH, Clifford, husband of Aline LIHOU, qv. Smith was VP of G Soc. in Hamilton, Ont., 1900s
SMITH, David, signed the Gaspe Petition in 1820
SMITH, Francis MOON, also signed the Petition. Moon is C.I. surname.
SMITH, ---, b G, mar Valerie BOUGOURD, res Chatham, Ont. Valerie related to ROBERT fam
SMITH, Augusta Barbara, 1880-1943, mar Frank James HOCQUARD, qv, bur United Ch, West Paspebiac, Gaspe (GLF)
SMITH, Alice, b Randow Island, Trinity Bay, Nfld., mar Rev. Ralph LE DREW, av.
SMOLLETT, in Perce, Gaspe, from C.I.? SNOW DATA IN CI COLL.
SNOW, byboat keeper from J in Nfld. (K. Mathews) To NFLD 1705
SNOWMAN, Henry Theodore, b 1907 St. Helier, J, son of Henry Theodore and Henrietta Gertz. He mar Jennifred LEGGO, b 1899, rem to Ontario.
A1. Lita Henrietta, b 1928, mar William Weston of Toronto
   B1. Carol Lee Weston, b 1947   B2. Paul Henry Weston, b 1949
A2. Gary Stuart, b 1937, mar Mary GIRARD, qv, b 1940
   B1. Donna, b 1958   B2. Wanda, b 1959   B3. Shane, b 1967
A3. Iris Sylvia, b 1932, mar Edmund Boyle, 8 chn
   B1. Patricia Boyle, b 1949   B5. Darlene Boyle, b 1959
   B2. Peggy Boyle, b 1951   B6. Easter Boyle, b 1961
   B3. Sharon Boyle b 1955   B7. Dwight Boyle, b 1966
   B4. Dean Boyle, b 1957   B8. Hearn Boyle, b 1968

A4. Lorne Henry Joseph, b 1941, mar Doris Ann McGregor, b 1942, 2 chn
B1. Peter Brent, b 1962   B2. Marlene Rose, b 1965
SOHIER, Pierre, b J, res Riv. Claude, Que., mar Henrietta PINEL of J (Remiggi)
A1. Joseph Wesley, b J, mar Sara Castonguay, bp 1858, dau of Charles Philipbert C. of Riv. Claude, Que. and Marguerite Henley
SOHIER, desc of C.I. fam of this name at Simcoe, Ont.
SOHIER, Wesley, was settled early in Marsoui, between Cap aux Renards and Mont Louis, Gaspe. With Wesley as surname, might be from C.I. (GLF)
SOHIER, U.E.L., to Ontario ca 1800 from where in U.S.?
SOHIER, George, from J, in Gaspe ca 1841
SOLEBY, Capt. from G in Nfld. (K. Mathews)
SOLWAY, R., Boy Scout Commissioner in 1940, Vancouver, BC, thought to have come from C.I.
SOLWAY, SALWAY, Eva, in Cardston, Alta., from C.I. fam SOLLOWS, in Yarmouth, NS 1773, poss name SELOUS? (Census; LOST IN CANADA)
SOMERVILLE, from C.I.?, in Perce (Cent. Bklt.)
SOPER, some from C.I. in western Canada? Very early in Nfld. late 1500s. (T. Peddle, Augusta, Maine; Seary)
SORMANY, Henry Armand, b 1833 St. Helier, J, son of Venetian born Edouard Sormand, and Henriette Jeanne de la Croix d'Erlanges, of Norman nobility. Orphan, arrived in Shippegan 1853 as clerk for Wm. Fruing & Co. Soon left, mar 1859, Virginie Hache, and settled in Lamecque. Just. of the Peace, school teacher, and customs officer.
A1. Amedee, d 1877, while attending college at St. Louis, NB
A2. Wilfred, parish priest in Bathurst, NB, at Ste. Therese, NB, 1906
A3. Alphonse, M.D., deputy for Gloucester Co. 1908-1912, d Shediac, NB 1943
A4. Amanda, b ca 1885?, nun, hospital in Tracadie, NB
A5. Isabel, nun, 1885   A7. Marie, mar Edouard Chiasson, Lameque
A6. Josephine, nun, Tracadie, NB (SORMANY DATA FROM D.ROBICHAUD,
A8. Alexandrine, mar Clement Chiasson, Lameque   OF BERESFORD,NB)
A9. Clementine, mar Andrew Chiasson, Lameque, a son, Livain (Robichaud)
A10. Malvina, mar Fabien Hache
A11. Albert, b 1885 Lameque, M.D., Edmundston, and Madawaska City, NB, mar Eva Fortier, Quebec City 1910. Chn: Raymonde, Annette, Armand, Marcel, Roger and Helene. Albert d Edmundston 1970. Extraordinary career in vars fields, education, religion, journalism, municipal affairs. Biography: UN DEMI-SIECLE D'HISTOIRE ACADIENNE, by Alexandre Savoie.
SORMANY, from J to Saguenay and Charlevois-Saguenay (Gingras)
SORSOLEIL, John, b 1812 J, mar Anse au Griffon, Gaspe 1837, Marie MARIN, poss MORIN?, dau of Joseph M. and Madeleine Gaudreau. John was a miller. (Remiggi; GLF; Census)
A1. Francois Joseph, bp 1837   A5. Abraham, b 1848
A2. Mary Ann, b 1840, mar Touet   A6. Isaac, b 1850
A3. Philip, bp 1842   A7. William, b 1856
A4. John, b 1843   A8. Rachel, b 1857
SORSOLEIL, from J to Gaspe 1800s (GLF) 2SORSOLEIL TO NFLD.(CIFHS)
SORSOLEIL, C.I. surname on S. coast of Nfld. (G.W. Le Messurier)
SORSOLEIL, Philip, in La Poile, Nfld. 1860s (Rev. Hammond)
SOUDER, see ALEXANDER and ROBIN
SPETTIGUE, related to CARTER of J, desc in London, Ont.
SPINGLE, in Nfld. (Seary) Cf SPIGOURNEL of J (Stevens)
SPRATT, C.I. in Maritimes Fisheries (J.H. Le Breton list)
SQUIRES. This fam said to have come to Nfld. from the W. coast of

SQUIRES

England, poss Bristol. They settled in Bay de Verde, Conc. Bay, and once had title to Bell Is. and the Wabana Mines. There has been a very long association between the LE GROS, LE GROW and the SQUIRE fams, with a great deal of intermarriage. Other surnames involved in this fam were BOTT, JANES, KING, and THISTLE, all of which in various forms have been found in the C.I. (See BOTT, JAMES, LE ROY, and TISSIER). "There are as many LE GROWS and SQUIRES around Boston today as in Nfld. There is reason to believe that travel between Nfld. and New England by the Squires and Le Gros began in the 1600s. Families by this name were living next door to each other in Salem and Marblehead in the late 1600s, and the same situation occurred in Nfld. It seems to indicate that there was a great deal of sailing done by Islanders and associated families between these two places at a very early time." (Susan Squires, Newburyport, Mass.)

SQUIRE, SQUIRES, cf PASQUIRE and PASQUIOU of J. The Squires below were probably related. (Susan Squires, Newburyport, Mass.)

SQUIRE, Pierre, d 1816 St. Georges Cove, Gaspe, age 52. Origin unver.

SQUIRE, John, and Patience, of Broad Cove, Nfld.
A1. John Boert, b 1829, d.y.?   A4. Elizabeth, b 1836
A2. Elizabeth, b 1831, d.y.?   A5. Catherine, b 1839
A3. John, b 1834

SQUIRES, John and Mary ---, a son William, b 1832, mar Mary ---

SQUIRES, Gregory, mar Sarah ---
A1. Henry Thomas, b 1866, mar Mary Ann ---, a son Joseph, b 1890
A2. Gregory?, mar 1. Elizabeth, and 2. ---
   B1. Gregory, b 1867, d.y.   B2. Gregory, b 1868, no issue
   B3. Alexander
     C1. Sydney Anderson?, poss half brother
       D1. Richard Anderson, b 1880?

SQUIRES, William and Susannah, of Broad Cove, Bay de Verde, Nfld.
A1. Edward, mar 1856, Jane Janes?
   B1. Edward, b 1857   B2. Cecilia, b 1860
   B3. James, b 1864
     C1. Frederick, rem to Calif?, son Frederick and dau Nancy
     C2. Lawson
   B4. Frederick, b 1866
     C1. Walter, mar Sadie ---, a son Walter res Boston, and a dau, Dorothy
     C2. George   C3. Ernest
   B5. Elfreda, d.y.
   B6. William, b 1871, mar Bertha LE GROW, qv, 3 chn
A2. John, mar Mary
   B1. George, drowned in Maine
   B2. William, mar Mary Ann Boggs
     C1. John Robert, b 1884   C3. Harry, b 1888, a son Frank res Calif.
     C2. Alice, b 1885   C4. Drucilla, b 1889
   B3. Jeremiah, b 1853, 5 chn
     C1. John, b 1896   C3. Herbert, b 1899   C5. Albert, b 1905
     C2. Benjamin, b 1897   C4. Arthur Rene, b 1901, res Maine
   B4. John, b 1856, 4 chn, George, Nott?, Frederick, Gladys
   B5. Elizabeth, b 1858   B8. Drucilla, b 1867
   B6. Alice, b 1860   B9. Susannah, b 1871
   B7. Sarah, b 1864   B10. Victoria, b 1872
A3. James, b ca 1829?, mar Selina?
   B1. John, b 1859, had 2 chn, at least; Ida and Charles
   B2. William James, b 1869   B4. Edward, b 1864, d.y.?
   B3. Maryann, b 1861   B5. Stephen or Leonard, perhaps both?

B6. Edward again, b 1868
A4. William, b 1838, mar Margaret ---
  B1. John Samuel, b 1864, d.y.?   B2. John, b 1868
STAGG, Charles, b 1834 Yeovil, Eng.?, d 1919 G, mar Susan Monkley, b
  1834, d 1904 G. Ten chn, most of whom emigrated to Canada (Arthur
  S. Gadd, Leamington, Ont.)
A1. Emily Stagg, b 1859 G, d Eng. 1934, mar John William CODE, qv, fam
    to Canada
A2. Charles, b 1858 G, unmar   A3. Lucy, b 1861 G, d 1955, unmar
A4. Frederick, b G, mar 3 times, at least 4 chn
  B1. Frederick B2. Lillian B3. Hedley B4. Florence
A5. Arthur, b G, d age 9 of TB
A6. Thomas, b G, d there as a young man, mar Agnes ---, son in G
A7. Henry, b G, mar ---, 3 chn: Edith, Ada Winifred and Owen.
A8. Joseph, unmar
A9. Albert, a least 6 chn
  B1. Margaret   B2. Elsie   B3. Herbert   B4. Mabel
A10. Ada Ellen, b 1877 G, unmar
STAGG, Mr. and Mrs. Richard, from G to Hamilton ca 1910
A1. Clinton, mar Freda MARETT of G, also to Canada
  B1. a dau, b Hamilton, Ont., res G, mar Dennis ---
STAGG, Edward Ernest, b 1885, unverified as C.I. From Oxford to Canada
  early 1900s. Served WWI, mar Mabel Hall, b 1894, 5 chn, 14 grchn.
A1. Kathleen, 3 sons   A3. Leon, 2 chn   A5. Rex, 3 chn
A2. Audrey, 4 chn   A4. Marie, 2 sons
STAINER, Channel Islander in the Maritimes. (J.H. Le Breton list)
STANBURY, Capt. from G in Nfld. (K. Mathews)
STANLEY, from C.I. in Canada? <u>MORE STANNAGE DATA IN CI COLL</u>.
STANNAGE, Rev. John, b J, ordained 1834 in N.S., res St. Margarets Bay
  1834-1857 (PANS) This man said to be cousin to Wm. Edward BRINE, qv.
  Rev. John mar Eliza LE CAIN, qv, 1840, dau of a merchant.
STARCH, STARCK, in Victoria, BC 1940, member of C.I. Society there
STARCK, C.P., commercial traveler, from C.I. 1898
STARK, in Nfld. (Seary) Cf STARCK of J (Stevens)
STARR, see QAAM, by Turk
STEDMAN, Philip, of C.I.?, bought block of land site of Dumfries, Ont.
  from Joseph Brant, early 1800s. Stedman in W. Canada.
STEEL, in Nfld. (Seary) Cf STEEL, STILLE of J (Stevens) STILLE said to
  be Huguenot.
STENYING, C.I. in Maritimes Fisheries (J.H. Le Breton list)
STEPHENS, STEVENS, in Nfld. lSeary) Cf same of C.I.
STEVENS, from J to Winnipeg, Man.
STEVENS, Capt., was a C.I. privateer 1692, desc of an old G fam named
  de St. Estienne
STEVENS, STEVENSON, curr Gaspe, poss some from C.I.
STEVENSON, Sydney, to Canada from Sark?
STINESS, Samuel. This old Amer fam orig connected with Ch Islanders
  in the Amer Colonies. He mar Rebecca Widger, of C.I. fam, in 1776.
  A son, Samuel, mar Ruth BESSOM, BISSON, 1797. (Turk)
STOCK, STOCKES, Capt. and agent from G in Nfld. (K. Mathews)
STONE, Tradesman from G in Nfld. (K. Mathews) Cf STONORE of J (Stevens)
STONELAKE, Guernsey, from C.I.?, in Ontario
STOODLEY, Gertrude Mary, b 1895 J, mar Frank LE FEUVRE, rem to Mich.
  A son, Frank George S. LE FEUVRE, b 1929, res Wyandotte, Mich.
  STOODLEY also in Nfld. (Seary)
STRATHY, Mrs. and Mr., in B.C., members of C.I. Society, 1940
STRONG, in Nfld. (Seary) Cf STRONG of J (Stevens)

STRONG, Francis, b J, age 21 in 1871, Butcher? in Cox., Bon. Co., Gaspe 1871
SULLIVAN, John, b J. John and Margaret Sullivan were related to the MACHONS of PEI, of the fams that settled there in 1806, 1907. Chn were registered by that name in the Methodist class in Murray Harb. in 1820.
SUMMERHAYS, George, age 33, at Perce 1871, from C.I.? Also noted in Cent. Bklt. Cf SAUMAREZ of the C.I. (Aldo Brochet)
SUNNERGEN, Edw., in Cupids, Conc. Bay, Nfld. 1789, from C.I.?
SUTTON, Victoria, b 1834 J, bur Perce 1861. Mar Philip LE BOUTILLIER, who was b 1825. Suttons of England and Jersey. (Harold Sutton, Petit Pabos) SEE EXTRA PAGES.
SWAISLAND, W., b G, rem to McKellar St., Glencoe, Ont. 1876, Deputy Registrar. (Cummings) (James Talman, London, Ont.)
SWYER, SWYERS, poss SQUIRES?, in Nfld. One from J settled at Sandy Pt., St. George's Bay, 1700s (Seary)
SWARTON, Mary, dau of "one Swarton, a Jerseyman, John and Hannah HUBERT?, bp New England, 1675, captured by Indians, mar in Canada 1697, John LAHAY, or Jean Laha, an Irishman, had eleven chn."
SWARTON, Jasper, bro of Mary, captured also, redeemed with his mother in 1695. See QAAM, by Turk. (Louise Swanton, Newton, Mass.)
SWEET, in Nfld. (Seary) Cf SWETE of C.I. See QAAM, by Turk
SYLVESTRE, from J to Gaspe, a Walter in Cap Chat, Que.
SYE, Augustus, in White Bear Bay, Nfld., West Coast, 1860s, said to be of C.I. origin. (Rev. Hammond)
SYMES, Capt. Edward, mar Elizabeth Williams in St. Heliers, J (1800s?)
A1. John, res Chatham, Ont.
A2. Bruce, mar Edmonson, res Saskatoon, Sask, two daus; Marjorie and Linda
SYVRET. Those in N.B. may have been from New England. (Reg. Savary, Kirkton, Ont.)
SYVRET, from J?, at Miscou, NB 1831 (Ganong)
SYVRET, ---, from J, mar Philip LE BOUTILLIER 1800. Name also listed by Betty Tardif and J.H. Le Breton, Channel Islanders in the Maritimes Fisheries.
SYVRET, 1824-1908, bur St. Peters, Malbaie, Gaspe (Marg. Syvret, Jersey)
SYVRET, George S., 1911-1941, bur Malbaie
SYVRET, Helena M., d age 11 months, Malbaie
SYVRET, Wm. E., 1868-1951, bur Malbaie
SYVRET, George of J, settled northern N.B. and the names of his descendands is now SIEVRY? (Reg. Savary)
SYVRET, James, b J, in Malbaie 1861 (Census) with Anne, b J, James and Ann, b Canada (Cent. Bklt.) (See art.in SPEC, NewCarlisle1976)
SYVRET, John, also SIVRET, b 1795 J, mar Newport, Gaspe, Mary Maher, and 2. in Newport, 1838, Virginia Grenier, dau of Francois G. and Victoire Grenier. A Mariner? (Brochet; Census)
A1. George, b 1841   A3. Joseph, b 1845   A5. Ann   A6. Simon
A2. Elie, b 1843   A4. William, b 1849 Newport   A7. Elizabeth
SYVRET, James, settled in Canada, related to Marguerite SYVRET of Jersey. See also, A GENEALOGICAL AND BIOGRAPHICAL RECORD OF THE SAVARY FAMILY AND THE SEVERY FAMILY, Boston, 1893.
TABB, Richard, b J, in Gaspe 1861 (Census) See also TAPP
TACHEY, C.I. name in Canada (Gingras; K.H. Annett, Gaspe)
TACKER, also see as THACKER. This fam of Nfld. and St. Helier, J. See THACKER. (Soc. Jers.)
TADIER, from C.I. to Ontario
TANGUY, TANGUAY, TANGY. TANGY tombstone in Annopolis, N.S. 1700s.

TAPP, some in Gaspe, said to be from C.I. very early
TAPP, John, Jean. There were two John Tapps in Gaspe at the same time,
both R.C., although at least one of them had been Prot. on arrival in
Gaspe. Poss some records unclear, in spite of much research. See
also TAPP fam under TOUZEL fam. (Church records; Census; Joyce
Buckland, No. Highlands, Calif.)
TAPP, John, Jean, chr 1805, age ca 25 in Gaspe, mar 1. Elizabeth HAYDEN
and 2. Angelique Chicoine, dau of Aubin C. and Anne David.
A1. Abraham, b ca 1802, bp 1821 Malbaie, mar Anne Chicoine 1825
   B1. Abraham, b 1829 Malbaie   B5. Antoine, b 1835
   B2. Jean Baptiste, b 1831   B6. Catherine, b 1838
   B3. Thomas Isaac, b 1832   B7. Suzanne, b 1840
   B4. John, b 1833   B8. Christine, b 1844
A2. Rodger, mar Anne BOND
A3. John, mar Genevieve Francoeur-Leclerc 1823, dau of Etienne F. and
Marie Chicoine
   B1. Jean, b 1824 Malbaie   B5. Genevieve, b 1832
   B2. Appoline, b 1825   B6. Mathilde, b 1835
   B3. Edouard, b 1827   B7. Magloire, b 1837
   B4. Elisabeth   B8. Suzanne, b 1839
A4. Thomas, b ca 1800, bp 1823 Malbaie, mar Emilie O'Connor 1827, dau of
Pierre O'C.and Anne Bergeron. He d 1878, bur St. Peters, Barachois,
Gaspe.
   B1. Angelique, b 1828 Malbaie   B4. Henriette, b 1835 Malbaie
   B2. Thomas, b 1830 Malbaie   B5. Andie Philippe, b 1837, mar
   B3. Philippe, b 1833, d 1837 Gaspe   Mary Jane LUCAS, qv.
   B4. John, b 1839, mar Elize Anne Ferguson
   B7. Henry, b 1841, mar Julie Ann TOUZEL
   B8. Emilie Madelaine, b 1844
   B9. Georges Abraham, b 1847, mar Angelique Hunt
   B10. Pierre Absolom, b 1849 Malbaie, mar Caroline TOUZEL, qv, 1870.
He d 1938, bur Notre Dame Cem, Ottawa, Ont. Caroline, b 1853
Gaspe, d 1905 Ottawa, Ont. See TOUZEL, Caroline, for this fam
of 8 chn.
A5. by second wife, Angelique Chicoine, John, bp 1805 Malbaie, mar
Marie Bond, dau of Aubin Bond, 12 chn
   B1. Marie, b 1828 Malbaie   B7. Jean Baptiste, b 1837 Malbaie
   B2. Aubin John, b 1829, mar Sophie B8. Thomas, b 1839, d 1848 Malbaie
       GIRARD, qv, 1850   B9. George Henry, b 184-
   B3. Hubert, b 1830   B10. Jean Baptiste, b 1844
   B4. Elisabeth, b 1831   B11. Caroline, b 1846
   B5. Mary Ann, b 1833   B12. Thomas Edward, b 1849 Malbaie
   B6. Julie, b 1835
A6. Christine, bp 1807 Malbaie, mar 1824, John BOND
A7. Charles, bp 1807, mar Catherine CLEMENT 1829, dau of Thomas CLEMENT,
qv, and Elizabeth BAKER
   B1. Sophie, b 1831 Malbaie   B3. Charles, b 1834
   B2. Nelly, b 1832   B4. Catherine, b 1836
A8. Aubin, b 1810, mar 1836, Marie McSweeney, d 1840 Gaspe
   B1. Jean, b 1833, illeg. son by Anne CLEMENT? B3. Ellen, b 1839
   B2. Eleonore, b 1838 Malbaie   B4. Suzanne, b 1841
A9. Guillaume, b 1812, d 1843
A10. Mathieu, b 1814, mar Jane BOND 1834, dau of Joseph B. and Marie
SYNNETT
   B1. John Aubertin, b 1836 Malbaie   B4. James, b 1839
   B2. Mathieu Ernessie, b 1835   B5. Elisabeth, b 1841
   B3. Angelique, b 1837   B6. Emilie, b 1843

B7. Emerentienne, b 1845   B8. Thomas, b 1846   B9. Nicholas, b 1849
A11. Helene, b 1816   A12. Edward, b 1818
A13. Suzanne, b 1820 Malbaie, mar Georges Hunt 1841
A14. Anne, b 1823 Malbaie, mar James GIRARD 1840, 4 chn
A15. Elisabeth, b 1824, mar Andre GIRARD 1841
A16. Emilie, b 1827, mar Joseph BOND 1845
TAPP, in Nfld. See TOUZEL, Caroline
TARA, in Nfld. (Seary) said to be of C.I. origin. Philip in Fortune Bay, 1877. (Rev. Hammond) John and Wm. in Moyambrose 1870s. (Rev. Hammond)
TARDIF, Capt. from G in Nfld. (K. Mathews)
TARDIF, John, b 1929, res Gaspe, mar Helen Beatrice Ascah 1952 (Ascah Gen.)
TARDIF, Alexander, b G, mar Amy LE NOURY before 1900? After his wife's death, he took dau Vera, age 6, to Mass., then to Haskell Place, NJ, where he remar before 1920, had 3 sons, one named Howard TARDIF. (Howard T. Falla, Agincourt, Ont.)
A1. Bernard, b ca 1905, rem to Toronto ca 1925
A2. Vera, b G, res Mass. and N.J. with father, but returned to G
A3. Harold, b ca 1910
TARDIF, Richardson, b St. Peter Port, G, or in J, 1859? In 1873, age 14, rem to Gaspe, where he worked for Robin Collas firm. In 1888, mar Elizabeth Higginson of Buckingham, Que., res Newport, Que., 3 daus. Eliz. d 1939, age 82, and he d 1943, age 84, bur St. Paul's, Perce, Que. (Cent. Bklt.; Brochet; Rev. d'Hist)
A1. Edith, b ca 1890, res Perce, mar Robert Gurnham of Montreal, res there
A2. Laura D. Tardif, mar Dumaresq C. VALPY, qv, res Perce. See VALPY
A3. Elizabeth, b ca 1892, organist at St. Pauls, Perce
TARDY, Eunice, dau of Capt. John Tardy of Halifax, mar Benjamin Pitman of Yarmouth, NS 1789 at Chebogue. At the same place, and by the same minister, a Mary Tardy and Nehimiah Porter were mar in 1776. This captain may have been a Tardif, several of whom settled in the Maritimes, or may have been a U.E.L. of Marblehead, Mass., who rem to Canada. See TARDY in QAAM, by Turk. (Alice Westmore, Yarmouth, NS)
TAUDVIN, John and Elizabeth, were in PEI in school in 1820. This fam from G in 1806 on G vessel, captained by Capt. Taudvin. (Census) This surname poss TOSTEVIN, qv.
TAUDVIN, Elizabeth, mar Daniel MACHON, qv, 7 chn
TAVENOR, in Nfld. (Seary) Cf TAVERNER of J (Stevens)
TAYLER, Cyrus, to Canada 1920 from Ruette Braye, G, 2 daus, res later Salt Lake City? Some in Canada and two in SLC. (See QAAM, by Turk) Cyrus poss mar Jennie Ronald in Canada.
TAYLER, Richard Charles, of Montville farm, Ruette Braye, mar Alice DOREY, qv, rem 1920 to SLC, Utah, 5 sons; 2 in Canada.
TAYLOR, Robert, in Brigus 1805, in Buck Cove 1788. Poss from C.I.? Others. See Seary.
TAYLOR, in Nfld. (Seary) Cf TAILLEUR of J (Stevens)
TAYLOR, Elizabeth B., of G?, mar Alfred MICHEL, qv (GLF)
TEMPLE, in Nfld. (Seary) Cf TEMPLIER of J (Stevens)
TENNIER, Anne, 1873-1948, mar Philip HOCQUARD, qv, bur United Ch Cem, W. Paspebiac, Gaspe. Origin unver.
TERRANT, TARRANT, Richard, in Burin, Nfld. 1860s, poss from C.I. (Rev. Hammond) This name also spelled TERREYEN in J. (Stevens)
TESSIER, TEXIER, THISTLE, S. coast of Nfld., from C.I. (Hug. Soc. Letter) See THISTLE (G.W. Le Messurier; Seary)
TWEKESBURY, two Englishmen mar two Alderney girls, rem to Chatham, Ont.

ca 1870s? (Luce) This fam related to the LE BER fam of Ont.
THACKER, TACKER, Thomas, of Nfld., res in St. Helier, J, mar 1748, Anne BOUDIER, connected with the INGOUVILLE fam of N.S.? and with STE. CROIX fam, and LE GALLAIS fam. (Soc. Jers.)
THELLAND, John and Francis, signed the Gaspe Petition 1820, from C.I.?
THELLAND, Francois, son of Wm. and of Esther Luce of J, mar Angelique Defoi 1823 at Newville, Que. (Pontbriand; Gingras)
THEOFAIR, Eunice?, dau of George and Amelia HACQUOIL, qv, of St. John, J, b ca 1890, to Lethbridge, Alta., 4 sons and a dau, mar Haynes, W.J.
THERIN, Francis, from J to Gaspe ca 1900 or before
THIBEAU, THIBEAUX, TIBBO, qv, said to be C.I., settled in Nfld. Current Stephenville, and St. John's, Nfld.
THISTLE, Nfld. surname, said to be derived from TISSIER of C.I. See also LE GROW. Poss to Harbor Grace, Nfld. 1600s? (Seary)
THOMAS, John and Elizabeth, from C.I. to Gaspe, 4 sons; John, Charles and Francis to Gaspe. Charles at Barachois, John and Francis at Paspebiac. (GLF)
THOMAS, Lillian, b 1893 St. Helier, J, mar 1914, Harry E. PAINTER, qv. She was the dau of Albert William Thomas and Elsie Courtney NOEL, qv, res St. Helier. First to Montreal 1913, then to McAdam, N.B.
THOMAS, John, Jersey trader in Sandy Pt., Nfld. 1871 (Lovell; Seary) Cf THOMAS of J (Stevens)
THOMEY, THOUME, C.I. name on S. coast of Nfld. (G.W. Le Messurier)
THOMEY, THOUME, Capt. and agent from G in Nfld. (K. Mathews) "Old Capt. Thomey gave us some interesting stories about the old Jersey foundations on which his grandfather had built their house at Mosquito, now Bristol's Hope, over 150 years ago." (Shortis-Munn)
THOMSON, Louisa Anne Ringler, of Ross Cottage, St. Helier, J, mar 1853, St. Saviour Ch, Thomas Robert Drummond Hay of Scotland (G.L.T. Drummond-Hay, Nanaimo, BC)
A1. Annie Louisa, b 1854, d 1938 St. Helier, J
A2. Charles Drummond-Hay, homesteaded in Belmont, Man., d 1926
THORBON, Capt. from G in Nfld. (K. Mathews)
THOREAU, THEREAU, Philip Edward, b ca 1840 J, to Canada in employ of Hudson Bay Co., in his youth, emigrated to N.Z. 1878, d 1920, age 75, 5 chn. His father, Edw. John Thoreau, b 1815, mar 1837, Sophie Calherne LERRIER in J. Mar Anne ---, 1843, b J, a son, Philip W., bp 1860, Methodists.
THORNE, agent for Newman and Co., from J?, in St. Lawrence Bay, Nfld. 1800s (Tocque)
THORNHILL, THORNELL, poss THOREL?, Hug surname in J (Lawton) See also QAAM, by Turk.
THORNHILL, THORNELL, James and Robert, in Fortune Bay, Nfld. 1860s. (Rev. Hammond; Seary) Cf THORNELL of J (Stevens) See NICHOLE, NICOLLE
THORP, Susan Marie, of J?, 1845-1865, wife of Philip LE BOUTILLIER, qv, bur St. Pauls, Perce, Gaspe (Cent. Bklt.; GLF)
THOUMINE, see GODDEN
THOURNE, Capt. from G in Nfld. (K. Mathews)
TIBBO, THIBAULT, from C.I. to Nfld. (Hug. Soc.; Seary)
TIBBO, THIBAULT, TIBBOT, agent, boatkeeper and others, from J to Nfld. (K. Mathews)
TIBBO, Jonathan, mar ---, 1779-1842, settled Nfld. ca 1770, one of three bros. The other two settled in Placentia Bay and Fortune Bay, Nfld. (Frank Tibbo, Gander, Nfld.) Tibbos from Jersey.
A1. George, 1807-1881
  B1. Jonathan
    C1. George W., b 1871

TOMS, Some in CI.
    D1. Gilbert, b 1912, mar Annie STOODLEY, b 1913
        E1. Frank, b 1933, mar Joyce Brownlee, b 1932 Ont.
            F1. Nancy, b 1955   F3. Beverly, b 1972, all b Grand
            F2. Barry, b 1957   Bank, Nfld.
            F3. Barbara, b 1962   TILLY, SCOTTISH SURNAME.
TILLER, TILLIER, TILLEY, from C.I. to Nfld. Cf TILLEY of J (Stevens)
TILLER, Robert, mar Mary Hussey in Trinity Bay, Nfld. 1764
TILLER, Thomas and wife, Catherine, in Trinity Bay, Nfld. 1764, with
    Brace, bp 1757 and Joseph, bp 1759
TILLER, George, and wife, Sarah, in Trinity, Nfld. 1764, with son,
    George, bp 1787
TILLER, John, said to be of C.I. origin, in Bonaventure Bay, Nfld.
    1860s (Rev. Hammond)
TILLERS, Wm. and Anne, with a Thomas, bp 1815, and Mary, bp 1815
TILLY, Sabina, mar James Hurdle in Bonavestia Bay, Nfld. 1787
TILLY, Thomas and wife, Anne, in Bonavista Bay, Nfld. 1787
    A1. George, bp 1828   A2. Jane, bp 1828   A3. John, bp 1835, age 6
    A4. Thomas, bp 1835, age 4   A5. Matilda, bp 1835, age 1½ years
TILLY, Joseph and Rebecca, with a Joseph, bp 1828
TILLY, Wm., Jr., son of the coroner, d 1846, age 15, bur Cape Cove
    Angl. Ch Cem (Brochet)
TINGLEY, from C.I. to Nfld. Sometimes variant and abbreviation of J
    surname MATTINGLEY. (Jers. Soc. Bull. Vol. 6)
TINNISWOOD, see BASSETT
TIPPET, James, John, and Robert, of C.I. origin, in Bay Roberts, Nfld.
    1801 (Rev. Hammond)
TIPPLE, prob THEBAULT, Thomas, in La Poile, Nfld. 1860s, said to be
    from C.I. (Rev. Hammond)   TISSIER, John, Montreal mar Wanda LE
TISSIER, see TESSIER, TEXIER and THISTLE   GRESLEY, qv. CHN.
TITFORD, James, in Bay Roberts, Con. Bay, Nfld. 1860s, said to be of
    C.I. origin (Rev. Hammond)
TIZZARD, in Nfld. (Seary) Cf TIZARD of J (Stevens) This name found
    very early in Carbonear, Old Perlican, etc., Nfld.
TOBIN, in Nfld. (Seary) Cf TOBIN of J (Stevens)
TOCQUE, Rev. Philip, b Nfld. of J fam, educated Hartford, Conn, and
    Appleton, U.S. Ordained 1851 in Conn. Priest 1854 by Bishop of N.S.
    Res Boston, Tusket, NS, and Kinmount. Arthur of NEWFOUNDLAND, AS IT
    WAS AND AS IT IS IN 1877. Served as traveling SPG missionary, 1850s
    and 1860s. In Hopetown, Gaspe 1863, and in Ontario 1868.
TOCQUE, Harold, b ca 1895 J?, rem to Canada early 1900s, served in Can.
    Army WWI. A half sister in St. Catherines, Ont. Their father was
    engaged in the operation of fishing ships to the Grand Banks, with
    offices in Jersey and Gaspe. Related to L'ARBALESTIER fam. (Letter
    from B. Arbalestier, Vancouver, BC)
TOCQUE, from C.I. to Carbonear, Nfld. (Shortis-Munn)
TOMPKINS, in Nfld. (Seary) Cf TOMPKINS of J (Stevens, in 1749)
TONERI, from J, in Victoria, BC, 1940 (Luce)
TORGETT, see TOURGET   MORE TORODE DATA IN CHAN.IS. COLL. from
TORODE, TORUDE, Capt. from G in Nfld. (K. Mathews) Anne Frazer,CALIF.
TORODE, Ella Louise, b 1873 G, d 1950, mar Jules LE GRAND, qv. She
    was dau of John T. of Anneville, and Long Rue, St. Saviours, G.
TOSTEVIN, John, b Quebec, age 39, and Eliza, age 38, with sev chn at
    Cape Cove, Gaspe 1871 (Census)
TOSTEVIN, Leonard, mar Olive FAUVEL, qv, Gaspe (Brochet)
TOSTEVIN, Cf TAUDVIN of PEI fam 1806
TOSTEVIN, bros and sisters from Vale, G to Canada and U.S. early 1900s,
    chn of Peter T. and Eliza Jane RADFORD of G. (Tanna Savident, Powell

Much TOSTEVIN data from E. T. Johnson, Hamilton, New Zealand inCI COLL River, BC; James Savident, San Mateo, Calif.)
A1. Eliza Jane, b 1882 Vale mar James E. SAVIDENT, qv, rem to Victoria, BC 1912, with others in fam. She d 1956, 3 sons, see SAVIDENT.
A2. Peter, b 1883 G, to New Zealand, d 1967
A3. Jack, b 1884, to New Hampshire, U.S. Stone mason, mar, 1 dau. He d 1974.
A4. William, b 1885 G, to New Zealand, d 1973
A5. Ada, b 1886, mar twice, once to Franklin LE NOURY, qv, a dau, Joyce Parsons
A6. Arthur, b 1887, rem to Milford, N.S. 1912, mar Jane Hyslop, b 1899, a son d.y.
A7. Ethel, b 1888, mar Joseph Marshall, rem to Victoria, BC 1917
  B1. --- Marshall, d WWII
  B2. Muriel, mar Len Walsh, res BC
    C1. Linda   C2. Mike   C3. Larry
A8. Harry, b 1889, rem to Milford, N.H., mar, a dau. He d 1973.
A9. Reta, b 1900, rem to Victoria, BC 1917, then to San Leandro, Calif. Mar DOREY, qv.
A10. Clifford, b 1901 G, rem to Victoria, BC, mar Lillian Tottman, b 1905 England, no issue

TOSTEVIN, James, in Gaspe 1820, signed Petition. Had son or grandson, James Jr., 1861-1926, mar Cape Cove, Gaspe, 1885, Eliza, Elizabeth, LENFESTY, who d 1951, both bur St. James Angl. Ch, Cape Cove, 9 chn. (Claudette Maroldo, Cherry Hill, NJ)
A1. John James, b 1885 Cape Cove, d 1922
A2. Francis Pearson, b 1887, mar Lilian Susan MERCIER, qv, of L'Anse au Beaufils 1918
  B1. Thornby Harold, b 1918 Cape Cove B4. Dorothy Lillian, b 1931
  B2. Donald Pearson, b 1920   B5. Mary Jane, b 1932
  B3. Iona Grace, b 1926, d 1943, age 17
A3. William Arthur, b 1889 Cape Cove
A4. Sarah Eliza, b 1891 Cape Cove, mar Frederick LENFESTY, 1887-1970, son of Wm. and Margaret Lenfesty of L'Anse au Beaufils and a second cousin.
A5. Mary Adelaide, b 1892 Cape Cove
A6. Alfred Harold, b 1895. Gravestone: "Harold Daniel Tostevin," 1895-1912, St. James Ch.
A7. Frederic Thomas, b 1896. A Fred. mar Grace Root, 1887-1974, bur Cape Cove, Gaspe. (GLF)
A8. Lilian Jane, b 1898, d 1917   A9. Laura May, b 1899

TOSTEVIN, Eliza Jane, 1870-1947, mar Philip MERCIER, qv, 1859-1947, bur Cape Cove (GLF)

TOSTEVIN, John James, b J?, related to James LENFESTY?, to Perce, mar there, Anna MAUGER, qv, b 1800 Perce, d ca 1845. Desc. He d young ca 1833, she remar twice; chn (Brochet)
A1. Rachel, b 1823   A2. Elizabeth, b 1825, mar James E. Flynn
A3. John James Jr., b 1828, mar _____COLLIN, Quebecoise.
A4. Mary Ann Judith, b 1833, mar Daniel DUMARESQ, qv

TOUCH, Capt. from J and G in Nfld. (K. Mathews)

TOUET, Philip Wesley, b 1850s J, rem to Gaspe 1870. In Quebec, mar Mary LE ROSSIGNOL of J, and later took his wife and three daus to Iowa. There, he was a construction worker on the Railroad, and son, Wesley, was born. Rem then to Oregon and finally to Vancouver Is., where they settled in Cordova Bay. Built a one room log cabin with a lean-to kitchen on one side, now the oldest house in the Bay. The Touet house still stands (record from some years back), remodeled, added to, but with the log cabin still at its center. Philip T.

became a dairy farmer and sold his produce in Victoria. His sideline was building barns. His two daus mar JEUNE bros, qv. Desc in Victoria and Saanich, B.C.(Article: Margaret Belford, B.C. Archives.)
A1. Philip Wesley, Jr., unmar   A3. Agnes, mar P. JEUNE, qv,
A2. Emily, mar Frederick JEUNE, qv, 3 chn   6 chn
A4. Mary Jane, mar --- Stockand
TOUET, John, had land grant at Cap Rosier, Gaspe 1865, Elias had grant 1866, and Philip had grant 1866. Philip in Cape Rosier 1861. (GLF; Sylvia Wilson)
TOUET, Edward, b J, in Gaspe 1861 (Census) with Mary Ann, b Gaspe
TOUET, Elia, b J, in Cap Rosier 1861 with Mary, b J and Elias, b J
TOUET, Capt. from J and G in Nfld. (K. Mathews)
TOUET, Elie, b ca 1805 J, res Anse au Griffon, Gaspe 1861, carpenter, with wife, Mary
A1. John, bp 1828, mar Mary Ann ---, bp 1826 J
    B1. John E., b 1851   B3. Edward W., b 1856   B5. Theophile, b 1860
    B2. Ann Mary, b 1854   B4. Jane, b 1858
A2. Edward, bp 1835 J, shoemaker, mar Mary Anne SANSOLEIL or SORSOLEIL?, qv, bp 1840. Mary Anne was the dau of John Sansoleil or Sorsoleil and Marie Marin.
A3. Elias, b 1838 J   A4. Philip, b 1840 J
TOURBON, Capt. from G in Nfld. (K. Mathews)
TOURGET, TORGETT, John, in Bonaventure Bay, Nfld. 1860s (Rev. Hammond)
TOURGIS, Esther, b J, mar Francis Philipp ROY, qv. A son b in Pte. aux Trembles, Montreal, 1855, Congregational or Evangelical Ch. (Therese Gravel, Montreal)
A1. George Peter ROY
TOURGIS, Charlotte, b J, mar William Gunn Hamilton of Aberdeen, Scotland, a dau, Elizabeth Hamilton, b AuxGres of Trois Riv., Pte. Aux Trembles, Que. (Gravel) Eliz·bp 29 July, 1855
TOURGIS, Jane, d Gr. Greve 1888, age 64, wife of Charles ENOUF, ESNOUF, bur St. George's Cove, Gaspe. (Brochet)
TOUSSAINT, Harry Alexander, b 1800s Alderney?, rem to Ontario. A dau, Barbara, b 1929, mar --- WILLIAMS, 3 sons and a dau. (B. Williams, Burlington, Ont.)
TOUZEAU, Mr. and Mrs. Ernest, from G in 1911 to B.C. A son Walter, Inspector of Agriculture, in Channel Islands Society in Vancouver, 1952.
TOUZEAU, Capt. from G in Nfld. (K. Mathews)
TOUZEAU, Peter Mahy, b G, son of Henry T. and Louise MARTEL, rem to Canada ca 1909, mar Janet McCann. (W.J. Touzeau, Delta, BC)
A1. Harry Peter, b 1911, mar --- Rise, no issue
A2. Arthur Eugene, b 1913, mar Hildur? ---
    B1. Phyllis Elaine, mar Gerry Kiernan
       C1. Michael Kiernan   C2. Cher Kiernan
A3. Edward Sidney, b 1917, mar Enid ---
    B1. Rochelle, mar Richard Wright
       C1. Richard Wright   C2. Raven Wright
    B2. Maureen Ruth, mar Garth Hutchinson   B3. Kenneth Edward
TOUZEAU, Ernest Martel, b G, bro of Peter above, rem to Canada 1911, mar Christine Elizabeth VAUDIN, qv (W.O. Touzeau, Delta, BC)
A1. Ernest George, b 1905 G, mar Elsa Pauline Cote
    B1. Marie Louise, mar Robert George Paterson
       C1. Robert Bruce Paterson   C3. Douglas Allan Paterson
       C2. Susan Marie Paterson   B2.<u>Valerie Lorraine mar Jos.Orth</u>
A2. Walter David, b 1913   <u>Chn: Michael and Michelle</u>
A3. Lillian Frances, b 1920, mar Andrew Wiloughby Manzer
    B1. Christine Ethyl, mar Wayne McConnell

B2. Julia Frances Manzer, mar Robin Lind, a son, Derek Martin Lind
B3. Patricia Elaine Manzer, mar Richard Bell
TOUZEL, TOUSEL, see also LE TOUZEL
TOUZEL, John, from J?, res Belle Anse, Gaspe 1800s (J.H. Le Breton and Tardif lists)
TOUZEL, Susan H., wife of Ronald GIRARD of G?, in Gaspe. She was b 1879, d 1949 (GLF)
TOUZEL, Willo Irene, wife of John G. BECQUET, qv, of Gaspe 1899-1949
TOUZEL, involved in Nfld. trade by 1717
TOUZEL, to Nfld. (Seary) Cf LE TOUZEL of J (Stevens, C.R. Fay)
TOUZEL, Edward John Buesnel, b Quebec, of J fam
TOUZEL, Henry, b J, in Gaspe Bay 1861 (Census) with Mary A., b NS; Adolphus, b J; Henry, b J; William; Selina, and Amelia, b Gaspe; poss related to Guignons of Gaspe.
TOUZEL, Philip, b St. Helier, J, mar 1854 Pt. St. Peter, Gaspe, Marguerite Maria LUCAS, qv, who d 1863 at Sheldrade, Saguenay, Que. Philip first to Gaspe, later settled Sheldrake. Brother of Thomas John below. (Joyce Buckland, No. Highlands, Calif.)
A1. Philip Edward, b 1854 Pt. St. Peter   A3. Philip John b 1860 Sheldrake
A2. Thomas George, b 1857   A4. Alfred, b 1863 Sheldrake
TOUZEL, Thomas John, shipbuilder, b 1820 J, d 1893. Rem to Gaspe. Mar ca 1841, Susan Elizabeth BEST. (Joyce Buckland, No. Highlands, Calif.)
A1. Elvina Susannah, b 1841 St. Helier, J, mar George S. Buckley 1861, son of Michael B., b 1840 Pt. St. Peter, Gaspe
  B1. Susan Maria, b 1862 Pt. St. Peter   B4. George Allan Buckley, b 1870
  B2. Thomas George Buckley, b 1865   B5. Maud Mary Buckley, b 1872
  B3. Esther Celeste, b 1868
A2. Esther Elizabeth, b 1845
A3. Thomas John, b 1846, mar Mary A. LE GRESLEY, qv
  B1. Thomas John, b 1872 Barachois, and others?
A4. Julianna and/or Jane?, b 1849 Pt. St. Peter, Gaspe
A5. Caroline Elzeda, b 1851, mar Peter Absolom TAPP, qv, 1870. She d 1905 Ottawa, Ont.
  B1. Peter Benjamin Tapp, b 1870 Barachois, Gaspe
  B2. Susanne Emilia, b 1872, mar Robert Johnson, d 1941 Ottawa
  B3. Esther Azilda, b 1874, mar James Dunn, bur Ottawa
  B4. Alexander Solomon, b 1877, d 1908
  B5. Rebecca Jane Tapp, b 1878 Barachois, mar Richard Smith, res Ottawa
  B6. Joseph George Tapp, b 1881, mar Eliza Ann Dolman, d 1964 Ottawa
  B7. Frank Tapp, b 1881, twin, mar Margaret Tighe, d 1965 Ottawa
  B8. Alice Desired, b 1883 Barachois, mar Joseph Edmond Patry, 1904, d 1911. He was the son of Esther AUBIN, qv.
    C1. Joseph Edmond Patry, b 1905 Ottawa, d.y.
    C2. Harold Peter Patry, b 1906 Ottawa, mar Catherine LAMBERT 1933, 3 chn
      D1. Anne Marie Patry, b 1935, d.y.
      D2. Mary Elizabeth Patry, b 1937, mar Philip Hort Smith
      D3. Anne Marie again, b 1940, mar --- Hebert?
    C3. Leola Caroline Patry, b 1908 Ottawa, mar James Wm. Buckland 1929, d 1971, bur Sacramento, Calif. She mar 2. W.C. Cox.
      D1. Vernon Edward Buckland, b 1930 Ottawa, mar Margaret Mackenzie 1955, b 1930 C'town, PEI
        E1. Edward George Buckland, b 1956 Carlton Place, Ont.
        E2. Carolyn Margaret, b 1957 Smiths Falls, Ont.
        E3. Sandra Elizabeth, b 1962, d.y., bur Ottawa
        E4. Pamela Jean Buckland, b 1963
      D2. Maynard Peter Buckland, b 1932 Ottawa, mar Joyce Gale Krans

1973
B9. Marie Julie Angele, b 1885 Barachois, mar Alfred John Orr 1906, d 1975 Ottawa
B10. John Thomas, b 1887 Barachois, rem to U.S.A.
B11. James, b Ottawa, mar Letitia ---, d 1975 Springfield, Ohio
A7. Mary Ann, b 1854 Quebec   A8. Edward John, b 1857
TOWER, Mrs. Gertrude, nee Leadbeater, b G, mar in Canada 1912 (Edw. Le Page)
TRACHY, Benjamin, b J, mar Elisabeth LE BRUN at St. Peters, J and rem to Gaspe (Gallant) (Signed the Gaspe Petition 1820)
A1. Edouard, b ca 1793 J, bp at Perce, age 26, mar there 1819, Suzanne BOURGET, dau of Charles B. and Louise Turcotte
  B1. Elisabeth, b 1820 Perce, mar 1837, Louis Cloutier, son of Louis C. and Madeleine St. Aubain
  B2. Jean, b 1822 Perce
  B3. Suzanne, b 1824 Perce, mar Bernard Chalifour, son of Frederic C. and Genevieve d'Anglande
  B4. Euphrosine, b 1826 Perce   B5. Genevieve, b 1826 Perce, twin
  B6. Margaret, b 1829 Perce, mar 1848, Charles Bouchard, son of Jos. B. and Marguerite Cote
  B7. Mary, b 1831 Perce
  B8. Victor, d Perce 1837, age 3   B9. Edouard, b 1837
A2. Abraham, mar Louise BOURGET, dau of Charles B., sister of Susanne BOURGET above
  B1. Elisabeth, b 1821 Paspebiac, mar Hugh-Louis BAKER, qv, dit Blondin
    C1. Aurelia Baker, mar Peter LE MOIGNAN 1875 (See LE MOIGNAN GENEALOGY)
  B2. Jeanne Marie, b 1822 Paspebiac, mar Perce 1843, Cesaire Turgeon, son of Francois T. and Cecile Bouchard of Beaumont
  B3. Abraham, b 1825 Paspebiac
  B4. Marguerite, b 1828   B5. Benjamin, b 1830 Anse du Cap
  B6. John, b 1832 B8. Louise, b 1835 B7. Philippe b 1838, in Gaspe 1861?
TRACHY, from C.I. to Cap d'Espoir? 1781 or 1871 (Syvret)
TRACHY, from C.I. to Saguenay and Charlevois-Saguenay areas of Quebec (Gingras) TRACHY, PH.of Trin.J, to Minn.,Minn.
TRACHY, "Daniel Trachy, from Guernsey, mar at Montmagny in 1826." Recueil de Genealogie de Beauce, Dorchester, Frontenac, Vol. III, by Frere Eloi-Gerard Talbot, p. 27.
TRACHY, TRECHY?, Edward, b J, in Gaspe 1861 (Census) with Susan, Mary, Edward, John, Marie, Jane, John Jr., Flora, all b Quebec.
TRACHY, Alvina, 1873-1959, widow of J.A. Boucher, 1863-1943, bur Cath. Ch, Perce (GLF)
TRACHY, Leonard and Raymond, desc of Jersey fam, res Gaspe
TRACHY, Carole Mary, b 1939 St. Peter Port, G, dau of G. Eric Charles Trachy and Gwendoline Mary Nearing, rem to Canada
TRACHY, Abraham, b J, res Gaspe, mar Mary Sullivan, res Cape Cove. A son, Edward, b 1874, desc in Douglastown, Que. and in Calif. (Eda T. Gaul, Douglastown, Que.)
TRACY, ---, mar G, --- LE CHEMINANT, qv, rem from G to Glencoe, Ont. See LE CHEMINANT.
TRACY, in Nfld. (Seary) Cf TRACHY and TRACY of J (Stevens)
TRAHY, John, origin unknown, had a shipyard at Five Mile River near Maitland, NS, and contracted to build for Capt. Lorway, a barque of between 700 and 800 tons, to be delivered in 1872. The ship was named ANNIE LORWAY. Typical of a 3 master Barque, square rigged on the fore and main masts, and had fore and aft rig on the mizzen, cost #34,000, ready for sea. Some interesting detail on the handling and

TUCKER,M.S. mar Pat.LAMBOTTE,St.Martin G, res Toronto,ONT.
commercial management of this ship. (Capt. Parker's CAPE BRETON SHIPS
AND MEN)
TRENCHARD, in Nfld. (Seary) Cf TRENCHARD of J (Stevens)
TRIBBLE, in Canada. Cf TRUBUIL of J.
TRICOT, J fam in Nfld. (Lady McKie) Cf TRIQUEL or TRICOT of J (Stevens)
TRIPP, Felicia M., wife of Amos ALEXANDRE, d at 55 in 1916, bur Sandy
Beach, Gaspe (GLF)
TROKE, in Nfld. (Seary) Cf TROGUER of J (Stevens) or poss TOCQUE?
TROY, in Nfld. (Seary) Cf TROY of J (Stevens)
TRUDEL, in Gaspe, origin uncertain. Cf TRUDEL of C.I.
TUCK, Mrs. A., from G to Burnaby, BC (Mr. Rattle, Toronto, Ont.)
TUCK, Byeboat keeper from J in Nfld. (K. Mathews)
TUCKER, gravestone in Annapolis, 1700s, origin unknown
TUCKER, in C.I., poss some in Canada
TUPPER, the large and noted Tupper family of N.S. has descent from a
Tupper of England who rem to the Island of Guernsey for a few years
before settling in America, early 1700s. (See Tupper Genealogy)
Origin TOUTPERT of France, or Henry Tupper rem from Hesse-Cassel, Germany, after edict against the Lutherans. (Carey-Wimbush) TUPPER,
C.I. name on S. coast of Nfld. (G.W. Le Messurier)
TUPPER, Capt. and merchants from J and G in Nfld. (K. Mathews)
TUPPER, Pt. Tupper, on the Strait of Canso, which divides the Island
of Cape Breton from Nova Scotia. Named for Ferdinand Brock Tupper,
Historian of G. (Review of Guernsey Society, Summer, 1975, T. Priaulx)
TURIFF, from C.I.?, in Canada
TURPIN, in Nfld. (Seary) Cf TURPIN of J (Stevens) See p. 45 and p. 491
TURPIN, see ROBERT, ROBERTS. Some from C.I. in U.S. and Canada.
TUZO. (Sources: Aldo Brochet, Perce; Cent. Bklt.; GLF; Census; F.M.
Gibaut, MEMOIRS OF A GASPESIAN, in Rev. d'Hist, March 1963; H.H.
Gibaut, Quebec, P.Q.) SEE EXTRA PAGES.
TUZO. "A family of Tuzos from Jersey, sent out by the S.P.G. to Bermuda,
and then made their way to Gaspe." (Lady McKie) This settler, an
Anglican, who came with wife and possibly with Pierre Du Val?, from
Bermuda. MORE DATA IN CHANNEL ISLAND COLLECTION.
TUZO, Joseph Stowe, missionary, and J.P., b 1791, d 1843, mar Bon. Is.
or in Bermuda, Mary Eve, 1794-1852. She was the first postmaster at
Perce, 6 chn. Cf TOUZEAU Ralph Tuzo, Chatham,NB has Chart of Family.
A1. Joseph Eve, b 1823, mar 1850, Louisa Languedoc, dau of Jos. L. and
Eliza Boyle. He was a gaoler and postmaster. He and descendants
contributed greatly to civic admin. of Gaspe area. D 1890 Perce.
She was b 1823, d 1914, bur St. Pauls, Perce.
B1. James Thomas, b ca 1852, mar ca 1875, Edith LE BRUN, qv, of Perce.
He was J.P., county sheriff, postmaster for 50 yrs., d 1935, bur
Perce.
C1. Lillian, mar Claude Johnson, res Ottawa, Ont.
C2. Florence, mar J. McCarthy, res Sept. Isles, Que.
C3. Muriel, mar L. Le MARQUANT, res Sept. Isles, Que.
C4. Eileen, mar Harold LE GRESLEY, qv, res Gaspe
C5. Ralph, res Shippegan, N.B., worked for W.S. Loggie Co. there
C6. Nelson De C., res Riverbend, Que.
C7. Capt. Harold, res Halifax, N.S.
C8. Reginald James, b 1891, res Ottawa, mar Irene LE MARQUAND, qv
C9. Francis, res Campbellton, N.B.
C10. etc. Others, such as Maria, Laura and John? These are in
Census, 1861.
B2. Alice Louisa, b 1854, d 1955, mar 1875, Francis GIBAUT, qv, bur
St. Pauls, Perce, 7 chn.

TUZO
VALPY, more in CI COLL. from Mrs.K.Thompson, Edmonton,ALTA.
  B3. Elizabeth, poss sometimes known as Henrietta?, 1856-1955. Or
    poss 2 persons.
  B4. Elias George, b 1858, d 1935, civil servant, Perce
  B5. Henry, b 1860, d 1915, bur Perce
  B6. Julia Vibert, b ca 1862, d 1934, mar Charles DE QUETTEVILLE, qv,
    rem to U.S.
  B7. Eva, b 1863, d 1947, mar Philip Syvret HAMON, qv
  B8. Druscilla Dill, b ca 1865, d ca 1917. Mar Dumaresq VALPY, qv,
    of Perce, his second wife
A2. Henry Francis, drowned 1845
A3. Thomas, res Annapolis Valley, N.S., mar, no issue
A4. son, d.y. A5. Alice, mar Samuel Pudden Watson.
A6. John D., b 1831, d 1878 Magdalen Islands, Que. Mar Maria Languedoc,
  b 1834 Gaspe. His chn returned to live at Gaspe Basin. He was
  gaoler and deputy sheriff in Magdalen Islands 1871.
  B1. Claude, b 1861   B3. Susan, b 1864   B5. John, b 1870
  B2. Edith, b 1863   B4. Thomas, b 1869
TUZO, John, mar Lillian BECHERVAISE, qv, b 1906. He was poss a grandson of John D.
TUZO, Elizabeth, b 1845 Perce, d there 1946, age 99, part of, or mar
into above family
TUZO, Joseph, b 1860, and James T., b 1890, both part of above fam
VAGUS, Robert, said to be from C.I. in Burin, Nfld. (Rev. Hammond) Poss
VAGUE, VAGG, from C.I.?
VAIL, VEAL, in Nfld. (Seary) Cf VEALE, VIEL of Ch. Islands
VALCOUR, La France, signed Gaspe Petition 1820, prob. French
VALLACK, Capt. from G in Nfld. (K. Mathews)
VALLAT, VALLET, VALLIT, VALLOT, Capt. from G in Nfld. (K. Mathews) Cf
similar names in J (Stevens)
VALLIS, in Nfld. Cf VALOIS (Stevens)
VALLOIS, Mr. and Mrs. F., from C.I. 1908, worked for BC Telephone.
Frank from St. Lawrence, J.
VALPY, VALPYAND LE BAS, Jersey Fishery firm at Perce ca 1860 to 1930.
In Bon. Is. ca 1890 to 1910. At Pabos ca 1880 to 1920. Prop. D.C.
Valpy and Charles Godfray Le Bas. Original name of firm VALPY, LE BAS
AND LE SUEUR. This firm may have been begun by Richard Valpy De
Lisle of Jersey and London, England, a merchant. Had some connection
with Fred. K. JANVRIN of Bath, England. (Brochet) See also JANVRIN.
VALPY. The following, Edward, Andrew, and Dumaresq, thought to be related. (Nancy Druscilla Dolbel, Milton, Ont.; Jennie Le Breton,
Belleville, Ont.; Aldo Brochet)   VALPY, SEE EXTRA PAGES.
VALPY, Edward, mar LE BAS? At Bonaventure Island 1871
VALPY, Andrew DU PRE, b J, son of --- Valpy and --- LE BAS. To Gaspe,
first for CRC, then for Robin, Jones and Whitman Co. Mar 1. Jane
DUMARESQ of Gaspe, dau of Frederick D. and of Mary BECHERVAISE, 2
chn. He mar 2. Charlotte Mae ---, 3 chn.
  A1. Ina Dumaresq, b Gaspe?, mar Alfred C. Miller
    B1. George Alfred Valpy Miller, mar Lois Flindell of Belleville, Ont.
      4 chn
      C1. Janet Miller   C3. Peter Miller
      C2. Debra Miller   C4. Scott Miller
  A2. Margaret Jane, mar Thomas LE BRETON, qv, no issue
  A3. Charles DU PRE, mar Vivian Markham of Vancouver, BC
    B1. David, mar ---, 2 chn, Randell and Catherine
    B2. Michael, mar Amanda ---, a dau, Leslie Amanda
  A4. Mildred Muir, mar Angus Sweeting of Montreal, no issue
  A5. Gordon Francis, d.y.

VALPY, Dumaresq, 1848 J, mar 1. --- TARDIF, qv, and 2. Drusilla Dill
TUZO, qv, 1867-1917, dau of Joseph Eve TUZO, and Louisa Languedoc.
Widow res Perce after Dumaresq was killed aboard ship on Atlantic
voyage, bur at sea. 1890, age 42
- A1. Edward LE MONTAIS, b 1886, res Poughkeepsie, NY, mar, d 1958. A son
res Vancouver, B.C. and dau, Dorothy? res Poughkeepsie, N.Y. Mar
--- Galle.
- A2. Marjorie Tuzo, b 1888, d 1937, mar 1911/Rev. Sydney Radley WALTERS of
Malbaie, bur St. Pauls, Perce
  - B1. Col. Radley Walters, D.S.O., MC, stationed at Camp Borden, Ont.,
res PerceB2.Ruth R.Walters,b1914
- A3. Lottie Dumaresq Valpy, b 1889, d 1927, mar A. Neil Somerville, bur
Perce. Mar in Bridgeport, CT. Alex S. from Glasgow,Sct.
  - B1. Geraldine Sommerville, res Montreal
- A4. Charles Dumaresq, b 1890 Perce, mar 1916, Laura D. TARDIF, qv, He
d 1968 Perce, dau of Richardson TARDIF of St. Peter Port, G, and
Elizabeth Higginson.
  - B1. Richardson D., b 1918, mar Mary Janet Donavan, res Riverside,
Saint John, N.B. Served in WWII, RCAF.
  - B2. Nancy Drusilla, b 1919, mar Alfred W. DOLBEL, res Milton, Ont.
Served in WWII, RCAF, 5 chn.
  - B3. Laura Joan Dumaresq, b 1922, mar Louis Brunner, res Geneva, Ohio,
3 chn, Medalist, WWII, B.C.
  - B4. Charles Dumaresq, b 1930, mar Paula Galbraith, res Saint John, NB,
no issue

VALPY, Edward, age 32, b J, agent at Bon. Is. 1871 (Brochet)
VALPY, Robert, from J to Gaspe town, a Robin manager in 1932 (Brideau)
VALPY, to Gaspe 1777 (Syvret)
VALPY, dit JANVRIN, Philippe. See JANVRIN, 1677-1721.
VALPY, WALPY, Benjamin, in Yarmouth, N.S. 1773 (Census; Lost in Canada)
VALPY. Some Valpys of J rem to Salem, Mass. and Dover, Maine in the
1600s. Several removed in the 1700s to N.S. as U.E.L.'s. Some re-
cords of the Canadian branch are in research by descendants. (Mar-
blehead, Mass. vital records; Maine and N.H. records; Francilia Nagle,
Yarmouth, N.S.) More info available, too late to include.
VALPY, Capt. John, of J?, ancestry, b ca 1773 Mass.?, mar ca 1795 Yarmouth, NS, Sarah Crocker, b 1774, dau of Daniel Crocker, UEL?, formerly of Plymouth, Mass. and of his second wife, Abigail ROBERTS, qv.
Capt. Valpy d at sea 1807, age 34, a monument in Chebogue, NS. Sarah
d 1865, 6 chn. She is bur at Kemptville, NS. Some of this fam rem
to Calif.
- A1. Abigail, b 1792?, mar Nathaniel Churchill, son of Ephraim C., 9
chn. She d 1871.
- A2. Hanna , b 1797, mar George T. Hunter, a son of Sheriff George H.
- A3. Benjamin, b 1802   A4. Capt. John, b 1804, mar --- MacLaren
- A5. Capt. Calvin, b 1806, mar Elizabeth Gardner, dau of Capt. Reuben G.
Capt. Calvin of the EAGLE, passed the Straits of Magellan in 1850
enroute for San Francisco.

VALPY, Emmeline, of above family?, mar James Prosser, 10 chn in N.S.
- A1. a dau Bethiah, b 1856, mar 1879, John Marshall. She d 1932, 4 chn.
Some desc res Quincy, Mass.

VARDON, Michael of J, had fishery lots at Perce ca 1784 (GLF: A. Brochet)
VARDON. Obadiah, of J fam, 1871-1951, res Malbaie, Que. 1930s. Mar Liza
LUCAS, qv. Order of chn not known.
- A1. Nelson, had a son   A2. Hudson   A3. Nickerson, res London, Ont.
- A4. Watson, mar Marion Helen Dow, res Gaspe
- A5. Kathie, mar 1. Vincent VIBERT, qv, and 2. Bob Waugh, res Guelph Ont.

A6. Lorinda, mar Frank Cartwright
A7. Bertha, mar 1. Clarence GIRARD, qv, and 2. --- HOTTON
A8. Jackson, res Malbaie, Gaspe
VARDON, Claude, mar Jessie ---, 1906-1959, bur St. Pauls, Perce, Gaspe (GLF)
VARDON, Nathan Jacob, 1874-1886, res Gaspe (GLF)
VARDON, John, b J, in Malbaie 1861 (Census) with Mary Jane, Jane, Elizabeth, Elias, Anna, and Allice, all b Quebec. He was age 54 in 1871. John mar Mary Jane LUCAS?
VARDON, Sutton, and Eliza Julia, b Que., were in Gaspe 1861 (Census)
VARDON, Hannah Sophia, b middle 1800s Malbaie, part of above family?
VARDY, in Nfld. prob originally AVERTY, of C.I. A Maj. R.J. in St. Johns, Nfld.
VASLET, in Nfld. (Seary) Cf VESLET of J (Stevens)
VATCHER, Hugh, of Grt. St. Lawrence, Nfld. 1871, from J? Cf VAUTIER of J (Stevens)
VAUMOREL, a J surname (Saunders)
VAUDIN, Edward Henry Osborn, b 1865 St. Helier, J, d 1921 Victoria, BC. Mar 1891 St. Heliers, Ellen McCreight, b 1855 Ireland. She d 1936 Victoria, BC. (Brian Young, Alderwood Manor, Wash.)
A1. Doris Eileen, b 1892 St. Helier, J, mar Victoria 1917, Chester Peter Pearson
B1. Peter Campbell Pearson, b 1918 Victoria, mar 1940, Bettina R.C. Healy, b 1919 Toronto, Ont.
C1. Richard John Pearson, b 1945 Kelowna, B.C., to U.S. 1963
C2. Rosemary Ann Pearson, b 1941 Victoria, B.C.
A2. Nancy, mar --- Armythe, res North Vancouver, B.C.
A3. V----, mar ?, res Kelowna, BC
VAUDIN, Christine Elizabeth, b G, mar Ernest MARTEL TOUZEAU, qv, 3 chn, to Canada 1911. VAUDIN, Elizabeth Mary, b 1821 J, dau of George Joshua V., b 1797 J. Eliz. mar Thomas Boyle of Ontario (Brian Young)
VAUDIN, C.I. name on the S. coast of Nfld. (G.W. Le Messurier)
VAUTIER, VOUCHER, VATCHER, VAUTHIER, VAUTER, etc. and other forms of Walter, in C.I. Current Shigawake and Paspebiac, Que.
VAUTIER, Philippe. Said to be from Val de la Mare, St. Ouen, J, in Que. early 1800s, a ship captain and/or a boat builder. Poss two Philippes there at that time. Mar Marie SYVRET. A son, John. (Jeanne Prevost, Ste. Foy, Que.)
A1. John, mar Bridget GLEEN, poss GLYN, a son, Edward
B1. Edward, b J?, mar Annie Sullivan, res Quebec. She was the dau of Richard S. and Eleanor Jones.
C1. Julia, mar 1909 St. Godfroi, New Carlisle, Que., James PREVOST, qv, a farmer of Port Daniel, Bon. Co., Que., 6 chn; see PREVOST.
C2. Jeanne, mar Neil Garrity in late life, res Cambridge, Mass., no issue
C3. Roland, drowned in St. Lawrence River as a young man. Mar Gladys --- of Douglastown, Que.
D1. Edward D2. Roland, res Shigawake, Que. D3. Elsie D4. Orva
D5. Emma, d ca 1966, mar Thomas Maher of Quebec, P.Q.
D6. Nellie, mar Alex McLellan, no issue
VAUTIER, in Maritimes Fisheries (J.H. Le Breton list)
VAUTIER, Richard, from J, in Gaspe with Martha?
VAUTIER, Capt. John, from C.I. to N.B. ca 1825 (Maurice Melanson, Robichaud, N.B.)
A1. John   A2. Hedley   A3. George
VAUTIER, Amos, Amice, b ca 1818 J, mar in Canada 1862, Cathleen Boyle, or Bayle of Ire.

VAUTIERS. Listed in Mercantile Navy List, edited by John J. Mayo for yrs. 1860-1863.
VAUTIER, John, master from Plymouth, England
VAUTIER, John, master, certified Hull, Quebec 1853, #8390 and 18393
VAUTIER, George, #15471, 2nd mate, examined Plymouth, England
VAUTIER, Charles William, #19226, and Charles, 1st mate, #19995
VAUTIER, Peter, #22085, 1st mate
VAUTIER, Philip, master, #23725
VAUTIER, Amice, mar Catherine Bail 1862, by Rev. Samuel Bacon 1862 in New Castle, North. Co., New Brunswick. (New Brunswick Museum, Saint John, N.B.) Poss same as Amos above. J.VAUTIER,ERROR BY GALLANT
VAUTIER, Jacques, son of Jacques Sr. and Elizabeth Godfrey of St. Aubin, J, mar 1822, Catherine Blake, widow of Wm. Smith of Perce (Brochet)
VAUTIER, Abraham, b J, ship Capt., mar 1829 Gaspe Bay, age 68 in 1871 there
VAUTIER, Capt. John, of J desc, mar Margaret E. Carter, qv, bur St. Paul Angl. Cem, Gaspe (GLF)
VAUTIER, Philippe, from St. Helier, J, boat builder in Quebec early 1800s, mar Marie-Angelique Bergeron
VAUTIER, VAUTHIER, from J to N.B. and Que. (Rev. Le Gresley; K.H. Annett)
VAUTIER, C.I. name on S. coast of Nfld. (G.W. Le Messurier) Peter in Nfld. 1856 (Seary)
VAUTIER, Francis, from J? in La Poile, Nfld. 1860s (Rev. Hammond)
VAUTIER, VATCHER, Emmanuel and Stephen Burgeo, Nfld. 1860s (Rev. Hammond)
VAUTIER, VAUTURE, Capt. from J in Nfld. 1800s? or earlier (K. Mathews)
VAUTIER, VOUCHER, Richard and Martha, members of St. Thomas Angl. Ch, S. coast and French shore area of Nfld. (Rev. Hammond, Bell Island, Nfld.)

A1. Stephen, b ca 1818, bp 1830   A4. Emanuel, age 5, bp 1830
A2. Deborah, age 9, bp 1830   A5. Joseph, age 1, bp 1830
A3. Richard, age 7, bp 1830

VAVASOUR, in Nfld. (Seary) Cf LE VAVASSEUR dit DURELL of J (Stevens)
VELLIS, poss VEILLEZ, James, Richard and Samuel in Fortune Bay, Nfld. 1860s (Rev. Hammond)
VEITCHE, fam from C.I.? in Nfld. (Lady McKie)
VENEMENT, James, Capt. in Gaspe 1871, age 45, b J (Census)
VENNEMENT, J.R., from C.I. to Vancouver, BC 1900s?
VENEMONT, James, of J, caretaker for Charles Robin 1772, Paspebiac (Rev. d'Hist)   VERGE, DU VERGEE,ETC. SEE ADDED PAGES.
VERDY, Wm. from C.I.?, in Channel, Nfld. 1860s (Rev. Hammond) Poss VERDIER or AVERTY from J. See also VERTEE in QAAM, by Turk.
VERROW, in Nfld., said to be of C.I. origin. (Rev. Hammond) Poss VERRIOUR of J.
VIBERT, Peter, Pierre, b 1795 J, rem to Corner of the Beach, Gaspe, ca 1830, mar 1831 Roseanne or Roxanne GALE, 1795-1880
VIBERT, Peter, Pierre, b J, to Corner of the Beach, Gaspe ca 1830, mar 1831, Judith INGROUVILLE, dau of Daniel I. of G, seven chn. Mar 2. Sara Bunton Cass. See BUNTON. (Nola Journeau, St. Eustache, Que. and Ellen Hill, Verdun, Que.; Bible; family records; GLF)
A1. Peter Daniel, b ca 1835, mar --- BUNTON
  B1. Adolphus, mar Emily Stewart of York Centre, Gaspe
    C1. Ruby, unmar   C2. Winnie, unmar
    C3. Rupert John, 1898-1940, mar Emilie Hutton, 2 sons, res Malbaie
    C4. Leopold, d.y.   C5. Stewart   C6. Wilfred
    C7. Harold, unmar, d 1975, bur Montreal
    C8. Vincent, mar Kathie VARDON, qv, d 1973

VIBERT 533

                D1. Shirley, mar --- ROBERTSON, res Montreal
            C9. Gertrude, unmar, res Montreal
            C10. Drucy, Drusillia, unmar, res Montreal
        B2. Frank, mar ---
            C1. Ruth, res Calif.   C3. Dewey   C5. Jessie
            C2. Edie   C4. Hattie   C6. Effie
            C7. Harry Clifford, mar Agnes ARBOUR, qv, 1891-1963, res Cannes des
                Roches, Gaspe
                D1. Norman, res Cannes des Roches, Gaspe
                D2. Ruth   D3. Edith
                D4. Jean, mar Maggie VIBERT, res Bridgeville, Gaspe, 5 chn
                D5. Arthur   D6. Agnes   D7. Mabel, res Montreal   D8. others?
    A2. George, had general store, mar Margaret BUNTON, qv, 1856-1918
        B1. Elias BUNTON, foster ch raised by George and wife, heir
    A3. Philip, 1837-1910, mar Frances Cass, 1836-1896, whose sister Ester
        mar Daniel Mabe, and res Corner of the Beach, Gaspe
        B1. Elias, 1874-1965, mar 1902, Margaret Ross, 1884-1962
            C1. Maud   C2. Marjorie, mar Wm. Staler of Toronto, res there
            C3. Elsie, mar Arthur SEALE of Shigawake, Gaspe
                D1. Brock Seale   D2. dau
            C4. Reginald, Vet WWII, mar and res Scotland
            C5. Alice   C6. Grace
            C7. Leslie, d late 1960s, mar Evelyn Patterson, res Sunny Bank,
                Gaspe
                D1. Ralph   D2. Kenneth   D3. Sandra   D4. Wendy
        B2. Arthur, mar Emily Nannette, res Gaspe, Que.
            C1. Olga   C2. Fred, res Gaspe, Que.   C3. Jenny
        B3. William Godfrey, 1864-1918, mar 1. Laura BECK, 1870-1902, and 2.
            Nancy LE GRESLEY, qv.
            C1. Harvey Godfrey, b 1895, mar 1927, Mabel ROBERTSON, 1898-1970
                D1. June Matilda, mar Robert Farmer, res Ottawa, Ont.
            C2. Herman Isaac, b 1896, d 1976, mar Helena JEAN, qv
                D1. Raymond, mar girl from Bridgeville, Gaspe. Raymond d age 30,
                    and wife soon after. Child raised by mother's sister.
                D2. Foster, mar girl from Cannes des Roches, res there, 6 chn
            C3. Clarence, b 1898, mar Hilda DEVOUGE, qv, of Bridgeville, Gaspe
                D1. Clifton, res England, mar English girl, WWII
                D2. Rexford, drowned after returning from WWII
                D3. Weston, mar a Rosebridge girl, res Moncton, no issue
                D4. Stanley, mar Kathleen Buckley of Barachois, Gaspe, 2 daus
                D5. Ross, b 1934, mar Laura Harrison, res Manitoba, no issue
                D6. Bruce, mar Margaret Small, of Barbados, 2 sons, res Montreal
                D7. Sonny, mar, res Toronto   D8. Rodney, mar, res Toronto
                D9. Beulah, mar Englishman, res Toronto, at least 3 chn
            C4. May Isabel, b 1901, mar Robert Mannan, no issue, res Rhode Is.
            C5. Laura Mabel, b 1902, mar 1. Ross Coffin, a dau Doris, mar 2.
                --- Colerick
        B4. John   B5. Alfred, mar Barbara Cass
        B6. Alice, mar Christopher Mabe
            C1. Ada Mabe, mar Duncan DEVOUGE
                D1. Grant DEVOUGE
            C2. Lydia Mabe, mar Sydney VIBERT, a first cousin, son of James,
                no issue
    A4. Edward, mar Mary Ann Hogan, d 1913, bur Corner of the Beach
        B1. Frederick Wilfred, 1869-1889 B2. Edward B3. Elma B4. Irma
    A5. May Ann, 1834-1929, mar Edward Packwood, 1826-1900, res Pt. St.
        Peter, Gaspe

B1. Edward Jr., 1862-1934, mar Mary JEAN, qv, 1882-1931
A6. Jane, 1841-1911, mar Peter Mabe, 1829-1907
A7. Elizabeth, 1848-1910, mar Henry Mabe, 1829-1907
  B1. William Mabe, owned general store, unmar
  B2. Sara, res Calif., unmar
  B3. Lucy Mabe, res Montreal and Corner of the Beach
A8. Elias, by second wife, shot accidentally while fishing, gun went off in boat. Age 16 in 1878.
A9. James, 1857-1928, by second wife, mar 1. Emily Miller, 1865-1905 and 2. Roxanne TAPP, qv, who d 1930. She was sister of Abacel Tapp, who mar Dr. McNally of Calumet Island, Que. and later of Barachois, Gaspe. Roxanne and Abacel were daus of James Tapp, qv, of Barachois, Gaspe. B1. to B16. by first wife.
  B1. Herbert, Bert, unmar, WWI Vet, 1884-1925, CNR conductor
  B2. Beatrice, mar, res New York, a son, 1886-1965
  B3. Sydney, 1890-1952, mar Lydia Mabe, no issue
  B4. Gladys, mar Jack Drouin, res Campbell's Bay, a son, Vibert Drouin
  B5. Ross, unmar   B6. Maud
  B7. Hilda, mar George Hamilton?, res Hamilton, Ont., deceased, no issue
  B8. Wilson, res Campbell's Bay, Que., general store, mar twice; 1. Jean, 5 chn, and 2. Ella, a dau, Lorraine.
  B9. Percy, unmar   B10. Grace   B11. Eleanor
  B12. Ida Muriel, res Ottawa, Ont., mar Sydney Peacock of Montreal, a son, Niel Peacock
  B13. Ada, mar Arthur Young, res Montreal, 1904-1966, no issue
  B14., 15., 16., others
  B17. James, by second wife, b 1907, d 1962, mar Ethel Cleary of Grand Cascapedia, Bon. Co., Que., b 1901, 4 chn
    C1. James Albert Lindy, b 1932, res Dorval, Que., pres. Lakeshore Motors, mar Marion Willett, 1958, 3 chn
      D1. Lindy, Jr., b 1960   D3. Douglas, b 1966
      D2. Belinda, b 1963
    C2. Mary Ellen Roxanna, b 1934, mar Harry Hill, res Montreal, divorced, 4 chn. Manager for Bell Canada.
      D1. Shawn George James Hill, b 1959
      D2. Dwayne Stephen Paul Hill, b 1960   D4. Todd Harry Michel
      D3. Karen Mary Ethel Hill, b 1962   Hill, b 1963
    C3. dau, stillborn   C4. Rudy, b 1936, res Lachine, Que.
  B18. Roxanna, b 1908, d 1966, mar Jack Landry of Quebec City
    C1. Betty, mar Guy LAMONTAGNE, qv, 3 chn, res Quebec City
    C2. Ellen, mar Mike McNichols, res Longueuil, Que.
  B19. Lewis, 1910-1913   B20. Cecil, 1912-1914   B21. son, d.y.
  B22. Grace Eleanor, Ella, b 1915, mar Maurice Plamondon of Que., res BC
    C1. Robert, mar Adele ---, 3 chn, works for Bell Canada
      D1. Eric Plamondon   D2. Julie Plamondon   D3. Lisa Plamondon
    C2. Carol, mar Harold ---, of Louisiana, res Seattle, 2 chn
    C3. Margaret, Peggy, mar John ---, of Washington, U.S., 2 chn
    C4. Gerald, mar Mimi LEPAGE, res Montreal
  B23. John, b 1917, d 1928
  B24. Leo, b 1920, mar Hazel Reid of England, and 2. Beatrice Miville of Quebec City. 3 chn by first wife. Leo a Vet of WWII
    C1. Lee, res Quebec City, b 1943
    C2. Hazel, b 1944, mar Lucien Pepin, 3 chn, res Quebec City
      D1. Josee   D2. Michel   D3. Nancy
    C3. boy, b 1946, d.y.

VIBERT. These four men may be part of family above. Uncertain and incomplete.
I. VIBERT, Philip, mar Harriet HAMMOND, qv. He was b 1878, d age 34.
   C1. Charles Henry, b 1905, d 1963, mar Grace Paulmert, b 1908, b Barachois, Gaspe. Charles was b in Bridgeville, Que. (Carole V. Rodgers, Laval, Que.)
      D1. Charles Paul Emmett, b 1934 Montreal, mar Rosalie TAPP, 5 chn
         E1. Lynn, b ca 1955   E4. Eric, b ca 1960
         E2. Gail, b ca 1957   E5. Lois, b ca 1962
         E3. Kevin, b ca 1958
      D2. Carole Mary Grace, b 1937, mar Bernard Rodgers, 2 chn
         E1. Carolyn Rodgers, b 1962   E2. Michael Rodgers, b 1966
      D3. Gloria Ann, b 1941, mar Harris Thomason, or Thompson, 3 chn.
         E1. Daniel Thompson, b 1961 E3. Tammy Jane Thompson, b 1964
         E2. Richard, b 1963
   C2. Percy, mar, 3 chn, res Malartic, Quebec 1970s
   C3. William, res Bridgeville, Gaspe, 7? children
II. Elias, unmar, d in his late 70s in Gaspe
III. Donald, mar late in life, no issue
IV. Hiram, res Niagara Falls, d Gaspe, no issue
V. Mae, mar Henry MARION, d early 40s, had 6 or 7 chn, res Montreal and Toronto

VIBERT. Sev. fams to Gaspe from J. Information plentiful on these, but sometimes chn of one fam confused with other fams. Some data uncertain and unverified. (Nola Journeau, St. Eustache, Que.; Ellen Hill, Verdun, Que.; Thorna Rountree, Westmount, Que.;)
VIBERT, Jean, bp 1793 St. Mary, J, son of Helier V. and Jeanne BALLEYNE, qv, rem to Gaspe, mar St. Mary, J, Marguerite ARTHUR, at least 7 chn. Some rem to Gaspe and Montreal. Spent at least part of his life in J and part in Gaspe. He d before 1862, and she d 1878, bur Gaspe town.
A1. Marguerite, bp 1819 St. Mary, J, mar and d in J, mar a cooper, or COOPER of J
A2. Ann Caroline, b ca 1823
A3. Mary Ann, b 1827 St. Brelade, J, mar Capt. Wood, poss d in Montreal
A4. John Arthur, b 1827, bp St. Brelade, J, mar Sybil SHAW, qv, of N.S. 1858. See JEAN fam. He was capt. of sev. vessels for different firms, the first being John LE BOUTILLIER AND CO. of Gaspe, later John and Elias COLLAS Co. His journal shows voyages to Italy, Spain, Caribean, Brazil, U.S. and northern Europe.
   B1. Arthur, b 1861   B5. George, b 1876
   B2. Jack   B6. Herbert, b 1878
   B3. Joseph   B7. Margaret
   B4. Sybil   B8. Mary Anne Thorne, b 1873, lived to age 100
A5. Eliza, bp 1829 St. Mary, J, mar DOLBEL, qv, res Perce, ran the Baker Hotel, rem to Mont Louis, Gaspe, where they had a fishing establishment.
A6. Jane Sarah, bp 1831, d unmar Montreal?
A7. Helier James, bp St. Mary, J 1833, d 1838 there
VIBERT, John James, b 1848 St. Peter, J, son of Jean V. and Jane LE GRESLEY, qv, mar 1877 Canada to Lydia Amelia HAMON. John d 1917, Lydia 1920 in Montreal.
A1. Rev. Arthur John, b 1878, d 1937   A6. Lillian Lydia
A2. Reginald Dumaresq   A7. Hilda Hamon
A3. Ethel Esther   A8. Amy Florence
A4. Stanley James   A9. Lydia Hamon
A5. Edwin Le Quesne   A10. Percy Philip
VIBERT, Philip, b early 1800s J, son of Jean V. and Jane LE GRESLEY, bro

of John James above. Mar 1877, Susan MERCIER, qv, res Canada. (Witnesses: Edward Beck, Mary Mercier)
- A1. Ernest, mar, at least 2 sons, Donald and Reginald
- A2. Earle, 4 chn, Raymond, Robert, Elizabeth, and Kathryn A3. Nelle

VIBERT, Philip, b 1804 Alderney, son of Rev. John V. and Susan Mary NICOLLE, qv. John was chaplain to H.M. forces at Alderney. Philip mar 1836 at St. Mary's, J, Susannah Dove, dau of Thomas Dove of Woolwich and widow of J. Thompson. Philip d 1886, bur St. Pauls, Gaspe. (GLF; Pat Vibert, Burnaby, BC) POSS.SAME AS PHILIP BELOW?

VIBERT, Philip, b ca 1795 Ald., sheriff of Perce, d ca 1880, mar --- GALE? Mentioned by Thomas Pye in 1866, CANADIAN SCENERY, Dist. of Gaspe. Pye wrote many articles for the Miramichi GLEANER, of NB, under pen name MERCATOR.

VIBERT, Philippe James, b J, son of Philippe V. and Marie Elizabeth LE CHEMINANT, qv, bp 1825 St. Brelade, J. Rem from J 1847 on the STE. ANNE. Worked for Robin firm, settled Cape Cove, Gaspe. Mar Martha LENFESTY, qv, 1848, dau of James L. and Susan MAUGER Dobson.
- A1. Philippe James Jr., b 1849, d 1907. Mar Eliza Jane LAWRENCE, 1857-1914, res Cape Cove, 9 chn, rem to Montreal later. (Brochet; Claudette Maroldo, Cherry Hill, NJ)
    - B1. James Philip, b 1879, d 1940, mar Nellie Willia, 2 daus; Ada and Edith
    - B2. Albert Henry, b 1886, d 1963. Mar Catherine LE BRETON, qv, 1886-1945
        - C1. Arthur, mar Ann Johnson
            - D1. Wayne Robert, mar Patricia Ann Smerek
        - C2. Lloyd   C3. Eliza
    - B3. Mary Elizabeth, b 1888 Cape Cove, d 1963. Mar Francis Cassidy, 1880-1946
        - C1. Albert Cassidy   C3. Ruth Cassidy   C5. Irene Cassidy
        - C2. Philip Cassidy   C4. Wilson Cassidy
    - B4. Emma Jane, b 1891, d 1968, mar Norman Beech
        - C1. Vera Beech   C2. Norman Beech
    - B5. Martin Gilbert, b 1893, mar Mabel Beagley, two daus; Thelma and Dorothy
    - B6. Oliver William, b 1896, d 1961, mar Dorothy LEE, qv
        - C1. Lawrence   C2. Sharon   C3. James   C4. Jane
    - B7. Herman Charles, b 1899, mar Belle Weldon, two chn; Duane and Dorothy
    - B8. Wilson George, b 1900, d 1918 B9. and 10. 2 chn, d.y.
- A2. John Peter, b 1851 Perce, d 1874, unmar
- A3. Peter, b 1853, twin, mar Rosanna GALE 1887. D 1943, carpenter.
    - B1. Ernest Franklin, b 1887 Cape Cove   B5. Leslie Edmond, b 1896
    - B2. Lillie Grace, b 1890   B6. Edward James, Edwin, b 1898
    - B3. Mildred Edith, b 1892   B7. Alexandra Lucy, b 1901
    - B4. John Albert, b 1894   B8. Florence May, b 1904 d 1917
- A4. Mary Magdalene, b 1853, twin, d 1874, unmar
- A5. Martha, b 1858, unmar
- A6. Frederick, b 1859 Perce, d 1931, mar Carrie Boldt
    - B1. Harry, b 1885, mar Elizabeth Braun, 1893-1967
        - C1. Harry   C2. Grace   C3. Eleanor
    - B2. Grace, b 1887, mar Earl Shaffer
        - C1. Arthur Shaffer   C3. Marjorie Shaffer   C5. Howard Shaffer
        - C2. Edward Shaffer   C4. Florence Shaffer
    - B3. Linnie Mae, b 1894, mar Murell Wolfe
    - B4. Carrie Florence, b 1890, mar Carl Schnubel   B5. Esther
- A7. Silas, b 1862, d 1881, unmar A8. Walter, b 1862, d 1938, unmar

VIBERT 537

A9. Louise, b 1865, d 1952, mar Leander Jones
   B1. Albert Jones   B3. Ethel Jones   B5. Melvin Jones
   B2. Walter Jones   B4. George Jones
VIBERT, Philip, b ca 1820 J, fisherman and farmer, Episcopal, mar Elizabeth ---, res Malbaie, Gaspe, 1861 Census. Wife, 30 yrs. old at that time, with 6 chn.
A1. Mary, b ca 1850 Que.   A3. Amy, b ca 1852   A5. Alice, b ca 1857
A2. Charles, b ca 1851   A4. Rachel, b ca 1854 A6. Susan, b ca 1859 Que.
VIBERT, 3 bros from J to Canada:
VIBERT, George William, b 1890 St. John, J, mar 1913 Trinity, J, Florence Amelia Henwood, rem to Sask 1953. George d 1973, Florence in J, 1929. (Lilliam Le Boutillier, Sask, Sask)
A1. Florence Amelia, b 1916 J, rem to Sask 1957
A2. Lilian May, b 1923 St. Helier, J, rem to Sask with husband, Walter Alfred LE BOUTILLIER, qv, 3 chn
VIBERT, Percy Charles, b J, bro of George William above, mar Ada Anne Rachel RONDEL, qv, rem to Canada
A1. Percy, res Arcadia, Calif.
A2. Una, mar --- ROBERTS, qv, res Richmond, BC
VIBERT, Edward Joseph, b 1868, d 1941, bur St. Pauls, Gaspe. Mar Bertha Sarah Suddard, 1869-1955 (GLF)
A1. Harold James, b 1893, d in mill accident
A2. George Christopher, b 1899, d.y.
A3. Eugene Percival, b 1903, d 1924   A4. Kenneth Arthur, b 1906, d.y.
A5. Wilfred, mar Eva BECHERVAISE
   B1. Wilma B2. Keith B3. Kathleen B4. Weston B5. Stanley
A6. Ella   A7. Erma   A8. Kathleen
VIBERT, John, b ca 1820 J, res Malbaie. Mar Peggy ---, 2 chn under two years in 1861? John and Mary Ann. C of E.
VIBERT, John, b ca 1815 J, fisherman and farmer in Malbaie, mar Ellen ---, R.C. She was 32 in 1861. Two chn, Philip and Mary Ann, also two elderly VIBERTS, Margaret S., age 77, unmar, and John, age 70, unmar. (Mrs. Claudette Maroldo, Cherry Hill, N.J.)
VIBERT, Edward, b J, mar Ada Mary LE QUESNE, qv, in Quebec?
A1. Edward John, b 1883, mar Eva De Langis
   B1. John Edward Raymond, b 1908 St. Jacques Des Piles, Que., mar Marie Olive Boudreau, res Montreal, Que.
VIBERT, James, poss John James, Jean Jacques, b 1819?, J, rem to Miscou Island, N.B., mar 1845, Esther Jane Ward, 4 chn. Mar 2. Sarah BROWN, qv, 1833-1895, 11 chn. (Nola Journeau, St. Eustache, Que.)
A1. John, b 1845 Miscou, lost at sea 1895. Mar Harriet McLean, 5 chn, res Gloucester, Mass.
   B1. Helen May, 1873-1936
   B2. Sumner Dana, mar Anna Belle Lawrence, 4 chn
      C1. Dorothy A. C2. Lawrence Dana C3. Harriet Allison C4. Virginia
   B3. Hattie V., 1879-1886
   B4. Edith Jane, b 1871, d.y. Edith Jane again, d.y.
A2. Philip, b 1849, drowned, mar 1872, Katherine Whittie, b 1854 Cape Hood, N.S.
   B1. Christiana Jane, mar Walter Doyle, 4 chn
      C1. Catherine Viola Doyle   C3. Mabel Doyle
      C2. Irene Doyle, mar Felix Favorite C4. Philip Doyle
A3. William, b 1856, mar 1. Isabella McConnell, at least one dau, Ludy, who mar --- Washburn, who had chn
A4. ---?, died from snake bite
A5. Charles, b 1851, d 1913, mar Margaret Chiasson, 3 sons
   B1. Frank C., b 1876, d 1940, mar Mary Ann BROWN, b 1895, 5 chn

C1. Violet, b ca 1911, mar --- Garcia, res Halifax, Mass., no issue
C2. Clifford, b ca 1919, mar Mildred Vibert, 3 chn, res Miscou, NB
    D1. Larry, b ca 1948   D3. Murray, b ca 1963
    D2. Ralph, b ca 1955
C3. Raymond, b ca 1922, mar Joyce Wilson, 2 chn, res Toronto, Ont.
    D1. Donna, b ca 1959   D2. Karen, b ca 1962
C4. Susan, b ca 1925, mar Hubert Wilson, 4 chn, res Montreal
    D1. Carol Anne, b 1947, a son, Andrew Wilson
    D2. Daniel Wilson, b 1953
    D3. Robert Wilson, b 1954   D4. Michael Wilson, b 1955
C5. Curtis, b 1936, mar Gayle BAKER, res Franklin, Mass., 2 chn
    D1. Curt Jr., b ca 1963   D2. Kimberly, b ca 1966
B2. Stillman, mar Edith Biseau, 3 chn
    C1. Lennie, dec   C2. Benson, rem to Vancouver, BC
    C3. Mabel, mar 1. Paul BEAUDIN, 1 ch, and 2. Aubrey Smith, 4 chn
        D1. Dalton Beaudin, mar ---, 4 chn
            E1. James Beaudin, b ca 1961   E3. Sandra Beaudin, b ca 1965
            E2. David Beaudin, b ca 1962   E4. John Beaudin, b ca 1970
        D2. Clayton Smith, b ca 1950
        D3. Carson Smith, b ca 1952   D4. Wilma Smith, b ca 1957
        D5. Phyllis Smith, b ca 1960, res Hamilton, Ont.
B3. Freeman, mar Grace Blakeley, 6 chn. Sons are tuna fishermen, Miscou.
    C1. Haviland, mar Edna Gregoire, res Miscou, dau, Debbie
    C2. Douglas, mar Doris Marks, res Miscou, dau, Donna
    C3. Morris, mar Pierrette Grey, 3 chn, Gayle, Beryl and Austin
    C4. Ethel, res Miscou, mar Harris VIBERT, 2 chn, Gary and Sharon, res Toronto
    C5. Preston, res Miscou, unmar
    C6. Leslie, b 1932, unmar, holds world record for largest tuna caught on sporting tackle
A6. Nancy, b 1853 Miscou, d 1919
    B1. Minn Vibert, mar --- Robinson, res U.S.   B2. Bobbie
A7. Thomas, b 1854 Miscou, mar Elizabeth Biseau, 5 chn
    B1. Rena, mar George Brown, 9 chn
        C1. Byron Brown, mar Blanche Brown, res Miscou
            D1. Milton Brown   D2. dau
        C2. Elmer   C5. Melinda   C8. Lettie
        C3. MacKenzie, res Ont.   C6. Lorna   C9. Carl
        C4. Jane, res St. John, NB C7. Della
    B2. Jane, mar John Brown, res Miscou, N.B.
        C1. Gladys Brown, res Mass.   C4. Mabel Brown
        C2. Elsie Brown   C5. Ellen Brown, mar --- Hayward,
        C3. Ambrose Brown   res Mass.
    B3. Mabel, mar Thomas Sterling, res Lawrence, Mass.
    B4. Lester, unmar   B4. Basil, unmar
A8. John, b 1857, d 1902. Mar Katie Wiseman Marks, Lettie Scott's mother
A9. James, b 1859, unmar
A10. George J., b 1861, mar Hannah Campbell, 12 chn, 4 d.y.
    B1. Bertha, mar Theo. Russel, a dau   B3. Grace, mar Thomas Robertson,
    B2. Gladys, mar Harry Storey, a son   3 chn
    B4. Alice, mar 1. M. McLean, a son Robert, and 2. Harry Branch
    B5. Ethel, mar Dave Stanton, a dau Eleanor. Ethel d 1974
    B6. Irene, mar Earl Doucet, no issue
    B7. Harris, mar Ethel VIBERT, 2 chn, Gary and Sharon
    B8. Howard Jordon, b 1904, mar Lela Marks, b 1907, mar 1926, 7 chn

           C1. Jeanette, b 1926, mar Roy Hunsley, b 1916, res Moncton, N.B.
              D1. Francis Hunsley, b 1955   D2. Gordon Hunsley, b 1953
           C2. Marjorie L., b 1929, mar Ronald E. Steeves, b 1928, 4 chn, res
               Moncton, NB
              D1. Brenda Joy Steeves, b 1949
              D2. Beverly Lynne Steeves, b 1951, mar Eric MacIntosh, 3 chn
                 E1. Heather MacIntosh, b 1970   E3. Ronnie MacIntosh, b 1974
                 E2. Scott MacIntosh, b 1971
              D3. Ronald Wayne Howard Steeves, b 1954
              D4. Crystal Holly Steeves, b 1960
           C3. Duncan, b 1928, d 1964, mar Maureen O'Toole, 1957, 3 chn, res
               Detroit, Mich.
              D1. Stephen   D2. Charlene   D3. Sheila
           C4. David, b 1936, mar Bernadette Bashman 1964, res Little Shippe-
               gan, NB
           C5. Mark Dean Vibert Stanton, b 1937, mar Annette Conway, 4 chn,
               res Vancouver, BC
              D1. Leslie Ann   D2. Mark Dean   D3. Susanne   D4. Jane
           C6. Ruth, b 1942, mar Ian Boyd, b 1935, 2 chn, res Edmundston, NB
              D1. Darcy Boyd, b 1973   D2. Craig Boyd, b 1974
           C7. Sharron Nancy, b 1952
       A11. Elizabeth, b 1863, d 1920, mar Robert Chiasson
          B1. Sadie Chiasson, mar George Brown, res Miscou, N.B.
             C1. Charles Byers Brown
             C2. Gertie Brown, mar Howard Biseau, 2 chn
                D1. Dennis Biseau   D2. Linda Biseau, mar, 1 ch
             C3. Mabel Brown, mar Gus. Dragon in Mass., 2 chn
                D1. Wayne Dragon, mar, a son   D2. Sheila Dragon, mar, a son
             C4. Emma, mar Earl Wilson, res Vancouver, BC, no issue
       A12. Edward Henderson, b 1864, d 1912. Mar Jessie Campbell, 10 chn.
            She d 1944.
          B1. Elizabeth, 1889-1965, mar Hamilton Harper, 8 chn
             C1. Estella Harper, b 1914, d 1944, mar Harold Archibald
                D1. Thomas Harper, b 1935, mar Bernice Gregoire, 3 chn
                   E1. Sandra Harper, b 1963   E3. Wendy Harper, b 1968
                   E2. Wayne Harper, b 1964
                D2. Margaret Archibald, b 1941
             C2. Windsor Harper, b 1917, mar Gertrude VIBERT, 12 chn
                D1. Jean Harper, b 1947, mar Gordon Ray, 4 chn
                D2. John Harper, b 1948   D3. Milton Harper, b 1950
                D4. Susan Harper, b 1951, mar Lindsay Harper, 1921-1976, 2 chn
                D5. Heather Harper   D6. Daniel Harper, b 1960
                D7. Kenneth Harper   D8. Laura Harper
                D9. Karen Harper   D10. Andrew Harper, 1966-1977
                D11. Hazel Harper   D12. William Harper, b 1967
             C3. Nellie Harper, b 1919, d 1970, unmar
             C4. Luella Harper, b 1921, mar Warren Biseau, 11 chn
                D1. Albert Biseau, b 1940, mar 1. Ada Chiasson, and 2. Kathy
                    VIBERT, res Miscou, 6 chn by first wife.
                D2. Jack, b 1942, d.y.
                D3. Ivan Biseau, b 1943, mar Patricia Godin, 4 daus
                D4. Jean Biseau, b 1944, mar Elmer Hachey, 4 chn
                D5. Rodney Biseau, b 1946, mar in Toronto, Pat ---, 2 chn
                D6. Edna Biseau, b 1947, mar Wm. McConnell, res Island River, NB
                   E1. Elizabeth McConnell, b 1974 E2. Holly McConnell, b 1975
                D7. Gerald Biseau, b 1949, mar Corinne Wilson, res Toronto, 2 chn
                D8. Linda Biseau, b 1951, mar Eugene Trepanier, 2 chn

D9. Joan Biseau, b 1956, 1 ch b 1976
D10. Nancy Biseau, b 1959, 1 ch b 1977 D11. Ina Biseau, b 1962
C5. Edward James Harper, b 1923, mar Lillian FILLIER, qv, from Nfld., res Sudbury, Ont., 4 chn
    D1. Geraldine Harper, b 1949, mar Ray Wilde, 2 chn
    D2. Brian Harper, b 1957
    D3. Karen Harper, b 1959   D4. Kenneth, b 1961
C6. Edna Harper, b 1927, mar Ernest Dee of Gaspe, b 1916, 5 chn, res Montreal
    D1. Harper Dee, b 1951   D4. Douglas Dee, b 1959
    D2. Alan Dee, b 1952, d 1954   D5. Trevor Dee, b 1966
    D3. Alvin Dee, b 1957
C7. Ella Harper, b 1930, d 1977, mar Gerald Adams of Gaspe, b 1916, 7 chn, res Montreal
    D1. Stephen Adams, b 1950, mar France Labonte, no issue
    D2. Hamilton Adams, b 1951, mar Brenda Goddard, res Ottawa, Ont., 2 chn
        E1. Cynthia Adams, b 1973   E2. Gerald Adams, b 1977
    D3. Barry Adams, b 1953, d 1958
    D4. Brenda Adams, b 1956, mar Martin Conlin, res Montreal, 1 ch
        E1. Tanya Conlin, b 1977
    D5. Wanda Adams, b 1958
    D6. Karen Adams, b 1963   D7. Cheryl Adams, b 1966
C8. Iola Harper, b 1932, d 1958
    D1. Mark Harper, b 1953, d 1960   D2. Ella Harper, b 1955
B2. Estella, b 1892, mar 1. Ralph Atkins, 2. Bert Shaw, and 3. Freemont Nickerson
C1. Ermond (AKA Edward) J. Vibert, b 1911 Auburn, ME, mar 1942 Verdun, Que., Cecilia G. Hall, b 1916 Louisa, Que., 3 chn. Res Westford, Mass.
    D1. Kevin Hall, b 1948 Lowell, Mass., mar Regina Perkins, no issue
    D2. Linda Cecilia, b 1949 Lowell, mar Danny Montoya of Calif, 1 ch
    D3. Calvin Ermond, b 1951, mar Dolores MARCHAND of Dracut, Mass.
C2. Edward Atkins, res Waterville, ME, 2 chn, Linda and Ralph
C3. Douglas Shaw, d in Calif.
C4. Idora Shaw, mar 1.? and 2. Charles Young, res Lawrence, Mass.
    D1. Joseph   D4. Kitty Young   D7. Lawrence Young
    D2. Donna   D5. Trudy Young
    D3. Thomas   D6. Randa Young
C5. Kathryn Shaw, mar 1.? and 2. Donald Sites, res Bangor, ME
    D1. Lawrence   D2. Kathy   D3. Julie   D4.?
C6. Doris Nickerson
B3. William Sumner, b 1896, d 1967, mar Katie Brune, b 1904, res Miscou, NB, 10 chn, 2 d.y.
C1. Milton, 1925-1945, WWII
C2. Eula, b 1926, mar Lawrence Adamson 1947, 3 daus, res Little Britain
    D1. Lynn Adamson, b 1948, mar Steven Keys, 1971, 2 chn
        E1. Jason Keys, b 1973   E2. Sarah Keys, b 1975
    D2. Vivian Adamson, b 1950, mar Richard Moore 1969, 2 chn
        E1. Vanessa Moore, b 1972   E2. Valerie Moore, b 1975
    D3. Jennifer Adamson, b 1958
C3. Merle T., b 1932, mar Shirley Sheriden Lang of Toronto, 4 chn
    D1. Kathy, b 1953, mar Steven Carter, a dau, Jennifer Carter, b 1976, res Calif.
    D2. John, b 1958   D3. Paul, b 1962   D4. Mathew, b 1966
C4. Donald, b 1934, mar Anne Butland of Nfld. 1953, res Toronto

          D1. Wayne, b 1954   D3. William, b 1959   D4. Judy, b 1965
          D2. Paul, b 1956   D4. Gregory, b 1963
      C5. Lewis, b 1937, unmar, res Vancouver and Miscou
      C6. Lyman, b 1940, res Miscou, mar Roselyn Beaudin 1967, 5 chn
          D1. Angela, b 1968   D3. Tracy, b 1971   D4. Neil, b 1973
          D2. Russel, b 1969   D4. Darryl, b 1972
      C7. Verna, b 1942, mar Al Gagnon 1964, 2 chn, res Whitby, Ont.
          D1. Glenn Gagnon, b 1969   D2. Cynthia Gagnon, b 1971
      C8. Elizabeth, Betty, b 1944, mar Ronald Thomas, 1967, res Whitby,
          Ont., 2 chn
          D1. Roanne Thomas, b 1969   D2. Bradley Thomas, b 1973
   B4. John, b 1898, d 1976, mar Christianna Ellis 1925, 1905-1975, b
       and d Miscou. He was prisoner in Hong Kong 4 yrs. See N.B.
       section, page 69.
       C1. Gertrude, b 1926, mar Windsor Harper, 12 chn. See page 539.

       C2. Arnold, b 1927, unmar
   B5. George Arthur, b 1901, d 1976, res Miscou, a mailman 42 years.
       Mar Freda Brune, b 1910, 2 chn.
       C1. Nola, b 1932, mar Ernest John JOURNEAU, qv, of Bon. Is. 1954
           D1. Gary George JOURNEAU, b 1960 Montreal
       C2. Ronald W., b 1937, res Miscou, mar 1. Jean MARKS, qv, and 2.
           Dianne Landry of Caraquet, NB
           D1. Cheryl, b 1960   D4. Noram b 1972   D6. Sandra, b 1977
           D2. Anthony, b 1962 D5. Cindy, b 1974
           D3. Mario, by second wife, b 1967
   B6. Clara, b 1903, mar Oscar Edgerly, 7 chn, res Dracut, Mass.
       C1. George Edgerly, mar twice
           D1. Frank Edgerly   D4. George Edgerly   D6. others?
           D2. Elizabeth Edgerly   D5. Roseanne Edgerly
           D3. by second wife, Oscar Edgerly
       C2. Geraldine Edgerly, mar 1. --- Cott and 2. John Ahern
           D1. Allen Cott   D4. Cindy Ahern
           D2. David Cott, twin of Allen D5. Cathy Ahern
           D3. Brenda Cott   D6. Sharon Ahern
       C3. Ruth, mar --- March, chn David and Patricia March
       C4. Beverly, mar --- Beese, chn Linda and David Beese
       C5. Virginia   C6. Clara
       C7. Marjorie, mar John Leighton, chn Debbie and Jennifer Leighton
   B7. Effie, b ca 1905, mar Charles Williams, rem to Maine, sons d in
       accident
       C1. John Williams   C2. Arthur Williams
   B8. Gertrude, b 1907, d 1916
   B9. Lillian, b 1911, mar Gerald Brooks, res New York, 5 chn
       C1. Phyllis L. Brooks, b 1929, mar Wm. C. Benedict
           D1. Sherry E. Benedict, mar Larry Verstraete
               E1. Christopher L. Verstraete, b 1974
               E2. Erick W. Verstraete, b 1977
           D2. Dawn, mar Robert Auerhahn
           D3. Gale Benedict, mar David Ellsworth, a son, Jason David, b 1977
           D4. William C. Benedict   D5. Wendy A. Benedict
       C2. Dorothy E. Brooks, b 1930, mar John Pitts
       C3. Gerald F. Brooks, b 1931, mar Joan Smith, res near Rochester,
           N.Y.

         D1. Pamela M. Brooks, b 1959   D4. Mary Brooks, b 1964
         D2. Gerald F. Brooks, b 1960   D5. Paul Brooks, b 1966
         D3. William Brooks, b 1963
      C4. John Arthur Brooks, b 1932, mar Ruth Bach
         D1. John M. Brooks, b 1955   D4. Craig J. Brooks, b 1962
         D2. James A. Brooks, b 1958   D5. Patricia A. Brooks, b 1966
         D3. Jeffrey A. Brooks, b 1958
      C5. Carole A. Brooks, b 1936
A13. Frank J., b 1866 Miscou, d 1942, mar 1. Sarah Campbell and 2. Mary
   Ann Burbridge, no issue
A14. Emily, 1870-1930, a son, Ernest Vibert, mar Gertie Blakeley, no
   issue
A15. Philip, b 1871, d 1948, mar Elizabeth McWilliams, 12 chn
   B1. Leonard, mar 1. Biseau?, a dau, and 2. Mary Early of Saint John,
      NB, no issue
      C1. Mildred, mar Clifford VIBERT, 3 chn, see Clifford
   B2. Lawrence, mar Catherine ---, no issue, res Miscou
   B3. Lescel, mar Ethel Wilson, res Pembroke, Ont., 3 chn
      C1. Marine, b 1934, mar J. Fitzgerald, res Toronto, no issue
      C2. Reginald, b 1937, mar, res Pembroke, Ont.
      C3. Norma, mar ---, res Pembroke, Ont. Chn, twins
   B4. Harold, res Pembroke, Ont., 2 chn, Donald and Debbie
   B5. Chester, mar Dorothy Banks of Saint John, NB, a dau, Shirley
   B6. Ruby, mar --- Sealy of Bathurst, NB, 4 chn
      C1. Ross Sealy   C2. Carole Sealy   C3. Dale Sealy   C4. Elaine Sealy
   B7. Lena, mar Allen Stokes, a son, Walter Stokes, res Montreal
   B8. Bert, mar Enid MARKS of Miscou, 12 chn
      C1. Kenneth   C5. Lynn   C9. Colin
      C2. Linda   C6. Terry   C10. Bruce
      C3. Catherine   C7. Kelly   C11. Paul
      C4. Robert   C8. Mark   C12. Donald
   B9. Fred, mar Mayme Davidson, a son Glenn, res Shippegan, NB
   B10. Melvin, res Miscou, mar Marion Chiasson, no issue
   B11. Stanton, res Miscou, mar Laura Davidson, 4 chn
      C1. Judy, mar D. Michaud C3. James Randolph, mar Holly Wiseman 1977
      C2. Sandra, mar C. SIVRIT C4. Wendy
   B12. Kerr, mar Gwen Brooks, no issue, res Montreal
VIBERT, Douglas, of Perce, mar Ellen Hollick (Claudette Maroldo, Cherry
   Hill, N.J.)
A1. Edgar Frank, b 1877, witness Mrs. F. Le BRUN
A2. Florence Mary, 1875-1876
VIBERT, William Godfrey, res Corner of the Beach, mar 1894, Luree BECK
VIBERT, Percival, son of Elias V. and Minnie Rose of Corner of the
   Beach, d 1908
VIBERT, Ida Isabelle, dau of Philip V. and Margaret BROWN, d in Chandler, Que. 1918
VIBERT, Ida May, dau of Philip V. Jr., d 1884 at Campbellton
VIBERT, P., from J to Victoria, BC 1940 (Luce)
VIBERT, Syvret, from J to Gaspe 1777
VIBERT, Capt., boat keeper and merchant from J and G to Nfld. (K.
   Mathews)
VICK, George, in Campbellton, NB, b ca 1902 Cf VICQ of J.
VICQ, John and Joseph, from C.I. fam?, in Gaspe Militia 1850s. Cf DE
   VIC of J (Stevens)
VICQ, Joshua, b J, carpenter at Cox, Que., age 59 in 1871. Carpenter,
   with wife, Mary Jane, age 51 in 1871, RC, John Joseph, age 30, George
   Francis, 19, Jane, 18, and Ann Rosalie, 14. (Census)

VIDAMOUR, Marguerite, b G, mar Jean HOPIN of G. Son John, mar Gr. Riviere, Gaspe 1843, Caroline Collins. Desc spell name AUPIN.
VIEL, George, age 30, in Gaspe 1871 with Marie Sophie, age 25, George Amos, age 5, and Sophie J. (Census)
VIEL, from C.I. to Perce (Cent. Bklt.) Also in Ontario.
VIGOT, Cyrille, b Grouville, J, to Canada ca 1905, age 17, worked for Wm. Fruing Co. and also for W.S. Loggie Co. at Shippegan, NB. D WWI, 1915, 26th Btn. (J.H. Le Breton list)
VIGOURS, boat keeper from J in Nfld. (K. Mathews)
VILLANEUVE, from J to Nfld. (Lady McKie; G.W. Le Messurier) Jersey firm estab at Placentia Bay and Burin. A Pierre V. res St. Brelade, J and mar Anne LE BRETON, who d 1744
VILLANEUVE, Capt., agent, merchant, and ship owner from J in Nfld. (K. Mathews)
VILLANEUVE, from C.I. to Gaspe, then to Alpena, Mich.?
VINCENT, in Nfld. (Seary) Cf same in J (Stevens)
VINCENT, Jean August. Frederic, known as Jean Vincent, master boat or ship builder for Peter John Duval, then for Charles Robin and Co. In New Brunswick for some time, and may have returned to J. (Donat Robichaud, Beresford, NB) Res Shippegan 1831. They named a vessel of Robins for him in 1836, a goelette, VINCENT. He launched in 1839 the brick PATRUUS, 216 tons. A John Vincent in Bon. Co., Gaspe, 1871, age 16.
VINCENT, John and Samuel, fishermen in Sandy Pt., Nfld. 1871 (Lovell)
VINCENT, Mrs. Phyllis, nee LE FEVRE, of Gaspe, and Osoyoos, BC
VINCENT, Betty and Douglas, in Vict., BC from J?
VINCENT, P.J., b J, d 1913, age 18 in Newport, Gaspe. Prob worked for the Le marquands (GLF)
VINCENT, John, servant in Bay de Verdes, Conc. Bay, Nfld. 1860s (Rev. Hammond)
VINCENT, Wm., in Greenspond, Bon. Bay, Nfld. 1860s (Rev. Hammond)
VINCENT, Capt. from J in Nfld. (K. Mathews)
VINCENT, Charles, Loyalist, of unknown origin, in Cumberland Co., NB 1783, of fam that settled in U.S. 1675, poss from C.I.? (Mrs. J.B. Owen of Peace River, Alta.)
VIXCOUNT, in Nfld. (Seary) Cf LE VESCONTE of J (Stevens)
VIVIAN, in Nfld. (Seary) Cf VIVYAN of J (Stevens)
VOISEY, VOISIN, in Canada, cf VOISIN of J (Stevens
VOKEY, Wm. of J, at Spaniards Bay, Nfld. ca 1775. Cf LE VOGUER of J (Stevens)
VOLTIGEURS. In the Canadian West, these men were a local militia organized by Mr. Douglas from retired Hudson Bay Co. men. They wore boots or moccasins, long woolen stockings, buckskin pants, blue caps and hats, and red belts. They earned a dollar a day and rations. (SEA UNTO SEA, Canada, 1850-1910, by W.G. Hardy, New York, 1959) It seems quite likely that among these men were some from Channel Island families.
VOTIER, prob VAUTIER, John, b ca 1818 J, carpenter, in Bon. Co., Gaspe 1871 (Census) with Bridget, age 46, b Ireland; also chn. See VAUTIER.
A1. John, b ca 1849 Que., carpenter
A2. Catherine, b ca 1850
A3. Elizabeth, b ca 1851
A4. William, b ca 1853
A5. Edward, b ca 1855
A6. Philip, b ca 1857
A7. Francis, b ca 1859
A8. Margaret, b ca 1861
A9. George, b ca 1863
VOUCHER, VOUTIER, see VAUTIER and VATCHER
WADE, Robert, from J early 1800s to Nfld., then to PEI. See A8. MESSERVY fam.

WAIDE, Capt. from J in Nfld. (K. Mathews)
WALDRON, in Nfld. (Seary) Cf WALDRAIN of J (Stevens)
WALKER, in Nfld. (Seary) Cf WALKER of C.I.
WALLIS, in Nfld. (Seary) Cf same of J (Stevens) In Alderney 1309 (Carey-Wimbush)
WALPY, see VALPY
WALTERS, in Gaspe, and Perce (Cent. Bklt.) from C.I.? John and George Radley W. were missionaries for SPG 1800s, Gaspe
WARREN, Mrs. and Mrs. F., said to be from Alderney to BC
WARREN, Robert, res Val d' Espoir, Gaspe. Others to Perce. (Cent. Bklt.) Origin unver.
WARR, some from C.I.?, in Canada. "name originated in Normandy...our ancestors came to Britain with Wm. the Conqueror in 1066." Other variants: DE GUERRE, GREER, GEER, GEAR, etc. (Ernest Warr, Willowdale, Ont.)
WARREN, G., from G to London, Ont. 1938? (Guernsey Club there)
WATERMAN, Mrs. Annie, from Alderney to BC 1906, related to LAW and PIKE
WATTS, Caroline Mary West, b 1856 Alderney, mar John White Turriff 1881, Toronto, Ont. She d 1940. Dau of John West Watts of Litchboro, Northants, Eng., and Mary Anne DINGLE, b 1831 J. See DINGLE. Emigrated to Coboconk, Ont., with parents, John and Mary Ann, and sister, Harriet, b 1858, in 1860s. (May Stone, Aurora, Ont.)
A1. Arthur Norman Turriff, b 1885 London, Ont., d 1926 Toronto. Mar 1. Rose ROBERTSON, who d 1911, and 2. Lillian Brough, Toronto, 1913.
 B1. Arthur Hugh, b 1909 Toronto, mar Catherine Chenault 1939, res Dallas, Texas
 B2. Marguerite L. Turriff, b 1914 Chatham, Ont., d 1962 Toronto, mar John Sykes 1932, Toronto
 B3. Gordon E. Turriff, b 1918, mar Jean H. MacCallum 1943, res Islington, Ont.
 B4. Jean W. Turriff, b 1921, Toronto, d there 1967, unmar
A2. Ann Guthrie Turriff, b 1882 London, Ont., d.y.
A3. May, b 1887 London, Ont., d 1928 Toronto, Ont., mar George Hutcheon 1913, Toronto
A4. John West Turriff, b 1890 London, Ont., mar Marion Mitchell 1916, res Rexdale, Ont.
 B1. John M. Turriff, b 1917 Hamilton, Ont., mar Norma Carlile Chadwick 1948, res Oak Ridge, Ont.
 B2. Elizabeth May Turriff, b 1918 Toronto, mar Richard Styles 1938, res Rexdale, Ont.
 B3. George Watts Turriff, b 1920 Toronto, mar Catherine McMeekin 1943 Toronto, res Cornwall, Ont.
 B4. James E. Turriff, b 1923 Toronto, mar Anna Carlile 1950, who d 1963, mar 2. Catherine Ellis Scraggs 1969, res Rexdale, Ont.
A5. Bessie Clark Turriff, b 1894 Havelock, Ont., mar Reuben Stone 1920, Toronto, d 1940. Res Aurora, Ont.
 B1. Elsie May Stone, b 1921, Toronto, res Aurora, Ont.
 B2. John Charles Stone, b 1929, Toronto, mar Elizabeth Heighington 1955, res Aurora
  C1. John Jay Stone, b 1956   C2. Dana Charles Stone, b 1960
WATTS, Harriet, sister of Caroline above, b 1858 Alderney?, mar Geo. A. POWLES, of Powles Corners, Ont.
A1. Percy Powles, b Orillia, Ont.   A5. Alice Powles
A2. Carrie Powles, b Gary, Indiana   A6. Edith Powles
A3. Carl Powles, b Chicago, ILL.   A7. Clarence Powles, adopted
A4. Howard Powles, b Chicago, ILL
WATTS, tradesman from J in Nfld. (K. Mathews)

WAYE, in Nfld. (Seary) Cf WAY of C.I.
WEARY, WEARE, George, age 30 in 1871, b J, clerk at Perce 1871 (Brochet) Settled in New Carlisle, Que. early 1800s. Mar Elizabeth Forsythe. (Sidney Weary, Beaconsfield, Que.; GLF)
A1. John S., b 1879 New Carlisle, mar 1904, Elizabeth ASSELS, dau of Daniel A. and Elizabeth GALLON. Elizabeth, 1883-1961, John d 1956.
  B1. George Daniel, b 1905, d.y.   B2. Hazel Dell, b 1906, d 1920
  B3. Sarah Elizabeth, b 1908, d 1975, mar Carl Chester Patterson, res Kitchener, Ont.
    C1. John Chester Patterson, b 1931, 5 chn
      D1. John Patterson, b 1953, dau, Tara, b 1975
      D2. Larry Patterson, b 1955   D4. Ross Patterson, b 1965
      D3. Mark Patterson, b 1961   D5. Stephen Patterson, b 1971
    C2. June Margaret Patterson, b 1933, mar --- Wagel
      D1. Daren Wagel, b 1965   D2. Derek Wagel, b 1975
    C3. Jarvis Patterson, b 1934, mar?, 2 sons; Gary and Kevin Patterson
    C4. Elizabeth, Betty, Patterson, b 1936, mar James Morris
      D1. Donna Morris, b 1955   D3. Todd Morris, b 1964
      D2. Allan Morris, b 1960
    C5. Beulah Janet Maria Patterson, b 1938
  B4. John Reginald, b 1912
  B5. Walter Franklin, b 1913, mar Amy Chisholm, res New Carlisle, Que.
  B6. Elmer Lewis, b 1917, d.y.
  B7. David Sidney, b 1922, mar Daphne Evelyn Bryden Smith, b London, Eng., res Beaconsfield, Que.
    C1. Sally Elizabeth Evelyn, b 1956 C2. Anne Rosamond Rhoda, b 1958
  B8. Alice Beulah, b 1923, mar Kenneth Alfred BURT, res Lasalle, Que.
    C1. George Sydney Burt, b 1949 C3. Donna Ann Burt, b 1956
    C2. Judy Carolyn Burt, b 1952
WEARY, E., Missionary, minister, SPG at Riviere Du Loup, Que., 1889-1892. An Edwin C.W. was also SPG missionary in Nfld. 1882.
WEBB, WEBBER, WEBER, in Nfld. Cf WEBBER of J (Stevens) Some in Nfld. 1677
WEBBER, merchant from J in Nfld. (K. Mathews)
WEEKS, Bert, b G, mar Louisa LE REVEREND, qv, rem to Orangeville, Ont. ca 1920s, no issue
WELCH, Reginald Charles, b 1905 Saumarez Rd., Castel, G, to Canada 1924, mar Nan Johnstone, b Calderbank, Scotland (R.C. Welch, Toronto, Ont.)
WELSH, from C.I. to Nfld. (Rev. Hammond) See also Seary. Cf WELCH of J (Stevens)
WEST, see John WATTS
WESTAWAY, found J and Canada. Origin unverified.
WESTLAKE, Capt. and ship owner from J in Nfld. (K. Mathews)
WESTON, Capt. from Alderney in Nfld. (K. Mathews)
WEYBOROUGH, Capt. from J in Nfld. (K. Mathews)
WHEADON, fam from Illminster, southern Eng., settled in St. Peter Port, G, 3 sons; Edward, William and George, chn of Wm. Henry W. and Harriet Margaret THOUMINE, mar 1870s? (Lloyd Wheadon, San Luis Obispo, Calif.)
WHEADON, William, to U.S., returned to G, then mar and settled in N.Z. ca 1885, where he d
WHEADON, Percy, b 1881 G, rem to Western Canada ca 1900 with friend, Walter BIRD, homesteaded for 10 yrs. Returned to G, mar Hilda BECKET BECQUET?, and brought her to Seattle, Wash. A son, Jack, b 1945, has greenhouse in Kirkland, Wash.
A1. Kenneth, b 1947   A2. Nora, b ?

WHEADON, Nora, b 1877 G, res there, mar --- GRUT
WHEADON, Albert, from G to Manitoba ca 1904. His only son lost in
 WWII over the Channel
WHEADON, Thomas, b ca 1885 G, rem to Auburn, Calif., mar Margaret
 ROLLANDS. A dau, Ruth, mar --- Jorgenson, and res Peace River, BC
A1. a son, Rolland, is a wheat farmer in Sask.
WHEADON, Edward, drowned on the Titanic, visiting a dau who lived in
 N.J. Has another dau, and three sons; Edward, Herbert, and George.
WHEADON, George, of same fam, mar Anita Julia Adcock, b 1880
A1. Hubert, rem to Canada, a son
  B1. Lloyd, b St. Peter Port 1900, mar Amanda MAHY, b 1894, dau of
    Ernest John MAHY, b 1870, and Marie Louise MARQUIS, b 1871
A2. James, killed over the Channel, WWII
A3. Albert, b G, rem to Manitoba A4,5,6,7. 4 daus
WHEATLEY, Jon James, Dean of Grad. Studies, Simon Fraser Univ., Burna-
 by, BC, b London, Eng., 1931, son of James E.W. and Marjorie Milicent
 May W., of Jersey, C.I. (Who's Who in Canada, 1977-8) Cf WHITELY of J
WHEELER, in Nfld. (Seary) Cf WHEELER, WHILEUR of J (Stevens)
WHITE, DE WHITING, C.I. at Carbonear, Conc. Bay, Nfld., very early,
 and in Gaspe area (Rev. Hammond; J.H. Le Breton list)
WHITCHURCH, F., member of G club in St. Thomas, Ont. 1938   SEE
WHITELY, in Nfld. (Seary) Cf WHITELY of J (Stevens)   EXTRA PAGES
WHITE. "All the Whites in western Newfoundland are descendants of
 families whose original surname was LE BLANC...it is generally
 assumed that the Le Blancs in western Nfld. came with other Acadian
 French during the Acadian expulsion from N.S." (Harold Horwood)
 He notes also that these WHITES spoke Jersiaise, as the Jersey traders
 dominated the south and west coasts of Nfld. for many years.
WHITING, Mrs. Doreen of J, rem to Vancouver, BC (Soc. Jers.) Others
 in Western Canada
WHITTLE. "Mr. and Mrs. John E.S. Whittle, Haultain St., will mark
 their golden wedding anniversary on Dec. 31 (1967) at an open house
 from 2 to 5 at their home...Mr. Whittle was born in Jersey...and his
 wife, Elsie Lee...England. Mr. Whittle came to Canada in 1907 and
 has lived in Victoria since 1908. There are two sons, Roy...and
 Stanley...and nine grandchildren." Mr. Whittle died in 1969 (Colon-
 ist) Roy res North Vancouver. This fam said to have come to Jersey
 from Huddersfield, southern England.
WIDGER, in Nfld. (Seary) Cf WIDGER in QAAM, by Turk
WIGNALL, from C.I.?, in Burlington, Ont.
WILKINS, Capt. from G in Nfld. (K. Mathews)
WILLET, George J., from J to Middleton Twp., Ont., farmer there in
 1857 (Cumming)
WILLETT, George, signed the Gaspe Petition in 1820
WILLETT, Samuel, mar Leah de Ste. CROIX, qv, in N.S. (Calnek)
WILLETT, from C.I. to Nfld. (Rev. Hammond)
WILLET, Bedell, age 46, res Ont. 1871 in Hallowel Twp. Farmer, Prot.,
 wife, Elizabeth, two chn, Ida age 19, and Herbert age 5. Origin un-
 known.
WILLETT, from C.I.?, to Victoria, BC
WILLIAMS, in Nfld. (Seary) Cf WILLIAMS, GILLAM and GUILLAUME of C.I.
WILSON, John Frederick, advocate of J in Perce, Gaspe 1843 (Brochet)
WINCHELL, VINCHELEZ, etc., of G. See WINCY below.
WINCY, Dr. George DE JERSEY, b 1800 G, to N.S. ca 1835, settled at
 L'Ardoise, mar Sophia Mombourquette? He was found beaten and drowned
 St. Peters Bay, 1858. Widow d ca 1903 (Stephen White, Moncton, NB)
A1. Louise Eliza, b 1842, mar 1863 at L'Ardoise, Patrice Pate, Pottie,

son of Raphael P. and Marguerite Biret, b 1840
A2. William, b 1843, d.y.   A3. Victoire, b 1845, d.y.
A4. William again, b 1847, mar 1876, Sabine Martel, dau of Simon M.
    and Marie Landry, b 1857
A5. Victoire again, b 1849, mar 1874, Remi Mombouquette, son of Pierre
    M. and Rufine Boucher, b 1847
A6. Sophia, b 1850, mar 1874, George MIDDLETON, son of John M. and
    Marguerite Bonin
A7. Daniel, b 1848, mar 1874, Anne Martel, dau of Simon and Marie Landry
    b 1848, 6 chn
  B1. Marie Sophie, b 1875, d 1879   B4. Daniel, b 1881
  B2. Eliza, b 1876   B5. John Henry, b 1883, d.y.
  B3. William, b 1879, mar Margaret Riled? B6. Marie Sophie again b 1885
A8. Marguerite Genevieve, b ca 1853
A9. Marie Henriette, b ca 1856, mar 1885 at L'Ardoise Jacques Pate, son
    of Marin P. and of Sabine TAYLOR, b ca 1856
A10. George, b ca 1842?, mar 1875, Martine Robichaud, dau of Joseph and
    Brigitte CLEMENTS, qv, of L'Ardoise, CB
  B1. Sophie Brigitte, b 1876   B3. Maria Ann, b 1883
  B2. George, b 1880
A11. Marie Anne, b ?, mar 1877, Maurice Martel, son of Simon M. and
    Marie Landry, b 1850
A12. Elizabeth May, b 1841
WOOD, WOODS, from C.I. to Ontario? (Wood in G 1750)
WOODS, Anne Elizabeth of J?, mar Charles FENTON, FAINTON? See BERTRAM
    fam of N.Z.
WOODS, Delahaye, mar John RENOUF at Auckland, N.Z. 1877, 6 boys and 4
    girls. She d at St. Helier, J 1894.
WOLFREY, said to be C.I. surname in Nfld. In J ca 1840, a WOLFREY mar
    a HACKING. (Backhurst)
WOLSTENHOLME. Has occurred in J, and in connection with some family
    charts. A Cape Wolstenholme is mentioned in the Grenfell book,
    ROMANCE OF THE LABRADOR.
WOOLDRIDGE. Capt. from J in Nfld. (K. Mathews)
WOTTON, present in N.S. 1783. This name found sometimes in conn with
    C.I. fams
WRIGHT, John, closely assoc with Jerseymen in Gaspe middle 1800s. Poss
    from C.I. (Brochet)
WRIXTON, Maria, b 1891 G, mar George DAVEY, qv
YEO, E., from C.I.?, in Victoria, BC 1940, member of Soc. there
YOUNG, Mr. and Mrs. J, from Ald. to BC (Luce)
YOUNG, in Nfld. (Seary) Cf LE JEUNE and YOUNG of J (Stevens) Cf also
    JEUNE of J.

SURNAME INDEX

The reader should note that Channel Island surnames included in this book constitute only a minor portion of the many thousands of Channel Island surnames known. Thousands more, not in this book, can be found in current Channel Island phone books. The CATALOGUE OF JERSEY FAMILY NAMES, by Charles Stevens, 1970, contains the oldest Island names up to about the first quarter of this century, about 1900 names. The Stevens book, however, lacks the family names of those "which fell into neither category, flourished in the early middle ages without betraying their existence on contemporary parchments...they are every bit as genuine Jerriais as the more expansive people whose names sparkle in the armorials and the history books." (Stevens)

The reader, when examining pages for surnames, should check the entire page, as there is sometimes more than one mention of the same surname on a page.

The surnames in this index may not include the following:
1. the surnames noted in the Bibliographies, starting on page 29.
2. the surnames noted in lists, such as the Quebec name lists on page 83, etc.
3. the surnames included in the family charts in parentheses, contributors to the information in this book

The Mc and Mac surnames: These two forms have not been separated in this index. If you are looking for Mac, and the index lists only the Mc, please check the page numbers given.

An asterisk (*) after or near a surname in the index means that the name appears in the new ADDITIONS AND CORRECTIONS pages.

ABBEY-419
ABBOT-127,415
ABEL-404
ABERCROMBIE-251
ACKERMAN-333
A'COURT-127
ACOU, HACQUOIL-277
ACTESON-127,158,195,438
ACTON-431
ADAIR-329,491
ADAMS-127,201,212,229,250,469,482, 483,484,514,540 *
ADAMSON-540
ADCOCK-546 Cf HADCOCK
ADEY,ADE-127
AGNES-127,141,168,187,258
AGNEW-96,97,128 to 131,323
AHERN-541
AHIER-31,131,133,137,164,195,196, 238,255,279,391,413,414,436, *
AIKEN-411
AIREY-267
ALBERT-227,343,438,481 &
ALBEURY-137
ALBRIGHT-367
ALCORN-323
ALDERSEY-421
ALEXANDER, ALEXANDRE-65,66,79,137, 138,236,245,247,307,316,345,350, 359,392,395,398,442,448,449,528
ALLAIN-137,139

ALLARD-131,474
ALBION-453
ALLEN-130,132,139,160,161,190,196, 241,292,350,390,396,421,464,494
ALLES-139. See ALLEZ
ALLEY-139 *
ALLEYRE-139   See also DALLAIRE
ALLEZ-138 *
ALLISON-322
ALMOND-25,132,138,164,168,348,*
ALSBERT-361
AMBERMAN-146
AMBROSE-489
AMESSE-180
AMICIS-490
AMIE, AMY-108. See AMY
AMIRAUX-59, *
AMOND-138
AMY-138,140,141,207,219,264,482
ANDERSON-105,128,141,157,160,161,170, 214,252,254,255,308,338,349,352, 375,382,383,395,396
ANDRE,ANDRES,ANDRESS-141
ANDREW,ANDREWS-141,155,287
ANDROS-141,240 *
ANEZ,AGNES-141 *
ANGEL-141
ANGIER-356
ANGLEHART-477
ANGOT-141   ANLEY-541
ANNANDALE-305

ANNET-141,142,152,153,176,348
ANQUETIL-142,421
ANTHOINE,ANTHONIE,ANTOINE,etc.-32,
  47,141,142,482
ANTEL,ANQUETIL?-50,142
ANTROBUS-174
APPLEBY-142,301,465
APSEY-441
ARBOUR-142,309,328,485,533,
ARCENEAU-378
ARCHBOLD-321
ARCHER-142,241
ARCHIBALD-539
ARDIEL-251
ARIS-337
ARKLEY-405
ARLESS-473
ARMEROD-391
AMRSTRONG-253,290,384,482
ARNE-352
ARNAULD-142
ARNESS-379
ARNETT-444
ARNOLD-142,222,268,273,504
ARNOTT-385
ARP-128
ARSENAULT-131,221,226,354,496
ARSENEAU-227
ARTANDI-495
ARTHUR-142,335,478,535
ASCAH-183,348,367
ASH-142
ASHER-495
ASHDOWN-96
ASHTON-323
ASHWORTH-467
ASPELL,ASPLET,ASPLEY-142
ASPIRAULT-162,429
ASSEL,ASSELS-142,545 *
ASSELIN-310   ASTEE *
ATHERTON-469
ATKINS-271,540
ATWELL-353
ATWOOD-334,385
AUBAIN-142
AUBERT-142,143,293,294,327,437
AUBERT DE GASPE-365
AUBIN-59,339,386,423,526 *
AUCLAIR-179,256
AUDET-136,239
AUDOIRE-150,407,408
AUERHAHN-541
AUGER,AUGRES-143
AUPIN,HOPIN, qv-278,543
AUSTIN-144,305
AUTOVINA-499
AVERY-144,160,472
AVERTY-144,531,532
AVRAMENKO-393

AYBORN-144
AYLEN-170
AYER-131   See AHIER-416
AYRE-143   See AHIER-416

BAAL-144 *
BABCOCK-251,459,496,497
BACH-442
BACHLEY-144,505
BACON-144,532
BADHAM-128
BAETZ-391
BAGG,BAGGS-435,441,472
BAGNALL,BAGNELL-258,442
BAGNOLD-348
BAILEY,BAYLEY-144,177,221,230,283,
  295,320,338,443
BAILHACHE-144,147,272,330
BAILIEU-144,217
BAILLIEUL-144
BAILLIE-144
BAINBRIDGE-144
BAKER-145,156,176,182,189,198,208,
  255,260,268,292,302,307,320,329,
  238,364,369,370,374,381,391,407,
  493,497,503,506,520,527,538
BAKKER-504
BALACHE-145   See BAILHACHE
BALCOM,BALCOMB-58,59,145 to 147,217,
  295,464
BALDING-252
BALDWIN-193,212,241,331,334,346
BALEMAN-435
BALESTIER, see L'ARBALESTIER
BALFOUR-341
BALIFF-474
BALIN-208
BALL-140,147,500
BALLACHEY-147
BALLAINE, see BALLEINE
BALLAM-60,147,186,438
BALLANTYNE-308
BALLEINE-59,60,147 to 149,186,208,
  268,287,326,429,435,535
BALLHAST, see BAILHACHE
BALLINGALL-186
BALTZOR-156
BANBURY-149
BANCROFT-320
BANDAGRIGGT-311
BANDINEL-45,149,225,228
BANKS-145,268,542
BANNATYNE-432
BANNIER-149
BAPTISTE-149   See also BATISTE
BARBER, BARBIER-149
BARBER-STARKEY-421,422

BARBISON-149
BARETT-149
BAREFOOT-165,184,214
BARGERT-489
BARK-271 BARKER-257,487,496 *
BARLOW-149,333,388,505
BARNERS-374
BARNES-149,249,288,304,376,453,*
  490 See LE BAS *
BARNHARD-499
BARNSON-250
BARRASIN-149
BARRETT-149,222,238,356
BARRINGHAM-149
BARSTAD *
BARTELS-452
BARTH-214
BARTLETT-129,149,150,201,241,257,
  491,481D
BARTLEY-487
BARTNICKI-259
BARTON-150,185,438
BARTRAM-150,157
BARWICK-406
BAS-150 See LE BAS
BASHFORD-150
BASHMAN-539
BASSETT-150,451,523
BATCHELOR-323
BATE,BATES-180,220,251,307 *
BATEMAN-444
BATH-290
BATHURST-345
BATISTE-94,150,327,423
BATTAM-438
BATTEN-150,151
BATTY-451
BAUCHE-39,151
BAUDAINS-279,309
BAUDIN,BEAUDIN-151
BAXTER-164,229,315
BAYFIELD-151
BEADLE-151
BEAGLEY-536
BEAKER-233,302,437
BEAL,BEALE-151,189,321
BEAMER-513
BEAMISH-151,334
BEAN-151,301,509
BEARD-151
BEARDSLEY-190
BEARE, cf LE BER-416,419
BEARSE-445
BEASLEY-433
BEASON,BEESON See BISSON-151,162
BEATTEN,BEATON-151,354,475 *
BEATY,BEATTY,BEATTIE,etc.-214,361,
  396,486
BEAUCAMP-151

BEAUCHAMP-151,154* See DE BEAUCHAMP
BEAUCHESNE-356
BEAUDIN,BAUDAIN,etc.-152,162 to 164,
  538,541
BEAUDRY-427
BEAULIEU-178,235,438
BEAUMONT-208-393
BEAUNE-497
BEAUPRE-148
BEAUREGARD-312
BEAUZEVAL-157
BEBE-201
BECHARD-152,158 See BICHARD
BECHERVAISE-152,153,154,236,529,537 481C
BECK-154,186,225,226,255,328,353,
  354,416,429,443,493,533,536,542
BECKSTROM-130
BECKETT,BECQUET-103,154,448,483,526,
  545
BECKWITH-161,313,420
BEDARD-394
BEDELL-494
BEECH-536
BEECHAN-154
BEECHER-171,420
BEEHAN,BIHAN?-154
BEESAW-154,165 See BISSON
BEESE-541
BEGGS-283
BEGIN-154
BEGLIN,BEGHIN-154
BEINTEMA-183
BELACHE, see BAILHACHE
BELANGER-288,333
BELFIELD-334
BELIN-208
BELIVEAU, see BELLIVEAU
BELKNAP-388
BELL-154,173,181,264,340,341,389,
  390,417,526   *
BELLAS-451
BELLEAU-140,309
BELLEFONTAINE-166,221
BELLENOY-514
BELLINJEUNE-154
BELLIVEAU,BELIVEAU-134,144,154,162,
  163,178,239,240,250
BELLOT-154
BENEDICT-541
BENEST-154,167,273
BENET-155
BENFIELD-408
BENNETT-154,155,157,175,248,254,450,
  491
BENOIT-155
BENSON-128,253,301
BENT-146,147,157,319
BENTLEY-354
BENTON-395

BERESFORD-155
BERGE-410
BERGER-203
BERGERON-190,239,506,520
BERGERON, dit L'AMBOISE-131
BERK-509
BERNACCI-168
BERNARD-155,262,369,384,497
BERNIE-481A
BERNIER-134,155,256,261
BERO-495
BERRIMAN-155,216
BERRY-321,322,326,417,451
BERTEAU, BERTEAUX-54,58,155,264,320
BERTHELOT-240,438
BERTIN-343
BERTON, LE BRETON-155,157
BERTRAM-157,237,256,279,547 *
BERTRAND-157,178
BERUBE-136
BERWICK-351
BESANT,BISSON-50,157,162,330
BESOM-162
BESSIN-157
BEST-157,160,526
BETHANKE-379
BETTS-284
BEVILL-157
BEVIS-153,157
BEXFIELD-157
BEZEAU-178 See BISEAU
BIBBER *
BIARD-157,158,187,311
BICHARD-152,158,159,221,236,259,
   428,485,500,503
BICKLE,BICKEL-270,385
BICKFORD-197
BICQUET-159
BIDWELL-409,500
BIENNON-153
BIETH-394
BIGARD-159
BIGELOW-130
BIGNELL-159
BIHAN-154
BILEICK-420
BILES-159
BILLARD-159
BILLOT-159,195
BILLOWS-454
BILODEAU-154,200,428
BILOZIR-405
BINET-41,159
BINGHAM-148
BINNET,BINNEY-159
BIRCH-159,193,314
BIRD-159,318,434,545
BIRDSELL-504
BIRECKI-271

BIRET-547
BIRKAN-267
BIRMINGHAM-288
BIRT-354 See BURT   BISSETTE,481D
BISEAU-538,539,540,542
BISHOP-41,58,59,159,160,161,162,170,
   173,177,271,388,396,407,472 *
BISSON-151,152,154,157,158,159,162,
   163,164,168,220,279,335,336,342,
   386,410,511,482,518
BITOT-165
BIXBY-511
BLACK-181,268,384,389,393
BLACKBURN-281,289,362
BLACKHALL-242,390,400
BLACKLER-165
BLACKWELL-231
BLACKMAN-384
BLAINEY-300
BLAIR-148,395
BLAIS-163
BLAKE-165,532 *
BLAKELEY-542
BLAMPIED,BLANCPIED,BAREFOOT,etc.-
   149,165,166,184,188,280,399
BLANC, see LE BLANC
BLANCHARD-343,344
BLANCHET,BLANCHETTE-261,294,488,481B
BLANCPIED-149,165,166,450 See
   BLAMPIED
BLANDYN-166
BLANDY-166
BLAYLOCK-514
BLEEKER-293   BLRERYY *
BLIAULT-166
BLIGHT-408
BLISS-352
BLOCK-378
BLOID-369
BLOM-492
BLONDEL-166,380,386,399
BLUE-418
BLUNDELL-166,242   Cf BLONDEL
BLUNDON-166,467
BOCCARDY-212
BODEN-151,167 See BAUDAIN,BEAUDIN
BOEHNER-461
BOGER-170
BOGGS-314,517
BOGLE-167
BOGEJI-167
BOHEN,BOHAN,BOHON-166
BOIS,DUBOIS-172
BOISSEL-316
BOIST-499
BOISVERT-393
BOIT,BOITEAU-166
BOKEY,LE BOSQUET-50,167
BOLANDER-317

BOLE-250
BOLDT-536
BOLGER-183,278
BOLEOR-167
BOLTER-240
BOLTON-291,395
BOMONT-510   See BEAUMONT
BONAMY-167
BONAVIA-453
BOND-143,145,167,255,260 to 262,
    427,428,485,506,520,521
BONDY-199
BONES-167
BONESTEEL-296
BONHEUR-167
BONIN-411,547
BONNELL-167,278 *
BONNER-167,222
BONOKOSKI-394
BONOVIEW-167
BONOVRIER-167
BOOKER-192,499
BOONE-167,355
BOORE-264
BOOTH-300,396,419,446
BORDEN-167
BORLASE-223
BOSDET-167,171,242,438
BOSSY-167
BOSTWICK-24
BOTSFORD-377,378
BOTT-167,168,517 *
BOUCANT-168
BOUCHARD-286,287,473
BOUCHER-53,154,168,211,368,438,494,
    547
BOUCHEY-367
BOUDIER-168,522
BOUDIN   See BOUTIN
BOUDINOT-167   See BOURINOT
BOUDREAU, BOUDROT-141,142,168,180,
    209,221,222,361,411,465,537
BOUGETT-168
BOUGHE-168
BOUGOURD-168,207,515
BOUILLON-164,168,169,310,413,420 *
BOULANGER-143
BOULARD-466
BOULAY-363,442
BOULE-143
BOULET-218,462,500
BOURDON-167,184
BOURGAISE, BOURGAIZE-169,170,248,
    300,348,436 *
BOURGEOIS-170
BOURGET-143,154,170,293,301,311,
    429,527
BOURNE-498
BOURNIEF-170

BOURQUE-135
BOURINOT-59,171,242
BOUTEVILLON-187
BOUTILLIER   See LE BOUTILLIER-171,
    172,282,etc.
BOUTIN-162,476
BOUTINEAU-225
BOUTON-172
BOUYER-185   BOUZANE *
BOWDEN-172
BOWEN, BOWENS-219,250,251,336
BOWER, BOWERS-158,172,288,316,338,
    339,493 *
BOWES-183,228
BOWKETT-350
BOWLBY-147,495
BOWLER-140
BOWLES-160
BOWMAN-335
BOY-172   See BOIT and BOIST
BOYCE-172
BOYD-140,539
BOYLE-153,172,226,342,515,531
BRABANT-435
BRACHE-172,214,295
BRADBURY-183,464
BRADY-475
BRADFORD-172
BRADLEY-499
BRADTHRAFT-172
BRADWIN-231
BRAGG-288,374,377
BRAID-362
BRAIN-172 See BRINE
BRAITHWAITE-467
BRANCH-538
BRANT-518
BRASSARD-179,309,448,449
BRAUN-536
BRAY-395,422
BRAZIL-459
BREAK-415,416
BRECHIN-217
BRECKEN-275
BREE-168   See BRAY
BREEN-253
BREEZE-350
BREHAUT, see also BURHOE-71,73,173,
    174,186,355,361,390,416,418 *
BRENNAN-153,482,488
BRENNAND-435
BRESSON-290
BRETON, see also LE BRETON-175,177,
    401
BRETT,BRITT-175
BREUGEM-441
BREWER-175
BRIAND-175
* BRIARD-137,175,243,340,341,410,506

BRIDEAU,BRIDEAUX-17,138,175,176,
    211,456 *
BRIDGEN-487
BRIDGNELL-369
BRIDLE-176,177
BRIEN-176,227   481D
BRIENT-506
BRIGGS-109,189,253,255,472,499
BRIGHAM-146
BRILLANT-175,260 BRIMAGE *
BRINE-41,59,60,172,177,178,288,
    334,518
BRISON-211
BRISSET-162
BRISTOL-178
BRISTOW-431
BROAD-305
BROATCH-384
BROCHET-178 to 182,207,218,232,293,
    302,303,437 *
BROCK,BROCQ, see also LE BROCQ-23,
    24,91,181,182,214,223,342,246,
    404,437,511, 481C
BROCKETT-178
BRODIE-418
BROMILOW-375
BROOKS-418,461,510,541
BROPHIE-206
BROTHERSTONE-233,247
BROTHERTON-132 to 137,179,429
BROUARD-182,387
BROUSSEAULT-182
BROUN-318
BROWARD, cf BROUARD-182,387
BROWN-89,130,153,156,157,177,182,
    188,253,254,256,271,273,284,289,
    291,294,323,324,325,367,379,400,
    410,424,428,464,478,488,491,494,
    509,511,514,537 to 539, 542
BROWNING-182,419
BROWNLEE-323,523
BRUDNICKI-449
BRUN, see LE BRUN, also BRUNE
BRUNE-183,540,541
BRUNET-180,182,338,339
BRUNNER-530
BRUSHATH-182
BRUSHETT-182,183,278
BRYAN-190
BRYANT-319,508
BRYSON-283
BUBAR,BUBER-183
BUCHANAN-284,419,488
BUCKART-338
BUCKINGHAM-168
BUCKLAND-526
BUCKLE,BUCKLEY-316,460,526,533
BUDD-187
BUELOW-413

BUESNEL-106,183,295,372,448,526 *
BUFFETT-183
BUFFINGTON-128
BUJOLD-136
BUKER-425
BULFORD-183
BULGER-183,316
BULL-443
BULLARD-183
BULLEN,BALLEINE-183   See BALLEINE
BULLER-406
BULLEY-183
BULLEYMENT-512
BULLOCK-375
BOLMAN-384
BUNGAY-183
BUNOET-183
BUNTAIN-183
BUNTLIN-292 *
BUNTON-183,184,233,292,373,374,532,
    533 *
BUOTE-355
BURBRIDGE-160,161,241,542
BURCH, see BIRCH
BURCHART-184
BURDEN-184
BURDETTE-325,349
BUREAU-424
BURFITT-184,214   BURFIELD-481A
BURGESS,BURGIS-184,362,465
* BURHOE,BREHAUT-72,73,173,184 to 186
BURKE-325,334
BURKWALT-495
BURMAN-186,290
BURNHAM-246   BURNESS-481B
BURNIE-129,481D   BURNETTE-481D
BURNS-422,474
BURRARD-286
BURSEY-488
BURT,BURTT-41,186,294,385,545
BURTIN-186
BURWELL-181,395
BURTON-254
BUSBY-190
BUSH-502
BUSHELL-186
BUSLEY-186
BUSSEY-186,187,271
BUTLAND-540
BUTLER, cf LE BOUTILLIER-155,187,
    231,307,428,445
BUTLIN-157,168,187,231,292,294,296,
    298,448,507
BUTT-45,187,346,441,458,459,471 *
BUTTER-355
BUTTON-28,45,296,494
BYATT-334
BYE
BYERS-220

BYRDE-371* See BIRD
BYRNE-460
BYSSE, see BUSSEY

CABLE-187
CABELDU-187,188,204,214,337,358
CABOT-66,134,189,190,269,381,400,
   414
CABOUR-436
CADEREL-190
CADORET-190,224
CADOTTE-378
CAEN,DE CAEN-191
CAHILL-327,404
CAIN-190
CAINES-428
CAIRNS-150
CAISSIE-497
CAKE,CAKETERRE-191   CALE *
CALDWELL-228,279,306,315,360,430
CALKIN-160
CALLAGHAN-186,227   CALLEN-481A
CALNEK-146
CAMBREY-191
CAMBRIDGE-73
CAMERON-109,170,251,395,415 *
CAMIOT-191,372,452
CAMMIADE-374
CAMPBELL-328,329,333,350,351,358,
   364,378,385,417,433,444,498,
   511,538,539,481 *
CAMPEAU-134,136
CAMPION-302
CANE-191
CANILLE-191
CANIVET. *   CANN *
CANNON-511
CANTELL-191
CAPELL-176
CAPILLERY-235
CAPLAN-322
CARAVAN-191
CARBONEAU-506
CARCAUD-191
CARDEN-499
CAREEN-191 See COREEN
CAREY-41,44,191,192,214,219,258,
   396,460 *
CARLISLE,CARLILE-544
CARLSON-379,417,444
CARLYONG-496
CARMICHAEL-275,354
CARON-226,261,294,311,400
CARPENTER-372
CARR,CARRE-171,193,379,475 *
CARRELL-80,193
CARRIE-193

CARRIERE-194,393
CARROL-232
CARRY-194
CARSWELL-194,497
CARTER-41,131,194,300,355,366,385,
   532,540, *
CARTERET,DE CARTERET-26,27,28,194,
   207,390
CARTIER-77,368
CARTWRIGHT-305,487
CARTY-147
CARVANA-411
CARVANEL-191,194
CARVER-355,469
CASEY-180 See also CAISSIE
CASGRAIN-259
CASGRAIN-GAGNON-474
CASH-285
CASS-148,184,186,277,373,374,380,
   532,533
CASSEL-194
CASSELMAN-187
CASSIDY-536
CASSIE-413
CASSIVI-134,179,477
CASSON-470
CASTELLAN,CASTILLON-327,360
CASTETS-134
CASTEL-194
CASTLE-194,238
CASTLEY-421
CASTONGUAY-516
CASWELL-194
CATTLE-197   CATHRAE *
CATTO-405
CAUDEY,CODEY,CODY, see CODY and
   LE CAUDEY
CAUGHILL-314
CAULFIELD-509
CAVANAUGH-460,506
CHACHA-195
CELY-417
CHADWICK-544
CHAFE-440
CHALKER-195
CHALMERS-268,338,363
CHAMBERLIN-195
CHAMBERS-177,195,223,503,504
CHAMPION-195,237
CHAMPLAIN-65
CHANCEY-195
CHANNON-497
CHANT-195
CHAPADOS-132,133,135,136
CHAPMAN-443
CHARDINE-195
CHARLES-195
CHARLTON-408   CHEOP-481E
CHARPENTIER-211,388 See CARPENTER

CHARRON-311
CHASE-195,452.456
CHASTRAY-195
CHASTY-504
CHATEL-195
CHATTERTON-196,429 *
CHECKLEY-422
CHEDORE-132,133,195,196,197,432,438
CHENALLE-221
CHENAULT-541   CHEOP-481E
CHERRY-197,267
CHESLEY-216
CHESTLE-176
CHEVALIER-154,197,296,299,462
CHIAPON-506
CHIASSON-138,212,261,328,343,515,
   537,539,542
CHICK-197
CHICOINE-216,260,261,262,298,347,
   368,428,520 *See COTON,COTTON
CHILDS-408,492
CHILTON-327
CHINCHILLA-185
CHINN-197
CHIPMAN-156,160
CHISHOLM-332.545
CHOQUETTE-170
CHORNEY-195
CHOUINARD-462,466,467
CHRICHTON-129,251,385
CHRISTIE-32,384
CHRISTESON-378
CHRISTIAN-197
CHRISTIANSON-378
CHRISTIE-371
CHRISTOPHERSON-130
CHRONZY-129
CHUPIK-241
CHURCHILL-144,202,273,530
CHURCHWARD-197
CHUTE-146,156,216,318,319
CICERELLA-367
CLANTER-197
CLARK,CLARKE-139,145,153,156,206,
   * 216,222,270,290,291,311,314,
   330,362,383,390,402,430 *81B
CLARKSON-214
CLAVET-392
CLAYPOOL-397
CLAYTON-283
CLEAL-197,264 *
CLEARY-534
CLEAVES-511
CLEGG-290
CLELLAND-193,254
CLEMENS,CLEMENT,CLEMENTS-32,74,138,
   161,197,198,209,297,333,343,349,
   356,417,418,443,506,520,547
CLERK,CLERKE-32,198

CLEUGH-406
CLIFFORD-198,306,365
CLOADE,COADE-198
CLOUGH-198,242,243 *
CLOUTIER-226,262,527
CLOWATER-279
CLUETT-198
CLUFF-198
COAKER-176
COAL-162
COASTES-243
COBAT-199
COBBAERT-456
COBBIDUCK, etc.-204
COCHRANE-188,465
COCK, see LE COCQ
CODE,CODEY-79,199,328,518   See CODY
CODERRE-405
CODDING-245
CODNER-199
CODVILLE-356
CODY-91,199,200,232,292,324,437
COFFIN-152,153,200,226,238,443,468,
   481,533,481 A,C,D.B.
COFRE-394
COGHLAN-200
COHOON-326
COHU-200,498
COLBECK-200
COLBORNE,COLBOURNE-200,256
COLCLOUGH-200
COLDWELL-160,161
COLE-200,222,232,494
COLERICK-533
COLES-250
COLINET-200
COLLARD-200
COLLAS-39,47,78,79,149,162,200,202,
   274,345,348,349,381,392,463,535
COLLENETT-200,202,324
COLLETON-27
COLLETT-202,385,493
COLLEY-41,202
COLLIER,COLYER,etc.-202
COLLINGS-202,439 *
COLLIN,COLLINS-32,144,199,202,312,
   377,429,451,509,543
COLOMBE,COULOMBE-202,347,506
COLPITTS-295
COMBER-202,481C
COMEAU-227,316
COMSTOCK-160
CONGDON-161
CONIAM-248   *
CONKLIN-427
CONLIN-540
CONN-415
CONNELL-494,495   CONRAD- *
CONNOR,CONNORS-238,271,335

CONWAY-539
COOBIE-471
COOK,COKE,COOKE-199,215,251,256,271, 272,297,301,321,342,381,388,405, 431,459,480,485
COOLMAN-380
COONEY *
COOMBE,COOMBES-202,203,391,410,479,
COOPER-203,298,344,348,356,358,380, 444,535 *
COPE-268
COPELAND-338
COPLEY-496
CORBEIT-512
CORBEL-410
CORBET,CORBETT-158,203,321
CORBIN-34,189,203,220,254,424,447, 448
CORBUIS-203
CORCORAN-203
CORDERY-489
CORDINER,CORDWAINER-199
COREEN,CORINNE,CAREEN-203,323
CORMIER-233,234,343,438,456,468
CORNELL-203
CORNEW,CORNU-195
CORNICK-203
CORNISH-203
CORY-236
COSGROVE-510
COSH,COISH-203
COSTARD-204
COTE-219,261,310,335,340,525
COTNAM-424
COTT-541
COTTER-203
COTTON,COTON-178,218,261,262,506, 508 See also CHICOINE
COTTRILL-220
COUDRE-203
COUGHLAN-44
COUILLIARD,COUILLARD-203
COUL,COULL-152,203,477
COULLARD-203
COULOMBE,* see COLOMBE
COULTER-299,451
COULTRY-414 COULTHURST *
COURAGE-203,204
COURAY-203
COURISH-204
COURT,A'COURT?-250
COURTOIS, see LE COURTOIS-303
COUSIN,COUSINS-185,432
COURROIT-131
COUTANGES,COUTANCE,COUSTANCHE,etc.- 204,205,211,361 *
COUTEUR, see LE COUTEUR
COUTTS-474
COUTEUR-162,300 See LE COUTEUR *
COUVET,LE COUVET-169 *

COVVYDUCK,etc.-204
COWDRIE-454
COWIE-157,255,407
COWLEY-194,288,340
COWLING-367 COWPER-481A
COWRIE-255 COYSH *
COX-161,204,324,396,423,526
CRABB-240 COXON-481A
CRAFFORD-204
CRAIG-129,201,267,271,396,434,474;
CRANDALL-499
CRANE-145
CRAPPER-411
CRAWFORD-204,267,323,353,419,482
CRANSTON-190,353,445
CRASWELL-469
CRAVEL-419
CRAVEN-510
CREIGHTON-79,421
CRESPEL-204
CRESSWELL-327
CRISBY-204
CROCKER-24,223,530*
CROCKETT-414
CROFT-204,290
CROMBIE-230,284
CRONE-448
CRONIER-300
CRONYN,CRONIN-205
CROIX, see DE STE. CROIX-205
CROSBIE,CROSBY-431,461,494 *
CROSIER-362
CROSS-205,505
CROSSLEY-183
CROSSMAN-186
CROSSWELL-355
CROTHERS-158
CROWE-188
CROWELL-222
CROZIER-196,315
CRUCHET-205
CRUICKSHANK-407
CUBIT-205
CUDDY-153
CULLEN,CULLENS-137,267,296
CULVERWELL-147
CUMBY-459
CUMMINGS-248,407
CUNNING-153
CUNNINGHAM-187,481B
CUPPS-419,443
CUQUS-205
CURNEW-205,480
CURRIE,CURRY-160,205,324,329,447
CURTIS-205,254
CURWARD-372
CUSACK-368
CUSHING-165
CUSSION-205

CUSTANCE-205
CUTHBERT-164 *
CUTLER-147,205,238,280,287,328,403
CYR-134,142,180,239

DACHEL- *
DACOSTA-205
DA ENCARNADOS-335
DAIGLE-262
DAIN-205
DALE,DALES-232,489
DALET-205
DALEY,DALY-205,322,355,423
DALLAIN-105,138,205
DALLAIRE-429
DALLEY-32,169
DAMON-405
DAMPIER-205
DANCY-205,294
DANIEL-205
DANSEREAU-477
DARAICHE-485,508,509
DARBY-202,452 *
DARKE-184
DARLING-366
DART-159,367
DAUBIGNY-35
D'AUFRESNE-451
DAUGER-405
DAUGHLREY-407
DAUKS-331
DAUSON-421 *
DAUVERGNE-36,205,281
DAVEY-205,206,291,317,389,419,444,
  502,547 *
DAVID-186,206,506,520 *
DAVIDSON-164,189,252,390,411,433,
  542
DAVIS-161,206,252,265,278,318,
  440,441,495,501,481C
DAVISON-179,449
DAWE-271,450
DAWES-364
DAWSON-32,192,206,397,401
DAY-312,496 * 481E
DAYTON *
DEA-294,477 See also DAY
DE ALDANA-230
DEAN-79,206,297,440
DEARING-206   DEARLE *
DE BARNEVILLE-149
DE BARRA-230,232,427
DE BARTOLOMA-230
DE BEAUCAMP-206
DE BEAUCHAMP-206,255,429
DE BEAUVOIR-191,206,258
DE BLANCHELANDE-206
DE BOIS-206

DE BOURCIER-204,206,207 *
DE BROCQ-297 See also BROCK
DE BRODER-200,207,256,479,501
DE CAEN,DE CANE-207
DE CARTERET-60,114,138,141,207,208,
  218,225,294,317,387,403,507,508,
  512 *
DE CASTRO-205
DE CAUX-204,208
DE CHAMPS-261
DE CHESNEY-208
DECKER-349
DE COSTA,DE COSTE-205,221
DE COSTER-205,208
DEE-208,540
DE FEU,DU FEU-208
DE FINTA-363
DE GALLIE-208
DE GARRETT-208,230,289
DE GARIE,DE GARIS-71,144,172,208,
  213,217,220,249,476,478 *
DE GARST-169
DE GAUDEMENT-309
DE GRACE-138,211,212,343,465
DE GRAVE-208
DE GRAY-208
DE GRUCHY-41,59,60,90,114,145,172,
  208 to 210,238,242,247,249,255,
  263,266,311,317,401,414,509 *
DE GUERNSEY-47,114
DE GUERRE,544
DE HAVILLAND-210
DEIDRECK-170
DEITRICK-380
DE JAUSSERAND-210
DE JERSEY-41,72,74,114,210,351,546
DE LA COUR-210
DE LA CROIX,CROSS-210,516
DE LA FONTENELLE-188
DE LA GARDE-210,212,249,423
DELAHANTY-178
DELAIN-212
DE LA HAYE-89,99,212,480
DE LA LANDE-298
DE LA MARE-41,212,213,221,299,368,
  381 *
DELANEY-32
DE LANGIS-537
DELAP-465   DELAREE *
DE LA PERELLE-78,148,200,213,225,
  301,457,458,481,512
DE LA ROCQUE,ROCK-213,501
DE LA RONDE-213,295
DE LA RUE-213,302,381
DE LA TASTE-213
DE LA TOUR-65
DELAUNEY-213
DE LAURENTIS-348
DE LISLE-214,286,511 *

DELONG-374
DE LOUCHE-188,214
DEMARSE-508
DEMERIT, see MERRITT
DEMMER-187
DEMONT-177
DE MOUILPIED-41,214,438 *
DE MOUNTENAY-230
DEMPSEY-474,492
DENNIS-172,214,218,260,405,432
DENNY-148
DENTITH-214
DENTON-215,245,443
DENTREMONT-221
DENTY-215
DENYS-65
DEPRE-215
DE PUTRON-41,215,257
DE QUETTEVILLE-42,54,215,249,356, 529,
DE RAICHE-261 See DARAICHE
D'ERLANGES-516
DE ROIS-261
DE ROSIER-216
DERRIEN-482
DERSH-397
DE RUE-216,224
DE SALABERRY-31
DE SAUMAREZ-216,240
DESBOIS-236
DES BRISAY-217
DES GARRIS-208,217,218
DE SILVA,DE SILVER-218
DES JARDINS-316
DES LANDES-178,218,404
DES LAURIERS-222
DESMOND-188
DESNEY-218
DESNOYERS-300
DESPERQUES
DESPRES-215,218,226,262 *
DES ROCHES-204,213
DE ST. AMAND-294,328
DE STE.CROIX-58,78,205,216,217*,505
DE ST. ESTIENNE-218,518
DESTERRE-218
DEUTSCH-323
DE VEAU-218
DEVERE-192 * DE VERGE,DES VERGES
DEVEREUX-218,252
DE VEULLE-218
DE VIC,VICQ-218,542
DEVINE-231
DEVLIN-429
DEVOE,de VEAUX-200,218
DE VOUGE-533
DE VOYER-26
DEWAR-331
DEWDNEY-219

DE WEERD-508
DEWEY-218
DE WHITING-546
DEWLANEY-332
DE WINTON-254
DE WOLFE-160,161
DE YOUNG-351
DIAMOND-218
DICE-331
DICK-43,218
DICKIE-171
DICKSON-160,319
DIELEMONT-219 *
DIETRICH-518
DIGGLES-322
DIGNEY-338
DIMOCKE-218
DIMOND-218
DINGLE-42,90,218,500,544
DINNEY-218
DINSOME,DINSMORE-251
DIONNE,DION-239,256,272,481C
DIOUVILLE-218
DI PESA-444
DITCHBURN-218,219,486
DITMARS-319
DIVENS-375,381
DIXON-129,219,222,223,319,320,424, 426,482
DOBERTY-279
DOBI-324
DOBREE-191,219
DOBSON-373,375,484 *
DOCKREE-504
DODDRIDGE-104
DODGE-219
DODMAN-395
DODSON-186,349
DOERR-284   DOGGETT-481A
DOHERTY-339,426
DOHN-403
DOIDGE-150,451
DOLBEL-158,219,257,436,530,535
DOLLAIRE,DALLAIRE-429
DOLMAN-526
DOLOMOUNT,etc.-219
DOMAILLE,DOMELLE-219,369
DOMINE-219
DONOHUE-327,366
DONALD-219
DONAVAN-530
DONCASTER-283
DONDIET-226
DOREEN-424
DOREY-42,170,208,220 to 223,229,353, 382,386,389,453,480,507,524 *
DORION-488
DORNBOUGH-367
DORSEY-385

DOUBLET-223
DOUCET-343,344,460,465,538
DOUGLAS-161,184,264,477
DOUVILLE-397
DON-196,223
DOVE-536
DOW-477,530,*
DOWN,DOWNS-223,224,353,386,413
DOWNEY-223
DOWNING-191,404
DOWNTON-224
DOYLE-128,222,349,537
DRAGON-539
DRAKE-354,356
DRAPER-106,176,224,334,335 *
DRAYTON-435
DRENTTEL-352
DRESSLER-254
DREW-216,224,388
DREYER-349
DRINKWATER-222
DRISCOLL-178,179 *
DROSS,DROS-224,485
DROUIN-131,534
DRUGGET-224
DRUMMOND-32,35,401
DRYNES-251
DUBE-163
DUBOIS-54,224
DU CHEMIN-224,388
DU CHESNAY-219
DU FEU,DU FEW-224,315
DUFFUS-366
DUFOUR-224,239 *
DU FRECY-383
DU FRESNE-224,227,244,506,508
DUGAN-157
DUGDALE-304
DUGAS-134,243,343,466
DUGIT-415
DUGUAY-132,144,180,193,196,208,
  217,262,276,316,477,485
DU HEAUME-54,210,224,275,337 *
DUKE-224,228,343
DUKEMAN-224
DUKESHIRE-322
DULMAGE-254
DUMAIS-310
DUMARESQ-31,33,78,79,114,153,154,
  218,224 to 228,262,317,338,373,
  380,463,524,529
DUMBLETON-372,478
DUNMAR-267
DUNBRACK-186
DUNCAN-186,193,335,410   *
DUNDAS-300
DUNHAM-504
DUNN-155,259,268,311,466,473,526
DUNNETT-338

DUNNINGTON-174
DUNSHEATHE-189
DUNVILLE-250
DU PARC-457
DUPEE-384   DUPUY *
DU PONT-476
DUPRES-79
DU PUIS-163,229,304,369
DUQUEMIN-224,229 *
DURAND-229
DURANT-253
DURELL-29,54,66,229,304,402,532
DURET-378,379
DURKEE-320
DURLAND-146,217
DURMAN-338
DURNFORD-192
DUTKA-491
DUTOT-229,230,243
DU VAL-30,32,42,65,79,80,157,180,
  230 to 235,249,277,280,286,294,
  307,312,324,328,335,374,375,377,
  381,427,428,429,528,543 *
DYER-235,434
DYKEMAN-431
DYMTRYSHAK-348
DYNE-290
DYSON-488,489
DYTTMER-483

EADE-464
EAGLE-511
EARLE-464
EARLY-542
EAST-324
EASTERBROOK-355,471,473
EATON-277
EBATA-140
EBDON-280
EBSWORTHY-235
ECCLES-313
ECKERT-220
ECOBICHON-235,272,280
EDEN-152,153,348
EDDIE-369
EDGAR-264
EDGE-290
EDGERLY-541
EDGINGTON-282
EDMOND,EDMONDS-235,289
EDMONSON-415,420
EDMUND,EDMUNDS-235,236 *
EDSON-353
EDWARD,EDWARDS-187,236,252,276,470
EFFARD-236
EGELTON-329
EGER,EGRE-236,446

EICHORN-298
EIDE-338
EISENHAUR-461
ELEMENT-226,227,256,260,436,513
ELFORD-336
ELKINGTON-496
ELKINS-433
ELLACOTT-400
ELLENS-441
ELLERY-395
ELLIOT-222,249,250,512
ELLIS-236,299,490,541
ELLSWORTH-541
ELY-236
EMERY-236
EMILY-236
EMOND-236   EMOSS *
ENEVOLDSEN-236   ENGLERT *
ENGLAND-129,236,252,291
ENGLISH-17,236,262,299,463,507,508
ENMAN-185
ENOUE-236
ENOUF,ESNOUF-131,525
ENRIGHT-466
ENS-405
EPSTEIN-333
EREAUT-137,236
ERDLE-499
ERICKSON-375,378
ERREY-207
ERVEN-349
ERWIN-498
ESCOTT-236
ESCULIER-311
ESNOUF-131,236,363,372,525
ESNOUF-DENIZE-236,392,429
EVANS-206,214,245,358,489
EVANSON-141
EVE-528
EVERARD-232
EVERSON-472
EVES-502
EWE-308
EWING-158
EYTON-176

FACEY-236
FAESAN-236
FAHYE-304
FAINTON-236,547   FAIRFIELD *
FAIRN-156
FAIRSERVICE-236
FAIRWEATHER-236,313
FALHABER-508
FALLA-53,224,237,386,480,509
FALLE-30,42,54,79,89,90,238,279,
  368,507 *

FALLIER-238
FALLON-478
FALLOW or FALLON-72,239,305
FALLU-72,178,239,240,372
FALOONA-393
FANNING-72,73,262
FARGO-161
FARLEY-452
FARMAN-328
FARMER-533
FARNCOMB-341
FARNELLE-441
FARQUHARSON-433,469
FARR-240,484,496   FARRELL-481C
FASHON-240
FAUVEL-178,240,308,310,523 *
FAVORITE-537
FAWNE-240
FAY-449
FAYIE,FAHEY-367
FEARON-240,371
FEAST-332
FEDERICO-424
FEENEY-496
FELKER-386
FELT-461
FENNELL-188,491
FENNET-509
FENTON, cf FAINTON-44,157,236,240,
  267,547   FEQUET *
FERBRACHE-206,301,369,387
FEREY-108,240,370
FERGUSON-173,211,212,238,240,353,
  373,375,376,443,462,511,520
FERMET-509
FERRINGTON-491
FERRIS-323
FEVER-240
FEWER-240
FIANDER-240
FICK-323
FICKETT-240 *   See also FEQUET
FIDLER-386
FIELD-421
FIEDLER-419
FILION-240,304,474
FILLETT-45
FILLEUL-42,45,240,241,288,307 *
FILLIATRE,LE FILLATRE,etc.-241,242,
  433 *
FILLIER-540   FINCH *
FINDLEY-242,387
FINLAY-314
FINLAYSON-390
FINN-403
FINNER-461
FINNIS-250
FIOTT-31,49,234,242,243,266,338,400
FIROIR-221

FISET-315
FISH-160,499
FISHER-242,393,415,416,441
FITCH-160
FITZGERALD-254,496,542
FITZPATRICK-157
FIXOTT-170,243,266,268
FLEET-320
FLEMING-322,367,FLEMMING-481A
FLETCHER-243,301,323,416,503
FLETT-198
FLEURY-47,104,105,108,243
FLINDELL-529
FLINT-132,475,496
FLIPPIN-163
FLOOD,FLOUD-243
FLOOK-488
FLOTO-358
FLOWERS-196,243 *
FLYNN-143,204,300,301,311,327,333
   339,428,429
FOARD-243,400
FOLEY,LAFFOLEY-244,460,481B
FONDA-222
FONTAINE-244
FOOTE-244,428
FORBES-515 *
FORBIN-201
FORD,FORDE-267,268,362
FORESTER-333
FORGEARD-333
FORGETT-244
FORDHAM-128
FOREMAN-244
FOREST-166,222,411
FORREST-258   FORRES *
FORSDYKE-274
FORSEY,FORSAY-233,244
FORSTER-25
FORSYTHE-160,161,545,481,481E
FORTIER-244,393,462,508,516,481C
FORTIN-244,294,506
FORTUNE-244
FOSSARD-133
FOSSE,FOSSEY-244
FOSTER-35,250,297,318,322,386,417
FOUGERE-221,222,411,450
FOULEAU-244
FOURNIE-189
FOURNIER-134,244,298,310,400,401,
   506
FOWLER-216,351   FOWLES *
FOWLOW-239,244   FOZARD *
FOX-28,307,308,407,408
FRAIZE,FRAISE-244
FRANCAIS-244
FRANCIS-244,496
FRANCOEUR-227,239,467,508
FRANCOEUR-LE CLERC-520

FRANKLIN-35
FRANKOVITCH-490
FRANKUM-504
FRASE-445
FRASER-177,237,241,294,321,472 *
FRAZER-157,158
FRECK,FRECKER-244
FREEBORN-363
FREED-507
FREEMAN-396
FRENCH-206,244,336,443,459
FRENETTE-421
FREWINS-245
FRICK-418
FRIEND-497
FRIESON-305
FRITOT-245,389,392
FRIZZELL-245
FROMENT-347
FROUD-245,470
FROOME-245
FROST-188,245,268
FROUING,FRUING-66,78,137,245,543
FRY-140,245,368
FULLER-49,140,245,246,363
FULLERTON-130
FURBER-459
FUREY,LE HURAY-50,246,445
FURGESON-271
FURNEAUX-246
FURSE,FURZE,FURZER-246

GABOUREL-246
GABRIEL-246,367
GADD-199
GADDEN-282
GAGNE-162,256,311,344, *
GAGNON-429,456,462,541
GAILLE-246   GAILLARD *
GAILBRAITH-530
GALE-246,247,302,433,456,532
GALIX-142
GALLAIS-247 See LE GALLAIS
GALLAGHER-290,491
GALLANT-212,247
GALLAUDET-216,217
GALLAWAY-370
GALLE-530   GALLEY *
GALLIARD-247,259
GALLICHAN-114,138,142,204,209,247,
   269,300,303,337,348,349,356,399,
   400,480
GALLICHAUD-204,247
GALLIE-187,233,247,248,265,364
GALLIENNE-170,248,249,263,381,420*
GALLO-491
GALLON-249,339,545 GALLUP *

GALOPIN,GALPIN-249
GAMMON-265,339
GANZ-361
GARCELON-249
GARCIA-538
GARDE-249 See DE LA GARDE
GARDEN,GARDNER,GARDINER-104,225,
  249,393,470,530
GARE-368
GAREAU-128
GARGET-387
GARIS-249 See DE GARIS
GARNER,GARNIER-249
GARRETT-208,249,264
GARRITY-530
GARSIN-249
GASNIER-152,278,349
GASPARD-398
GASSEAULT-370
GASSET-270
GATECLIFFE-489
GATES-245,320
GAUDEN,GAUDIN-42,104,105,109,131,
  153,154,216,250 to 257,263,
  339,372
GAUDET-221,293
GAUDIEBNE-248
GAUDION-248,256,257,263,484,514
GAUDREAU-294,516
GAUGHELL-494
GAUTHIER,GAUTIER-249,257,370,462,
  466
GAUTREAU-193
GAUTRON-312
GAUVIN-257
GAVEY-41,150,194,211,219,257,
  350,478,515 * 481 C
GAVRY- *   GAVIT *
GAWRYLUK-253
GEAR-215,257
GEARY-214,257,544
GEER-544
GEIGER-267
GENDREAU-178,180
GENDRON-257
GENGE-99,229,256,258,301,336
GEORGE-316
GERARD-178
GERDES-387
GERJEAU-294

GERMAIN-370
GERRY-219
GERTZ-515
GERVAISE-287,393
GEZEQUEL-326
GHIGHI-263
GIASSON-506
GIBAUT,GIBEAUT-258,288,304,455,528 *
GIBBENS-290
GIBBONS-171,201,209,281 to 284,420 *
GIBNEY-405
GIBSON-143,158,241,259,362,455,498
GIFFARD-127,181,259,289,332
GIFFORD-199
GIGNAC-133
GIGUERE-259
GIGUET-259
GILBERT-161,241,259,362,397,417,434
GILBERTSON-415
GILCHRIST-494 *
GILE,GILES-259,311,332
GILL,GILLES,GILLIS-259,368,465,496
GILLESPIE-397,549 *
GILLETT-259
GILLAM,GUILLIAM,GUILLAUME,etc.-27,
  152,259,546 See WILLIAMS
GILLFILLING,GILLFILLAN-259
GILLIARD-247,259
GILLIAT-147,217
GILLES-382
GILLINGS,GELLANCE-259,260
GILLIS-221
GILMORE-147,391,446,491
GILPIN-492
GIBSON-391,443
GIONET-438

GIOT-259
GIRARD-180,193,226,260 to 262,366, 368,429,515,520 to 521,531
GIROUX-394
GIVENS-277
GLAHOLM-487
GLASS-367
GLAVENWHITE-331
GLAVINE-467
GLEASON-393
GLEETON-298
GLEN,GLENN-251
GLORY-204
GLOVER-198,339,355,419
GLUGSTON-251
GLYN,GLYNN,GLEEN-262,531
GOASDOUE-262
GODBOUT-392
GODDARD-540
GODDEN, cf GAUDIN-32,42,262,263, 522
GODFRAY-30,237,258,263,307
GODFREY-43,65,78,258,263,337, 372,532
GODIN-227,263,276,539
GODION-394   GODNER-441
GOENS-394
GOFF-189
GOGO-291
GOLDSMITH-192
GOLLEDGE-263
GOMM-456
GONNEVILLE-129
GOOBIE-263
GOOCH-264 *
GOOD,GOODE-265,284,340
GOODENUFF-428   GOODERHAM-481A
GOODFELLOW-250
GOODLOE-499
GOODMAN-481E
GOODRICH-217
GOODRUM,GOODERHAM?-211
GOODWIN-376,431
GOOTE-263
GORDEN-263
GORDON-172,206,418,435,488
GORE-23,263
GORGERON-222
GORMAN-367
GORSKI-433
GORT-379
GOSLIN-290
GOSLING-263
GOSS,GOSSE-263,459
GOSSELIN-128,263,264
GOSSET,GOSSETT-39,127,264,307,467 *
GOUBERT-141,207,264,265
GOUCHER-216   GOTTWALD *
GOUDREAU-266
GOUGEON-163
GOULD-264
GOULDRUP,GOLDRUP-264,265
GOULET-257,325,467
GOUPY-263,269
GOURBVILLE-265
GOURDEAU-260
GOURLEY-258
GOUSHON-265
GOUSHOU-271
GOVER,GOUVERT-265
GRACE-508 See DE GRACE
GRAHAM,GRAHAME-130,170,214,265,296, 355,356,386,394,396
GRANDIN-45,265 *
GRANDY-265
GRANT-145,179,180,265,291,431 *
GRANVILLE-265
GRASETT-365
GRASSIE-213
GRAUVETT-169
GRAVELLE-484
GRAVES-186
GRAVET-212
GRAY-41,181,263,265,268,300,305,337, 394 to 396 * GRAYBEAL *
GREALEY-265   GREENING *
GREER-330
GREECHY, see GRUCHY and DE GRUCHY
GREELEY-66,266
GREEN,GREENE-32,164,216,266,347,484, 494   GREENING *
GREENMAN-495
GREENWOOD- *
GREENSLADE-266
GREER-544
GREFFARD-265
GREGG-266,434,440
GREGOIRE-538,539 See GREGORY
GRENFELL-53
GRENIER-135,136,310,317,519
GRESHUE-266
GRESLEY-265,266 See LE GRESLEY
GRETTEAU-184
GREY-221
GRIBER-254
GRIEVE-334
GRIFFIN-300
GRIFFITH-492
GRIMSHAW-266
GRIMWOOD-274
GRISSINGER *
GRIVEL-263
GROGAN-309
GROOM-266
GROSSEILLIERS-26 to 28
GROSSET-441
GROSVALET-448
GROUCHY,GRUCHY-169,266 See DE GRUCHY

GROVE-362
GROVER-148,443
GROVES-362 *
GRUCHY-43,148,165,190,243,266 to 269,288 See DE GRUCHY
GRUT-174,359,450,514,546 *
GUEDARD-269
GUEGAN-269
GUERIN-269
GUERNIER-269
GUERNSEY-269
GUEROUT-365
GUEST-396
GUGE-269
GUIGNARD-171,276
GUIGNON,GUIGNION-481,502,526 *
GUIGNION-152,175,269,381,401,481E
GUILBERT,GILBERT-269,487,508
GUILLAN-269
GUILLARD-269
GUILLAT-261
GUILLAUME,GUILLIAM,GILLAM-27,47, 241,546
GUILLE-269,408
GUILLET-89,91,142,269,270,394
GUIMONT-294
GUITE-131,134
GUITON-270
GULLICKSON-379
GUNBY-364
GUNTON-90,270
GUPPY-263,269
GURBA-224
GURLEY-145
GUSHUE,GUSHEE,etc.-270,450
GUSTIN-89,271,398
GUTHRIE-179,353
GUY-271

HAAS *
HACAULT-272
HACHEY,HACHE-138,211,272,342,344, 438,465,516,639
HACHEZ-199
HACKETT-272
HACKING-272,547
HACKWELL,HACQUOIL-148,522
HACOU-272
HACQUOIL-79,272,274,325,377
HADCOCK-511   HADLOCK-481E
HAFEY-272
HAHN-501   HAIGHT-481B
HAILES-258
HAINLEY-267
HAIN,HAINS,HAINES-272,281,321*
HAKE-272
HALE-401
HALENAN-272

HALL-25,129,130,153,197,216,252,289, 431,473,518,540
HALLAN-404
HALLETT-272,387
HALLIDAY-230
HAMEL-272,392
HAMELIN-272,392
HAMEN-272
HAMER-168
HAMILTON-160,191,201,223,290,434, 525,534
HAMON,HAMMON,HAMMOND-43,59,169,261, 272 to 274,280,293,295,332,348, 356,386,389,399,485,529 *
HAMPSHIRE-424
HAMPTON-274
HANCOCK-319
HAND,HANDY-201,274,340,446
HANLON-273
HANNAN,HANNON-321,460
HANSEN,HANSON-131,174,219,241,387, 455 *
HARCOE-274
HARDELEY-397
HARDING-273,352,402 * 481A
HARDOUIN-235
HARDWICK-147,155,156,320,321
HARDY-31,274,275,441
HARKER-383 *   HARGROVE 481C
HARLOW-472
HARPER-232,275,408,435,541
HARQUAIL,HACQUOIL-79,272,274,325 *
HARRINGTON-275
HARRIS-147,156,160,172,216,217,254, 275,318,331,417,418,434,445
HARRISON-264,290,348,350,497,533
HART-224,411 *
HARTERY-164
HARTMAN-254
HARTWELL-341
HARVEY,HARVIE-176,255,256,273,275, 355,367,415,481 B
HASKELL-275
HASKETT-275
HASKINS-470
HASLAM-284
HASSARD-380
HASTINGS-145,323
HASZARD-380,433
HATCH-375
HATCHER-275
HATFIELD-481A
HATT-241,410
HAVILLAND,DE HAVILLAND-210,275
HAWCOE,HACOUOIL-50,272,275
HAWKE-170
HAWKES-304
HAWKINS-353,415 *
HAWKESWORTH-146

HAWLEY-275,326
HAY-129, see also LAHAY,
    DE LA HAY
HAYDEN,HAYDON-261,275,315,475,
    520
HAYE,HAYES-133,275,397
HAYNES-275,281,295
HAZARD-433
HAZELTON-336
HEACOCK-148
HEAD-275
HEADLEY?
HEADON-325
HEALD-414
HEALY-431
HEANEY,HENEY-275
HEARN-222,489
HEATON-411
HEAUME,DU HEAUME-275
HEBERT-526
HEFFORD-458
HEIGHINGTON-544
HELIER, see HILLIER-356 *
HELLER,HELLEUR,etc.-275,276 *
HELM-505,481A
HELSON-407
HEMERY-276
HEMSTREET-383
HENDERSON-276,296,329,397,398,404
HENLEY-104,227,366,367,402,485,
    508,516
HENNIGAR-319
HENNING-415
HENNIQUEN-236
HENRY-66,276,279,418,419,442,453,
    480
HENSHAW-321,431
HENSLEY-185
HENWOOD-537
HEPNER-350
HERALD-277
HERAULT,L'HERAULT,etc.-276,292 *
HERBERT-526
HERD-252
HERIOT-31,32,276
HERITAGE-277
HERIVEL-277
HERMAN-469
HERON-277
HERPE-277
HERRING-352,418
HERRO,HERAULT-277
HERRON-436
HESKETH-139
HEULIN,HUELIN-277,391
HEWGILL-250,251
HEWITSON-277
HEWLIN, see HEULIN,HUELIN-280
HIBBS-277,305,450

HIBERT,HUBERT-277,392,488
HICKEY-129,133,430
HICKLING-187
HICKOX-383
HICKS-206,216,251,267,277,317
HIGGINS-445,459
HIGGINSON-504,530
HILDUR-525
HILL-159,279,297,418,434,471,504,
    508,534
HILLDRETH-215
HILLIER,HILLIAR,HILLYER,etc.-32 to
    43,277,361 *
HILLIS-332,475
HILLMAN-468
HILLSON-265
HILLYARD,HILLIARD,etc.-277,460
HIMBURG-413
HIND-250,395
HINGLEY-419
HISCOCK-155
HOARE-174
HOBBS-277,327
HOCART,HOCQUARD-233,235,246,248,277,
    278,297,335,370,439,493,513,515*
HODDENOT,HODINET-278
HODGART-255
HODGE,HODGES-238,278
HODGINS-481A HODGDON *
HODGSON-236-355
HOGUE-497
HOLDEN-378,549 *
HOLDER
HOLLAND-214,296,310,375,497
HOLLETT-183,278
HOLLEY-278
HOLLICK-542
HOLLINS-325
HOLLON-364
HOLMAN-278
HOLMES-144,163,278,323,335,405,420,
    495
  HOLNESS-494
HOLROYD-352
HOLT-251,296
HOLTON-438
HOMER,HOMMART-278,461
HONELL-279
HONNER-253
HOOEY-408
HOOFT-510
HOOKER-314
HOOKEY,LE HUQUET-50,278,351
HOOPER-146,278,353,363,417
HOPIN,HOPKINS,AUPIN,etc.-143,202,278,
    461,543
HOPKINS-407
HOPKINSON-486
HORMAN-278 *

HORNE-278,296,297,387
HORNER-348
HORNIBROOK-265,341
HORPIN-278
HORRELL,HORRILL,etc.-278,279,387
HORSEFALL-320
HORTON-416,443,449
HORWOOD-317
HOSKIN-290
HOSKING-206,278
HOTTON-249,278,279,303,350,368, 481
HOUDE-282
HOUGHTALIN-264
HOUGOURD
HOUGUEZ-278,279,453
HOUSE,HOUZE-279,472
HOUSMANT-339
HOUSTON-383
HOWARD-147,279,406,414,417 *
HOWATT-104
HOWE-253,303,356,417,418
HOWELL-147,243,279,478 *
HOWLETT,HOLLETT-279
HOXIE-417
HOYLE,HOYLES-43,79,165,238,271, 279,326 *
HOYT-231,320
HOZEN-352
HUARD-133,135,142,162,279
HUBERT-165,230,242,243,277,279, 280,293,398,454
HUDDLESON-344
HUDON-134
HUDSON-32,280,321,473
HUE-273,280,438
HUET,HUOT-281
HUELIN-231,235,249,280,281,294, 312,360 *
HUGEN-490
HUGGARD-267
HUGH-353,417
HUGHES-140,241,255,280,470
HULD-314
HULEN-281,514
HULL-281,411
HUME,HEAUME?-148,419
HUNSLEY-539
HUNSON-171
HUNT-132,192,217,319,334,379,410, 495,497,520,521,481B
HUNTER-250,251,416,530 8
HUNTINGTON-195,283,360,429,446
HUNTON,HUNTOON-66,281
HUOT-233,241,281
HURDLE,HURDLEY-281,523
HURE-281
HUREAU-166
HURLBUT-253,254

HURLEY-265,271
HURST-391
HURTAULT-281
HUSBAND-445
HUSSEY-197,281
HUSTINS-281
HUTCHESON-144
HUTCHEON-544
HUTCHINSON-134,483,497,525
HUTTON-432
HUXTER-281
HUYCK-349   HUYETT *
HYDE-218,418,448
HYMAN-368,412
HYNES-281,430
HYSLOP-127,524

IMRIE-205
INGLIS-291,361,366,440
INGOLDSBY-252
INGOUVILLE,INGROUVILLE,etc.-59,145, 171,209,281,285,295,499,522,532 *
INGRAM-185,295,305,449
INKPEN-183
INNISWOOD-451
INSLEY-106,224,313   INWOOD-481C
IRELAND-209,405
IRISH-386
IRVINE-97
IRVING-442
IRWIN-371,495
ISABEL,ISABELLE-243,285
ISLES-322
IVANY-144
IVES- *   See also EVES-502
IVEY-489

JACCKI-511
JACK,JACQUES-285
JACKLYN-382
JACKMAN-285,432
JACKSON-144,285,334,355,416,490
JACKSON-CLARKE-413
JACQUES-217,285,332,506,481C
JACOBS-145,160,433,498
JACOBSON-129
JALBERT-261,348,467
JAMES-28,184,210,285,322,340 *
JAMIESON-129,285,424,425
JANAWAY-210
JANDRON-285,289,370
JANES-346,517
JANOWISC-499

JANVRIN-30,54,59,60,147,177,285 to
   288,328,359,365,447,529,530 *
JARDIN-287
JARDINE-186
JARNET-287
JARVES,JARVIS-251,287
JEAN-44,59,60,89,166,172,177,209,
   211,226,243,258,266,268,286,
   289,344,368,398,403,533,534,
   535 *
JEANDRON-257,289,340
JEAN-LOUIS-334
JEANOTTE-481 A
JEAUROND-408
JEFFARD-289
JEFFRIES-289,504
JEFFERY-289,469
JEFFERS-395
JEFFERSON-487
JELLISON-229
JENKS-419
JENKINS-186,289,317,355,380,445,469
JENNIEX-289
JENNINGS-289,353
JENSON,JENSEN-148,291,377,378
JEPSON-282
JERRARD-289
JERRETT-208,249,258,289   JERRY *
JERSEY,DE JERSEY-289
JERVIS-503
JESS-315
JESSUP-328
JESTINGS-321
JEUNAIX-289,290
JEUNE, see LE JEUNE-43,107,109,174,
   289 to 292,448,525,547 *
JEWELL-434,515,481D
JEZEQUEL-292
JOCELYN,JOSSLYN-241
JODOIN-268
JOHNCOX-468
JOHN,JOHNS-292,386
JOHNSON-128,198,267,271,292,301,
   314,339,352,367,370,379,422,
   430,434,526,528,536
JOHNSTON-79,182,292,353,383,445,510
JOLI-292
JOLLY-139,292
JONCAS-162
JONES-39,131,156,184,241,274,297,
   319,324,353,367,389,405,435,
   460,531,537,481A
JONSON-148
JORDAN,JORDEN-174,292,354,419
JORGENSON-546
JOSEPHSON-480
JOSSLYN-241
JOST-321
JOUAN-94,292,426

JOUDRIE,JOUDRY-357,443
JOUINOIX-295
JOURDAINE-486
JOURDON-292
JOURNEAULX,JOURNEAU,etc.-54,69,143,
   179,181,200,231,292 to 295,327,
   328,391,481,510,511,541 *
JOURNEAY-241
JOWINOIX-289,290,295
JOYCE-295
JOYNT-411
JUDGE-254
JUDSON-185
JUNE *

KAGIHARI-346
KAIL-253
KALOTTE-474
KANE-423   KAPASI-481D
KAPUSTA-251
KARATHANOS-179
KARTELL-295
KASTELL-295
KATCHER-497
KAULBACH-321,449
KAY-238,327
KAYTER-404
KEATES-326,367
KEAYS-180
KEEFER-381
KEEPING-354
KEIKKEN-377
KELLER-289,511
KELLEY,KELLY-219,222,232,241,395,
   423,481C
KELLING-295
KELSEY-307
KELM-479
KEMENS-400
KEMISH-408
KEMLEUR,KEMNEUR-300,327
KEMP-270,433,512
KEMPSTER-295
KENDALL-345,349,440
KENDRICK-284
KENNEDY-139,147,262,305,440,441,
   444,469,490 *
KENNETT-295
KENNIE-161
KENT-450
KENTNOR-250
KERAUTRET-295
KERBY-59,296,299
KERCHEVAL-445
KERNAGHAN-404
KERR-338,345,411,451,453,482
KEYHO-172,299

KEYS-259,332,499,540
KEYSER-267
KIDD-128,267,324
KIDVILLE-54
KIEGAN-200
KIER-417
KIERNAN-525
KILBURN-161
KILEY-284
KILNER-296
KILPATRICK-340,489
KILVINGTON-361
KIM-404   KIMBERLEY *
KINDER-434
KING-145,148,181,190,254,296,321,
   346,347,367,390,496,517
KINGSLAND-139
KINGSLEY-362
KINGSWOOD-341
KINNEAR-387
KINNEY-296
KINSELA-296   KIPP *
KIRBY-188,296
KIRK-148,178,252,296,489
KIRKHAM-503
KIRKPATRICK-294,395
KISSAM-148
KITCHEN-187
KLEIN-364
KLEISINGER-241
KLIENSCHROTH-449
KLITTE-489
KLIZ-254
KLUGHART-130
KNAPP-296
KNELL-507
KNIGHT, CHEVALIER?-32,154,185,192,
   214,296,323,331,382 *
KNOTT-148
KNOX-334
KNOWLES-239,416
KNUDSEN-313,479
KOEHLER-499
KOEN-421
KOLENSKI-426
KONAR-474
KONDEY-433
KORVIN-396
KOSMO-378
KRAFT-499
KRANZ-526
KROGEL-130   KROPF *
KRUPP-267
KRUSE-187,296   *
KURTZ-396,434
KURZ-433,434
KYLE-168,434
KWASNY-252

LABAT-207
LABBEE,LABEY-287,296,467
LA BARGE,LA BARGY,etc.-297
LABEY-141,155,255,296,297,335,467
LA BILLOIS-297
LA BLANC-297
LA BONTE-540
LA BOSSIERE-264
LABOU-297
LA BRAVE-223
LABRIE-462
LA BRUE-297
LACHEUR, see LE LACHEUR
LACKIE-490
LA CLOCHE, BELL-154,297
LA COGNES-297
LA COSTA-297
LA COURS,etc.-297
LA COUTURE-298
LA COUVET,COUVEE-298,427,481B
LA CROIX-298,301
LA DOUCEUR-455
LA DROS-298
LAEL,LISLE?-407
LA FAVE-408
LAFFOLEY-244,298,299
LA FLAMME-143,258,300,327,485,506
LA FLEUR-299
LA FONTAINE-163,402
LA FORET,LA FOREST-239
LA FORTUNE-433
LA FOSSE-299
LA FOUR-299
LA FRANCE-293,299
LAGADU-299
LAGDEN-487,492
LA GERCHE-287,299,462
LAHAY-519
LAHNER-379
LAINCHBURY-291
LAINE,LAINEY-299,387
LAING-264,404,415
LAIRD-383
LAJOIE-325
LAKE-299,300,320,464
LALIBERT-164   LALONDE- *
LAMARR-299
LA MARCH,LA MARSH-94,299,424
LA MASURIER-299 See LE MASURIER
LAMB-130,142,186,299
LAMBERT-140,163,176,209,299,301,
   379,393,526
LAMBLEY-474   LAMBOTTE *
LAMBRETTE-163
LA MONTAGNE-267,534
LAMOREAUX-267
LAMPMAN-314
LAMY-299 See AMY
LANDELL-129

LANDRY-131,166,191,221,227,239,
  257,342,343,404,429,450,465,466,
  490,534,541,547
LANE-219
LANG-465,540
LANGDON-299
LANGIN-299
LANGLAIS,LANGLEY-163,299,409
LANGLOIS-17,32,43,162,166,169,204,
  226,262,272,299,300,301,311,350,
  369,387,428,502,508,509 * 481B
LANGRISH-43,337
LANGTRY-90,106,224,301,316
LANGUEDOC-152,153,528,529,530
LANKIN-494
LANNIGAN,LANIGAN-166,287,288
LANNEL-251
LANNON-301
LANTEIGNE-438
LANTIN-151
LA PERELLE-301
LA PIERRE-310,370
LA POINTE-485
LARAIX-94,301
LARAWAY,LE RUEZ-302,409 *
LARAY-429
L'ARBALESTIER-142,257,301,302,523
L'ARMOUR-314
LAROCQUE-343,501
LARSON-379
LAREAU-213
LARRAWAY, etc.-302,399
LARRIBEE-229
LA RUE-213,302,356,368
LA SALIR-222,223
LA SERRE, etc.-302
LA SIEUR-302
LASKEY-482
LATHMER-373
LATHROP-145
LATIMER-171,222,223,302,355,430
LATTIMORE-223
LAUGHLIN-352
LAUGA-302
LAURENCE-302
LAURENS-179,292,302
LAURIE-435
LAURSEN-491
LAUX-479
LA VACHE-287,302   LA VAIL-481B
LA VALLEE-246,302,394
L'AVENTURE-302
LA VIELLE-302
LAVIGNE-456
LAVOIE-134,310,474
LAW-176,302,314,491,544
LAWLOR-274
LAWRENCE-178,179,278,300,302,303,
  314,339,382,387,428,479,536,537

LAWRENTZ- *
LAWSON-390,433
LAWTON-303
LAYTON-422
LEADBEATER-303,527
LEAHY-223
LEALE-303
LEAMAN,LEAMON-283,332
LEAMY-303,404
LEAR-303,399
LEARY-327
LEARNING,LAURNEYS-303
LEASON-308
LE BAILLEY-303
LE BAIRE,LE BER?-303
LE BARGE,LE BARGY,LA BARGE,etc.-303,
  479
LE BAS-303,304,529 *
LE BASTART-304
LE BEL-304,465
LE BELIER,LE BELLIER-304
LE BER-240,304,305,436,480,522
LE BEUF-306
LE BLANC,LE BLANCQ-134,142,163,216,
  228,239,304,306,318,425,450,546
LE BLOND-306
LE BOEUF-306
LE BONTEVUE-167
LE BORGNE-306
LE BOSIGNET-306
LE BOSQUET-306   LE BOSSIERE *
LE BOURVEAU-306
LE BOURGNON-306 LE BOUTHILLIER *
LE BOUTILLIER-18,32,37,54,59,78,80,
  108,149,158,170,187,191,193,208,
  210,234,240,286,306 to 318,336,
  341,514,519,522,535,537 *
LE BOYER-312,484
LE BOW,LE BEAU-312
LE BRASSEUR-312,477
LE BRETON-32,33,47,90,172,274,288,*
  293,301,311 to 313,316,529,536,543
LE BREAUX-297,316
LE BROCK,LE BROCQ-137,191,199,234,
  297,316,334,342,350,462 *
LE BROSSAULT-316
LE BREUILLY-316
LE BRUN-194,206,209,307,308,316,317,
  318,324,397,404,414,485,527,528,
  542
LE CAIN,LE QUESNE-58,59,156,191,317
  to 322,389,485 *
LE CAPPELAIN-127,290,322,323,324
LE CASSE,LA CASSE-324
LE CAUDEY,LE CODY-199,324
LE CAUX-324
LE CERF-324
LE CHARPENTIER See CARPENTER-372
LE CHASSEUR-324

LE CHEMINANT-301,324,387,527,536
LE CHESNE-401
LE CLAIR-324
LE CLERC,LE CLERCQ-143,263,324,325
LE COCQ-204,325,326,342,371
LE COIGNET-297
LE CONTE-326
LE CORE,LE CORRE-325
LE CORNU-79,148,188,203,205,258,
  278,279,326,474
LE COUILLIARD-132,485
LE COUTEUR-33,65,73,106,108,142,
  143,147,199,203,205,229,231,292,
  327,328,329,340,403,439 *
LE COURTOIS-94,144,150,326,327,
  442,457,477,479,486
LE COUVET, etc.-329 *
LE COZ-203
LE CRAS,LE CRAW-45,301,329,330 *
L'ECRIVAIN-330
LE CRONIER-330
LE CUCU-205
LE DAIN-205,234,330
LE DEZ-297
LE DREW-157,224,330,331,515
LEDGERWOOD-431
LE DROIT-224,331
LE DROW-330,331
LE DUC-224,331
LEE-231,264,331,332,413,436,546
LEEK-295
LEEPER-308
LE FEBVRE-237,240,332
LE FEUVRE-168,239,240,259,273,274,
  316,332 to 335,345,398,486,518
LE FEVER,LE FEVRE-32,43,239,334,
  335,543
LEFFLER-499
LE FILLIATRE,LE FILLATRE-235,241,
  242 *
LE FLOCH-164,336
LE FOLLET See LAFFOLEY
LE FRANCOIS-244
LE FRESNE-335
LEGACE-343,429
LE GALLAIS-43,44,59,99,127,133, *
  142,163,187,212,223,233,235,247,
  257,277,281,297,303,335,336,337,
  364,420,426,436,439,455,515,522
LE GALLE-247
LE GALLEZ-337
LE GALLIENNE-248,450 *
LE GALLIS-337
LE GALLOIS-337
LE GARIGNON-337 *
LE GASSE-337
LE GAULT-180
LE GELLUS-337
LE GEOFFREY-258,263,337

LEGER,LEGERE-227,438,456
LE GEYT-242,337,338
LEGGE,LEGG-45,436,460 *
LEGGETT-337
LEGGO-515
LE GOUPIL-263,269
LE GRAISEY-337,464
LE GRAND-149,153,164,175,201,225,
  255,289,303,338 to 341,439,452,
  466,523 *
LE GRANDAIS-341
LE GRESLEY-151,159,164,212,266,278,
  316,325,341 to 344,347,360,373,
  381,399,414,423,438,439,446,463,
  464,526,528,533,535 *
LE GROS-45,78,94,137,201,256,298,
  328,342,344,345,348,429,445,471,
  509,517
LE GROW-345 to 347,472,517,522
LE GRUIEC-304   LE GUEDARD-347 *
LE GUERRIER-438   LE GUILCHER-347
LE GUY-272   LE GUYADER-347
LE HARDI,LE HARDY,HARDY-31,274,368
LE HARVIE,LE ARVIE-275
LE HERISSIER-347
LE HERON See HERON
LEHMAN-284
LE HOUGUEZ-278
LE HOUILLIER-347
LE HUQUET-137,145,169,200,201,209, *
  247,257,269,278,300,316,344,348,
  349,350,351,368,369,388,455,478
LE HURAY-246,351
LE HUREL-278
L'HEREAULT, etc.-394 *
LEIGH-234,351,386
LEIGHTON-140,541
LE JERSEY-351 See DE JERSEY
LE JEUNE, see also JEUNE*44,351,541,
LE LACHEUR-33,72,73,215,223,240,272,
  * 276,351 to 358,399,401,417,418,451A
  436,443,446,453,477,481,498,499,491E
LE LIEVRE-163,313,315,358,370,457
LE MAIN, see MAIN-420
LE MAISTRE,LE MAITRE-137,174,188,
  287,358,359,370,389,398,426,477 *
LE MAITRE-359,365,388,420,510   *
LE MAN-303
LE MARCHAND-359
LE MARCHANT-34,44,192,359,477
LE MARINEL-473
LE MARQUAND,LE MARQUANT-74,108,109,
  137,164,204,359 to 362,386,392,
  413,424,425,437,528 *
LE MARREC-362
LE MASURIER-210,234,236,248,299,336,
  362 to 364,451   *
LEMEE,LE MAY-358,364
LEMERILL-146

LE MERCIER-364,432
LE MESSURIER-34,66,127,238,273,363, 364,365,454 *
LE MESURIER-34,44,114,144,238,269, 274,276,301,347,348,350,364 to 369,401 *
LE MIERE-168
LE MIEUX-133,199,304,310,508
LEMME-303
LEMMING-263
LE MOIGNAN-144,145,285,317,359,369, 370,371,527
LE MOINE-303,371
LE MOIR-402
LEMON-418 Cf LE MOINE
LE MONNIER-371,437
LE MONTAIS-66,316,390,437,438,461, 530
LE MOTTEE-229,325,326,371,398,437, 438,475,476
LE MOUSTRE-371,514
LE MOYNE-258
LEMPRIERE-31,37,39,114,183,191,239, 280,371,372
LENDREAU-399
LE NEVEU-106,371 to 373,439
LENFESTEY,LENFESTY-114,157,158,174, 190,200,201,216,225,228,230,231, 272,296,373 to 382,410,429,432, 524,536 *
LENGER-477
LE NOBLE-447
LE NOIR-293,423
LE NORMAN-450
LE NOURY-220,296,382,383,389,451, 452,479,524 *
LENT-147
LEONARD-300,383,
LE PAGE-34,73,94,127,143,207,220 * to 224,256,292,324,360,383 to 387,389,436,447,453,454,462,534
LE PARNEAU-238
LE PATOUREL-98,182,277,301,387
LE PELLEY-141,345,347,348,386,387, 388,460
LE PENNEC-388
LE PETIT-388,458
LE POIDEVIN-224,302,*388,389,436,453
LEPPARD-128
LE PREVOST-205,220,237,248,273,382, 386,389
LE QUELENEC-389
LE QUESNE-58,59,78,138,155,191,205, 207,245,303,318,320,321,322,325, 389,390,466,537 *
LE QUIN-390
LE RAY-390,429,465 *
LE REGLE-397,482
LE RENDU-390
LE RETILLIE, see RETTY-485
LE REVEREND-390,545
LE RHE-174,390
LE RICHE-275,294,315,390 to 392,485
LE ROCKE,LE ROCHE,etc.-398,501
LE ROSSIGNOL-79,234,235,358,369,392 to 398,447,524
LE ROUGETEL-132,398
LE ROUSSET-398
LE ROUX-398,399,435
LE ROY,LE ROI-176,231,296,399,517
LERRIER-303,399,522
LE RUE-300
LE RUEZ-399,409,483
LE SARRE, etc.-399
LE SAUTEUR-399,455
LE SAUVAGE-94,399
LE SCELLIEUR, LE SEELEUR,etc.-242, 246,247,392,399,400,401,483 *
LESBIREL, see also SEBIRE-140,356, 399,512,513,188
LESEBIRE-399
LE SERRE,LE SARRE-96
LE SHANE-401
LESLIE-129,401
LE SUCCEUR-401
LE SUEUR-34,44,73,108,234,237,402, 414,529
LETACNOUX-401
LE TALIVERE-401
LE TEMPLIER-401
LE TEXIER-401
LE TIEC-401
LE TIRANT-312
LE TISSIER-401,420,499
LE TOURNEAU-256,298,310,401,485
LE TOUZEL-175,208,269,296,357,401, 402,481,493,502,526,527,481A&E
LETSON-151
LE VALLIANT-402
LE VAIN-402
LE VALLEE,LE VALLEY-402,510
LE VATT-402
LE VASSEUR,LE VAVASSEUR-402,442,453, 532
LE VECQUE-178
LE VEILLEZ-402
LE VER,LEVER-283,402
LEVERSON-250
LE VESCONTE-35,59,60,166,177,207, 287,288,401 to 407,507,543
LEVESQUE-180
LEVIN-250
LE VOGUER-543
LEVY-271
LE WEG-450
LEWIS-147,161,171,222,254,256,283, 377,407,449,510,481C
L'HERAULT-276,407 *

LIBBY-214
LIETJEN-440
LIEVRE,LE LIEVRE-407
LIGHTFOOT-331
LIHOU-143,144,154,269,407,408,409,
    464,515
LILLY-94,409
LILLYCROP-409
LILOIS-261
LIND-526
LINDSEY,LINDSAY-181,363,409,449,
    471,484   LING *
LINFESTY,LENFESTY-375,376
LIPPERT-364   LINNINGTON-481 D
LISLE-407
LISSACK-379
LITTLE-314,315,409,495
LITTLEJOHN-329
LIVERNOIS-311
LIVINGSTONE-307,444
LIZOT-316
LIZYNESS-183
LOCKE-409
LOCKHART-380
LOCKWOOD-348
LODGE-432
LOFTGREN-377
LOGAN-338
LOGGIE-528,543   Cf LOUGEE
LONG-216,409   LOMAS *
LONGLEY-146,216,409
LONGMIRE-317
LONGMORE-422   LOREE- *
LORD-265,349,373,409
LORWAY-330,409,527
LOSIER-211,227,316
LOUGEE-302,452
LOUGHEED-182,251,451
LOUIS-409
LOUVEL-409
LOVE-264,435,503
LOVELY-455
LOVELL-181,497
LOVERIDGE-409
LOVERING-300
LOVETT-160
LOVETT-FRASER-451
LOW,LOWE-89,147,249,410,445
LOWREY-177,468
LOWTHER-410
LUBNER-267
LUCAN-53,410
LUCAS-130,164,260,262,381,410,520,
    526,530,531 *
LUCE-66,78,103,168,175,212,214,410
    to 413,428,463,484,522 *
LUCEY-433
LUDD-413
LUDLOW-413

LUET-188
LUMSDEN-444
LUNDY-153,452
LUNNEY-127
LUOME-252
LUSCOMBE-257
LUSH-413,479,510
LUYBEN-332
LYLE-252
LYNCH-503
LYNN-488
LYS-413
LYSTER *

MABE,MABEY-184,308,374,534 *
MABERY-397
MACAULEY-355
MACE-413,421
MACHON-72,73,97,154,165,210,279,331,
    354,355,356,413,414 to 420,442,
    447,478,481 * 481A,481C
MACHULSON-325
MACKLEM-ROBERT-292,472
MADDEN-243
MADER-396
MADSEN-224,495
MAGEE-330
MAGER-420
MAGILL-391
MAGOWAN-296
MAGUIRE-129
MAHAN-191,226,345,373,376,381,509,
MAHER-519,531
MAHIE,MAHE,MAHY-154,220,221,256,
    296,408,420,425,546
MAHLER-304
MAHON-396,432
MAICH-478
MAIDENS-492
MAILHOT-337 *
MAILLARD-413,414
MAILLOUX-465
MAIN-420
MAINDONALD-248,420,421 *
MAINGAY-214
MAINGUY-245,421 to 423
MAINVILLE-304,423
MAINWARING-423   MAIONI-481D
MAISONEUVE-206
MAITLAND-277,294
MAJOR-81,144,150,423,428 *
MALCOLM-246,290,396
MALINS-509
MALLARD-422
MALLET,MALET,MALLETT-94,137,143,
    184,211,225,423 *
MALLICK-282
MALLOU-429

MALOWNEY-212
MALLOY-489
MALONEY-163,178,179,181,260,262, 293,302,303
MALOUIN-368
MALTBY,MALTHOUSE,MALTWOOD-423
MAIZARD-403
MANDER-368
MANGER-408
MANLEY-229
MANN-217,442,451
MANNAN-533 ✷
MANNING-165,192,341,423 *
MANSEL-423,424,498
MANTHA-189
MANTON-291
MANUEL-424
MANZER-525,526
MARCEAU-136,474
MARCHAND-94,424,450,540
MARCHANT, see MARCHAND and LE MARCHANT
MARCHE,MARCH-424,541
MARCOTTE-224
MARCUS-232
MARDELEY-424
MARETT,MARET-285,360,424,425,462, 465,518 *
MARGISON-453
MARIE-424
MARIN-462,516,525
MARINEL,LE MARINEL-473
MARION-424,535
MARKHAM-529
MARKS-424,425,481,538,541,542
MARLING-334
MARLTON-191
MARMAUD,MARMO-285,425
MAROLDO-378,379 *
MARON-238
MAROONEY-228
MARQUAND,LE MARQUAND-72,360,425, 432,450 *
MARQUIS-387,420,425,546
MARR-254,417,435
MARRETT-425 ✷
MARRIE-425
MARRIETTE-33,357,425,426,503
MARRYMAN-364
MARSH-252,426   MARSKELL-481C
MARSHALL-147,170,209,242,268,275, 389,426,494,509,510,524,530
MARTEL-158,412,426,495,525,531,547 *
MARTIN-145,160,186,281,282,305,352, 416,426,432,448,449,488,489,493
MARTINDALE-256
MARTINEAU-426
MARTRET-426
MASON-184,214,426   MASABKI *

MASSE-130,219

MASSON-475
MASTEL-426
MASTERS, cf LE MAISTRE-426
MASURY See LE MASURIER
MATHESON-184,468
MATHEW,MATTHEWS,etc.-292,426,478
MATIGIAN-489
MATSON-179
MATTE-397
MATTESON-259
MATTHEAU-311
MATTICE-313
MATTINGLY-426,523
MATZ-379
MAUDE-188,294
MAUGER-36,80,81,142,144,145,150, 159,171,180,222,225,230,232,233, 235,287,295,298,301,315,373,404, 420,423,426 to 430,437,439,481, 502,507,524,536 * 481A
MAUNDER-454   MAVINS *
MAXWELL-200,240,251,263,337,406, 430,508
MAY-430,494
MAYBEE-430
MAYNARD-234,253,254,386
MAYNE-430
MAYO-73,384,430,532
MAZEROLLE-211,212 MCAFEE 481C&D
MC ALPIN-183
MC ANULTY-295
MC ARTHUR-148
MC AULEY-480 See MC CAULEY, MC COLLEY
MC AUSLEN-251,253
MC BETH-323
MC BREARTY-239
MC BRIDE-157
MC CABE-171,185,189,495
MC CAFFERY-487
MC CAIG-495
MC CALL-190
MC CALLUM-337,404,544
MC CARTHY-171,309,402,460,528,481B
MC CARTHNEY-232
MC CARTNEY-351,452
MC CAULEY-406
MC CLEAN-266
MC CLEARY-394   MC CLELLAN *
MC CLENAHAN-395   MC CLENNAN *
MC CLOCKLIN-430,431
MC CLURE-487
MC COLLY-319
MC COMB-388
MC CONAGHY-462
MC CONNELL-170,499,525,537,539
MC CORKINGDALE-334

MC CORMICK,MC CORMACK-146,241,317,
   324,386
MC COUBREY-186,360,361
MC COY-506
MC CRAE-105,222,438,484
MC CREIGHT-531
MC CULLOUGH,MC CULLOCH-192,350
MC CUTCHEON-356
MC DADE-455
MC DAVID-250
MC DEEN-474
MC DERMOTT-129
MC DONALD,MACDONALD,etc.-104,128,
   150,177,228,231,245,282 to 284,
   363,376,384,386,403,415,419,442,
   443,450,468,471,490 *
MC DONNELL-25,246
MC DORMAND-318
MC DOUGAL,MC DOUGALL,etc.-288,290,
   403
MC DOWELL-140
MC DUFF-353,417,419
MC EACHERN-414 *
MC FARLAN,MC FARLAND,etc.-171,282,
   380,403,414,443
MC FAYDEN-503
MC FETTRIDGE-230
MC GEORGE-297
MC GINNIS-429,465,495 *
MC GLONE-498
MC GLYNN-306
MC GORLICK-199   MC GOWN-481 C
MC GRATH-496
MC GREGOR-185,395,468,470,516
MC GUIGAN-434
MC GUIRE-431
MC HARD-153
MC ILROY-186
MC, MAC INTOSH-138,245,355,396,414,
   420,539
MC INTYRE-169,239,265,441
MC ISAAC-221
MC KAME,MC KANE-431
MC KAY,MACKAY-131,291,416,419,444
MC DEAN-388
MC KEAUGH-148
MC KEIVER *
MC KEIGAN-282,318,472
MC KELVEY-393   MC KELLEHER *
MAC KENDRICK-435
MC KENNA-496
MAC KENZIE,MC KENZIE-131,168,169,*
   192,288,313,336,394,403,419,422,
   431,444,469,472,493,502,510,526,

MC KIE-36
MC KIM-188
MC KINNEL-431

MAC KINNON-173,176,219,266,283,356,
   433,445,469,487
MC KNIGHT-416,472
MC KOY-301
MC LACHIAN-306,411
MC LAREN-355,453,530
MC LEAN-160,219,266,293,403,445,
   537,538
MC LEAY-146
MC LELLAN-175,228,383,416,511,531
MC LENNAN-185,390
MC LEOD-148,153,177,198,333,383,388,
   403,404,414,416 to 419,422,445 to
   447,470,490,508
MC LOUGHLIN-455
MC MAHAN,MC MAHON-314,331,379,421
MC MANUS-411
MC MEEKIN
MC, MAC MILLAN-384,417,446,512 *
MC MULLEN-313,368
MC MURCHY-251,413
MC MURRICH-314
MC NAB-251,337,411
MC NABOW-362
MC NAIR-375
MC NALLY-138,534
MC NAMARA-221,384
MC NAUGHT-265
MC NAUGHTON-135
MC NEIL-211,221,377,428 *
MC NEILL-140,232,291,383,385,443,
   483
MC NEILLY-179
MC NICHOLS-534
MC NISH-198
MC PETRIE-483
MC PHAIL-250
MC PHEE-128
MC PHERSON-185,283,355,360,469
MC QUILLAN-325,468   MAC QUERRIE-313
MC RAE-196,222 *
MC RAILD-489
MC SWEENEY-509,520
MC TAGUE-423

MC TEIR-140
MC VEAN-454
MC VICAR-193
MC WHA-183
MC WHINNEY-279
MC WHIRTER-331
MC WILLIAMS-354,542
MEAGHER-446
MEASURE,MEASURER, see LE MESURIER,
   etc.
MEECHAM-188,492
MEGGISON-489
MELLISH-184,385
MENARD-393

MENCE-320
MENCHINTON-430
MERCATOR-536
MERCER, see   MERCIER-431,432
MERCHANT-470
MERCIER-162,197,239,364,423,432,
   524,536
MEREDITH-222
MERELA-495,496
MERRITT-24,147,321,322,512
MERRY-432
MESITI-402,481A
MESSINGER-254
MESSERVY-36,57,114,151,242,431 to
   435,466,543 *
MESSURIER-387, see LE MESSURIER,
   etc.
METCALFE-372
METHOT-162,163
METIVIER-262
METZ-441
MEUNIER-221,453
MEYER,MEYERS-311,374,411
MICHAEL-435
MICHAUD-436,506,542   MICHIEL *
MICHEL-149,183,435,482
MICHNIAK-333
MIDDLETON-435,469,547
MIFFLIN-325
MIFTARAJ-189
MIGNAULT,MIGNOT-193,234,235,436
MILLAIS-436
MILLAR-275
MILLARD-94
MILLEN-271
MILLER-152,164,176,208,232,282,308,
   335,336,363,386,408,418,436,470,
   481,490,509,534,481A,481B,481D
MILES-435
MILLEY,MILLAIS?-361,436
MILLFORD-443
MILLIGAN-497
MILLMAN-338,388,433,436
MILLS-131,146,436
MILNER-322
MILSON-459
MILTON-413
MINCHINTON-219,431,436, see
   MENCHINTON
MINK-140
MINNVILLE, see MAINVILLE-298
MINOR-161
MISCHAUD-436
MISSEN,MISSIN,MISSON-386,436,503
MITCHELL-194,219,251,270,273,307,
   368,395,436,459,472,489,497,544
MITCHELMORE-436
MIVILLE-534
MOFFITT,MOFFET-436,488

MOIR-377
MOKER-307
MOLLET-108,407,436,439,484 *
MOLLOY-133,298,429
MOLSEUR-327
MOMBOURQUETTE-547
MONAHAN-189
MONAMY-436
MONET-437
MONTAIS, see LE MONTAIS
MONGER-437
MONK-108
MONKLEY-518
MONNIER-437
MONROE-448
MONSTER-437
MONTAYE-437
MONTGOMERY-291,495
MONTOYA-540
MONUMENT-328
MOODY-437,469
MOON-94,361,400,437,515
MOONEY-377,379
MOORE,MOORES,MOORS-139,184,287,314,
   322,334,347,369,385,403,419,437,
   447,479,540
MOORHOUSE-140
MORAND-171
MORANT,MOURANT-437
MORCOMBE-437,446 *
MOREAU-200,294,328,379,461
MOREHOUSE-156
MORENZE-189
MORGAN-271,290,465,497
MORICE-437
MORIN-132,133,135,136,216,221,361,
   506,516
MORLEY-294,441
MORRELL,MORRILL-214,419,420,437
MORRIS-224,261,337,369,370,455,468,
   545
MORRISH-210
MORRISON-31,174,190,430,437,446,495,
   514,478 *
MORRISSEY-79,142,178,199,232,292,
   293,437,438,478,502 *
MORSE-146,160,320,326,378
MORTON-350
MORVAL-175
MOSDELL-282,283
MOSER-438
MOSES-438
MOSHIER-502   MOSHER *
MOSS-438
MOSSING-415
MOTE-494
MOTT-321,371,438
MOTTEE, see LE MOTTEE-371
MOTYKA-140

MOUCHET-215
MOUILPIED,DE MOUILPIED-184,438*
MOULAND,MOULIN-438
MOUNT-313
MOUNTAIN-328,447
MOUNTENAY-232
MOUNTJOY-314
MOUNTNEY-199
MOURANT-196,212,294,296,297,307,
    438,439 *
MOUSSEAU-323
MOWATT-356,358
MOYSE-438,439
MUELLER-355
MUGFORD-270,340,439
MUIRHEAD-435
MULCAHY-311
MULLEY-439   MULLEN *,
MULLIN,MOULIN-309,439,481C,481E
MULMICHAEL-200
MUMFORD-411
MUNGER-439 8
MUNNING-192
MUNRO,MUNROE,MONROE-181,233,248,
    252,261,277,335,342,439,448
MUNRO-WILSON-434
MUNCELL-439
MURCELL-439
MURCHISON-255,280
MURDOCH-366,492
MURFORD-313
MURLEY-353,417
MURPHY-296,477
MURRAY-133,355,396
MUTCH-184,468
MYALL-512
MYCROFT-494
MYERS-186,469
MYLES-241

NAASCHO-499
NADEAU-474
NADSGOOD-140
NAFTEL-182,439,448 *
NAIDOO-439
NANNETTE-533
NASH-232,293
NASTEL-439
NATHE-397

NASON-337
NAUFFTS-171

NEARING-527
NEARY-273,464
NEEDHAM-250
NEEL-328,439

NEEVE-422
NEIF-309
NEILY-146
NELSON-212,250,378,470,498
NESBITT-224,303,507
NESS-434
NETTLE-173
NETTOT-439
NEVE-262
NEVEU-439
NEVELLE,NEVILLE-422,439
NEWBERRY-315 *
NEWCOMB-160
NEWLEY-253
NEWMAN-133,279,449
NEWRICK-474
NEWSOME-128
NEWTON-439
NIBLOCK-257
NICHOLAS-180,426
NICHOL,NICHOLLE,NICHOLS,etc.-45,235,
    348,395,440,459,460,475,484
NICHOLSON-144,354,435
NICKERSON-540
NICKOLSON-419
NICHOLAS,NICHOLAS-180,370,440
NICOL,NICOLE,NICOLLE,etc.-18,74,78,
    229,307,355,357,400,418,423,441 to
    447,490,491,492,509,522,536 *
NIELSON,NIELSEN-294
NIGHTINGALE,LE ROSSIGNOL-392,447
NILES-292,386,447
NISBET-192
NIXON-176
NOBLE-161,173,447
NOEL-44,187,226,260,261,400,447,448,
    459,483,522
NOFTAL,NAFTEL-448
NOGET-458
NOON-199
NORMAN-128,189,271,448 to 450,475
NORMAND-131,166
NORMANDEAU-327
NORMORE-154,277,450,468,492
NORRIS-259,261
NORTH-333,492
NORTON-512
NORWOOD-210
NORSWORTHY,NOSEWORTHY-440,450,459
NOTTINGHAM-290
NOURY,LE NOURY-94,169,202,450,451,
    510
NOWLAND-428
NOYAN-451
NUSSEY-387
NYE-510 *

OAKES-246,363,451
OAKLEY-246   OBEN *
O'BRIEN-129,252,330
O'CONNOR-132,190,499,506,520
ODLUM-451
ODOIRE-451
O'DONOHUE-231,378
ODRUIT-462
OFFRAY-451
O'FLYNN-282
OGIER-220,382,452,478
OGILVIE-452
OGLETREE-274
O'HARA-153,157,200,201,230,367,442
OLAND-147
OLDNALL-291
OLDRING-433
OLEARY-146,328
OLESEN-452
OLIVER-92,304,315,452 *
OLIVIER,OLLIVIER-47,340,452
OLMSTEAD-394
OLSEN-508   OLSON-481B
OMER,HOMER?,HOMMART?-310
O'NEILL-231
OOSTEMA-511
ORANGE-149,286,452
ORDE-216,217,290,321
ORDISH-194
O'REILLY-306,307,345
ORGAN-452
ORMANDY-307 *   ORMOND *
ORMEROD-496
O'ROURKE-178,393
ORR-527
ORVIS-452
OSBORNE,OSBOURNE-174,215,388,404,
  407,452,492
OSHIER-231
OSLER-391
OSMENT-452
OSMOND-452   OSTRANDER *
OSTREN-183
OSTRINSKI-491
O'SULLIVAN-428
OTIS-452
O'TOOLE-452,539
OUEDART-191 OUELLET,OUILLET-285,
  304,347,452,477,508
OUGIER-452
OULESS-224
OURAY-452
OUVEN-452
OWEN-276,408
OXNER-321,469
OZANNE-221,452,453,509
OZARD-326,387,453 *
OZONG-453

PACKWOOD-79,453,462,506,533
PACQUET,PAQUET-211,212,454
PADDE-454
PADDEN-94
PADDY-215
PAGE-162,261,262,454
PAGEOT-454
PAGET-79,143,218,454
PAIN,PAINE-454
PAINCHAUD-131,309,312
PAINT-280,373,454
PAINTER-92,454,455,522
PAISNEL-455
PALET-455
PALFREY-348,455
PALING-195
PALLAH-455
PALLOT-106,399,402,455,456,483
PALMER-156,217,246,457,471
PALUSZAK-483
PALYCIA-173
PANE-310
PANEK-474
PAON-166,450
PAPE-476
PAPINEAU-181
PAQUET-211,212,454,457
PAQUIN-136
PAQUOR-457
PARADIS-191,393
PARDY-440,457
PARE-308
PARENT-239
PARES-457
PARISE-133,429
PARK-306,494
PARKER-146,147,337,346,354,356
PARKES-490
PARKMAN-383
PARLETT-491
PARMEITER-408
PARNELL,PARNALL-332,496
PARODY-457
PAROUTY-457
PARRETT,PARROTT-457
PARRIS-457,481D
PARRY-375
PARSONS-350,362,382,410,433,457,524
PARTRIDGE-265
PASCAL-457
PASHA,PERCHARD-50,457,462
PASQUIRE-154,221,457,517
PASSFIELD-497
PASSMORE-384
PATCH, see LE PATOUREL
PATE,PATEY,POTTIE-457,546,547
PATRIARCHE-457   PATTON-481C
PATRY-526
PATTEN-457 See also PETTEN

PATERSON,PATTERSON-152,153,180,197,
  219,226,331,356,363,413,481,525,
  533,545,481A & C
PAULE,PAUL-94,240,326,327,457
PAULET-476
PAULIN-226,234,456
PAULMERT-535
PAULSON-329
PAWLEY-457
PAYETTE-408
PAYN,PAYNE-78,237,255,270,458,465
PAYNTER-458
PAYZANT-59,458
PEACHE-458
PEACOCK-534
PEARCEY-129
PEARCHE,PEARCE-458
PEARDON-355
PEARL-458
PEARSON-347,434,458
PEATTY-458
PECHARD-458
PECHE-128
PECHT-352
PEDDLE-17,441,458 to 461,466
PEDVIN, see POIDEVIN, LE POIDEVIN
PEEL-393
PEGG-250
PEINTEUR-476
PELCHAT-256
PELHAM-173* See also PULHAM
PELLETIER-462,481B
PELLEY-441,460,479 See PEDDLE and
  LE PELLEY
PELLIER-460
PELOQUIN-370
PENDEXTER,POINDEXTER-66
PENISTON-313
PENMAN-357
PENNEC-461
PENNEL,PINEL-433,460,461
PENNER-293
PENNINGTON-139
PENNY,PENNEY-290,352,418,419,443 to
  445,458,461
PENOYER-490
PEPER-511
PEPIN-461,534
PEPPER-461
PEPPERDENE-170
PEPPERELL-461
PEPPY,PEPPYS,PIPPY-467
PERCEY-461
PERCHARD-78,328,457,462
PERCY-270
PERELLE,DE LA PERELLE-459,462,513
PEREWAY, see PIROUET
PERICHON-476
PERKINS-216,229,462,540 *

PERREE,PERRY-201,202,225,227,250,
  251,268,287,341,342,353,425,457,
  462,463
PERRETT-463
PERREWAY,PIROUET-463
PERRIER-231,393,463
PERRIN-239,332,463
PERROCHON-476
PERRON-339,393
PERROT-463
PERRY, see PERREE *
PERRYMAN-329
PESET-463
PETEL-458,463,466
PETERS-194,333,469
PETERSON-431 8
PETFORD-446
PETHIC-463
PETHERIC-453
PETITPAS-151,221
PETITE,LE PETIT-464
PETRIE-488,491
PETTES,PETTIS-464
PETTINDALE-255
PETTEN,PETTON-463
PETTIT-270,380
PEYTON-464,474 * See also PITON.*
PEZET,PESET-463
PFAU-237
PFLUGER-313
PHILATRE, see LE FILLATRE
PHILIBERT-311
PHILIP,PHILIPPE,PHILLIPS,etc.-178,
  220,249,408,427,434,443,444,464
PHIPPERD-464 Cf VIBERT
PHIPPS-352,464,477
PICARD-314,366
PICCO-464
PICOTT, see PICOT
PICHETTE-293
PICKETT,PICQUET,etc.-464
PICKLES-426
PICKNEL-466
PICKUP-147,217,464,465
PICOT,PICCOTT-138,142,338,342,370,
  405,464,465,466
PIDDLE-466
PIDGEON-309,466
PIERCE,PIERCY,PIERCEY-451,461
PIEROWAY,PIROUET-466
PIERPOINT,PIERPONT-161,466
PIERSON-466
PIGDEN-338

PIKE-448,466,510,544
PILLSBURY-170
PIMM-309
PINABEL-466
PINAULT-234

PINCHARD-467
PINCOTT-128
PINEL-78,414,433,461,466,467
PINET-456
PINEO-488
PINK,PINGLAUX-467   PINK-481 D
PINKERTON-362
PINNEY-461
PINOS-467
PINSENT-467
PIPER-220
PIPON-38
PIPPY-155,345,450,461,467 to 474
PIQUET-473
PIROUET,PEREWAY,etc.-176,463,473
PITHON-475
PITON-79,230,281,298,326,394,464, 473 to 475 *
PITRE-343
PITTMAN-216   PITMAN *
PITTON-298
PITTS-541
PLAMONDON-534
PLANTS-370
PLEDGER-255
PLETZER-305
PLEVEN-448,475
PLOURDE-178,261
PLOWMAN-475
PLUMMER-350
PLUMRIDGE-488

POCOCK-334
POFF-421 *
POFFENROTH-208
POIDEVIN, see LE POIDEVIN-91,93, 475,476
POINDEXTER,POIGNDESTRE,PENDEXTER, etc.-66,108,371,476,479,482
POIRIER-463,476
POIRAS-463
POITIER-476
POLLARD-130,329
POLLETT-476
POLLIS-476
POLLOCK-476
POLWESKI-346
PONCARD-476
POND-476
PONTSORM-476
PONTBRIAND-179
POPE-422,476
PORTER-182,186,252,282,290,362,476, 487
PORTSEA-31,237
POTTER-147,318 to 320,476,487
POTTLE-314
POTTS-194,296
POTVIN-476

POULE-476
POULIN,POULAIN,etc.-193,223,227, 476,480
POULSON-471
POUNTNEY-431
POVEY-329
POWELL-181,185,476
POWER,POWERS-137,166,211
POWLES-544
POWLEY-476
POYNES-476
POYNTER-476
PRATT-250,323,476,479,481C
PRAUGHT-185,468
PREAUTY-476
PREDHAM,PRIDHAM-476
PRENTICE-367,368,477
PRESHYON-476
PRESS-477,479
PRESCOTT-498
PRESTON-496
PREUDHOMME-476
PREVEL,PREVIL-94,137,203,476
PREVOST-24,94,262,312,389,477,531, *
PRIAULX-208,407,413,477,478,481A
PRICE-81,152,192,201,254,257,293, 350,394,395,404,478
PRIDDLE-478
PRIEST-303,382,452,478,479
PRIMROSE-321
PRINCE-478
PRINGLE-385
PRIOR-267,395,396
PRITCHARD-131   PROUD *
PROUINGS-478
PROCTOR-194,393
PROPERT-479
PROSSER-465,530
PROVIDENCE-318
PROULX-327,344,366,367,474,477
PROVOST-256
PRUNTY-208
PRYNE-445
PUDDISTER,PUDDESTER,POINDEXTER,etc.- 50,66,479,480

PULASKI-346
PULHAM-71,173
PULLEN,etc.-416,479,480,481D
PULSFORD-480   PUNCH *
PURCELL-480
PURCHASE
PURDY-147,321,472
PURNELL-505
PUTNAM-451
PYE-153
PYKE-367,368
PYNCHON-467

PYNN-480
PYNTRER-476

QUEENTON-480
QUENALT,QUENAULT-195,205,480
QUENTIN-481
QUEREE-212,262,413,414
QUERIPEL-221,234,237,480
QUERRIE,QUERRY-480
QUERTIER-480
QUESNEL-304,480

QUETTEVILLE, see DE QUETTEVILLE
QUICK-499
QUIGLEY-273,472
QUILLIAN-146
QUINLAN-407
QUIN,QUINN-214,250,269,323,475,480
QUINTON-293,480,481

RAAB-421
RABASSE-481
RABBITS-481
RABE,RABEY-157,176,401,402,407,
   413,481,502,481A,481B,481C,D,E.
RABEL-130
RABIN-481
RADCLIFFE-455
RADFORD-481,523
RADISSON-26 to 28
RADKE-300
RAE-496
RAFUSE-186,445,454
RAIL-136,145,148,162,163,278
RAINY-200
RALPH-459
RAMIER,RAMIE-481
RAMSDEN-364
RAMSAY-489
RANCH-128
RANCON-221,411
RANCOURT-226
RANDALL,RANDELL-464,481
RANDLES-369
RANKIN-493
RAPLEY-250
RATTIE,RETTIE,RATTUE-481
RAULAND-208
RAULT-481,505
RAUTENSTRAUCH-483
RAVEN-174
RAWDING-322
RAWLINS-481
RAY-539 * See LE RAY
RAYBURN-431

RAYMOND-481
RAYNER-327
READ-481   READER-481C
REBASS-481
REBIC-481
REBOURG,REBOURS-481
REBY, see RABEY
RECCORD,RECORD-481
RECEUVER-129
REDDY-248,418
REDFOOT-506
REDHEAD-490
REDMAN-482
REDMOND-482
REED-216,248,296,344
REEVES-301
REGINATTO-283
REGLE-482
REGULAR-482
REHEL-162,366
REID-290,325,334,419,420,445,534
RELF-333
REMO-482
REMON-140,480,482
REMPHREY-482
REMSON-146
RENAUD-482
RENAULT-209,219,435,476,482,483,514
RENCIT-251
RENOUF-59,103,105,108,145,188,209,
   237,306,312,325,341,387,436,453,
   483,484,485,493,510,547 *
REPP-251
RETTIE,RETILLEY,etc.-485
REVANS-485
REVEL-487
REVENU-485
REYNARD-485
REYNOLDS-132,418,420,485
REYNOSO-191
RHEAUME-129   RHINES- *
RHODDA-321,485
RHODES-326,406
RICE-197,266,318,319,320
RICHARD,RICHARDS-152,158,161,236,
   256,273,361,413,419,485,497
RICHARDSON-108,147,348,408,446,455,
   485,489,511
RICHE,LE RICHE-485
RICHER-151,334
RICHMOND-434
RICHTER-308
RICKABY-356,485
RICKARD-263
RICKER-66,485
RICO,RICOU-486
RICOURDEAU-481
RIDDLE,RIDALL,RIDDALS,RIDDELL,etc.-
   188,305,306,323

RIDEOUT-486
RIEVE-486
RIFOU,RIFFOU-332,506
RIGG-495
RILEY-220,511
RINFRET-MALOUIN-506
RINGLER-522
RIOU,RIOUX-211,227,311,344,486
RIPLEY-150,326,486
RIPPEY-272,356
RISE-525
RITCHIE-258,318,322
RITER-400
RITHET-486
RIVE-108,218,292,486
RIVERS-210
ROACH-318
ROBBINS-486
ROBERGE-486
ROBERT,ROBERTS-32,72,94,154,169,
    182,220,269,296,363,387,419,
    443,450,462,472,487 to 493,
    489,515,528,530,537,538 *
ROBERTSON-194,222,297,328,329,383,
    533,544
ROBICHAUD-137,138,193,211,227,228,
    274,372,438,493,547 *
ROBILLIARD,ROBILLARD-94,150,159,
    168,183,202,224,229,291,373,
    382,407
ROBIN-17,32,37 to 39,53,65,66,78 to
    80,137,200,207,245,285,309,353,
    386,403,450,481,483,495 to 500,
    503,543 *
ROBINS-32,486
ROBINSON-27,155,156,158,214,251,
    355,362,378,386,455,473,474,
    489,500,481B
ROBISON-283
ROBISSON-499
ROBLEY-295
ROBSON-152,215
ROCHE-501 See ROCK
ROCHFORD-211
ROCK-213,501
ROCKLAND-461
RODDA-206,278,321,485,501
RODGERS-193,220,326,427,429,501,535
ROEMER-130
ROGERS,ROGER-366,403,434
ROHERTY-79
ROLFE-453
ROLITEZ-470
ROLLAND,ROLAND-501,546
ROLLINGS-383,386
ROMAINE-501
ROMBOUGH-415
ROMERIL-73,207,255,300,304,483,501,
    502 *

ROMONOFF-73,351
RONDEL-502,537
RONEY-336
ROONEY-367
ROOP-465
ROOT-524
ROPER-502
ROPERT-502
ROSE-145,206,275,300,327,479,481,
    494,502,542 * 481A,   .481D.
ROSEWARNE-383
ROSIER-502
ROSS-186,189,195,253,259,314,315,
    320,351,397,423,437,456
ROSSIER-501,502
ROSSIGNOL, see LE ROSSIGNOL-234,502
ROTH-291, *
ROTHERA-337
ROUET-233,234,503 *
ROUGEAU-203
ROUGET-503
ROULEAU-134
ROUNDS-503
ROUSE-327
ROUSSEL-316,366,426,465,499,503,504,
    505,512.* See also RUSSEL
ROUSSY-135,145,429
ROUTANT-394
ROUTLEDGE-324
ROUTLEY-255
ROWAN-283
ROWBOTHAM-509
ROWE-390,504,505
ROWLAND-208,418,505
ROWLEY-191
ROWSELL,ROUSSELL-505
ROY-161,211,226,234,311,316,336,
    343,390,505,525
RUALT,RAULT-94
RUDD-505
RUDDERHAM-282
RUDOLPH-461
RUFFOLO-264
RUGG-420,505
RUGGLE,RUGGLES, see LE PATOUREL
RUMSEY-505
RUNDLE
RUSHWORTH-384
RUSSEL,RUSSELL-270,283,384,486,430,
    505,538 See also ROUSSEL
RUTHERFORD-174,467
RUTLEDGE-289
RUTTAN-148
RYAN-274,440,450
RYERSE-415
RYERSON-318,320

SABIN-302,510
SABOURIN-339
SACKETT-505
SACRY,SACRE-505
SADLER-143
SAICH-490
SAILS-350   SAINT-505
ST.AMAND,DE ST.AMAND-293
ST.CHARLES-212   ST.CLAIR-505
ST.CROIX,DE ST.CROIX-132,260,463,
ST.GEORGE-506   505,506,522 *
ST.JOHN-506   ST.LAURENT *
SALISBURY-319
SALLE-506
SALLENEUVE-506
SALM-375
SALMON-506
SALT,SALTER-371,507
SALVAS-310
SALVIDOR-507
SALWAY,SOLWAY-504,505
SAMSON,SAMPSON-166,187,221,266,
    404,507
SAMUEL-226,261,506
SANDERS-32,216,291,321
SANDLIAM-220
SANFORD-400
SANGSTER-388,433
SANQUA-507
SANS SANS, cf SANSAENS,etc.-507
SANSOLEIL-525
SARCHET-507
SARE, cf SARRE-174
SARGENT-507
SARK- 507
SARRE,SERRE,LE SARRE,etc.-507
SARTIN-508
SASIER-227
SASSEVILLE-134
SATTERLEE-349
SAULL-490
SAUMAREZ-29,225,508,519
SAUNDERS-78,249,262,377,391,413,
    513
SAUVAGE-508,509 *
SAUVAGEAU-133
SAUVARY-151,301,509
SAVAGE-78,509 *
SAVARD-134,367
SAVARY-302,509,510
SAVIDENT-450,507,510,524
SAVOIE,SAVOY-134,211,212,393
SAWYER,SAWYERS, cf SOHIER-490,510
SAYRE-508,510   SAXTON-481A
SCAMMEL-294,510,511
SCHEFER,SCHAFER-128,404
SCHEURMAN-250
SCHELL-431
SCHIER-188

SCHLACHTER-228
SCHMEARER-508
SCHNEIDER-181
SCHNUBEL-536
SCHORSE-482
SCHOTT-170,235
SCHREDER-352
SCHREIBER-182,213,214,511,512
SCHULTZ-253,254,267,396
SCHUMACHER-266
SCHURCOTTE-499
SCHUYLER-240
SCHWEGMAN-394
SCHWERDFAGER-231
SCOTT-153,170,196,207 to 210,247,270,
 * 271,306,322,335,337,411,490,512,538
SCRAGGS-544
SCRUTTON-509
SEAGER-159
SEALE-512,533
SEALY-542
SEAMAN-160 *
SEARLE-218,356,450,512
SEARS-319
SEAWARD-271,512
SEBIRE,SEBIREL,etc.-188,399,503,512,
    513
SEDGELEY-503,513
SEED-489

SEIFERT-139
SEIPP-487
SEIVRY-513
SELBY-411
SELK-193
SELLERS-479
SELOUS-513,515,516
SENAY-209
SENCABAUGH,etc.-173,210,351,416,419,
    443
SENIOR-206
SENNETT-236
SENNOTT,SYNNETT,etc.-513,515
SENTNER-185
SERAVO-488
SERGEANT,SERGENT-513
SERGERIE-133
SERRE,LE SARRE,LE SERRE-507
SERELLE-513
SERRICK-271   SEVEREID *
SEVERY,SEIVRET,SYVRET,etc.-513
SEWARD-512,513
SEWELL-180
SEYMOUR-140
SHADDUCK-*
SHADY-254
SHAEFER-322
SHAEFFE-24
SHAFFER-536

SHAFTO-129
SHANAHAN-497
SHANNEY-513
SHANTZ-253
SHARAM-443
SHARP-159,233,282,289,340,394,395
SHAW-44,161,222,253,287,318,323,
    404,444,445,456,513,535,540,481C
SHAY-319
SHEA-298,314,339
SHEARER-252,361
SHEEHAN-200,315
SHEFFER-349
SHEIMAN-349
SHELLEY-293   SHEPARD *
SHEPHERD-277,281,323,513,481B
SHEPPARD-32,174,359,459,513,514 *
SHERIDAN-377
SHERRY-361
SHERWOOD-170,505
SHIELD,SHIELDS-302,379,514
SHIELS-379
SHINE-469
SHINSKI-396
SHIRLEY-375   SHIRRA- *
SHIRREF-154
SHOESMITH-514
SHORE-282
SHORT-189,251,252
SHOUP-323
SHUERT-511
SHURMAN-441
SHURR-377
SIEGRIST-487,488
SIEVREY,SIVRET,SYVRET,etc.-514,519
    See SYVRET
SIGNAC-514
SILLARS-256
SILVA,DE SILVA,SILVER-218

SILVRAY-151
SIMARD-143,199,474
SIMMONDS,SIMMONS-358,514
SIMM,SIMMS-128,271,323
SIMON-78,368,453,481,514,515,481E
SIMONEAU-141,143,178,392
SIMONS-145

SIMPSON-314,319,353,397,400,507,515
SIMS-405   481A,481D,481B
SINCLAIR-217
SINDEN-220,445,446
SINGLETON-419
SINNOT, see SENNOTT,SYNNOT-515
SIOUVILLE-515
SISCOE-415
SISSON-268
SITES-540

SIVRAIS,SIVRET, see SYVRET-294,515,
    542,etc.
SKAGEN-267
SKELLDING-327
SKELLY-189
SKELTON-318,515
SKENE-402
SKETTON-515
SKIDMORE-182   SKILL- *
SKIMMINGS-454
SKINNER-312
SKULL-501
SLAUGHTER-354,377
SLEEMAN,etc.-515
SLINGERLAND-408
SLOCUM,SLOCOMB-156,291,356
SLOOT-415
SLOTSVE-393,394
SLOUS, see SELOUS-467
SLY-515
SMALL-422,451,533
SMART-442
SMEREK-536
SMELLIE-289
SMIRL-282
SMITH-129,130,132,137,168,185,189,
    192,222,233,235,238,250,277,290
    to 292,297,302,318,327,330,336,
    345,349,352,356,362,366,377,379,
    383,384,386,391,411,415,416,430,
    434,435,441,463,487,488,498,512,
    526,532,538,541,545 * 481A,E.
SMOLLETT-515
SMYE-410
SMYTHE-129,481E
SNELGROVE-144,384
SNODDOW-323
SNODGRASS-386
SNOW-515 *
SNOWMAN-338,515,516
SNYDER-268
SOHIER-273,510,516 *
SOLEBY-516
SOLLOM-377
SOLLOWS-516
SOLOJUK-444
SOLOMON-296
SOLWAY,SALWAY-516
SOMERTON-197,273
SOMMERVILLE,SOMERVILLE-193,510,516,
    530
SOONER-419
SOPER-488,516
SORENSON-379,487 *
SORMANY-66,516
SORSDAHL-446
SORSOLEIL-516,525
SOUDER-483,516
SOUTH-153

SOUTHALL-492
SOUTHERN-353,506
SOUTHWARD-267
SOWLES-285
SPAEDER-271

SPAULDING-418,422
SPEIGHT-489   SPENCER *
SPETTIGUE-516
SPIGOURNEL-516
SPINGLE-516
SPINNEY-481 A
SPOONER-271
SPRACKLIN-271,272
SPRATT-384,385,516
SPRUEN-260   SPRENGER *
SPURR-156,318 to 320,322
SPURRELL-271,459
SQUIRE,SQUIRES-154,197,273,346,
    464,516 to 518
STABLER-488
STACEY-291
STACK-335   STAFFORD-481A
STAGG-199,518
STAILING-321
STAINER-518
STAINS-190
STAIRS-185
STAITON,STANTON-308
STALER-533
STAMFORD-241
STAMPER-470
STANBURY-518
STANFIELD-404
STANFORTH-308
STANLEY-201,246,294,348,409,518,
STANNAGE-44,177,321,518   481 B
STANNARD-28
STANTON-245,538
STAPLES-158
STARCH,STARCK,STARK-518
STARKS-446
STARRATT-146

STEAD-192,193,363,448

STEDMAN-518
STEELE-127,442,451,518 *
STEER-244
STEEVES-539
STEHR-395
STENYING-518
STEPLER-491
STERLING-538
STEVE-495

STEVENS,STEPHENS-143,207,268,497,518
STEVENS-GUILLE-269,349
STEVENSON-284,387,402,518
STEWARD-445
STEWART-152,186,227,308,320,365,372,
    445,469,488,510,532
STICKINGS-354

STILLE-518 * see also STEELE *
STINESS-518
STOCK-518
STOCKDALE-71
STOCKLEY-417
STOKES-252,542
STONE-197,246,273,305,327,356,379,
    464,518,544 *
STONEHOUSE-292
STONELAKE-518
STONORE-518
STOODLEY-333,518,523
STORY-331,538
STOVER-170
STOVIN-256
STOW-273   STRATH *
STRATHY-518
STRAUSS-333
STREET-470
STREETER-140   STREIGHT *
STRICKERT-267
STRICKLAND-245,337

STRONG-514,518,519
STROOMER-158
STOVALL-231
STRUDWICK-268
STUART-320,358
STUBBS-440
STUDWICK-494
STUTTART-419
STYLES-301,544
SUCHASKI-137
SUCKLING-228
SUDDARD-176,190,219,401,537
SULATYCKA-323
SULIS-319
SULLIVAN-132,189,190,196,370,442,
    447,488,496,497,519,527,531
SUMMERHAYES, cf SAUMAREZ-376,519
SUNNERGEN-519
SUTCLIFFE-419
SUTHERLAND-190,223,262,549 *
SUTTON-191,309,519
SVENDSEN-179
SWAISLAND-519
SWAN-179
SWANDERS-491
SWANEK-373
SWANSON-214,303
SWARTON-519

SWEENEY-301,321,489
SWEET,SWETE-519
SWEETING-529
SWEETMAN-410,428
SWIFFEN-414
SWINARTON-497
SWITZER-250
SWORD-305
SWYER-519
SYE-519
SYKES-252,512
SYLVAIN-369
SYLVESTRE-94,519
SYKES-544
SYMES-519
SYMONS-290,514
SYNETT-467,509,515,520
SYNOTT,SYNNOTT,etc.-261,513,515
SYPHER-319
SYVRET,etc.-65,225,509,513,514,
 515,519,531,542
SZEZECH-354

TABB-519
TACHEY-519
TACKER,THACKER-519
TADIER-519
TAGG-505
TAILLEY-475
TAIT-230
TALBOT-307
TANGUY,TANGY,etc.-404,519
TANTON-186
TAPP-198,260,261,285,520,521,526,
 534,535
TARA-521
TARDIF-237,485,521,530
TARDY-521
TARGETT-135
TATE-334
TATO-222
TAUDVIN, see TOSTEVIN-72,74,416,
 419,521,523
TAVENOR-521
TAYLER-521
TAYLOR-132,169,219,271,301,327,
 346,384,432,435,441,454,459,
 521,547 *
TEED-435
TEMPLE-521
TENNANT-193,396,548 *
TENNIER-277,521 *
TENNYSON-308
TERNAN-488
TERRANT,TARRANT-521
TERRIO, see THERIAULT-221
TERRISS-187

TESSIER, see TISSIER and THISTLE-
 167,521
TETLAW-264
TETTRIDGE, see MC FETTRIDGE
TETU-163,310
TEWKESBURY-421
THACKER-168,522   THACHER *
THACKERY,THRACKRAY-395,449
THAYER-49
THELLAND-522
THEOFAIR-522
THERIN,THEREIN-191
THERRIEN-446
THERRIER-121
THERIAULT, see also TERRIO-227,343,
 344,450,465
THIBEAU,THIBEAULT,TIBBO,etc.-193,
 261,392,394,522,523
THISTLE,TISSIER-346,471,517,521,522,
 523
THOM-344,394
THOMAS-138,192,320,327,393,454,522,
 541 * 481C
THOMASON-217,535
THOMASSIN-393,394
THOMEY,THOUME-50,522
THOMPSON-153,157,247,250,252,279,
 283,291,332,340,348,368,380,396,
 404,413,420,427,431,448,451,477,
 487,503,535,536 *   ,481C
THOMSON-447,522
THORBON-522
THOREAU-91,269,299,486,522
THOREL-522
THORNE-173,186,504,522,535
THORNELL,THORNHILL-440,522
THORPE-282,309,522   THORNTON-481A
THORSEN-251
THOUME-454,522
THOUMINE-263,522,545 *
THOURNE-522
THREAPLETON-289
THUR-378
THURSTON-253
TIBBO, see THIBEAU, etc.
TIGHE-209,526
TILDESLY-333
TILLER,TILLIER,TILLEY,TILLY,etc.-
 523
TILLY-380,481A
TIMBERLAKE-465
TIMLOCK-496
TINGLEY-426,523 See MATTINGLY
TINNISWOOD-150,523
TIPPET-523
TIPPLE-523
TISSIER-517,522,523 See THISTLE
TITFORD-523
TIZZARD-523

TOASE-41
TOBIN-523
TOCQUE-44,195,523
TODD-365
TODHUNTER-431
TOGERSON-182
TOLLES-141
TOMLINSON-321
TOMPKINS-523   TOMS *
TONERI-108,523
TOOPE-399
TOPE-183 *
TORGETT, see TOURGIS
TORODE-114,340,523 *
TORREY-275
TOSTEVIN-174,208,220,225,373,376,
  377,382,416,428,432,499,510,
  523,524
TOTTMAN-524
TOUCHETTE-393
TOUET-109,204,290,397,525
TOURBON-525   TOUMINE, THOUMINE *
TOURGET,TORGETT-525
TOURGIS-44,437
TOURTEL-386
TOUSEAU-198
TOUSSAINT-198,525
TOUT-331
TOUZEAU,TUZO-525,526,531
TOUZEL,LE TOUZEL-154,269,401,520,
  521,527
TOWER-303,527
TOWN-548
TOWNER-512
TOWNSEND,TOWNSHEND-189,265
TRACHY-144,145,204,206,288,317,
  369,370,527
TRACY-314,324,496,527
TRAHY-527,528
TRAINER-488
TRAPNELL-144
TRAVAT-148
TRAVERS-336,429 *
TREBLE-189
TREEN-470
TREFRY-461
TRELUICK-282
TREMANIER-163
TREMBLAY-179,310,465,481B
TRENCHARD-431,528
TRENTADUE-211
TREPANIER-539
TRIBBLE,TRUBUIL-528
TRICOT-528
TRIMARCHI-179
TRIPP-137,528
TRIVENTI-293
TROKE-528
TROOP-146,216

TROTTIER-211
TROWBRIDGE-259
TROY-528   TRUDEAU *
TUCK,TOCQUE-528
TUCKER-405,497,498,528 *
TUFTS-146
TUMMON-494
TUPHOLME-490
TUPPER-25,44,147,191,528
TURGEON-527
TURIFF,TURRIFF-168,528,544,481C
TURK-416
TURNBALL-319
TURNBULL-327
TURNER-32,160,292
TURPIN-45,491,528
TUZO, see TOUZEAU-45,152,153,215, *
  258,273,317,340,360,528,529,530
TWEEDY-180,417
TWELLS-396
TWIGG-385,386
TYRE-488
TYRRELL-170
TYSON-210
TYWAINEN-128

ULOTH-415
UNGURAN-448
UPSHAW-140
URQUHART-153
URSIC-128
UZILLE-409

VADER-455
VAGUE,VAGG-529
VAGUS-529
VAIL-529
VALENTINE-147
VALLAT,VALLOT,etc.-529
VALLEE-395
VALLIS,VALLOIS,etc.-529
VALPY-147,219,226,304,432,438,529,
  530,544 *
VALPY DIT JANVRIN-432
VAN ANTWERP-352
VAN ARNUM *
VAN BUSKIRK-146   VAN COURT *
VANDERBYLE-374
VANDRAY-323
VAN IDERSTINE-416,419
VAN OOSTROM-289
VAN ORDER-187
VANSLYKE-407
VARDON-152,357,410,530,531,532
VARDY-531

VAREY-415
VARIOUF-269,487
VARLEY-484
VARNEY-352
VASLET-531
VASSELIN-138 *
VATCHER-531   See VAUTIER
VAUDIN-45,114,525,531
VAUGHT-323
VAUMOREL-531
VAUTIER-194,262,477,531,532 *
VAVASOUR,VAVASSOR,LE VAVASSEUR,
   etc.-402,500,532
VEAL-529
VEILLEUX-204,532
VELLIS,VEILLEZ-532
VEITCHE-532
VENEMENT,VENNEMENT,VENEMONT-532
VERCOE-254
VERDIER-532
VERDY,AVERTY-532   VERGE *
VERMETTE-325
VERREAULT,VERROW?-226,532
VER STRAETE-541
VERVOORN-483
VESCONTE, see LE VESCONTE
VEZINA-293
VIBBER, see VIBERT-160
VIBERT-18,19,65 to 69,108,142,152,
   154,160,184,215,247,270,284,
   293,307,308,367,380,464,532 to
   542 *
VICK,VICQ-542
VICKERS-369,488
VICKERY-325
VICTORSON-384
VIDAL-108,476
VIDAMOUR-229,278,542,543
VIEL-529,543
VIENS-397
VIERIN-473
VIERKOETTER-341
VIGNEAU-166,248
VIGOT-543
VIGOURS-543
VILLANEUVE-543
VILLETTE-362
VINCENT-238,255,279,433,543
VINCHELEZ-546
VINING-254
VIXCOUNT-543
VIVIAN,VYVYAN-543
VLAD-259
VODEN, see VAUDIN
VOIGT-333
VOISE,VOISEY-361,543
VOISIN-543
VOKES-312
VOKEY-543

VOLTIGEURS-31,543
VOSIKA-349
VOSS-239
VOTIER-543   See VAUTIER
VOUCHER-543   See VAUTIER
VYNER-27

WADDELL-128
WADDINGHAM-496
WADDINGTON-212
WADE-146,543
WADIE-418
WADLEIGH -348
WAFER-300
WAGEL-545
WAGG-440
WAGNER-450
WAGGENER,WAGONER,etc.-32,445,450
WAIDE-544
WAINWRIGHT-254,422
WAKEFIELD-229
WALDER-268
WALDRON-544
WALKER-43,172,186,199,214,217,254,
   327,329,364,393,431,445,451,453,
   544 *
WALL-143,293,328
WALLBERG-472
WALLEGHAN-512
WALLENDER-252
WALLER-291
WALLIS-208,544
WALSH-162,200,336,366
WALPY-544   See VALPY
WALTERS-45,352,530,544
WARCUP-198
WARD-217,344,345,355,383,457,537 *
WARDEN-90
WARNE-147,245
WARNEHOLTZ-238
WARNER-478
WARNSDORFER-445
WARR-544
WARREN-94,231,264,544
WARSABA-140
WARWICK-29
WASHBURN-537
WATERMAN-302,489,490,544
WATERTON-501
WATKINS-494,481A
WATKINSON-284
WATSON-416,529
WATT,WATTS-90,159,164,218,249,363,
   466,470,544,545
WAUGH-289,530
WAYE-545
WEARE,WEARY-45,66,156,545

WEATHERALL-332
WEATHERHEAD-183
WEATHERILL-282
WEAVER-493
WEAYMOUTH-503
WEBB-322,336,397,405,482,545,481A
WEBBER,WEBER-435,545
WEBSTER-145,217,290
WEEKS-246,266,545
WEIL-387
WEINMAN-331
WEIR-441
WEISBRODT-395
WEISMILLER-274,275
WELCH-545

WELLER-473
WELLING-177
WELLS-160,188,320,350,395,458
WELSH-396,545
WESBROOK,WESTBROOK-251
WESSENGER-254
WEST-90,247,331,333,545,481A,481C
WESTAWAY-545
WESTLAKE-545
WESTON-515,545
WESTRA-422
WESTWOOD-354
WETMORE-491
WEYBOROUGH-545
WHALEN-271,309,323,332,463   See WHELAN
WHEADON-154,545,546
WHEATLEY-546
WHEELER-264,383,443,546,481B
WHELAN-246,406,479
WHEELOCK-156,217,461
WHERRY-252
WHIBLEY-475
WHILEUR-546
WHILLOCK *
WHIPPLE-160,161
WHITAKER-232,374,375
WHITCHURCH-94,546
WHITCOMBE-208
WHITE-130,243,254,322,418,443,450, 479,490,493,546 *
WHITEFOOT-164
WHITEHEAD-346
WHITELAW-305,306
WHITELY-546 *
WHITEMAN-130
WHITESIDE-407
WHITING-546
WHITMAN-156,217,377 ✳
WHITNUM-415
WHITTIE-537
WHITTLE-108,546
WHITTOM,WHITTON-164,248,413

WICKHAM-352
WICKS-494
WIDGER-518,546
WIELAND-339
WIGHT-223
WIGNALL-382,479,546
WILBECQUE-308
WILBY-255
WILDE-540
WILDERMUTH-223   WILKES-481D
WILKIE,WILKE-174,319,321
WILKINS-546
WILKINSON-236
WILLET,WILLETT-146,176,217,348,465, 534,546
WILLIAMS-23,24,156,158,201,232,241, 320,321,323,375,401,404,417,471, 482,494,503,519,525,541,546
WILLIAMSON-160,327,502
WILLIS-192,352,382,479
WILLS-350,406,407
WILSAR-170
WILSEY-489
WILSON-127,150,153,217,222,232,305, 314,315,329,333,339,349,353,355, 362,411,423,433,504,512,538,539, 542,546 *
WILTON-251,333
WILTSHIRE-425
WINCHELL-546 See VINCHELEZ
WINCY-546,547 ✗
WINDISH-241
WINDSOR-72,223,351
WINFIELD-353
WINSHIP-456
WINSLOW-416
WINSOR-448
WINTER-246
WINTERFLOOD-151
WINTON-254
WISEMAN-542
WISENER-415
WITHERS-146
WITHROW-289
WITT-147,189
WITTEN-284
WITTEWRONG-29
WOLANSKI-410
WOLCOTT-431
WOLF,WOLFE-178,498,536
WOLFREY-547
WOLLENHAUPT-177
WONNACOTT-341,386
WOOD-135,184 to 186,194,219,265, 267,290,296,352,385,445,482,535
WOODARD-396
WOODBRIDGE-267
WOODBURY-216,217
WOODS-433,513,547

WOODSIDE-139
WOODWARD-318,384
WOOLDRIDGE-547
WOLFE-390
WOLFREY-547
WOLSTENHOLME-547
WOOLNER-32,383,384
WOOTTEN,WOOTEN,WOTTEN,etc.-188,547
WORMINGTON-339
WORMOLD-350
WRIGHT-147,305,307,333,367,406,
    414,423,490,525,547 *
WRIXTON-206,547
WYATT-426
WYLIE-296

YATES-291
YEO-547
YODER-254
YOKOYAMA-291
YONKERS-249
YOUNG-164,184,186,196,208,221,250,
    251,253,295,322,351,440,459,
    509,534,540,547   See also JEUNE
    and LE JEUNE
YVON-506

ZAGNI-271
ZAZULAK-231,232
ZIMMERMAN-251
ZOFFEL-130
ZONA-375
ZUCK-130
ZUURBIER-148

www.ingramcontent.com/pod-product-compliance
Lightning Source LLC
Chambersburg PA
CBHW071131300426
44113CB00009B/944